Strategic Management

University of
Chester

CHESTER CA
LIF

Seventh Edition

Strategic Management

An Integrated Approach

Charles W. L. Hill
University of Washington

Gareth R. Jones
Texas A&M University

Houghton Mifflin Company

Boston   New York

For my children, Elizabeth, Charlotte, and Michelle
Charles W. L. Hill

For Nicholas and Julia and Morgan and Nia
Gareth R. Jones

Vice-President and Publisher: George T. Hoffman
Senior Sponsoring Editor: Lise Johnson
Associate Editor: Julia Perez
Editorial Assistant: Amy Galvin
Senior Project Editor: Kerry Falvey
Manufacturing Manager: Karen Fawcett
Executive Marketing Manager: Steven W. Mikels
Marketing Associate: Lisa Boden

Cover image: © Medioimages/Imagestate

Library of Congress Control Number: 2005935203

ISBNs:
Instructor's Exam Copy:
ISBN-13: 978-0-618-73166-4
ISBN-10: 0-618-73166-0

For orders, use student text ISBNs:
ISBN-13: 978-0-618-64162-8
ISBN-10: 0-618-64162-9

1 2 3 4 5 6 7 8 9—DOW—10 09 08 07 06

Brief Contents

Contents

2   External Analysis: The Identification of Opportunities and Threats   42

PART 2   The Nature of Competitive Advantage

3   Internal Analysis: Distinctive Competencies, Competitive Advantage, and Profitability   75

---

4 Building Competitive Advantage Through Functional-Level Strategy   109

PART 3   Strategies

5   Building Competitive Advantage Through Business-Level Strategy   149

6   Business-Level Strategy and the Industry Environment   187

7   Strategy in High-Technology Industries   229

8 Strategy in the Global Environment

9 Corporate-Level Strategy: Horizontal Integration, Vertical Integration, and Strategic Outsourcing   304

10 Corporate-Level Strategy: Formulating and Implementing Related and Unrelated Diversification   336

PART 4   Implementing Strategy

11   Corporate Performance, Governance, and Business Ethics   373

12 Implementing Strategy in Companies That Compete in a Single Industry   411

Part 5   Cases in Strategic Management

| Introduction: Analyzing a Case Study and Writing a Case Study Analysis | C1 |

Cases

Section A: Business Level Cases: Domestic and Global

Preface

The significant revisions we made to the sixth edition of *Strategic Management: An Integrated Approach* have been well received by instructors and students alike. Our book has strengthened its position as the most widely used strategic management textbook on the market. This tells us that we continue to meet the expectations of existing users and attract many new users to our book. It is clear that most strategy instructors share with us a concern for currency in text and examples to ensure that cutting-edge issues and new developments in strategic management are continually addressed.

Just as in the last edition, our objective in rewriting the seventh edition has been to maintain all that was good about prior editions, while refining our approach to discussing established strategic management issues and adding new material to the text to present a more complete, clear, and current account of strategic management in the 2000s. We believe that the result is a book that is more closely aligned with the needs of today's professors and students and the realities of competition in the new global environment.

Comprehensive and Up-to-Date Coverage

Users of our book enjoyed the major chapter additions and changes we made to the sixth edition of *Strategic Management*. In particular, Chapter 7, which discusses strategy in high-technology industries characterized by markets driven by rapid technological change, was well received. Users also liked Chapter 11, which expands coverage of organizational stakeholders, business ethics, and corporate governance in light of the continuing ongoing examples of unethical behavior by corporate managers in organizations such as WorldCom, Adelphia, and Enron, many of whom received long prison sentences in 2005. Finally, our new streamlined approach to strategy implementation in single- and multi-business companies in Chapters 12 and 13 proved easier for students to understand and appreciate—and to use in developing the case studies that many instructors require their students to write.

In this revision we have made no changes to the number or sequencing of our chapters. However, we have made many significant changes inside each chapter and between chapters to refine and update our presentation of strategic management. Continuing real-world changes in strategic management practices such as the increased use of cost reduction strategies, including global outsourcing and lean production, and a renewed emphasis on the "business model" as the driver of differentiation and competitive advantage have led to many changes in our approach. Thus although the overall organization of this edition, depicted in Figure 1.4 on page 12, is similar to the sixth edition, the additional material (in particular our increased use of the concept of the "business model" as a way of framing the issue of competitive advantage) has changed our presentation to reflect current thinking in the field of strategic management.

Major Content Changes Within Chapters

- In Chapter 1 there is a new emphasis on strategic leadership and a new section entitled "Strategic Leadership, Competitive Advantage, and Superior Performance" that highlights the goals of strategic leadership and shows how competitive advantage results in superior performance. Chapter 1 also contains an important new section entitled "Competitive Advantage and a Company's Business Model" that discusses in depth the role of a company's business model in the strategy-making process. A business model is managers' conception of how the set of strategies their company pursues should mesh together into a congruent whole to enable a company to gain a competitive advantage and achieve superior performance. A business model is a mental model or gestalt of how the set of strategies and investments a company makes should fit together if it is to achieve superior performance. The use of the business model concept changes the way we approach the analysis of functional-, business-, and corporate-level strategy and provides us with an additional tool to drive home the message of strategic management to students.

■ In Chapter 3 there is a new section explaining the connection between a company's business model, the value chain, and distinctive competencies. We have also revised and expanded the discussion of competitive advantage and profitability. This section explains in detail how an analysis of financial statements can reveal the financial impact of major differences in strategic choices. It also explains how strategic managers must think through the impact of their decisions on the financial position of the company.

■ Chapter 5 presents a whole new approach to examining the issues and tradeoffs in the choice of a generic business-level competitive strategy. Today, the growing ability of companies to pursue both a differentiation and low-cost strategy simultaneously requires that business-level strategy be conceptualized in a new and more sophisticated way. We offer an approach that does this by using the concepts of the business model and value frontier to outline the choices facing companies in pursuing a viable competitive strategy. We believe our new approach offers students additional insights into the competitive issues facing companies today.

■ Chapter 6 continues with this analysis and has been revised to focus on the way in which the nature of competition changes as companies pursue business models based on both differentiation and low-cost strategies, especially as industries pass through different stages of growth.

■ Chapter 7, which focuses on high-tech issues such as the importance of technological standards in industries, the nature of "network economics," and strategies for winning "format wars" has been streamlined and updated given the rapidly changing events in industries such as cell phones, flat-screen TVs, microprocessors, and videogames.

■ Chapter 8 on strategy in the global environment has also been significantly revised and updated to reflect the rapid integration of the global economy, the emergence of new industrial powers such as China and India, and the implication of these developments for strategic management.

■ In Chapter 9, the growing importance of strategic outsourcing as a way of building competitive advantage is reflected in expanded coverage of the issues involved. Also covered is the increase in horizontal integration that has taken place in the last few years as companies seek to offer a wider range of bundled products and to streamline their product offerings to reduce their level of diversification.

■ Chapter 10 has been significantly revised and streamlined to offer new coverage of the advantages and disadvantages of diversification. It also contains a new section called "The Web of Corporate-Level Strategy" that makes it quite clear that a company can potentially pursue each and every strategy if this would strengthen its business model and lead to increased profitability and profit growth. On the other hand, a company should not be afraid to refocus its resources and move back to its core business if changes in the competitive environment make this the most appropriate way to strengthen its business model.

■ Chapter 11, which looks at corporate performance, governance, and business ethics, has been substantially revised to include considerably more material on business ethics and strategy. The chapter explains how poor corporate performance can be caused by a combination of poor corporate governance systems and unethical behavior. The chapter reviews the strategic importance of managing stakeholders, putting strong corporate governance mechanisms in place, and making ethical decisions. Agency theory is used to explain failures of corporate governance and poor managerial ethics. There is an extended look at different approaches to business ethics. The chapter draws heavily on recent examples of corporate fraud at companies such as Enron, WorldCom, and Tyco to illustrate the main points.

■ Finally, Chapters 12 and 13 have been revised to make them compatible with our new treatment of the business model and business- and corporate-level strategy.

Once again, throughout the revision process we have been careful to preserve the *balanced and integrated* nature of our account of strategic management. Moreover, as we have continued to add new material, we have also shortened or deleted coverage of out-of-date or less important models and concepts to help students identify and focus on the core concepts and issues in the field. We have also paid close attention to retaining the book's readability.

Finally, it is important to emphasize that we have overhauled the case selection. There are 34 cases in this edition, and 26 of these cases are new to this edition. The remaining cases have been updated and revised. For example, the home videogame and Nucor cases have been revised to include material through to early 2005. As always, we have used a tight screen to weed out poor-quality cases and we believe that the selection we offer is the best on the market.

Practicing Strategic Management: An Interactive Approach

We have received a lot of positive feedback about the usefulness of the end-of-chapter exercises/assignments in the *Practicing Strategic Management* sections in our book. They offer a wide range of different kinds of hands-on learning experiences for students. Following the Chapter Summary and Discussion Questions, each chapter contains the following assignments/exercises:

■ *Small-Group Exercise.* This short (20-minute) experiential exercise asks students to divide into groups and discuss a scenario concerning some aspect of strategic management. For example, the scenario in Chapter 11 asks students to identify the stakeholders of their educational institution and evaluate how stakeholders' claims are being and should be met.

■ *Exploring the Web.* The Internet exercise requires students to explore a particular website and answer chapter-related questions. For example, the Chapter 8 assignment is to go to the website of IBM and analyze its strategy for competing in the global marketplace. This section also asks students to explore the Web for relevant sites of their own choosing and answer questions.

■ *Article File.* As in the last edition, this exercise requires students to search business magazines to identify a company that is facing a particular strategic management problem. For instance, students are asked to locate and research a company pursuing a low-cost or a differentiation strategy, and to describe this company's strategy, its advantages and disadvantages, and the core competencies required to pursue it. Students' presentations of their findings lead to lively class discussions.

■ **Strategic Management Project.** Students, in small groups, choose a company to study for the whole semester and then analyze the company using the series of questions provided at the end of every chapter. For example, students might select Ford Motor Co. and, using the series of chapter questions, collect information on Ford's top managers, mission, ethical position, domestic and global strategy and structure, and so on. Eventually, students write a case study of their company and present it to the class at the end of the semester. Normally, we also have students present one or more of the cases in the book early in the semester, but in our classes we now treat the students' own projects as the major class assignment and their case presentations as the climax of the semester's learning experience.

■ **Closing Case study.** A short closing case provides an opportunity for a short class discussion of a chapter-related theme.

In creating these exercises it is not our intention to suggest that they should *all* be used for *every* chapter. For example, over a semester an instructor might combine a group Strategic Management Project with five to six Article File assignments and five to six Exploring the Web exercises, while doing eight to ten Small-Group Exercises in class.

We have found that our interactive approach to teaching strategic management appeals to students. It also greatly improves the quality of their learning experience. Our approach is more fully discussed in the *Instructor's Resource Manual.*

Strategic Management Cases

The 34 cases that we have selected for this edition will appeal, we are certain, to students and professors alike, both because these cases are intrinsically interesting and because of the number of strategic management issues they illuminate. The organizations discussed in the cases range from large, well-known companies, for which students can do research in order to update the information, to small, entrepreneurial businesses that illustrate the uncertainty and challenge of the strategic management process. In addition, the selections include many international cases, and most of the other cases contain some element of global strategy. Refer to the table of contents for a complete listing of the cases with brief descriptions.

We feel that our entire selection is unrivaled in breadth and depth, and we are grateful to the other case authors who have contributed to this edition:

Vincent Amanor-Boadu, *Kansas State University*
Sally Baack, *San Francisco State University*
Frank C. Barnes, *University of North Carolina–Charlotte*
Christopher A. Bartlett, *Harvard Business School*
David Barton, *Kansas State University*
Mike Boland, *Kansas State University*
Lew Brown, *University of North Carolina, Greensboro*
Isaac Cohen, *San Jose State University*
Christina Darwall, *Harvard Business School California Research Center*
S.S. George, *ICFAI Center for Management Research*
Armand Gilinsky, Jr., *Sonoma State University*
Robert H. Girling, *Sonoma State University*
Debra Glassman, *University of Washington*

Jeffrey A. Krug, *Appalachian State University*
Suresh Kotha, *University of Washington*
Anne T. Lawrence, *San Jose State University*
Robert J. Mockler, *St. John's University*
Rebecca J. Morris, *University of Nebraska at Omaha*
Susan L. Peters, *Texas A&M University*
Murray Silverman, *San Francisco State University*
Beverly B. Tyler, *North Carolina State University*
Meg Wozny, *Harvard Business School*
Jie Xu, *Sonoma State University*
Pai-Ling Yin, *Harvard Business School California Research Center*
David Yoffie, *Harvard Business School California Research Center*

To help students learn how to effectively analyze and write a case study, we continue to include a special section on this subject. This section includes a checklist and explanation of areas to consider, suggested research tools, and tips on financial analysis.

Teaching and Learning Aids

Taken together, the teaching and learning features of *Strategic Management* provide a package that is unsurpassed in its coverage and that supports the integrated approach that we have taken throughout the book.

For the Instructor

- The **Instructor's Resource Manual** has been completely revised. For each chapter we provide a clearly focused synopsis, a list of teaching objectives, a comprehensive lecture outline, suggested answers to discussion questions, and comments on the end-of-chapter activities. Each chapter opening case, Strategy in Action boxed feature, and chapter closing case has a synopsis and a corresponding teaching note to help guide class discussion.

- The **Test Bank** has been revised and offers a set of comprehensive true/false and multiple-choice questions, and new essay questions for each chapter in the book. The mix of questions has been adjusted to provide fewer fact-based or simple memorization items and to provide more items that rely on synthesis or application. Also, more items now reflect real or hypothetical situations in organizations. Every question is keyed to the teaching objectives in the *Instructor's Resource Manual* and includes an answer and page reference to the textbook.

- The **Instructor's Resource Manual: Cases** includes a complete list of Case Discussion Questions as well as a *comprehensive teaching note* for each case, which gives a complete analysis of case issues. It is written in a user-friendly question-and-answer format.

- **HM ClassPrep™ with HMTesting CD** provides a variety of teaching resources in electronic format allowing for easy customization to meet specific instructional needs. Included in ClassPrep are electronic *Instructor's Resource Manual* files, Premium and Basic PowerPoint slides, Classroom Response System content, and much more. The computerized version of the Test Bank allows instructors to select, edit, and add questions, or generate randomly selected questions to produce a test master for easy duplication. Online Testing and Gradebook functions allow instructors to administer tests via their local area network or the World Wide Web, set up classes, record grades from tests or assignments, analyze grades, and produce/compile class and individual statistics.

- The **video program** highlights many issues of interest and can be used to spark class discussion. It offers a compilation of footage from the Videos for Humanities series.

- An extensive **website** contains many features to aid instructors including downloadable files for the text and case materials from the *Instructor's Resource Manual*, the downloadable Premium and Basic PowerPoint slides, the Video Guide, and sample syllabi. Additional materials on the student website may also be of use to instructors.

- **Eduspace®**, powered by Blackboard®, is a course management tool that includes downloadable MP3 audio chapter summaries and quizzes, chapter outlines, visual glossaries, all questions from the textbook with suggested answers, Debate Issues, ACE self-test questions, auto-graded quizzes, Premium and Basic PowerPoint slides, Classroom Response System content, links to content on the websites, video activities, and Test Bank content. A Getting Started Guide is also available.

- **Blackboard®/Web CT®** includes course material, downloadable MP3 audio chapter summaries and quizzes, chapter outlines, visual glossaries, all questions from the textbook with suggested answers, Premium and Basic PowerPoint slides, Classroom Response System content, links to content on the websites, video activities, and Test Bank content.

For the Student

- The **student website** includes downloadable MP3 audio chapter summaries and quizzes, chapter overviews, Internet exercises (repeated from the textbook, with updates as necessary), ACE self-tests, links to the companies highlighted in the chapter opening and closing cases and the Strategy in Action boxed features as well as to the cases featured in the second half of the book, case discussion questions to help guide student case analysis, glossaries, visual glossaries, flashcards for studying the key terms, a section with guidelines on how to do case study analysis, and much more.

Acknowledgments

This book is the product of far more than two authors. We are grateful to Lise Johnson, our sponsor, Julia Perez, our editor, and Steve Mikels, our marketing manager, for their help in promoting and developing the book and for providing us with timely feedback and information from professors and reviewers that have allowed us to shape the book to meet the needs of its intended market. We are also grateful to Kerry Falvey, senior project editor, and Sarah Driver, editorial assistant, for their adept handling of production. We are also grateful to the case authors for allowing us to use their materials. We also want to thank the departments of management at the University of Washington and Texas A&M University for providing the setting and atmosphere in which the book could be written, and the students of these universities who reacted to and provided input for many of our ideas. In addition, the following reviewers of this and earlier editions gave us valuable suggestions for improving the manuscript from its original version to its current form:

Ken Armstrong, *Anderson University*
Kunal Banerji, *West Virginia University*
Kevin Banning, *Auburn University–Montgomery*
Glenn Bassett, *University of Bridgeport*
Thomas H. Berliner, *The University of Texas at Dallas*
Richard G. Brandenburg, *University of Vermont*

Steven Braund, *University of Hull*
Philip Bromiley, *University of Minnesota*
Geoffrey Brooks, *Western Oregon State College*
Lowell Busenitz, *University of Houston*
Charles J. Capps III, *Sam Houston State University*
Gene R. Conaster, *Golden State University*
Steven W. Congden, *University of Hartford*
Catherine M. Daily, *Ohio State University*
Robert DeFillippi, *Suffolk University Sawyer School of Management*
Helen Deresky, *SUNY–Plattsburgh*
Gerald E. Evans, *The University of Montana*
John Fahy, *Trinity College, Dublin*
Patricia Feltes, *Southwest Missouri State University*
Mark Fiegener, *Oregon State University*
Isaac Fox, *Washington State University*
Craig Galbraith, *University of North Carolina at Wilmington*
Scott R. Gallagher, *Rutgers University*
Eliezer Geisler, *Northeastern Illinois University*
Gretchen Gemeinhardt, *University of Houston*
Lynn Godkin, *Lamar University*
Robert L. Goldberg, *Northeastern University*
James Grinnell, *Merrimack College*
Todd Hostager, *University of Wisconsin–Eau Claire*
Graham L. Hubbard, *University of Minnesota*
Tammy G. Hunt, *University of North Carolina at Wilmington*
James Gaius Ibe, *Morris College*
W. Grahm Irwin, *Miami University*
Jonathan L. Johnson, *University of Arkansas Walton College of Business Administration*
Marios Katsioloudes, *St. Joseph's University*
Robert Keating, *University of North Carolina at Wilmington*
Geoffrey King, *California State University–Fullerton*
Rico Lam, *University of Oregon*
Robert J. Litschert, *Virginia Polytechnic Institute and State University*
Franz T. Lohrke, *Louisiana State University*
Paul Mallette, *Colorado State University*
Lance A. Masters, *California State University–San Bernardino*
Robert N. McGrath, *Embry-Riddle Aeronautical University*
Charles Mercer, *Drury College*
Van Miller, *University of Dayton*
Tom Morris, *University of San Diego*
Joanna Mulholland, *West Chester University of Pennsylvania*
Francine Newth, *Providence College*
Paul R. Reed, *Sam Houston State University*
Rhonda K. Reger, *Arizona State University*
Malika Richards, *Indiana University*
Stuart Rosenberg, *Dowling College*
Ronald Sanchez, *University of Illinois*
Joseph A. Schenk, *University of Dayton*
Brian Shaffer, *University of Kentucky*

Leonard Sholtis, *Eastern Michigan University*
Pradip K. Shukla, *Chapman University*
Dennis L. Smart, *University of Nebraska at Omaha*
Barbara Spencer, *Clemson University*
Lawrence Steenberg, *University of Evansville*
Kim A. Stewart, *University of Denver*
Ted Takamura, *Warner Pacific College*
Bobby Vaught, *Southwest Missouri State*
Robert P. Vichas, *Florida Atlantic University*
Edward Ward, *St. Cloud State University*
Kenneth Wendeln, *Indiana University*
Daniel L. White, *Drexel University*
Edgar L. Williams, Jr., *Norfolk State University*
Jun Zhao, *Governors State University*

Charles W. L. Hill
Gareth R. Jones

Strategic Management

Chapter 1

Strategic Leadership: Managing the Strategy-Making Process for Competitive Advantage

Opening Case

Wal-Mart

Wal-Mart is one of the most extraordinary success stories in business history. Started in 1962 by Sam Walton, Wal-Mart has grown to become the world's largest corporation. In the financial year ending January 31, 2004, the discount retailer whose mantra is "every day low prices" had sales of nearly $256 billion, five thousand stores in ten countries (almost three thousand are in the United States), and 1.3 million employees. Some 8 percent of all retail sales in the United States are made at a Wal-Mart store. Wal-Mart is not only large but also very profitable. In 2003, the company earned a return on invested capital of 14.7 percent, significantly better than rivals Costco and Target, which earned 9.4 percent and 10 percent, respectively (another major rival, Kmart, emerged from bankruptcy protection in 2004). As shown in the accompanying figure, Wal-Mart has been consistently more profitable than its rivals for years.

Wal-Mart's superior profitability reflects a competitive advantage that is based on the successful implementation of a number of strategies. In 1962 Wal-Mart was one of the first companies to apply the self-service supermarket business model developed by grocery chains to general merchandise (two of its rivals, Kmart and Target, were established in the same year). Unlike its rivals, who focused on urban and suburban locations, Sam Walton's Wal-Mart concentrated on small southern towns that were ignored by its rivals. Wal-Mart grew quickly by pricing lower than local mom-and-pop retailers, often putting them out of business. By the time Kmart and Target realized that small towns could support a large discount general merchandise store, Wal-Mart had preempted them. These towns, which were large enough to support one discount retailer, but not two, provided a secure profit base for Wal-Mart.

However, there is far more to the Wal-Mart story than location strategy. The company was also an innovator in information systems, logistics, and human resource practices. Taken together, these strategies resulted in higher productivity and lower costs than rivals, which enabled the company to earn a high profit while charging low prices. Wal-Mart led the way among American retailers in developing and implementing sophisticated product-tracking systems using bar-code technology and checkout scanners. This information technology enabled Wal-Mart to track what was selling and adjust its inventory accordingly so that the products found in a store matched local demand. By avoiding overstocking, Wal-Mart

Profitability in the U.S. Retail Industry, 1994–2003

Data Source: Value Line Investment Survey.

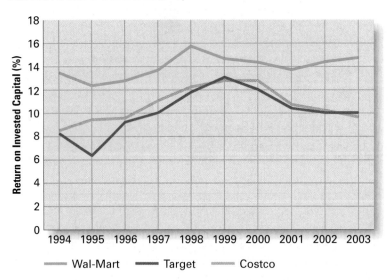

did not have to hold periodic sales to shift unsold inventory. Over time, it linked this information system to a nationwide network of distribution centers where inventory was stored and then shipped to stores within a 300-mile radius on a daily basis. The combination of distribution centers and information centers enabled Wal-Mart to reduce the amount of inventory it held in stores and devote more of that valuable space to selling and reducing the amount of capital it had tied up in inventory.

With regard to human resources, the tone was set by Sam Walton, who believed that employees should be respected and rewarded for helping to improve the profitability of the company. Underpinning this belief, Walton referred to employees as "associates." He established a profit sharing scheme for all employees, and after the company went public in 1970, he initiated a program that allowed employees to purchase Wal-Mart stock at a discount to its market value. Wal-Mart was rewarded for this approach by high employee productivity, which translated into lower operating costs and higher profitability.

As Wal-Mart grew larger, the sheer size and purchasing power of the company enabled it to drive down the prices that it paid suppliers and to pass on those savings to customers in the form of lower prices, which enabled Wal-Mart to gain more market share and hence demand even lower prices. To take the sting out of the persistent demands for lower prices, Wal-Mart shared its sales information with suppliers on a daily basis, enabling them to gain efficiencies by configuring their own production schedules to sales at Wal-Mart.

Already by the 1990s, Wal-Mart was the largest general seller of general merchandise in America. To sustain its growth, Wal-Mart started to diversify into the grocery business, opening 200,000-square-foot supercenter stores that sold groceries and general merchandise under the same roof. Wal-Mart also diversified into the warehouse club business with the establishment of Sam's Club. With its entry into Mexico in 1991, the company began expanding internationally. By pursuing these expansion strategies, Wal-Mart aims to increases sales to over $400 billion by 2010, up from $40 billion today, thereby solidifying its scale-based advantage.

Despite all of its success, Wal-Mart has experienced problems. In some parts of America, such as California and the Northeast, there has been a backlash against Wal-Mart, particularly by small town residents who see Wal-Mart as a threat to local retailers. Increasingly, Wal-Mart has found it difficult to get planning permission to open up new stores in these towns. In addition, despite the long-held belief that employees should be treated well, Wal-Mart has been the target of lawsuits from employees who claim that they were pushed to work long hours without overtime pay, and from female employees claiming that the culture of Wal-Mart discriminates against them. While some observers believe that these complaints have little merit, others argue that they are signs that the company has become too large and may be encountering limits to profitable growth.[1]

Overview

Why do some companies succeed while others fail? Why has Wal-Mart been able to do so well in the fiercely competitive retail industry, while others like Kmart have struggled? In the personal computer industry, what distinguishes Dell from less successful companies such as Gateway? In the airline industry, how is it that Southwest Airlines has managed to keep increasing its revenues and profits through both good times and bad, while rivals such as US Airways and United Airlines have had to seek bankruptcy protection? How did Sony come to dominate the market for videogames with its highly successful PlayStation, while former industry leader Sega saw its market share slump from 60 percent in the early 1990s to less than 10 percent by 2000, and finally pulled out of the market in 2001? What explains the persistent growth and profitability of Nucor Steel, now the largest steel market in America, during a period when many of its once larger rivals disappeared into bankruptcy?

In this book, we argue that the strategies that a company's managers pursue have a major impact on its performance relative to its competitors. A **strategy** is a set of related actions that managers take to increase their company's performance. For most, if not all, companies, achieving superior performance relative to rivals is the ultimate challenge. If a company's strategies result in superior performance, it is said to have a *competitive advantage*. Wal-Mart's strategies produced superior performance from 1994 to 2003; as a result, Wal-Mart has enjoyed a competitive advantage over its rivals. How did Wal-Mart achieve this competitive advantage? As explained in the *Opening Case*, it was due to the successful pursuit of a number of strategies by Wal-Mart's managers, most notably the company's founder, Sam Walton. These strategies enabled the company to lower its cost structure, charge low prices, gain market share, and become more profitable than its rivals. (We will return to the example of Wal-Mart several times throughout this book in a *Running Case* that examines various aspects of Wal-Mart's strategy and performance.)

This book identifies and describes the strategies that managers can pursue to achieve superior performance and provide their company with a competitive advantage. One of its central aims is to give you a thorough understanding of the analytical techniques and skills necessary to identify and implement strategies successfully. The first step toward achieving this objective is to describe in more detail what *superior performance* and *competitive advantage* mean and to explain the pivotal role that managers play in leading the strategy-making process.

Strategic leadership is about how to most effectively manage a company's strategy-making process to create competitive advantage. The **strategy-making process** is the process by which managers select and then implement a set of strategies that aim to achieve a competitive advantage. **Strategy formulation** is the task of selecting strategies, whereas **strategy implementation** is the task of putting strategies into action, which includes designing, delivering, and supporting products; improving the efficiency and effectiveness of operations; and designing a company's organization structure, control systems, and culture. Paraphrasing the well-known saying that "success is 10 percent inspiration and 90 percent perspiration," in the strategic management arena we might say that "success is 10 percent formulation and 90 percent implementation." The task of selecting strategies is relatively easy (but requires good analysis and some inspiration); the hard part is putting those strategies into effect.

By the end of this chapter, you will understand how strategic leaders can manage the strategy-making process by formulating and implementing strategies that enable a company to achieve a competitive advantage and superior performance. Moreover, you will learn how the strategy-making process can go wrong and what managers can do to make this process more effective.

Strategic Leadership, Competitive Advantage, and Superior Performance

Strategic leadership is concerned with managing the strategy-making process to increase the performance of a company, thereby increasing the value of the enterprise to its owners, its shareholders. As shown in Figure 1.1, to increase shareholder value, managers must pursue strategies that increase the profitability of the company *and* ensure that profits grow (for more details, see the Appendix to this chapter). To do this, a company must be able to outperform its rivals; it must have a competitive advantage.

■ Superior Performance

Maximizing shareholder value is the ultimate goal of profit-making companies, for two reasons. First, shareholders provide a company with the risk capital that enables managers to buy the resources needed to produce and sell goods and services. Risk capital is capital that cannot be recovered if a company fails and goes bankrupt. In the case of Wal-Mart, for example, shareholders provided Sam Walton's company with capital to build stores and distribution centers, invest in information systems, purchase inventory to sell to customers, and so on. Had Wal-Mart failed, its shareholders would have lost their money; their shares would have been worthless. Thus, shareholders will not provide risk capital unless they believe that managers are committed to pursuing strategies that give them a good return on their capital investment. Second, shareholders are the legal owners of a corporation, and, their shares therefore represent a claim on the profits generated by a company. Thus, managers have an obligation to invest those profits in ways that maximize shareholder value. Of course (as explained later in this book), managers *must* behave in a legal, ethical, and socially responsible manner while working to maximize shareholder value.

By **shareholder value**, we mean the returns that shareholders earn from purchasing shares in a company. These returns come from two sources: (a) capital appreciation in the value of a company's shares and (b) dividend payments. For example, between January 2 and December 31, 2003, the value of one share in the bank JPMorgan increased from $23.96 to $35.78, which represents a capital appreciation of $11.82. In addition, JPMorgan paid out a dividend of $1.30 a share during 2003. Thus, if an investor had bought one share of JPMorgan on January 2 and held on to it for the entire year, her return would have been $13.12 ($11.82 + $1.30), an impressive 54.8 percent return

FIGURE 1.1

Determinants of Shareholder Value

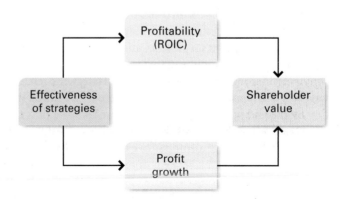

on her investment. One reason JPMorgan's shareholders did so well during 2003 was that investors came to believe that managers were pursuing strategies that would both increase the long-term profitability of the company and significantly grow its profits in the future.

One way of measuring the **profitability** of a company is by the return that it makes on the capital invested in the enterprise.[2] The return on invested capital (ROIC) that a company earns is defined as its net profit over the capital invested in the firm (profit/capital invested). By *net profit*, we mean net income after tax. By *capital*, we mean the sum of money invested in the company: that is, stockholders' equity plus debt owed to creditors. So defined, profitability is the result of how efficiently and effectively managers use the capital at their disposal to produce goods and services that satisfy customer needs. A company that uses its capital efficiently and effectively makes a positive return on invested capital.

The **profit growth** of a company can be measured by the increase in net profit over time. A company can grow its profits if it sells products in markets that are growing rapidly, gains market share from rivals, increases the amount it sells to existing customers, expands overseas, or diversifies profitably into new lines of business. For example, between 1994 and 2004 Wal-Mart increased its net profit from $2.68 billion to $10.1 billion. It was able to do this because the company (a) took market share from rivals such as Kmart, (b) established stores in nine foreign nations that collectively generated $41 billion in sales by 2004, and (c) entered the grocery business. Because of the increase in net profit, Wal-Mart's earnings per share increased from $0.59 to $2.35; as a result, each share became more valuable.

Together profitability and profit growth are the principal drivers of shareholder value (see the Appendix to this chapter for details). To both boost profitability and to grow profits over time, managers must formulate and implement strategies that give their company a competitive advantage over rivals. Wal-Mart's strategies have done this. As a result, investors who purchased Wal-Mart's stock in January 1994, when the shares were trading at $11 each, would have made a 500 percent return if they had held on to them through until December 2004, when they were trading at $55 each. By pursuing strategies that lead to high and sustained profitability and profit growth, Wal-Mart's managers have thus rewarded shareholders for their decisions to invest in the company.

One of the key challenges managers face is to simultaneously generate high profitability *and* increase the profits of the company. Companies that have high profitability but whose profits are not growing will not be as highly valued by shareholders as a company that has both high profitability and rapid profit growth (see the Appendix for details). At the same time, managers need to be aware that if they grow profits but profitability declines, that too will not be as highly valued by shareholders. What shareholders want to see, and what managers must try to deliver through strategic leadership, is *profitable growth*: that is, high profitability and sustainable profit growth. This is not easy, but some of the most successful enterprises of our era have achieved it—companies such as Dell, Microsoft, Intel, and Wal-Mart.

■ **Competitive Advantage and a Company's Business Model**

Managers do not make strategic decisions in a competitive vacuum. Their company is competing against other companies for customers. Competition is a rough-and-tumble process in which only the most efficient and effective companies win out. It is a race without end. To maximize shareholder value, managers must formulate and implement strategies that enable their company to outperform rivals—that give it a competitive advantage. A company is said to have a **competitive advantage** over its rivals when its profitability is greater than the average profitability of all other companies competing for the same set of customers. The higher its profitability relative to rivals, the greater its competitive advantage will be. A company has a **sustained competitive advantage** when its strategies enable it to maintain above-average profitability for a number of years. As discussed in the *Opening Case*, Wal-Mart had a significant and sustained competitive advantage over rivals such as Target, Costco, and Kmart between 1994 and 2003.

If a company has a sustained competitive advantage, it is likely to gain market share from its rivals, and thus grow its profits more rapidly than those of rivals. Thus, competitive advantage will also lead to higher profit growth than rivals.

The key to understanding competitive advantage is appreciating how the different strategies managers pursue over time can create activities that fit together to make a company unique or different from its rivals and able to persistently outperform them. A **business model** is managers' conception of how the set of strategies their company pursues should mesh together into a congruent whole, enabling the company to gain a competitive advantage and achieve superior profitability and profit growth. In essence, a business model is a kind of mental model, or gestalt, of how the various strategies and capital investments made by a company *should* fit together to generate above-average profitability and profit growth. A business model encompasses the totality of how a company will:

- Select its customers
- Define and differentiate its product offerings
- Create value for its customers
- Acquire and keep customers
- Produce goods or services
- Deliver those goods and services to the market
- Organize activities within the company
- Configure its resources
- Achieve and sustain a high level of profitability
- Grow the business over time

The business model at discount stores such as Wal-Mart, for example, is based on the idea that costs can be lowered by replacing a full-service retail format with a self-service format and providing a wider selection of products that are sold in a large-footprint store that contains minimal fixtures and fittings. These savings can then be passed on to consumers in the form of lower prices, which in turn grow revenues and help the company to achieve further cost reductions from economies of scale. Over time, this business model has proved superior to the business models adopted by smaller full-service mom-and-pop stores and by traditional high-service department stores such as Sears. The business model, known as the self-service supermarket business model, was first developed by grocery retailers in the 1950s and was later refined and improved by general merchandisers such as Wal-Mart. More recently, the same basic business model has been applied to toys (Toys "R" Us), office supplies (Staples, Office Depot), and home improvement supplies (Home Depot and Lowe's).

Wal-Mart outperformed close rivals, like Kmart, who adopted the same basic business model because Wal-Mart's strategies differed in key areas and because it implemented the business model more effectively. As a result, over time Wal-Mart created unique activities that have become the foundation of its competitive advantage. For example, Wal-Mart was one of the first retailers to make strategic investments in distribution centers and information systems, which lowered the costs of managing inventory (see the *Opening Case*). This gave Wal-Mart a competitive advantage over rivals such as Kmart, which suffered from poor inventory controls and thus higher costs. So although Wal-Mart and Kmart pursued a similar business model, key differences in the choice of strategies and the effectiveness of implementation created two unique organizations: one that attained a competitive advantage and one that ended up with a competitive disadvantage.

The business model that managers develop may not only lead to higher profitability and thus competitive advantage at a point in time, but it may also help the firm to grow its profits over time, thereby maximizing shareholder value while maintaining or even increasing profitability. Wal-Mart's business model was so efficient and effective that it enabled the company to take market share from rivals like Kmart and thereby increase its profits over time. In addition, Wal-Mart was able to grow profits further by applying its business model to new international markets and opening stores in nine different countries, as well as by adding groceries to its product mix in large Wal-Mart supercenters.

■ Industry Differences in Performance

It is important to recognize that in addition to its business model and associated strategies, a company's performance is also determined by the characteristics of the industry in which it competes. Different industries are characterized by different competitive conditions. In some, demand is growing rapidly, and in others it is contracting. Some might be beset by excess capacity and persistent price wars, others by excess demand and rising prices. In some, technological change might be revolutionizing competition. Others might be characterized by a lack of technological change. In some industries, high profitability among incumbent companies might induce new companies to enter the industry, and these new entrants might depress prices and profits in the industry. In other industries, new entry might be difficult, and periods of high profitability might persist for a considerable time. Thus, the different competitive conditions prevailing in different industries might lead to differences in profitability and profit growth. For example, average profitability might be higher in some industries and lower in other industries because competitive conditions vary from industry to industry.

Figure 1.2 shows the average profitability, measured by ROIC, among companies in several different industries between 1997 and 2003. The drug industry had a favorable competitive environment: demand for drugs was high and competition was generally not based on price. Just the opposite was the case in the steel and air transport industries: both are extremely price competitive. In addition, the steel industry was characterized by declining demand, excess capacity, and price wars. Exactly how industries differ is discussed in detail in Chapter 2. For now, the important point to remember is that the profitability and profit growth of a company are determined by two main factors: its relative success in its industry and the overall performance of its industry relative to other industries.[3]

■ Performance in Nonprofit Enterprises

A final point concerns the concept of superior performance in the nonprofit sector. By definition, nonprofit enterprises such as government agencies, universities, and charities are not in "business" to make profits. Nevertheless, they are expected to use their resources efficiently and operate effectively, and their managers set goals to

Return on Invested
Capital in Selected
Industries, 1997–2003

Data Source: Value Line Investment Survey.

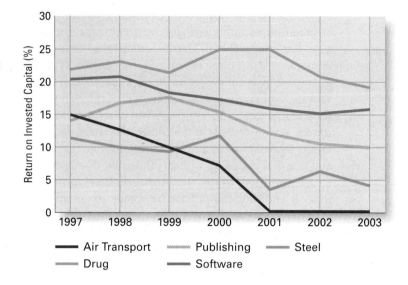

measure their performance. The performance goal for a business school might be to
get its programs ranked among the best in the nation. The performance goal for a
charity might be to prevent childhood illnesses in poor countries. The performance
goal for a government agency might be to improve its services while not exceeding
its budget. The managers of nonprofits need to map out strategies to attain these
goals. They also need to understand that nonprofits compete with each other for
scarce resources, just as businesses do. For example, charities compete for scarce donations, and their managers must plan and develop strategies that lead to high performance and demonstrate a track record of meeting performance goals. A successful strategy gives potential donors a compelling message as to why they should
contribute additional donations. Thus, planning and thinking strategically are as
important for managers in the nonprofit sector as they are for managers in profit-
seeking firms.

Strategic Managers

Managers are the lynchpin in the strategy-making process. It is individual managers
who must take responsibility for formulating strategies to attain a competitive advantage and for putting those strategies into effect. They must lead the strategy-making
process. The strategies that made Wal-Mart so successful were not chosen by some
abstract entity know as the company; they were chosen by the company's founder,
Sam Walton, and the managers he hired. Wal-Mart's success, like the success of any
company, was based in large part upon how well the company's managers performed
their strategic roles. In this section we look at the strategic roles of different managers. Later in the chapter we discuss strategic leadership, which is how managers can
effectively lead the strategy-making process.

In most companies, there are two main types of managers: **general managers**,
who bear responsibility for the overall performance of the company or for one of its
major self-contained subunits or divisions, and **functional managers**, who are re-

FIGURE 1.3

Levels of Strategic
Management

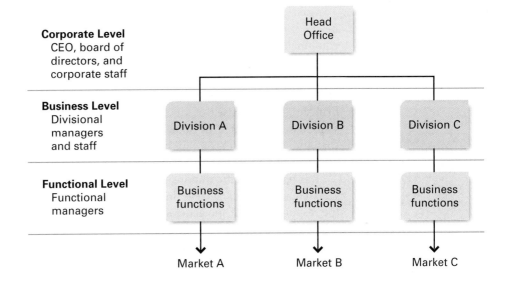

FIGURE 1.3

Levels of Strategic
Management

sponsible for supervising a particular function, that is, a task, activity, or operation, such as accounting, marketing, R&D, information technology, or logistics.

A company is a collection of functions or departments that work together to bring a particular product or service to the market. If a company provides several different kinds of products or services, it often duplicates these functions and creates a series of self-contained divisions (each of which contains its own set of functions) to manage each different product or service. The general managers of these divisions then become responsible for their particular product line. The overriding concern of general managers is for the health of the whole company or division under their direction; they are responsible for deciding how to create a competitive advantage and achieve high profitability with the resources and capital they have at their disposal. Figure 1.3 shows the organization of a **multidivisional company**, that is, a company that competes in several different businesses and has created a separate self-contained division to manage each of these. As you can see, there are three main levels of management: corporate, business, and functional. General managers are found at the first two of these levels, but their strategic roles differ depending on their sphere of responsibility.

■ **Corporate-Level Managers**

The corporate level of management consists of the chief executive officer (CEO), other senior executives, and corporate staff. These individuals occupy the apex of decision making within the organization. The CEO is the principal general manager. In consultation with other senior executives, the role of *corporate-level managers* is to oversee the development of strategies for the whole organization. This role includes defining the goals of the organization, determining what businesses it should be in, allocating resources among the different businesses, formulating and implementing strategies that span individual businesses, and providing leadership for the entire organization.

Consider General Electric as an example. GE is active in a wide range of businesses, including lighting equipment, major appliances, motor and transportation equipment, turbine generators, construction and engineering services, industrial electronics, medical systems, aerospace, aircraft engines, and financial services. The main strategic responsibilities of its CEO, Jeffrey Immelt, are setting overall strategic goals, allocating resources among the different business areas, deciding whether the firm should divest itself of any of its businesses, and determining whether it should acquire any new ones. In other words, it is up to Immelt to develop strategies that span individual businesses; his concern is with building and managing the corporate portfolio of businesses to maximize corporate profitability.

It is *not* his specific responsibility to develop strategies for competing in the individual business areas, such as financial services. The development of such strategies is the responsibility of the general managers in these different businesses, or *business-level managers*. However, it is Immelt's responsibility to probe the strategic thinking of business-level managers to make sure that they are pursuing robust business models and strategies that will contribute toward the maximization of GE's long-run profitability, to coach and motivate those managers, to reward them for attaining or exceeding goals, and to hold them to account for poor performance.

Corporate-level managers also provide a link between the people who oversee the strategic development of a firm and those who own it (the shareholders). Corporate-level managers, and particularly the CEO, can be viewed as the agents of shareholders.[4] It is their responsibility to ensure that the corporate and business strategies that the company pursues are consistent with maximizing profitability and profit growth. If they are not, then ultimately the CEO is likely to be called to account by the shareholders.

■ Business-Level Managers

A **business unit** is a self-contained division (with its own functions—for example, finance, purchasing, production, and marketing departments) that provides a product or service for a particular market. The principal general manager at the business level, or the business-level manager, is the head of the division. The strategic role of these managers is to translate the general statements of direction and intent that come from the corporate level into concrete strategies for individual businesses. Thus, whereas corporate-level general managers are concerned with strategies that span individual businesses, business-level general managers are concerned with strategies that are specific to a particular business. At GE, a major corporate goal is to be first or second in every business in which the corporation competes. Then the general managers in each division work out for their business the details of a business model that is consistent with this objective.

■ Functional-Level Managers

Functional-level managers are responsible for the specific business functions or operations (human resources, purchasing, product development, customer service, and so on) that constitute a company or one of its divisions. Thus, a functional manager's sphere of responsibility is generally confined to *one* organizational activity, whereas general managers oversee the operation of a *whole* company or division. Although they are not responsible for the overall performance of the organization, functional managers nevertheless have a major strategic role: to develop functional strategies in their area that help fulfill the strategic objectives set by business- and corporate-level general managers.

In GE's aerospace business, for instance, manufacturing managers are responsible for developing manufacturing strategies consistent with corporate objectives. Moreover, functional managers provide most of the information that makes it possible for business- and corporate-level general managers to formulate realistic and attainable strategies. Indeed, because they are closer to the customer than the typical general manager is, functional managers themselves may generate important ideas that subsequently may become major strategies for the company. Thus, it is important for general managers to listen closely to the ideas of their functional managers. An equally great responsibility for managers at the operational level is strategy implementation: the execution of corporate- and business-level plans.

The Strategy-Making Process

We can now turn our attention to the process by which managers formulate and implement strategies. Many writers have emphasized that strategy is the outcome of a formal planning process and that top management plays the most important role in this process.[5] Although this view has some basis in reality, it is not the whole story. As we shall see later in the chapter, valuable strategies often emerge from deep within the organization without prior planning. Nevertheless, a consideration of formal, rational planning is a useful starting point for our journey into the world of strategy. Accordingly, we consider what might be described as a typical formal strategic planning model for making strategy.

■ A Model of the Strategic Planning Process

The formal strategic planning process has five main steps:

1. Select the corporate mission and major corporate goals.

2. Analyze the organization's external competitive environment to identify *opportunities* and *threats*.

3. Analyze the organization's internal operating environment to identify the organization's *strengths* and *weaknesses*.

4. Select strategies that build on the organization's strengths and correct its weaknesses in order to take advantage of external opportunities and counter external threats. These strategies should be consistent with the mission and major goals of the organization. They should be congruent and constitute a viable business model.

5. Implement the strategies.

The task of analyzing the organization's external and internal environment and then selecting appropriate strategies constitutes strategy formulation. In contrast, as noted earlier, strategy implementation involves putting the strategies (or plan) into action. This includes taking actions consistent with the selected strategies of the company at the corporate, business, and functional levels, allocating roles and responsibilities among managers (typically through the design of organization structure), allocating resources (including capital and money), setting short-term objectives, and designing the organization's control and reward systems. These steps are illustrated in Figure 1.4 (which can also be viewed as a plan for the rest of this book).

Each step in Figure 1.4 constitutes a *sequential* step in the strategic planning process. At step 1, each round or cycle of the planning process begins with a statement of the corporate mission and major corporate goals. This statement is shaped by the existing business model of the company. The mission statement is followed by the foundation of strategic thinking: external analysis, internal analysis, and strategic choice. The strategy-making process ends with the design of the organizational structure and the culture and control systems necessary to implement the

Main Components of
the Strategic Planning
Process

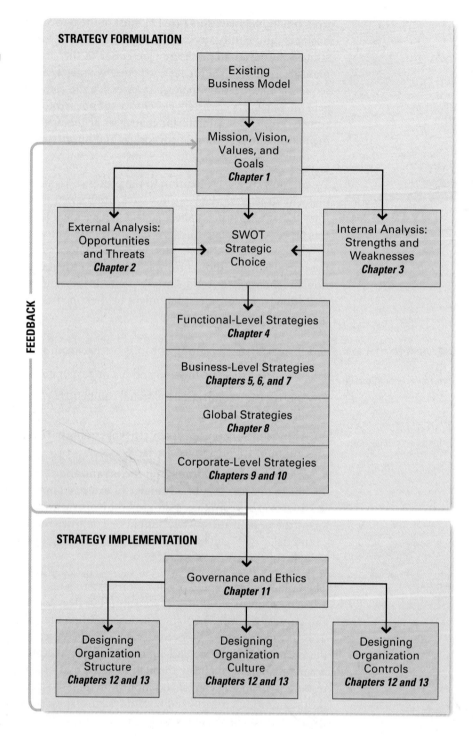

organization's chosen strategy. This chapter discusses how to select a corporate mission and choose major goals. Other parts of strategic planning are reserved for later chapters, as indicated in Figure 1.4.

Some organizations go through a new cycle of the strategic planning process every year. This does not necessarily mean that managers choose a new strategy each year. In many instances, the result is simply to modify and reaffirm a strategy and structure already in place. The strategic plans generated by the planning process generally look out over a period of one to five years, with the plan being updated, or *rolled forward*, every year. In most organizations, the results of the annual strategic planning process are used as input into the budgetary process for the coming year so that strategic planning is used to shape resource allocation within the organization. Strategy in Action 1.1 looks at how Microsoft uses strategic planning to drive its resource allocation decisions.

■ **Mission Statement**

The first component of the strategic management process is crafting the organization's mission statement, which provides the framework or context within which strategies are formulated. A mission statement has four main components: a statement of the *raison d'être* of a company or organization—its reason for existence—which is normally referred to as the *mission*; a statement of some desired future state, usually referred to as the *vision*; a statement of the key *values* that the organization is committed to; and a statement of *major goals*.

■ **The Mission** A company's **mission** describes what it is that the company does. For example, the mission of Kodak is to provide "customers with the solutions they need to capture, store, process, output, and communicate images—anywhere, anytime."[6] In other words, Kodak exists to provide imaging solutions to consumers. In its mission statement, Ford Motor Company describes itself as a company that is "passionately committed to providing personal mobility for people around the world.... We anticipate consumer need and deliver outstanding products and services that improve people's lives."[7] In short, Ford is a company that exists to satisfy consumer needs for personal mobility; that is its mission. Both of these missions focus on the customer needs that the company is trying to satisfy rather than on particular products (imaging and personal mobility rather than conventional film or cameras and automobiles). These are customer-oriented rather than product-oriented missions.

An important first step in the process of formulating a mission is to come up with a definition of the organization's business. Essentially, the definition answers these questions: "What is our business? What will it be? What should it be?"[8] The responses guide the formulation of the mission. To answer the question, "What is our business?" a company should define its business in terms of three dimensions: who is being satisfied (what customer groups), what is being satisfied (what customer needs), and how customers' needs are being satisfied (by what skills, knowledge, or distinctive competencies).[9] Figure 1.5 illustrates these dimensions.

This approach stresses the need for a *customer-oriented* rather than a *product-oriented* business definition. A product-oriented business definition focuses on the characteristics of the products sold and the markets served, not on which kinds of customer needs the products are satisfying. Such an approach obscures the company's true mission because a product is only the physical manifestation of applying a particular skill to satisfy a particular need for a particular customer group. In

Strategy in Action   1.1

Strategic Planning at Microsoft

There is a widespread belief that strategic planning does not apply to high-tech industries. "You can't plan for the unpredictable," the argument goes, "and technology markets are characterized by rapid and unpredictable change, so why bother with planning?" Nevertheless, the world's most successful high-tech company, Microsoft, has had a formal strategic planning process in place for many years. The genesis of Microsoft's planning process goes back to 1994 when the rapidly growing company hired Bob Herbold from Procter & Gamble as Microsoft's chief operations officer. Herbold was hired to bring some operating discipline to Microsoft's fluid, freewheeling culture but to do so without undermining the entrepreneurial values and passion for innovation that had made Microsoft so successful. Microsoft's top managers, Bill Gates and Steve Balmer, had been growing increasingly frustrated with the lack of operating efficiency and coherence at Microsoft, and they wanted to do something about it.

One area that Herbold focused on was strategic planning, which was almost nonexistent when he arrived. What did exist was "a rat's nest of incompatible planning approaches used by the different units and divisions.... Bill [Gates] wanted a more formal planning process because, as he said, 'We have no sense of where we will be in two years except for the product guys saying they have great new products coming along.'" At the very least, Gates felt that Microsoft needed some sense of its financial outlook for the next year or two that it could communicate to investors.

Herbold, Gates, and Balmer understood that any assumptions underlying a plan could be made invalid by unforeseen changes in the business environment, and such changes were commonplace in the software industry. At the same time, they acknowledged that Microsoft had some fairly traditional businesses with established revenue streams, such as Microsoft Office and Windows, and the company needed a plan for the future to craft a strategy for these businesses, focus product development efforts, and allocate resources to these businesses. Moreover, the company needed to plan for the future of its newer businesses, such as MSN, the videogame business (Xbox), and its hand-held computer business.

What has emerged at Microsoft is a three-year planning process that compares the subsequent performance of divisions and units against the strategies and goals outlined in the plan to determine future resource allocation. The planning process is built on a standard format that makes it easy to compare the performance data obtained from each of Microsoft's different businesses or divisions. Planning data include projections for market share, revenues, and profits three years into the future, as well as a statement of major strategies and goals. These projections are updated every year in a rolling plan because the industry changes so much.

Unit strategies are hashed out over the year in strategic planning review meetings between top managers (Gates and Balmer) and division managers. Typically, the unit managers develop strategies, and the top managers probe the strategic thinking of unit managers, asking them to justify their assumptions and ultimately approving, amending, or not approving the unit strategy. Unit strategies are also debated at regular strategy conferences, which Gates and Balmer normally attend.

The strategies that result from these processes are the product of an intense dialogue between top management and unit managers. Unit managers are held accountable for any commitments made in the plan. Thus, the plan not only drives resource allocation, it is also used as a control mechanism. Gates and Balmer determine the overall strategy of Microsoft in consultation with the board of directors, although many of the ideas for new businesses, new products, and acquisitions do not come from the top. Instead, they are proposed by employees within the units and approved if they survive scrutiny.

The planning process is formal, decentralized, and flexible. It is formal insofar as it is a regular process that uses standard information to help drive resource allocation for the coming year and holds managers accountable for their performance. It is decentralized insofar as unit managers propose many of the strategies that make up the plan, and those plans are accepted only after scrutiny by the top managers. It is flexible in that top managers do not see the plan as a straitjacket, but as a document that helps to map out where Microsoft may be going over the next few years. All managers recognize that the assumptions contained in the plan may be invalidated by unforeseen events, and they are committed to rapidly changing strategies if the need arises, as it has often in the past.[a]

FIGURE 1.5

Defining the Business

Source: D. F. Abell, *Defining the Business: The Starting Point of Strategic Planning* (Englewood Cliffs, N.J.: Prentice-Hall, 1980), p. 7.

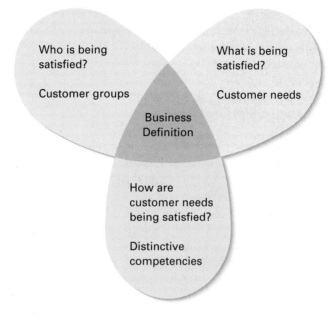

practice, that need may be served in many different ways, and a broad customer-oriented business definition that identifies these ways can safeguard companies from being caught unaware by major shifts in demand.

By helping anticipate demand shifts, a customer-oriented mission statement can also assist companies in capitalizing on changes in their environment. It can help answer the question, "What will our business be?" Kodak's mission statement—to provide "*customers* with the *solutions* they need to capture, store, process, output, and communicate images"—is a customer-oriented statement that focuses on customer needs rather than a particular product (or solution) for satisfying those needs, such as chemical film processing. For this reason, it is helping to drive Kodak's current investments in digital imaging technologies, which are starting to replace its traditional business based on chemical film processing.

The need to take a customer-oriented view of a company's business has often been ignored. History is littered with the wreckage of once-great corporations that did not define their business or defined it incorrectly so that ultimately they declined. In the 1950s and 1960s, many office equipment companies such as Smith Corona and Underwood defined their businesses as being the production of typewriters. This product-oriented definition ignored the fact that they were really in the business of satisfying customers' information-processing needs. Unfortunately for those companies, when a new technology came along that better served customer needs for information processing (computers), demand for typewriters plummeted. The last great typewriter company, Smith Corona, went bankrupt in 1996, a victim of the success of computer-based word-processing technology.

In contrast, IBM correctly foresaw what its business would be. In the 1950s, IBM was a leader in the manufacture of typewriters and mechanical tabulating equipment using punch-card technology. However, unlike many of its competitors, IBM defined its business as *providing a means for information processing and storage*, rather than just supplying mechanical tabulating equipment and typewriters.[10] Given this definition, the company's subsequent moves into computers, software systems, office systems, and printers seem logical.

■ **Vision** The **vision** of a company lays out some desired future state; it articulates, often in bold terms, what the company would like to achieve. The vision of Ford, for example, is "to become the world's leading consumer company for automotive products and services." This vision is challenging; judged by size, Ford is currently the world's number 3 company behind General Motors and Toyota. Attaining this vision will thus be a stretch for Ford, but that is the point. Good vision statements are meant to challenge a company by articulating some ambitious but attainable future state that will help to motivate employees at all levels and to drive strategies.[11]

Nokia, the world's largest manufacturer of mobile (wireless) phones, operates with a very simple but powerful vision: "If it can go mobile, it will!" This vision implies that not only will voice telephony go mobile (it already has), but so will a host of other services based on data, such as imaging and Internet browsing. This vision has led Nokia to develop multimedia mobile handsets that not only can be used for voice communication but that also take pictures, browse the Internet, play games, and manipulate personal and corporate information.

■ **Values** The **values** of a company state how managers and employees should conduct themselves, how they should do business, and what kind of organization they should build to help a company achieve its mission. Insofar as they help drive and shape behavior within a company, values are commonly seen as the bedrock of a company's **organizational culture**: the set of values, norms, and standards that control how employees work to achieve an organization's mission and goals. An organization's culture is commonly seen as an important source of its competitive advantage.[12] (We discuss the issue of organization culture in depth in Chapter 12.) For example, Nucor Steel is one of the most productive and profitable steel firms in the world. Its competitive advantage is based in part on the extremely high productivity of its work force, something, the company maintains, that is a direct result of its cultural values, which determine how it treats its employees. These values are as follow:

■ "Management is obligated to manage Nucor in such a way that employees will have the opportunity to earn according to their productivity."

■ "Employees should be able to feel confident that if they do their jobs properly, they will have a job tomorrow."

■ "Employees have the right to be treated fairly and must believe that they will be."

■ "Employees must have an avenue of appeal when they believe they are being treated unfairly."[13]

At Nucor, values emphasizing pay for performance, job security, and fair treatment for employees help to create an atmosphere within the company that leads to high employee productivity. In turn, this has helped to give Nucor one of the lowest cost structures in its industry, which helps to explain the company's profitability in a very price-competitive business.

In one study of organizational values, researchers identified a set of values associated with high-performing organizations that help companies achieve superior financial performance through their impact on employee behavior.[14] These values included respect for the interests of key organizational **stakeholders**: individuals or groups that have an interest, claim, or stake in the company, in what it does, and in how well it performs.[15] They include stockholders, bondholders, employees, customers, the communities in which the company does business, and the general public. The study found that deep respect for the interests of customers, employees, suppliers, and shareholders was associated with high performance. The study also noted that the encouragement of leadership and entrepreneurial behavior by mid- and lower-level managers and a willingness to support change efforts within the organization contributed to high performance. Companies found to emphasize such values consistently throughout their organization include Hewlett-Packard, Wal-Mart, and PepsiCo. The same study identified the values of poorly performing companies—values that, as might be expected, are *not* articulated in company mission statements: (1) arrogance, particularly to ideas from outside the company; (2) a lack of respect for key stakeholders; and (3) a history of resisting change efforts and "punishing" mid- and lower-level managers who showed "too much leadership." General Motors was held up as an example of one such organization. According to the authors, a mid- or lower-level manager who showed too much leadership and initiative there was not promoted!

■ **Major Goals** Having stated the mission, vision, and key values, strategic managers can take the next step in the formulation of a mission statement: establishing major goals. A **goal** is a *precise* and *measurable* desired future state that a company attempts to realize. In this context, the purpose of goals is to specify with precision what must be done if the company is to attain its mission or vision.

Well-constructed goals have four main characteristics:[16]

1. They are *precise and measurable*. Measurable goals give managers a yardstick or standard against which they can judge their performance.

2. They *address crucial issues*. To maintain focus, managers should select a limited number of major goals to assess the performance of the company. The goals that are selected should be crucial or important ones.

3. They are *challenging but realistic*. They give all employees an incentive to look for ways of improving the operations of an organization. If a goal is unrealistic in the challenges it poses, employees may give up; a goal that is too easy may fail to motivate managers and other employees.[17]

4. They *specify a time period* in which they should be achieved when that is appropriate. Time constraints tell employees that success requires a goal to be attained by a given date, not after that date. Deadlines can inject a sense of urgency into goal attainment and act as a motivator. However, not all goals require time constraints.

Well-constructed goals also provide a means by which the performance of managers can be evaluated.

As noted earlier, although most companies operate with a variety of goals, the central goal of most corporations is to maximize shareholder returns, and doing this requires both high profitability and sustained profit growth. Thus, most companies operate with goals for profitability and profit growth. However, it is important that top managers do not make the mistake of overemphasizing current profitability to the detriment of long-term profitability and profit growth.[18] The overzealous pursuit of current profitability to maximize short-term ROIC can encourage such misguided managerial actions as cutting expenditures judged to be nonessential in the short run—for instance, expenditures for research and development, marketing, and new capital investments. Although cutting current expenditure increases current profitability, the resulting underinvestment, lack of innovation, and diminished marketing can jeopardize long-run profitability and profit growth. These expenditures are vital if a company is to pursue its long-term mission and sustain its competitive advantage and profitability over time. Despite these negative consequences, managers may make such decisions because the adverse effects of a short-run orientation may not materialize and become apparent to shareholders for several years or because they are under extreme pressure to hit short-term profitability goals.[19] It is also worth noting that pressures to maximize short-term profitability may drive managers to act unethically. This apparently occurred during the late 1990s at Enron Corporation, Tyco, WorldCom, and Computer Associates, where managers systematically inflated profits by manipulating financial accounts in a manner that misrepresented the true performance of the firm to shareholders. (Chapter 11 provides a detailed discussion of the issues.)

To guard against short-run behavior, managers need to ensure that they adopt goals whose attainment will increase the long-run performance and competitiveness of their enterprise. Long-term goals are related to such issues as product development, customer satisfaction, and efficiency, and they emphasize specific objectives or targets concerning such things as employee and capital productivity, product quality, and innovation. The *Opening Case* mentioned how managers at Wal-Mart used information technology to track sales of individual items at individual stores; this information then enabled them to reduce inventory costs. To achieve long-run performance goals, Wal-Mart had to improve its efficiency, and reducing inventory was one of many steps in that direction. Only by paying constant attention to their processes and operations can companies improve their customer satisfaction, productivity, product quality, and innovation over the long run. Managers' ability to make the right decisions gives their companies a competitive advantage and boosts *long-term* performance. Both analysts and shareholders watch how well a company makes these decisions and attains its goals, and its stock price fluctuates according to the perception of how well it has succeeded. Positive shareholder perceptions boost stock price and help maximize the returns from holding a company's stock.

■ **External Analysis**

The second component of the strategic management process is an analysis of the organization's external operating environment. The essential purpose of the external analysis is to identify strategic *opportunities* and *threats* in the organization's operating environment that will affect how it pursues its mission. Three interrelated environments should be examined at this stage: the *industry environment* in which the company operates, the country or *national environment*, and the wider socioeconomic or *macroenvironment*.

Analyzing the industry environment requires an assessment of the competitive structure of the company's industry, including the competitive position of the company and its major rivals. It also requires analysis of the nature, stage, dynamics, and history of the industry. Because many markets are now global markets, analyzing the industry environment also means assessing the impact of globalization on competition within an industry. Such an analysis may reveal that a company should move some production facilities to another nation, that it should aggressively expand in emerging markets such as China, or that it should beware of new competition from emerging nations. Analyzing the macroenvironment consists of examining macroeconomic, social, government, legal, international, and technological factors that may affect the company and its industry.

■ Internal Analysis

Internal analysis, the third component of the strategic planning process, serves to pinpoint the *strengths* and *weaknesses* of the organization. Such issues as identifying the quantity and quality of a company's resources and capabilities and ways of building unique skills and company-specific or distinctive competencies are considered here when we probe the sources of competitive advantage. Building and sustaining a competitive advantage requires a company to achieve superior efficiency, quality, innovation, and responsiveness to its customers. Company strengths lead to superior performance in these areas, whereas company weaknesses translate into inferior performance.

■ SWOT Analysis and the Business Model

The next component of strategic thinking requires the generation of a series of strategic alternatives, or choices of future strategies to pursue, given the company's internal strengths and weaknesses and its external opportunities and threats. The comparison of **s**trengths, **w**eaknesses, **o**pportunities, and **t**hreats is normally referred to as a **SWOT analysis**.[20] Its central purpose is to identify the strategies that will create a company-specific business model that will best *align, fit,* or *match* a company's resources and capabilities to the demands of the environment in which it operates. Managers compare and contrast the various alternative possible strategies against each other and then identify the set of *strategies* that will create and sustain a competitive advantage:

- *Functional-level strategy,* directed at improving the effectiveness of operations within a company, such as manufacturing, marketing, materials management, product development, and customer service

- *Business-level strategy,* which encompasses the business's overall competitive theme, the way it positions itself in the marketplace to gain a competitive advantage, and the different positioning strategies that can be used in different industry settings—for example, *cost leadership, differentiation, focusing on a particular niche or segment of the industry,* or some *combination* of these

- *Global strategy,* addressing how to expand operations outside the home country to grow and prosper in a world where competitive advantage is determined at a global level

- *Corporate-level strategy,* which answers the primary questions: What business or businesses should we be in to maximize the long-run profitability and profit growth of the organization, and how should we enter and increase our presence in these businesses to gain a competitive advantage?

The strategies identified through a SWOT analysis should be congruent with each other. Thus, functional-level strategies should be consistent with, or support, the company's business-level strategy and global strategy. Moreover, as we explain later in this book, corporate-level strategies should support business-level strategies. When taken together, the various strategies pursued by a company constitute a viable business model. In essence a SWOT analysis is a methodology for choosing between competing business models and for fine-tuning the business model that managers choose. Thus, at Wal-Mart a SWOT analysis might be used to fine-tune and improve aspects of the self-service supermarket business model. In contrast, when Microsoft entered the videogame market with its Xbox offering, it had to settle on the best business model for competing in this market. Microsoft used a SWOT type of analysis to compare alternatives and settled on a "razor and razor blades" business model in which the Xbox console is priced below cost to build sales (the "razor"), while profits are made from royalties on the sale of games for the Xbox (the "blades").

■ Strategy Implementation

Having chosen a set of congruent strategies to achieve a competitive advantage and increase performance, managers must put those strategies into action: Strategy has to be implemented. Strategy implementation involves taking actions at the functional, business, and corporate levels to execute a strategic plan. Thus implementation can include, for example, putting quality improvement programs into place, changing the way a product is designed, positioning the product differently in the marketplace, segmenting the marketing and offering different versions of the product to different consumer groups, implementing price increases or decreases, expanding through mergers and acquisitions, or downsizing the company by closing down or selling off parts of the company. These and other topics are discussed in detail in Chapters 4 through 10.

Strategy implementation also entails designing the best organization structure and the best culture and control systems to put a chosen strategy into action. In addition, senior managers need to put a governance system in place to make sure that all within the organization act in a manner that is not only consistent with maximizing profitability and profit growth but also legal and ethical. In this book we look at the topic of governance and ethics in Chapter 11, we discuss the organization structure, culture, and controls required to implement business-level strategies in Chapter 12, and the structure, culture, and controls required to implement corporate-level strategies in Chapter 13.

■ The Feedback Loop

The feedback loop in Figure 1.4 indicates that strategic planning is ongoing; it *never* ends. Once a strategy has been implemented, its execution must be monitored to determine the extent to which strategic goals and objectives are actually being achieved and to what degree competitive advantage is being created and sustained. This information and knowledge pass back up to the corporate level through feedback loops and become the input for the next round of strategy formulation and implementation. Top managers can then decide whether to reaffirm the existing business model and the existing strategies and goals or suggest changes for the future. For example, if a strategic goal proves too optimistic, the next time a more conservative goal is set. Or feedback may reveal that the business model is not working, so managers may seek ways to change it.

Strategy as an Emergent Process

The basic planning model suggests that a company's strategies are the result of a plan, that the strategic planning process itself is rational and highly structured, and that the process is orchestrated by top management. Several scholars have criticized the formal planning model for three main reasons: the unpredictability of the real world, the role that lower-level managers can play in the strategic management process, and the fact that many successful strategies are often the result of serendipity, not rational strategizing. They have advocated an alternative view of strategy making.[21]

■ **Strategy Making in an Unpredictable World**

Critics of formal planning systems argue that we live in a world in which uncertainty, complexity, and ambiguity dominate, and in which small chance events can have a large and unpredictable impact on outcomes.[22] In such circumstances, they claim, even the most carefully thought out strategic plans are prone to being rendered useless by rapid and unforeseen change. In an unpredictable world, there is a premium on being able to respond quickly to changing circumstances and to alter the strategies of the organization accordingly.

A dramatic example of this occurred in 1994 and 1995 when Microsoft CEO Bill Gates shifted the company strategy after the unanticipated emergence of the World Wide Web (see Strategy in Action 1.2). According to critics of formal systems, such a flexible approach to strategy making is not possible within the framework of a traditional strategic planning process, with its implicit assumption that an organization's strategies need to be reviewed only during the annual strategic planning exercise.

■ **Autonomous Action: Strategy Making by Lower-Level Managers**

Another criticism leveled at the rational planning model of strategy is that too much importance is attached to the role of top management, particularly the CEO.[23] An alternative view now gaining wide acceptance is that individual managers deep within an organization can and often do exert a profound influence over the strategic direction of the firm.[24] Writing with Robert Burgelman of Stanford University, Andy Grove, the former CEO of Intel, noted that many important strategic decisions at Intel were initiated not by top managers but by the **autonomous action** of lower-level managers deep within Intel who, on their own initiative, formulated new strategies and worked to persuade top-level managers to alter the strategic priorities of the firm.[25] These strategic decisions included the decision to exit an important market (the DRAM memory chip market) and to develop a certain class of microprocessors (RISC-based microprocessors) in direct contrast to the stated strategy of Intel's top managers. Strategy in Action 1.2 details how autonomous action by two young employees drove the evolution of Microsoft's strategy toward the Internet. In addition, the prototype for another Microsoft product, the Xbox videogame system, was developed by four lower-level engineering employees on their own initiative. They then successfully lobbied top managers to dedicate resources toward commercializing their prototype. Another famous example of autonomous action, in this case at 3M, is given in Strategy in Action 1.3.

Autonomous action may be particularly important in helping established companies deal with the uncertainty created by the arrival of a radical new technology that changes the dominant paradigm in an industry.[26] Top managers usually rise to preeminence by successfully executing the established strategy of the firm. Therefore, they may have an emotional commitment to the status quo and are often unable to see things from a different perspective. In this sense, they are a conservative force that promotes inertia. Lower-level managers, however, are less likely to have the same commitment to the status quo and have more to gain from promoting new technologies and strategies. They may be the ones to first recognize new strategic opportunities (as was the case at both Microsoft and 3M) and lobby for strategic change.

Strategy in Action

1.2

A Strategic Shift at Microsoft

The Internet has been around since the 1970s, but prior to the early 1990s, it was a drab place, lacking the color, content, and richness of today's environment. What changed the Internet from a scientific tool to a consumer-driven media environment was the invention of hypertext markup language (HTML) and the related invention of a browser for displaying graphics-rich webpages based on HTML. The combination of HTML and browsers effectively created the World Wide Web (WWW). This was an unforeseen development.

A young programmer at the University of Illinois in 1993, Mark Andreesen, had developed the first browser, known as Mosaic. In 1994, he left Illinois and joined a start-up company, Netscape, which produced an improved browser, the Netscape Navigator, along with software that enabled organizations to create webpages and host them on computer servers. These developments led to a dramatic and unexpected growth in the number of people connecting to the Internet. In 1990, the Internet had 1 million users. By early 1995, the number had exceeded 80 million and was growing exponentially.

Prior to the emergence of the Web, Microsoft did have a strategy for exploiting the Internet, but it was one that emphasized set-top boxes, video on demand, interactive TV, and an online service, MSN, modeled after AOL and based on proprietary standards. In early 1994, Gates received e-mails from two young employees, Jay Allard and Steve Sinofsky, who argued that Microsoft's current strategy was misguided and ignored the rapidly emerging

Web. In companies with a more hierarchical culture, such action might have been ignored, but in Microsoft, which operates as a meritocracy in which good ideas trump hierarchical position, it produced a very different response. Gates convened a meeting of senior executives in April 1994 and then wrote a memo to senior executives arguing that the Internet represented a sea change in computing and that Microsoft had to respond.

What ultimately emerged was a 180-degree shift in Microsoft's strategy. Interactive TV was placed on the back burner, and MSN was relaunched as a Web service based on HTML. Microsoft committed to developing its own browser technology and within a few months had issued Internet Explorer to compete with Netscape's Navigator (the underlying technology was gained by an acquisition). Microsoft licensed Java, a computer language designed to run programs on the Web, from a major competitor, Sun Microsystems. Internet protocols were built into Windows 95 and Windows NT, and Gates insisted that henceforth Microsoft's applications, such as the ubiquitous Office, embrace the WWW and have the ability to convert documents into an HTML format. The new strategy was given its final stamp on December 7, 1995, Pearl Harbor Day, when Gates gave a speech arguing that the Internet was now pervasive in everything Microsoft was doing. By then, Microsoft had been pursuing the new strategy for a year. In short, Microsoft quickly went from a proprietary standards approach to one that embraced the public standards on the WWW.[b]

■ **Serendipity and Strategy**

Business history is replete with examples of accidental events that help to push companies in new and profitable directions. What these examples suggest is that many successful strategies are not the result of well-thought-out plans but of serendipity, that is, of stumbling across good things unexpectedly. One such example occurred at 3M during the 1960s. At that time, 3M was producing fluorocarbons for sale as coolant liquid in air-conditioning equipment. One day, a researcher working with fluorocarbons in a 3M lab spilled some of the liquid on her shoes. Later that day when she spilled coffee over her shoes, she watched with interest as the coffee formed into little beads of liquid and then ran off her shoes without leaving a stain. Reflecting on this phenomenon, she realized that a fluorocarbon-based liquid might turn out to be useful for protecting fabrics from liquid stains, and so the idea for Scotch Guard was born. Subsequently, Scotch Guard became one of 3M's most profitable

Strategy in Action   1.3

The Genesis of Autonomous Action at 3M

In the 1920s, the Minnesota Mining and Manufacturing Company (3M) was a small manufacturer of sandpaper. Its best-selling product, wet-and-dry sandpaper, was introduced in 1921 and was sold primarily to automobile companies, which used it to sand auto bodies between paint coats because it produced a smooth finish. A problem with wet and dry, however, was that the grit did not always stay bound to the sandpaper, and bits of grit that had detached from the paper could ruin an otherwise perfect paint job. To deal with this problem in the early 1920s, the CEO, a young William McKnight, hired 3M's first research scientist, Richard Drew. Drew was straight out of college; this was his first job. McKnight charged Drew with developing a stronger adhesive to better bind the grit to the paper backing.

While experimenting with adhesives, Drew developed a weak adhesive that had an interesting quality: if placed on the back of a strip of paper and stuck to a surface, the strip of paper could be peeled off the surface it was adhered to without leaving any adhesive residue on that surface. This serendipitous discovery gave Drew an epiphany. He had been visiting auto body paint shops to see how 3M's sandpaper was used and noticed a problem with paint running. His epiphany was to cover the back of a strip of paper with his weak adhesive and use it as "masking tape" to cover parts of the auto body that were not to be painted. An excited Drew took his idea to McKnight and explained how masking tape might create an entirely new business for 3M. McKnight reminded Drew that he had been hired to fix a specific problem and pointedly suggested that he concentrate on doing that and not on dreaming up other business ideas.

Chastised, Drew went back to his lab but could not get the idea out of his mind, so he continued to work on it at night, long after everyone else had gone home. He succeeded in perfecting the masking tape product and then went to visit several auto body shops to show them his innovation. He quickly received several commitments for orders. Drew then went to McKnight again. He told him that he had continued to work on the masking tape idea on his own time, had perfected the product, and had several customers interested in purchasing it. This time it was McKnight's turn to be chastised. Realizing that he had almost killed a good business idea, McKnight reversed his original position and gave Drew the go-ahead to pursue the idea.

Sticky tape subsequently became a huge business for 3M. Moreover, McKnight went on to become a long-serving CEO and then chairman of 3M's board until 1966. Drew became the chief science officer and also served until the 1960s. Together they helped build 3M and shaped its organization culture. One of the main principles of that culture came out of the original incident between Drew and McKnight: top management should "delegate responsibility and encourage men and women to exercise their initiative." According to McKnight, as business grows, "it becomes increasingly necessary to delegate responsibility and to encourage men and women to exercise their initiative…. Mistakes will be made. But if a person is essentially right, the mistakes he or she makes are not as serious in the long run as the mistakes management will make if it undertakes to tell those in authority exactly how they must do their jobs…. Management that is destructively critical when mistakes are made kills initiative. And it's essential that we have many people with initiative if we are to continue to grow." Based on their own experience, McKnight and Drew established a culture at 3M that encourages autonomous action.[c]

products and took the company into the fabric protection business, an area it had never planned to participate in.[27]

Serendipitous discoveries and events can open up all sorts of profitable avenues for a company. But some companies have missed out on profitable opportunities because serendipitous discoveries or events were inconsistent with their prior (planned) conception of what their strategy should be. In one of the classic examples of such myopia, a century ago the telegraph company Western Union turned down an opportunity to purchase the rights to an invention made by Alexander Graham

Bell. The invention was the telephone, a technology that subsequently made the telegraph obsolete.

Intended and Emergent Strategies

Henry Mintzberg's model of strategy development provides a more encompassing view of what strategy actually is. According to this model, illustrated in Figure 1.6, a company's *realized strategy* is the product of whatever planned strategies are actually put into action (the company's deliberate strategies) *and* of any unplanned, or emergent, strategies. In Mintzberg's view, many planned strategies are not implemented because of unpredicted changes in the environment (they are unrealized). **Emergent strategies** are the unplanned responses to unforeseen circumstances. They arise from autonomous action by individual managers deep within the organization, from serendipitous discoveries or events, or from an unplanned strategic shift by top-level managers in response to changed circumstances. They are *not* the product of formal top-down planning mechanisms.

Mintzberg maintains that emergent strategies are often successful and may be more appropriate than intended strategies. Richard Pascale has described how this was the case for the entry of Honda Motor Co. into the U.S. motorcycle market.[28] When a number of Honda executives arrived in Los Angeles from Japan in 1959 to establish a U.S. operation, their original aim (intended strategy) was to focus on selling 250-cc and 350-cc machines to confirmed motorcycle enthusiasts rather than 50-cc Honda Cubs, which were a big hit in Japan. Their instinct told them that the Honda 50s were not suitable for the U.S. market, where everything was bigger and more luxurious than in Japan.

However, sales of the 250-cc and 350-cc bikes were sluggish, and the bikes themselves were plagued by mechanical failure. It looked as if Honda's strategy was going to fail. At the same time, the Japanese executives who were using the Honda 50s to run errands around Los Angeles were attracting a lot of attention. One day they got a

FIGURE 1.6

Emergent and Deliberate Strategies

Data Source: Adapted from H. Mintzberg and A. McGugh, *Administrative Science Quarterly,* Vol. 30. No. 2, June 1985.

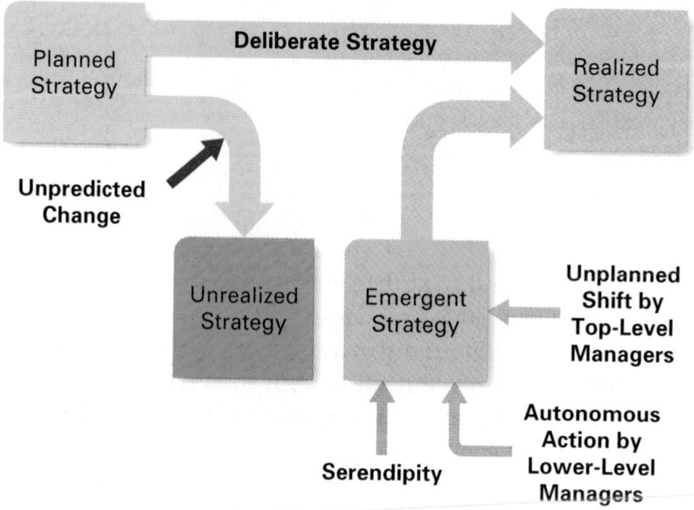

call from a Sears, Roebuck buyer who wanted to sell the 50-cc bikes to a broad market of Americans who were not necessarily motorcycle enthusiasts. The Honda executives were hesitant to sell the small bikes for fear of alienating serious bikers, who might then associate Honda with "wimpy" machines. In the end, however, they were pushed into doing so by the failure of the 250-cc and 350-cc models.

Honda had stumbled onto a previously untouched market segment that was to prove huge: the average American who had never owned a motorbike. Honda had also found an untried channel of distribution: general retailers rather than specialty motorbike stores. By 1964, nearly one out of every two motorcycles sold in the United States was a Honda.

The conventional explanation for Honda's success is that the company redefined the U.S. motorcycle industry with a brilliantly conceived *intended* strategy. The fact was that Honda's intended strategy was a near disaster. The strategy that *emerged* did so not through planning but through unplanned action in response to unforeseen circumstances. Nevertheless, credit should be given to the Japanese management for recognizing the strength of the emergent strategy and for pursuing it with vigor.

The critical point demonstrated by the Honda example is that successful strategies can often emerge within an organization without prior planning in response to unforeseen circumstances. As Mintzberg has noted, strategies can take root virtually wherever people have the capacity to learn and the resources to support that capacity.

In practice, the strategies of most organizations are probably a combination of the intended (planned) and the emergent. The message for management is that it needs to recognize the process of emergence and to intervene when appropriate, killing off bad emergent strategies but nurturing potentially good ones.[29] To make such decisions, managers must be able to judge the worth of emergent strategies. *They must be able to think strategically.* Although emergent strategies arise from within the organization without prior planning—that is, without going through the steps illustrated in Figure 1.4 in a *sequential* fashion—top management still has to evaluate emergent strategies. Such evaluation involves comparing each emergent strategy with the organization's goals, external environmental opportunities and threats, and internal strengths and weaknesses. The objective is to assess whether the emergent strategy fits the company's needs and capabilities. In addition, Mintzberg stresses that an organization's capability to produce emergent strategies is a function of the kind of corporate culture that the organization's structure and control systems foster. In other words, the different components of the strategic management process are just as important from the perspective of emergent strategies as they are from the perspective of intended strategies.

Strategic Planning in Practice

Despite criticisms, research suggests that formal planning systems do help managers make better strategic decisions. A study that analyzed the results of twenty-six previously published studies came to the conclusion that, on average, strategic planning has a positive impact on company performance.[30] Another study of strategic planning in 656 firms found that formal planning methodologies and emergent strategies both form part of a good strategy formulation process, particularly in an unstable environment.[31] For strategic planning to work, it is important that top-level managers plan not just in the context of the *current* competitive environment but also in the context of the *future* competitive environment. To try to forecast what that future will look like, managers can use scenario planning techniques to plan for different possible futures. They can also involve operating managers in the planning process and seek to shape the future competitive environment by emphasizing strategic intent.

■ **Scenario Planning**

One reason that strategic planning may fail over the long run is that strategic managers, in their initial enthusiasm for planning techniques, may forget that the future is inherently unpredictable. Even the best-laid plans can fall apart if unforeseen contingencies occur, and that happens all the time in the real world. The recognition that uncertainty makes it difficult to forecast the future accurately led planners at Royal Dutch Shell to pioneer the *scenario approach* to planning.

In the scenario approach, managers are given a set of possible future scenarios for the development of competition in their industry. Some scenarios are optimistic and some pessimistic, and then teams of managers are asked to develop specific strategies to cope with each different scenario. A set of industry-specific indicators are chosen and used as signposts to track the development of the industry and to determine the probability that any particular scenario is coming to pass. The idea is to get managers to understand the dynamic and complex nature of their environment, think through problems in a strategic fashion, and generate a range of strategic options that might be pursued under different circumstances.[32]

The scenario approach to planning has spread rapidly among large companies. According to one survey, over 50 percent of the *Fortune 500* companies use some form of scenario planning.[33]

■ **Decentralized Planning**

A serious mistake that some companies have made in constructing their strategic planning process has been to treat planning as an exclusively top management responsibility. This *ivory tower* approach can result in strategic plans formulated in a vacuum by top managers who have little understanding or appreciation of current operating realities. Consequently, top managers may formulate strategies that do more harm than good. For example, when demographic data indicated that houses and families were shrinking, planners at GE's appliance group concluded that smaller appliances were the wave of the future. Because they had little contact with home builders and retailers, they did not realize that kitchens and bathrooms were the two rooms that were *not* shrinking. Nor did they appreciate that working women wanted big refrigerators to cut down on trips to the supermarket. GE ended up wasting a lot of time designing small appliances with limited demand.

The ivory tower concept of planning can also lead to tensions between corporate-, business-, and functional-level managers. The experience of GE's appliance group is again illuminating. Many of the corporate managers in the planning group were recruited from consulting firms or top-flight business schools. Many of the functional managers took this pattern of recruitment to mean that corporate managers did not think they were smart enough to think through strategic problems for themselves. They felt shut out of the decision-making process, which they believed to be unfairly constituted. Out of this perceived lack of procedural justice grew an us-versus-them mindset that quickly escalated into hostility. As a result, even when the planners were right, operating managers would not listen to them. For example, the planners correctly recognized the importance of the globalization of the appliance market and the emerging Japanese threat. However, operating managers, who then saw Sears Roebuck as the competition, paid them little heed.

Finally, ivory tower planning ignores the important strategic role of autonomous action by lower-level managers and serendipity.

Correcting the ivory tower approach to planning requires recognizing that successful strategic planning encompasses managers at *all* levels of the corporation. Much of the best planning can and should be done by business and functional managers who are closest to the facts; in other words, planning should be decentralized. The role of corporate-level planners should be that of *facilitators* who help business and functional managers do the planning by setting the broad strategic goals of the organization and providing the resources required to identify the strategies that might be required to attain those goals.

It is not enough to involve lower-level managers in the strategic planning process, however; they also need to perceive that the decision-making process is fair, a concept that Chan Kim and Renee Mauborgne refer to as *procedural justice*.[34] If people perceive the decision-making process to be unjust, they are less likely to be committed to any resulting decisions and to cooperate voluntarily in activities designed to implement those decisions. Consequently, the strategy chosen might fail for lack of support among those who must implement it at the operating level.

■ Strategic Intent

The formal strategic planning model has been characterized as the *fit model* of strategy making. This is because it attempts to achieve a fit between the internal resources and capabilities of an organization and external opportunities and threats in the industry environment. Gary Hamel and C. K. Prahalad have criticized the fit model because it can lead to a mindset in which management focuses too much on the degree of fit between the *existing* resources of a company and *current* environmental opportunities, and not enough on building *new* resources and capabilities to create and exploit *future* opportunities.[35] Strategies formulated with only the present in mind, argue Prahalad and Hamel, tend to be more concerned with today's problems than with tomorrow's opportunities. As a result, companies that rely exclusively on the fit approach to strategy formulation are unlikely to be able to build and maintain a competitive advantage. This is particularly true in a dynamic competitive environment, where new competitors are continually arising and new ways of doing business are constantly being invented.

As Prahalad and Hamel note, again and again, companies using the fit approach have been surprised by the ascent of competitors that initially seemed to lack the resources and capabilities needed to make them a real threat. This happened to Xerox, which ignored the rise of Canon and Ricoh in the photocopier market until they had become serious global competitors; to General Motors, which initially overlooked the threat posed by Toyota and Honda in the 1970s; and to Caterpillar, which ignored the danger Komatsu posed to its heavy earthmoving business until it was almost too late to respond.

The secret of the success of companies like Toyota, Canon, and Komatsu, according to Prahalad and Hamel, is that they all had bold ambitions that outstripped their existing resources and capabilities. All wanted to achieve global leadership, and they set out to build the resources and capabilities that would enable them to attain this goal. Consequently, top management created an obsession with winning at all levels of the organization that they sustained over a ten- to twenty-year quest for global leadership. It is this obsession that Prahalad and Hamel refer to as **strategic intent**. They stress that strategic intent is more than simply unfettered ambition. It encompasses an active management process, which includes "focusing the organization's attention on the essence of winning; motivating people by communicating the value of the target; leaving room for individual and team contributions; sustaining enthusiasm by providing new operational definitions as circumstances change; and using intent consistently to guide resource allocations."[36]

Thus, underlying the concept of strategic intent is the notion that strategic planning should be based on setting an ambitious vision and ambitious goals that stretch a company and then finding ways to build the resources and capabilities necessary to attain that vision and those goals. As Prahalad and Hamel note, in practice the two approaches to strategy formulation are not mutually exclusive. All the components of the strategic planning process that we discussed earlier (see Figure 1.4) are important.

In addition, say Prahalad and Hamel, the strategic management process should begin with a challenging vision, such as attaining global leadership, that stretches the organization. Throughout the subsequent process, the emphasis should be on finding ways (strategies) to develop the resources and capabilities necessary to achieve these goals rather than on exploiting *existing* strengths to take advantage of *existing* opportunities. The difference between strategic fit and strategic intent, therefore, may just be one of emphasis. Strategic intent is more internally focused and is concerned with building new resources and capabilities. Strategic fit focuses more on matching existing resources and capabilities to the external environment.

Strategic Decision Making

Even the best-designed strategic planning systems will fail to produce the desired results if managers do not use the information at their disposal effectively. Consequently, it is important that strategic managers learn to make better use of the information they have and understand why they sometimes make poor decisions. One important way in which managers can make better use of their knowledge and information is to understand how common cognitive biases can result in good managers making bad decisions.[37]

■ Cognitive Biases and Strategic Decision Making

The rationality of human decision makers is bounded by our own cognitive capabilities.[38] We are not supercomputers, and it is difficult for us to absorb and process large amounts of information effectively. As a result, when making decisions, we tend to fall back on certain rules of thumb, or heuristics, that help us to make sense out of a complex and uncertain world. However, sometimes these rules lead to severe and systematic errors in the decision-making process.[39] Systematic errors are those that appear time and time again. They seem to arise from a series of **cognitive biases** in the way that human decisionmakers process information and reach decisions. Because of cognitive biases, many managers end up making poor strategic decisions.

A number of biases have been verified repeatedly in laboratory settings, so we can be reasonably sure that they exist and that we are all prone to them.[40] The **prior hypothesis bias** refers to the fact that decisionmakers who have strong prior beliefs about the relationship between two variables tend to make decisions on the basis of these beliefs, even when presented with evidence that their beliefs are wrong. Moreover, they tend to seek and use information that is consistent with their prior beliefs, while ignoring information that contradicts these beliefs. To put this bias in a strategic context, it suggests that a CEO who has a strong prior belief that a certain strategy makes sense might continue to pursue that strategy, despite evidence that it is inappropriate or failing.

Another well-known cognitive bias, **escalating commitment**, occurs when decisionmakers, having already committed significant resources to a project, commit even more resources even if they receive feedback that the project is failing.[41] This may be an irrational response; a more logical response would be to abandon the project and move on (that is, to cut your losses and run), rather than escalate commitment. Feelings of personal responsibility for a project apparently induce decision-makers to stick with a project despite evidence that it is failing.

A third bias, **reasoning by analogy**, involves the use of simple analogies to make sense out of complex problems. The problem with this heuristic is that the analogy may not be valid. A fourth bias, **representativeness**, is rooted in the tendency to generalize from a small sample or even a single vivid anecdote. This bias violates the statistical law of large numbers, which says that it is inappropriate to generalize from a small sample, let alone from a single case. In many respects, the dot-com boom of the late 1990s was based on reasoning by analogy and representativeness. Prospective entrepreneurs saw some of the early dot-com companies such Amazon and Yahoo! achieve rapid success, at least judged by some metrics. Reasoning by analogy from a very small sample, they assumed that any dot-com could achieve similar success. Many investors reached similar conclusions. The result was a massive wave of start-ups that jumped into the Internet space in an attempt to capitalize on the perceived opportunities. That the vast majority of these companies subsequently went bankrupt is testament to the fact that the analogy was wrong and the success of the small sample of early entrants was no guarantee that all dot-coms would succeed.

The final cognitive bias is referred to as the **illusion of control**: the tendency to overestimate one's ability to control events. General or top managers seem to be particularly prone to this bias: having risen to the top of an organization, they tend to be overconfident about their ability to succeed. According to Richard Roll, such overconfidence leads to what he has termed the *hubris hypothesis* of takeovers.[42] Roll argues that top managers are typically overconfident about their ability to create value by acquiring another company. Hence, they end up making poor acquisition decisions, often paying far too much for the companies they acquire. Subsequently, servicing the debt taken on to finance such an acquisition makes it all but impossible to make money from the acquisition.

■ Groupthink and Strategic Decisions

Because most strategic decisions are made by groups, the group context within which decisions are made is clearly an important variable in determining whether cognitive biases will operate to adversely affect the strategic decision-making process.

The psychologist Irvin Janis has argued that many groups are characterized by a process known as groupthink and as a result make poor strategic decisions.[43] **Groupthink** occurs when a group of decisionmakers embarks on a course of action without questioning underlying assumptions. Typically, a group coalesces around a person or policy. It ignores or filters out information that can be used to question the policy and develops after-the-fact rationalizations for its decision. Commitment to the mission or goals becomes based on an emotional rather than an objective assessment of the "correct" course of action. The consequences can be poor decisions.

This phenomenon may explain, at least in part, why companies often make poor strategic decisions in spite of sophisticated strategic management. Janis traced many historical fiascoes to defective policymaking by government leaders who received social support from their in-group of advisers. For example, he suggested that President John F. Kennedy's inner circle suffered from groupthink when the members of this group supported the decision to launch the Bay of Pigs invasion of Cuba in 1961, even though available information showed that it would be an unsuccessful venture and would damage U.S. relations with other countries. Janis has observed that groupthink-dominated groups are characterized by strong pressures toward uniformity, which make their members avoid raising controversial issues, questioning weak arguments, or calling a halt to soft-headed thinking. As discussed in Strategy in Action 1.4, the Senate Intelligence Committee believed that groupthink biased CIA and other reports on Iraq's weapons of mass destruction that the Bush Administration subsequently used to justify the 2003 invasion of that nation.

■ Techniques for Improving Decision Making

The existence of cognitive biases and groupthink raises the issue of how to bring critical information to bear on the decision-making mechanism so that a company's strategic decisions are realistic and based on thorough evaluation. Two techniques known to enhance strategic thinking and counteract groupthink and cognitive biases are devil's advocacy and dialectic inquiry (Figure 1.7).[44] **Devil's advocacy** requires the generation of both a plan and a critical analysis of the plan. One member of the decision-making group acts as the devil's advocate, bringing out all the reasons that might make the proposal unacceptable. In this way, decisionmakers can become aware of the possible perils of recommended courses of action.

Dialectic inquiry is more complex, for it requires the generation of a plan (a thesis) and a counterplan (an antithesis) that reflect *plausible but conflicting* courses of

Strategy in Action   1.4

Was Intelligence on Iraq Biased by Groupthink?

In October 2002 intelligence agencies in the United States issued a National Intelligence Estimate on Iraq's efforts to procure and build weapons of mass destruction (WMDs). The report concluded that there was good evidence that Iraq was actively pursuing a nuclear weapons program and, furthermore, had tried to procure uranium for its bomb-making efforts from the African nation of Niger. In addition, the report claimed that Iraq was stockpiling chemical weapons, including mustard, saran, and nerve gas, and was actively pursuing a research program to produce biological weapons, including anthrax and smallpox viruses. The report was used by the Bush administration to help justify the 2003 invasion of Iraq, which culminated in the removal of Saddam Hussein's regime. The report also helped convince the U.S. Senate that Iraq was violating United Nations conditions imposed after the first Gulf War in 1991. On the basis of this intelligence, seventy-five senators voted to authorize the 2003 war.

By late 2003, however, it was becoming increasingly apparent that if there were WMDs in Iraq, they were very few in number and extremely well hidden. Had the pre-war intelligence been wrong? In mid 2004, the Senate Intelligence Committee published a report evaluating the information contained in the October 2002 National Intelligence Estimate. The findings of the Senate report were endorsed by all seventeen members of the committee, nine Republicans and eight Democrats. In total, they constituted a damning indictment of the prewar intelligence provided by the CIA and others to the Bush administration and Congress.

The Senate report concluded that a "groupthink" dynamic inside American intelligence agencies generated a "collective presumption that Iraq had an active and growing weapons program." This internal bias, according to the senators, prompted analysts, collectors, and managers in the CIA and other agencies to "interpret ambiguous evidence as being conclusively indicative of a WMD program as well as ignore or minimize evidence that Iraq did not have active or expanding weapons of mass destruction programs." As a consequence, most of the key judgments in the October 2002 National Intelligence Estimate were "either overstated, or were not supported by the underlying intelligence reporting."

One of the most critical parts of the Senate report dealt with the prewar assessment of Iraq's nuclear weapons program. The report stated that the 2002 National Intelligence Estimate represented a sharp break from previous assessments, which had concluded that Iraq had not reconstituted its nuclear weapons program. The Senate report stated that the CIA made a significant shift in its assessment shortly after Vice President Dick Cheney began stating publicly that Iraq had actively reconstituted its nuclear weapons program. The implication was that the CIA gave the administration the information it thought it wanted, rather than accurate information. Moreover, the Senate report claimed that the CIA's leading advocate of the Iraqi nuclear weapons threat withheld evidence from analysts who disagreed with him, misstated the analysis and information produced by others, and distributed misleading information both inside and outside the agency. The committee also concluded that the CIA overstated what it knew about Iraq's attempts to procure uranium from Niger and that it delayed for months examining documents pertaining to those attempts that would later prove to be forgeries.

On the topic of biological weapons, the Senate report concluded that none of the claims about Iraq's biological weapons or capabilities was supported by intelligence and that claims that Iraq had restarted its chemical weapons program were the results of "analytical judgments" and not based on hard evidence. The intelligence on biological weapons came from a single Iraqi defector code-named "Curve Ball" who was apparently an alcoholic and, in the opinion of the one person who had interviewed him, a Pentagon analyst, "utterly useless as a source." When the same analyst saw information provided by Curve Ball included in a speech that Colin Powell made to the United Nations to justify war with Iraq, he contacted the CIA to express his concerns. A CIA official quickly responded in an e-mail: "Let's keep in mind the fact that this war's going to happen regardless of what Curve Ball said or didn't say. The powers that be probably aren't terribly interested in whether Curve Ball knows what he is talking about."

In sum, the Senate report painted a picture of intelligence institutions that selectively interpreted information to support what they thought administration policy was, while ignoring or dismissing contradictory information—sure signs of groupthink. At the same time, the report concluded that there was no evidence of undue political pressure by policymakers in the administration or Congress. Instead, the committee blamed intelligence leaders "who did not encourage analysts to challenge their assumptions, fully consider alternative arguments, accurately characterize the intelligence reporting, or council analysts who lost their objectivity." Be this as it may, an objective observer might also wonder why neither the Senate nor the administration asked hard questions about the quality and source of the intelligence information in the run-up to the war.[d]

action.[45] Strategic managers listen to a debate between advocates of the plan and counterplan and then decide which plan will lead to the higher performance. The purpose of the debate is to reveal the problems with definitions, recommended courses of action, and assumptions of both plans. As a result of this exercise, strategic managers are able to form a new and more encompassing conceptualization of the problem, which then becomes the final plan (a synthesis). Dialectic inquiry can promote strategic thinking.

Another technique for countering cognitive biases is the outside view, which has been championed by Nobel Prize winner Daniel Kahneman and his associates.[46] The **outside view** requires planners to identify a reference class of analogous past strategic initiatives, determine whether those initiatives succeeded or failed, and evaluate the project at hand against those prior initiatives. According to Kahneman, this technique is particularly useful for countering biases such as the illusion of control (hubris), reasoning by analogy, and representativeness. Thus, for example, when considering a potential acquisition, planners should look at the track record of acquisitions made by other enterprises (the reference class), determine if they succeeded or failed, and objectively evaluate the potential acquisition against that reference class.

FIGURE 1.7

Processes for
Improving Decision
Making

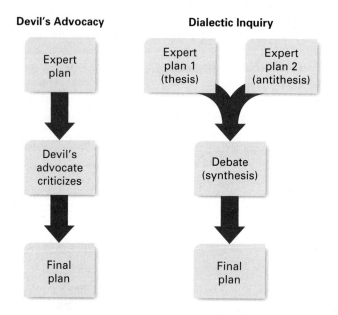

Devil's Advocacy

Expert
plan

↓

Devil's
advocate
criticizes

↓

Final
plan

Dialectic Inquiry

Expert
plan 1
(thesis)

Expert
plan 2
(antithesis)

↓

Debate
(synthesis)

↓

Final
plan

Kahneman argues that such a "reality check" against a large sample of prior events tends to constrain the inherent optimism of planners and produce more realistic assessments and plans.

Strategic Leadership

One of the key strategic roles of both general and functional managers is to use all their knowledge, energy, and enthusiasm to provide strategic leadership for their subordinates and develop a high-performing organization. Several authors have identified a few key characteristics of good strategic leaders that do lead to high performance: (1) vision, eloquence, and consistency; (2) articulation of a business model; (3) commitment; (4) being well informed; (5) willingness to delegate and empower; (6) astute use of power; and (7) emotional intelligence.[47]

■ Vision, Eloquence, and Consistency

One of the key tasks of leadership is to give an organization a sense of direction. Strong leaders seem to have a clear and compelling vision of where the organization should go, are eloquent enough to communicate this vision to others within the organization in terms that energize people, and consistently articulate their vision until it becomes part of the organization's culture.[48]

In the political arena, John F. Kennedy, Winston Churchill, Martin Luther King Jr., and Margaret Thatcher have all been held up as examples of visionary leaders. Think of the impact of Kennedy's sentence, "Ask not what your country can do for you, ask what you can do for your country," of King's "I Have a Dream" speech, and of Churchill's "we will never surrender." Kennedy and Thatcher were able to use their political office to push for governmental actions that were consistent with their vision. Churchill's speech galvanized a nation to defend itself against an aggressor, and King was able to pressure the government from outside to make changes in society.

Examples of strong business leaders include Microsoft's Bill Gates; Jack Welch, the former CEO of General Electric; and Sam Walton, Wal-Mart's founder. For years, Bill Gates's vision of a world in which there would be a Windows-based personal computer on every desk was a driving force at Microsoft. More recently, the vision has evolved into one of a world in which Windows-based software can be found on any computing device, from PCs and servers to videogame consoles (Xbox), cell phones, and hand-held computers. At GE, Jack Welch was responsible for articulating the simple but powerful vision that GE should be first or second in every business in which it competed, or exit from that business. Similarly, it was Sam Walton who established and articulated the vision that has been central to Wal-Mart's success: passing on cost savings from suppliers and operating efficiencies to customers in the form of everyday low prices.

■ **Articulation of the Business Model**

Another key characteristic of good strategic leaders is their ability to identify and articulate the business model the company will use to attain its vision. A business model is managers' conception of how the various strategies that the company pursues fit together into a congruent whole. At Wal-Mart, for example, it was Sam Walton who identified and articulated the basic business model of the company: the self-service supermarket business model. The various strategies that Wal-Mart has pursued over the years have refined this basic model, creating one that is now unique in terms of its efficiency and effectiveness. Although individual strategies can take root in many different places in an organization, and although their identification is not the exclusive preserve of top management, only strategic leaders have the perspective required to make sure that the various strategies fit together into a congruent whole and form a valid and compelling business model. If strategic leaders lack a clear conception of what the business model of the company is or should be, it is likely that the strategies the firm pursues will not fit together, and the result will be lack of focus and poor performance.

■ **Commitment**

Strong leaders demonstrate their commitment to their vision and business model by actions and words, and they often lead by example. Consider Nucor's former CEO, Ken Iverson. Nucor is a very efficient steel maker with perhaps the lowest cost structure in the steel industry. It has turned in thirty years of profitable performance in an industry where most other companies have lost money because of a relentless focus on cost minimization. In his tenure as CEO, Iverson set the example: he answered his own phone, employed only one secretary, drove an old car, flew coach class, and was proud of the fact that his base salary was the lowest of the *Fortune 500* CEOs (Iverson made most of his money from performance-based pay bonuses). This commitment was a powerful signal to employees that Iverson was serious about doing everything possible to minimize costs. It earned him the respect of Nucor employees and made them more willing to work hard. Although Iverson has retired, his legacy lives on in the cost-conscious organization culture that has been built at Nucor, and like all other great leaders, his impact will last beyond his tenure.

■ **Being Well Informed**

Effective strategic leaders develop a network of formal and informal sources who keep them well informed about what is going on within their company. Herb Kelleher at Southwest Airlines, for example, was able to find out much about the health of his company by dropping in unannounced on aircraft maintenance facilities and helping workers perform their tasks; McDonald's Ray Kroc and Wal-Mart's Sam Walton routinely dropped in unannounced to visit their restaurants and stores. Using informal and unconventional ways to gather information is wise because formal channels can be captured by special interests within the organization or by gatekeepers, managers who may misrepresent the true state of affairs to the leader, such as may have happened at Enron. People like Kelleher who constantly interact with employees at all levels are better able to build informal information networks than leaders who closet themselves and never interact with lower-level employees.

■ Willingness to Delegate and Empower

High-performance leaders are skilled at delegation. They recognize that unless they learn how to delegate effectively, they can quickly become overloaded with responsibilities. They also recognize that empowering subordinates to make decisions is a good motivation tool and often results in decisions being made by those who must implement them. At the same time, astute leaders recognize that they need to maintain control over certain key decisions. Thus, although they will delegate many *important* decisions to lower-level employees, they will not delegate those that they judge to be of *critical importance* to the future success of the organization, such as articulating the company's vision and business model.

■ The Astute Use of Power

In a now classic article on leadership, Edward Wrapp noted that effective leaders tend to be very astute in their use of power.[49] He argued that strategic leaders must often play the power game with skill and attempt to build consensus for their ideas rather than use their authority to force ideas through; they must act as members of a coalition or its democratic leaders rather than as dictators. Jeffery Pfeffer has articulated a similar vision of the politically astute manager who gets things done in organizations through the intelligent use of power.[50] In Pfeffer's view, power comes from control over resources that are important to the organization: budgets, capital, positions, information, and knowledge. Politically astute managers use these resources to acquire another critical resource: critically placed allies who can help them attain their strategic objectives. Pfeffer stresses that one does not need to be a CEO to assemble power in an organization. Sometimes quite junior functional managers can build a surprisingly effective power base and use it to influence organizational outcomes.

■ Emotional Intelligence

Emotional intelligence is a term that Daniel Goldman coined to describe a bundle of psychological attributes that many strong and effective leaders exhibit:[51]

- Self-awareness—the ability to understand one's own moods, emotions, and drives, as well as their effect on others

- Self-regulation—the ability to control or redirect disruptive impulses or moods, that is, to think before acting

- Motivation—a passion for work that goes beyond money or status and a propensity to pursue goals with energy and persistence

- Empathy—the ability to understand the feelings and viewpoints of subordinates and to take those into account when making decisions

- Social skills—friendliness with a purpose

According to Goldman, leaders who possess these attributes—who exhibit a high degree of emotional intelligence—tend to be more effective than those who lack these attributes. Their self-awareness and self-regulation help to elicit the trust and confidence of subordinates. In Goldman's view, people respect leaders who, because they are self-aware, recognize their own limitations and, because they are self-regulating, consider decisions carefully. Goldman also argues that self-aware and self-regulating individuals tend to be more self-confident and therefore better able to cope with ambiguity and more open to change. A strong motivation exhibited in a passion for work can also be infectious, helping to persuade others to join together in pursuit of a common goal or organizational mission. Finally, strong empathy and social skills can help leaders earn the loyalty of subordinates. Empathetic and socially adept individuals tend to be skilled at managing disputes between managers, better able to find common ground and purpose among diverse constituencies, and better able to move people in a desired direction than leaders who lack these skills. In short, Goldman argues that the psychological makeup of a leader matters.

Summary of Chapter

1. A strategy is an action that a company takes to attain one or more of its goals.

2. The major goal of companies is to maximize the returns that shareholders get from holding shares in the company. To maximize shareholder value, managers must pursue strategies that result in high and sustained profitability and also in profit growth.

3. The profitability of a company can be measured by the return that it makes on the capital invested in the enterprise. The profit growth of a company can be measured by the growth in earnings per share. Profitability and profit growth are determined by the strategies managers adopt.

4. A company has a competitive advantage over its rivals when it is more profitable than the average for all firms in its industry. It has a sustained competitive advantage when it is able to maintain above-average profitability over a number of years. In general, a company with a competitive advantage will grow its profits more rapidly than rivals.

5. General managers are responsible for the overall performance of the organization or for one of its major self-contained divisions. Their overriding strategic concern is for the health of the total organization under their direction.

6. Functional managers are responsible for a particular business function or operation. Although they lack general management responsibilities, they play a very important strategic role.

7. Formal strategic planning models stress that an organization's strategy is the outcome of a rational planning process.

8. The major components of the strategic management process are defining the mission, vision, and major goals of the organization; analyzing the external and internal environments of the organization; choosing a business model and strategies that align an organization's strengths and weaknesses with external environmental opportunities and threats; and adopting organizational structures and control systems to implement the organization's chosen strategies.

9. Strategy can emerge from deep within an organization in the absence of formal plans as lower-level managers respond to unpredicted situations.

10. Strategic planning often fails because executives do not plan for uncertainty and because ivory tower planners lose touch with operating realities.

11. The fit approach to strategic planning has been criticized for focusing too much on the degree of fit between existing resources and current opportunities, and not enough on building new resources and capabilities to create and exploit future opportunities.

12. Strategic intent refers to an obsession with achieving an objective that stretches the company and requires it to build new resources and capabilities.

13. In spite of systematic planning, companies may adopt poor strategies if their decision-making processes are vulnerable to groupthink and if individual cognitive biases are allowed to intrude into the decision-making process.

14. Devil's advocacy, dialectic inquiry, and the outside view are techniques for enhancing the effectiveness of strategic decision making.

15. Good leaders of the strategy-making process have a number of key attributes: vision, eloquence, and consistency; ability to craft a business model; commitment; being well informed; a willingness to delegate and empower; political astuteness; and emotional intelligence.

Discussion Questions

1. What do we mean by *strategy*? How is a business model different from a strategy?
2. What do you think are the sources of sustained superior profitability?
3. Between 1997 and 2004 Microsoft's ROIC fell from 32 percent to 17.5 percent. Over the same period, Microsoft's profits grew from $3.45 billion to $11.33 billion. How can a company have declining profitability (as measured by ROIC) but growing profits? What do you think explains this situation at Microsoft? For 2004, analysts predicted that Microsoft's ROIC would jump to 35 percent. Why do you think this was the case? Was it due to any change in the company's strategy?
4. What are the strengths of formal strategic planning? What are its weaknesses?
5. Discuss the accuracy of this statement: Formal strategic planning systems are irrelevant for firms competing in high-technology industries where the pace of change is so rapid that plans are routinely made obsolete by unforeseen events.
6. Pick the current or a past president of the United States and evaluate his performance against the leadership characteristics discussed in the text. On the basis of this comparison, do you think that the president was/is a good strategic leader? Why?

Practicing Strategic Management

■ SMALL-GROUP EXERCISE
Designing a Planning System

Break up into groups of three to five people each, and discuss the following scenario. Appoint one group member as a spokesperson for the group, who will communicate your findings to the class when called on to do so by the instructor.

You are a group of senior managers working for a fast-growing computer software company. Your product allows users to play interactive role-playing games over the Internet. In the past three years, your company has gone from being a start-up enterprise with 10 employees and no revenues to a company with 250 employees and revenues of $60 million. It has been growing so rapidly that you have not had time to create a strategic plan, but now your board of directors is telling you that they want to see a plan, and they want it to drive decision making and resource allocation at the company. They want you to design a planning process that will have the following attributes:

1. It will be democratic, involving as many key employees as possible in the process.
2. It will help to build a sense of shared vision within the company about how to continue to grow rapidly.
3. It will lead to the generation of three to five key strategies for the company.
4. It will drive the formulation of detailed action plans, and these plans will be subsequently linked to the company's annual operating budget.

Design a planning process to present to your board of directors. Think carefully about who should be included in this process. Be sure to outline the strengths and weaknesses of the approach you choose, and be prepared to justify why your approach might be superior to alternative approaches.

■ ARTICLE FILE 1

At the end of every chapter in this book is an article file task. The task requires you to search newspapers or magazines in the library for an example of a real company that satisfies the task question or issue.

Your first article file task is to find an example of a company that has recently changed its strategy. Identify whether this change was the outcome of a formal planning process or whether it was an emergent response to unforeseen events occurring in the company's environment.

■ STRATEGIC MANAGEMENT PROJECT
Module 1

To give you practical insight into the strategic management process, we provide a series of strategic modules; one is at the end of every chapter in this book. Each module asks you to collect and analyze information relating to the material discussed in that chapter. By completing these strategic modules, you will gain a clearer idea of the overall strategic management process.

The first step in this project is to pick a company to study. We recommend that you focus on the same company throughout the book. Remember also that we will be asking you for information about the corporate and international strategy of your company, as well as its structure. We strongly recommend that you pick a company for which such information is likely to be available.

There are two approaches that can be used to select a company to study, and your instructor will tell you which one to follow. The first approach is to pick a well-known company that has a lot of information written about it. For example, large publicly held companies such as IBM, Microsoft, and Southwest Airlines are routinely covered in the business and financial press. By going to the library at your university, you should be able to track down a great deal of information on such companies. Many libraries now have comprehensive Web-based electronic data search facilities such as *ABI/ Inform*, the *Wall Street Journal Index*, the *F&S Index*, and the *Nexis-Lexis* databases. These enable you to identify any article that has been written in the business press on the company of your choice within the past few years. A number of nonelectronic data sources are also available and useful. For example, *F&S Predicasts* publishes an annual list of articles relating to major companies that appeared in the national and international business press. *S&P Industry Surveys* is also a great source for basic industry data, and *Value Line Ratings and Reports* contains good summaries of a firm's financial position and future prospects. Collect full financial information on the company that you pick. This can be accessed from Web-based electronic databases such as the Edgar database, which archives all forms that publicly quoted companies have to file with the Securities and Exchange Commission (SEC); for example, 10-K filings can be accessed from the SEC's Edgar database. Most SEC forms for public companies can now be accessed from Internet-based financial sites, such as Yahoo!'s finance site (**www.finance.yahoo.com/**).

A second approach is to pick a smaller company in your city or town to study. Although small companies are not routinely covered in the national business press, they may be covered in the local press. More important, this approach can work well if the management of the company will agree to talk to you at length about the strategy and structure of the company. If you happen to know somebody in such a company or if you have worked there at some point, this approach can be very worthwhile. However, we *do not* recommend this approach unless you can get a *substantial* amount of guaranteed access to the company of your choice. If in doubt, ask your instructor before making a decision. The key issue is to make sure that you have access to enough interesting information to complete a detailed and comprehensive analysis.

Your assignment for Module 1 is to choose a company to study and to obtain enough information about it to carry out the following instructions and answer the questions:

1. Give a short account of the history of the company, and trace the evolution of its strategy. Try to determine whether the strategic evolution of your company is the product of intended strategies, emergent strategies, or some combination of the two.
2. Identify the mission and major goals of the company.
3. Do a preliminary analysis of the internal strengths and weaknesses of the company and the opportunities and threats that it faces in its environment. On the basis of this analysis, identify the strategies that you think the company should pursue. (You will need to perform a much more detailed analysis later in the book.)
4. Who is the CEO of the company? Evaluate the CEO's leadership capabilities.

■ EXPLORING THE WEB
Visiting 3M

Go to the website of 3M (**www.3m.com**) and visit the section that describes its history (**www.3m.com/profile/looking/index.jhtml**). Using the information contained there, map out the evolution of strategy at 3M from its establishment to the present day. To what degree do you think that this evolution was the result of detailed long-term strategic planning, and to what degree was it the result of unplanned actions taken in response to unpredictable circumstances?

General Task Search the Web for a company site with sufficient information to map out the evolution of that company's strategy over a significant period of time. What drove this evolution? To what degree was it the result of detailed long-term strategic planning, and to what degree the result of unplanned actions taken in response to unpredictable circumstances?

Closing Case

Shattered Dreams: Level 3 Communications

In 1996 Jim Crowe sold MFS Communications, the local exchange telecommunications company that he had built up from scratch, to WorldCom for $14.3 billion. As part of that sale, WorldCom got MFS's UUNet, which at the time was the owner of the largest fiber-optic network in the nation. The business at UUNet was booming, primarily because of explosive growth in the Internet and a surge in the volume of digital data that was pumped through UUNet's fiber-optic pipes. As for Jim Crowe, at over $150 million his take from the sale of MFS elevated him to the ranks of the superrich. He had no reason to ever work again, but Jim Crowe was not the kind of man to sit back and relax. He wanted back in the game. Like many others at the time, he was convinced that the growth of the Internet was the mother of all business opportunities.

In 1997, Crowe's belief seemed to get validation when UUNet's chief scientist, Michael O'Dell, stated that Internet traffic was doubling every hundred days. This implied a growth rate of over 1,000 percent a year. O'Dell went on to say that there was not enough fiber-optic capacity to go around and that "demand will far outstrip supply for the foreseeable future." Electrified by the potential opportunity, Crowe quickly established a company to build a state-of-the-art fiber-optic network. Called Level 3 Communications, the company was funded by a number of wealthy investors, including Crowe and Walter Scott Jr., an Omaha-based construction billionaire, Crowe's former boss, and a close friend of the legendary investor Warren Buffet. Scott himself had been dazzled by a talk given by Microsoft's Bill Gates in 1995 in which Gates stated that "the Internet was going to radically change the world." Moreover, Scott had funded the establishment of MFS Communications, which started off its life as a subsidiary of Scott's construction company. Not surprisingly, Scott saw Crowe as a strategic visionary.

With Crowe as CEO and Scott as chairman, Level 3 quickly raised $3 billion. In 1998 the company went public and immediately started building its fiber-optic network. By 2001, Level 3 had raised some $13 billion, much of it in the form of debt. Crowe had a very clear strategic plan. The goal was to raise money, rapidly build a high-capacity fiber-optic network that linked major cities in the United States, and then cut prices to attract demand from major users of fiber-optic networks, including corporations, Internet service providers like AOL, and

traditional telecommunications companies. Crowe believed that demand for his network would be highly price elastic: a 1 percent cut in price would increase demand significantly more than 1 percent. He argued that if he cut prices, revenues would surge, quickly using the massive capacity that Level 3 was putting in the ground. Crowe was also a big advocate of strategic focus, believing that Level 3 should concentrate exclusively on carrying Internet traffic for service providers and corporations. The business model was straightforward: Since most of the costs of the business were fixed (the costs of building out the network), profitability would be highly leveraged to volume. Once the fixed costs were covered, it would be like printing money.

Level 3 was not alone. Around the same time there was a rush of companies entering the business or expanding their networks, including 360 Networks, Global Crossing, Qwest Communications, WorldCom, Williams Communications Group, Genuity Inc., and XO Communications. In all cases, the strategic plans were remarkably similar: raise the money, build the networks, cut prices, and they will come. Surging demand would soon catch up with capacity, resulting in a profit bonanza for those who had the foresight to build out their networks. It was a gold rush, and the first into the field would stake the best claims.

However, there were dissenting voices. As early as October 1998 an Internet researcher at AT&T Labs named Andrew Odlyzko published a paper that debunked the assertion that demand for Internet traffic was growing at 1,000 percent a year. Odlyzko's careful analysis came to the conclusion that growth was much slower, only 100 percent a year. While still large, that growth rate was not nearly large enough to fill the massive flood of fiber-optic capacity that was entering the market. Moreover, Odlyzko noted that new technologies were increasing the amount of data that could be sent down existing fibers, reducing the need for new fiber. But with investment money flooding into the market, few paid any attention to him. UUNet was still using the 1,000 percent figure as late as September 2000.

As it turned out, Odlyzko was right. Capacity rapidly outstripped demand, and by late 2002 less than 3 percent of the fiber that had been laid in the ground was actually being used. While prices tumbled, the surge in volume that Crowe had bet on did not materialize. Unable to service the debt they had taken on to build out their networks, company after company tumbled into bankruptcy, including WorldCom, 360 Networks, XO Communications, and Global Crossing. Level 3's stock fell by more than 95 percent, but the company avoided bankruptcy because of an infusion of $500 million in cash from a group of investors led by Warren Buffet and some quick-footed work by Jim Crowe.

Crowe's strategic shift involved the purchase of two software distribution companies, Software Spectrum and Corporate Software, that specialized in selling, installing, and maintaining software made by companies such as Microsoft on the PCs and servers of some nine thousand corporate clients. The logic underlying the acquisitions was that Level 3 could ultimately use its fiber-optic network to distribute and maintain the software, as opposed to doing that manually, thereby reducing costs. While neither business was profitable, Crowe was able to use the acquisitions to convince investors that Level 3 still had a viable long-term strategic vision. At the same time, with the balance sheet strengthened by a cash infusion, Level 3 purchased a bankrupt competitor, Genuity, for under $300 million, helping to consolidate the industry and acquiring Genuity's customers. Finally, in early 2004 Level 3 announced that it would use its network to offer Voice over Internet Protocol services to consumers and corporations (voice telephone calls over the Internet, as opposed to over a traditional telecommunications network), thereby taking aim at the market currently dominated by traditional wire line telephone companies.

While none of these strategic moves guarantees the survival of Level 3, the trends are encouraging. Revenues expanded to $4 billion in 2003, up from $1.53 billion in 2002, while losses fell from $4.4 billion in 2002 to $721 million in 2003. Half of 2003 revenues came from the software distribution business. Crowe still believes that ultimately his original vision will be vindicated but that the current industry structure is unsustainable and there are still too many suppliers in the marketplace. Andrew Odlyzko, who debunked the original estimates of Internet growth, believes that the excess capacity situation in the industry will not be resolved until the end of the current decade.[52]

Case Discussion Questions

1. What was the planned strategy of Level 3 Communications in the late 1990s?

2. Why was Level 3 Communications able to raise so much capital?

3. Was that strategy unrealized, or is it still part of the intended strategy of the firm?

4. What have been the emergent strategies of Level 3 over the last few years? How do these emergent strategies fit with Level 3's original plans?

5. Were any cognitive biases at work at Level 3, other communications companies, and the investment community during 1997–2001? What were those biases? What were the effects of those biases? How might an entrepreneur like Jim Crowe have avoided them?

Appendix to Chapter 1

Enterprise Valuation, ROIC, and Growth

The ultimate goal of strategy is to maximize the value of a company to its shareholders (subject to the important constraints that this is done in a legal, ethical, and socially responsible manner). The two main drivers of enterprise valuation are return on invested capital (**ROIC**) and the growth rate of profits, g.[53]

ROIC is defined as net operating profits less adjusted taxes (NOPLAT) over the invested capital of the enterprise (IC), where IC is the sum of the company's equity and debt (the method for calculating adjusted taxes need not concern us here). That is:

$$\text{ROIC} = \text{NOPLAT/IC}$$

Where

$$\begin{aligned} \text{NOPLAT} = \text{ } & \text{revenues} - \text{cost of goods sold} \\ & - \text{operating expenses} \\ & - \text{depreciation charges} \\ & - \text{adjusted taxes} \end{aligned}$$

$$\text{IC} = \text{value of shareholders' equity} + \text{value of debt}$$

The growth rate of profits, g, can be defined as the percentage increase in net operating profits (NOPLAT) over a given time period. More precisely:

$$g = [(\text{NOPLAT}_{t+1} - \text{NOPLAT}_t)/\text{NOPLAT}_t] \times 100$$

Note that if NOPLAT is increasing over time, earnings per share will also increase so long as (a) the number of shares stays constant, or (b) the number of shares outstanding increases more slowly than NOPLAT.

The valuation of a company can be calculated using discounted cash flow analysis and applying it to future expected free cash flows (free cash flow in a period is defined as NOPLAT − net investments).

It can be shown that the valuation of a company so calculated is related to the company's weighted average cost of capital (WACC), which is the cost of the equity and debt that the firm uses to finance its business, and the company's ROIC. Specifically:

If ROIC > WACC, the company is earning more than its cost of capital and it is creating value.

If ROIC = WACC, the company is earning its cost of capital and its valuation will be stable.

If ROIC < WACC, the company is earning less than its cost of capital and it is therefore destroying value.

A company that earns more than its cost of capital is even more valuable if it can grow its net operating profits less adjusted taxes (NOPLAT) over time. Conversely, a firm that is not earning its cost of capital destroys value if it grows its NOPLAT. This critical relationship between ROIC, g, and value is shown in Table A1.

In Table A1, the figures in the cells of the matrix represent the discounted present values of future free cash flows for a company that has a starting NOPLAT of $100, invested capital of $1,000, a cost of capital of 10 percent, and a 25-year time horizon after which ROIC = cost of capital.

The important points revealed by this exercise are as follows:

1. A company with an already high ROIC can create more value by increasing its profit growth rate rather than pushing for an even higher ROIC. Thus a company with an ROIC of 15 percent and a 3 percent growth rate can create more value by increasing its profit growth rate from 3 percent to 9 percent than it can by increasing ROIC to 20 percent.

TABLE A1

ROIC, Growth, and Valuation

NOPLAT Growth, g	ROIC 7.5%	ROIC 10.0%	ROIC 12.5%	ROIC 15%	ROIC 20%
3%	887	1,000	1,058	1,113	1,170
6%	708	1,000	1,117	1,295	1,442
9%	410	1,000	1,354	1,591	1,886

2. A company with a low ROIC destroys value if it grows. Thus, if ROIC = 7.5 percent, a 9 percent growth rate for 25 years will produce less value than a 3 percent growth rate. This is because unprofitable growth requires capital investments, the cost of which cannot be covered. Unprofitable growth destroys value.

3. The best of both worlds is high ROIC and high growth.

Very few companies are able to maintain an ROIC > WACC and grow NOPLAT over time, but there are some notable examples, including Dell, Microsoft, and Wal-Mart. Because these companies have generally been able to fund their capital investment needs from internally generated cash flows, they have not had to issue more shares to raise capital. Thus growth in NOPLAT has translated directly into higher earnings per share for these companies, making their shares more attractive to investors and leading to substantial share price appreciation. By successfully pursuing strategies that result in a high ROIC and growing NOPLAT, these firms have maximized shareholder value.

Chapter 2

External Analysis: The Identification of Opportunities and Threats

Opening Case

Why Is the Pharmaceutical Industry So Profitable?

The pharmaceutical industry is highly profitable. Between 2000 and 2003 the average rate of return on invested capital for firms in the industry was 22.6 percent. Put differently, for every dollar of capital invested in the industry, the average pharmaceutical firm generated 22.6 cents of profit. This compares with an average return on invested capital of 15.9 percent for firms in the software industry, 11.9 percent for publishing firms, 11.2 percent for retail firms, 6.6 percent for steel firms, and 1.8 percent for firms in the air transportation industry.

The high profitability of the pharmaceutical industry can be best understood by looking at several aspects of its underlying economic structure. First, demand for pharmaceuticals is strong and has been growing steadily for decades. Between 1990 and 2003 there was a 12.5 percent annual increase in spending on prescription drugs in the United States. This strong growth was driven by favorable demographics. As people grow older, they tend to need and consume more prescription medicines, and the population in most advanced nations has been growing older as the post–World War II babyboom generation ages.

Second, successful new prescription drugs can be extraordinarily profitable. Lipitor, the cholesterol-lowering drug sold by Pfizer, was introduced in 1997, and by 2003 this drug had generated a staggering $9.23 billion in annual sales for Pfizer. The costs of manufacturing, packing, and distributing Lipitor amounted to only about 10 percent of revenues, or under $1 billion. Pfizer spent close to $400 million on promoting Lipitor and perhaps as much again on maintaining a sales force to sell the product. That still left Pfizer with a gross profit of perhaps $7 billion. Since the drug is protected from direct competition by a twenty-year patent, Pfizer has a temporary monopoly and can charge a high price. Once the patent expires, other firms will be able to produce "generic" versions of Lipitor, and the price will fall—typically by 80 percent within a year—but that is some way off.

Competing firms can produce drugs that are similar (but not identical) to a patent-protected drug. Drug firms patent a specific molecule, and competing firms can patent similar, but not identical, molecules that have a similar pharmacological effect. Thus Lipitor does have competitors in the market for cholesterol-lowering drugs, such as Zocor sold by Merck and Crestor sold by AstraZeneca. But these competing drugs are also patent protected. Moreover, the high costs and risks associated with developing a new drug and bringing it to market constitute a formidable barrier to entry, limiting competition. Out of every five thousand compounds tested in the laboratory by a drug company, only five enter clinical trials, and only one of these will ultimately make it to the market. On average, estimates suggest that it costs some $800 million and takes anywhere from ten to fifteen years to bring a new drug to market. Once on the market, only three out of ten drugs ever recoup their R&D and marketing costs and turn a profit. Thus the high profitability of the pharmaceutical industry rests on a handful of blockbuster drugs. To produce a blockbuster, a drug company must spend large amounts of money on research, most of which fails to produce a product. Only very large companies can shoulder the costs and risks of doing this, and it is very difficult for new companies to enter the industry. Pfizer, for example, spent some $7.13 billion on R&D in 2003 alone, equivalent to almost 18 percent of its total revenues. In a testament to just how difficult it is to get into the industry, although a large number of companies have been started in the last twenty years in the hope that they might develop new pharmaceuticals, only one of these companies, Amgen, was ranked among the top twenty in the industry in terms of sales in 2003. Most have failed to bring a product to market.

In addition to R&D spending, the incumbent firms in the pharmaceutical industry spend large amounts of money on advertising and sales promotion. While the $400 million a year that Pfizer spends promoting Lipitor is small relative to the drug's revenues, it is a large amount for a new competitor to match, making market entry very difficult unless the competitor has a significantly better product. Thus promotional spending constitutes another formidable barrier to entry.

In sum, patent protection that grants a temporary monopoly to some firms, high R&D costs, significant risk of failure, and high marketing costs make it very difficult for new firms to enter the pharmaceutical market. The industry tends to be dominated by large established enterprises that have the scale required to bear the considerable costs and risks associated with developing new drugs and can afford to spend large amounts of money to promote those drugs in the marketplace.

Furthermore, there are some big opportunities on the horizon for firms in the industry. New scientific breakthroughs in genomics are holding out the promise that within the next decade pharmaceutical firms might be able to bring new drugs to market that treat some of the most intractable medical conditions, including Alzheimer's, Parkinson's disease, cancer, heart disease, stroke, and AIDS. But there are also some threats to the long-term dominance and profitability of industry giants like Pfizer. Most notably, as spending on health care rises, politicians are looking for ways to limit health care costs, and one possibility is some form of price control on prescription drugs. Price controls are already in effect in most developed nations, and although they have not yet been introduced in the United States, they could be.[1]

Overview

Strategy formulation begins with an analysis of the forces that shape competition in the industry in which a company is based. The goal is to understand the opportunities and threats confronting the firm and to use this understanding to identify strategies that will enable the company to outperform its rivals. **Opportunities** arise when a company can take advantage of conditions in its environment to formulate and implement strategies that enable it to become more profitable. For example, as noted in the *Opening Case*, as scientific understanding of the underlying causes of Alzheimer's advances, pharmaceutical companies have an opportunity to make enormous profits by developing patented medicines that can treat this debilitating condition. **Threats** arise when conditions in the external environment endanger the integrity and profitability of the company's business. One such threat in the pharmaceutical industry is price controls, which, if imposed, will reduce the ability of pharmaceutical firms to charge high prices and earn high profits. Another threat many pharmaceutical firms face is patent expiration and generic competition. When the patent on Eli Lilly's blockbuster antidepressant Prozac expired in 2001, the company was quickly faced by generic competitors and sales of Prozac fell from $2.6 billion in 2000 to $645 million in 2003.

This chapter begins with an analysis of the industry environment. First, it examines concepts and tools for analyzing the competitive structure of an industry and identifying industry opportunities and threats. Second, it analyzes the competitive implications that arise when groups of companies *within* an industry pursue similar and different kinds of competitive strategies. Third, it explores the way an industry evolves over time and the accompanying changes in competitive conditions. Fourth, it looks at the way in which forces in the macroenvironment affect industry structure and influence opportunities and threats. By the end of the chapter, you will understand that to succeed, a company must either fit its strategy to the external environment in which it operates or be able to reshape the environment to its advantage through its chosen strategy.

Defining an Industry

An **industry** can be defined as a group of companies offering products or services that are close substitutes for each other—that is, products or services that satisfy the same basic customer needs. A company's closest **competitors,** its rivals, are those that serve the same basic customer needs. For example, carbonated drinks, fruit punches, and bottled water can be viewed as close substitutes for each other because they serve the same basic customer needs for refreshing and cold nonalcoholic beverages. Thus, we can talk about the soft drink industry, whose major players are Coca-Cola, PepsiCo, and Cadbury Schweppes. Similarly, desktop computers and notebook computers satisfy the same basic need that customers have for computer hardware on which to run personal productivity software, browse the Internet, send e-mail, play games, and store, display, and manipulate digital images. Thus, we can talk about the personal computer industry, whose major players are Dell, Hewlett-Packard, Lenovo (the Chinese company which purchased IBM's personal computer business), Gateway, and Apple Computer.

The starting point of external analysis is to identify the industry that a company competes in. To do this, managers must begin by looking at the basic customer needs their company is serving—that is, they must take a customer-oriented view of their business as opposed to a product-oriented view (see Chapter 1). An industry is the *supply side* of a market, and companies in the industry are the suppliers. Customers are the *demand side* of a market and are the buyers of the industry's products. *The basic customer needs that are served by a market define an industry's boundary.* It is very important for managers to realize this, for if they define industry boundaries incorrectly, they may be caught flat-footed by the rise of competitors that serve the same basic customer needs with different product offerings. For example, Coca-Cola long saw itself as being in the soda industry—meaning carbonated soft drinks—whereas in fact it was in the soft drink industry, which includes noncarbonated soft drinks. In the mid-1990s, Coca-Cola was caught by surprise by the rise of customer demand for bottled water and fruit drinks, which began to cut into the demand for sodas. Coca-Cola moved quickly to respond to these threats, introducing its own brand of water, Dasani, and acquiring orange juice maker Minute Maid. By defining its industry boundaries too narrowly, Coke almost missed the rapid rise of the noncarbonated soft drinks segment of the soft drinks market.

■ Industry and Sector

An important distinction that needs to be made is between an *industry* and a **sector.** A **sector** is a group of closely related industries. For example, as illustrated in Figure 2.1, the computer sector comprises several related industries: the computer component industries (for example, the disk drive industry, the semiconductor industry, and the modem industry), the computer hardware industries (for example, the personal computer industry, the hand-held computer industry, and the mainframe computer industry), and the computer software industry. Industries within a sector may be involved with each other in many different ways. Companies in the computer component industries are the *suppliers* of firms in the computer hardware industries. Companies in the computer software industry provide important *complements* to computer hardware: the software programs that customers purchase to run on their hardware. And companies in the personal, hand-held, and mainframe industries are in indirect *competition* with each other because all provide products that are to a degree *substitutes* for each other.

■ **Industry and Market Segments**

It is also important to recognize the difference between an *industry* and the *market segments* within that industry. **Market segments** are distinct groups of customers within a market that can be differentiated from each other on the basis of their distinct attributes and specific demands. In the soft drink industry, for example, although all customers demand refreshing and cold nonalcoholic beverages, there is a group within this market who in addition demand (need) sodas that do not contain caffeine. Coca-Cola has recognized the existence of this caffeine-free market segment and sought to satisfy the needs of customers within it by producing and marketing noncaffeinated colas. Similarly, in the personal computer industry, there are different segments where customers desire desktop machines, lightweight portable machines, and servers that sit at the center of a network of personal computers (see Figure 2.1). Personal computer makers recognize the existence of these different segments by producing a range of product offerings that appeal to customers in different segments. Customers in all of these different segments, however, share a common need for PCs on which to run personal software applications.

FIGURE 2.1

The Computer Sector: Industries and Segments

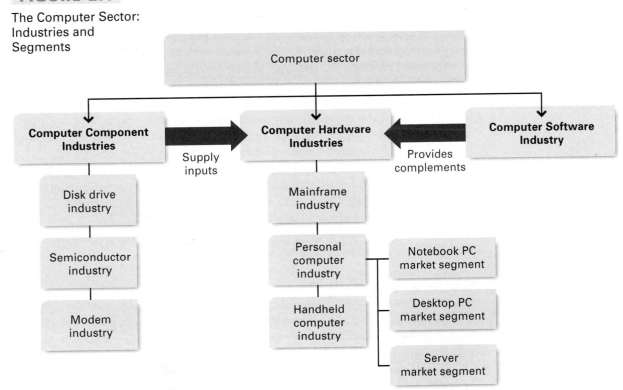

■ **Changing Industry Boundaries**

Industry boundaries may change over time as customer needs evolve or new technologies emerge that enable companies in hitherto unrelated industries to satisfy established customer needs in new ways. We have noted that during the 1990s, as consumers of soft drinks began to develop a taste for bottled water and noncarbonated fruit-based drinks, Coca-Cola found itself in direct competition with the manufacturers of bottled water and fruit-based soft drinks: all were in the same industry.

For an example of how technological change can alter industry boundaries, consider the convergence that is currently taking place between the computer and telecommunications industries. Historically, the telecommunications equipment industry has been considered a distinct entity from the computer hardware industry. However, as telecommunications equipment has moved from traditional analog technology to digital technology, so telecommunications equipment has increasingly come to resemble computers. The result is that the boundaries between these different industries are blurring. A digital wireless phone, for example, is nothing more than a small hand-held computer with a wireless connection, and small hand-held computers often now come with wireless capabilities, transforming them into phones. Thus, Nokia and Motorola, which manufacture wireless phones, are now finding themselves competing directly with Palm, which manufactures hand-held computers.

Industry competitive analysis begins by focusing on the overall industry in which a firm competes before market segments or sector-level issues are considered. Tools that managers can use to perform such industry analysis are discussed in the following sections: Porter's five forces model, strategic group analysis, and industry life cycle analysis.

Porter's Five Forces Model

Once the boundaries of an industry have been identified, the task facing managers is to analyze competitive forces in the industry environment to identify opportunities and threats. Michael E. Porter's well-known framework, known as the five forces model, helps managers with this analysis.[2] His model, shown in Figure 2.2, focuses on five forces that shape competition within an industry: (1) the risk of entry by potential competitors, (2) the intensity of rivalry among established companies within an industry, (3) the bargaining power of buyers, (4) the bargaining power of suppliers, and (5) the closeness of substitutes to an industry's products.

Porter argues that the stronger each of these forces is, the more limited is the ability of established companies to raise prices and earn greater profits. Within Porter's framework, a *strong* competitive force can be regarded as a *threat* because it depresses profits. A *weak* competitive force can be viewed as an *opportunity* because it allows a company to earn greater profits. The strength of the five forces may change through time as industry conditions change. The task facing managers is to recognize how changes in the five forces give rise to new opportunities and threats and to formulate appropriate strategic responses. In addition, it is possible for a company, *through its choice of strategy,* to alter the strength of one or more of the five forces to its advantage. This is discussed in the following chapters.

■ **Risk of Entry by Potential Competitors**

Potential competitors are companies that are not currently competing in an industry but have the capability to do so if they choose. For example, cable television companies have recently emerged as potential competitors to traditional phone companies. New digital technologies have allowed cable companies to offer telephone service over the same cables that transmit television shows.

Established companies already operating in an industry often attempt to discourage potential competitors from entering the industry because the more companies

RE 2.2

Five Forces
Model

that enter, the more difficult it becomes for established companies to protect their share of the market and generate profits. A high risk of entry by potential competitors represents a threat to the profitability of established companies. But if the risk of new entry is low, established companies can take advantage of this opportunity to raise prices and earn greater returns.

The risk of entry by potential competitors is a function of the height of **barriers to entry,** that is, factors that make it costly for companies to enter an industry. The greater the costs that potential competitors must bear to enter an industry, the greater are the barriers to entry and the *weaker* this competitive force. High entry barriers may keep potential competitors out of an industry even when industry profits are high. Important barriers to entry include economies of scale, brand loyalty, absolute cost advantages, customer switching costs, and government regulation.[3] An important strategy is building barriers to entry (in the case of incumbent firms) or finding ways to circumvent those barriers (in the case of new entrants). We shall discuss this topic in more detail in subsequent chapters.

■ **Economies
of Scale**

Economies of scale arise when unit costs fall as a firm expands its output. Sources of scale economies include (1) cost reductions gained through mass-producing a standardized output, (2) discounts on bulk purchases of raw material inputs and component parts, (3) the advantages gained by spreading fixed production costs over a large production volume, and (4) the cost savings associated with spreading marketing and advertising costs over a large volume of output. If these cost advantages are significant, a new company that enters the industry and produces on a small scale suffers a significant cost disadvantage relative to established companies. If the new company decides to enter on a large scale in an attempt to obtain these economies of scale, it

has to raise the capital required to build large-scale produc~~tion~~ **FIGU~~RE~~**
high risks associated with such an invest~~m~~ent. A further risk ~~of~~ Porter's
that the increased supply of products will depress pri~~ces~~ ~~and~~ result in vig~~orous~~ ~~retali~~-
ation by established companies. For these reasons, the thre~~at~~ ~~of~~ entry is reduced
when established companies have economies of scale.

■ **Brand Loyalty**

Brand loyalty exists when consumers have a preference for the products of established companies. A company can create brand loyalty through continuous advertising of its brand-name products and company name, patent protection of products,
product innovation achieved through company research and development programs, an emphasis on high product quality, and good after-sales service. Significant
brand loyalty makes it difficult for new entrants to take market share away from established companies. Thus it reduces the threat of entry by potential competitors
since they may see the task of breaking down well-established customer preferences
as too costly. In the market for colas, for example, consumers have a strong preference for the products of Coca-Cola and PepsiCo, which makes it difficult for other
enterprises to enter this market (nevertheless, the Cott Corporation has succeeded
in entering the soft drink market: see Strategy in Action 2.1).

■ **Absolute Cost Advantages**

Sometimes established companies have an **absolute cost advantage** relative to potential entrants, meaning that entrants cannot expect to match the established companies'
lower cost structure. Absolute cost advantages arise from three main sources: (1) superior production operations and processes due to accumulated experience, patents, or
secret processes; (2) control of particular inputs required for production, such as labor,
materials, equipment, or management skills, that are limited in their supply; and (3)
access to cheaper funds because existing companies represent lower risks than new
entrants. If established companies have an absolute cost advantage, the threat of
entry as a competitive force is weaker.

■ **Customer Switching Costs**

Switching costs arise when it costs a customer time, energy, and money to switch
from the products offered by one established company to the products offered by a
new entrant. When switching costs are high, customers can be *locked in* to the product offerings of established companies, even if new entrants offer better products.[4] A
familiar example of switching costs concerns the costs associated with switching
from one computer operating system to another. If a person currently uses
Microsoft's Windows operating system and has a library of related software applications (for example, word-processing software, spreadsheet, games) and document
files, it is expensive for that person to switch to another computer operating system.
To effect the change, this person would have to buy a new set of software applications
and convert all existing document files to run with the new system. Faced with such
an expense of money and time, most people are unwilling to make the switch *unless*
the competing operating system offers a *substantial* leap forward in performance. Thus,
the higher the switching costs are, the higher is the barrier to entry for a company
attempting to promote a new computer operating system.

■ **Government Regulation**

Historically, government regulation has constituted a major entry barrier into many
industries. For example, until the mid-1990s, U.S. government regulation prohibited
providers of long-distance telephone service from competing for local telephone service and vice versa. Other potential providers of telephone service, including cable television service companies such as Time Warner and Comcast (which could in theory

Strategy in Action

Circumventing Entry Barriers into the Soft Drink Industry

The soft drink industry has long been dominated by two companies, Coca-Cola and PepsiCo. By spending large sums of money on advertising and promotion, both companies have created significant brand loyalty and made it very difficult for new competitors to enter the industry and take market share away from these two giants. When new competitors do try to enter, both companies have responded by cutting prices and thus forcing the new entrant to curtail expansion plans.

However, in the early 1990s the Cott Corporation, then a small Canadian bottling company, worked out a strategy for entering the soft drink market. Cott's strategy was deceptively simple. The company initially focused on the cola segment of the soft drink market. Cott signed a deal with Royal Crown Cola for exclusive global rights to its cola concentrate. RC Cola was a small player in the U.S. cola market. Its products were recognized as having a high quality, but RC Cola had never been able to effectively challenge Coke or Pepsi. Next, Cott signed a deal with a Canadian grocery retailer, Loblaw, to provide the retailer with its own private-label brand of cola. Priced low, the Loblaw private-label brand, known as President's Choice, was very successful and took share from both Coke and Pepsi.

Emboldened by this success, Cott decided to try to convince other retailers to carry private-label cola. To retailers, the value proposition was simple because, unlike its major rivals, Cott spent almost nothing on advertising and promotion. This constituted a major source of cost savings, which Cott passed on to retailers in the form of lower prices. For their part, the retailers found that they could significantly undercut the price of Coke and Pepsi colas and still make better profit margins on private-label brands than on branded colas.

Despite this compelling value proposition, few retailers were willing to sell private-label colas for fear of alienating Coca-Cola and Pepsi, whose products were a major draw of grocery store traffic. Cott's breakthrough came in 1992 when it signed a deal with Wal-Mart to supply the retailing giant with a private-label cola, called "Sam's Choice" (named after Wal-Mart founder Sam Walton). Wal-Mart proved to be the perfect distribution channel for Cott. The retailer was just starting to get into the grocery business, and consumers went to Wal-Mart not to buy branded merchandise but to get low prices.

As Wal-Mart's grocery business grew, so did Cott's sales. Cott soon added other flavors to its offering, such as lemon lime soda, which would compete with Seven Up and Sprite. Moreover, pressured by Wal-Mart, by the late 1990s other U.S. grocers had also started to introduce private-label sodas, often turning to Cott to supply their needs.

By 2003, Cott had grown to become a $1.4 billion company. Its 2003 volume growth in an otherwise stagnant U.S. market for sodas was 12.6 percent. Private-label companies, of which Cott was by far the largest, captured 7.9 percent of the U.S. soda market in 2003, up from almost nothing a decade earlier. The losers in this process were Coca-Cola and PepsiCo, who were now facing the steady erosion of their brand loyalty and market share as consumers increasingly came to recognize the high quality and low price of private-label sodas.[a]

use their cables to carry telephone traffic as well as TV signals), were prohibited from entering the market altogether. These regulatory barriers to entry significantly reduced the level of competition in both the local and long-distance telephone markets, enabling telephone companies to earn higher profits than might otherwise have been the case. All this changed in 1996 when the government deregulated the industry significantly. In the months that followed this announcement, local, long-distance, and cable TV companies all announced their intention to enter each other's markets, and a host of new players entered the market. The five forces model predicts that falling entry barriers due to government deregulation will result in significant new entry, an increase in the intensity of industry competition, and lower industry profit rates, and indeed, that is what occurred.

In summary, if established companies have built brand loyalty for their products, have an absolute cost advantage with respect to potential competitors, have significant scale economies, are the beneficiaries of high switching costs, or enjoy regulatory protection, the risk of entry by potential competitors is greatly diminished; it is a weak competitive force. Consequently, established companies can charge higher prices, and industry profits are higher. Evidence from academic research suggests that the height of barriers to entry is one of the most important determinants of profit rates in an industry.[5] Clearly, it is in the interest of established companies to pursue strategies consistent with raising entry barriers to secure these profits. By the same token, potential new entrants have to find strategies that allow them to circumvent barriers to entry.

Even when entry barriers are very high, new firms may still enter an industry if they perceive that the benefits outweigh the substantial costs of entry. This is what appears to have occurred in the telecommunications industry following deregulation in 1996. Deregulation led to a flood of new entrants such as Level 3 Communications, 360networks, and Global Crossing, who built fiber-optic networks to serve what they perceived as explosive growth in the amount of Internet traffic. These entrants had to undertake billions of dollars in capital expenditure to build out their networks and match the scale advantages of established companies such as World-Com. However, the new entrants were able to raise the capital to do so from investors who shared management's euphoric vision of future demand in the industry (Level 3 alone raised $13 billion). As it turned out, the euphoric vision of demand growth was based on the erroneous assumption that Internet traffic was growing at 1,000 percent a year when in fact it was only growing at 100 percent a year. When the euphoric vision proved to be false, many of the new entrants went bankrupt, but not before their investments had created excess capacity in the industry and sparked intense price competition that depressed the returns for all players, new entrants and established companies alike (see the *Closing Case* to Chapter 1 for further details).

■ **Rivalry Among Established Companies**

The second of Porter's five competitive forces is the intensity of rivalry among established companies within an industry. **Rivalry** refers to the competitive struggle between companies in an industry to gain market share from each other. The competitive struggle can be fought using price, product design, advertising and promotion spending, direct selling efforts, and after-sales service and support. More intense rivalry implies lower prices or more spending on non-price-competitive weapons, or both. Because intense rivalry lowers prices and raises costs, it squeezes profits out of an industry. Thus, intense rivalry among established companies constitutes a strong threat to profitability. Alternatively, if rivalry is less intense, companies may have the opportunity to raise prices or reduce spending on non-price-competitive weapons, which leads to a higher level of industry profits. The intensity of rivalry among established companies within an industry is largely a function of four factors: (1) industry competitive structure, (2) demand conditions, (3) cost conditions, and (4) the height of exit barriers in the industry.

■ **Industry Competitive Structure**

The *competitive structure* of an industry refers to the number and size distribution of companies in it, something that strategic managers determine at the beginning of an industry analysis. Industry structures vary, and different structures have different implications for the intensity of rivalry. A **fragmented industry** consists of a large number of small or medium-sized companies, none of which is in a position to determine industry price. A **consolidated industry** is dominated by a small number of large companies (an **oligopoly**) or, in extreme cases, by just one company (a **monopoly**), and companies often are in a position to determine industry prices. Examples of fragmented industries are agriculture, dry cleaning, video rental, health clubs, real estate brokerage, and sun tanning parlors. Consolidated industries include the aerospace, soft drink, automobile, pharmaceutical, and stockbrokerage industries.

Many fragmented industries are characterized by low entry barriers and commodity-type products that are hard to differentiate. The combination of these traits tends to result in boom-and-bust cycles as industry profits rise and fall. Low entry barriers imply that whenever demand is strong and profits are high, new entrants will flood the market, hoping to profit from the boom. The explosion in the number of video stores, health clubs, and sun tanning parlors during the 1980s and 1990s exemplifies this situation.

Often the flood of new entrants into a booming fragmented industry creates excess capacity, so companies start to cut prices in order to use their spare capacity. The difficulty companies face when trying to differentiate their products from those of competitors can exacerbate this tendency. The result is a price war, which depresses industry profits, forces some companies out of business, and deters potential new entrants. For example, after a decade of expansion and booming profits, many health clubs are now finding that they have to offer large discounts in order to hold on to their membership. In general, the more commodity-like an industry's product is, the more vicious will be the price war. This bust part of the cycle continues until overall industry capacity is brought into line with demand (through bankruptcies), at which point prices may stabilize again.

A fragmented industry structure, then, constitutes a threat rather than an opportunity. Most booms are relatively short-lived because of the ease of new entry and will be followed by price wars and bankruptcies. Because it is often difficult to differentiate products in these industries, the best strategy for a company is to try to minimize its costs so it will be profitable in a boom and survive any subsequent bust. Alternatively, companies might try to adopt strategies that change the underlying structure of fragmented industries and lead to a consolidated industry structure in which the level of industry profitability is increased. Exactly how companies can do this is something we shall consider in later chapters.

In consolidated industries, companies are interdependent, because one company's competitive actions or moves (with regard to price, quality, and so on) directly affect the market share of its rivals, and thus their profitability. When one company makes a move, this generally "forces" a response from its rivals, and the consequence of such competitive interdependence can be a dangerous competitive spiral. Rivalry increases as companies attempt to undercut each other's prices or offer customers more value in their products, pushing industry profits down in the process. The fare wars that have periodically created havoc in the airline industry provide a good illustration of this process.

Companies in consolidated industries sometimes seek to reduce this threat by following the prices set by the dominant company in the industry.[6] However, companies must be careful, for explicit face-to-face price-fixing agreements are illegal. (Tacit, indirect agreements, arrived at without direct or intentional communication, are legal.) Instead, companies set prices by watching, interpreting, anticipating, and responding to each other's behavior (something discussed in detail in Chapter 5 when the competitive dynamics of game theory are examined). However, tacit price-leadership agreements often break down under adverse economic conditions, as has occurred in the breakfast cereal industry, profiled in Strategy in Action 2.2.

Strategy in Action

2.2

Price Wars in the Breakfast Cereal Industry

For decades, the breakfast cereal industry was one of the most profitable in the United States. The industry has a consolidated structure dominated by Kellogg, General Mills, and Kraft Foods with its Post brand. Strong brand loyalty, coupled with control over the allocation of supermarket shelf space, helped to limit the potential for new entry. Meanwhile, steady demand growth of around 3 percent per annum kept industry revenues expanding. For years, Kellogg, which accounted for over 40 percent of the market share, acted as the price leader in the industry. Every year Kellogg increased cereal prices, its rivals followed, and industry profits remained high.

This favorable industry structure started to change in the early 1990s when growth in demand slowed and then stagnated as a latte and bagel or muffin replaced cereal as the morning fare for many American adults. Then came the rise of powerful discounters such as Wal-Mart, which entered the grocery industry in the early 1990s and began to promote aggressively its own brand of cereal, priced significantly below the brand-name cereals. As the decade progressed, other grocery chains such as Kroger's started to follow suit, and brand loyalty in the industry began to decline as customers realized that a $2.50 bag of wheat flakes from Wal-Mart tasted about the same as a $3.50 box of Cornflakes from Kellogg. As sales of cheaper store-brand cereals began to take off, supermarkets, no longer as dependent on brand names to bring traffic into their stores, began to demand lower prices from the branded cereal manufacturers.

For several years, the manufacturers of brand cereals tried to hold out against these adverse trends, but in the mid-1990s the dam broke. In 1996, Kraft (then owned by Philip Morris) aggressively cut prices by 20 percent for its Post brand in an attempt to gain market share. Kellogg

soon followed with a 19 percent price cut on two-thirds of its brands, and General Mills quickly did the same. The decades of tacit price collusion were officially over.

If the breakfast cereal companies were hoping that the price cuts would stimulate demand, they were wrong. Instead, demand remained flat while revenues and margins followed prices down and Kellogg's operating margins dropped from 18 percent in 1995 to 10.2 percent in 1996, a trend experienced by the other brand cereal manufacturers.

By 2000, conditions had only worsened. Private-label sales continued to make inroads, gaining over 10 percent of the market. Moreover, sales of breakfast cereals started to contract at 1 percent per annum. To cap it off, an aggressive General Mills continued to launch expensive price and promotion campaigns in an attempt to take share away from the market leader. Kellogg saw its market share slip to just over 30 percent in 2001, *behind* the 31 percent now held by General Mills. For the first time since 1906, Kellogg no longer led the market. Moreover, profits at all three major producers remained weak in the face of continued price discounting.

In mid-2001, General Mills finally blinked and raised prices a modest 2 percent in response to its own rising costs. Competitors followed, signaling perhaps that after a decade of costly price warfare, pricing discipline might once more emerge in the industry. Both Kellogg and General Mills tried to move further away from price competition by focusing on brand extensions, such as Special K containing berries and new varieties of Cheerios. Kellogg's efforts with Special K helped the company recapture market leadership from General Mills. More importantly, the renewed emphasis on nonprice competition halted years of damaging price warfare, at least for the time being.[b]

■ **Industry Demand** The level of industry demand is a second determinant of the intensity of rivalry among established companies. Growing demand from new customers or additional purchases by existing customers tend to moderate competition by providing greater scope for companies to compete for customers. Growing demand tends to reduce rivalry because all companies can sell more without taking market share away from other companies. High industry profits are often the result. Conversely, declining demand results in more rivalry as companies fight to maintain market share and revenues (as in the breakfast cereal industry). Demand declines when customers are leaving the marketplace or each customer is buying less. Now a company can grow only by taking market share away from other companies. Thus, declining demand constitutes a major threat, for it increases the extent of rivalry between established companies.

■ **Cost Conditions**

The cost structure of firms in an industry is a third determinant of rivalry. In industries where fixed costs are high, profitability tends to be highly leveraged to sales volume and the desire to grow volume can spark intense rivalry. **Fixed costs** are the costs that must be borne before the firm makes a single sale. For example, before they can offer service, cable TV companies have to lay cable in the ground; the cost of doing so is a fixed cost. Similarly, to offer air express service, a company like FedEx must invest in planes, package-sorting facilities, and delivery trucks—all fixed costs that require significant capital investments. In industries where the fixed costs of production are high, if sales volume is low firms cannot cover their fixed costs and will not be profitable. They thus have an incentive to cut their prices and/or increase promotion spending to drive up sales volume so that they can cover their fixed costs. In situations where demand is not growing fast enough and too many companies are engaged in the same actions (cutting prices and/or raising promotion spending in an attempt to cover fixed costs), the result can be intense rivalry and lower profits. Research suggests that it is often the weakest firms in an industry that initiate such actions, precisely because they are the ones struggling to cover their fixed costs.[7]

■ **Exit Barriers**

Exit barriers are economic, strategic, and emotional factors that prevent companies from leaving an industry.[8] If exit barriers are high, companies become locked into an unprofitable industry where overall demand is static or declining. The result is often excess productive capacity, which leads to even more intense rivalry and price competition as companies cut prices in the attempt to obtain the customer orders needed to use their idle capacity and cover their fixed costs.[9] Common exit barriers include the following:

■ Investments in assets such as specific machines, equipment, and operating facilities that are of little or no value in alternative uses or cannot be sold off. If the company wishes to leave the industry, it has to write off the book value of these assets.

■ High fixed costs of exit, such as the severance pay, health benefits, and pensions that have to be paid to workers who are being made redundant when a company ceases to operate.

■ Emotional attachments to an industry, as when a company's owners or employees are unwilling to exit from an industry for sentimental reasons or because of pride.

■ Economic dependence on the industry because a company relies on a single industry for its revenue and profit.

■ The need to maintain an expensive collection of assets at or above some minimum level in order to participate effectively in the industry.

■ Bankruptcy regulations, particularly in the United States, where Chapter 11 bankruptcy provisions allow insolvent enterprises to continue operating and reorganize themselves under bankruptcy protection. These regulations can keep unprofitable assets in the industry, result in persistent excess capacity, and lengthen the time required to bring industry supply in line with demand.

As an example of the effect of exit barriers in practice, consider the express mail and parcel delivery industry. The key players in this industry, such as Federal Express and UPS, rely on the delivery business entirely for their revenues and profits. They have to be able to guarantee their customers that they will deliver packages to all major localities in the United States, and much of their investment is specific to this purpose. To meet this guarantee, they need a nationwide network of air routes and ground routes, an asset that is required in order to participate in the industry. If excess capacity develops in this industry, as it does from time to time, Federal Express cannot incrementally reduce or minimize its excess capacity by deciding not to fly to and deliver packages in, say, Miami because that proportion of its network is underused. If it did that, it would no longer be able to guarantee to its customers that it would be able to deliver packages to all major locations in the United States, and its customers would switch to some other carrier. Thus, the need to maintain a nationwide network is an exit barrier that can result in persistent excess capacity in the air express industry during periods of weak demand. Finally, both UPS and Federal Express managers and employees are emotionally tied to this industry because they both were first movers, in the ground and air segments of the industry, respectively, and because their employees are also major owners of their companies' stock and they are dependent financially on the fortunes of the delivery business.

■ The Bargaining Power of Buyers

The third of Porter's five competitive forces is the bargaining power of buyers. An industry's buyers may be the individual customers who ultimately consume its products (its end-users) or the companies that distribute an industry's products to end-users, such as retailers and wholesalers. For example, while soap powder made by Procter & Gamble and Unilever is consumed by end-users, the principal buyers of soap powder are supermarket chains and discount stores, which resell the product to end-users. The **bargaining power of buyers** refers to the ability of buyers to bargain down prices charged by companies in the industry or to raise the costs of companies in the industry by demanding better product quality and service. By lowering prices and raising costs, powerful buyers can squeeze profits out of an industry. Thus, powerful buyers should be viewed as a threat. Alternatively, when buyers are in a weak bargaining position, companies in an industry can raise prices and perhaps reduce their costs by lowering product quality and service, thus increasing the level of industry profits. Buyers are most powerful in the following circumstances:

- When the industry that is supplying a particular product or service is composed of many small companies and the buyers are large and few in number. These circumstances allow the buyers to dominate supplying companies.

- When the buyers purchase in large quantities. In such circumstances, buyers can use their purchasing power as leverage to bargain for price reductions.

- When the supply industry depends on the buyers for a large percentage of its total orders.

- When switching costs are low so that buyers can play off the supplying companies against each other to force down prices.

- When it is economically feasible for buyers to purchase an input from several companies at once so that buyers can play off one company in the industry against another.

- When buyers can threaten to enter the industry and produce the product themselves and thus supply their own needs, also a tactic for forcing down industry prices.

The auto component supply industry, whose buyers are large automobile manufacturers such as GM, Ford, and DaimlerChrysler, is a good example of an industry in which buyers have strong bargaining power and thus a strong competitive threat.

Why? The suppliers of auto components are numerous and typically small in scale; their buyers, the auto manufacturers, are large in size and few in number. Daimler-Chrysler, for example, does business with nearly two thousand different component suppliers in the United States and normally contracts with a number of different companies to supply the same part. Additionally, to keep component prices down, both Ford and GM have used the threat of manufacturing a component themselves rather than buying it from auto component suppliers. The automakers have used their powerful position to play off suppliers against each other, forcing down the price they have to pay for component parts and demanding better quality. If a component supplier objects, the automaker uses the threat of switching to another supplier as a bargaining tool.

Another issue is that the relative power of buyers and suppliers tends to change in response to changing industry conditions. For example, because of changes now taking place in the pharmaceutical and health care industries, major buyers of pharmaceuticals (hospitals and health maintenance organizations) are gaining power over the suppliers of pharmaceuticals and have been able to demand lower prices. The *Running Case* discusses how Wal-Mart's buying power has changed over the years as the company has become larger.

■ The Bargaining Power of Suppliers

The fourth of Porter's five competitive forces is the bargaining power of suppliers—the organizations that provide inputs into the industry, such as materials, services, and labor (which may be individuals, organizations such as labor unions, or companies that supply contract labor). The **bargaining power of suppliers** refers to the ability of suppliers to raise input prices, or to raise the costs of the industry in other ways—for example, by providing poor-quality inputs or poor service. Powerful suppliers squeeze profits out of an industry by raising the costs of companies in the industry. Thus, powerful suppliers are a threat. Alternatively, if suppliers are weak, companies in the industry have the opportunity to force down input prices and demand higher-quality inputs (such as more productive labor). As with buyers, the ability of suppliers to make demands on a company depends on their power relative to that of the company. Suppliers are most powerful in these situations:

- The product that suppliers sell has few substitutes and is vital to the companies in an industry.

- The profitability of suppliers is not significantly affected by the purchases of companies in a particular industry, in other words, when the industry is not an important customer to the suppliers.

- Companies in an industry would experience significant switching costs if they moved to the product of a different supplier because a particular supplier's products are unique or different. In such cases, the company depends on a particular supplier and cannot play suppliers off against each other to reduce price.

- Suppliers can threaten to enter their customers' industry and use their inputs to produce products that would compete directly with those of companies already in the industry.

- Companies in the industry cannot threaten to enter their suppliers' industry and make their own inputs as a tactic for lowering the price of inputs.

An example of an industry in which companies are dependent on a powerful supplier is the personal computer industry. Personal computer firms are heavily dependent on Intel, the world's largest supplier of microprocessors for PCs. The industry

Running Case

Wal-Mart's Bargaining Power over Suppliers

When Wal-Mart and other discount retailers began in the 1960s, they were small operations with little purchasing power. To generate store traffic, they depended in large part on stocking nationally branded merchandise from well-known companies such as Procter & Gamble and Rubbermaid. Since the discounters did not have high sales volume, the nationally branded companies set the price. This meant that the discounters had to look for other ways to cut costs, which they typically did by emphasizing self-service in stripped-down stores located in the suburbs where land was cheaper (in the 1960s the main competitors for discounters were full-service department stores like Sears that were often located in downtown shopping areas).

Discounters such as Kmart purchased their merchandise through wholesalers, who in turned bought from manufacturers. The wholesaler would come into a store and write an order, and when the merchandise arrived, the wholesaler would come in and stock the shelves, saving the retailer labor costs. However, Wal-Mart was located in Arkansas and placed its stores in small towns. Wholesalers were not particularly interested in serving a company that built its stores in such out-of-the-way places. They would do it only if Wal-Mart paid higher prices.

Wal-Mart's Sam Walton refused to pay higher prices. Instead he took his fledgling company public and used the capital raised to build a distribution center to stock merchandise. The distribution center would serve all stores within a 300-mile radius, with trucks leaving the distribution center daily to restock the stores. Because the distribution center was serving a collection of stores and thus buying in larger volumes, Walton found that he was able to cut the wholesalers out of the equation and order directly from manufacturers. The cost savings generated by not having to pay profits to wholesalers were then passed on to consumers in the form of lower prices, which helped Wal-Mart continue growing. This growth increased its buying power and thus its ability to demand deeper discounts from manufacturers.

Today Wal-Mart has turned its buying process into an art form. Since 8 percent of all retail sales in the United States are made in a Wal-Mart store, the company has enormous bargaining power over its suppliers. Suppliers of nationally branded products, such as Procter & Gamble, are no longer in a position to demand high prices. Instead, Wal-Mart is now so important to Procter & Gamble that it is able to demand deep discounts from them. Moreover, Wal-Mart has itself become a brand that is more powerful than the brands of manufacturers. People don't go to Wal-Mart to buy branded goods; they go to Wal-Mart for the low prices. This simple fact has enabled Wal-Mart to bargain down the prices it pays, always passing on cost savings to consumers in the form of lower prices.

Since 1991 Wal-Mart has provided suppliers with real-time information on store sales through the use of individual Stock Keeping Units (SKUs). These have allowed suppliers to optimize their own production processes, matching output to Wal-Mart's demands and avoiding under- or overproduction and the need to store inventory. The efficiencies that manufacturers gain from such information are passed on to Wal-Mart in the form of lower prices, which then passes on those cost savings to consumers.[c]

standard for personal computers runs on Intel's microprocessor chips. Intel's competitors, such as Advanced Micro Devices (AMD), must develop and supply chips that are compatible with Intel's standard. Although AMD has developed competing chips, Pentium still supplies about 85 percent of the chips used in PCs primarily because only Intel has the manufacturing capacity required to serve a large share of the market. It is beyond the financial resources of Intel's competitors, such as AMD, to match the scale and efficiency of Intel's manufacturing systems. This means that while PC manufacturers can buy some microprocessors from Intel's rivals, most notably AMD, they still have to turn to Intel for the bulk of their supply. Because Intel is in a powerful bargaining position, it can charge higher prices for its microprocessors than would be the case if its competitors were more numerous and stronger (that is, if the microprocessor industry were fragmented).

■ **Substitute Products**

The final force in Porter's model is the threat of **substitute products**: the products of different businesses or industries that can satisfy similar customer needs. For example, companies in the coffee industry compete indirectly with those in the tea and soft drink industries because all three serve customer needs for nonalcoholic drinks. The existence of close substitutes is a strong competitive threat because this limits the price that companies in one industry can charge for their product, and thus industry profitability. If the price of coffee rises too much relative to that of tea or soft drinks, coffee drinkers may switch to those substitutes.

If an industry's products have few close substitutes, so that substitutes are a weak competitive force, then, other things being equal, companies in the industry have the opportunity to raise prices and earn additional profits. Thus, there is no close substitute for microprocessors, which gives companies like Intel and AMD the ability to charge higher prices than would be the case if there were a substitute for microprocessors.

■ **A Sixth Force: Complementors**

Andrew Grove, the former CEO of Intel, has argued that Porter's five forces model ignores a sixth force: the power, vigor, and competence of complementors.[10] **Complementors** are companies that sell products that add value to (complement) the products of companies in an industry because when used *together,* the products better satisfy customer demands. For example, the complementors to the personal computer industry are the companies that make software applications to run on those machines. The greater the supply of high-quality software applications to run on personal computers, the greater is the value of personal computers to customers, the greater the demand for PCs, and the greater the profitability of the personal computer industry.

Grove's argument has a strong foundation in economic theory, which has long argued that *both* substitutes and complements influence demand in an industry.[11] Moreover, recent research has emphasized the importance of complementary products in determining demand and profitability in many high-technology industries, such as the computer industry in which Grove made his mark.[12] The issue, therefore, is that when complements are an important determinant of demand for an industry's products, industry profits depend critically on there being an adequate supply of complementary products. When the number of complementors is increasing and they produce attractive complementary products, this boosts demand and profits in the industry and can open up many new opportunities for creating value. Conversely, if complementors are weak and are not producing attractive complementary products, this can be a threat that slows industry growth and limits profitability.

Summary

The systematic analysis of forces in the industry environment using the Porter framework is a powerful tool that helps managers to think strategically. It is important to recognize that one competitive force often affects the others, so that all forces need to be considered and thought about when performing industry analysis. Indeed, industry analysis leads managers to think systematically about how their strategic choices will be affected by the forces of industry competition and also about how their choices will affect the five forces and change conditions in the industry.

Strategic Groups Within Industries

Companies in an industry often differ significantly from each other with respect to the way they strategically position their products in the market in terms of such factors as the distribution channels they use, the market segments they serve, the quality of their products, technological leadership, customer service, pricing policy, advertising policy, and promotions. As a result of these differences, within most industries, it is

FIGURE 2.3

Strategic Groups in
the Pharmaceutical
Industry

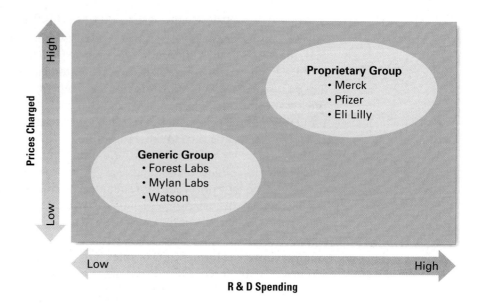

possible to observe groups of companies in which each company follows a business
model that is similar to that pursued by other companies in the group, but *different*
from the business model followed by companies in other groups. These different
groups of companies are known as **strategic groups.**[13]

Normally, the basic differences between the business models that companies in
different strategic groups use can be captured by a relatively small number of strategic factors. For example, in the pharmaceutical industry, two main strategic groups
stand out (see Figure 2.3).[14] One group, which includes such companies as Merck, Eli
Lilly, and Pfizer, is characterized by a business model based on heavy R&D spending
and a focus on developing new, proprietary, blockbuster drugs. The companies in
this *proprietary* strategic group are pursuing a high-risk, high-return strategy. It is a
high-risk strategy because basic drug research is difficult and expensive. As discussed in the *Opening Case*, bringing a new drug to market can cost up to $800 million
in R&D money and a decade of research and clinical trials. The risks are high because
the failure rate in new drug development is very high: only one out of every five drugs
entering clinical trials is ultimately approved by the U.S. Food and Drug Administration. However, the strategy is also a high-return one because a single successful drug
can be patented, giving the innovator a twenty-year monopoly on its production and
sale. This lets these proprietary companies charge a high price for the patented drug,
allowing them to earn millions, if not billions, of dollars over the lifetime of the
patent.

The second strategic group might be characterized as the *generic drug* strategic
group. This group of companies, which includes Forest Labs, Mylan Labs, and Watson
Pharmaceuticals, focuses on the manufacture of generic drugs: low-cost copies of
drugs that were developed by companies in the proprietary group whose patents have
now expired. Low R&D spending, production efficiency, and an emphasis on low
prices characterize the business models of companies in this strategic group. They
are pursuing a low-risk, low-return strategy. It is low risk because they are not investing millions of dollars in R&D. It is low return because they cannot charge high prices.

■ Implications of Strategic Groups

The concept of strategic groups has a number of implications for the identification of opportunities and threats within an industry. First, because all the companies in a strategic group are pursuing a similar business model, customers tend to view the products of such enterprises as *direct substitutes* for each other. Thus, a company's *closest* competitors are those in its strategic group, not those in other strategic groups in the industry. The most immediate threat to a company's profitability comes from rivals within its own strategic group. For example, in the retail industry, there is a group of companies that might be characterized as discounters. Included in this group are Wal-Mart, Kmart, Target, and Fred Meyer. These companies compete most vigorously with each other, rather than with other retailers in different groups, such as Nordstrom or The Gap. Kmart, for example, was driven into bankruptcy in late 2001, not because Nordstrom or The Gap took business from it, but because Wal-Mart and Target gained share in the discounting group by virtue of their superior strategic execution of the discounting business model.

A second competitive implication is that different strategic groups can have a different standing with respect to each of the competitive forces; thus, *each strategic group may face a different set of opportunities and threats.* The risk of new entry by potential competitors, the degree of rivalry among companies within a group, the bargaining power of buyers, the bargaining power of suppliers, and the competitive force of substitute and complementary products can each be a relatively strong or weak competitive force depending on the competitive positioning approach adopted by each strategic group in the industry. For example, in the pharmaceutical industry, companies in the proprietary group have historically been in a very powerful position in relation to buyers because their products are patented and there are no substitutes. Also, rivalry based on price competition within this group has been low because competition in the industry revolves around being the first to patent a new drug (so-called patent races), not around drug prices. Thus, companies in this group have been able to charge high prices and earn high profits. In contrast, companies in the generic group have been in a much weaker position because many companies are able to produce different versions of the same generic drug after patents expire. Thus, in this strategic group, products are close substitutes, rivalry has been high, and price competition has led to lower profits for this group as compared to companies in the proprietary group.

■ The Role of Mobility Barriers

It follows from these two issues that some strategic groups are more desirable than others because competitive forces open up greater opportunities and present fewer threats for those groups. Managers, after having analyzed their industry, might identify a strategic group where competitive forces are weaker and higher profits can be made. Sensing an opportunity, they might contemplate changing their business model and move to compete in that strategic group. However, taking advantage of this opportunity may be difficult because of mobility barriers between strategic groups.

Mobility barriers are within-industry factors that inhibit the movement of companies between strategic groups. They include the barriers to entry into a group and the barriers to exit from a company's existing group. For example, Forest Labs would encounter mobility barriers if it attempted to enter the proprietary group in the pharmaceutical industry because it lacks R&D skills, and building these skills would be an expensive proposition. Essentially, over time, companies in different groups develop different cost structures and skills and competencies that give them different pricing options and choices. A company contemplating entry into another strategic group must evaluate whether it has the ability to imitate, and indeed outperform, its potential competitors in that strategic group. Managers must determine if it is cost-effective to overcome mobility barriers before deciding whether the move is worthwhile.

In summary, an important task of industry analysis is to determine the sources of the similarities and differences among companies in an industry and to work out the broad themes that underlie competition in an industry. This analysis often reveals new opportunities to compete in an industry by developing new kinds of products to meet the needs of customers better. It can also reveal emerging threats that can be countered effectively by changing competitive strategy. This issue is taken up in Chapters 5, 6, and 7, which examine crafting competitive strategy in different kinds of markets to build a competitive advantage over rivals and best satisfy customer needs.

Industry Life Cycle Analysis

An important determinant of the strength of the competitive forces in an industry (and thus of the nature of opportunities and threats) is the changes that take place in it over time. The similarities and differences between companies in an industry often become more pronounced over time, and its strategic group structure frequently changes. The strength and nature of each of the competitive forces also change as an industry evolves, particularly the two forces of risk of entry by potential competitors and rivalry among existing firms.[15]

A useful tool for analyzing the effects of industry evolution on competitive forces is the **industry life cycle** model, which identifies five sequential stages in the evolution of an industry that lead to five distinct kinds of industry environment: embryonic, growth, shakeout, mature, and decline (see Figure 2.4). The task facing managers is to *anticipate* how the strength of competitive forces will change as the industry environment evolves and to formulate strategies that take advantage of opportunities as they arise and that counter emerging threats.

■ Embryonic Industries

An *embryonic* industry is just beginning to develop (for example, personal computers and biotechnology in the 1970s, and nanotechnology today). Growth at this stage is slow because of such factors as buyers' unfamiliarity with the industry's product,

FIGURE 2.4

Stages in the Industry Life Cycle

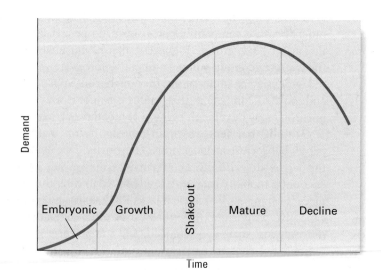

high prices due to the inability of companies to reap any significant scale economies, and poorly developed distribution channels. Barriers to entry tend to be based on access to key technological know-how rather than cost economies or brand loyalty. If the core know-how required to compete in the industry is complex and difficult to grasp, barriers to entry can be quite high, and established companies will be protected from potential competitors. Rivalry in embryonic industries is based not so much on price as on educating customers, opening up distribution channels, and perfecting the design of the product. Such rivalry can be intense, and the company that is the first to solve design problems often has the opportunity to develop a significant market position. An embryonic industry may also be the creation of one company's innovative efforts, as happened with microprocessors (Intel), vacuum cleaners (Hoover), and photocopiers (Xerox). In such circumstances, the company has a major opportunity to capitalize on the lack of rivalry and build a strong hold on the market.

■ **Growth Industries**

Once demand for the industry's product begins to take off, the industry develops the characteristics of a growth industry. In a *growth* industry, first-time demand is expanding rapidly as many new customers enter the market. Typically, an industry grows when customers become familiar with the product, prices fall because experience and scale economies have been attained, and distribution channels develop. The U.S. cellular telephone industry was in the growth stage for most of the 1990s. In 1990, there were only 5 million cellular subscribers in the nation. By 2004, this figure had increased to over 130 million, and overall demand was still growing at a healthy rate.

Normally, the importance of control over technological knowledge as a barrier to entry has diminished by the time an industry enters its growth stage. Because few companies have yet achieved significant scale economies or built brand loyalty, other entry barriers tend to be relatively low as well, particularly early in the growth stage. Thus, the threat from potential competitors generally is highest at this point. Paradoxically, however, high growth usually means that new entrants can be absorbed into an industry without a marked increase in the intensity of rivalry. Thus, rivalry tends to be relatively low. Rapid growth in demand enables companies to expand their revenues and profits without taking market share away from competitors. A strategically aware company takes advantage of the relatively benign environment of the growth stage to prepare itself for the intense competition of the coming industry shakeout.

■ **Industry Shakeout**

Explosive growth cannot be maintained indefinitely. Sooner or later, the rate of growth slows, and the industry enters the shakeout stage. In the *shakeout* stage, demand approaches saturation levels: most of the demand is limited to replacement because there are few potential first-time buyers left.

As an industry enters the shakeout stage, rivalry between companies becomes intense. Typically, companies that have become accustomed to rapid growth continue to add capacity at rates consistent with past growth. However, demand is no longer growing at historic rates, and the consequence is the emergence of excess productive capacity. This condition is illustrated in Figure 2.5, where the solid curve indicates the growth in demand over time and the broken curve indicates the growth in productive capacity over time. As you can see, past point t_1, demand growth becomes slower as the industry becomes mature. However, capacity continues to grow until time t_2. The gap between the solid and broken lines signifies excess capacity. In an attempt to use this capacity, companies often cut prices. The result can be a price war,

FIGURE 2.5

Growth in Demand
and Capacity

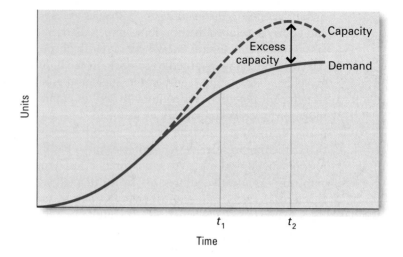

which drives many of the most inefficient companies into bankruptcy, which is
enough to deter any new entry.

■ **Mature** The shakeout stage ends when the industry enters its *mature* stage: the market is to-
Industries tally saturated, demand is limited to replacement demand, and growth is low or zero.
What growth there is comes from population expansion that brings new customers
into the market or an increase in replacement demand.

As an industry enters maturity, barriers to entry increase, and the threat of entry
from potential competitors decreases. As growth slows during the shakeout, companies can no longer maintain historic growth rates merely by holding on to their
market share. Competition for market share develops, driving down prices and
often producing a price war, as has happened in the airline and personal computer
industry. To survive the shakeout, companies begin to focus on minimizing costs
and building brand loyalty. The airlines, for example, tried to cut operating costs by
hiring nonunion labor and to build brand loyalty by introducing frequent-flyer
programs. Personal computer companies have sought to build brand loyalty by providing excellent after-sales service and working to lower their cost structures. By the
time an industry matures, the surviving companies are those that have brand loyalty
and efficient low-cost operations. Because both these factors constitute a significant
barrier to entry, the threat of entry by potential competitors is greatly diminished.
High entry barriers in mature industries give companies the opportunity to increase
prices and profits.

As a result of the shakeout, most industries in the maturity stage have consolidated and become oligopolies. In mature industries, companies tend to recognize
their interdependence and try to avoid price wars. Stable demand gives them the opportunity to enter into price-leadership agreements. The net effect is to reduce the
threat of intense rivalry among established companies, thereby allowing greater
profitability. Nevertheless, the stability of a mature industry is always threatened
by further price wars. A general slump in economic activity can depress industry
demand. As companies fight to maintain their revenues in the face of declining demand,

price-leadership agreements break down, rivalry increases, and prices and profits fall. The periodic price wars that occur in the airline industry seem to follow this pattern.

■ **Declining Industries**

Eventually, most industries enter a *decline* stage: growth becomes negative for a variety of reasons, including technological substitution (for example, air travel for rail travel), social changes (greater health consciousness hitting tobacco sales), demographics (the declining birthrate hurting the market for baby and child products), and international competition (low-cost foreign competition pushing the U.S. steel industry into decline). Within a declining industry, the degree of rivalry among established companies usually increases. Depending on the speed of the decline and the height of exit barriers, competitive pressures can become as fierce as in the shakeout stage.[16] The main problem in a declining industry is that falling demand leads to the emergence of excess capacity. In trying to use this capacity, companies begin to cut prices, thus sparking a price war. The U.S. steel industry experienced these problems because steel companies tried to use their excess capacity despite falling demand. The same problem occurred in the airline industry in the 1990–1992 period and again in 2001–2003, as companies cut prices to ensure that they would not be flying with half-empty planes (that is, that they would not be operating with substantial excess capacity). Exit barriers play a part in adjusting excess capacity. The greater the exit barriers, the harder it is for companies to reduce capacity and the greater is the threat of severe price competition.

Summary

In summary, a third task of industry analysis is to identify the opportunities and threats that are characteristic of different kinds of industry environments in order to develop an effective business model and competitive strategy. Strategic managers have to tailor their strategies to changing industry conditions. And they have to learn to recognize the crucial points in an industry's development so that they can forecast when the shakeout stage of an industry might begin or when an industry might be moving into decline. This is also true at the level of strategic groups, for new embryonic groups may emerge because of shifts in customer needs and tastes or some groups may grow rapidly because of changes in technology and others will decline as their customers defect. Thus, for example, companies in the upscale retail group such as Macy's, Dillard's, and Nordstrom are facing declining sales as customers defect to discount retailers like Target and Wal-Mart and online companies like amazon.com and landsend.com.

Limitations of Models for Industry Analysis

The competitive forces, strategic groups, and life cycle models provide useful ways of thinking about and analyzing the nature of competition within an industry to identify opportunities and threats. However, each has its limitations, and managers need to be aware of their shortcomings.

■ **Life Cycle Issues**

It is important to remember that the industry life cycle model is a generalization. In practice, industry life cycles do not always follow the pattern illustrated in Figure 2.4. In some cases, growth is so rapid that the embryonic stage is skipped altogether. In others, industries fail to get past the embryonic stage. Industry growth can be revitalized after long periods of decline through innovation or social change. For example, the health boom brought the bicycle industry back to life after a long period of decline.

The time span of the stages can also vary significantly from industry to industry. Some industries can stay in maturity almost indefinitely if their products become basic necessities of life, as is the case for the car industry. Other industries skip the mature stage and go straight into decline, as in the case of the vacuum tube industry. Transistors replaced vacuum tubes as a major component in electronic products even though the vacuum tube industry was still in its growth stage. Still other industries may go through several shakeouts before they enter full maturity, as appears to be happening in the telecommunications industry.

■ Innovation and Change

Over any reasonable length of time, in many industries competition can be viewed as a process driven by innovation.[17] Indeed, innovation is frequently the major factor in industry evolution and causes the movement through the industry life cycle. Innovation is attractive because companies that pioneer new products, processes, or strategies can often earn enormous profits. Consider the explosive growth of Toys "R" Us, Dell Computer, and Wal-Mart. In a variety of different ways, all of these companies were innovators. Toys "R" Us pioneered a new way of selling toys (through large discount warehouse-type stores), Dell pioneered a whole new way of selling personal computers (by mail order), and Wal-Mart pioneered the low-price discount superstore concept.

Successful innovation can transform the nature of industry competition. In recent decades, one frequent consequence of innovation has been to lower the fixed costs of production, thereby reducing barriers to entry and allowing new, and smaller, enterprises to compete with large established organizations. For example, two decades ago, large integrated steel companies such as US Steel, LTV, and Bethlehem Steel dominated the steel industry. The industry was a typical oligopoly, dominated by a small number of large producers, in which tacit price collusion was practiced. Then along came a series of efficient mini-mill producers such as Nucor and Chaparral Steel, which used a new technology: electric arc furnaces. Over the past twenty years, they have revolutionized the structure of the industry. What was once a consolidated industry is now much more fragmented and price competitive. The successor company to US Steel, USX, now has only a 12 percent market share, down from 55 percent in the mid-1960s, and both Bethlehem and LTV went bankrupt. In contrast, the mini-mills as a group now hold over 40 percent of the market, up from 5 percent twenty years ago.[18] Thus, the mini-mill innovation has reshaped the nature of competition in the steel industry.[19] A competitive forces model applied to the industry in 1970 would look very different from a competitive forces model applied in 2004.

Michael Porter, the originator of the competitive forces and strategic group concepts, has explicitly recognized the role of innovation in revolutionizing industry structure. Porter now talks of innovations as "unfreezing" and "reshaping" industry structure. He argues that after a period of turbulence triggered by innovation, the structure of an industry once more settles down into a fairly stable pattern, and the five forces and strategic group concepts can once more be applied.[20] This view of the evolution of industry structure is often referred to as *punctuated equilibrium*.[21] The punctuated equilibrium view holds that long periods of equilibrium, when an industry's structure is stable, are punctuated by periods of rapid change when industry structure is revolutionized by innovation; there is an unfreezing and refreezing process.

Figure 2.6 shows what punctuated equilibrium might look like for one key dimension of industry structure: competitive structure. From time t_0 to t_1, the competitive

FIGURE 2.6

Punctuated
Equilibrium and
Competitive Structure

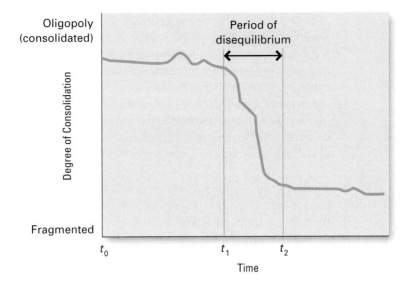

structure of the industry is a stable oligopoly, with a few companies sharing the market. At time t_1, a major new innovation is pioneered by either an existing company or a new entrant. The result is a period of turbulence between t_1 and t_2. After a while, the industry settles down into a new state of equilibrium, but now the competitive structure is far more fragmented. Note that the opposite could have happened: the industry could have become more consolidated, although this seems to be less common. In general, innovations seem to lower barriers to entry, allow more companies into the industry, and as a result lead to fragmentation rather than consolidation.

During a period of rapid change when industry structure is being revolutionized by innovation, value typically migrates to business models based on new positioning strategies.[22] In the stockbrokerage industry, value migrated away from the full-service broker model to the online trading model. In the steel industry, the introduction of electric arc technology led to a migration of value away from large, integrated enterprises and toward small mini-mills. In the book-selling industry, value has migrated away from small boutique "bricks and mortar" booksellers toward large bookstore chains like Barnes & Noble and online bookstores such as amazon.com.

Because the competitive forces and strategic group models are static, they cannot adequately capture what occurs during periods of rapid change in the industry environment when value is migrating. Similarly, a simple view of the industry life cycle does not allow for an industry to repeat a stage or even jump stages that technological upheavals can lead to. Nevertheless, they are useful tools for analyzing industry structure during periods of stability.

Some scholars question the validity of the punctuated equilibrium approach. Richard D'Avani has argued that many industries are **hypercompetitive,** meaning that they are characterized by permanent and ongoing innovation and competitive change (the computer industry is often cited as an example of a hypercompetitive industry).[23] The structure of such industries is constantly being revolutionized by innovation, so there are no periods of equilibrium or stability. When this is the case, some might argue that the competitive forces and strategic group models are of limited value because they represent no more than snapshots of a constantly changing situation. Thus, managers must constantly repeat industry analysis and pay attention to changes in the forces of competition. Moreover, D'Avani and others claim that markets have become more hypercompetitive in the modern era, although recent research evidence seems to suggest that this is not the case, and many industries are characterized by long periods of relative stability.[24]

■ Company Differences

Another criticism of industry models is that they overemphasize the importance of industry structure as a determinant of company performance and underemphasize the importance of variations or differences among companies within an industry or a strategic group.[25] As we discuss in the next chapter, there can be enormous variance in the profit rates of individual companies within an industry. Research by Richard Rumelt and his associates, for example, suggests that industry structure explains only about 10 percent of the variance in profit rates across companies.[26] The implication is that individual company differences explain much of the remainder. Other studies have put the explained variance closer to 20 percent, which is still not a large figure.[27] Similarly, a growing number of studies have found only weak evidence of a link between strategic group membership and company profit rates, despite the fact that the strategic group model predicts a strong link.[28] Collectively, these studies suggest that the individual resources and capabilities of a company are far more important determinants of its profitability than is the industry or strategic group of which the company is a member. Although these findings do not make the five forces and strategic group models irrelevant, they do mean that the models have limited usefulness. A company will not be profitable just because it is based in an attractive industry or strategic group. As we discuss in Chapters 3 and 4, more is required.

The Macroenvironment

Just as the decisions and actions of strategic managers can often change an industry's competitive structure, so too can changing conditions or forces in the wider **macroenvironment**—that is, the broader economic, global, technological, demographic, social, and political context in which companies and industries are embedded (see Figure 2.7). Changes in the forces in the macroenvironment can have a direct impact on any or all of the forces in Porter's model, thereby altering the relative strength of these forces and, with it, the attractiveness of an industry.

■ Macroeconomic Forces

Economic forces affect the general health and well-being of a nation or the regional economy of an organization, which in turn affect companies' and industries' ability to earn an adequate rate of return. The four most important factors in the macroenvironment are the growth rate of the economy, interest rates, currency exchange rates, and inflation (or deflation) rates. Economic growth, because it leads to an expansion in customer expenditures, tends to produce a general easing of competitive pressures within an industry. This gives companies the opportunity to expand their operations and earn higher profits. Because economic decline (a recession) leads to a reduction in customer expenditures, it increases competitive pressures. Economic decline frequently causes price wars in mature industries.

The level of interest rates can determine the demand for a company's products. Interest rates are important whenever customers routinely borrow money to finance their

FIGURE 2.7

The Role of the
Macroenvironment

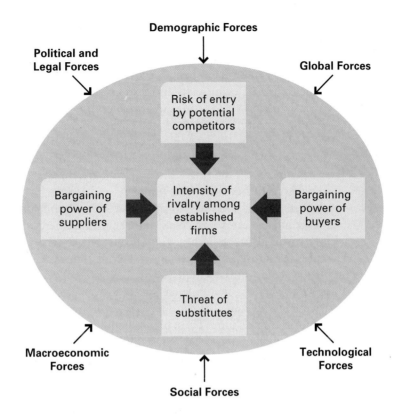

purchase of these products. The most obvious example is the housing market, where mortgage rates directly affect demand. Interest rates also have an impact on the sale of autos, appliances, and capital equipment, to give just a few examples. For companies in such industries, rising interest rates are a threat and falling rates an opportunity.

Interest rates are also important insofar as they influence a company's cost of capital, and therefore its ability to raise funds and invest in new assets. The lower that interest rates are, the lower the cost of capital for companies will be, and the more investment there will be. This is not always a good thing. In the late 1990s, the very low cost of capital allowed dot-com and telecommunications companies with questionable business plans to raise large amounts of money and invest those funds in computers and telecommunications gear (the low cost of capital lowered barriers to entry by enabling start-ups to raise the capital required to circumvent entry barriers). This was initially good for the manufacturers of telecommunications equipment and computers, but the demand signal that was being sent was not sustainable: many of the dot-com and telecommunications start-ups of the 1990s went bankrupt between 2000 and 2002. Secondhand computers and telecommunications equipment from these bankrupt companies flooded the market, depressing first-time demand for that equipment and helping to plunge the computer and telecommunications equipment businesses into a deep slowdown. (For example, in January 2002, Internet auction house eBay listed more than three thousand Cisco products that were being auctioned for much less than their initial prices.)

Currency exchange rates define the value of different national currencies against each other. Movement in currency exchange rates has a direct impact on the competitiveness of a company's products in the global marketplace. For example, when the value of the dollar is low compared with the value of other currencies, products made in the United States are relatively inexpensive and products made overseas are relatively expensive. A low or declining dollar reduces the threat from foreign competitors while creating opportunities for increased sales overseas. For example, the fall in the value of the dollar against the Japanese yen that occurred between 1985 and 1995, when the dollar-to-yen exchange rate declined from 240 yen per dollar to 85 yen per dollar, sharply increased the price of imported Japanese cars, giving U.S. car manufacturers some protection against those imports.

Price inflation can destabilize the economy, producing slower economic growth, higher interest rates, and volatile currency movements. If inflation keeps increasing, investment planning becomes hazardous. The key characteristic of inflation is that it makes the future less predictable. In an inflationary environment, it may be impossible to predict with any accuracy the real value of returns that can be earned from a project five years hence. Such uncertainty makes companies less willing to invest. Their holding back in turn depresses economic activity and ultimately pushes the economy into a slump. Thus, high inflation is a threat to companies.

Price deflation also has a destabilizing effect on economic activity. If prices are deflating, the real price of fixed payments goes up. This is particularly damaging for companies and individuals with a high level of debt who must make regular fixed payments on that debt. In a deflationary environment, the increase in the real value of debt consumes more of household and corporate cash flows, leaving less for other purchases and depressing the overall level of economic activity. Although significant deflation has not been seen since the 1930s, in the 1990s it started to take hold in Japan.

■ **Global Forces**   Over the last half-century there have been enormous changes in the world economic system. We review these changes in some detail in Chapter 8 when we discuss global strategy. For now, the important points to note are that barriers to international trade and investment have tumbled, and more and more countries are enjoying sustained economic growth. Economic growth in places like Brazil, China, and India is creating large new markets for companies' goods and services and is giving companies an opportunity to grow their profits faster by entering these nations. Falling barriers to international trade and investment have made it much easier to enter foreign nations. For example, twenty years ago, it was almost impossible for a Western company to set up operations in China. Today, Western and Japanese companies are investing over $50 billion a year in China. By the same token, however, falling barriers to international trade and investment have made it easier for foreign enterprises to enter the domestic markets of many companies (by lowering barriers to entry), thereby increasing the intensity of competition and lowering profitability. Because of these changes, many formally isolated domestic markets have now become part of a much larger, and more competitive, global marketplace, creating a myriad threats and opportunities for companies. We shall return to this topic and discuss it in more detail in Chapter 8.

■ **Technological Forces**   Since World War II, the pace of technological change has accelerated.[29] This has unleashed a process that has been called a "perennial gale of creative destruction."[30] Technological change can make established products obsolete overnight and simultaneously create a host of new product possibilities. Thus, technological change is both creative and destructive—both an opportunity and a threat.

One of the most important impacts of technological change is that it can affect the height of barriers to entry and therefore radically reshape industry structure. The Internet, because it is so pervasive, has the potential for changing the competitive structure of many industries. It often lowers barriers to entry and reduces customer switching costs, changes that tend to increase the intensity of rivalry in an industry and lower both prices and profits.[31] For example, the Internet has lowered barriers to entry into the news industry. Providers of financial news now have to compete for advertising dollars and customer attention with new Internet-based media organizations that sprang up during the 1990s, such as TheStreet.com, the Motley Fool, and Yahoo!'s financial section. The resulting increase in rivalry has given advertisers more choices, enabling them to bargain down the prices that they must pay to media companies. Similarly, in the automobile industry, the ability of customers to comparison-shop for cars online and purchase cars online from a number of distributors such as Auto Nation has increased the ability of customers to find the best value for money. Customers' increased bargaining power enables them to put downward pressure on car prices and squeeze profits out of the automobile industry.

◼ Demographic Forces

Demographic forces are outcomes of changes in the characteristics of a population, such as age, gender, ethnic origin, race, sexual orientation, and social class. Like the other forces in the general environment, demographic forces present managers with opportunities and threats and can have major implications for organizations. Over the past thirty years, for example, women have entered the work force in increasing numbers. Between 1973 and 2002, the percentage of women in the work force increased from 44 to 60 percent in the United States, 48 to 68 percent in Canada, and 51 to 68 percent in Britain.[32] This dramatic increase has brought issues such as equal pay for equal work and sexual harassment at work to the forefront of issues that managers must address if they are to attract and make full use of the talents of female workers.

Changes in the age distribution of a population are another example of a demographic force that affects managers and organizations. Currently, most industrialized nations are experiencing the aging of their populations as a consequence of falling birth and death rates and the aging of the babyboom generation. In Germany, for example, the percentage of the population over age sixty-five is expected to rise from 15.4 percent in 1990 to 20.7 percent in 2010. Comparable figures for Canada are 11.4 and 14.4 percent; for Japan, 11.7 and 19.5 percent; and for the United States, 12.6 and 13.5 percent.[33]

The aging of the population is increasing opportunities for organizations that cater to older people; the home health care and recreation industries, for example, are seeing an upswing in demand for their services. As the babyboom generation from the late 1950s to the early 1960s has aged, it has created a host of opportunities and threats. During the 1980s, many baby boomers were getting married and creating an upsurge in demand for the customer appliances normally bought by couples marrying for the first time. Companies such as Whirlpool Corporation and General Electric capitalized on the resulting upsurge in demand for washing machines, dishwashers, dryers, and the like. In the 1990s, many of these same baby boomers were starting to save for retirement, creating an inflow of money into mutual funds and creating a boom in the mutual fund industry. In the next twenty years, many of these same baby boomers will retire, creating a boom in retirement communities.

■ **Social Forces**

Social forces refer to the way in which changing social mores and values affect an industry. Like the other macroenvironmental forces discussed here, social change creates opportunities and threats. One of the major social movements of recent decades has been the trend toward greater health consciousness. Its impact has been immense, and companies that recognized the opportunities early have often reaped significant gains. Philip Morris, for example, capitalized on the growing health consciousness trend when it acquired Miller Brewing Company and then redefined competition in the beer industry with its introduction of low-calorie beer (Miller Lite). Similarly, PepsiCo was able to gain market share from its rival, Coca-Cola, by being the first to introduce diet colas and fruit-based soft drinks. At the same time, the health trend has created a threat for many industries. The tobacco industry, for example, is in decline as a direct result of greater customer awareness of the health implications of smoking.

■ **Political and Legal Forces**

Political and legal forces are outcomes of changes in laws and regulations. They result from political and legal developments within society and significantly affect managers and companies.

Political processes shape a society's laws, which constrain the operations of organizations and managers and thus create both opportunities and threats.[34] For example, throughout much of the industrialized world, there has been a strong trend toward deregulation of industries previously controlled by the state and privatization of organizations once owned by the state. In the United States, deregulation of the airline industry in 1979 allowed twenty-nine new airlines to enter the industry between 1979 and 1993. The increase in passenger-carrying capacity after deregulation led to excess capacity on many routes, intense competition, and fare wars. To respond to this more competitive task environment, airlines have had to look for ways to reduce operating costs. The development of hub-and-spoke systems, the rise of nonunion airlines, and the introduction of no-frills discount service are all responses to increased competition in the airlines' task environment. Despite these innovations, the airline industry still experiences intense fare wars, which have lowered profits and caused numerous airline company bankruptcies. The global telecommunications service industry is now experiencing the same kind of turmoil following the deregulation of that industry in the United States and elsewhere.

In most countries, the interplay between political and legal forces, on the one hand, and industry competitive structure, on the other, is a two-way process in which the government sets regulations that influence competitive structure, and firms in an industry often seek to influence the regulations that governments enact by a number of means. First, when permitted, they may provide financial support to politicians or political parties that espouse views favorable to the industry and lobby government legislators directly to shape government regulations. For example, during the 1990s and early 2000s, the now-bankrupt energy trading company Enron lobbied government legislators to persuade them to deregulate energy markets in the United States, an action that Enron would benefit from. Second, companies and industries may lobby the government through industry associations. In 2002, the United States Steel Industry Association was a prime mover in persuading President Bush to enact a 30 percent tariff on imports of foreign steel into the United States. The purpose of the tariff was to protect American steel makers from foreign competitors, thereby reducing the intensity of rivalry in the United States steel markets.

Summary of Chapter

1. An industry can be defined as a group of companies offering products or services that are close substitutes for each other. Close substitutes are products or services that satisfy the same basic customer needs.

2. The main technique used to analyze competition in the industry environment is the five forces model. The five forces are (1) the risk of new entry by potential competitors, (2) the extent of rivalry among established firms, (3) the bargaining power of buyers, (4) the bargaining power of suppliers, and (5) the threat of substitute products. The stronger each force is, the more competitive the industry and the lower the rate of return that can be earned.

3. The risk of entry by potential competitors is a function of the height of barriers to entry. The higher the barriers to entry are, the lower is the risk of entry and the greater are the profits that can be earned in the industry.

4. The extent of rivalry among established companies is a function of an industry's competitive structure, demand conditions, cost conditions, and barriers to exit. Strong demand conditions moderate the competition among established companies and create opportunities for expansion. When demand is weak, intensive competition can develop, particularly in consolidated industries with high exit barriers.

5. Buyers are most powerful when a company depends on them for business but they themselves are not dependent on the company. In such circumstances, buyers are a threat.

6. Suppliers are most powerful when a company depends on them for business but they themselves are not dependent on the company. In such circumstances, suppliers are a threat.

7. Substitute products are the products of companies serving customer needs similar to the needs served by the industry being analyzed. The more similar the substitute products are to each other, the lower is the price that companies can charge without losing customers to the substitutes.

8. Some argue for a sixth competitive force of some significance: the power, vigor, and competence of complementors. Powerful and vigorous complementors may have a strong positive impact on demand in an industry.

9. Most industries are composed of strategic groups: groups of companies pursuing the same or a similar strategy. Companies in different strategic groups pursue different strategies.

10. The members of a company's strategic group constitute its immediate competitors. Because different strategic groups are characterized by different opportunities and threats, it may pay a company to switch strategic groups. The feasibility of doing so is a function of the height of mobility barriers.

11. Industries go through a well-defined life cycle: from an embryonic stage, through growth, shakeout, and maturity, and eventually decline. Each stage has different implications for the competitive structure of the industry, and each gives rise to its own set of opportunities and threats.

12. The five forces, strategic group, and industry life cycles models all have limitations. The five forces and strategic group models present a static picture of competition that deemphasizes the role of innovation. Yet innovation can revolutionize industry structure and completely change the strength of different competitive forces. The five forces and strategic group models have been criticized for deemphasizing the importance of individual company differences. A company will not be profitable just because it is based in an attractive industry or strategic group; much more is required. The industry life cycle model is a generalization that is not always followed, particularly when innovations revolutionize an industry.

13. The macroenvironment affects the intensity of rivalry within an industry. Included in the macroenvironment are the macroeconomic environment, the global environment, the technological environment, the demographic and social environment, and the political and legal environment.

Discussion Questions

1. Under what environmental conditions are price wars most likely to occur in an industry? What are the implications of price wars for a company? How should a company try to deal with the threat of a price war?

2. Discuss Porter's five forces model with reference to what you know about the U.S. airline industry. What does the model tell you about the level of competition in this industry?

3. Identify a growth industry, a mature industry, and a declining industry. For each industry, identify the following: (a) the number and size distribution of companies, (b) the nature of barriers to entry, (c) the height of barriers to entry, and (d) the extent of product differentiation. What do these factors tell you about the nature of competition in each industry? What are the implications for the company in terms of opportunities and threats?

4. Assess the impact of macroenvironmental factors on the likely level of enrollment at your university over the next decade. What are the implications of these factors for the job security and salary level of your professors?

Practicing Strategic Management

SMALL-GROUP EXERCISE
Competing with Microsoft

Break up into groups of three to five people, and discuss the following scenario. Appoint one group member as a spokesperson who will communicate your findings to the class.

You are a group of managers and software engineers at a small start-up. You have developed a revolutionary new operating system for personal computers that offers distinct advantages over Microsoft's Windows operating system: it takes up less memory space on the hard drive of a personal computer; it takes full advantage of the power of the personal computer's microprocessor, and in theory can run software applications much faster than Windows; it is much easier to install and use than Windows; and it responds to voice instructions with an accuracy of 99.9 percent, in addition to input from a keyboard or mouse. The operating system is the only product offering that your company has produced.

Complete the following exercises:

1. Analyze the competitive structure of the market for personal computer operating systems. On the basis of this analysis, identify what factors might inhibit adoption of your operating system by customers.
2. Can you think of a strategy that your company might pursue, either alone or in conjunction with other enterprises, in order to "beat Microsoft"? What will it take to execute that strategy successfully?

ARTICLE FILE 2

Find an example of an industry that has become more competitive in recent years. Identify the reasons for the increase in competitive pressure.

STRATEGIC MANAGEMENT PROJECT
Module 2

This module requires you to analyze the industry environment in which your company is based using the information you have already gathered:

1. Apply the five forces model to the industry in which your company is based. What does this model tell you about the nature of competition in the industry?
2. Are any changes taking place in the macroenvironment that might have an impact, positive or negative, on the industry in which your company is based? If

so, what are these changes, and how might they affect the industry?

3. Identify any strategic groups that might exist in the industry. How does the intensity of competition differ across these strategic groups?
4. How dynamic is the industry in which your company is based? Is there any evidence that innovation is reshaping competition or has done so in the recent past?
5. In what stage of its life cycle is the industry in which your company is based? What are the implications of this for the intensity of competition both now and in the future?
6. Is your company based in an industry that is becoming more global? If so, what are the implications of this change for competitive intensity?
7. Analyze the impact of national context as it pertains to the industry in which your company is based. Does national context help or hinder your company in achieving a competitive advantage in the global marketplace?

EXPLORING THE WEB
Visiting Boeing and Airbus

Visit the websites of the Boeing Corporation (**www.boeing.com**) and Airbus Industrie (**www.airbus.com**). Go to the news features of both sites, and read through the press releases issued by both companies. Also look at the annual reports and company profile (or history features) contained on both sites. With this material as your guide:

1. Use Porter's five forces model to analyze the nature of competition in the commercial jet aircraft market.
2. Assess the likely outlook for competition over the next ten years in this market. Try to establish whether new entry into this industry is likely, whether demand will grow or shrink, how powerful buyers are likely to become, and what the implications of all this are for the nature of competition ten years out.

General Task   Search the Web for information that allows you to assess the current state of competition in the market for personal computers. Use that information to perform an analysis of the structure of the market in the United States. (Hint: Try visiting the websites of personal computer companies. Also visit *Electronic Business Today* at **www.ebtmag.com**).

Closing Case

Plane Wreck: The Airline Industry in 2001–2004

Between 2001 and 2003, players in the global airline industry lost some $30 billion, more money than the industry had made since its inception. The losses were particularly severe among the big six airlines in the United States (American Airlines, United, Delta, Continental, US Airways, and Northwest). In 2002 these major airlines lost $7.4 billion and another $5.3 billion in 2003. Both US Airways and United were forced to seek Chapter 11 bankruptcy protections. Although forecasts suggest the six major airlines will break even in 2004, a return to the boom years of 1995–2000, when the airlines posted record profits, seems unlikely anytime soon.

The dramatic slump in airline profits began in early 2001 when business travel started to fall off in the wake of the rapidly deflating technology and dot-com bubble of the 1990s. Then, in the aftermath of the terrorist attacks of September 11, demand dropped through the floor. The airlines began cutting prices to try to maintain their passenger loads in the face of declining demand. However, the tactic didn't work. When one airline serving a particular route cut its prices, its competitors, desperate to cover their fixed costs, quickly followed. The result was a downward price spiral. In the fourth quarter of 2001, prices fell by 15 percent as airlines tried to induce people to fly. Despite this effort, passenger traffic fell by 19 percent, and revenue at major airlines fell by over 30 percent.[35]

Even though demand and profits plummeted at the big six airlines, some carriers continued to make profits during 2001–2003, most notably the budget airline Southwest. In addition, other newer budget airlines, including AirTran and JetBlue (which was started in 2000), gained market share during this period. Indeed, between 2000 and 2003 the budget airlines in the United States expanded capacity by 44 percent even as the majors slashed their carrying capacity and parked unused planes in the desert. In 1998 the budget airlines held a 16 percent share of the U.S. market, and by mid 2004 their share had risen to 29 percent.

The key to the success of the budget airlines is their business model, which gives them a 30 to 50 percent cost advantage over traditional airlines. The budget airlines all follow the same basic script: They purchase just one type of aircraft (some standardize on Boeing 737s, others on Airbus 320s). They also hire nonunion labor and cross-train employees to perform multiple jobs (for example, to help meet turnaround times, the pilots might help check

tickets at the gate). As a result of such flexible work rules, Southwest needs only 80 employees to support and fly an aircraft, compared to 115 at the big six airlines. The budget airlines also favor flying "point to point" rather than through hubs, and they often use cheap secondary airports rather than major hubs. They focus on large markets with large traffic volume (such as up and down the East Coast). To cut costs further, they offer no frills on the flights: no in-flight food or complementary drinks. Finally, prices are set low to fill up the seats.

In contrast, the business model of the six major airlines is based on the network or hub-and-spoke system. Under this system, the network airlines route their flights through major hubs. Often a single airline will dominate a hub (thus United dominates Chicago O'Hare airport). This system was developed because it was a way of efficiently using airline capacity when there wasn't enough demand to fill a plane flying point to point. By using a hub-and-spoke system, the major network airlines have been able to serve some 38,000 city pairs, some of which generate fewer than fifty passengers per day. But the budget airlines seem to have found a way around this constraint by focusing on a few hundred city pairs where there is sufficient demand to fill their planes and flying directly between them (point to point). The network carriers also suffer from a higher cost structure because of their legacy of a unionized work force. In addition, their costs are pushed higher by their superior in-flight service. In good times, the network carriers can recoup their costs by charging higher prices than the discount airlines, particularly for business travelers, who pay more to book late and to fly business or first class. In the weak demand environment of the early 2000s, however, this was no longer the case.

To make matters worse for the network airlines, the budget airlines have started to enter the lucrative coast-to-coast markets. The major airlines long dominated these markets and kept fares high. However, by taking advantage of new long-range versions of their favorite aircraft, such as the Boeing 737–800, to fly these routes nonstop, budget airlines have been able to directly compete with the network airlines. JetBlue, for example, has over 50 percent of its capacity on coast-to-cost routes. To protect their turf, the network airlines have responded by adding more flights in an attempt to squeeze the budget carriers out. As a result, between June 2003 and June 2004, capacity on coast-to-coast routes increased anywhere from 14 to 100 percent. With all these extra seats to fill, airlines have had to slash fares, which have fallen by as much as 60 to 70 percent on some routes.

The major network airlines have also moved to cut their operating costs. Between 2001 and 2004, they cut their operating costs by $13.4 billion and reduced payrolls by 100,000. Yet it has not been enough to check the expansion of the budget airlines or to close the cost advantage the discounters enjoy. To make matters worse, in 2004 prices for jet fuel soared as oil peaked at over $40 a barrel. Some of the major airlines responded by trying to raise prices, only to give up within days. Some observers have also commented that the industry's problems are exacerbated by bankruptcy laws that keep troubled airlines such as United in the industry by allowing them time to reorganize under Chapter 11 bankruptcy protection rules.[36]

Case Discussion Questions

1. Use the competitive forces model to analyze the structure of the airline industry during 2001–2004. How well does this analysis explain the low profitability of the industry?

2. Are the budget airlines in a different strategic group than the major network airlines?

3. Compare and contrast the business models of the network and budget airlines. What are the strengths and weaknesses of each model?

4. What is required for the industry to return to profitability?

5. What must the major network airlines do to respond to the competitive threat posed by the budget airlines? Have they taken steps in this direction? Have they done enough?

Chapter 3

Internal Analysis: Distinctive Competencies, Competitive Advantage, and Profitability

Opening Case

Dell's Competitive Advantage

Dell Computer has a sustained history of very high profitability. Between 1998 and 2003 its average return on invested capital (ROIC) was a staggering 39 percent, far ahead of the profitability of competing manufacturers of personal computers. For comparison, Apple Computer earned an average ROIC of 7 percent over the same period, Gateway 10 percent, and Hewlett-Packard 13 percent. Moreover, Dell managed to maintain a very high ROIC even in the tough selling environment for personal computers that existed in 2001–2003, while the profitability of its competitors fell sharply during this same period (see the figure on page 76). Clearly, Dell has a sustained competitive advantage over its rivals. Where does this competitive advantage come from?

The answer can be found in Dell's business model: selling directly to customers. Michael Dell reasoned that by cutting out wholesalers and retailers he could obtain the profits they would otherwise receive and give part of those profits to customers in the form of lower prices. Initially, Dell sold directly through mailings and telephone contacts, but since the mid 1990s most of its sales have been made through its web site. By 2001, 85 percent of Dell's sales were made through the Internet. Dell's sophisticated interactive web site allows customers to mix and match product features such as microprocessors, memory, monitors, internal hard drives, CD and DVD drives, keyboard and mouse format, and so on to customize their own computer system. The ability to customize orders keeps customers coming back to Dell. This strong customer loyalty helped to drive sales up to a record $41.5 billion in fiscal 2004.

Another major reason for Dell's high performance is that Dell minimizes the cost structure of its supply chain, in particular, the costs of holding inventory, yet it can still build a computer to individual customer specifications within three days. Dell has about two hundred suppliers, over half of them located outside the United States. It uses the Internet to feed real-time information about order flow to its suppliers so they have up-to-the-minute information about demand trends for the components they produce, along with volume expectations for the upcoming four to twelve weeks. Dell's suppliers use this information to adjust their own production schedules, manufacturing just enough components for Dell's needs and shipping them by the

Profitability in the U.S. Personal Computer Industry, 1998–2003

Data Source: Value Line Investment Survey.

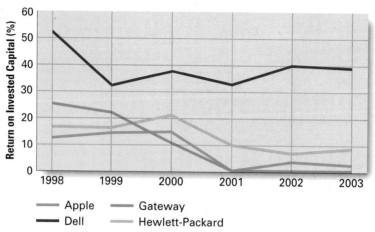

most appropriate mode so that they arrive just in time for production. This tight coordination is pushed back even further down the supply chain because Dell shares this information with its suppliers' biggest suppliers. For example, Selectron Technologies builds motherboards for Dell that incorporate digital signal processing chips from Texas Instruments. To coordinate the supply chain, Dell passes information to both Texas Instruments and Selectron. Texas Instruments then adjusts its schedules to Selectron's needs, and Selectron adjusts its schedule to fit the order data it receives from Dell. All of this coordination results in lower costs along the supply chain.

Dell's ultimate goal is to drive all inventories out of the supply chain apart from those actually in transit between suppliers and Dell, effectively replacing inventory with information. Although it has not yet achieved this goal, it has succeeded in driving down inventory to the lowest level in the industry. Dell has about three days of inventory on hand, compared to twenty to thirty at competitors such as Hewlett-Packard and Gateway. This is a major source of competitive advantage in the computer industry, where component costs account for 75 percent of revenues and typically fall by 1 percent per week due to rapid obsolescence.

In sum, Dell's competitive advantage is based on a direct selling business model that eliminates wholesalers and retailers and allows the company to lower prices. This, combined with strong customer loyalty and efficient internal operations, particularly in supply-chain management, has given Dell the lowest cost structure in the industry. When demand for personal computers fell in 2001, Dell was able to take advantage of its cost-leadership position to cut prices aggressively and gain market share while still maintaining high profitability through economies of scale and other efficiencies. By early 2004 Dell had 16.5 percent of the global market for PCs, up from 14.6 percent a year earlier. Hewlett-Packard, which held second place, had a 14 percent share in early 2004.[1]

Overview

Why, within a particular industry or market, do some companies outperform others? What is the basis of their (sustained) competitive advantage? The *Opening Case* provides some clues. The competitive advantage of Dell Computer comes from its direct selling business model, which lowers costs and enables the company to respond to customer demands, and also from its focus on efficient supply-chain management. As you will see in this chapter, efficiency and customer responsiveness are two of the four main building blocks of competitive advantage. The other two are *innovation* and the *quality of product or service offering*.

This chapter focuses on internal analysis, which is concerned with identifying the *strengths* and *weaknesses* of the company. Together with an analysis of the company's external environment, internal analysis gives managers the information they need to choose the business model and strategies that will enable their company to attain a sustained competitive advantage. Internal analysis is a three-step process. First, managers must understand the process by which companies create value for customers and profit for themselves, and they need to understand the role of *resources, capabilities,* and *distinctive competencies* in this process. Second, they need to understand how important superior *efficiency, innovation, quality,* and *responsiveness to customers* are in creating value and generating high profitability. Third, they must be able to analyze the sources of their company's competitive advantage to identify what is driving the profitability of their enterprise and where opportunities for improvement might lie. In other words, they must be able to identify how the *strengths* of the enterprise boost its profitability and how any *weaknesses* lead to lower profitability.

Three more critical issues in internal analysis are addressed in this chapter. First, what factors influence the *durability* of competitive advantage? Second, why do successful companies often lose their competitive advantage? Third, how can companies avoid competitive failure and sustain their competitive advantage over time?

After reading this chapter, you will understand the nature of competitive advantage and why managers need to perform internal analysis, just as they must conduct industry analysis, to achieve superior performance and profitability.

Competencies, Resources, and Competitive Advantage

A company has a *competitive advantage* over its rivals when its profitability is greater than the average profitability of all companies in its industry. It has a *sustained competitive advantage* when it is able to maintain above-average profitability over a number of years (as Dell has done in the personal computer industry). What are the sources of competitive advantage and superior profitability, and what is the link between strategy, competitive advantage, and profitability?

■ Strategy, Distinctive Competencies, and Competitive Advantage

The primary objective of strategy is to achieve a sustained competitive advantage, which in turn will result in superior profitability and profit growth. All the levels of strategy identified in Chapter 1—functional, business, global, and corporate—are involved in creating a competitive advantage, and they are discussed in detail in the next chapters. No matter what the level, however, to use strategy to achieve a competitive advantage, a company must create distinctive competencies.

Distinctive competencies are firm-specific strengths that allow a company to *differentiate* its products and/or achieve substantially *lower costs* than its rivals and thus gain a competitive advantage. It can be argued, for example, that Toyota has distinctive competencies in the development and operation of manufacturing processes. Toyota pioneered a whole range of manufacturing techniques, such as just-in-time inventory systems, self-managing teams, and reduced setup times for complex equipment. These competencies, collectively known as the Toyota *lean production* system, helped it attain superior efficiency and product quality, which are the basis of its competitive advantage in the global automobile industry.[2] Distinctive competencies arise from two complementary sources: *resources* and *capabilities.*[3]

■ **Resources**   **Resources** are financial, physical, social or human, technological, and organizational factors that allow a company to create value for its customers. Company resources can be divided into two types: tangible and intangible resources. **Tangible resources** are physical entities, such as land, buildings, plant, equipment, inventory, and money. **Intangible resources** are nonphysical entities that are created by managers and other employees, such as brand names, the reputation of the company, the knowledge that employees have gained through experience, and the intellectual property of the company, including that protected through patents, copyrights, and trademarks.

The more *firm specific* and *difficult to imitate* is a resource, the more likely a company is to have a distinctive competency. For example, Polaroid's distinctive competency in instant photography was based on a firm-specific and valuable intangible resource: technological know-how in instant film processing that was protected from imitation by a thicket of patents. Once a process can be imitated, as when patents expire, or a superior technology, such as digital photography, comes along, the distinctive competency disappears, as has happened to Polaroid. Another important quality of a resource that leads to a distinctive competency is that it is *valuable*: in some way, it helps to create strong *demand* for the company's products. Thus, Polaroid's technological know-how was valuable while it created strong demand for its photographic products; it became far less valuable when superior digital technology came along.

■ **Capabilities** Capabilities refer to a company's skills at coordinating its resources and putting them to productive use. These skills reside in an organization's rules, routines, and procedures, that is, the style or manner through which it makes decisions and manages its internal processes to achieve organizational objectives. More generally, a company's capabilities are the product of its organizational structure, processes, and control systems. They specify how and where decisions are made within a company, the kind of behaviors the company rewards, and the company's cultural norms and values. (We discuss how organizational structure and control systems help a company obtain capabilities in Chapters 12 and 13.) Capabilities are intangible. They reside not so much in individuals as in the way individuals interact, cooperate, and make decisions within the context of an organization.[4]

■ **A Critical Distinction** The distinction between resources and capabilities is critical to understanding what generates a distinctive competency. A company may have firm-specific and valuable resources, but unless it has the capability to use those resources effectively, it may not be able to create a distinctive competency. It is also important to recognize that a company may not need firm-specific and valuable resources to establish a distinctive competency so long as it *does have* capabilities that no competitor possesses. For example, the steel mini-mill operator Nucor is widely acknowledged to be the most cost-efficient steel maker in the United States. Its distinctive competency in low-cost steel making does not come from any firm-specific and valuable resources. Nucor has the same resources (plant, equipment, skilled employees, know-how) as many other mini-mill operators. What distinguishes Nucor is its unique capability to manage its resources in a highly productive way. Specifically, Nucor's structure, control systems, and culture promote efficiency at all levels within the company.

In sum, for a company to have a distinctive competency it must at a minimum have either (1) a firm-specific and valuable resource and the capabilities (skills) necessary to take advantage of that resource (as illustrated by Polaroid) or (2) a firm-specific capability to manage resources (as exemplified by Nucor). A company's distinctive competency is strongest when it possesses *both* firm-specific and valuable resources and firm-specific capabilities to manage those resources.

Figure 3.1 illustrates the relationship of a company's strategies, distinctive competencies, and competitive advantage. Distinctive competencies shape the strategies that the company pursues, which lead to competitive advantage and superior profitability. However, it is also very important to realize that the strategies a company adopts can build new resources and capabilities or strengthen the existing resources and capabilities of the company, thereby enhancing the distinctive competencies of the enterprise. Thus, the relationship between distinctive competencies and strategies is not a linear one; rather, it is a reciprocal one in which distinctive competencies shape strategies, and strategies help to build and create distinctive competencies.[5]

FIGURE 3.1

Strategy, Resources, Capabilities, and Competencies

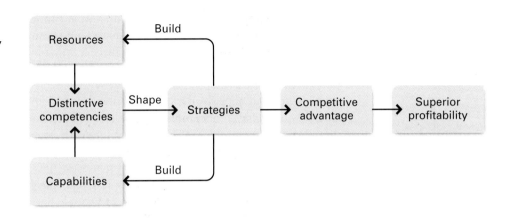

The history of The Walt Disney Company since the 1980s illustrates the way this process works. In the early 1980s, Disney suffered a string of poor financial years that culminated in a 1984 management shakeup when Michael Eisner was appointed CEO. Four years later, Disney's sales had increased from $1.66 billion to $3.75 billion, its net profits from $98 million to $570 million, and its stock market valuation from $1.8 billion to $10.3 billion. What brought about this transformation was the company's deliberate attempt to use its resources and capabilities more aggressively: Disney's enormous film library, its brand name, and its filmmaking skills, particularly in animation. Under Eisner, many old Disney classics were re-released, first in movie theaters and then on video, earning the company millions in the process. Then Eisner reintroduced the product that had originally made Disney famous: the full-length animated feature. Putting together its brand name and in-house animation capabilities, Disney produced a stream of major box office hits, including *The Little Mermaid, Beauty and the Beast, Aladdin, Pocahontas*, and *The Lion King*. Disney also started a cable television channel, the Disney Channel, to use this library and capitalize on the company's brand name. In other words, Disney's existing resources and capabilities shaped its strategies.

Through his choice of strategies, Eisner also developed new competencies in different parts of the business. In the filmmaking arm of Disney, for example, Eisner created a new low-cost film division under the Touchstone label, and the company had a string of low-budget box office hits. It entered into a long-term agreement with the computer animation company Pixar to develop a competency in computer-generated animated films. This strategic collaboration has produced several hits, including *Toy Story* and *Monsters Incorporated*. In sum, Disney's transformation was based not only on strategies that took advantage of the company's existing resources and capabilities, but also on strategies that built new resources and capabilities, such as those that underlie the company's competency in computer-generated animated films.

■ **Competitive Advantage, Value Creation, and Profitability**

Competitive advantage leads to superior profitability. At the most basic level, how profitable a company becomes depends on three factors: (1) the *value* customers place on the company's products, (2) the *price* that a company charges for its products, and (3) the *costs* of creating those products. The value customers place on a product reflects the *utility* they get from a product, the happiness or satisfaction gained from consuming or owning the product. *Utility* must be distinguished from *price*. Utility is something that customers get from a product. It is a function of the attributes of the product, such as its performance, design, quality, and point-of-sale and after-sale service. For example, most customers would place a much higher utility value on a top-end Lexus car from Toyota than on a low-end basic economy car from General Motors (they would value it more), precisely because they perceive the Lexus to have better performance and superior design, quality, and service. A company that strengthens the utility (or value) of its products in the eyes of customers has more *pricing options:* it can raise prices to reflect that utility (value) or hold prices lower to induce more customers to purchase its products, thereby expanding unit sales volume.

Whatever pricing option a company chooses, however, the price a company charges for a good or service is typically less than the utility value placed on that good or service by the customer. This is so because the customer captures some of that utility in the form of what economists call a *consumer surplus.*[6] The customer is able to do this because the company is competing with other companies for the customer's business, so the company must charge a lower price than it could were it a monopoly supplier. Moreover, it is normally impossible to segment the market to such a degree that the company can charge each customer a price that reflects that individual's unique assessment of the utility of a product—what economists refer to as a customer's *reservation price*. For these reasons, the price that gets charged tends to be less than the utility value placed on the product by many customers. Nevertheless, remember the basic principle here: *the more utility that consumers get from a company's products or services, the more pricing options it has.*

These concepts are illustrated in Figure 3.2: *U* is the average utility value per unit of a product to a customer, *P* is the average price per unit that the company decides to charge for that product, and *C* is the average unit cost of producing that product (including actual production costs and the cost of capital investments in production systems). The company's average profit per unit is equal to $P - C$, and the consumer surplus is equal to $U - P$. In other words, $U - P$ is a measure of the value the consumer captures, and $P - C$ is a measure of the value the company captures. The company makes a profit so long as *P* is more than *C*, and its profitability will be greater the lower *C* is *relative* to *P*. Bear in mind that the difference between *U* and *P* is in part determined by the intensity of competitive pressure in the marketplace; the lower the intensity of competitive pressure is, the higher the price that can be charged relative to *U*, but the difference between *U* and *P* is also determined by the company's pricing

FIGURE 3.2

Value Creation
per Unit

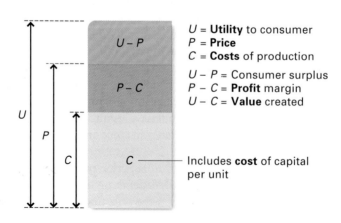

U = **Utility** to consumer
P = **Price**
C = **Costs** of production

U – *P* = Consumer surplus
P – *C* = **Profit** margin
U – *C* = **Value** created

Includes **cost** of capital per unit

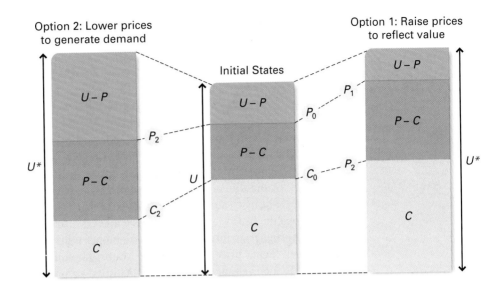

FIGURE 3.3

Value Creation and Pricing Options

choice.[7] As we shall see, a company may choose to keep prices low relative to volume because lower prices enable the company to sell more products, attain scale economies, and boost its profit margin by lowering C relative to P.

Note also that the *value created* by a company is measured by the difference between the utility a consumer gets from the product (U) and the costs of production (C), that is, $U - C$. A company creates value by converting factors of production that cost C into a product from which customers gets a utility of U. A company can create more value for its customers by lowering C or making the product more attractive through superior design, performance, quality, service, and the like. When customers assign a greater utility to the product (U increases), they are willing to pay a higher price (P increases). This discussion suggests that a company has a competitive advantage and high profitability when it creates more value for its customers than do rivals.[8]

The company's pricing options are captured in Figure 3.3. Suppose a company's current pricing option is the one pictured in the middle column of Figure 3.3. Imagine that the company decides to pursue strategies to increase the utility of its product offering from U to U^* in order to boost its profitability. Increasing utility initially raises production costs because the company has to spend money to increase product performance, quality, service, and other factors. Now there are two different pricing options that the company can pursue. Option 1 is to raise prices to reflect the higher utility: the company raises prices more than its costs increase, and profit per unit ($P - C$) increases. Option 2 involves a very different set of choices: the company *lowers* prices in order to expand unit volume. Basically, what is happening here is that customers recognize that they are getting a great bargain because price is now much lower than utility (the *consumer surplus* has increased), so they rush out to buy more (*demand* has increased). As unit volume expands due to increased demand, the company is able to realize scale economies and reduce its average unit costs. Although creating the extra utility initially cost more and prices are now lowered, profit margins widen because the average unit costs of production fall as volume increases and scale economies are attained.

Managers need to understand the dynamic relationships among *utility, pricing, demand,* and *costs* and make decisions on the basis of that understanding to maximize competitive advantage and profitability. Option 2 in Figure 3.3, for example, might not be a viable strategy if demand did not increase rapidly with lower prices or if there are few economies of scale to be had by increasing volume. Managers must understand how value creation and pricing decisions affect demand and also how unit costs change with increases in volume. In other words, they must have a good grasp of the demand for the company's product and its cost structure at different levels of output if they are to make decisions that maximize profitability.

Consider the automobile industry. According to a 2004 study by Harbour & Associates, in 2003 Toyota made $2,402 in profit on every vehicle it manufactured in North America. General Motors, in contrast, made only $178 profit per vehicle.[9] What accounts for the difference? First, Toyota has the best reputation for quality in the industry. According to annual surveys issued by J.D. Power and Associates, Toyota consistently tops the list in terms of quality, while GM cars are at best in the middle of the pack. The higher quality translates into a higher utility and allows Toyota to charge 5 to 10 percent higher prices than General Motors for equivalent cars. Second, Toyota has a lower cost per vehicle than General Motors, in part because of its superior labor productivity. For example, in Toyota's North American plants, it took an average of 31.06 employee hours to build a car, compared to 40.52 at GM plants in North America. That 9.5-hour productivity advantage translates into much lower labor costs for Toyota and, hence, a lower overall cost structure. Therefore, as summarized in Figure 3.4, Toyota's advantage over GM derives from greater utility (U), which has allowed the company to charge a higher price (P) for its cars, and from a lower cost structure (C), which taken together implies significantly greater profitability per vehicle ($P - C$).

Toyota's decisions with regard to pricing are guided by its managers' understanding of the relationship of utility, prices, demand, and costs. Given its ability to build more utility into its products, Toyota could have charged even higher prices than illustrated in Figure 3.4, but that might have led to lower sales volume, fewer scale economies, higher unit costs, and lower profit margins. Toyota's managers have sought to find the pricing option that enables the company to maximize its profits given their assessment of demand for its products and its cost function. Thus, to create superior value a company does not have to have the lowest cost structure in an industry or create the product with the highest utility in the eyes of customers. All that is necessary is that the gap between perceived utility (U) and costs of production (C) is greater than the gap attained by competitors.

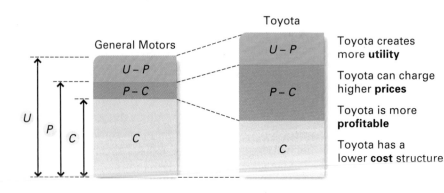

FIGURE 3.4

Comparing Toyota and General Motors

■ **Differentiation and Cost Structure**

Note that Toyota has *differentiated* itself from General Motors by its superior quality, which allows it to charge higher prices, and its superior productivity translates into a *lower cost structure*. Thus, its competitive advantage over General Motors is the result of strategies that have led to distinctive competencies, resulting in greater *differentiation* and a *lower cost structure*.

Indeed, at the heart of any company's business model is the combination of congruent strategies aimed at creating distinctive competencies that (1) *differentiate* its products in some way so that its consumers derive more utility from them, which gives the company more pricing options, and (2) result in a *lower cost structure*, which also gives it a broader range of pricing choices.[10] Achieving a sustained competitive advantage and superior profitability requires the right choices with regard to utility through differentiation and pricing given the demand conditions in the company's market and the company's cost structure at different levels of output. This issue is addressed in detail in the following chapters.

The Value Chain

All of the functions of a company—such as production, marketing, R&D, service, information systems, materials management, and human resources—have a role in lowering the cost structure and increasing the perceived utility (value) of the products through differentiation. As the first step in examining this concept, consider the value chain, which is illustrated in Figure 3.5.[11] The term **value chain** refers to the idea that a company is a chain of activities for transforming inputs into outputs that customers value. The transformation process involves a number of primary activities and support activities that add value to the product.

■ **Primary Activities**

Primary activities have to do with the design, creation, and delivery of the product, its marketing, and its support and after-sales service. In the value chain illustrated in Figure 3.5, the primary activities are broken down into four functions: research and development, production, marketing and sales, and customer service.

■ **Research and Development** **Research and development** (R&D) is concerned with the design of products and production processes. Although we think of R&D as being associated with the design of physical products and production processes in manufacturing enterprises, many service companies also undertake R&D. For example, banks compete with each other by developing new financial products and new ways of delivering those products to customers. Online banking and smart

FIGURE 3.5

The Value Chain

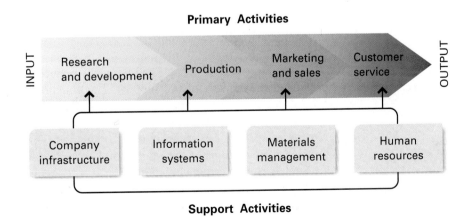

debit cards are two recent examples of the fruits of new-product development in the banking industry. Earlier examples of innovation in the banking industry were ATM machines, credit cards, and debit cards.

By creating superior product design, R&D can increase the functionality of products, which makes them more attractive to customers, thereby adding value. Alternatively, the work of R&D may result in more efficient production processes, thereby lowering production costs. Either way, the R&D function can help to lower costs or raise the utility of a product and permit a company to charge higher prices. At Intel, for example, R&D creates value by developing ever more powerful microprocessors and helping to pioneer ever more efficient manufacturing processes (in conjunction with equipment suppliers).

■ **Production**   **Production** is concerned with the creation of a good or service. For physical products, when we talk about production, we generally mean manufacturing. For services such as banking or retail operations, "production" typically takes place when the service is delivered to the customer, as when a bank makes a loan to a customer. By performing its activities efficiently, the production function of a company helps to lower its cost structure. For example, the efficient production operations of Honda and Toyota help those automobile companies achieve higher profitability relative to competitors such as General Motors. The production function can also perform its activities in a way that is consistent with high product quality, which leads to differentiation (and higher value) and lower costs.

■ **Marketing and Sales**   There are several ways in which the **marketing and sales** functions of a company can help to create value. Through brand positioning and advertising, the marketing function can increase the value that customers perceive to be contained in a company's product (and thus the utility they attribute to the product). Insofar as these help to create a favorable impression of the company's product in the minds of customers, they increase utility. For example, in the 1980s, the French company Perrier persuaded U.S. customers that slightly carbonated bottled water was worth $1.50 per bottle rather than a price closer to the $0.50 that it cost to collect, bottle, and distribute the water. Perrier's marketing function essentially increased the perception of utility that customers ascribed to the product.

Marketing and sales can also create value by discovering customer needs and communicating them back to the R&D function of the company, which can then design products that better match those needs. For another example of value creation by the marketing function of an enterprise, see Strategy in Action 3.1, which looks at how Pfizer's sales force increased the perception of the utility associated with one of its main pharmaceuticals, Zoloft.

■ **Customer Service**   The role of the **service** function of an enterprise is to provide after-sales service and support. This function can create superior utility by solving customer problems and supporting customers after they have purchased the product. For example, Caterpillar, the U.S.-based manufacturer of heavy earth-moving equipment, can get spare parts to any point in the world within twenty-four hours, thereby minimizing the amount of downtime its customers have to face if their Caterpillar equipment malfunctions. This is an extremely valuable support capability in an industry where downtime is very expensive. It has helped to increase the utility that customers associate with Caterpillar products, and thus the price that Caterpillar can charge for its products.

Strategy in Action   3.1

Value Creation at Pfizer

The antidepressant drug Prozac, introduced by Eli Lilly & Company in 1988, was one of the most lucrative mental health drugs in history. In 1995, U.S. customers alone filled almost 19 million prescriptions for Prozac, which was used to mitigate the effects of a wide range of mental disorders, including chronic depression, bulimia, and obsessive disorders. Worldwide sales of the drug topped $2 billion in 1995, making it a gold mine for Lilly.

During the 1990s, Prozac's market position came under attack from an aggressive marketing and sales campaign by rival pharmaceutical company Pfizer. In 1992, Pfizer introduced its own antidepressant, Zoloft. According to medical experts, the differences between Prozac and Zoloft are slight at best. Both drugs function in the same basic manner, by boosting serotonin, a brain chemical believed to be in short supply in many depressed people. Both drugs also have a similar list of possible side effects. Prozac's label cites nausea, nervousness, anxiety, insomnia, and drowsiness as possible side effects. Zoloft's label lists nausea and other stomach problems, diarrhea, sexual dysfunction, and sleepiness. As one expert noted, "These drugs are so similar that you have to be kidding yourself if you think one drug is going to be consistently superior to the other in treating patients."

Despite the similarity between the two products, Pfizer gained share from Lilly in the antidepressant market. By 1998, Zoloft accounted for 40 percent of the market, up from little more than zero in 1992. The main reason for this success seems to have been Pfizer's aggressive marketing and sales campaign, which created an impression in the eyes of physicians that Zoloft is a safer drug. Pfizer sales representatives bill their product as just as effective as Prozac but without its occasional downside, anxiety. The

reference to anxiety seems carefully designed to remind doctors of a spate of failed lawsuits alleging that Prozac caused suicides and other violent acts. Pfizer's sales force also logged more "face time" with physicians than Lilly's. According to Scott-Levin and Associates, in 1995 Zoloft sales representatives made 660,000 sales visits to doctors, 70,000 more than the Prozac sales force logged. About three-quarters of these were not to psychiatrists but to basic primary care physicians, who increasingly prescribe antidepressants but presumably are less familiar with their more subtle properties than psychiatrists are. Doctors also claim that Pfizer salespeople play up Prozac's clinical reputation for being more agitating than Zoloft. They also emphasize that unlike Zoloft, Prozac remains in the bloodstream for weeks after a patient stops taking it, raising the possibility of adverse drug interaction if a patient switches to other medications.

The important point here is that Pfizer's marketing and sales force altered physicians' perceptions of the relative utility of Prozac and Zoloft. For Pfizer, the payoff came in terms of rapidly increasing revenues and market share and, of course, a greater return on the company's investment in developing Zoloft. Just how successful Pfizer had been was demonstrated in August 2001 when Prozac came off patent, allowing generic competitors to enter the market. Sales of Prozac fell by 80 percent within months as low-priced generic versions of Prozac grabbed market share. However, despite the fact that Zoloft is chemically very similar to Prozac, sales of Zoloft remained robust and hit a record $3.12 billion in 2003, up from $2.74 billion in the prior year. The Zoloft brand was strong enough to ward off competition from low-priced generic versions of Prozac.[a]

■ **Support Activities**   The **support activities** of the value chain provide inputs that allow the primary activities to take place. These activities are broken down into four functions: materials management (or logistics), human resources, information systems, and company infrastructure (see Figure 3.5).

■ **Materials Management (Logistics)**   The **materials-management** (or logistics) function controls the transmission of physical materials through the value chain, from procurement through production and into distribution. The efficiency with which this is carried out can significantly lower cost, thereby creating more value. As noted in the *Running Case*, Wal-Mart has the most efficient materials-management setup in the retail industry. By tightly controlling the flow of goods from its suppliers through its stores and into the hands of customers, Wal-Mart has eliminated the need to hold large inventories of goods. Lower inventories mean lower costs, and hence greater value creation.

■ **Human Resources** There are a number of ways in which the **human resource** function can help an enterprise to create more value. This function ensures that the company has the right mix of skilled people to perform its value creation activities effectively. It is also the job of the human resource function to ensure that people are adequately trained, motivated, and compensated to perform their value creation tasks. If the human resources are functioning well, employee productivity rises (which lowers costs) and customer service improves (which raises utility), thereby enabling the company to create more value.

■ **Information Systems** **Information systems** are the largely electronic systems for managing inventory, tracking sales, pricing products, selling products, dealing with customer service inquiries, and so on. Information systems, when coupled with the communications features of the Internet, are holding out the promise of being able to improve the efficiency and effectiveness with which a company manages its other value creation activities. As noted in the *Running Case,* Wal-Mart uses information systems to alter the way it does business. By tracking the sale of individual items very closely, its materials-management function has enabled it to optimize its product mix and pricing strategy. Wal-Mart is rarely left with unwanted merchandise on its hands, which saves on costs, and the company is able to provide the right mix of goods to customers, which increases the utility that customers associate with Wal-Mart.

■ **Company Infrastructure** **Company infrastructure** is the companywide context within which all the other value creation activities take place: the organizational structure, control systems, and company culture. Because top management can exert considerable influence in shaping these aspects of a company, top management should also be viewed as part of the infrastructure of a company. Indeed, through strong leadership, top management can shape the infrastructure of a company and, through that, the performance of all other value creation activities that take place within it.

The Building Blocks of Competitive Advantage

The four factors that build and sustain competitive advantage—superior efficiency, quality, innovation, and customer responsiveness—are the product of the company's distinctive competencies. Indeed, in a very real sense they are "generic" distinctive competencies. These generic competencies allow a company to (1) differentiate its product offering, and hence offer more utility to its customers, and (2) lower its cost structure (see Figure 3.6). These factors can be considered *generic* distinctive competencies because any company, regardless of its industry or the products or services it produces, can pursue them. Although they are discussed sequentially below, they are highly interrelated, and the important ways they affect each other should be noted. For example, superior quality can lead to superior efficiency, and innovation can enhance efficiency, quality, and responsiveness to customers.

■ Efficiency

In one sense, a business is simply a device for transforming inputs into outputs. Inputs are basic factors of production such as labor, land, capital, management, and technological know-how. Outputs are the goods and services that the business produces. The simplest measure of efficiency is the quantity of inputs that it takes to

Running Case

Support Activities as a Source of Value Creation at Wal-Mart

One of the foundations of Wal-Mart's competitive advantage is the way it uses information systems and logistics to manage its massive supply chain and closely match what customers want with what its suppliers are producing. Wal-Mart's goal is to have goods from a manufacturer arrive at a store and be placed on shelves just before consumers walk into the store to purchase them. This would eliminate the need to hold extensive inventory either in the store or at distribution centers. Moreover, by anticipating what customers want and supplying just enough goods to each store, Wal-Mart is striving to eliminate the twin evils of the retail business: understocking and overstocking. Understocking implies that a sale is not made because the product a customer wants is not in stock. Overstocking requires the retailers to cut prices to shift unsold or slow-moving merchandise.

As measured by inventory turnover, Wal-Mart is probably closer to attaining this goal than any other major retailer. In 2003 Wal-Mart turned over its inventory 7.72 times. Target, another discount retailer, turned over its inventory 6.29 times, and Kmart just 5.51 times. Sears, the department store, turns over its inventory 5.02 times a year. Because Wal-Mart turns its inventory over more rapidly, it has less capital tied up in inventory. This reduces the capital Wal-Mart needs to generate sales and boosts the company's profitability as measured by return on invested capital. How does Wal-Mart do this?

Wal-Mart's high inventory turnover rests on the twin foundations of leading-edge information systems and efficient logistics. Wal-Mart stores its inventory in massive distribution centers, of which there are over one hundred in the United States alone. Each distribution center serves two hundred to three hundred stores within a 300-mile radius. Manufacturers deliver their products to the distribution centers, where they are sorted, stored, and then shipped out to Wal-Mart stores on a fleet of company-owned trucks.

The key to this process is Wal-Mart's information systems. Wal-Mart was one of the first retailers to introduce bar-coding scanners at its checkouts and also one of the first to require manufacturers to place bar codes on their products. The scanning system enables Wal-Mart to track what is selling in a particular store, right down to individual items. This information is then uploaded from the stores to Wal-Mart's central headquarters, where it is communicated on a real-time basis to distribution centers. There merchandise is loaded onto a Wal-Mart truck and shipped out to the store on a daily basis. Because stores are clustered closely together, each truck may serve several stores. Moreover, since many of Wal-Mart's suppliers have manufacturing plants located close to a Wal-Mart store, a truck will often stop at a plant on the way back to a distribution center to pick up merchandise. As a result, by the time the truck arrives at the distribution center, it is 60 to 70 percent full. Thus, not only does Wal-Mart replenish store inventory on a daily basis, but it also uses its trucking capacity efficiently.

To gain further supply-chain efficiencies, Wal-Mart also transmits sales information to manufacturers on a real-time basis. This allows the manufacturers to optimize their own production schedules and deliver products to a Wal-Mart distribution center just when they are needed. Over the years, Wal-Mart has refined this process by introducing a process known as *cross-docking*. With cross-docking, the merchandise from the supplier's truck is unloaded and then immediately transferred to Wal-Mart trucks that are ready to head out to stores. Cross-docking reduces the need to sort and store inventory at a distribution center. This technique boosts profitability in two ways: it reduces labor costs, and it also allows Wal-Mart to operate with smaller distribution centers, thereby lowering capital requirements.

Wal-Mart continues to look for ways to improve the efficiency of its logistics and information systems. In July 2003, it announced that, starting January 1, 2005, it would require its one hundred top suppliers to affix radio frequency identification tags (RFID tags) on all cases and pallets delivered to a distribution center. Radio tags eliminate the need to manually scan inventory with a bar-code scanner, reducing labor costs. Moreover, with radio tags inventory can be automatically scanned at multiple points in a supply chain. This gives Wal-Mart more information and thus more ability to optimize its inventory position. Many observers believe that it is only a matter of time before Wal-Mart requires RFID tags on individual items. When this is achieved, products can be scanned automatically as a customer walks up to a checkout, reducing checkout time and thus labor costs.[b]

FIGURE 3.6

Building Blocks of
Competitive
Advantage

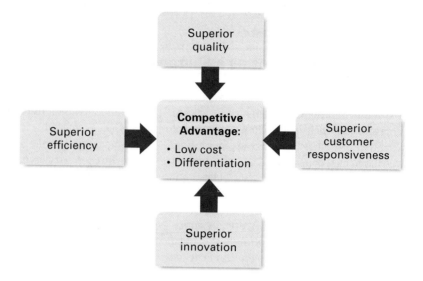

produce a given output—that is, efficiency = outputs/inputs. The more efficient a company is, the fewer the inputs required to produce a given output. For example, if it takes General Motors thirty hours of employee time to assemble a car and it takes Ford twenty-five hours, we can say that Ford is more efficient than GM. And as long as other things are equal, such as wage rates, we can assume from this information that Ford will have a lower cost structure than GM. Thus, efficiency helps a company attain a competitive advantage through a lower cost structure. Similarly, an analysis of financial statements suggests that in 2003 Wal-Mart generated $4.02 of sales for every dollar of capital it invested in its business, whereas its competitor Target generated $2.26 of sales for every dollar of capital it invested in its business (capital is used to build stores, purchase equipment, buy inventory, and so forth). Clearly Wal-Mart is more efficient in its use of capital: it needs less capital (the input) to generate a dollar of sales (the output) than Target.

As these examples suggest, two of the most important components of efficiency for many companies are employee productivity and capital productivity. *Employee productivity* is usually measured by output per employee and *capital productivity* by output per unit of invested capital (this is discussed in depth in the next section). Holding all else constant, the company with the highest labor and capital productivity in an industry will typically have the lowest cost structure and therefore a cost-based competitive advantage. The concept of productivity is not limited to employee and capital productivity. Pharmaceutical companies, for example, often talk about the productivity of their R&D spending, by which they mean how many new drugs they develop from their investment in R&D. Other companies talk about their sales force productivity, which means how many sales they generate from every sales call, and so on. The important point to remember is that high productivity leads to greater efficiency and lower costs.

Strategy in Action 3.2 looks at how Southwest Airlines has attained its low-cost position in the U.S. airline industry. As you will see, its competitive advantage derives from its superior labor productivity.

Strategy in Action   3.2

Southwest Airlines' Low Cost Structure

Southwest Airlines has long been one of the standout performers in the U.S. airline industry. It is famous for its low fares, which are generally some 30 percent below those of its major rivals, and these are balanced by an even lower cost structure, which has enabled it to record superior profitability even in bad years such as 2003, when the industry faced slumping demand. Southwest was the only airline among the top eight in the United States to show a profit for the quarter immediately following the September 11 terrorist attacks on the World Trade Center and the Pentagon.

A major source of Southwest's low cost structure seems to be its very high employee productivity. One way the airlines measure employee productivity is by the ratio of employees to passengers carried. According to figures from company 10-K statements, in 2003 Southwest had an employee-to-passenger ratio of 1 to 1,999, one of the best in the industry. By comparison, the ratio at one of the better major airlines, Continental, was 1 to 1,420. These figures suggest that, holding size constant, Southwest runs its operation with far fewer people than competitors. How does it do this?

First, Southwest devotes enormous attention to the people it hires. On average, the company hires only 3 percent of those interviewed in a year. When hiring, it emphasizes teamwork and a positive attitude. Southwest rationalizes that skills can be taught but a positive attitude and a willingness to pitch in cannot. Southwest also creates incentives for its employees to work hard. All employees are covered by a profit-sharing plan, and at least 25 percent of an employee's share of the profit-sharing plan has to be invested in Southwest Airlines stock. This gives rise to a simple formula: the harder employees work, the more profitable Southwest becomes, and the richer the employees get. The results are clear. At other airlines, one would never see a pilot helping to check passengers onto the plane. At Southwest, pilots and flight attendants have been known to help clean the aircraft and check in passengers at the gate. They do this to turn around an aircraft as quickly as possible and get it into the air again, because an aircraft doesn't make money when it is sitting on the ground.

Southwest also reduces its costs by striving to keep its operations as simple as possible. By operating only one type of plane, the Boeing 737, it reduces training costs, maintenance costs, and inventory costs while increasing efficiency in crew and flight scheduling. The operation is nearly ticketless, which reduces cost and back-office accounting functions. Because there is no seat assignment, costs are again reduced. There are no meals or movies in flight, and the airline will not transfer baggage to other airlines, reducing the need for baggage handlers. Another major difference between Southwest and most other airlines is that Southwest flies point to point rather than operating from congested airport hubs. As a result, its costs are lower because there is no need for dozens of gates and thousands of employees to handle banks of flights that come in and then disperse within a two-hour window, leaving the hub empty until the next flights a few hours later.

However, success can bring its own problems, and this is starting to occur at Southwest. While other airlines have been able to get significant pay concessions from their employees in recent years, employees at Southwest have successfully lobbied for higher pay. After two years of sometimes bitter disputes, which have damaged the once harmonious culture at Southwest, in mid 2004 the company's airlines attendants won a 31 percent pay increase spread out over five years. With mechanics and pilots set to enter negotiations next, some observers are now worrying that Southwest's cost structure will rise, eroding the airline's cost-based competitive advantage.[c]

■ **Quality as Excellence and Reliability**   A product can be thought of as a bundle of attributes.[12] The attributes of many physical products include their form, features, performance, durability, reliability, style, and design.[13] A product is said to have *superior quality* when customers perceive that its attributes provide them with higher utility than the attributes of products sold by rivals. For example, a Rolex watch has attributes—such as design, styling, performance, and reliability—that customers perceive as being superior to the same attributes in many other watches. Thus, we can refer to a Rolex as a high-quality product: Rolex has *differentiated* its watches by these attributes.

When customers evaluate the quality of a product, they commonly measure it against two kinds of attributes: those related to *quality as excellence* and those related to *quality as reliability*. From a quality-as-excellence perspective, the important attributes are things such as a product's design and styling, its aesthetic appeal, its features and functions, the level of service associated with the delivery of the product, and so on. For example, customers can purchase a pair of imitation leather boots for $20 from Wal-Mart, or they can buy a handmade pair of butter-soft leather boots from Nordstrom for $500. The boots from Nordstrom will have far superior styling, feel more comfortable, and look much better than those from Wal-Mart. The utility consumers will get from the Nordstrom boots will in all probability be much greater than the utility derived from the Wal-Mart boots, but of course, they will have to pay far more for them. That is the point: when excellence is built into a product offering, consumers have to pay more to own or consume it.

With regard to *quality as reliability*, a product can be said to be *reliable* when it consistently does the job it was designed for, does it well, and rarely, if ever, breaks down. As with excellence, reliability increases the utility a consumer gets from a product, and thus the price the company can charge for that product. Toyota's cars, for example, have the highest reliability ratings in the automobile industry, and therefore consumers are prepared to pay more for them than for cars that are very similar in other attributes. As we shall see, increasing product reliability has been the central goal of an influential management philosophy that came out of Japan in the 1980s and is commonly referred to as **total quality management.**

The position of a product against two dimensions, *reliability* and *other attributes*, can be plotted on a map similar to Figure 3.7. For example, a Lexus has attributes—such as design, styling, performance, and safety features—that customers perceive as demonstrating excellence in quality and that are viewed as being superior to those of most other cars. Lexus is also a very reliable car. Thus, the overall level of quality of the Lexus is very high, which means that the car offers consumers significant utility, and that gives Toyota the option of charging a premium price for the Lexus. Toyota also produces another very reliable vehicle, the Toyota Corolla, but this is aimed at less wealthy

FIGURE 3.7

A Quality Map for Automobiles

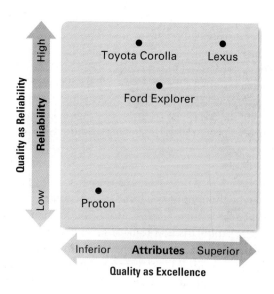

customers and it lacks many of the superior attributes of the Lexus. Thus, although this is also a high-quality car in the sense of being reliable, it is not as high quality as a Lexus in the sense of being an excellent product. At the other end of the spectrum, we can find poor-quality products that have both low reliability and inferior attributes, such as poor design, performance, and styling. An example is the Proton, which is built by the Malaysian car firm of the same name. The design of the car is over a decade old and has a dismal reputation for styling and safety. Moreover, Proton's reliability record is one of the worst of any car, according J.D. Power.[14]

The concept of quality applies whether we are talking about Toyota automobiles, clothes designed and sold by the Gap, the customer service department of Citibank, or the ability of airlines to arrive on time. Quality is just as relevant to services as it is to goods.[15] The impact of high product quality on competitive advantage is twofold.[16] First, providing high-quality products increases the utility those products provide to customers, which gives the company the option of charging a higher price for them. In the automobile industry, for example, Toyota can charge a higher price for its cars because of the higher quality of its products. Thus, compared with General Motors, Toyota has had both lower costs and the ability to charge higher prices. As a result, historically it has been more profitable than GM.

The second impact of high quality on competitive advantage comes from the greater efficiency and the lower unit costs associated with *reliable* products. When products are reliable, less employee time is wasted making defective products or providing substandard services and less time has to be spent fixing mistakes, which translates into higher employee productivity and lower unit costs. Thus, high product quality not only enables a company to differentiate its product from that of rivals, but if the product is reliable, it also lowers costs.

The importance of reliability in building competitive advantage has increased dramatically over the past decade. Indeed, so crucial is the emphasis placed on reliability by many companies that achieving high product reliability can no longer be viewed as just one way of gaining a competitive advantage. In many industries, it has become an absolute imperative for survival.

■ **Innovation**   **Innovation** refers to the act of creating new products or processes. There are two main types of innovation: product innovation and process innovation. **Product innovation** is the development of products that are new to the world or have superior attributes to existing products. Examples are Intel's invention of the microprocessor in the early 1970s, Cisco's development of the router for routing data over the Internet in the mid 1980s, and Palm's development of the PalmPilot, the first commercially successful hand-held computer, in the mid 1990s. **Process innovation** is the development of a new process for producing products and delivering them to customers. Examples include Toyota, which developed a range of new techniques collectively known as the Toyota *lean production system* for making automobiles: just-in-time inventory systems, self-managing teams, and reduced setup times for complex equipment. Wal-Mart pioneered efforts to use information systems to manage its logistics and inventory (see the *Running Case*), and Staples applied the supermarket business model to the retail office supplies business.

Product innovation creates value by creating new products, or enhanced versions of existing products, that customers perceive as having more utility, thus increasing the company's pricing options. Process innovation often allows a company to create more value by lowering production costs. Toyota's lean production system, for example, helped to boost employee productivity, thus giving Toyota a cost-based competitive advantage.[17] Similarly, Staples' application of the supermarket business model to retail office supplies dramatically lowered the cost of selling office supplies. Staples passed on some of this cost saving to customers in the form of lower prices, which enabled the company to increase its market share rapidly.

In the long run, innovation of products and processes is perhaps the most important building block of competitive advantage.[18] Competition can be viewed as a process driven by innovations. Although not all innovations succeed, those that do can be a major source of competitive advantage because, by definition, they give a company something **unique**—something its competitors lack (at least until they imitate the innovation). Uniqueness can allow a company to differentiate itself from its rivals and charge a premium price for its product or, in the case of many process innovations, reduce its unit costs far below those of competitors.

■ **Responsiveness to Customers**

To achieve superior responsiveness to customers, a company must be able to do a better job than competitors of identifying and satisfying its customers' needs. Customers will then attribute more utility to its products, creating a differentiation based on competitive advantage. Improving the quality of a company's product offering is consistent with achieving responsiveness, as is developing new products with features that existing products lack. In other words, achieving superior quality and innovation is integral to achieving superior responsiveness to customers.

Another factor that stands out in any discussion of responsiveness to customers is the need to customize goods and services to the unique demands of individual customers or customer groups. For example, the proliferation of soft drinks and beers can be viewed partly as a response to this trend. Automobile companies have become more adept at customizing cars to the demands of individual customers. For instance, following the lead of Toyota, the Saturn division of General Motors builds cars to order for individual customers, letting them choose from a wide range of colors and options.

An aspect of responsiveness to customers that has drawn increasing attention is **customer response time**: the time that it takes for a good to be delivered or a service to be performed.[19] For a manufacturer of machinery, response time is the time it takes to fill customer orders. For a bank, it is the time it takes to process a loan or that a customer must stand in line to wait for a free teller. For a supermarket, it is the time that customers must stand in checkout lines. Customer survey after customer survey has shown slow response time to be a major source of customer dissatisfaction.[20]

Other sources of enhanced responsiveness to customers are superior design, superior service, and superior after-sales service and support. All of these factors enhance responsiveness to customers and allow a company to differentiate itself from its less responsive competitors. In turn, differentiation enables a company to build brand loyalty and charge a premium price for its products. Consider how much more people are prepared to pay for next-day delivery of Express Mail, as opposed to delivery in three to four days. In 2004, a two-page letter sent by overnight Express Mail within the United States cost about $14, compared with 37 cents for regular mail. Thus, the price premium for express delivery (reduced response time) was $13.63, or a premium of 3,684 percent over the regular price.

■ **Business Models, the Value Chain, and Generic Distinctive Competencies**

As noted in Chapter 1, a business model is managers' conception, or gestalt, of how the various strategies that a firm pursues fit together into a congruent whole, enabling the firm to achieve a competitive advantage. More precisely, a business model represents the way in which managers configure the value chain of the firm through strategy, as well as the investments they make to support that configuration, so that they can build the distinctive competencies necessary to attain the efficiency, quality,

FIGURE 3.8

Competitive Advantage and the Value Creation Cycle

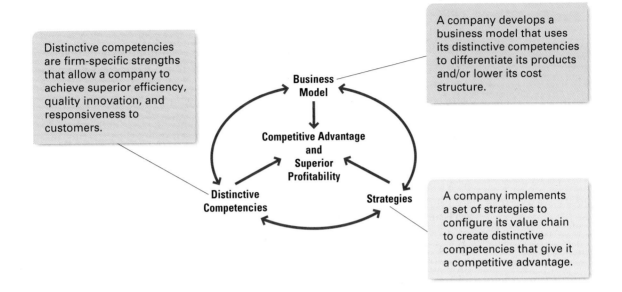

innovation, and customer responsiveness required to support the firm's low-cost or differentiated position, thereby achieving a competitive advantage and generating superior profitability (see Figure 3.8).

For example, the main strategic goal of Wal-Mart is to be the lowest-cost operator offering a wide display of general merchandise in the retail industry. Wal-Mart's business model involves offering general merchandise in a self-service supermarket type of setting. As discussed in the *Running Case*, Wal-Mart's strategies flesh out this business model and help the company to attain its strategic goal. For example, to reduce costs, Wal-Mart limits investments in the fittings and fixtures of its stores. One of the keys to generating sales and lowering costs in this setting is rapid inventory turnover, which is achieved through strategic investments in logistics and information systems. Wal-Mart in fact makes major investments in process innovation to improve the effectiveness of its information and logistics systems, which enables the company to respond to customer demands for low-priced goods when they walk in the door and to do so in a very efficient manner.

Wal-Mart's business model is very different from that found at a retailer such as Nordstrom. Nordstrom's business model is to offer high quality, and high-priced apparel, in a full-service and sophisticated setting. This implies differences in the way the value chain is configured. Nordstrom devotes far more attention to in-store customer service than Wal-Mart does, which implies significant investments in its salespeople. Moreover, Nordstrom invests far more in the furnishings and fittings for its stores, as opposed to Wal-Mart, whose stores have a basic warehouse feel to them. Nordstrom recaptures the costs of this investment by charging higher prices for higher-quality merchandise. Thus, even though Wal-Mart and Nordstrom both sell apparel (Wal-Mart is in fact the biggest seller of apparel in the United States), their business models imply a very different positioning in the marketplace, and a very different configuration of value chain activities and investments.

Analyzing Competitive Advantage and Profitability

If a company's managers are to perform a good internal analysis, they need to be able to analyze the financial performance of their company, identifying how its strategies contribute (or not) to profitability. To identify strengths and weaknesses effectively, they need to be able to compare, or *benchmark,* the performance of their company against that of competitors and the historic performance of the company itself. This will help them determine whether they are more or less profitable than competitors and whether the performance of the company has been improving or deteriorating through time; whether their company strategies are maximizing the value being created; whether their cost structure is out of line with those of competitors; and whether they are using the resources of the company to the greatest effect.

As we noted in Chapter 1, the key measure of a company's financial performance is its profitability, which captures the return that a company is generating on its investments. Although several different measures of profitability exist, such as return on assets and return on equity, many authorities on the measurement of profitability argue that return on invested capital (ROIC) is the best measure because "it focuses on the true operating performance of the company."[21] (However, return on assets is very similar in formulation to return on invested capital.)

ROIC is defined as net profit over invested capital, or ROIC = net profit/invested capital. Net profit is calculated by subtracting the total costs of operating the company away from its total revenues (total revenues–total costs). *Net profit* is what is left over after the government takes its share in taxes. *Invested capital* is the amount that is invested in the operations of a company: property, plant, equipment, inventories, and other assets. Invested capital comes from two main sources: interest-bearing debt and shareholders' equity. Interest-bearing debt is money the company borrows from banks and those who purchase its bonds. Shareholders' equity is the money raised from selling shares to the public, *plus* earnings that the company has retained in prior years and are available to fund current investments. ROIC measures the effectiveness with which a company is using the capital funds that it has available for investment. As such, it is recognized to be an excellent measure of the value a company is creating.[22]

A company's ROIC can be algebraically decomposed into two major components: *return on sales* and *capital turnover.*[23] Specifically:

$$ROIC = \text{net profits/invested capital}$$
$$= \text{net profits/revenues} \times \text{revenues/invested capital}$$

where net profits/revenues is the return on sales, and revenues/invested capital is capital turnover. Return on sales measures how effectively the company converts revenues into profits. Capital turnover measures how effectively the company employs its invested capital to generate revenues. These two ratios can be further decomposed into some basic accounting ratios, as shown in Figure 3.9 (these ratios are defined in Table 3.1).[24]

The decomposition of ROIC shown in Figure 3.9 was first developed by managers at the DuPont Company in the early 1900s as a methodology for identifying the drivers of profitability, and the decomposition formula is sometimes referred to as "the DuPont Formula." Figure 3.9 says that a company's managers can increase ROIC by pursuing strategies that increase the company's return on sales. To increase the company's return on sales, they can pursue strategies that reduce the cost of goods sold (COGS) for a given level of sales revenues (COGS/sales); reduce the level of spending on sales force, marketing, general, and administrative expenses (SG&A) for a given level of sales revenues (SG&A/sales); and reduce R&D spending for a given level of sales revenues (R&D/sales). Alternatively, they can increase return on sales by pursuing strategies that increase sales revenues more than they increase the costs of the

FIGURE 3.9

Drivers of Profitability (ROIC)

business, as measured by COGS, SG&A, and R&D expenses. That is, they can increase the return on sales by pursuing strategies that *lower costs* or increase value through *differentiation,* and thus allow the company to increase its prices more than its costs.

Figure 3.9 also tells us that a company's managers can boost the profitability of their company by getting greater sales revenues from their invested capital, thereby increasing capital turnover. They do this by pursuing strategies that reduce the

TABLE 3.1

Definitions of Basic Accounting Terms

Term	Definition	Source
Cost of goods sold (COGS)	Total costs of manufacturing products	Income statement
Sales, general, and administrative expenses (SG&A)	Costs associated with selling products and administering the company	Income statement
R&D expenses (R&D)	Research and development expenditure	Income statement
Working capital	The amount of money the company has to work with in the short term: current assets minus current liabilities	Balance sheet
Property, plant, and equipment (PPE)	The value of investments in the property, plant, and equipment that the company uses to manufacture and sell its products; also known as *fixed capital*	Balance sheet
Return on sales (ROS)	Net profit expressed as a percentage of sales; measures how effectively the company converts revenues into profits	Ratio
Capital turnover	Revenues divided by invested capital; measures how effectively the company uses its capital to generate revenues	Ratio
Return on invested capital (ROIC)	Net profit after tax divided by invested capital	Ratio
Net profit	Total revenues minus total costs after tax	Income statement
Invested capital	Interest-bearing debt plus shareholders' equity	Balance sheet

amount of *working capital*, such as the amount of capital invested in inventories, needed to generate a given level of sales (working capital/sales) and then pursuing strategies that reduce the amount of *fixed capital* that they have to invest in plant, property, and equipment (PPE) to generate a given level of sales (PPE/sales). That is, they pursue strategies that reduce the amount of capital that they need to generate every dollar of sales, and thus their cost of capital. Now recall that cost of capital is part of the cost structure of a company (see Figure 3.2), so strategies designed to increase capital turnover also *lower the cost structure.*

To see how these basic drivers of profitability help us to understand what is going on in a company and to identify its strengths and weaknesses, let us compare the financial performance of Wal-Mart against one of its closest and more efficient competitors, Target. For the financial year ending January 2004, Wal-Mart earned an ROIC of 14.21 percent, while Target earned a respectable 8.65 percent. Wal-Mart's superior profitability can be understood in terms of the impact of its strategies on the various ratios identified in Figure 3.9. These are summarized in Figure 3.10.

First, note that Wal-Mart has a *lower* return on sales than Target. The main reason for this is that Wal-Mart's cost of goods sold (COGS) as a percentage of sales is higher than Target's (76.8 percent against 66 percent). For a retailer, the COGS reflects the price that Wal-Mart pays to its suppliers for merchandise. The lower COGS/sales ratio implies that Wal-Mart does not mark up prices as much as Target: its profit margin on each item sold is lower. Consistent with its long-time strategic goal, Wal-Mart passes on the low prices it gets from suppliers to customers. Wal-Mart's higher COGS/sales ratio reflects its strategy of being the lowest-price retailer.

On the other hand, Wal-Mart spends significantly less on sales, general, and administrative expenses (SG&A) as a percentage of sales than Target (17.36 percent against 23.95 percent). There are three reasons for this difference. First, Wal-Mart's early strategy

FIGURE 3.10

Comparing Wal-Mart and Target

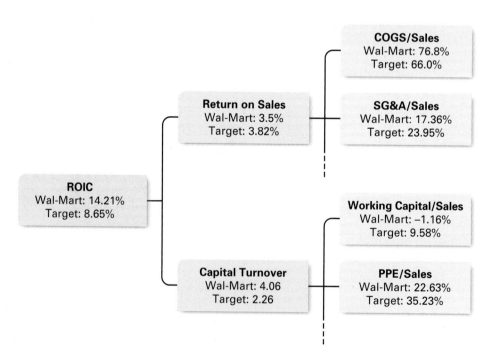

was to focus on small towns that could only support one discounter. In small towns, the company does not have to advertise heavily because it is not competing against other discounters. Second, Wal-Mart has become such a powerful brand that the company does not need to advertise as heavily as its competitors, even when its stores are located close to them in suburban areas. Third, because Wal-Mart sticks to its low-price philosophy, and because the company manages its inventory so well, it does not usually have an overstocking problem. Thus, the company does not have to hold periodic sales, nor does it have to bear the costs of promoting those sales (such as by sending out advertisements and coupons in local newspapers). These factors reduce Wal-Mart's SG&A/sales ratio.

In addition, Wal-Mart operates with a flat organization structure that has very few layers of management between the head office and store managers (the company has no regional headquarters). This reduces administrative expenses (which are a component of SG&A) and hence the SG&A/sales ratio. Wal-Mart can operate with this flat structure because its information systems allow the company's top managers to monitor and control individual stores directly, rather than rely on intervening layers of subordinates to do that for them.

It is when we consider the capital turnover side of the ROIC equation, however, that the financial impact of Wal-Mart's competitive advantage in information systems and logistics becomes apparent. Wal-Mart generates $4.06 for every dollar of capital invested in the business, whereas Target generates only $2.26 for every dollar of capital invested. Wal-Mart is much more efficient in its use of capital than Target. Why?

One crucial reason is that Wal-Mart has a much lower working capital/sales ratio than Target. In fact, Wal-Mart has a *negative* ratio (–1.16 percent), while Target has a positive ratio (9.58 percent). The negative working capital ratio implies that Wal-Mart does not need any capital to finance its day-to-day operations. In fact, it is using its suppliers' capital to finance these operations, a rare accomplishment. Wal-Mart is able to do this for two reasons. First, Wal-Mart is so powerful that it can demand and get very favorable payment terms from its suppliers. It does not have to pay for merchandise for sixty days after it is delivered. Second, Wal-Mart turns over its inventory so rapidly—7.72 times a year, or every 47 days—that it typically sells merchandise *before* it has to pay its suppliers. Thus, suppliers finance Wal-Mart's inventory and the company's short-term capital needs. As you will recall from the *Running Case*, Wal-Mart's high inventory turnover is the result of strategic investments in information systems and logistics. It is these value chain activities more than any other that explain Wal-Mart's competitive advantage.

Finally, Wal-Mart has a significantly lower PPE/sales ratio than Target: 22.63 percent versus 35.23 percent. There are several explanations for this lower ratio. First, many of Wal-Mart's stores are still located in small towns where land is cheap, whereas most of Target's stores are located in more expensive suburban mall locations. Thus, on average, Wal-Mart needs to spend less on a store than Target. Again, strategy has a clear impact on financial performance. Second, because Wal-Mart turns its inventory over so rapidly, it does not need to devote as much in-store space to storing inventory. This means that more floor space can be devoted to selling merchandise. Other things being equal, this will result in a higher PPE/sales ratio. By the same token, efficient inventory management means that less space is needed at a distribution center to support a store, which again reduces total capital spending on property, plant, and equipment. Third, the higher PPE/sales ratio may also reflect the fact that Wal-Mart's brand is so powerful, and its commitment to low pricing so strong, that store traffic is higher than at comparable discounters such as Target. The stores are simply busier. Hence the PPE/sales ratio is higher.

In sum, Wal-Mart's high profitability is a function of its strategy and the distinctive competencies that strategic investments have built over the years, particularly in information systems and logistics. As in the Wal-Mart example, the methodology described in this section can be a very useful tool for analyzing why and how well a company is achieving and sustaining a competitive advantage. It highlights a company's strengths and weaknesses, showing where there is room for improvement and where a company is excelling. As such, it can drive strategy formulation. Moreover, the same methodology can be used to analyze the performance of competitors and gain a greater understanding of their strengths and weakness. This understanding can then inform strategy.

The Durability of Competitive Advantage

The next question we must address is how long a competitive advantage will last once it has been created. In other words, what is the *durability* of competitive advantage given that other companies are also seeking to develop distinctive competencies that will give them a competitive advantage? The answer depends on three factors: barriers to imitation, the capability of competitors, and the general dynamism of the industry environment.

■ Barriers to Imitation

A company with a competitive advantage will earn higher-than-average profits. These profits send a signal to rivals that the company has some valuable distinctive competency that allows it to create superior value. Naturally, its competitors will try to identify and imitate that competency, and insofar as they are successful, ultimately their increased success may whittle away the company's superior profits.[25]

How quickly rivals will imitate a company's distinctive competencies is an important issue, because the speed of imitation has a bearing on the durability of a company's competitive advantage. Other things being equal, the more rapidly competitors imitate a company's distinctive competencies, the less durable its competitive advantage will be, and the more important it is that the company endeavor to improve its competencies to stay one step ahead of the imitators. It is important to stress at the outset that ultimately almost any distinctive competency can be imitated by a competitor. The critical issue is *time:* the longer it takes competitors to imitate a distinctive competency, the greater the opportunity the company has to build a strong market position and reputation with customers, which are then more difficult for competitors to attack. Moreover, the longer it takes to achieve an imitation, the greater is the opportunity for the imitated company to improve on its competency or build other competencies, thereby staying one step ahead of the competition.

Barriers to imitation are a primary determinant of the speed of imitation. **Barriers to imitation** are factors that make it difficult for a competitor to copy a company's distinctive competencies; the greater the barriers to imitation, the more sustainable is a company's competitive advantage.[26] Barriers to imitation differ depending on whether a competitor is trying to imitate resources or capabilities.

■ Imitating Resources
In general, the easiest distinctive competencies for prospective rivals to imitate tend to be those based on possession of firm-specific and valuable tangible resources, such as buildings, plant, and equipment. Such resources are visible to competitors and can often be purchased on the open market. For example, if a company's competitive advantage is based on sole possession of efficient-scale manufacturing facilities, competitors may move fairly quickly to establish similar facilities. Although Ford gained a competitive advantage over General Motors in the 1920s by being the first to adopt an assembly line manufacturing technology to produce automobiles, General Motors quickly imitated that innovation, competing away Ford's distinctive competency in the process. A similar process is occurring in the auto industry now, as companies try to imitate Toyota's famous production system.

Intangible resources can be more difficult to imitate. This is particularly true of brand names, which are important because they symbolize a company's reputation. In the heavy earthmoving equipment industry, for example, the Caterpillar brand name is synonymous with high quality and superior after-sales service and support. Similarly, the St. Michael's brand name used by Marks & Spencer, Britain's largest retailer, symbolizes high-quality but reasonably priced clothing. Customers often display a preference for the products of such companies because the brand name is an important guarantee of high quality. Although competitors might like to imitate well-established brand names, the law prohibits them from doing so.

Marketing and technological know-how are also important intangible resources and can be relatively easy to imitate. The movement of skilled marketing personnel between companies may facilitate the general dissemination of marketing know-how. For example, in the 1970s, Ford was acknowledged as the best marketer among the big three U.S. auto companies. In 1979, it lost a lot of its marketing know-how to Chrysler when its most successful marketer, Lee Iacocca, joined Chrysler and subsequently hired many of Ford's top marketing people to work with him at Chrysler. More generally, successful marketing strategies are relatively easy to imitate because they are so visible to competitors. Thus, Coca-Cola quickly imitated PepsiCo's Diet Pepsi brand with the introduction of its own brand, Diet Coke.

With regard to technological know-how, the patent system in theory should make technological know-how relatively immune to imitation. Patents give the inventor of a new product a twenty-year exclusive production agreement. For example, the biotechnology company Immunex discovered and patented Enbrel, which is capable of halting the disease-causing mechanism that leads to rheumatoid arthritis. All prior treatments simply provided patients with some relief from the symptoms of rheumatoid arthritis. Approved by the Food and Drug Administration in 1998, Enbrel racked up sales of over $400 million in its first year on the market and may ultimately generate annual revenues of $4 billion. (In 2002, Immunex was acquired by Amgen.) Despite the large market, Immunex's patent stops potential competitors from introducing their own version of Enbrel. However, whereas it is relatively easy to use the patent system to protect a biological product from imitation, this is not true of many other inventions. In electrical and computer engineering, for example, it is often possible to invent around patents: that is, produce a product that is functionally equivalent but does not rely on the patented technology. One study found that 60 percent of patented innovations were successfully invented around in four years.[27] This suggests that, in general, distinctive competencies based on technological know-how can be relatively short-lived.

■ **Imitating Capabilities** Imitating a company's capabilities tends to be more difficult than imitating its tangible and intangible resources, chiefly because capabilities are based on the way in which decisions are made and processes managed deep within a company. It is hard for outsiders to discern them.

On its own, the invisible nature of capabilities would not be enough to halt imitation; competitors could still gain insights into how a company operates by hiring people away from that company. However, a company's capabilities rarely reside in a single individual. Rather, they are the product of how numerous individuals interact within a unique organizational setting.[28] It is possible that no one individual within a company may be familiar with the totality of a company's internal operating routines and procedures. In such cases, hiring people away from a successful company in order to imitate its key capabilities may not be helpful.

■ Capability of Competitors

According to work by Pankaj Ghemawat, a major determinant of the capability of competitors to imitate a company's competitive advantage rapidly is the nature of the competitors' prior strategic commitments.[29] By **strategic commitment**, Ghemawat means a company's commitment to a particular way of doing business—that is, to developing a particular set of resources and capabilities. Ghemawat's point is that once a company has made a strategic commitment, it will have difficulty responding to new competition if doing so requires a break with this commitment. Therefore, when competitors have long-established commitments to a particular way of doing business, they may be slow to imitate an innovating company's competitive advantage. Its competitive advantage will thus be relatively durable.

The U.S. automobile industry again offers an example. From 1945 to 1975, the industry was dominated by the stable oligopoly of General Motors, Ford, and Chrysler, all of which geared their operations to the production of large cars, which American customers demanded at the time. When the market shifted from large cars to small, fuel-efficient ones during the late 1970s, U.S. companies lacked the resources and capabilities required to produce these cars. Their prior commitments had built the wrong kind of skills for this new environment. As a result, foreign producers, and particularly the Japanese, stepped into the market breach by providing compact, fuel-efficient, high-quality, and low-cost cars. The failure of U.S. auto manufacturers to react quickly to the distinctive competency of Japanese auto companies gave the latter time to build a strong market position and brand loyalty, which subsequently have proved difficult to attack.

Another determinant of the ability of competitors to respond to a company's competitive advantage is the absorptive capacity of competitors.[30] **Absorptive capacity** refers to the ability of an enterprise to identify, value, assimilate, and use new knowledge. For example, in the 1960s and 1970s, Toyota developed a competitive advantage based on its innovation of lean production systems. Competitors such as General Motors were slow to imitate this innovation, primarily because they lacked the necessary absorptive capacity. General Motors was such a bureaucratic and inward-looking organization that it was very difficult for the company to identify, value, assimilate, and use the knowledge that underlay lean production systems. Indeed, long after General Motors had identified and understood the importance of lean production systems, it was still struggling to assimilate and use that new knowledge. Put differently, internal inertia forces can make it difficult for established competitors to respond to a rival whose competitive advantage is based on new products or internal processes—that is, on innovation.

Taken together, factors such as existing strategic commitments and low absorptive capacity limit the ability of established competitors to imitate the competitive advantage of a rival, particularly when that competitive advantage is based on innovative products or processes. This is why when innovations reshape the rules of competition in an industry, value often migrates away from established competitors and toward new enterprises that are operating with new business models.

■ Industry Dynamism

A dynamic industry environment is one that is changing rapidly. We examined the factors that determine the dynamism and intensity of competition in an industry in Chapter 2 when we discussed the external environment. The most dynamic industries tend to be those with a very high rate of product innovation—for instance, the customer electronics industry and the personal computer industry. In dynamic industries, the rapid rate of innovation means that product life cycles are shortening and that competitive advantage can be fleeting. A company that has a competitive advantage today may find its market position outflanked tomorrow by a rival's innovation.

In the personal computer industry, the rapid increase in computing power during the past two decades has contributed to a high degree of innovation and a turbulent environment. Reflecting the persistence of innovation, Apple Computer in the late 1970s and early 1980s had an industrywide competitive advantage due to its innovation. In 1981, IBM seized the advantage by introducing its first personal computer. By the mid 1980s, IBM had lost its competitive advantage to high-power "clone" manufacturers such as Compaq that had beaten IBM in the race to introduce a computer based on Intel's 386 chip. In turn, in the 1990s, Compaq subsequently lost its competitive advantage to Dell, which pioneered new low-cost ways of delivering computers to customers using the Internet as a direct selling device.

Summary

The durability of a company's competitive advantage depends on the height of barriers to imitation, the capability of competitors to imitate its innovation, and the general level of dynamism in the industry environment. When barriers to imitation are low, capable competitors abound, and the environment is dynamic, with innovations being developed all the time, then competitive advantage is likely to be transitory. But even within such industries, companies can build a more enduring competitive advantage if they are able to make investments that build barriers to imitation.

During the 1980s, Apple Computer built a competitive advantage based on the combination of a proprietary disk operating system and an intangible product image. The resulting brand loyalty enabled Apple to carve out a fairly secure niche in an industry where competitive advantage has otherwise proven to be very fleeting. However, by the mid 1990s its strategy had been imitated, primarily because of the introduction of Microsoft's Windows operating system, which imitated most of the features that had enabled Apple to build brand loyalty. By 1996, Apple was in financial trouble, providing yet another example that no competitive advantage lasts forever. Ultimately, anything can be imitated. However, Apple has shown remarkable resilience; in the late 1990s, it clawed its way back from the brink of bankruptcy to establish a viable position within its niche once again, a position it still held on to by the mid 2000s.

Avoiding Failure and Sustaining Competitive Advantage

How can a company avoid failure and escape the traps that have snared so many once successful companies? How can managers build a sustainable competitive advantage? Much of the remainder of this book deals with these issues. Here, we make a number of key points that set the scene for the coming discussion.

■ Why Companies Fail

When a company loses its competitive advantage, its profitability falls. The company does not necessarily fail; it may just have average or below-average profitability and can remain in this mode for a considerable time, although its resource and capital base is shrinking. Failure implies something more drastic. A failing company is one whose profitability is now substantially lower than the average profitability of its competitors; it has lost the ability to attract and generate resources so that its profit margins and invested capital are shrinking rapidly.

Why does a company lose its competitive advantage and fail? The question is particularly pertinent because some of the most successful companies of the twentieth century have seen their competitive position deteriorate at one time or another. IBM, General Motors, American Express, Digital Equipment, and Sears, among many others, which all at one time were held up as examples of managerial excellence, have gone through periods where their financial performance was poor and they clearly lacked any competitive advantage. We explore three related reasons for failure: inertia, prior strategic commitments, and the Icarus paradox.

■ **Inertia** The inertia argument says that companies find it difficult to change their strategies and structures in order to adapt to changing competitive conditions.[31] IBM is a classic example of this problem. For thirty years, it was viewed as the world's most successful computer company. Then in the space of a few years, its success turned into a disaster: it lost $5 billion in 1992, leading to layoffs of more than 100,000 employees. IBM's troubles were caused by a dramatic decline in the cost of computing power as a result of innovations in microprocessors. With the advent of powerful low-cost microprocessors, the locus of the computer market shifted from mainframes to small, low-priced personal computers, leaving IBM's huge mainframe operations with a diminished market. Although IBM had, and still has, a significant presence in the personal computer market, it had failed to shift the focus of its efforts away from mainframes and toward personal computers. This failure meant deep trouble for one of the most successful companies of the twentieth century (although IBM has now executed a successful turnaround with a repositioning as a provider of e-commerce infrastructure and solutions).

One reason that companies find it so difficult to adapt to new environmental conditions seems to be the role of capabilities in causing inertia. Organizational capabilities—the way a company makes decisions and manages its processes—can be a source of competitive advantage, but they are difficult to change. IBM always emphasized close coordination among operating units and favored decision processes that stressed consensus among interdependent operating units as a prerequisite for a decision to go forward.[32] This capability was a source of advantage for IBM during the 1970s, when coordination among its worldwide operating units was necessary to develop, manufacture, and sell complex mainframes. But the slow-moving bureaucracy that it had spawned was a source of failure in the 1990s, when organizations had to adapt readily to rapid environmental change.

Capabilities are difficult to change because a certain distribution of power and influence is embedded within the established decision-making and management processes of an organization. Those who play key roles in a decision-making process clearly have more power. It follows that changing the established capabilities of an organization means changing its existing distribution of power and influence, and those whose power and influence would diminish resist such change. Proposals for change trigger turf battles. This power struggle and the political resistance associated with trying to alter the way in which an organization makes decisions and manages its process—that is, trying to change its capabilities—bring on inertia. This is not to say that companies cannot change. However, because change is so often resisted by those who feel threatened by it, change in most cases has to be induced by a crisis. By then, the company may already be failing, as happened at IBM.

■ **Prior Strategic Commitments** Ghemawat has argued that a company's prior strategic commitments not only limit its ability to imitate rivals but may also cause competitive disadvantage.[33] IBM, for instance, had major investments in the mainframe computer business, so when the market shifted, it was stuck with significant resources specialized to that particular business: its manufacturing facilities were geared to the production of mainframes, its research organization was similarly specialized, and so was its sales force. Because these resources were not well suited to the newly emerging personal computer business, IBM's difficulties in the early 1990s were in a sense inevitable. Its prior strategic commitments locked it into a business that was shrinking. Shedding these resources was bound to cause hardship for all organization stakeholders.

■ **The Icarus Paradox** Danny Miller has postulated that the roots of competitive failure can be found in what he termed the *Icarus paradox*.[34] Icarus is a figure in Greek mythology who used a pair of wings, made for him by his father, to escape from an island where he was being held prisoner. He flew so well that he went higher and higher, ever closer to the sun, until the heat of the sun melted the wax that held his wings together and he plunged to his death in the Aegean Sea. The paradox is that his greatest asset, his ability to fly, caused his demise. Miller argues that the same paradox applies to many once successful companies. According to Miller, many companies become so dazzled by their early success that they believe more of the same type of effort is the way to future success. As a result, they can become so specialized and inner directed that they lose sight of market realities and the fundamental requirements for achieving a competitive advantage. Sooner or later, this leads to failure.

Miller identifies four major categories among the rising and falling companies, which he labels "craftsmen," "builders," "pioneers," and "salesmen." The "craftsmen," such as Texas Instruments and Digital Equipment Corporation (DEC), achieved early success through engineering excellence. But then they became so obsessed with engineering details that they lost sight of market realities. (The story of DEC's demise is summarized in Strategy in Action 3.3.) Among the "builders" are Gulf & Western and ITT. Having built successful, moderately diversified companies, they then became so enchanted with diversification for its own sake that they continued to diversify far beyond the point at which it was profitable to do so. Miller's third group are the "pioneers" like Wang Labs. Enamored of their own originally brilliant innovations, managers here continued to search for additional brilliant innovations and ended up producing novel but completely useless products. The final category comprises the "salesmen," exemplified by Procter & Gamble and Chrysler. They became so convinced of their ability to sell anything that they paid scant attention to product development and manufacturing excellence and as a result spawned a proliferation of bland, inferior products.

■ Steps to Avoid Failure

Given that so many traps wait for companies, the question arises as to how strategic managers can use internal analysis to find them and escape them. We now look at several tactics that managers can use.

■ Focus on the Building Blocks of Competitive Advantage

Maintaining a competitive advantage requires a company to continue focusing on all four generic building blocks of competitive advantage—efficiency, quality, innovation, and responsiveness to customers—and to develop distinctive competencies that contribute to superior performance in these areas. One of the messages of Miller's Icarus paradox is that many successful companies become unbalanced in their pursuit of distinctive competencies. DEC, for example, focused on engineering quality at the expense of almost everything else, including, most importantly, responsiveness to customers. Other companies forget to focus on any distinctive competency at all.

■ Institute Continuous Improvement and Learning

The only constant in the world is change. Today's source of competitive advantage may soon be rapidly imitated by capable competitors or made obsolete by the innovations of a rival. In such a dynamic and fast-paced environment, the only way that a company can maintain a competitive advantage over time is to continually improve its efficiency, quality, innovation, and responsiveness to customers. The way to do this is to recognize the importance of learning within the organization.[35] The most successful companies are not those that stand still, resting on their laurels. They are those that are always seeking out ways of improving their operations and in the process are constantly upgrading the value of their distinctive competencies or creating new competencies. Companies such as General Electric and Toyota have a reputation for being learning

Strategy in Action

3.3

The Road to Ruin at DEC

Digital Equipment Corporation (DEC) was one of the premier computer companies of the 1970s and 1980s. DEC's original success was founded on the minicomputer, a cheaper, more flexible version of its mainframe cousins that Ken Olson and his brilliant team of engineers invented in the 1960s. They then improved on their original minicomputers until they could not be beat for quality and reliability. In the 1970s, their VAX series of minicomputers was widely regarded as the most reliable series of computers ever produced, and DEC was rewarded by high profit rates and rapid growth. By 1990, it was number 27 on the *Fortune 500* list of the largest corporations in America.

Buoyed by its success, DEC turned into an engineering monoculture: its engineers became idols; its marketing and accounting staff, however, were barely tolerated. Component specs and design standards were all that senior managers understood. Technological fine-tuning became such an obsession that the needs of customers for smaller, more economical, user-friendly computers were ignored. DEC's personal computers, for example, bombed because they were out of touch with the needs of customers, and the company failed to respond to the threat to its core market presented by the rise of computer workstations and client-server architecture. Indeed, Ken Olson was known for dismissing such new products. He once said, "We always say that customers are right, but they are not always right." Perhaps. But DEC, blinded by its early success, failed to remain responsive to its customers and changing market conditions.

By the early 1990s, DEC was in deep trouble. Olson was forced out in July 1992, and the company lost billions of dollars between 1992 and 1995. It returned to profitability in 1996, primarily because of the success of a turnaround strategy aimed at reorienting the company to serve precisely those areas that Olson had dismissed. In 1998, the company was acquired by Compaq Computer Corporation and disappeared from the business landscape as an independent entity.[d]

organizations. This means that they are continually analyzing the processes that underlie their efficiency, quality, innovation, and responsiveness to customers. Their objective is to learn from prior mistakes and to seek out ways to improve their processes over time. This has enabled Toyota, for example, to continually upgrade its employee productivity and product quality, and thus stay ahead of imitators.

■ **Track Best Industrial Practice and Use Benchmarking** One of the best ways to develop distinctive competencies that contribute to superior efficiency, quality, innovation, and responsiveness to customers is to identify and adopt best industrial practice. Only in this way will a company be able to build and maintain the resources and capabilities that underpin excellence in efficiency, quality, innovation, and responsiveness to customers. (We discuss what constitutes best industrial practice in some depth in Chapter 4.) It requires tracking the practice of other companies, and perhaps the best way to do so is through **benchmarking**: measuring the company against the products, practices, and services of some of its most efficient global competitors. For example, when Xerox was in trouble in the early 1980s, it decided to institute a policy of benchmarking to identify ways to improve the efficiency of its operations. Xerox benchmarked L. L. Bean for distribution procedures, Deere & Company for central computer operations, Procter & Gamble for marketing, and Florida Power & Light for total quality management processes. By the early 1990s, Xerox was benchmarking 240 functions against comparable areas in other companies. This process has been credited with helping it dramatically improve the efficiency of its operations.[36]

■ **Overcome Inertia** Overcoming the internal forces that are a barrier to change within an organization is one of the key requirements for maintaining a competitive advantage, and an entire chapter, Chapter 14, is spent discussing this issue. Suffice it to say here that identifying barriers to change is an important first step. Once this step has been taken, implementing change requires good leadership, the judicious use of power, and appropriate changes in organizational structure and control systems.

■ The Role of Luck

A number of scholars have argued that luck plays a critical role in determining competitive success and failure.[37] In its most extreme version, the luck argument devalues the importance of strategy altogether. Instead, it states that, in the face of uncertainty, some companies just happen to pick the correct strategy.

Although luck may be the reason for a company's success in particular cases, it is an unconvincing explanation for the persistent success of a company. Recall our argument that the generic building blocks of competitive advantage are superior efficiency, quality, innovation, and responsiveness to customers. Keep in mind also that competition is a process in which companies are continually trying to outdo each other in their ability to achieve high efficiency, superior quality, outstanding innovation, and quick responsiveness to customers. It is possible to imagine a company getting lucky and coming into possession of resources that allow it to achieve excellence on one or more of these dimensions. However, it is difficult to imagine how *sustained* excellence on any of these four dimensions could be produced by anything other than conscious effort, that is, by strategy. Luck may indeed play a role in success, and managers must always exploit a lucky break (Strategy in Action 3.4 discusses the role of luck in the early history of Microsoft and how Bill Gates exploited that luck). However, to argue that success is entirely a matter of luck is to strain credibility. As the great banker of the early twentieth century, J. P. Morgan, once said, "The harder I work, the luckier I seem to get." Managers who strive to formulate and implement strategies that lead to a competitive advantage are more likely to be lucky.

Strategy in Action 3.4

Bill Gates's Lucky Break

The product that launched Microsoft into its leadership position in the software industry was MS-DOS, the operating system for IBM and IBM-compatible PCs. The original DOS program, however, was developed not by Microsoft but by Seattle Computer, where it was known as Q-DOS (which stood for "quick and dirty operating system"). When IBM was looking for an operating system to run its original PC, it talked to a number of software companies, including Microsoft, asking whether they could develop such a system. Seattle Computer was not one of those companies. Bill Gates, already a player in the emerging Seattle computer community, knew that Seattle Computer had developed a disk operating system and took action: he borrowed $50,000 from his father, a senior partner in a prominent Seattle law firm, and then went to see the CEO of Seattle Computer and offered to purchase the rights to the company's Q-DOS system. He did not, of course, reveal that IBM was looking for a disk operat-

ing system. Seattle Computer, short of cash, quickly agreed. Gates then renamed the system MS-DOS, upgraded it somewhat, and licensed it to IBM. The rest, as they say, is history.

So was Gates lucky? Of course he was. It was lucky that Seattle Computer had not heard about IBM's request. It was lucky that IBM approached Microsoft. It was lucky that Gates knew about Seattle Computer's operating system. And it was lucky that Gates had a father wealthy enough to lend him $50,000 on short notice. Nevertheless, to attribute all of Microsoft's subsequent success to luck would be wrong. Although MS-DOS gave Microsoft a tremendous head start in the industry, it did not guarantee that Microsoft would continue to enjoy the kind of worldwide success that it has. To do that, Microsoft had to build the appropriate set of resources and capabilities required to produce a continual stream of innovative software, which is precisely what the company did with the cash generated from MS-DOS.[e]

Summary of Chapter

1. Distinctive competencies are the firm-specific strengths of a company. Valuable distinctive competencies enable a company to earn a profit rate that is above the industry average.

2. The distinctive competencies of an organization arise from its resources (its financial, physical, human, technological, and organizational assets) and capabilities (its skills at coordinating resources and putting them to productive use).

3. In order to achieve a competitive advantage, a company needs to pursue strategies that build on its existing resources and capabilities and formulate strategies that build additional resources and capabilities (develop new competencies).

4. The source of a competitive advantage is superior value creation.

5. To create superior value, a company must lower its costs or differentiate its product so that it creates more value and can charge a higher price, or do both simultaneously.

6. Managers must understand how value creation and pricing decisions affect demand and how costs change with increases in volume. They must have a good grasp of the demand conditions in the company's market and the cost structure of the company at different levels of output if they are to make decisions that maximize the profitability of their enterprise.

7. The four building blocks of competitive advantage are efficiency, quality, innovation, and responsiveness to customers. These are generic distinctive competencies. Superior efficiency enables a company to lower its costs; superior quality allows it to charge a higher price and lower its costs; and superior customer service lets it charge a higher price. Superior innovation can lead to higher prices, particularly in the case of product innovations, or lower unit costs, particularly in the case of process innovations.

8. If a company's managers are to perform a good internal analysis, they need to be able to analyze the financial performance of their company, identifying how the strategies of the company relate to its profitability, as measured by the return on invested capital.

9. The durability of a company's competitive advantage depends on the height of barriers to imitation, the capability of competitors, and environmental dynamism.

10. Failing companies typically earn low or negative profits. Three factors seem to contribute to failure: organizational inertia in the face of environmental change, the nature of a company's prior strategic commitments, and the Icarus paradox.

11. Avoiding failure requires a constant focus on the basic building blocks of competitive advantage, continuous improvement, identification and adoption of best industrial practice, and victory over inertia.

Discussion Questions

1. What are the main implications of the material discussed in this chapter for strategy formulation?

2. When is a company's competitive advantage most likely to endure over time?

3. It is possible for a company to be the lowest-cost producer in its industry and simultaneously have an output that is the most valued by customers. Discuss this statement.

4. Why is it important to understand the drivers of profitability, as measured by the return on invested capital?

5. Which is more important in explaining the success and failure of companies: strategizing or luck?

Practicing Strategic Management

▬ SMALL-GROUP EXERCISE

Analyzing Competitive Advantage

Break up into groups of three to five people. Drawing on the concepts introduced in this chapter, analyze the competitive position of your business school in the market for business education. Then answer the following questions:

1. Does your business school have a competitive advantage?

2. If so, on what is this advantage based, and is this advantage sustainable?

3. If your school does not have a competitive advantage in the market for business education, identify the inhibiting factors that are holding it back.

4. How might the Internet change the way in which business education is delivered?

5. Does the Internet pose a threat to the competitive position of your school in the market for business education, or is it an opportunity for your school to enhance its competitive position? (Note that it can be both.)

ARTICLE FILE 3

Find a company that has sustained its competitive advantage for more than ten years. Identify the source of the competitive advantage, and explain why it has lasted so long.

STRATEGIC MANAGEMENT PROJECT

Module 3

This module deals with the competitive position of your company. With the information you have at your disposal, perform the tasks and answer the questions listed:

1. Identify whether your company has a competitive advantage or disadvantage in its primary industry. (Its primary industry is the one in which it has the most sales.)

2. Evaluate your company against the four generic building blocks of competitive advantage: efficiency, quality, innovation, and responsiveness to customers. How does this exercise help you understand the performance of your company relative to its competitors?

3. What are the distinctive competencies of your company?

4. What role have prior strategies played in shaping the distinctive competencies of your company? What has been the role of luck?

5. Do the strategies your company is pursuing now build on its distinctive competencies? Are they an attempt to build new competencies?

6. What are the barriers to imitating the distinctive competencies of your company?

7. Is there any evidence that your company finds it difficult to adapt to changing industry conditions? If so, why do you think this is the case?

EXPLORING THE WEB

Visiting Johnson & Johnson

Visit the website of Johnson & Johnson (**www.jnj.com**). Read through the material contained on the site, paying particular attention to the features on company history, Johnson & Johnson's credo, innovations, and company news. On the basis of the information contained here, answer the following questions:

1. Do you think that Johnson & Johnson has a distinctive competence?

2. What is the nature of this competence? How does it help the company to attain a competitive advantage?

3. What are the resources and capabilities that underlie this competence? Where do these resources and capabilities come from?

4. How imitable is Johnson & Johnson's distinctive competence?

General Task   Search the Web for a company site that goes into depth about the history, products, and competitive position of that company. On the basis of the information you collect, answer the following questions:

1. Does the company have a distinctive competence?

2. What is the nature of this competence? How does it help the company to attain a competitive advantage?

3. What are the resources and capabilities that underlie this competence? Where do these resources and capabilities come from?

4. How imitable is the company's distinctive competence?

Closing Case

Google

In 1996 two computer science PhD students at Stanford University, Sergey Brin and Larry Page, were wondering how they could sort through the massive amount of information that was starting to appear on the Web in order to find specific and useful information on a topic. While there were several different technologies, or search engines, available to search the Web for information,

none of them seemed particularly useful to Brin and Page. The basic problem was that existing search engines did a poor job of distinguishing between useful and trivial websites. Brin and Page decided to build a search engine that would not only examine the words on webpages and then index them as other search engines did, but would also look at how and where these words were being used, and also at the number of other websites linked to a page. The goal was to have the search engine return a list of webpages, with the most useful appearing at the top.

The first iteration of their search engine, which relied on a proprietary algorithm developed by Brin and Page, was known as BackRub. BackRub soon created a buzz among other computer science students at Stanford, but it was the encouragement of another former Stanford student, David Filo, one of the founders of yahoo.com, that persuaded Brin and Page to start their own company.

By July 1998 Brin and Page had put their PhD studies on hold and were actively raising money from family, friends, and angel investors. Initially they found it very difficult to raise money, but in mid 1998 they had a chance encounter with another former Stanford student, Andy Bechtolsheim, who had been one of the founders of Sun Microsystems. Impressed by a demonstration of BackRub, Bechtolsheim wrote Brin and Page a check for $100,000 on the spot. By September 1998 they had raised $1 million, enough to capitalize their company, which they called Google.

By December 1998 the beta version of Google's search engine had been up and running on the Web for months and was answering over 10,000 search queries a day. From that point on, growth was exponential. By December 2000, Google's index included more than 1.3 billion webpages, and the company was answering some 60 million search inquiries a day. By 2004 the number of webpages indexed by Google exceeded 4 billion and the search engine was handling more than 300 million inquiries a day. Google's technology quickly became pervasive. Soon most major Web portals were using Google's search engine technology, including Yahoo! and AOL Time Warner. Estimates suggested that in 2003 some 75 percent of Internet searches were made using Google.

What was most impressive about Google, however, was that, unlike many other dot-com businesses of the 1990s, Google found a way to make money. In 2003 the company made $967 million in revenues and $105 million in net profit. In the first six months of 2004 alone, revenues surged to $1.35 billion and net income to $143 million. The basic business model is simple. Google sells to advertisers the words that people enter when they search for something on the Web. This means that whoever bids the most for a particular term, say, *digital cameras*, gets their link put at the top of a Google-generated list. Google distinguishes between independent search results and those that are paid for by listing "sponsored links" on the right side of its page. However, a sponsor does not pay Google unless a user clicks through to it from a Google-generated link.

To determine the price to charge advertisers for a term, Google uses an automated bidding process known as a Vickery second price auction. Under this bidding methodology, winning bidders pay only 1 cent more than the bidder below them. Thus if there are three bids for the term *digital cameras*—say, $1 a click, $0.50 a click, and $0.25 click—the winner will pay $0.51 a click to Google.

In August 2004, Google went public and raised over $1.5 billion. With no debt and flush with cash, the company looks set to build on its lead in the search engine business. However, competitors have not been sitting on the sidelines. In 2003 Yahoo! purchased a rival search engine company, Overture Services, for some $1.6 billion. Then in February 2004 Yahoo! replaced Google as the search engine on its site with a proprietary search engine based on Overture's technology. Microsoft, too, seems to have its sights set on Google. Microsoft is reportedly working on its own search engine technology, which it plans to integrate with its technology, including Microsoft Office and Longhorn, the next version of the Windows operating system that is due for release in 2006. [38]

Case Discussion Questions

1. What is the value that Google creates for (a) customers and (b) advertisers? How does this value translate into higher revenues and profits?
2. What are the sources of Google's competitive advantage? How secure are these advantages from imitation by competitors? What must Google do to keep the competitors at bay?
3. Do competitors such as Yahoo! and Microsoft potentially have assets and capabilities that give them an advantage over Google in the search engine business?

Chapter 4

Building Competitive Advantage Through Functional-Level Strategy

Opening Case

Verizon Wireless

In the wireless telecommunications industry one metric above all others determines a company's profitability: customer churn, or the number of subscribers who leave a service within a given time period. Churn is important because it costs between $300 and $400 to acquire a customer. With monthly bills in the United States averaging $50, it can take six to eight months just to recoup the fixed costs of a customer acquisition. If churn rates are higher, profitability is eaten up by the costs of acquiring customers who do not stay long enough to provide a profit to the service provider.

The risk of churn increased significantly in the United States after November 2003 when the Federal Communications Commission allowed wireless subscribers to take their numbers with them when they switched to a new service provider. Over the next six months, a clear winner emerged in the battle to limit customer defections: Verizon Wireless. Between November 2003 and May 2004 the churn rate at Verizon Wireless averaged 1.6 percent a month, implying that 20 percent of the company's customers were leaving the service each year. While this might sound high, it was considerably lower than the churn rate at AT&T Wireless, whose monthly churn rate of 3.7 percent was the highest among the big six wireless service providers in the United States, or T-Mobile, which had a 3.2 percent monthly churn rate.

Verizon's low churn rate has enabled the company to grow its subscriber base faster than rivals, which allows the company to better achieve economies of scale by spreading the fixed costs of building a wireless network over a larger customer base. In the quarter ending June 30, 2004, Verizon added 1.5 million customers, bringing its total up to 40.4 million. These customer additions easily outpaced those of its rivals. Sprint, for example, added 505,000 subscribers in the quarter, Cingular 428,000, and AT&T Wireless just 15,000.

There are several reasons for Verizon's success. First, in its early years the company invested heavily in building a high-quality nationwide wireless network. It has the largest coverage area of any wireless provider and has successfully differentiated itself on the quality of its service. Customers report clearer connections and fewer dropped calls on the Verizon network than on any other network.

A technological choice has also played into this advantage. Verizon is one of two U.S. wireless companies that took a chance and bet on a new wireless technology know as CDMA (the other was Sprint). CDMA is less costly to install than a competing wireless technology, known as GSM, and is well suited to providing broadband services, such as wireless connections to the Internet. When Verizon chose to build a nationwide CDMA network, the technology was unproven and critics questioned its reliability and cost. But the critics were wrong, and Verizon now has an advantage over most of its competitors, who opted for the more established GSM technology. Utilizing the broadband capabilities of its CDMA network, in 2005 Verizon was the first wireless provider to offer a nationwide "broadband" service that will allow subscribers to connect to the Internet in major metropolitan areas via a laptop or cell phone. This may well prove to be another source of differential advantage.

Verizon has communicated its coverage and quality advantage to customers with its "Test Man" advertisements. In these ads, a Verizon Test Man wearing horn-rimmed glasses and a Verizon uniform wanders around remote spots in the nation asking on his Verizon cell phone, "Can you hear me now?" Verizon says that the Test Man is actually the personification of a crew of fifty Verizon employees who each drive some 100,000 miles annually in specially outfitted vehicles to test the reliability of Verizon's network.

To further reduce customer churn, Verizon has invested heavily in its customer care function. Almost as soon as new customers receive their first monthly bill, Verizon Wireless representatives are on the phone, asking how they like the service. In that same call, a Verizon representative will ask what parts of the service a customer isn't using. If someone isn't yet using voice mail, for example, the representative will offer to set it up and get it working.

In addition, Verizon's automated software programs analyze the call habits of individual customers. Using that information, Verizon representatives will contact customers and suggest alternative calling plans that might better suit their needs. For example, Verizon might contact a customer and say, "We see that because of your heavy use on weekends, an alternative calling plan might make more sense for you and help reduce your monthly bills." The goal is to anticipate customer needs and proactively satisfy them, rather than have the customer take the initiative and possibly switch to another service provider.[1]

Overview

In this chapter, we take a close look at **functional-level strategies**: those aimed at improving the effectiveness of a company's operations and thus its ability to attain superior efficiency, quality, innovation, and customer responsiveness.

It is important to keep in mind the relationships among functional strategies, distinctive competencies, differentiation, low cost, value creation, and profitability (see Figure 4.1). Note that distinctive competencies shape the functional-level strategies that a company can pursue and that managers, through their choices with regard to functional-level strategies, can build resources and capabilities that enhance a company's distinctive competencies. Note also that the ability of a company to attain superior efficiency, quality, innovation, and customer responsiveness will determine if its product offering is *differentiated* from that of rivals and if it has a *low cost structure*. Recall that companies that increase the utility consumers get from their products through differentiation, while simultaneously lowering their cost structure, create more value than their rivals, and this leads to a competitive advantage and superior profitability and profit growth.

The *Opening Case* illustrates some of these relationships. Verizon Wireless has differentiated itself from its competitors through the reliability and coverage of its wireless network (a tangible resource) and through its superior after-sales service and support, or customer care (a capability). Verizon's network advantages have been communicated to customers through the "Can you hear me now?" advertisement campaign. Its successful differentiation, which is based on quality and customer responsiveness and is achieved through actions taken at the functional level, has reduced customer churn rates to the lowest level in the industry, boosting profitability and enabling Verizon to capture more market share, which implies greater profit growth. Consistent with the Verizon case, much of this chapter is devoted to looking

FIGURE 4.1

The Roots of Competitive Advantage

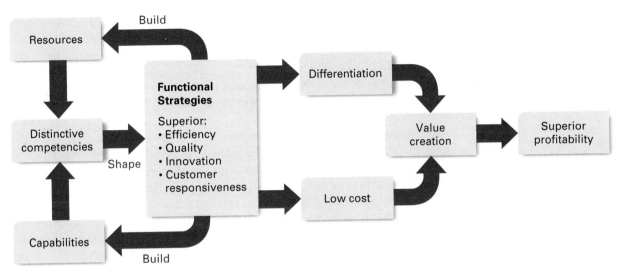

at the basic strategies that can be adopted at the operating level to improve competitive position. By the end of this chapter, you will understand how functional-level strategies can be used to build a sustainable competitive advantage.

Achieving Superior Efficiency

A company is a device for transforming inputs (labor, land, capital, management, and technological know-how) into outputs (the goods and services produced). The simplest measure of efficiency is the quantity of inputs that it takes to produce a given output; that is, efficiency = outputs/inputs. The more efficient a company is, the fewer the inputs required to produce a given output and therefore the lower its cost structure will be. Put another way, an efficient company has higher productivity, and therefore lower costs, than its rivals. Here we review the steps that companies can take at the functional level to increase their efficiency and thereby lower their cost structure.

■ Efficiency and Economies of Scale

Economies of scale are unit cost reductions associated with a large scale of output. You will recall from the last chapter that it is very important for managers to understand how the cost structure of their enterprise varies with output because this understanding should help to drive strategy. For example, if unit costs fall significantly as output is expanded—that is, if there are significant economies of scale—a company may benefit by keeping prices down and increasing volume.

One source of economies of scale is the ability to spread fixed costs over a large production volume. *Fixed costs* are costs that must be incurred to produce a product whatever the level of output; examples are the costs of purchasing machinery, setting up machinery for individual production runs, building facilities, and advertising and R&D. For example, Microsoft spent approximately $1 billion to develop the latest version of its Windows operating system, Windows XP. It can realize substantial scale economies by spreading the fixed costs associated with developing the new operating system over the enormous unit sales volume it expects for this system (95 percent of the world's personal computers use a Microsoft operating system). These scale economies are significant because of the trivial incremental (or marginal) cost of producing additional copies of Windows XP: once the master copy has been produced, additional CDs containing the operating system can be produced for a few cents. The key to Microsoft's efficiency and profitability (and that of other companies with high fixed costs and trivial incremental or marginal costs) is to increase sales rapidly enough that fixed costs can be spread out over a large unit volume and substantial scale economies can be realized.

Another source of scale economies is the ability of companies producing in large volumes to achieve a greater division of labor and specialization. Specialization is said to have a favorable impact on productivity, mainly because it enables employees to become very skilled at performing a particular task. The classic example of such economies is Ford's Model T car. The world's first mass-produced car, the Model T Ford was introduced in 1923. Until then, Ford had made cars using an expensive hand-built craft production method. By introducing mass-production techniques, the company achieved greater division of labor (it split assembly into small, repeatable tasks) and specialization, which boosted employee productivity. Ford was also able to spread the fixed costs of developing a car and setting up production machinery over a large volume of output. As a result of these economies, the cost of manufacturing a car at Ford fell from $3,000 to less than $900 (in 1958 dollars).

These examples illustrate that economies of scale can boost profitability, as measured by return on invested capital (ROIC), in a number of ways. Economies of scale exist in production, sales and marketing, and R&D, and the overall effect of realizing scale economies is to reduce spending as a percentage of revenues on cost of goods sold (COGS); sales, general, and administrative expenses (SG&A); and R&D expenses, thereby boosting return on sales and, by extension, ROIC (see Figure 3.9). Moreover, by making more intensive use of existing capacity, a company can increase the amount of sales generated from its property, plant, and equipment (PPE), thereby reducing the amount of capital it needs to generate a dollar of sales, and thus increasing its capital turnover and its ROIC.

The concept of scale economies is illustrated in Figure 4.2, which shows that as a company increases its output, unit costs fall. This process comes to an end at an output of Q_1, where all scale economies are exhausted. Indeed, at outputs of greater than Q_1, the company may encounter **diseconomies of scale**, which are the unit cost increases associated with a large scale of output. Diseconomies of scale occur primarily because of the increasing bureaucracy associated with large-scale enterprises and the managerial inefficiencies that can result.[2] Larger enterprises have a tendency to develop extensive managerial hierarchies in which dysfunctional political behavior is commonplace, information about operating matters is accidentally and deliberately distorted by the number of managerial layers through which it has to travel to reach top decisionmakers, and poor decisions are the result. As a result, past some point (such as Q_1 in Figure 4.2), the inefficiencies that result from such developments outweigh any additional gains from economies of scale, and unit costs start to rise as output expands.

Managers must know not only the extent of economies of scale, but also where diseconomies of scale begin to occur. At Nucor Steel, for example, the realization that diseconomies of scale exist has led to a decision not to build plants that employ more

FIGURE 4.2

Economies and
Diseconomies of
Scale

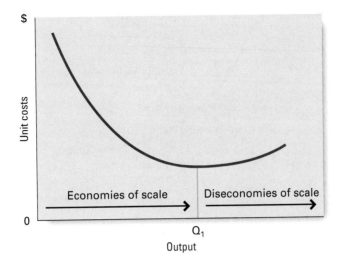

**Efficiency and
Learning Effects**

than 300 individuals. The belief is that it is more efficient to build two plants, each
employing 300 people, than one plant employing 600 people. Although the larger
plant might theoretically be able to reap greater scale economies, Nucor's management believes that these would be swamped by the diseconomies of scale that come
with larger organizational units.

Learning effects are cost savings that come from learning by doing. Labor, for example, learns by repetition how best to carry out a task. Therefore, labor productivity
increases over time, and unit costs fall as individuals learn the most efficient way to
perform a particular task. Equally important, management in new manufacturing
facilities typically learns over time how best to run the new operation. Hence, production costs decline because of increasing labor productivity and management efficiency. Japanese companies like Toyota are noted for making learning a central part
of their operating philosophy.

Learning effects tend to be more significant when a technologically complex task
is repeated because there is more to learn. Thus, learning effects will be more significant in an assembly process that has 1,000 complex steps than in one with 100 simple
steps. Although learning effects are normally associated with the manufacturing
process, there is every reason to believe that they are just as important in service industries. For example, one famous study of learning in the context of the health care
industry found that more experienced medical providers posted significantly lower
mortality rates for a number of common surgical procedures, suggesting that learning effects are at work in surgery.[3] The authors of this study used the evidence to
argue for establishing regional referral centers for the provision of highly specialized
medical care. These centers would perform many specific surgical procedures (such
as heart surgery), replacing local facilities with lower volumes and presumably higher
mortality rates. Another recent study found strong evidence of learning effects in a
financial institution. The study looked at a newly established document-processing
unit with one hundred staff members and found that, over time, documents were
processed much more rapidly as the staff learned the process. Overall, the study

FIGURE 4.3

The Impact of Learning and Scale Economies on Unit Costs

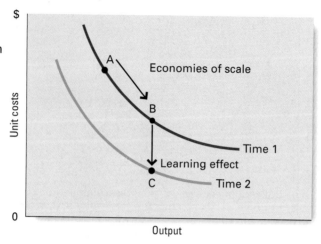

concluded that unit costs fell every time the cumulative number of documents processed doubled.[4]

In terms of the unit cost curve of a company, although economies of scale imply a movement along the curve (say, from A to B in Figure 4.3), the realization of learning effects implies a downward shift of the *entire* curve (B to C in Figure 4.3) as both labor and management become more efficient over time at performing their tasks at every level of output. In accounting terms, learning effects in a production setting will reduce the cost of goods sold as a percentage of revenues, enabling the company to earn a higher return on sales and return on invested capital.

No matter how complex the task is, however, learning effects typically die out after a limited period of time. Indeed, it has been suggested that they are really important only during the start-up period of a new process and cease after two or three years.[5] When changes occur to a company's production system—as a result of merger or the use of new information technology, for example—the learning process has to begin again.

■ **Efficiency and the Experience Curve**

The experience curve refers to the systematic lowering of the cost structure, and consequent unit cost reductions, that have been observed to occur over the life of a product.[6] According to the experience-curve concept, unit manufacturing costs for a product typically decline by some characteristic amount each time *accumulated* output of the product is doubled (accumulated output is the total output of a product since its introduction). This relationship was first observed in the aircraft industry, where it was found that each time accumulated output of airframes was doubled, unit costs declined to 80 percent of their previous level.[7] Thus, the fourth airframe typically costs only 80 percent of the second airframe to produce, the eighth airframe only 80 percent of the fourth, the sixteenth only 80 percent of the eighth, and so on. The outcome of this process is a relationship between unit manufacturing costs and accumulated output similar to that illustrated in Figure 4.4. Economies of scale and learning effects underlie the experience-curve phenomenon. Put simply, as a company increases the accumulated volume of its output over time, it is able to realize both economies of scale (as volume increases) and learning effects. Consequently, unit costs and cost structure fall with increases in accumulated output.

FIGURE 4.4

The Experience Curve

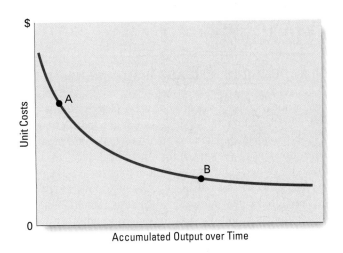

The strategic significance of the experience curve is clear: increasing a company's product volume and market share will lower its cost structure relative to its rivals. Thus, company B in Figure 4.4, because it is farther down the experience curve, has a cost advantage over company A because of its lower cost structure. The concept is perhaps most important in industries that mass-produce a standardized output (for example, the manufacture of semiconductor chips). A company that wishes to become more efficient and lower its cost structure must try to ride down the experience curve as quickly as possible. This means constructing efficient scale manufacturing facilities even before it has generated demand for the product and aggressively pursuing cost reductions from learning effects. It might also need to adopt an aggressive marketing strategy, cutting prices to the bone and stressing heavy sales promotions and extensive advertising in order to build up demand, and hence accumulated volume, as quickly as possible. The need to be aware of the relationship of demand, price options, and costs noted in Chapter 3 is clear.

Once down the experience curve because of its superior efficiency, the company is likely to have a significant cost advantage over its competitors. For example, it has been argued that Intel uses such tactics to ride down the experience curve and gain a competitive advantage over its rivals in the market for microprocessors. Similarly, one reason Matsushita came to dominate the global market for VHS videotape recorders is that it based its strategy on the experience curve.[8] The early success of Texas Instruments was also based on exploiting the experience curve, as Strategy in Action 4.1 details.

The company farthest down the experience curve cannot become complacent about its cost advantage. Strategy in Action 4.1 explains how obsession with the experience curve at Texas Instruments harmed the company. More generally, there are three reasons that managers should not become complacent about their efficiency-based cost advantages derived from experience effects. First, since neither learning effects nor economies of scale go on forever, the experience curve is likely to bottom out at some point; indeed, it must do so by definition. When this occurs, further unit cost reductions from learning effects and economies of scale will be hard to come by. Thus, in time, other companies can lower their cost structures and match

Strategy in Action   4.1

Too Much Experience at Texas Instruments

Texas Instruments (TI) was an early user of the experience-curve concept. TI was a technological innovator, first in silicon transistors and then in semiconductors. The company discovered that with every doubling of accumulated production volume of a transistor or semiconductor, unit costs declined to 73 percent of their previous level. Building on this insight, when TI first produced a new transistor or semiconductor, it would slash the price of the product to stimulate demand. The goal was to drive up the accumulated volume of production and so drive down costs through the realization of experience-curve economies. As a result, during the 1960s and 1970s, TI hammered its competitors in transistors and moved on to prevail in semiconductors and, ultimately, in hand-held calculators and digital watches. Until 1982, TI enjoyed rapid growth, with sales quadrupling between 1977 and 1981 alone.

After 1982, things began to go wrong for TI. The company's single-minded focus on cost reductions, an outgrowth of its strategic reliance on the experience curve, left it with a poor understanding of customer needs and market trends. Competitors such as Casio and Hewlett-Packard began to make major inroads into TI's hand-held calculator business by focusing on features in addition to cost and price that customers demanded. TI was slow to react to this trend and lost substantial market share as a result. In the late 1970s, it also decided to focus on semiconductors for watches and calculators, where it had gained substantial experience-curve-based cost economies, rather than developing metal oxide semiconductors for computer memories and advanced semiconductors. As it turned out, with the growth in minicomputers and personal computers in the early 1980s, the market shifted toward high-power metal oxide semiconductors. Consequently, TI found itself outflanked by Intel and Motorola. In sum, TI's focus on realizing experience-curve economies initially benefited the company, but then it seems to have contributed toward a myopia that cost the company dearly.[a]

the cost leader. Once this happens, a number of low-cost companies can have cost parity with each other. In such circumstances, a sustainable competitive advantage must rely on strategic factors besides the minimization of production costs by using existing technologies—factors such as better responsiveness to customers, product quality, or innovation.

Second, as noted in Chapter 2, changes that are always taking place in the external environment disrupt a company's business model, so cost advantages gained from experience effects can be made obsolete by the development of new technologies. The price of television picture tubes followed the experience-curve pattern from the introduction of television in the late 1940s until 1963. The average unit price dropped from $34 to $8 (in 1958 dollars) in that time. However, the advent of color TV interrupted the experience curve. To make picture tubes for color TVs, a new manufacturing technology was required, and the price of color TV tubes shot up to $51 by 1966. Then the experience curve reasserted itself. The price dropped to $48 in 1968, $37 in 1970, and $36 in 1972.[9] In short, technological change can alter the rules of the game, requiring that former low-cost companies take steps to reestablish their competitive edge.

A further reason for avoiding complacency is that producing a high volume of output does not necessarily give a company a lower cost structure. Different technologies have different cost structures. For example, the steel industry has two alternative manufacturing technologies: an integrated technology, which relies on the basic oxygen furnace, and a mini-mill technology, which depends on the electric arc furnace. Whereas the basic oxygen furnace requires high volumes to attain maximum efficiency, mini-mills are cost efficient at relative low volumes. Moreover, even when both technologies are producing at their most efficient output levels, steel companies with basic oxygen furnaces do not have a cost advantage over mini-mills. Consequently, the pursuit of experience economies by an integrated company using basic oxygen technology may not bring the kind of cost advantages that a naive reading of the experience-curve phenomenon would lead the company to expect. Indeed, there have been significant periods of time when integrated companies have not been able to get enough orders to run at optimum capacity. Hence, their production costs have been considerably higher than those of mini-mills.[10] As we discuss next, in many industries new flexible manufacturing technologies hold out the promise of allowing small manufacturers to produce at unit costs comparable to those of large assembly-line operations.

Efficiency, Flexible Manufacturing, and Mass Customization

Central to the concept of economies of scale is the idea that the best way to achieve high efficiency and a lower cost structure is through the mass production of a standardized output. The tradeoff implicit in this idea is between unit costs and product variety. Producing greater product variety from a factory implies shorter production runs, which implies an inability to realize economies of scale and higher costs. That is, a wide product variety makes it difficult for a company to increase its production efficiency and thus reduce its unit costs. According to this logic, the way to increase efficiency and achieve a lower cost structure is to limit product variety and produce a standardized product in large volumes (see Figure 4.5a).

This view of production efficiency has been challenged by the rise of flexible manufacturing technologies. The term **flexible manufacturing technology**—or **lean production**, as it is sometimes called—covers a range of manufacturing technologies designed to reduce setup times for complex equipment, increase the use of individual

FIGURE 4.5

Tradeoff Between Costs and Product Variety

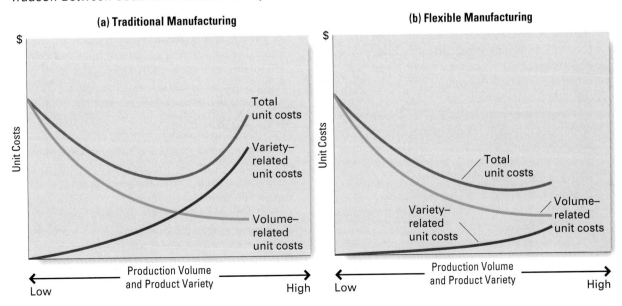

machines through better scheduling, and improve quality control at all stages of the manufacturing process.[11] Flexible manufacturing technologies allow the company to produce a wider variety of end products at a unit cost that at one time could be achieved only through the mass production of a standardized output (see Figure 4.5b). Indeed, research suggests that the adoption of flexible manufacturing technologies may increase efficiency and lower unit costs relative to what can be achieved by the mass production of a standardized output, while at the same time enabling the company to customize its product offering to a much greater extent than was once thought possible. The term **mass customization** has been coined to describe the ability of companies to use flexible manufacturing technology to reconcile two goals that were once thought to be incompatible: *low cost* and *differentiation through product customization.*[12]

Flexible manufacturing technologies vary in their sophistication and complexity. One of the most famous examples, Toyota's production system, is relatively unsophisticated, but it has been credited with making Toyota the most efficient auto company in the global industry. Toyota's flexible manufacturing system is profiled in Strategy in Action 4.2. **Flexible machine cells** are another common flexible manufacturing technology. A flexible machine cell is a grouping of various types of machinery, a common materials handler, and a centralized cell controller (a computer). Each cell normally contains four to six machines capable of performing a variety of operations but dedicated to producing a family of parts or products. The settings on the machines are computer controlled, which allows each cell to switch quickly between the production of different parts or products.

Strategy in Action   4.2

Toyota's Lean Production System

Toyota's flexible manufacturing system was developed by one of the company's engineers, Ohno Taiichi. After working at Toyota for five years and visiting Ford's U.S. plants, Ohno became convinced that the mass-production philosophy for making cars was flawed. He saw numerous problems, including three major drawbacks. First, long production runs created massive inventories, which had to be stored in large warehouses. This was expensive because of the cost of warehousing and because inventories tied up capital in unproductive uses. Second, if the initial machine settings were wrong, long production runs resulted in the production of a large number of defects (that is, waste). And third, the mass-production system was unable to accommodate consumer preferences for product diversity.

In looking for ways to make shorter production runs economical, Ohno developed a number of techniques designed to reduce setup times for production equipment, a major source of fixed costs. By using a system of levers and pulleys, he was able to reduce the time required to change dies on stamping equipment from a full day in 1950 to three minutes by 1971. This advance made small production runs economical, which allowed Toyota to respond better to consumer demands for product diversity. Small production runs also eliminated the need to hold large inventories, thereby reducing warehousing costs. Furthermore, small production runs and the lack of inventory meant that defective parts were produced only in small numbers and entered the assembly process immediately. This reduced waste and made it easier to trace defects to their source and fix the problem. In sum, Ohno's innovations enabled Toyota to produce a more diverse product range at a lower unit cost than was possible with conventional mass production.[b]

Improved capacity utilization and reductions in work-in-progress (that is, stockpiles of partly finished products) and waste are major efficiency benefits of flexible machine cells. Improved capacity utilization arises from the reduction in setup times and from the computer-controlled coordination of production flow between machines, which eliminates bottlenecks. The tight coordination between machines also reduces work-in-progress. Reductions in waste are due to the ability of computer-controlled machinery to identify ways to transform inputs into outputs while producing a minimum of unusable waste material. Freestanding machines might be in use 50 percent of the time; the same machines when grouped into a cell can be used more than 80 percent of the time and produce the same end product with half the waste, thereby increasing efficiency and resulting in lower costs.

The effects of installing flexible manufacturing technology on a company's cost structure can be dramatic. Ford Motor Company is currently introducing flexible manufacturing technologies into its automotive plants around the world. These new technologies should allow Ford to produce multiple models from the same line and to switch production from one model to another much more quickly than in the past. In total, Ford hopes to take $2 billion out of its cost structure by 2010.[13]

More generally, in terms of the profitability framework developed in Chapter 3, flexible manufacturing technology should boost profitability (measured by ROIC) by reducing the cost of goods sold as a percentage of revenues, reducing the working capital needed to finance work-in-progress (because there is less of it), and reducing the amount of capital that needs to be invested in property, plant, and equipment to generate a dollar of sales (because less space is needed to store inventory).

■ Marketing and Efficiency

The marketing strategy that a company adopts can have a major impact on efficiency and cost structure. **Marketing strategy** refers to the position that a company takes with regard to pricing, promotion, advertising, product design, and distribution. Some of the steps leading to greater efficiency are fairly obvious. For example, riding down the experience curve to achieve a lower cost structure can be facilitated by aggressive pricing, promotions, and advertising, all of which are the task of the marketing function. Other aspects of marketing strategy have a less obvious but no less important impact on efficiency. One important aspect is the relationship of customer defection rates, cost structure, and unit costs, which was touched on in the *Opening Case* on Verizon.[14]

Customer defection rates (churn rates) are the percentage of a company's customers who defect every year to competitors. Defection rates are determined by customer loyalty, which in turn is a function of the ability of a company to satisfy its customers. Because acquiring a new customer entails certain one-time fixed costs for advertising, promotions, and the like, there is a direct relationship between defection rates and costs. The longer a company holds on to a customer, the greater is the volume of customer-generated unit sales that can be set against these fixed costs and the lower the average unit cost of each sale. Thus, lowering customer defection rates allows a company to achieve a lower cost structure.

One consequence of the defection-cost relationship depicted is illustrated in Figure 4.6. Because of the relatively high fixed costs of acquiring new customers, serving customers who stay with the company only for a short time before switching to competitors often leads to a loss on the investment made to acquire those customers. The longer a customer stays with the company, the more the fixed costs of acquiring that customer can be spread out over repeat purchases, boosting

FIGURE 4.6

The Relationship Between Customer Loyalty and Profit per Customer

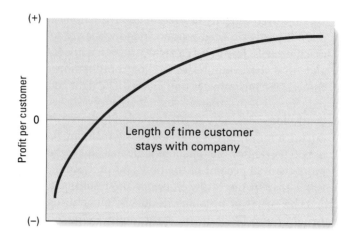

the profit per customer. Thus, there is a positive relationship between the length of time that a customer stays with a company and profit per customer. If a company can reduce customer defection rates, it can make a much better return on its investment in acquiring customers and thereby boost its profitability. In terms of the profitability framework developed in Chapter 3, reduced customer defection rates mean that the company needs to spend less on sales, general, and administrative expenses to generate a dollar of sales revenue, which increases both return on sales and return on invested capital.

We discussed one example of the importance of customer defection rates in the *Opening Case*, when we looked at customer churn in the wireless industry. For another example, consider the credit card business.[15] Most credit card companies spend an average of $50 to recruit a customer and set up a new account. These costs come from the advertising required to attract new customers, the credit checks required for each customer, and the mechanics of setting up an account and issuing a card. These one-time fixed costs can be recouped only if a customer stays with the company for at least two years. Moreover, when customers stay a second year, they tend to increase their use of the credit card, which raises the volume of revenues generated by each customer over time. As a result, although the credit card business loses $50 per customer in year 1, it makes a profit of $44 in year 3 and $55 in year 6.

Another economic benefit of long-time customer loyalty is the free advertising that customers provide for a company. Loyal customers can dramatically increase the volume of business through referrals. A striking example is Britain's largest retailer, the clothing and food company Marks & Spencer, whose success is built on a well-earned reputation for providing its customers with high-quality goods at reasonable prices. The company has generated such customer loyalty that it does not need to advertise in Britain, a major source of cost saving.

The key message, then, is that reducing customer defection rates and building customer loyalty can be major sources of a lower cost structure. One study has estimated that a 5 percent reduction in customer defection rates leads to the following increases in profits per customer over average customer life: 75 percent in the credit card business, 50 percent in the insurance brokerage industry, 45 percent in the industrial laundry business, and 35 percent in the computer software industry.[16]

A central component of developing a strategy to reduce defection rates is to identify customers who have defected, find out why they defected, and act on that information so that other customers do not defect for similar reasons in the future. To take these measures, the marketing function must have information systems capable of tracking customer defections.

■ Materials Management, Just-in-Time, and Efficiency

The contribution of materials management (logistics) to boosting the efficiency of a company can be just as dramatic as the contribution of production and marketing. **Materials management** encompasses the activities necessary to get inputs and components to a production facility (including the costs of purchasing inputs), through the production process, and out through a distribution system to the end-user.[17] Because there are so many sources of cost in this process, the potential for reducing costs through more efficient materials-management strategies is enormous. For a typical manufacturing company, materials and transportation costs account for 50 to 70 percent of its revenues, so even a small reduction in these costs can have a substantial impact on profitability. According to one estimate, for a company with revenues of $1 million, a return on invested capital of 5 percent, and materials-management costs that amount to 50 percent of sales revenues (including purchasing costs), increasing total profits by $15,000 would require either a 30 percent increase in sales revenues or a 3 percent reduction in materials costs.[18] In a typical competitive market, reducing materials costs by 3 percent is usually much easier than increasing sales revenues by 30 percent.

Improving the efficiency of the materials-management function typically requires the adoption of a just-in-time (JIT) inventory system, designed to economize on inventory holding costs by having components arrive at a manufacturing plant just in time to enter the production process or to have goods arrive at a retail store only when stock is almost depleted. The major cost saving comes from increasing inventory turnover, which reduces inventory holding costs, such as warehousing and storage costs, and the company's need for working capital. For example, through efficient logistics Wal-Mart can replenish the stock in its stores at least twice a week; many stores receive daily deliveries if they are needed. The typical competitor replenishes its stock every two weeks, so it has to carry a much higher inventory and needs more working capital per dollar of sales. Compared to its competitors, Wal-Mart can maintain the same service levels with a lower investment in inventory, a major source of its lower cost structure. Thus, faster inventory turnover has helped Wal-Mart achieve an efficiency-based competitive advantage in the retailing industry.[19] More generally, in terms of the profitability model developed in Chapter 3, JIT inventory systems reduce the need for working capital (since there is less inventory to finance) and the need for fixed capital to finance storage space (since there is less to store), which reduces capital needs, increases capital turnover, and, by extension, boosts the return on invested capital.

The drawback of JIT systems is that they leave a company without a buffer stock of inventory. Although buffer stocks are expensive to store, they can help tide a company over shortages on inputs brought about by disruption among suppliers (for instance, a labor dispute at a key supplier) and can help a company respond quickly to increases in demand. However, there are ways around these limitations. For example, to reduce the risks linked to dependence on just one supplier for an important input, a company might decide to source inputs from multiple suppliers.

Recently, the efficient management of materials and inventory has been recast in terms of **supply-chain management**: the task of managing the flow of inputs and components from suppliers into the company's production processes to minimize inventory holding and maximize inventory turnover. One of the exemplary companies in terms of supply-chain management is Dell, whose goal is to streamline its supply chain to such an extent that it "replaces inventory with information." Strategy in Action 4.3 looks at how the three major office superstores—Office Depot, Staples, and Office Max—are competing against each other by trying to manage their supply chains more efficiently.

Strategy in Action   4.3

Supply-Chain Management at Office Superstores

Over the past decade, Office Depot, Staples, and Office Max have been engaged in an intense race to dominate the office superstore business. Office superstores have adopted a supermarket approach to selling office supplies and equipment, which includes everything from paper and printer ink to computers and office furniture. Like all other supermarket-type retailers, their margins are razor thin. So to boost their profitability, all three have been looking at ways of managing their supply chains more efficiently. The goal is to coordinate the flow of materials from vendors to such a degree that inventory turns over more rapidly and so less store space needs to be devoted to storing inventory, which allows for smaller, less expensive stores. To the extent that they are successful, this strategy should produce higher sales per square foot, require less investment in store real estate, and tie up less working capital in inventory. All of this will boost profitability as measured by the return on invested capital.

Using inventory turnover as a metric, Office Depot is the clear leader, with a 7.1 inventory turn rate; its inventory turns over (is replaced) 7.1 times per year. Staples is next, with 4.2 inventory turns, followed by Office Max, with 3.2 inventory turns. Office Depot attributes its high inventory turnover to an early investment in information systems, which allow it to track the sales of individual items closely and link them to an optimal reordering cycle. In addition, these systems have helped it to identify slow-moving, low-margin items. Over the past few years, Office Depot has scaled back the number of products it keeps in stock—its stock keeping units (SKUs)—by about 20 percent by removing slow-moving, low-margin items from its stores. As a result, it can operate with slightly smaller stores and still generate comparable sales levels; its new stores are 25,000 square feet, compared to 30,000 square feet in older stores. As it has grown larger, Office

Depot has also been able to use its buying power to persuade vendors to drop-ship supplies at Office Depot warehouses on a just-in-time basis, thereby removing the need to hold expensive inventory.

For its part, Staples announced in 2001 that more efficient supply-chain management was one of its top priorities. Staples has put some thirty initiatives in place in recent years in an attempt to manage its inventory better. Among them is working closely with its top thirty suppliers to develop joint processes for streamlining the supply process. Regular meetings with Hewlett-Packard, for example, have prompted the retailer to move ink cartridges, one of its major categories, to the front of the store to yield faster inventory turns. Staples credits this action with a $6 million to $8 million reduction in inventory. More generally, Staples maintains that between 1998, when it started work on these initiatives, and 2001, the average inventory per store has fallen by some 30 percent. One of the most dramatic steps Staples has taken has been to eliminate the in-store stock of personal computers from some two hundred stores and to replace the product displays and on-floor inventory with a web-based display that allows Staples customers to enter a customized order for a PC, which a Staples vendor then builds.

Office Max too is investing aggressively in supply-chain management initiatives in an attempt to take inventory out of its system. Like its competitors, it has invested in information systems to track the sale of individual items and to link that information to reordering cycles. It is in the process of reducing its SKUs, removing slow-selling, low-margin items from stores, and downscaling the size of its stores while planning to boost sales per square foot. As a result, the average size of a new Office Max store has fallen by 15 percent over the last few years.[c]

■ R&D Strategy and Efficiency

The role of superior research and development (R&D) in helping a company achieve a greater efficiency and a lower cost structure is twofold. First, the R&D function can boost efficiency by designing products that are easy to manufacture. By cutting down on the number of parts that make up a product, R&D can dramatically decrease the required assembly time, which translates into higher employee productivity, lower costs, and higher profitability. For example, after Texas Instruments redesigned an infrared sighting mechanism that it supplies to the Pentagon, it found that it had reduced the number of parts from 47 to 12, the number of assembly steps from 56 to 13, the time spent fabricating metal from 757 minutes per unit to 219 minutes per unit, and unit assembly time from 129 minutes to 20 minutes. The result was a substantial decline in production costs. Design for manufacturing requires close coordination between the production and R&D functions of the company, of course. Cross-functional teams that contain production and R&D personnel who work jointly on the problem best achieve this.

The second way in which the R&D function can help a company achieve a lower cost structure is by pioneering process innovations. A *process innovation* is an innovation in the way production processes operate that improves their efficiency. Process innovations have often been a major source of competitive advantage. Toyota's competitive advantage is based partly on the company's invention of new flexible manufacturing processes that dramatically reduced setup times. This process innovation enabled it to obtain efficiency gains associated with flexible manufacturing systems years ahead of its competitors.

■ Human Resource Strategy and Efficiency

Employee productivity is one of the key determinants of an enterprise's efficiency, cost structure, and profitability.[20] Productive manufacturing employees can lower the cost of goods sold as a percentage of revenues, a productive sales force can increase sales revenues for a given level of expenses, and productive employees in the company's R&D function can boost the percentage of revenues generated from new products for a given level of R&D expenses. Thus, productive employees lower the costs of generating revenues, increase the return on sales, and by extension boost the company's return on invested capital. The challenge for a company's human resource function is to devise ways to increase employee productivity. Among the choices it has are using certain hiring strategies, training employees, organizing the work force into self-managing teams, and linking pay to performance. The *Running Case* looks at the steps Wal-Mart has taken to boost employee productivity.

■ Hiring Strategy Many companies that are well known for their productive employees devote considerable attention to hiring. Southwest Airlines hires people who have a positive attitude and work well in teams because it believes that people who have a positive attitude will work hard and interact well with customers, therefore helping to create customer loyalty. Nucor hires people who are self-reliant and goal oriented, because its employees work in self-managing teams where they have to be self-reliant and goal oriented to perform well. As these examples suggest, it is important to make sure that the hiring strategy of the company is consistent with its own internal organization, culture, and strategic priorities. The people a company hires should have attributes that match the strategic objectives of the company.

Running Case

Human Resource Strategy and Productivity at Wal-Mart

Wal-Mart has one of the most productive work forces in the retail industry. In 2002, for example, it generated $175,000 in sales for every employee, compared to $144,000 at Target and $141,000 at Sears. The roots of Wal-Mart's high productivity go back to the company's early days and the business philosophy of the company's founder, Sam Walton.

Sam Walton began his career in 1940 as a management trainee at J.C. Penney. There he noticed that all employees were called associates, and moreover, that treating them with respect seemed to reap dividends in the form of high employee productivity. Twenty-two years later, when he founded Wal-Mart, Walton decided to call all employees "associates" to symbolize their importance to the company. He reinforced this policy by emphasizing that, at Wal-Mart, "our people make the difference." Unlike many managers who have stated this mantra, Walton believed it and put it into action. He believed that if you treat people well, they will return the favor by working hard, and that if you empower them, then ordinary people can work together to achieve extraordinary things. These beliefs formed the basis for a decentralized organization that operated with an open door policy and open books, allowing associates to see how their store and the company were doing.

Consistent with the open door policy, Walton continually emphasized that management needed to listen to associates and their ideas. As he noted in his 1992 book, "The folks on the front lines—the ones who actually talk to the customer—are the only ones who really know what's going on out there. You'd better find out what they know. This really is what total quality is all about. To push responsibility down in your organization, and to force good ideas to bubble up within it, you must listen to what your associates are trying to tell you."

Despite his belief in empowerment, however, Walton was notoriously tight on salaries. Walton opposed unionization, fearing that it would lead to higher pay and restrictive work rules that would sap productivity. The culture of Wal-Mart also encouraged people to work hard. One of Walton's favorite homilies was the "sundown rule," which stated that one should never leave until tomorrow what can be done today. The sundown rule was enforced by senior managers, including Walton, who would drop in unannounced at a store and pepper store managers and employees with questions, at the same time praising them for a job well done and celebrating the "heroes" who took the sundown rule to heart.

The key to getting extraordinary effort out of employees while paying them meager salaries was to reward them with profit sharing plans and stock ownership schemes. Long before it became fashionable in American business, Walton was placing a chunk of Wal-Mart's profits into a profit sharing plan for associates and the company was putting matching funds into employee stock ownership programs. The idea was simple: reward associates by giving them a stake in the company, and they will work hard for low pay because they know they will make it up in profit sharing and stock price appreciation.

For years this formula worked extraordinarily well, but there are now signs that Wal-Mart's very success is creating problems. In 2004 the company, with a staggering 1.4 million associates, was the largest private employer in the world. As the company has grown, it has become increasingly difficult to hire the kinds of people that Wal-Mart has traditionally relied on: those willing to work long hours for low pay based on the promise of advancement and reward through profit sharing and stock ownership. The company has come under attack for paying its associates low wages and pressuring them to work long hours without overtime pay. Labor unions have made a concerted but so far unsuccessful attempt to unionize stores, and the company is the target of lawsuits from employees alleging sexual discrimination. Wal-Mart claims that the negative publicity is based on faulty data, and perhaps that is right, but if the company has indeed become too big to put Walton's principles into practice, the glory days may be over.[d]

■ **Employee Training** Employees are a major input into the production process. Those who are highly skilled can perform tasks faster and more accurately and are more likely to learn the complex tasks associated with many modern production methods than individuals with lesser skills. Training upgrades employee skill levels, bringing the company productivity-related efficiency gains from learning and experimentation.[21]

■ **Self-Managing Teams** The use of **self-managing teams**, whose members coordinate their own activities and make their own hiring, training, work, and reward decisions, has been spreading rapidly. The typical team comprises five to fifteen employees who produce an entire product or undertake an entire task. Team members learn all team tasks and rotate from job to job. Because a more flexible work force is one result, team members can fill in for absent coworkers and take over managerial duties such as scheduling work and vacation, ordering materials, and hiring new members. The greater responsibility thrust on team members and the empowerment it implies are seen as motivators. (Empowerment is the process of giving lower-level employees decision-making power.) People often respond well to being given greater autonomy and responsibility. Performance bonuses linked to team production and quality targets work as an additional motivator.

The effect of introducing self-managing teams is reportedly an increase in productivity of 30 percent or more and a substantial increase in product quality. Further cost savings arise from eliminating supervisors and creating a flatter organizational hierarchy, which also lowers the cost structure of the company. In manufacturing companies, perhaps the most potent way to lower the cost structure is to combine self-managing teams with flexible manufacturing cells. For example, after the introduction of flexible manufacturing technology and work practices based on self-managing teams, a General Electric plant in Salisbury, North Carolina, increased productivity by 250 percent compared with GE plants that produced the same products four years earlier.[22]

Still, teams are no panacea; in manufacturing companies, self-managing teams may fail to live up to their potential unless they are integrated with flexible manufacturing technology. Also, teams put a lot of management responsibilities on team members, and helping team members to cope with these responsibilities often requires substantial training—a fact that many companies often forget in their rush to drive down costs, with the result that the teams don't work out as well as planned.[23]

■ **Pay for Performance** It is hardly surprising that linking pay to performance can help increase employee productivity, but the issue is not quite so simple as just introducing incentive pay systems. It is also important to define what kind of job performance is to be rewarded and how. Some of the most efficient companies in the world, mindful that cooperation among employees is necessary to realize productivity gains, link pay to group or team (rather than individual) performance. Nucor divides its work force into teams of thirty or so, with bonus pay, which can amount to 30 percent of base pay, linked to the ability of the team to meet productivity and quality goals. This link creates a strong incentive for individuals to cooperate with each other in pursuit of team goals; that is, it facilitates teamwork.

■ **Information Systems and Efficiency** With the rapid spread of computers, the explosive growth of the Internet and corporate intranets (internal corporate computer networks based on Internet standards), and the spread of high-bandwidth fiber optics and digital wireless technology, the information systems function is moving to center stage in the quest for operating efficiencies and a lower cost structure.[24] The impact of information systems on productivity is wide ranging and potentially affects all other activities of a company. For example, Cisco Systems has been able to realize significant cost savings by moving its ordering and customer service functions online. The company has just 300 service agents handling all of its customer accounts, compared to the 900 it would need if sales were not handled online. The difference represents an annual saving of $20 million a year. Moreover, without automated customer service functions, Cisco calculates that it would need at least 1,000 additional service engineers, which would cost around $75 million.[25]

Like Cisco, many companies are using web-based information systems to reduce the costs of coordination between the company and its customers and the company and its suppliers. By using web-based programs to automate customer and supplier interactions, they can substantially reduce the number of people required to manage these interfaces, thereby reducing costs. This trend extends beyond high-tech companies. Banks and financial service companies are finding that they can substantially reduce costs by moving customer accounts and support functions online. Such a move reduces the need for customer service representatives, bank tellers, stockbrokers, insurance agents, and others. For example, it costs an average of about $1.07 to execute a transaction at a bank, such as shifting money from one account to another; executing the same transaction over the Internet costs $0.01.[26]

Similarly, the theory behind Internet-based retailers such as amazon.com is that by replacing physical stores and their supporting personnel with an online virtual store and automated ordering and checkout processes, a company can take significant costs out of the retailing system. Cost savings can also be realized by using web-based information systems to automate many internal company activities, from managing expense reimbursements to benefits planning and hiring processes, thereby reducing the need for internal support personnel.

■ **Infrastructure and Efficiency**

A company's infrastructure—that is, its structure, culture, style of strategic leadership, and control system—determines the context within which all other value creation activities take place. It follows that improving infrastructure can help a company increase efficiency and lower its cost structure. Above all, an appropriate infrastructure can help foster a companywide commitment to efficiency and promote cooperation among different functions in pursuit of efficiency goals. These issues are addressed at length in later chapters.

For now, it is important to note that strategic leadership is especially important in building a companywide commitment to efficiency. The leadership task is to articulate a vision that recognizes the need for *all* functions of a company to focus on improving efficiency. It is not enough to improve the efficiency of production, or of marketing, or of R&D in a piecemeal fashion. Achieving superior efficiency requires a companywide commitment to this goal that must be articulated by general and functional managers. A further leadership task is to facilitate the cross-functional cooperation needed to achieve superior efficiency. For example, designing products that are easy to manufacture requires that production and R&D personnel communicate; integrating JIT systems with production scheduling requires close communication between materials management and production; designing self-managing teams to perform production tasks requires close cooperation between human resources and production; and so on.

Table 4.1 summarizes the primary roles that various functions must take to achieve superior efficiency. Bear in mind that achieving superior efficiency is not something that can be tackled on a function-by-function basis. It requires an organization-wide commitment and an ability to ensure close cooperation among functions. Top management, by exercising leadership and influencing the infrastructure, plays a major role in this process.

TABLE 4.1

Primary Roles of Value Creation Functions in Achieving Superior Efficiency

Value Creation Function	Primary Roles
Infrastructure (leadership)	1. Provide companywide commitment to efficiency. 2. Facilitate cooperation among functions.
Production	1. Where appropriate, pursue economies of scale and learning economics. 2. Implement flexible manufacturing systems.
Marketing	1. Where appropriate, adopt aggressive marketing to ride down the experience curve. 2. Limit customer defection rates by building brand loyalty.
Materials management	1. Implement JIT systems. 2. Implement supply-chain coordination.
R&D	1. Design products for ease of manufacture. 2. Seek process innovations.
Information systems	1. Use information systems to automate processes. 2. Use information systems to reduce costs of coordination.
Human resources	1. Institute training programs to build skills. 2. Implement self-managing teams. 3. Implement pay for performance.

Achieving Superior Quality

In Chapter 3, we noted that quality can be thought of in terms of two dimensions: *quality as reliability* and *quality as excellence*. High-quality products are reliable, in the sense that they do the job they were designed for and do it well, and are also perceived by consumers to have superior attributes. We also noted that superior quality gives a company two advantages. First, a strong reputation for quality allows a company to *differentiate* its products from those offered by rivals, thereby creating more utility in the eyes of customers, which gives the company the option of charging a premium price for its products. Second, eliminating defects or errors from the production process reduces waste, increases efficiency, and lowers the cost structure of the company and increases its profitability. For example, reducing the number of defects in a company's manufacturing process will lower the cost of goods sold as a percentage of revenues, thereby raising the company's return on sales and return on invested capital. In this section, we look in more depth at what managers can do to enhance the reliability and other attributes of the company's product offering.

■ Attaining Superior Reliability

The principal tool that most managers now use to increase the reliability of their product offering is the Six Sigma quality improvement methodology. The Six Sigma methodology is a direct descendant of the total quality management (TQM) philosophy that was widely adopted, first by Japanese companies and then by American companies, during the 1980s and early 1990s.[27] The TQM concept was developed by a number of American management consultants, including W. Edwards Deming, Joseph Juran, and A. V. Feigenbaum.[28] Originally, these consultants won few converts in the United States. However, managers in Japan embraced their ideas enthusiastically and even named their premier annual prize for manufacturing excellence after Deming. The philosophy underlying TQM, as articulated by Deming, is based on the following five-step chain reaction:

1. Improved quality means that costs decrease because of less rework, fewer mistakes, fewer delays, and better use of time and materials.
2. As a result, productivity improves.
3. Better quality leads to higher market share and allows the company to raise prices.
4. This increases the company's profitability and allows it to stay in business.
5. Thus the company creates more jobs.[29]

Deming identified a number of steps that should be part of any quality improvement program:

- A company should have a clear business model to specify where it is going and how it is going to get there.
- Management should embrace the philosophy that mistakes, defects, and poor-quality materials are not acceptable and should be eliminated.
- Quality of supervision should be improved by allowing more time for supervisors to work with employees and giving them appropriate skills for the job.
- Management should create an environment in which employees will not fear reporting problems or recommending improvements.
- Work standards should not only be defined as numbers or quotas but should also include some notion of quality to promote the production of defect-free output.
- Management is responsible for training employees in new skills to keep pace with changes in the workplace.
- Achieving better quality requires the commitment of everyone in the company.

It took the rise of Japan to the top rank of economic powers in the 1980s to alert Western business to the importance of the TQM concept. Since then, quality improvement programs have spread rapidly throughout Western industry. Strategy in Action 4.4 describes one of the most successful implementations of a quality improvement process, General Electric's Six Sigma program.

Despite such instances of spectacular success, quality improvement practices are not universally accepted. A study by the American Quality Foundation found that only 20 percent of U.S. companies regularly review the consequences of quality performance, compared with 70 percent of Japanese companies.[30] Another study, this one by Arthur D. Little, of five hundred American companies using TQM found that only 36 percent believed that TQM was increasing their competitiveness.[31] A prime reason for this, according to the study, was that many companies had not fully understood or embraced the TQM concept. They were looking for a quick fix, whereas implementing a quality improvement program is a long-term commitment.

■ **Implementing Reliability Improvement Methodologies**

Among companies that have successfully adopted quality improvement methodologies, certain imperatives stand out. These are discussed below in the order in which they are usually tackled in companies implementing quality improvement programs. What needs to be stressed first, however, is that improvement in product reliability is a cross-functional process. Its implementation requires close cooperation among all

Strategy in Action   4.4

General Electric's Six Sigma Quality Improvement Process

Six Sigma, a quality and efficiency program adopted by several major corporations, including Motorola, General Electric, and Allied Signal, aims to reduce defects, boost productivity, eliminate waste, and cut costs throughout a company. "Sigma" comes from the Greek letter that statisticians use to represent a standard deviation from a mean: the higher the number of sigmas, the smaller the number of errors. At 6 sigma, a production process would be 99.99966 percent accurate, creating just 3.4 defects per million units. Although it is almost impossible for a company to achieve such perfection, several companies strive toward that goal.

General Electric is perhaps the most fervent adopter of Six Sigma programs. Under the direction of long-serving CEO Jack Welch, GE spent nearly $1 billion between 1994 and 1998 to convert all of its divisions to the Six Sigma faith. Welch credits the program with raising GE's operating profit margins to 16.6 percent in 1998, up from 14.4 percent three years earlier.

One of the first products designed from start to finish using Six Sigma processes was a $1.25 million diagnostic computer tomography (CT) scanner, the Lightspeed, which produces rapid three-dimensional images of the human body. The new scanner captures multiple images simultaneously, requiring only twenty seconds to do full-body scans that once took three minutes—important because patients must remain perfectly still during the scan. GE spent $50 million to run 250 separate Six Sigma analyses designed to improve the reliability and lower the manufacturing cost of the new scanner. Its efforts were rewarded when the Lightspeed's first customers soon noticed that it ran without downtime from the start, a testament to the reliability of the product.

Achieving that reliability took a lot of work. GE's engineers deconstructed the scanner into its basic components and tried to improve the reliability of each component through a detailed step-by-step analysis. For example, the most important part of CT scanners is vacuum tubes that focus x-ray waves. The tubes that GE used in previous scanners, which cost $60,000 each, suffered from low reliability. Hospitals and clinics wanted the tubes to operate for twelve hours a day for at least six months, but typically they lasted only half that long. Moreover, GE was scrapping some $20 million in tubes each year because they failed preshipping performance tests, and a disturbing number of faulty tubes were slipping past inspection, only to be pronounced dead on arrival.

To try to solve the reliability problem, the Six Sigma team took the tubes apart. They knew that one problem was a petroleum-based oil used in the tube to prevent short circuits by isolating the anode, which has a positive charge, from the negatively charged cathode. The oil often deteriorated after a few months, leading to short circuits, but the team did not know why. By using statistical "what-if" scenarios on all parts of the tube, the researchers learned that the lead-based paint on the inside of the tube was adulterating the oil. Acting on this information, the team developed a paint that would preserve the tube and protect the oil.

By pursuing this and other improvements, the Six Sigma team was able to extend the average life of a vacuum tube in the CT scanner from three months to over a year. Although the improvements increased the cost of the tube from $60,000 to $85,000, the increased cost was outweighed by the reduction in replacement costs, making it an attractive proposition for customers.[e]

functions in the pursuit of the common goal of improving quality; it is a process that cuts across functions. The roles played by the different functions in implementing reliability improvement methodologies are summarized in Table 4.2.

■ **Build Organizational Commitment to Quality** There is evidence that quality improvement programs will do little to improve the performance of a company unless everyone in the organization embraces it.[32] When Xerox launched its quality program, its first step was to educate the entire work force, from top management down, in the importance and operation of the program. It did so by forming

TABLE 4.2

Roles Played by Different Functions in Implementing Reliability Improvement Methodologies

Value Creation Function	Primary Roles
Infrastructure (leadership)	1. Provide leadership and commitment to quality.
	2. Find ways to measure quality.
	3. Set goals, and create incentives.
	4. Solicit input from employees.
	5. Encourage cooperation among functions.
Production	1. Shorten production runs.
	2. Trace defects back to source.
Marketing	1. Focus on the customer.
	2. Provide customers' feedback on quality.
Materials management	1. Rationalize suppliers.
	2. Help suppliers implement quality improvement methodologies.
	3. Trace defects back to suppliers.
R&D	1. Design products that are easy to manufacture.
Information systems	1. Use information systems to monitor defect rates.
Human resources	1. Institute quality improvement training programs.
	2. Identify and train "black belts."
	3. Organize employees into quality teams.

groups, beginning with a group at the top of the organization that included the CEO. The top group was the first to receive basic TQM training. Each member of this group was then given the task of training a group at the next level in the hierarchy, and so on down throughout the organization until all 100,000 employees had received basic TQM training. Both top management and the human resource function of the company can play a major role in this process. Top management has the responsibility of exercising the leadership required to make a commitment to quality an organization-wide goal. The human resource function must take on responsibility for companywide training in TQM techniques.

■ **Create Quality Leaders** If a quality improvement program is to be successful, individuals must be identified to lead the program. Under the Six Sigma methodology, exceptional employees are identified and put through a "black belt" training course on the Six Sigma methodology. The black belts are taken out of their normal job roles and assigned to work solely on Six Sigma projects for the next two years. In effect, they become internal consultants and project leaders. Because they are dedicated to Six Sigma programs, they are not distracted from the task at hand by day-to-day operating responsibilities. To make a black belt assignment attractive, many companies now use it as a step in a career path. Successful black belts may not return to their prior job after two years, but instead are promoted and given more responsibility.

■ **Focus on the Customer** Quality improvement practitioners see a focus on the customer as the starting point, and indeed, the raison d'être, of the whole quality philosophy.[33] The marketing function, because it provides the primary point of contact with the customer, should play a major role here. It needs to identify what customers want from the good or service that the company provides, what the company actually provides to customers, and the gap between what customers want and what they get, which could be called the quality gap. Then, together with the other functions of the company, it needs to formulate a plan for closing the quality gap.

■ **Identify Processes and the Source of Defects** One of the hallmarks of the Six Sigma quality improvement methodology is identifying discrete repetitive processes that can be improved. This is normally done by using flow chart methodology to break an operation into its constituent parts. Thus, as noted in Strategy in Action 4.4, to improve its Lightspeed CT scanner, GE's engineers deconstructed the scanner into its basic components and tried to improve the reliability of each component through a detailed step-by-step analysis.

Quality improvement methodologies preach the need to identify defects that arise from processes, trace them to their source, find out what caused them, and make corrections so that they do not recur. Production and materials management typically have primary responsibility for this task.

To uncover defects, Deming advocated the use of statistical procedures to pinpoint variations in the quality of goods or services. Deming viewed variation as the enemy of quality.[34] The Six Sigma methodology also relies heavily on statistical analysis of variation. Once variations have been identified, they must be traced to their source and eliminated. One technique that helps greatly in tracing defects to their source is reducing lot sizes for manufactured products. With short production runs, defects show up immediately. Consequently, they can be quickly traced to the source, and the problem can be addressed. Reducing lot sizes also means that, when defective products are produced, their number will not be large, thus decreasing waste. Flexible manufacturing techniques, discussed earlier, can be used to reduce lot sizes without raising costs. Consequently, adopting flexible manufacturing techniques is an important aspect of a TQM program.

JIT inventory systems also play a part. Under a JIT system, defective parts enter the manufacturing process immediately; they are not warehoused for several months before use. Hence, defective inputs can be quickly spotted. The problem can then be traced to the supply source and corrected before more defective parts are produced. Under a more traditional system, the practice of warehousing parts for months before they are used may mean that many defects are produced by a supplier before they enter the production process.

■ **Find Ways to Measure Quality** Another imperative of any quality improvement program is to create a metric that can be used to measure quality. This is relatively easy in manufacturing companies, where quality can be measured by criteria such as defects per million parts. It tends to be more difficult in service companies, but with a little creativity, suitable metrics can be devised. For example, one of the metrics Florida Power & Light uses to measure quality is meter-reading errors per month. Another is the frequency and duration of power outages. L. L. Bean, the Freeport, Maine, mail-order retailer of outdoor gear, uses the percentage of orders that are correctly filled as one of its quality measures. For some banks, the key measures are the number of customer defections per year and the number of statement errors per thousand customers. The common theme that runs through all these examples is identifying what quality means from a customer's perspective and devising a method to gauge this.

■ **Set Goals and Create Incentives** Once a metric has been devised, the next step is to set a challenging quality goal and create incentives for reaching it. Xerox again provides an example. When it introduced its TQM program, its initial goal was to reduce defective parts from 25,000 per million to 1,000 per million. Under Six Sigma programs the goal is 3.4 defects per million units. One way of creating incentives to attain such a goal is to link rewards, like bonus pay and promotional opportunities, to the goal. Thus, within many companies that have adopted self-managing teams, the bonus pay of team members is determined in part by their ability to attain quality goals. Setting goals and creating incentives are key tasks of top management.

■ **Solicit Input from Employees** Employees can be a vital source of information regarding the sources of poor quality. Therefore, a framework must be established for soliciting employee suggestions for improvements. Quality circles, which are meetings of groups of employees, have often been used to achieve this goal. Other companies have used self-managing teams as forums for discussing quality improvement ideas. Whatever forum is used, soliciting input from employees requires that management be open to receiving, and acting on, bad news and criticism from employees. According to Deming, one problem with U.S. management is that it has grown used to "killing the bearer of bad tidings." But, he argues, managers who are committed to the quality concept must recognize that bad news is a gold mine of information.[35]

■ **Build Long-Term Relationships with Suppliers** A major source of poor-quality finished goods is poor-quality component parts. To decrease product defects, a company has to work with its suppliers to improve the quality of the parts they supply. The primary responsibility in this area falls on the materials-management function, which interacts with suppliers.

To implement JIT systems with suppliers and to get suppliers to adopt their own quality improvement programs, two steps are necessary. First, the number of suppliers has to be reduced to manageable proportions. Second, the company must commit to building a cooperative long-term relationship with the suppliers that remain. Asking suppliers to invest in JIT and quality improvement programs is asking them to make major investments that tie them to the company. For example, in order to implement a JIT system fully, the company may ask a supplier to relocate its manufacturing plant so that it is next-door to the company's assembly plant. Suppliers are likely to be hesitant about making such investments unless they feel that the company is committed to an enduring, long-term relationship with them.

■ **Design for Ease of Manufacture** The more assembly steps a product requires, the more opportunities there are for making mistakes. Designing products with fewer parts should make assembly easier and result in fewer defects. Both R&D and manufacturing need to be involved in designing products that are easy to manufacture.

■ **Break Down Barriers Among Functions** Implementing quality improvement methodologies requires organization-wide commitment and substantial cooperation among functions. R&D has to cooperate with production to design products that are easy to manufacture, marketing has to cooperate with production and R&D so that customer problems identified by marketing can be acted on, human resource management has to cooperate with all the other functions of the company in order to devise suitable quality-training programs, and so on. The issue of achieving cooperation among subunits within a company is explored in Chapter 12. What needs stressing at this point is that ultimately it is the responsibility of top management to ensure that such cooperation occurs. Strategy in Action 4.5 describes the efforts of a service company to put quality improvement programs into practice and the benefits it has gained as a result.

■ Improving Quality as Excellence

As we stated in Chapter 3, a product is a bundle of different attributes, and reliability is just one of them, albeit an important one. Products can also be *differentiated* by attributes that collectively define product excellence. These attributes include the form, features, performance, durability, and styling of a product. In addition, a company can create quality as excellence by emphasizing attributes of the service associated with the product, such as ordering ease, prompt delivery, easy installation, the availability of customer training and consulting, and maintenance services. Dell Computer, for example, differentiates itself on ease of ordering (via the Web), prompt delivery, easy installation, and the ready availability of customer support and maintenance services. Differentiation can also be based on the attributes of the people in the company whom customers interact with when making a product purchase, such as their

Strategy in Action   4.5

Six Sigma at Mount Carmel Health

Following the lead of General Electric, a number of health care organizations have adopted the Six Sigma approach or similar quality improvement tools as a way of trying to improve the quality of their service offerings. One of them is Mount Carmel Health, a health care provider in Ohio. Mount Carmel Health implemented a Six Sigma program after suffering from poor financial performance in 2000. It was initiated in late 2000, and by early 2001 forty-four employees had been trained in Six Sigma principles. These "black belts" were pulled out of their original positions and were not replaced. By the second half of 2001 they were leading some sixty projects in different phases of implementation.

One of the first projects focused on a simple and common problem among health care providers: timely and accurate reimbursement of costs. Mount Carmel discovered that it was writing off large amounts of potential revenues from the government-run Medicare programs as uncollectible because the charges were denied by

Medicare administrators. Mount Carmel had low expectations for this business anyway so had never analyzed why the write-offs were so high. After conducting a careful analysis as part of a Six Sigma project, it discovered that a significant portion of the denials were due to the incorrect coding of reports submitted to Medicare. If the reports were coded correctly—that is, if fewer errors were made in the "production" of forms—the Six Sigma team estimated that annual income would be some $300,000 higher, so they devised improved processes for coding the forms to reduce the error rate. The result was that net income rose by over $800,000. It appeared that improving the coding process for this one parameter improved the reporting of many other parameters and led to a reimbursement rate much higher than anticipated.

Mount Carmel now estimates that Six Sigma projects saved the organization some $1 million in 2001, $6.5 million in 2002, and $9 million in 2003.[f]

TABLE 4.3

Attributes Associated with a Product Offering

Product Attributes	Service Attributes	Associated Personnel Attributes
Form	Ordering ease	Competence
Features	Delivery	Courtesy
Performance	Installation	Credibility
Durability	Customer training	Reliability
Reliability	Customer consulting	Responsiveness
Style	Maintenance and repair	Communication

competence, courtesy, credibility, responsiveness, and communication. Singapore Airlines, for example, enjoys an excellent reputation for quality service, largely because passengers perceive their flight attendants as competent, courteous, and responsive to their needs. Thus, we can talk about the product attributes, service attributes, and personnel attributes associated with a company's product offering (see Table 4.3).

For a product to be regarded as high in the excellence dimension, a company's product offering must be seen as superior to that of rivals. Achieving a perception of high quality on any of these attributes requires specific actions by managers. First, it is important for managers to collect marketing intelligence indicating which of these attributes are most important to customers. For example, consumers of personal computers may place a low weight on durability because they expect their PC to be made obsolete by technological advances within three years, but they may place a high weight on features and performance. Similarly, ease of ordering and timely delivery may be very important attributes for customers of online booksellers (as they indeed are for customers of amazon.com), whereas customer training and consulting may be very important attributes for customers who purchase complex business-to-business software to manage their relationships with suppliers.

Second, once the company has identified the attributes that are important to customers, it needs to design its products, and the associated services, so that those attributes are embodied in the product, and it needs to make sure that personnel in the company are appropriately trained so that the correct attributes are emphasized. This requires close coordination between marketing and product development (the topic of the next section) and the involvement of the human resource management function in employee selection and training.

Third, the company must decide which of the significant attributes to promote and how best to position them in the minds of consumers, that is, how to tailor the marketing message so that it creates a consistent image in the minds of customers.[36] At this point, it is important to recognize that although a product might be differentiated on the basis of six attributes, covering all of those attributes in the company's communication messages may lead to an unfocused message. Many marketing experts advocate promoting only one or two central attributes to customers. For example, Volvo consistently emphasizes the safety and durability of its vehicles in all marketing messages, creating the perception in the minds of consumers (backed by product design) that Volvo cars are safe and durable. Volvo cars are also very reliable and have high performance, but the company does not emphasize these attributes in its marketing messages. In contrast, Porsche emphasizes performance and styling in all of its marketing messages; thus, a Porsche is positioned differently in the minds of consumers than a Volvo is. Both are regarded as high-quality products because both have superior attributes, but the attributes that the two companies have chosen to emphasize are very different. They are differentiated from the average car in different ways.

Finally, it must be recognized that competition does not stand still, but instead produces continual improvement in product attributes and often the development of new-product attributes. This is obvious in fast-moving high-tech industries where product features that were considered leading edge just a few years ago are now obsolete, but the same process is also at work in more stable industries. For example, the rapid diffusion of microwave ovens during the 1980s required food companies to build new attributes into their frozen food products: they had to maintain their texture and consistency while being microwaved. A product could not be considered high quality unless it could do that. This speaks to the importance of having a strong R&D function in the company that can work with marketing and manufacturing to continually upgrade the quality of the attributes that are designed into the company's product offerings. Exactly how to achieve this is covered in the next section.

Achieving Superior Innovation

In many ways, building distinctive competencies that result in innovation is the most important source of competitive advantage. This is because innovation can result in new products that better satisfy customer needs, can improve the quality (attributes) of existing products, or can reduce the costs of making products that customers want. Thus, the ability to develop innovative new products or processes gives a company a major competitive advantage that allows it to (1) *differentiate* its products and charge a premium price and/or (2) *lower its cost structure* below that of its rivals. Competitors, however, attempt to imitate successful innovations and often succeed. Therefore, maintaining a competitive advantage requires a continuing commitment to innovation.

Robert Cooper found that successful new-product launches are major drivers of superior profitability. Cooper looked at more than two hundred new-product introductions and found that of those classified as successes, some 50 percent achieve a return on investment in excess of 33 percent, half have a payback period of two years or less, and half achieve a market share in excess of 35 percent.[37] Many companies have established a track record for successful innovation. Among them are DuPont, which has produced a steady stream of successful innovations, such as cellophane, Nylon, Freon, and Teflon; Sony, whose successes include the Walkman, the Compact Disc, and the PlayStation; Nokia, which has been a leader in the development of wireless phones; Pfizer, a drug company that during the 1990s and early 2000s produced eight blockbuster new drugs; 3M, which has applied its core competency in tapes and adhesives to developing a wide range of new products; Intel, which has consistently managed to lead in the development of innovative new microprocessors to run personal computers; and Cisco Systems, whose innovations helped to pave the way for the rapid growth of the Internet.

■ The High Failure Rate of Innovation

Although promoting innovation can be a source of competitive advantage, the failure rate of innovative new products is high. One study of product development in the chemical, drug, petroleum, and electronics industries suggested that only about 20 percent of major R&D projects ultimately result in a commercially successful product or process.[38] An in-depth case study of product development in three companies (one in chemicals and two in drugs) reported that about 60 percent of R&D projects reached technical completion, 30 percent were commercialized, and only 12 percent earned a profit that exceeded the company's cost of capital.[39] Along the same lines, another study concluded that one in nine major R&D projects, or about 11 percent, produced commercially successful products.[40] In sum, the evidence suggests that only 10 to 20 percent of major R&D projects give rise to a commercially successful product. Well-publicized product failures include Apple Computer's Newton, a personal digital assistant; Sony's Betamax format in the video player and recorder market; and Sega's Dreamcast videogame console. While many reasons have been advanced to explain why so many new products fail to generate an economic return, five explanations for failure appear on most lists: uncertainty, poor commercialization, poor positioning strategy, technological myopia, and being slow to market.[41]

■ **Uncertainty** New-product development is an inherently risky process. It requires testing a hypothesis whose answer is impossible to know prior to market introduction: Have we tapped an unmet customer need? Is there sufficient market demand for this new technology? Although good market research can reduce the uncertainty about likely future demand for a new technology, uncertainty cannot be eradicated, so a certain failure rate is to be expected.

The failure rate is higher for quantum product innovations than for incremental innovations. A **quantum innovation** represents a radical departure from existing technology—the introduction of something that is new to the world. The development of the World Wide Web can be considered a quantum innovation in communications technology. Other quantum innovations include the development of the first photocopier by Xerox, the first contact lenses by Bausch and Lomb, and the first microprocessor by Intel in 1971. **Incremental innovation** refers to an extension of existing technology. For example, Intel's Pentium Pro microprocessor is an incremental product innovation because it builds on the existing microprocessor architecture of Intel's X86 series. The uncertainty of future demand for a new product is much greater if that product represents a quantum innovation that is new to the world than if it is an incremental innovation designed to replace an established product whose demand profile is already well known. Consequently, the failure rate tends to be higher for quantum innovations.

■ **Poor Commercialization** A second reason frequently cited to explain the high failure rate of new-product introductions is **poor commercialization**—something that occurs when there is definite customer demand for a new product, but the product is not well adapted to customer needs because of factors such as poor design and poor quality. For instance, many of the early personal computers failed to sell because customers needed to understand computer programming to use them. Steve Jobs at Apple Computer understood that if the technology could be made user friendly (if it could be *commercialized*), there would be an enormous market for it. Hence, the original personal computers that Apple marketed incorporated little in the way of radically new technology, but they made existing technology accessible to the average person. Paradoxically, the failure of Apple Computer to establish a market for the Newton, the hand-held personal digital system that Apple introduced in the summer of 1993, can be traced to poor commercialization of a potentially attractive technology. Apple predicted a $1 billion market for the Newton, but sales failed to materialize when it became clear that the Newton's handwriting software, an attribute that Apple chose to emphasize in its marketing promotions, could not adequately recognize messages written on the Newton's message pad.

■ **Poor Positioning Strategy** Poor positioning strategy arises when a company introduces a potentially attractive new product, but sales fail to materialize because it is poorly positioned in the marketplace. **Positioning strategy** is the specific set of options a company adopts for a product on four main dimensions of marketing: price, distribution, promotion and advertising, and product features. Apart from poor product quality, another reason for the failure of the Apple Newton was poor positioning strategy. The Newton was introduced at such a high initial price (close to $1,000) that there would probably have been few buyers even if the technology had been adequately commercialized.

■ **Technological Myopia** Another reason that many new-product introductions fail is that companies often make the mistake of marketing a technology for which there is not enough customer demand. **Technological myopia** occurs when a company gets blinded by the wizardry of a new technology and fails to examine whether there is customer demand for the product. This problem may have been a factor in the failure of the desktop computer introduced by NeXT in the late 1980s (NeXT was founded by Steve Jobs, the founder of Apple Computer). Technologically, the NeXT machines were clearly ahead of their time with advanced software and hardware features that would not be incorporated into most PCs for another decade. However, customer acceptance was very slow, primarily because of the complete lack of applications software such as spreadsheet and word processing programs to run on the machines. Management at NeXT was so enthused by the technology incorporated in their new computer that they ignored this basic market reality. After several years of slow sales, NeXT eventually withdrew the machines from the marketplace.

■ **Being Slow to Market** Finally, companies fail when they are slow to get their products to market. The more time that elapses between initial development and final marketing—that is, the slower the "cycle time"—the more likely it is that someone else will beat the company to market and gain a first-mover advantage.[42] By and large, slow innovators update their products less frequently than fast innovators do. Consequently, they can be perceived as technical laggards relative to the fast innovators. In the car industry, General Motors has suffered from being a slow innovator. Its product development cycle has been about five years, compared with two to three years at Honda, Toyota, and Mazda and three to four years at Ford. Because they are based on five-year-old technology and design concepts, GM cars are already out of date when they reach the market.

■ **Building Competencies in Innovation** Companies can take a number of steps to build a competency in innovation and avoid failure. Five of the most important steps seem to be (1) building skills in basic and applied scientific research, (2) developing a good process for project selection and project management, (3) achieving cross-functional integration, (4) using product development teams, and (5) using partly parallel development processes.[43]

■ **Skills in Basic and Applied Research** Building skills in basic and applied research requires the employment of research scientists and engineers and the establishment of a work environment that fosters creativity. A number of top companies try to achieve this by setting up university-style research facilities, where scientists and engineers are given time to work on their own research projects, in addition to projects that are linked directly to ongoing company research. At Hewlett-Packard, for example, company labs are open to engineers around the clock. Hewlett-Packard even encourages its corporate researchers to devote 10 percent of company time to exploring their own ideas and does not penalize them if they fail. 3M allows researchers to spend 15 percent of the workweek researching any topic that intrigues them, as long as there is the potential of a payoff for the company. The most famous outcome of this policy is the ubiquitous Post-its. The idea for them evolved from a researcher's desire to find a way to keep the bookmark from falling out of his hymnal. Post-its are now a major 3M business, with annual revenues of around $300 million.

■ **Project Selection and Management** Project management is the overall management of the innovation process, from generation of the original concept, through development, and into final production and shipping. Project management requires three important skills: the ability to generate as many good ideas as possible, the ability to select among competing projects at an early stage of development so that the most promising receive funding and potential costly failures are killed off, and the ability to minimize time to market. The concept of the development funnel, divided into three phases, summarizes what is required to build these skills (see Figure 4.7).[44]

The objective in phase I is to widen the mouth of the tunnel to encourage as much idea generation as possible. To this end, a company should solicit input from all its functions, as well as from customers, competitors, and suppliers. At gate 1, the funnel narrows. Here ideas are reviewed by a cross-functional team of managers who did not participate in the original concept development. Concepts that are ready to proceed then move to phase II, where the details of the project proposal are worked out. Note that gate 1 is not a go/no-go evaluation point. At this screen, ideas may be sent back for further concept development and then resubmitted for evaluation.

During phase II, which typically lasts only one or two months, the data and information from phase I are put into a form that will enable senior management to

FIGURE 4.7

The Development Funnel

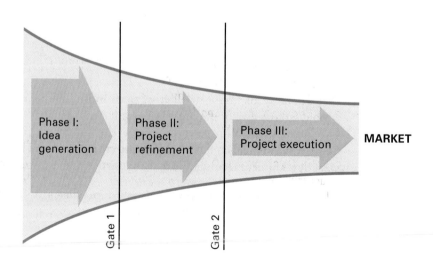

evaluate proposed projects against competing projects. Normally, this requires the development of a careful project plan, complete with details of the proposed target market, attainable market share, likely revenues, development costs, production costs, key milestones, and the like. The next big selection point, gate 2, is a go/no-go evaluation point. Senior managers review the projects under consideration and select those that seem likely winners and make most sense from a strategic perspective given the long-term goals of the company. The overriding objective is to select projects whose successful completion will help to maintain or build a competitive advantage for the company. A related objective is to ensure that the company does not spread its scarce capital and human resources too thinly over too many projects and instead concentrates resources on projects where the probability of success and potential returns is most attractive. Any project selected to go forward at this stage will be funded and staffed, the expectation being that it will be carried through to market introduction. In phase III, the project development proposal is executed by a cross-functional product development team.

■ **Cross-Functional Integration** Tight cross-functional integration between R&D, production, and marketing can help a company to ensure that:

1. Product development projects are driven by customer needs.

2. New products are designed for ease of manufacture.

3. Development costs are kept in check.

4. Time to market is minimized.

5. Close integration between R&D and marketing is achieved to ensure that product development projects are driven by the needs of customers.

A company's customers can be one of its primary sources of new-product ideas. The identification of customer needs, and particularly unmet needs, can set the context within which succ essful product innovation takes place. As the point of contact with customers, the marketing function can provide valuable information. Moreover, integrating R&D and marketing is crucial if a new product is to be properly commercialized. Otherwise, a company runs the risk of developing products for which there is little or no demand.

The case of Techsonic Industries illustrates the benefits of integrating R&D and marketing. This company manufactures depth finders—electronic devices that fishermen use to measure the depth of water beneath a boat and to track their prey. Techsonic had weathered nine new-product failures in a row when the company decided to interview sportspeople across the country to identify what it was they needed. They discovered an unmet need for a depth finder with a gauge that could be read in bright sunlight, so that is what Techsonic developed. In the year after the $250 depth finder hit the market, Techsonic's sales tripled to $80 million, and its market share surged to 40 percent.[45]

Integration between R&D and production can help a company to ensure that products are designed with manufacturing requirements in mind. Design for manufacturing lowers manufacturing costs and leaves less room for mistakes and thus can lower costs and increase product quality. Integrating R&D and production can help lower development costs and speed products to market. If a new product is not designed with manufacturing capabilities in mind, it may prove too difficult to build, given existing manufacturing technology. In that case, the product will have to be redesigned, and both overall development costs and time to market may increase significantly. For example, making design changes during product planning could increase overall development costs by 50 percent and add 25 percent to the time it takes to bring the product to market.[46] Moreover, many quantum product innovations require new processes to manufacture them, which makes it all the more important to achieve close integration between R&D and production, since minimizing time to market and development costs may require the simultaneous development of new products and new processes.[47]

■ **Product Development Teams** One of the best ways to achieve cross-functional integration is to establish cross-functional product development teams, composed of representatives from R&D, marketing, and production. The objective of a team should be to take a product development project from the initial concept development to market introduction. A number of attributes seem to be important in order for a product development team to function effectively and meet all its development milestones.[48]

First, a heavyweight project manager—one who has high status within the organization and the power and authority required to get the financial and human resources that the team needs to succeed—should lead the team and be dedicated primarily, if not entirely, to the project. The leader should believe in the project (a champion) and be skilled at integrating the perspectives of different functions and helping personnel from different functions work together for a common goal. The leader should also be able to act as an advocate of the team to senior management.

Second, the team should be composed of at least one member from each key function. The team members should have a number of attributes, including an ability to contribute functional expertise, high standing within their function, a willingness to share responsibility for team results, and an ability to put functional advocacy aside. It is generally preferable if core team members are 100 percent dedicated to the project for its duration. This ensures that their focus is on the project, not on the ongoing work of their function.

Third, the team members should be physically co-located to create a sense of camaraderie and facilitate communication. Fourth, the team should have a clear plan and clear goals, particularly with regard to critical development milestones and development budgets. The team should have incentives to attain those goals, such as pay bonuses when major development milestones are hit. Fifth, each team needs to develop its own processes for communication and conflict resolution. For example, one product development team at Quantum Corporation, a California-based manufacturer of disk drives for personal computers, instituted a rule that all major decisions would be made and conflicts resolved at meetings that were held every Monday afternoon. This simple rule helped the team to meet its development goals.[49]

■ **Partly Parallel Development Processes** One way in which a product development team can compress the time it takes to develop a product and bring it to market is to use a partly parallel development process. Traditionally, product development processes have been organized on a sequential basis, as illustrated in Figure 4.8a. A problem with this kind of process is that product development proceeds without manufacturing issues in mind. Most significant, because the basic design of a product is completed prior to the design of a manufacturing process and full-scale commercial production, there is no early warning system to indicate manufacturability.

Sequential and Partly Parallel Development Processes

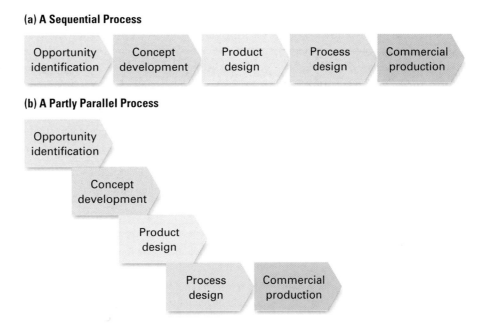

(a) A Sequential Process

Opportunity identification → Concept development → Product design → Process design → Commercial production

(b) A Partly Parallel Process

Opportunity identification
Concept development
Product design
Process design
Commercial production

As a consequence, the company may find that it cannot cost-efficiently manufacture the product and may have to send it back to the design stage for redesign. The cycle time lengthens as the product bounces back and forth between stages.

To solve this problem, companies typically use a process similar to that illustrated in Figure 4.8b. In the partly parallel development process, development stages overlap so that, for example, work starts on the development of the production process before the product design is finalized. By reducing the need for expensive and time-consuming product redesigns, such a process can significantly reduce the time it takes to develop a new product and bring it to market.

For an example, consider what occurred after Intel Corporation introduced its 386 microprocessor in 1986. A number of companies, including IBM and Compaq, were racing to be the first to introduce a 386-based personal computer. Compaq beat IBM by six months and gained a major share of the high-power market mainly because it used a cross-functional team and a partly parallel process to develop the product. The team included engineers (R&D) and marketing, production, and finance people. Each function worked in parallel rather than sequentially. While engineers were designing the product, production people were setting up the manufacturing facilities, marketing people were working on distribution and planning marketing campaigns, and finance people were working on project funding.

The primary role that the various functions play in achieving superior innovation is summarized in Table 4.4. The table makes two matters clear. First, top management must bear primary responsibility for overseeing the whole development process. This entails both managing the development funnel and facilitating cooperation among the functions. Second, the effectiveness of R&D in developing new products and processes depends on its ability to cooperate with marketing and production.

TABLE 4.4

Functional Roles for Achieving Superior Innovation

Value Creation Function	Primary Roles
Infrastructure (leadership)	1. Manage overall project (i.e., manage the development function). 2. Facilitate cross-functional cooperation.
Production	1. Cooperate with R&D on designing products that are easy to manufacture. 2. Work with R&D to develop process innovations.
Marketing	1. Provide market information to R&D. 2. Work with R&D to develop new products.
Materials management	1. No primary responsibility.
R&D	1. Develop new products and processes. 2. Cooperate with other functions, particularly marketing and manufacturing, in the development process.
Information systems	1. Use information systems to coordinate cross-functional and cross-company product development work.
Human resources	1. Hire talented scientists and engineers.

Achieving Superior Responsiveness to Customers

To achieve superior responsiveness to customers, a company must give customers what they want, when they want it, and at a price they are willing to pay—so long as the company's long-term profitability is not compromised in the process. Customer responsiveness is an important *differentiating* attribute that can help to build brand loyalty. Strong product differentiation and brand loyalty give a company more pricing options; it can charge a premium price for its products or keep prices low to sell more goods and services to customers. Either way, the company that is more responsive to its customers' needs than rivals will have a competitive advantage, all else being equal.

Achieving superior responsiveness to customers means giving customers value for money, and steps taken to improve the efficiency of a company's production process and the quality of its products should be consistent with this aim. In addition, giving customers what they want may require the development of new products with new features. *In other words, achieving superior efficiency, quality, and innovation are all part of achieving superior responsiveness to customers.* There are two other prerequisites for attaining this goal. First, a company has to develop a competency in listening to and focusing on its customers and in investigating and identifying their needs. Second, it constantly needs to seek better ways to satisfy those needs.

■ Focusing on the Customer

A company cannot be responsive to its customers' needs unless it knows what those needs are. Thus, the first step to building superior responsiveness to customers is to motivate the whole company to focus on the customer. The means to this end are demonstrating leadership, shaping employee attitudes, and using mechanisms for bringing customers into the company.

■ **Demonstrating Leadership** Customer focus must start at the top of the organization. A commitment to superior responsiveness to customers brings attitudinal changes throughout a company that ultimately can be built only through strong leadership. A mission statement that puts customers first is one way to send a clear message to employees about the desired focus. Another avenue is top management's own actions. For example, Tom Monaghan, the founder of Domino's Pizza, stayed close to the customer by visiting as many stores as possible every week, running some deliveries himself, insisting that other top managers do the same, and eating Domino's pizza regularly.[50]

■ **Shaping Employee Attitudes** Leadership alone is not enough to attain a superior customer focus. All employees must see the customer as the focus of their activity and be trained to focus on the customer, whether their function is marketing, manufacturing, R&D, or accounting. The objective should be to make employees think of themselves as customers—to put themselves in customers' shoes. At that point, employees will be better able to identify ways to improve the quality of a customer's experience with the company.

To reinforce this mindset, incentive systems within the company should reward employees for satisfying customers. For example, senior managers at the Four Seasons hotel chain, who pride themselves on their customer focus, like to tell the story of Roy Dyment, a doorman in Toronto who neglected to load a departing guest's briefcase into his taxi. The doorman called the guest, a lawyer, in Washington, D.C., and found that he desperately needed the briefcase for a morning meeting. Dyment hopped on a plane to Washington and returned it—without first securing approval from his boss. Far from punishing Dyment for making a mistake and for not checking with management before going to Washington, the Four Seasons responded by naming Dyment Employee of the Year.[51] This action sent a powerful message to Four Seasons employees about the importance of satisfying customer needs.

■ **Bringing Customers into the Company** "Know thy customer" is one of the keys to achieving superior responsiveness to customers. Knowing the customer not only requires that employees think like customers themselves; it also demands that they listen to what their customers have to say and, as much as possible, bring them into the company. Although this may not involve physically bringing customers into the company, it does mean bringing in customers' opinions by soliciting feedback from customers on the company's goods and services and by building information systems that communicate the feedback to the relevant people.

For an example, consider direct selling clothing retailer Lands' End. Through its catalog, the Internet, and customer service telephone operators, Lands' End actively solicits comments from its customers about the quality of its clothing and the kind of merchandise they want it to supply. Indeed, it was customers' insistence that initially prompted the company to move into the clothing segment. Lands' End used to supply equipment for sailboats through mail-order catalogs. However, it received so many requests from customers to include outdoor clothing in its offering that it responded by expanding the catalog to fill this need. Soon clothing became the main business, and Lands' End dropped the sailboat equipment. Today, the company still pays close attention to customer requests. Every month, a computer printout of customer requests and comments is given to managers. This feedback helps the company to fine-tune the merchandise it sells. Indeed, frequently new lines of merchandise are introduced in response to customer requests.[52]

■ Satisfying Customer Needs

Once a focus on the customer is an integral part of the company, the next requirement is to satisfy the customer needs that have been identified. As already noted, efficiency, quality, and innovation are crucial competencies that help a company satisfy customer needs. Beyond that, companies can provide a higher level of satisfaction if they differentiate their products by (1) customizing them, where possible, to the requirements of individual customers and (2) reducing the time it takes to respond to or satisfy customer needs.

■ Customization

Customization is varying the features of a good or service to tailor it to the unique needs or tastes of groups of customers or, in the extreme case, individual customers. Although extensive customization can raise costs, the development of flexible manufacturing technologies has made it possible to customize products to a much greater extent than was feasible ten to fifteen years ago without experiencing a prohibitive rise in cost structure (particularly when flexible manufacturing technologies are linked with web-based information systems). For example, online retailers such as amazon.com have used web-based technologies to develop a homepage customized for each individual user. When a customer accesses amazon.com, he or she is offered a list of recommendations for books or music to purchase based on an analysis of prior buying history, a powerful competency that gives amazon.com a competitive advantage.

The trend toward customization has fragmented many markets, particularly customer markets, into ever smaller niches. An example of this fragmentation occurred in Japan in the early 1980s when Honda dominated the motorcycle market there. Second-place Yamaha decided to go after Honda's lead. It announced the opening of a new factory that, when operating at full capacity, would make Yamaha the world's largest manufacturer of motorcycles. Honda responded by proliferating its product line and stepping up its rate of new-product introduction. At the start of what became known as the "motorcycle wars," Honda had 60 motorcycles in its product line. Over the next eighteen months, it rapidly increased its range to 113 models, customizing them to ever smaller niches. Honda was able to accomplish this without bearing a prohibitive cost penalty because it has a competency in flexible manufacturing. The flood of Honda's customized models pushed Yamaha out of much of the market, effectively stalling its bid to overtake Honda.[53]

■ Response Time

Giving customers what they want when they want it requires speed of response to customer demands. To gain a competitive advantage, a company must often respond to customer demands very quickly, whether the transaction is a furniture manufacturer's delivery of a product once it has been ordered, a bank's processing of a loan application, an automobile manufacturer's delivery of a spare part for a car that broke down, or the wait in a supermarket checkout line. We live in a fast-paced society, where time is a valuable commodity. Companies that can satisfy customer demands for rapid response build brand loyalty, differentiate their products, and can charge higher prices for them.

Increased speed often lets a company choose a premium pricing option, as the mail delivery industry illustrates. The air express niche of the mail delivery industry is based on the notion that customers are often willing to pay considerably more for overnight Express Mail as opposed to regular mail. Another example of the value of rapid response is Caterpillar, the manufacturer of heavy earthmoving equipment, which can get a spare part to any point in the world within twenty-four hours.

TABLE 4.5

Primary Roles of Different Functions in Achieving Superior Responsiveness to Customers

Value Creation Function	Primary Roles
Infrastructure (leadership)	1. Through leadership by example, build a companywide commitment to responsiveness to customers.
Production	1. Achieve customization through implementation of flexible manufacturing. 2. Achieve rapid response through flexible manufacturing.
Marketing	1. Know the customer. 2. Communicate customer feedback to appropriate functions.
Materials management	1. Develop logistics systems capable of responding quickly to unanticipated customer demands (JIT).
R&D	1. Bring customers into the product development process.
Information systems	1. Use web-based information systems to increase responsiveness to customers.
Human resources	1. Develop training programs that get employees to think like customers themselves.

Downtime for heavy construction equipment is very costly, so Caterpillar's ability to respond quickly in the event of equipment malfunction is of prime importance to its customers. As a result, many of them have remained loyal to Caterpillar despite the aggressive low-price competition from Komatsu of Japan.

In general, reducing response time requires (1) a marketing function that can quickly communicate customer requests to production, (2) production and materials-management functions that can quickly adjust production schedules in response to unanticipated customer demands, and (3) information systems that can help production and marketing in this process.

Table 4.5 summarizes the steps different functions must take if a company is to achieve superior responsiveness to customers. Although marketing plays the critical role in helping a company attain this goal, primarily because it represents the point of contact with the customer, Table 4.5 shows that the other functions also have major roles. Moreover, like achieving superior efficiency, quality, and innovation, achieving superior responsiveness to customers requires top management to lead in building a customer orientation within the company.

Summary of Chapter

1. A company can increase efficiency through a number of steps: exploiting economies of scale and learning effects, adopting flexible manufacturing technologies, reducing customer defection rates, implementing just-in-time systems, getting the R&D function to design products that are easy to manufacture, upgrading the skills of employees through training, introducing self-managing teams, linking pay to performance, building a companywide commitment to efficiency through strong leadership, and designing structures that facilitate cooperation among different functions in pursuit of efficiency goals.

2. Superior quality can help a company lower its costs, differentiate its product, and charge a premium price.

3. Achieving superior quality demands an organization-wide commitment to quality and a clear focus on the customer. It also requires metrics to measure quality

goals and incentives that emphasize quality, input from employees regarding ways in which quality can be improved, a methodology for tracing defects to their source and correcting the problems that produce them, a rationalization of the company's supply base, cooperation with the suppliers that remain to implement total quality management programs, products that are designed for ease of manufacturing, and substantial cooperation among functions.

4. The failure rate of new-product introductions is high because of factors such as uncertainty, poor commercialization, poor positioning strategy, slow cycle time, and technological myopia.

5. To achieve superior innovation, a company must build skills in basic and applied research; design good processes for managing development projects; and achieve close integration between the different functions of the company, primarily through the adoption of cross-functional product development teams and partly parallel development processes.

6. To achieve superior responsiveness to customers often requires that the company achieve superior efficiency, quality, and innovation.

7. To achieve superior responsiveness to customers, a company needs to give customers what they want when they want it. It must ensure a strong customer focus, which can be attained by emphasizing customer focus through leadership; training employees to think like customers; bringing customers into the company through superior market research; customizing products to the unique needs of individual customers or customer groups; and responding quickly to customer demands.

Discussion Questions

1. How are the four generic building blocks of competitive advantage related to each other?
2. What role can top management play in helping a company achieve superior efficiency, quality, innovation, and responsiveness to customers?
3. In the long run, will adoption of Six Sigma quality improvement processes give a company a competitive advantage, or will it be required just to achieve parity with competitors?
4. In what sense might innovation be called the single most important building block of competitive advantage?

Practicing Strategic Management

■ SMALL-GROUP EXERCISE
Identifying Excellence

Break up into groups of three to five people, and appoint one group member as a spokesperson who will communicate your findings to the class.

You are the management team of a start-up company that will produce disk drives for the personal computer industry. You will sell your product to manufacturers of personal computers (original equipment manufacturers). The disk drive market is characterized by rapid technological change, product life cycles of only six to nine months, intense price competition, high fixed costs for manufacturing equipment, and substantial manufacturing economies of scale. Your customers, the original equipment manufacturers, issue very demanding technological specifications that your product has to comply with. They also pressure you to deliver

your product on time so that it fits in with their own product introduction schedule.

1. In this industry, what functional competencies are the most important for you to build?
2. How will you design your internal processes to ensure that those competencies are built within the company?

■ ARTICLE FILE 4

Choose a company that is widely regarded as excellent. Identify the source of its excellence, and relate it to the material discussed in this chapter. Pay particular attention to the role played by the various functions in building excellence.

■ STRATEGIC MANAGEMENT PROJECT
Module 4

This module deals with the ability of your company to achieve superior efficiency, quality, innovation, and responsiveness to customers. With the information you have at your disposal, answer the questions and perform the tasks listed:

1. Is your company pursuing any of the efficiency-enhancing practices discussed in this chapter?

2. Is your company pursuing any of the quality-enhancing practices discussed in this chapter?

3. Is your company pursuing any of the practices designed to enhance innovation discussed in this chapter?

4. Is your company pursuing any of the practices designed to increase responsiveness to customers discussed in this chapter?

5. Evaluate the competitive position of your company in the light of your answers to questions 1–4. Explain what, if anything, the company needs to do to improve its competitive position.

■ EXPLORING THE WEB
Visiting Applied Materials

Visit the website of Applied Materials, the world's largest manufacturer of semiconductor fabrication equipment (**www.appliedmaterials.com**). Go to the section titled "About" Applied Materials, and read the company's mission statement. What does this mission statement tell you about the kind of competitive advantage that Applied Materials is trying to build? How important are efficiency, quality, innovation, and responsiveness to customers to this company?

Now go to the sections of Applied's website that detail the company's financial results, products, and press releases. Read through these sections and try to establish how successful Applied has been at meeting the objectives set down in its mission statement. What do you think the company has done at the functional level to increase its efficiency, responsiveness to customers, innovative ability, and product quality?

General Task   Search the Web for a company whose homepage describes in some detail its approach to achieving one of the following: superior productivity, product quality, customer service, or innovation. Using this information, document the company's functional-level strategy and assess whether the strategy makes sense given what you have learned so far in this book.

Closing Case

Redesigning the American Car

In 2003 Detroit's big three carmakers, GM, Ford, and DaimlerChrysler, accounted for only 60.2 percent of the vehicles sold in the United States, the lowest number ever. The market share loss has been greatest in the U.S. passenger car market, where foreign producers walked away with 55 percent of the market in 2003, up from 34 percent in 1993. For most of the last decade, strong sales of sports utility vehicles, where Detroit dominates, have held overall market share losses in check, but now foreign producers such as Toyota, Honda, and Kia are going after that segment too, creating huge potential problems for Detroit.

The American automobile makers have responded by trying to reinvigorate their passenger car business and coming out with a host of new designs. Just as importantly, they are trying to cut the costs of developing and producing those cars. The old rule of thumb was that it took four years and cost $1 billion to design a new car and tool a factory to produce it. To recoup these costs, Detroit would typically sell a car for seven years before developing a new design. Unfortunately for the American producers, the Japanese shortened the life cycle of a typical vehicle to five years, and by lowering development and tooling costs, they have been able to make good money on their car models.

Now the American producers are trying to strike back. Typical is Ford, which has reduced its product development time by a quarter since the late 1990s and continues to reduce it by 10 percent per year. Ford now designs almost one-third of its models in less than thirty months. One reason for this progress has been the increased communication among designers. Ford designers used to work in different teams and did not share enough knowledge about parts and platform design. Now teams get together to see how they can share the design work.

Moreover, design teams are trying to use the same parts in a wider variety of car models and, where appropriate, use parts from old models in new cars. Detroit auto designers used to boast that new models were completely redesigned from the floor up with all new parts. Now that is seen as costly and time consuming. At General Motors, for example, the goal is now to reuse 40 to 60 percent of parts from one car generation to the next, thereby reducing design time and tooling costs. At Ford, the number of parts has been slashed. For example, Ford engineers now choose from just four steering wheels, instead of contemplating fourteen different designs.

Another important trend has been to reduce the number of platforms used for car models, as Japanese producers have long been doing. Honda, for example, builds its Odyssey minivan and its Pilot and Acura MDX sports utility vehicles on the same platform, and it has added a pickup truck to the mix. Currently Chrysler bases its vehicle fleet on thirteen distinct platforms. The company is trying to bring this down to just four platforms, reducing the product development budget from $42 billion to $30 billion in the process. Ford and General Motors have similar aims. The platform for GM's new small car offering, the Pontiac Solstice, will also be used for its new Saturn coupe and perhaps one more GM car. As GM develops its next generation of Chevy Silverado and GMC Sierra pickups, it plans to reuse much of the existing platform, cutting development costs in half to nearly $3 billion. Over the next eight years, Ford plans to use its Mazda 6 sedan platform (Ford owns Mazda) as the basis for ten new vehicles. The idea, according to Ford's head of operations, is to engineer it once and use it often.

Hand in hand with changes in design philosophy, the Detroit companies are retooling their factories to reduce costs and make them capable of producing several car models from the same line. By doing so, they hope to be able to reduce the breakeven point for a new car model. GM's Solstice, for example, is forecast to sell around 25,000 units a year—too few to recoup fixed costs under the old design-and-build philosophy. But GM has cut design costs by using a common platform and common parts, and it has cut tooling costs by investing in flexible manufacturing technologies that can be used to produce multiple designs based on the Solstice platform from the

same basic line. GM has also worked hard to get unions to agree to changes in inflexible work rules. Assembly line workers now perform several different jobs, which reduces waste and boosts productivity. Similarly, Ford hopes to have 75 percent of its production built on flexible assembly lines by 2010, and, if successful, its investments in flexible factories could reduce annual costs by some $2 billion a year.

Critics say that the new vision coming out of Detroit is not that new. Although the techniques being discussed will reduce development time and tooling costs, Japanese automakers have been pursuing the same techniques for years. The critics fear that Detroit automakers are chasing a moving target and that when they arrive in the promised land, it will be too late, since their global competitors will have already taken competition to the next level.[54]

Case Discussion Questions

1. How have lower development and tooling costs given Japanese auto manufacturers an advantage in the marketplace?

2. What steps are the Detroit automobile makers taking to reduce product development time and tooling costs? If they are successful, what are the implications of these initiatives for (a) the number of car models they can sell and (b) breakeven volumes for an individual model? Will these initiatives benefit Detroit's customers? How?

3. The Japanese producers have been pursuing for years many of the methodologies now being introduced in Detroit. Why do you think it has taken the Detroit automakers so long to respond to their foreign competitors?

4. If the Detroit companies successfully implement their new operating strategies, do you think they will gain a competitive advantage in the marketplace?

Chapter 5

Building Competitive Advantage Through Business-Level Strategy

Opening Case

Samsung Changes Its Business Model Again and Again

In the last five years Samsung, based in Seoul, Korea, has risen to become the most profitable consumer electronics company in the world. Since 1999 its revenues have doubled, and in 2004 it made a record $12 billion profit, thus becoming the second most profitable global technology company after Microsoft.[1] The story of how Samsung's business model has changed over time explains how the company has reached its enviable position.

In the 1980s, Samsung watched as Japanese companies like Sony and Matsushita (the maker of Panasonic and JVC products) turned out thousands of innovative new consumer electronics such as the Walkman, home video recorders, high-quality televisions, and compact disk players. Samsung's strategy was to see which of these products and which of their specific features, such as a TV with a hard disk that can store movies, customers liked the best. Then Samsung's engineers would find ways to imitate this technology, just as Japanese companies had imitated U.S. electronics companies in the 1950s when they were the world's leading electronics makers. Samsung would make a low-cost copy of these products and sell them at lower prices than Japanese companies. However, while this strategy was profitable, Samsung was not in the league of Japanese companies like Sony, which could charge premium prices for their electronics and then continually plow their enormous profits back into research to make ever more advanced state-of-the-art electronics—and thus increase their profitability.

Samsung continued to pursue its low-cost strategy until the mid 1990s, when its chairman, Lee Kun Hee, made a major decision. Sensing the emerging threat posed by China and other Asian countries whose cheap labor would rob Samsung of its low-cost advantage, Lee realized that Samsung needed to find a way to enter the big league and compete directly against the Japanese giants. The question was how to do this, given that companies like Sony, Panasonic, and Hitachi were leaders in electronics research and development.

Lee began his new strategy by closing down thirty-two unprofitable product divisions and laying off 40 percent of Samsung's work force. Having lowered its cost structure, Samsung could now invest much more of its capital in research and development activities. Lee decided to concentrate Samsung's research budget on new-product opportunities in areas like microprocessors, LCD screens, and other new kinds of digital components that he sensed would be in demand in the coming digital revolution. Today, Samsung is a major supplier of chips and LCD screens to all global electronics makers, and it can produce these components at a much lower cost than they can because it is farther down the experience curve.[2]

The focus of Lee's new strategy, however, was on developing research and engineering skills that would allow the company to quickly capitalize on the technology being innovated by Sony, Matsushita, Phillips, and Nokia. His engineers would take this technology and rapidly develop and improve it to create new and improved products that were more advanced than those offered by Japanese competitors. Samsung would produce a wider variety of products than competitors but only in relatively small quantities. Then, as its new products were sold in stores, newer electronic models that were still more advanced would replace them. One advantage of speeding products to market is that inventory does not sit in Samsung's warehouses or stores, nor does Samsung need to stock large quantities of components because it needs only enough to make its budgeted output of a particular product. So, by making speed the center of its differentiation strategy, Samsung was able to make more efficient use of its capital even as it introduced large numbers of new products to the market.

At the same time, Samsung's ability to innovate a large number of advanced products attracts customers and has allowed it to build its market share. Today, for example, while Nokia can claim to be a leading cell phone innovator, Samsung was the first to realize that customers wanted a color screen for their phone to allow them to play games and a built-in camera that would allow them to send photographs to their friends. Both these incremental advances have allowed Samsung to dramatically increase its share of the cell phone market, while Nokia's has fallen just as dramatically. To compete with Samsung, Nokia has had to learn how to innovate new models of cell phones rapidly. In 2004, while Nokia introduced only a score of new phones, Samsung brought out ninety new models; however, Nokia announced that it would be introducing over fifty new phones in 2005 to meet Samsung's challenge.[3]

By making speed of new-product development the center of its business model, Samsung also was able to move ahead of its other major competitors like Sony. Sony, because of its focus on developing new technology and because of the slow speed of decision making typical in Japanese companies, was hard hit by Samsung's success, and its profitability and stock price declined sharply in the 2000s. Moreover, today Samsung is not just imitating Sony's leading-edge technology but is also developing its own, as shown by the fact that in 2004 Sony and Samsung announced a major agreement to share the costs of basic research into improving LCDs, which run into billions of dollars.

Today, Samsung is in the first tier of electronics makers and is regarded by many as one of the most innovative companies in the world. Almost a quarter of Samsung's 80,000 employees work in one of its four research divisions—semiconductors, telecommunications, digital media, and flat-screen panels. Because many of its products require components developed by all four divisions, it brings researchers, designers, engineers, and marketers from all its divisions together in teams at its research facility outside of Seoul to spur the innovation that is the major source of its success. At the same time, it can still make many electronic components at a lower cost than its competitors, which has further contributed to its high profitability. Given the rapid technological advances in China, however, it appears that Chinese companies may soon be able to make some of their components at a lower cost than Samsung, thus doing to Samsung what Samsung did to companies like Sony. Samsung is relying on the speed of its research and engineering to fight off their challenge, but all global electronics makers are now in a race to speed their products to market.

Overview

As the *Opening Case* suggests, this chapter examines how a company selects and pursues a business model that will allow it to compete effectively in an industry and grow its profits and profitability. A successful business model results from business-level strategies that create a competitive advantage over rivals and achieve superior performance in an industry.

In Chapter 2 we examined how the competitive forces at work inside an industry affect its profitability. As industry forces change, so they change the profitability of an industry, and thus the profitability of any particular business model. Industry analysis is vital in formulating a successful business model because it determines (1) how existing companies will decide to change their business-level strategies to improve the performance of their business model over time, (2) whether or not established companies outside an industry may decide to create a business model to enter it, and (3) whether entrepreneurs can devise a business model that will allow them to compete successfully against existing companies in an industry.

In Chapter 3, we examined how competitive advantage depends on a company developing a business model that allows it to achieve superior efficiency, quality, innovation, and customer responsiveness, the building blocks of competitive advantage. And in Chapter 4, we discussed how every function must develop the distinctive competencies that allow a company to implement a business model that will lead to superior performance and competitive advantage in an industry.

In this chapter we examine the competitive decisions involved in creating a business model that will attract and retain customers, and continue to do so over time so that a company enjoys growing profits and profitability. To create a successful business model, strategic managers must (1) formulate business-level strategies that will allow a company to attract customers away from other companies in the industry (its competitors), and (2) implement those business-level strategies, which also involves the use of functional-level strategies to increase responsiveness to customers, efficiency, innovation, and quality.

By the end of this chapter, you will be able to distinguish between the principal generic business models and business-level strategies that a company uses to obtain a competitive advantage over its rivals. You will also understand why, and under what circumstances, strategic leaders like Samsung's Lee Kun Hee change their company's strategies over time to pursue different kinds of business models.

Competitive Positioning and the Business Model

To create a successful business model, managers must choose a set of business-level strategies that work together to give a company a competitive advantage over its rivals; that is, they must optimize **competitive positioning**. As we noted in Chapter 1, to craft a successful business model a company must first define its business, which entails decisions about (1) customers' needs, or what is to be satisfied, (2) customer groups, or who is to be satisfied, and (3) distinctive competencies, or how customer needs are to be satisfied.[4] The decisions managers make about these three issues determine which set of strategies they formulate and implement to put a company's business model into action and create value for customers. Consequently, we need to examine the principal choices facing managers as they make these three decisions.

■ Formulating the Business Model: Customer Needs and Product Differentiation

Customer needs are desires, wants, or cravings that can be satisfied by means of the attributes or characteristics of a product—a good or service. For example, a person's craving for something sweet can be satisfied by a box of Godiva chocolates, a carton of Ben & Jerry's ice cream, a Snickers bar, or a spoonful of sugar. Two factors determine which product a customer chooses to satisfy these needs: (1) the way a product is differentiated from other products of its type so that it appeals to customers, and (2) the price of the product. All companies must differentiate their products to a certain degree to attract customers. Some companies, however, decide to offer customers a low-priced product and do not engage in much product differentiation. Companies that seek to create something unique about their product differentiate their products to a much greater degree than others so that they satisfy customers' needs in ways other products cannot.

Product differentiation is the process of designing products to satisfy customers' needs. A company obtains a competitive advantage when it creates, makes, and sells a product in a way that better satisfies customer needs than its rivals do. It is here that the four building blocks of competitive advantage come into play, for a company's decision to pursue one or more of these building blocks determines its approach to product differentiation. If managers devise strategies to differentiate a product by innovation, excellent quality, or responsiveness to customers, they are choosing a business model based on offering customers differentiated products. On the other hand, if managers base their business model on finding ways to increase efficiency and reliability to reduce costs, they are choosing a business model based on offering customers low-priced products.

Creating unique or distinctive products can be achieved in countless different ways, which explains why there are usually many different companies competing in an industry. Distinctiveness obtained from the physical characteristics of a product commonly results from pursuing innovation or quality, such as when a company focuses on developing state-of-the-art car safety systems or on engineering an SUV to give it sports-car-like handling. Similarly, companies might try to design their cars with features such as butter-soft hand-sewn leather interiors, fine wood fittings, and sleek, exciting body styling to appeal to customers' psychological needs, such as a personal need for prestige, status, or to declare a particular "lifestyle."[5]

Differentiation has another important aspect. Companies that invest their resources to create something distinct or different about their products can often charge a *higher,* or *premium, price* for their product. For example, superb design or technical sophistication allows companies to charge more for their products because customers are willing to pay these higher prices. Mercedes-Benz buyers pay a high premium price to enjoy their sophisticated vehicles, as do customers of Godiva chocolates, which retail for about $26 a pound—much more than, say, a box of Whitman's candies or a Hershey bar.

Consider the high-price segment of the car market, where customers are willing to pay more than $35,000 to satisfy their needs for a "personal luxury vehicle." In this segment, Cadillac, Mercedes-Benz, Infiniti, BMW, Jaguar, Lexus, Lincoln, Audi, Volvo, Acura, and others are engaged in a continuing battle to design the "perfect" luxury vehicle—the one that best meets the needs of those who want such a vehicle. Over time, the companies that attract the most luxury car buyers—because they have designed the cars that possess the innovative features or excellent quality and reliability these customers desire the most—are the ones that achieve a sustained competitive advantage over rivals. For example, some customers value a sporty ride and performance handling; Mercedes-Benz and BMW, because of their cutting-edge technical design, can offer this driving experience better than any other maker. Toyota's Lexus division is well known for the smoothness and quietness of its cars and their exceptional reliability. Lexus cars consistently outrank all other cars in published reliability rankings, and this excellence appeals to a large group of customers who appreciate these qualities. Volvo has a reputation for producing safe cars, and Rolls-Royce has a reputation for prestige cars. Other luxury carmakers have not fared so well. Cadillac, Lincoln, Audi, Acura, and Infiniti have found it more difficult to differentiate their cars, which sometimes compare unfavorably to their rivals in terms of ride, comfort, safety, or reliability. Although these less successful companies still sell many cars, customers often find their needs better satisfied by the attributes and qualities of their rivals' cars.

Even in the luxury car segment, however, carmakers must be concerned with efficiency, because price affects a buying decision even for highly differentiated products. Luxury carmakers compete to offer customers the car with the ride, performance, and features that provide them with the most value (satisfy their needs) given the price of the car. Thus, Lexus cars are always several thousand dollars less than comparable cars, and Toyota can price these cars lower because of its low cost structure. For example, the Lexus ES300, introduced in 2003 at around $35,000, is about $10,000 less than the BMW 5 Series and Mercedes E Class, its nearest rivals. Most customers are discriminating and match price to differentiation even in the luxury car segment of the market, so BMW and Mercedes have to offer customers something that justifies their vehicles' higher prices.

At every price range in the car market—under $15,000, from $15,000 to $25,000, $25,000 to $35,000, and the luxury segment above $35,000—many models of cars compete to attract customers. For each price range a carmaker has to decide how best to differentiate a particular car model to suit the needs of customers in that price range. Typically, the more differentiated a product is, the more it will cost to design and produce, and so differentiation leads to a higher cost structure. Thus, if a carmaker is to stay within the $15,000 to $25,000 price range and yet design and produce a differentiated car that will give it a competitive advantage and allow it to outperform its rivals in the same price range, its strategic managers have to make crucial and difficult decisions. They have to forecast what features customers will most value; for example, they may decide to trade off styling, safety, and performance so that the car will not cost too much to produce, enabling them to make a profit and to still sell the car for less than $25,000.

In sum, in devising a business model, strategic managers are always constrained by the need to differentiate their products against the need to keep their cost structure under control so that they can offer the product at a competitive price—a price that offers customers as much or more value than the products of its rivals. Companies that have built a competitive advantage through innovation, quality, and reliability can differentiate their products more successfully than their rivals. In turn, because customers perceive there is more value in their products, these companies can charge a premium price.

■ Formulating the Business Model: Customer Groups and Market Segmentation

The second main choice involved in formulating a successful business model is to decide which kind of product(s) to offer to which customer group(s). Customer groups are the sets of people who share a similar need for a particular product. Because a particular product usually satisfies several different kinds of desires and needs, many different customer groups normally exist in a market. In the car market, for example, some customers want basic transportation, some want top-of-the-line luxury, and others want the thrill of driving a sports car: these are three of the customer groups in the car market.

In the athletic shoe market, the two main customer groups are those people who use them for sporting purposes and those who like to wear them because they are casual and comfortable. Within each customer group there are often subgroups composed of people who have an even more specific need for a product. Inside the group of people who buy athletic shoes for sporting purposes, for example, are subgroups of people who buy shoes suited to a specific kind of activity, such as running, aerobics, walking, and tennis (see Figure 5.1).

A company searching for a successful business model has to group customers according to the similarities or differences in their needs to discover what kinds of

FIGURE 5.1

Identifying Customer
Groups and Market
Segments

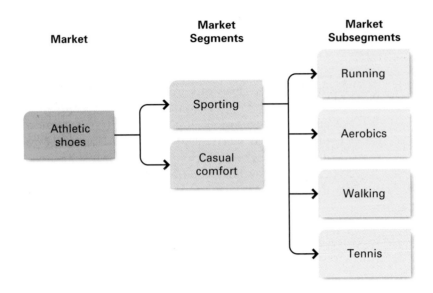

products to develop for different kinds of customers. The marketing function performs research to discover a group of customers' primary need for a product, how they will use it, and their income or buying power (to determine the balance between differentiation and price). Other important attributes of a customer group are then identified that more narrowly target their specific needs. Once a group of customers who share a similar or specific need for a product has been identified, this group is treated as a market segment. Companies then decide whether to make and sell a product designed to satisfy the specific needs of this customer segment.

■ **Three Approaches to Market Segmentation** Market segmentation is the way a company decides to group customers, based on important differences in their needs or preferences, in order to gain a competitive advantage.[6] First, the company must segment the market according to how much customers are able and willing to pay for a particular product—such as the different price ranges for cars mentioned above. Once price has been taken into consideration, customers can be segmented according to the specific needs that are being satisfied by a particular product, such as the economy, luxury, or speed of cars mentioned above.

In crafting a business model, managers have to think strategically about which segments they are going to compete in and how they will differentiate their products for each segment. In other words, once market segments have been identified, a company has to decide how *responsive it should be to the needs of customers in the different segments*. This decision determines a particular company's product range. There are three main approaches toward market segmentation in devising a business model (Figure 5.2):

■ First, a company might choose not to recognize that different market segments exist and make a product targeted at the average or typical customer. In this case customer responsiveness is at a *minimum*, and the focus is on price, not differentiation.

■ Second, a company can choose to recognize the differences between customer groups and make a product targeted toward most or all of the different market

FIGURE 5.2

Three Approaches to
Market Segmentation

No Market Segmentation	High Market Segmentation	Focused Market Segmentation
A product is targeted at the "average customer."	A different product is offered to each market segment.	A product is offered to one or a few market segments.

segments. In this case customer responsiveness is *high* and products are being *customized* to meet the specific needs of customers in each group, so the emphasis is on differentiation, not price.

■ Third, a company might choose to target just *one or two market segments* and devote its resources to developing products for customers in just these segments. In this case, it may be highly responsive to the needs of customers in only these segments, or it may offer a bare-bones product to undercut the prices charged by companies who do focus on differentiation.

Since a company's cost structure and operating costs increase when it makes a different product for each market segment rather than just one product for the whole market, why would a company devise a business model based on serving customers in multiple market segments? The answer is that although operating costs increase, the decision to produce a range of products that are closely aligned with the needs of customers in different market segments attracts many more customers (because responsiveness to customers increases), and therefore sales revenues and profits increase. Recall from the *Opening Case* that Samsung's revenues have increased because of its ability to offer customers a continual supply of new and improved cell phones that it can sell at a premium price. As long as a company's revenues increase faster than its operating costs as its product range expands, profitability increases.

This does not mean that all companies should decide to produce a wide range of products aimed at each market segment to increase their profitability. It depends on how much customer needs for a product differ in a particular market or industry. In some industries, like cars, customer needs differ widely. There are considerable differences in buyers' primary needs for a car, income levels, lifestyles, ages, and so on. For this reason, major global carmakers broaden their product range and make vehicles to serve most market segments. A company that produces just one car model, compared to a company that produces twenty-five models, may find itself at a serious competitive disadvantage.

On the other hand, in some markets customers have similar needs for a product and so the relative price of competing products drives their buying choices. In this situation, a company that chooses to use its resources to make and sell a single product as inexpensively as possible might gain a major competitive advantage. The average customer buys the product because it's "OK" and good "value for the money." This is the business model followed by companies that specialize in making a low-cost product, such as BIC, which makes low-cost razors and ballpoint pens, and Arm & Hammer, which makes baking soda. These are products that most people use in the same way. This is also the business model followed by companies like Wal-Mart, with its mission to buy products from suppliers as cheaply as possible and then sell them to customers at the lowest possible prices. BIC and Wal-Mart do not segment the market; they decide to serve the needs of customers who want to buy products as inexpensively as possible. Wal-Mart promises everyday low prices and price rollbacks; BIC promises the lowest-priced razor blades that work acceptably.

The third approach to market segmentation is to target a product just at one or two market segments. To pursue this approach a company must develop something very special or distinctive about its product to attract a large share of customers in those particular market segments. In the car market, for example, Rolls-Royce and Porsche target their products at specific market segments. Porsche, for example, targets its well-known sports cars at buyers in the high-priced sports car segment. In a similar way, specialty retailers compete for customers in a particular market segment, such as the segment composed of affluent people who can afford to buy expensive hand-made clothing, or people who enjoy wearing "trendy" shoes such as Nike's Converse brand. A retailer might also specialize in a particular style of clothing, such as western wear, beachwear, or accessories. In many markets these are enormous opportunities for small companies to specialize in satisfying the needs of a specific market segment. Often, these companies can better satisfy their customers' needs because they are so close to them and understand how their needs are changing over time.

Market segmentation is an evolving, ongoing process that presents considerable opportunities for strategic managers to improve their company's business model. For example, in the car industry, savvy strategists often identify a "new" customer group whose specific needs have not been met and who have had to "satisfice" and buy a model that does not meet their needs exactly but is a reasonable compromise. Now a car company can decide to treat this group as a market segment and create a product designed to meet their specific needs; if it makes the right choice, it has a blockbuster product. This was the origin of the minivan, sports utility vehicle, and all the recently introduced "hybrid" vehicles like the Honda Pilot, Toyota Scion, or Dodge Magnum. In the case of SUVs, many car buyers wanted a more rugged and powerful vehicle capable of holding many people or towing heavy loads. They liked the comfort of a car but also the qualities of a pickup; by combining these two, carmakers created the SUV market segment. If managers make mistakes, however, and design a product for a market segment that is much smaller than they expected, the opposite can occur. In 2004, for example, Ford announced that it was ending production of its expensive luxury Lincoln truck and Excursion SUV because sales had been only in the hundreds a year, not the thousands a year it had projected.

■ **Implementing the Business Model: Building Distinctive Competencies**

To develop a successful business model, strategic managers have to devise a set of strategies that determine (1) how to differentiate and price their product and (2) how much to segment a market and how wide a range of products to develop. Whether these strategies will result in a profitable business model now depends on strategic managers' ability to implement their business model, that is, to choose strategies that will create products that provide customers with the most value, while keeping their cost structure viable (because of the need to be price competitive).

In practice, this involves deciding how to invest a company's capital to build and shape distinctive competencies that result in a competitive advantage based on superior efficiency, quality, innovation, and/or responsiveness to customers. Hence, implementing a company's business model sets in motion *the specific set of functional-level strategies needed to create a successful differentiation and low cost business strategy.* We discussed how functional strategies can build competitive advantage in Chapter 4. The better the fit between a company's business strategy and its functional-level strategies, the more value and profit a company creates.

Figure 5.3 illustrates Wal-Mart's business model. As we discuss in previous chapters, Sam Walton, the company's founder, devised a business model based on the strategy of keeping operating costs to a minimum so that he could offer customers everyday low prices and continuous price rollbacks. To this end, Walton chose business-level strategies to increase efficiency, such as having low product differentiation (Wal-Mart chooses minimal advertising and low responsiveness to customers) and targeting the mass market. His discount retail business model was based on the idea that lower costs mean lower prices.

Having devised a way to compete for customers, Walton's task was now to implement the business model in ways that would create a low-cost structure to allow

FIGURE 5.3

Wal-Mart's Business Model

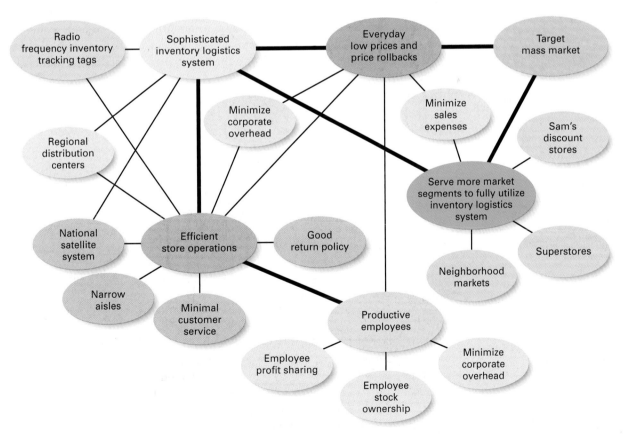

him to charge lower prices. One business-level strategy he implemented was to locate his stores outside large cities in small towns where there were no low-cost competitors; a second was to find ways to manage the value chain to reduce the costs of getting products from manufacturers to customers; and a third was to design and staff store operations to increase efficiency. The task of all functional managers in logistics, materials management, sales and customer service, store management, and so on was to implement specific functional-level strategies that supported the low-cost/low-price business model. Figure 5.3 illustrates some of the thousands of specific choices that Wal-Mart has made to allow it to implement its business model successfully.

Competitive Positioning and Business-Level Strategy

Figure 5.4 presents a way of thinking about the competitive positioning decisions that strategic managers make to create a successful business model.[7] The decision to differentiate a product increases its perceived value to the customer so that market demand for the product increases. However, differentiation is expensive; for example, additional expenditures on resources are needed to improve product quality or support a higher level of service. Therefore, the decision to increase product differentiation also raises a company's cost structure and results in a higher unit cost. (In some cases, however, if increased demand for the product allows a company to make large volumes of the product and achieve economies of scale, these economies can offset some of these extra costs; this effect is showed by the dotted line in Figure 5.4.)[8]

To maximize profitability, managers must choose a premium pricing option that compensates for the extra costs of product differentiation but is not so high it chokes off the increase in expected demand (to prevent customers from deciding that the extra differentiation is not worth the higher price). Once again, to increase

FIGURE 5.4

Competitive Positioning at the Business Level

Source: Copyright © C. W. L. Hill and G. R. Jones, "The Dynamics of Business-Level Strategy" (unpublished manuscript, 2005).

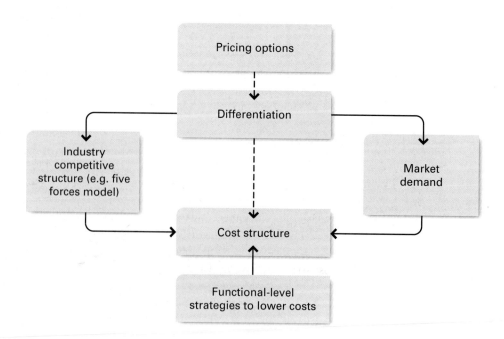

profitability, managers must also search for other ways to reduce the cost structure, but not in ways that will harm the differentiated appeal of its products. There are many specific functional strategies a company can adopt to achieve this. For example, Nordstrom, the luxury department store retailer, differentiates itself in the retail clothing industry by providing a high-quality shopping experience with elegant store operations and a high level of customer service, all of which raise Nordstrom's cost structure. However, Nordstrom can still lower its cost structure by, for example, managing its inventories efficiently and increasing inventory turnover. Also, its strategy of being highly responsive to customers results in more customers and higher demand, which means that sales per square foot increase, and this revenue enables it to make more intensive use of its facilities and salespeople, which leads to scale economies and lower costs. Thus, no matter what the level of differentiation is that a company chooses to pursue in its business model, it always has to recognize the way its cost structure will vary as a result of its choice of differentiation and the other specific strategies it adopts to lower its cost structure; in other words, *differentiation and cost structure decisions affect one another.*

The last main dynamic shown in Figure 5.4 concerns the impact of the industry's competitive structure on a company's differentiation, cost structure, and pricing choices. Recall that strategic decision making takes place in an environment where watchful and agile competitors exist; therefore, one company's choice of competitive positioning is always made *with reference to those of its competitors.* If, for example, competitors start to offer products with new or improved features, a company may be forced to increase its level of differentiation to remain competitive, even if this reduces its profitability. Similarly, if competitors decide to develop products for new market segments, the company will have to follow suit or become uncompetitive. Thus, because differentiation increases costs, increasing industry competition can drive up a company's cost structure. When that happens, a company's ability to charge a premium price to cover these high costs depends on whether its profitability increases or decreases.

In sum, maximizing the profitability of a company's business model is about making the right choices with regard to value creation through differentiation, costs, and pricing given both the demand conditions in the company's market and the competitive conditions in the company's industry. Because *all the different variables in Figure 5.4 change as the others change,* managers can never accurately predict the outcome of their decisions. This is why devising and managing a successful business model is such a difficult thing to do.

Competitive Positioning: Generic Business-Level Strategies

As we discuss above, a successful business model is the result of the way a company formulates and implements a set of business-level strategies to achieve a fit between its differentiation, cost, and pricing options. While no diagram can ever model all the complexities involved in business-level strategy decisions, Figure 5.5 represents a way to bring together the three issues involved in developing a successful business model. In the figure, the vertical and horizontal axes represent the decisions of strategic managers to position a company's products with respect to the tradeoff between differentiating products (higher costs/higher prices) and achieving the lowest cost structure or cost leadership (lower costs/lower prices). In Figure 5.5 the curve connecting the axes represents the "value creation frontier," meaning the maximum amount of value that the products of different companies in an industry can provide at any one time with different business models. In other words, companies on

FIGURE 5.5

Competitive
Positioning and the
Value Creation
Frontier

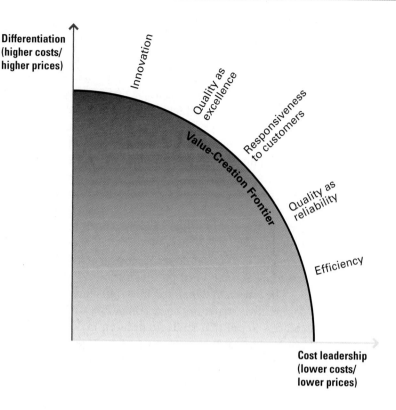

the value frontier are those that have the most successful business models in a particular industry.

As Figure 5.5 illustrates, the value creation frontier is reached by pursuing one or more of the four building blocks of competitive advantage (quality has been split into two), which have been listed from top to bottom according to how much they can contribute to the creation of a differentiation or cost-leadership advantage. Thus innovation, a costly process that results in unique products, is nearest the differentiation axis, followed by quality as excellence, customer responsiveness, and quality as reliability; efficiency is closest to the cost-leadership axis.

To reach the value creation frontier and so achieve above-average profitability, a company must formulate and implement a business model using a consistent set of business-level strategies that give it a *specific competitive position vis-à-vis its rivals*. A **generic competitive strategy** is a specific business-level strategy that gives a company a competitive advantage, and four principal ones can be identified: cost leadership, focused cost leadership, differentiation, and focused differentiation.[9] *Generic* means that all companies can potentially pursue these strategies regardless of whether they are manufacturing, service, or nonprofit enterprises; they are also generic because they can be pursued across different kinds of industries.

■ Cost Leadership

A company's business model in pursuing a cost-leadership strategy is based on doing everything it can to lower its cost structure so it can make and sell goods or services at a lower cost than its competitors. In essence, a company seeks to achieve a competitive advantage and above-average profitability by developing a cost-leadership business model that positions it on the value creation frontier as close as possible to the lower costs/lower prices axis.

Two advantages accrue from a cost-leadership strategy. First, if a company's closest rivals, such as those that compete in the same price range or for the same customer group, charge similar prices for their products, the cost leader will be more profitable than its competitors because of its lower costs. Second, and more commonly, the cost leader gains a competitive advantage by being able to charge a lower price than its competitors because of its lower cost structure. As discussed earlier, offering customers the same kind of value from a product but at a lower price attracts many more customers, so that even though the company has chosen a lower price option, the increased volume of sales will cause profits to surge. If its competitors try to get lost customers back by reducing their prices and all companies start to compete on price, the cost leader will still be able to withstand competition better than the other companies because of its lower costs. It is likely to win any competitive struggle. For these reasons, cost leaders are likely to earn above-average profits. A company becomes a cost leader when its strategic managers develop a business model that is based on the following business-level strategic choices.

■ **Strategic Choices** The cost leader chooses a low to moderate level of product differentiation relative to its competitors. Differentiation is expensive; the more a company expends resources to make its products distinct, the more its costs rise.[10] The cost leader aims for a level of differentiation obtainable at low cost.[11] Wal-Mart, for example, does not spend hundreds of millions of dollars on store design to create an attractive shopping experience as chains like Macy's, Dillard's, or Saks Fifth Avenue have done. As Wal-Mart explains in its mission statement, "We think of ourselves as buyers for our customers and we apply our considerable strengths to get the best value for you," and such value is not obtained by building lavish stores.[12] Cost leaders often wait until customers want a feature or service before providing it, as Samsung did in the *Opening Case.* For example, a cost leader is never the first to offer theater-quality sound in a DVD player; instead, it adds such sound quality only when it is obvious that customers demand it.

The cost leader also ignores the many different market segments in an industry and positions its products to appeal to the "average" customer to reduce the costs of developing and selling many different products tailored to the needs of different market segments. In targeting the average customer, strategic managers try to produce or provide the least or smallest number of products that will be desired by the highest number of customers, something at the heart of Wal-Mart's approach to stocking its stores. Thus, although customers may not get exactly the products they want, they are attracted by the lower prices.

To implement cost leadership, the overriding goal of the cost leader must be to choose strategies to increase its efficiency and lower its cost structure compared with its rivals. The development of distinctive competencies in manufacturing, materials management, and information technology is central to achieving this goal. For example, manufacturing companies pursuing a cost-leadership strategy concentrate on doing all they can to continually ride down the experience curve so that their cost structure keeps getting lower and lower. Achieving a cost-leadership position requires that a company develop skills in flexible manufacturing, adopt efficient materials-management techniques, and do all it can to increase inventory turnover and reduce the cost of goods sold. (Table 4.1 outlined the ways in which a company's functions can be used to increase efficiency.)

Consequently, for companies that make products, the manufacturing and materials-management functions are the center of attention, and the other functions shape their distinctive competencies to meet the needs of manufacturing and materials management.[13] The sales function, for example, may develop the competency of capturing large, stable sets of customers' orders. In turn, this allows manufacturing to make longer production runs and so achieve economies of scale and reduce costs. At Dell, for example, online customers are provided with a limited set of choices so that Dell can customize PCs to a customer's needs at low cost. Finding ways to customize products at low cost is an important task for managers pursuing a cost-leadership strategy. The human resource function may focus on instituting training programs and compensation systems that lower costs by improving employees' productivity, and the research and development function may specialize in process improvements to lower the manufacturing costs.

By contrast, companies supplying services, such as retail stores like Wal-Mart, must develop distinctive competencies in whatever functions contribute most to their cost structure. In Wal-Mart this is the cost of purchasing products, so the logistics or materials-management function becomes of central importance. Wal-Mart has taken advantage of advances in information technology to lower the costs associated with getting goods from manufacturers to customers, just as Dell, the cost leader in the PC industry, uses the Internet to lower the cost of selling its computers. Another major source of cost savings in pursuing cost leadership is to choose an organizational structure and culture to implement this strategy in the most cost-efficient way. Thus, a low-cost strategy implies minimizing the number of managers in the hierarchy and the rigorous use of budgets to control production and selling costs. An interesting example of the way a company can craft a business model to become the cost leader in an industry is Ryanair, discussed in Strategy in Action 5.1.

■ **Advantages and Disadvantages** Porter's five forces model, introduced in Chapter 2, explains why each of the business models allows a company to reach the value creation frontier shown in Figure 5.5.[14] The five forces are threats from competitors, powerful suppliers, powerful buyers, substitute products, and new entrants. The cost leader is protected from industry competitors by its cost advantage. Its lower costs also mean that it will be less affected than its competitors by increases in the price of inputs if there are powerful suppliers, and less affected by a fall in the prices it can charge if there are powerful buyers. Moreover, since cost leadership usually requires a large market share, the cost leader purchases in relatively large quantities, increasing its bargaining power over suppliers. If substitute products begin to come onto the market, the cost leader can reduce its price to compete with them and retain its market share. Finally, the leader's cost advantage constitutes a barrier to entry because other companies are unable to enter the industry and match the leader's costs or prices. The cost leader is therefore relatively safe as long as it can maintain its low-cost advantage.

The principal dangers of the cost-leadership approach lurk in competitors' ability to find ways to lower their cost structures and beat the cost leader at its own game. For instance, if technological change makes experience-curve economies obsolete, new companies may apply lower-cost technologies that give them a cost advantage. The steel mini-mills discussed in Chapter 4 gained this advantage. Competitors may also draw a cost advantage from labor-cost savings. Global competitors located in countries overseas often have very low labor costs; wage costs in the United States are

Strategy in Action

Ryanair Takes Control over the Sky in Europe

Ryanair, based in Dublin, Ireland, imitated and improved on the cost-leadership business model pioneered by Southwest Airlines in the United States and used it to become a leading player in the European air travel market. Ryanair's CEO, the flamboyant Michael O'Leary, saw the specific strategies Southwest had developed to cut costs and used the same strategies to position Ryanair as the lowest-cost, lowest-priced European airline. Today, the average cost of a Ryanair ticket within Europe is $48, compared to $330 on British Airways and $277 on Lufthansa, which have long dominated the European air travel market. The result is that Ryanair now flies more passengers inside Britain than British Airways, and its share of the European market is growing as fast as it can gain access to new landing spots and buy the new planes needed to service its expanding route structure.

O'Leary has managed to improve on Southwest's low-cost business model. Ryanair imitated the main elements of Southwest's model, such as only using one plane, the 737, to reduce maintenance costs, selling tickets directly to customers, and eliminating seat assignments and free in-flight meals. It also avoids high-cost airports like Heathrow and chooses smaller ones outside big cities, such as Luton, its London hub, just as Wal-Mart chose to move into smaller towns. However, to reduce clean-up costs, O'Leary also eliminated the seat-back pockets that often contain trash left by previous passengers, as well as blankets, pillows, free sodas or snacks, and even "sick" bags—anything at all a passenger might expect to receive on a more differentiated airline. "You get what you pay for" is Ryanair's philosophy. To implement his cost-leadership strategy, O'Leary and all employees are expected to find ways to wipe out or reduce the small, incremental expenses that arise in performing the tens of thousands of specific operations needed to run an airline. His goal is to eliminate all the differentiated qualities of an airline that can raise costs. Through all these tactics

Ryanair has lowered its cost structure so far that no other European airline can come close to offering its low-cost fares and break even, let alone make a profit.

The other side of Ryanair's business model is to add to its revenues by getting its customers to spend as much as possible while they are on its flights. To this end, Ryanair offers snacks, meals, and a variety of drinks to encourage customers to open their wallets. In addition, to cut costs his planes have no back-seat LCD screens for viewing movies and playing games. In 2004 Ryanair introduced a new digital hand-held device that passengers can rent for $6 a flight to watch movies and sitcoms or play games or music. Fourteen percent of its revenues come from these sources, and they are so important that in 2003 the airline gave away over 1 million of its unsold seats free to customers so that it could at least get some revenue from passengers sitting in what otherwise would be empty seats.

How have competitors reacted to Ryanair's cost-leadership strategy? Some airlines have started a low-price subsidiary, just as United's Song division was created to compete with Southwest in the United States. However, this often results in cannibalization as their passengers move from the high-price to the low-price service. Some airlines that pursue the differentiation strategy, like British Airways, are not suffering because they are solidly profitable in the business segment of the market. However, other airlines, such as Italy's flagship airline, Alitalia, are close to bankruptcy, and the Irish carrier Aer Lingus has had to cut its costs by 50 percent in the last few years just to survive. O'Leary sees brutal price wars ahead: new low-cost entrants like easyJet have entered the market, and more will do so. The lower-cost, lower-fare business model will fare well if price wars develop, and if the large national airlines are going to prosper they will have to offer customers something that makes them willing to pay higher prices.[a]

roughly 600 percent more than they are in Malaysia, China, or Mexico. Most U.S. companies now assemble their products abroad as part of their low-cost strategy; many are forced to do so simply to compete and stay in business.

Competitors' ability to imitate the cost leader's methods easily is another threat to the cost-leadership strategy. For example, companies in Hong Kong and China routinely take apart the electronic products of Japanese companies like Sony and Panasonic to see how they are designed and assembled. Then, using Chinese-made components and a huge pool of inexpensive domestic labor, they manufacture clones of these products and flood the U.S. market with inexpensive tape players, radios, phones, and DVD players. This was part of Samsung's early strategy.

Finally, the cost-leadership strategy carries a risk that strategic managers in their single-minded desire to reduce costs might make decisions that decrease costs but then drastically affect demand for the product. This happened to Gateway in the early 2000s when, to reduce the costs of customer service, customer support people were instructed not to help customers who were experiencing problems with their new Gateway computers if they had installed their own new software on the machines. New buyers, most of whom install their own software, began to complain vociferously, and Gateway's sales began to fall as word spread. Within six months, managers had reversed their decision, and once again Gateway began offering full customer support.

■ Focused Cost Leadership

A cost leader is not always a large, national company that targets the average customer. Sometimes a company can target one or a few market segments and successfully pursue cost leadership by developing the right strategies to serve those segments. These companies pursue a business model based on **focused cost leadership**. They compete for customers in a narrow market segment, which can be defined geographically, by type of customer, or by segment of the product line.[15] In Figure 5.6, focus cost leaders are represented by the smaller circles next to the cost leader's circle. For example, since a geographic niche can be defined by region or even by locality, a cement-making company, a carpet-cleaning business, or a pizza chain could pursue a cost-leadership

FIGURE 5.6

Generic Business Models and the Value Creation Frontier

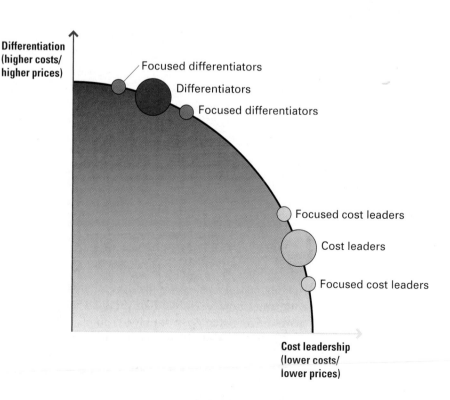

FIGURE 5.7

Why Focus Strategies
Are Different

strategy in one or more cities in a region. Figure 5.7 compares a focused cost-leadership business model with a pure cost-leadership model.

If a company uses a focused cost-leadership approach, it competes against the cost leader in the market segments where it can operate at no cost disadvantage. For example, in local lumber, cement, bookkeeping, or pizza delivery markets, the focuser may have lower materials or transportation costs than the national cost leader. The focuser may also have a cost advantage because it is producing complex or custom-built products that do not lend themselves easily to economies of scale in production and therefore offer few cost-saving possibilities. Pursuing a focus strategy, a cost leader concentrates on small-volume custom products, for which it has a cost advantage, and leaves the large-volume standardized market to the national cost leader—for example, low-priced Mexican food specials versus Big Macs.

Because it has no cost disadvantage in its market segments, a focused cost leader also operates on the value creation frontier and so earns above-average profits. Such a company has great opportunity to develop its own niche and compete against companies pursuing cost-leadership or differentiated strategies. Ryanair, for example, began as a focus company because at first it only operated flights between Dublin and London. Since there was no cost leader in the European market, it was able to quickly expand its operations, and today it is the cost leader. Similarly, Southwest began as a focused cost leader within the Texas market but is now a national air carrier and competes against new companies that pursue focused cost leadership, such as Jet Blue and Song.[16]

Because a focused company only makes and sells a relatively small quantity of a product, its cost structure will often be higher than that of the cost leader. In some industries, like cars, this can make it very difficult or impossible to compete with the cost leader. However, sometimes, by targeting some new market segment or by implementing a business model in a superior way—such as by adopting a more advanced technology—focused companies can be a threat to large cost leaders. For example, flexible manufacturing systems have opened up many new opportunities for focused companies because small production runs become possible at a lower cost. Increasingly, small, specialized companies are competing with large companies in specific market segments in which they have no cost disadvantage. The steel mini-mills discussed in Chapter 4 provide another good example of how a focused company, in this case Nucor, by specializing in one market can grow so efficient that it becomes the cost leader. Similarly, the growth of the Internet has opened up many new opportunities for focused companies to develop business models based on being the cost leader compared to bricks-and-mortar companies. Amazon.com shows how effectively a company can craft a business model to become the cost leader.

■ **Implications and Conclusions** To pursue a cost-leadership strategy, strategic managers need to devote enormous efforts to incorporate all the latest information, materials management, and manufacturing technology into their operations to find new ways to reduce costs. Often, as we saw in Chapter 4, using new technology will also raise quality and increase responsiveness to customers. A low-cost approach requires ongoing strategic thinking to make sure the business model is aligned with changing environmental opportunities and threats.

Strategic managers in companies throughout the industry are watching the cost leader and will move quickly to imitate its innovations because they also want to reduce their costs. Today, a differentiator cannot let a cost leader get too great a cost advantage because the leader might then be able to use its high profits to invest more in product differentiation and beat the differentiator at its own competitive game. For example, Toyota and Honda began as cost leaders, manufacturing simple low-priced cars. Their cars sold well, and they then invested their profits to design and make new models of cars that became increasingly differentiated in features and quality. Today, Toyota and Honda, with cars in every market segment, pursue a differentiation strategy, although Toyota also has the lowest cost structure of any global car company.

A cost leader must also respond to the strategic moves of its differentiated competitors and increase the quality and features of its products if it is to prosper in the long run. Even low-priced products, such as Timex watches and BIC razors, cannot be too inferior to the more expensive Seiko watches or Gillette razors if the lower-costs/lower-prices policy is to succeed. All business-level strategies play out with rivals closely watching each other's strategic moves. If Seiko brings out a novel kind of LCD watch dial or Gillette a three- or four-bladed razor, managers at Timex and BIC will respond within months by incorporating these innovations in their low-priced products if required. This situation is also very common in the high-priced women's fashion industry. As soon as the famous designers like Gucci and Dior have shown their spring and fall collections, their designs are copied and the plans transmitted to factories in Malaysia, where workers are ready to manufacture low-priced imitations that within months will reach low-price clothing retail stores around the world.

A business model like cost leadership should be thought of as a specific set of strategies that helps strategic managers stay focused on how to compete most effectively over time. It is all too easy for strategic managers, flush with the success of their cost-leadership strategy, to become less vigilant and lose sight of changes in the five forces of competition and in the macroenvironment that change the rules of the competitive game. McDonald's, long the cost leader in the fast-food industry, was surprised when rivals like Taco Bell began to offer 99-cent daily specials. McDonald's had to learn how to make fast food more cheaply to compete, and its managers have adopted new cooking techniques and food management practices that have ratcheted it down the experience curve, so that today 99-cent meals are a permanent fixture on McDonald's menu.

■ **Differentiation** A **differentiation** business model is based on pursuing a set of generic strategies that allows a company to achieve a competitive advantage by creating a product that customers perceive as different or distinct in some important way. A differentiator (that is, a differentiated company) has the ability to satisfy customers' needs in a way that its competitors cannot. This means that it can charge a premium price (one higher than that charged by its closest rivals). The ability to increase revenues by charging premium prices (rather than by reducing costs, as the cost leader does) allows the differentiator to reach the value frontier, outperform its competitors, and achieve superior profitability, as shown in Figure 5.6. As noted earlier, customers pay a premium price when they believe the product's differentiated qualities are worth the extra money. Consequently, differentiated products are often priced on the basis of what the market will bear.[17]

Mercedes-Benz cars are more expensive than the cars of its closest rivals because customers believe they offer more features and confer more status on their owners. Similarly, a BMW is not much more expensive to produce than a Honda, but its high price is determined by customers who want its distinctive sporty ride and the prestige of owning a BMW. (In fact, in Japan, BMW prices its entry cars quite modestly to attract young, well-heeled Japanese customers from Honda.) Similarly, Rolex watches do not cost much to produce, their design has not changed very much for years, and their gold content represents only a small fraction of the price. Customers, however, buy a Rolex because of the distinct qualities they perceive in it: its beautiful design, its intrinsic value, and its ability to confer status on its wearer.

■ **Strategic Choices** A differentiator invests its resources to gain a competitive advantage from superior innovation, excellent quality, and responsiveness to customer needs—the three principal routes to high product differentiation. For example, Procter & Gamble claims that its product quality is high and that Ivory soap is 99.44 percent pure. Maytag stresses reliability and the best repair record of any other washer on the market. IBM promotes the quality service provided by its well-trained sales force. Innovation is commonly the source of differentiation for technologically complex products, and many people pay a premium price for new and innovative products, such as a state-of-the-art computer, DVD player, or car.

When differentiation is based on responsiveness to customers, a company offers comprehensive after-sales service and product repair. This is an especially important consideration for complex products such as cars and domestic appliances, which are likely to break down periodically. Maytag, Dell Computer, and BMW all excel in responsiveness to customers. In service organizations, quality-of-service attributes are also very important. Neiman Marcus, Nordstrom, and FedEx can charge premium prices because they offer an exceptionally high level of service. Firms of lawyers, accountants, and consultants stress the service aspects of their operations to clients: their knowledge, professionalism, and reputation.

Finally, a product's appeal to customers' psychological desires is a source of differentiation. The appeal can be prestige or status, as it is with BMWs and Rolex watches; safety of home and family, as with Aetna or Prudential Insurance; or simply providing a superior shopping experience, as with Target and Macy's. Differentiation can also be tailored to age groups and socioeconomic groups. Indeed, the bases of differentiation are endless.

A company pursuing a business model based on differentiation frequently strives to differentiate itself along as many dimensions as possible. The less it resembles its rivals, the more it is protected from competition and the wider is its market appeal. Thus, BMWs offer more than prestige; they also offer technological sophistication, luxury, reliability, and good, although very expensive, repair service. All these bases of differentiation help increase sales.

Generally, a differentiator chooses to segment its market into many segments and niches, just as Samsung does. Strategic managers recognize the revenue-enhancing ability of being able to attract more customers willing to pay a premium price in each market segment. Some companies base their business models on offering a product designed for most market segments, but a company might choose to serve just the handful of segments in which it has a specific differentiation advantage. For example, Sony produces twenty-four models of television sets, filling all the niches from mid-priced to high-priced sets. However, its lowest-priced model is always priced about $60 above that of its competitors, bringing into play the premium-price factor. Consumers have to pay extra for a Sony. Similarly, although Mercedes-Benz has filled niches below its high-priced models with its S and C series, recently it has produced a car for the low-priced market segment. It sells this car only in Europe because it fears that introducing it in the United States would dilute its exclusive image and affect its differentiated appeal.

Finally, in choosing how to implement its business model, a differentiated company concentrates on developing distinctive competencies in the functions that provide the source of its competitive advantage. Differentiation on the basis of innovation and technological competency depends on the R&D function, as discussed in Chapter 4. Efforts to improve service to customers depend on the quality of the sales and customer service function.

Because developing a differentiation advantage is expensive, a differentiator has a higher cost structure than the cost leader does. However, building new competencies in the functions that sustain a company's differentiated appeal does not mean neglecting the cost structure. As noted earlier, the differentiator studies how the cost leader operates and attempts to copy cost-saving innovations that will reduce its costs while preserving the source of its competitive advantage. The differentiator must control all costs that do not contribute to its differentiation advantage so that the price of the product does not exceed what customers are willing to pay, as noted in Nordstrom's case. Otherwise, it risks letting the cost leader go upmarket and steal its customers. Also, since superior profitability is the result of controlling costs as well as maximizing value and revenues, it pays to watch costs closely. The key is not to minimize them to the point of losing the source of differentiation.[18] The owners of the famous Savoy Hotel in London, England, face just this problem. The Savoy's reputation has always been based on the incredibly high level of service it offers its customers. Three hotel employees serve the needs of each guest, and in every room, a guest can summon a waiter, maid, or valet by pressing a button at bedside. The cost of offering this level of service has been so high that the hotel makes less than 1 percent net profit every year.[19] Its owners try to find ways to reduce costs to increase profits, but if they reduce the number of hotel staff (the main source of the Savoy's high costs), they may destroy the main source of its differentiated appeal.

■ **Advantages and Disadvantages** The advantages of the differentiation strategy can also be discussed in the context of the five forces model. Differentiation safeguards a company against competitors to the degree that customers develop brand loyalty for its products, a valuable asset that protects the company on all fronts. Powerful suppliers are rarely a problem because the differentiated company's strategy is geared more toward the price it can charge than toward costs. Also, differentiators can often pass on price increases to customers because they are willing to pay the premium price. Thus, a differentiator can tolerate moderate increases in input prices better than the cost leader can. Differentiators are unlikely to experience problems with powerful buyers because they offer a distinct product. Only they can supply the product, and it commands brand loyalty. Differentiation and brand loyalty also create a barrier to entry for other companies seeking to enter the industry. New companies are forced to develop their own distinctive competency to be able to compete, an expensive undertaking.

Finally, the threat of substitute products depends on the ability of competitors' products to meet the same customers' needs as the differentiator's products and to break customers' brand loyalty. This can happen; phone companies are suffering as alternative ways of making phone calls through digital fiber-optic cable, satellite, and the Internet are becoming increasingly available. The issue is how much of a premium price a company can charge for distinctness before customers switch products. In the phone industry, the answer is "not much"; the large carriers were forced to reduce prices drastically so that 2.5 cents a minute is a common rate, down from 37 cents just a decade ago.

The main problems with a differentiation strategy center on strategic managers' long-term ability to maintain a product's perceived difference or distinctness in customers' eyes. What has become increasingly apparent is how quickly agile competitors move to imitate and copy successful differentiators. This has happened across many industries, such as retailing, computers, autos, home electronics, telecommunications, and pharmaceuticals. Patents and first-mover advantages (the advantages of being the first to market a product or service) last only so long, and as the overall quality of products produced by all companies goes up, brand loyalty declines. The problems L.L. Bean has had in maintaining its competitive advantage, described in Strategy in Action 5.2, highlight many of the threats that face a differentiator.

■ **Implications and Conclusions** A business model based on differentiation requires a company to formulate and implement business-level strategies that reinforce each other and together increase the value of a good or service in the eyes of customers. When a product has distinctness in customers' eyes, differentiators can charge a premium price. The disadvantages of a differentiation strategy are the ease with which competitors can imitate a differentiator's product and the difficulty of maintaining a premium price. When differentiation stems from the design or physical features of the product, differentiators are at great risk because imitation is easy. The risk is that, over time, products such as DVD players or televisions become commodity-like products, for which the importance of differentiation diminishes as customers become more price sensitive. However, when differentiation stems from functional-level strategies that lead to superior service or reliability, or from any intangible source, such as FedEx's guarantee or the prestige of a Rolex, a company is much more secure. It is difficult to imitate intangibles, and the differentiator can reap the benefits of this strategy for a long time. Nevertheless, all differentiators must watch out for imitators and be careful that they do not charge a price higher than the market will bear.

■ **Focused Differentiation**   As in the case of the focused cost leader, a company that pursues a business model based on **focused differentiation** chooses to specialize in serving the needs of one or two market segments or niches. Once it has chosen its market segment, a focused company positions itself using differentiation. If a company uses a focused differentiation approach, then all the means of differentiation that are open to the differentiator are available to the focused company. The point is that the focused company develops a business model that allows it to successfully position itself to compete with the differentiator in just one or a few segments. For example, Porsche, a focused company, competes against GM in the sports car and luxury SUV segments of the car market.

Strategy in Action

L.L. Bean's New Business Model

In 1911, Leon Leonwood Bean, a hunter who grew weary of walking miles with wet feet in search of game, decided he would invent a waterproof boot with leather uppers attached to a large rounded rubber base and sole. Soon he began selling his shoes through mail order, and as word spread about their reliability, backed by his policy of being responsive to customers who complained (often replacing their boots years after a sale), his company's reputation spread. As the years went by, L.L. Bean expanded its now well-known product line to include products such as its canvas tote bags and, of course, its flannel dog bed. By 2000 the company's mail order revenues exceeded $1 billion a year, and L.L. Bean became known for offering one of the broadest and highest-quality product lines of sporting clothes and accessories.

To display its product line, the company built a 160,000-square-foot signature store in Freeport, Maine, that stocks hundreds of versions of its backpacks, fleece vests, shirts, moccasins, tents, and other items, and over 3 million visitors a year shop its store. L.L. Bean established this store partly to give customers hands-on access to its products so that they would have a better understanding of the high quality they were being offered. Of course, L.L. Bean expects to command a premium price for offering such a wide variety of high-quality products, and historically it has enjoyed high profit margins. Customers buy its products for their personal use but also as gifts for friends and relatives.

Bean's business model began to suffer in the mid 1990s, however, when there was an explosion in the number of companies touting high-quality, high-priced products to customers, and Bean's catalogue lost its unique appeal. Furthermore, the growth of the Internet through the 1990s gave customers access to many more companies that offered quality products, often at much lower prices, such as

Lands' End, which also began to feature fleece vests, dog baskets, and so on in its product lineup. The problem facing any differentiator is how to protect or defend the uniqueness of its products from imitators, who will always be seeking to steal away its customers by offering them similar kinds of products at reduced prices.

Finding ways to protect Bean's business model has proved to be a major challenge. Its catalogue sales have been stagnant for several years because customers have switched loyalty to lower-priced companies, just as Ryanair stole away business from its well-known but much higher-cost competitors, the national airlines. Bean's current CEO, Chris McCormick, is trying to craft some new strategies to help the company build its competitive advantage. One of these is to build a chain of L.L. Bean stores in major urban locations to show more customers the quality of its products and so attract them to either buy them there or to use its website; it hopes to have ten stores open by 2010. This has not proved easy to date, however, because physical retail stores have a high cost structure, and Bean has had to search for the right way to implement its strategy. It has also had to lower the price of its sporting clothes and accessories in these stores; it can longer charge premium prices. Another strategy has been to launch an aggressive advertising campaign aimed at younger customers who may not know the Bean story. Then, with physical stores, the Internet, and its catalogues it may have a better chance of getting their business.

The jury is out, however. Not only are other differentiated sporting goods chains expanding, such as Dick's Sporting Goods and Gander Mountain, but sites like amazon.com and landsend.com, now owned by Sears, are offering lower-priced products. Whether McCormick will be able to successfully change L.L. Bean's business model to allow it to reach the value creation frontier remains to be seen.[b]

For the focused differentiator, selecting a niche often means focusing on one type of customer, such as serving only the very rich, the very young, or the very adventurous; or focusing on only a segment of the product line, such as only on vegetarian foods or very fast automobiles, designer clothes, or sunglasses. Focused differentiators are able to reach the value frontier because they are frequently able to develop a differentiated product that better meets the needs of customers in a particular segment than a differentiator (Figure 5.6). For example, a focused differentiator may gain better knowledge of the needs of a small customer set (such as sports car buyers), knowledge of a region, or expertise in a particular field (such as corporate law, management consulting, or website management for retail customers or restaurants). Alternatively, it might develop superior skills in responsiveness to customers, based on its ability to serve the particular needs of regional or industry customers in ways that a national differentiator would find very expensive. Similarly, concentration on a narrow range of products sometimes allows a focuser to develop innovations more quickly than a large differentiator can.

The focuser does not attempt to serve all market segments because that would bring it into direct competition with the differentiator. Instead, it concentrates on building market share in one market segment; if it is successful, it may begin to serve more and more market segments and chip away at the differentiator's competitive advantage. However, if it is too successful at what it does, or if it does try to compete with the differentiator, it may run into trouble because the differentiator has the resources to imitate the focused company's business model. For example, when Ben & Jerry's innovated a luxury ice cream, their huge success led other companies like Haagen-Dazs and Godiva to bring out their own competing products. A good example of another luxury product made by a focused differentiator is profiled in Strategy in Action 5.3.

Strategy in Action   5.3

Up, Up, and Away in the Restaurant Business

The restaurant business is crowded with thousands of companies, ranging from giant fast-food chains like McDonald's and Taco Bell, through more upscale chains like The Outback and Chili's, all the way up to expensive gourmet restaurants, which typically are found in major cities. Some of these expensive restaurants also have several branches in different cities, such as Brennan's or Ruth's Chris Steak House, but many are just single-establishment operations, run by a well-trained and sometimes well-known chef, that attract customers because of the quality of their food or the ingenuity of their cuisine.

In this top echelon of restaurants, which compete by the quality of their food and the impeccable way in which their waiters anticipate, not just respond to, customer needs, the drive to excel and beat the competition is ever present. The world-famous chef Alaine Ducasse opened a restaurant called the Essex House in New York in 2000. He deliberately set out to design a prix fixe menu (one that offers a number of different courses at a fixed price) that was the most expensive one in the world. He charged $160 a person for his meals, and his restaurant has been packed every day by rich people wishing to taste his mouth-watering cuisine.

In adopting this focused approach, however, Ducasse simply seemed to be opening the door to a new wave of specialized competitors in this most expensive of all market niches. In 2003, Japanese chef Masayoshi Takayama decided to offer his exquisite sushi at a prix fixe price that starts at $300. Not to be outdone, Chef Ducasse then appointed another world-famous chef, Christian Delouvrier, to take over at the Essex House, and he has now designed a menu that starts with a prix fixe of $225 a person but can go up to $400, serving such dishes as baby sea scallops topped with caviar, pâté de foie gras (a luxurious duck paté), and the freshest possible exotic seafood cooked to perfection.

How can these restaurants attract customers when they ask such exorbitant prices? The answer is that they limit the number of seats in their restaurants, often serving just a hundred or fewer people a night, and customers often book months in advance. By limiting the supply of seats, they create a scarcity for their products that drives up the prices they can charge and allows them to make high profits in this tiny market segment.

As in the case of cost leadership, many companies that started with a focus differentiation strategy have grown to become the leading differentiators in their industry. Sometimes they have achieved this through internal growth and by issuing stocks and building debt to raise the capital they needed to expand their businesses—as amazon.com and Google have done. At other times, a focus company may expand quickly by taking over other focused companies and combining their resources. For example, Cisco Systems, the largest Internet router maker, grew to be the leading differentiator in its industry by buying over fifty small specialist software and hardware companies. Its managers believed these companies possessed the products and knowledge that would allow it to become the leader, and despite the downturn in e-commerce, Cisco remains the dominant industry competitor.

In summary, a focused differentiator can protect its competitive advantage and niche to the extent that it can provide a product or service that its rivals cannot, for example, by being close to its customers and responding to their changing needs. However, if the focuser's niche disappears over time because of technological change or changes in customers' tastes, it cannot move easily to new niches, and this can be a major danger. For example, clothing store chain Brooks Brothers, whose focus was on providing formal business attire, ran into great difficulty in the 1990s when business casual became the clothing norm at most companies. It found it hard to adapt to the changing market and was bought out in 2001. Similarly, corner diners have become almost a thing of the past because they are unable to compete with the low prices and speed of fast-food chains like McDonald's and the upscale atmosphere of Starbuck's. The disappearance of niches is one reason that so many small companies fail.

The Dynamics of Competitive Positioning

So far we have discussed the differences between the kinds of generic strategies companies use to formulate and implement a particular business model. Each of the four models just discussed can be thought of as an "ideal" type of competitive positioning that results in competitive advantage and above-average profitability. The companies that are able to use these models to position themselves at the frontier are the most successful in their industry. In most industries, however, while some companies are able to pursue business-level strategies that allow them to reach the value creation frontier and obtain superior performance, other companies are unable to reach this frontier and have average or below-average profitability. As Figure 5.8 shows, companies in the retail industry such as Neiman Marcus, Foley's, Target, Wal-Mart, and Costco reach this frontier, but others like Nordstrom, Dillard's, Sears, and Kmart do not. The question is, why are some companies in an industry able to reach this frontier while others fail—even when they seem to be using the same business model, such as Wal-Mart and Kmart? Moreover, companies that can continually outperform their rivals, such as Dell and Wal-Mart, are rare. Many successful companies lose their position on the frontier at some point in their history, and to turn around their declining performance they need to change their business models.

To understand why some companies perform better than others and why the performance of one company can change over time, it is necessary to understand the dynamics involved in positioning a company's business model so it can successfully compete in the long term. In this section we first explore why some companies are able to sustain superior performance. Then we examine why differences in performance among companies in an industry are to be expected and why some companies run into major problems that can affect their survival.

FIGURE 5.8

The Dynamics
of Competitive
Positioning

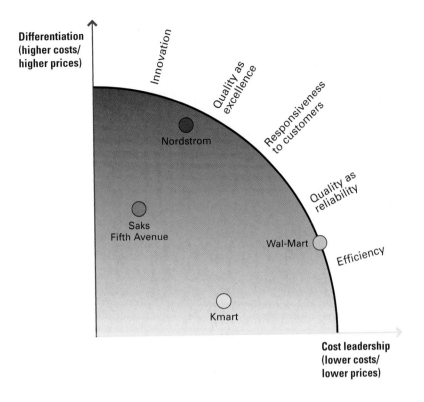

■ **Competitive**
Positioning
for Superior
Performance

Both differentiation and cost leadership are business models that can result in superior performance; many of the most successful companies in an industry are well known because they offer luxurious, excellent products or products that can be bought at a rock-bottom price. However, as we have emphasized throughout this chapter, no company can afford to ignore its cost structure. Managers must always try to find ways to reduce costs in this era of intense global competition in which new (focused) companies might appear with some kind of differentiation or cost advantage and use it to become a dominant competitor, as Toyota and Wal-Mart have done. At the same time, companies need to increase their market share to grow their profits over time, and this requires differentiation—finding new ways to increase product differentiation and market segmentation.

For these reasons, in the middle of the value creation frontier is an area occupied by companies whose intent is to develop business-level strategies to improve their differentiation and cost structure simultaneously. These **broad differentiators** also operate on the value frontier because they have chosen a level of differentiation that gives them a competitive advantage in the market segments they have targeted but have also pursued this strategy *in a way that has allowed them to lower their cost structure over time* (see Figure 5.9). Thus, although they may have higher costs than cost leaders, and offer a less differentiated product than differentiators, they have found a competitive position that offers their customers as much value as their industry rivals, and sometimes more. Broad differentiators continually use their distinctive competencies to increase the range of their products, and they are constantly seeking to enter new market segments to increase their market share to grow their profits.

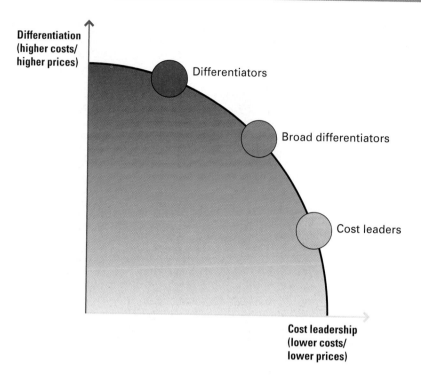

FIGURE 5.9

The Broad
Differentiation
Business Model

At the same time they also work continuously to find ways to lower their cost structure and increase their ROIC.

Importantly, the companies that have formulated and implemented the business-level strategies that enable them to get to this middle, or broadly differentiated, position may pose serious threats to both differentiators and cost leaders over time. These companies make a differentiated product that allows them to charge a premium price for their product compared to a cost leader. However, because of their low cost structure, they can choose to price their product with just *some "small" premium* over the price charged by cost leaders—and of course a much lower price than a differentiator has to charge to cover its higher cost structure. As a result, customers may now perceive the value offered by the broad differentiator's products to be well worth the premium price and so are attracted away from the cost leader's product. At the same time, those customers who are reluctant to pay the high premium price differentiators command may decide that the qualities of the broad differentiator's product (and its price) more than make up for the loss of the "extra" differentiated features of the luxury premium-priced products—such as a Mazda RX7 versus a Mercedes sports coupe or a regular pint of ice cream on sale versus a pint of Godiva.

Essentially, when they pursue their business model successfully, broad differentiators may steadily increase their market share over time; thus they grow their profits and gain increasing capital to reinvest in their business and continually improve their business model. And, in a dynamic, changing, competitive environment, this leads to a second problem for their rivals. Over time, their growing profits allow broad differentiators to invest in new technology that may both increase their differentiation advantage and lower their cost structure. As they build their competitive advantage, they become able to offer customers more and more value for money, which means that they push the value creation frontier to the right.

As broad differentiators constantly improve their business-level strategy to formulate and implement their broad differentiation business model, industry differentiators and cost leaders may find over time that they have lost the distinctive competencies that led to their superior performance. Toyota, profiled in Strategy in Action 5.4, provides a good example of a company that used a broad differentiation business model to put its rivals at a competitive disadvantage, with the result that today it is the second largest global carmaker by sales after GM, but many times as profitable as GM and most other global carmakers.

Strategy in Action   5.4

Toyota's Goal? A High-Value Vehicle to Match Every Customer Need

The car industry has always been one of the most competitive in the world because of the huge revenues and profits that are at stake: in 2004, annual global car sales were over $300 billion. It is small wonder, then, that industry rivalry has been increasing as carmakers have been fighting to develop new car models that better satisfy the needs of particular groups of buyers. One company at the forefront of these endeavors is Toyota.

Toyota, which pioneered lean production, produced its first car thirty years ago, an ugly, boxy affair that was, however, inexpensive. As the quality of its car became apparent, sales increased, and Toyota, which was then a focused cost leader, plowed back its profits into improving the styling of its vehicles and into efforts to continually reduce production costs. Over time, it used its low cost structure, including its efficient design processes, to produce an ever increasing range of reasonably priced vehicles tailored to different segments of the car market. By the 1980s its ability to go from the initial design stage to the production stage in two to three years allowed it to bring out new models faster than its competitors and to capitalize on the development of new market segments. Low costs and fast time to market have also allowed it to correct mistakes quickly if it designs a car that proves to have little market appeal—and Toyota has made mistakes.

In 1999, for example, Toyota brought out the Echo, a subcompact car that featured state-of-the-art engineering to deliver exceptional fuel economy: around fifty to sixty miles per gallon. The Echo was designed to be inexpensive to run and buy, and Toyota targeted this vehicle at buyers in their twenties, expecting them to appreciate these qualities. Its designers were disappointed when this age group displayed little enthusiasm for the car; its styling did not appeal to them even if its performance did fit their budget. The Echo's buyers turned out to be individuals in their forties who appreciated its economy and found it a useful second car to get around in.

Recognizing that they failed to position their product to hit the important market segment of young adults, the main car buyers of the future, Toyota's designers went back to the drawing board. Analyzing changing market trends and demographics, they sought to find the styling and features that would offer a car that was good-looking and fun to drive for this market segment and that could be sold for $16,000 to $18,000. Toyota (and several other carmakers) realized that perhaps the time was ripe for the return to the hatchback, but an updated version of it. Hatchbacks had been very popular in the early 1980s; however, the cars then were small and often had an ungainly appearance. Sales of hatchbacks had dropped off quickly when carmakers began to offer new sports utility vehicles and updated small sedans; by 1995, relatively few were available.

Drawing on its design and manufacturing competencies, Toyota's engineers updated and shaped the hatchback to suit the needs of the young adults in their twenties: the result was the Toyota Matrix, introduced in 2002 at a price starting at $17,000. The Matrix features revolutionary body styling reflective of much more expensive, sporty cars. It is spacious inside and geared to the needs of its intended young buyers; for example, seats fold back to allow for carrying a large cargo volume, and many storage bins and two-prong plugs for power outlets allow for the use of VCRs, MP3 players, and other devices. The message is that the Matrix is designed to be functional, fun, and a sporty ride. Then in 2003 Toyota introduced a new car, the Scion, once again a hybrid car designed to appeal to young people.

Toyota has also been a leader in positioning its whole range of vehicles to take advantage of emerging market segments. In the sports utility segment, its first offering was the expensive Toyota Land Cruiser, priced at over $35,000. Realizing the need for sports utility vehicles in other price ranges, it next introduced the 4Runner, priced at $20,000 and designed for the average sports utility customer; the RAV4, a small sports utility vehicle in the low $20,000 range, followed; then came the Sequoia, a bigger, more powerful version of the 4Runner in the upper $20,000 range. Finally, taking the technology from its Lexus R3000 vehicle, it introduced the luxury Highlander sports utility vehicle in the low $30,000 range. It now offers six models of sports utility vehicles, each offering a particular combination of price, size, performance, styling, and luxury to appeal to a particular customer group within the sports utility segment of the car market. Toyota also positions its sedans to appeal to different sets of buyers. For example, the Camry, one of the best-selling cars in the United States, is targeted toward the middle of the market, to customers who can afford to pay about $25,000 and want a balance of luxury, performance, safety, and reliability. The Camry also has a small premium price relative to similar cars of its U.S. competitors, such as the Ford Taurus and the GM Impala.

Toyota's broad differentiation business model is based, on the demand side, at making a range of vehicles that optimizes the amount of value it can create for different groups of customers. On the supply side, the number of models it makes is constrained by the need to maintain a low cost structure and to choose the car-pricing options that will generate maximum sales revenues and profits. The decision about how many kinds of vehicles to produce is also affected by the strategies of its rivals, for they are also trying to determine the optimum range of cars to produce. Toyota was not alone in its decision to produce a hatchback in 2002; other noticeable competitors included BMW, which introduced the redesigned Mini Cooper; Honda's new Civic hatchbacks; the already well-received PT Cruiser from DaimlerChrysler; and Ford's Focus. In fact, the number of hatchback models doubled between 2000 and 2002, as did the expected number of sales (to 650,000 vehicles). Competition in this market segment is now intense. Each car company needs to anticipate the actions of its rivals, and each hopes, like Toyota, that it has made the right choices to obtain a large share of customers in this important market segment.[c]

Why has Toyota been so successful in pursuing a business model based on broad differentiation? Toyota is a leader in continuously improving manufacturing techniques to lower its cost structure. Recall that changes in technology, such as the constantly improving flexible manufacturing technologies we discussed in Chapter 4, as well as new digital, electronic, and information technologies (which we examine in detail in Chapter 7), have made it possible for all companies to reduce their cost structure if they can implement it in the right way. New technologies also provide many opportunities to increase product differentiation while maintaining a low cost structure. Technological developments often provide many ways for a company that has traditionally pursued a pure differentiation strategy to do so at a significantly lower cost so that it can choose a lower pricing option and build demand.

Companies like Toyota are continuously experimenting with new ways to reduce costs and segment their markets. The use of robots and flexible manufacturing cells reduces the costs of retooling the production line, and the costs associated with small production runs make it much easier to produce a wide variety of vehicle models and maintain an efficient cost structure. Today, flexible manufacturing enables a company pursuing differentiation to manufacture a range of products at a cost comparable to that of the cost leader. BMW, for example, has taken advantage of flexible manufacturing technologies to reduce its costs, and it has also chosen to charge only a modest premium price to boost its sales revenues. This new strategy has worked: its market share and profitability have increased in recent years.

Indeed, the ability of flexible manufacturing to substantially reduce the costs of differentiating products has promoted the trend toward market fragmentation and niche marketing in many consumer goods industries, such as mobile phones, computers, and appliances. Another way that a differentiated producer may be able to realize significant economies of scale is by standardizing many of the component parts used in its end products. Toyota's various models of sports utility vehicles are built on only three different car platforms. As a result, Toyota is able to realize significant economies of scale in the manufacture and bulk purchase of standardized component parts, despite its high level of market segmentation.

The way in which a business model based on broad differentiation can disrupt industry competition and change the rules of the competitive game is illustrated in Figure 5.10, which contrasts the car industry as it was in the days of mass production with the industry in the days of lean production. The value frontier (V_0) represents the most value that could be produced using mass-production technology, and at this time GM was the broad differentiator, with its five divisions producing cars that gave it an 80 percent share of the U.S. car market. Toyota is shown as the focused cost leader on the value creation frontier because it was learning the skills involved in lean production. On the other hand, Porsche and Jaguar are shown as

FIGURE 5.10

Using a Business Model to Push Out the Value Creation Frontier

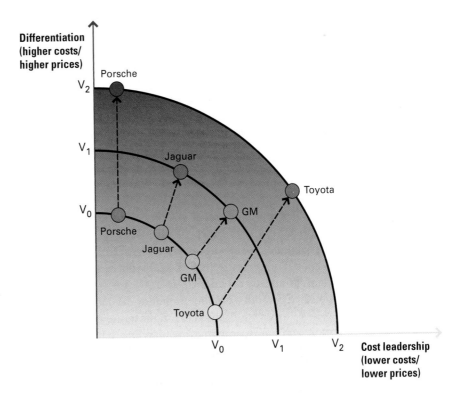

the differentiators on the value frontier: their pricey cars sold because of their innovative features, exceptional styling, and European origin.

On the V_0 frontier GM was the dominant company, but as Toyota grew, its continuous ability to make high-quality cars in an efficient way and then to expand into more and more market segments changed the rules of the competitive game. Today, in an era of lean production, Toyota is the successful broad differentiator and has pushed out the value frontier to V_2, meaning that customers now receive substantially more performance, safety, and luxury from their cars than they did ten or twenty years ago; in essence, they get more "value for their money." Where is GM today? To survive, GM has had to develop skills in lean manufacturing, and these have allowed it to move up to the V_1 frontier. However, GM cannot match Toyota's low cost structure, and it has also had to dramatically cut the number of models it offers customers because it cannot sell its cars at profitable prices. By 2004 its market share had fallen to 26 percent, and today it is creating far less value than Toyota, something reflected in its ROIC and stock price.

Jaguar, now owned by Ford, is also in a desperate position. Ford has tried to reduce Jaguar's cost structure and strengthen its styling and image, which has always been the key to its cars' differentiated appeal. By 2004, it was clear its strategies had not worked: demand for Jaguars has been falling while demand for BMWs, Mercedes, and Lexus's has been soaring. As for Porsche, it also had to learn lean production skills; however, its task is a little easier because it only produces a few sports car models. In addition, its engineers have kept their performance and handling at the leading edge of technological developments, so that today Porsche enjoys record sales and profits. Toyota and Porsche are on the value frontier at V_2; although GM and Jaguar have moved forward to V_1, their enormous losses in the last twenty years because of their failure to reach the value creation frontier have led to major falls in their market share and profits. Intense competition from ever advancing technology and from countries like China that have low-cost labor has been transforming competition in many industries, including the car industry. Increasingly carmakers have been trying to find ways to compete with Toyota and reach the new value frontier—however, Toyota is continually pushing the frontier out to the right.

One set of business-level strategies a broad differentiator commonly uses to maintain a low cost structure is to make a vehicle targeted at one segment of the global market and then allow only limited customization of that vehicle. Increasingly, for example, carmakers throughout the world are offering customers a mid-priced sedan with an economy, luxury, or sports package to appeal to this principal market segment. Package offerings substantially lower manufacturing costs because long production runs of the various packages are possible. Once again, the company is getting gains from differentiation and from low cost at the same time. Just-in-time inventory systems can also help reduce costs and improve the quality and reliability of a company's products. Toyota's cost of goods sold is the lowest of any carmaker, and although Ford and Chrysler have spent billions to lower their costs, Toyota continues to push the value frontier out to the right, as already mentioned. In 2004, for example, its hybrid car, the Prius, which is powered by both a gasoline engine and a battery, became popular because of rising gas prices. Toyota has licensed the rights to use its hybrid technology to Ford and GM, and more and more companies are planning to bring out a range of hybrid vehicles.

Finally, many companies, such as Dell and amazon.com, have been using the Internet and e-commerce as a way of becoming a broad differentiator. Both of these companies have been rapidly expanding the range of products they offer customers and taking advantage of their highly efficient materials-management systems to drive down costs compared to bricks-and mortar retailers. The Internet is a highly cost-effective way to inform millions of potential customers about the nature and quality of a company's products. Also, when customers do their own work on the Internet, such as by managing their own finances, stock trades, bill paying, travel booking, and purchasing, a company has shifted these costs to the customer and is no longer bearing them. Direct selling to the customer also avoids the need to use wholesalers and other intermediaries, which results in great cost savings. It has been estimated that 40 percent of the profit in a new car goes to the dealership that sells the car and for costs such as those associated with marketing the car.

■ **Competitive Positioning and Strategic Groups**   As the preceding discussion suggests, competition in an industry is dynamic. New developments such as (1) technological innovations that permit increased product differentiation, (2) the identification of new customer groups and market segments, and (3) the continual discovery of better ways to implement a business model to lower the cost structure continually change the competitive forces at work in an industry. In such a dynamic situation, the competitive position of companies can change rapidly. Some companies are able to gain from positioning themselves competitively to pursue broad differentiation. On the other hand, companies that are slow to recognize how their competitive position is changing because of the actions of their rivals may find their competitive advantage and ability to make above-average profits disappearing. Strategic-group analysis, which we discuss in Chapter 2, is a useful tool to help companies in an industry better understand the dynamics of competitive positioning so they can position themselves to achieve superior performance.

A company's business model determines how it will compete for customers in a particular market segment, market, or industry, and typically several companies are competing for the same set of customers. This means that the business-level strategies pursued by one company affect the strategies pursued by the others, and over time companies competing for the same customers become rivals locked in a competitive struggle. The goal is to be the company that reaches or pushes out the value frontier to obtain a competitive advantage and achieve above-average profitability.

Within most industries, strategic groups emerge, with all companies within each group pursuing a similar business model.[20] All companies in an industry competing to be the cost leader form one strategic group, all those seeking some form of differentiation advantage form another, and companies that have developed a broad differentiation strategy constitute another strategic group. Companies pursuing focused differentiation or focused cost leadership form yet other strategic groups.

The concept of strategic groups has a number of implications for competitive positioning. First, strategic managers must map their competitors according to their choice of business model. They can then identify the sets of strategies their rivals have decided to pursue, such as what customers' needs to satisfy, which customer groups to serve, and which distinctive competencies to develop. They can then use this knowledge to position themselves closer to customers and differentiate themselves from their competitors. In other words, careful strategic-group analysis allows managers to uncover the most important bases of competition in an industry and to identify products and market segments where they can compete most successfully for customers. Such analysis also helps to reveal what competencies are likely to be most valuable in the future so that companies can make the right investment decision. For example, the need to develop new models of cars that can be sold across the world and are assembled reliably by low-cost labor has dominated competitive positioning in the global car industry. U.S. car companies have bought or formed alliances with almost every foreign car manufacturer to obtain marketing, design, or manufacturing knowledge.

Second, once a company has mapped its competitors, it can better understand how changes taking place in the industry are affecting its relative standing vis-à-vis differentiation and cost structure, as well as identify opportunities and threats. Often a company's nearest competitors are those companies in its strategic group that are pursuing a similar business model. Customers tend to view the products of such companies as direct substitutes for each other. Thus, a major threat to a company's profitability can arise from within its own strategic group when one or more companies find ways to either improve product differentiation and get closer to customers or lower their cost structure. This is why today companies benchmark their closest competitors on major performance dimensions to determine if they are falling behind in some important respect. For example, UPS and FedEx are constantly examining each other's performance.

Because strategic-group analysis also forces managers to focus on the activities of companies in other strategic groups, it helps them to identify emerging threats from companies outside their strategic group, such as when a focused company has devised a business model that will bring sweeping changes to the industry. It also helps them understand opportunities that might be arising because of changes in the environment; in response to these changes, they might purchase a focused company and implement its business model across the entire company to absorb the threat.

Recall from Chapter 2 that different strategic groups can have a different standing with respect to each of Porter's five competitive forces because these forces affect companies in different ways. In other words, the risk of new entry by potential competitors, the degree of rivalry among companies within a group, the bargaining power of buyers, the bargaining power of suppliers, and the competitive force of substitute products can all vary in intensity among different strategic groups within the same industry. In the global car industry, for example, the smaller focused differentiators and cost leaders ran into trouble in the 1990s. Their input costs were rising, and they could not afford billions of dollars to design new models and build the new flexible manufacturing plants needed to produce them. Indeed, some European, Korean, and even Japanese companies started to lose billions of dollars. Large U.S. and European carmakers, which were also suffering from the emergence of Toyota and Honda as broad differentiators, realized that they had to reduce their cost structure to survive. The need to compete with Toyota and Honda led to a huge wave of global merger activity that has left just a handful of global giants to compete in the 2000s. For example, Daimler Benz took over Chrysler Suzuki, GM took control of Isuzu and Saab, Ford merged with Mazda and took over Jaguar and Volvo, and Renault took a controlling stake in Nissan to learn lean production techniques. Thus, the strategic group map in the global car industry changed dramatically. Today, only a handful of focused companies like BMW and Porsche remain, and even they have forged alliances with other carmakers. If they make a mistake in managing their business models, they will also become a target for one of the large global companies seeking to increase product differentiation.

In sum, strategic-group analysis involves identifying and charting the business models and business-level strategies that industry rivals are pursuing. Managers can then determine which strategies are successful and unsuccessful and why a certain business model is working or not. Importantly, they can also analyze how the relative competitive position of industry rivals, both those pursuing the same business model and those pursuing different business models, is changing over time. This knowledge allows them to either fine-tune or radically alter their business models and strategies to improve their competitive position.

■ Failures in Competitive Positioning

Successful competitive positioning requires that a company achieve a fit between its strategies and its business model. Thus, a cost leader cannot strive for a high level of market segmentation, as a differentiator does, and provide a wide range of products because those choices would raise its cost structure too much and the company would lose its low-cost advantage. Similarly, a differentiator with a competency in innovation that tries to reduce its expenditures on research and development, or one with a competency in after-sales service that seeks to economize on its sales force to decrease costs, is asking for trouble because it has implemented its business model in the wrong way.

To pursue a successful business model, managers must be careful to ensure that the set of business-level strategies they have formulated and implemented are working in harmony to support each other and do not result in conflicts that ruin the competitive position a company is aiming for through its choice of business model. Many companies, through neglect, ignorance, or error—perhaps because of the Icarus paradox discussed in Chapter 1—do not work to continually improve their business model, do not perform strategic-group analysis, and often fail to identify and respond to changing opportunities and threats in the industry environment. As a result, the company's business model starts to fail because its business-level strategies do not work together and its profitability starts to decline. Sometimes its performance can decline so quickly that the company is taken over by other companies or goes bankrupt.

These companies have lost their position on the value frontier, either because they have lost the source of their competitive advantage or because their rivals have found ways to push out the value creation frontier and leave them behind. Sometimes these companies initially pursued a successful cost-leadership or differentiation business model but then gradually began to pursue business-level strategies that worked against them. Unfortunately, it seems that most companies lose control of their business models over time, often because they become large, complex companies that are difficult to manage or because the environment is changing faster than they can change their business model—such as by adjusting product and market choices to suit changing industry conditions. This is why it is so important that managers *think strategically*.

In Chapter 1, we defined *strategic intent* as the way managers think about where they want their organization to be in the future and what kinds of resources and capabilities they will need to achieve this vision. Strategic intent provides a company with a sense of direction and stretches managers at all levels to be more inventive or innovative and to think how to make better use of resources. Moreover, it "implies a competitive distinct point of view about the future; it holds out to employees the promise of exploring new competitive territory."[21] The experience of Holiday Inns described in Strategy in Action 5.5 shows how a company can lose control of its business model, but also how managers can change it to suit the changing competitive landscape.

There are many factors that can cause a company to make competitive positioning errors. While some focused companies may succeed spectacularly for a time, a focuser can also make a major error when, in its rush to implement its business

Strategy in Action   5.5

Holiday Inns on Six Continents

The history of the Holiday Inns motel chain is one of the great success stories in U.S. business. Its founder, Kemmons Wilson, vacationing in the early 1950s, found motels to be small, expensive, and of unpredictable quality. This discovery, along with the prospect of unprecedented highway travel that would come with the new interstate highway program, triggered a realization: there was an unmet customer need—a gap in the market for quality accommodations. Holiday Inns was founded to meet that need. From the beginning, Holiday Inns set the standard for offering motel features such as air conditioning and icemakers while keeping room rates reasonable. These amenities enhanced the motels' popularity, and motel franchising, Wilson's invention, made rapid expansion possible. By 1960, Holiday Inns could be found in virtually every city and on every major highway. Before the 1960s ended, more than one thousand of them were in full operation, and occupancy rates averaged 80 percent. The concept of mass accommodation had arrived.

The service Holiday Inns offered appealed to the average traveler, who wanted a standardized product (a room) at an average price—the middle of the hotel room market. But by the 1970s, travelers were beginning to make different demands on hotels and motels. Some wanted luxury and were willing to pay higher prices for better accommodations and service. Others sought low prices and accepted rock-bottom quality and service in exchange. As the market fragmented into different groups of customers with different needs, Holiday Inns was still offering an undifferentiated, average-cost, average-quality product.

Although Holiday Inns missed the change in the market and thus failed to respond appropriately to it, the competition did not. Companies such as Hyatt siphoned off the top end of the market, where quality and service sold rooms. Chains such as Motel 6 and Days Inns captured the basic-quality, low-price end of the market. In between were many specialty chains that appealed to business travelers, families, or self-caterers (people who

want to be able to cook in their hotel rooms). Holiday Inns' position was attacked from all sides. As occupancy rates dropped drastically with increasing competition, profitability declined.

Wounded but not dead, Holiday Inns began a counterattack. The original chain was upgraded to suit quality-oriented travelers. Then to meet the needs of different kinds of travelers, Holiday Inns created new hotel and motel chains: the luxury Crowne Plazas; the Hampton Inns serving the low-priced end of the market; and the all-suite Embassy Suites. Thus Holiday Inns attempted to meet the demands of the many niches, or segments, of the hotel market that have emerged as customers' needs have changed over time. These moves were successful in the early 1990s, and Holiday Inns grew to become one of the largest suppliers of hotel rooms in the industry. However, by the late 1990s, falling revenues made it clear that with intense competition in the industry from other chains such as Marriott, Holiday Inns was once again losing its differentiated appeal.

In the fast-changing hotel and lodging market, positioning each hotel brand or chain to maximize customer demand is a continuing endeavor. In 2000, the pressure on all hotel chains to adapt to the challenges of global competition and become globally differentiated brands led to the takeover of Holiday Inns and its incorporation into the international Six Continents Hotels chain. Today, around the globe, more than 3,200 hotels flying the flags of Holiday Inn, Holiday Inn Express, Crowne Plaza, Staybridge Suites by Holiday Inn, and luxury Inter-Continental Hotels and Resorts are positioning themselves to offer the services, amenities, and lodging experiences that will cater to virtually every travel occasion and guest need. In the 2000s, the company has undertaken a massive modernization campaign in the United States to take existing full-service Holiday Inns to their next evolution. Holiday Inns plans to have a room to meet the need of every segment of the lodging market anywhere in the world.[d]

model, it overexpands and so loses control of its business model. Take People Express, a U.S. airline that was the first cost leader to emerge after deregulation of the U.S. airline industry. It started out as a specialized air carrier serving a narrow market niche: low-priced travel on the eastern seaboard. In pursuing focused cost leadership, it was very successful, but in its rush to expand to other geographic regions it decided to take over other airlines. These airlines were differentiators that had never pursued cost leadership, and the move raised the company's cost structure and it lost its competitive advantage against the other national carriers. In the end, People Express was swallowed up by Texas Air and incorporated into Continental Airlines. Herb Kelleher, the founder of Southwest Airlines, watched how People Express had failed, and he stuck to the cost-leadership business model. He took *twenty* years to build his national airline, but he never deviated from the strategies necessary to pursue cost leadership.

Interestingly, in 2004 Southwest announced it might do away with its strategy of no seat reservations and might make other changes to deal with its expanding route structure. This means that its top managers need to be vigilant in managing its cost structure. Another focus differentiator that ran into problems in 2004 was Krispy Kreme Doughnuts, which began to expand the number of its stores rapidly in the 2000s as demand for its tasty product soared. By 2004, its cost structure was out of control, and its failure to implement its business model, combined with the fall in the demand for doughnuts because of the Atkins diet craze, resulted in its first loss. By the end of 2004 the value of its stock had declined by 80 percent. The question is, can it recover?

Differentiators can also fail in the market and end up stuck in the middle if focused competitors attack their markets with more specialized or low-cost products that blunt their competitive edge. This happened to IBM in the large-frame computer market as PCs became more powerful and able to do the job of the much more expensive mainframes. Of course, the increasing movement toward flexible manufacturing has aggravated the problems facing both cost leaders and differentiators. No company is safe in the jungle of competition, and each must be constantly on the lookout to take advantage of competitive advantages as they arise.

In sum, strategic managers must employ the tools discussed in this book to continually monitor how well the business-level strategies that formulate and implement their company's business model are working. There is no more important task than ensuring that their company is optimally positioned against its rivals to compete for customers. And, as we have discussed, the constant changes occurring in the external environment, as well as through the actions of competitors who work to push out the value frontier, make competitive positioning a complex, demanding task that requires the highest degree of strategic thinking. This is why companies pay tens of millions of dollars a year to CEOs and other top managers who have demonstrated their ability to create and sustain successful business models.

Summary of Chapter

1. To create a successful business model, managers must choose business-level strategies that give a company a competitive advantage over its rivals; that is, they must optimize competitive positioning. They must first decide on (1) customer needs, or what is to be satisfied, (2) customer groups, or who is to be satisfied, and (3) distinctive competencies, or how customer needs are to be satisfied. These decisions determine which strategies they formulate and implement to put a company's business model into action.

2. Customer needs are desires, wants, or cravings that can be satisfied through the attributes or characteristics of a product. Customers choose a product based on (1) the way a product is differentiated from other products of its type and (2) the price of the product. Product differentiation is the process of designing products to satisfy customers' needs in ways that competing

products cannot. Companies that create something distinct or different can often charge a higher, or premium, price for their product.

3. If managers devise strategies to differentiate a product by innovation, excellent quality, or responsiveness to customers, they are choosing a business model based on offering customers differentiated products. If managers base their business model on finding ways to reduce costs, they are choosing a business model based on offering customers low-priced products.

4. The second main choice in formulating a successful business model is to decide which kind of product(s) to offer to which customer group(s). Market segmentation is the way a company decides to group customers, based on important differences in their needs or preferences, in order to gain a competitive advantage.

5. There are three main approaches toward market segmentation. First, a company might choose to ignore differences and make a product targeted at the average or typical customer. Second, a company can choose to recognize the differences between customer groups and make a product targeted toward most or all of the different market segments. Third, a company might choose to target just one or two market segments.

6. To develop a successful business model, strategic managers have to devise a set of strategies that determine (1) how to differentiate and price their product, and (2) how much to segment a market and how wide a range of products to develop. Whether these strategies will result in a profitable business model now depends on strategic managers' ability to provide customers with the most value while keeping their cost structure viable.

7. The value creation frontier represents the maximum amount of value that the products of different companies inside an industry can give customers at any one time by using different business models. Companies on the value frontier are those that have the most successful business models in a particular industry.

8. The value creation frontier can be reached by choosing among four *generic competitive strategies:* cost leadership, focused cost leadership, differentiation, and focused differentiation.

9. A cost-leadership business model is based on lowering the company's cost structure so it can make and sell goods or services at a lower cost than its rivals. A cost leader is often a large, national company that targets the average customer. Focused cost leadership is developing the right strategies to serve just one or two market segments.

10. A differentiation business model is based on creating a product that customers perceive as different or distinct in some important way. Focused differentiation is providing a differentiated product for just one or two market segments.

11. The middle of the value creation frontier is occupied by broad differentiators, which have pursued their differentiation strategy in a way that has also allowed them to lower their cost structure over time.

12. Strategic-group analysis helps companies in an industry better understand the dynamics of competitive positioning. In strategic-group analysis, managers identify and chart the business models and business-level strategies their industry rivals are pursuing. Then they can determine which strategies are successful and unsuccessful and why a certain business model is working or not. In turn, this allows them to either fine-tune or radically alter their business models and strategies to improve their competitive position.

13. Many companies, through neglect, ignorance, or error, do not work to continually improve their business model, do not perform strategic-group analysis, and often fail to identify and respond to changing opportunities and threats. As a result, their business-level strategies do not work together, their business model starts to fail, and their profitability starts to decline. There is no more important task than ensuring that one's company is optimally positioned against its rivals to compete for customers.

Discussion Questions

1. Why does each generic business model require a different set of business-level strategies? Give examples of pairs of companies in (a) the computer industry, (b) the electronics industry, and (c) the fast-food industry that pursue different types of business models.

2. How do changes in the environment affect the success of a company's business model?

3. What is the value creation frontier? How does each of the four generic business models allow a company to reach this frontier?

4. How can companies pursuing cost leadership and differentiation lose their place on the value frontier? In what ways can they regain their competitive advantage?

5. How can a focused company push the value frontier to the right? How does this affect other industry competitors? On the other hand, how can changes in the value frontier threaten focused companies?

6. Why is strategic-group analysis important for superior competitive positioning?

7. What are some of the reasons companies lose control over their business models, and thus their competitive advantage, over time?

Practicing Strategic Management

■ SMALL-GROUP EXERCISE
Finding a Strategy for a Restaurant

Break up into groups of three to five people, and discuss the following scenario. You are a group of partners contemplating opening a new restaurant in your city. You are trying to decide how to position your restaurant to give it the best competitive advantage.

1. Create a strategic-group map of the restaurants in your city by analyzing their generic business models and strategies. What are the similarities or differences between these groups?
2. Identify which restaurants you think are the most profitable and why.
3. On the basis of this analysis, decide what kind of restaurant you want to open and why.

■ ARTICLE FILE 5

Find an example (or several examples) of a company pursuing one of the generic business models. What set of business-level strategies does the company use to formulate and implement its business model? How successful has the company been?

■ STRATEGIC MANAGEMENT PROJECT
Module 5

This part of the project focuses on the nature of your company's business model and business-level strategies. If your company operates in more than one business, concentrate on either its core, or most central, business or on its most important businesses. Using all the information you have collected on your company so far, answer the following questions:

1. How differentiated are the products or services of your company? What is the basis of their differentiated appeal?

2. What is your company's strategy toward market segmentation? If it segments its market, on what basis does it do so?
3. What distinctive competencies does your company have? (Use the information on functional-level strategy in the last chapter to answer this question.) Is efficiency, quality, innovation, responsiveness to customers, or a combination of these factors the main driving force in your company?
4. What generic business model is your company pursuing? How has it formulated and implemented a set of business-level strategies to pursue this business model?
5. What are the advantages and disadvantages associated with your company's choice of business model and strategies?
6. Is your company a member of a strategic group in an industry? If so, which one?
7. How could you improve your company's business model and strategies to strengthen its competitive advantage?

■ EXPLORING THE WEB
Visiting the Luxury Car Market

Enter the websites of three luxury carmakers, such as Lexus (**www.lexususa.com**), BMW (**www.bmw.com**), and Cadillac (**www.cadillac.com, www.gm.com**), all of which compete in the same strategic group. Scan the sites to determine the key features of each company's business model and strategies. In what ways are their business models and strategies similar and different? Which of these companies do you think has a competitive advantage over the others?

General Task Search the Web for a company that is a differentiator, cost leader, or broad differentiator. What specific set of strategies does the company use to pursue its business model? How successful has it been in its industry? Has it reached the value frontier?

Closing Case

How E*TRADE Uses the Internet to Gain a Low-Cost Advantage

In many industries, new entrants have taken advantage of the opportunities opened up by the Internet to overcome barriers to entry and compete successfully against market leaders. Consider the situation of E*TRADE, the online brokerage company. For many years, large, established brokerages like Merrill Lynch had dominated the industry and used their protected positions to charge high brokerage fees. E*TRADE's managers bought and developed software and hardware that allowed their customers to make their own trades and to do so at a price as low as $19.95.

The low-cost competition story in the brokerage industry did not stop there. By 1999, E*TRADE itself had come under pressure from a new generation of online brokerage houses such as Suretrade, Ameritrade, and DLJ, which began offering customers trades for only $9.95 and even $7.95, undercutting E*TRADE's prices by 100 percent. How could E*TRADE, which had made its reputation by being the low-cost leader in the industry, compete against companies boasting that they were the new cost leaders?

The answer for E*TRADE was to enhance its differentiated appeal to its customers by offering a higher quality of service and a broader product line. E*TRADE introduced a new software package that made it even easier for customers to use the Internet to trade shares. Very importantly, the new software was more reliable in that customers were able to make their trades when they wanted. Previously, E*TRADE, like other brokerage companies, had experienced many problems when too many customers made trades at once; often the overloaded system simply crashed, and customers were unable to buy or sell shares. In addition, E*TRADE's new package offered customers more financial research tools and gave them access to more information about specific companies to aid in their investment decisions. E*TRADE also offered customers increased access to real-time stock quotes so that they could take advantage of second-to-second changes in stock prices. Finally, it offered customers the opportunity to invest in initial public offerings of shares from new companies, where both potential risks and returns are high.

In 1999, E*TRADE decided to merge with an online bank, TeleBank, so that it could offer its customers a broad range of online banking services, such as bill paying online, and thus become a one-stop online shopping site for all of a customer's financial needs. It also took over a variety of other insurance and financial service companies to offer its customers a broad financial service product line.

The realization that it could not just be a low-cost company but also had to create a differentiation advantage in the quickly evolving online financial services industry has paid off for E*TRADE. Its customers did not switch to the new low-cost leaders because they perceived that they were receiving extra value in terms of service and reliability for the $19.95 price. E*TRADE's customer accounts have increased steadily, and its stock price has risen as investors perceive that the company's competitive advantage is sustainable and that it is likely to remain a dominant player in the changed industry environment. Indeed, E*TRADE has shown the other companies in the industry that, to remain viable, they must all pursue a differentiation strategy to attract customers, even as they do all they can to control their cost structure.[22]

Case Discussion Questions

1. How have E*TRADE's business model and business-level strategies changed over time?

2. What is happening in the stockbrokerage industry today? How has E*TRADE been altering its business model and strategies to compete?

Chapter 6

Business-Level Strategy and the Industry Environment

Opening Case

Nike's Winning Ways

Nike, headquartered in Beaverton, Oregon, was founded over thirty years ago by Bill Bowerman, a former University of Oregon track coach, and Phil Knight, an entrepreneur in search of a profitable business opportunity. Bowerman's goal was to dream up a new kind of sneaker tread that would enhance a runner's traction and speed, and he came up with the idea for Nike's "waffle tread" after studying the waffle iron in his home. Bowerman and Knight made their shoe and began by selling it out of the trunks of their car at track meets. From this small beginning Nike has grown into a company that sold over $12 billion worth of shoes in the $35 billion athletic footwear and apparel industries in 2004.[1]

Nike's amazing growth came from its business model, which has always been based on two original functional strategies: to innovate state-of-the-art athletic shoes and then to publicize the qualities of its shoes through dramatic "guerrilla" marketing. Nike's marketing is designed to persuade customers that its shoes are not only superior but also a high fashion statement and a necessary part of a lifestyle based on sporting or athletic interests. A turning point came in 1987 when Nike increased its marketing budget from $8 million to $48 million to persuade customers its shoes were the best. A large part of this advertising budget soon went to pay celebrities like Michael Jordan millions of dollars to wear and champion its products. The company has consistently pursued this strategy: in 2003 it signed basketball star LeBron James to a $90 million endorsement contract, and many other sporting stars, such as Tiger Woods and Serena Williams, are already part of its charmed circle.

Nike's strategy to emphasize the uniqueness of its product has obviously paid off; its market share soared and its revenues hit $9.6 billion in 1998. However, 1998 was also a turning point, for in that year sales began to fall. Nike's $200 Air Jordans no longer sold like they used to, and inventory built up in stores and warehouses. Suddenly it seemed much harder to design new shoes that customers perceived to be significantly better. Nike's stunning growth in sales was actually reducing its profitability; somehow it had lost control of its business model. Phil Knight, who had resigned his management position, was forced to resume the helm and lead the company out of its troubles. He recruited a team of talented top managers from leading consumer products companies to help him improve Nike's business model. As a result, Nike has changed its business model in some fundamental ways.

In the past, Nike shunned sports like golf, soccer, rollerblading, and so on and focused most of its efforts on making shoes for the track and basketball market to build its market share in this area. However, when its sales started to fall, it realized that using marketing to increase sales in a particular market segment can only grow sales and profits so far; it needed to start to sell more types of shoes to more segments of the athletic shoe market. So Nike took its design and marketing competencies and began to craft new lines of shoes for new market segments. For example, it launched a line of soccer shoes and perfected their design over time, and by 2004 it had won the biggest share of the soccer market from its archrival Adidas.[2] In addition, in 2004 it launched its Total 90 III shoes, which are aimed at the millions of casual soccer players throughout the world who want a shoe they can just "play" in. Once more, Nike's dramatic marketing campaigns aim to make their shoes part of the "soccer lifestyle," to persuade customers that traditional sneakers do not work because soccer shoes are sleeker and fit the foot more snugly.

To take advantage of its competencies in design and marketing, Nike then decided to enter new market segments by purchasing other footwear companies that offered shoes that extended or complemented its product lines.[3] For example, it bought Converse, the maker of retro-style sneakers; Hurley International, which makes skateboards and Bauer in-line and hockey skates; and Official Starter, a licensor of athletic shoes and apparel whose brands include the low-priced Shaq brand. Allowing Converse to take advantage of Nike's in-house competencies has resulted in dramatic increases in the sales of its sneakers, and Converse has made an important contribution to Nike's profitability.[4]

Nike had also entered another market segment when it bought Cole Haan, the dress shoemaker, in the 1980s. Now it is searching for other possible acquisitions. It decided to enter the athletic apparel market to use its skills there, and by 2004 sales were over $1 billion. In making all these changes to its business model, Nike was finding ways to invest its capital in new products where it could increase its market share and profitability. Its new focus on developing new and improved products for new market segments is working. Nike's ROIC has soared from 14 percent in 2000 to 21 percent in 2004, and in 2004 it made over $1 billion in profits.

Overview

As Nike's success story suggests, a company's business model cannot just be created and left to take care of itself. If strategic managers do create a successful business model, they still face another challenge: the need to continually formulate and implement business-level strategies to sustain their competitive advantage over time in different kinds of industry environments. Different industry environments present particular kinds of opportunities and threats for companies, and a company's business model and strategies have to adapt and change to meet the changing environment.

This chapter first examines how companies in fragmented industries can develop new kinds of business-level strategies to strengthen their business models. It then considers the challenges of developing and sustaining a competitive advantage in embryonic, growth, mature, and declining industries. By the end of this chapter, you will understand how forces in the changing industry environment require managers to pursue new kinds of business-level strategies to strengthen their company's business model and keep it at the value creation frontier.

Strategies in Fragmented Industries

A *fragmented industry* is one composed of a large number of small and medium-sized companies—for example, the dry cleaning, restaurant, health club, and legal services industries. There are several reasons that an industry may consist of many small companies rather than a few large ones.[5]

First, fragmented industries are characterized by low barriers to entry because of the lack of economies of scale. Many homebuyers, for example, prefer dealing with local real estate agents, whom they perceive as having better local knowledge than national chains. Second, in some industries, there may even be diseconomies of scale. In the restaurant business, for example, customers often prefer the unique food and style of a popular local restaurant rather than the standardized offerings of some national chain. Third, low entry barriers that permit constant entry by new companies also serve to keep an industry fragmented. The restaurant industry exemplifies this situation. The costs of opening a restaurant are moderate and can be borne by a single entrepreneur. High transportation costs, too, can keep an industry fragmented, and local or regional production may be the only efficient way to satisfy customers' needs, as in the cement business. Finally, an industry may be fragmented because customers' needs are so specialized that only small job lots of products are required, and thus there is no room for a large mass-production operation to satisfy the market.

For some fragmented industries, these factors dictate that the focus business model will be the most profitable to pursue. Companies may specialize by customer group, customer need, or geographic region, so that many small specialty companies operate in local or regional markets. All kinds of custom-made products—furniture, clothing, hats, boots, and so on—fall into this category, as do all small service operations that cater to particular customers' needs, such as laundries, restaurants, health clubs, and furniture rental stores. Indeed, service companies make up a large proportion of the enterprises in fragmented industries because they provide personalized service to clients and therefore need to be responsive to their needs.

However, strategic managers are eager to gain the cost advantages of pursuing cost leadership or the sales-revenue-enhancing advantages of differentiation by circumventing the competitive conditions that have allowed focus companies to dominate an industry. Essentially, companies have searched for new business-level strategies that will allow them to consolidate a fragmented industry in order to enjoy the much higher potential returns possible in a consolidated industry. These companies include large retailers such as Wal-Mart and Target, fast-food chains such as McDonald's and Burger King, video rental chains such as Blockbuster Video and Hollywood Video (which announced a plan to merge in 2004), chains of health clubs such as Bally's and President and First Lady, repair shops like Midas Muffler, and even lawyers, consultants, and tax preparers.

To grow, consolidate their industries, and become the industry leaders, these companies have developed strategies such as chaining, franchising, creating a horizontal merger, and also using the Internet and information technology (IT) in order to realize the advantages of a cost-leadership or differentiation business model. In doing so, these companies have pushed out the value creation frontier to the right, with the result that many focus companies have lost their competitive advantage and have disappeared.

Many of the new leaders pioneered a new business model in an industry that lowers costs or confers a differentiation advantage (or both). They do this by competing in a very different way from established rivals. Managers in a fragmented industry must seek out cost or differentiation advantages that others have not recognized.

■ **Chaining**   Companies such as Wal-Mart and Midas International pursue a **chaining** strategy to obtain the advantages of cost leadership. They establish networks of linked merchandising outlets that are so interconnected by advanced IT that they function as one large business entity. The consolidated buying power that these companies possess through their nationwide store chains allows them to negotiate large price reductions with their suppliers, which promotes their competitive advantage. They overcome the barrier of high transportation costs by establishing sophisticated regional distribution centers, which can economize on inventory costs and maximize responsiveness to the needs of stores and customers. They also realize economies of scale from sharing managerial skills across the chain and from using nationwide, rather than local, advertising.

The U.S. food retail business during the 1950s, when supermarkets revolutionized the business model behind the selling of food products, is a good example of the advantages of chaining. Prior to the development of supermarkets, the food retail industry was fragmented, with many small mom-and-pop retailers selling a limited range of products and providing full service to customers, including home delivery. The first supermarkets were usually regionally based, with fewer than a hundred stores, and they differentiated themselves by offering a much larger selection of items in a big store layout. At the same time, they lowered their costs by moving from a full-service to a self-service strategy (they needed far fewer employees to run a store), and they passed on those cost savings to customers in the form of lower prices. In other words, the supermarkets competed in a very different way from established food retailers: they adopted a new business model.

As the supermarkets started to grow, opening hundreds of more stores, they were able to capture scale economies that were not available to smaller retailers. For example, by clustering their stores around central distribution warehouses in different cities and eventually regions, they were able to gain distribution efficiencies and reduce the amount of inventory they had to hold in a store. Also, by buying from vendors in large quantities, they were able to demand deep price discounts that they passed on to customers in the form of lower prices, enabling them to gain even more market share from smaller retailers. In the 1970s and 1980s, the supermarkets were also the first to introduce information systems based on point-of-sale terminals that tracked the sale of individual items. The information provided enabled the supermarkets to optimize their stocking of items, quickly cutting back on items that were not selling and devoting more shelf space to items that were selling faster. Reducing the need to hold inventory took even more costs out of the systems and ensured a good match between customer demands and items in the supermarket, which further differentiated the supermarkets from smaller retailers. Although these information systems were expensive to implement, the supermarkets could spread the costs over a large volume of sales. The small mom-and-pop retailers could not afford such systems because their sales base was too small. As a consequence of these developments, the food retail industry was becoming consolidated by the 1980s, a trend that is accelerating today. The small mom-and-pop food retailer is now almost extinct.

The new supermarket business model that provided cost and differentiation advantages over the old established mom-and-pop model has been applied to a wide range of retail industries, consolidating one after the other. Barnes & Noble and Borders applied the supermarket business model to book retailing, Staples applied it to office supplies, Best Buy to electronic retailing, Home Depot to building supplies, and so on. In each case, the companies that pursued a business model based on cost leadership or differentiation changed the competitive structure of the industry to its advantage, consolidating the industry and weakening the five forces of competition in the process.

◼ Franchising

Like chaining, franchising is a business-level strategy that allows companies, particularly service companies such as McDonald's or Century 21 Real Estate, to enjoy the competitive advantages that result from cost leadership or differentiation. In franchising, the franchisor (parent) grants to its franchisees the right to use the parent's name, reputation, and business model in a particular location or area in return for a sizable franchise fee and often a percentage of the profits.[6]

One particular advantage of this strategy is that because franchisees essentially own their businesses, they are strongly motivated to make the companywide business model work effectively and make sure that quality and standards are consistently high so that customers' needs are always satisfied. Such motivation is particularly critical for a differentiator that must continually work to maintain its unique or distinctive appeal. In addition, franchising lessens the financial burden of swift expansion and so permits rapid growth of the company. Finally, a nationwide franchised company can reap the advantages of large-scale advertising, as well as economies in purchasing, management, and distribution, as McDonald's does very efficiently in pursuing its cost-leadership model.

■ **Horizontal Merger**

Companies such as Anheuser-Busch, Dillard's, and Blockbuster have been choosing a strategy of *horizontal merger* to consolidate their respective industries. For example, Dillard's arranged the merger of regional store chains in order to form a national company. By pursuing horizontal merger, companies are able to obtain economies of scale or secure a national market for their product. As a result, they are able to pursue a cost-leadership or a differentiation business model (although, as we noted in Chapter 5, Dillard's has not been pursuing its differentiation model effectively). The many important strategic implications of horizontal merger are discussed in detail in Chapter 9.

■ **Using Information Technology and the Internet**

The arrival of new technology often gives a company the opportunity to develop new business strategies to consolidate a fragmented industry. eBay and amazon.com, for example, used the Internet, and the associated strategies e-commerce makes possible, to pursue a cost-leadership model and consolidate the fragmented auction and bookselling industries. Before eBay, the auction business was extremely fragmented, with local auctions in cities being the principal way in which people could dispose of their antiques and collectibles. By harnessing the Internet, eBay can now assure sellers that they are getting wide visibility for their collectibles and are likely to receive a higher price for their product. Similarly, amazon.com's success in the book market has accelerated the consolidation of the book retail industry, and many small bookstores have closed because they cannot compete by price or selection. Clear Channel Communications, profiled in Strategy in Action 6.1, has used many of the strategies discussed above to become the biggest radio broadcaster in the United States.

The challenge in a fragmented industry is to figure out the best set of strategies to overcome a fragmented market so that the competitive advantages associated with pursuing one of the different business models can be realized. It is difficult to think of any major service activities—from consulting and accounting firms to businesses satisfying the smallest customer need, such as beauty parlors and car repair shops—that have not been consolidated by companies seeking to pursue a more profitable business model.

Strategies in Embryonic and Growth Industries

As Chapter 2 discusses, an embryonic industry is one that is just beginning to develop, and a growth industry is one in which first-time demand is expanding rapidly as many new customers enter the market. In choosing the strategies needed to pursue a business model, embryonic and growth industries pose special challenges because the *attributes of customers change* as market demand expands and *new groups of customers* who have different and evolving needs emerge. Also, other factors affect the rate at which a market grows and expands. Strategic managers have to be aware of the way competitive forces in embryonic and growth industries change over time because they

Strategy in Action

6.1

Clear Channel Creates a National Chain of Local Radio Stations

In 2004, Clear Channel Communications, Inc., based in San Antonio, Texas, operated over 1,200 U.S. radio stations, far more than its largest competitors: Viacom with 220 and Citadel with 205. The company started out with only one station in San Antonio in 1995, following a pattern that used to be typical of the radio broadcasting industry. Historically, the industry was fragmented because a federal law prevented any company from owning more than 40 stations nationwide; as a result, a large proportion of the local radio stations were independently owned and operated.

Clear Channel took advantage of the repeal of this law in 1996 to start to buy up radio stations and, most importantly, to develop a business model (which today is one of *broad differentiation*) that would allow it to obtain the gains from consolidating this fragmented industry. Its strategic managers recognized from the beginning that the major way to increase the profitability of city and small town radio stations was to obtain economies of scale from operating and marketing on a national level. The issue was to find ways to raise the quality of its programming to increase its value to listeners, increase the number of listeners, and thus increase advertising revenues (because advertising rates are based on the number of listeners). At the same time, it needed to find ways to reduce each station's high operating costs, that is, lower its cost structure. How to do both simultaneously was the challenge.

On the value side of the equation, an important issue was how to achieve economies of scale from having a national reach while maintaining local ties to the community. Many listeners like to feel they are listening to a local station that understands who they are and what their needs are. Yet if all programming and service are handled on a local level, how can economies of scale from a national base be achieved? Most cost savings come from standardizing service across stations, from broadcasting uniform content. In addition, local listeners often become used to the glitzy, slick productions put on by national cable television broadcasting companies such as MTV and the main TV networks. Because they are national, these companies can afford to pay large sums to stars and celebrities and invest heavily in developing quality products. Such large expenditures are beyond most radio stations' budgets and simply increase the cost of goods sold too much. Moreover, advertising rates had to be kept at a level that both large national

companies and small local ones would find acceptable; they could not simply be raised to cover higher costs.

Clear Channel's managers began to experiment with information technology and the Internet and took advantage of emerging digital technology that allowed for the easy and rapid manipulation and transfer of large volumes of data. By the late 1990s, music and programming could easily be recorded, stored in digital format, and edited. Its managers hit on a strategy called "voice tracking." To obtain economies of scale, Clear Channel employed popular regional or national DJs to record its daily programs, and these same DJs customized their productions to suit the needs of local markets. For example, one technology allows DJs to isolate and listen to the end of one track and the beginning of the next; then they can insert whatever talk, news, or information is appropriate between tracks as and when they like. The local stations supply this local information; after they have customized their program, the DJs send it over the Internet, where the local operators handle it. This practice has enormous advantages. On the cost side, the programming costs of a limited number of popular DJs are much lower than the cost of employing an army of local DJs. On the differentiation side, the quality of programming is much higher because Clear Channel can invest more in its programming and because the appeal of some DJs is much higher than others. Over time, higher-quality programming increases the number of listeners, and this attracts more national advertisers, whose digital advertisements can be easily inserted in the programming by local operators.

In addition, Clear Channel is developing its own proprietary brand name, KISS, across its radio stations so that when people travel, they will be attracted to its local stations wherever they are. It also hopes this move will stimulate word-of-mouth advertising. As its brand becomes national, this widened scope will attract larger advertisers and boost its sales revenues. To speed this process, Clear Channel is also linking its different businesses—for example, it is the largest billboard and concert operator in the United States—to its KISS label. It hopes that the resulting increased customer demand will drive up advertising revenues, which will allow it to start or buy more radio stations and expand its reach, thereby lowering its cost structure and increasing its future profitability.[a]

commonly have to build and develop new kinds of competencies and refine their business models to compete effectively in the long term.

Most embryonic industries emerge when a technological innovation creates new product or market opportunities. For example, a century ago, the car industry was born following the development of a new technology, the internal combustion engine, which gave rise to many new products, including the motorcar and motorbus. In 1975, the PC industry was born after new microprocessor technology was developed to build the world's first commercially available PC, the Altair 8800, sold by MITS. Shortly afterward, the PC software industry was born when a Harvard dropout, Bill Gates, and his old school friend, Paul Allen, wrote a version of a popular computer language, BASIC, that would run on the Altair 8800.[7] In 1986, the Internet protocol (IP) network equipment industry was born following the development of the router, an IP switch, by an obscure California start-up, Cisco Systems.

Customer demand for the products of an embryonic industry is frequently limited at first, for a variety of reasons. Moreover, strategic managers who understand how markets develop are in a much better position to pursue a business model and strategies that will lead to a sustained competitive advantage. Reasons for slow growth in market demand include (1) the limited performance and poor quality of the first products, (2) customer unfamiliarity with what the new product can do for them, (3) poorly developed distribution channels to get the product to customers, (4) a lack of complementary products to increase the value of the product for customers, and (5) high production costs because of small volumes of production.

Customer demand for the first cars, for example, was limited by their poor performance (they were no faster than a horse, far noisier, and frequently broke down), a lack of important complementary products such as a network of paved roads and gas stations, and high production costs, which made them a luxury item. Similarly, demand for the first PCs was limited because buyers had to be able to program a computer to use it, and there were no software application programs that could be purchased to run on the PCs. Because of such problems, early demand for the products of embryonic industries comes from a small set of technologically sophisticated customers who are willing to put up with, and may even enjoy, imperfections in the product. Computer hobbyists, who got great joy out of tinkering with their imperfect machines and finding ways to make them work, bought the first PCs.

An industry moves from an embryonic to a growth stage when a *mass market* starts to develop for the industry's product (a mass market is one in which large numbers of customers enter the market). Mass markets typically start to develop when three things occur: (1) ongoing technological progress makes a product easier to use and increases the value of the product to the average customer, (2) key complementary products are developed that do the same, and (3) companies in the industry strive to find ways to reduce production costs so they can lower their cost structure and choose a low price option, and this stimulates high demand.[8] For example, a mass market for cars emerged when (1) technological progress increased the performance of cars, (2) a network of paved roads and gas stations was established (which meant a car could go more places and thus had more value), and (3) Henry Ford began to mass-produce cars, which dramatically lowered production costs and allowed him to reduce prices, causing the demand for cars to surge. Similarly, the mass market for PCs started to emerge when technological advances made them easier to use, a supply of complementary software such as spreadsheets and word processing programs was developed that increased the value of owning a PC, and companies in the industry started to use mass production to build PCs at low cost.

FIGURE 6.1

Market Development
and Customer Groups

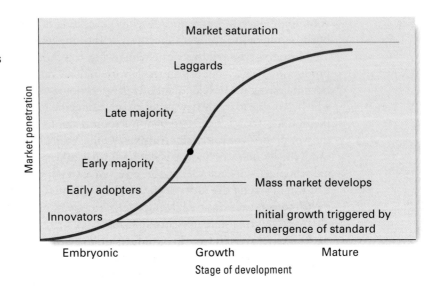

The development of most markets follows an **S**-shaped growth curve similar to that illustrated in Figure 6.1.

Strategic managers who understand how the demand for a product is affected by changing customer needs and groups can focus their energies on developing new strategies to protect and strengthen their business models, such as building competencies in low-cost manufacturing or speedy product development. One strategy, for example, would be to share information about new products under development with the companies that supply complementary products so that customers will be convinced the new product is worth buying. Another strategy would be to involve customers in the product development process to gain their input and their acceptance of a new product.

■ **The Changing Nature of Market Demand**

The development of most markets follows an **S**-shaped growth curve similar to that illustrated in Figure 6.1. As the stage of market development moves from embryonic to mature, customer demand first accelerates and then decelerates as a market approaches saturation. As we note in Chapter 2, in a saturated market, most customers have already bought the product, and demand is limited to replacement demand; the market is mature. Figure 6.1 shows that different groups of customers who have different needs enter the market over time—and this has major implications for a company's product differentiation and market segmentation decisions.

The first group of customers to enter the market are referred to as the *innovators*. Innovators are "technocrats" who get great delight from being the first to purchase and experiment with products based on a new technology, even though that technology is imperfect and expensive. They often have an engineering mindset and want to own the technology for its own sake. In the PC industry, the first customers were software engineers and computer hobbyists who wanted to write computer code at home.[9]

The *early adopters* are the second group of customers to enter the market. Early adopters understand that the technology might have important future applications and are willing to experiment with it to see if they can pioneer uses for it, often by finding new ways to satisfy customer needs. Early adopters are often visionaries who appreciate how the technology may be used in the future and try to be the first to profit from its use. Jeff Bezos, the founder of amazon.com, was an early adopter of the Internet and web-based technology, who saw in 1994 that the Internet could be used in innovative ways to sell books. He saw this possibility before anyone else and was one of the first dot-com pioneers to purchase web servers and related software and use it to sell products over the Internet. Amazon was thus an early adopter.

Both innovators and early adopters enter the market while the industry is in its embryonic stage. The next group of customers, the *early majority,* represents the leading wave or edge of the mass market; their entry signifies the beginning of the growth stage. Customers in the early majority are comfortable with the new technology and products. However, they are pragmatists: they weigh the benefits of adopting new products against their costs and wait to enter the market until they are confident that products will offer them tangible benefits. Once they start to enter the market, however, they do so in large numbers. This is what happened in the PC market after IBM's introduction of the PC in 1981. For the early majority, IBM's entry into the market legitimized the technology and signaled that the benefits of adoption would be worth the costs of purchasing and learning to use the product. The growth of the PC market was then given further impetus by the development of important applications that added value to it, such as new spreadsheet and word processing programs. These applications transformed the PC from a hobbyist's toy into a business productivity tool.

Once the mass market attains a critical mass, with something like 30 percent of the potential market penetrated, the next wave of customers enters the market. This wave is characterized as the *late majority:* the customers who purchase a new technology or product only when it is clear it will be around for a long time. A typical late majority customer group is the customers who started to enter the PC market in the mid 1990s who were older and somewhat intimidated by computers. However, watching others similar to themselves buying PCs to send e-mail and browse the Web, they overcame their hesitancy and started to purchase PCs. By 2002, some 65 percent of homes in the United States had at least one PC, suggesting that the product was well into the late majority group and thus the market was approaching saturation. Indeed, the entry of the late majority signals the end of the growth stage.

Laggards, the last group of customers to enter the market, are inherently conservative and technophobic. They often refuse to adopt a new technology even if its benefits are obvious or unless they are forced by circumstances—to reply to a colleague's e-mail, for example—to do so. People who stick to using typewriters rather than computers to write letters and books could be considered laggards today.

Figure 6.2 looks at the differences among these groups of consumers in a somewhat different way. The bell-shaped curve represents the total market, and the divisions in the curve show the percentage of customers who on average fall into each customer group. The early adopters are a very small percentage of the total customers who will ultimately buy the product. Thus, the figure illustrates a vital competitive fact: *Most market demand and industry profits arise when the early and late majority enter the market.* And research has found that although many of the early pioneering companies do well in attracting innovators and early adopters, many of these companies often *fail* to attract a significant share of early and late majority customers and ultimately go out of business.

■ Strategic Implications: Crossing the Chasm

Why are pioneering companies often unable to create a business model that allows them to be successful over time and remain the market leaders? *Innovators and early adopters have very different customer needs from the early majority.* In an influential book, Geoffrey Moore argues that because of the differences in customer needs

FIGURE 6.2

Market Share of
Different Customer
Segments

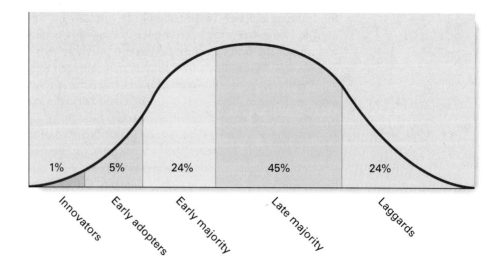

between these groups, the business-level strategies required for companies to succeed in the emerging mass market are quite different from those required to succeed in the embryonic market.[10] Pioneering companies that do not change the strategies they use to pursue their business model will therefore lose their competitive advantage to those companies that implement new strategies that push the value creation frontier out to the right. Different strategies are often required to support and strengthen a company's business model as a market develops over time, for the following reasons:

- Innovators and early adopters are technologically sophisticated individuals who are willing to tolerate engineering imperfections in the product. The early majority, however, value ease of use and reliability. Companies competing in an embryonic market typically pay more attention to increasing the performance of a product than to its ease of use and reliability. Those competing in a mass market need to make sure that the product is reliable and easy to use. Thus, the product development strategies required for success are different as a market develops over time.

- Innovators and early adopters are typically reached through specialized distribution channels, and products are often sold by word of mouth. Reaching the early majority requires mass-market distribution channels and mass media advertising campaigns that require a different set of marketing and sales strategies.

- Because innovators and the early majority are relatively few in number and are not particularly price sensitive, companies serving them typically pursue a focus model and produce small quantities of a product. To serve the rapidly growing mass market, a cost-leadership model based on large-scale mass production may be critical to ensure that a high-quality product can be produced reliably at a low price point.

In sum, the business model and strategies required to compete in an embryonic market populated by early adopters and innovators are very different from those required to compete in a high-growth mass market populated by the early majority.

FIGURE 6.3

The Chasm: AOL and
Prodigy

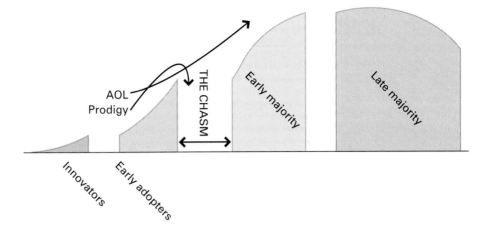

As a consequence, the transition between the embryonic market and the mass market is not a smooth, seamless one. Rather, it represents a *competitive chasm,* or gulf, that companies must cross. According to Moore, many companies do not or cannot develop the right business model; they fall into the chasm and go out of business. This insight is consistent with the observation that although embryonic markets are frequently populated by large numbers of small companies, once the mass market begins to develop, the number of companies in the marketplace drops off sharply.[11]

Figure 6.3, which compares the strategies of AOL Time Warner and Prodigy, illustrates Moore's thesis by showing that a wide chasm exists between innovators and the early majority, that is, between the embryonic market and the rapidly growing mass market. Note also that other smaller chasms exist between other sets of customers, and that these too represent important, although less dramatic, breaks in the nature of the market that require changes in business-level strategy (for example, a different approach to market segmentation). The implication of Moore's thesis is that a company must often formulate and implement new strategies, and build new competencies, if it is to create a business model that can successfully cross the chasm. Strategy in Action 6.2 describes how the early leader in online services, Prodigy, fell into the chasm, while AOL successfully built a business model to cross it.

To cross this chasm successfully, managers must correctly identify the customer needs of the first wave of early majority users—the leading edge of the mass market. Once companies have identified these customers needs, they must alter their business model by developing new strategies to redesign products and create distribution channels and marketing campaigns to reach the early majority. In this way, they will have ready a suitable product, at a reasonable price, that they can sell to the early majority as they start to enter the market in large numbers. In sum, industry pioneers must abandon their old focused business model that was directed solely on the needs of their early or initial customers, because this focus may lead them to ignore the needs of the early majority and the need to pursue a differentiation or cost-leadership model to become the dominant competitor in the future.

Strategy in Action 6.2

How Prodigy Fell into the Chasm

Before America Online (AOL) became a household name, Prodigy Communications was a market leader. Founded in 1984, Prodigy was a joint venture between Sears, IBM, and CBS. CBS soon dropped out, but IBM and Sears stuck with it, investing $500 million in developing the network and finally launching it in 1990. Prodigy's business model was differentiation, and the goal was to build the largest proprietary online shopping network: the system would give its customers the ability to buy anything, even plane tickets, online. IBM knew about computers, and Sears knew about retail. It seemed like the perfect marriage.

Launched in the fall of 1990, the service quickly accumulated half a million users. There was little sense of competition at the time. The largest competitor, CompuServe, was conservatively managed, and it pursued a focused business model based on servicing the needs of technical users and financial services (CompuServe was owned by H&R Block, America's largest tax return service). There was another small competitor, AOL, but in the words of one Prodigy executive, "It was just a little thing off to the side." Ten years later, the little thing had become the largest online service in the world, with 33 million members, and Prodigy had exited the online business altogether after IBM and Sears had invested, and lost, some $1.2 billion on the venture.

Why did Prodigy fail? The company appeared to be focusing on the mass market. Its target customers were not computer-oriented early adopters but typical middle-class Americans. And its business model to sell products online seemed correct; surely this ultimately had to become a major application of the Internet. The problem was that Prodigy's managers did not choose the right set of strategies to formulate the business model; in particular, they did not understand the full range of needs customers were trying to satisfy by using the Internet.

One of the surprise early drivers of customer demand for online services, and a major factor in creating the mass market, was e-mail. AOL's strategy was to offer its members unlimited e-mail, but Prodigy charged members a fee for sending more than thirty e-mails per month—a big difference in business models. Another important application of online service was chatrooms, a service that customers were increasingly embracing. AOL saw chatrooms as one of the unique possibilities of online service for satisfying customer needs, and its strategy was to quickly implement the software that would soon make chatrooms one of its most popular features.

The lawyers at Prodigy's corporate headquarters, however, feared that Prodigy might be held legally liable for comments made in chatrooms or events that arose from them, and they discouraged Prodigy from offering this service. This censorship, lack of chatrooms, and charges for e-mail rankled members, who soon started to switch in droves to AOL.

The nature of the software interface used to allow customers to connect to an online service also became a critical competitive issue as the market developed. When it was introduced, Prodigy's primitive graphical user interface was acceptable by the PC standards of the time, which were based on Microsoft's MS-DOS operating system. When Microsoft introduced its much more user-friendly Windows 3.0 systems in 1990, AOL moved quickly to redesign its software interface to be compatible with Windows, and this made AOL much easier to use. Prodigy, however, was part owned by IBM, which at that time was trying to promote its own new PC operating system, the ill-fated OS/2. So Prodigy dragged its feet. It waited to implement a Windows version of its own interface until December 1993, by which time it had lost the majority of Windows users to AOL.

By 1996, the battle was effectively over: AOL was growing by leaps and bounds and Prodigy was losing customers at a rapid pace because its strategies had pushed out the value frontier. AOL, by correctly sensing the way customer needs were changing and then providing a differentiated product that met those needs, crossed the chasm with ease.[b]

■ Strategic Implications of Market Growth Rates

A final important issue that strategic managers must understand in embryonic and growth industries is that different markets develop at different rates. The speed at which a market develops can be measured by its growth rate, that is, the rate at which the industry's product is bought by customers in that market. Figure 6.4 charts the growth rates of a number of important products in the United States

FIGURE 6.4

Differences in Diffusion Rates

Source: Peter Brimelow, "The Silent Boom," *Forbes,* July 7, 1997, pp. 170–171. Reprinted by permission of Forbes Magazine © 2002 Forbes, Inc.

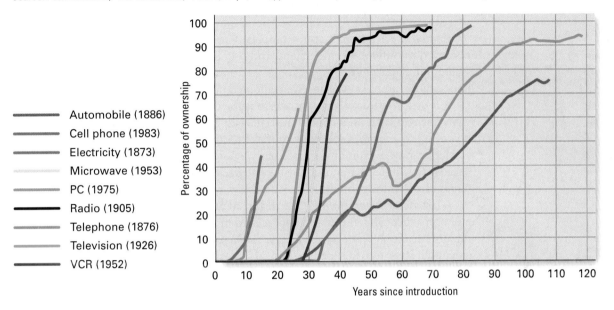

from their initial introduction to the present time. Although many of these products display the classic **S**-shaped growth curve, their markets have grown at different rates. For example, demand for TVs has grown more rapidly than demand for cars. The market growth rates for new kinds of products seem to have accelerated over time, probably because the increasing use of the mass media and low-cost mass production help to accelerate the demand for new products. However, there are also differences in the growth rate for new products introduced at around the same time. For example, the cell phone was introduced somewhat later than the PC, and yet market demand has grown more rapidly.

■ **Factors Affecting Market Growth Rates**

A number of factors explain the variation in market growth rates for different products and thus the speed with which a particular industry develops. It is important for strategic managers to understand the source of these differences, for by their choice of business model and strategies, they can accelerate or retard the rate at which a particular market grows.[12] *In other words, business-level strategy is a major determinant of industry profitability.*

The first factor that accelerates customer demand is a new product's *relative advantage*, that is, the degree to which a new product is perceived as better at satisfying customer needs than the product it supersedes. For example, the early growth in demand for cell phones was partly driven by their economic benefits. Studies showed that because business customers could always be reached by cell phone, they made better use of their time—for example, by not showing up at a meeting that had been cancelled at the last minute—and saved two hours per week in time that would otherwise have been wasted. For busy executives, the early adopters, the productivity benefits of owning a cell phone outweighed the costs. Cell phones also diffused rapidly for social reasons, in particular, because they conferred glamour or prestige on their users (something that also drives demand for advanced kinds of hand-held computers and smart phones).

Another factor driving growth in demand is *compatibility*, the degree to which a new product is perceived as being consistent with the current needs or existing values of potential adopters. Demand for cell phones grew rapidly because their operation was compatible with the prior experience of potential adopters who used traditional wire-line phones.

Complexity is a third factor. Complexity is the degree to which a new product is perceived as difficult to understand and use. Early PCs with their clunky operating system interfaces were complex to use and so were slow to be adopted. The first cell phones were simple to use and were adopted quickly.

A fourth factor is *trialability*, which is the degree to which a new product can be experimented with on a hands-on trial basis. Many people first used cell phones by borrowing one from a colleague to make a call, and this positive experience helped accelerate growth rates. In contrast, early PCs were more difficult to experiment with because they were rare and expensive and because some training was needed in how to use them. These complications led to slower growth rates.

A last factor is *observability*, the degree to which the results of using and enjoying a new product can be seen and appreciated by other people. The PalmPilot diffused rapidly because it was easy to observe how easily its users could schedule meetings, enter addresses, record expenses, and so on. The convenience of the device was clear, and the same was true of the cell phone, so they were rapidly adopted.

Young companies must be sure to use devise strategies that address these issues if they are to grow their market share. Nike, for example, worked hard to show how its new sneakers offered customers major advantages in sports performance and how its new shoes were compatible with the sporting lifestyle that was sweeping the United States. Obviously, trialability was easy and complexity was low, for its shoes were conveniently displayed and could be tried on in stores. Nike also used its guerrilla marketing to increase the observability of its products, and as people watched others wearing Nike shoes, a kind of contagion effect took over as people just had to have a pair of its shoes. Thus Nike was highly successful in using these strategies to pursue its differentiation business model.

■ Strategic Implications of Differences in Growth Rates

From a strategic perspective, companies can increase the demand for a new product if they develop business-level strategies to clearly show its relative advantage, make it as compatible as possible with customers' prior needs and experiences, reduce its complexity, and make it possible for customers to try out or observe others using the product. These considerations must drive the product development process that takes a product from the design stage and puts it into customers' hands. Companies that develop the distinctive competencies needed to do this gain a competitive advantage and thus increased market share.

Apple Computer succeeded at first because the less complex design of its Apple II PC made it easier to use than competing designs, and also because some key complements (particularly VisiCalc, the first business spreadsheet) soon became available for the machine. Similarly, the first Sony PlayStation was very popular because Sony pioneered the marketing strategy of setting up displays in retail stores where potential customers could try a PlayStation and others could observe them enjoying it.

Another important strategic issue at the growth stage is that the popularity of a new product often increases or spreads in a way that is analogous to a *viral model of infection*. Lead adopters (the first customers who buy a product) in a market become "infected" or enthused with the product. Subsequently, they infect other people by telling them about its advantages, and after having observed the benefits of the product, these people also adopt it. A good example of this model of diffusion occurred with Hotmail, when its developers decided to add a tag line on the bottom of an e-mail that read "get your free e-mail at Hotmail.com." This tag line proved to be remarkably effective in recruiting new members. Someone would sign on at one institution, say, the University of Washington, and send e-mail via Hotmail to friends. Some of the recipients would also sign on. Within a few days, there would be ten members at the University of Washington, then one hundred, and within a month a thousand—all "infected" from the original user.

Companies promoting new products can take advantage of this viral diffusion phenomenon by identifying and aggressively courting potential opinion leaders in a community—customers whose views command respect. For example, when the manufacturers of new high-tech medical equipment, such as an MRI scanner, start to sell a new product, they first try to get well-known doctors at major research and teaching hospitals to use the product. They may give these opinion leaders free machines for their research purposes and work closely with them in developing the technology. Once these opinion leaders commit to the product and give it their stamp of approval, doctors at many other hospitals often follow.

In sum, understanding competitive dynamics in embryonic and growth industries is an important strategic issue. The ways in which different kinds of customer groups emerge and customer needs change are important determinants of the strategies that need to be pursued to make a business model successful over time. Similarly, understanding the factors that affect a market's growth rate allows managers to tailor their business model to a changing industry environment. (Much more is said about competition in dynamic, changing, high-tech industries in the next chapter.)

Navigating Through the Life Cycle to Maturity

Another crucial decision that faces strategic managers at each stage of the industry life cycle is which investment strategy to pursue. An investment strategy determines the amount and type of resources and capital—human, functional, and financial—that must be spent to configure a company's value chain so that it can pursue a business model successfully over time.[13] In deciding on an investment strategy, managers must evaluate the potential return (on invested capital) from investing in a generic business model against the cost. In this way, they can determine whether pursuing a certain business model strategy is likely to be profitable and how the profitability of a particular business model will change as competition within the industry changes.

Two factors are crucial in choosing an investment strategy: the competitive advantage a company's business model gives it in an industry relative to its competitors, and the stage of the industry's life cycle in which the company is competing.[14] In determining the strength of a company's relative competitive position, market share and distinctive competencies become important. A large market share signals greater potential returns from future investment because it suggests a company has brand loyalty and is in a strong position to grow its profits in the future. Similarly, the more difficult it is to imitate a company's distinctive competencies, such as those in R&D or manufacturing and marketing, the more sustainable is the competitive advantage supplied by its business model and the greater the likelihood that investment in it will lead to a higher ROIC. These two attributes also reinforce one another; for example, a large market share may help a company to create and develop distinctive competencies that strengthen its business model over time because high demand allows it to ride down the experience curve and lower its cost structure. Also, a large market share can create a large cash flow, which may allow for more investment to develop competencies in R&D or elsewhere. In general, companies with the largest market share and the strongest distinctive competencies are in the best position to build and sustain their competitive advantage. Companies with a small market share and little potential for developing a distinctive competency are in a much weaker competitive position.[15]

Because different kinds of opportunities and threats are found in each life cycle stage, the stage of the industry life cycle also influences a company's choice of how much to invest in its business model. Each stage therefore has different implications for the investment of resources needed to obtain a competitive advantage. Competition is strongest in the shakeout stage of the life cycle and least important in the embryonic stage, for example. The *risks* associated with pursuing a certain business model therefore change over time. The difference in risk explains why the potential returns from investing in a particular business model depend on the life cycle stage.

■ **Embryonic Strategies**

In the embryonic stage, all companies, weak and strong, emphasize the development of a distinctive competency and an associated business model. During this stage, investment needs are great because a company has to establish a competitive advantage. Many fledgling companies in the industry are seeking resources to develop a distinctive competency. Thus, the appropriate business-level investment strategy is a **share-building strategy**. The aim is to build market share by developing a stable and distinct competitive advantage to attract customers who have no knowledge of the company's products.

Companies require large amounts of capital to develop R&D or sales and service competencies. They cannot generate much of this capital internally. Thus, a company's success depends on its ability to demonstrate a distinctive competency to attract outside investors, or venture capitalists. If a company gains the resources to develop a distinctive competency, it will be in a relatively stronger competitive position. If it fails, its only option may be to exit the industry. In fact, companies in weak competitive positions at all stages in the life cycle may choose to exit the industry to cut their losses.

■ **Growth Strategies**

At the growth stage, the task facing a company is to strengthen its business model to provide the base it needs to survive the coming shakeout. Thus, the appropriate investment strategy is the **growth strategy**. The goal is to maintain its relative competitive position in a rapidly expanding market and, if possible, to increase it—in other words, to grow with the expanding market. However, other companies are entering the market and catching up with the industry's innovators. As a result, the companies first into the market with a particular kind of product often require successive waves of capital infusion to maintain the momentum generated by their success in the embryonic stage. For example, differentiators need to engage in extensive research and development to maintain their technological lead, and cost leaders need to invest in state-of-the-art machinery and computers to obtain new experience-curve economies. All this investment to strengthen their business model is very expensive. And, as we discuss above, many companies fail to recognize the changing needs of customers in the market and invest their capital in ways that do not lead to the distinctive competencies required for long-term success.

The growth stage is also the time when companies attempt to secure their grip over customers in existing market segments and enter new segments so that they can increase their market share. Increasing the level of market segmentation to become a broad differentiator is expensive as well. A company has to invest resources to develop a new sales and marketing competency, for example. Consequently, at the growth stage, companies must make investment decisions about the relative advantages of differentiation, cost-leadership, or focus business models given their financial needs and relative competitive position. If one or a few companies have emerged as the clear cost leaders, for example, other companies might realize that it is futile to compete head-to-head with these companies and instead decide to pursue a growth strategy using a differentiation or focus approach and invest resources in developing other competencies. As a result, strategic groups start to develop in an industry as each company seeks the best way to invest its scarce resources to maximize its competitive advantage.

Companies must spend a lot of money just to keep up with growth in the market, and finding additional resources to develop new skills and competencies is a difficult task for strategic managers. Consequently, companies in a weak competitive position at this stage engage in a **market concentration** strategy to find a viable competitive position. They seek to specialize in some way and adopt a focus business model to reduce their investment needs. If they are very weak, they may also choose to exit the industry and sell out to a stronger competitor.

■ **Shakeout Strategies**

By the shakeout stage, demand is increasing slowly, and competition by price or product characteristics becomes intense. Companies in strong competitive positions need resources to invest in a **share-increasing strategy** to attract customers from weak companies exiting the market. In other words, companies attempt to maintain and increase market share despite fierce competition. The way companies invest their resources depends on their business model.

For cost leaders, because of the price wars that can occur, investment in cost control is crucial if they are to survive the shakeout stage; they must do all they can to reduce costs. Differentiators in a strong competitive position choose to forge ahead and increase their market share by investing in marketing, and they are likely to develop a sophisticated after-sales service network. Differentiators in a weak position reduce their investment burden by withdrawing to a focused model, the market concentration strategy, to specialize in a particular market segment. A market concentration strategy generally indicates that a company is trying to turn around its business so that it can survive in the long run.

Weak companies exiting the industry engage in a harvest strategy. A company using a **harvest strategy** must limit or decrease its investment in a business and extract, or milk, the investment as much as it can. For example, a company reduces to a minimum the assets it employs in the business and forgoes investment to reduce its cost structure.[16] Then the company "harvests" all the sales revenues it can profitably obtain before it liquidates all its assets and exits the industry. Companies that have lost their cost-leadership position to more efficient companies are more likely to pursue a harvest strategy because a smaller market share means higher costs and they are unable to move to a focus strategy. Differentiators, in contrast, have a competitive advantage in this stage if they can move to a focus model.

■ **Maturity Strategies**

By the maturity stage, companies want to reap the rewards of their previous investments in developing the business models that have made them dominant industry competitors. Until now, profits have been reinvested in the business, and dividends have been small. Investors in leading companies have obtained their rewards through the appreciation of the value of their stock, because the company has reinvested most of its capital to maintain and increase market share. As market growth slows in the maturity stage, a company's investment strategy depends on the level of competition in the industry and the source of the company's competitive advantage.

In environments in which competition is high because of technological change or low barriers to entry, companies need to defend their competitive position. Strategic managers need to continue to invest heavily in maintaining the company's competitive advantage. Both cost leaders and differentiators adopt a **hold-and-maintain strategy** to defend their business models and to ward off threats from focused companies who might be appearing. They expend resources to develop their distinctive competency so as to remain the market leaders. For example, differentiated companies may invest in improved after-sales service, and low-cost companies may invest in the latest production technologies.

It is at this point too that many companies realize the benefits that can be obtained by investing resources to become broad differentiators to protect themselves from aggressive competitors (both at home and abroad) that are watching for any opportunity or perceived weakness to take the lead in the industry. Differentiators enter new market segments to increase their market share; they also take advantage of their growing profits to develop flexible manufacturing systems to reduce their production costs. Cost leaders also begin to enter more market segments and increase product differentiation to expand their market share. For example, Gallo moved from the bulk wine segment and began marketing premium wines and wine coolers to take advantage of its low production costs. Soon Gallo's new premium brands, like Falling Leaf chardonnay, became the best-selling wines in the United States. As time goes on, the competitive positions of the leading differentiators and cost leaders become closer, and the pattern of industry competition changes yet again, as we discuss in the next section.

Strategy in Mature Industries

As a result of fierce competition in the shakeout stage, an industry becomes consolidated, and so a mature industry is often dominated by a small number of large companies. Although it may also contain many medium-sized companies and a host of small, specialized ones, the large companies determine the nature of competition in the industry because they can influence the five competitive forces. Indeed, these large companies owe their leading positions to the fact that they have developed the most successful business models and strategies in the industry.

By the end of the shakeout stage, companies have learned how important it is to analyze each other's business model and strategies. They also know that if they change their strategies, their actions are likely to stimulate a competitive response from industry rivals. For example, a differentiator that starts to lower its prices because it has adopted a more cost-efficient technology not only threatens other differentiators but may also threaten cost leaders that see their competitive advantage being eroded. Hence, by the mature stage of the life cycle companies have learned the meaning of competitive independence.

As a result, in mature industries, business-level strategy revolves around understanding how established companies *collectively* try to reduce the strength of industry competition to preserve both company and industry profitability. Interdependent companies can help protect their competitive advantage and profitability by adopting

FIGURE 6.5

Strategies for
Deterring Entry
of Rivals

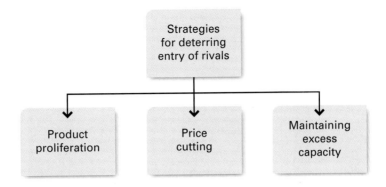

strategies and tactics, first, to deter entry into an industry, and second, to reduce the level of rivalry within an industry.

■ **Strategies to Deter Entry: Product Proliferation, Price Cutting, and Maintaining Excess Capacity**

Companies can use three main methods to deter entry by potential rivals and hence maintain and increase industry profitability: product proliferation, price cutting, and maintaining excess capacity (see Figure 6.5). Of course, *potential entrants* will try to circumvent such entry-deterring strategies by incumbent companies. Competition is rarely a one-way street.

■ **Product Proliferation** As we note above, in the maturity stage most companies move to increase their market share by producing a wide range of products targeted at different market segments. Sometimes, however, to reduce the threat of entry, existing companies ensure that they are offering a product targeted at every segment in the market. This creates a barrier to entry because potential competitors find it hard to break into an industry and establish a "beachhead" when there is no obvious group of customers whose needs are not being met by existing companies.[17] This strategy of "filling the niches," or catering to the needs of customers in all market segments to deter entry, is known as **product proliferation**.

Because the large U.S. carmakers were so slow to fill the small-car niches (they did *not* pursue a product proliferation strategy), they were vulnerable to the entry of the Japanese into these market segments in the United States in the 1980s. Ford and GM really had no excuse for this situation, for in their European operations, they had a long history of small-car manufacturing. Managers should have seen the opening and filled it ten years earlier, but the (mistaken) view was that "small cars mean small profits." Better small profits than no profits! In the soap and detergent industry, on the other hand, competition is based on the production of new kinds of soaps and detergents to satisfy or create new desires by customers. Thus, the number of soaps and detergents, and especially the way they are packaged (powder, liquid, or tablets), proliferates, making it very difficult for prospective entrants to attack a new market segment.

Figure 6.6 indicates how product proliferation can deter entry. It depicts product space in the restaurant industry along two dimensions: atmosphere, which ranges from fast food to candlelight dining, and quality of food, which ranges from average to gourmet. The circles represent product spaces filled by restaurants located along the

FIGURE 6.6

Product Proliferation in the Restaurant Industry

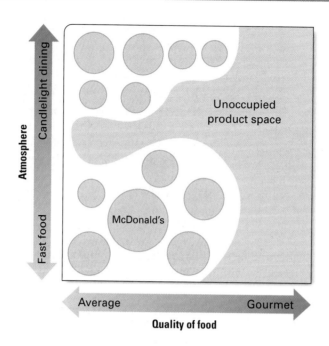

two dimensions. Thus, McDonald's is situated in the average quality/fast food area. A gap in the product space gives a potential entrant or an existing rival an opportunity to enter the market and make inroads. The shaded unoccupied product space represents areas where new restaurants can enter the market. When all the product spaces are filled, this barrier to entry makes it much more difficult for a new company to gain a foothold in the market and differentiate itself.

■ **Price Cutting** In some situations, pricing strategies can be used to deter entry by other companies, thus protecting the profit margins of companies already in an industry. One entry-deterring strategy is to cut prices every time a new company enters the industry or, even better, every time a potential entrant is *contemplating* entry, and then raise prices once the new or potential entrant has withdrawn. The goal here is to send a signal to potential entrants that new entry will be met with price cuts. If incumbent companies in an industry consistently pursue such a strategy, potential entrants will come to understand that their entry will spark off a price war, the threat of new entry will be reduced, average prices will be higher, and industry profitability will increase.

However, a price-cutting strategy will not keep out an entrant that plans to adopt a new technology that will give it a cost advantage over established companies or that has pioneered a new business model that its managers expect will also give it a competitive advantage. In fact, many of the most successful entrants into mature industries are companies that have done just this. For example, the Japanese car companies were able to enter the U.S. market because they had pioneered new lean manufacturing technologies that gave them a cost and quality advantage over established U.S. companies. Today, Japanese car companies' share of the U.S. market is limited only by an informal trade agreement; it could easily double if they were allowed to import all the cars they wished and sell them at lower prices, which might drive one or more U.S. car companies out of the market.

A second price-cutting strategy is to charge a high price initially for a product and seize short-term profits but then to cut prices aggressively in order to build market share *and* deter potential entrants simultaneously.[18] The incumbent companies thus signal to potential entrants that if they enter the industry, the incumbents will use their competitive advantage to drive down prices to a level at which new companies will be unable to cover their costs. This pricing strategy also allows a company to ride down the experience curve and obtain substantial economies of scale. Since costs fall with prices, profit margins could still be maintained.

Still, this strategy is unlikely to deter a strong potential competitor—an established company that is trying to find profitable investment opportunities in other industries. It is difficult, for example, to imagine 3M's being afraid to enter an industry because companies there threaten to drive down prices. A company such as 3M has the resources to withstand any short-term losses. Dell also had few worries about entering the highly competitive electronics industry and starting to sell televisions, digital cameras, and so on because of its powerful set of distinctive competencies. Hence, when faced with such a scenario, it may be in the interests of incumbent companies to accept new entry gracefully, giving up market share gradually to the new entrants to prevent price wars from developing and thus saving their profits, if this is feasible. As Strategy in Action 6.3 details, Toys "R" Us has been forced to give up market share in the toy market, and it has lost much of its prominence as a result.

■ **Maintaining Excess Capacity** A third competitive technique that allows companies to deter entry involves maintaining excess capacity, that is, maintaining the physical capability to produce more of a product than customers currently demand. Existing industry companies may deliberately develop some limited amount of excess capacity to warn potential entrants that if they enter the industry, existing firms can retaliate by increasing output and forcing down prices until entry would become unprofitable. However, the threat to increase output has to be *credible*; that is, companies in an industry must collectively be able to raise the level of production quickly if entry appears likely.

■ **Strategies to Manage Rivalry**

Beyond seeking to deter entry, companies also wish to develop strategies to manage their competitive interdependence and decrease price rivalry. Unrestricted competition over prices reduces both company and industry profitability. Several strategies are available to companies to manage industry rivalry. The most important are price signaling, price leadership, nonprice competition, and capacity control (Figure 6.7).

■ **Price Signaling** A company's ability to choose the price option that leads to superior performance is a function of several factors, including the strength of demand for a product and the intensity of competition between rivals. Price signaling is a first means by which companies attempt to control rivalry among competitors so as to allow the *industry* to choose the most favorable pricing option.[19] **Price signaling** is the process by which companies increase or decrease product prices to convey their intentions to other companies and so influence the way they price their products.[20] Companies use price signaling to improve industry profitability.

Companies may use price signaling to announce that they will respond vigorously to hostile competitive moves that threaten them. For example, they may signal that if one company starts to cut prices aggressively, they will respond in kind. A **tit-for-tat strategy** is a well-known price signaling strategy in which a company does

Strategy in Action   6.3

Toys "R" Us's New Competitors

Toys "R" Us, based in Paramus, New Jersey, grew at an astonishing 25 percent annual rate to become the market leader in the retail toy market in 1990 with a 20 percent share. To reach its dominant position, the company consolidated the fragmented toy market by developing a nationwide chain of retail outlets so that it could pursue a cost-leadership strategy. To lower its cost structure, Toys "R" Us developed efficient materials-management techniques for ordering and distributing toys to its stores, and it provided a low level of customer service compared to traditional small toy shops. This business model allowed it to achieve a low expense-to-sales ratio of 17 percent, and it then used this favorable cost structure to promote a philosophy of everyday low pricing. The company deliberately set out to undercut the prices of its rivals, and it succeeded: two of its largest competitors, Child World and Lionel, went bankrupt.

With its dominant position in the industry established, Toys "R" Us continued to build its chain of toy stores, and it began stocking an ever larger and more complex array of products. This would raise its costs; nevertheless, its managers reasoned that they could afford to do so since they were in the driver's seat, and customers would find more value in a wider toy selection. Moreover, raising prices to customers could offset any cost increases, or perhaps the company could negotiate higher price discounts from toy makers like Mattel or Parker Bros.

The company received a shock in 1995 when its commanding position was threatened by the entry of a new set of rivals. Recognizing the high profits that Toys "R" Us was earning, rapidly expanding companies such as Wal-Mart, Kmart, and Target began to make toy selling a major part of their business model. What could Toys "R" Us do to stop them? Not much. Because of its failure to control costs, Toys "R" Us could not stop their entry into its business by reducing its prices; in other words, by failing to pursue its cost-leadership strategy faithfully, it had lost its ability to

play pricing games as it had done with its earlier rivals. The entry of these other companies also reduced its power over its suppliers, the toy makers, because they now had important new customers. Finally, some of the new entrants, Wal-Mart in particular, were now the cost leaders in the retail industry, and their size gave them the resources to withstand any problems if Toys "R" Us attempted to start a price war. In fact, Wal-Mart simply imitated the Toys "R" Us earlier approach and began selling toys at prices that were below those of Toys "R" Us! Indeed, Toys "R" Us's sales fell from 25 percent in 1990 to 17 percent by 1999, when Wal-Mart became the market leader with 18 percent.

To survive, Toys "R" Us has tried to lower its cost structure in its core toy business. It installed new IT to increase the efficiency of its purchasing and distribution operations. It reduced the number of items its stores carry by over 30 percent to slash its cost structure. At the same time, recognizing that it will never be able to match Wal-Mart's low costs, it changed its business model to try to create customer value by developing other kinds of stores for related market segments, such as Kids "R" Us and Babies "R" Us. It also went online and attempted to develop a major Web presence. However, faced with the high costs of online selling today, it partnered with amazon.com; toys bought in its shop on amazon's website can be picked up at any Toys "R" Us store.

By 2004, it was clear that these moves had not halted the decline in the company's market share and profitability. In fact, in 2004 it made the surprise announcement that it was thinking of getting out of the toy business and would henceforth focus on its specialty Kids "R" Us and Babies "R" Us stores, which are making money. However, in November 2004 it still had not found a buyer for its toy stores, and it was not clear if its managers felt that liquidating its toy store assets was a better solution than staying in the toy business and hoping for a turnaround.[c]

exactly what its rivals do: if its rivals cut prices, the company follows; if its rivals raise prices, the company follows. By pursuing this strategy consistently over time, a company sends a clear signal to its rivals that it will match any pricing moves they make, the idea being that, sooner or later, rivals will learn that the company will always pursue a tit-for-tat strategy. Because rivals now know that the company will match any

Strategies for Managing Industry Rivalry

price reductions and cutting prices will only reduce profits, price cutting becomes less common in the industry. Moreover, a tit-for-tat strategy also signals to rivals that price increases will be immitated, increasing the probability that rivals will initiate price increases to raise profits. Thus, a tit-for-tat strategy can be a useful way of shaping pricing behavior in an industry.[21]

The airline industry is a good example of the power of price signaling when prices typically rise and fall depending on the current state of customer demand. If one carrier signals the intention to lower prices, a price war frequently ensues as other carriers copy each other's signals. If one carrier feels demand is strong, it tests the waters by signaling an intention to increase prices, and price signaling becomes a strategy to obtain uniform price increases. Nonrefundable tickets, another strategy adopted to obtain a more favorable pricing option, originated as a market signal by one company that was quickly copied by all other companies in the industry. Carriers recognized that they could stabilize their revenues and earn interest on customers' money if they collectively acted to force customers to assume the risk of buying airline tickets in advance. In essence, price signaling allows companies to give one another information that enables them to understand each other's competitive product or market strategy and make coordinated, price-competitive moves.

■ **Price Leadership** **Price leadership**—in which one company assumes the responsibility for choosing the most favorable industry pricing option—is a second tactic used to reduce price rivalry and thus enhance the profitability of companies in a mature industry.[22] Formal price leadership, or price setting by companies jointly, is illegal under antitrust laws, so the process of price leadership is often very subtle. In the car industry, for example, prices are set by imitation. The price set by the weakest company—that is, the one with the highest cost structure—is often used as the basis for competitors' pricing. Thus, U.S. carmakers set their prices, and Japanese carmakers then set theirs with reference to the U.S. prices. The Japanese are happy to do this because they have lower costs than U.S. companies, so they make higher profits than U.S. carmakers without competing with them by price. Pricing is done by market segment. The prices of different auto models in the model range indicate the customer segments that the companies are aiming for and the price range they believe the market segment can tolerate. Each manufacturer prices a model in the segment with reference to the prices charged by its competitors, not by reference to competitors' costs. Price leadership also allows differentiators to charge a premium price.

Although price leadership can stabilize industry relationships by preventing head-to-head competition and thus raise the level of profitability within an industry, it has its dangers. It helps companies with high cost structures, allowing them to survive without having to implement strategies to become more productive and efficient. In the long term, such behavior makes them vulnerable to new entrants that have lower costs because they have developed new low-cost production techniques. That is what happened in the U.S. car industry after the Japanese entered the market. After years of tacit price fixing, with GM as the price leader, the carmakers were subjected to growing low-cost Japanese competition, to which they were unable to respond. Indeed, most U.S. carmakers survived only because the Japanese carmakers were foreign firms. Had the foreign firms been new U.S. entrants, the government would probably not have taken steps to protect Chrysler, Ford, or GM.

■ **Nonprice Competition** A third very important aspect of product and market strategy in mature industries is the use of **nonprice competition** to manage rivalry within an industry. The use of strategies to try to prevent costly price cutting and price wars does not preclude competition by product differentiation. Indeed, in many industries, product differentiation strategies are the principal tool companies use to deter potential entrants and manage rivalry within their industry. Nike, the broad differentiator profiled in the *Opening Case*, offers an excellent example of such a company.

Product differentiation allows industry rivals to compete for market share by offering products with different or superior features or by applying different marketing techniques. In Figure 6.8, product and market segment dimensions are used to identify four nonprice competitive strategies based on product differentiation: market penetration, product development, market development, and product proliferation. (Notice that this model applies to new market segments, not new markets.)[23]

■ **Market Penetration** When a company concentrates on expanding market share in its existing product markets, it is engaging in a strategy of **market penetration**.[24] Market penetration involves heavy advertising to promote and build product differentiation, which Nike has actively pursued through its guerrilla marketing, for example. In a mature industry, advertising aims to influence customers' brand choice and create a brand-name reputation for the company and its products; hence

FIGURE 6.8

Four Nonprice
Competitive Strategies

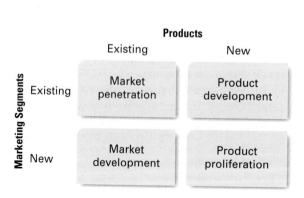

Nike's use of famous sportspeople. In this way, a company can increase its market share by attracting the customers of its rivals. Because brand-name products often command premium prices, building market share in this situation is very profitable.

In some mature industries—for example, soap and detergent, disposable diapers, and brewing—a market-penetration strategy becomes a way of life.[25] In these industries, all companies engage in intensive advertising and battle for market share. Each company fears that, by not advertising, it will lose market share to rivals. Consequently, in the soap and detergent industry, Proctor & Gamble spends more than 20 percent of sales revenues on advertising, with the aim of maintaining and perhaps building market share. These huge advertising outlays constitute a barrier to entry for prospective entrants.

■ **Product Development** **Product development** is the creation of new or improved products to replace existing ones.[26] The wet-shaving industry depends on product replacement to create successive waves of customer demand, which then create new sources of revenue for companies in the industry. Gillette, for example, periodically comes out with a new and improved razor, such as its new vibrating razor that competes with Schick's four-bladed razor, to try to boost its market share. Similarly, in the car industry, each major car company replaces its models every three to five years to encourage customers to trade in their old models and buy the new one.

Product development is crucial for maintaining product differentiation and building market share. For instance, the laundry detergent Tide has gone through more than fifty changes in formulation during the past forty years to improve its performance. The product is always advertised as Tide, but it is a different product each year. Refining and improving products is a crucial strategy companies use to fine-tune and improve their business models in a mature industry, but this kind of competition can be as vicious as a price war because it is very expensive and can dramatically increase a company's cost structure. One of Nike's central strategies is product development, and in the early 2000s its cost structure started to soar because its managers had not realized how much the attempt to develop literally thousands of new models of shoes a year was affecting its bottom line.

■ **Market Development** **Market development** finds new market segments for a company's products. A company pursuing this strategy wants to capitalize on the brand name it has developed in one market segment by locating new market segments in which to compete—just as Nike has done in many segments of the shoe market. In this way, it can exploit the product differentiation advantages of its brand name. The Japanese auto manufacturers provide an interesting example of the use of market development. When they entered the market, each Japanese manufacturer offered a car such as the Toyota Corolla and the Honda Accord aimed at the economy segment of the auto market. Then they upgraded each car over time, and now each is directed at a more expensive market segment. The Accord is a leading contender in the midsize car segment, and the Corolla fills the small-car segment that used to be occupied by the Celica, which is now aimed at a sportier market segment. By redefining their product offerings, Japanese manufacturers have profitably developed their market segments and successfully attacked their industry rivals, wresting market share from these companies. Although the Japanese used to compete primarily as cost leaders, market development has allowed them to become differentiators as well. In fact, as we noted in the last chapter, Toyota has used market development to be-

FIGURE 6.9

Toyota's Product
Lineup

Price	Sports Utility Vehicles	Passenger/ Sports Sedans	Passenger Vans	Personal Luxury Vehicles	Sporty Cars	Pickup Trucks
$11–20K	RAV4, Scion xB	Echo, Matrix, Corolla, Prism, Scion xA			Celica GT	Tacoma
$21–30K	4-Runner, Highlander	Camry, Avalon	Sienna	Avalon	MR2, Spyder	Tundra
$31–45K	Sequoia, RX330	GS 300, IS 300		ES 330	Camry, Solara	Tundra Double Cab
$46–75K	Land Cruiser, GX, LX	GS 430		LS 430	SC 430	

come a broad differentiator. Figure 6.9 illustrates how, over time, Toyota has used market development to develop a vehicle for almost every main segment of the car market.[27]

■ **Product Proliferaton** **Product proliferation** can be used to manage rivalry within an industry and to deter entry. The strategy of product proliferation generally means that large companies in an industry all have a product in each market segment or niche and compete head-to-head for customers. If a new niche develops, such as sports utility vehicles, designer sunglasses, or Internet websites, then the leader gets a first-mover advantage, but soon all the other companies catch up. Once again, competition is stabilized, and rivalry within the industry is reduced. Product proliferation thus allows the development of stable industry competition based on product differentiation, not price—that is, nonprice competition based on the development of new products. The battle is over a product's perceived quality and uniqueness, not over its price. Once again, this is the strategy adopted by Nike in its battle with Adidas. Today Nike offers shoes to most of the major subsegments of the athletic shoe segment and uses the power of advertising to promote the Nike "lifestyle" across all these segments.

■ **Capacity Control** Although nonprice competition helps mature industries avoid the cutthroat price cutting that reduces company and industry levels of profitability, price competition does periodically break out when excess capacity exists in an industry. Excess capacity arises when companies collectively produce too much output and, to dispose of it, they cut prices. When one company cuts prices, the others quickly follow (a game theory prediction; see the discussion in a later section of this chapter) because they fear that the price cutter will be able to sell its entire inventory while they will be left with unwanted goods. The result is that a price war develops.

Excess capacity may be caused by a shortfall in demand, as when a recession lowers the demand for cars and causes car companies to give customers price incentives to purchase a new car. In this situation, companies can do nothing except wait for better times. By and large, however, excess capacity results from companies within an industry simultaneously responding to favorable conditions: they all invest in new plants to be able to take advantage of the predicted upsurge in demand. Paradoxically, each individual company's effort to outperform the others means that, collectively, the companies create industry overcapacity, which hurts them all. Although demand is rising, the consequence of each company's decision to increase capacity is a surge in industry capacity, which drives down prices. To prevent the accumulation of costly excess capacity, companies must devise strategies that let them control—or at least benefit from—capacity expansion programs. Before we examine these strategies, however, we need to consider in greater detail the factors that cause excess capacity.[28]

■ **Factors Causing Excess Capacity** The problem of excess capacity often derives from technological developments. Sometimes new low-cost technology is the culprit because all companies invest in it simultaneously to prevent being left behind. Excess capacity occurs because the new technology can produce more than the old. In addition, new technology is often introduced in large increments, which generate overcapacity. For instance, an airline that needs more seats on a route must add another plane, thereby adding hundreds of seats even if only fifty are needed. To take another example, a new chemical process may operate efficiently only at the rate of a 1,000 gallons a day, whereas the previous process was efficient at 500 gallons a day. If all companies within an industry change technologies, industry capacity may double and enormous problems can result.

Overcapacity may also be caused by competitive factors within an industry. Entry into an industry is one such a factor. The entry of South Korean companies into the global semiconductor industry in the 1990s caused massive overcapacity and price declines. Similarly, the entry of steel producers from the former Soviet Union countries into the global steel market produced excess capacity and plunging prices in the world steel market in the late 1990s and early 2000s. Sometimes the age of a company's plant is the source of the problem. For example, in the hotel industry, given the rapidity with which the quality of hotel furnishings declines, customers are always attracted to new hotels. When new hotel chains are built alongside the old chains, excess capacity can result. Often companies are simply making simultaneous competitive moves based on industry trends, but those moves eventually lead to head-to-head competition. Most fast-food chains, for instance, establish new outlets whenever demographic data show population increases. However, the companies seem to forget that all other chains use the same data (they are not fully anticipating their rivals' actions). Thus, a locality that has no fast-food outlets may suddenly see several being built at the same time. Whether they can all survive depends on the growth rate of demand relative to the growth rate of the chains.

■ **Choosing a Capacity-Control Strategy** Given the various ways in which capacity can expand, companies clearly need to find some means of controlling it. If they are always plagued by price cutting and price wars, they will be unable to recoup the investments in their generic strategies. Low profitability within an industry caused by overcapacity forces not just the weakest companies but also sometimes the major players to exit the industry. In general, companies have two strategic choices: either (1) each company individually must try to preempt its rivals and seize the initiative, or (2) the companies collectively must find indirect means of coordinating with each other so that they are all aware of the mutual effects of their actions.

To *preempt* rivals, a company must forecast a large increase in demand in the product market and then move rapidly to establish large-scale operations that will be able to satisfy the predicted demand. By achieving a first-mover advantage, the company may deter other firms from entering the market since the preemptor will usually be able to move down the experience curve, reduce its costs and therefore its prices as well, and threaten a price war if necessary.

This strategy, however, is extremely risky, for it involves investing resources before the extent and profitability of the future market are clear. Wal-Mart, with its strategy of locating in small rural towns to tap an underexploited market for discount goods, preempted Sears and Kmart. Wal-Mart has been able to engage in market penetration and market expansion because of the secure base it established in its rural strongholds.

A preemptive strategy is also risky if it does not deter competitors and they decide to enter the market. If the competitors have a stronger generic strategy or more resources, such as Microsoft or Intel, they can make the preemptor suffer. Thus, for the strategy to succeed, the preemptor must generally be a credible company with enough resources to withstand a possible price war.

To *coordinate* with rivals as a capacity-control strategy, caution must be exercised since collusion on the timing of new investments is illegal under antitrust law. However, tacit coordination is practiced in many industries as companies attempt to understand and forecast one another's competitive moves. Generally, companies use market signaling to secure coordination. They make announcements about their future investment decisions in trade journals and newspapers. In addition, they share information about their production levels and their forecasts of demand within an industry to bring supply and demand into equilibrium. Thus, a coordination strategy reduces the risks associated with investment in the industry. This is very common in the chemical refining and oil business, where new capacity investments frequently cost hundreds of millions of dollars.

■ Game Theory

As we have discussed, companies are in a constant competitive struggle with rivals in their industry to gain more business from customers. A useful way of viewing this struggle is as a competitive game between companies, in which companies are continually using competitive moves and tactics to compete effectively in an industry. Companies that understand the nature of the competitive game they are playing can often improve their competitive positioning and increase the profitability of their business models. For example, managers can implement better strategies to pursue cost leadership or differentiation.

A branch of work in the social sciences known as *game theory* can be used to model competition between a company and its rivals and help managers improve their business models and strategies.[29] From a game theory perspective, companies in an industry can be viewed as players that are all simultaneously making choices about which business models and strategies to pursue to maximize their profitability. The problem strategic managers face is that the potential profitability of each business model is not some fixed amount; it varies depending on the strategies one company selects and also the strategies that its rivals select. There are two basic types of game: sequential move games and simultaneous move games. In a *sequential move game*, such as chess, players move in turn, and one player can select a strategy to pursue after considering its rival's choice of strategies. In a *simultaneous move game*, the players act at the same time, in ignorance of their rival's current actions. The classic game of rock-paper-scissors is a simultaneous move game.

In the business world, both sequential and simultaneous move games are commonplace as strategic managers jockey for competitive position in the industry. Indeed, game theory is particularly useful in analyzing situations in which a company is competing against a limited number of rivals and there is a considerable level of interdependence in the industry, as occurs in a mature industry. Several of the basic principles that underlie game theory are examined below; these principles can be useful in determining which business model and strategies managers should pursue.

■ **Look Forward and Reason Back** One of the most basic messages of game theory is that managers need to think strategically in two related ways: (1) look forward, think ahead, and anticipate how rivals will respond to whatever strategic moves they make, and (2) reason backward to determine which strategic moves to pursue today given their assessment of how the company's rivals will respond to various future strategic moves. Managers who do both of these things should be able to discover the specific competitive strategy that will lead to the greatest potential returns. This cardinal principle of game theory is known as *look forward and reason back*. To understand its importance, consider this scenario.

Two large companies, UPS and FedEx, which specialize in next-day delivery of packages, dominate the U.S. air express industry. They have a very high fixed cost structure because they need to invest in a capital-intensive nationwide network of aircraft, trucks, and package-sorting facilities. The key to their profitability is to increase volume sufficiently so that these fixed costs can be spread out over a large number of packages, reducing the unit cost of transporting each package.

Imagine that a bright young manager at UPS calculates that if UPS cuts prices for next-day delivery service by 15 percent, the volume of packages the company ships will grow by over 30 percent, and so will UPS's total revenues and profitability. Is this a smart move? The answer depends on whether the bright young manager has remembered to look forward and reason back and think through how FedEx would respond to UPS's price cuts.

Because UPS and FedEx are competing directly against each other, their strategies are interdependent. If UPS cuts prices, FedEx will lose market share, its volume of shipments will decline, and its profitability will suffer. Because FedEx is unlikely to accept this result, if UPS cuts prices by 15 percent, FedEx is likely to follow and cut its prices by 15 percent to hold on to market share. The net result is that the average level of prices in the industry will fall by 15 percent, as will revenues, and both players will see their profitability decline—a lose-lose situation. By looking forward and reasoning back, the new manager discovers that the strategy of cutting prices is not a good one.

Decision trees can be used to help in the process of looking forward and reasoning back. Figure 6.10 maps out the decision tree for the simple game analyzed above from the perspective of UPS. (Note that this is a sequential move game.) UPS moves first, and then FedEx must decide how to respond. Here, you see that UPS has to

FIGURE 6.10

A Decision Tree for
UPS's Pricing Strategy

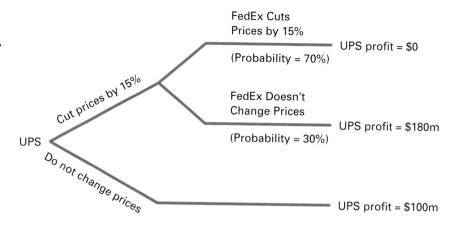

choose between two strategies: cutting prices by 15 percent or leaving them unchanged. If it leaves prices unchanged, it will continue to earn its current level of profitability, which is $100 million. If it cuts prices by 15 percent, one of two things can happen: FedEx matches the price cut, or FedEx leaves its prices unchanged. If FedEx matches UPS's price cut (FedEx decides to fight a price war), profits are competed away and UPS's profit will be $0. If FedEx does not respond and leaves its prices unaltered, UPS will gain market share and its profits will rise to $180 million. So the best pricing strategy for UPS to pursue depends on its assessment of FedEx's likely response.

Figure 6.10 assigns probabilities to the different responses from FedEx: specifically, there is a 70 percent chance that FedEx will match UPS's price cut and a 30 percent chance that it will do nothing. These probabilities come from an assessment of how UPS's price cut will affect FedEx's sales volume and profitability. The bigger the negative impact of UPS's price cut is on FedEx's sales volume and profitability, the more likely it is that FedEx will match UPS's price cuts. This is another example of the principle of looking forward and reasoning backward. Assigning a 70 percent probability to the top branch in Figure 6.10 assumes that the price cut from UPS will have a significant negative impact on FedEx's business and will force the company to respond with a price cut of its own. The probabilities can also come from looking at the history of FedEx's responses to UPS's price moves. If FedEx has a long history of matching UPS's price cuts, the probability that it will do so this time is high. If FedEx does not have a history of matching UPS's price cuts, the probability will be lower.

Now let us revisit the question of what strategy UPS should pursue. If UPS does not cut prices, its profits are $100 million. If it cuts prices, its expected profits are $(.70) \times \$0 + (.30) \times \$180 = \$60$ million. Since $60 million is less than $100 million, UPS should not pursue the price-cutting strategy. If it did, FedEx would probably respond, and the net effect would be to depress UPS's profitability. Another way of looking at this scenario is to ask under what assumptions about the probability of FedEx's responding it would be worthwhile for UPS to cut prices by 15 percent. For UPS to move forward with its price cuts, the expected profits from doing so must be greater than $100 million, which is the profit from doing nothing. The way to work this out is to find the probability for which UPS is indifferent between leaving prices unaltered or changing them. Signifying probability by p, $100\,m = p \times \$180\,m$, and solving for p, $p = \$100\,m/\$180\,m = 0.556$. In other words, for UPS to go ahead with the proposed price cut, the probability that FedEx will do nothing must be greater than 55.6 percent.

■ **Know Thy Rival** At this juncture, the question of whether this example is rather contrived might arise. After all, could UPS managers *really* anticipate how FedEx's profits could be affected if UPS cut its prices by 15 percent? And could UPS really assign a probability to FedEx's likely response? The answer is that although UPS's managers cannot calculate exactly what the profit impact and probabilities would be, they can make an informed decision by collecting competitive information and thinking strategically. For example, they could estimate FedEx's cost structure by looking at FedEx's published financial accounts. And because they are in the same business as FedEx, they can assess the effect of falling demand on FedEx's cost structure and bottom line. Moreover, by looking at the history of FedEx's competitive behavior, they can assess how FedEx will respond to a price cut.

This illustrates a second basic principle of game theory: know thy rivals. In other words, in thinking strategically, managers put themselves in the position of a rival to answer the question of how that rival is likely to act in a particular situation. If a company's managers are to be effective at looking forward and reasoning back, they must have a good understanding of what their rival is likely to do under different scenarios, and they need to be able to extrapolate their rival's future behavior based on this understanding.

■ **Find the Dominant Strategy** A **dominant strategy** is one that makes you better off than you would be if you played any other strategy, *no matter what strategy your opponent uses.* To grasp this concept, consider a simultaneous move game based on a situation that developed in the U.S. car industry in the early 1990s (so far we have been considering a sequential move game). Two car companies, Ford and GM, both differentiators, have to decide whether to introduce cash-back rebate programs in November to move unsold inventory that is building up on the lots of car dealers nationwide. Each company can make one of two moves: offer rebates or do not offer rebates. Because the advanced planning associated with launching such a strategy is fairly extensive, both companies must make a decision about what to do by mid-October, which is before they have had a chance to see what their rival is doing.

In each of the previous four years, both companies have introduced just such programs on November 1 and kept them in place until December 31. Customers have become conditioned to expect these programs and increasingly have held back their new car purchases in anticipation of the cash rebate programs beginning in November. This learned behavior by customers has increased the strategic importance of the rebate programs and made the rebate programs themselves increasingly expensive for the automobile companies. Figure 6.11 lays out a payoff matrix associated with each strategy.

The four cells in this matrix represent the four possible outcomes of pursuing or not pursuing a cash rebate strategy. The numbers in parentheses in the center of

FIGURE 6.11

A Payoff Matrix for
GM and Ford

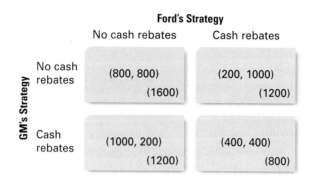

each cell represent the profit that General Motors and Ford, respectively, will get in
each case (in millions of dollars). If both General Motors and Ford decide not to
introduce cash rebates (cell 1), each will get $800 million in profit for the November 1–
December 31 period. If GM introduces a cash rebate program but Ford doesn't,
GM will gain market share at Ford's expense, and GM will get $1,000 million in
profit, while Ford gets just $200 million (cell 2). The converse holds if Ford intro-
duces a rebate program but GM doesn't (cell 3). If both companies introduce rebate
programs, both get $400 million (remember, the rebates are expensive and essen-
tially represent deep price discounting to move unsold inventory)(cell 4). Finally,
the figures in parentheses in the lower-right-hand corner of each cell represent the
joint profit associated with each outcome.

   If you look at this payoff matrix, you will see that GM's dominant strategy is to
offer cash rebates, because whatever strategy Ford pursues, GM does better if it offers cash rebates than if it doesn't. If Ford's strategy is to offer no cash rebates,
GM's best strategy is to offer rebates and capture a profit of $1,000 million. If
Ford's strategy is to offer cash rebates, GM's best strategy is again to offer cash rebates
and get a profit of $400 million. So whatever Ford does, GM's best strategy is to offer
cash rebates.

   An interesting aspect of this game is that Ford also goes through the same reasoning process. Indeed, the payoff matrix shows that Ford's dominant strategy is also to
offer cash rebates. The net result is that while both players get $400 million profit, the
combined payoff of $800 million is the lowest of any combination! Clearly, both au-
tomakers could have done better if they had cooperated and jointly decided not to
offer cash rebates. Why didn't they do this? There are two reasons. First, cooperation
to set prices is illegal under U.S. antitrust law. Second, even though neither party will
gain from offering rebates, *it cannot trust the other party not to offer a cash rebate since
then it would be even worse off.* As the payoff matrix shows, if Ford does not offer cash
rebates, GM has a very big incentive to do so, and vice versa. So both companies assume that the other will offer rebates, both end up doing so, and customers receive
the value and are the winners!

   The payoff structure in this game is very famous. It is known as the *prisoner's
dilemma game* because it was first explained using an example of two suspects, or
"prisoners," who are being interrogated for possible involvement in a crime. In the
original exposition, the prisoners could confess to the crime and also implicate their
partner in the crime to get a reduced sentence, or not confess or implicate the other. If

the other prisoner also either doesn't confess or implicate the other, they both end up going free. The problem is that neither prisoner can trust the other not to implicate the other in order to get a reduced sentence. So to reduce their losses (length of jail time), both end up confessing and implicate the other, and both go to jail.

The prisoner's dilemma is thought to capture the essence of many situations where two or more companies are competing against each other and their dominant strategy is to fight a price war, even if they would collectively be better off by *not* doing so. In other words, the prisoner's dilemma can be used to explain the mutually destructive price competition that breaks out in many industries from time to time. It also raises the question of whether companies can do anything to extricate themselves from such a situation. This brings us to the final principle of game theory explored here.

■ **Strategy Shapes the Payoff Structure of the Game** An important lesson of game theory is that through its choice of strategy, a company can alter the payoff structure of the competitive game being played in the industry. To understand this, consider once more the cash rebate game played by Ford and GM in which both companies are compelled to choose a dominant strategy that depresses total payoffs. How can they extricate themselves from this predicament? They can do it by changing the behavior of customers.

Recall that rebates were necessary only because customers had come to expect them and held off purchasing a car until the rebates were introduced. In a self-fulfilling prophecy, this depresses demand and forces the companies to introduce rebates to move unsold inventory on the lots of car dealers. If these expectations could be changed, customers would not hold off their purchases in anticipation of the rebates being introduced in November of each year, and companies would no longer have to introduce rebates to move unsold inventory on the lots of car dealers. A company can change customer behavior through its choice of strategy.

This is what GM actually did. After several years of rebate wars, GM decided to issue a new credit card that allowed cardholders to apply 5 percent of their charges toward buying or leasing a new GM car, up to $500 a year with a maximum of $3,500. The credit card launch was one of the most successful in history: within two years, there were 9 million GM credit card holders, and the card had replaced the other incentives that GM offered, principally the end-of-year cash rebates. Because of the card, price-sensitive customers who typically waited for the rebates could purchase a reduced price car any time of the year. Moreover, once they had the card, they were much more likely to buy from GM than Ford. This strategy changed customer behavior. Customers no longer waited for rebates at the end of the year before buying, an inventory of unsold cars did not build up on the lots of dealers, and GM was not forced into fighting a rebate war to clear inventory.

If this strategy was so successful, what was to stop Ford from imitating it? Nothing! Ford began to offer its own credit card soon after GM. In this case, however, imitation of the strategy led to increased profitability because both GM and Ford had found a clever way to differentiate themselves from each other: by issuing credit cards that created stronger brand loyalty. With the new cards, a GM cardholder was more likely to buy a GM car and a Ford cardholder was more likely to buy a Ford car. By reducing the tendency of customers to play GM and Ford dealers off against each other, the card also had the effect of enabling both GM and Ford to raise their prices. Figure 6.12 illustrates how strategy can change the payoff matrix.

Altered Payoff Matrix
for GM and Ford

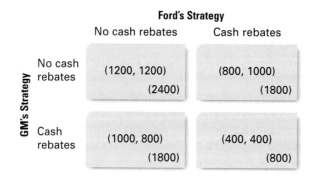

By issuing credit cards and strengthening the differentiation component of their strategy, both Ford and GM reduced the value of cash rebates and made it less likely that customers would switch to the company that offers rebates. The payoff structure of the game changed, and so did the dominant strategy. Now that GM's dominant strategy is to not offer cash rebates, for whatever Ford does, GM is better off by not offering rebates. The same is true for Ford. In other words, by their choice of strategy, General Motors and Ford have changed their dominant strategy in a way that boosts their profitability.

More generally, this example suggests that the way out of mutually destructive price competition associated with a prisoner's dilemma type of game is for the players to change their business models and differentiate their product offerings in the minds of customers, thereby reducing their sensitivity to price competition. In other words, by their choice of strategy and business model (one principally based on differentiation), companies can alter the payoff structure associated with the game, alter their dominant strategy, and move it away from a prisoner's dilemma type of game structure.

This insight also points to the need for companies to think through how their choice of business strategy might change the structure of the competitive game they are playing. Although we have looked at how strategy can transform the payoff structure of the game in a way that is more favorable, the opposite can and does occur. Companies often unintentionally change their business models and pursue strategies that change the payoff structure of the game in a way that is much less favorable to them and comes to resemble a prisoner's dilemma, as the competitive dynamics between Coca-Cola and PepsiCo in the soft drink industry suggests in Strategy in Action 6.4.

In retrospect, what happened was that the Pepsi challenge changed the long-established competitive rules in the industry. As the basis of competition shifted from differentiation by abstract lifestyle advertising to direct product comparisons, and then to price competition, the payoff structure associated with their game changed and became more of a prisoner's dilemma type of structure. Had Pepsi's managers looked ahead and reasoned back, they might have realized that price competition would be the outcome of its new aggressive strategy and might not have launched the Pepsi challenge, especially because the company was gaining market share from Coke, albeit slowly. However, because Pepsi's strategy changed the nature of differentiation in the industry, it led to a lose-lose situation.

Strategy in Action 6.4

Coca-Cola and PepsiCo Go Head-to-Head

For thirty years, until the late 1970s, the cola segment of the soft drink industry went through a golden age in which the main players, Coca-Cola and PepsiCo, were very profitable. These two companies competed against each other on the basis of advertising their products, Coke and Pepsi, based on abstract lifestyle product attributes. PepsiCo would introduce advertisements showing that it was cool to drink Pepsi, and Coca-Cola would produce advertisements with catchy jingles such as "things go better with Coke." Neither company competed on price. Coke led the market throughout the period, although by the mid-1970s, Pepsi was closing in.

It was at this juncture that Pepsi launched a new and innovative strategy: the Pepsi challenge. The Pepsi challenge was a taste test in which customers were blindfolded and asked which drink they preferred, Pepsi or Coke. In the test, about 55 percent of customers consistently said they preferred Pepsi, a significant result given that Pepsi trailed Coke in market share. Pepsi test-marketed the Pepsi challenge in Dallas, and it was so successful that in the late 1970s Pepsi rolled out the challenge nationally, a situation that presented a real dilemma for Coke. It could

not respond with its own blind taste test, because in the tests, the majority of people preferred Pepsi. Moreover, the Pepsi challenge had changed the nature of competition in the industry. After thirty years of competition through product differentiation based on lifestyle product attributes with no direct (and aggressive) product comparisons, Pepsi had shifted to a direct product comparison based on a real attribute of the product: taste.

PepsiCo had altered its business model and changed how it chose to differentiate its product from Coke. As Pepsi was now gaining market share, Coca-Cola's managers decided to make an aggressive response: deep price discounts for Coke in local markets where they controlled the Coke bottler and the local Pepsi bottler was weak. This was a successful move; in markets where price discounting was used, Coke started to gain its share back. PepsiCo then decided to respond in kind and cut prices too. Before long, price discounting was widespread in the industry. Customers were coming to expect price discounting, brand loyalty had been eroded, and the value associated with differentiation had been reduced. Both Coke and Pepsi experienced declining profitability.[d]

So how did the soft drink manufacturers try to extricate themselves from this situation? Over the course of a few years, they once more shifted the way in which they differentiated their products. They introduced new products, such as Diet Coke and Cherry Coke, to rebuild brand loyalty, and they reemphasized abstract advertising by using celebrities to help create a brand image for their soda, thus differentiating it from their competitors' offerings and reducing customer price sensitivity. They are still doing this today—advertising Pepsi, for example, using the gyrations and music of Britney Spears as a device for building a brand image that differentiates its offering from Coke. However, it took several years for Pepsi and Coke to do this, and in the interim they had to grapple with a payoff structure that reduced profitability in the industry; moreover, price discounting is still common today.

Strategies in Declining Industries

Sooner or later, many industries enter into a decline stage, in which the size of the total market starts to shrink. Examples are the railroad industry, the tobacco industry, and the steel industry. Industries start declining for a number of reasons, including technological change, social trends, and demographic shifts. The railroad and steel industries began to decline when technological changes brought viable substitutes for their

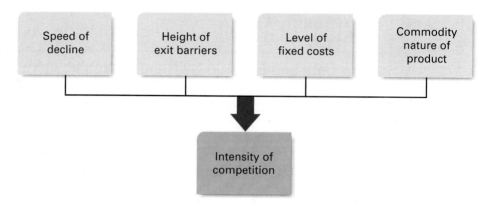

FIGURE 6.13

Factors that Determine the Intensity of Competition in Declining Industries

products. The advent of the internal combustion engine drove the railroad industry into decline, and the steel industry fell into decline with the rise of plastics and composite materials. As for the tobacco industry, changing social attitudes toward smoking, which are themselves a product of growing concerns about the health effects of smoking, have caused decline.

■ **The Severity of Decline**

When the size of the total market is shrinking, competition tends to intensify in a declining industry and profit rates tend to fall. The intensity of competition in a declining industry depends on four critical factors, which are indicated in Figure 6.13. First, the intensity of competition is greater in industries in which decline is rapid as opposed to industries, such as tobacco, in which decline is slow and gradual.

Second, the intensity of competition is greater in declining industries in which exit barriers are high. As you recall from Chapter 2, high exit barriers keep companies locked into an industry even when demand is falling. The result is the emergence of excess productive capacity and, hence, an increased probability of fierce price competition.

Third, and related to the previous point, the intensity of competition is greater in declining industries in which fixed costs are high (as in the steel industry). The reason is that the need to cover fixed costs, such as the costs of maintaining productive capacity, can make companies try to use any excess capacity they have by slashing prices, which can trigger a price war.

Finally, the intensity of competition is greater in declining industries in which the product is perceived as a commodity (as it is in the steel industry) in contrast to industries in which differentiation gives rise to significant brand loyalty, as was true until very recently of the declining tobacco industry.

Not all segments of an industry typically decline at the same rate. In some segments, demand may remain reasonably strong despite decline elsewhere. The steel industry illustrates this situation. Although bulk steel products, such as sheet steel, have suffered a general decline, demand has actually risen for specialty steels, such as those used in high-speed machine tools. Vacuum tubes provide another example. Although demand for them collapsed when transistors replaced them as a key component in many electronics products, vacuum tubes still had some limited applications in radar equipment for years afterward. Consequently, demand in this vacuum tube segment remained strong despite the general decline in the demand for vacuum tubes. The point, then, is that there may be pockets of demand in an industry in which demand is declining more slowly than in the industry as a whole or not declining at all. Price competition thus may be far less intense among the companies serving such pockets of demand than within the industry as a whole.

■ **Choosing a Strategy** There are four main strategies that companies can adopt to deal with decline: (1) a **leadership strategy**, by which a company seeks to become the dominant player in a declining industry; (2) a **niche strategy**, which focuses on pockets of demand that are declining more slowly than the industry as a whole; (3) a **harvest strategy**, which optimizes cash flow; and (4) a **divestment strategy**, by which a company sells off the business to others. Figure 6.14 provides a simple framework for guiding strategic choice. Note that the intensity of competition in the declining industry is measured on the vertical axis and that a company's strengths relative to remaining pockets of demand are measured on the horizontal axis.

■ **Leadership Strategy** A leadership strategy aims at growing in a declining industry by picking up the market share of companies that are leaving the industry. A leadership strategy makes most sense (1) when the company has distinctive strengths that allow it to capture market share in a declining industry and (2) the speed of decline and the intensity of competition in the declining industry are moderate. Philip Morris has pursued such a strategy in the tobacco industry. Through aggressive marketing, Philip Morris has increased its market share in a declining industry and earned enormous profits in the process.

The tactical steps companies might use to achieve a leadership position include using aggressive pricing and marketing to build market share, acquiring established

FIGURE 6.14

Strategy Selection in a Declining Industry

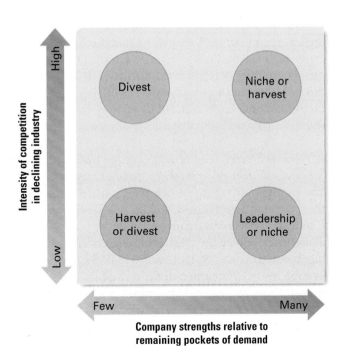

Strategy in Action   6.5

How to Make Money in the Vacuum Tube Business

At its peak in the early 1950s, the vacuum tube business was a major industry in which companies such as Westinghouse, General Electric, RCA, and Western Electric had a large stake. Then along came the transistor, making most vacuum tubes obsolete, and one by one all the big companies exited the industry. One company, however, Richardson Electronics, not only stayed in the business but also demonstrated that high returns are possible in a declining industry. Primarily a distributor (although it does have some manufacturing capabilities), Richardson bought the remains of a dozen companies in the United States and Europe as they exited the vacuum tube industry, and it now has a warehouse that stocks more than 10,000 different types of vacuum tubes. The company is the world's only supplier of many of them, which helps explain why its gross margin is in the 35 to 40 percent range.

Richardson survives and prospers because vacuum tubes are vital parts of some older electronic equipment that would be costly to replace with solid-state equipment. In addition, vacuum tubes still outperform semiconductors in some limited applications, including radar and welding machines. The U.S. government and General Motors are big customers of Richardson.

Speed is the essence of Richardson's business. The company's Illinois warehouse offers overnight delivery to some 40,000 customers, and it processes 650 orders a day at an average price of $550. Customers such as GM do not really care whether a vacuum tube costs $250 or $350; what they care about is the $40,000 to $50,000 downtime loss that they face when a key piece of welding equipment isn't working. By responding quickly to the demands of such customers and being the only major supplier of many types of vacuum tubes, Richardson has placed itself in a position that many companies in growing industries would envy: a monopoly position. However, a new company, Westrex, was formed to take advantage of the growing popularity of vacuum tubes in high-end stereo systems, and today it is competing head-to-head with Richardson in some market segments. Clearly, competition can be found even in a declining industry.[e]

competitors to consolidate the industry, and raising the stakes for other competitors— for example, by making new investments in productive capacity. Such competitive tactics signal to other competitors that the company is willing and able to stay and compete in the declining industry. These signals may persuade other companies to exit the industry, which would further enhance the competitive position of the industry leader. Strategy in Action 6.5 offers an example of a company, Richardson Electronics, that has prospered by taking a leadership position in a declining industry. It is one of the last companies in the vacuum tube business.

■ **Niche Strategy** A niche strategy focuses on pockets of demand in the industry in which demand is stable or declining less rapidly than the industry as a whole. The strategy makes sense when the company has some unique strengths relative to those niches where demand remains relatively strong. As an example, consider Naval, a company that manufactures whaling harpoons and small guns to fire them and makes money doing so. This might be considered rather odd, since the world community has outlawed whaling. However, Naval survived the terminal decline of the harpoon industry by focusing on the one group of people who are still allowed to hunt whales, although only in very limited numbers: North American Eskimos. Eskimos are permitted to hunt bowhead whales, provided that they do so only for food and not for commercial purposes. Naval is the sole supplier of small harpoon whaling guns to

Eskimo communities, and its monopoly position allows it to earn a healthy return in this small market.

■ **Harvest Strategy** As we noted earlier, a harvest strategy is the best choice when a company wishes to get out of a declining industry and optimize cash flow in the process. This strategy makes the most sense when the company foresees a steep decline and intense future competition or lacks strengths relative to remaining pockets of demand in the industry. A harvest strategy requires the company to cut all new investments in capital equipment, advertising, R&D, and the like. The inevitable result is that it will lose market share, but because it is no longer investing in this business, initially its positive cash flow will increase. Essentially, the company is taking cash flow in exchange for market share. Ultimately, cash flows will start to decline, and at this stage it makes sense for the company to liquidate the business. Although this strategy is very appealing in theory, it can be somewhat difficult to put into practice. Employee morale in a business that is being run down may suffer. Furthermore, if customers catch on to what the company is doing, they may defect rapidly. Then market share may decline much faster than the company expected.

■ **Divestment Strategy** A divestment strategy rests on the idea that a company can recover the most of its investment in an underperforming business by selling it early, before the industry has entered into a steep decline. This strategy is appropriate when the company has few strengths relative to whatever pockets of demand are likely to remain in the industry and when the competition in the declining industry is likely to be intense. The best option may be to sell out to a company that is pursuing a leadership strategy in the industry. The drawback of the divestment strategy is that it depends for its success on the ability of the company to spot its industry's decline before it becomes serious and to sell out while the company's assets are still valued by others.

Summary of Chapter

1. In fragmented industries composed of a large number of small and medium-sized companies, the principal forms of competitive strategy are chaining, franchising, and horizontal merger, as well as using the Internet.

2. In embryonic and growth industries, strategy is determined partly by market demand. The innovators and early adopters have different needs from the early and the late majority, and a company must be prepared to cross the chasm between the two. Similarly, managers must understand the factors that affect a market's growth rate so they can tailor their business model to a changing industry environment.

3. Companies need to navigate the difficult road from growth to maturity by choosing an investment strategy that supports their business model. In choosing this strategy, managers must consider the company's competitive position in the industry and the stage of the industry's life cycle. Some main types of investment strategy are share building, growth, market concentration, share increasing, harvest, and hold-and-maintain.

4. Mature industries are composed of a few large companies whose actions are so highly interdependent that the success of one company's strategy depends on the responses of its rivals.

5. The principal strategies used by companies in mature industries to deter entry are product proliferation, price cutting, and maintaining excess capacity.

6. The principal strategies used by companies in mature industries to manage rivalry are price signaling,

price leadership, nonprice competition, and capacity control.

7. Game theory suggests several management principles: look forward and reason back, know thy rival, pursue your dominant strategy, remember that strategy can alter the payoff structure of the game, and use strategy to change the payoff structure in a way that increases the profitability of your dominant strategy.

8. In declining industries, in which market demand has leveled off or is falling, companies must tailor their price and nonprice strategies to the new competitive environment. They also need to manage industry capacity to prevent the emergence of capacity expansion problems.

9. There are four main strategies a company can pursue when demand is falling: leadership, niche, harvest, and divestment. The choice is determined by the severity of industry decline and the company's strengths relative to the remaining pockets of demand.

Discussion Questions

1. Why are industries fragmented? What are the main ways in which companies can turn a fragmented industry into a consolidated one?

2. What are the key problems in maintaining a competitive advantage in embryonic and growth industry environments? What are the dangers associated with being the leader?

3. In managing their growth through the life cycle, what investment strategies should be made by (a) differentiators in a strong competitive position and (b) differentiators in a weak competitive position?

4. Discuss how companies can use (a) product differentiation and (b) capacity control to manage rivalry and increase an industry's profitability.

5. What insights would game theory offer (a) a small pizza place operating in a crowded college market and (b) a detergent manufacturer seeking to bring out new products in established markets?

Practicing Strategic Management

■ SMALL-GROUP EXERCISE
How to Keep the Hot Sauce Hot

Break up into groups of three to five people, and discuss the following scenario. Appoint one group member as a spokesperson who will communicate your findings to the class. You are the managers of a company that has pioneered a new kind of hot sauce for chicken that has taken the market by storm. The hot sauce's differentiated appeal has been based on a unique combination of spices and packaging that has allowed you to charge a premium price. Over the past three years, your hot sauce has achieved a national reputation, and now major food companies such as Kraft and Nabisco, seeing the potential of this market segment, are beginning to introduce hot sauces of their own, imitating your product.

1. Describe your business model and the strategies you are pursuing.

2. Describe the industry's environment in which you are competing.

3. What kinds of competitive strategies could you adopt to strengthen your business model in this kind of environment?

■ ARTICLE FILE 6

Choose a company or group of companies in a particular industry environment, and explain how it has adopted a competitive strategy to protect or enhance its business-level strategy.

■ STRATEGIC MANAGEMENT PROJECT
Module 6

This part of the project considers how conditions in the industry environment affect the success of your company's business model and strategies. With the information you have at your disposal, perform the tasks and answer the questions listed:

1. In what kind of industry environment (for example, embryonic, mature) does your company operate? Use the information from Strategic Management Project: Module 2 to answer this question.

2. Discuss how your company has attempted to develop strategies to protect and strengthen its business model. For example, if your company is operating in an embryonic industry, how has it attempted to increase its competitive advantage over time? If it operates in a mature industry, discuss how it has tried to manage industry competition.

3. What new strategies would you advise your company to pursue to increase its competitive advantage? For example, how should it attempt to differentiate its products in the future or lower its cost structure?

4. On the basis of this analysis, do you think your company will be able to maintain its competitive advantage in the future? Why or why not?

EXPLORING THE WEB
Visiting Wal-Mart

Enter the website of retailer Wal-Mart (**www.walmartstores.com**). Click on "About Wal-Mart," and then click on "Timeline." Study the events in Wal-Mart's timeline, and then outline the development of Wal-Mart's business model and strategies in the retailing industry over time.

General Task   Search the Web for a company that has recently changed its business model and strategy in some way. What precipitated the change? What changes did the company make?

Closing Case

Information Technology, the Internet, and Changing Strategies in the Fashion World

Well-known fashion houses like Chanel, Dior, Gucci, and Armani charge thousands of dollars for the fashionable suits and dresses that they introduce twice yearly in the fall and spring. Since only the very rich can afford such differentiated and expensive clothing, to expand demand for its luxury products most luxury designers produce less expensive lines of clothing and accessories that are sold in upscale fashion retailers such as Neiman Marcus, Nordstrom, and Saks Fifth Avenue.

Both fashion clothes designers and retailers have experienced enormous problems in the past decade. New kinds of competitors have taken advantage of the opportunities opened by the Internet and advances in information technology (IT) to enter the high fashion market segment and compete head-to-head with them by offering high-quality clothes at significantly lower prices. Essentially, all of these new competitors have developed capabilities in using IT that allow them to pursue a focused differentiation strategy but at a much lower cost than the luxury fashion houses. This has allowed them to circumvent barriers to entry into the high fashion segment and develop well-received brand names.

First, upscale department stores and retail chains like Dillard's and Macy's, which target the middle of the fashion clothing market, have developed their own store-specific prestigious clothing labels. These well-made clothes are often sold at a significant price discount from luxury brands and thus attract customers away. Second, many small, agile fashion designers such as England's Jaeger and Laura Ashley and Spain's Zara now produce fashionable clothes at lower prices and sell them in their own chains of clothing stores. Zara, in particular, has achieved significant success, and its sales have soared. It has managed to position itself as the low-price cost leader in the fashion segment of the clothing market because it has created innovative information systems that lower costs and speed time to market.

Zara uses IT to manage the interface between its design and manufacturing operations efficiently. Major fashion houses like Dior and Gucci can take six or more months to design their collections and then three to six more before their moderately priced lines become available in upscale retailers. Zara's designers closely watch the trends in the high fashion industry and the kinds of innovations that the major houses are introducing. Then, using their information systems, which are linked to their suppliers and the low-cost manufacturers the company uses abroad, they can create a new collection in only five weeks, and these clothes can then be made in a week and delivered to stores soon after.

This short time to market gives Zara great flexibility and has allowed it to compete effectively in the rapidly changing fashion market, where customer tastes evolve quickly.

IT also gives Zara instant feedback on which of its clothes are selling well and in which countries. This information enables Zara to engage in continual product development and remain at the cutting edge of fashion, a major source of differentiation advantage. For example, Zara can manufacture more of a particular kind of dress or suit to meet high customer demand, and it can keep up with fashion by constantly changing its mix of clothes in its rapidly expanding network of global stores. Moreover, since it is following a focused strategy, it can do this at relatively small output levels.

Indeed, IT has allowed Zara to minimize the inventory it has to carry, which is the major cost of goods sold for a clothing maker/retailer. For this reason, IT is a major driver of profitability. Because of the quick manufacturing-to-sales cycle and just-in-time fashion, Zara has been able to offer its collections at comparatively low prices and still make profits that are the envy of the fashion clothing industry. In fact, pricing has become the major competitive tool for managing competition in the fashion industry. When Zara offered its shares to the public for the first time in 2001, they soared in price because of the company's high return on invested capital. Investors believe that there will soon be a chain of Zara stores in most major cities around the world as its name becomes as common as those of well-known designers.

Many of the other clothing design and retail companies have awakened to the threat posed by companies like Zara and have pioneered their own proprietary lines of clothes (Dillard's Daniel Cremieux line is one), using a similar strategy to Zara's. Clothing designers like Ralph Lauren and Tommy Hilfiger have been forced to adopt similar approaches, bringing out new clothes collections several times a year and instituting price markdowns to sell inventory quickly. Even the major fashion houses have taken note of what is happening. Gucci, for example, which began to experience problems in the 1990s, brought in Thomas Ford, an American, as its chief designer and invested its resources to produce a new Ford-designed clothes line for both men and women to attract back Gucci's customers. Using IT, Gucci has also been able to design, manufacture, and distribute its clothing at a faster rate.

Increasingly, these companies are realizing that a competitive advantage and superior profitability cannot be maintained by brand image alone; all clothing companies must learn to use new strategies to defend their differentiated appeal, something that can be quickly lost in today's fast-changing global marketplace.[30]

Case Discussion Questions

1. What business model and strategies is Zara pursuing?

2. How has Zara's business model changed the nature of industry competition?

3. What new strategies have emerged in the fashion industry as a result?

Chapter 7

Strategy in High-Technology Industries

Opening Case

The Smart Phone Format War

At the present time the cell phone business is witnessing a format war. Symbian, a consortium led by Finnish cell phone maker Nokia, is engaged in a winner-takes-all struggle with Microsoft and PalmSource to establish its software as the operating system that will run applications on smart phones. Smart phones are hand-held devices that combine traditional cell phone functions with functions once only found on hand-held computers or PCs. Leading-edge smart phones are in effect powerful hand-held computers and communicators that come with a full range of personal information and management applications such as addresses and date books; the ability to browse the Internet; the ability to send and receive e-mail and digital photos; and the ability to run a growing number of other software programs ranging from pocket-sized versions of Microsoft Office to videogames.

Although the global market for such software is still relatively small—valued at $250 million a year in 2004—sales of smart phones are growing rapidly and may exceed 30 million units worldwide in 2005, up from a mere 5 million in 2003. Ultimately, many analysts believe that the development of the market for smart phone operating systems will mirror the development of the market for personal computer operating systems, where Microsoft dominates with a share of over 90 percent. They argue that independent software developers will write programs for whichever operating system is found on the largest number of smart phones. Thus if Symbian is outselling its rivals 2 to 1, developers will write applications for Symbian first. This will make Symbian smart phones more attractive to customers, and thus demand for smart phones with a Symbian operating system will increase. As demand grows, even more applications will become available for smart phones with a Symbian operating system, and Symbian's lead over its rivals will increase until its rivals are marginalized in the industry. Symbian could in effect become the Microsoft of the smart phone business.

Symbian has some big advantages on its side. In addition to Nokia, with about 48 percent of Symbian's equity, members of the consortium include some of the world's largest cell phone manufacturers, most notably Ericsson, Sony, Matsushita, and Siemens. These manufacturers clearly have an incentive to push smart phones that use the Symbian operating system. Perhaps for this reason, as of mid 2004 Symbian held a 41 percent share of the market for smart phone operating systems, up from 37 percent a year earlier. Symbian is followed by PalmSource and Microsoft, each with a 23 percent share. However, Symbian's influence is constrained by the fact that ultimately it is smart phone service providers, such as Verizon, that place orders for smart phones on behalf of their customers, and the service providers may request a Microsoft

229

or Palm operating system. PalmSource's operating system is based in the software originally developed for the Palm series of personal digital assistants, while Microsoft uses its Pocket PC software, which is derived from and compatible with Microsoft Windows. Both PalmSource and Microsoft have an advantage in that there are already a wide range of applications written to run on their operating systems. Moreover, many people are already familiar with the Palm and Microsoft user interfaces (for example, the interface on a Microsoft smart phone is similar to that on a Microsoft Windows PC). Still, these advantages have not been sufficient to halt the rise of Symbian. While Microsoft's market share held steady between 2003 and 2004, PalmSource saw its share fall to 23 percent from 31 percent a year earlier. Neither company is ready to concede defeat to Symbian just yet, however. Microsoft claims that a range of new phones based on its operating system will hit the market in 2005, while PalmSource has just introduced a more powerful version of its operating system, which it hopes will halt its declines in market share.[1]

Overview

In this chapter, we look at the nature of competition and strategy in high-technology industries. **Technology** refers to the body of scientific knowledge used in the production of goods or services. **High-technology (high-tech) industries** are those in which the underlying scientific knowledge that companies in the industry use is advancing rapidly, and by implication so are the attributes of the products and services that result from its application. The computer industry is often thought of as the quintessential example of a high-technology industry. Other industries often considered high tech are telecommunications, where new technologies based on wireless and the Internet have proliferated in recent years; consumer electronics, where the digital technology underlying products from DVD players to videogame terminals and digital cameras is advancing rapidly; pharmaceuticals, where new technologies based on cell biology, recombinant DNA, and genomics are revolutionizing the process of drug discovery; power generation, where new technologies based on fuel cells and cogeneration may change the economics of the industry; and aerospace, where the combination of new composite materials, electronics, and more efficient jet engines may give birth to a new era of near-supersonic commercial aircraft.

This chapter focuses on high-technology industries for a number of reasons. First, technology is accounting for an ever larger share of economic activity. Estimates suggest that 12 to 15 percent of total economic activity in the United States is accounted for by information technology industries.[2] This figure actually underestimates the true impact of technology on the economy, because it ignores the other high-technology areas we just mentioned. Moreover, as technology advances, many low-technology industries are becoming more high tech. For example, the development of biotechnology and genetic engineering transformed the production of seed corn, long considered a low-technology business, into a high-technology business. Moreover, high-technology products are making their way into a wide range of businesses; today a Ford Taurus contains more computing power than the multimillion-dollar mainframe computers used in the Apollo space program, and the competitive advantage of physical stores, such as Wal-Mart, is based on their use of information technology.[3] The circle of high-technology industries is both large and expanding, and even in industries not thought of as high tech, technology is revolutionizing aspects of the product or production system.

Although high-tech industries may produce very different products, when it comes to developing a business model and strategies that will lead to a competitive advantage and superior profitability and profit growth, they often face a similar situation. This chapter examines the competitive features found in many high-tech industries and the kinds of strategies that companies must adopt to build business models that will allow them to achieve superior profitability and profit growth.

By the time you have completed this chapter, you will have an understanding of the nature of competition in high-tech industries and the strategies that companies can pursue to succeed in those industries.

Technical Standards and Format Wars

Especially in high-tech industries, ownership of **technical standards**—a set of technical specifications that producers adhere to when making the product or a component of it—can be an important source of competitive advantage.[4] *Indeed, the source of product differentiation is based on the technical standard.* Often, only one standard will come to dominate a market, so many battles in high-tech industries revolve around companies competing to be the one that sets the standard.

Battles to set and control technical standards in a market are referred to as **format wars**; they are essentially battles to control the source of differentiation and thus the value that such differentiation can create for the customer. Because differentiated products often command premium prices and are often expensive to develop, the competitive stakes are enormous. The profitability and very survival of a company may depend on the outcome of the battle. For example, the outcome of the battle now being waged over the establishment and ownership of the operating system used by smart phones will help determine which companies will be leaders for decades to come in that marketplace (see the *Opening Case*).

■ Examples of Standards

A familiar example of a standard is the layout of a computer keyboard. No matter what keyboard you buy, the letters are all in the same pattern.[5] The reason is quite obvious. Imagine if each computer maker changed the ways the keys were laid out—if some started with QWERTY on the top row of letters (which is indeed the format used and is known as the QWERTY format), some with YUHGFD, and some with ACFRDS. If you learned to type on one layout, it would be irritating and time-consuming to have to relearn on a YUHGFD layout. The standard format (QWERTY) makes it easy for people to move from computer to computer because the input medium, the keyboard, is set out in a standard way.

Another example of a technical standard concerns the dimensions of containers used to ship goods on trucks, railcars, and ships: all have the same basic dimensions—the same height, length, and width—and all make use of the same locking mechanisms to hold them onto a surface or to bolt against each other. Having a standard ensures that containers can easily be moved from one mode of transportation to another—from trucks, to railcars, to ships, and back to railcars. If containers lacked standard dimensions and locking mechanisms, it would suddenly become much more difficult to ship containers around the world. Shippers would have to make sure that they had the right kind of container to go on the ships and trucks and railcars scheduled to carry a particular container around the world—very complicated indeed.

Consider, finally, the personal computer. Most share a common set of features: an Intel or Intel-compatible microprocessor, random access memory (RAM), a Microsoft operating system, an internal hard drive, a floppy disk drive, a CD drive, a keyboard, a monitor, a mouse, a modem, and so on. We call this set of features the dominant design for personal computers (a **dominant design** refers to a common set of features or design characteristics). Embedded in this design are several technical standards (see Figure 7.1). For example, there is the Wintel technical standard based on an Intel microprocessor

FIGURE 7.1

Technical Standards
for Personal
Computers

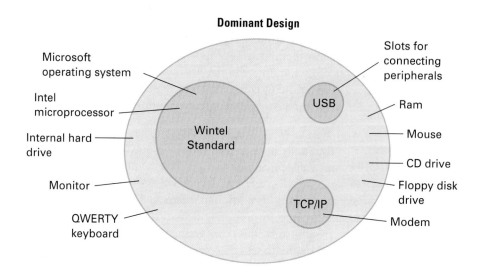

and a Microsoft operating system. Microsoft and Intel own that standard, which is central to the personal computer. Developers of software applications, component parts, and peripherals such as printers adhere to this standard when developing their own products because this guarantees that their products will work well with a personal computer based on the Wintel standard. Another technical standard for connecting peripherals to the PC is the Universal Serial Bus (or USB), established by an industry standards-setting board. No one owns it; the standard is in the public domain. A third technical standard is for communication between a PC and the Internet via a modem. Known as TCP/IP, this standard was also set by an industry association and is in the public domain. Thus, as with many other products, the PC is actually based on several technical standards. It is also important to note that when a company owns a standard, as Microsoft and Intel do with the Wintel standard, it may be a source of competitive advantage and high profitability.

■ **Benefits of**   Standards emerge because there are economic benefits associated with them. First,
Standards   having a technical standard helps to guarantee *compatibility* between products and their complements—other products used with them. For example, containers are used with railcars, trucks, and ships, and PCs are used with software applications. Compatibility has the tangible economic benefit of reducing the costs associated with making sure that products work well with each other.

Second, having a standard can help to *reduce confusion* in the minds of consumers. A few years ago, several consumer electronics companies were vying with each other to produce and market the first DVD players, and they were championing different variants of the basic DVD technology—different standards—that were incompatible with each other; a DVD disk designed to run on a DVD player made by Toshiba would not run on a player made by Sony, and vice versa. The companies feared that selling these incompatible versions of the same technology would produce confusion in the minds of consumers, who would not know which version to purchase and might decide to wait and see which technology ultimately dominated the marketplace. With lack of demand, the technology might fail to gain traction in the marketplace and would not be successful. To avoid this possibility, the developers of DVD equipment established a standard-setting body for the industry, the DVD Forum, which established a common technical standard for DVD players and disks that all companies adhered to. The result was that when DVDs were introduced, there was a common standard and no confusion in consumers' minds. This helped to boost demand for DVD players, making this one of the fastest-selling technologies of the late 1990s and early 2000s. First introduced in 1997, by 2001 some 13 million DVD players were sold in the United States, and they are now in one in four homes in the country.[6] However, so far the DVD Forum has not been able to agree on a common standard for the next version of DVDs, DVD recorders, which is slowing diffusion and adoption of the technology (see Strategy in Action 7.1).

Third, the emergence of a standard can help to *reduce production costs*. Once a standard emerges, products based on that standard design can be mass-produced, enabling the manufacturers to realize substantial economies of scale and lower their cost structures. The fact that there is a central standard for PCs (the Wintel

Strategy in Action   7.1

Where Is the Standard for DVD Recorders?

A few years ago, the 200-member DVD Forum achieved something of a coup when it managed to broker an agreement among some of its most important members on a common set of standards for DVD players. This common standard reduced consumer confusion and helped to propel DVD players into a mass-market phenomenon, replacing VHS video players in living rooms. Nevertheless, the DVD players found in most homes currently lack one attribute of VHS technology: they cannot record. It's not that a technology for making DVD recorders does not exist; in fact, several do, and therein lies the problem. The DVD Forum has been unable to get some of its most powerful members to agree on a common technical standard for DVD recorders, primarily because different companies want to see their variant of the technology become the industry standard.

There are at least three versions of DVD recorders now on offer: Hewlett-Packard is pushing one format, Sony and Philips are sponsoring another, and Matsushita yet another. And most important, DVD disks recorded using one format may not play on widely used DVD players or on computers that use another recording format.

First introduced in 1999, by 2003 some 1 million DVD recorders had been sold in the United States, many of them incorporated into new personal computers. But

industry observers feel that sales could have been much higher had there been harmonization of standards. By way of comparison, some 40 million CD recorders were sold in 2001, making CD recording technology solidly mainstream (DVDs can hold ten times as many data as CDs and are thus better suited to recording video). One reason for the slow takeup of DVD recorders has been the confusion over standards, and it's not just consumers who are confused. Many retailers are hesitant about stocking the technology until the battle over standards is resolved.

Another reason for the slow market growth has been the high price of DVD recorders. As of early 2004, a stand-alone DVD recorder still cost around $500. Although down from $1,500, the price tag for a DVD recorder is still substantially above that of a DVD player, which often can be purchased for under $100. For the price to fall lower, producers need to be able to manufacture in high volume and realize significant scale economies. But here lies the catch: to generate significant demand to support mass production and bring prices down, it may first be necessary to harmonize standards and reduce consumer confusion—and that is something that the producers currently seem unwilling to do. For the time being, the different companies are continuing to push their own proprietary standard in the hope that they establish it as the leading standard in the industry and reap the associated gains.[a]

standard) means that the component parts for a PC can be mass-produced. A manufacturer of internal hard drives, for example, can mass-produce drives for Wintel PCs, and so can realize substantial scale economies. If there were several competing and incompatible standards, each of which required a unique type of hard drive, production runs for hard drives would be shorter, unit costs would be higher, and the cost of PCs would go up.

Fourth, the emergence of standards can help to reduce the *risks associated with supplying complementary products* and thus increase the supply for those complements. Consider the risks associated with writing software applications to run on personal computers. This is a risky proposition, requiring the investment of considerable sums of money for developing the software before a single unit is sold. Imagine what would occur if there were ten different operating systems in use for PCs, each with only 10 percent of the market, rather than the current situation, where 95 percent of the world's PCs adhere to the Wintel standard. Software developers would be faced with the need to write ten different versions of the same software application, each for a much smaller market segment. This would change the economics of software development, increase its risks, and reduce potential profitability. Moreover, because of their higher cost structure and fewer economies of scale, the price of software programs would increase.

Thus, although many people complain about the consequences of Microsoft's near monopoly of PC operating systems, that monopoly does have at least one good effect: it substantially reduces the risks facing the makers of complementary products and the costs of those products. In fact, standards lead to both low-cost and differentiation advantages for individual companies and can help raise the level of industry profitability.

■ Establishment of Standards

Standards emerge in an industry in three main ways. First, recognizing the benefits of establishing a standard, companies in an industry might lobby the government to mandate an industry standard. In the United States, for example, the Federal Communications Commission (FCC), after detailed discussions with broadcasters and consumer electronics companies, has mandated a single technical standard for digital television broadcasts (DTV) and is requiring broadcasters to have capabilities in place for broadcasting digital signals based on this standard by 2006. The FCC took this step because it believed that without government action to set the standard, the rollout of DTV would be very slow. With a standard set by the government, consumer electronics companies can have greater confidence that a market will emerge, and this should encourage them to develop DTV products.

Second, technical standards are often set by cooperation among businesses, without government help, often through the medium of an industry forum, such as the DVD Forum. Companies cooperate in this way when they decide that competition among them to create a standard might be harmful because of the uncertainty that it would create in the minds of consumers.

When standards are set by the government or an industry association, they fall into the **public domain**, meaning that any company can freely incorporate the knowledge and technology on which the standard is based into its products. For example, no one owns the QWERTY format, and therefore no one company can profit from it directly. Similarly, the language that underlies the presentation of text and graphics on the Web, hypertext markup language (HTML), is in the public domain; it is free for all to use. The same is true for TCP/IP, the communications standard used for transmitting data on the Internet.

Often, however, the industry standard is selected competitively by the purchasing patterns of customers in the marketplace—that is, by *market demand*. In this case, the strategy and business model a company has developed for promoting its technological standard are of critical importance because ownership of an industry standard that is protected from imitation by patents and copyrights is a valuable asset—a source of sustained competitive advantage and superior profitability. Microsoft and Intel, for example, both owe their competitive advantage to their ownership of format wars, which exist between two or more companies competing against each other to get their designs adopted as the industry standard. Format wars are common in high-tech industries because of the high stakes. The Wintel standard became the dominant standard for PCs only after Microsoft and Intel won format wars against Apple Computer's proprietary system and later against IBM's OS/2 operating system. Microsoft and Real Networks are currently competing head-to-head in a format war to establish rival technologies—Windows Media Player and RealPlayer—as the standard for streaming video and audio technology on the Web. The *Opening Case* tells how Symbian, Microsoft, and PalmSource are engaged in a format war in the wireless business as they try to get their respective operating systems established as the standard for smart phones.

■ Network Effects, Positive Feedback, and Lockout

There has been a growing realization that when standards are set by competition between companies promoting different formats, network effects are a primary determinant of how standards are established.[7] **Network effects** arise in industries where the size of the "network" of *complementary* products is a primary determinant of demand for an industry's product. For example, the demand for automobiles early in the twentieth century was an increasing function of the *network* of paved roads and gas stations. Similarly, the demand for telephones is an increasing function of the number of other numbers that can be called with that phone; that is, of the size of the telephone network (the telephone network is the complementary product). When the first telephone service was introduced in New York City, only a hundred numbers could be called. The network was very small because of the limited number of wires and telephone switches, which made the telephone a relatively useless piece of equipment. As more and more people got telephones and as the network of wires and switches expanded, the value of a telephone connection increased. This led to an increase in demand for telephone lines, which further increased the value of owning a telephone, setting up a positive feedback loop. The same type of positive feedback loop is now at work in the Internet.

To understand why network effects are important in the establishment of standards, consider the classic example of a format war: the battle between Sony and Matsushita to establish their respective technology for videocassette recorders (VCRs) as the standard in the marketplace. Sony was first to market with its Betamax technology, followed by Matsushita with its VHS technology. Both companies sold VCR recorder-players, and movie studios issued films prerecorded on VCR tapes for rental to consumers. Initially, all tapes were issued in Betamax format to play on Sony's machine. Sony *did not* license its Betamax technology, preferring to make all of the player-recorders itself. When Matsushita entered the market, it realized that to make its VHS format players valuable to consumers, it would have to encourage movie studios to issue movies for rental on VHS tapes. The only way to do that, Matsushita's managers reasoned, was to increase the installed base of VHS players as rapidly as possible. They believed that the greater the installed base of VHS players, the greater the incentive would be for movie studios to issue movies for

Positive Feedback in the Market for VCRs

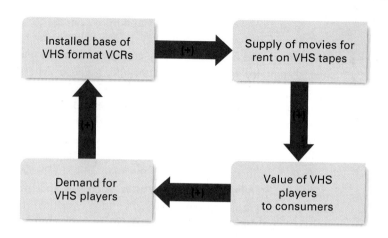

rental on VHS format tapes. The more prerecorded VHS tapes were available for rental, the greater the value of a VHS player became to consumers, and therefore, the greater the demand would be for VHS players (see Figure 7.2). Matsushita wanted to exploit a positive feedback loop.

To do this, Matsushita chose a licensing strategy under which any consumer electronics company was allowed to manufacture VHS format players under license. The strategy worked. A large number of companies signed on to manufacture VHS players, and soon far more VHS players were available for purchase in stores than Betamax players. As sales of VHS players started to grow, movie studios issued more films for rental in VHS format, and this stoked demand. Before long, it was clear to anyone who walked into a video rental store that there were more and more VHS tapes available for rent and fewer and fewer Betamax tapes. This served to reinforce the positive feedback loop, and ultimately Sony's Betamax technology was shut out of the market. The pivotal difference between the two companies was strategy: Matsushita chose a licensing strategy, and Sony did not. As a result, Matsushita's VHS technology became the de facto standard for VCRs, while Sony's Betamax technology was locked out.

The general principle that emerges from this example is that when two or more companies are competing with each other to get their technology adopted as a standard in an industry, and when network effects and positive feedback loops are important, the company that wins the format war will be the one whose strategy best exploits positive feedback loops. It turns out that this is a very important strategic principle in many high-technology industries, particularly computer hardware, software, telecommunications, and consumer electronics. Microsoft is where it is today because it exploited a positive feedback loop. So did Dolby (see Strategy in Action 7.2).

An important implication of the positive feedback process is that as the market settles on a standard, companies promoting alternative standards can become **locked out** of the market when consumers are unwilling to bear the switching costs required for them to abandon the established standard and adopt the new standard. In this context, **switching costs** are the costs that consumers must bear to switch from a product based on one technological standard to a product based on another.

Strategy in Action

7.2

How Dolby Became the Standard in Sound Technology

Inventor Ray Dolby's name has become synonymous with superior sound in homes, movie theaters, and recording studios. The technology produced by his company, Dolby Laboratories, is part of nearly every music cassette and cassette recorder, prerecorded videotape, and, most recently, DVD movie disk and player. Since 1976, close to 1.5 billion audio products that use Dolby's technology have been sold worldwide. More than 44,000 movie theaters now show films in Dolby Digital Surround Sound, and some 40 million Dolby Digital home theater receivers have been sold since 1999. Dolby technology has become the industry standard for high-quality sound in the music and film industry. Any company that wants to promote its products as having superior technology licenses sound technology from Dolby. How did Dolby build this technology franchise?

The story goes back to 1965 when Dolby Laboratories was founded in London by Ray Dolby (the company's headquarters moved to San Francisco in 1976). Dolby, who had a PhD in physics from Cambridge University in England, had invented a technology for reducing the background hiss in professional tape recording without compromising the quality of the material being recorded. Dolby manufactured the sound systems incorporating his technology, but sales to professional recording studios were initially slow. Then in 1968 Dolby had a big break. He met Henry Kloss, whose company, KLH, was a highly regarded American producer of audio equipment (record players and tape decks) for the consumer market. Dolby reached an agreement to license his noise-reduction technology to KLH, and soon other manufacturers of consumer equipment started to approach Dolby to license the technology. Dolby briefly considered manufacturing record players and tape decks for the consumer market, but as he later commented, "I knew that if we entered that market and tried to make something like a cassette deck, we would be in competition with any licensee that we took on. . . . So we had to stay out of manufacturing in that area in order to license in that area."

Dolby adopted a licensing business model and then had to determine what licensing fee to charge. He knew his technology was valuable, but he also understood that charging a high licensing fee would encourage manufacturers to invest in developing their own noise-reduction

technology. He decided to charge a modest fee to reduce the incentive that manufacturers would have to develop their own technology. Then there was the question of which companies to license to. Dolby wanted the Dolby name associated with superior sound, so he needed to make sure that licensees adhered to quality standards. Therefore, the company set up a formal quality control program for its licensees' products. Licensees have to agree to have their products tested by Dolby, and the licensing agreement states that they cannot sell products that do not pass Dolby's quality tests. By preventing products with substandard performance from reaching the market, Dolby has maintained the quality image of products featuring Dolby technology and trademarks. Today, Dolby Laboratories tests samples of hundreds of licensed products every year under this program. By making sure that the Dolby name is associated with superior sound quality, Dolby's quality assurance strategy has increased the power of the Dolby brand, making it very valuable to license.

Another key aspect of Dolby's strategy was born in 1970 when Dolby began to promote the idea of releasing prerecorded cassettes encoded with Dolby noise-reduction technology so that they would have low noise when played on players equipped with Dolby noise-reduction technology. Dolby decided to license the technology on prerecorded tapes for free, instead collecting licensing fees just from the sales of tape players that used Dolby technology. This strategy was hugely successful and set up a positive feedback loop that helped to make Dolby technology ubiquitous. Growing sales of prerecorded tapes encoded with Dolby technology created a demand for players that contained Dolby technology, and as the installed base of players with Dolby technology grew, the proportion of prerecorded tapes that were encoded with Dolby technology surged, further boosting demand for players incorporating Dolby technology. By the mid 1970s, virtually all prerecorded tapes were encoded with Dolby noise-reduction technology. This strategy remains in effect today for all media recorded with Dolby technology and encompasses not only videocassettes but also videogames and DVD releases encoded with Dolby Surround or Dolby Digital.

As a result of its licensing and quality assurance strategies, Dolby has become the standard for high-quality sound in the music and film industries. Although the company is small—its revenues were around $250 million in 2004—its influence is large. It continues to push the boundaries of sound-reduction technology (it has been a leader in digital sound since the mid 1980s) and has successfully extended its noise-reduction franchise, first into films, then into DVD and videogame technology, and finally onto the Web, where it has licensed its digital technology to a wide range of media companies for digital music delivery and digital audio players, such as those built into personal computers and hand-held music players.[b]

For illustration, imagine that a company developed an operating system for personal computers that was both faster and more stable (crashed less) than the current standard in the marketplace, Microsoft Windows. Would this company be able to gain significant market share from Microsoft? Only with great difficulty. Consumers buy personal computers not for their operating system but for the applications that run on that system. A new operating system would initially have a very small installed base, so few developers would be willing to take the risks in writing word processing programs, spreadsheets, games, and other applications for that operating system. Because there would be very few applications available, consumers who did make the switch would have to bear the switching costs associated with giving up some of their applications—something that they might be unwilling to do. Moreover, even if applications were available for the new operating system, consumers would have to bear the costs of purchasing those applications, another source of switching costs. In addition, they would have to bear the costs associated with learning to use the new operating system, yet another source of switching costs. Thus, many consumers would be unwilling to switch even if the new operating system performed better than Windows, and the company promoting the new operating system would be locked out of the market.

Consumers *will* bear switching costs if the benefits of adopting the new technology outweigh the costs of switching. For example, in the late 1980s and early 1990s, millions of people switched from analog record players to digital CD players even though the switching costs were significant: they had to purchase the new player technology, and many people purchased duplicate copies of their favorite music recordings. They nevertheless made the switch because for many people, the perceived benefit—the incredibly better sound quality associated with CDs—outweighed the costs of switching.

As this process started to get under way, a positive feedback started to develop, with the growing installed base of CD players leading to an increase in the number of music recordings issued on CDs, as opposed to or in addition to vinyl records. Past some point, the installed base of CD players got so big that music companies started to issue recordings only on CDs. Once this happened, even those who did not want to switch to the new technology were required to if they wished to purchase new music recordings. The industry standard had shifted: the new technology had locked in as the standard, and the old technology was locked out. It follows that despite its dominance, the Wintel standard for personal computers could one day be superseded if a competitor finds a way of providing sufficient benefits that enough consumers are willing to bear the switching costs associated with moving to a new operating system.

Strategies for Winning a Format War

From the perspective of a company pioneering a new technological standard in a marketplace where network effects and positive feedback loops operate, the key question becomes, "What strategy should we pursue to establish our format as the dominant one?"

The various strategies that companies should adopt to win format wars revolve around *finding ways to make network effects work in their favor and against their competitors*. Winning a format war requires a company to build the installed base for its standard as rapidly as possible, thereby leveraging the positive feedback loop, inducing consumers to bear switching costs, and ultimately locking the market into its technology. It requires the company to jump-start and then accelerate demand for its technological standard or format such that it becomes established as quickly as possible as the industry standard, thereby locking out competing formats. There are a number of key strategies and tactics that can be adopted to try to achieve this.[8]

■ Ensure a Supply of Complements

It is important for the company to make sure that, in addition to the product itself, there is an adequate supply of complements. For example, no one will buy the Sony PlayStation 2 unless there is an adequate supply of games to run on that machine. And no one will purchase a Palm hand-held computer unless there are enough software applications to run on it. Companies normally take two steps to ensure an adequate supply of complements.

First, they may diversify into the production of complements and seed the market with sufficient supply to help jump-start demand for their format. Before Sony produced the original PlayStation in the early 1990s, it established its own in-house unit to produce videogames for the PlayStation. When it launched the PlayStation, Sony also simultaneously issued sixteen games to run on the machine, giving consumers a reason to purchase the format. Second, companies may create incentives or make it easy for independent companies to produce complements. Sony also licensed the right to produce games to a number of independent game developers, charged the developers a lower royalty rate than they had to pay to competitors such as Nintendo and Sega, and provided them with software tools that made it easier for them to develop the games. Thus, the launch of the Sony PlayStation was accompanied by the simultaneous launch of thirty or so games, which quickly helped to stimulate demand for the machine.

■ Leverage Killer Applications

Killer applications are applications or uses of a new technology or product that are so compelling that they persuade customers to adopt the new format or technology in droves, thereby "killing" demand for competing formats. Killer applications often help to jump-start demand for the new standard. For example, in the late 1990s, hand-held computers based on the Palm operating system became the dominant format in the market for personal digital assistants (PDAs). The killer applications that drove adoption of the Palm format were the personal information management functions and a pen-based input medium (based on **Graffiti**) that Palm bundled with its original PalmPilot, which it introduced in 1996. There had been PDAs before the PalmPilot, including Apple Computer's ill-fated Newton, but it was the applications and ease of use of the PalmPilot that persuaded many consumers to enter this market. Within eighteen months of its initial launch, more than 1 million PalmPilots had been launched, making for a faster demand ramp-up than the first cell phones and pagers. Similarly, the killer applications that induced consumers to sign up to online services such as AOL were e-mail, chatroom, and the ability to browse the Web.

Ideally, the company promoting a technological standard will want to develop the killer applications itself—that is, develop the appropriate complementary products—as Palm did with the PalmPilot. However, it may also be able to leverage the applications that others develop. For example, the early sales of the IBM PC following its 1981 introduction were driven primarily by IBM's decision to license two important software programs for the PC, VisiCalc (a spreadsheet program) and Easy Writer (a word processing program), both developed by independent companies. IBM saw that they were driving rapid adoption of rival personal computers, such as the Apple II, so it quickly licensed them, produced versions that would run on the IBM PC, and sold them as complements to the IBM PC, a strategy that was to prove very successful.

■ Aggressively Price and Market

A common tactic to jump-start demand is to adopt a **razor-and-razor-blades strategy:** pricing the product (razor) low in order to stimulate demand and increase the installed base, and then trying to make high profits on the sale of complements (razor blades), which are priced relatively high. This strategy owes its name to the fact that it was pioneered by Gillette to sell its razors and razor blades. Many other companies have followed this strategy—for example, Hewlett-Packard typically sells its printers at cost but makes significant profits on the subsequent sale of its replacement cartridges. In this case, the printer is the "razor," and it is priced low to stimulate demand and induce consumers to switch from their existing printer, while the cartridges are the "blades," which are priced high to make profits. The inkjet printer represents a proprietary technological format because only Hewlett-Packard cartridges can be used with the printers, and not cartridges designed for competing inkjet printers, such as those sold by Canon. A similar strategy is used in the videogame industry: manufacturers price videogame consoles at cost to induce consumers to adopt their technology, while making profits on the royalties they receive from the sales of games that run on their system.

Aggressive marketing is also a key factor in jump-starting demand to get an early lead in an installed base. Substantial upfront marketing and point-of-sales promotion techniques are often used to try to get potential early adopters to bear the switching costs associated with adopting the format. If these efforts are successful, they can be the start of a positive feedback loop. Again, the Sony PlayStation provides a good example. Sony colinked the introduction of the PlayStation with nationwide television advertising aimed at its primary demographic (eighteen- to thirty-four-year-olds) and in-store displays that allowed potential buyers to play games on the machine before making a purchase. More recently, Microsoft earmarked $500 million for marketing its new Xbox in 2002. Successful marketing can set the ball rolling and create a positive feedback loop.

■ Cooperate with Competitors

Companies have been close to simultaneously introducing competing and incompatible technological standards a number of times. A good example is the compact disk. Initially four companies—Sony, Philips, JVC, and Telefunken—were developing CD players using different variations of the underlying laser technology. If this situation had persisted, they might have ultimately introduced incompatible technologies into the marketplace, so a CD made for a Philips CD player would not play on a Sony CD player. Understanding that the nearly simultaneous introduction of such incompatible technologies can create significant confusion among consumers and often leads them to delay their purchases, Sony and Philips decided to join forces with each other and cooperate on developing the technology. Sony contributed its error correction technology, and Philips contributed its laser technology. The result of this cooperation was that momentum among other players in the industry shifted toward the Sony-Philips alliances; JVC and Telefunken were left with little support. Most important, recording labels announced that they would support the Sony-Philips format but not the Telefunken or JVC format. Telefunken and JVC subsequently decided to abandon their efforts to develop CD technology. The cooperation between Sony and Philips was important because it reduced confusion in the industry and allowed a single format to rise to the fore, which speeded up adoption of the technology. The cooperation was a win-win situation for both Philips and Sony, eliminating their competitors and allowing them to share in the success of the format.

■ **License the Format**

Another strategy often adopted is to license the format to other enterprises so that they can produce products based on it. The company that pioneered the format gains from the licensing fees that flow back to it and from the enlarged supply of the product, which can stimulate demand and help accelerate market adoption. This was the strategy that Matsushita adopted with its VHS format for the videocassette recorder. In addition to producing VCRs at its own factory in Osaka, Matsushita let a number of other companies produce VHS format players under license (Sony decided not to license its competing Betamax format and produced all Betamax format players itself), and so VHS players were more widely available. More people purchased VHS players, which created an incentive for film companies to issue more films on VHS tapes (as opposed to Betamax tapes), which further increased demand for VHS players, and hence helped Matsushita to lock in VHS as the dominant format in the marketplace. Sony, ironically the first to market, saw its position marginalized by the reduced supply of the critical complement, prerecorded films, and ultimately withdrew Betamax players from the consumer marketplace.

Dolby, we saw in Strategy in Action 7.2, adopted a similar licensing strategy to get its noise-reduction technology adopted as the technological standard in the music and film industries. By charging a modest licensing fee for use of the technology in recording equipment and forgoing licensing fees on media recorded using Dolby technology, Dolby deliberately sought to reduce the financial incentive that potential competitors might have to develop their own, possibly superior, technology. Dolby calculated that its long-run profitability would be maximized by adopting a licensing strategy that limited the incentive of competitors to enter the market.

The correct strategy to pursue in a particular scenario requires that the company consider all of these different strategies and tactics and pursue those that seem most appropriate given the competitive circumstances prevailing in the industry and the likely strategy of rivals. Although there is no one best mix of strategies and tactics, the company must keep the goal of rapidly increasing the installed base of products based on its standard at the front of its mind. By helping to jump-start demand for its format, a company can induce consumers to bear the switching costs associated with adopting its technology and leverage any positive feedback process that might exist. Also important is not pursuing strategies that have the opposite effect. For example, pricing high to capture profits from early adopters, who tend not to be as price sensitive as later adopters, can have the unfortunate effect of slowing demand growth and letting a more aggressive competitor pick up share and establish its format as the industry standard.

Costs in High-Technology Industries

In many high-tech industries, the fixed costs of developing the product are very high, but the costs of producing one extra unit of the product are very low. This is most obvious in the case of software. For example, it reportedly cost Microsoft $1 billion to develop Windows XP, the latest version of its Windows operating system, but the cost of producing one more copy of Windows XP is virtually zero. Once Windows XP was completed, Microsoft produced master disks that it sent out to PC manufacturers, such as Dell Computer, which then loaded a copy of Windows XP onto every PC it sold. The cost to Microsoft was effectively zero, and yet it receives a significant licensing fee for each copy of Windows XP installed on a PC.[9] For Microsoft, the *marginal cost* of making one more copy of Windows XP is close to zero, although the *fixed costs* of developing the product are $1 billion.

Many other high-technology products have similar cost economics: very high fixed costs and very low marginal costs. Most software products share these features, although if the software is sold through stores, the costs of packaging and distribution will raise the marginal costs, and if it is sold by a sales force direct to end-users, this too will raise the marginal costs. Many consumer electronics products have the same basic economics. The fixed costs of developing a DVD player or a videogame console can be very expensive, but the costs of producing an incremental unit are very low. The costs of developing a new drug, such as Viagra, can run to over $500 million, but the marginal cost of producing each additional pill is at most a few cents.

■ **Comparative Cost Economics**

To grasp why this cost structure is strategically important, it must be understood that, in many industries, marginal costs *rise* as a company tries to expand output (economists call this the *law of diminishing returns*). To produce more of a good, a company has to hire more labor and invest in more plant and machinery. At *the margin,* the additional resources used are not as productive, so this leads to increasing marginal costs. However, the law of diminishing returns often does not apply in many high-tech settings, such as the production of software or sending one more bit of data down a digital telecommunications network.

Consider two companies, α and β (see Figure 7.3). Company α is a conventional producer and faces diminishing returns, so as it tries to expand output, its marginal

FIGURE 7.3

Cost Structures in High-Technology Industries

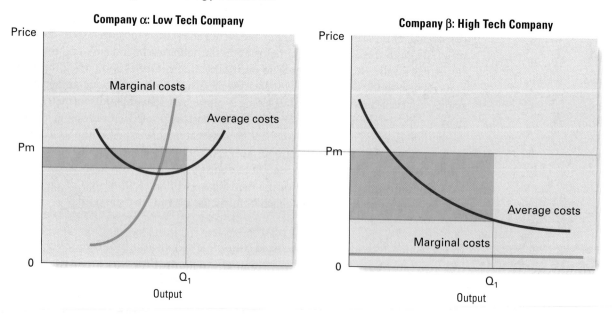

costs rise. Company β is a high-tech producer, and its marginal costs do not rise at all as output is increased. Note that in Figure 7.3, company β's marginal cost curve is drawn as a straight line near to the horizontal axis, implying that marginal costs are close to zero and do not vary with output, whereas company α's marginal costs rise as output is expanded, illustrating diminishing returns. Company β's flat and low marginal cost curve means that its average cost curve will fall continuously over all ranges of output as it spreads its fixed costs out over greater volume. In contrast, the rising marginal costs encountered by company α mean that its average cost curve is the U-shaped curve familiar from basic economics texts. For simplicity, assume that both companies sell their product at the same price, P_m, and both sell exactly the same quantity of output, $0 - Q_1$. You will see from Figure 7.3 that at an output of Q_1, company β has much lower average costs than company α and as a consequence is making far more profit (profit is the blue shaded area in Figure 7.3).

■ **Strategic Significance**

If a company can shift from a cost structure where it encounters increasing marginal costs to one where fixed costs may be high but marginal costs are much lower, its profitability may increase. In the consumer electronics industry, such a shift has been playing out for two decades. Music recordings used to be based on analog technology where marginal costs rose as output expanded due to diminishing returns (as in the case of company α in Figure 7.3). Since the 1980s, digital systems such as CD players have replaced analog systems. Digital systems are software based, and this implies much lower marginal costs of producing one more copy of a recording. As a result, the music labels have been able to lower prices, expand demand, and see their profitability increase (their production system has more in common with company β in Figure 7.3).

This process is still unfolding. The latest technology for making copies of music recordings is based on distribution over the Internet (for example, by downloading onto an MP3 player). Here, the marginal costs of making one more copy of a recording are lower still. In fact, they are close to zero and do not increase with output. The only problem is that the low costs of copying and distributing music recordings have created a major copyright problem that the major music labels have yet to solve (we discuss this in more detail shortly when we consider intellectual property rights). The same shift is now beginning to affect other industries. Some companies are building their strategies around trying to exploit and profit from this shift. For an example, Strategy in Action 7.3 looks at SonoSite.

Another implication of its cost structure is that when a high-tech company faces high fixed costs and low marginal costs, its strategy should emphasize the low-cost option: deliberately drive prices down to drive volume up. Look again at Figure 7.3 and you will see that *the high-tech company's average costs fall rapidly as output expands.* This implies that prices can be reduced to stimulate demand, and so long as prices fall less rapidly than average costs, per unit profit margins will expand as prices fall. This is a consequence of the fact that the firm's marginal costs are low and do not rise with output. This strategy of pricing low to drive volume and reap wider profit margins is central to the business model of some very successful high-technology companies, including Microsoft. When Microsoft founder Bill Gates was called into a U.S. Senate hearing during the Microsoft antitrust investigation in 2000, he explained to the bemused senators that Microsoft did not behave like a classic monopolist, raising prices and restricting output to maximize profits. Rather, he said, Microsoft cut prices to stimulate sales and thus increase its profit margins. Gates claimed that the strategy was good for consumers—they got cheaper software—and good for Microsoft's

Strategy in Action   7.3

Lowering Costs Through Digitalization

The ultrasound unit has been an important piece of diagnostic equipment in hospitals for some time. Ultrasound units use the physics of sound to produce images of soft tissues in the human body. They can produce detailed three-dimensional color images of organs and, by using contrast agents, track the flow of fluids through an organ. A cardiologist, for example, can use an ultrasound in combination with contrast agents injected into the bloodstream to track the flow of blood through a beating heart. In additional to the visual diagnosis, ultrasound also produces an array of quantitative diagnostic information of great value to physicians.

Modern ultrasound units are sophisticated instruments that cost around $250,000 to $300,000 each for a top-line model. They are fairly bulky instruments, weighing some three hundred pounds, and are wheeled around hospitals on carts.

A few years back, a group of researchers at ATL, one of the leading ultrasound companies, came up with an idea for reducing the size and cost of a basic unit. They theorized that it might be possible to replace up to 80 percent of the solid circuits in an ultrasound unit with software, in the process significantly shrinking the size and reducing the weight of machines and thereby producing portable ultrasound units. Moreover, by digitalizing much of the ultrasound, replacing hardware with software, they could considerably drive down the marginal costs of making additional units, and would thus be able to make a good profit at much lower price points.

The researchers reasoned that a portable and inexpensive ultrasound unit would find market opportunities in totally new niches. For example, a small, inexpensive ultrasound unit could be placed in an ambulance or carried into battle by an army medic, or purchased by family physicians for use in their offices. Although they realized that it would be some time, perhaps decades, before such small, inexpensive machines could attain the image quality and diagnostic sophistication of top-of-the-line machines, they saw the opportunity in terms of creating market niches that previously could not be served by ultrasound companies because of the high costs and bulk of the product.

The researchers ultimately became a project team within ATL and were then spun out of ATL as an entirely new company, SonoSite. In late 1999, they introduced their first portable product, weighing just six pounds and costing around $25,000. SonoSite targeted niches that full-sized ultrasound products could not reach: ambulatory care and foreign markets that could not afford the more expensive equipment. In 2003, the company sold $85 million worth of its product. In the long run, SonoSite plans to build more features and greater image quality into the small hand-held machines, primarily by improving the software. This could allow the units to penetrate U.S. hospital markets that currently purchase the established technology, much as client-server systems based on PC technology came to replace mainframes for some functions in business corporations.[c]

profit margins. It was clear from the questioning that the senators had trouble believing this explanation, but for Gates and his company, it has been a central aspect of their strategy since the early 1980s.

Managing Intellectual Property Rights

Ownership of a technology can be a source of sustained competitive advantage and superior profitability, particularly when the company owns a technology that is the standard in an industry, such as Microsoft and Intel's Wintel standard for personal computers and Dolby's ownership of the standard for noise-reduction technology in the music and film recording industries. Even if a technology is not standard but is valued by a sufficient number of consumers, ownership of that technology can still be very profitable. Apple's current personal computer technology is by no means the standard in the marketplace, much as Apple would like it to be. In fact,

the company's iMac technology accounts for less th
computers sold every year. But that small slice of a v
able niche for Apple.

■ Intellectual Property Rights

Because new technology is the product of intellectual a
tellectual property. The term **intellectual property** refe
lectual and creative effort and includes not only new
range of intellectual creations, including music, films,
society, we value the products of intellectual and creati
erty is seen as a very important driver of economic prog....... and social wealth.[10] But
it is also often expensive, risky, and time-consuming to create intellectual property.

For example, a new drug to treat a dangerous medical condition such as cancer
can take twelve to sixteen years to develop and cost as much as $800 million. More-
over, only 20 percent of new drugs that are tested in humans actually make it to the
market.[11] The remainder fail because they are found to be unsafe or ineffective.
Given the costs, risks, and time involved in this activity, few companies would be
willing to embark on the road required to develop a new drug and bring it to market
unless they could be reasonably sure that if they were successful in developing the
drug, their investment would be profitable. If the minute they introduced a successful cancer drug, their competitors produced imitations of that drug, no company
would even consider making the initial investment.

To make sure that this does not happen, we grant the creators of intellectual
property certain rights over their creation. These rights, which stop competitors from
copying or imitating the creation for a number of years, take the legal forms of
patents, copyrights, and trademarks, which all serve the same basic objective: to give
individuals and companies an incentive to engage in the expensive and risky business
of creating new intellectual property.

The creation of intellectual property is a central endeavor in high-technology industries, and the management of intellectual property rights has moved to center
stage in many of these companies. Developing strategies to protect and enforce intellectual property rights can be an important aspect of competitive advantage. For
many companies, this amounts to making sure that their patents and copyrights are
respected. It is not uncommon, therefore, to see high-technology companies bringing lawsuits against their competitors for patent infringement. In general, companies
often use such lawsuits not only to sanction those they suspect of violating the company's intellectual property rights, but also to signal to potential violators that the
company will aggressively defend its property. Legal action alone suffices to protect
intellectual property in many industries, but in others, such as software, the low costs
of illegally copying and distributing intellectual property call for more creative
strategies to manage intellectual property rights.

■ Digitalization and Piracy Rates

Protecting intellectual property has become more complicated in the past few
decades because of **digitalization,** that is, the rendering of creative output in digital
form. This can be done for music recordings, films, books, newspapers, magazines,
and computer software. Digitalization has dramatically lowered the cost of copying
and distributing digitalized intellectual property or digital media. As we have seen,
the marginal cost of making one more copy of a software program is very low, and
the same is true for any other intellectual property rendered in digital form. Moreover,
digital media can be distributed at a very low cost (again, almost zero), for example, by
distributing over the Internet. Reflecting on this, one commentator has described the

Internet as a "giant out-of-control copying machine."[12] The low marginal costs of copying and distributing digital media have made it very easy to sell illegal copies of such property. In turn, this has helped to produce a high level of piracy (in this context, **piracy** refers to the theft of intellectual property).

The International Federation of the Phonographic Industry claims that around one-third of all CDs and cassettes around the globe were illegally produced and sold in 2002, suggesting that piracy cost the industry over $4.6 billion per annum.[13] The computer software industry also suffers from lax enforcement of intellectual property rights. Estimates suggest that violations of intellectual property rights cost computer software firms revenues equal to $13.08 billion in 2002.[14] According to the Business Software Alliance, a software industry association, in 2002 some 39 percent of all software applications used in the world were pirated. The worst region was Eastern Europe, where the piracy rate was 71 percent. One of the worst countries was China, where the piracy rate in 2002 ran 92 percent and cost the industry over $2.4 billion in lost sales, up from $444 million in 1995. Although the piracy rate was much lower in the United States, the value of sales lost was more significant because of the size of the market, reaching an estimated $2.0 billion in 2002.[15]

The scale of this problem is so large that simply resorting to legal tactics to enforce intellectual property rights has amounted to nothing more than a partial solution to the piracy problem. Many companies now build sophisticated encryption software into their digital products, which can make it more difficult for pirates to copy digital media and thereby can raise the costs of stealing. But the pirates too are sophisticated and often seem to be able to find their way around encryption software. This raises the question of whether there are additional strategies that can be adopted to manage digital rights, and thereby limit piracy.

■ **Strategies for Managing Digital Rights**

One strategy is simply to recognize that while the low costs of copying and distributing digital media make some piracy inevitable, the same attributes can be used to the company's advantage. The basic strategy here represents yet another variation of the basic razor-and-razor-blades principle: give something away for free to boost the sales of a complementary product. A familiar example concerns Adobe Acrobat Reader, the software program for reading documents formatted by Adobe Acrobat (that is, PDF formatted documents). Adobe developed Adobe Acrobat to allow people to format documents in a manner that resembled a high-quality printed page and to display and distribute these documents over the Web. Moreover, Adobe documents are formatted in a read-only format, meaning that they cannot be altered by individuals, nor can parts of those documents be copied and pasted to other documents. Its strategy has been to give away Adobe Acrobat Reader for free and then make money by selling its Acrobat software for formatting documents. The strategy has worked extremely well. Anyone can download a copy of Acrobat Reader from Adobe's website. Because the marginal costs of copying and distributing this software over the Web are extremely low, the process is almost costless for both Adobe and its customers. The result is that the Acrobat Reader has diffused very rapidly and is now the dominant format for viewing high-quality documents distributed and downloaded over the Web. As the installed base of Acrobat Readers has grown, sales of Adobe Acrobat software have soared as more and more organizations and individuals realize that formatting their digital documents in Acrobat format makes sense.

Another strategy is to take advantage of the low costs of copying and distributing digital media to drive down the costs of purchasing those media, thereby reducing the incentive that consumers have to steal. When coupled with encryption software that makes piracy more difficult and vigorous legal actions to enforce intellectual property regulations, this can slow the piracy rate and generate incremental revenues that cost little to produce.

Several music companies are now experimenting with variants of this strategy. Roxio, a manufacturer of software for copying, or "burning," music onto CDs, has begun to partner with several music labels to develop just such a strategy.[16] In 2001, Roxio's Easy CD Creator and Toast software accounted for 70 percent of the CD burning software sold. The software is now preloaded onto most new personal computers. However, Roxio's sales growth has been hampered by opposition from music labels, which argue that Roxio's software is promoting music piracy and hurting CD sales. In response, Roxio persuaded several music companies to start experimenting with a service that allows users to burn music onto CDs. In January 2002, Pressplay, a service backed by Sony, Universal Music, and EMI, began to allow users to download songs digitally and burn them onto CDs. Users pay $25 a month to burn twenty songs, although they can burn only two tracks from a single artist each month. This business model allows subscribers to customize a CD, which is what many do anyway when pirating CDs by burning them. However, in theory, the service saves customers money because they do not have to purchase the original CDs. Pressplay and Roxio hope that the strategy will reduce piracy rates, while generating incremental revenues that cost very little to produce because of the extremely low marginal costs of copying and distributing music in this manner (in 2003 Pressplay was sold to Roxio).

Capturing First-Mover Advantages

In high-technology industries, companies often compete by striving to be the first to develop revolutionary new products, that is, to be a **first mover**. By definition, the first mover with regard to a revolutionary product is in a monopoly position. If the new product satisfies unmet consumer needs and demand is high, the first mover can capture significant revenues and profits. Such revenues and profits signal to potential rivals that there is money to be made by imitating the first mover. As illustrated in Figure 7.4, in the absence of strong barriers to imitation, this implies that imitators will rush into the market created by the first mover, competing away the first mover's monopoly profits and leaving all participants in the market with a much lower level of returns.

FIGURE 7.4

The Impact of Imitation on Profits of a First Mover

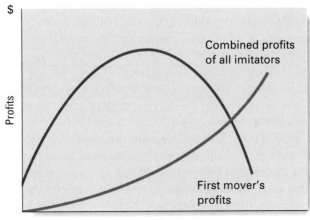

Despite imitation, some first movers have the ability to capitalize on and reap substantial **first-mover advantages**—the advantages of pioneering new technologies and products that lead to an enduring competitive advantage. Intel introduced the world's first microprocessor in 1971 and today still dominates the microprocessor segment of the semiconductor industry. Xerox introduced the world's first photocopier and for a long time enjoyed a leading position in the industry. Cisco introduced the first Internet protocol network router in 1986 and still dominates the market for that equipment today. Some first movers can reap substantial advantages from their pioneering activities that lead to an enduring competitive advantage. They can, in other words, limit or slow the rate of imitation.

But there are plenty of counterexamples suggesting that first-mover advantages might not be easy to capture and, in fact, that there might be **first-mover disadvantages**—the competitive *disadvantages* associated with being first. For example, Apple Computer was the first company to introduce a hand-held computer, the Apple Newton, but the product failed; a second mover, Palm, succeeded where Apple had failed. In the market for commercial jet aircraft, DeHavilland was first to market with the Comet, but it was the second mover, Boeing, with its 707 jetliner, that went on to dominate the market.

Clearly being a first mover does not by itself guarantee success. As we shall see, the difference between innovating companies that capture first-mover advantages and those that fall victim to first-mover disadvantages in part turns on the strategy that the first mover pursues. Before considering the strategy issue, however, we need to take a closer look at the nature of first-mover advantages and disadvantages.[17]

■ **First-Mover Advantages**

There are five main sources of first-mover advantages.[18] First, the first mover has an opportunity to *exploit network effects* and positive feedback loops, locking consumers into its technology. In the VCR industry, Sony could have exploited network effects by licensing its technology, but instead the company ceded its first-mover advantage to the second mover, Matsushita.

Second, the first mover may be able to establish significant *brand loyalty*, which is expensive for later entrants to break down. Indeed, if the company is successful in this endeavor, its name may become closely associated with the entire class of products, including those produced by rivals. People still talk of "Xeroxing" when they are going to make a photocopy or "FedExing" when they are going to send a package by overnight mail.

Third, the first mover may be able to ramp up sales volume ahead of rivals and thus reap cost advantages associated with the realization of *scale economies and learning effects* (see Chapter 4). Once the first mover has these cost advantages, it can respond to new entrants by cutting prices in order to hold on to its market share and still earn significant profits.

Fourth, the first mover may be able to create *switching costs* for its customers that subsequently make it difficult for rivals to enter the market and take customers away from the first mover. Wireless service providers, for example, will give new customers a "free" wireless phone, but customers must sign a contract agreeing to pay for the phone if they terminate the service contract within a specified time period, such as a year. Because the real cost of a wireless phone may run from $100 to $200, this represents a significant switching cost that later entrants have to overcome.

Finally, the first mover may be able to *accumulate valuable knowledge* related to customer needs, distribution channels, product technology, process technology, and so on. This accumulated knowledge gives it a knowledge advantage that later entrants might find difficult or expensive to match. Sharp, for example, was the first mover in the commercial manufacture of active matrix liquid crystal displays used in laptop computers. The process for manufacturing these displays is very difficult, with a high reject rate for flawed displays. Sharp has accumulated such an advantage with regard to production processes that it has been very difficult for later entrants to match it on product quality, and thus costs.

■ First-Mover Disadvantages

Balanced against these first-mover advantages are a number of disadvantages.[19] First, the first mover has to bear significant *pioneering costs* that later entrants do not. The first mover has to pioneer the technology, develop distribution channels, and educate customers about the nature of the product. All of this can be expensive and time-consuming. Later entrants, by way of contrast, might be able to *free-ride* on the first mover's investments in pioneering the market and customer education.

Related to this, first movers are more prone to *make mistakes* because there are so many uncertainties in a new market. Later entrants may be able to learn from the mistakes made by first movers, improve on the product or the way in which it is sold, and come to market with a superior offering that captures significant market share from the first mover. For example, one of the reasons that the Apple Newton failed was that the handwriting software in the hand-held computer failed to recognize human handwriting. The second mover in this market, Palm, learned from Apple's error. When it introduced the PalmPilot, it used software that recognized letters written in a particular way, Graffiti, and then persuaded customers to learn this method of inputting data into the hand-held computer.

Third, first movers run the risk of *building the wrong resources and capabilities* because they are focusing on a customer set that is not going to be characteristic of the mass market. This is the *crossing the chasm* problem that we discussed in the previous chapter. You will recall that the customers in the early market—those we categorized as innovators and early adopters—have different characteristics from the first wave of the mass market, the early majority. The first mover runs the risk of gearing its resources and capabilities to the needs of innovators and early adopters and not being able to switch when the early majority enters the market. As a result, first movers run a greater risk of plunging into the chasm that separates the early market from the mass market.

Finally, the first mover may invest in *inferior or obsolete technology*. This can happen when its product innovation is based on underlying technology that is advancing rapidly. By basing its product on an early version of the technology, it may lock itself into something that rapidly becomes obsolete. In contrast, later entrants may be able to leapfrog the first mover and introduce products that are based on later versions of the underlying technology. This happened in France during the 1980s when, at the urging of the government, France Telecom introduced the world's first consumer online service, Minitel. France Telecom distributed crude terminals to consumers for free, which they could hook up to their phone line and use to browse phone directories. Other simple services were soon added, and before long the French could carry out online shopping, banking, travel, weather, and news—all years before the Web was invented. The problem was that by the standards of the Web, Minitel was very crude and inflexible, and France Telecom, as the first mover, suffered. The French were very slow to adopt personal computers and then the Internet primarily because Minitel had such a presence. As late as 1998, only a fifth of French households had a computer, compared with two-fifths in the United States, and only 2 percent of households were connected to the Internet, compared to over 30 percent in the United States. As the result of a government decision, France Telecom, and indeed an entire nation, was slow to adopt a revolutionary new online medium, the Web, because they were the first to invest in a more primitive version of the technology.[20]

■ **Strategies for Exploiting First-Mover Advantages**

The task facing a first mover is how to exploit its lead to capitalize on first-mover advantages and build a sustainable long-term competitive advantage while simultaneously reducing the risks associated with first-mover disadvantages. There are three basic strategies available: (1) develop and market the innovation itself, (2) develop and market the innovation jointly with other companies through a strategic alliance or joint venture, and (3) license the innovation to others and let them develop the market.

The optimal choice of strategy depends on the answers to three questions:

1. Does the innovating company have the *complementary assets* to exploit its innovation and capture first-mover advantages?

2. How difficult is it for imitators to copy the company's innovation? In other words, what is the *height of barriers to imitation?*

3. Are there *capable competitors* that could rapidly imitate the innovation?

■ **Complementary Assets** Complementary assets are the assets required to exploit a new innovation and gain a competitive advantage.[21] Among the most important complementary assets are competitive manufacturing facilities capable of handling rapid growth in customer demand while maintaining high product quality. State-of-the-art manufacturing facilities enable the first mover to move quickly down the experience curve without encountering production bottlenecks or problems with the quality of the product. The inability to satisfy demand because of these problems, however, creates the opportunity for imitators to enter the marketplace. For example, in 1998, Immunex was the first company to introduce a revolutionary new biological treatment for rheumatoid arthritis. Sales for this product, Enbrel, ramped up very rapidly, hitting $750 million in 2001. However, Immunex had not invested in sufficient manufacturing capacity. In mid-2000, it announced that it lacked the capacity to satisfy demand and that bringing additional capacity on line would take at least two years. This manufacturing bottleneck gave the second mover in the market, Johnson & Johnson, the opportunity to expand demand for its product rapidly, which by early 2002 was outselling Enbrel. Immunex's first-mover advantage had been partly eroded because it lacked an important complementary asset, the manufacturing capability required to satisfy demand.

Complementary assets also include marketing know-how, an adequate sales force, access to distribution systems, and an after-sales service and support network. All of these assets can help an innovator build brand loyalty and achieve market penetration more rapidly.[22] In turn, the resulting increases in volume facilitate more rapid movement down the experience curve and the attainment of a sustainable cost-based advantage due to scale economies and learning effects. One of the reasons that EMI, the first mover in the market for CT scanners, ultimately lost out to established medical equipment companies, such as GE Medical Systems, was that it lacked the marketing know-how, sales force, and distribution systems required to compete effectively in the world's largest market for medical equipment, the United States.

Developing complementary assets can be very expensive, and companies often need large infusions of capital for this purpose. That is why first movers often lose out to late movers that are large, successful companies in other industries with the resources to develop a presence in the new industry quickly. Microsoft and 3M exemplify companies that can move quickly to capitalize on the opportunities when other companies open up new product markets, such as compact disks or floppy disks. For example, although Netscape pioneered the market for Internet browsers with Netscape Navigator, Microsoft's Internet Explorer ultimately dominated the market for Internet browsers.

■ **Height of Barriers to Imitation** Recall from Chapter 3 that **barriers to imitation** are factors that prevent rivals from imitating a company's distinctive competencies and innovations. Although ultimately any innovation can be copied, the higher the barriers are, the longer it takes for rivals to imitate, and the more time the first mover has to build an enduring competitive advantage.

Barriers to imitation give an innovator time to establish a competitive advantage and build more enduring barriers to entry in the newly created market. Patents, for example, are among the most widely used barriers to imitation. By protecting its photocopier technology with a thicket of patents, Xerox was able to delay any significant imitation of its product for seventeen years. However, patents are often easy to "invent around." For example, one study found that this happened to 60 percent of patented innovations within four years.[23] If patent protection is weak, a company might try to slow imitation by developing new products and processes in secret. The most famous example of this approach is Coca-Cola, which has kept the formula for Coke a secret for generations. But Coca-Cola's success in this regard is an exception. A study of one hundred companies has estimated that proprietary information about a company's decision to develop a major new product or process is known to its rivals within about twelve to eighteen months of the original development decision.[24]

■ **Capable Competitors** **Capable competitors** are companies that can move quickly to imitate the pioneering company. Competitors' capability to imitate a pioneer's innovation depends primarily on two factors: (1) R&D skills and (2) access to complementary assets. In general, the greater the number of capable competitors with access to the R&D skills and complementary assets needed to imitate an innovation, the more rapid imitation is likely to be.

In this context, R&D skills refer to the ability of rivals to reverse-engineer an innovation in order to find out how it works and quickly develop a comparable product. As an example, consider the CT scanner. GE bought one of the first CT scanners produced by EMI, and its technical experts reverse-engineered it. Despite the product's technological complexity, GE developed its own version, which allowed it to imitate EMI quickly and ultimately to replace EMI as the major supplier of CT scanners.

With regard to complementary assets, the access that rivals have to marketing, sales know-how, or manufacturing capabilities is one of the key determinants of the rate of imitation. If would-be imitators lack critical complementary assets, not only do they have to imitate the innovation, but they may also have to imitate the innovator's complementary assets. This is expensive, as AT&T discovered when it tried to enter the personal computer business in 1984. AT&T lacked the marketing assets (sales force and distribution systems) necessary to support personal computer products. The lack of these assets and the time it takes to build them partly explain why, four years after it entered the market, AT&T had lost $2.5 billion and still had not emerged as a viable contender. It subsequently pulled out of this business.

TABLE 7.1

Strategies for Profiting from Innovation

Strategy	Does the Innovator Have the Required Complementary Assets?	Likely Height of Barriers to Imitation	Number of Capable Competitors
Going it alone	Yes	High	Very few
Entering into an alliance	No	High	Moderate number
Licensing the innovation	No	Low	Many

■ **Three Innovation Strategies** The way in which these three factors—complementary assets, height of barriers to imitation, and the capability of competitors—influence the choice of innovation strategy is summarized in Table 7.1. The competitive strategy of *developing and marketing the innovation alone* makes most sense when (1) the innovator has the complementary assets necessary to develop the innovation, (2) the barriers to imitating a new innovation are high, and (3) the number of capable competitors is limited. Complementary assets allow rapid development and promotion of the innovation. High barriers to imitation buy the innovator time to establish a competitive advantage and build enduring barriers to entry through brand loyalty or experience-based cost advantages. The fewer the capable competitors there are, the less likely it is that any one of them will succeed in circumventing barriers to imitation and quickly imitating the innovation.

The competitive strategy of *developing and marketing the innovation jointly with other companies through a strategic alliance or joint venture* makes most sense when (1) the innovator lacks complementary assets, (2) barriers to imitation are high, and (3) there are several capable competitors. In such circumstances, it makes sense to enter into an alliance with a company that already has the complementary assets—in other words, with a capable competitor. Theoretically, such an alliance should prove to be mutually beneficial, and each partner can share in high profits that neither could earn on its own. Moreover, such a strategy has the benefit of co-opting a potential rival. For example, had EMI teamed up with a capable competitor to develop the market for CT scanners, such as GE Medical Systems, instead of going it alone, the company might not only have been able to build a more enduring competitive advantage, but it would also have co-opted a potentially powerful rival into its camp.

The third strategy, *licensing*, makes most sense when (1) the innovating company lacks the complementary assets, (2) barriers to imitation are low, and (3) there are many capable competitors. The combination of low barriers to imitation and many capable competitors makes rapid imitation almost certain. The innovator's lack of complementary assets further suggests that an imitator will soon capture the innovator's competitive advantage. Given these factors, because rapid diffusion of the innovator's technology through imitation is inevitable, the innovator can at least share in some of the benefits of this diffusion by licensing out its technology.[25] Moreover, by setting a relatively modest licensing fee, the innovator may be able to reduce the incentive that potential rivals have to develop their own competing, and possibly superior, technology. This seems to have been the strategy Dolby adopted to get its technology established as the standard for noise reduction in the music and film businesses (see Strategy in Action 7.2).

Technological Paradigm Shifts

Technological paradigm shifts occur when new technologies come along that revolutionize the structure of the industry, dramatically alter the nature of competition, and require companies to adopt new strategies in order to survive. A good example of a paradigm shift that is currently unfolding is the shift from chemical to digital photography (another example of *digitalization*). For over half a century, the large incumbent enterprises in the photographic industry such as Kodak and Fuji film have generated most of their revenues from selling and processing film using traditional silver halide technology. The rise of digital photography is a huge threat to their business models. Digital cameras do not use film, the mainstay of Kodak's and Fuji's business. Moreover, these cameras are more like specialized computers than conventional cameras and are thus based on scientific knowledge that Kodak and Fuji have little knowledge of. Although both Kodak and Fuji are investing heavily in the development of digital cameras, they are facing intense competition from companies such as Sony, Canon, and Hewlett-Packard, which have developed their own digital cameras; from software developers such as Adobe and Microsoft, which make the software for manipulating digital images; and from printer companies such as Hewlett-Packard and Canon, which are making the printers that consumers can use to print out their own high-quality pictures at home. As digital substitution gathers speed in the photography industry, it is not clear that the traditional incumbents will be able to survive this shift; the new competitors might well rise to dominance in the new market.

If Kodak and Fuji do decline, they will not be the first large incumbents to be felled by a technological paradigm shift in their industry. In the early 1980s, the computer industry was revolutionized by the arrival of personal computer technology, which gave rise to client-server networks that replaced traditional mainframe and minicomputers for many business uses. Many incumbent companies in the mainframe era, such as Wang, Control Data, and DEC, ultimately did not survive, and even IBM went through a decade of wrenching changes and large losses before it reinvented itself as a provider of e-business solutions. In their place, new entrants such as Microsoft, Intel, Dell, and Compaq rose to dominance in this new computer industry.

Examples such as these raise four questions:

1. When do paradigm shifts occur, and how do they unfold?

2. Why do so many incumbents go into decline following a paradigm shift?

3. What strategies can incumbents adopt to increase the probability that they will survive a paradigm shift and emerge on the other side of the market abyss created by the arrival of new technology as a profitable enterprise?

4. What strategies can new entrants into a market adopt to profit from a paradigm shift?

We shall answer each of these questions in the remainder of this chapter.

■ Paradigm Shifts and the Decline of Established Companies

Paradigm shifts appear to be more likely to occur in an industry when one, or both, of the following conditions are in place.[26] First, the established technology in the industry is mature and approaching or at its "natural limit," and second, a new "disruptive technology" has entered the marketplace and is taking root in niches that are poorly served by incumbent companies using the established technology.

■ The Natural Limits to Technology
Richard Foster has formalized the relationship between the performance of a technology and time in terms of what he

FIGURE 7.5

The Technology
S-Curve

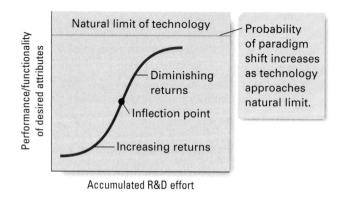

calls the technology S-curve (see Figure 7.5).[27] This curve shows the relationship over time of *cumulative* investments in R&D and the performance (or functionality) of a given technology. Early in its evolution, R&D investments in a new technology tend to yield rapid improvements in performance as basic engineering problems are solved. After a time, diminishing returns to cumulative R&D begin to set in, the rate of improvement in performance slows, and the technology starts to approach its natural limit, where further advances are not possible. For example, one can argue that there was more improvement in the first fifty years of the commercial aerospace business following the pioneering flight by the Wright Brothers than there has been in the second fifty years. Indeed, the world's largest commercial jet aircraft, the Boeing 747, is based on a 1960s design, as is the world's fastest commercial jet aircraft, the Concorde. In commercial aerospace, therefore, we are now in the region of diminishing returns and may be approaching the natural limit to improvements in the technology of commercial aerospace.

Similarly, it can be argued that we are approaching the natural limit to technology in the performance of silicon-based semiconductor chips. Over the past two decades, the performance of semiconductor chips has been increased dramatically by packing ever more transistors onto a single small silicon chip. This process has helped to increase the power of computers, lower their cost, and shrink their size. But we are starting to approach limits to the ability to shrink the width of lines on a chip and therefore pack ever more transistors onto a single chip. The limit is imposed by the natural laws of physics. Light waves are used to help etch lines onto a chip, and one cannot etch a line that is smaller than the wavelength of light being used. Semiconductor companies are already using light with very small wavelengths, such as extreme ultraviolet, to etch lines onto a chip, but there are limits to how far this technology can be pushed, and many believe that we will reach those limits within the decade. Does this mean that our ability to make smaller, faster, cheaper computers is coming to an end? Probably not. It is more likely that we will find another technology to replace silicon-based computing and enable us to continue building smaller, faster, cheaper computers. In fact, several exotic competing technologies are already being developed that may replace silicon-based computing. These include self-organizing molecular computers, three-dimensional microprocessor technology, quantum computing technology, and using DNA to perform computations.[28]

FIGURE 7.6

Established and
Successor
Technologies

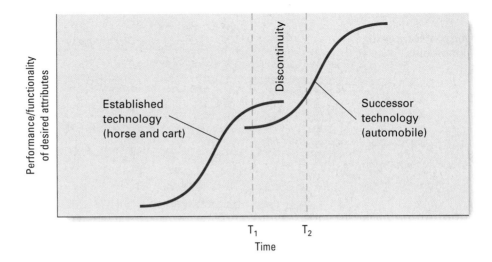

What does all of this have to do with paradigm shifts? According to Foster, when a technology approaches its natural limit, research attention turns to possible alternative technologies, and sooner or later one of those alternatives might be commercialized and replace the established technology. That is, the probability that a paradigm shift will occur increases. Thus, sometime in the next decade or two, another paradigm shift might shake the very foundations of the computer industry as exotic computing technology replaces silicon-based computing. If history is any guide, if and when this happens, many of the incumbents in today's computer industry will go into decline, and new enterprises will rise to dominance.

Foster pushes this point a little further, noting that, initially, the contenders for the replacement technology are not as effective as the established technology in producing the attributes and features that consumers demand in a product. For example, in the early years of the twentieth century, automobiles were just starting to be produced. They were valued for their ability to move people from place to place, but so was the horse and cart (the established technology). When automobiles originally appeared, the horse and cart was still quite a bit better than the automobile at doing this (see Figure 7.6). After all, the first cars were slow, noisy, and prone to breakdown. Moreover, they needed a network of paved roads and gas stations to be really useful, and that network didn't exist, so for most applications, the horse and cart was still the preferred mode of transportation—to say nothing of the fact that it was cheaper.

However, this comparison ignored the fact that in the early twentieth century, automobile technology was at the very start of its S-curve and was about to experience dramatic improvements in performance as major engineering problems were solved (and those paved roads and gas stations were built). In contrast, after 3,000 years of continuous improvement and refinement, the horse and cart was almost definitely at the end of its technological S-curve. The result was that the rapidly improving automobile soon replaced the horse and cart as the preferred mode of transportation. At time T_1 in Figure 7.6, the horse and cart was still superior to the automobile. By time T_2, the automobile had surpassed the horse and cart.

FIGURE 7.7

Swarm of Successor
Technologies

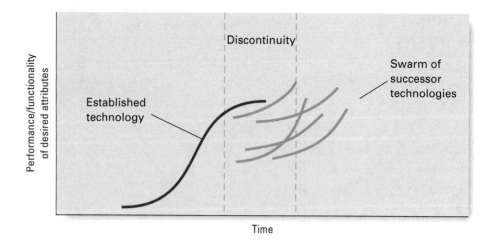

Foster notes that because the successor technology is initially less efficient than the established technology, established companies and their customers often make the mistake of dismissing it, only to be taken off-guard by its rapid performance improvement. A final point here is that often there is not one potential successor technology but a swarm of potential successor technologies, only one of which might ultimately rise to the fore (see Figure 7.7). When this is the case, established companies are put at a disadvantage. Even if they recognize that a paradigm shift is imminent, they may not have the resources to invest in all the potential replacement technologies. If they invest in the wrong one, something that is easy to do given the uncertainty that surrounds the entire process, they may be locked out of subsequent development.

■ **Disruptive Technology** Clayton Christensen has built on Foster's insights and his own research to develop a theory of disruptive technology that has become very influential in high-technology circles.[29] Christensen uses the term **disruptive technology** to refer to a new technology that gets its start away from the mainstream of a market and then, as its functionality improves over time, invades the main market. Such technologies are disruptive because they revolutionize industry structure and competition, often causing the decline of established companies. They cause a technological paradigm shift.

Christensen's greatest insight is that established companies are often aware of the new technology but do not invest in it because they listen to their customers, and their customers do not want it. Of course, this arises because the new technology is early in its development, and thus only at the beginning of the **S**-curve for that technology. Once the performance of the new technology improves, customers *do* want it, but by this time it is new entrants, as opposed to established companies, that have accumulated the knowledge required to bring the new technology into the mass market. Christensen supports his view by several detailed historical case studies, one of which is summarized in Strategy in Action 7.4.

In addition to listening too closely to their customers, Christensen also identifies a number of other factors that make it very difficult for established companies to adopt a

Strategy in Action   7.4

Disruptive Technology in Mechanical Excavators

Excavators are used to dig out foundations for large buildings, trenches to lay large pipes for sewers and the like, and foundations and trenches for residential construction and farm work. Prior to the 1940s, the dominant technology used to manipulate the bucket on a mechanical excavator was based on a system of cables and pulleys. Although these mechanical systems could lift large buckets of earth, the excavators themselves were quite large, cumbersome, and expensive. Thus, they were rarely used to dig small trenches for house foundations, irrigation ditches for farmers, and the like. In most cases, these small trenches were dug by hand.

In the 1940s, a new technology made its appearance: hydraulics. In theory, hydraulic systems had certain advantages over the established cable and pulley systems. Most important, their energy efficiency was higher: for a given bucket size, a smaller engine would be required using a hydraulic system. However, the initial hydraulic systems also had drawbacks. The seals on hydraulic cylinders were prone to leak under high pressure, effectively limiting the size of bucket that could be lifted using hydraulics. Notwithstanding this drawback, when hydraulics first appeared, many of the incumbent firms in the mechanical excavation industry took the technology seriously enough to ask their primary customers whether they would be interested in products based on hydraulics. Since the primary customers of incumbents needed excavators with large buckets to dig out the foundations for buildings and large trenches, their reply was negative. For this customer set, the hydraulic systems of the 1940s were not reliable or powerful enough. Consequently, after consulting with their customers, these established companies in the industry made the strategic decision not to invest in hydraulics. Instead, they continued to produce excavation equipment based on the dominant cable and pulley technology.

It was left to a number of new entrants, which included J. I. Case, John Deere, J. C. Bamford, and Caterpillar, to pioneer hydraulic excavation equipment. Because of the limits on bucket size imposed by the seal problem, these companies initially focused on a poorly served niche in the market that could make use of small buckets: residential contractors and farmers. Over time, these new entrants were able to solve the engineering problems associated with weak hydraulic seals, and as they did this, they manufactured excavators with larger buckets. Ultimately, they invaded the market niches served by the old-line companies: general contractors that dug the foundations for large buildings, sewers, and so on. At this point, Case, Deere, Caterpillar, and their kin rose to dominance in the industry, while the majority of established companies from the prior era lost share. Of the thirty or so manufacturers of cable-actuated equipment in the United States in the late 1930s, only four survived to the 1950s.[d]

new disruptive technology. He notes that many established companies declined to invest in new disruptive technologies because initially they served such small market niches that it seemed unlikely that they would have an impact on the company's revenues and profits. As the new technology started to improve in functionality and invade the main market, their investment was often hindered by the fact that exploiting the new technology required a new business model totally different from the company's established model, and thus very difficult to implement.

Both of these points can be illustrated by reference to one more example: the rise of online discount stockbrokers during the 1990s such as Ameritrade and E*TRADE, which made use of a new technology, the Internet, to allow individual investors to trade stocks for a very low commission fee, whereas full-service stockbrokers, such as Merrill Lynch, where orders had to be placed through a stockbroker who earned a commission for performing the transaction, did not.

Christensen also notes that a new network of suppliers and distributors typically grows up around the new entrants. Not only do established companies initially ignore disruptive technology, but so do their suppliers and distributors. This creates an opportunity for new suppliers and distributors to enter the market to serve the new entrants. As the new entrants grow, so does the associated network. Ultimately, Christensen suggests, the new entrants and their network may replace not only established enterprises, but also the entire network of suppliers and distributors associated with established companies. Taken to its logical extreme, this view suggests that disruptive technologies may result in the demise of the entire network of enterprises associated with established companies in an industry.

The established companies in an industry that is being rocked by a technological paradigm shift often have to cope with internal inertia forces that limit their ability to adapt, but the new entrants do not and thereby have an advantage. They do not have to deal with an established and conservative customer set and an obsolete business model. Instead, they can focus on optimizing the new technology, improving its performance, and riding the wave of disruptive technology into new market segments until they invade the main market and challenge the established companies, by which time they may be well equipped to beat them.

■ **Strategic Implications for Established Companies**

Although Christensen has uncovered an important tendency, it is by no means written in stone that all established companies are doomed to fail when faced with disruptive technologies, as we have seen with IBM and Merrill Lynch. Established companies must meet the challenges created by the emergence of disruptive technologies.[30]

First, having access to the knowledge about how disruptive technologies can revolutionize markets is itself a valuable strategic asset. Many of the established companies that Christensen examined failed because they took a myopic view of the new technology and asked their customers the wrong question. Instead of asking, "Are you interested in this new technology?" they should have recognized that the new technology was likely to improve rapidly over time and instead have asked, "Would you be interested in this new technology if it improves its functionality over time?" If they had done this, they may have made very different strategic decisions.

Second, it is clearly important for established enterprises to invest in newly emerging technologies that may ultimately become disruptive technologies. Companies have to hedge their bets about new technology. As we have noted, at any time, there may be a swarm of emerging technologies, any one of which might ultimately become a disruptive technology. Large, established companies that are generating significant cash flows can and often should establish and fund central R&D operations to invest in and develop such technologies. In addition, they may wish to acquire newly emerging companies that are pioneering potentially disruptive technologies or enter into alliances with them to develop the technology jointly. The strategy of acquiring companies that are developing potentially disruptive technology is one that Cisco Systems, a dominant provider of Internet network equipment, is famous for pursuing. At the heart of this strategy must be a recognition on the part of the incumbent enterprise that it is better for the company to develop disruptive technology and then cannibalize its established sales base than to have that sales base taken away by new entrants.

However, Christensen makes the very important point that even when established companies do undertake R&D investments in potentially disruptive technologies, they often fail to commercialize those technologies because of internal forces that suppress change. For example, managers in the parts of the business that are currently generating the most cash may claim that they need the greatest R&D investment to maintain their market position and may lobby top management to delay investment in a new technology. Early on in the S-curve, when it is very unclear what the long-term prospects of a new technology may be, this can be a powerful argument. The consequence, however, may be that the company fails to build a competence in the new technology and will suffer accordingly.

In addition, Christensen argues that the commercialization of new disruptive technology often requires a radically different value chain with a completely different cost structure—a new business model. For example, it may require a different manufacturing system, a different distribution system, and different pricing options and involve very different gross margins and operating margins. Christensen argues that it is almost impossible for two distinct business models to coexist within the same organization. When they try to do that, almost inevitably the established business model will suffocate the business model associated with the disruptive technology.

The solution to this problem is to separate out the disruptive technology and place it in its own autonomous operating division. For example, during the early 1980s Hewlett-Packard (HP) built a very successful laser jet printer business. Then along came ink jet technology. Some in the company believed that ink jet printers would cannibalize sales of laser jets and consequently argued that HP should not produce ink jets. Fortunately for HP, senior management at the time saw ink jet technology for what it was: a potential disruptive technology. Far from not investing in it, they allocated significant R&D funds toward its commercialization. Furthermore, when the technology was ready for market introduction, they established an autonomous ink jet division at a different geographic location with its own manufacturing, marketing, and distribution activities. They accepted that the ink jet division might take sales away from the laser jet division and decided that it was better to have an HP division cannibalize the sales of another HP division than have those sales cannibalized by another company. Happily for HP, it turns out that ink jets cannibalize sales of laser jets only on the margin and that both have profitable market niches. This felicitous outcome, however, does not detract from the message of the story: if your company is developing a potentially disruptive technology, the chances of success will be enhanced if it is placed in a stand-alone product division and given its own mandate.

■ **Strategic Implications for New Entrants**

This work just discussed also holds implications for new entrants. The new entrants, or attackers, have several advantages over established enterprises. Pressures to continue the existing out-of-date business model do not hamstring new entrants, which do not have to worry about product cannibalization issues. They do not have to worry about their established customer base or relationships with established suppliers and distributors. Instead, they can focus all their energies on the opportunities offered by the new disruptive technology, ride the S-curve of technology improvement, and grow rapidly with the market for that technology. This does not mean that the new entrants have no problems to solve. They may be constrained by a lack of capital or have to manage the organizational problems associated with rapid growth; most important, they may need to find a way to take their technology from a small out-of-the-way niche into the mass market.

Perhaps one of the most important issues facing new entrants is the choice of whether to partner with an established company or go it alone in their attempt to develop and profit from a new disruptive technology. Although a new entrant may enjoy all of the advantages of the attacker, it may lack the resources required to exploit them fully. In such a case, it might want to consider forming a strategic alliance with a larger, established company to gain access to those resources. The main issues here are the same as those that we discussed earlier when examining the three strategies that a company can pursue to capture first-mover advantages: go it alone, enter into a strategic alliance, or license its technology.

Summary of Chapter

1. Technical standards are important in many high-tech industries: they guarantee compatibility, reduce confusion in the minds of customers, allow for mass production and lower costs, and reduce the risks associated with supplying complementary products.
2. Network effects and positive feedback loops often determine which standard comes to dominate a market.
3. Owning a standard can be a source of sustained competitive advantage.
4. Establishing a proprietary standard as the industry standard may require the company to win a format war against a competing and incompatible standard. Strategies for doing this include producing complementary products, leveraging killer applications, using aggressive pricing and marketing, licensing the technology, and cooperating with competitors.
5. Many high-tech products are characterized by high fixed costs of development but very low or zero marginal costs of producing one extra unit of output. These cost economics create a presumption in favor of strategies that emphasize aggressive pricing to increase volume and drive down average total costs.
6. Many digital products suffer from very high piracy rates because of the low marginal costs of copying and distributing such products. Piracy can be reduced by the appropriate combination of strategy, encryption software, and vigorous defense of intellectual property rights.
7. It is very important for a first mover to develop a strategy to capitalize on first-mover advantages. A company can choose from three strategies: develop and market the technology itself, do so jointly with another company, or license the technology to existing companies. The choice depends on the complementary assets required to capture a first-mover advantage, the height of barriers to imitation, and the capability of competitors.

8. Technological paradigm shifts occur when new technologies come along that revolutionize the structure of the industry, dramatically alter the nature of competition, and require companies to adopt new strategies in order to survive.
9. Technological paradigm shifts are more likely to occur when progress in improving the established technology is slowing because it is giving diminishing returns and a new disruptive technology is taking root in a market niche.
10. Established companies can deal with paradigm shifts by hedging their bets with regard to technology or setting up a stand-alone division to exploit the technology.

Discussion Questions

1. What is different about high-tech industries? Were all industries once high tech?
2. Why are standards so important in many high-tech industries? What are the competitive implications of this?
3. You work for a small company that has the leading position in an embryonic market. Your boss believes that the company's future is ensured because it has a 60 percent share of the market, the lowest cost structure in the industry, and the most reliable and highest-valued product. Write a memo to him outlining why his assumptions might be incorrect.
4. You are working for a small company that has developed an operating system for PCs that is faster and more stable than Microsoft's Windows operating system. What strategies might the company pursue to unseat Windows and establish its new operating system as the dominant technical standard in the industry?
5. You are a manager for a major music record label. Last year, music sales declined by 10 percent, primarily because of very high piracy rates for CDs. Your boss has asked you to develop a strategy for reducing piracy rates. What would you suggest that the company do?

Practicing Strategic Management

▦ SMALL-GROUP EXERCISE
Burning DVDs

Break up into groups of three to five people, and discuss the following scenario. Appoint one group member as a spokesperson who will communicate your findings to the class.

You are a group of managers and software engineers at a small start-up that has developed software that enables customers with PCs to copy films from one DVD to another (that is, to "burn" DVDs).

1. How do you think the market for this software is likely to develop? What factors might inhibit adoption of this software?
2. Can you think of a strategy that your company might pursue in combination with film studios that will enable your company to increase revenues and the film companies to reduce piracy rates?

▦ ARTICLE FILE 7

Find an example of an industry that has undergone a technological paradigm shift in recent years. What happened to the established companies as that paradigm shift unfolded?

▦ STRATEGIC MANAGEMENT PROJECT
Module 7

This module requires you to analyze the industry environment in which your company is based and determine if it is vulnerable to a technological paradigm shift. With the information you have at your disposal, answer the following questions:

1. What is the dominant product technology used in the industry in which your company is based?
2. Are technical standards important in your industry? If so, what are they?
3. What are the attributes of the majority of customers purchasing the product of your company (for example, early adopters, early majority, late majority)? What does this tell you about the strategic issues that the company is likely to face in the future?
4. Did the dominant technology in your industry diffuse rapidly or slowly? What drove the speed of diffusion?
5. Where is the dominant technology in your industry on its S-curve? Are alternative competing technologies

being developed that might give rise to a paradigm shift in your industry?
6. Are intellectual property rights important to your company? If so, what strategies is it adopting to protect those rights? Is it doing enough?

▦ EXPLORING THE WEB
Visiting Kodak

Visit the website of Kodak (**www.kodak.com**), and search it to find out what Kodak is doing in the area of digital photography. Use this information to answer the following questions:

1. How important do you think digital photography is in Kodak's total revenues?
2. How is this likely to change over the next decade?
3. Where is digital photography on the S-curve? Where is traditional photography? What are the implications of this comparison for Kodak?
4. Identify Kodak's competitors in (a) its traditional film business and (b) the digital photography business. What are the implications of the change in the set of competitors confronting Kodak?
5. How does the switch from traditional to digital photography change the economics of the photography business?
6. Do you think that Kodak is pursuing the correct strategies to deal with digital substitution? What do you think is the long-term outlook for Kodak's business if it continues pursuing its current strategies? Do you think the company should make some changes? If so, what?

General Task Search the Web for information that allows you to assess the current state of competition in the market for hand-held computers such as those produced by Palm, Handspring, and Compaq. Use that information to perform an analysis of the market in the United States. Answer the following questions:

1. What is the leading standard for operating systems in this market?
2. How did this standard emerge to become the market leader?
3. How secure is this standard? Could it be supplanted by another standard over the next few years?

Closing Case

Battling Piracy in the Videogame Market

Over the last decade the videogame industry has grown into a global colossus worth more than $22 billion a year in revenues. For the three biggest players in the industry—Sony with its PlayStation 2, Microsoft with Xbox, and Nintendo—this potentially represents a huge growth engine. But the engine is threatened by a rise in piracy, which in 2004 cost the industry close to $4 billion.

The piracy problem is particularly serious in East Asia (excluding Japan), where videogame consoles are routinely "chipped"—sold with modified chips, called "mod chips," that override the console's security system, allowing it to play illegally copied games and CDs. Importers or resellers, who charge a small markup for making the modification, illegally install the mod chips. In some regions, such as Hong Kong, it is almost impossible to find a console that hasn't been modified.

Because they allow users to play illegally copied games, consoles with mod chips installed offer a gaping gateway for software pirates, and they directly threaten the profitability of console and game makers. The big three in the industry all follow a razor-and-razor-blades business model, where the console (razor) is sold at a loss and profit is made on the sale of the games (razor blades). In the case of Microsoft's Xbox, estimates suggest that the company loses as much as $200 on each Xbox it sells. To make profits, Microsoft collects royalties on the sale of games developed under license, in addition to producing and selling some games itself. Each game typically retails for around $50, and Microsoft must sell six to twelve games to each Xbox user to recoup the $200 loss on the initial sale and start making a profit. If those users are purchasing pirated games and playing them on "chipped" Xbox consoles, Microsoft collects nothing in royalties and may never reach the breakeven point. Sony and Nintendo face similar problems. In East Asia, some 70 percent of game software sold in the region may be pirated thanks to the popularity of "chipped" consoles and the low price of pirated games, which may sell for one-third the price of a legal game.

Historically, all of the big videogame companies tried to deal with the piracy problem in East Asia by ignoring the market. Sony launched its PlayStation 2 in East Asia two years after its Japanese launch, and Microsoft delayed its East Asian launch for a year after it launched it elsewhere in the world. But this tactic is increasingly questionable in a region where there may soon be more gamers than in the United States. Industry estimates suggest that Asian gamers will spend some $7.6 billion on videogame software in 2004, much of it on low-priced pirated games, compared to $7.4 billion in the United States.

Another tactic that both Sony and Microsoft are now using is to regularly alter the hardware specifications of its consoles, rendering the existing mod chips useless. But the companies have found that this is just a temporary solution, for within a few weeks the new system is cracked and mod chips are available on the market that are tailor-made to override the new specifications.

A third tactic is to push the local authorities to legally enforce existing intellectual property rights law, which in theory outlaws the mod chip practice. In late 2002, Microsoft, Sony, and Nintendo joined forces to sue a Hong Kong company called Lik-Sang, which sold mod chips through its website and which is one of the world's largest distributors of the chips. Some observers question the value of this move, however, for they argue that if Lik-Sang is shut down, there are many others in Hong Kong that may be willing to take its place. What is needed, they argue, is concerted government action to stop the pirates, and so far East Asian governments have not been quick to act.[31]

Case Discussion Questions

1. Why do the console manufacturers in the videogame industry all adopt a "razor-and-razor-blades" strategy?

2. Why is piracy rampant in the videogame industry? What are the implications of high piracy rates for (a) the profitability of the console manufacturers and (b) the supply of new videogames?

3. What impact do you think the spread of peer-to-peer file-sharing networks, such as Kazaa, might have on the rate of software piracy in the videogame industry?

4. What strategies and tactics are Microsoft, Sony, and Nintendo adopting to reduce the rate of piracy? What are the limitations of these strategies and tactics? Do you think they will be successful at limiting piracy?

5. Can you think of any other steps that Microsoft, Sony, and Nintendo might take to limit piracy? Could they change their business model in some way so that piracy would be less of a problem?

6. How might a shift to online gaming change the piracy rate?

Chapter 8

Strategy in the Global Environment

Opening Case

The Evolution of Global Strategy at Procter & Gamble

Founded in 1837, Cincinnati-based Procter & Gamble has long been one of the world's most international of companies. Today P&G is a global colossus in the consumer products business with annual sales in excess of $50 billion, some 54 percent of which are generated outside of the United States. P&G sells over three hundred brands—including Ivory Soap, Tide, Pampers, IAM pet food, Crisco, and Folgers—to consumers in 160 countries. It has operations in 80 countries and employs close to 100,000 people globally. P&G established its first foreign factory in 1915 when it opened a plant in Canada to produce Ivory Soap and Crisco. This was followed in 1930 by the establishment of the company's first foreign subsidiary in Britain. The pace of international expansion quickened in the 1950s and 1960s as P&G expanded rapidly in Western Europe, and then again in the 1970s when the company entered Japan and other Asian nations. Sometimes P&G entered a nation by acquiring an established competitor and its brands, as occurred in Britain and Japan, but more typically the company set up operations from the ground floor.

By the late 1970s the business model at P&G was well established. The company developed new products in Cincinnati and then relied on semiautonomous foreign subsidiaries to manufacture, market, and distribute those products in different nations. In many cases, foreign subsidiaries had their own production facilities and tailored the packaging, brand name, and marketing message to local tastes and preferences. For years this business model delivered a steady stream of new products and reliable growth in sales and profits. By the 1990s, however, profit growth at P&G was slowing down.

The essence of the problem was simple: P&G's costs were too high primarily because of extensive duplication of manufacturing, marketing, and administrative facilities in different national subsidiaries. The duplication of assets made sense in the world of the 1960s, when national markets were segmented from each other by barriers to cross-border trade. Products produced in Britain, for example, could not be sold economically in Germany because of the high tariff duties levied on imports into Germany. By the 1980s, however, barriers to cross-border trade were falling rapidly worldwide and fragmented national markets were merging into larger regional or global markets. Moreover, the retailers through which P&G distributed its products were themselves growing larger and more global, such as Wal-Mart from the United States, Tesco from the United Kingdom, and Carrefour from France. These emerging global retailers were demanding price discounts from P&G.

In 1993 P&G embarked on a major reorganization in an attempt to control its cost structure and recognize the new reality of emerging global markets. The company shut down some thirty manufacturing plants around the globe, laid off 13,000 employees, and concentrated production in fewer plants that could better realize economies of scale and serve regional markets. These actions cut some $600 million a year out of P&G's cost structure. It wasn't enough: profit growth remained sluggish.

In 1998 P&G launched its second reorganization of the decade. Named "Organization 2005," the goal was to transform P&G into a truly global company. The company tore up its old organization, which was based on countries and regions, and replaced it with one based on seven self-contained global business units, ranging from baby care to food products. Each business unit was given complete responsibility for generating profits from its products, as well as for manufacturing, marketing, and developing the products. Each business unit was also told to concentrate production in fewer larger facilities to try to build global brands wherever possible, thereby eliminating marketing differences between countries,

and to accelerate the development and launching of new products. In 1999 P&G announced that, as a result of this initiative, it would close down another ten factories and lay off 15,000 employees, mostly in Europe, where there was still extensive duplication of assets. The annual cost savings were estimated to be about $800 million. P&G planned to use the savings to cut prices and increase marketing spending in an effort to gain market share and thus further lower costs through the attainment of scale economies.

This time the strategy seemed to work. In 2003 and then again in 2004, P&G reported strong growth in both sales and profits. Between 2002 and 2004 revenues surged 28 percent, from $40.2 billion to $51.4 billion, while profits increased an impressive 46 percent, from $4.35 billion to $6.34 billion. Significantly, P&G's global competitors, such as Unilever, Kimberley-Clark, and Colgate-Palmolive, were struggling in 2003 and 2004.[1]

Overview

Procter & Gamble has a long history as one of the world's most successful multinational companies. As described in the *Opening Case*, it was one of the first companies to expand internationally and for decades profited handsomely from this strategy. By the early 1990s, however, it found itself out of step with the rapid emergence of a global marketplace. To improve the company's profitability and profit growth, P&G had to change its strategy, moving from a strategic posture that granted considerable autonomy to operations in individual countries to one that recognized that markets were becoming more global. P&G is not alone in having to make this shift. Many other companies, large and small, have had to struggle with the same issue and have changed their strategy as a result.

This chapter begins with a discussion of ongoing changes in the global competitive environment and discusses models managers can use for analyzing competition in different national markets. Next, the chapter discusses the various ways in which international expansion can increase a company's profitability and profit growth. It also looks at the advantages and disadvantages of different strategies companies can pursue to gain a competitive advantage in the global marketplace. This is followed by a discussion of two related strategic issues: (1) how managers decide which foreign markets to enter, when to enter them, and on what scale and (2) what kind of vehicle or means a company should use to expand globally and enter a foreign country. Once a company has entered a foreign market, it becomes a **multinational company,** that is, a company that does business in two or more national markets. The vehicles that companies can employ to enter foreign markets and become multinationals include exporting, licensing, setting up a joint venture with a foreign company, and setting up a wholly owned subsidiary. The chapter closes with a discussion of the benefits and costs of entering into strategic alliances with other global companies.

By the time you have completed this chapter, you will have a good understanding of the various strategic issues that companies face when they decide to expand their operations abroad to achieve competitive advantage and superior profitability.

The Global and National Environments

Fifty years ago most national markets were isolated from each other by significant barriers to international trade and investment. In those days, managers could focus on analyzing just those national markets in which their company competed. They did not need to pay much attention to entry by global competitors, for there were few and entry was difficult. Nor did they need to pay much attention to entering foreign markets, since that was often prohibitively expensive. All of this has now changed. Barriers to international trade and investment have tumbled, huge global markets for goods and services have been created, and companies from different nations are entering each other's home markets on a hitherto unprecedented scale, increasing the intensity of competition. Rivalry can no longer be understood merely in terms of what happens within the boundaries of a nation; managers now need to consider how globalization is impacting the environment in which their company competes and what strategies their company should adopt to exploit the unfolding opportunities and counter competitive threats. In this section we look at the changes ushered in by falling barriers to international trade and investment, and we discuss a model for analyzing the competitive situation in different nations.

■ The Globalization of Production and Markets

The past half-century has seen a dramatic lowering of barriers to international trade and investment. For example, the average tariff rate on manufactured goods traded between advanced nations has fallen from around 40 percent to under 4 percent. Similarly, in nation after nation, regulations prohibiting foreign companies from entering domestic markets and establishing production facilities, or acquiring domestic companies, have been removed. As a result of these two developments, there has been a surge in both the volume of international trade and the value of foreign direct investment. The volume of world-merchandised trade has been growing faster than the world economy since 1950.[2] From 1970 to 2003, the volume of world-merchandised trade expanded twenty-fivefold, outstripping world production, which grew about 7.5 times in real terms. Moreover, between 1992 and 2003 the total flow of foreign direct investment from all countries increased about 279 percent, while world trade grew by some 69 percent and world output by 28 percent.[3] These two trends have led to the globalization of production and the globalization of markets.[4]

The globalization of production has been increasing as companies take advantage of lower barriers to international trade and investment to disperse important parts of their production processes around the globe. Doing so enables them to take advantage of national differences in the cost and quality of factors of production such as labor, energy, land, and capital, which allow them to lower their cost structures and boost profits. For example, the Boeing Company's commercial jet aircraft, the 777, uses 132,500 engineered parts that are produced around the world by 545 suppliers. Eight Japanese suppliers make parts of the fuselage, doors, and wings; a supplier in Singapore makes the doors for the nose landing gear; three suppliers in Italy manufacture wing flaps; and so on. Part of Boeing's rationale for outsourcing so much production to foreign suppliers is that these suppliers are the best in the world at performing their particular activity. Therefore, the result of having foreign suppliers build specific parts is a better final product and higher profitability for Boeing.[5]

As for the globalization of markets, it has been argued that the world's economic system is moving from one in which national markets are distinct entities, isolated from each other by trade barriers and barriers of distance, time, and culture, toward a system in which national markets are merging into one huge global marketplace. Increasingly, customers around the world demand and use the same basic product offerings. Consequently, in many industries, it is no longer meaningful to talk about the German market, the U.S. market, or the Japanese market; there is only the global market. The global acceptance of Coca-Cola, Citigroup credit cards, blue jeans, the Sony PlayStation, McDonald's hamburgers, the Nokia wireless phone, and Microsoft's Windows operating system are examples of this trend.[6]

The trend toward the globalization of production and markets has several important implications for competition within an industry. First, industry boundaries do not stop at national borders. Because many industries are becoming global in scope, actual and potential competitors exist not only in a company's home market but also in other national markets. Managers who analyze only their home market can be caught unprepared by the entry of efficient foreign competitors. The globalization of markets and production implies that companies around the globe are finding their home markets under attack from foreign competitors. For example, in Japan, Merrill Lynch and Citicorp are making inroads against Japanese financial service institutions. In the United States, Finland's Nokia has taken the lead from Motorola in the market for wireless phone handsets (see Strategy in Action 8.1). In the European Union, the once dominant Dutch company Philips has seen its market share in the customer electronics industry taken by Japan's JVC, Matsushita, and Sony.

Second, the shift from national to global markets has intensified competitive rivalry in industry after industry. National markets that once were consolidated oligopolies, dominated by three or four companies and subjected to relatively little foreign competition, have been transformed into segments of fragmented global industries in which a large number of companies battle each other for market share in country after country. This rivalry has threatened to drive down profitability and made it all the more critical for companies to maximize their efficiency, quality, customer responsiveness, and innovative ability. The painful restructuring and downsizing that has been going on at companies such as Motorola and Kodak is as much a response to the increased intensity of global competition as it is to anything else. However, not all global industries are fragmented. Many remain consolidated oligopolies, except that now they are consolidated global, rather than national, oligopolies. In the videogame industry, for example, three companies are battling for global dominance, Microsoft from the United States and Nintendo and Sony from Japan. In the market for wireless handsets, Nokia of Finland does global battle against Motorola of the United States and Samsung from South Korea.

Finally, although globalization has increased both the threat of entry and the intensity of rivalry within many formerly protected national markets, it has also created enormous opportunities for companies based in those markets. The steady decline in barriers to cross-border trade and investment has opened up many once protected markets to companies based outside them. Thus, for example, in recent years, western European, Japanese, and U.S. companies have accelerated their investments in the nations of eastern Europe, Latin America, and Southeast Asia as they try to take advantage of growth opportunities in those areas.

Strategy in Action   8.1

Finland's Nokia

The wireless phone market is one of the great growth stories of the last decade. Starting from a very low base in 1990, annual global sales of wireless phones surged to reach 440 million units in 2003. By the end of 2003, there were over 1.2 billion wireless subscribers worldwide, up from less than 10 million in 1990. Nokia is a dominant player in the market for mobile telephone sales. Nokia's roots are in Finland, not normally a country that comes to mind when one talks about leading-edge technology companies. In the 1980s, Nokia was a rambling Finnish conglomerate with activities that embraced tire manufacturing, paper production, consumer electronics, and telecommunications equipment. By 2004 it had transformed itself into a focused telecommunications equipment manufacturer with a global reach, sales of over $30 billion, earnings of more than $5 billion, and a 38 percent share of the global market for wireless phones. How has this former conglomerate emerged to take a global leadership position in wireless telecommunications equipment? Much of the answer lies in the history, geography, and political economy of Finland and its Nordic neighbors.

In 1981 the Nordic nations cooperated to create the world's first international wireless telephone network. They had good reason to become pioneers: it cost far too much to lay down a traditional wire line telephone service in those sparsely populated and inhospitably cold countries. The same features made telecommunications all the more valuable: people driving through the Arctic winter and owners of remote northern houses needed a telephone to summon help if things went wrong. As a result, Sweden, Norway, and Finland became the first nations in the world to take wireless telecommunications seriously. They found, for example, that although it cost up to $800 per subscriber to bring a traditional wire line service to remote locations, the same locations could be linked by wireless cellular for only $500 per person. As a consequence, 12 percent of people in Scandinavia owned cellular phones by 1994, compared with less than 6 percent in the United States, the world's second most developed market. This lead continued over the next decade. By the end of 2003, 85 percent of the population in Finland owned a wireless phone, compared with 55 percent in the United States.

Nokia, a long-time telecommunications equipment supplier, was well positioned to take advantage of this development from the start, but there were also other forces at work that helped Nokia develop its competitive edge. Unlike virtually every other developed nation, Finland has never had a national telephone monopoly. Instead, the country's telephone services have long been provided by about fifty or so autonomous local telephone companies whose elected boards set prices by referendum (which naturally means low prices). This army of independent and cost-conscious telephone service providers prevented Nokia from taking anything for granted in its home country. With typical Finnish pragmatism, its customers were willing to buy from the lowest-cost supplier, whether that was Nokia, Ericsson, Motorola, or some other company. This situation contrasted sharply with that prevailing in most developed nations until the late 1980s and early 1990s, where domestic telephone monopolies typically purchased equipment from a dominant local supplier or made it themselves. Nokia responded to this competitive pressure by doing everything possible to drive down its manufacturing costs while staying at the leading edge of wireless technology.

The consequences of these forces are clear. Nokia is now the leader in digital wireless technology, which is the wave of the future. Many now regard Finland as the lead market for wireless telephone services. If you want to see the future of wireless, you don't go to New York or San Francisco; you go to Helsinki, where Finns use their wireless handsets not just to talk to each other but also to browse the Web, execute e-commerce transactions, control household heating and lighting systems, or purchase Coke from a wireless-enabled vending machine. Nokia has gained this lead because Scandinavia started switching to digital technology five years before the rest of the world. Spurred on by its cost-conscious Finnish customers, Nokia now has the lowest cost structure of any cellular phone equipment manufacturer in the world, and thus is a more profitable enterprise than Motorola, its leading global rival. It cost Nokia an average of $114 to make and sell each phone in 2002, compared with about $131 a year earlier. Its closest rival, Motorola Inc. of Schaumburg, Illinois, spent an average of $139 to make and sell each phone.[a]

■ National Competitive Advantage

Despite the globalization of production and markets, many of the most successful companies in certain industries are still clustered in a small number of countries. For example, many of the world's most successful biotechnology and computer companies are based in the United States, and many of the most successful customer electronics companies are based in Japan and South Korea. Germany is the base for many successful chemical and engineering companies. These facts suggest that the nation-state within which a company is based may have an important bearing on the competitive position of that company in the global marketplace.

In a study of national competitive advantage, Michael Porter identified four attributes of a national or country-specific environment that have an important impact on the global competitiveness of companies located within that nation:[7]

- ■ *Factor endowments:* A nation's position in factors of production such as skilled labor or the infrastructure necessary to compete in a given industry
- ■ *Local demand conditions:* The nature of home demand for the industry's product or service
- ■ *Competitiveness of related and supporting industries:* The presence or absence in a nation of supplier industries and related industries that are internationally competitive
- ■ *Intensity of rivalry:* The conditions in the nation governing how companies are created, organized, and managed and the nature of domestic rivalry

Porter speaks of these four attributes as constituting the *diamond,* arguing that companies from a given nation are most likely to succeed in industries or strategic groups in which the four attributes are favorable (see Figure 8.1). He also argues that the diamond's attributes form a mutually reinforcing system in which the effect of one attribute is dependent on the state of others.

FIGURE 8.1

National Competitive Advantage

Source: Adapted from M. E. Porter, "The Competitive Advantage of Nations," *Harvard Business Review,* March–April 1990, page 77.

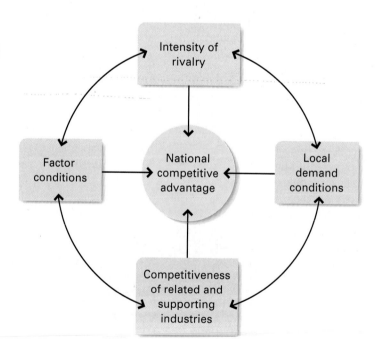

■ Factor Endowments **Factor endowments**—the cost and quality of factors of production—are a prime determinant of the competitive advantage that certain countries might have in certain industries. Factors of production include **basic factors**, such as land, labor, capital, and raw materials, and **advanced factors**, such as technological know-how, managerial sophistication, and physical infrastructure (roads, railways, and ports). The competitive advantage that the United States enjoys in biotechnology might be explained by the presence of certain advanced factors of production—for example, technological know-how—in combination with some basic factors, which might be a pool of relatively low-cost venture capital that can be used to fund risky start-ups in industries such as biotechnology.

■ Local Demand Conditions Home demand plays an important role in providing the impetus for "upgrading" competitive advantage. Companies are typically most sensitive to the needs of their closest customers. Thus, the characteristics of home demand are particularly important in shaping the attributes of domestically made products and creating pressures for innovation and quality. A nation's companies gain competitive advantage if their domestic customers are sophisticated and demanding and pressure local companies to meet high standards of product quality and produce innovative products. Japan's sophisticated and knowledgeable buyers of cameras helped stimulate the Japanese camera industry to improve product quality and introduce innovative models. A similar example can be found in the cellular phone equipment industry, where sophisticated and demanding local customers in Scandinavia helped push Nokia of Finland and Ericsson of Sweden to invest in cellular phone technology long before demand for cellular phones took off in other developed nations. As a result, Nokia and Ericsson, together with Motorola, are significant players in the global cellular telephone equipment industry. The case of Nokia is reviewed in more depth in Strategy in Action 8.1.

■ Competitiveness of Related and Supporting Industries The third broad attribute of national advantage in an industry is the presence of internationally competitive suppliers or related industries. The benefits of investments in advanced factors of production by related and supporting industries can spill over into an industry, thereby helping it achieve a strong competitive position internationally. Swedish strength in fabricated steel products (such as ball bearings and cutting tools) has drawn on strengths in Sweden's specialty steel industry. Switzerland's success in pharmaceuticals is closely related to its previous international success in the technologically related dye industry. One consequence of this process is that successful industries within a country tend to be grouped into clusters of related industries. Indeed, this was one of the most pervasive findings of Porter's study. One such cluster is the German textile and apparel sector, which includes high-quality cotton, wool, synthetic fibers, sewing machine needles, and a wide range of textile machinery.

■ Intensity of Rivalry The fourth broad attribute of national competitive advantage in Porter's model is the intensity of rivalry of firms within a nation. Porter makes two important points here. First, different nations are characterized by different management ideologies, which either help them or do not help them to build national competitive advantage. For example, Porter noted the predominance of engineers in top management at German and Japanese firms. He attributed this to these firms' emphasis on improving manufacturing processes and product design. In contrast, Porter noted a predominance of people with finance backgrounds leading many U.S. firms. He linked this to U.S. firms' lack of attention to improving manufacturing processes and product design. He argued that the dominance of finance led to an overemphasis on maximizing short-term financial returns. According to Porter, one consequence of these different management ideologies was a relative loss of U.S. competitiveness in those engineering-based industries where manufacturing processes and product design issues are all-important (such as the automobile industry).

Porter's second point is that there is a strong association between vigorous domestic rivalry and the creation and persistence of competitive advantage in an industry. Rivalry induces companies to look for ways to improve efficiency, which makes them better international competitors. Domestic rivalry creates pressures to innovate, improve quality, reduce costs, and invest in upgrading advanced factors. All this helps to create world-class competitors. The stimulating effects of strong domestic competition are clear in the story of the rise of Nokia of Finland in the market for wireless handsets and telephone equipment (see Strategy in Action 8.1).

■ **Using the Framework** The framework just described can help managers to identify where their most significant global competitors are likely to come from. For example, there is an emerging cluster of computer service and software companies in Bangalore, India, that includes two of the fastest-growing information technology companies in the world, Infosys and Wipro. These companies might soon emerge as aggressive competitors on the global stage. Indeed, there are signs that this is now happening, since both companies have recently opened up offices in the European Union and United States so they can better compete against the likes of IBM and EDS.

The framework can also be used to help managers decide where they might want to locate certain productive activities. Seeking to take advantage of U.S. expertise in biotechnology, many foreign companies have set up research facilities in San Diego, Boston, and Seattle, where U.S. biotechnology companies tend to be clustered. Similarly, in an attempt to take advantage of Japanese success in customer electronics, many U.S. electronics companies have set up research and production facilities in Japan, often in conjunction with Japanese partners.

Finally, the framework can help a company assess how tough it might be to enter certain national markets. If a nation has a competitive advantage in certain industries, it might be challenging for foreigners to enter those industries. For example, the highly competitive retailing industry in the United States has proved to be a very difficult one for foreign companies to enter. Successful foreign retailers such as Britain's Marks & Spencer and IKEA from Sweden have found it tough going in the United States, precisely because the U.S. retailing industry is the most competitive in the world.

Increasing Profitability and Profit Growth Through Global Expansion

Here we look at a number of ways in which expanding globally can enable companies to increase their profitability and grow their profits more rapidly. At the most basic level, global expansion increases the size of the market a company is addressing, thereby boosting profit growth. Moreover, as we shall see, global expansion offers opportunities for reducing the cost structure of the enterprise or adding value through differentiation, thereby potentially boosting profitability.

■ Expanding the Market: Leveraging Products

A company can increase its growth rate by taking goods or services developed at home and selling them internationally. Indeed, almost all multinationals started out doing just this. Procter & Gamble, for example, developed most of its best-selling products at home and then sold them around the world (Pampers and Ivory Soap being cases in point). Similarly, from its earliest days, Microsoft has always focused on selling its software around the world. Automobile companies like Ford, Volkswagen, and Toyota also grew by developing products at home and then selling them in international markets. The returns from such a strategy are likely to be greater if indigenous competitors in the nations a company enters lack comparable products. Thus Toyota has grown its profits by entering the large automobile markets of North America and Europe and by offering products that are differentiated from those offered by local rivals (Ford and GM) by their superior quality and reliability.

It is important to note that the success of many multinational companies is based not just on the goods or services that they sell in foreign nations, but also on the distinctive competencies (unique skills) that underlie the production and marketing of those goods or services. Thus Toyota's success is based on its distinctive competency in manufacturing automobiles, and expanding internationally can be seen as a way of generating greater returns from this competency. Similarly, Procter & Gamble's global success was based on more than its portfolio of consumer products; it was also based on the company's skills in mass-marketing consumer goods. P&G grew rapidly in international markets between 1950 and 1990 because it was one of the most skilled mass-marketing enterprises in the world and could "outmarket" indigenous competitors in the nations it entered. Global expansion was thus a way of generating higher returns from its competency in marketing.

Pushing this further, one could say that since distinctive competencies are in essence the most valuable aspects of a company's business model, the successful global expansion by manufacturing companies like Toyota and P&G was based on their ability to transfer aspects of their business model and apply it to foreign markets.

The same can be said of companies engaged in the service sectors of an economy, such as financial institutions, retailers, restaurant chains, and hotels. Expanding the market for their services often means replicating their business model in foreign nations (albeit with some changes to account for local differences, which we will discuss in more detail shortly). Starbucks, for example, is expanding rapidly outside of the United States by taking the basic business model it developed at home and using that as a blueprint for establishing international operations. As explained in the *Running Case*, Wal-Mart has done the same thing, establishing stores in nine other nations since 1992 following the blueprint it developed in the United States. Similarly, McDonald's is famous for its international expansion strategy, which has taken the company into more than 120 nations that collectively generate over half of the company's revenues.

■ Realizing Cost Economies from Global Volume

In addition to growing profits more rapidly, by expanding its sales volume through international expansion a company can realize cost savings from economies of scale, thereby boosting profitability. Such scale economies come from several sources. First, by spreading the fixed costs associated with developing a product and setting up production facilities over its global sales volume, a company can lower its average unit cost. Thus, Microsoft can garner significant scale economies by spreading the $1 billion it cost to develop Windows XP over global demand. Second, by serving a

Running Case

Wal-Mart's Global Expansion

In the early 1990s managers at Wal-Mart realized that the company's opportunities for growth in the United States were becoming more limited. By 1995 the company would be active in all fifty states, and management calculated that by the early 2000s domestic growth opportunities would be constrained because of market saturation. So the company decided to expand globally. Initially, the critics scoffed. Wal-Mart, they said, was too American a company. While its business model was well suited to America, it would not work in other countries where infrastructure was different, where consumer tastes and preferences varied, and where established retailers already dominated.

Unperturbed, in 1991 Wal-Mart started to expand internationally with the opening of its first stores in Mexico. The Mexican operation was established as a joint venture with Cifera, the largest local retailer. Initially, Wal-Mart made a number of missteps that seemed to prove the critics right. It had problems replicating its efficient distribution system in Mexico. Poor infrastructure, crowded roads, and a lack of leverage with local suppliers, many of whom could not or would not deliver directly to Wal-Mart's stores or distribution centers, resulted in stocking problems and raised costs and prices. Initially, prices at Wal-Mart in Mexico were some 20 percent above prices for comparable products in the company's U.S. stores, which limited Wal-Mart's ability to gain market share. There were also problems with merchandise selection. Many of the stores in Mexico carried items that were popular in the United States. These included ice skates, riding lawn mowers, leaf blowers, and fishing tackle. Not surprisingly, these items did not sell well in Mexico, so managers would slash prices to move inventory, only to find that the company's automated information systems would immediately order more inventory to replenish the depleted stock.

By the mid 1990s, however, Wal-Mart had learned from its early mistakes and had adapted its operations in Mexico to match the local environment. A partnership with a Mexican trucking company dramatically improved the distribution system, while more careful stocking practices meant that the Mexican stores sold merchandise that appealed more to local tastes and preferences. As Wal-Mart's presence grew, many of Wal-Mart's suppliers built factories close by its Mexican distribution centers so that they could better serve the company, which helped to further drive down inventory and logistics costs. Today, Mexico is a leading light in Wal-Mart's international operations. In 1998, Wal-Mart acquired a controlling interest in Cifera. By 2003, Wal-Mart was more than twice the size of its nearest rival in Mexico, with 623 stores and revenues of over $11 billion.

The Mexican experience proved to Wal-Mart that it could compete outside of the United States. It has subsequently expanded into nine other countries. In Canada, Britain, Germany, Japan, and South Korea, Wal-Mart entered by acquiring existing retailers and then transferring its information systems, logistics, and management expertise. In Puerto Rico, Brazil, Argentina, and China, Wal-Mart established its own stores. As a result of these moves, by 2003 the company had over 1,350 stores outside the United States, employed 330,000 associates, and generated international revenues of more than $46 billion.

In addition to greater growth, expanding internationally brought Wal-Mart two other major benefits. First, Wal-Mart has also been able to reap significant economies of scale from its global buying power. Many of Wal-Mart's key suppliers have long been international companies; for example, GE (appliances), Unilever (food products), and Procter & Gamble (personal care products) are all major Wal-Mart suppliers that have long had their own global operations. By building international reach, Wal-Mart has been able to use its enhanced size to demand deeper discounts from the local operations of its global suppliers, increasing the company's ability to lower prices to consumers, gain market share, and ultimately earn greater profits. Second, Wal-Mart has found that it is benefiting from the flow of ideas across the eleven countries in which it now competes. For example, a two-level store in New York State came about because of the success of multilevel stores in South Korea. Other ideas, such as wine departments in its stores in Argentina, have now been integrated into layouts worldwide.

Wal-Mart realized that if it didn't expand internationally, other global retailers would beat it to the punch. In fact, Wal-Mart does face significant global competition from Carrefour of France, Ahold of Holland, and Tesco from the United Kingdom. Carrefour, the world's second largest retailer, is perhaps the most global of the lot. This pioneer of the hypermarket concept now operates in twenty-six countries and generates more than 50 percent of its sales outside France. Compared to Carrefour, Wal-Mart is a laggard, with just 18.5 percent of its sales in 2003 generated from international operations. However, there is still room for significant global expansion because the global retailing market is still very fragmented. In 2003 the top twenty-five retailers controlled less than 20 percent of worldwide retail sales, although forecasts suggest the figure could reach 40 percent by 2009, with Latin America, Southeast Asia, and eastern Europe being the main battlegrounds.[b]

global market, a company can potentially utilize its production facilities more intensively, which leads to higher productivity, lower costs, and greater profitability. For example, if Intel sold microprocessors only in the United States, it might only be able to keep its factories open for one shift, five days a week. But by serving a global market from the same factories, it might be able to utilize those assets for two shifts, seven days a week. In other words, the capital invested in those factories is used more intensively if Intel sells to a global as opposed to a national market, which translates into higher capital productivity and a higher return on invested capital. Third, as global sales increase the size of the enterprise, so its bargaining power with suppliers increases, which may allow it to bargain down the cost of key inputs and boost profitability that way. Wal-Mart has been able to use its enormous sales volume as a lever to bargain down the price it pays suppliers for merchandise sold through its stores.

In addition to the cost savings that come from economies of scale, companies that sell to a global as opposed to local marketplace may be able to realize further cost savings from learning effects. We first discussed learning effects in Chapter 4, where we noted that employee productivity increases with cumulative increases in output over time (for example, it costs considerably less to build the one-hundredth aircraft off a Boeing assembly line than the tenth because employees learn how to perform their tasks more efficiently over time). By selling to a global market, a company may be able to increase its sales volume more rapidly, and thus the cumulative output from its plants, which in turn should result in quicker learning, higher employee productivity, and a cost advantage over competitors that are growing more slowly because they lack international markets.

■ **Realizing Location Economies**   Earlier in this chapter we discussed how countries differ from each other along a number of dimensions, including differences in the cost and quality of factors of production. These differences imply that some locations are more suited than others for producing certain goods and services.[8] **Location economies** are the economic benefits that arise from performing a value creation activity in the optimal location for that activity, wherever in the world that might be (transportation costs and trade barriers permitting). Locating a value creation activity in the optimal location for that activity can have one of two effects: (1) it can lower the costs of value creation, helping the company achieve a low-cost position, or (2) it can enable a company to differentiate its product offering, which gives it the option of charging a premium price or keeping price low and using differentiation as a means of increasing sales volume. Thus, efforts to realize location economies are consistent with the business-level strategies of low cost and differentiation. In theory, a company that realizes location economies by dispersing each of its value creation activities to the optimal location for that activity should have a competitive advantage over a company that bases all of its value creation activities at a single location. It should be able to differentiate its product offering better and lower its cost structure more than its single-location competitor. In a world where competitive pressures are increasing, such a strategy may well become an imperative for survival.

For an example of how this works in an international business, consider Clear Vision, a manufacturer and distributor of eyewear. Started in the 1970s by David Glassman, the firm now generates annual gross revenues of more than $100 million. Not exactly small, but no corporate giant either, Clear Vision is a multinational firm with production facilities on three continents and customers around the world. Clear Vision began its move toward becoming a multinational in the early 1980s. The strong dollar at that time made U.S.-based manufacturing very expensive. Low-priced imports were taking an ever larger share of the U.S. eyewear market, and Clear Vision realized it could not survive unless it also began to import. Initially the firm bought from independent overseas manufacturers, primarily in Hong Kong. However, it became dissatisfied with these suppliers' product quality and delivery. As Clear Vision's volume of imports increased, Glassman decided that the best way to guarantee quality and delivery was to set up Clear Vision's own manufacturing operation overseas. Accordingly, Clear Vision found a Chinese partner, and together they opened a manufacturing facility in Hong Kong, with Clear Vision being the majority shareholder.

The choice of the Hong Kong location was influenced by its combination of low labor costs, a skilled work force, and tax breaks given by the Hong Kong government. The firm's objective at this point was to lower production costs by locating value creation activities at an appropriate location. After a few years, however, the increasing industrialization of Hong Kong and a growing labor shortage had pushed up wage rates to the extent that it was no longer a low-cost location. In response, Glassman and his Chinese partner moved part of their manufacturing to a plant in mainland China to take advantage of the lower wage rates there. Again, the goal was to lower production costs. The parts for eyewear frames manufactured at this plant are shipped to the Hong Kong factory for final assembly and then distributed to markets in North and South America. The Hong Kong factory now employs 80 people and the China plant between 300 and 400.

At the same time, Clear Vision was looking for opportunities to invest in foreign eyewear firms with reputations for fashionable design and high quality. Its objective was not to reduce production costs but to launch a line of high-quality, differentiated, "designer" eyewear. Clear Vision did not have the design capability in-house to support such a line, but Glassman knew that certain foreign manufacturers did. As a result, Clear Vision invested in factories in Japan, France, and Italy, holding a minority shareholding in each case. These factories now supply eyewear for Clear Vision's Status Eye division, which markets high-priced designer eyewear.[9]

■ **Some Caveats** Introducing transportation costs and trade barriers complicates this picture somewhat. New Zealand might have a comparative advantage for low-cost car assembly operations, but high transportation costs make it an uneconomical location from which to serve global markets. Factoring transportation costs and trade barriers into the cost equation helps explain why many U.S. companies have been shifting their production from Asia to Mexico. Mexico has three distinct advantages over many Asian countries as a location for value creation activities: low labor costs; Mexico's proximity to the large U.S. market, which reduces transportation costs; and the North American Free Trade Agreement (NAFTA), which has removed many trade barriers between Mexico, the United States, and Canada, increasing Mexico's attractiveness as a production site for the North American market. Thus, although the relative costs of value creation are important, transportation costs and trade barriers also must be considered in location decisions.

Another caveat concerns the importance of assessing political and economic risks when making location decisions. Even if a country looks very attractive as a production location when measured against cost or differentiation criteria, if its government is unstable or totalitarian, companies are usually well advised not to base production there. Similarly, if a particular national government appears to be pursuing inappropriate social or economic policies, this might be another reason for not basing production in that location, even if other factors look favorable.

■ Leveraging the Skills of Global Subsidiaries

Initially, many multinational companies develop the valuable competencies and skills that underpin their business model in their home nation and then expand internationally, primarily by selling products and services based on those competencies. Thus, Wal-Mart honed its retailing skills in the United States before transferring them to foreign locations. However, for more mature multinational enterprises that have already established a network of subsidiary operations in foreign markets, the development of valuable skills can just as well occur in foreign subsidiaries.[10] Skills can be created anywhere within a multinational's global network of operations, wherever people have the opportunity and incentive to try new ways of doing things. The creation of skills that help to lower the costs of production, or to enhance perceived value and support higher product pricing, is not the monopoly of the corporate center.

Leveraging the skills created within subsidiaries and applying them to other operations within the firm's global network may create value. For example, McDonald's increasingly is finding that its foreign franchisees are a source of valuable new ideas. Faced with slow growth in France, its local franchisees have begun to experiment not only with the menu but also with the layout and theme of restaurants. Gone are the ubiquitous Golden Arches; gone too are many of the utilitarian chairs and tables and other plastic features of the fast-food giant. Many McDonald's restaurants in France now have hardwood floors, exposed brick walls, and even armchairs. Half of the 930 or so outlets in France have been upgraded to a level that would make them unrecognizable to an American. The menu, too, has been changed to include premier sandwiches, such as chicken on focaccia bread, priced some 30 percent higher than the average hamburger. In France at least, the strategy seems to be working. Following the change, increases in same-store sales rose from 1 percent annually to 3.4 percent. Impressed with the impact, McDonald's executives are now considering adopting similar changes at other McDonald's restaurants in markets where same-store sales growth is sluggish, including the United States.[11]

For the managers of a multinational enterprise, this phenomenon creates important new challenges. First, they must have the humility to recognize that valuable skills can arise anywhere within the firm's global network, not just at the corporate center. Second, they must establish an incentive system that encourages local employees to acquire new competencies. This is not as easy as it sounds. Creating new competencies involves a degree of risk. Not all new skills add value. For every valuable idea created by a McDonald's subsidiary in a foreign country, there may be several failures. The management of the multinational must install incentives that encourage employees to take the necessary risks, and the company must reward people for successes and not sanction them unnecessarily for taking risks that did not pan out. Third, managers must have a process for identifying when valuable new skills have been created in a subsidiary, and finally, they need to act as facilitators, helping to transfer valuable skills within the firm.

Cost Pressures and Pressures for Local Responsiveness

Companies that compete in the global marketplace typically face two types of competitive pressures: *pressures for cost reductions* and *pressures to be locally responsive* (see Figure 8.2).[12] These competitive pressures place conflicting demands on a company. Responding to pressures for cost reductions requires that a company try to minimize its unit costs. To attain this goal, it may have to base its productive activities at the most favorable low-cost location, wherever in the world that might be. It may also have to offer a standardized product to the global marketplace in order to realize the cost savings that come from economies of scale and learning effects. On the other hand, responding to pressures to be locally responsive requires that a company differentiate its product offering and marketing strategy from country to country in an effort to accommodate the diverse demands arising from national differences in consumer tastes and preferences, business practices, distribution channels, competitive conditions, and government policies. Because differentiation across countries can involve significant duplication and a lack of product standardization, it may raise costs.

While some companies, such as Company A in Figure 8.2, face high pressures for cost reductions and low pressures for local responsiveness, and others, such as Company B, face low pressures for cost reductions and high pressures for local responsiveness, many companies are in the position of Company C. They face high pressures for *both* cost reductions and local responsiveness. Dealing with these conflicting and contradictory pressures is a difficult strategic challenge, primarily because being locally responsive tends to raise costs.

FIGURE 8.2

Pressures for Cost Reductions and Local Responsiveness

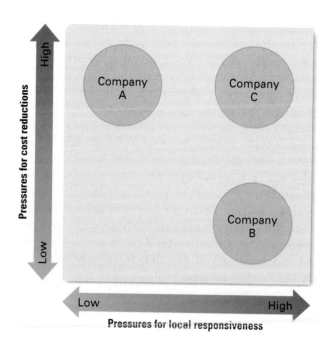

■ **Pressures for Cost Reductions**

In competitive global markets, international businesses often face pressures for cost reductions. To respond to these pressures, a firm must try to lower the costs of value creation. A manufacturer, for example, might mass-produce a standardized product at the optimal location in the world, wherever that might be, to realize economies of scale and location economies. Alternatively, it might outsource certain functions to low-cost foreign suppliers in an attempt to reduce costs. Thus, many computer companies have outsourced their telephone-based customer service functions to India, where qualified technicians who speak English can be hired for a lower wage rate than in the United States. In the same vein, a retailer like Wal-Mart might push its suppliers (who are manufacturers) to also lower their prices. (In fact, the pressure that Wal-Mart has placed on its suppliers to reduce prices has been cited as a major cause of the trend among North American manufacturers to shift production to China.)[13] A service business, such as a bank, might move some back-office functions, such as information processing, to developing nations where wage rates are lower.

Cost reduction pressures can be particularly intense in industries producing commodity-type products where meaningful differentiation on nonprice factors is difficult and price is the main competitive weapon. This tends to be the case for products that serve universal needs. Universal needs exist when the tastes and preferences of consumers in different nations are similar if not identical, such as for bulk chemicals, petroleum, steel, sugar, and the like. They also exist for many industrial and consumer products: for example, hand-held calculators, semiconductor chips, personal computers, and liquid crystal display screens. Pressures for cost reductions are also intense in industries where major competitors are based in low-cost locations, where there is persistent excess capacity, and where consumers are powerful and face low switching costs. Many commentators have argued that the liberalization of the world trade and investment environment in recent decades, by facilitating greater international competition, has generally increased cost pressures.[14]

■ **Pressures for Local Responsiveness**

Pressures for local responsiveness arise from differences in consumer tastes and preferences, infrastructure and traditional practices, distribution channels, and host government demands. Responding to pressures to be locally responsive requires that a company differentiate its products and marketing strategy from country to country to accommodate these factors, all of which tends to raise a company's cost structure.

■ **Differences in Customer Tastes and Preferences** Strong pressures for local responsiveness emerge when customer tastes and preferences differ significantly between countries, as they may for historic or cultural reasons. In such cases, a multinational company's products and marketing message have to be customized to appeal to the tastes and preferences of local customers. The company is then typically pressured to delegate production and marketing responsibilities and functions to a company's overseas subsidiaries.

For example, the automobile industry in the 1980s and early 1990s moved toward the creation of "world cars." The idea was that global companies such as General Motors, Ford, and Toyota would be able to sell the same basic vehicle the world over, sourcing it from centralized production locations. If successful, the strategy would have enabled automobile companies to reap significant gains from global scale economies. However, this strategy frequently ran aground upon the hard rocks of consumer reality. Consumers in different automobile markets seem to have different tastes and preferences, and these require different types of vehicles. North American consumers show a strong demand for pickup trucks. This is particularly true in the South and West where many families have a pickup truck as a second or third car. But in European countries, pickup trucks are seen purely as utility vehicles and are purchased primarily by firms rather than individuals. As a consequence, the product mix and marketing message need to be tailored to take into account the different nature of demand in North America and Europe. Another example of the need to respond to national differences in tastes and preferences is given in Strategy in Action 8.2, which looks at the experience of MTV Networks in foreign markets.

Notwithstanding the experiences of companies such as MTV, some commentators have argued that customer demands for local customization are on the decline worldwide.[15] According to this argument, modern communications and transport technologies have created the conditions for a convergence of the tastes and preferences of customers from different nations. The result is the emergence of enormous global markets for standardized consumer products. The worldwide acceptance of McDonald's hamburgers, Coca-Cola, Gap clothes, Nokia cell phones, and Sony television sets, all of which are sold globally as standardized products, is often cited as evidence of the increasing homogeneity of the global marketplace.

Others, however, consider this argument to be extreme. For example, Christopher Bartlett and Sumantra Ghoshal have observed that in the consumer electronics industry, buyers reacted to an overdose of standardized global products by showing a renewed preference for products that are differentiated to local conditions.[16]

■ Differences in Infrastructure and Traditional Practices

Pressures for local responsiveness also arise from differences in infrastructure or traditional practices among countries, creating a need to customize products accordingly. To meet this need, companies may have to delegate manufacturing and production functions to foreign subsidiaries. For example, in North America, consumer electrical systems are based on 110 volts, whereas in some European countries 240-volt systems are standard. Thus, domestic electrical appliances have to be customized to take this difference in infrastructure into account. Traditional practices also often vary across nations. For example, in Britain, people drive on the left-hand side of the road, creating a demand for right-hand-drive cars, whereas in France (and the rest of Europe), people drive on the right-hand side of the road and therefore want left-hand-drive cars. Obviously, automobiles have to be customized to take this difference in traditional practices into account.

Although many of the country differences in infrastructure are rooted in history, some are quite recent. For example, in the wireless telecommunications industry, different technical standards are found in different parts of the world. A technical standard known as GSM is common in Europe, and an alternative standard, CDMA, is more common in the United States and parts of Asia. The significance of these different standards is that equipment designed for GSM will not work on a CDMA network, and vice versa. Thus, companies such as Nokia, Motorola, and Ericsson, which manufacture wireless handsets and infrastructure such as switches, need to customize their product offering according to the technical standard prevailing in a given country.

■ Differences in Distribution Channels

A company's marketing strategies may have to be responsive to differences in distribution channels among countries, which may necessitate delegating marketing functions to national subsidiaries. In the pharmaceutical industry, for example, the British and Japanese

Strategy in Action

MTV Goes Global, with a Local Accent

8.2

MTV Networks has become a symbol of globalization. Established in 1981, the U.S.-based music TV network has been expanding outside its North American base since 1987, when it opened MTV Europe. Now owned by media conglomerate Viacom, MTV Networks, which includes siblings Nickelodeon and VH1, the music station for the aging baby boomers, generates more than $1 billion in revenues outside the United States. Since 1987, MTV has become the most ubiquitous cable programmer in the world. By 2004 the network had seventy-two channels, or distinct feeds, that reached a combined total of 321 million households in 140 countries.

While the United States still leads in number of households, with 70 million, the most rapid growth is elsewhere, particularly in Asia, where nearly two-thirds of the region's 3 billion people are under thirty-five, the middle class is expanding quickly, and TV ownership is spreading rapidly. MTV Networks figures that every second of every day almost 2 million people are watching MTV around the world, the majority outside the United States.

Despite its international success, MTV's global expansion got off to a weak start. In 1987, it piped a single feed across Europe almost entirely composed of American programming with English-speaking veejays. Naively, the network's U.S. managers thought Europeans would flock to the American programming. But while viewers in Europe shared a common interest in a handful of global superstars, who at the time included Madonna and Michael Jackson, their tastes turned out to be surprisingly local. What was popular in Germany might not be popular in Great Britain. Many staples of the American music scene left Europeans cold, and MTV suffered as a result. Soon local copycat stations were springing up in Europe that focused on the music scene in individual countries. These stations took viewers and advertisers away from MTV. As explained by Tom Freston, chairman of MTV Networks, "We were going for the most shallow layer of what united viewers and brought them together. It didn't go over too well."

In 1995, MTV changed its strategy and broke Europe into regional feeds, of which there are now eight: one for the United Kingdom and Ireland; another for Germany, Austria, and Switzerland; one for Scandinavia; one for Italy; one for France; one for Spain; one for Holland; and a feed for other European nations, including Belgium and Greece. The network adopted the same localization strategy elsewhere in the world. For example, in Asia it has an English-Hindi channel

for India, separate Mandarin feeds for China and Taiwan, a Korean feed for South Korea, a Bahasa-language feed for Indonesia, a Japanese feed for Japan, and so on. Digital and satellite technology have made the localization of programming cheaper and easier. MTV Networks can now beam half a dozen feeds off one satellite transponder.

While MTV Networks exercises creative control over these different feeds, and while all the channels have the same familiar frenetic look and feel of MTV in the United States, a significant share of the programming and content is now local. When MTV opens a local station now, it first asks expatriates from elsewhere in the world to do a "gene transfer" of company culture and operating principles—in other words, its business model. But once these are established, the network switches to local employees and the expatriates move on. The idea is to "get inside the heads" of the local population and produce programming that matches their tastes. Although as much as 60 percent of the programming still originates in the United States, with staples such as *The Real World* having equivalents in different countries, an increasing share of programming is local in conception. In Italy, *MTV Kitchen* combines cooking with a music countdown. *Erotica* airs in Brazil and features a panel of youngsters discussing sex. The Indian channel produces twenty-one homegrown shows hosted by local veejays who speak "Hinglish," a city-bred mix of Hindi and English. Hit shows include *MTV Cricket in Control*, appropriate for a land where cricket is a national obsession, *MTV Housefull*, which hones in on Hindi film stars (India has the biggest film industry outside of Hollywood), and *MTV Bakra*, which is modeled after *Candid Camera*.

This localization push has reaped big benefits for MTV, capturing viewers back from local imitators. In India, ratings increased by more than 700 percent between 1996, when the localization push began, and 2000. In turn, localization helps MTV to capture more of those all-important advertising revenues, even from other multinationals such as Coca-Cola, whose own advertising budgets are often locally determined. In Europe, MTV's advertising revenues increased by 50 percent between 1995 and 2000. While the total market for pan-European advertising is valued at just $200 million, the total market for local advertising across Europe is a much bigger pie, valued at $12 billion. MTV now gets 70 percent of its European advertising revenue from local spots, up from 15 percent in 1995. Similar trends are evident elsewhere in the world.[c]

distribution system is radically different from the U.S. system. British and Japanese doctors will not accept or respond favorably to a U.S.-style high-pressure sales force. Thus, pharmaceutical companies have to adopt different marketing practices in Britain and Japan compared with the United States—soft sell versus hard sell.

■ **Host Government Demands** Finally, economic and political demands imposed by host country governments may require local responsiveness. For example, pharmaceutical companies are subject to local clinical testing, registration procedures, and pricing restrictions, all of which make it necessary that the manufacturing and marketing of a drug should meet local requirements. Moreover, because governments and government agencies control a significant proportion of the health care budget in most countries, they are in a powerful position to demand a high level of local responsiveness.

More generally, threats of protectionism, economic nationalism, and local content rules (which require that a certain percentage of a product should be manufactured locally) dictate that international businesses manufacture locally. As an example, consider Bombardier, the Canadian-based manufacturer of railcars, aircraft, jet boats, and snowmobiles. Bombardier has twelve railcar factories across Europe. Critics of the company argue that the resulting duplication of manufacturing facilities leads to high costs and helps explain why Bombardier makes lower profit margins on its railcar operations than on its other business lines. In reply, managers at Bombardier argue that in Europe, informal rules with regard to local content favor people who use local workers. To sell railcars in Germany, they claim, you must manufacture in Germany. The same goes for Belgium, Austria, and France. To try to address its cost structure in Europe, Bombardier has centralized its engineering and purchasing functions, but it has no plans to centralize manufacturing.[17]

Choosing a Global Strategy

Pressures for local responsiveness imply that it may not be possible for a firm to realize the full benefits from economies of scale and location economies. It may not be possible to serve the global marketplace from a single low-cost location, producing a globally standardized product, and marketing it worldwide to achieve economies of scale. In practice, the need to customize the product offering to local conditions may work against the implementation of such a strategy. For example, automobile firms have found that Japanese, American, and European consumers demand different kinds of cars, and this necessitates producing products that are customized for local markets. In response, firms like Honda, Ford, and Toyota are pursuing a strategy of establishing top-to-bottom design and production facilities in each of these regions so that they can better serve local demands. Although such customization brings benefits, it also limits the ability of a firm to realize significant scale economies and location economies.

In addition, pressures for local responsiveness imply that it may not be possible to leverage skills and products associated with a firm's distinctive competencies wholesale from one nation to another. Concessions often have to be made to local conditions. Despite being depicted as "poster boy" for the proliferation of standardized global products, even McDonald's has found that it has to customize its product offerings (its menu) in order to account for national differences in tastes and preferences.

Given the need to balance the cost and differentiation (value) sides of a company's business model, how do differences in the strength of pressures for cost reductions versus those for local responsiveness affect the choice of a company's strategy? Companies typically choose among four main strategic postures when competing

FIGURE 8.3

Four Basic Strategies

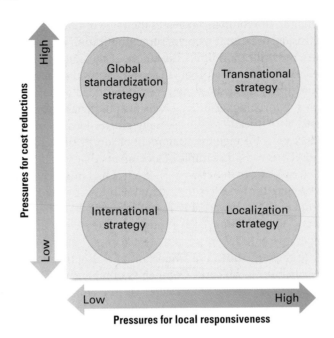

internationally: a global standardization strategy, a localization strategy, a transnational strategy, and an international strategy.[18] The appropriateness of each strategy varies with the extent of pressures for cost reductions and local responsiveness. Figure 8.3 illustrates the conditions under which each of these strategies is most appropriate.

■ Global Standardization Strategy

Companies that pursue a **global standardization strategy** focus on increasing profitability by reaping the cost reductions that come from economies of scale and location economies; that is, their business model is based on pursuing a low-cost strategy on a global scale. The production, marketing, and R&D activities of companies pursuing a global strategy are concentrated in a few favorable locations. These companies try not to customize their product offering and marketing strategy to local conditions because customization, which involves shorter production runs and the duplication of functions, can raise costs. Instead, they prefer to market a standardized product worldwide so that they can reap the maximum benefits from economies of scale. They also tend to use their cost advantage to support aggressive pricing in world markets.

This strategy makes most sense when there are strong pressures for cost reductions and demand for local responsiveness is minimal. Increasingly, these conditions prevail in many industrial goods industries, whose products often serve universal needs. In the semiconductor industry, for example, global standards have emerged, creating enormous demands for standardized global products. Accordingly, companies such as Intel, Texas Instruments, and Motorola all pursue a global strategy.

In many consumer goods markets, however, demands for local responsiveness remain high. In these markets the global standardization strategy is inappropriate.

■ Localization Strategy

A localization strategy focuses on increasing profitability by customizing the company's goods or services so that they provide a good match to tastes and preferences in different national markets. Localization is most appropriate when there are substantial differences across nations with regard to consumer tastes and preferences and where cost pressures are not too intense. By customizing the product offering to local demands, the company increases the value of that product in the local market. On the downside, because it involves some duplication of functions and smaller production runs, customization limits the ability of the company to capture the cost reductions associated with mass-producing a standardized product for global consumption. The strategy may make sense, however, if the added value associated with local customization supports higher pricing, which would enable the company to recoup its higher costs, or if it leads to substantially greater local demand, enabling the company to reduce costs through the attainment of some scale economies in the local market.

MTV is a good example of a company that has had to pursue a localization strategy (see Strategy in Action 8.2). If MTV had not localized its programming to match the demands of viewers in different nations, it would have lost market share to local competitors, its advertising revenues would have fallen, and its profitability would have declined. Thus, even though it raised costs, localization became a strategic imperative at MTV.

At the same time, it is important to realize that companies like MTV still have to keep a close eye on costs. Companies pursuing a localization strategy still need to be efficient and, whenever possible, capture some scale economies from their global reach. As noted earlier, many automobile companies have found that they have to customize some of their product offerings to local market demands—for example, by producing large pickup trucks for U.S. consumers and small fuel-efficient cars for Europeans and Japanese. At the same time, these companies try to get some scale economies from their global volume by using common vehicle platforms and components across many different models and by manufacturing those platforms and components at efficiently scaled factories that are optimally located. By designing their products in this way, these companies have been able to localize their product offering, yet simultaneously capture some scale economies.

■ Transnational Strategy

We have argued that a global standardization strategy makes most sense when cost pressures are intense and demands for local responsiveness limited. Conversely, a localization strategy makes most sense when demands for local responsiveness are high but cost pressures are moderate or low. What happens, however, when the company simultaneously faces both strong cost pressures and strong pressures for local responsiveness? How can managers balance out such competing and inconsistent demands? According to some researchers, the answer is by pursuing what has been called a transnational strategy.

Two of these researchers, Christopher Bartlett and Sumantra Ghoshal, argue that in today's global environment, competitive conditions are so intense that, to survive, companies must do all they can to respond to pressures for both cost reductions and local responsiveness. They must try to realize location economies and economies of scale from global volume, transfer distinctive competencies and skills within the company, and simultaneously pay attention to pressures for local responsiveness.[19] Moreover, Bartlett and Ghoshal note that, in the modern multinational enterprise, distinctive competencies and skills do not reside just in the home country but can develop in any of the company's worldwide operations. Thus, they maintain that the flow of skills and product offerings should not be all one way, from home company to foreign subsidiary. Rather, the flow should also be from foreign subsidiary to home country and from foreign subsidiary to foreign subsidiary. Transnational companies, in other words, must also focus on leveraging subsidiary skills.

In essence, companies that pursue a transnational strategy are trying to develop a business model that simultaneously achieves low costs, differentiates the product offering across geographic markets, and fosters a flow of skills between different subsidiaries in the company's global network of operations. As attractive as this may sound, the strategy is not an easy one to pursue because it places conflicting demands on the company. Differentiating the product to respond to local demands in different geographic markets raises costs, which runs counter to the goal of reducing costs. Companies like Ford and ABB (one of the world's largest engineering conglomerates) have tried to embrace a transnational strategy and have found it difficult to implement in practice.

Indeed, how best to implement a transnational strategy is one of the most complex questions that large global companies are grappling with today. It may be that few if any companies have perfected this strategic posture. But some clues to the right approach can be derived from a number of companies. Consider, for example, the case of Caterpillar. The need to compete with low-cost competitors such as Komatsu of Japan forced Caterpillar to look for greater cost economies. However, variations in construction practices and government regulations across countries meant that Caterpillar also had to be responsive to local demands. Therefore, Caterpillar confronted significant pressures for cost reductions *and* for local responsiveness.

To deal with cost pressures, Caterpillar redesigned its products to use many identical components and invested in a few large-scale component-manufacturing facilities, sited at favorable locations, to fill global demand and realize scale economies. At the same time, the company augments the centralized manufacturing of components with assembly plants in each of its major global markets. At these plants, Caterpillar adds local product features, tailoring the finished product to local needs. Thus, Caterpillar is able to realize many of the benefits of global manufacturing while reacting to pressures for local responsiveness by differentiating its product among national markets.[20] Caterpillar started to pursue this strategy in 1979, and by 1997 it had succeeded in doubling output per employee, significantly reducing its overall cost structure in the process. Meanwhile, Komatsu and Hitachi, which are still wedded to a Japan-centric global strategy, have seen their cost advantages evaporate and have been steadily losing market share to Caterpillar.

However, building an organization capable of supporting a transnational strategy is a complex and challenging task. Indeed, some would say it is too complex, because the strategy implementation problems of creating a viable organizational structure and control systems to manage this strategy are immense. We shall return to this issue in Chapter 13.

■ International Strategy

Sometimes it is possible to identify multinational companies that find themselves in the fortunate position of being confronted with low cost pressures and low pressures for local responsiveness. Typically these enterprises are selling a product that serves universal needs, but because they do not face significant competitors, they are not confronted with pressures to reduce their cost structure. Xerox found itself in this position in the 1960s after its invention and commercialization of the photocopier. The technology underlying the photocopier was protected by strong patents, so for several years Xerox did not face competitors—it had a monopoly. Since the product was highly valued in most developed nations, Xerox was able to sell the same basic product the world over and charge a relatively high price for it. At the same time, because it did not face direct competitors, the company did not have to deal with strong pressures to minimize its costs.

Historically, companies like Xerox have followed a similar developmental pattern as they build their international operations. They tend to centralize product development functions such as R&D at home. However, they also tend to establish manufacturing and marketing functions in each major country or geographic region in which they do business. Although they may undertake some local customization of product offering and marketing strategy, this tends to be rather limited in scope. Ultimately, in most international companies, the head office retains tight control over marketing and product strategy.

Other companies that have pursued this strategy include Procter & Gamble, which historically always developed innovative new products in Cincinnati and then transferred them wholesale to local markets. Another company that has followed a similar strategy is Microsoft. The bulk of Microsoft's product development work takes place in Redmond, Washington State, where the company is headquartered. Although some localization work is undertaken elsewhere, this is limited to producing foreign-language versions of popular Microsoft programs such as Office.

■ **Changes in Strategy over Time**

The Achilles heel of the international strategy is that, over time, competitors inevitably emerge, and if managers do not take proactive steps to reduce their cost structure, their company may be rapidly outflanked by efficient global competitors. This is exactly what happened to Xerox. Japanese companies such as Canon ultimately invented their way around Xerox's patents, produced their own photocopiers in very efficient manufacturing plants, priced them below Xerox's products, and rapidly took global market share from Xerox. Xerox's demise was not due to the emergence of competitors, for ultimately that was bound to occur, but rather to its failure to proactively reduce its cost structure in advance of the emergence of efficient global competitors. The message in this story is that an international strategy may not be viable in the long term, and to survive companies that are able to pursue it need to shift toward a global standardization strategy, or perhaps a transnational strategy, in advance of competitors (see Figure 8.4).

FIGURE 8.4

Changes over Time

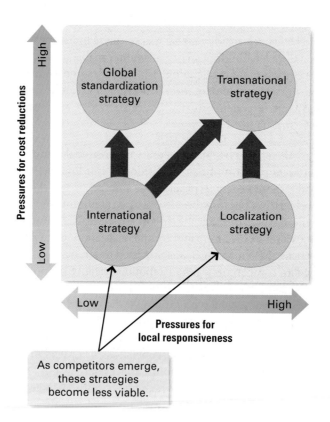

The same can be said about a localization strategy. Localization may give a company a competitive edge, but if it is simultaneously facing aggressive competitors, the company will also have to reduce its cost structure, and the only way to do that may be to adopt more of a transnational strategy. Thus, as competition intensifies, international and localization strategies tend to become less viable, and managers need to orient their companies toward either a global standardization strategy or a transnational strategy.

Basic Entry Decisions

A company contemplating foreign expansion must make three basic decisions: which overseas markets to enter, when to enter those markets, and on what scale.

■ Which Overseas Markets to Enter

There are over two hundred nation-states in the world, and they do not all hold out the same profit potential for a company contemplating foreign expansion. The choice of foreign markets must be based on an assessment of their long-run profit potential. The attractiveness of a country as a potential market for international business depends on balancing the benefits, costs, and risks associated with doing business in that country. The long-run economic benefits of doing business in a country are a function of factors such as the size of a market (in terms of demographics), the existing wealth (purchasing power) of consumers in that market, and the likely future wealth of consumers. Some markets are very large when measured by numbers of consumers (such as China and India), but low living standards may imply limited purchasing power and therefore a relatively small market when measured in economic terms. The costs and risks associated with doing business in a foreign country are typically lower in economically advanced and politically stable democratic nations and greater in less developed and politically unstable nations.

By performing benefit-cost-risk calculations, a company can come up with a ranking of countries in terms of their attractiveness and long-run profit potential.[21] Obviously, preference is given to entering markets that rank highly. For an example, consider the case of the American financial services company Merrill Lynch, whose situation is profiled in Strategy in Action 8.3. During the past decade, Merrill Lynch greatly expanded its operations in the United Kingdom, Canada, and Japan. All three of these countries have a large pool of private savings and exhibit relatively low political and economic risks, so it makes sense that they would be attractive to Merrill Lynch. By offering its financial service products, such as mutual funds and investment advice, Merrill Lynch should be able to capture a large enough proportion of the private savings pool in each country to justify its investment in setting up business there. Of the three countries, Japan is probably the riskiest given the fragile state of its financial system, which is still suffering from a serious bad debt problem. However, the large size of the Japanese market and the fact that its government seems to be embarking on significant reform explain why Merrill has been attracted to this nation.

One other factor of importance is the value that a company's business model can create in a foreign market. This depends on the suitability of its business model to that market and the nature of indigenous competition.[22] Most important, if the company can offer a product that has not been widely available in that market and satisfies an unmet need, the value of that product to consumers is likely to be much greater than if the company simply offers the same type of product that indigenous competitors and other foreign entrants are already offering. Greater value translates into an ability to charge higher prices or build up unit sales volume more rapidly (or both). Again, on this count, Japan is clearly very attractive to Merrill Lynch.

Strategy in Action

8.3

Merrill Lynch in Japan

Merrill Lynch, the U.S.-based financial services institution, is an investment banking titan. It is the world's largest underwriter of debt and equity and the third largest adviser on mergers and acquisitions behind Morgan Stanley and Goldman Sachs. As one might expect, its investment banking operations have long had a global reach. The company has a dominant presence not only in New York but also in London and Tokyo. However, until recently, Merrill's international presence was limited to the investment banking side of its business. In contrast, its private client business, which offers banking, financial advice, and stockbrokerage services to individuals, has historically been concentrated in the United States. This is now changing rapidly. In 1995 Merrill purchased Smith New Court, the largest stockbrokerage firm in Britain, and in 1997 it acquired Mercury Asset Management, the U.K.'s leading manager of mutual funds. Then in 1998 Merrill acquired Midland Walwyn, Canada's last major independent stockbrokerage firm. The company's boldest moves, however, have probably been in Japan.

Merrill started to establish a private client business in Japan in the 1980s but met with limited success. At the time, it was the first foreign firm to enter Japan's private client investment market, and it had great difficulty in attracting employee talent and customers away from Japan's four big stockbrokerage firms, which traditionally had monopolized the Japanese market. Moreover, restrictive regulations made it almost impossible for Merrill to offer its Japanese private clients the range of services it offered clients in the United States. For example, foreign exchange regulations meant that it was very difficult for Merrill to sell non-Japanese stocks, bonds, and mutual funds to Japanese investors. In 1993, Merrill admitted defeat, closed down its six retail branches in Kobe and Kyoto, and withdrew from the private client market in Japan.

Over the next few years, however, things started to change. In the mid 1990s, Japan embarked on a wide-ranging deregulation of its financial services industry. Among other things, this led to the removal of many of the restrictions that had made it so difficult for Merrill to do business in Japan. For example, the relaxation of foreign exchange controls meant that by 1998 it was possible for Japanese citizens to purchase foreign stocks, bonds, and mutual funds. Meanwhile, Japan's four big stockbrokerage firms continued to struggle with serious financial problems, the result of the 1991 crash of that country's stock market. In November 1997, in what was a dramatic shock to many Japanese, one of these firms, Yamaichi Securities, declared that it was bankrupt: it had $2.2 billion in accumulated "hidden losses" and would shut its doors. Recognizing the country's financial system was strained and in need of fresh capital, know-how, and the stimulus of greater competition, the Japanese government signaled that it would adopt a much more relaxed attitude to foreign entry into its financial services industry. This attitude underlay Japan's wholehearted endorsement of a 1997 deal brokered by the World Trade Organization (WTO) to liberalize global financial services. Among other things, the WTO deal made it much easier for foreign firms to sell financial service products to Japanese investors.

By 1997, it had become clear to Merrill Lynch that the climate in Japan had changed significantly. The big attraction of the market was still the same: the financial assets owned by Japanese households are huge, amounting to a staggering 1,220 trillion yen in late 1997, with only 3 percent invested in mutual funds (most are invested in low-yielding bank accounts and government bonds). However, attitudes were changing, and it looked as if it would be much easier to do business in Japan.

Accordingly, in mid 1997, Merrill started to consider reentering the Japanese private client market. Initially, it considered a joint venture with Sanwa Bank to sell Merrill's mutual fund products to Japanese consumers through Sanwa's four hundred retail branches. The proposed alliance had the advantage of allowing Merrill to leverage Sanwa's existing distribution system rather than having to build a distribution system of its own from scratch. However, in the long run, the strategy would not have given Merrill the presence that it felt it needed to build a solid financial services business in Japan. Merrill's executives reasoned that it was important for them to make a major commitment to the Japanese market in order to establish its brand name as a premier provider of investment products and financial advice to individuals. This would enable the company to entrench itself as a major player before other foreign institutions entered the market—and before Japan's own stockbrokerages rose to the challenge. At the same time, given their prior experience in Japan, Merrill's executives were hesitant to go down this road because of the huge costs and risks.

The problem of how best to enter the Japanese market was solved by the bankruptcy of Yamaichi Securities. Suddenly Yamaichi's nationwide network of offices and 7,000 employees were up for grabs. In late December 1997, Merrill announced that it would hire some 2,000 of Yamaichi's employees and acquire up to fifty of Yamaichi's branch offices. The deal, enthusiastically endorsed by the Japanese government, significantly lowered Merrill's costs of establishing a retail network in Japan. Merrill's goal for the new subsidiary was to have $20 billion under management by 2000 and to break even by 2001.

The company got off to a quick start. In February 1998, Merrill Lynch launched its first mutual fund in Japan and saw the value of its assets swell to $1 billion by April. By mid 2002, it announced it had $12.9 billion under management in Japan. However, the collapse in global stock markets in 2001–2002 hit Merrill's Japanese unit hard. After losing $500 million in Japan on its investment, in January 2002 the company fired 75 percent of its Japanese work force and closed all but eight of its retail locations. Despite this costly downsizing, the company held on to almost all of the assets under management, continued to attract new accounts, and by mid 2002 was reportedly making a profit in Japan.[d]

■ Timing of Entry

Once a set of attractive national markets has been identified, it is important to consider the timing of entry: *early* (before other overseas companies) or *late* (after other international businesses have already established themselves in the market).

Several first-mover advantages are frequently associated with entering a market early.[23] One advantage is the ability to preempt rivals and capture demand by establishing a strong brand name. A second is the ability to build up demand, sales revenue, and market share in that country and ride down the experience curve ahead of future rivals. Both factors give the early entrant a cost advantage over later entrants, which may enable it to respond to later entry by cutting prices below those of later entrants and drive them out of the market. A third advantage is the ability of early entrants to create switching costs that tie customers into their products or services. Such switching costs make it difficult for later entrants to win business.

The case of Merrill Lynch illustrates these ideas. By entering the private client market in Japan early, Merrill hoped to establish a brand name that later entrants would find difficult to match. Moreover, by entering early with a valuable product offering, Merrill hoped to build up its sales volume rapidly, which will enable it to realize scale economies from establishing a network of Japanese branches. In addition, as Merrill trains its Japanese staff, their productivity should rise because of learning economies, which again translates into lower costs. Thus, Merrill should be able to ride down the experience curve and achieve a lower cost structure than later entrants.

Finally, Merrill's business model is based on establishing close relationships between its financial advisers (that is, stockbrokers) and private clients. Merrill's financial advisers are taught to get to know the needs of their clients and help manage their finances more effectively. Once these relationships are established, people rarely change. In other words, because of switching costs, they are unlikely to shift their business to later entrants. This effect is likely to be particularly strong in a country like Japan, where long-term relationships have traditionally been very important in business and social settings. For all of these reasons, Merrill Lynch may be able to capture first-mover advantages that will enable it to enjoy a strong competitive position in Japan for years to come.

There can also be first-mover disadvantages associated with entering a foreign market before other global companies.[24] These disadvantages are associated with *pioneering costs*, which an early entrant has to bear and which a later entrant can avoid. Pioneering costs arise when the business system in a foreign country is so different from that in a company's home market that a company has to devote considerable effort, time, and expense to learning the rules of the game. Pioneering costs also include the costs of business failure if the company, because of its ignorance of the overseas environment, makes major strategic mistakes. Thus, a global company that is one of the first to enter a national market has a certain liability.[25] Research evidence suggests that the probability of survival increases if an international business enters a national market *after* several other overseas companies have already done so.[26] The late entrant, it would appear, benefits by observing and learning from the mistakes made by early entrants.

Pioneering costs also include the costs of promoting and establishing a product offering, including the costs of educating customers. These costs can be particularly significant when the product being promoted is one that local customers are unfamiliar with. In many ways, Merrill Lynch will have to bear such pioneering costs in Japan. Most Japanese are not familiar with the type of investment products and services that it intends to sell, so Merrill will have to invest significant resources in customer education. In contrast, later entrants may be able to free-ride on an early entrant's investments in learning and customer education by watching how the early entrant proceeded in the market, avoiding costly mistakes made by the early entrant, and exploiting the market potential created by the early entrant's investments in customer education.

Scale of Entry and Strategic Commitments

The final issue that a company needs to consider when contemplating market entry is the scale of entry. Entering a market on a large scale involves the commitment of significant resources to that venture. Not all companies have the resources necessary to enter on a large scale, and even some large companies prefer to enter overseas markets on a small scale and then build their presence slowly over time as they become more familiar with the market. The original entry by Merrill Lynch into the private client market in Japan was on a small scale, involving only a handful of branches. In contrast, Merrill's reentry into the Japanese market in 1997 was on a significant scale.

The consequences of entering on a significant scale are associated with the value of the resulting strategic commitments.[27] A *strategic commitment* is a decision that has a long-term impact and is difficult to reverse. Deciding to enter a foreign market on a significant scale is a major strategic commitment. Strategic commitments, such as large-scale market entry, can have an important influence on the nature of competition in a market. For example, by entering Japan's private client business on a significant scale, Merrill has signaled its commitment to the market. This will have several effects. On the positive side, it will make it easier for Merrill to attract clients. The scale of entry gives potential clients reason for believing that Merrill will remain in the market for the long run. It may also give other overseas institutions considering entry into Japan's market pause for thought, since now they will have to compete not only against Japan's indigenous institutions but also against an aggressive and successful U.S. institution. On the negative side, the move may wake up Japan's financial institutions and elicit a vigorous competitive response from them. Moreover, by committing itself heavily to Japan, Merrill may have fewer resources available to support expansion in other desirable markets. In other words, Merrill's commitment to Japan limits its strategic flexibility.

As this example suggests, significant strategic commitments are neither unambiguously good nor bad. Rather, they tend to change the competitive playing field and unleash a number of changes, some of which may be desirable and some of which will not. It is therefore important for a company to think through the implications of large-scale entry into a market and act accordingly. Of particular relevance is trying to identify how actual and potential competitors might react to large-scale entry into a market. It is also important to bear in mind a connection between large-scale entry and first-mover advantages. Specifically, the large-scale entrant is more likely than the small-scale entrant to be able to capture first-mover advantages associated with demand preemption, scale economies, and switching costs.

Balanced against the value and risks of the commitments associated with large-scale entry are the benefits of entering on a small scale. Small-scale entry has the advantage of allowing a company to learn about a foreign market while simultaneously limiting the company's exposure to that market. In this sense, small-scale entry can be seen as a way of gathering more information about a foreign market before deciding whether to enter on a significant scale and how best to enter that market. In other words, by giving the company time to collect information, small-scale entry reduces the risks associated with a subsequent large-scale entry. On the other hand, the lack of commitment associated with small-scale entry may make it more difficult for the small-scale entrant to build market share and capture first-mover or early-mover advantages. The risk-averse company that enters a foreign market on a small scale may limit its potential losses, but it may also lose the chance to capture first-mover advantages.

The Choice of Entry Mode

The issue of when and how to enter a new national market raises the question of how to determine the best mode or vehicle for such entry. There are five main choices of entry mode: exporting, licensing, franchising, entering into a joint venture with a host country company, and setting up a wholly owned subsidiary in the host country. Each mode has its advantages and disadvantages, and managers must weigh these carefully when deciding which mode to use.[28]

■ Exporting

Most manufacturing companies begin their global expansion as exporters and only later switch to one of the other modes for serving a foreign market. Exporting has two distinct advantages: it avoids the costs of establishing manufacturing operations in the host country, which are often substantial, and it may be consistent with scale economies and location economies. By manufacturing the product in a centralized location and then exporting it to other national markets, the company may be able to realize substantial scale economies from its global sales volume. That is how Sony came to dominate the global television market, how Matsushita came to dominate the VCR market, and how many Japanese auto companies originally made inroads into the U.S. auto market.

There are also a number of drawbacks to exporting. First, exporting from the company's home base may not be appropriate if there are lower-cost locations for manufacturing the product abroad (that is, if the company can realize location economies by moving production elsewhere). Thus, particularly in the case of a company pursuing a global standardization or transnational strategy, it may pay to manufacture in a location where conditions are most favorable from a value creation perspective and then export from that location to the rest of the globe. This is not so much an argument against exporting as an argument against exporting from the company's home country. For example, many U.S. electronics companies have moved some of their manufacturing to Asia because low-cost but highly skilled labor is available there. They export from that location to the rest of the globe, including the United States.

Another drawback is that high transport costs can make exporting uneconomical, particularly in the case of bulk products. One way of getting around this problem is to manufacture bulk products on a regional basis, thereby realizing some economies from large-scale production while limiting transport costs. Many multinational chemical companies manufacture their products on a regional basis, serving several countries in a region from one facility.

Tariff barriers, too, can make exporting uneconomical, and a government's threat to impose tariff barriers can make the strategy very risky. Indeed, the implicit threat from the U.S. Congress to impose tariffs on Japanese cars imported into the United States led directly to the decision by many Japanese auto companies to set up manufacturing plants in the United States.

Finally, a common practice among companies that are just beginning to export also poses risks. A company may delegate marketing activities in each country in which it does business to a local agent, but there is no guarantee that the agent will act in the company's best interest. Often foreign agents also carry the products of competing companies and thus have divided loyalties. Consequently, they may not do as good a job as the company would if it managed marketing itself. One way to solve this problem is to set up a wholly owned subsidiary in the host country to handle local marketing. In this way, the company can reap the cost advantages that arise from manufacturing the product in a single location and exercise tight control over marketing strategy in the host country.

■ Licensing

International licensing is an arrangement whereby a foreign licensee buys the rights to produce a company's product in the licensee's country for a negotiated fee (normally, royalty payments on the number of units sold). The licensee then puts up most of the capital necessary to get the overseas operation going.[29] The advantage of licensing is that the company does not have to bear the development costs and risks associated with opening up a foreign market. Licensing therefore can be a very attractive option for companies that lack the capital to develop operations overseas. It can also be an attractive option for companies that are unwilling to commit substantial financial resources to an unfamiliar or politically volatile foreign market where political risks are particularly high.

Licensing has three serious drawbacks, however. First, it does not give a company the tight control over manufacturing, marketing, and strategic functions in foreign countries that it needs to have in order to realize scale economies and location economies—as companies pursuing both global standardization and transnational strategies try to do. Typically, each licensee sets up its own manufacturing operations. Hence, the company stands little chance of realizing scale economies and location economies by manufacturing its product in a centralized location. When these economies are likely to be important, licensing may not be the best way of expanding overseas.

Second, competing in a global marketplace may make it necessary for a company to coordinate strategic moves across countries so that the profits earned in one country can be used to support competitive attacks in another. Licensing, by its very nature, severely limits a company's ability to coordinate strategy in this way. A licensee is unlikely to let a multinational company take its profits (beyond those due in the form of royalty payments) and use them to support an entirely different licensee operating in another country.

A third problem with licensing is the risk associated with licensing technological know-how to foreign companies. For many multinational companies, technological know-how forms the basis of their competitive advantage, and they would want to maintain control over the use to which it is put. By licensing its technology, a company can quickly lose control over it. RCA, for instance, once licensed its color television technology to a number of Japanese companies. The Japanese companies quickly assimilated RCA's technology and then used it to enter the U.S. market. Now the Japanese have a bigger share of the U.S. market than the RCA brand does.

There are ways of reducing this risk. One way is by entering into a cross-licensing agreement with a foreign firm. Under a **cross-licensing agreement**, a firm might license some valuable intangible property to a foreign partner and, in addition to a royalty payment, also request that the foreign partner license some of its valuable know-how to the firm. Such agreements are reckoned to reduce the risks associated with licensing technological know-how, since the licensee realizes that if it violates the spirit of a licensing contract (by using the knowledge obtained to compete directly with the licensor), the licensor can do the same to it. Put differently, cross-licensing agreements enable firms to hold each other hostage, thereby reducing the probability that they will behave opportunistically toward each other.[30] Such cross-licensing agreements are increasingly common in high-technology industries. For example, the U.S. biotechnology firm Amgen has licensed one of its key drugs, Nuprogene, to Kirin, the Japanese pharmaceutical company. The license gives Kirin the right to sell Nuprogene in Japan. In return, Amgen receives a royalty payment, and through a licensing agreement it gains the right to sell certain of Kirin's products in the United States.

■ **Franchising**

In many respects, franchising is similar to licensing, although franchising tends to involve longer-term commitments than licensing. **Franchising** is basically a specialized form of licensing in which the franchiser not only sells intangible property to the franchisee (normally a trademark), but also insists that the franchisee agree to abide by strict rules as to how it does business. The franchiser will also often assist the franchisee to run the business on an ongoing basis. As with licensing, the franchiser typically receives a royalty payment, which amounts to some percentage of the franchisee revenues.

Whereas licensing is a strategy pursued primarily by manufacturing companies, franchising, which resembles it in some respects, is a strategy employed chiefly by service companies. McDonald's provides a good example of a firm that has grown by using a franchising strategy. McDonald's has set down strict rules as to how franchisees should operate a restaurant. These rules extend to control over the menu, cooking methods, staffing policies, and restaurant design and location. McDonald's also organizes the supply chain for its franchisees and provides management training and financial assistance.[31]

The advantages of franchising are similar to those of licensing. Specifically, the franchiser does not have to bear the development costs and risks of opening up a foreign market on its own, for the franchisee typically assumes those costs and risks. Thus, using a franchising strategy, a service company can build up a global presence quickly and at a low cost.

The disadvantages are less pronounced than in the case of licensing. Because franchising is a strategy used by service companies, a franchiser does not have to consider the need to coordinate manufacturing to achieve scale economies and location economies. Nevertheless, franchising may inhibit a company's ability to achieve global strategic coordination.

A more significant disadvantage of franchising is the lack of quality control. The foundation of franchising arrangements is the notion that the company's brand name conveys a message to consumers about the quality of the company's product. Thus, a traveler booking into a Hilton International hotel in Hong Kong can reasonably expect the same quality of room, food, and service as she would receive in New York; the Hilton brand name is a guarantee of the consistency of product quality. However, foreign franchisees may not be as concerned about quality as they should be, and poor quality may mean not only lost sales in the foreign market but also a decline in the company's worldwide reputation. For example, if the traveler has a bad experience at the Hilton in Hong Kong, she may never go to another Hilton hotel and may steer her colleagues away as well. The geographic distance separating it from its foreign franchisees and the sheer number of individual franchisees—tens of thousands in the case of McDonald's—can make it difficult for the franchiser to detect poor quality. Consequently, quality problems may persist.

To reduce this problem, a company can set up a subsidiary in each country or region in which it is expanding. The subsidiary, which might be wholly owned by the company or a joint venture with a foreign company, then assumes the rights and obligations to establish franchisees throughout that particular country or region. The combination of proximity and the limited number of independent franchisees that have to be monitored reduces the quality control problem. Besides, since the subsidiary is at least partly owned by the company, the company can place its own managers in the subsidiary to ensure the kind of quality monitoring it wants. This organizational arrangement has proved very popular in practice. It has been used by McDonald's, KFC, and Hilton Hotels Corp. to expand their international operations, to name just three examples.

Joint Ventures

Establishing a joint venture with a foreign company has long been a favored mode for entering a new market. One of the most famous long-term joint ventures is the Fuji-Xerox joint venture to produce photocopiers for the Japanese market. The most typical form of joint venture is a 50/50 joint venture, in which each party takes a 50 percent ownership stake and operating control is shared by a team of managers from both parent companies. Some companies have sought joint ventures in which they have a majority shareholding (for example, a 51 percent to 49 percent ownership split), which permits tighter control by the dominant partner.[32]

Joint ventures have a number of advantages. First, a company may feel that it can benefit from a local partner's knowledge of a host country's competitive conditions, culture, language, political systems, and business systems. Second, when the development costs and risks of opening up a foreign market are high, a company might gain by sharing these costs and risks with a local partner. Third, in some countries, political considerations make joint ventures the only feasible entry mode.[33] For example, historically many U.S. companies found it much easier to get permission to set up operations in Japan if they went in with a Japanese partner than if they tried to enter on their own. This is why Xerox originally teamed up with Fuji to sell photocopiers in Japan.

Despite these advantages, joint ventures can be difficult to establish and run because of two main drawbacks. First, as in the case of licensing, a company that enters into a joint venture risks losing control over its technology to its venture partner.

To minimize this risk, it can seek a majority ownership stake in the joint venture, and then as the dominant partner it would be able to exercise greater control over its technology. The trouble with this strategy is that it may be difficult to find a foreign partner willing to accept a minority ownership position.

The second disadvantage is that a joint venture does not give a company the tight control over its subsidiaries that it might need in order to realize scale economies or location economies—as both global standardization and transnational companies try to do—or to engage in coordinated global attacks against its global rivals. Consider the entry of Texas Instruments (TI) into the Japanese semiconductor market. When TI established semiconductor facilities in Japan, part of its objective was to limit Japanese manufacturers' market share and the amount of cash available to them to invade TI's global market. In other words, TI was engaging in global strategic coordination. To implement this strategy, TI's Japanese subsidiary had to be prepared to take instructions from the TI corporate headquarters regarding competitive strategy. The strategy also required that the Japanese subsidiary be run at a loss if necessary. Clearly, a Japanese joint venture partner would have been unlikely to accept such conditions since they would have meant a negative return on investment. Thus, in order to implement this strategy, TI set up a wholly owned subsidiary in Japan instead of entering this market through a joint venture.

■ Wholly Owned Subsidiaries

A **wholly owned subsidiary** is one in which the parent company owns 100 percent of the subsidiary's stock. To establish a wholly owned subsidiary in a foreign market, a company can either set up a completely new operation in that country or acquire an established host country company and use it to promote its products in the host market (as Merrill Lynch did when it acquired various assets of Yamaichi Securities; see Strategy in Action 8.3).

Setting up a wholly owned subsidiary offers three advantages. First, when a company's competitive advantage is based on its control of a technological competency, a wholly owned subsidiary will normally be the preferred entry mode, since it reduces the company's risk of losing this control. Consequently, many high-tech companies prefer wholly owned subsidiaries to joint ventures or licensing arrangements. Wholly owned subsidiaries tend to be the favored entry mode in the semiconductor, computer, electronics, and pharmaceutical industries. Second, a wholly owned subsidiary gives a company the kind of tight control over operations in different countries that it needs if it is going to engage in global strategic coordination—taking profits from one country to support competitive attacks in another.

Third, a wholly owned subsidiary may be the best choice if a company wants to realize location economies and the scale economies that flow from producing a standardized output from a single or limited number of manufacturing plants. When pressures on costs are intense, it may pay a company to configure its value chain in such a way that value added at each stage is maximized. Thus, a national subsidiary may specialize in manufacturing only part of the product line or certain components of the end product, exchanging parts and products with other subsidiaries in the company's global system. Establishing such a global production system requires a high degree of control over the operations of national affiliates. Different national operations have to be prepared to accept centrally determined decisions as to how they should produce, how much they should produce, and how their output should be priced for transfer between operations. A wholly owned subsidiary would have to comply with these mandates, whereas licensees or joint venture partners would most likely shun such a subservient role.

On the other hand, establishing a wholly owned subsidiary is generally the most costly method of serving a foreign market. The parent company must bear all the costs and risks of setting up overseas operations—in contrast to joint ventures, where the costs and risks are shared, or licensing, where the licensee bears most of the costs and risks. But the risks of learning to do business in a new culture diminish if the company acquires an established host country enterprise. Acquisitions, though, raise a whole set of additional problems, such as trying to marry divergent corporate cultures, and these problems may more than offset the benefits. (The problems associated with acquisitions are discussed in Chapter 10.)

■ Choosing an Entry Strategy

The advantages and disadvantages of the various entry modes are summarized in Table 8.1. Inevitably, there are tradeoffs in choosing one entry mode over another. For example, when considering entry into an unfamiliar country with a track record of nationalizing foreign-owned enterprises, a company might favor a joint venture with a local enterprise. Its rationale might be that the local partner will help it establish operations in an unfamiliar environment and speak out against nationalization should the possibility arise. But if the company's distinctive competency is based on proprietary technology, entering into a joint venture might mean risking loss of control over that technology to the joint venture partner, which would make this strategy unattractive. Despite such hazards, some generalizations can be offered about the optimal choice of entry mode.

TABLE 8.1

The Advantages and Disadvantages of Different Entry Modes

Entry Mode	Advantages	Disadvantages
Exporting	■ Ability to realize location- and scale-based economies	■ High transport costs ■ Trade barriers ■ Problems with local marketing agents
Licensing	■ Low development costs and risks	■ Inability to realize location- and scale-based economies ■ Inability to engage in global strategic coordination ■ Lack of control over technology
Franchising	■ Low development costs and risks	■ Inability to engage in global strategic coordination ■ Lack of control over quality
Joint ventures	■ Access to local partner's knowledge ■ Shared development costs and risks ■ Political dependency	■ Inability to engage in global strategic coordination ■ Inability to realize location- and scale-based economies ■ Lack of control over technology
Wholly owned subsidiaries	■ Protection of technology ■ Ability to engage in global strategic coordination ■ Ability to realize location- and scale-based economies	■ High costs and risks

■ **Distinctive Competencies and Entry Mode** When companies expand internationally to earn greater returns from their differentiated product offerings, entering markets where indigenous competitors lack comparable products, the companies are pursuing an international strategy. The optimal entry mode for such companies depends to some degree on the nature of their distinctive competency. In particular, we need to distinguish between companies with a distinctive competency in technological know-how and those with a distinctive competency in management know-how.

If a company's competitive advantage—its distinctive competency—derives from its control of proprietary *technological know-how*, licensing and joint venture arrangements should be avoided if possible to minimize the risk of losing control of that technology. Thus, if a high-tech company is considering setting up operations in a foreign country in order to profit from a distinctive competency in technological know-how, it should probably do so through a wholly owned subsidiary.

However, this rule should not be viewed as a hard and fast one. For instance, a licensing or joint venture arrangement might be structured in such a way as to reduce the risks that a company's technological know-how will be expropriated by licensees or joint venture partners. We consider this kind of arrangement in more detail later in the chapter when we discuss the issue of structuring strategic alliances. To take another exception to the rule, a company may perceive its technological advantage as being only transitory and expect rapid imitation of its core technology by competitors. In this situation, the company might want to license its technology as quickly as possible to foreign companies in order to gain global acceptance of its technology before imitation occurs.[34] Such a strategy has some advantages. By licensing its technology to competitors, the company may deter them from developing their own, possibly superior, technology. It also may be able to establish its technology as the dominant design in the industry (as Matsushita did with its VHS format for VCRs), ensuring a steady stream of royalty payments. Such situations apart, however, the attractions of licensing are probably outweighed by the risks of losing control of technology, and therefore licensing should be avoided.

The competitive advantage of many service companies, such as McDonald's or Hilton Hotels, is based on *management know-how*. For such companies, the risk of losing control of their management skills to franchisees or joint venture partners is not that great. The reason is that the valuable asset of such companies is their brand name, and brand names are generally well protected by international laws pertaining to trademarks. Given this fact, many of the issues that arise in the case of technological know-how do not arise in the case of management know-how. As a result, many service companies favor a combination of franchising and subsidiaries to control franchisees within a particular country or region. The subsidiary may be wholly owned or a joint venture. In most cases, however, service companies have found that entering into a joint venture with a local partner in order to set up a controlling subsidiary in a country or region works best because a joint venture is often politically more acceptable and brings a degree of local knowledge to the subsidiary.

■ **Pressures for Cost Reduction and Entry Mode** The greater the pressures for cost reductions are, the more likely it is that a company will want to pursue some combination of exporting and wholly owned subsidiaries. By manufacturing in the locations where factor conditions are optimal and then exporting to the rest of the world, a company may be able to realize substantial location economies and substantial scale economies. The company might then want to export the finished product to marketing subsidiaries based in various countries. Typically, these subsidiaries would be wholly owned and have the responsibility for overseeing distribution in a particular country. Setting up wholly owned marketing subsidiaries is preferable to a joint venture arrangement or using a foreign marketing agent because it gives the company the tight control over marketing that might be required to coordinate a globally dispersed value chain. In addition, tight control over a local operation enables the company to use the profits generated in one market to improve its competitive position in another market. Hence companies pursuing global or transnational strategies prefer to establish wholly owned subsidiaries.

Global Strategic Alliances

Global strategic alliances are cooperative agreements between companies from different countries that are actual or potential competitors. Strategic alliances run the range from formal joint ventures, in which two or more companies have an equity stake, to short-term contractual agreements, in which two companies may agree to cooperate on a particular problem (such as developing a new product).

■ Advantages of Strategic Alliances

Companies enter into strategic alliances with competitors to achieve a number of strategic objectives.[35] First, strategic alliances may be a way of *facilitating entry into a foreign market*. For example, Motorola initially found it very difficult to gain access to the Japanese cellular telephone market. In the mid 1980s, it complained loudly about formal and informal Japanese trade barriers. The turning point for Motorola came in 1987, when it formed its alliance with Toshiba to build microprocessors. As part of the deal, Toshiba provided Motorola with marketing help, including some of its best managers. This aided Motorola in the political game of winning government approval to enter the Japanese market and obtaining allocations of radio frequencies for its mobile communications systems. Since then, Motorola has played down the importance of Japan's informal trade barriers. Although privately the company still admits they exist, with Toshiba's help Motorola has become skilled at getting around them.[36]

Second, many companies enter into strategic alliances to share the *fixed costs and associated risks* that arise from the development of new products or processes. Motorola's alliance with Toshiba was partly motivated by a desire to share the high fixed costs associated with setting up an operation to manufacture microprocessors. The microprocessor business is so capital intensive (it cost Motorola and Toshiba close to $1 billion to set up their facility) that few companies can afford the costs and risks of going it alone. Similarly, an alliance between Boeing and a number of Japanese companies to build Boeing's latest commercial jetliner, the 787, was motivated by Boeing's desire to share the estimated $8 billion investment required to develop the aircraft.

Third, many alliances can be seen as a way of bringing together *complementary skills and assets* that neither company could easily develop on its own. In 2003, for example, Microsoft and Toshiba established an alliance aimed at developing embedded microprocessors (essentially tiny computers) that can perform a variety of entertainment functions in an automobile (such as run a back-seat DVD player or a wireless Internet connection). The processors will run a version of Microsoft's Windows CE operating system. Microsoft brings its software engineering skills to the alliance and Toshiba its skills in developing microprocessors.[37]

Finally, it may make sense to enter into an alliance if it helps the company *set technological standards for its industry* and if those standards benefit the company. For example, in 1999 Palm Computer, the leading maker of personal digital assistants (PDAs), entered into an alliance with Sony under which Sony agreed to license and use Palm's operating system in Sony PDAs. The motivation for the alliance was in part to help establish Palm's operating system as the industry standard for PDAs, as opposed to a rival Windows-based operating system from Microsoft.[38]

■ Disadvantages of Strategic Alliances

The various advantages can be very significant. Nevertheless, some commentators have criticized strategic alliances on the grounds that they give competitors a low-cost route to gain new technology and market access.[39] For example, a few years ago some commentators argued that many strategic alliances between U.S. and Japanese firms were part of an implicit Japanese strategy to keep higher-paying, higher-value-added jobs in Japan while gaining the project engineering and production process skills that underlie the competitive success of many U.S. companies.[40] They argued that Japanese success in the machine tool and semiconductor industries was built on U.S. technology acquired through strategic alliances. And they argued that U.S. managers were aiding the Japanese in achieving their goals by entering alliances that channel new inventions to Japan and provide a U.S. sales and distribution network for the resulting products. Although such deals may generate short-term profits, so the argument goes, in the long run the result is to "hollow out" U.S. firms, leaving them with no competitive advantage in the global marketplace.

These critics have a point: alliances do have risks. Unless it is careful, a company can give away more than it gets in return. Nevertheless, there are so many examples of apparently successful alliances between companies, including alliances between U.S. and Japanese companies, that this criticism seems extreme. It is difficult to see how the Motorola-Toshiba alliance or the long-standing alliance between Fuji Film and Xerox to manufacture photocopiers (Fuji-Xerox) fits their thesis. In all of these cases, both partners seemed to have gained from the alliance. Thus, we might ask: *Why do some alliances benefit the company, whereas in others, it can end up giving away technology and market access and get very little in return?* The next section provides an answer to this question.

Making Strategic Alliances Work

The failure rate for international strategic alliances is quite high. For example, one study of forty-nine international strategic alliances found that two-thirds run into serious managerial and financial troubles within two years of their formation, and that although many of these problems are ultimately solved, 33 percent are ultimately rated as failures by the parties involved.[41] The success of an alliance seems to be a function of three main factors: partner selection, alliance structure, and the manner in which the alliance is managed.

■ Partner Selection

One of the keys to making a strategic alliance work is to select the right kind of partner. A good partner has three principal characteristics. First, a good partner helps the company achieve strategic goals such as achieving market access, sharing the costs and risks of new-product development, or gaining access to critical core competencies. In other words, the partner must have capabilities that the company lacks and that it values. Second, a good partner shares the firm's vision for the purpose of the alliance. If two companies approach an alliance with radically different agendas, the chances are great that the relationship will not be harmonious and will end in divorce.

Third, a good partner is unlikely to try to exploit the alliance opportunistically for its own ends—that is, to expropriate the company's technological know-how while giving away little in return. In this respect, firms with reputations for fair play probably make the best partners. For example, IBM is involved in so many strategic alliances that it would not pay the company to trample over individual alliance partners (in early 2003 IBM reportedly had more than 150 major strategic alliances).[42] This would tarnish IBM's reputation of being a good ally and would make it more difficult for IBM to attract alliance partners. Because IBM attaches great importance to its alliances, it is unlikely to engage in the kind of opportunistic behavior that critics highlight. Similarly, their reputations make it less likely (but by no means impossible) that such Japanese firms as Sony, Toshiba, and Fuji, which have histories of alliances with non-Japanese firms, would opportunistically exploit an alliance partner.

To select a partner with these three characteristics, a company needs to conduct some comprehensive research on potential alliance candidates. To increase the probability of selecting a good partner, the company should collect as much pertinent publicly available information about potential allies as possible; collect data from informed third parties, including companies that have had alliances with the potential partners, investment bankers who have had dealings with them, and some of their former employees; and get to know potential partners as well as possible before committing to an alliance. This last step should include face-to-face meetings between senior managers (and perhaps middle-level managers) to ensure that the chemistry is right.

■ **Alliance Structure**

Having selected a partner, the alliance should be structured so that the company's risk of giving too much away to the partner is reduced to an acceptable level. Figure 8.5 depicts the four safeguards against opportunism by alliance partners that we discuss here. (**Opportunism** includes the "expropriation" of technology or markets.) First, alliances can be designed to make it difficult (if not impossible) to transfer technology not meant to be transferred. Specifically, the design, development, manufacture, and service of a product manufactured by an alliance can be structured so as to "wall off" sensitive technologies to prevent their leakage to the other participant. In the alliance between General Electric and Snecma to build commercial aircraft engines, for example, GE reduced the risk of "excess transfer" by walling off certain sections of the production process. The modularization effectively cut off the transfer of what GE regarded as key competitive technology while permitting Snecma access to final assembly. Similarly, in the alliance between Boeing and the Japanese to build the 767, Boeing walled off research, design, and marketing functions considered central to its competitive position, while allowing the Japanese to share in production technology. Boeing also walled off new technologies not required for 767 production.[43]

Second, contractual safeguards can be written into an alliance agreement to guard against the risk of opportunism by a partner. For example, TRW has three strategic alliances with large Japanese auto component suppliers to produce seat belts, engine valves, and steering gears for sale to Japanese-owned auto assembly plants in the

FIGURE 8.5

Structuring Alliances to Reduce Opportunism

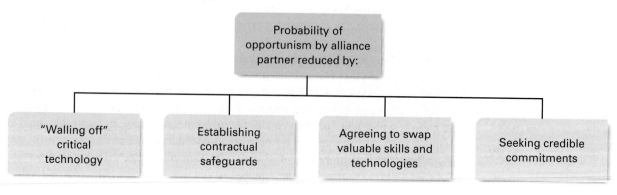

United States. TRW has clauses in each of its alliance contracts that bar the Japanese firms from competing with TRW to supply U.S.-owned auto companies with component parts. By doing this, TRW protects itself against the possibility that the Japanese companies are entering into the alliances merely as a means of gaining access to the North American market to compete with TRW in its home market.

Third, both parties to an alliance can agree in advance to swap skills and technologies, thereby ensuring a chance for equitable gain. Cross-licensing agreements are one way to achieve this goal. For example, in the alliance between Motorola and Toshiba, Motorola has licensed some of its microprocessor technology to Toshiba, and in return Toshiba has licensed some of its memory chip technology to Motorola.

Fourth, the risk of opportunism by an alliance partner can be reduced if the firm extracts a significant credible commitment from its partner in advance. The long-term alliance between Xerox and Fuji to build photocopiers for the Asian market perhaps best illustrates this. Rather than enter into an informal agreement or some kind of licensing arrangement (which Fuji Photo initially wanted), Xerox insisted that Fuji invest in a 50/50 joint venture to serve Japan and East Asia. This venture constituted such a significant investment in people, equipment, and facilities that Fuji Photo was committed from the outset to making the alliance work in order to earn a return on its investment. By agreeing to the joint venture, Fuji essentially made a credible commitment to the alliance. Given this commitment, Xerox felt secure in transferring its photocopier technology to Fuji.[44]

Managing the Alliance

Once a partner has been selected and an appropriate alliance structure agreed on, the task facing the company is to maximize the benefits from the alliance. One important ingredient of success appears to be sensitivity to cultural differences. Many differences in management style are attributable to cultural differences, and managers need to make allowances for these in dealing with their partner. Beyond this, maximizing the benefits from an alliance seems to involve building trust between partners and learning from partners.[45]

Managing an alliance successfully requires building interpersonal relationships between the firms' managers, or what is sometimes referred to as *relational capital*.[46] This is one lesson that can be drawn from a successful strategic alliance between Ford and Mazda. Ford and Mazda set up a framework of meetings within which their managers not only discuss matters pertaining to the alliance but also have time to get to know each other better. The belief is that the resulting friendships help build trust and facilitate harmonious relations between the two firms. Personal relationships also foster an informal management network between the firms. This network can then be used to help solve problems arising in more formal contexts (such as in joint committee meetings between personnel from the two firms).

A major factor determining how much a company gains from an alliance is its ability to learn from alliance partners. Gary Hamel, Yves Doz, and C. K. Prahalad reached this conclusion after a five-year study of fifteen strategic alliances between major multinationals. They focused on a number of alliances between Japanese companies and Western (European or American) partners. In every case in which a Japanese company emerged from an alliance stronger than its Western partner, the Japanese company had made a greater effort to learn. Indeed, few Western companies seemed to want to learn from their Japanese partners. They tended to regard the alliance purely as a cost-sharing or risk-sharing device rather than as an opportunity to learn how a potential competitor does business.[47]

For an example of an alliance in which there was a clear learning asymmetry, consider the agreement between General Motors and Toyota Motor Corp. to build the Chevrolet Nova. This alliance was structured as a formal joint venture, New United Motor Manufacturing, in which both parties had a 50 percent equity stake. The venture owned an auto plant in Fremont, California. According to one of the Japanese managers, Toyota achieved most of its objectives from the alliance: "We learned about U.S. supply and transportation. And we got the confidence to manage U.S. workers." All that knowledge was then quickly transferred to Georgetown, Kentucky, where Toyota opened a plant of its own in 1988. By contrast, although General Motors got a new product, the Chevrolet Nova, some GM managers complained that their new knowledge was never put to good use inside GM. They say that they should have been kept together as a team to educate GM's engineers and workers about the Japanese system. Instead, they were dispersed to different GM subsidiaries.[48]

When entering an alliance, a company must take some measures to ensure that it learns from its alliance partner and then puts that knowledge to good use within its own organization. One suggested approach is to educate all operating employees about the partner's strengths and weaknesses and make clear to them how acquiring particular skills will bolster their company's competitive position. For such learning to be of value, the knowledge acquired from an alliance has to be diffused throughout the organization—as did not happen at GM. To spread this knowledge, the managers involved in an alliance should be used as a resource in familiarizing others within the company about the skills of an alliance partner.

Summary of Chapter

1. For some companies, international expansion represents a way of earning greater returns by transferring the skills and product offerings derived from their distinctive competencies to markets where indigenous competitors lack those skills. As barriers to international trade have fallen, industries have expanded beyond national boundaries and industry competition and opportunities have increased.

2. Because of national differences, it pays a company to base each value creation activity it performs at the location where factor conditions are most conducive to the performance of that activity. This strategy is known as focusing on the attainment of location economies.

3. By building sales volume more rapidly, international expansion can help a company gain a cost advantage through the realization of scale economies and learning effects.

4. The best strategy for a company to pursue may depend on the kind of pressures it must cope with: pressures for cost reductions or for local responsiveness. Pressures for cost reductions are greatest in industries producing commodity-type products, where price is the main competitive weapon. Pressures for local responsiveness arise from differences in consumer tastes and preferences, as well as from national infrastructure and traditional practices, distribution channels, and host government demands.

5. Companies pursuing an international strategy transfer the skills and products derived from distinctive competencies to foreign markets, while undertaking some limited local customization.

6. Companies pursuing a localization strategy customize their product offering, marketing strategy, and business strategy to national conditions.

7. Companies pursuing a global standardization strategy focus on reaping the cost reductions that come from scale economies and location economies.

8. Many industries are now so competitive that companies must adopt a transnational strategy. This involves a simultaneous focus on reducing costs, transferring skills and products, and being locally responsive. Implementing such a strategy may not be easy.

9. The most attractive foreign markets tend to be found in politically stable developed and developing nations that have free market systems.

10. Several advantages are associated with entering a national market early, before other international businesses have established themselves. These advantages

must be balanced against the pioneering costs that early entrants often have to bear, including the greater risk of business failure.

11. Large-scale entry into a national market constitutes a major strategic commitment that is likely to change the nature of competition in that market and limit the entrant's future strategic flexibility. The firm needs to think through the implications of such commitments before embarking on a large-scale entry. Although making major strategic commitments can yield many benefits, there are also risks associated with such a strategy.

12. There are five different ways of entering a foreign market: exporting, licensing, franchising, entering into a joint venture, and setting up a wholly owned subsidiary. The optimal choice among entry modes depends on the company's strategy.

13. Strategic alliances are cooperative agreements between actual or potential competitors. The advantages of alliances are that they facilitate entry into foreign markets, enable partners to share the fixed costs and risks associated with new products and processes, facilitate the transfer of complementary skills between companies, and help companies establish technical standards.

14. The drawbacks of a strategic alliance are that the company risks giving away technological know-how and market access to its alliance partner while getting very little in return.

15. The disadvantages associated with alliances can be reduced if the company selects partners carefully, paying close attention to reputation, and structures the alliance so as to avoid unintended transfers of know-how.

Discussion Questions

1. Plot the position of the following companies on Figure 8.3: Procter & Gamble, IBM, Coca-Cola, Dow Chemicals, Pfizer, and McDonald's. In each case, justify your answer.

2. Are the following global standardization industries or industries where localization is more important: bulk chemicals, pharmaceuticals, branded food products, moviemaking, television manufacture, personal computers, airline travel, and Internet online services such as AOL and MSN?

3. Discuss how the need for control over foreign operations varies with the strategy and distinctive competencies of a company. What are the implications of this relationship for the choice of entry mode?

4. Licensing proprietary technology to foreign competitors is the best way to give up a company's competitive advantage. Discuss.

5. What kind of companies stand to gain the most from entering into strategic alliances with potential competitors? Why?

Practicing Strategic Management

■ SMALL-GROUP EXERCISE
Developing a Global Strategy

Break into groups of three to five people, and discuss the following scenario. Appoint one group member as a spokesperson who will communicate your findings to the class. You work for a company in the soft drink industry that has developed a line of carbonated fruit-based drinks. You have already established a significant presence in your home market, and now you are planning the global strategy development of the company in the soft drink industry. You need to decide the following:

1. What overall strategy to pursue: a global standardization strategy, a localization strategy, an international strategy, or a transnational strategy

2. Which markets to enter first

3. What entry strategy to pursue (e.g., franchising, joint venture, wholly owned subsidiary)

4. What information do you need to make this kind of decision? On the basis of what you do know, what strategy would you recommend?

■ ARTICLE FILE 8

Find an example of a multinational company that in recent years has switched its strategy from a localization, international, or global standardization strategy to a transnational strategy. Identify why the company made the switch and any problems that the company may be encountering while it tries to change its strategic orientation.

STRATEGIC MANAGEMENT PROJECT
Module 8

This module requires you to identify how your company might profit from global expansion, the strategy that your company should pursue globally, and the entry mode that it might favor. With the information you have at your disposal, answer the questions regarding the following two situations:

Your company is already doing business in other countries.

1. Is your company creating value or lowering the costs of value creation by realizing location economies, transferring distinctive competencies abroad, or realizing cost economies from the economies of scale? If not, does it have the potential to?

2. How responsive is your company to differences among nations? Does it vary its product and marketing message from country to country? Should it?

3. What are the cost pressures and pressures for local responsiveness in the industry in which your company is based?

4. What strategy is your company pursuing to compete globally? In your opinion, is this the correct strategy, given cost pressures and pressures for local responsiveness?

5. What major foreign market does your company serve, and what mode has it used to enter this market? Why is your company active in these markets and not others? What are the advantages and disadvantages of using this mode? Might another mode be preferable?

Your company is not yet doing business in other countries.

1. What potential does your company have to add value to its products or lower the costs of value creation by expanding internationally?

2. On the international level, what are the cost pressures and pressures for local responsiveness in the industry in which your company is based? What implications do these pressures have for the strategy that your company might pursue if it chose to expand globally?

3. What foreign market might your company enter, and what entry mode should it use to enter this market? Justify your answer.

EXPLORING THE WEB
Visiting IBM

IBM stands for International Business Machines. Using the significant resources located at IBM's corporate website (**www.ibm.com**), including annual reports and company history, explain what the "International" means in IBM. Specifically, how many countries is IBM active in? How does IBM create value by expanding into foreign markets? What entry mode does IBM adopt in most markets? Can you find any exceptions to this? How would you characterize IBM's strategy for competing in the global marketplace? Is IBM pursuing a transnational, global standardization, international, or localization strategy?

General Task Search the Web for a company site where there is a good description of that company's international operations. On the basis of this information, try to establish how the company enters foreign markets and what overall strategy it is pursuing (global standardization, international, localization, transnational).

Closing Case

Planet Starbucks

Thirty years ago Starbucks was a single store in Seattle's Pike Place Market selling premium roasted coffee. Today it is a global roaster and retailer of coffee with more than 7,600 retail stores, some 2,000 of which are to be found in thirty-four countries outside the United States. Starbucks set out on its current course in the 1980s when the company's director of marketing, Howard Schultz, came back from a trip to Italy enchanted with the Italian coffeehouse experience. Schultz, who later became CEO, persuaded the company's owners to experiment with the coffeehouse format—and the Starbucks experience was born. The basic business model was to sell the company's own premium roasted coffee, along with freshly brewed espresso-style coffee beverages, a variety of pastries, coffee accessories, teas, and other products, in a tastefully designed coffeehouse setting. The company also stressed providing superior customer service. Reasoning that motivated employees provide the best customer service, Starbucks executives devoted much attention to employee hiring and training programs and progressive compensation policies that gave even part-time employees stock option grants and medical benefits. The formula met with spectacular success in the United States, where Starbucks went from obscurity to one of the best-known brands in the country in a decade.

In 1995, with almost 700 stores across the United States, Starbucks began exploring foreign opportunities. The company established a joint venture with a local retailer, Sazaby Inc. Each company held a 50 percent stake in the venture, Starbucks Coffee of Japan. Starbucks initially invested $10 million in this venture, its first foreign direct investment. The Starbucks format was then licensed to the venture, which was charged with taking over responsibility for growing Starbucks' presence in Japan.

To make sure the Japanese operations replicated the North American "Starbucks experience," Starbucks transferred some employees to the Japanese operation. All Japanese store managers and employees were required to attend training classes similar to those given to U.S. employees. Stores also had to adhere to some basic design parameters established in the United States. In 2001, the company introduced a stock option plan for all Japanese employees, making it the first company in Japan to do so. Skeptics doubted that Starbucks would be able to replicate its North American success overseas, but by early 2004 Starbucks had more than 500 stores in Japan and the Japanese unit was predicted to make a healthy profit for the year.

After getting its feet wet in Japan, the company embarked on an aggressive foreign investment program. In 1998, it purchased Seattle Coffee, a British coffee chain with 60 retail stores, for $84 million. An American couple, originally from Seattle, had started Seattle Coffee with the intention of establishing a Starbucks-like chain in Britain. Also in the late 1990s, Starbucks opened stores throughout Asia, including Taiwan, China, Singapore, Thailand, South Korea, and Malaysia. By the end of 2002, with more than 1,200 stores in twenty-seven countries outside of North America, Starbucks was initiating aggressive expansion plans in continental Europe. The company's target was to open some 650 stores in six European countries, including the coffee cultures of France and Italy, by 2005.

As in Japan, much of Starbucks' international expansion has been undertaken with local joint venture partners, to whom the company licenses the Starbucks' format (the U.K. is an exception to this). In general, Starbucks only transfers small numbers of Americans to international markets, preferring foreign operations to be run by local managers who understand the market better. To cater to local tastes, Starbucks has introduced some novel products:

a green tea Frappuccino in Taiwan and Japan, for example, where it has rapidly become the largest-selling Frappuccino. Sometimes these local products have made it back into the United States: a strawberries and cream Frappuccino first sold in the United Kingdom was introduced into the United States in 2004. In some locations outside of the United States, such as China, Japan, and the United Kingdom, food is much more important in the product mix. Internationally, far more of what is ordered is consumed on the premises—about 85 percent—which requires more instore seating and porcelain cups for those inclined to linger. In North America the pattern is exactly the opposite, with some 86 percent of items ordered to go, usually in paper cups. Real estate strategy has also been adjusted to cater to local conditions. In the United States, the strategy has been to find the best street corner locations in the best markets. This strategy did not work in the United Kingdom, where the best corners are on busy shopping streets where the rents are too high for even high-volume Starbucks stores.

Despite such local differences, however, the biggest surprise to Starbucks' management has been how well the basic Starbucks formula has succeeded in international markets. Lattes are becoming standard fare the world over, from noncoffee cultures such as China and tea cultures such as Japan, to the long established coffee cultures of western Europe. Starbucks is fast becoming one of the best-known global brands. In 2004, the magazine *Brandchannel* named Starbucks as one of the ten most impactful global brands for the third year in a row. Building on its international success, in April 2004 the company stated that it ultimately planned to have 10,000 stores in North America and some 15,000 in other counties, which would make Starbucks almost as globally ubiquitous as that other American restaurant icon, McDonald's.[49]

Case Discussion Questions

1. How has Starbucks' strategy of expanding overseas created value for the company's shareholders?

2. Using the global strategy framework outlined in this chapter, would you classify Starbucks as a localization, international, global standardization, or transnational enterprise? Do you think it has the right strategic posture?

3. Why do you think Starbucks has used joint ventures with local companies to enter many foreign markets?

4. Why do you think that Starbucks chose Japan as its first foreign market? Why did it pick Britain as its second? Why did the company wait until 2002 to open its first stores on the European mainland?

Chapter 9

Corporate-Level Strategy: Horizontal Integration, Vertical Integration, and Strategic Outsourcing

Opening Case

Read All About News Corp

Before television and the Internet, "Read all about it" was the cry of street vendors eager to persuade news-hungry customers to buy the most recent version of their newspaper. Now, TV channels like CNN and Web portals like Yahoo! and Google provide almost instantaneous news from around the world. "Read the latest" might also describe the growth of News Corporation Limited, or News Corp, the company headed by controversial CEO Rupert Murdoch, who every year for the last several decades has engineered some kind of acquisition or divestiture that has created one of the four largest and most powerful entertainment media companies in the world. What is the news about News Corp? What kinds of strategies did Murdoch use to create his media empire?

Rupert Murdoch was born into a newspaper family; his father owned and ran the *Adelaide News,* an Australian regional newspaper, and when his father died in 1952 Murdoch gained control of the paper. He quickly enlarged his customer base by acquiring more Australian newspapers. One of these had connections to a major British "pulp" newspaper, the *Mirror,* a paper similar to the *National Enquirer,* and Murdoch recognized he had an opportunity to copy the *Mirror's* business model but make his paper even more sensational. His business model worked, and Murdoch established the *Sun* as a leading British tabloid.

Murdoch's growing reputation as an entrepreneur showed that he could create a much higher return from the assets he controlled (ROIC) than his competitors and enabled him to borrow increasing amounts of money from investors. With this money he bought well-known newspapers such as the *British Sunday Telegraph* and then his first U.S. newspaper, the *San Antonio Express.* Pursuing his sensational business model further, he launched the *National Star.* His growing profits and reputation allowed him to continue to borrow money, and in 1977 he bought the *New York Post.* Four years later, in 1981, he engineered a new coup when he bought the *Times* and *Sunday Times,* Britain's leading conservative publications—a far cry from the *Sun* tabloid.

Murdoch's strategy of horizontal integration through merger allowed him to create one of the world's biggest newspaper empires. However, he also realized that industries in the entertainment and media sector can be divided into those that provide media content or "software" (books, movies, and television programs) and those that provide the media channels or "hardware" necessary to bring software to customers (movie theaters, TV channels, TV cable, and satellite broadcasting). Murdoch decided that he could create the most profit by becoming involved in both the media software *and* hardware industries—that is, the entire value chain of the entertainment and media sector. This strategy of vertical integration gave him control over all the different industries, joined together like links in a chain that converted inputs such as stories into finished products like newspapers or books.

In the 1980s, Murdoch began purchasing global media companies in both the software and hardware stages of the entertainment sector. He also launched new ventures of his own. For example, sensing the potential of satellite broadcasting, in 1983 he launched Sky, the first satellite TV channel, in the United Kingdom. He also began a new strategy of horizontal integration by purchasing companies that owned television stations; for Metromedia, which owned seven stations that reached over 20 percent of U.S. households, he paid $1.5 billion. He scored another major coup in 1985 when he bought Twentieth Century Fox Movie Studios, a premium content provider. Now he had Fox's huge film library and its creative talents to make new films and TV programming.

In 1986, Murdoch decided to create the FOX Broadcasting Company and buy or create his own U.S. network of FOX affiliates that would show programming developed by his own FOX movie studios. After a slow start, the FOX network gained popularity with sensational shows like *The Simpsons*, which became FOX's first blockbuster program. Then in 1994 FOX purchased the sole rights to broadcast all NFL games for over $1 billion,

thereby shutting out NBC and becoming the "fourth network." The FOX network has never looked back and, with Murdoch's sensational business model, was one of the first to create the "reality" programming that has proved so popular in the 2000s.

Realizing that he could create even more value by transmitting his growing media content over new channels, Murdoch also began to increase his company's presence in satellite broadcasting. In 1990, Murdoch merged his Sky satellite channel with British Satellite Broadcasting to form BSkyB, which has since become the leading satellite provider in the United Kingdom. Then, in 2003, News Corp announced it would buy DIRECTV, one of the two largest satellite TV providers, for $6.6 billion. At the same time, News Corp was also acquiring many other companies in both stages of the entertainment value chain to strengthen its competitive position in those industries.

By 2004, Murdoch's business model, based on strategies of horizontal and vertical integration, had created a global media empire. The company's profitability has ebbed and flowed because of the massive debt needed to fund Murdoch's acquisitions, debt that has frequently brought his company near to financial ruin. However, banks that understand the value of his assets, such as Citibank, have provided the money needed to service those debts. Meanwhile, New Corps's ROIC has been increasing. Indeed, in November 2004, it appeared that one of its largest investors, Liberty Media, sensing that News Corp's assets might be worth much more if they were combined with its own media assets or sold off to other companies, seemed ready to start a hostile takeover bid to gain control of News Corp's media empire.

Overview   Over the last decades Rupert Murdoch has acquired or started scores of companies in order to create a media empire, that is, a collection of businesses in different industries in the media sector. The overriding goal of managers is to maximize the value of a company for its shareholders, and theoretically Murdoch embarked on his quest because he believes that, by combining all these different businesses into one entity, he could increase their profitability. In other words, he believed that the value of the empire as a whole would be greater than the value of each part separately. Clearly, the scale of Murdoch's mission and vision for News Corp takes the issue of strategy formulation to a new level of complexity.

The News Corp story illustrates the use of corporate-level strategy to identify (1) which businesses and industries a company should compete in, (2) which value creation activities it should perform in those businesses, and (3) how it should enter or leave businesses or industries to maximize its long-run profitability. In formulating corporate-level strategy, managers must adopt a long-term perspective and consider how changes taking place in an industry and in its products, technology, customers, and competitors will affect their company's current business model and its future strategies. They then decide how to implement specific corporate-level strategies to redefine their company's business model so that it can achieve a competitive position in the changing industry environment by taking advantage of the opportunities and countering the threats. Thus the principal goal of corporate-level strategy is to enable a company to sustain or promote its competitive advantage and profitability in its present business and in any new businesses or industries that it enters.

This chapter is the first of two that deals with the role of corporate-level strategy in repositioning and redefining a company's business model. We discuss three corporate-level strategies—horizontal integration, vertical integration, and strategic outsourcing—that are primarily directed toward improving a company's competitive advantage and profitability in its present business or product market. Diversification, which entails entry into new kinds of markets or industries, is examined in the next chapter, along with guidelines for choosing the most profitable way to enter new markets or industries or to exit others. By the end of this and the next chapter, you will understand how the different levels of strategy contribute to the creation of a successful and profitable business or multibusiness model. You will also be able to differentiate between the types of corporate strategies managers use to maximize long-term company profitability.

Corporate-Level Strategy and the Multibusiness Model

The formulation of corporate-level strategies is the final part of the strategy formulation process. These strategies drive a company's business model over time and determine the kinds of business- and functional-level strategies that will maximize long-run profitability. The relationship between business-level strategy and functional-level strategy was discussed in Chapter 5. Strategic managers develop a business model and strategies that use their company's distinctive competencies to strive for a cost-leadership position and/or to differentiate its products. Chapter 8 described how global strategy is also an extension of these basic principles. Throughout this chapter and the next, we repeatedly stress that, to succeed, corporate-level strategies are also based on the choice of business-level strategies that increase profitability. To understand what this means, we must return to the concepts of profitability and the value chain introduced in Chapter 3.

To increase profitability, a corporate strategy should enable a company, or one or more of its business divisions or units, to perform one or more value-chain activities or functions (1) at a lower cost, and/or (2) in a way that allows for differentiation. A company can then choose the pricing option (lowest, average, or premium price) that allows it to maximize revenues and profitability. In addition, corporate-level strategy will boost profitability if it helps a company achieve a better competitive position, such as by reducing industry rivalry and lowering the threat of damaging price competition.

Thus, a company's corporate-level strategies should be chosen to promote the success of a company's business model and to allow it to achieve a sustainable competitive advantage at the business level. Competitive advantage leads to higher profitability.

Like News Corp, many companies choose to expand their business activities beyond one market or industry and enter others. When a company decides to expand in this way, it must construct its business model at two levels. First, it must develop a business model and strategies for each business unit or division in every industry in which it competes. Second, it must also develop a higher-level *multibusiness model* that justifies its entry into different businesses and industries. This model should explain how and why the company's current competencies and business strategies would increase its return on investment in the value chain of a new industry. For example, Dell used elements of its PC business model, such as direct selling over the Internet, to guide the business model developed for a new unit in the consumer electronics industry. News Corp used its expertise in sensational marketing that it learned from its involvement in the newspaper business and applied it to its FOX network to create reality TV programs and "racy" sitcoms.

A multibusiness model should also explain any other ways in which a company's involvement in more than one business or industry can increase its profitability. Dell, for example, might argue that its entry into computer consulting and the sale of printers and high-powered servers will enable it to offer its customers a complete line of computer products and services and thus better compete with HP or IBM. News Corp might argue that its entry into the satellite broadcasting industry will give it access to more viewers for its television programming, which will generate important advertising revenues. Much of what follows is a discussion of why some companies are better off staying within one industry while others may profit from entering other industries.

Horizontal Integration: Single-Industry Strategy

Managers use corporate-level strategy to identify which industries their company should compete in to maximize its long-run profitability. For many companies, profitable growth and expansion often entail competing successfully within a single market or industry. Examples of such companies include McDonald's, with its focus on the global fast-food restaurant business, and Wal-Mart, with its focus on global discount retailing.

Staying inside an industry allows a company to focus its total managerial, financial, technological, and functional resources and capabilities on competing successfully in one area. This is important in fast-growing and changing industries, where demands on a company's resources and capabilities are likely to be substantial but where the long-term profits from establishing a competitive advantage are also likely to be significant.

A second advantage of staying inside a single industry is that a company "sticks to the knitting," meaning that it stays focused on what it knows and does best. It does not make the mistake of entering new industries where its existing resources and capabilities add little value and/or where a whole new set of competitive industry forces—new competitors, suppliers, and customers—present unanticipated threats. Both Coca-Cola and Sears, like many other companies, have committed this strategic error. Coca-Cola once decided to expand into the movie business and acquired Columbia Pictures, and it also acquired a large wine-producing business. Sears, the clothing seller, once decided to become a one-stop shopping place and bought Allstate Insurance, Coldwell Banker (a real estate company), and Dean Witter (a financial services enterprise). Both companies found they not only lacked the competencies to compete successfully in their new industries but also that they had not foreseen the different kinds of competitive forces that existed in these industries. They concluded that entry into these new industries dissipated, rather than created, value and lowered their profitability, and they ultimately sold off their new businesses for a loss.

Even when a company stays inside one industry, sustaining a successful business model and strategies over time can be difficult because of changing conditions in the environment, such as advances in technology that allow new competitors into the market and blur the boundaries between different products or markets. A decade ago, when most telecommunications service companies were competing in the local and/or long-distance phone service market, the strategic issue was how to shape the company's line of phone service products to best meet customer demand and reduce industry rivalry. However, a new kind of product, wireless phone service, was emerging. At first it was so expensive that only business customers who really needed it could afford it. Within five years, however, wireless phone companies had developed a business model to lower the cost and price of wireless phone service, and many customers began to switch to the new product, a trend that has accelerated.

At the same time, the use of the Internet began to grow. At first it was not regarded as a substitute for wire line phone service, but today millions of people are using VOIP technology to make phone calls over the Internet, and companies that want to attract customers must now include services like digital messaging and wireless e-mail in their product line. Many of the leading phone companies did not sense how these changes in technology would affect industry competition and were late in changing their business models to add these new products and services. As a result, many have been swallowed up and acquired by companies like SBC, WorldCom, and Verizon, which did sense the emerging threats.

Thus, even inside one industry, it is all too easy for strategic managers to fail to see the "forest" (changing nature of the industry that results in new product/market opportunities) for the "trees" (focus on positioning current products). A focus on corporate-level strategy can help managers forecast future trends and position their company so it can compete successfully in a changing environment. Strategic managers must avoid becoming so immersed in positioning their company's *existing* product lines that they fail to consider new opportunities and threats. The task for corporate-level managers is to analyze how new emerging technologies might impact their business models, how and why these might change customer needs and customer groups in the future, and what kinds of new distinctive competencies will be needed to respond to these changes.

One corporate-level strategy that has been widely used to help managers better position their companies is horizontal integration. **Horizontal integration** is the process of acquiring or merging with industry competitors in an effort to achieve the competitive advantages that come with large scale and scope. An **acquisition** occurs when one company uses its capital resources, such as stock, debt, or cash, to purchase another company, and a **merger** is an agreement between equals to pool their operations and create a new entity. The *Opening Case* discusses how Rupert Murdoch made scores of acquisitions in the newspaper industry so that all his newspapers could take advantage of the stories written by News Corp journalists anywhere in the world, thus reducing costs.

Mergers and acquisitions have occurred in many industries. In the automobile industry, Chrysler merged with Daimler Benz to create DaimlerChrysler; in the aerospace industry, Boeing merged with McDonald Douglas to create the world's largest aerospace company; in the pharmaceutical industry, Pfizer acquired Warner-Lambert to become the largest pharmaceutical firm; in the financial services industry, Citicorp and Travelers merged to create Citigroup, the world's largest financial services company; and in the computer hardware industry, Compaq acquired Digital Equipment Corporation and then itself was acquired by Hewlett-Packard. The most recent wave of mergers and acquisitions peaked in 2000, when U.S. firms spent some $1.6 trillion on 11,000 mergers and acquisitions, up from $300 billion in 1991. Although not all of these acquisitions and mergers involved horizontal integration (some entailed vertical integration or diversification), the vast majority appear to have been horizontal.[1] Moreover, many of these mergers and acquisitions were cross-border affairs as companies raced to acquire foreign companies in the same industry. In 2000, companies from all nations spent around $1.1 trillion on 7,900 cross-border mergers and acquisitions, over 70 percent of them horizontal mergers and acquisitions.[2] In 2001, the number and value of both domestic and international mergers and acquisitions fell by 20 to 30 percent, although the figure remained high by historic standards.

The net result of this wave of mergers and acquisitions has been to increase the level of concentration in a wide range of industries. Consolidated oligopolies have been replacing more fragmented industry structures. For example, twenty years ago, cable television was dominated by a patchwork of thousands of small, family-owned businesses, but by 2002, three companies controlled nearly two-thirds of the market. In 1990, the three big publishers of college textbooks accounted for 35 percent of the market; by 2004, they accounted for over 65 percent. In the manufacture of basic DRAM semiconductor chips, because of mergers and acquisitions the four largest firms accounted for 83 percent of the global market in early 2002, up from 45 percent in 1995.[3] Why is this happening? An answer can be found by looking at the way horizontal integration can improve the competitive advantage and profitability of companies who choose to stay inside one industry.

■ Benefits of Horizontal Integration

In pursuing horizontal integration, managers have decided to invest their company's capital to purchase the assets of industry competitors as a way to increase the profitability of its business model. Profits and profitability increase when horizontal integration (1) lowers the cost structure, (2) increases product differentiation, (3) replicates the business model, (4) reduces rivalry within the industry, and (5) increases bargaining power over suppliers and buyers.

■ Lower Cost Structure Horizontal integration can lower a company's cost structure because it creates increasing *economies of scale*. Suppose there are five major competitors, each operating a manufacturing plant in some region of the United States, and none of these plants is operating at full capacity. If one competitor buys up another and shuts down that plant, it can operate its own plant at full capacity and so reduce its manufacturing costs. Achieving economies of scale is very important in industries that have a high fixed-cost structure. In such industries, large-scale production allows companies to spread their fixed costs over a large volume and in this way drive down average unit costs. In the telecommunications industry, for example, the fixed costs of building a fiber-optic or wireless network are very high, and to make such an investment pay off, a company needs a large volume of customers. Thus companies like SBC and Verizon acquired other telecommunications companies to get their customers. These new customers increased its utilization rate and thus reduced the costs of serving each customer. Similarly, mergers and acquisitions in the pharmaceutical industry have in part been driven by a desire to realize scale economies in sales and marketing. The fixed costs of building a nationwide pharmaceutical sales force are very high, and pharmaceutical companies need a good portfolio of products to effectively use that sales force. Pfizer acquired Warner-Lambert because its salespeople would then have more products to sell when they visited physicians and their productivity would therefore increase.

A company can also lower its cost structure when horizontal integration allows it to *reduce the duplication of resources* between two companies, such as by eliminating the need for two sets of corporate head offices, two separate sales forces, and so on. Thus, one way HP justified its strategy to acquire rival computer maker Compaq was that the acquisition would save the combined company $2.5 billion in annual expenses by eliminating redundant functions, as discussed in Strategy in Action 9.1.

Strategy in Action

9.1

Beating Dell: Why Hewlett-Packard Wanted to Acquire Compaq

In 2001, Hewlett-Packard (HP) shocked the business world when its CEO, Carly Fiorina, announced that rival computer maker Compaq had agreed to be acquired by HP. The announcement came at the end of a year in which slumping demand and strong competition from Dell had buffeted both companies. The merged company would have annual revenues of about $87.4 billion, putting it in the same league as IBM, and would be able to provide customers with a full range of computer products and services. With the exception of printers, where HP is the market leader, there was significant product overlap between HP and Compaq.

To justify the acquisition, Fiorina claimed that it would yield a number of benefits. First, there would be significant cost savings. Some $2.5 billion a year would be taken out of annual expenses by eliminating redundant administrative functions and cutting 15,000 employees. In addition, combining the PC businesses of HP and Compaq would enable HP to capture significant scale economies and compete more efficiently with Dell. The same would be true in the computer server and storage businesses, areas where Dell was gaining share. Critics, however, were quick to point out that Dell's competitive advantage was based on its cost-leadership business model, which was based on the efficient management of its supply chain— an area where both HP and Compaq lagged behind Dell. Although achieving economies of scale is desirable, would the merger allow the new HP to reduce its cost structure, such as by increasing its supply-chain efficiency? If the new

HP could not change its PC business model to match Dell's low costs, then the merger would not provide any real benefit.

In addition to the cost advantages of the merger, Fiorina argued that the acquisition would give HP a critical mass in the computer service and consultancy business, where it lagged behind leader IBM significantly. By being able to offer customers a total solution to their information technology needs, both hardware *and* services, Fiorina argued that HP could gain new market share among corporate customers, who would now buy its PCs as part of the total "computer package"; moreover, HP would be entering the higher-margin service business. Here too, however, critics were quick to perceive flaws. They argued that HP would still be a minnow in the service and consultancy area, with under 3 percent of market share.

In 2004, HP announced that it had achieved its cost savings target and that it was continuing to find ways to reduce the duplication of resources in the merged company. However, it also announced that Dell's entry into the printer business had hurt its profit margins and that the profit margins on the sales of its PCs were still well below those obtained by Dell. Thus HP has not been able to lower its cost structure to match Dell, while Dell has applied its cost-leadership model to a growing number of computer and electronic products and announced record profits. The result is that Dell's stock price has soared while HP's has sunk; it still has to find ways to realize the gains from its decision to pursue horizontal integration.[a]

Another example of using horizontal integration to reduce operating costs occurred in 2004 when Kmart and Sears announced that they were merging their companies to better position themselves to compete against Wal-Mart. They hope to share common purchasing and distribution facilities and combine their HRM functions to reduce costs. Some Kmart stores might be converted to Sears stores and vice versa, and in some areas the stores may be sold off to realize the value of the real estate. In addition, Kmart stores may carry some of Sears's well-known product lines, such as its appliances and Craftsman tools. This move would also result in differentiation advantages, which we discuss next.

■ **Increased Product Differentiation** Horizontal integration may also increase profitability when it increases product differentiation, for example, by allowing a company to combine the product lines of merged companies so that it can offer customers a wider range of products that can be bundled together. **Product bundling** involves offering customers the opportunity to buy a complete range of products at a single combined price. This increases the value of a company's product line because customers often obtain a price discount from buying a set of products and also become used to dealing with just one company and its representatives. A company may obtain a competitive advantage from increased product differentiation. A famous example of the value of product bundling is Microsoft Office, which is a bundle of different software programs, including a word processor, spreadsheet, and presentation program. In the early 1990s, Microsoft was number 2 or 3 in each of these product categories, behind companies such as WordPerfect (which led in the word processing category), Lotus (which had the best-selling spreadsheet), and Harvard Graphics (which had the best-selling presentation software). By offering all three programs in a single-price package, Microsoft presented consumers with a superior value proposition, and its product bundle quickly gained market share, ultimately accounting for more than 90 percent of all sales of word processors, spreadsheets, and presentation software.

A variation on the bundling theme is providing a "total solution." Becoming a total solution provider is an important rationale for horizontal integration in the computer sector, where companies have tried to increase the value of their offerings by providing all of the hardware and service needs of corporate customers. This was also one of the justifications for the HP-Compaq merger. Providing a total solution saves customers time and money (because they do not have to deal with several suppliers) and ensures that different parts of a customer's information technology system work seamlessly together. By increasing the value of the company's product line, the total solution provider gains market share, and developing this differentiated business model is one of the main reasons for IBM's current success in the computer industry.

Another way to increase product differentiation is through **cross-selling**, which involves a company taking advantage of or "leveraging" its established relationship with customers by acquiring additional product lines or categories that it can sell to them. This is a popular business-level strategy in the financial services industry and has been a major factor driving horizontal integration there. The concept behind cross-selling is that customers prefer to purchase all of their financial service products from a single provider—their checking account, mortgage loans, insurance policies, and investment services—in a sort of *financial services supermarket.* A major rationale for the creation of Citigroup from the merger of Citicorp and Travelers was to create a company that could sell insurance products directly to banking customers and banking services to insurance customers. Once again, product differentiation increases because customers prefer to do business with a single provider of such services and thus place a higher value on purchasing from a company that can provide such services.

■ **Replicating the Business Model** Given the ways in which horizontal integration can lead to both product differentiation and low-cost advantages, there is clearly great strategic value to finding ways to use horizontal integration to replicate a company's successful business model in new market segments within its industry. In the retail industry, for example, Wal-Mart took its low-cost/low-price discount retail business model to enter into the even lower-priced warehouse segment. It has also expanded the range of products it offers customers by entering the supermarket business and establishing a nationwide chain of Wal-Mart superstores that sell groceries and produce. It has replicated this business model globally by acquiring supermarket chains in several countries, such as the United Kingdom, Germany, and, most recently, Japan, where it can use its efficient global materials-management processes to pursue its cost-leadership strategy. In the United States, Wal-Mart launched an unsuccessful bid to acquire the Safeway supermarket chain to expand its presence in the supermarket segment. In the meantime, however, it is experimenting with new small-size supermarkets it calls "neighborhood markets" to expand its presence in the supermarket segment (see the *Running Case*)—perhaps until a new opportunity arises to acquire a national supermarket chain.

Running Case

Wal-Mart's New Chain of "Neighborhood Markets"

Wal-Mart has long recognized that its huge supercenters and discount stores do not serve the needs of customers who want a quick and convenient shopping experience, for example, when they want to pick up food for an evening meal. It has also recognized that places like neighborhood supermarkets, drugstores, and convenience stores are a very lucrative segment of the food retailing market and that customers spend billions of dollars shopping in these locations. So, in the late 1990s, Wal-Mart decided to explore the concept of opening a chain of what it calls "neighborhood markets." Each of these supermarkets is around 40,000 square feet, about a quarter of the size of a superstore, and stocks 20,000 to 30,000 items, as opposed to the over 100,000 items available in Wal-Mart's larger stores. According to the plan, the neighborhood markets would be positioned to compete directly with supermarkets like Kroger and Albertsons and would be open twenty-four hours a day. They would also have a pharmacy and film-processing unit to draw off trade from drugstores, since customers could shop for food while they waited for their prescriptions to be filled or their film to be developed. In addition, the stores would have a large health and beauty products section, which is a high-profit-margin business that encourages impulse buying.

To test whether its cost-leadership model would work at this small scale of operations, Wal-Mart opened stores slowly in good locations. Margins are small in the supermarket business, often between 1 and 2 percent, which is lower than Wal-Mart is accustomed to. To keep costs low, it located its new stores in areas where it has an efficient warehouse food preparation and delivery system. Its plan is to prepare items like bakery goods and meat and deli items in a central location and then ship them to supermarkets in prepackaged containers. Each neighborhood market store is also tied in by satellite to

Wal-Mart's retail link network so that food service managers know what kind of food is selling and what is not. They can then adjust the food each store sells by changing the mix that is trucked fresh each day. In addition, because the stores have no butcher or baker, labor costs are reduced by 10 percent.

As a result of these measures, the sixty-plus U.S. stores that were opened by 2004 have been able to undercut the prices charged by supermarkets such as Publix, Winn-Dixie, Kroger, and Albertsons by 10 percent. A typical neighborhood market generates around $20 million a year in sales, has a staff of ninety, and obtains a 2.3 percent profit margin, which is significantly higher than average in the supermarket industry.

Wal-Mart has been opening stores in widely different locations, such as Manhattan, Dallas, Salt Lake City, Tampa, and Ogden, apparently to see if its business model for the new store will work in different kinds of urban settings. If it does, then it can roll out sixty to one hundred new stores each year and so build the neighborhood market chain in the way it has built its other chains. While Wal-Mart has been reticent to comment on how well its new chain is doing, perhaps for fear of alerting its competitors to the growing threat, there are reports that its new stores are even more profitable per square foot than its supercenters. If this is true, investing its capital to rapidly expand its chain will increase Wal-Mart's ROIC and further contribute to its growth and profitability. At the same time, the weaker of its rivals, such as Winn-Dixie and Albertsons, will find their revenues and profits falling, so a continuing shakeout in the supermarket industry is likely in the years ahead. Indeed, it is possible that growing competition from Wal-Mart may induce these companies to agree to be acquired by Wal-Mart.

■ **Reduced Industry Rivalry** Horizontal integration can help to reduce industry rivalry in two ways. First, acquiring or merging with a competitor helps to *eliminate excess capacity* in an industry, which, as we discuss in Chapter 6, often triggers price wars. By taking excess capacity out of an industry, horizontal integration creates a more benign environment in which prices might stabilize or even increase.

In addition, by reducing the number of players in an industry, horizontal integration often makes it easier to implement *tacit price coordination* between rivals, or coordination reached without communication (explicit communication to fix prices is illegal). In general, the larger the number of players in an industry, the more difficult it is to establish informal pricing agreements, such as price leadership by a dominant firm, that reduce the possibility that a price war will erupt. By increasing industry concentration and an oligopoly, horizontal integration can make it easier to establish tacit coordination among rivals.

Both of these motives also seem to have been behind the acquisition of Compaq by Hewlett-Packard in 2002. The PC industry was suffering from significant excess capacity and a serious price war, triggered by Dell's desire to gain market share. By acquiring Compaq, Hewlett-Packard hoped to be able to remove excess capacity in the industry, and by reducing the number of large players, the company hoped to be able to impose some pricing discipline. In fact, Dell continued to price aggressively throughout 2003, but in 2004 it increased the price of many of its PCs by 10 percent or more, signaling to HP that it should not start a new price war.

■ **Increased Bargaining Power** A final reason that some companies use horizontal integration is that it allows them to obtain bargaining power over suppliers or buyers and so increase their profitability at the expense of suppliers or buyers. By consolidating the industry through horizontal integration, a company becomes a much larger buyer of suppliers' products and uses this as leverage to bargain down the price it pays for its inputs, thereby lowering its cost structure. Similarly, by acquiring its competitors, a company gains control over a greater percentage of an industry's product or output. Other things being equal, it then has more power to raise prices and profits because customers have less choice of supplier and are more dependent on the company for their products.

When a company has greater ability to raise prices to buyers or bargain down the price paid for inputs, it has increased **market power**. For an example of how the process of consolidation through horizontal integration can play out, see Strategy in Action 9.2, which looks at the way in which health care providers in eastern Massachusetts have pursued horizontal integration to gain bargaining power, and hence market power, over insurance providers.

■ **Problems with Horizontal Integration**

Although horizontal integration can clearly strengthen a company's business model in several ways, there are problems and limitations associated with this strategy. One problem concerns the numerous dangers associated with using mergers and acquisitions to pursue horizontal integration. We discuss these dangers in detail in Chapter 10, but for now the important issue is that a wealth of data suggests that the majority of mergers and acquisitions *do not* create value and that many actually *destroy* value.[4] For example, a recent study by KPMG, a large accounting and management consulting company, looked at seven hundred large acquisitions between 1996 and 1998 and found that although some 30 percent of these did increase the profitability of the acquiring company, 31 percent reduced profitability, and the remainder had little impact

Strategy in Action   9.2

Horizontal Integration in Health Care

In the United States, health maintenance organizations (HMOs) have become a powerful force in the health care sector. HMOs are health insurance companies that provide people with health care coverage, and often companies contract with HMOs on behalf of their employees for health insurance coverage. The HMOs then "supply" patients to health care providers. Thus, HMOs can be viewed as the suppliers of the critical input—patients—to health care providers. In turn, the revenues of health care providers are dependent on the number of patients who pass through their system. Clearly, it is in the interests of HMOs to bargain down the price they must pay health care providers for coverage, and to gain bargaining power HMOs have used horizontal integration to merge with each other until, today, they control a large volume of patients. However, to fight back, health care providers have also resorted to horizontal integration, and the battle is raging.

As an example of how this process plays out, consider how the relationship between HMOs and hospitals has evolved in eastern Massachusetts over the past decade. In the early 1990s, three big HMOs controlled 75 percent of the market for health insurance in eastern Massachusetts. In contrast, there were thirty-four separate hospital networks in the region. Thus, the insurance providers were consolidated, while the health care providers were fragmented, giving the insurance providers considerable bargaining power. The HMOs used their bargaining power to demand deep discounts from health care providers. If a hospital wouldn't offer discounts to an HMO, the HMO would threaten to remove it from its list of providers. Because losing all of those potential patients would severely damage the revenues that a hospital could earn, the hospitals had little choice but to comply with the request.

This began to change in 1994 when two of the most prestigious hospitals in the region, Massachusetts General and Brigham & Women's Hospital, merged with each other to form Partners HealthCare System. Since then, Partners has continued to pursue the strategy of acquiring other hospitals in order to gain power over HMOs. By 2002, it had seven hospitals and some 5,000 doctors in its system. Other regional hospitals pursued a similar strategy, and the number of independent hospital networks in the region fell from thirty-four in 1994 to twelve by 2002.

In 2000, Partners started to exercise its strengthened bargaining power by demanding that HMOs accept a fee increase for services offered by Partners hospitals. One of the biggest HMOs, Tufts, refused to accept the increase and informed nearly 200,000 of its 900,000 subscribers that they would no longer be able to use Partners hospitals or physicians affiliated with Partners. There was an enormous uproar from subscribers. So many employers threatened to pull out of the HMO and switch to another if the policy was not changed that Tufts quickly realized it had little choice but to accept the fee increase. Tufts went back to Partners and agreed to a 30 percent fee increase over three years. Thus, bargaining power in the system had shifted away from the HMOs and toward the hospital networks. However, the Massachusetts attorney general received so many complaints from employers about rising health care premiums that an investigation into market power and anticompetitive behavior among health care providers in eastern Massachusetts was started. Clearly, the battle is not over yet.[b]

on it.[5] The implication is that *implementing* a horizontal integration strategy is not an easy task for managers.

As we discuss in Chapter 10, mergers and acquisitions often fail to produce the anticipated gains, for a number of reasons: problems associated with merging very different company cultures, high management turnover in the acquired company when the acquisition was a hostile one, and a tendency of managers to overestimate the benefits to be had from a merger or acquisition and underestimate the problems involved in merging their operation. For example, much of the opposition to the merger between HP and Compaq was based on the belief that Carly Fiorina was glossing over the difficulties and costs associated with merging the operations of these two companies, especially since they had very different cultures.

Another problem with horizontal integration is that, when a company uses it to become a dominant industry competitor, an attempt to keep using the strategy to grow even larger brings a company into conflict with the Federal Trade Commission, the government agency responsible for enforcing antitrust law. Antitrust authorities are concerned about the potential for abuse of market power; they believe that more competition is generally better for consumers than less competition. They worry that large companies that dominate their industry may be in a position to abuse their market power and raise prices to consumers above the level that would exist in more competitive situations. They also believe that dominant companies can use their market power to crush potential competitors by, for example, cutting prices whenever new competitors enter a market and so forcing them out of business, and then raising prices again once the threat has been eliminated. Because of these concerns, any merger or acquisition that is perceived by the antitrust authorities as creating too much consolidation and the *potential* for future abuse of market power may be blocked. This happened when WorldCom tried to acquire Sprint because it realized it needed to have a strong presence in the wireless phone market. The Justice Department was concerned that the proposed acquisition would reduce the number of major long-distance providers in the United States from three to two and gives these companies too much market power. WorldCom was obliged to drop the acquisition bid.

Vertical Integration: Entering New Industries to Strengthen the "Core" Business Model

Many companies that use horizontal integration to strengthen their business model and improve their competitive position also use the corporate-level strategy of vertical integration for the same purpose. In pursuing vertical integration, however, a company is entering new industries to support the business model of its "core" industry, the one that is the primary source of its competitive advantage and profitability. At this point, therefore, a company has to formulate a multibusiness model that explains how entry into a new industry will enhance its long-term profitability. The multibusiness model justifying vertical integration is based on a company entering industries that *add value* to its core products because this increases product differentiation and/or lowers its cost structure.

A company pursuing a strategy of **vertical integration** expands its operations either backward into an industry that produces inputs for the company's products (*backward vertical integration*) or forward into an industry that uses, distributes, or sells the company's products (*forward vertical integration*). To enter an industry, it may establish its own operations and build the value chain needed to compete effectively in that industry, or it may acquire or merge with a company that is already in the industry. A steel company that supplies its iron ore needs from company-owned iron ore mines exemplifies backward integration. A PC maker that sells its PCs through company-owned retail outlets illustrates forward integration. For example, in 2001 Apple Computer entered the retail industry when it decided to set up a chain of Apple Stores to sell its computers and later iPods. IBM is a highly vertically integrated company; for example, it integrated backward into the disk drive industry to produce the disk drives that go into its computers and forward into the computer software and consulting services industries.

Figure 9.1 illustrates four *main* stages in a typical raw-materials-to-customer value-added chain. For a company based in the final assembly stage, backward integration means moving into component parts manufacturing and raw materials

FIGURE 9.1

Stages in the Raw-Materials-to-Customer Value-Added Chain

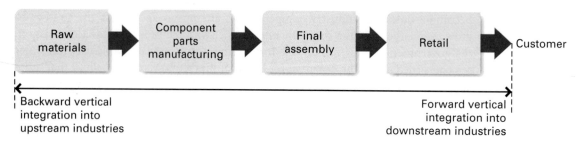

production. Forward integration means moving into distribution and sales (retail). At each stage in the chain, *value is added* to the product, meaning that a company at that stage takes the product produced in the previous stage and transforms it in some way so that it is worth more to a company at the next stage in the chain and, ultimately, to the customer. It is important to note that each stage of the value-added chain is a separate industry or industries in which many different companies may be competing. Moreover, within each industry, every company has a value chain composed of the value creation activities we discussed in Chapter 3: R&D, production, marketing, customer service, and so on. In other words, we can think of a value chain that runs *across* industries, and embedded within that are the value chains of companies *within* each industry.

As an example of the value-added concept, consider how companies in each industry involved in the production of a personal computer contribute to the final product (Figure 9.2). At the first stage in the chain are the raw materials companies that make specialty ceramics, chemicals, and metal, such as Kyocera of Japan, which manufactures the ceramic substrate for semiconductors. These companies sell their products to the makers of PC component products, such as Intel and Micron Technology, which transform the ceramics, chemicals, and metals they purchase into computer components such as microprocessors, disk drives, and memory chips. In the process, they *add value* to the raw materials they purchase. At the third stage, these components are then sold to companies that assemble PCs, such as Gateway, Apple, Dell, and HP, which take these components and transform them into PCs—that is, *add value* to the components they purchase. At stage 4 the finished PCs are then either

FIGURE 9.2

The Raw-Materials-to-Customer Value-Added Chain in the Personal Computer Industry

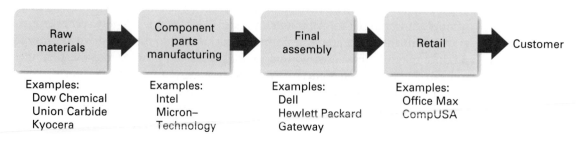

FIGURE 9.3

Full and Taper
Integration

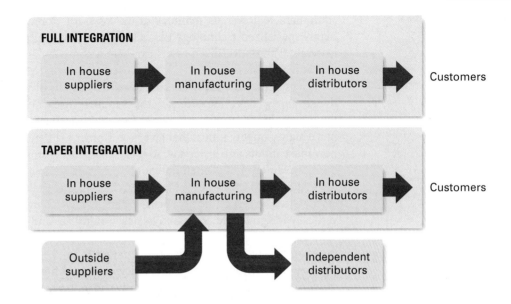

sold directly to the final customer, as Dell and Gateway do, or sold to companies such as OfficeMax and CompUSA that distribute and sell them to the final customer. Companies that distribute and sell PCs also *add value* to the product because they make it accessible to customers and provide customer service and support.

Thus companies in different industries add value at each stage in the raw-materials-to-customer chain. Viewed in this way, vertical integration presents companies with a choice about which industries in the raw-materials-to-customer chain to operate and compete in. This choice is determined by how much establishing operations at a stage in the value chain will increase product differentiation or lower costs, as we discuss below.

Finally, it is also important to distinguish between full integration and taper integration (see Figure 9.3).[6] A company achieves **full integration** when it produces *all* of a particular input needed for its processes or disposes of *all* of its completed products through its own operations. In **taper integration**, company buys from independent suppliers in addition to company-owned suppliers or disposes of its completed products through independent outlets in addition to company-owned outlets. The advantages of taper integration over full integration are discussed later in the chapter.

■ Increasing Profitability Through Vertical Integration

As noted earlier, a company pursues vertical integration to strengthen the business model of its original or core business and to improve its competitive position.[7] Vertical integration increases product differentiation, lowers costs, or reduces industry competition when it (1) facilitates investments in efficiency-enhancing specialized assets, (2) protects product quality, and (3) results in improved scheduling.

■ Facilitating Investments in Specialized Assets
A specialized asset is one that is designed to perform a specific task and whose value is significantly reduced in its next-best use.[8] The asset may be a piece of equipment that has a firm-specific use or the know-how or skills that a company or employees have acquired through training and experience. Companies invest in specialized assets because these assets allow them to lower their cost structure or to better differentiate their products, which facilitates premium pricing. A company might invest in specialized

equipment to lower its manufacturing costs, for example, or it might invest in a highly specialized technology that allows it to develop better-quality products than its rivals. Thus, specialized assets can help a company achieve a competitive advantage at the business level.

Just as a company invests in specialized assets in its own industry to build competitive advantage, it is often necessary that suppliers invest in specialized assets to produce the inputs that a specific company needs. By investing in these assets, a supplier can make higher-quality inputs that give its customer a differentiation advantage, or it can now make inputs at a lower cost so it can charge its customer a lower price to keep its business. However, it is often difficult to persuade companies in adjacent stages of the raw-materials-to-customer value-added chain to undertake investments in specialized assets. Often, to realize the benefits associated with such investments, a company has to vertically integrate and enter into adjacent industries and make the investments itself. Why does this happen?

Imagine that Ford has developed a unique high-performance fuel injection system that will dramatically increase fuel efficiency and differentiate Ford's cars from those of its rivals, giving it a major competitive advantage. Ford has to decide whether to make the system in-house (vertical integration) or contract with an independent supplier to make the system. Manufacturing these new systems requires a substantial investment in specialized equipment that can be used only for this purpose. In other words, because of its unique design, the equipment cannot be used to manufacture any other type of fuel injection system for Ford or any other automaker. Thus this is an investment in specialized assets.

Consider this situation from the perspective of an independent supplier deciding whether or not to make this investment. The supplier might reason that once it has made the investment, it will become dependent on Ford for business because *Ford is the only possible customer for the fuel injection system made by this specialized equipment.* The supplier realizes that this puts Ford in a strong bargaining position and that Ford might use its power to demand lower prices for the fuel injection systems. Given the risks involved, the supplier declines to make the investment in specialized equipment.

Now consider Ford's position. Ford might reason that if it contracts out production of these systems to an independent supplier, it might become too dependent on that supplier for a vital input. Because specialized equipment is required to produce the fuel injection systems, Ford cannot switch its order to other suppliers. Ford realizes that this increases the bargaining power of the independent supplier and that the supplier might use its power to demand higher prices.

The situation of *mutual dependence* that would be created by the investment in specialized assets makes Ford hesitant to allow efficient suppliers to make the product, and makes suppliers hesitant to undertake such a risky investment. The problem is a lack of trust—neither Ford nor the supplier can trust the other to play fair in this situation. The lack of trust arises from the risk of **holdup**; that is, being taken advantage of by a trading partner after the investment in specialized assets has been made.[9] Because of this risk, Ford reasons that the only safe way to get the new fuel injection systems is to manufacture them itself.

To generalize from this example, if achieving a competitive advantage requires one company to make investments in specialized assets so it can trade with another, the risk of holdup may serve as a deterrent and the investment may not take place. Consequently, the potential for higher profitability from specialization will be lost. To prevent such loss, companies vertically integrate into adjacent stages in the value

Strategy in Action 9.3

Specialized Assets and Vertical Integration in the Aluminum Industry

The metal content and chemical composition of bauxite ore, used to produce aluminum, vary from deposit to deposit, so each type of ore requires a specialized refinery—that is, the refinery must be designed for a particular type of ore. Running one type of bauxite through a refinery designed for another type reportedly increases production costs by 20 percent to 100 percent. Thus, the value of an investment in a specialized aluminum refinery and the cost of the output produced by that refinery depend on receiving the right kind of bauxite ore.

Imagine that an aluminum company has to decide whether to invest in an aluminum refinery designed to refine a certain type of ore. Also assume that this ore is extracted by a company that owns a single bauxite mine. Using a different type of ore would raise production costs by 50 percent. Therefore, the value of the aluminum company's investment is dependent on the price it must pay the bauxite company for this bauxite. Recognizing this, once the aluminum company has made the investment in a new refinery, what is to stop the bauxite company from raising bauxite prices? Nothing. Once it has

made the investment, the aluminum company is locked into its relationship with its bauxite supplier. The bauxite supplier can increase prices because it knows that as long as the increase in the total production costs of the aluminum company is less than 50 percent, the aluminum company will continue to buy its ore. Thus, once the aluminum company has made the investment, the bauxite supplier can *hold up* the aluminum company.

How can the aluminum company reduce the risk of holdup? The answer is by purchasing the bauxite supplier. If the aluminum company can purchase the bauxite supplier's mine, it need no longer fear that bauxite prices will be increased after the investment in an aluminum refinery has been made. In other words, vertical integration, by eliminating the risk of holdup, makes the specialized investment worthwhile. In practice, it has been argued that these kinds of considerations have driven aluminum companies to pursue vertical integration to such a degree that, according to one study, 91 percent of the total volume of bauxite is transferred within vertically integrated aluminum companies.[c]

chain. Historically, the problems surrounding specific assets have driven automobile companies to vertically integrate backward into the production of component parts, steel companies to vertically integrate backward into the production of iron, computer companies to vertically integrate backward into chip production, and aluminum companies to vertically integrate backward into bauxite mining. The way specific asset issues have led to vertical integration in the aluminum industry is discussed in Strategy in Action 9.3.

■ **Enhancing Product Quality** By entering industries at other stages of the value-added chain, a company can often enhance the quality of the products in its core business, and so strengthen its differentiation advantage. For example, the ability to control the reliability and performance of components such as fuel injection systems may increase a company's competitive advantage in the luxury sedan market and enable it to charge a premium price. Conditions in the banana industry also illustrate the importance of vertical integration in maintaining product quality. Historically, a problem facing food companies that import bananas has been the variable quality of delivered bananas, which often arrive on the shelves of U.S. supermarkets too ripe or not ripe enough. To correct this problem, major U.S. food companies such as General Foods have integrated backward and now own banana plantations so they have control over the supply of bananas. As a result, they can now distribute and sell bananas of a standard quality at the optimal time to better satisfy customers. Knowing they can rely on the quality of these brands, customers are also willing to pay more for them. Thus, by vertically integrating backward into plantation ownership, banana companies have built customer confidence, which in turn has enabled them to charge a premium price for their product.

The same considerations can promote forward vertical integration. Ownership of retail outlets may be necessary if the required standards of after-sales service for complex products are to be maintained. For example, in the 1920s, Kodak owned retail outlets for distributing photographic equipment. The company felt that few established retail outlets had the skills necessary to sell and service its photographic equipment. By the 1930s, Kodak decided that it no longer needed to own its retail outlets because other retailers had begun to provide satisfactory distribution and service for Kodak products. It then withdrew from retailing.

■ **Improved Scheduling** Sometimes important strategic advantages can be obtained when vertical integration makes it quicker, easier, and more cost effective to plan, coordinate, and schedule the transfer of a product, such as raw materials or component parts, between adjacent stages of the value-added chain.[10] Such advantages can be crucial when a company wants to realize the benefits of just-in-time inventory systems. For example, in the 1920s, Ford profited from the tight coordination and scheduling that are possible with backward vertical integration. Ford integrated backward into steel foundries, iron ore shipping, and iron ore mining. Deliveries at Ford were coordinated to such an extent that iron ore unloaded at Ford's steel foundries on the Great Lakes was turned into engine blocks within twenty-four hours, which helped to lower Ford's cost structure.

Very often, the improved scheduling that vertical integration makes possible also enables a company to respond better to sudden changes in demand. For example, if demand drops, a company can quickly cut production of components, or when demand increases, a company can quickly increase production capacity to get its products into the marketplace faster.[11]

■ **Problems with Vertical Integration** Vertical integration can often be used to strengthen a company's business model and increase profitability. However, the opposite can occur when vertical integration results in (1) an increasing cost structure, (2) disadvantages that arise when technology is changing fast, and (3) disadvantages that arise when demand is unpredictable. Sometimes these disadvantages are so great that vertical integration, rather than increasing profitability, may actually reduce it—in which case companies **vertically disintegrate** and exit industries adjacent in the industry value chain. For example, Ford, which was highly vertically integrated, sold all its companies involved in mining iron ore and making steel when more efficient and specialized steel producers emerged that were able to supply lower-priced steel.

■ **Increasing Cost Structure** Although vertical integration is often undertaken to lower a company's cost structure, it can raise costs if, over time, a company makes mistakes, such as continuing to purchase inputs from company-owned suppliers when low-cost independent suppliers that can supply the same inputs exist. During the early 1990s, for example, General Motors's (GM) company-owned suppliers made 68 percent of the component parts for its vehicles; this figure was higher than for any other major carmaker and made GM the highest-cost global carmaker. In 1992, it was paying $34.60 an hour in United Auto Workers wages and benefits to its employees at company-owned suppliers for work that rivals could get done by independent nonunionized suppliers at half these rates.[12] Thus, vertical integration can be a disadvantage when company-owned suppliers develop a higher cost structure than those of independent suppliers. Why would a company-owned supplier develop such a high cost structure?

One explanation is that company-owned or "in-house" suppliers know that they can always sell their components to the car-making divisions of their company—they have a "captive customer." When company-owned suppliers do not have to compete with independent suppliers for orders, they have much less *incentive* to look for new ways to reduce operating costs or increase quality. Indeed, in-house suppliers may simply pass on any cost increases to the car-making divisions in the form of higher **transfer prices**, the prices one division of a company charges other divisions for its products. Unlike independent suppliers, which constantly have to increase their efficiency to protect their competitive advantage, in-house suppliers face no such competition, and the resulting rising cost structure reduces a company's profitability.

The term *bureaucratic costs* refers to the costs of solving the transaction difficulties that arise from managerial inefficiencies and the need to manage the handoffs or exchanges between business units to promote increased differentiation or to lower a company's cost structure. Bureaucratic costs become a component of a company's cost structure because considerable managerial time and effort must be spent to reduce or eliminate managerial inefficiencies such as those that result when company-owned suppliers lose their incentive to increase efficiency.

This problem can be partially solved when a company pursues taper, rather than full, integration, because now in-house suppliers do have to compete with independent suppliers. In essence, independent suppliers provide a benchmark against which a company can measure the relative efficiency of its in-house suppliers, providing an incentive for company-owned suppliers to find ways to lower their cost structure.

■ **Technological Change** When technology is changing fast, vertical integration may lock a company into an old, inefficient technology and prevent it from changing to a new one that would strengthen its business model.[13] Consider a radio manufacturer that in the 1950s integrated backward and acquired a manufacturer of vacuum tubes to reduce costs. When transistors replaced vacuum tubes as a major component in radios in the 1960s, this company found itself locked into a technologically outdated business. However, if it had switched to transistors, the company would have had to write off its investment in vacuum tubes, and so managers were reluctant to adopt the new technology. Instead, they continued to use vacuum tubes in their radios while competitors that were not in the vacuum tube industry rapidly switched to the new technology. As a result, the company lost its competitive advantage, and its failing business model led to a rapid loss in market share. Thus, vertical integration can pose a serious disadvantage when it prevents a company from adopting new technology or changing its suppliers or distribution systems to match the requirements of changing technology.

■ **Demand Unpredictablility** Suppose the demand for a company's core product, such as cars or washing machines, is predictable and a company knows how many units it needs to make each month or year. Under these conditions vertical integration, by allowing the company to schedule and coordinate the flow of products along the value-added chain, may result in major cost savings. However, suppose the demand for cars or washing machines fluctuates wildly and is unpredictable. Now, if demand for cars suddenly plummets, the carmaker may find itself burdened with ware-houses full of component parts it now no longer needs, and this is a major drain on profitability. Thus, vertical integration can be risky when demand is unpredictable because it is hard to manage the volume or flow of products along the value-added chain.

For example, an auto manufacturer might vertically integrate backward to acquire a supplier of fuel injection systems that can make exactly the number of systems the carmaker needs each month. However, if demand for cars now falls because gas prices soar, the carmaker finds itself locked into a business that is now inefficient because it is not producing at full capacity. Its cost structure then starts to rise. When demand is unpredictable, taper integration might be less risky than full integration because a company can keep its in-house suppliers running at full capacity and increase or reduce its orders from independent suppliers to match changing demand conditions.

The Limits of Vertical Integration

Thus, although there are many ways that vertical integration can strengthen a company's business model, it may weaken it (1) when bureaucratic costs increase because company-owned suppliers lack the incentive to reduce operating costs and (2) when changing technology or uncertain demand reduces a company's ability to change its business model to protect its competitive advantage. It is clear that strategic managers have to carefully assess the advantages and disadvantages of expanding the boundaries of their company by entering adjacent industries, either backward (upstream) or forward (downstream), in the value-added chain. Moreover, while the decision to enter a new industry to make crucial component parts might have been profitable in the past, it might make no economic sense today, when many low-cost global component parts suppliers exist that can compete for a company's business. The risks and returns on investing in vertical integration have to be continually evaluated, and companies should be as willing to vertically disintegrate as vertically integrate to strengthen their core business model. Finally, it is worth noting that taper integration rather than full vertical integration may decrease bureaucratic costs because it creates an incentive for in-house suppliers to reduce operating costs. There are other ways of achieving this, however, as we discuss next.

Alternatives to Vertical Integration: Cooperative Relationships

Is it possible to obtain the differentiation and cost advantages associated with vertical integration without having to bear the problems associated with this strategy? In other words, is there another corporate-level strategy that managers can use to obtain the advantages of vertical integration while allowing other companies to perform upstream and downstream activities? Today, many companies have found that they can realize many of the benefits associated with vertical integration by entering into long-term cooperative relationships with companies in industries along the value-added chain. **Strategic alliances** are long-term agreements between two or more companies to jointly develop new products that benefit all companies concerned; they were discussed in Chapter 8. The advantages of strategic alliances can be clarified by contrasting them with the benefits obtained if a company decides to enter into short-term contracts with other companies.

Short-Term Contracts and Competitive Bidding

Many companies use short-term contracts, which last for a year or less, to establish the price and conditions under which they will purchase raw materials or components from suppliers or sell their final products to distributors. A classic example is the carmaker that uses a *competitive bidding strategy* in which independent component suppliers compete to be the company that will be chosen to supply a particular part, made to agreed-upon specifications, at the lowest price. For example, GM typically solicits bids from global suppliers to produce a particular component and awards a one-year contract to the supplier submitting the lowest bid. At the end of the year, the contract is put out for competitive bid again. There is no guarantee that the company that wins the contract one year will hold on to it the next.

The advantage of this strategy for GM is that it forces suppliers to compete over price, which drives the cost of its inputs down. However, GM has no long-term commitment to individual suppliers, and it drives a hard bargain. For this reason, prospective suppliers will likely be unwilling to make the expensive investment in specialized assets that are needed to produce higher-quality or better-designed component parts. In addition, they will be reluctant to agree on tight scheduling, because that would allow GM to obtain the benefits from a just-in-time inventory system but would increase the suppliers' operating costs and so reduce their profitability. With no guarantee it will retain GM's business, the supplier may refuse to invest in specialized assets, and so to realize differentiation and cost gains GM will have to vertically integrate backward.

In other words, the strategy of short-term contracting and competitive bidding, *because it signals a company's lack of long-term commitment to its suppliers,* will make it difficult or impossible for that company to realize the gains associated with vertical integration. Of course, this is not a problem when there is minimal need for close cooperation and no need to invest in specialized assets to improve scheduling or product quality. In such cases, competitive bidding may be optimal. However, when this need is significant, a competitive bidding strategy can be a serious drawback.

Interestingly enough, in the past GM did place itself at a competitive disadvantage when it used a competitive bidding approach to negotiate with its suppliers. In 1992, the company instructed its parts suppliers to cut their prices by 10 percent, regardless of prior pricing agreements. In effect, GM tore up existing contracts and threatened to stop doing business with suppliers that did not agree to the price reduction. Although its action gave it a short-term benefit from lower costs, in the longer term the loss of trust and the hostility created between the company and its suppliers resulted in problems for GM. According to press reports, several suppliers claimed that they reduced the R&D spending necessary to design GM parts in the future, a form of specialized investment. They also indicated that they would first impart their new design knowledge to Chrysler (now DaimlerChrysler) and Ford, which both focused on forging cooperative long-term relationships with their suppliers.[14]

■ Strategic Alliances and Long-Term Contracting

As opposed to short-term contracts, strategic alliances are long-term cooperative relationships between two or more companies who agree to commit resources to develop new products. Typically, one company agrees to supply the other, and the other company agrees to continue purchasing from that supplier; both make a commitment to jointly seek ways to lower costs or increase input quality. A strategic alliance, by creating a stable long-term relationship, becomes a *substitute* for vertical integration; it allows both companies to share in the same kinds of benefits that result from vertical integration but avoids the problems linked with having to manage a company located in an adjacent industry in the value-added chain, such as lack of incentives or changing technology.

Consider the cooperative relationships, which often go back decades, that many Japanese carmakers have with their components suppliers (the *keiretsu* system), which exemplifies successful long-term contracting. Together, carmakers and suppliers work out ways to increase the value added—for example, by implementing just-in-time inventory systems or cooperating on component-parts designs to improve quality and lower assembly costs. As part of this process, the suppliers make substantial investments in specialized assets to better serve the needs of a particular carmaker. Any cost savings that result are shared by carmakers and suppliers. Thus, Japanese carmakers have been able to capture many of the benefits of vertical integration without having to enter and own companies in new industries. Similarly, the component suppliers also benefit because their business and profitability grow as the companies they supply grow.[15]

In contrast to their Japanese counterparts, U.S. carmakers have historically pursued vertical integration.[16] And, according to several studies, the result is that the ever increasing cost of managing scores or even hundreds of companies in different industries has put GM and Ford at a significant cost disadvantage relative to their Japanese competitors.[17] Moreover, even when U.S. auto companies decided not to integrate vertically, they tended to use their powerful position to pursue an aggressive competitive bidding strategy, playing off component suppliers against each other.[18] This mindset now seems to be changing. For details on how Daimler-Chrysler has attempted to build long-term cooperative relationships with suppliers, see Strategy in Action 9.4.

■ Building Long-Term Cooperative Relationships

The interesting question raised by the preceding section is, how does a company create a stable long-term strategic alliance with another company given the fear of holdup, and the possibility of being cheated, that arise when one company makes an investment in specialized assets to trade with another? How have companies like Toyota managed to develop such enduring relationships with their suppliers?

There are several steps companies can take to ensure the success of a long-term cooperative relationship and to lessen the chance that one company will renege on its agreement and try to cheat the other. One of those steps is for the company that makes the investment in specialized assets to demand a *hostage* from its partner. Another is to establish a *credible commitment* on both sides to build a trusting long-term relationship.[19]

■ Hostage Taking
Hostage taking is essentially a means of guaranteeing that a partner will keep its side of the bargain. The cooperative relationship between Boeing and Northrop illustrates this type of situation. Northrop is a major subcontractor for Boeing's commercial airline division, providing many components for the 747 and 767 aircraft. To serve Boeing's special needs, Northrop has had to make substantial investments in specialized assets. In theory, because of the sunk costs associated with such investments, Northrop is dependent on Boeing, and Boeing is in a position to renege on previous agreements and use the threat to switch orders to other suppliers as a way of driving down prices. In practice, however, Boeing is highly unlikely to do this because it is a major supplier to Northrop's defense division and provides many parts for the Stealth bomber. Boeing also has had to make substantial investments in specialized assets to serve Northrop's needs. Thus, the companies are *mutually dependent*. Boeing is unlikely to renege on any pricing agreements with Northrop because it knows that Northrop could respond in kind. Each company holds a hostage—the specialized investment the other has made—as insurance against any attempt by the other company to renege on its prior pricing agreements.

■ Credible Commitments
A credible commitment is a believable promise or pledge to support the development of a long-term relationship between companies.

Strategy in Action

9.4

DaimlerChrysler's U.S. *Keiretsu*

For most of its history, Chrysler (now DaimlerChrysler) managed suppliers through a competitive bidding process: suppliers were selected on the basis of their ability to supply components at the lowest possible cost to Chrysler. A supplier's track record on performance and quality was relatively unimportant in this process. Contracts were renegotiated every two years, with little or no commitment from Chrysler to continuing to do business with a particular supplier. As a result, the typical relationship between Chrysler and its suppliers was characterized by mutual distrust, suspicion, and a reluctance on the part of suppliers to invest too much in their relationship with Chrysler.

Since the early 1990s, Chrysler has systematically reorganized its dealings with suppliers in an attempt to build stable long-term relationships. The aim of this new approach has been to try to get suppliers to help Chrysler develop new products and improve its production processes. To encourage suppliers to cooperate and make investments specific to Chrysler's needs, the company has moved sharply away from its old adversarial approach. The average contract with suppliers has been lengthened from two years to over four and a half years. Furthermore, Chrysler has given 90 percent of its suppliers commitments that business will be extended for at least the life of a model, if not beyond. The company has also committed itself to sharing with suppliers the benefits of any process improvements they might suggest. The basic thinking behind offering suppliers such credible commitments is to align incentives between Chrysler and its suppliers to create a sense of "shared destiny" and encourage mutual cooperation to increase the size of the financial pie that they will share in the future.

By 1996 the fruits of this new approach were beginning to appear. By involving suppliers early on in product development and giving them greater responsibility for design and manufacturing, DaimlerChrysler was able to compress its product development cycle and substantially reduce the costs of the product development effort. DaimlerChrysler's U.S. division reduced the time it took to develop a new vehicle from 234 weeks during the mid-1980s to about 160 weeks by 1996. The total cost of developing a new vehicle also dropped by 20 to 40 percent, depending on the model. With development costs in the automobile industry running at between $1 and $2 billion, that translates into a huge financial saving. Many of these savings were the direct result of engineering improvements suggested by suppliers or of improved coordination between the company and suppliers in the design process. To facilitate this process, the number of resident engineers from suppliers who work side by side with DaimlerChrysler engineers in cross-company design teams increased from 30 in 1989 to more than 300 by 1996.

In 1990, Chrysler began implementing a program known internally as the supplier cost reduction effort (SCORE), which focuses on cooperation between DaimlerChrysler and suppliers to identify opportunities for process improvements. In its first two years of operation, SCORE generated 875 ideas from suppliers that were worth $170.8 million in annual savings to suppliers. In 1994, suppliers submitted 3,786 ideas that produced $504 million in annual savings. By December 1995, Chrysler had implemented 5,300 ideas that have generated more than $1.7 billion in annual savings. One supplier alone, Magna International, submitted 214 proposals; Chrysler adopted 129 of them for a total cost saving of $75.5 million. Many of the ideas themselves have a relatively small financial impact; for example, a Magna suggestion to change the type of decorative wood grain used on minivans saved $0.5 million per year. But the cumulative impact of thousands of such ideas has had a significant impact on DaimlerChrysler's bottom line.

DaimlerChrysler has continued to pursue this approach aggressively, so much so that in 2004 it announced that its long-term goal was for its suppliers to take over a much higher percentage of actual car production—which includes making the car body and assembling most of its major components. Chrysler believes that this will give suppliers greater motivation than its own car divisions to control quality and reduce costs. Thus it has a radical long-term business model: it wants to be a car designer and not a carmaker. The cars that come off the assembly line may have Chrysler's name on them, but it will have only designed them, not built them.[d]

To understand the concept of credibility in this context, consider the following relationship between General Electric and IBM. GE is one of the major suppliers of advanced semiconductor chips to IBM, and many of the chips are customized to IBM's requirements. To meet IBM's specific needs, GE has had to make substantial investments in specialized assets that have little other value. As a consequence, GE is dependent on IBM and faces a risk that IBM will take advantage of this dependence to demand lower prices. In theory, IBM could back up its demand by threatening to switch its business to another supplier. However, GE reduced this risk by having IBM enter into a contractual agreement that committed IBM to purchase chips from GE for a ten-year period. In addition, IBM agreed to share the costs of the specialized assets needed to develop the customized chips, thereby reducing GE's investment. Thus, by publicly committing itself to a long-term contract and putting some money into the chip development process, IBM essentially made a *credible commitment* to continue purchasing those chips from GE.

■ **Maintaining Market Discipline** Just as a company pursuing vertical integration faces the problem that its in-house suppliers might become lazy and inefficient, so a company that forms a strategic alliance with another to make its components runs the risk that the other company's costs will rise as it becomes progressively more lax or inefficient over time. This happens because the supplier knows it does not have to compete with other suppliers for the company's business. Consequently, a company seeking to form a long-term strategic alliance needs to possess some kind of power that it can use to discipline its partner should the need arise.

The company holds two strong cards over its supplier. First, even long-term contracts are periodically renegotiated, generally every four to five years, so the supplier knows that if it fails to live up to its commitments, the company may refuse to renew the contract. Second, some companies engaged in long-term relationships with suppliers use a **parallel sourcing policy**—that is, they enter into a long-term contract with *two* suppliers for the same part (as is the practice at Toyota, for example).[20] This arrangement gives the company a hedge against an uncooperative supplier because it knows that if it fails to comply with the agreement, the company can switch all its business to the other supplier. This threat rarely needs to be actualized because the mere fact that the company and its suppliers know that parallel sourcing is being used and that a supplier can be replaced at short notice injects an element of market discipline into their relationship.

The growing importance of just-in-time inventory systems as a way to reduce costs and enhance quality and so differentiation is increasing the pressure on companies to form strategic alliances in a wide range of industries. The number of strategic alliances formed each year, especially global strategic alliances, is increasing, and the popularity of vertical integration may be falling because so many low-cost global suppliers now exist in countries like Malaysia, Korea, and China.

Strategic Outsourcing

Vertical integration and strategic alliances are alternative ways of managing the value chain *across industries* to strengthen a company's core business model. However, just as low-cost suppliers of component parts exist, so today many *specialized companies* exist that can perform one of a company's *own value-chain activities* in a way that contributes to a company's differentiation advantage or that lowers its cost structure.

Strategic outsourcing is the decision to allow one or more of a company's value-chain activities or functions to be performed by independent specialist companies that focus all their skills and knowledge on just one kind of activity. The activity to be outsourced may encompass an entire function, such as the manufacturing function, or it may be just one kind of activity that a function performs. For example, many companies outsource the management of their pension systems while keeping other human resource activities within the company. When a company chooses to outsource a value-chain activity, it is choosing to focus on a *fewer* number of value-creation activities to strengthen its business model.

There has been a clear move among many companies to outsource activities that managers regard as being "noncore" or "nonstrategic," meaning they are not a source of a company's distinctive competencies and competitive advantage.[21] One survey found that some 54 percent of the companies polled had outsourced manufacturing processes or services in the past three years.[22] Another survey estimates that some 56 percent of all global product manufacturing is outsourced to manufacturing specialists.[23] Companies that outsource include Nike, which does not make its athletic shoes, and The Gap, which does not make its jeans and clothing; these products are made under contract at low-cost global locations. Similarly, many high-technology companies outsource much of their manufacturing activity to contract manufacturers that specialize in low-cost assembly. Cisco, which is in the router and switch business, does not actually manufacture routers and switches. Rather, they are made by contract manufacturers such as Flextronics and Jabil Circuit. What Cisco does is design the routers and switches, sell the routers and switches, and coordinate the supply chain to match demand for routers and switches with the supply of routers and switches (see Strategy in Action 9.5).

While manufacturing is probably the most popular form of strategic outsourcing, as we note earlier, many other kinds of noncore activities are also outsourced. Microsoft has long outsourced its entire customer technical support operation to an independent company, as does Dell. Both companies have extensive customer support operations in India that are staffed by skilled operatives who are paid a fraction of what their U.S. counterparts earn. BP Amoco outsourced almost all of its human resource function to Exult, a San Antonio company, in a five-year deal worth $600 million, and a few years later Exult won a ten-year $1.1 billion contract to handle HRM activities for all Bank of America's 150,000 employees. Similarly, in 2002, American Express outsourced its entire information technology function to IBM in a seven-year deal worth $4 billion.[24] The Gartner Group, a market research company, estimated that the information technology outsourcing market in North America was worth $101 billion in 2000 and would grow to $160 billion by 2005.[25]

Companies engage in strategic outsourcing to strengthen their business models and increase their profitability. The process of strategic outsourcing typically begins with strategic managers identifying the value-chain activities that form the basis of a company's competitive advantage; these are obviously kept within the company to protect them from competitors. Managers then systematically review the noncore functions to assess whether they can be performed more effectively and efficiently by independent companies that specialize in those activities. Because these companies specialize in a particular activity, they can perform it in ways that lower costs or improve differentiation. If managers decide there are differentiation or cost advantages, these activities are outsourced to those specialists.

Strategy in Action

Cisco's $2 Billion Blunder

9.5

During the late 1990s, Cisco Systems became famous for the way it focused on developing distinctive competencies in a few key value-chain activities while outsourcing the remainder to specialist companies. Cisco was known as the "hardware maker that didn't make hardware." While it dominated the market for Internet protocol (IP) routers and switches, critical components of IP networks, these products were actually made by several contract manufacturers. Cisco focused its energies on just three main activities: product innovation, marketing and selling (primarily through Cisco's website), and managing the supply chain. Cisco claimed that this speeded the development of new products and allowed it to avoid expensive investment in manufacturing facilities, which reduced its need for capital and boosted its return on invested capital. Moreover, Cisco boasted that, under its outsourcing strategy, it did not have to deal with the hassle and expense of holding inventory, which was the responsibility of the contract manufacturer that shipped the finished products directly to customers.

Cisco's supply chain was structured like a four-tier pyramid with Cisco at the pinnacle. The contract manufacturers responsible for final assembly of Cisco's products formed the second tier of the pyramid. These manufacturers were fed by a third tier that supplied components such as processor chips and optical gear. The third-tier companies drew on an even larger base of suppliers of commodity inputs. According to Cisco CEO John Chambers, the system was very responsive to shifts in demand, and Cisco could immediately transmit product orders it received through its website down the supply chain, which allowed contract manufacturers and component suppliers to optimize their production schedules in real time. This dramatically reduced the amount of inventory in the supply chain, which further reduced Cisco's capital requirements (since the company did not have to finance extensive inventories) and boosted the company's ROIC.

In May 2001, however, it became apparent that major problems had arisen with Cisco's vaunted outsourcing strategy. The company announced that it would take a $2.2 billion charge against earnings to write down the value of inventory in the supply chain that had been ordered but could not be used. The problem was that demand for routers and switches had collapsed, but Cisco's systems had not detected this until it was too late. How did this happen? Why did a system that has been praised for being responsive to shifts in demand fail to detect a major fall in demand?

There was a major flaw in the way in which Cisco managed its supply chain. During the boom years up to 2000, demand for routers and switches rocketed as almost every kind of company, from large established firms to new telecommunications companies and dot-coms, invested in IP networks. However, these customers had not been able to get Cisco's products quickly enough, so they had started to double- and triple-book orders for Cisco and its competitors products, knowing that they would ultimately make purchases from just one company. Cisco, however, did not detect this. As far as it knew, it couldn't produce products fast enough. Moreover, the problem was amplified as orders moved down the supply chain. Suppose Cisco ordered 10,000 units of a particular router. Each of the contract manufacturers would compete to fill the entire order, and to gain an edge they often tried to lock up supplies of scarce components. If three contract manufacturers were competing to build the same 10,000 routers, it would look like sudden demand for 30,000 routers, so component makers too would increase their output. The result was a huge surge in inventory that far outstripped underlying demand. When the telecommunications and dot-com bubble burst in early 2001, demand from these customers plunged and Cisco was left with a bloated supply chain full of inventory no longer needed.

To reduce the risk of this problem occurring again, Cisco reconfigured the way it manages its supply chain. It created a central Internet-based repository of information, known as eHub, that *all* participants in the supply chain can access. Now, if contract manufacturers get an order for 10,000 routers and all turn around and place orders for 10,000 chips each (for a total of 30,000) to try to tie up scarce components, the chip makers can access eHub and see that the true order is for just 10,000 routers, not 30,000, and plan accordingly.[e]

FIGURE 9.4

Strategic Outsourcing
of Primary Value
Creation Functions

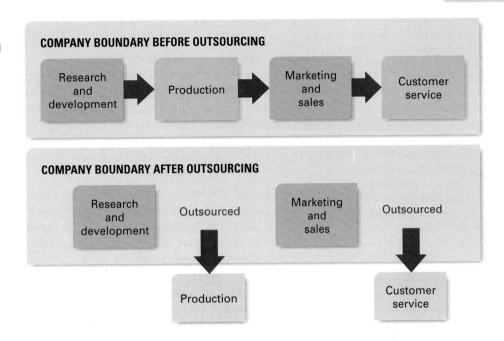

One possible outcome of this process is illustrated in Figure 9.4, which shows the primary value-chain activities and boundaries of a company before and after it has pursued strategic outsourcing. In this example, the company decided to outsource its production and customer service functions, leaving just R&D and marketing and sales within the company.

Once outsourcing has been executed, the relationships between the company and its specialists are then often structured as long-term contractual relationships with rich information sharing between the company and the specialist organization to which it has contracted the activity. The term **virtual corporation** has been coined to describe companies that have pursued extensive strategic outsourcing.[26]

■ **Benefits of Outsourcing**   Strategic outsourcing has several advantages. It can help a company to (1) lower its cost structure, (2) better differentiate its products in the market,[27] and (3) focus on the distinctive competencies that are vital to its long-term competitive advantage and profitability.

■ **Reducing the Cost Structure**   Outsourcing will reduce costs when the price that must be paid to a specialist company to perform a particular value-chain activity is less than what it would cost the company to perform that activity internally. Specialists are often able to perform an activity at a lower cost than the company because they are able to realize scale economies or other efficiencies not available to the company. For example, performing basic personnel activities, such as managing pay and benefit systems, requires a significant investment in developing a sophisticated information technology system. Purchasing this system represents a considerable fixed cost for one company. Moreover, the average cost of performing a personnel transaction can be driven down only if the IT system handles a large volume of transactions, and one company may not have the volume that allows this. By aggregating the demand from many different companies, a company that specializes in this activity, such as Exult and Paycheck, can obtain huge economies of scale that any one company could not hope to achieve by itself. Some of these cost savings are then passed on to client companies in the form of lower prices, which reduces their cost structure. A similar dynamic is at work in the contract manufacturing business. Once again, manufacturing specialists like Solectron, Flextronics, and Jabil Circuit make large capital investments to build efficient-scale manufacturing facilities, but then are able to spread those capital costs over a huge volume of outputs, thereby driving down unit costs so that they can make a product for less than the company can itself. In 2002, for example, IBM announced that it would no longer make PCs, although it would continue to design and sell them under the IBM brand name. Instead, it entered into an agreement with a contract manufacturer, Sanmina-SCI, to manufacture all of its PCs. As part of the agreement, IBM sold its PC manufacturing operations in the United States and Scotland to Sanmina for $200 million. IBM benefits from the lower prices it pays Sanmina for PCs because it can resell them under its own differentiated brand name, boosting its profitability.

In addition to the gains from scale economies, the greater acceleration in *cumulative* volume handled by specialists means that they are likely to obtain the cost savings associated with learning effects much more rapidly than a company that performs an activity just for itself (see Chapter 4 for a review of learning effects). For example, because a company like Flextronics is manufacturing similar products for several different companies, it is able to build up *cumulative* volume more rapidly, and it learns how to manage and operate the manufacturing process more efficiently than any of its clients could. This drives down the specialists' cost structure and allows them to charge client companies a lower price for a product than if they made it in-house.

The specialist may also be able to perform an activity at a lower cost than the company because it is based in a low-cost global location. Nike, for example, outsources the manufacture of its running shoe to companies based in China because of the much lower wage rates in China. The Chinese-based specialist can now assemble shoes, which is a very labor-intensive activity, at a much lower cost than if Nike performed the same activity itself in the United States. In theory, Nike could establish its own operations in China to manufacture running shoes. However, that would require a major capital investment and would limit its ability to switch production to an even lower-cost location later, say, Vietnam. So for Nike and most other consumer goods companies, the most efficient choice is to outsource manufacturing activity to both lower costs and give it the flexibility to switch to a more favorable location should labor costs change.

■ **Enhanced Differentiation** A company may also be able to differentiate its final products better by outsourcing certain noncore activities to specialists. For this to occur, the *quality* of the activity performed by specialists must be greater than if that same activity was performed by the company. On the reliability dimension of quality, for example, a specialist may be able to achieve a lower error rate in performing an activity, precisely because it focuses solely on that activity and has developed a strong distinctive competency in it. Again, this is one advantage claimed for contract manufacturers. Companies like Flextronics have adopted Six Sigma methodologies (see Chapter 4) and driven down the defect rate associated with manufacturing a product. This means they can provide more reliable products to their clients, which can now differentiate their products on the basis of their superior quality.

A company can also improve product differentiation by outsourcing to specialists when they stand out on the excellence dimension of quality. For example, the excellence of Dell's customer service, which is outsourced to an Indian specialist company, is a differentiating factor, and Dell stands at the top of customers' satisfaction ratings. Inside the United States, Dell also outsources its PC maintenance and repair function to specialist companies. A customer who has a problem with a product purchased from Dell can get excellent help over the phone. If it turns out that there is a defective part in the computer, a maintenance person will be dispatched to replace the part within twenty-four hours. The excellence of this service clearly differentiates Dell and helps to guarantee repeat purchases. In a similar way, carmakers often outsource specific kinds of vehicle component design activities, such as microchips or headlights, to specialists that have earned a reputation for design excellence in this particular activity.

■ **Focus on the Core Business** A final advantage of strategic outsourcing is that it allows managers to focus their energies and their company's resources on performing those core activities that have the most potential to create value and competitive advantage. In other words, companies can enhance their core competencies and so are able to push out the value frontier and create more value for their customers. Despite its mistakes, for example, Cisco remains the dominant competitor in the Internet router industry because it has focused on building its competencies in product design, marketing and sales, and supply-chain management. Companies that focus on the core activities essential for competitive advantage in their industry are better able to drive down the costs of performing those activities, and better differentiate their final products.

■ **Risks of Outsourcing** Although outsourcing noncore activities has many benefits, there are also risks associated with it, risks such as holdup and the possible loss of important information when an activity is outsourced. Managers must assess these risks before they decide to outsource a particular activity, although, as we discuss below, these risks can be reduced when the appropriate steps are taken.

■ **Holdup** In the context of outsourcing, holdup refers to the risk that a company will become too dependent on the specialist provider of an outsourced activity and that the specialist will use this fact to raise prices beyond some previously agreed-on rate. As with strategic alliances, the risk of holdup can be reduced by outsourcing to several suppliers and pursuing a parallel sourcing policy, as Cisco does. Moreover, when an activity can be performed well by any one of several different providers, the threat that a contract will not be renewed in the future is normally sufficient to keep the chosen provider from exercising bargaining power over the company. For example, although IBM enters into long-term contracts to provide information technology services to a wide range of companies, it would be highly unlikely to try to raise prices after the contract has been signed because it knows full well that such an action would reduce its chance of getting the contract renewed in the future. Moreover, the fact that IBM has many strong competitors in the IT services business, such as EDS and Computer Sciences, gives it a very strong incentive to deliver significant value to its client and not to practice holdup.

■ **Loss of Information** A company that is not careful can lose important competitive information when it outsources an activity. For example, many computer hardware and software companies have outsourced their customer technical support function to specialists. Although this makes good sense from a cost and differentiation perspective, it may also mean that a critical point of contact with the customer, and a source of important feedback, is lost. Customer complaints can be a useful piece of information and a valuable input into future product design, but if those complaints are not clearly communicated to the company by the specialists performing the technical support activity, the company can lose that information. Again, this is not an argument against outsourcing. Rather, it is an argument for making sure that there is good communication flow between the outsourcing specialist and the company. At Dell, for example, a great deal of attention is paid to making sure that the specialist responsible for providing technical support and on-site maintenance collects and communicates all relevant data regarding product failures and other problems to Dell, so that Dell can design better products.

Summary of Chapter

1. A corporate strategy should enable a company, or one or more of its business units, to perform one or more of the value creation functions at a lower cost or in a way that allows for differentiation and a premium price.

2. Horizontal integration can be understood as a way of trying to increase the profitability of a company by (a) reducing costs, (b) increasing the value of the company's products through differentiation, (c) replicating the business model, (d) managing rivalry within the industry to reduce the risk of price warfare, and (e) increasing bargaining power over suppliers and buyers.

3. There are two drawbacks associated with horizontal integration: the numerous pitfalls associated with mergers and acquisitions and the fact that the strategy can bring a company into direct conflict with antitrust authorities.

4. Vertical integration can enable a company to achieve a competitive advantage by helping build barriers to entry, facilitating investments in specialized assets, protecting product quality, and helping to improve scheduling between adjacent stages in the value chain.

5. The disadvantages of vertical integration include increasing bureaucratic costs if a company's internal or in-house supplier becomes inefficient and a lack of flexibility when technology is changing fast or demand is uncertain.

6. Entering into a long-term contract can enable a company to realize many of the benefits associated with vertical integration without having to bear the same level of bureaucratic costs. However, to avoid the risks associated with becoming too dependent on its partner, it needs to seek a credible commitment from its partner or establish a mutual hostage-taking situation.

7. The strategic outsourcing of noncore value creation activities may allow a company to lower its costs, better differentiate its products, and make better use of scarce resources, while also enabling it to respond rapidly to changing market conditions. However, strategic outsourcing may have a detrimental effect if the company outsources important value creation activities or becomes too dependent on the key suppliers of those activities.

Discussion Questions

1. Why was it profitable for General Motors and Ford to integrate backward into component-parts manufacturing in the past, and why are both companies now trying to buy more of their parts from outside?

2. Under what conditions might horizontal integration be inconsistent with the goal of maximizing profitability?

3. What value creation activities should a company outsource to independent suppliers? What are the risks involved in outsourcing these activities?

4. What steps would you recommend that a company take in order to build long-term cooperative relationships with its suppliers that are mutually beneficial?

Practicing Strategic Management

■ SMALL-GROUP EXERCISE
Comparing Vertical Integration Strategies

Break up into small groups of three to five people, and discuss the following scenario. Appoint one group member as a spokesperson who will communicate your findings to the class when called on to do so by the instructor. Then read the following description of the activities of Seagate Technologies and Quantum Corporation, both of which manufacture computer disk drives. On the basis of this description, outline the pros and cons of a vertical integration strategy. Which strategy do you think makes most sense in the context of the computer disk drive industry?

Quantum Corporation and Seagate Technologies are major producers of disk drives for personal computers and workstations. The disk drive industry is characterized by sharp fluctuations in the level of demand, intense price competition, rapid technological change, and product life cycles of no more than twelve to eighteen months. In recent years, Quantum and Seagate have pursued very different vertical integration strategies.

Seagate is a vertically integrated manufacturer of disk drives, both designing and manufacturing the bulk of its own disk drives. Quantum specializes in design, while outsourcing most of its manufacturing to a number of independent suppliers, including, most importantly, Matsushita Kotobuki Electronics (MKE) of Japan. Quantum makes only its newest and most expensive products in-house. Once a new drive is perfected and ready for large-scale manufacturing, Quantum turns over manufacturing to MKE. MKE and Quantum have cemented their partnership over eight years. At each stage in designing a new product, Quantum's engineers send the newest drawings to a production team at MKE. MKE examines the drawings and is constantly proposing changes that make new disk drives easier to manufacture. When the product is ready for manufacture, eight to ten Quantum engineers travel to MKE's plant in Japan for at least a month to work on production ramp-up.

■ ARTICLE FILE 9

Find an example of a company whose horizontal or vertical integration strategy appears to have dissipated rather than created value. Identify why this has been the case and what the company should do to rectify the situation.

■ STRATEGIC MANAGEMENT PROJECT
Module 9

This module requires you to assess the horizontal and vertical integration strategy being pursued by your company. With the information you have at your disposal, answer the questions and perform the tasks listed:

1. Has your company ever pursued a horizontal integration strategy? What was the strategic reason for pursuing this strategy?
2. How vertically integrated is your company? If your company does have vertically integrated operations, is it pursuing a strategy of taper or full integration?
3. Assess the potential for your company to create value through vertical integration. In reaching your assessment, also consider the bureaucratic costs of managing vertical integration.
4. On the basis of your assessment in question 3, do you think your company should (a) outsource some operations that are currently performed in-house or (b) bring some operations in-house that are currently outsourced? Justify your recommendations.
5. Is your company involved in any long-term cooperative relationships with suppliers or buyers? If so, how are these relationships structured? Do you think that these relationships add value to the company? Why?
6. Is there any potential for your company to enter into (additional) long-term cooperative relationships with suppliers or buyers? If so, how might these relationships be structured?

■ EXPLORING THE WEB
Visiting Motorola

Visit Motorola's website (**www.motorola.com**), and review its various business activities. Using this information, answer the following questions:

1. To what extent is Motorola vertically integrated?
2. Does vertical integration help Motorola establish a competitive advantage, or does it put the company at a competitive disadvantage?

General Task Search the Web for an example of a company that has pursued a strategic outsourcing strategy. Describe that strategy, and assess whether the strategy has increased the profitability of the company.

Closing Case

The Rise of WorldCom

In 1983, WorldCom was a small reseller of long-distance telephone service. By 2001, the company had generated sales of $40 billion, making it the second largest provider of telecommunications services behind AT&T. WorldCom entered 2001 as the number 2 provider of long-distance phone service in the United States, with 19 percent of the market; the largest single carrier of Internet data in the country, with an estimated 37 percent of the market; and a dazzling array of strategic assets, including a 300,000-mile fiber-optic network that was global in its reach.

WorldCom was very much the creation of its swaggering cowboy CEO, Bernie Ebbers, whose strategy for growth was quite simple: acquire competitors. An apparently savvy dealmaker, over seventeen years Ebbers acquired some sixty other telecommunication service providers, capping off the spree with the acquisition of MCI Communications, which at the time was larger than WorldCom and the number 2 long-distance telephone company in the nation. Ebbers's deal making was financed by a combination of WorldCom stock and debt. As long as the stock continued to rise—and it increased by a staggering 7,000 percent during the 1990s—WorldCom could use its "currency" to buy other companies in the industry. In addition, WorldCom borrowed large amounts of money from the debt markets, some $30 billion by late 2001. The debt markets proved only too willing to lend to WorldCom given the company's glittering growth prospects.

Driving the buying spree were two strategic objectives that were central to WorldCom's business model: (1) the desire to reap scale economies in order to drive down costs and (2) the desire to capture and retain customers by bundling together telecommunications services, such as long-distance service and Internet access, and selling them under a single contract. Ebbers reasoned that the scale economies would come from assembling a nationwide and international network to transmit data and voice traffic. The costs of assembling such a network are primarily fixed and include the costs of laying fiber-optic networks and installing switches. Once the network has been built, the costs of sending additional traffic down the network are virtually zero. This gives the company with the largest volume of traffic a huge cost advantage, because it can spread the fixed costs of building and maintaining its network over a very large volume, driving down the average costs of serving each customer. In addition, Ebbers believed that customers would want only

one telecommunications service provider, and one bill, for all services they used, including long-distance and local phone service, Internet access, and wireless phone service. By assembling a company that could provide all of those services to consumers in a single bundle with a single bill, Ebbers believed that WorldCom would have a competitive advantage in the marketplace that would help it to increase volume more rapidly than rivals and thus better realize potential scale economies.

WorldCom grew through acquisition, as opposed to organically, because it was quicker to grow this way and cheaper to use a mix of WorldCom's high-flying stock and long-term debt to buy competitors than to build the network entirely on its own. Moreover, when WorldCom made an acquisition, it applied a fairly standard formula: cut the overhead, eliminate any duplication, and drive the traffic of the acquired customers through WorldCom's network to realize scale economies.

The strategy seemed to work well until 2000, when WorldCom made a bid to acquire Sprint for $115 billion. Sprint was the number 3 long-distance company in the United States with 8 percent of the market, operated the second largest data network in the country with 16 percent of the market, and was one of the largest providers of wireless service in the United States. The acquisition made perfect strategic sense. It would enable WorldCom to reap additional scale economies and bundle wireless service with its long-distance and Internet access service. Unfortunately for WorldCom, antitrust authorities in both the United States and the European Union thought that it would also give WorldCom substantial monopoly power, and both indicated that they would oppose the acquisition. The U.S. Justice Department claimed that the acquisition would create an unacceptable level of concentration in the long-distance phone business, with AT&T and WorldCom controlling 80 percent of the market after the acquisition. The Department of Justice also claimed that the acquisition would result in the monopolization of high-speed Internet data lines, creating a company that controlled 53 percent of Internet traffic and giving the expanded WorldCom the ability to discriminate against rivals and "irrevocably tip the market" toward a monopoly outcome.

In mid 2000, WorldCom announced that in the face of opposition from antitrust authorities, it would abandon the acquisition. This proved to be a turning point in the company's fortunes. During the next two years the company's stock plummeted from over $50 a share to under $1. A number of factors contributed to the implosion in the stock price. First, a price war erupted in the long-distance telephone service business. A combination of slowing growth and the entry of new competitors, particularly the Baby Bells that had been allowed by the 1996 Telecommunications Act to start offering long-distance telephone service, conspired to drive down prices for long-distance service. Second, in the data area, many of WorldCom's largest customers were other telecommunications providers, particularly new companies that had entered the market in the aftermath of the 1996 act. By mid 2001, many of these companies were in trouble. They had taken on too much debt to build out their own networks ahead of demand and now were unable to generate the cash flow to meet their debt obligations. As they crumbled into bankruptcy, WorldCom lost business that it had counted on to generate its own growth and service its debt commitments. It also started to lose the customers who had come with the acquisition of other carriers, such as MCI, and who complained that the quality of customer service had declined markedly under WorldCom.

The net result was that, by 2002, WorldCom was looking at declining revenues and steep losses, a far cry from the double-digit earnings growth it had been predicting eighteen months earlier. Suddenly the company was struggling to generate the cash flow required to service its debt commitments. Moreover, a May 2002 financial audit ordered by WorldCom's board of directors discovered that the company had understated expenses by $3 billion during 2001 and inflated its income by $1.4 billion in the quarter ending March 31, 2002. This revelation led to the resignation of several senior executives, including CEO Bernie Ebbers. The news of possible accounting fraud, taken together with WorldCom's sudden losses, led rating agencies to downgrade WorldCom's debt. This pushed up the interest rate on that debt, making it more expensive for WorldCom to serve. The company was now caught in a vice—on one side, due to unexpectedly poor business conditions its cash flow was plunging, and on the other, the price of serving its debt was surging. In July 2002, WorldCom bowed to the inevitable and declared bankruptcy. Bernie Ebbers's grand strategic vision lay in ruins.[28]

Case Discussion Questions

1. What was the rationale for WorldCom pursuing a strategy of horizontal integration?

2. Why did the strategy fail?

Chapter 10

Corporate-Level Strategy: Formulating and Implementing Related and Unrelated Diversification

Opening Case

United Technologies Has an "ACE in Its Pocket"

United Technologies Corporation (UTC), based in Hartford, Connecticut, is a *conglomerate*, a company that owns a wide variety of other companies that operate in different businesses and industries. Some of the companies in UTC's portfolio are more well known than UTC itself, such as Sikorsky Aircraft Corporation; Pratt & Whitney, the aircraft engine and component maker; Otis Elevator Company; Carrier air conditioning; and Chubb, the security and lock maker that UTC acquired in 2003. Today, investors frown upon companies like UTC that own and operate companies in widely different industries. There is a growing perception that managers can better manage a company's business model when the company operates as an independent or stand-alone entity. How can UTC justify holding all these companies together in a conglomerate? Why would this lead to a greater increase in their long-term profitability than if they operated as separate companies? In the last decade the boards of directors and CEOs of many conglomerates, such as Greyhound-Dial, ITT Industries, and Textron, have realized that by holding diverse companies together they were reducing, not increasing, the profitability of their companies. As a result, many conglomerates have been broken up and their companies spun off to allow them to operate as separate, independent entities.

UTC's CEO George David claims that he has created a unique and sophisticated multi-business model that adds value across UTC's diverse businesses. David joined Otis Elevator as an assistant to its CEO in 1975, but within one year Otis was acquired by UTC, during a decade when "bigger is better" ruled corporate America and mergers and acquisitions, of whatever kind, were seen as the best way to grow profits. UTC sent David to manage its South American operations and later gave him responsibility for its Japanese operations. Otis had formed an alliance with Matsushita to develop an elevator for the Japanese market, and the resulting "Elevonic 401," after being installed widely in Japanese buildings, proved to be a disaster. It broke down much more often than elevators made by other Japanese companies, and customers were concerned about its reliability and safety.

Matsushita was extremely embarrassed about the elevator's failure and assigned one of its leading total quality management (TQM) experts, Yuzuru Ito, to head a team of Otis engineers to find out why it performed so poorly. Under Ito's direction all the employees—managers, designers, and production workers—who had produced the elevator analyzed why the elevators were malfunctioning. This intensive study led to a total redesign of the elevator, and when their new and improved elevator was launched worldwide, it met with great success. Otis's share of the global elevator market increased dramatically, and one result was that David was named president of UTC in 1992. He was given the responsibility to cut costs across the entire corporation, including its important Pratt & Whitney division, and his success in reducing UTC's cost structure and increasing its ROIC led to his appointment as CEO in 1994.

Now responsible for all of UTC's diverse companies, David decided that the best way to increase UTC's profitability, which had been falling, was to find ways to improve efficiency and quality in all its constituent companies. He convinced Ito to move to Hartford and take responsibility for championing the kinds of improvements that had by now transformed the Otis division, and Ito began to develop UTC's TQM system, which is known as *Achieving Competitive Excellence*, or ACE.

ACE is a set of tasks and procedures that are used by employees from the shop floor to top managers to analyze all aspects of the way a product is made. The goal is to find ways to improve *quality and reliability*, to *lower the costs* of making the product, and especially to find ways to make the next generation of a particular product perform better—in other words, to encourage *technological innovation*. David makes every employee in every function and at every level take responsibility for achieving the incremental, step-by-step gains that can result in innovative and efficient products that enable a company to dominate its industry—to push back the value creation frontier.

David calls these techniques "process disciplines," and he has used them to increase the performance of all UTC companies. Through these techniques he has created the extra value for UTC that justifies it owning and operating such a diverse set of businesses. David's success can be seen in the performance that his company has achieved in the decade since he took control: he has quadrupled UTC's earnings per share, and in the first six months of 1994 profit grew by 25 percent to $1.4 billion, while sales increased by 26 percent to $18.3 billion. UTC has been in the top three performers of the companies that make up the Dow Jones industrial average for the last three years, and the company has consistently outperformed GE, another huge conglomerate, in its returns to investors.

David and his managers believe that the gains that can be achieved from UTC's process disciplines are never-ending because its own R&D—in which it invests over $2.5 billion a year—is constantly producing product innovations that can help all its businesses. Indeed, recognizing that its skills in creating process improvements are specific to manufacturing companies, UTC's strategy is to only acquire companies that make products that can benefit from the use of its ACE program—hence its Chubb acquisition. At the same time, David only invests in companies that have the potential to remain leading companies in their industries and so can charge above-average prices. His acquisitions strengthen the competencies of UTC's existing businesses. For example, he acquired a company called Sunderstrand, a leading aerospace and industrial systems company, and combined it with UTC's Hamilton aerospace division to create Hamilton Sunderstrand, which is now a major supplier to Boeing and makes products that command premium prices.

Overview   George David utilizes ACE to increase the ROIC of UTC's companies or divisions, recognizing that UTC must own companies that are well positioned in their industries to maintain and grow their market share and protect their profit margins. David has developed a *multibusiness model* that (1) allows each company to pursue its own, industry-specific business model, (2) supplies each division with corporate support through its ACE performance-enhancing set of skills, and (3) uses the financial power of the UTC empire to make acquisitions and divestitures to allow companies to better position themselves vis-à-vis their competitors. As we discuss later, UTC is pursuing the corporate-level strategy of unrelated diversification to strengthen the business models of its individual companies and so increase their individual profitability—and thus the total profitability of the whole conglomerate.

In this chapter we continue our discussion of how companies can utilize their distinctive competencies, and the business models that are based on them, by formulating and implementing new corporate-level strategies to grow their profits and their free cash flow. Companies cannot stand still; they must continually search for ways to use their capital more efficiently and effectively. In a competitive environment, resources such as capital move to their most highly valued use, which means they are invested in companies that are expected to be the most profitable in the future. If a company's managers do not strive to build its distinctive competencies and competitive advantage, they will ultimately lose out to those companies that have found successful business models.

This chapter discusses the corporate-level strategy of **diversification,** which is a company's decision to enter one or more new industries to take advantage of its existing distinctive competencies and business model. We discuss two different types of diversification, related diversification and unrelated diversification, and we examine the different kinds of distinctive competencies and multibusiness models on which they are based. Then we look at three different methods or strategies companies can use to implement a diversification strategy: internal new ventures, acquisitions, and joint ventures. By the end of this chapter you will understand why some companies decide to diversify and enter new markets and industries and why they select a particular strategy to implement a diversification strategy in the most profitable way.

Expanding Beyond a Single Industry

The role of managers in corporate-level strategy is to identify which industries a company should compete in to maximize its long-run profitability. As we discuss in Chapter 9, for many companies, profitable growth and expansion often entail concentrating on a single market or industry. For example, McDonald's focuses on the global fast-food restaurant business and Wal-Mart on global discount retailing. Companies that stay inside one industry pursue horizontal integration and strategic outsourcing to strengthen their business models, expand their business, and increase their profitability. Even though vertical integration leads a company to enter industries at adjacent stages of the value chain, the intent is still to strengthen its core business model.

As a result of these strategies, a company's fortunes are tied closely to the profitability of its *original industry*—and this can be dangerous if that industry goes into decline. As an industry matures, the opportunities to grow profits often fall. Moreover, companies that concentrate on just one industry sometimes miss out on opportunities to increase their profitability by leveraging their distinctive competencies to make and sell products in *new industries*. There is compelling evidence to suggest that companies that rest on their laurels, do not engage in constant learning, and do not force themselves to stretch can lose out to agile new competitors that come along with superior business models.[1] For these reasons, many argue that companies must *leverage*, that is, find new ways to take advantage of their distinctive competencies and core business model in new markets and industries.

■ A Company as a Portfolio of Distinctive Competencies

Gary Hamel and C. K. Prahalad have developed a model that can help managers assess how and when they should expand beyond their current market or industry. According to these authors, a fruitful approach to identifying new product market opportunities is to think of a company not as a portfolio of products, but as a *portfolio of distinctive competencies*, and then consider how those competencies might be leveraged, that is, used to create more value and profit in new industries.[2]

Industry

Existing — New

Competence

New

Premier plus 10

What new competencies will we need to build to protect and extend our franchise in current industries?

Mega-opportunities

What new competencies will we need to build to participate in the most exciting industries of the future?

Existing

Fill in the blanks

What is the opportunity to improve our position in existing industries and better leverage our existing competencies?

White spaces

What new products or services could we create by creatively redeploying or recombining our current competencies?

Recall from Chapter 3 that a distinctive competency is a company-specific resource or capability that gives a company a competitive advantage. Hamel and Prahalad argue that when managers want to identify a profitable opportunity for diversification, they must first define and classify the company's *current* set of distinctive competencies. Then they can use a matrix like that illustrated in Figure 10.1 to establish an agenda for entering new markets or industries. This matrix distinguishes between existing competencies and new ones that would have to be developed to allow a company to compete in a new industry. It also distinguishes between the existing industries in which a company operates and new industries in which it might operate in the future. Each quadrant in the matrix has different strategic implications.

■ **Fill in the Blanks**   The lower-left quadrant of Figure 10.1 represents the company's existing portfolio of competencies and products. In the 1900s, for example, Canon had distinctive competencies in precision mechanics, fine optics, and microelectronics and was active in two industries, cameras and photocopiers. It used its competencies in precision mechanics and fine optics to produce mechanical cameras. These two competencies plus an additional competency it had developed in microelectronics allowed it to produce photocopiers. The term *fill in the blanks* refers to the opportunity to improve a company's competitive position in its existing industries by sharing its current competencies between divisions. Canon, for example, realized that it could strengthen its camera business by giving it the microelectronics skills it had developed in its copier business. Then the camera division could make advanced cameras with electronic features such as auto-focusing.

■ **Premier Plus 10**   The upper-left quadrant in Figure 10.1 is referred to as *premier plus 10.* The term is used to suggest another important question: What *new* distinctive competencies must be developed now to ensure that a company remains a *premier* provider of its existing products in *ten* years' time? To strengthen the business model of its copier business, Canon decided that it needed to build a new competency in electronic imaging (the ability to capture and store images in a digital format as opposed to the more traditional chemical-based photographic processes). By developing this new competency, Canon was able to protect its competitive advantage and make advanced products like laser copiers, color copiers, and digital cameras.

■ **White Spaces**   The lower-right quadrant of Figure 10.1 is referred to as *white spaces* because the issue managers must address is how can it fill "white spaces," that is, opportunities to creatively redeploy or recombine its current distinctive competencies to produce new products in new industries. Canon was able to recombine its established competencies in precision mechanics and fine optics and its recently acquired competency in electronic imaging to produce fax machines and laser jet printers, thereby entering the fax and printer industries. In other words, it leveraged its distinctive competencies to take advantage of opportunities in other industries and create valuable new products.

■ **Mega-Opportunities**   Opportunities represented by the upper-right quadrant of Figure 10.1 do not overlap with the company's current industries or its current competencies. Rather, they imply entry into new industries where the company currently has none of the competencies required to succeed. Nevertheless, a company may choose to pursue such opportunities if they are seen to be particularly attractive, significant, or relevant to its existing product market activities. For example, in 1979, Monsanto was primarily a manufacturer of chemicals, including fertilizers. However, the company saw enormous opportunities in the emerging biotechnology industry. Senior research scientists felt that it might be possible to produce genetically engineered crop seeds that would produce their own "organic" pesticides. In that year, the company embarked on a massive investment, which ultimately amounted to several hundred million dollars, to build a world-class competence in biotechnology. This investment was funded by cash flows generated from Monsanto's operations in the chemical industry. The investment paid off in the 1990s when Monsanto introduced a series of genetically engineered crop seeds that were resistant to many common pests. Roundup, a Monsanto herbicide that can be used to kill weeds but that will not kill its genetically engineered plants, became the industry leader.[3]

A focus on using or recombining existing competencies or building new competencies to enter new industries helps managers think strategically about how industry boundaries might change over time and how this will affect their current business models. By helping managers think about how to transfer and leverage competencies across industries, Prahalad and Hamel's model can help managers avoid the strategic mistake of entering new markets where their business model will fail to give them a competitive advantage, as many companies, such as Coca-Cola and Sears, discussed in the last chapter, have done.

Increasing Profitability Through Diversification

Diversification is the process of adding new businesses to the company that are distinct from its core industry. A multibusiness model then focuses on finding ways to use the company's distinctive competencies to increase the value of products in those new industries that it has entered. A **diversified company** is one that operates in two or more industries. In each industry a company enters, it establishes an operating division or business unit, which is essentially a self-contained company that makes and sells products for its particular market. To increase profitability, a diversification strategy should enable the company or one or more of its business units to perform one or more of the value-chain functions (1) at a lower cost, (2) in a way that allows for differentiation and gives the company pricing options, or (3) in a way that helps the company to manage industry rivalry better.

The managers of most companies first consider diversification when they are generating **free cash flow**, that is, cash *in excess* of that required to fund investments in the company's existing industry and to meet any debt commitments.[4] In other words, free cash flow is cash in excess of that which can be profitably reinvested in an existing business (*cash* is simply *capital* by another name). When a company is generating free cash flow, managers must decide whether to return that capital to shareholders in the form of higher dividend payouts or invest it in diversification. Technically, any free cash flow belongs to the company's owners—its shareholders. For diversification to make sense, the return on investing free cash flow to pursue diversification opportunities, that is, the return on invested capital (ROIC), *must* exceed the return that stockholders could get by investing that capital in a diversified portfolio of stocks and bonds. If this were not the case, it would be in the best interests of shareholders for the company to return any excess cash to them through higher dividends rather than pursue a diversification strategy. Thus, a diversification strategy is *not* consistent with maximizing returns to shareholders unless the multibusiness model managers use to justify entry into a new industry will significantly increase the value a company can create.

Six main justifications for pursuing a multibusiness model based on diversification can be identified. Diversification can increase company profitability when managers (1) transfer competencies between business units in different industries, (2) leverage competencies to create business units in new industries, (3) share resources between business units to realize economies of scope, (4) use product bundling, (5) use diversification to reduce rivalry in one or more industries, and (6) utilize *general* organizational competencies that increase the performance of all the company's business units.

■ **Transferring Competencies Across Industries**

Transferring competencies involves taking a distinctive competency developed in one industry and implanting it in an existing business unit in another industry. This business unit might be a company that the diversified company has acquired. Companies that base their diversification strategy on transferring competencies believe that they can use one or more of their distinctive competencies in a value-chain activity—for example, manufacturing, marketing, materials management, and R&D—to significantly strengthen the business model of the acquired company. For example, over time Philip Morris developed distinctive competencies in product development, consumer marketing, and brand positioning that had made it a leader in the tobacco industry. Sensing an opportunity, it acquired Miller Brewing, which at the time was a relatively small player in the brewing industry. Then, to create value in Miller, Philip Morris transferred some of its best marketing experts to Miller, where they applied the skills acquired at Philip Morris to turn around Miller's lackluster brewing business (see Figure 10.2). The result was the creation of Miller Light, the first light beer, and a marketing campaign that helped to push Miller from the number 6 to the number 2 company in the brewing industry in terms of market share.

Companies that base their diversification strategy on transferring competencies tend to acquire businesses *related* to their existing activities because of commonalities between one or more of their value-chain functions. A *commonality* is some kind of attribute shared by two or more business units that allows them to create more

FIGURE 10.2

Transfer of
Competencies at
Philip Morris

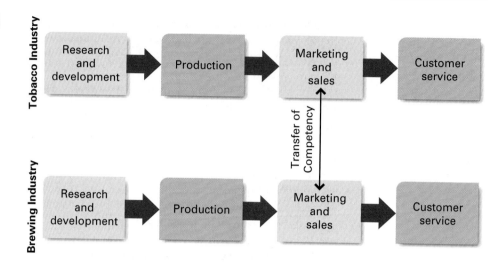

value when they operate together cohesively. For example, Miller Brewing was related to Philip Morris's tobacco business by marketing commonalities; both beer and tobacco are mass market consumer goods where brand positioning, advertising, and product development skills are important. In general, such competency transfers can increase profitability when they lower the cost structure of one or more of a diversified company's business units or enable one or more of its business units to better differentiate their products, which also gives that business unit pricing options.

For such a strategy to work, the competencies being transferred must involve value-chain activities that will become the source of a particular business unit's competitive advantage in the future. In other words, the distinctive competency being transferred must have real strategic value. However, all too often companies assume that *any* commonality between their value chains is sufficient for creating value. When they attempt to transfer competencies, they find the anticipated benefits are not forthcoming because the different business units did not share some important attribute in common. General Motors's acquisition of Hughes Aircraft, made simply because autos and auto manufacturing were "going electronic" and Hughes was an electronics company, demonstrates the folly of overestimating the commonalities among businesses. The acquisition failed to realize any of the anticipated gains for GM, whose competitive position did not improve, and GM subsequently sold off Hughes.

■ **Leveraging
Competencies**

Leveraging competencies involves taking a distinctive competency developed by a business in one industry and using it to create a *new* business unit in a different industry. The central idea here is that the set of distinctive competencies that are the source of competitive advantage in one industry might also be applied to create a differentiation- or cost-based competitive advantage for a new business unit in a different industry. For example, Canon used its distinctive competencies in precision mechanics, fine optics, and electronic imaging to produce laser jet printers, which for Canon was a new business in a new industry. Its competitive advantage in laser printers came from the fact that its competencies enabled it to produce high-quality (differentiated) printers that could be manufactured at a low cost.

The difference between leveraging competencies and transferring competencies is that in the case of leveraging competencies an entirely *new* business is being created, whereas transferring competencies involves a transfer between *existing* businesses. Although the distinction may seem subtle, it is actually very important, because different managerial processes are involved. Companies that leverage competencies to establish new businesses tend to be technology-based enterprises that use their R&D competencies to create new business opportunities in diverse industries. In contrast, companies that transfer competencies typically enter new industries by acquiring established businesses. They then transfer competencies to the acquired businesses in order to enhance their profitability, as Philip Morris did with Miller Brewing.

A number of companies have based their diversification strategy on leveraging competencies and using them to create new businesses in different industries. Microsoft leveraged its skills in software development and marketing to create two new businesses, its online network MSN and the Xbox videogame business. Microsoft's managers believed that the company's diversification strategy was in the best interests of shareholders because the company's competencies would enable it to attain a competitive advantage in the videogame and online industries. In fact, they were wrong. In 2003, when Microsoft broke its profits down by business unit, it turned out that the software business was generating almost all the profit and most other business units were making a loss. Realizing that entry into new industries was not a way it could increase the value of the company for its shareholders, Microsoft decided it would give back over $30 billion, or half its $60 billion cash hoard, to shareholders in the form of a dividend in 2004. Microsoft still hopes its Xbox business will be a success in the future, however.

A company that is famous for its ability to leverage competencies to create *new* businesses in diverse industries is 3M, which among other things leveraged its skills in adhesives to create new business opportunities (see Strategy in Action 10.1). From a humble beginning as a manufacturer of sandpaper, 3M has become one of the most diversified corporations in the United States. Most of this diversification came about not through acquisitions but by internally venturing and creating new business units itself (a topic discussed later in the chapter).

■ Sharing Resources: Economies of Scope

When two or more business units in different industries share resources and capabilities, they may be able to realize economies of scope.[5] **Economies of scope** arise when one or more of a diversified company's business units are able to realize cost-saving or differentiation advantages because they can more effectively pool, share, and utilize expensive resources or capabilities, such as skilled people, equipment, manufacturing facilities, distribution channels, advertising campaigns, and R&D laboratories. If business units in different industries can share a common resource or function, they can collectively lower their cost structure.[6] For example, the costs of GE's consumer products advertising, sales, and service activities are spread over a wide range of products, such as small and large appliances, air conditioning, and furnaces, reducing unit costs. These cost reductions have two major sources.

First, companies that can share resources across business units have to invest proportionately less in the shared resource than companies that cannot share. For example, Procter & Gamble makes both disposable diapers and paper towels, paper-based products valued for their ability to absorb liquid without disintegrating. Because both products need the same attribute—absorbency—Procter & Gamble can share the R&D costs associated with producing an absorbent paper-based product across the two businesses. Similarly, because both products are sold to the same customer

Strategy in Action

10.1

Diversification at 3M: Leveraging Technology

3M is a 100-year-old industrial colossus that in 2004 generated over $16 billion in revenues and $1.4 billion in profits from a portfolio of more than 50,000 individual products ranging from sandpaper and sticky tape to medical devices, office supplies, and electronic components. The company has consistently created new businesses by leveraging its scientific knowledge to find new applications for its proprietary technology. Today, the company is composed of more than forty discrete business units grouped into six major sectors: transportation, health care, industrial, consumer and office, electronics and communications, and specialty materials. The company has consistently generated 30 percent of sales from products introduced within the prior five years and currently operates with the goal to produce 40 percent of sales revenues from products introduced within the previous four years.

The process of leveraging technology to create new businesses at 3M can be illustrated by the following quotation from William Coyne, head of R&D at 3M: "It began with sandpaper: mineral and glue on a substrate. After years as an abrasives company, it created a tape business. A researcher left off the mineral, and adapted the glue and substrate to create the first sticky tape. After creating many varieties of sticky tape—consumer, electrical, medical— researchers created the world's first audio and videotapes. In their search to create better tape backings, other researchers happened on multilayer films that, surprise, have remarkable light management qualities. This multi-player film technology is being used in brightness enhancement films, which are incorporated in the displays of virtually all laptops and palm computers."

How does 3M do it? First, the company is a science-based enterprise with a strong tradition of innovation and risk taking. Risk taking is encouraged, and failure is not punished but seen as a natural part of the process of creating new products and business. Second, 3M's management is relentlessly focused on the company's customers and the problems they face. Many of 3M's products have come from helping customers to solve difficult problems. Third, managers set *stretch goals* that require the company to create new products and businesses at a rapid pace (such as the current goal that 40 percent of sales should come from products introduced within the last four years). Fourth, employees are given considerable autonomy to pursue their own ideas. An employee can spend 15 percent of his or her time working on a project of his or her own choosing without management approval. Many products have resulted from this autonomy, including the ubiquitous Post-it Notes. Fifth, while products belong to business units and it is business units that are responsible for generating profits, the technologies belong to every unit within the company. Anyone at 3M is free to try to develop new applications for a technology developed by its business units. Sixth, 3M has implemented an IT system that promotes the sharing of technological knowledge between business units so that new opportunities can be identified. Also, it hosts many in-house conferences where researchers from different business units are brought together to share the results of their work. Finally, 3M uses numerous mechanisms to recognize and reward those who develop new technologies, products, and businesses, including peer-nominated award programs, a corporate hall of fame, and of course, monetary rewards.[a]

group (supermarkets), it can use the same sales force to sell both products (see Figure 10.3). In contrast, competitors that make just paper towels or just disposable diapers cannot achieve the same economies and have to invest proportionately more in R&D and in maintaining a sales force. The net result is that, other things being equal, P&G will have lower expenses and earn a higher return on invested capital than companies that lack the ability to share resources.

Second, resource sharing across businesses may enable a company to use the shared resource more intensively, thereby realizing *economies of scale* (in other words, economies of scale are a source of economies of scope). For example, one of the motives behind the 1998 merger of Citicorp and Travelers to form Citigroup was that the

FIGURE 10.3

Sharing Resources at
Procter & Gamble

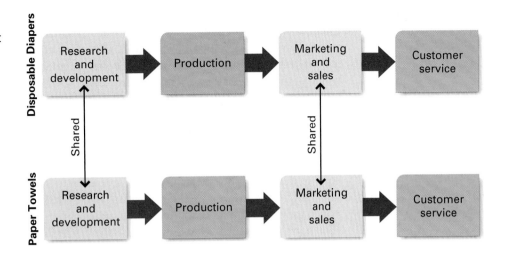

merger would allow Travelers to sell its insurance products and financial services
through Citicorp's retail banking network. The merger allows the expanded group
to better use an existing asset—its retail banking network—and thereby realize
economies of scale. Because economies of scale lower the cost structure of one or more
businesses, the net result is to increase the profitability of the diversified company.

Diversification to attain economies of scope is possible only when there are significant commonalities between one or more of the value-chain functions of a company's existing and new business units. Moreover, managers need to be aware that
the costs of coordination necessary to achieve economies of scope within a company
often outweigh the value that can be created by such a strategy.[7] Consequently, the
strategy should be pursued only when sharing is likely to generate a *significant* competitive advantage in one or more of a company's business units.

**■ Using Product
Bundling**

Increasingly, in their search for ways to differentiate their products, companies are
entering into related industries in order to expand their product lines and so be able
to satisfy customers' needs for a package of related products. This is currently happening in telecommunications, where customers are increasingly seeking a package
price for wired phone service, wireless phone service, high-speed access to the Internet,
VOIP phone service, television programming, online gaming, video on demand, or any
combination of these services. To meet this need, many Baby Bell phone companies
have been acquiring companies that provide one or more of these services, while cable
companies such as Comcast Corporation have acquired or formed strategic alliances
with companies that allow them to offer their customers phone service, and so on. In
2004, Microsoft announced an alliance with SBC whereby SBC would use its new
software to allow it to provide television service and video on demand over DSL
phone connections, as well as its other services. Similarly, EchoStar Communications
Corp., the satellite broadcaster, formed an alliance with Verizon to offer its TV service with Verizon's phone service.

Just as companies like to reduce the number of their component suppliers, so the
final customer wants to obtain the convenience, and reduced price, of bundled products. Another example of product bundling comes from the medical equipment
industry, where the companies that used to produce different kinds of products, such

as operating equipment, ultrasound devices, magnetic imaging, and x-ray equipment, have been merging to be able to offer hospitals a complete range of medical equipment. This development has been driven by hospitals because they want the convenience of dealing with a single supplier. In addition, because of the increased value of their orders, they also have increased bargaining power with the supplier.

■ Managing Rivalry: Multipoint Competition

Sometimes a company benefits by diversifying into an industry in order to hold a competitor in check that has either entered its industry or has the potential to do so. For example, if an aggressive company based in another industry enters a company's market and tries to gain market share by cutting prices, the company can respond in kind and diversify into the aggressor's home industry and also cut prices. In this way, the company sends a signal: "If you attack me, I'll respond in kind and make things tough for you." (This is an example of the strategy of tit-for-tat discussed in Chapter 6.) The hope is that such a move will cause the aggressor to pull back from its attack, thus moderating rivalry in the company's home industry and permitting higher prices and profits. Of course, for the tit-for-tat strategy to have its desired effect, the company would then need to pull back from its competitive attack in the aggressor's home market.

An example of diversification to keep a potential competitor in check occurred in the late 1990s when Microsoft awoke to the fact that Sony might emerge as a rival. Although Sony was in a different industry (consumer electronics as opposed to software), Microsoft realized that the Sony PlayStation was in essence nothing more than a specialized computer and, moreover, one that did not use a Microsoft operating system. Microsoft's fear was that Sony might use the PlayStation 2, which came equipped with web-browsing potential, as a "Trojan horse" to gain control of web browsing and computing from the living room, ultimately taking customers away from PCs with Microsoft operating systems. The desire to keep Sony's ambitions in check was another part of the rationale for Microsoft's diversification into the videogame industry with the launch of the Xbox.

Many diversified companies compete against each other in several different industries. Canon and Kodak compete against each other in photocopiers and digital cameras, for example. Similarly, Unilever and Procter & Gamble compete against each other in laundry detergents, personal care products, and packaged foods. When companies compete against each other in different industries, we refer to it as **multipoint competition.** Companies that are engaged in multipoint competition might be better able to manage rivalry by signaling that competitive attacks in one industry will be met by retaliatory attacks in another industry. If successful, such signaling might lead to *mutual forbearance,* and thus less intense rivalry and higher profit in each industry in which a company competes. It follows that the desire to manage rivalry better through multipoint competition might be a motive for diversification that increases profitability.

■ Utilizing General Organizational Competencies

By **general organizational competencies,** we mean competencies that transcend individual functions or business units and are found at the top or corporate level of the multibusiness company. Typically, these general competencies are the skills of a company's top managers and functional experts, such as George David and Yuzuru Ito of UTC. When these general competencies are present—and many times they are not—they help each business unit within a company perform at a higher level than it could if it operated as an independent company, thus increasing the profitability of the whole corporation.[8] We discuss three kinds of general organizational competencies that can result in superior performance: (1) entrepreneurial capabilities, (2) organizational design capabilities, and (3) strategic capabilities. These managerial skills are often not present because they are rare and difficult to develop and put into action.

■ **Entrepreneurial Capabilities** The example of 3M, profiled in Strategy in Action 10.1 above, provides many clues as to why entrepreneurial capabilities are important if the process of diversification is to increase profitability. A company may generate considerable excess cash flow, but to take advantage of it managers must identify new opportunities and act on them to create a stream of new and improved products in both existing and new industries. It appears that some companies are better able to stimulate their managers to act entrepreneurially than are others; examples are 3M, Hewlett-Packard, IBM, Canon, Sony, and Matsushita.[9]

These companies are able to promote entrepreneurship because they have an organization culture that stimulates managers to act entrepreneurially. The consequence is that these companies are able to create profitable new business units at a much higher rate than most other companies, which helps promote their diversification. We will highlight some of the systems required to generate profitable new businesses later in this chapter when we discuss internal new ventures. For now, note that the management systems of an entrepreneurial company must (1) encourage managers to take risks, (2) give them the time and resources to pursue novel ideas, (3) not punish managers when a new idea fails, but also (4) make sure the company does not waste resources pursuing too many risky ventures that have a low probability of generating a decent return on investment. Obviously, a difficult organizational balancing act is required here, for the company has to simultaneously encourage risk taking while limiting the amount of risk being undertaken.

Companies with entrepreneurial capabilities are able to achieve this balancing act. 3M's corporate goal of generating 40 percent of revenues from products introduced within the past four years focuses the organization on developing new products and businesses. The company's famous 15 percent rule, which has been copied by many companies, gives employees the time to pursue novel ideas. Its long-standing commitment to helping customers solve problems helps ensure that ideas for new businesses are customer focused. The company's celebration of employees who have created successful new businesses helps to reinforce the norm of entrepreneurship and risk taking. Similarly, there is a norm that failure should not be punished but viewed as a learning experience.

■ **Capabilities in Organizational Design** One of the main sources of entrepreneurial capabilities, as well as an important determinant of whether a company can obtain competencies at the functional level, is organizational design, a company's ability to create a structure, culture, and control systems that motivate and coordinate employees. The degree of autonomy the structure of an organization provides its managers, the kinds of norms and values present in its culture, and even the design of its headquarters buildings to encourage the free flow of ideas are important determinants of a diversified company's ability to reap the gains from its multibusiness model. Effective organizational structure and controls create incentives that encourage business unit (divisional) managers to maximize the efficiency and effectiveness of their units. Moreover, a good organizational design helps prevent the inertia that afflicts so many organizations, when employees become so absorbed in protecting their company's competitive position in existing markets that they lose sight of new or improved ways to do business or changing industry boundaries.

The last three chapters of this book take an in-depth look at these issues. To succeed in diversification, a company must have the structure and culture that enable it to rapidly change the way it motivates and coordinates its resources and capabilities. Companies that seem to be successful at managing their structures and cultures to further the diversification process share a number of features.[10] First, their different business units tend to be placed into self-contained divisions. Second, these business units tend to be managed by senior executives in a decentralized fashion. Rather than get involved in day-to-day operations, they set challenging financial goals for each unit, probe the managers of each unit about their strategies for attaining these goals, monitor their performance, and hold them accountable for that performance. Third, these internal monitoring and control mechanisms are linked with incentive pay systems that reward business unit managers who attain or surpass performance goals. Achieving these three things, and aligning a company's structure with its strategy, is a complex, never-ending task in a changing environment, and only top managers with superior organizational design skills can do it.

■ **Superior Strategic Capabilities** For diversification to increase profitability, a company's top managers must have superior strategic capabilities. Specifically, they must have certain intangible governance skills to manage different business units in a way that enables those units to perform better than they would if they were independent companies.[11] Simply put, the business of top management in the diversified company is to manage the managers of business units. This is not an easy thing to do well; governance skills are a rare and valuable capability. However, certain senior executives seem to have developed a skill for managing businesses and pushing the heads of business units to achieve superior performance. Examples include Jack Welch at General Electric, Bill Gates and Steve Ballmer at Microsoft, and George David of UTC, profiled in the *Opening Case.*

A flair for entrepreneurship is often found in top managers who have developed superior strategic capabilities or governance skills. As important, if not more so, is the ability to recognize ways to enhance the performance of individual managers, functions, and business units. Jack Welch, for example, was a master in improving the skills of his managers across the board in GE. He created organization-wide management development programs focusing on change management and created procedures to make middle managers question top management actions. At the functional and business levels, he instituted many of the techniques discussed in Chapter 4 to promote superior efficiency and quality, such as the Six Sigma quality improvement methodology, and he pushed hard to make sure that business unit managers used these techniques to improve the efficiency of their operations.

An especially important governance skill in the diversified company is the ability to diagnose the real source of performance problems in an underperforming business unit and take the appropriate steps to fix those problems, whether by pushing the top managers of the unit to take certain strategic actions or by replacing top managers with individuals better able to fix the problems. Top managers who have such governance skills tend to be very good at probing business unit managers for information and helping them think through strategic problems.

Related to this skill, an important way in which a diversified company can increase its profitability is by recognizing inefficient and poorly managed companies, acquiring them, and then restructuring them to improve their performance. The acquired company does not have to be in the same industry as the acquiring company for the strategy to work; thus, the strategy often leads to diversification. Improvements in the performance of the acquired company can come from a number of sources. First, the acquiring company usually replaces the top managers of the acquired company with a more aggressive management team. Second, the new managers of the acquired business are encouraged to sell off any unproductive assets, such as executive jets and elaborate corporate headquarters, and to reduce staffing levels. Third, the new management team is encouraged to intervene in the operations of the acquired business to seek out ways to improve the unit's efficiency, quality, innovativeness, and customer responsiveness. Fourth, to motivate the new management team and other employees of the acquired unit to undertake such actions, increases in their pay are typically linked to increases in the performance of the acquired unit. In addition, the acquiring company often establishes performance goals for the acquired company that cannot be met without significant improvements in operating efficiency. It also makes the new top managers aware that failure to achieve performance improvements consistent with these goals within a given amount of time will probably result in their being replaced.

Thus, the system of rewards and sanctions established by the acquiring company gives the new managers of the acquired unit strong incentives to look for ways to improve the performance of the unit under their charge. UTC has pursued the strategy of acquiring and restructuring underperforming companies with considerable success.

Two Types of Diversification

In the last section we discussed six principal ways in which companies can use diversification to implant their business models and strategies in other industries to increase their long-run profitability. It is possible to differentiate between two types of diversification based on their ability to realize these benefits: related diversification and unrelated diversification.[12]

■ Related Diversification

Related diversification is the strategy of establishing a business unit in a new industry that is *related* to a company's existing business units by some form of linkage or commonality between one or more components of each business unit's value chain. The goal is to obtain the benefits from transferring and leveraging distinctive competencies, sharing resources, and bundling products. These linkages are most commonly formed to take advantage of business models that have strong technological, manufacturing, marketing, and sales commonalities, meaning that the business model can be successfully "tweaked" to provide a competitive advantage in a new industry. Figure 10.4 provides some examples of the different kinds of linkages.

As an additional advantage, the related diversification process allows a company to use any general organizational competencies it possesses to increase overall business unit performance, such as by creating a culture that encourages entrepreneurship across units. The diversification of Philip Morris into the brewing industry with the acquisition of Miller Brewing is an example of related diversification because there are marketing and sales commonalities between the brewing and tobacco businesses: both are mass market consumer product businesses in which competitive success depends on brand-positioning skills and whose products can be sold and distributed together. 3M is another example of a company that has long pursued a strategy of related diversification. In 3M's case, the commonality is in the development of a set of core technologies, which are then shared among different kinds of business units. Improvements in technologies are also shared, and, as we discussed earlier, 3M

FIGURE 10.4

Commonalities Between the Value Chains of Three Business Units

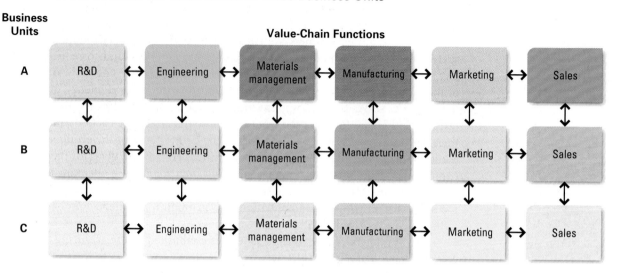

has a general organizational competency in promoting cross-unit learning. Another example of related diversification is given in Strategy in Action 10.2, which looks at Intel's recent diversification into the communications chip business and the problems surrounding it.

■ **Unrelated Diversification**

The multibusiness model underlying **unrelated diversification** aims to enhance profits by implanting general organizational competencies in new business units, and perhaps to capture the benefits of multipoint competition. Companies pursuing a strategy of unrelated diversification have no intention of transferring or leveraging competencies between business units; their focus is on developing a multibusiness model that will strengthen the business model of each individual business unit.

UTC provides an excellent example of a company pursuing unrelated diversification. Its CEO George David uses all three kinds of general organizational competencies to improve the profitability of UTC's business units. First, UTC focuses only on basic manufacturing businesses where it can apply its ACE quality improvement tools. Then, it uses these ACE skills to encourage and build an entrepreneurial focus in its business units. Managers at all levels are charged with finding ways to increase innovation, and UTC spends $2.5 billion on R&D. Second, David makes acquisitions to strengthen an existing business unit's competitive position, such as when he combined Sunderstrand with Hamilton and combined their distinctive competencies. Then he practices good organizational design skills by restructuring the acquired company and streamlining its activities to reduce its cost structure; he also has a companywide incentive system in place to reward high-performing business units. Finally, from a strategic point of view, he only wants UTC to be in businesses that have pricing power and are not at the mercy of powerful buyers and suppliers, and he divests businesses that are in a weak competitive position. He also continually monitors the performance of UTC's business units through the ACE system and looks for ways to increase their performance.

Strategy in Action   10.2

Related Diversification at Intel

Although Intel has had a small presence in the communications chip business since the 1980s, the company focused most of its attention and resources on the booming business of making microprocessors for personal computers. According to managers at Intel, "feeding the processor monster" was a way to boost profitability, and the company invested all its substantial free cash flows into designing new generations of ever more powerful microprocessors and building the large-scale, and expensive, fabrication facilities necessary to manufacture them efficiently. The decision seemed logical: Intel had the dominant position in the microprocessor market, its primary customers (PC makers like Dell) were growing by leaps and bounds, and demand for its microprocessors was soaring. Indeed, if Intel had not made these investments to strengthen its core business model, it would have opened the door to competitors such as AMD.

This strategy of staying in a single business changed at a contentious strategy meeting of Intel's top executives in 1996. Intel's executives came away from that meeting with two important insights. First, the PC industry would approach market saturation in the early 2000s. This meant that the growth in demand for Intel's microprocessors would slow down. To maintain its profit growth, Intel needed to find a new "growth driver." Second, its executives decided that because of the growing use of the Internet, "communications was going to be the driver for everything in the future, that all computing was connected computing, and that connectivity had as important and strategic a role to play as the microprocessor did." Moreover, it was clear that demand for products of the communications industry such as communications network gear, which needed advanced communications chips, was accelerating rapidly.

Intel's executives decided that they could boost the company's ROIC by diverting some cash flow from new PC chip development and using Intel's competencies to build a new business model in the rapidly growing communications chip industry. This was a different industry: the production technology was different, the customers were different, and the competitors were different. Intel believed, however, that because the communications chip industry was related to the microprocessor industry, it could obtain a competitive advantage by transferring its leading-edge PC microprocessor technology, as well as its

manufacturing and marketing capabilities, to the communications chip industry.

Once the decision was made to enter the communications chip industry on a significant scale, Intel had to decide how best to execute the strategy. The company's managers decided that the only way they could get big enough fast enough to gain scale economies and establish a sustainable competitive advantage in this booming market was for the company to buy the required technology, fabrication facilities, and sales force. It could then improve the performance of the acquired businesses by transferring its competencies to them. So Intel went on an acquisition binge. Between January 1997 and June 2001, it made eighteen major acquisitions of companies in the communications chip industry for a combined total of $8 billion. As a result of these acquisitions, by mid 2001 Intel became the fourth largest global company in the communications chip industry, behind only Lucent, Motorola, and Texas Instruments, with revenues of $2.5 billion. Unfortunately, Intel and all these other companies were hard hit by the slump in global demand for telecommunications equipment in the early 2000s.

Then, to make matters worse, Intel's push into communications chips had launched it on the road to designing chips that were faster and faster because speed was seen as the most vital ingredient in communication. By 2003, however, it was clear that what customers wanted was chips that could support high bandwidth and could process vast amounts of information *simultaneously*. Both these capabilities are needed for high-quality music, movie viewing, and other multimedia applications such as video telephone conferencing. Intel lacked such a chip, but in the meantime Advanced Micro Devices (AMD), its major competitor, had perceived the need to develop it. Suddenly Intel found itself at a competitive disadvantage. In 2004, it announced plans to abandon its high-speed communications chips to focus on those that could support the bandwidth needed for sophisticated multimedia applications. Intel had made the mistake of not focusing on what PC users and digital content providers needed in next-generation chips. It was so concerned with the need to increase speed that it entered a new industry assuming there was a commonality based on speed, but it was not there. Intel should have focused on customer needs, not its own distinctive competencies.[b]

In sum, the multibusiness model in unrelated diversification is primarily based on using general organizational competencies to increase the profitability of each business unit in the diversified company. By contrast, the multibusiness model in related diversification is based on transferring and leveraging competencies, sharing resources, and bundling products. In addition, companies that pursue related diversification are far more likely to encounter each other in different industries than are those pursuing unrelated diversification. Thus, they are far more likely to use multipoint competition to manage industry rivalry.

Disadvantages and Limits of Diversification

As we have discussed, many companies, such as 3M, UTC, Intel, and GE, have reaped enormous advantages from pursuing a strategy of diversification and have consistently increased their profitability over time. Nevertheless, many companies that have pursued diversification have enjoyed far less success, and for some companies diversification has actually dissipated or reduced their profitability. As a result, over the last few decades many companies have *de-diversified* and sold off their constituent businesses to focus on their core business. Clearly, there must be important disadvantages associated with diversification that can make it a dangerous strategy to pursue over time. Three conditions can make diversification disadvantageous: changing industry- and firm-specific conditions, diversification for the wrong reasons, and the increasing bureaucratic costs of extensive diversification.

■ Changing Industry- and Firm-Specific Conditions

Diversification is a complex strategy to pursue, and top managers must have the entrepreneurial ability to sense profitable new opportunities and the ability to implement the strategies needed to make diversification pay off. Over time, however, a company's top management team changes: sometimes the most able executives join other companies and become their CEOs, and sometimes successful CEOs decide to retire or step down. When they leave, these managers often take their vision with them, and their successors may lack the skills or commitment needed to implement and manage diversification successfully over time. Thus, the multibusiness model loses its ability to create value, and, as we discuss below, the cost structure of the diversified company often starts to increase, swallowing up the gains the strategy produces.

Over time, too, the environment can change rapidly and in unpredictable ways. We discuss earlier how blurring industry boundaries can destroy the source of a company's competitive advantage. If this happens in its core business, then clearly benefits from transferring or leveraging distinctive competencies will disappear and a company will now be saddled with a collection of businesses that have all become poor performers in their respective industries. When the computer industry changed, for example, and PCs and servers became the dominant product, IBM was left with unprofitable operations in the mainframe hardware and software industries that almost led to its bankruptcy. Thus one major problem with diversification is that the future success of this strategy is hard to predict; therefore, if a company is to profit from it over time, managers should be as willing to divest businesses as they are to acquire them. Unfortunately, research suggests that managers do not behave in this way.

■ Diversification for the Wrong Reasons

As we have discussed, different multibusiness models justify a company pursuing either related or unrelated diversification. If a company pursues diversification, its managers must have a clear vision of how their entry into new industries will allow them to create more value. Over time, however, as the profitability of their diversification strategy falls for reasons just noted, managers, rather than divesting their businesses, often use false or mistaken justifications for keeping their collection of businesses together. There are many famous historical examples of this behavior.

For example, one justification for diversification that once was widely used was that diversification could be used to obtain the benefits of risk pooling. Many CEOs argued that diversification, particularly unrelated diversification into industries that have different business cycles so that their revenues rise and fall in different cycles, would allow them to create a more stable companywide income stream over time—one that avoids the sharp swings up and down that can make the value of a company's stock volatile and unpredictable. An example of risk pooling might be the diversification by U.S. Steel into the oil and gas industry in an attempt to offset the adverse effects of cyclical downturns in the steel industry. According to advocates of risk pooling, a more stable income stream reduces the risk of bankruptcy and is in the best interests of the company's stockholders.

This simple argument ignores two facts. First, stockholders can easily eliminate the risks inherent in holding an individual stock by diversifying their own portfolios, and they can do so at a much lower cost than the company can. Thus, far from being in the best interests of stockholders, attempts to pool risks through diversification represent an unproductive use of resources; instead, profits should be returned to shareholders in the form of increased dividends. Second, research on this topic suggests that corporate diversification is not an effective way to pool risks because the business cycles of different industries are *inherently difficult to predict* and a diversified company might just find that a general economic downturn hits all its industries simultaneously. If this happens, the company's profitability will plunge.[13]

When the core business is in trouble, another mistaken justification for diversification is that the new industries will rescue it. An example of a company that made this mistake is Kodak. In the 1980s, increased competition from low-cost Japanese competitors like Fuji, combined with the beginnings of the digital revolution, led its revenues and profits first to plateau and then to fall. Its managers should have done all they could to reduce its cost structure; instead they took its still huge free cash flow and spent tens of billions of dollars to enter new industries such as health care, biotechnology, and computer hardware in a desperate attempt to find ways to increase profitability.

This was a disaster, because every industry Kodak entered was populated by strong companies such as 3M, Canon, and Xerox, and Kodak's corporate managers lacked any general competencies to give their new business units a competitive advantage. Moreover, the more industries they entered, the greater the range of threats they encountered and the more time they had to spend dealing with these threats. As a result, they could spend much less time improving the performance of their core film business, which continued to decline. In reality, Kodak's diversification was just for growth itself, but *growth does not create value*; growth is just the byproduct, not the objective, of a diversification strategy. However, in desperation companies diversify for reasons of growth alone rather than to gain any well-thought-out strategic advantage.

A large number of academic studies suggest that *extensive* diversification tends to reduce rather than improve company profitability.[14] For example, in a study that looked at the diversification of thirty-three major U.S. corporations over thirty-five years, Michael Porter observed that the track record of corporate diversification has been poor.[15] Porter found that most of the companies had divested many more diversified acquisitions than they had kept. He and others have concluded that the corporate diversification strategies pursued by most companies can dissipate value instead of creating it.[16]

■ The
Bureaucratic
Costs of
Diversification

A company diversifies to boost its profitability from higher product differentiation or a lower cost structure, but to achieve this it has to invest valuable resources. One reason that diversification often fails to boost profitability is that all too often the *bureaucratic costs* of diversification exceed the value created by the strategy. As we mentioned in the last chapter, **bureaucratic costs** are the costs associated with solving the transaction difficulties that arise between a company's business units, and between business units and corporate headquarters, as the company attempts to obtain the benefits from transferring, sharing, and leveraging competencies. They also include the costs of using general organizational competencies to solve managerial and functional inefficiencies. The level of bureaucratic costs in a diversified organization is a function of two factors: (1) the number of business units in a company's portfolio and (2) the extent to which coordination is required between these different business units to realize the benefits of diversification

■ **Number of Businesses** The greater the number of business units in a company's portfolio, the more difficult it is for corporate managers to remain informed about the complexities of each business. Managers simply do not have the time to assess the business model of each unit. This problem began to occur at GE in the 1970s when its growth-hungry CEO Reg Jones acquired many new businesses. As Jones commented,

> I tried to review each plan [of each business unit] in great detail. This effort took untold hours and placed a tremendous burden on the corporate executive office. After a while I began to realize that no matter how hard we would work, we could not achieve the necessary in-depth understanding of the 40-odd business unit plans.[17]

The inability of top managers in extensively diversified companies to maintain a superior multibusiness model over time may lead them to base important resource allocation decisions on only the most superficial analysis of each business unit's competitive position. Thus, for example, a promising business unit may be starved of investment funds while other business units receive far more cash than they can profitably reinvest in their operations. Furthermore, because they are distant from the day-to-day operations of the business units, corporate managers may find that business unit managers try to hide information on poor performance to save their own jobs. For example, business unit managers might blame poor performance on difficult competitive conditions even when it is the result of their inability to craft a successful business model. One reason that ACE is so effective at UTC is that it is a standardized set of rules and procedures that can be applied easily across all its divisions so that George David and his top managers understand exactly what is happening throughout the company. But when inefficiencies such as the suboptimal allocation of capital within the company and a failure by corporate executives to successfully encourage and reward aggressive profit-seeking behavior by business unit managers become extensive, the time and effort top managers must devote to solve such problems cancel out the value created by diversification.

FIGURE 10.5

Coordination Among
Related Business
Units

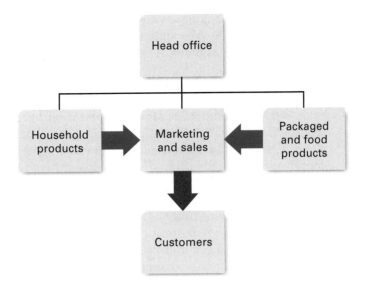

■ **Coordination Among Businesses** The coordination required to realize value from a diversification strategy based on transferring, sharing, or leveraging competencies is a major source of bureaucratic costs. The bureaucratic mechanisms needed to oversee and manage this coordination to reduce managerial inefficiencies, such as cross-business-unit teams and management committees, are one source of these costs. A second source is the costs associated with accurately measuring the performance, and therefore the unique profit contribution, of a business unit that is transferring or sharing resources with another. Consider a company that has two business units, one producing household products (such as liquid soap and laundry detergent) and another producing packaged food products. The products of both units are sold through supermarkets. To lower the costs of value creation, the parent company decides to pool the marketing and sales functions of each business unit using an organizational structure similar to that illustrated in Figure 10.5. The company is organized into three divisions: a household products division, a food products division, and a marketing division.

Although such an arrangement may result in substantial cost savings, it can also give rise to substantial control problems and hence bureaucratic costs. For example, if the performance of the household products business begins to slip, identifying who is to be held accountable—managers in the household products division or managers in the marketing division—may prove difficult. Indeed, each may blame the other for poor performance. Although these kinds of problems can be resolved if corporate management performs an in-depth audit of both divisions, the bureaucratic costs (managers' time and effort) involved in doing so may once again cancel out any value achieved from diversification.

In sum, diversification is the most complex and difficult strategy that a company can pursue. Changing conditions both in the external environment and inside a company can reduce the value creation advantages from pursuing this strategy, either because they rob business units of their competitive advantage or because they increase the bureaucratic costs associated with pursuing this strategy, which then also cancel out its advantages. Thus the existence of bureaucratic costs places a limit on the amount of diversification that can profitably be pursued. It makes sense for a company to diversify only as long as the value created by such a strategy exceeds the bureaucratic costs associated with expanding the boundaries of the organization to incorporate additional business activities.

Choosing a Strategy

■ **Related Versus Unrelated Diversification**

Because related diversification involves more sharing of competencies, one might say it can boost profitability in more ways than unrelated diversification and so is the better diversification strategy. However, some companies, such as UTC, can create as much or more value from pursuing unrelated diversification, so that approach must also have some substantial benefits. An unrelated company does *not* have to achieve coordination between business units, and so it has to cope only with the bureaucratic costs that arise from the number of businesses in its portfolio. In contrast, a related company has to achieve coordination *between* business units if it is to realize the gains that come from utilizing its distinctive competencies. Consequently, it has to cope with the bureaucratic costs that arise *both* from the number of business units in its portfolio *and* from coordination among business units. Thus, although it is true that related diversified companies can create value in more ways than unrelated companies, they also have to bear higher bureaucratic costs in order to do so. These higher costs may cancel out the higher benefits, making the strategy no more profitable than one of unrelated diversification.

How then does a company choose between these strategies? The choice depends on a comparison of the benefits of each strategy against the bureaucratic costs of pursuing it. It pays a company to pursue related diversification when (1) the company's competencies can be applied across a greater number of industries and (2) the company does have superior strategic capabilities that allow it to keep bureaucratic costs under close control—perhaps by encouraging entrepreneurship or by developing a value-creating organizational culture. Using the same logic, it pays a company to pursue unrelated diversification when (1) each business unit's functional competencies have few useful applications across industries but the company's top managers are skilled at raising the profitability of poorly run businesses; and (2) the company's managers have good organizational design skills to build distinctive competencies and keep bureaucratic costs in control and even to reduce them.

■ **The Web of Corporate-Level Strategy**

Finally, it is important to note that while some companies may choose to pursue a strategy of related or unrelated diversification, there is nothing that stops them from pursuing both of these strategies at the same time—*as well as all the other corporate-level strategies we have discussed.* The purpose of corporate-level strategy is to increase long-term profitability. A company should pursue any and all strategies as long as strategic managers have weighed the advantages and disadvantages of those strategies and arrived at a multibusiness model that justifies them. Figure 10.6 shows how Sony has entered into industries that have led it to pursue various strategies.

First, Sony's core business is its electronic consumer products business, which is well known for its generic distinctive competencies of innovation and marketing (it has one of the best-known brand names in the world). To protect the quality of its electronic products, Sony manufactures a high percentage of the component parts for its televisions, DVD players, and so on, and in this sense it has pursued a strategy of backward vertical integration. Sony also engages in forward vertical integration: after having acquired Columbia Pictures and MGM in 2004, it now operates in the movie industry and has opened several Sony stores in exclusive shopping malls. Sony also shared and leveraged its distinctive competencies by developing its own business

FIGURE 10.6

Sony's Web of
Corporate-Level
Strategy

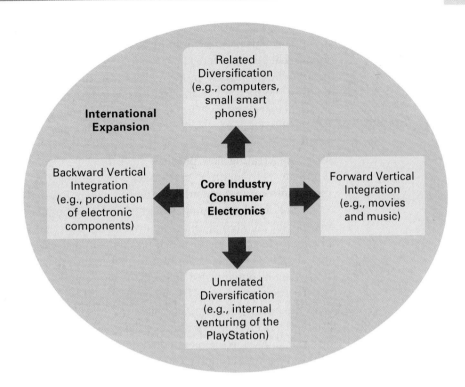

FIGURE 10.6

Sony's Web of Corporate-Level Strategy

units that operate in the computer and smart phone industries, a strategy of related diversification. Finally, in deciding to enter the home videogame industry and developing its PlayStation to compete with Nintendo, it is also pursuing a strategy of unrelated diversification. Today this division contributes more to Sony's total profits than its core electronics business.

While Sony has had enormous success pursuing all these strategies in the past, in the last few years its profitability has fallen. Analysts claim that its multibusiness model, which led it to diversify extensively and focus on innovating high-quality products, led it to neglect its cost structure. They also claim that its strategy of giving each business unit great autonomy has led each unit to pursue its own goals at the expense of the company's "multibusiness model." Sony's escalating bureaucratic costs have been draining its profitability and slowing innovation, which has allowed competitors like Samsung to catch up and even overtake it in areas like cell phones and flat-screen LCDs. Sony has been responding to these problems: it has taken major steps to reduce bureaucratic costs, speed innovation, and lower its cost structure, including exiting industries like PDAs and videocassette recorders. The next few years will show whether the company has been able to better implement its corporate strategies to improve its profitability.

Entry Strategy: Internal New Ventures

Having discussed all the corporate-level strategies managers can use to formulate the multibusiness model, we can examine the three main strategies that can be used to implement it: internal new ventures, acquisitions, and joint ventures. In this section we look at pros and cons of using internal new ventures. In the following sections we look at acquisitions and joint ventures.

■ The Attractions of Internal New Venturing

Internal new venturing is typically used to implement corporate-level strategies when a company possesses one or more generic distinctive competencies in its core business model that can be leveraged or recombined to enter a new industry. As a rule, companies whose business model is based on using their technology to innovate new kinds of products for related markets or industries tend to favor internal new venturing as an entry strategy. Thus technology-based companies that pursue related diversification, like DuPont, which has created new markets with products such as cellophane, nylon, Freon, and Teflon, tend to use internal new venturing. 3M has a near-legendary knack for creating new products from internally generated ideas that enable it to dominate new markets (see Strategy in Action 10.1). Similarly, Hewlett-Packard moved into computers and peripherals through internal new venturing.

Even if it lacks the competencies required to compete in a new industry, a company may pursue an internal venturing strategy when it is entering a newly emerging or embryonic industry—one in which no company has yet developed the business model that gives it a dominant position in that industry. This was Monsanto's situation in 1979 when it contemplated entering the biotechnology field to produce herbicides and pest-resistant crop seeds. The biotechnology field was young at that time, and there were no incumbent companies focused on applying biotechnology to agricultural products. Accordingly, Monsanto established an internal new venture to enter the industry and develop the required competencies. Indeed, Monsanto's whole venturing strategy was built around creating a business model that would allow it to build competencies ahead of other potential competitors and so establish a strong competitive position in this newly emerging industry.

■ Pitfalls of New Ventures

Despite the popularity of the internal new-venture strategy, there is a high risk of failure. Research suggests that somewhere between 33 and 60 percent of all new products that reach the marketplace do not generate an adequate economic return,[18] and most of these products were the result of internal new ventures. Three reasons are often put forward to explain the relatively high failure rate of internal new ventures: (1) market entry on too small a scale, (2) poor commercialization of the new-venture product, and (3) poor corporate management of the venture process.[19]

■ Scale of Entry

Research suggests that large-scale entry into a new industry is often a critical precondition for the success of a new venture. This means that in the short run large-scale entry requires a substantial capital investment to develop the product—and thus the prospect of substantial losses. But, in the long run, which can be as long as five to twelve years, depending on the industry, such a large investment results in far greater returns than if a company enters on a small scale and limits its investment to reduce its potential losses.[20] Large-scale entrants can more rapidly realize scale economies, build brand loyalty, and gain access to distribution channels, all of which increase the probability of a new venture's success. In contrast, small-scale entrants may find themselves handicapped by high costs due to a lack of scale economies and a lack of market presence that limits their ability to build brand loyalty and gain access to distribution channels. These scale effects are particularly significant when a company is entering an established industry where incumbent companies do possess scale economies, brand loyalty, and access to distribution channels. Now, the new entrant has to make a major investment in order to succeed.

Figure 10.7 plots the relationship between scale of entry and profitability over time for successful small-scale and large-scale ventures. The figure shows that successful

FIGURE 10.7

Scale of Entry and
Profitability

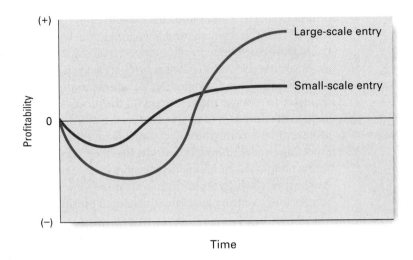

small-scale entry is associated with lower initial losses but that in the long run large-scale entry generates greater returns. However, because of the costs of large-scale entry and the huge potential losses if the venture fails, many companies make the mistake of choosing a small-scale entry strategy, which often means they fail to build the market share necessary for long-term success.

■ **Commercialization** Many internal new ventures are driven by the use of new or high technology to make better products, but to be commercially successful the products must be developed with customer requirements in mind. Many internal new ventures fail when a company ignores the needs of customers in a market and instead becomes blinded by the technological possibilities of a new product.[21] Thus, a new venture may fail because it is marketing a product based on a technology for which there is no demand, or because the company fails to commercialize or position the product correctly in the market.

For example, consider the desktop computer marketed by NeXT, the company started by the founder of Apple, Steven Jobs. The NeXT system failed to gain market share because the computer incorporated an array of expensive technologies that consumers simply did not want, such as optical disk drives and hi-fidelity sound. The optical disk drives, in particular, turned off customers because they made it tough to switch work from a PC with a floppy drive to a NeXT machine with an optical drive. In other words, NeXT failed because its founder was so dazzled by leading-edge technology that he ignored customer needs. However, Jobs redeemed himself when he successfully commercialized Apple's iPod, which dominated the MP3 player market in 2004.

■ **Poor Implementation** Managing the new-venture process raises difficult organization issues.[22] For example, one common mistake some companies make is to try to increase their chance of making a successful product by establishing many different internal new-venture projects at the same time. This "shotgun approach" of spreading the risks between projects places great demands on a company's cash flow and can result in the best ventures being starved of the cash they need to succeed.[23] Another common mistake is the failure of corporate managers to carefully develop upfront all the aspects of the business model that will be needed for the new-venture project to succeed—and to include scientists in the model-building process. Taking a team of research scientists and giving them the resources they need to do research in their favorite field may produce novel results, but these results may have little strategic or commercial value. Managers must clarify how and why the project will lead to a product that has a competitive advantage and establish strategic objectives and a timetable to manage the venture until the product reaches the market. Failure to anticipate the time and costs involved in the new-venture process constitutes a further mistake. Many companies have unrealistic expectations regarding the time frame, expecting profits to flow in quickly. Research suggests that some companies operate with a philosophy of killing new businesses if they do not turn a profit by the end of the third year, which is clearly an unrealistic view given that it can take five to twelve years before a venture generates substantial profits.

■ Guidelines for Successful Internal New Venturing

To avoid these pitfalls, a company should adopt a well-thought-out, structured approach to manage internal new venturing. New venturing begins with R&D, *exploratory research* to advance basic science and technology (the "R" in R&D), and *development research* to find and refine the commercial applications for a technology (the "D" in R&D). Companies with a strong track record of internal new venturing excel at both kinds of R&D: they help to advance basic science and then they find commercial applications for it.[24] To advance basic science, it is important for companies to (1) have strong links with universities, where much of the scientific knowledge that underlies new technologies is discovered, and (2) to make sure that significant research funds are under the control of researchers who can pursue "blue-sky" projects that might ultimately yield unexpected and commercially valuable technologies and products. For example, 3M has close links with several universities, including the University of Minnesota in its hometown, and funds basic research at those universities. And, as already mentioned, 3M's researchers spend 15 percent of their time on projects of their own choosing, many of which are basic research projects.

However, if the pursuit of basic research is all that a company does well, it will probably generate few successful commercial ventures. To translate good science into good products, it is critical that a major proportion of R&D funding be directed toward commercial ventures. Companies can take a number of steps to ensure that this happens. First, many companies place much of the funding for research in the hands of business unit managers who are responsible for narrowing down and then selecting the small number of research projects they believe have the best chance of a significant commercial payoff. Second, to make effective use of its R&D skills, a company's top managers must continually spell out the strategic objectives in its business model and communicate them clearly to scientists and engineers. Research must be in the pursuit of strategic goals.[25] For example, one of the biggest research projects at Microsoft has been language recognition software because a central objective of the company is to make computers easy to use. Researchers reason that if computers can understand spoken language, commands can be inputted by voice rather than through a keyboard, thus making computers easier to use and strengthening the Windows platform.

A company must also foster close links between R&D and marketing to increase the probability of a new product's commercial success, for this is the best way to ensure that research projects address the needs of the market. Also, a company should foster close links between R&D and manufacturing to ensure that it has the ability to make a proposed new product. Many companies successfully integrate the activities of different functions by creating cross-functional project teams to oversee the development of new products, from their inception to their market introduction. This approach can significantly reduce the time this process takes. For example, while R&D is working on the design, manufacturing is setting up facilities and is developing a campaign to show customers how much the new product will benefit them.

Finally, because large-scale entry often leads to greater long-term profits, a company can promote the success of internal new venturing by "thinking big." Well in advance, a company should construct efficient-scale manufacturing facilities and establish a large marketing program to develop a campaign for building a market presence and brand loyalty quickly. Corporate managers should not panic; they should accept that there will be initial losses and realize that, as long as market share is expanding, the product will eventually succeed.

Entry Strategy: Acquisitions

In Chapter 9 we explain that acquisitions are the main vehicle that companies use to implement a horizontal integration strategy, as well as vertical integration and diversification. In the *Opening Case*, we saw how UTC acquires new profitable businesses to pursue unrelated diversification. However, Chapter 9 also discusses how acquisitions may fail, and so it is necessary to understand both the benefits and risks associated with using acquisitions to implement a corporate-level strategy.

■ The Attractions of Acquisitions

Acquisitions are the principal strategy used to implement horizontal integration. With vertical integration or diversification, acquisitions are used when a company lacks the distinctive competencies to compete in an industry and therefore uses its capital to purchase an established company that has those competencies. A company is particularly likely to use acquisitions when it needs to move fast to establish a presence in an industry. Entering a new industry through internal venturing is a relatively slow process; acquisition is a much quicker way for a company to establish a significant market presence. A company can purchase a leading company with a strong competitive position in months rather than spend years building up a market leadership position through internal venturing. Thus, when speed is important, acquisition is the favored entry mode. Intel, for example, used acquisitions to build its communications chip business because it sensed that the market was developing very quickly and it would take too long to develop the required competencies internally (see Strategy in Action 10.2).

In addition, acquisitions are often perceived as somewhat less risky than internal new ventures, primarily because they involve less commercial uncertainty. Because of the risks associated with an internal new venture, it is difficult to predict its future profitability and cash flows. In contrast, when a company makes an acquisition it is acquiring a company with a reputation whose market share and profitability can be easily evaluated.

Finally, acquisitions are an attractive way to enter an industry that is protected by high barriers to entry. Recall from Chapter 2 that barriers to entry arise from factors associated with product differentiation (brand loyalty), absolute cost advantages, and economies of scale. When these barriers are substantial, a company may find it very difficult to enter an industry through internal new venturing because it will have to construct large-scale manufacturing facilities and invest in a massive advertising campaign to establish brand loyalty—difficult goals that require large capital expenditures. In contrast, if a company acquires an established company in the industry, it can circumvent most entry barriers because it has acquired a market leader that already has substantial scale economies and brand loyalty. In general, the greater the barriers to entry, the more likely it is that acquisitions will be the favored entry mode.

■ Acquisition Pitfalls

For these reasons, acquisitions have long been a popular vehicle for executing corporate-level strategies. However, despite this popularity, there is ample evidence that many acquisitions fail to add value for the acquiring company and, indeed, often end up dissipating value. For example, a study by Mercer Management Consulting looked at 150 acquisitions worth more than $500 million each that were undertaken between January 1990 and July 1995.[26] The Mercer study concluded that 50 percent of these acquisitions ended up eroding, or substantially eroding, shareholder value, and another 33 percent created only marginal returns. Only 17 percent of these acquisitions were judged to be successful. Similarly, a study by KPMG, an accounting and management consulting company, looked at 700 large acquisitions between 1996 and 1998 and found that although some 30 percent of these actually created value for the acquiring company, 31 percent destroyed value, and the remainder had little impact.[27]

More generally, a wealth of evidence from academic research suggests that many acquisitions fail to realize their anticipated benefits.[28] In a major study of the post-acquisition performance of acquired companies, David Ravenscraft and Mike Scherer concluded that the profitability and market shares of acquired companies often declined after acquisition.[29] They also noted that a smaller but substantial subset of acquired companies experienced traumatic difficulties that ultimately led to their being sold off by the acquiring company. This evidence suggests that many acquisitions destroy rather than create value.

Acquisitions may fail to create value for four reasons: (1) companies often experience difficulties when trying to integrate different organizational structures and cultures, (2) companies overestimate the potential economic benefits from an acquisition, (3) acquisitions tend to be very expensive, and (4) companies often do not adequately screen their acquisition targets.

■ Integrating the Acquired Company

Once an acquisition has been made, the acquiring company has to integrate the acquired company and combine in with its own organizational structure and culture. Integration involves the adoption of common management and financial control systems, the joining together of operations from the acquired and the acquiring company, the establishment of bureaucratic mechanisms to share information and personnel, and the need to create a common culture. Experience has shown that many problems can occur as companies attempt to integrate their activities.

After an acquisition, many acquired companies experience high management turnover because their employees do not like the acquiring company's way of operating—its structure and culture.[30] Research suggests that the loss of management talent and expertise, to say nothing of the damage from constant tension between the businesses, can materially harm the performance of the acquired unit.[31] Strategy in Action 10.3 describes what happened at Boston Co. after it was acquired by Mellon Bank.

■ Overestimating Economic Benefits

Even when companies find it easy to integrate their activities, they often overestimate the potential for creating value by joining together different businesses. They overestimate the competitive advantages that can be derived from the acquisition and so pay more for the target company than it is worth. Richard Roll has attributed this tendency to hubris on the part of top management. According to Roll, top managers typically overestimate their ability to create value from an acquisition, primarily because rising to the top of a corporation has given them an exaggerated sense of their own capabilities.[32] Coca-Cola's

Strategy in Action 10.3

Postacquisition Problems at Mellon Bank

In the search for a profitable way to expand his company's business, Frank Cahouet, the CEO of Philadelphia-based Mellon Bank, decided to reduce the large swings in Mellon's earnings because of changes in interest rates by diversifying into financial services to gain access to a steady flow of fee-based income from money management operations. As part of this strategy, he acquired Boston Co. for $1.45 billion. Boston is a high-profile money management company that manages investments for major institutional clients, such as state and corporate pension funds. Mellon followed up its Boston acquisition with the acquisition of mutual fund provider Dreyfus Corp., for $1.7 billion. As a result, almost half of Mellon's income was now generated from fee-based financial services.

Problems at Boston Co. began to surface soon after the Mellon acquisition. From the beginning there was a clash of corporate cultures. At Mellon, many managers arrived at their mundane offices by 7 A.M. and put in twelve-hour days for modest pay by banking industry standards. They were also accustomed to Frank Cahouet's management style, which emphasized cost containment and frugality. Boston Co. managers also put in twelve-hour days, but they expected considerable autonomy, flexible work schedules, high pay, ample perks, and large performance bonuses. In most years, the top twenty executives at Boston earned between $750,000 and $1 million each. Mellon executives who visited the Boston Co. unit were dumbstruck by its country club atmosphere and opulence. In its move to streamline Boston, Mellon insisted that Boston cut expenses and introduced new regulations for restricting travel, entertainment, and perks.

Things started to go wrong when the Wisconsin state pension fund complained to Mellon of lower returns on a portfolio run by Boston Co. Mellon was forced to liquidate the portfolio and take a $130 million charge against earnings; it also fired the responsible portfolio manager, claiming that this manager was making "unauthorized trades." At Boston Co., however, many managers saw Mellon's action as violating the guarantees of operating autonomy that it had given Boston at the time of the acquisition. They blamed Mellon for prematurely liquidating a portfolio whose strategy, they claimed, Mellon executives had approved and that, moreover, could still prove a winner if interest rates fell (which they subsequently did).

Infuriated by Mellon's interference, seven of Boston Co.'s asset unit managers, including the unit's CEO, Desmond Heathwood, proposed a management buyout to Mellon. This unit was one of the gems in Boston's crown, with over $26 billion in assets under management. Heathwood had been openly disdainful of Mellon's bankers, believing that they were out of their league in the investment business. Mellon rejected the buyout proposal, and Heathwood promptly left to start his own investment management company. A few days later, Mellon asked employees at Boston to sign employment contracts that limited their ability to leave and work for Heathwood's competing business. Thirteen senior employees refused to sign and then quit to join Heathwood's new money management operation.

The defection of Heathwood and his colleagues was followed by a series of high-profile client defections. The Arizona State Retirement System, for example, pulled $1 billion out of Mellon and transferred it to Heathwood's firm, and the Fresno County Retirement System transferred $400 million in assets over to Heathwood. As one client stated, "We have a relationship with the Boston Co. that goes back over 30 years, and the people who worked on the account are the people who left—so we left too."

Reflecting on the episode, Frank Cahouet noted, "We've clearly been hurt. . . . But this episode is very manageable. We are not going to lose our momentum." Others were not so sure. In this incident, they saw yet another example of how difficult it can be to merge two divergent corporate cultures and how the management turnover that results from such attempts can deal a serious blow to any attempt to create value out of an acquisition.[c]

acquisition of a number of medium-sized wine-making companies illustrates this situation. Reasoning that a beverage is a beverage, Coca-Cola thought it would be able to use its distinctive competence in marketing to dominate the U.S. wine industry. But after buying three wine companies and enduring seven years of marginal profits, Coca-Cola finally conceded that wine and soft drinks are very different products, with different kinds of appeal, pricing systems, and distribution networks. It subsequently sold the wine operations to Joseph E. Seagram & Sons at a substantial loss when adjusted for inflation.[33]

■ **The Expense of Acquisitions** Perhaps the most important reason for the failure of acquisitions is that the acquisition of companies whose stock is publicly traded tends to be very expensive—and the expense of the acquisition cancels out the prospective value-creating gains from the acquisition described earlier. One reason is that the management of the target company is not likely to agree to an acquisition unless there is a substantial premium over its current market value. Another reason is that the stockholders of the acquired company are unlikely to sell their stock unless they are paid a significant premium over its current market value—and premiums tend to run *25 to 50 percent over a company's stock price prior to a takeover bid.* Therefore, the acquiring company must be able to increase the value of the acquired company after it has been integrated by at least the same amount to make the acquisition pay, a tall order. This is a major reason why acquisitions are frequently unprofitable for the acquiring company.

The problem for the acquiring company is that the stock price of the acquisition target gets bid up enormously during the acquisition process. This frequently occurs in the case of a contested bidding contest where two or more companies simultaneously bid to acquire the target company. In addition, when many acquisitions are happening in a particular sector or industry, the price of *potential* target companies gets bid up by investors who speculate that a bid for these companies will be made at some future point, which further increases the cost of making acquisitions. This happened in the telecommunications sector when, to make sure they could meet the needs of customers who were demanding leading-edge equipment, many large companies went on acquisition binges. JDS Uniphase, Cisco Systems, Nortel, Corning, and Lucent all raced each other to buy up smaller companies that were developing promising new telecommunications equipment. The result was that stock prices for these companies got bid up by investors. When the telecommunications boom turned to bust, the acquiring companies found that they had vastly overpaid for their acquisitions and had to take large accounting write-downs. In 2001, Nortel Networks wrote down $12.3 billion in goodwill on its balance sheet to reflect a reduction in the value of the assets it had acquired during the boom. Another telecom equipment supplier, Corning, wrote down $4.8 billion, and JDS Uniphase wrote down a staggering *$40 billion.*

■ **Inadequate Preacquisition Screening** Obviously, as these enormous losses suggest, many companies do a poor job of evaluating the value-creating potential of potential acquisitions. After researching acquisitions made by twenty different companies, a study by Philippe Haspeslagh and David Jemison came to the conclusion that one reason for acquisitions failure is management's inadequate attention to preacquisition screening.[34] They found that many companies decide to acquire other firms without thoroughly analyzing the potential benefits and costs. After the acquisition has been completed, many acquiring companies discover that, instead of buying a well-run business, they have purchased a troubled organization. Moreover, they often have to take on an enormous amount of debt to fund these acquisitions, and they frequently are unable to pay it once the weaknesses of the acquired company's business model become clear.

■ Guidelines for
Successful
Acquisition

To avoid pitfalls and make successful acquisitions, companies need to take a structured approach to purchasing companies based on four components: (1) target identification and preacquisition screening, (2) bidding strategy, (3) integration, and (4) learning from experience.[35]

■ Identification and Screening

Thorough preacquisition screening increases a company's knowledge about a potential takeover target and lessens the risk of purchasing a potential problem business—one with a weak business model. It also leads to a more realistic assessment of the problems involved in executing a particular acquisition so that a company can plan how to integrate the new business and blend the organizational structures and cultures. The screening process should begin with a detailed assessment of the strategic rationale for making the acquisition, an identification of the kind of company that would make an ideal acquisition candidate, and a thorough analysis of the strengths and weaknesses of its business model by comparing it to other possible acquisition targets.

Indeed, an acquiring company should scan a target population of potential acquisition candidates and evaluate each according to a detailed set of criteria, focusing on (1) its financial position, (2) its distinctive competencies and competitive advantage, (3) the changing industry boundaries, (4) its management capabilities, and (5) its corporate culture. Such an evaluation will help the company identify the strengths and weaknesses of each target and the potential economies of scale and scope between the acquiring and the acquired companies. It will also help it to recognize potential integration problems and the problems that might exist when it is necessary to integrate the corporate cultures of the acquiring and the acquired companies. In 2004, for example, Microsoft and SAP, the world's leading provider of enterprise resource planning software, sat down together to discuss a possible acquisition by Microsoft. Both companies decided that even though there was a strong strategic rationale for a merger—together they would dominate the global computing market for most large global companies—the problems of creating an organizational structure that could successfully integrate their hundreds of thousands of employees throughout the world and blend two very different cultures were insurmountable.

Once a company has reduced the list of potential acquisition candidates to the most favored one or two, it needs to contact expert third parties, such as investment bankers like Goldman Sachs and Merrill Lynch, that may be able to provide valuable insights about the attractiveness of the potential acquisition and that will also handle the many issues surrounding the acquisition, such as the process of establishing the bidding strategy for acquiring the company's stock.

■ Bidding Strategy

The objective of bidding strategy is to reduce the price that a company must pay for the target company. The most effective way a company can acquire another is to make a friendly takeover bid, which means the two companies work out an amicable way to merge the two companies that satisfies the needs of stockholders and top managers. A friendly takeover helps prevent speculators from bidding up stock prices. By contrast, in a hostile bid, such as the one between Oracle and PeopleSoft, the price of the target company often gets bid up by speculators who expect that the offer price will be raised by the acquirer or that another company, sometimes called a *white knight*, might come in with a counteroffer more favorable to the management of the target company.

Another essential element of a good bidding strategy is timing. For example, Hanson PLC, one of the most successful companies to pursue unrelated diversification, searched for essentially sound companies suffering from short-term problems due to cyclical industry factors or one underperforming division. Such companies are typically undervalued by the stock market and so can be acquired without the standard 25 to 50 percent stock premium. With good timing, a company can make a bargain purchase. UTC also seems to follow this practice: it buys essentially sound manufacturing companies that are underperforming their peers because of short-term problems and then uses its ACE business processes to build their distinctive competencies and so establish a competitive business model.

■ **Integration** Despite good screening and bidding, an acquisition will fail unless the acquiring company possesses the essential organizational design skills needed to integrate the acquired company into its operations and so quickly develop a viable multibusiness model. Integration should center on the source of the potential strategic advantages of the acquisition—for instance, opportunities to share marketing, manufacturing, logistics, R&D, financial, or management resources. Integration should also involve steps to eliminate any duplication of facilities or functions. In addition, any unwanted business units of the acquired company should be divested.

■ **Learning from Experience** Research suggests that although many acquisitions do fail to create value for the acquiring company, companies that acquire many companies over time—such as UTC—become expert in this process and so can generate significant value from their acquisitions.[36] One reason may be that they learn from their experience and develop a "playbook" of how to execute an acquisition most efficiently and effectively. Tyco, profiled in the *Closing Case*, has a playbook that includes not making hostile acquisitions, auditing the accounts of the target company in detail, acquiring companies that will help Tyco achieve critical mass in an industry, moving quickly to realize cost savings after an acquisition, promoting managers one or two layers down to lead the newly acquired entity, and introducing profit-based incentive pay systems in the acquired unit. UTC's playbook includes only buying manufacturing companies where it can apply its ACE skills, insisting that managers from the top down work hard to put these ACE principles into practice, evaluating and rewarding these managers on their ability to do so, and divesting companies that are developing a weak competitive position because of powerful buyers or some other competitive force. Nevertheless, experience alone does not guarantee success, and it is important for managers to always perform postacquisition audits and review what worked and what did not and how things might be improved next time.[37]

Entry Strategy: Joint Ventures

Joint ventures are not used as much as acquisitions and internal new ventures to establish business units in another industry. Rather, they are used to strengthen the business models of a company's existing divisions, such as when Sony formed an alliance with Samsung to work together to become dominant partners in the flat-screen LCD industry. However, suppose a company is contemplating a new internal venture to establish a business unit in an embryonic or growth industry. Such a move involves substantial risks and costs because the company must establish the set of value-chain activities needed to operate in that new market. In this situation a joint venture might be the right strategy because it allows a company to share the risks and costs associated with establishing the new business unit, especially when the companies share *complementary* skills or distinctive competencies. A joint venture with another company may increase the probability of success.

Consider the 50/50 equity joint venture between UTC and Dow Chemical to build plastic-based composite parts for the aerospace industry. UTC was already involved in the aerospace industry (it builds Sikorsky helicopters), and Dow Chemical had skills in the development and manufacture of plastic-based composites. The alliance called for UTC to contribute its advanced aerospace skills and Dow to contribute its skills in developing and manufacturing plastic-based composites. Through the venture, both companies would become involved in new activities and would be able to realize the benefits associated with related diversification without having to merge their activities into one company or bear the costs and risks of developing new products on their own. Thus both companies would enjoy the value-creating benefits of entering a new market without having to bear the increased bureaucratic costs.

Although in some situations joint ventures can benefit both companies, they have three main drawbacks. First, a joint venture allows companies to share the risks and costs of developing a new business, but it also requires that they share in the profits if it succeeds. Then, if one company's skills are more important, it will have to "give away" profits to the other party because of the 50/50 agreement. This can create conflict and sour the working relationship as time goes on. Second, the joint venture partners may have different business philosophies, time horizons, or investment preferences, and so once again substantial problems can arise. Conflicts over how to run the joint venture can tear it apart and result in business failure.

Third, a company that enters into a joint venture always runs the risk of giving critical know-how away to its partner, which might then take that know-how and use it to compete with the other partner in the future. For example, having gained access to Dow's expertise in plastic-based composites, UTC might have dissolved the alliance and produced these materials on its own. As discussed earlier, such a risk can be minimized if Dow gets a *credible commitment* from UTC, which is what it did. UTC had to invest in asset-specific investments to make the products the joint venture was formed to create.

In sum, when deciding whether to go it alone and internally venture a new business unit or cooperate with another company in a joint venture, strategic managers need to assess the pros and cons of the alternatives carefully. While joint ventures allow companies to share risks and returns in changing environments, how much the joint venture will benefit one company versus another is unclear. Today, as in the Sony example, joint ventures are probably most useful when companies need to cooperate to improve the quality or reduce the cost of components, such as LCD screens. They might both use the same screen in their final products, but ultimately the company that can design the product that customers want to buy will become the market leader.

Restructuring

Many companies expand into new markets and industries to increase profitability; however, sometimes they also need to exit markets and industries to achieve the same goal. **Restructuring**, the process of divesting businesses and exiting industries to focus on core distinctive competencies, has become an increasingly popular strategy.[38] Why are so many companies restructuring, and what are the strategies they use to exit markets and industries?

Why Restructure?

One main reason that diversified companies have restructured in recent years is that the stock market has valued their stock at a **diversification discount**, meaning that the stock of highly diversified companies is valued lower, relative to their earnings, than the stock of less diversified enterprises.[39] Investors see highly diversified companies as less attractive investments for four reasons. First, as we discuss earlier, investors often feel these companies do not have a multibusiness model that justifies their participation in many different industries; companies like UTC may be the exception rather than the norm. Second, the complexity of the consolidated financial statements of highly diversified enterprises does not provide good evidence of how the individual business units in the company are performing and thus whether the multibusiness model is succeeding for the reasons that the company claims. As a result, investors perceive the company as being riskier than companies that operate in one industry, whose competitive advantage and financial statements are more easily understood. In these cases restructuring can be an attempt to boost the returns to shareholders by splitting up the multibusiness company into separate and independent parts.

The third reason for the diversification discount is that many investors have learned from experience that managers often have a tendency to pursue too much diversification, or diversify for the wrong reasons: they may pursue growth for its own sake, rather than diversify for greater profitability.[40] Some top managers are empire builders: they cannot be trusted not to expand the scope of their company beyond that point where the additional value created by the diversification exceeds its bureaucratic costs. Restructuring is thus a response to declining financial performance.

A final factor leading to restructuring is that innovations in strategic management have diminished the advantages of vertical integration or diversification. For example, a few decades ago there was little understanding of how long-term cooperative relationships, or strategic alliances, between a company and its suppliers could be a viable alternative to vertical integration. Most companies considered only two alternatives for managing the supply chain: vertical integration or competitive bidding. As we discuss in Chapter 9, in many situations long-term cooperative relationships can create the most value, especially because they avoid the need to incur bureaucratic costs or dispense with market discipline. As this strategic innovation has spread throughout the business world, the relative advantages of vertical integration have declined.

Summary of Chapter

1. Managers often first consider diversification when their company is generating free cash flow, which are financial resources in excess of those necessary to maintain a competitive advantage in the company's original, or core, business.

2. A diversified company can create value by (a) transferring competencies among existing businesses, (b) leveraging competencies to create new businesses, (c) sharing resources to realize economies of scope, (d) using product bundling, (e) using diversification as a means of managing rivalry in one or more industries, and (f) exploiting general organizational competencies that enhance the performance of all business units

within a diversified company. The bureaucratic costs of diversification are a function of the number of independent business units within the company and the extent of coordination between those business units.

3. Diversification motivated by a desire to pool risks or achieve greater growth is often associated with the dissipation of value.

4. There are three vehicles that companies use to enter new business areas: internal ventures, acquisition, and joint ventures.

5. Internal new venturing is typically employed as an entry strategy when a company has a set of valuable competencies in its existing businesses that can be leveraged or recombined to enter the new business area.

6. Many internal ventures fail because of entry on too small a scale, poor commercialization, and poor corporate management of the internal venture process. Guarding against failure involves a structured approach toward project selection and management, integration of R&D and marketing to improve commercialization of a venture idea, and entry on a significant scale.

7. Acquisitions are often favored as an entry strategy when the company lacks important competencies (resources and capabilities) required to compete in an area, but it can purchase an incumbent company that has those competencies and do so at a reasonable price. Acquisitions also tend to be favored when the barriers to entry into the target industry are high and the company is unwilling to accept the time frame, development costs, and risks of internal new venturing.

8. Many acquisitions fail because of poor postacquisition integration, overestimation of the value that can be created from an acquisition, the high cost of acquisition, and poor preacquisition screening. Guarding against acquisition failure requires structured screening, good bidding strategies, positive attempts to integrate the acquired company into the organization of the acquiring one, and learning from experience.

9. Joint ventures may be the preferred entry strategy when (a) the risks and costs associated with setting up a new business unit are more than the company is willing to assume on its own and (b) the company can increase the probability of successfully establishing a new business by teaming up with another company that has skills and assets complementing its own.

10. Restructuring is often a response to (a) an inadequate multibusiness model, (b) the complexity of consolidated financial statements, (c) excessive diversification due to top managers' empire building, and (c) innovations in the strategic management process that have reduced the advantages of vertical integration and diversification.

Discussion Questions

1. When is a company likely to choose related diversification and when unrelated diversification? Discuss with reference to an electronics manufacturer and an ocean shipping company.

2. Under what circumstances might it be best to enter a new business area by acquisition, and under what circumstances might internal new venturing be the preferred entry mode?

3. Imagine that IBM has decided to diversify into the cellular telecommunication provider business. What entry strategy would you recommend that the company pursue? Why?

4. Look at Honeywell's portfolio of businesses (described in Honeywell's 10-K statements, which can be accessed on the Web at **www.honeywell.com**). How many different industries is Honeywell involved in? Would you describe Honeywell as a related or unrelated diversification company? How do you think that Honeywell's diversification strategy increases profitability?

Practicing Strategic Management

■ SMALL-GROUP EXERCISE
Dun & Bradstreet

Break into small groups of three to five people, and discuss the following scenario. Appoint one group member as a spokesperson who will communicate your findings to the class. Then read the following news release from Dun & Bradstreet. On the basis of this information, identify the strategic rationale for the split and evaluate how the split might affect the performance of the three successor companies. If you were a stockholder in the old Dun & Bradstreet Corporation, would you approve of this split? Why?

Dun & Bradstreet CEO Robert E. Weissman today announced a sweeping strategy that will transform the 155-year-old business information giant into three publicly traded, global corporations. "This important action is designed to increase shareholder value by unlocking D&B's substantial underlying franchise strengths," said Weissman.

Building on preeminent Dun & Bradstreet businesses, the reorganization establishes three independent companies focused on high-growth information markets; financial information services; and consumer-product market research.

"Since the 1800s, D&B has grown by effectively managing a portfolio of businesses and gaining economies of scale," stated Weissman. "But the velocity of change in information markets has dramatically altered the rules of business survival. Today, market focus and speed are the primary drivers of competitive advantage. This plan is our blueprint for success in the 21st century," said Weissman.

The plan, approved today at a special meeting of D&B's board of directors, calls for D&B to create three separate companies by spinning off two of its businesses to shareholders. "D&B is the leader in business information," said Weissman. "By freeing our companies to tightly focus on our core vertical markets, we can more rapidly leverage this leadership position into emerging growth areas." The three new companies are:

■ Cognizant Corporation, a new high-growth company, including IMS International, the leading global supplier of marketing information to the pharmaceutical and healthcare industries; Nielsen Media Research, the leader in audience measurement for electronic media; and Gartner Group, the premier provider of advisory services to high-tech users, vendors and suppliers, in which Cognizant will hold a majority interest.

■ The Dun & Bradstreet Corporation, consisting of Dun & Bradstreet Information Services, the world's largest source of business-to-business marketing and commercial-credit information; Moody's Investors Service, a global leader in rating debt; and Reuben H. Donnelley, a premier provider of Yellow Pages marketing and publishing.

■ A. C. Nielsen, the global leader in marketing information for the fast-moving consumer packaged goods industry.

"These three separate companies will tailor their strategies to the unique demands of their markets, determining investments, capital structures and policies that will strengthen their respective global capabilities. This plan also clarifies D&B from an investor's perspective by grouping the businesses into three logical investment categories, each with distinct risk/reward profiles," said Weissman.

The Dun & Bradstreet Corporation is the world's largest marketer of information, software and services for business decision-making, with worldwide revenue of $4.9 billion in 1994.

■ ARTICLE FILE 10

Find an example of a diversified company that made an acquisition that apparently failed to create any value. Identify and critically evaluate the rationale that top management used to justify the acquisition when it was made. Explain why the acquisition subsequently failed.

■ STRATEGIC MANAGEMENT PROJECT
Module 10

This module requires you to assess your company's use of acquisitions, internal new ventures, and joint ventures as strategies for entering a new business area or as attempts to restructure its portfolio of businesses.

A. Your company has entered a new industry during the past decade.

1. Pick one new industry that your company has entered during the past ten years.
2. Identify the rationale for entering this industry.
3. Identify the strategy used to enter this industry.
4. Evaluate the rationale for using this particular entry strategy. Do you think that this was the best entry strategy to use? Justify your answer.
5. Do you think that the addition of this business unit to the company has added or dissipated value? Again, justify your answer.

B. Your company has restructured its corporate portfolio during the past decade.

1. Identify the rationale for pursuing a restructuring strategy.
2. Pick one industry that your company has exited from during the past ten years.
3. Identify the strategy used to exit from this particular industry. Do you think that this was the best exit strategy to use? Justify your answer.
4. In general, do you think that exiting from this industry has been in the company's best interest?

■ EXPLORING THE WEB
Visiting General Electric

Visit the website of General Electric Company of the United States (**www.ge.com**). Using the information contained on that website, answer the following questions.

1. Review GE's portfolio of major businesses. Does this portfolio make sense from a value creation perspective? Why?
2. What (if any) changes would you make to GE's portfolio of businesses? Why would you make these changes?
3. What (if any) core competencies do you think are held in common by one or more of GE's major business units? Is there any evidence that GE creates new business units by leveraging its core competencies?

General Task By searching through information sources on the Web, find an example of a company that has recently restructured its portfolio of businesses. Identify and evaluate the strategic rationale behind this restructuring to determine whether it makes sense.

Closing Case

Tyco International

Tyco International has been one of the great growth stories of the past decade. Under the leadership of Dennis Kozlowski, who became CEO in 1992, Tyco's sales expanded from $3.1 billion in 1992 to $38 billion in 2001, when it earned some $5.12 billion in after-tax profits. Much of this growth was driven by acquisitions that took Tyco into a diverse range of businesses, including medical supplies, security equipment, electronic components, plastics, financial services, and telecommunications. Between 1996 and 2001, Tyco spent some $45 billion in cash (much of it raised from debt offerings) and stock to purchase more than one hundred companies. With the acquisitions fueling growth, Tyco's earnings expanded by 35 percent each year between 1996 and 2001.

Tyco's success has been attributed to the consistent application of a business model that comprises a number of elements. First, although the company is diversified, it seeks to attain a critical mass in the industries in which it competes. Through acquisitions, it has become one of the largest providers of security systems, basic medical supplies, and electronic components in the United States. Indeed, it sees itself as using acquisitions to consolidate fragmented industries and attain economies of scale, which give it a cost-based advantage over smaller rivals. Second, the company *never* makes hostile acquisitions, which would be too expensive and could result in bad feelings among the managers of an acquired company. Third, Tyco deliberately seeks out companies that make basic products that have a strong market franchise but have been underperforming relative to their peers in recent years. Tyco's management believes that this indicates there is substantial room for improvement. Once it identifies a potential target, Tyco approaches management to see if they are interested in backing a sale of the company. If they express interest in supporting an acquisition, Tyco sends in teams of independent auditors to carefully go through the books of the target and identify the potential for improving performance. If the target company has potential, Tyco makes a formal bid. As a precondition of the bid, the top managers of the target company normally agree to step down (with a substantial severance package). Tyco typically replaces them with up-and-coming managers two or three layers below.

Once an acquisition has been completed, Tyco sets to work improving the performance of the acquired unit. Typically excess capacity is shut down, corporate overhead slashed, unprofitable product lines sold off or discontinued, plants and sales forces merged with those of similar operations within Tyco to attain scale economies, and head count reduced. For example, in 1999, Tyco acquired AMP, the world's largest manufacturer of electronic components, for $12 billion in Tyco stock. Within months, Tyco had identified close to $1 billion in cost savings that could be implemented by 2002 by closing unprofitable plants and reducing the work force by 8,000. On average, Tyco finds cost savings in an acquisition that amount to about 11 percent of the target company's revenues.

In addition to taking excess costs out of a newly acquired company, Tyco gives the employees of the acquired unit incentives to boost profitability. No bonuses are paid to anyone at Tyco unless annual net income growth exceeds 10 percent. However, bonuses quickly ramp up for each increment above that minimum and are unlimited for senior managers. In the best years, senior managers receive bonuses that are multiples of their salaries, supervisors at the plant level can receive cash or stock options worth as much as 40 percent of their salary, and hourly factory workers receive two to three weeks of extra pay.

Tyco's corporate structure is also very lean. While he was CEO, Kozlowski ran operations on an arm's-length basis, and this approach is still used. There are only seventy employees at the head office, most of whom focus on tax and legal issues. Performance goals for the coming year are set by negotiation between top management and the management of operating units. Once targets are set, the policy is one of management by exception, with operating managers being given considerable autonomy so long as they hit or exceed their targets.

Despite Tyco's impressive track record, the stock price underperformed the general market during much of 1998–2001. The stock was given a "diversification discount" by investors, who were put off by the complexity of Tyco's financial accounts and the lack of transparency with regard to the profitability of individual operations. In 1999, Tyco was the target of criticism by analysts who accused the company of inappropriate accounting methods. However, a subsequent investigation by the Securities and Exchange Commission gave Tyco's accounting practices a clean bill of health. Despite this, the criticisms persisted, and in late 2001 the company came under renewed attack from critics who argued that it had systematically inflated its profitability to make its performance look better than it actually was. According to the critics, the management at several companies Tyco acquired all artificially depressed the profitability of their companies in the final months before the deals were completed. This was done by taking numerous charges, slowing sales, and pushing up expenses. Consequently, Tyco's operating results were "spring-loaded" for a quarter or two after the acquisition closed as sales and profit margins suddenly expanded. They also argued that the debt that Tyco had taken on to finance some of its acquisitions, which by early 2002 totaled some $23 billion, left the company excessively leveraged and potentially vulnerable should cash flow projections fall short.

Tyco dismissed the charges of accounting tricks and pointed out that it would generate over $4 billion in free cash flow during 2002, more than enough to cover all of its short-term debt commitments. Nevertheless, the attacks persisted, and the stock price slid to under $20 by May 2002. To try to halt the slide, Kozlowski floated a number of ideas, including splitting up the company into four independent units and selling off its plastics and financial services unit, then using the proceeds to pay down the company's debt. However, with none of these ideas seeming to help the stock price, Kozlowski ultimately stated that he would continue to run the company as a diversified entity and focus on generating cash flow to pay down the company's debt load. Tyco would sell off some of its acquired businesses,

but only if it could get a decent price for them, and it would use the proceeds to pay down debt. Whatever the ultimate outcome, it seems clear that after a decade of success, investors had turned sour on Tyco's business model, recognizing, belatedly perhaps, that Tyco's growth had been bought at the price of accumulating tremendous debt.

To complicate matters, in June 2002 Kozlowski resigned after being charged with tax evasion. He was replaced by John Fort, Tyco's CEO between 1982 and 1992. One of Fort's first actions was to complete a spinoff of CIT Group, Tyco's finance arm, for $4.6 billion, significantly less than the $11 billion Tyco had paid to acquire CIT in 2000. With this cash in hand, however, Tyco appeared to have enough funds to service its debt commitments, and since the company continued to generate positive cash flow, its survival seemed assured.[41]

Case Discussion Questions

1. What kind of corporate-level strategy is Tyco pursuing? What is Tyco's multibusiness model, and in what ways could it create value?

2. What are the dangers and disadvantages of this business model?

3. Collect some recent information on Tyco from sources like Yahoo! Finance. How successful has it been in pursuing its strategy?

Chapter 11

Corporate Performance, Governance, and Business Ethics

Opening Case

Nike: The Sweatshop Debate

Nike is in many ways the quintessential global corporation. Established in 1972 by former University of Oregon track star Phil Knight, Nike is now one of the leading marketers of athletic shoes and apparel in the world. By 2004 the company had more than $12 billion in annual revenues, had a return on invested capital of 17.5 percent, and sold its products in some 140 countries. Nike does not do any manufacturing. Rather, it designs and markets its products and contracts for their manufacture from a global network of 600 factories owned by subcontractors scattered around the globe that together employ some 550,000 people. This huge corporation has made founder Phil Knight into one of the richest people in America. Nike's marketing phrase, "Just Do It!" has become as recognizable in popular culture as its "swoosh" logo or the faces of its celebrity sponsors, such as Tiger Woods.

For all of its successes, the company has been dogged for more than a decade by repeated and persistent accusations that its products are made in "sweatshops" where workers, many of them children, slave away in hazardous conditions for wages that are below subsistence level. Nike's wealth, its detractors claim, has been built upon the backs of the world's poor. Many see Nike as a symbol of the evils of globalization: a rich Western corporation exploiting the world's poor to provide expensive shoes and apparel to the pampered consumers of the developed world. Nike's "Niketown" stores have become standard targets for antiglobalization protestors. Several nongovernmental organizations, such as San Francisco–based Global Exchange, a human rights organization dedicated to promoting environmental, political, and social justice around the world, have targeted Nike for repeated criticism and protests. News organizations such as CBS's *48 Hours*, hosted by Dan Rather, have run exposés on working conditions in foreign factories that supply Nike. And students on the campuses of several major U.S. universities with which Nike has lucrative sponsorship deals have protested against those deals, citing Nike's use of sweatshop labor.

Typical of the allegations were those detailed in the CBS news program *48 Hours* in 1996. The report painted a picture of young women at a Vietnamese subcontractor who worked six days a week, in poor working conditions with toxic materials, for only 20 cents an hour. The report also stated that a living wage in Vietnam was at least $3 a day, an income that could not be achieved without working substantial overtime. Nike was not breaking any laws, and nor were its subcontractors, but this report and others like it raised questions about the ethics of using "sweatshop labor" to make what were essentially fashion accessories. It may have been legal, it may have helped the company to increase its profitability, but was it ethical to use subcontractors who by Western standards clearly exploited their work force? Nike's critics thought not, and the company found itself the focus of a wave of demonstrations and consumer boycotts.

Adding fuel to the fire, in November 1997 Global Exchange obtained and leaked a confidential report by Ernst & Young of an audit that Nike had commissioned of a Vietnam factory owned by a Nike subcontractor. The factory had 9,200 workers and made 400,000 pairs of shoes a month. The Ernst & Young report painted a dismal picture of thousands of young women, most under age twenty-five, laboring ten and a half hours a day, six days a week, in excessive heat and noise and foul air, for slightly more than $10 a week. The report also found that workers with skin or breathing problems had not been transferred to departments free of chemicals. More than half the workers who dealt with dangerous chemicals did not wear protective masks or gloves. The report stated that in parts of the plant workers were exposed to carcinogens that exceeded local legal standards by 177 times and that 77 percent of the employees suffered from respiratory problems.

These exposés surrounding Nike's use of subcontractors forced the company to reexamine its policies. Realizing that its subcontracting policies were perceived as unethical, Nike's management took a number of steps. These included establishing a code of conduct for Nike subcontractors and setting up a scheme whereby all subcontractors would be monitored annually by independent auditors. Nike's code of conduct required that all employees at footwear factories be at least eighteen years old and that exposure to potentially toxic materials would not exceed the permissible exposure limits established by the U.S. Occupational Safety and Health Administration (OSHA) for workers in the United States. In short, Nike concluded that behaving ethically required going beyond the requirements of the law. It required the establishment and enforcement of rules that adhere to accepted moral principles of right and wrong.[1]

Overview

The Nike story detailed in the *Opening Case* is an important one because it illustrates what should be a cardinal principle of business: that the quest to maximize profitability should be constrained not just by the law but also by ethical obligations. In Chapter 1 we note that the goal of managers should be to pursue strategies that maximize long-run shareholder value, but we also note that managers *must* behave in an ethical and socially responsible manner when pursuing this goal.

In this chapter we take a close look at the governance mechanisms that shareholders put in place to make sure that managers are acting in their interests, that is, pursuing strategies that maximize shareholder value. But we also discuss how managers need to pay attention to other stakeholders as well, such as employees, suppliers, and customers. Balancing the needs of different stakeholder groups is in the long-run interests of the company's owners, its shareholders. Good governance mechanisms recognize this truth. In addition, we will spend some time discussing the ethical implications of strategic decisions, and we will discuss how managers can make sure that their strategic decisions are founded on strong ethical principles.

Stakeholders and Corporate Performance

A company's **stakeholders** are individuals or groups with an interest, claim, or stake in the company, in what it does, and in how well it performs.[2] They include stockholders, creditors, employees, customers, the communities in which the company does business, and the general public. Stakeholders can be divided into internal stakeholders and external stakeholders (see Figure 11.1). **Internal stakeholders** are stockholders and employees, including executive officers, other managers, and board members. **External stakeholders** are all other individuals and groups that have some claim on the company. Typically, this group comprises customers, suppliers, creditors (including banks and bondholders), governments, unions, local communities, and the general public.

All stakeholders are in an exchange relationship with the company. Each of the stakeholder groups listed in Figure 11.1 supplies the organization with important

FIGURE 11.1

Stakeholders and the
Enterprise

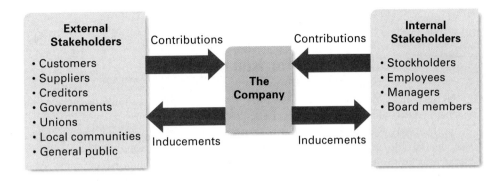

resources (or contributions), and in exchange each expects its interests to be satisfied
(by inducements).[3] Stockholders provide the enterprise with risk capital and in exchange expect management to try to maximize the return on their investment. Creditors, and particularly bondholders, also provide the company with capital in the
form of debt, and they expect to be repaid on time with interest. Employees provide
labor and skills and in exchange expect commensurate income, job satisfaction, job
security, and good working conditions. Customers provide a company with its revenues and in exchange want high-quality reliable products that represent value for
money. Suppliers provide a company with inputs and in exchange seek revenues and
dependable buyers. Governments provide a company with rules and regulations that
govern business practice and maintain fair competition. In exchange they want companies that adhere to these rules. Unions help to provide a company with productive
employees, and in exchange they want benefits for their members in proportion to
their contributions to the company. Local communities provide companies with
local infrastructure and in exchange want companies that are responsible citizens.
The general public provides companies with national infrastructure and in exchange
seeks some assurance that the quality of life will be improved as a result of the company's existence.

A company must take these claims into account when formulating its strategies, or
else stakeholders may withdraw their support. For example, stockholders may sell their
shares, bondholders may demand higher interest payments on new bonds, employees
may leave their jobs, and customers may buy elsewhere. Suppliers may seek more dependable buyers. Unions may engage in disruptive labor disputes. Government may
take civil or criminal action against the company and its top officers, imposing fines
and in some cases jail terms. Communities may oppose the company's attempts to locate its facilities in their area, and the general public may form pressure groups, demanding action against companies that impair the quality of life. Any of these reactions
can have a damaging impact on an enterprise. A detailed example is given in Strategy in
Action 11.1, which looks at how Bill Agee, the former CEO of Morrison Knudsen, lost
his job because the strategies he pursued failed to satisfy the interests of two important
stakeholder groups: the company's employees and its stockholders.

■ **Stakeholder
Impact Analysis**

A company cannot always satisfy the claims of all stakeholders. The goals of different
groups may conflict, and in practice few organizations have the resources to manage all stakeholders.[4] For example, union claims for higher wages can conflict with
consumer demands for reasonable prices and stockholder demands for acceptable
returns. Often the company must make choices. To do so, it must identify the most

Strategy in Action

11.1

Bill Agee at Morrison Knudsen

Bill Agee made his name as a whiz kid who became the chief financial officer of paper maker Boise Cascade during the 1970s while he was in his early thirties. He left Boise Cascade after the company was forced to write down its profits by $250 million because of earlier overstatements of the value of timberland sales. At the time, the write-downs were the largest in corporate history, but this did not stop Agee from being appointed CEO of defense contractor Bendix in 1976 when he was only thirty-eight years old. At Bendix, Agee became involved in a famous corporate soap opera that began when he promoted a young manager, Mary Cunningham, to a senior post over the heads of many other more experienced executives. At the time, many felt the promotion occurred because the two were romantically involved. Both denied this, but in 1982 Agee divorced his wife and married Cunningham, who by this time had left Bendix.

In 1988, Agee became CEO of Idaho-based Morrison Knudsen (MK), a seventy-five-year-old construction company that had made its name as the prime contractor on a number of large western construction projects, including the Hoover Dam and the Trans Alaska pipeline. By the time Agee joined the company, MK was perceived as a venerable institution that wasn't quite living up to its performance potential. Agee's strategy for improving performance was to sell off certain of MK's assets and invest the proceeds in the securities of other companies. At the same time, he pushed MK to pursue large construction projects aggressively and to develop its rail car manufacturing business. At one time, the rail car manufacturing business had been a major success story at MK, but it had fallen on hard times, unable to hold its own in the face of aggressive competition.

On the surface, MK appeared to be prospering under Agee's leadership. In 1993, MK earned $35.8 million, and Agee proclaimed it a "banner year" and a "watershed period" for the company's drive into railroad and mass transit industries. Underneath the surface, however, things were unraveling for Bill Agee. For one thing, 62 percent of MK's profits in 1993 came from Agee's financial plays in securities trading and capital gains on asset sales. Strip out these one-time gains, and it was clear that the operating performance of MK was poor. A prime reason seems to have been Agee's insistence that, in order to win new business,

MK should be the low bidder on large contracts. For instance, when MK bid on a contract to build eighty transit cars for the Bay Area Rapid Transit District (BART) in Oakland, California, Agee knocked down the bid to $142 million. According to one insider, the result was that "we were looking at a $14 million loss on the contract the day we won it." In the second quarter of 1994, MK announced a $40.5 million loss after taking a $59.4 million charge for underbidding various transit car contracts. Similarly, in the third quarter of 1994, MK took a $9.2 million charge against profits for underbidding on a $100 million contract to rebuild locomotives for Southern Pacific.

To compound matters, there had been significant employee opposition to Agee's leadership. An anonymous letter sent to MK's board in November 1994 by a group of MK executives calling themselves the MK Committee for Excellence leveled a large number of charges at Agee. They claimed that Agee irked subordinates immediately by removing the portrait of MK's founder from the headquarters and replacing it with a nearly life-sized portrait of himself and his wife, Mary Cunningham, paid for by the company. Agee further estranged insiders by quietly moving the CEO's office to his Pebble Beach estate in California and by scoffing at the company's engineering-oriented culture. Several old-hand MK engineering executives, who had top reputations in their field, were fired, usually after crossing swords with Agee over his policies.

There was also the matter of Agee's pay and perks. At $2.4 million, Agee's 1993 compensation was equal to 6.8 percent of MK's net income, more than any other CEO of a company with earnings in that range, according to a *Forbes* magazine list. According to insiders, MK paid $4 million a year for a corporate jet for Agee, equal to 13 percent of the company's general and administrative budget. The company also paid for landscaping services at Agee's Pebble Beach estate.

Things came to a head on February 1, 1995, when MK's board announced that the company would record a large loss for 1994. The board also announced that Agee would be stepping down as CEO, although initial indications were that he would stay on as chairman of the board. Preliminary figures suggested that MK would have to take a $179.6 million pretax charge in its 1994 fourth quarter, which would result in a net loss of $141 million for the quarter. At the same time, Standard & Poor's downgraded MK's long-term debt to junk bond rating, signaling that a significant risk of default existed.

The announcement gave rise to a blizzard of shareholder lawsuits and criticism, not only of Agee, but also of MK's board for acting so slowly. Many commentators wondered why it took a huge loss and an anonymous letter from MK employees to prod the board into action. Privately, several board members, most of whom were appointees and long-time friends of Agee, indicated that they were led astray by Agee, who repeatedly urged them not to worry about poor results. Still, many felt that the audit committee of the board of directors had not done a good job of vetting MK's financial accounts under Agee's

leadership. Stung by this criticism, the growing evidence of financial mismanagement under Agee's leadership, and the downgrade of MK's debt by Standard & Poor's, the board reversed its earlier position and decided to strip Agee of all posts at MK.

The shareholder lawsuits were settled in September 1995. Under the agreement, MK was to pay out $63 million in cash and stock to shareholders. The settlement also required the company to strengthen its board by adding seven new directors over the next two years. As part of the settlement, Agee agreed to relinquish rights to about $3 million in severance pay and to a cut in his MK pension from $303,000 a year for life to $99,750 a year for life.[a]

important stakeholders and give highest priority to pursuing strategies that satisfy their needs. Stakeholder impact analysis can provide such identification. Typically, stakeholder impact analysis follows these steps:

1. Identify stakeholders.

2. Identify stakeholders' interests and concerns.

3. As a result, identify what claims stakeholders are likely to make on the organization.

4. Identify the stakeholders who are most important from the organization's perspective.

5. Identify the resulting strategic challenges.[5]

Such an analysis enables a company to identify the stakeholders most critical to its survival and to make sure that the satisfaction of their needs is paramount. Most companies that have gone through this process quickly come to the conclusion that three stakeholder groups must be satisfied above all others if a company is to survive and prosper: customers, employees, and stockholders. Bill Agee, for example, lost his position because he failed to satisfy the demands of stockholders for a good return on their investment and the demands of employees for income, job satisfaction, job security, and good working conditions. More generally, companies that fail to satisfy the needs of their customers soon see their revenues fall and ultimately go out of business. Interestingly, Agee probably was satisfying the needs of customers because he was insisting on low prices; however, at the prices Agee was requiring, Morrison Knudsen could not possibly have been profitable.

■ **The Unique Role of Stockholders**

A company's stockholders are usually put in a different class from other stakeholder groups, and for good reason. Stockholders are legal owners and the providers of risk capital, a major source of the capital resources that allow a company to operate its business. The capital that stockholders provide to a company is seen as **risk capital** because there is no guarantee that stockholders will ever recoup their investment and or earn a decent return.

Recent history demonstrates all too clearly the nature of risk capital. Many investors who bought shares in companies that went public during the late 1990s and early 2000s through an initial public offering (IPO) subsequently saw the value of their holdings decline to zero, or something close to it. For example, in early 2000, Oniva.com, a provider of an online business-to-business marketplace aimed at small businesses, went public. On the first day of trading, the shares hit $25. They fell steadily afterward, and two years later, having lost 99 percent of their value, they were trading at $0.25, effectively wiping out the investment many made in the company. Of course, there are also some spectacular successes: investors who purchased shares of Dell, Microsoft, or Intel at their IPO have done extraordinarily well. But this is the nature of risk capital: the variance of returns is very high. To reward stockholders for providing the company with risk capital, management is obligated to pursue strategies that maximize the returns that stockholders get from their investment in the company's stock.

Over the past decade, maximizing returns to stockholders has taken on added importance as more and more employees have themselves become stockholders in the company for which they work through an employee stock ownership plan (ESOP). At Wal-Mart, for example, all employees who have served for more than one year are eligible for the company's ESOP. Under an ESOP, employees are given the opportunity to purchase stock in their company, sometimes at a discount to the market value of the stock. The company may also contribute to a certain proportion of the purchase price. By making employees stockholders, ESOPs tend to increase the already strong emphasis on maximizing returns to stockholders, for they now help to satisfy two key stakeholder groups: stockholders and employees.

■ Profitability, Profit Growth, and Stakeholder Claims

Because of the unique position assigned to stockholders, managers normally seek to pursue strategies that maximize the returns that stockholders receive from holding shares in the company. As we noted in Chapter 1, stockholders receive a return on their investment in a company's stock in two ways: from dividend payments and from capital appreciation in the market value of a share (that is, by increases in stock market prices). The best way for managers to generate the funds for future dividend payments and to keep the stock price appreciating is for them to pursue strategies that maximize the company's long-run profitability (as measured by the return on invested capital or ROIC) and grow the profits of the company over time.[6]

As we saw in Chapter 3, ROIC is an excellent measure of the profitability of a company. It tells managers how efficiently they are using the capital resources of the company (including the risk capital provided by stockholders) to generate profits. A company that is generating a positive ROIC is covering all of its ongoing expenses and has money left over, which is then added to shareholders' equity, thereby increasing the value of a company and thus the value of a share of stock in the company. The value of each share will increase further if a company can grow its profits over time, because then the profit that is attributable to every share (that is, the company's earning per share) will also grow. As we have seen in this book, to grow their profits companies must be doing one or more of the following: (a) participating in a market that is growing, (b) taking market share from competitors, (c) consolidating the industry through horizontal integration, and (d) developing new markets through international expansion, vertical integration, or diversification.

While managers should strive for profit growth if they are trying to maximize shareholder value, the relationship between profitability and profit growth is a complex one because attaining future profit growth may require investments that reduce the current rate of profitability. The task of managers is to find the right balance between profitability and profit growth.[7] Too much emphasis on current profitability at the expense of future profitability and profit growth can make an enterprise less attractive to shareholders. Too much emphasis on profit growth can reduce the profitability of the enterprise and have the same effect. In an uncertain world where the future is unknowable, finding the right balance between profitability and profit growth is certainly as much art as it is science, but it is something that managers must try to do.

In addition to maximizing returns to stockholders, boosting a company's profitability and profit growth rate is also consistent with satisfying the claims of several other key stakeholder groups. When a company is profitable and its profits are growing, it can pay higher salaries to productive employees and can also afford benefits such as health insurance coverage, all of which help to satisfy employees. In addition, companies with a high level of profitability and profit growth have no problem meeting their debt commitments, which provides creditors, including bondholders, with a measure of security. More profitable companies are also better able to undertake philanthropic investments, which can help to satisfy some of the claims that local communities and the general public place on a company. Pursuing strategies that maximize the long-run profitability and profit growth of the company is therefore generally consistent with satisfying the claims of various stakeholder groups.

There is an important cause-and-effect relationship here. It is pursuing strategies to maximize profitability and profit growth that helps a company to better satisfy the demands that several stakeholder groups place on it, not the other way around. The company that overpays its employees in the current period, for example, may have very happy employees for a short while, but such action will raise the company's cost structure and limit its ability to attain a competitive advantage in the marketplace, thereby depressing its long-run profitability and hurting its ability to award future pay increases. As far as employees are concerned, the way many companies deal with this situation is to make future pay increases contingent on improvements in labor productivity. If labor productivity goes up, labor costs as a percentage of revenues will fall, profitability will rise, and the company can afford to pay its employees more and offer greater benefits.

Of course, not all stakeholder groups want the company to maximize its long-run profitability and profit growth. Suppliers are more comfortable about selling goods and services to profitable companies because they can be assured that the company will have the funds to pay for those products. Similarly, customers may be more willing to purchase from profitable companies because they can be assured that those companies will be around in the long run to provide after-sales services and support. But neither suppliers nor customers want the company to maximize its profitability *at their expense.* Rather, they would like to capture some of these profits from the company in the form of higher prices for their goods and services (in the case of suppliers) or lower prices for the products they purchase from the company (in the case of customers). Thus, the company is in a bargaining relationship with some of its stakeholders, which was a phenomenon we discussed in Chapter 2.

Moreover, despite the argument that maximizing long-run profitability and profit growth is the best way to satisfy the claims of several key stakeholder groups, it should be noted that a company must do so within the limits set by the law and in a manner consistent with societal expectations. The unfettered pursuit of profit can lead to behaviors that are outlawed by government regulations, opposed by important public constituencies, or simply unethical. Governments have enacted a wide range of regulations to govern business behavior, including antitrust laws, environmental laws, and laws pertaining to health and safety in the workplace. It is incumbent on managers to make sure that the company is in compliance with these laws when pursuing strategies.

Unfortunately, there is plenty of evidence that managers can be tempted to cross the line between the legal and illegal in their pursuit of greater profitability and profit growth. For example, in mid 2003 the air force stripped Boeing of $1 billion in contracts to launch satellites when it was discovered that Boeing had obtained thousand of pages of proprietary information from rival Lockheed Martin. Boeing had used that information to prepare its winning bid for the satellite contract. This was followed by the revelation that Boeing's CFO, Mike Sears, had offered a government official, Darleen Druyun, a lucrative job at Boeing while Druyun was still involved in evaluating whether Boeing should be awarded a $17 billion contract to build tankers for the air force. Boeing won the contract against strong competition from Airbus, and Druyun was hired by Boeing. It was clear that the job offer may have had an impact on the air force decision. Boeing fired the CFO and Druyun, and shortly afterwards Boeing CEO Phil Condit resigned in a tacit acknowledgment that he bore responsibility for the ethics violations that had occurred at Boeing during his tenure as leader.[8] In another example, the chief executive of Archer Daniels Midland, one of the world's largest producers of agricultural products, was sent to jail after an FBI investigation revealed that the company had systematically tried to fix the price for lysine by colluding with other manufacturers in the global marketplace. In another case of price fixing, the seventy-six-year-old chairman of Sotheby's auction house was sentenced to a jail term and the former CEO to house arrest for fixing prices with rival auction house Christie's over a six-year period (see Strategy in Action 11.2).

Examples such as these beg the question of why managers would engage in such risky behavior. A body of academic work collectively known as agency theory

Strategy in Action 11.2

Price Fixing at Sotheby's and Christie's

Sotheby's and Christie's are the two largest fine art auction houses in the world. In the mid 1990s, the two companies controlled 90 percent of the fine art auction market, which at the time was worth some $4 billion a year. Traditionally, auction houses make their profit by the commission they charge on auction sales. In good times, these commissions can range as high as 10 percent on some items, but in the early 1990s, the auction business was in a slump, with the supply of art for auction drying up. With Sotheby's and Christie's desperate for works of art, sellers played the two houses off against each other, driving commissions down to 2 percent or even lower.

To try to control this situation, Sotheby's CEO, Dede Brooks, met with her opposite number at Christie's, Christopher Davidge, in a series of clandestine meetings held in car parking lots that began in 1993. Brooks claims that she was acting on behalf of her boss, Alfred Taubman, the chairman and controlling shareholder of Sotheby's. According to Brooks, Taubman had agreed with the chairman of Christie's, Anthony Tennant, to work together in the weak auction market and limit price competition. In their meetings, Brooks and Davidge agreed to a fixed and nonnegotiable commission structure. Based on a sliding scale, the commission structure would range from 10 percent on a $100,000 item to 2 percent on a $5 million item. In effect, Brooks and Davidge were agreeing to eliminate price competition between them, thereby guaranteeing both auction houses higher profits. The price-fixing agreement started in 1993 and continued unabated for six years until federal investigators uncovered the arrangement and brought charges against Sotheby's and Christie's.

With the deal out in the open, lawyers filed several class action lawsuits on behalf of sellers who had been defrauded by Sotheby's and Christie's. Ultimately, some 100,000 sellers signed on to the class action lawsuits, which the auction houses settled with a $512 million payment. The auction houses also pleaded guilty to price fixing and paid $45 million in fines to U.S. antitrust authorities. As for the key players, the chairman of Christie's, as a British subject, was able to avoid prosecution in the United States (price fixing is not an offense for which someone can be extradited). Christie's CEO, Davidge, struck a deal with prosecutors and in return for amnesty handed over incriminating documents to the authorities. Brooks also cooperated with federal prosecutors and avoided jail (in April 2002 she was sentenced to three years' probation, six months' home detention, 1,000 hours of community service, and a $350,000 fine). Taubman, ultimately isolated by all his former co-conspirators, was sentenced to a year in jail and fined $7.5 million.[b]

provides an explanation for why managers might engage in behavior that is either illegal or, at the very least, not in the interest of the company's shareholders.

Agency Theory

Agency theory looks at the problems that can arise in a business relationship when one person delegates decision-making authority to another. It offers a way of understanding why managers do not always act in the best interests of stakeholders and why they might sometimes behave unethically, and perhaps also illegally.[9] Although agency theory was originally formulated to capture the relationship between management and stockholders, the basic principles have also been extended to cover the relationship with other key stakeholders, such as employees, as well as relationships between different layers of management within a corporation.[10] While the focus of attention in this section is on the relationship between senior management and stockholders, some of the same language can be applied to the relationship between other stakeholders and top managers and between top management and lower levels of management.

■ Principal-Agent Relationships

The basic propositions of agency theory are relatively straightforward. First, an **agency relationship** is held to arise whenever one party delegates decision-making authority or control over resources to another. The **principal** is the person delegating authority, and the **agent** is the person to whom authority is delegated. The relationship between stockholders and senior managers is the classic example of an agency relationship. Stockholders, who are the *principals,* provide the company with risk capital, but they delegate control over that capital to senior managers, and particularly the CEO, who as their *agent* is expected to use that capital in a manner that is consistent with the best interests of stockholders. As we have seen, this means using that capital to maximize the company's long-run profitability and profit growth rate.

The agency relationship continues on down within the company. For example, in the large, complex, multibusiness company, top managers cannot possibly make all important decisions, so they delegate some decision-making authority and control over capital resources to business unit (divisional) managers. Thus, just as senior managers such as the CEO are the *agents* of stockholders, business unit managers are the *agents* of the CEO (and in this context, the CEO is the *principal*). The CEO entrusts business unit managers to use the resources over which they have control in the most effective manner so that they maximize the performance of their units, which helps the CEO to make sure that he or she maximizes the performance of the entire company, thereby discharging agency obligation to stockholders. More generally, whenever managers delegate authority to managers below them in the hierarchy and give them the right to control resources, an agency relation is established.

■ The Agency Problem

While agency relationships often work well, problems may arise if agents and principals have different goals and if agents take actions that are not in the best interests of their principals. Agents may be able to do this because there is an **information asymmetry** between the principal and agent: agents almost always have more information about the resources they are managing than the principal does. Unscrupulous agents can take advantage of any information asymmetry to mislead principals and maximize their own interests at the expense of principals.

In the case of stockholders, the information asymmetry arises because they delegate decision-making authority to the CEO, their agent, who by virtue of his or her position inside the company is likely to know far more than stockholders do about the company's operations. Indeed, there may be certain information about the company that the CEO is unwilling to share with stockholders because it would also help competitors. In such a case, withholding some information from stockholders may be in their best interests. More generally, the CEO, involved in the day-to-day running of the company, is bound to have an information advantage over stockholders, just as the CEO's subordinates may well have an information advantage over the CEO with regard to the resources under their control.

The information asymmetry between principals and agents is not necessarily a bad thing, but it can make it difficult for principals to measure how well an agent is performing, and thus hold the agent accountable for how well he or she is using the entrusted resources. There is a certain amount of performance ambiguity inherent in the relationship between a principal and agent: principals cannot know for sure if the agent is acting in his or her best interests. They cannot know for sure if the agent is using the resources to which he or she has been entrusted as effectively and efficiently as possible. To an extent, principals have to *trust* the agent to do the right thing.

Of course, this trust is not blind: principals do put mechanisms in place whose purpose is to monitor agents, evaluate their performance, and if necessary, take corrective action. As we shall see shortly, the board of directors is one such mechanism, for in part the board exists to monitor and evaluate senior managers on behalf of stockholders. Other mechanisms serve a similar purpose. In the United States, publicly owned companies must regularly file detailed financial statements with the Securities and Exchange Commission (SEC) that are in accordance with generally agreed-upon accounting principles (GAAP). This requirement exists to give stockholders consistent and detailed information about how well management is using the capital with which it has been entrusted. Similarly, internal control systems within a company are there to help the CEO make sure that subordinates are using the resources with which they have been entrusted as efficiently and effectively as possible.

Despite the existence of governance mechanisms and comprehensive measurement and control systems, a degree of information asymmetry will always remain between principals and agents, and there is always an element of trust involved in the relationship. Unfortunately, not all agents are worthy of this trust. A minority will deliberately mislead principals for personal gain, sometimes behaving unethically or breaking laws in the process. The interests of principals and agents are not always the same; they diverge, and some agents may take advantage of information asymmetries to maximize their own interests at the expense of principals and to engage in behaviors that the principals would never condone.

For example, some authors have argued that, like many other people, senior managers are motivated by desires for status, power, job security, and income.[11] By virtue of their position within the company, certain managers, such as the CEO, can use their authority and control over corporate funds to satisfy these desires at the cost of returns to stockholders. CEOs might use their position to invest corporate funds in various perks that enhance their status—executive jets, lavish offices, and expense-paid trips to exotic locations—rather than investing those funds in ways that increase stockholder returns. Economists have termed such behavior *on-the-job consumption.*[12] Bill Agee is an example of a CEO who appeared to engage in excessive on-the-job consumption (see Strategy in Action 11.1).

Besides engaging in on-the-job consumption, CEOs, along with other senior managers, might satisfy their desires for greater income by using their influence or control over the board of directors to get the compensation committee of the board to grant pay increases. Critics of U.S. industry claim that extraordinary pay has now become an endemic problem and that senior managers are enriching themselves at the expense of stockholders and other employees. They point out that CEO pay has been increasing far more rapidly than the pay of average workers, primarily because of very liberal stock option grants that enable a CEO to earn huge pay bonuses in a rising stock market, even if the company underperforms the market and competitors.[13] In 1950, when *Business Week* started its annual survey of CEO pay, the highest-paid executive was General Motors CEO Charles Wilson, whose $652,156 pay packet translates into $4.5 million in inflation-adjusted dollars in 2003. In contrast, the highest-paid executive in *Business Week*'s 2003 survey, Reuben Mark of Colgate-Palmolive, earned $141.1 million, primarily from exercising stock options.[14] In 1980, the average CEO in *Business Week*'s survey earned forty-two times what the average blue collar-worker earned. By 1990, this figure had increased to eighty-five times. Today, the average CEO in the survey earns more than two hundred times the pay of the average blue-collar worker.[15]

What rankles critics is the size of some CEO pay packages and their apparent lack of relationship to company performance.[16] In 1998, for example, Disney CEO Michael Eisner earned $575 million, mostly in the form of stock options, despite the fact that Disney did not do particularly well that year and the stock price fell 10 percent. A big gainer in 2001, Jozef Straus, earned $150 million from stock options in a year when the company he serves as CEO, JDS Uniphase, recorded a $50 billion loss related to the writing down of goodwill for companies acquired at premium prices during the booming 1990s. Critics feel that the size of these pay awards was out of all proportion to the achievement of the CEOs.[17] If so, this represents a clear example of the agency problem.

A further concern is that in trying to satisfy a desire for status, security, power, and income, a CEO might engage in *empire building,* buying many new businesses in an attempt to increase the size of the company through diversification.[18] Although such growth may depress the company's long-run profitability and thus stockholder returns, it increases the size of the empire under the CEO's control and, by extension, the CEO's status, power, security, and income (there is a strong relationship between company size and CEO pay). Instead of trying to maximize stockholder returns by

FIGURE 11.2

The Tradeoff Between
Profitability and
Revenue Growth
Rates

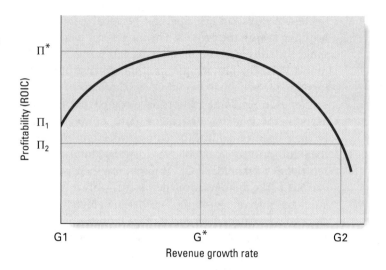

seeking the right balance between profitability and profit growth, some senior managers may trade long-run profitability for greater company growth by buying new
businesses. Figure 11.2 graphs long-run profitability against the rate of growth in
company revenues. A company that does not grow is probably missing out on some
profitable opportunities.[19] A moderate revenue growth rate of G^* allows a company
to maximize long-run profitability, generating a return of Π^*. Thus, a growth rate of
$G1$ in Figure 11.2 is not consistent with maximizing profitability ($\Pi1 < \Pi^*$). By the
same token, however, attaining growth in excess of G^* requires diversification into
areas that the company knows little about. Consequently, it can be achieved only by
sacrificing profitability; that is, past G^*, the investment required to finance further
growth does not produce an adequate return and the company's profitability declines. Yet $G2$ may be the growth rate favored by an empire-building CEO, for it will
increase his or her power, status, and income. At this growth rate, profitability is
equal only to $\Pi2$. Because $\Pi^* > \Pi2$, a company growing at this rate is clearly not
maximizing its long-run profitability or the wealth of its stockholders.

For an example of this kind of excessive growth, consider the case of Tyco International, profiled in the *Closing Case* in Chapter 10. Under the leadership of Dennis
Kozlowski, who became CEO of the company in 1992, Tyco's revenues expanded
from $3.1 billion in 1992 to $38 billion in 2001. Most of this growth was due to a series of acquisitions that took Tyco into a diverse range of unrelated businesses. Tyco
financed the acquisitions by taking on significant debt commitments, which by
2002 exceeded $23 billion. As Tyco expanded, some questioned Tyco's ability to
service its debt commitments and claimed that the company was engaging in "accounting tricks" to pad its books and make the company appear more profitable
than it actually was. These criticisms, which were ignored for several years, were finally shown to have some validity in 2002 when Kozlowski was forced out by the
board and subsequently charged with tax evasion by federal authorities. Among
other charges, it has been claimed that Kozlowski treated Tyco as his personal treasury, drawing on company funds to purchase an expensive Manhattan apartment
and a world-class art collection that he obviously thought were befitting of the CEO
of a major corporation. Kozlowski even used company funds to help pay for an
expensive birthday party for his wife that included toga-clad women, gladiators,

chariots, and other over-the-top scenarios. Kozlowski was replaced by a company outsider, Edward Breen. In 2003 Tyco took a $1.5 billion charge against earnings for accounting errors made during the Kozlowski era (in other words, Tyco's profits had been overstated by $1.5 billion during Kozlowski's tenure). Breen also set about dismantling parts of the empire that Kozlowski had built, divesting several businesses.[20]

Just how serious agency problems could be was emphasized in the early 2000s when a series of scandals swept through the corporate world, many of which could be attributed to self-interest seeking by senior executives and a failure of corporate governance mechanisms to hold the largess of those executives in check. Between 2001 and 2004 accounting scandals unfolded at a number of major corporations, including Enron, WorldCom, Tyco, Computer Associates, HealthSouth, Adelphia Communications, Dynegy, Royal Dutch Shell, and most recently, the major Italian food company, Parmalat. At Enron, some $27 billion in debt was hidden from shareholders, employees, and regulators in special partnerships that were kept off the balance sheet. At Parmalat, managers apparently "invented" some $8 to $12 billion in assets to shore up the company's balance sheet, assets that never existed. In the case of Royal Dutch Shell, senior managers knowingly inflated the value of the company's oil reserves by one-fifth, which amounted to 4 billion barrels of oil that never existed, making the company appear much more valuable than it actually was. At the other companies, earnings were systematically overstated, often by hundreds of millions of dollars, or even billions of dollars in the case of Tyco (see above) and WorldCom, which understated its expenses by $3 billion in 2001. Strategy in Action 11.3 discusses accounting fraud at Computer Associates. In all of these cases, the prime motivation seems to have been an effort to present a more favorable view of corporate affairs to shareholders than was actually the case, thereby securing senior executives significantly higher pay packets.[21]

It is important to remember that the agency problem is not confined to the relationship between senior managers and stockholders. It can also bedevil the relationship between the CEO and subordinates and between them and their subordinates. Subordinates might use control over information to distort the true performance of their unit in order to enhance their pay, increase their job security, or make sure their unit gets more than its fair share of company resources.

Confronted with agency problems, the challenge for principals is to (1) shape the behavior of agents so that they act in accordance with the goals set by principals, (2) reduce the information asymmetry between agents and principals, and (3) develop mechanisms for removing agents who do not act in accordance with the goals of principals and mislead them. Principals try to deal with these challenges through a series of governance mechanisms.

Governance Mechanisms

Governance mechanisms are mechanisms that principals put in place to align incentives between principals and agents and to monitor and control agents. The purpose of governance mechanisms is to reduce the scope and frequency of the agency problem: to help ensure that agents act in a manner that is consistent with the best interests of their principals. In this section, the primary focus is on the governance mechanisms that exist to align the interests of senior managers (as agents) with their principals, stockholders. It should not be forgotten, however, that governance mechanisms also exist to align the interests of business unit managers with those of their superiors, and so on down within the organization.

Strategy in Action   11.3

Did Computer Associates Inflate Revenues to Enrich Managers?

Computer Associates is one of the world's largest software companies. During the 1990s, its stock price appreciated at a rapid rate, driven in large part by surging revenues and a commensurate rise in profits. Because its revenues were growing more rapidly than those of rivals during the late 1990s, investors assumed that the company was gaining market share and that high profitability would follow, so they bid up the price of the company's stock. The senior managers of Computer Associates were major beneficiaries of this process.

Under a generous incentive program given to the company's three top managers by the board of directors—Charles Wang, then CEO and chairman of the board; Sanjay Kumar, the chief operating officer; and Russell Artzt, the chief technology officer—if the stock price stayed above $53.13 for sixty days, they would receive a special incentive stock award amounting to some 20 million shares. In May 1998, Kumar announced that Computer Associates had "record" revenues and earnings for the quarter. The stock price surged over the $53.13 trigger and stayed there long enough for all three to receive the special incentive stock award, then valued at $1.1 billion.

In late July 1998, after all three had received the award, Kumar announced that the effect of Asian economic turmoil and the year 2000 bug "leads us to believe that our revenue and earnings growth will slow over the next few quarters." The stock price promptly fell from the high 50s to under $40 a share. What followed was a series of class action lawsuits, undertaken on behalf of stockholders, that claimed that management had misled stockholders to enrich themselves. As a result of the lawsuits, the three were compelled to give back some of their gains, and the size of the award was reduced to 4.5 million shares. Wang stepped down as CEO, although he retained his position as chairman of the board, and Kumar became the CEO.

This was not the end of matters, however, for Computer Associates had attracted the attention of both the Justice Department and the SEC, which launched a joint investigation into the company's accounting practices. By 2002, they were reportedly focusing on a little-noticed action the company had taken in May 2000 to reduce its revenues by 10 percent, or $1.76 billion, below what it had previously reported for the three fiscal years that ended March 2000. The downward revisions, detailed in the company's 10-K filings with the SEC, retroactively

took hundreds of millions of dollars away from the top line in the fourteen months preceding the May 1998 stock award to senior managers, including some $513 million for the year ending March 1998. According to the company, earnings were unaffected by the revision because the lost revenue was offset by a commensurate downward revision of expenses. The downward revision reportedly came at the urging of auditor KPMG, which replaced Ernst & Young as the company's accountant in June 1999.

The implication that some observers were drawing was that Computer Associates deliberately overstated its revenues in the period prior to May 1998 to enrich the three top managers. The losers in this process were stockholders who purchased shares at the inflated price and longer-term shareholders who saw the value of their holdings diluted by the stock awarded to Wang, Kumar, and Artzt. In a statement issued after a report of the ongoing investigation was published in the *Wall Street Journal*, Computer Associates stated that it changed how it classified revenue and expenses at the advice of its auditors. "We continue to believe CA has acted appropriately," the company said. "This change in presentation had no impact on reported earnings, earnings per share, or cash flows."

By 2004, it was clear that Computer Associates had been acting anything but appropriately. According to the SEC investigation, between 1998 and 2000 the company adopted a policy of backdating contracts to boost revenues. For example, in January 2000 Computer Associates negotiated a $300 million contract with a customer but backdated the contract so that the revenues appeared in 1999. Although initially this may have been done to help secure the $1.1 billion special stock award, by 2000 the practice represented an increasingly desperate attempt to meet financial projects that the company was routinely missing.

Under increasing pressure, in 2002 Charles Wang stepped down as chairman, and in 2004 Kumar was forced to resign as CEO by the board of Computer Associates, which had belatedly come to recognize that the company's financial statements were fraudulent. Matters culminated in September 2004 when Kumar was indicted by federal prosecutors on charges of obstruction of justice and securities fraud.[c]

Here we look at four main types of governance mechanisms for aligning stockholder and management interests: the board of directors, stock-based compensation, financial statements, and the takeover constraint. The section closes with a discussion of governance mechanisms within a company to align the interest of senior and lower-level managers.

■ The Board of Directors

The board of directors is the centerpiece of the corporate governance system in the United States and the United Kingdom. Board members are directly elected by stockholders, and under corporate law they represent the stockholders' interests in the company. Hence, the board can be held legally accountable for the company's actions. Its position at the apex of decision making within the company allows it to monitor corporate strategy decisions and ensure that they are consistent with stockholder interests. If the board's sense is that corporate strategies are not in the best interest of stockholders, it can apply sanctions, such as voting against management nominations to the board of directors or submitting its own nominees. In addition, the board has the legal authority to hire, fire, and compensate corporate employees, including, most importantly, the CEO.[22] The board is also responsible for making sure that audited financial statements of the company present a true picture of its financial situation. Thus, the board exists to reduce the information asymmetry between stockholders and managers and to monitor and control management actions on behalf of stockholders.

The typical board of directors is composed of a mix of inside and outside directors. *Inside directors* are senior employees of the company, such as the CEO. They are required on the board because they have valuable information about the company's activities. Without such information, the board cannot adequately perform its monitoring function. But because insiders are full-time employees of the company, their interests tend to be aligned with those of management. Hence, outside directors are needed to bring objectivity to the monitoring and evaluation processes. *Outside directors* are not full-time employees of the company. Many of them are full-time professional directors who hold positions on the boards of several companies. The need to maintain a reputation as competent outside directors gives them an incentive to perform their tasks as objectively and effectively as possible.[23]

There is little doubt that many boards perform their assigned functions admirably. For example, one factor that led to the dismissal of Morrison Knudsen's CEO, Bill Agee, was that his strategies lost the support of the board (see Strategy in Action 11.1). Similarly, when the board of Sotheby's discovered that the company had been engaged in price fixing with Christie's, board members moved quickly to oust both the CEO and the chairman of the company (see Strategy in Action 11.2). But not all boards perform as well as they should. The board of now bankrupt energy company Enron signed off on that company's audited financial statements, which were later shown to be grossly misleading.

Critics of the existing governance system charge that inside directors often dominate the outsiders on the board. Insiders can use their position within the management hierarchy to exercise control over what kind of company-specific information the board receives. Consequently, they can present information in a way that puts them in a favorable light. In addition, because insiders have intimate knowledge of the company's operations and because superior knowledge and control over information are sources of power, they may be better positioned than outsiders to influence boardroom decision making. The board may become the captive of insiders and merely rubber-stamp management decisions instead of guarding stockholder interests.

Some observers contend that many boards are dominated by the company CEO, particularly when the CEO is also the chairman of the board.[24] To support this view, they point out that both inside and outside directors are often the personal nominees of the CEO. The typical inside director is subordinate to the CEO in the company's hierarchy and therefore unlikely to criticize the boss. Because outside directors are frequently the CEO's nominees as well, they can hardly be expected to evaluate the CEO objectively. Thus, the loyalty of the board may be biased toward the CEO, not the stockholders. Moreover, a CEO who is also chairman of the board may be able to control the agenda of board discussions in such a manner as to deflect any criticisms of his or her leadership. This was a problem in the case of Bill Agee: he was both CEO and chairman of the board at Morrison Knudsen.

In the aftermath of a wave of corporate scandals that hit the corporate world in the early 2000s, there are clear signs that many corporate boards are moving away from merely rubber-stamping top management decisions and are beginning to play a much more active role in corporate governance. In part they have been prompted by new legislation, such as the 2002 Sarbanes-Oxley Act in the United States, which tightened rules governing corporate reporting and corporate governance. Also important has been a growing trend on the part of the courts to hold directors liable for corporate misstatements. Powerful institutional investors such as pension funds have also been more aggressive in exerting their power, often pushing for more outside representation on the board of directors and for a separation between the roles of chairman and CEO, with the chairman role going to an outsider. Partly as a result, over 50 percent of big companies had outside directors in the chairman's role by the early 2000s, up from less than half of that number in 1990. Separating the role of chairman and CEO limits the ability of corporate insiders, and particularly of the CEO, to exercise control over the board. It is notable that the removal of Robert Stempel as the CEO of General Motors in the late 1990s followed the appointment of an outside director, John Smale, as chairman of the GM board. Still, when all is said and done, it must be recognized that boards of directors do not work as well as they should in theory, and other mechanisms are need to align the interests of stockholders and managers.

■ Stock-Based Compensation

According to agency theory, one of the best ways to reduce the scope of the agency problem is for principals to establish incentives for agents to behave in their best interest through pay-for-performance systems. In the case of stockholders and top managers, stockholders can encourage top managers to pursue strategies that maximize a company's long-run profitability and profit growth, and thus the gains from holding its stock, by linking the pay of those managers to the performance of the stock price.

The most common pay-for-performance system has been to give managers stock options: the right to buy the company's shares at a predetermined (strike) price at some point in the future, usually within ten years of the grant date. Typically, the strike price is the price that the stock was trading at when the option was originally granted. The idea behind stock options is to motivate managers to adopt strategies that increase the share price of the company, for in doing so they will also increase the value of their own stock options.

Several academic studies suggest that stock-based compensation schemes for executives, such as stock options, can align management and stockholder interests. For instance, one study found that managers were more likely to consider the effects of their acquisition decisions on stockholder returns if they themselves were significant shareholders.[25] According to another study, managers who were significant stockholders were less likely to pursue strategies that would maximize the size of the company rather than its profitability.[26] More generally, it is difficult to argue with the proposition that the chance to get rich from exercising stock options is the primary reason for the fourteen-hour days and six-day workweeks that many employees of fast-growing companies put in.

Many top managers often earn huge bonuses from exercising stock options that were granted several years previously. While not denying that these options do motivate managers to improve company performance, critics claim that they are often too generous. A particular cause for concern is that stock options are often granted at such low strike prices that the CEO can hardly fail to make a significant amount of money by exercising them, even if the company underperforms the stock market by a significant margin.

Other critics, including the famous investor Warren Buffett, complain that huge stock option grants increase the outstanding number of shares in a company and therefore dilute the equity of stockholders; accordingly, they should be shown in company accounts as an expense against profits. Under current accounting regulations, stock options, unlike wages and salaries, were not expensed until 2005, when new accounting regulations came into force. Buffett has noted that when his investment company, Berkshire Hathaway, "acquires an option issuing company, we promptly substitute a cash compensation plan having an economic value equivalent to that of the previous option plan. The acquiree's true compensation cost is therefore brought out of the closet and charged, as it should be, against earnings."[27] Buffett's point is that stock options are accounted for incorrectly in company financial statements. Table 11.1 details the amount that reported profits would have been reduced during the 1996–2000 period for several high-profile companies if stock options had been accounted for as an expense and deducted from profits. As can be seen, the impact would have been to depress profits severely at some of these companies, and by extension, profitability.

In theory, stock options and other stock-based compensation methods are a good idea; in practice, they have been abused. To limit the abuse, Alan Greenspan, chairman of the U.S. Federal Reserve, has joined Warren Buffett in arguing that accounting

TABLE 11.1

How Options Skew the Bottom Line

Company	Reduction in Net Profit If Options Had Been Expensed
AOL Time Warner	75 percent
Viacom	66 percent
NVIDIA	40 percent
MedImmune	31 percent
Lucent	30 percent
Pharmacia	28 percent
Cisco Systems	26 percent
Boise Cascade	17 percent

Source: D. Henry and M. Conlin, "Too Much of a Good Incentive?" *Business Week,* March 4, 2002, pp. 38–39.

rules should be changed to treat options as an expense that must be charged against profits. Some companies have taken matters into their own hands even without a change in accounting rules. Microsoft, for example, stopped issuing options to employees in 2003, replacing them with smaller stock grants. Since 2002, Boeing has expensed options in its accounts. In an effort to align management and stockholder interests, the aerospace company has also gone an important step further by issuing what it calls "performance share" units that are convertible into common stock only if its stock appreciates at least 10 percent annually for five years. Similarly, Unilever has created a system in which stock options do not vest unless the company achieves total shareholder returns over a rolling three-year period that are above the median for the group of twenty peer companies, including Coca-Cola, Nestlé, and Procter & Gamble. What all of these companies are trying to do in their own way is to limit the free ride that many holders of stock options enjoyed during the boom of the 1990s, while continuing to maintain a focus on aligning management and stockholder interests through stock-based compensation schemes.[28]

■ Financial Statements and Auditors

Publicly trading companies in the United States are required to file quarterly and annual reports with the SEC that are prepared according to GAAP. The purpose of this requirement is to give consistent, detailed, and accurate information about how efficiently and effectively the agents of stockholders, the managers, are running the company. To make sure that managers do not misrepresent this financial information, the SEC also requires that the accounts be audited by an independent and accredited accounting firm. Similar regulations exist in most other developed nations. If the system works as intended, stockholders can have a lot of faith that the information contained in financial statements accurately reflects the state of affairs at a company. Among other things, such information can enable a stockholder to calculate the profitability (ROIC) of a company in which he or she invests and to compare its ROIC against that of competitors.

Unfortunately, in the United States at least, this system has not been working as intended. Although the vast majority of companies do file accurate information in their financial statements and although most auditors do a good job of reviewing that information, there is substantial evidence that a minority of companies have abused the system, aided in part by the compliance of auditors. This was clearly an issue at bankrupt energy trader Enron, where the CFO and others misrepresented the true financial state of the company to investors by creating off-balance-sheet partnerships that hid the true state of Enron's indebtedness from public view. Enron's auditor, Arthur Andersen, also apparently went along with this deception, in direct violation of its fiduciary duty. Arthur Anderson also had lucrative consulting contracts with Enron that it did not want to jeopardize by questioning the accuracy of the company's financial statements. The losers in this mutual deception were shareholders, who had to rely on inaccurate information to make their investment decisions.

There have been numerous examples in recent years of managers' gaming financial statements to present a distorted picture of their company's finances to investors. The typical motive has been to inflate the earnings or revenues of a company, thereby generating investor enthusiasm and propelling the stock price higher, which gives managers an opportunity to cash in stock option grants for huge personal gain, obviously at the expense of stockholders who have been mislead by the reports. Another alleged example of such behavior is given in Strategy in Action 11.3, which discusses how top managers at Computer Associates may have managed that company's financial statements to present a rosy picture and cash in very lucrative stock awards.

The gaming of financial statements by companies such as Enron and Computer Associates raises serious questions about the accuracy of the information contained in audited financial statements. In response, in 2002 the United States passed the Sarbanes-Oxley bill into law, which represents the biggest overhaul of accounting rules and corporate governance procedures since the 1930s. Among other things, Sarbanes-Oxley set up a new oversight board for accounting firms, required CEOs and CFOs to endorse their company's financial statements, and barred companies from hiring the same accounting firm for auditing and consulting services. However, many critics felt that this legislation did not go far enough and that it should have contained other elements, such as a requirement that stock options be treated as an expense. Some companies took matters into their own hands even before the 2005 change in accounting rules requiring stock options to be expensed.

■ The Takeover Constraint

Given the imperfections in corporate governance mechanisms, it is clear that the agency problem may still exist at some companies. However, stockholders still have some residual power, for they can always sell their shares. If they start doing so in large numbers, the price of the company's shares will decline. If the share price falls far enough, the company might be worth less on the stock market than the book value of its assets. At this point, it may become an attractive acquisition target and runs the risk of being purchased by another enterprise, against the wishes of the target company's management.

The risk of being acquired by another company is known as the **takeover constraint.** The takeover constraint limits the extent to which managers can pursue strategies and take actions that put their own interests above those of stockholders. If they ignore stockholder interests and the company is acquired, senior managers typically lose their independence and probably their jobs as well. So the threat of takeover can constrain management action and limit the worst excesses of the agency problem.

During the 1980s and early 1990s, the threat of takeover was often enforced by **corporate raiders**: individuals or corporations that buy up large blocks of shares in companies that they think are pursuing strategies inconsistent with maximizing stockholder wealth. Corporate raiders argue that if these underperforming companies pursued different strategies, they could create more wealth for stockholders. Raiders buy stock in a company either to take over the business and run it more efficiently, or to precipitate a change in the top management, replacing the existing team with one more likely to maximize stockholder returns. Raiders are motivated not by altruism but by gain. If they succeed in their takeover bid, they can institute strategies that create value for stockholders, including themselves. Even if a takeover bid fails, raiders can still earn millions, for their stockholdings will typically be bought out by the defending company for a hefty premium. Called **greenmail**, this source of gain stirred much controversy and debate about its benefits. While some claim that the threat posed by raiders has had a salutary effect on enterprise performance by pushing corporate management to run their companies better, others claim there is little evidence of this.[29]

Although the incidence of hostile takeover bids has fallen off significantly since the early 1990s, this should not be taken to imply that the takeover constraint is no longer operating. Unique circumstances exist in the early 2000s that have made it more difficult to execute hostile takeovers. The boom years of the 1990s left many corporations with excessive debt (corporate America entered the new century with record levels of debt on its balance sheets), which limits the ability of companies to finance acquisitions, particularly hostile acquisitions, which are often particularly expensive. In addition, the market valuations of many companies got so out of line with underlying fundamentals during the stock market bubble of the 1990s that even after a substantial fall in certain segments of the stock market, such as the technology sector, valuations are still high relative to historic norms, making the hostile acquisition of even poorly run and unprofitable companies expensive. However, takeovers tend to go in cycles, and it seems likely that once excesses are worked out of the stock market and worked off corporate balance sheets, the takeover constraint will begin to reassert itself. It should be remembered that the takeover constraint is the governance mechanism of last resort and is often invoked only when other governance mechanisms have failed.

■ Governance Mechanisms Inside a Company

So far this section has focused on the governance mechanisms designed to reduce the agency problem that potentially exists between stockholders and managers. Agency relationships also exist within a company, and the agency problem can thus arise *between* levels of management. In this section, we explore how the agency problem can be reduced within a company by using two complementary governance mechanisms to align the incentives and behavior of employees with those of upper-level management: strategic control systems and incentive systems.

■ Strategic Control Systems

Strategic control systems are the primary governance mechanisms established within a company to reduce the scope of the agency problem between levels of management. These systems are the formal target setting, measurement, and feedback systems that allow managers to evaluate whether a company is executing the strategies necessary to maximize its long-run profitability and, in particular, whether the company is achieving superior efficiency, quality, innovation, and customer responsiveness. They are discussed in more detail in subsequent chapters.

The purpose of strategic control systems is to (1) establish standards and targets against which performance can be measured, (2) create systems for measuring and monitoring performance on a regular basis, (3) compare actual performance against the established targets, and (4) evaluate results and take corrective action if necessary. In governance terms, their purpose is to make sure that lower-level managers, as the agents of top managers, are acting in a way that is consistent with top managers' goals, which should be to maximize the wealth of stockholders, subject to legal and ethical constraints.

One increasingly influential model that guides managers through the process of creating the right kind of strategic control systems to enhance organizational performance is the balanced scorecard model.[30] According to the **balanced scorecard model**, traditionally managers have primarily used financial measures of performance such as return on invested capital to measure and evaluate organizational performance. Financial information is extremely important, but it is not enough by itself. If managers are to obtain a true picture of organizational performance, financial information must be supplemented with performance measures that indicate how well an organization has been achieving the four building blocks of competitive advantage: efficiency, quality, innovation, and responsiveness to customers. This is so because financial results simply inform strategic managers about the results of decisions they have *already taken*; the other measures balance this picture of performance by informing managers about how accurately the organization has put in place the building blocks that drive *future performance*.[31]

One version of the way the balanced scorecard operates is presented in Figure 11.3. Based on an organization's mission and goals, strategic managers develop a set of

FIGURE 11.3

A Balanced Scorecard
Approach

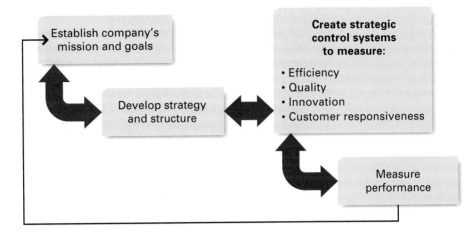

strategies to build competitive advantage to achieve these goals. They then establish an organizational structure to use resources to obtain a competitive advantage.[32] To evaluate how well the strategy and structure are working, managers develop specific performance measures that assess how well the four building blocks of competitive advantage are being achieved:

- *Efficiency* can be measured by the level of production costs, the productivity of labor (such as the employee hours needed to make a product), the productivity of capital (such as revenues per dollar invested in property, plant, and equipment), and the cost of raw materials.

- *Quality* can be measured by the number of rejects, the number of defective products returned from customers, and the level of product reliability over time.

- *Innovation* can be measured by the number of new products introduced, the percentage of revenues generated from new products in a defined period, the time taken to develop the next generation of new products versus the competition, and the productivity of R&D (how much R&D spending is required to produce a successful product).

- *Responsiveness to customers* can be measured by the number of repeat customers, customer defection rates, level of on-time delivery to customers, and level of customer service.

As Kaplan and Norton, the developers of this approach, suggest, "Think of the balanced scorecard as the dials and indicators in an airplane cockpit. For the complex task of navigating and flying an airplane, pilots need detailed information about many aspects of the flight. They need information on fuel, air speed, altitude, learning, destination, and other indicators that summarize the current and predicted environment. Reliance on one instrument can be fatal. Similarly, the complexity of managing an organization today requires that managers be able to view performance in several areas simultaneously."[33]

The way in which managers' ability to build a competitive advantage translates into organizational performance is then measured using financial measures such as the return on invested capital, the return on sales, and the capital turnover ratio (see Chapter 3). Based on an evaluation of the complete set of measures in the balanced scorecard, strategic managers are in a good position to reevaluate the company's mission and goals and take corrective action to rectify problems, limit the agency problem, or exploit new opportunities by changing the organization's strategy and structure—which is the purpose of strategic control.

■ **Employee Incentives** Control systems alone may not be sufficient to align incentives between stockholders, senior management, and the rest of the organization. To help do this, positive incentive systems are often put into place to motivate employees to work toward goals that are central to maximizing long-run profitability. As already noted, employee stock ownership plans (ESOPs) are one form of positive incentive, as are stock option grants. In the 1990s, ESOPs and stock ownership grants were pushed down deep within many organizations. The logic behind such systems is straightforward: recognizing that the stock price, and therefore their own wealth, is dependent on the profitability of the company, employees will work toward maximizing profitability.

In addition to stock-based compensation systems, employee compensation can also be tied to goals that are linked to the attainment of superior efficiency, quality, innovation, and customer responsiveness. For example, the bonus pay of a manufacturing employee might depend on attaining quality and productivity targets, which if reached will lower the costs of the company, increase customer satisfaction, and boost profitability. Similarly, the bonus pay of a salesperson might be dependent on surpassing sales targets, and of an R&D employee on the success of new products he or she had a hand in developing.

Ethics and Strategy

The term **ethics** refers to accepted principles of right or wrong that govern the conduct of a person, the members of a profession, or the actions of an organization. **Business ethics** are the accepted principles of right or wrong governing the conduct of businesspeople. Ethical decisions are in accordance with those accepted principles, whereas unethical decisions violate accepted principles. This is not as straightforward as it sounds. Managers may be confronted with **ethical dilemmas**, which are situations where there is no agreement over exactly what the accepted principles of right and wrong are, or where none of the available alternatives seems ethically acceptable.

In our society many accepted principles of right and wrong are not only universally recognized but also codified into law. In the business arena there are laws governing product liability (*tort laws*), contracts and breaches of contract (*contract law*), the protection of intellectual property (*intellectual property law*), competitive behavior (*antitrust law*), and the selling of securities (*securities law*). Not only is it unethical to break these laws, it is illegal.

In this book we argue that the preeminent goal of managers in a business should be to pursue strategies that maximize the long-run profitability and profit growth of the enterprise, thereby boosting returns to stockholders. Strategies, of course, must be consistent with the laws that govern business behavior: managers must act legally while seeking to maximize the long-run profitability of the enterprise. Unfortunately, as we have already seen in this chapter, there are examples of managers breaking the law. Moreover, managers may take advantage of ambiguities and gray areas in the law, of which there are many in our common law system, to pursue actions that are at best legally suspect and, in any event, clearly unethical. It is important to realize, however, that behaving ethically goes beyond staying within the bounds of the law. There are many examples of strategies and actions that, while legal, do not seem to be ethical. As we saw in the *Opening Case* on Nike's use of "sweatshop" labor in developing nations, while Nike was not breaking any laws, and neither were its subcontractors, many considered it unethical to use subcontractors who by Western standards clearly exploited their work force.

In this section we take a closer look at the ethical issues that managers may confront when developing strategy and at the steps managers can take to ensure that strategic decisions are not only legal, but also ethical.

■ **Ethical Issues in Strategy**

The ethical issues that strategic managers confront cover a wide range of topics, but most are due to a potential conflict between the goals of the enterprise, or the goals of individual managers, and the fundamental rights of important stakeholders, including stockholders, customers, employees, suppliers, competitors, communities, and the general public. Stakeholders have basic rights that should be respected, and it is unethical to violate those rights.

Stockholders have the right to timely and accurate information about their investment (in accounting statements), and it is unethical to violate that right. Customers have the right to be fully informed about the products and services they purchase, including the right to information about how those products might cause harm to them or others, and it is unethical to restrict their access to such information. Employees have the right to safe working conditions, fair compensation for the work they perform, and just treatment by managers. Suppliers have the right to expect contracts to be respected, and the firm should not take advantage of a power disparity between itself and a supplier to opportunistically rewrite a contract. Competitors have the right to expect that the firm will abide by the rules of competition and not violate the basic principles of antitrust laws. Communities and the general public, including their political representatives in government, have the right to expect that a firm will not violate the basic expectations that society places on enterprises: for example, by dumping toxic pollutants into the environment or overcharging for work performed on government contracts.

Those who take the stakeholder view of business ethics often argue that it is in the enlightened self-interest of managers to behave in an ethical manner that recognizes and respects the fundamental rights of stakeholders, because doing so will ensure the support of stakeholders and thus ultimately benefit the firm and its managers. Others go beyond this instrumental approach to ethics to argue that, in many cases, acting ethically is simply the right thing to do. They argue that businesses need to recognize their *noblesse oblige* and give something back to the society that made their success possible. *Noblesse oblige* is a French term that refers to honorable and benevolent behavior that is considered the responsibility of people of high (noble) birth. In a business setting, it is taken to mean benevolent behavior that is the moral responsibility of successful enterprises.

Unethical behavior often arises in a corporate setting when managers decide to put the attainment of their own personal goals, or the goals of the enterprise, above the fundamental rights of one or more stakeholder groups (in other words, unethical behavior may arise from agency problems). The most common examples of such behavior involve self-dealing, information manipulation, anticompetitive behavior, opportunistic exploitation of other players in the value chain in which the firm is embedded (including suppliers, complement providers, and distributors), the maintenance of substandard working conditions, environmental degradation, and corruption.

Self-dealing occurs when managers find a way to feather their own nests with corporate monies, and we have already discussed several examples in this chapter (such as Tyco and Computer Associates). **Information manipulation** occurs when managers use their control over corporate data to distort or hide information in order to enhance their own financial situation or the competitive position of the firm. As we have seen, many of the recent accounting scandals involved the deliberate manipulation of financial information. Information manipulation can also occur with regard to nonfinancial data. This occurred when managers at the tobacco companies suppressed internal research that linked smoking to health problems, violating the rights of consumers to accurate information about the dangers of smoking. When evidence of this came to light, lawyers brought class action suits against the tobacco companies, claiming that they had intentionally caused harm to smokers: they had broken tort law by promoting a product that they knew did serious harm to consumers. In 1999, the tobacco companies settled a lawsuit brought by the states who sought to recover health care costs associated with tobacco-related illnesses; the total payout to the states was $260 billion.

Anticompetitive behavior covers a range of actions aimed at harming actual or potential competitors, most often by using monopoly power, and thereby enhancing the long-run prospects of the firm. For example, in the 1990s the Justice Department claimed that Microsoft used its monopoly in operating systems to force PC makers to bundle Microsoft's web browser, Internet Explorer, with Windows and to display Internet explorer prominently on the computer desktop (the screen you see when you start a personal computer). Microsoft reportedly told PC makers that it would not supply them with Windows unless they did this. Since the PC makers had to have Windows to sell their machines, this was a powerful threat. The alleged aim of the action, which is an example of "tie-in-sales," which is illegal under antitrust laws, was to drive a competing browser maker, Netscape, out of business. The courts ruled that Microsoft was indeed abusing its monopoly power in this case, and under a 2001 consent decree the company agreed to stop the practice.

Putting the legal issues aside, action such as that allegedly undertaken by managers at Microsoft is unethical on at least three counts; first, it violates the rights of end-users by unfairly limiting their choice; second, it violates the rights of downstream participants in the industry value chain, in this case PC makers, by forcing them to incorporate a particular product in their design; and third, it violates the rights of competitors to free and fair competition.

Opportunistic exploitation of other players in the value chain in which the firm is embedded is another example of unethical behavior. Exploitation of this kind typically occurs when the managers of a firm seek to unilaterally rewrite the terms of a contract with suppliers, buyers, or complement providers in a way that is more favorable to the firm, often using their power to force the revision through. For example, in the late 1990s Boeing entered into a $2 billion contract with Titanium Metals Corporation to buy certain amounts of titanium annually for ten years. In 2000, after Titanium Metals had already spent $100 million to expand its production capacity to fulfill the contract, Boeing demanded that the contract be renegotiated, asking for lower prices and an end to minimum purchase agreements. As a major purchaser of titanium, managers at Boeing probably thought they had the power to push this contract revision through, and the investment by Titanium meant that they would be unlikely to walk away from the deal. Titanium promptly sued Boeing for breach of contract. The dispute was settled out of court, and under a revised agreement Boeing agreed to pay monetary damages to Titanium Metals (reported to be in the $60 million range) and entered into an amended contract to purchase titanium. Irrespective of the legality of this action, it was arguably unethical because it violated the rights of suppliers to have buyers who deal with them in a fair and open way.

Substandard working conditions arise when managers underinvest in working conditions, or pay employees below-market rates, in order to reduce their costs of production. The most extreme examples of such behavior occur when a firm establishes operations in countries that lack the workplace regulations found in developed nations such as the United States. The example of Nike, which was given earlier, falls into this category. However, many companies have also been accused of maintaining substandard working conditions at home. As noted in the *Running Case*, in recent years Wal-Mart has been the target of numerous lawsuits alleging that, among other things, the company discriminates against female employees and requires employees to work overtime for no additional pay.

Environmental degradation occurs when the firm takes actions that directly or indirectly result in pollution or other forms of environmental harm. Environmental degradation can violate the rights of local communities and the general public for such things as clean air and water, land that is free from pollution by toxic chemicals, and properly managed forests (because forests absorb rainfall, improper deforestation results in land erosion and floods).

Finally, **corruption** can arise in a business context when managers pay bribes to gain access to lucrative business contracts. For example, it was alleged that Halliburton was part of a consortium that paid some $180 million in bribes to win a lucrative contract to build a natural gas plant in Nigeria. Corruption is clearly unethical because it violates a bundle of rights, including the right of competitors to a level playing field when bidding for contracts and, when government officials are involved, the right of citizens to expect that government officials act in the best interest of the local community or nation and not in response to corrupt payments that feather their own nests.

■ The Roots of Unethical Behavior

Why do some managers behave unethically? What motivates them to engage in actions that violate accepted principals of right and wrong, trample on the rights of one or more stakeholder groups, or simply break the law? While there is no simple answer to this question, a few generalizations can be made. First, it is important to recognize that business ethics are not divorced from *personal ethics*, which are the generally accepted principles of right and wrong governing the conduct of individuals. As individuals we are taught that it is wrong to lie and cheat and that it is right to behave with integrity and honor and to stand up for what we believe to be right and true. The personal ethical code that guides our behavior comes from a number of sources, including our parents, our schools, our religion, and the media. Our personal ethical code will exert a profound influence on the way we behave as businesspeople. An individual with a strong sense of personal ethics is less likely to behave in an unethical manner in a business setting; in particular, he or she is less likely to engage in self-dealing and more likely to behave with integrity.

Second, many studies of unethical behavior in a business setting have come to the conclusion that businesspeople sometimes do not realize that they are behaving unethically, primarily because they simply fail to ask the relevant question: Is this decision or action ethical? Instead, they apply a straightforward business calculus to what they perceive to be a business decision, forgetting that the decision may also have an important ethical dimension. The fault here lies in processes that do not incorporate ethical considerations into business decision making. This may have been the case at Nike when managers originally made subcontracting decisions (see the *Opening Case*). Those decisions were probably made on the basis of good economic logic. Subcontractors were probably chosen on the basis of business variables such as cost, delivery, and product quality, and key managers simply failed to ask, "How does this subcontractor treat its work force?" If they thought about the question at all, they probably reasoned that it was the subcontractor's concern, not theirs.

Running Case

Working Conditions at Wal-Mart

When Sam Walton founded Wal-Mart, one of his core values was that if you treated employees with respect, tied compensation to the performance of the enterprise, trusted them with important information and decisions, and provided ample opportunities for advancement, they would repay the company with dedication and hard work. For years the formula seemed to work. Employees were called "associates" to reflect their status within the company, even the lowest hourly employee was eligible to participate in profit sharing schemes and could use profit sharing bonuses to purchase company stock at a discount to its market value, and the company made a virtue of promoting from within (two-thirds of managers at Wal-Mart started as hourly employees). At the same time, Walton and his successors always demanded loyalty and hard work from employees. For example, managers were expected to move to a new store on very short notice, and base pay for hourly workers was very low. Still, as long as the upside was there, little grumbling was heard from employees.

In the last ten years, however, the relationship between the company and its employees has been strained by a succession of lawsuits claiming that Wal-Mart pressures hourly employees to work overtime without compensating them, systematically discriminates against women, and knowingly uses contractors who hire undocumented immigrant workers to clean its stores, paying them below minimum wage.

For example, a class action lawsuit in Washington State claims that Wal-Mart routinely (a) pressured hourly employees not to report all their time worked, (b) failed to keep true time records, sometimes shaving hours from employee logs, (c) failed to give employees full rest or meal breaks, (d) threatened to fire or demote employees who would not work off the clock, and (e) required workers to attend unpaid meetings and computer training sessions. Moreover, the suit claims that Wal-Mart has a strict "no overtime" policy, punishing employees who work more than forty hours a week, but that the company also gives employees more work than can be completed in a forty-hour week. The Washington suit is one of more than thirty suits that have been filed around the nation in recent years.

With regard to discrimination against women, complaints date back to 1996, when an assistant manager in a California store, Stephanie Odle, came across the W2 of a male assistant manager who worked in the same store. The W2 showed that he was paid $10,000 more than Odle. When she asked her boss to explain the disparity, she was told that her coworker had "a wife and kids to support." When Odle, who is a single mother, protested, she was asked to submit a personal household budget. She was then granted a $2,080 raise. She was subsequently fired, she claims for speaking up. In 1998 she filed a discrimination suit against the company. Others began to file suits around the same time, and by 2004 the legal action had evolved into a class action suit that covered 1.6 million current and former female employees at Wal-Mart. The suit claims that Wal-Mart did not pay female employees the same as their male counterparts and did not provide them with equal opportunities for promotion.

In the case of both undocumented overtime and discrimination, Wal-Mart admits to no wrongdoing. The company does recognize that, with some 1.4 million employees, some problems are bound to arise, but it claims that there is no systematic companywide effort to get hourly employees to work without pay or to discriminate against women. Indeed, the company claims that this could not be the case since hiring and promotion decisions are made at the store level.

For their part, critics charge that while the company may have no policies that promote undocumented overtime or discrimination, its hard-driving cost-containment culture has created an environment where abuses can thrive. Store managers, for example, are expected to meet challenging performance goals, and in an effort to do so they may be tempted to pressure subordinates to work additional hours without pay. Similarly, company policy requiring managers to move to new stores at short notice unfairly discriminates against women, who lack the flexibility to uproot their families and move them to another state at short notice.

While the lawsuits are still ongoing and may take years to resolve, Wal-Mart has taken steps to change its employment practices. For example, the company has created a director of diversity and a diversity compliance team, and it has restructured its pay scales to promote equal pay regardless of gender.[d]

Unfortunately, the climate in some businesses does not encourage people to think through the ethical consequences of business decisions. This brings us to the third cause of unethical behavior in businesses: an organizational culture that de-emphasizes business ethics and considers all decisions to be purely economic ones. A related fourth cause of unethical behavior may be pressure from top management to meet performance goals that are unrealistic and can only be attained by cutting corners or acting in an unethical manner. As explained in the *Running Case*, this may have been an issue at Wal-Mart, where the pressure to meet performance goals may have encouraged store managers to pressure their subordinates to work extra hours without pay.

An organizational culture can "legitimize" behavior that society would judge as unethical, particularly when this is mixed with a focus on unrealistic performance goals, such as maximizing short-term economic performance regardless of the costs. In such circumstances, there is a greater-than-average probability that managers will violate their own personal ethics and engage in behavior that is unethical. By the same token, an organization culture can do just the opposite and reinforce the need for ethical behavior. At Hewlett-Packard, for example, Bill Hewlett and David Packard, the company's founders, propagated a set of values known as "The HP Way." These values, which shape the way business is conducted both within and by the corporation, have an important ethical component. Among other things, they stress the need for confidence in and respect for people, open communication, and concern for the individual employee.

This brings us to a fifth root cause of unethical behavior: *unethical leadership*. Leaders help to establish the culture of an organization, and they set the example that others follow. Other employees in a business often take their cues from business leaders, and if those leaders do not behave in an ethical manner, employees might not either. It is not what leaders say that matters, but what they do. A good example is Ken Lay, the former CEO of the failed energy company Enron. While constantly referring to Enron's code of ethics in public statements, Lay simultaneously engaged in behavior that was ethically suspect. Among other things, he failed to discipline subordinates who had inflated earnings by engaging in corrupt energy trading schemes. Such behavior sent a very clear message to Enron's employees—unethical behavior would be tolerated if it boosted earnings.

■ Philosophical Approaches to Ethics

In this section we take a look at the philosophical underpinnings of business ethics, for ultimately it is a philosophy that can provide managers with a moral compass that will help them to navigate their way through difficult ethical issues. We will start with the approach suggested by the Nobel Prize–winning economist Milton Friedman.

■ The Friedman Doctrine
In 1970 Milton Friedman wrote an article that has since become a classic straw man that business ethics scholars outline only to then tear down. Friedman's basic position is that the only social responsibility of business is to increase profits, so long as the company stays within the rules of law. He explicitly rejects the idea that businesses should undertake social expenditures beyond those mandated by the law and required for the efficient running of a business. For example, his arguments suggest that improving working conditions beyond the level required by the law *and* necessary to maximize employee productivity will reduce profits and are therefore not appropriate. His belief is that a firm should maximize its profits, since that is the way to maximize the returns that accrue to the owners of the

firm, its stockholders. If stockholders then wish to use the proceeds to make social investments, that is their right, according to Friedman, but managers of the firm should not make that decision for them.

Although Friedman is talking about social responsibility, rather than business ethics per se, most business ethics scholars equate social responsibility with ethical behavior, and thus believe Friedman is also arguing against business ethics. However, the assumption that Friedman is arguing against ethics is not quite true, for Friedman does state the following:

> There is one and only one social responsibility of business—to use its resources and engage in activities designed to increase its profits so long as it stays within the rules of the game, which is to say that it engages in open and free competition without deception or fraud.

In other words, Friedman does state that businesses should behave in an ethical manner, and not engage in deception and fraud.

Nevertheless, Friedman's arguments break down under closer examination. This is particularly true where the "rules of the game" are not well established, are ambiguous and open to different interpretations, or differ substantially from country to country. Consider again the case of sweatshop labor: using child labor may not be against the law in a developing nation, but it is still immoral to employee children because the practice conflicts with widely held views about what is the right thing to do. Similarly, there may be no rules against pollution in a developed nation, and spending money on pollution control may reduce the profit rate of the firm, but generalized notions of morality hold that it is still unethical to dump toxic pollutants into rivers or foul the air with gas releases. In addition to the local consequences of such pollution, which may have serious health effects for the surrounding population, there is also a global consequence because pollutants degrade those two global environments that we all have a stake in: the atmosphere and the oceans.

■ **Utilitarian and Kantian Ethics** Utilitarian and Kantian approaches to business ethics were developed in the eighteenth and nineteenth centuries. Utilitarian approaches to ethics hold that the moral worth of actions or practices is determined by their consequences. An action is judged to be desirable if it leads to the best possible balance of good consequences over bad consequences. Utilitarianism is committed to the maximization of good and the minimization of harm. It recognizes that actions have multiple consequences, some of which are good in a social sense, and some of which are harmful. As a philosophy for business ethics, it focuses attention on the need to carefully weigh all of the social benefits and costs of a business action and to only pursue those actions where the benefits outweigh the costs. The best decisions, from a utilitarian perspective, are those that produce the greatest good for the greatest number of people.

Many businesses have adopted specific tools, such as cost-benefit analysis and risk assessment, that are firmly rooted in a utilitarian philosophy. Managers often weigh the benefits and costs of a course of action before deciding whether to pursue it. An oil company considering drilling in the Alaskan wildlife preserve must weigh the economic benefits of increased oil production and the creation of jobs against the costs of environmental degradation in a fragile ecosystem.

For all of its appeal, however, the utilitarian philosophy has some serious drawbacks. One problem is measuring the benefits, costs, and risks of a course of action. In the case of an oil company considering drilling in Alaska, how does one measure the potential harm done to the fragile ecosystem of the region? In general, utilitarian philosophers recognize that benefits, costs, and risks often cannot be measured because of limited knowledge.

The second problem with utilitarianism is that the philosophy does not consider justice. The action that produces the greatest good for the greatest number of people may result in the unjustified treatment of a minority. Such action cannot be ethical, precisely because it is unjust. For example, suppose that in the interests of keeping down health insurance costs the government decides to screen people for the HIV virus and deny insurance coverage to those who are HIV positive. By reducing health costs, such action might produce significant benefits for a large number of people, but the action is unjust because it discriminates unfairly against a minority.

Kantian ethics are based on the philosophy of Immanuel Kant (1724–1804). Kant argued that people should be treated as ends and never purely as *means* to the ends of others. People are not instruments, like a machine. People have dignity and need to be respected as such. Employing people in sweatshops where they work long hours for low pay in poor work conditions is a violation of ethics according to Kantian philosophy because it treats people as mere cogs in a machine and not as conscious moral beings that have dignity. Although contemporary moral philosophers tend to view Kant's ethical philosophy as incomplete—for example, his system has no place for moral emotions or sentiments such as sympathy or caring—the notion that people should be respected and treated with dignity still resonates in the modern world.

■ **Rights Theories** Developed in the twentieth century, **rights theories** recognize that human beings have fundamental rights and privileges. Rights establish a minimum level of morally acceptable behavior. One well-known definition of a fundamental right construes it as something that takes precedence over or "trumps" a collective good. Thus we might say that the right to free speech is a fundamental right that takes precedence over all but the most compelling collective goals; for example, it overrides the interest of the state in civil harmony or moral consensus. Moral theorists argue that fundamental human rights form the basis for the *moral compass* managers should navigate by when making decisions that have an ethical component. In a business setting, stakeholder theory provides a useful way for managers to frame any discussion of rights. As noted earlier, stakeholders have basic rights that should be respected, and it is unethical to violate those rights.

It is important to note that along with *rights* come *obligations*. Because we have the right to free speech, we are also obligated to make sure that we respect the free speech of others. Within the framework of a theory of rights, certain people or institutions are obligated to provide benefits or services that secure the rights of others. Such obligations also fall upon more than one class of moral agent (a moral agent is any person or institution that is capable of moral action, such as a government or corporation).

For example, in the late 1980s, to escape the high costs of toxic waste disposal in the West, several firms shipped their waste in bulk to African nations, where it was disposed of at a much lower cost. In 1987 five European ships unloaded toxic waste containing dangerous poisons in Nigeria. Workers wearing thongs and shorts unloaded the barrels for $2.50 a day and placed them in a dirt lot in a residential area. They were not told about the contents of the barrels. Who bears the obligation for protecting the safety rights of workers and residents in a case like this? According to rights theorists, the obligation rests not on the shoulders of one moral agent but on the shoulders of all moral agents whose actions might harm, or contribute to the harm of, the workers and residents. Thus it was the obligation not just of the Nigerian government, but also of the multinational firms that shipped the toxic waste, to make sure that it did no harm to residents and workers. In this case, both the government and the multinationals obviously failed to recognize their basic obligation to protect the fundamental human rights of others.

■ **Justice Theories** Justice theories focus on the attainment of a just distribution of economic goods and services. A **just distribution** is one that is considered fair and equitable. The most famous theory of justice is attributed to philosopher John Rawls. Rawls argues that all economic goods and services should be distributed equally except when an unequal distribution would work to everyone's advantage.

According to Rawls, valid principles of justice are those to which all persons would agree with if they could freely and impartially consider the situation. Impartiality is guaranteed by a conceptual device that Rawls calls the *veil of ignorance*. Under the veil of ignorance, everyone is imagined to be ignorant of all of his or her particular characteristics, for example, his or her race, sex, intelligence, nationality, family background, and special talents. Rawls then asks, what system would people design under a veil of ignorance? His answer is that, under these conditions, people would unanimously agree on two fundamental principles of justice.

The first principle is that each person should be permitted the maximum amount of basic liberty compatible with a similar liberty for others. Roughly speaking, Rawls takes these liberties to be political liberty (the right to vote), freedom of speech and assembly, liberty of conscience and freedom of thought, the freedom and right to hold personal property, and freedom from arbitrary arrest and seizure. The second principle is that once equal basic liberty is ensured, inequality in basic social goods—such as income, wealth, and opportunities—is to be allowed *only* if it benefits everyone. Rawls believes that inequalities can be just as long as the system that produces them is to the advantage of everyone. More precisely, he formulates what he calls the *difference principle*, which is that inequalities are justified if they benefit the position of the least advantaged person. So, for example, the wide variations in income and wealth that we see in the United States can be considered "just" if the market-based system that produces this unequal distribution also benefits the least advantaged members of society.

In the context of business ethics, Rawls's theory creates an interesting perspective. Managers could ask themselves whether the policies they adopt would be considered "just" under Rawls's *veil of ignorance*. Is it "just," for example, to pay foreign workers less than workers in the firm's home country? Rawls's second principle would suggest that it is, as long as the inequality benefits the least advantaged members of the global society (which is what economic theory suggests). Alternatively, it is difficult to imagine that managers operating under a veil of ignorance would design a system where employees are paid subsistence wages to work long hours in sweatshop conditions and be exposed to toxic materials. Such working conditions are clearly unjust in Rawls's framework, and therefore it is unethical to adopt them. Similarly, operating under a veil of ignorance, most people would probably design a system that imparts protection from environmental degradation, preserves a free and fair playing field for competition, and prohibits self-dealing. Thus Rawls's veil of ignorance is a conceptual tool that helps define the moral compass managers can use to navigate through difficult ethical dilemmas.

■ Behaving Ethically

What then is the best way for managers to ensure that ethical considerations are taken into account? In many cases, there is no easy answer to this question, for many of the most vexing ethical problems involve very real dilemmas and suggest no obvious right course of action. Nevertheless, managers can and should do at least seven things to ensure that basic ethical principles are adhered to and that ethical issues are routinely considered when making business decisions. They can (1) favor hiring and promoting people with a well-grounded sense of personal ethics; (2) build an organizational culture that places a high value on ethical behavior; (3) make sure that leaders within the business not only articulate the rhetoric of ethical behavior but also act in a manner that is consistent with that rhetoric; (4) put decision-making processes in place that require people to consider the ethical dimension of business decisions; (5) use ethics officers; (6) put strong governance processes in place; and (7) act with moral courage.

■ Hiring and Promotion It seems obvious that businesses should strive to hire people who have a strong sense of personal ethics and would not engage in unethical or illegal behavior. Similarly, you would rightly expect a business to not promote people, and perhaps fire people, whose behavior does not match generally accepted ethical standards. But doing so is actually very difficult. How do you know that someone has a poor sense of personal ethics? In our society, if someone lacks personal ethics, he or she may hide this fact to retain people's trust.

Is there anything that businesses can do to make sure that they do not hire people who turn out to have poor personal ethics, particularly given that people have an incentive to hide this from public view (indeed, unethical people may well lie about their nature)? Businesses can give potential employees psychological tests to try to discern their ethical predisposition, and they can check with prior employees regarding someone's reputation, such as by asking for letters of reference and talking to people who have worked with the prospective employee. The latter approach is certainly not uncommon and does indeed influence the hiring process. As for promoting people who have displayed poor ethics, that should not occur in a company where the organization culture values ethical behavior and where leaders act accordingly.

■ Organization Culture and Leadership To foster ethical behavior, businesses need to build an organization culture that places a high value on ethical behavior. Three actions are particularly important. First, businesses must explicitly articulate values that place a strong emphasis on ethical behavior. Many companies now do this by drafting a **code of ethics**, a formal statement of the ethical priorities a business adheres to. Others have incorporated ethical statements into documents that articulate the values or mission of the business. For example, the food and consumer products giant Unilever has a code of ethics that includes the following points: "We will not use any form of forced, compulsory or child labor" and "No employee may offer, give or receive any gift or payment which is, or may be construed as being, a bribe. Any demand for, or offer of, a bribe must be rejected immediately and reported to management." Unilever's principles send a very clear message to managers and employees within the organization.

Having articulated values in a code of ethics or some other document, it is important that leaders in the business give life and meaning to those words by repeatedly emphasizing their importance *and then acting on them*. This means using every relevant opportunity to stress the importance of business ethics and making sure that key business decisions not only make good economic sense but also are ethical.

Many companies have gone a step further and hired independent firms to audit them and make sure that they are behaving in a manner consistent with their ethical code. Nike, for example, has in recent years hired independent auditors to make sure that its subcontractors are living up to Nike's code of conduct.

Finally, building an organization culture that places a high value on ethical behavior requires incentive and reward systems, including promotion systems, that reward people who engage in ethical behavior and sanction those who do not.

■ **Decision-Making Processes** In addition to establishing the right kind of ethical culture in an organization, businesspeople must be able to think through the ethical implications of decisions in a systematic way. To do this, they need a moral compass, and both rights theories and Rawls's theory of justice help to provide such a compass. Beyond these theories, some experts on ethics have proposed a straightforward practical guide, or ethical algorithm, to determine whether a decision is ethical. A decision is acceptable on ethical grounds if a businessperson can answer "yes" to each of these questions:

1. Does my decision fall within the accepted values or standards that typically apply in the organizational environment (as articulated in a code of ethics or some other corporate statement)?

2. Am I willing to see the decision communicated to all stakeholders affected by it—for example, by having it reported in newspapers or on television?

3. Would the people with whom I have a significant personal relationship, such as family members, friends, or even managers in other businesses, approve of the decision?

■ **Ethics Officers** To make sure that a business behaves in an ethical manner, a number of firms now have ethics officers. These individuals are responsible for making sure that all employees are trained to be ethically aware, that ethical considerations enter the business decision-making process, and that the company's code of ethics is adhered to. Ethics officers may also be responsible for auditing decisions to make sure that they are consistent with this code. In many businesses, ethics officers act as an internal ombudsperson with responsibility for handling confidential inquiries from employees, investigating complaints from employees or others, reporting findings, and making recommendations for change.

United Technologies, a large aerospace company with worldwide revenues of over $28 billion, has had a formal code of ethics since 1990. There are now some 160 "business practice officers" within United Technologies (this is the company's name for ethics officers) who are responsible for making sure that the code is adhered to. United Technologies also established an ombudsperson program in 1986 that lets employees inquire anonymously about ethics issues. The program has received some 56,000 inquiries since 1986, and 8,000 cases have been handled by an ombudsperson.

■ **Strong Corporate Governance** Strong corporate governance procedures are needed to make sure that managers adhere to ethical norms, in particular, that senior managers do not engage in self-dealing or information manipulation. The key to strong corporate governance procedures is an independent board of directors that is willing to hold top managers to account for self-dealing and is able to question the information provided to them by managers. If companies like Tyco, WorldCom, and Enron had had a strong board of directors, it is unlikely that they would have been racked by accounting scandals or that top managers would have been able to view the funds of these corporations as their own personal treasuries.

There are five cornerstones of strong governance. The first is a board of directors that is composed of a majority of outside directors who have no management responsibilities in the firm, are willing and able to hold top managers to account, and do not have business ties with important insiders. The outside directors should be individuals of high integrity whose reputation is based on their ability to act independently. The second cornerstone is a board where the positions of CEO and chairman are held by separate individuals and the chairman is an outside director. When the CEO is also chairman of the board of directors, he or she can control the agenda, thereby furthering his or her own personal agenda (which may include self-dealing) or limiting criticism against current corporate policies. The third cornerstone is a compensation committee formed by the board that is composed entirely of outside directors. It is the compensation committee that sets the level of pay for top managers, including stock option grants and the like. By making sure that the compensation committee is independent of managers, one reduces the scope of self-dealing. Fourth, the audit committee of the board, which reviews the financial statements of the firm, should also be composed of outsiders, thereby encouraging vigorous independent questioning of the firm's financial statements. Finally, the board should use outside auditors who are truly independent and do not have a conflict of interest. This was not the case in many recent accounting scandals, where the outside auditors were also consultants to the corporation and therefore less likely to ask hard questions of management for fear that doing so would jeopardize lucrative consulting contracts.

■ **Moral Courage** It is important to recognize that sometimes managers and others need significant *moral courage*. It is moral courage that enables managers to walk away from a decision that is profitable but unethical, that gives employees the strength to say no to superiors who instruct them to behave unethically, and that gives employees the integrity to go to the media and blow the whistle on persistent unethical behavior in a company. Moral courage does not come easily; there are well-known cases where individuals have lost their jobs because they blew the whistle on corporate behaviors.

Companies can strengthen the moral courage of employees by committing themselves to not take retribution on employees that exercise moral courage, say no to superiors, or otherwise complain about unethical actions. For example, Unilever's code of ethics includes the following:

> Any breaches of the Code must be reported in accordance with the procedures specified by the Joint Secretaries. The Board of Unilever will not criticize management for any loss of business resulting from adherence to these principles and other mandatory policies and instructions. The Board of Unilever expects employees to bring to their attention, or to that of senior management, any breach or suspected breach of these principles. Provision has been made for employees to be able to report in confidence and no employee will suffer as a consequence of doing so.

This statement gives "permission" to employees to exercise moral courage. Companies can also set up ethics hotlines that allow employees to anonymously register a complaint with a corporate ethics officer.

■ **Final Words** The steps discussed here can help to ensure that, when managers make business decisions, they are fully cognizant of the ethical implications and do not violate basic ethical prescripts. At the same time, not all ethical dilemmas have a clean and obvious solution—that is why they are dilemmas. At the end of the day, there are clearly things that a business should not do, and there are things that they should do, but there are also actions that present managers with true dilemmas. In these cases a premium is placed on the ability of managers to make sense out of complex, messy situations and to make balanced decisions that are as just as possible.

Summary of Chapter

1. Stakeholders are individuals or groups that have an interest, claim, or stake in the company, in what it does, and in how well it performs.
2. Stakeholders are in an exchange relationship with the company. They supply the organization with important resources (or contributions) and in exchange expect their interests to be satisfied (by inducements).
3. A company cannot always satisfy the claims of all stakeholders. The goals of different groups may conflict. The company must identify the most important stakeholders and give highest priority to pursuing strategies that satisfy their needs.
4. A company's stockholders are its legal owners and the providers of risk capital, a major source of the capital resources that allow a company to operate its business. As such, they have a unique role among stakeholder groups.
5. Maximizing long-run profitability and profit growth is the route to maximizing returns to stockholders, and it is also consistent with satisfying the claims of several other key stakeholder groups.
6. When pursuing strategies that maximize profitability, a company has the obligation to do so within the limits set by the law and in a manner consistent with societal expectations.
7. An agency relationship is held to arise whenever one party delegates decision-making authority or control over resources to another.
8. The essence of the agency problem is that the interests of principals and agents are not always the same, and some agents may take advantage of information asymmetries to maximize their own interests at the expense of principals.
9. A number of governance mechanisms serve to limit the agency problem between stockholders and managers. These include the board of directors, stock-based

compensation schemes, financial statements and auditors, and the threat of a takeover.
10. The term **ethics** refers to accepted principles of right or wrong that govern the conduct of a person, the members of a profession, or the actions of an organization. **Business ethics** are the accepted principles of right or wrong governing the conduct of businesspeople, and an ethical strategy is one that does not violate these accepted principles.
11. Unethical behavior is rooted in poor personal ethics; the inability to recognize that ethical issues are at stake, as when there are psychological and geographical distances between a foreign subsidiary and the home office; failure to incorporate ethical issues into strategic and operational decision making; a dysfunctional culture; and failure of leaders to act in an ethical manner.
12. Philosophies underlying business ethics include the Friedman doctrine, utilitarianism, Kantian ethics, rights theories, and justice theories such as that proposed by Rawls.
13. To make sure that ethical issues are considered in business decisions, managers should (a) favor hiring and promoting people with a well-grounded sense of personal ethics; (b) build an organizational culture that places a high value on ethical behavior; (c) make sure that leaders within the business not only articulate the rhetoric of ethical behavior but also act in a manner that is consistent with that rhetoric; (d) put decision-making processes in place that require people to consider the ethical dimension of business decisions; (e) use ethics officers; (f) have strong corporate governance procedures; and (g) be morally courageous and encourage others to be the same.

Discussion Questions

1. How prevalent was the agency problem in corporate America during the late 1990s?

2. During the late 1990s there was a boom in initial public offerings of Internet companies (dot.com companies). The boom was supported by sky high valuations often assigned to Internet start-ups that had no revenues or earnings. The boom came to an abrupt end in 2001 when the NASDAQ stock market collapsed, losing almost 80% of its value. Who do you think benefited most from this boom: investors (stockholders) in those companies, managers, or investment bankers?

3. Why is maximizing return on invested capital consistent with maximizing returns to stockholders?

4. How might a company configure its strategy-making processes to reduce the probability that managers will pursue their own self-interest at the expense of stockholders?

5. Should stock options be treated as an expense? If they were, what impact would this have on a company?

6. Under what conditions is it ethically defensible to outsource production to producers in the developing world who have much lower labor costs when such actions involve laying off long-term employees in the firm's home country?

Practicing Strategic Management

■ SMALL-GROUP EXERCISE
Evaluating Stakeholder Claims

Break up into groups of three to five people, and appoint one group member as a spokesperson who will communicate your findings to the class when called on by the instructor. Discuss the following:

1. Identify the key stakeholders of your educational institution. What claims do they place on the institution?

2. Strategically, how is the institution responding to those claims? Do you think the institution is pursuing the correct strategies in view of those claims? What might it do differently, if anything?

3. Prioritize the stakeholders in order of their importance for the survival and health of the institution. Do the claims of different stakeholder groups conflict with each other? If claims conflict, whose should be tackled first?

■ ARTICLE FILE 11

Find an example of a company that ran into trouble because it failed to take into account the rights of one of its stakeholder groups when making an important strategic decision.

■ STRATEGIC MANAGEMENT PROJECT
Module 11

This module deals with the relationships your company has with its major stakeholder groups. With the information you have at your disposal, perform the tasks and answer the questions that follow:

1. Identify the main stakeholder groups in your company. What claims do they place on the company? How is the company trying to satisfy those claims?

2. Evaluate the performance of the CEO of your company from the perspective of (a) stockholders, (b) employees, (c) customers, and (d) suppliers. What does this evaluation tell you about the ability of the CEO and the priorities that he or she is committed to?

3. Try to establish whether the governance mechanisms that operate in your company do a good job of aligning the interests of top managers with those of stockholders.

4. Pick a major strategic decision made by your company in recent years, and try to think through the ethical implications of that decision. In light of your review, do you think that the company acted correctly?

■ EXPLORING THE WEB
Visiting Merck

Visit the website of Merck, the world's largest pharmaceutical company (**www.merck.com/overview/philosophy.html**), and read the mission statement posted there. Then answer the following questions:

1. Evaluate this mission statement in light of the material contained in this chapter. Does the mission statement clearly state what Merck's basic strategic goal is? Do the values listed provide a good guideline for managerial action at Merck? Do those values recognize stakeholder claims?

2. Read the section on Merck's corporate responsibility and code of conduct. How does Merck attempt to balance

the goals of providing stockholders with an adequate rate of return on their investment while at the same time developing medicines that benefit humanity and that can be acquired by people in need at an affordable price? Do you think that Merck does a good job of balancing these goals?

3. In late September 2004 Merck recalled one of its best drugs, Vioxx, after research showed that people who used Vioxx had an elevated risk of suffering a heart at-

tack. To what extent do you think Merck's values and code of conduct played a part in this decision? Do you think Merck pulled the drug from the market quickly enough? (You may want to take a look at press reports on this issue.)

General Task Using the Web, find an example of a company where there was overt conflict between principals and agents over the future strategic direction of the organization.

Closing Case

The Collapse of Enron

In early December 2001, the Enron Corporation filed for Chapter 11 bankruptcy protection. Enron, which started off as a natural gas pipeline operator and independent power producer, had emerged during the late 1990s as the principal player in the rapidly expanding market for energy trading. At its height in 2000, the company had boasted revenues of $101 billion, a stock market capitalization of $63 billion, and a chairman, Kenneth Lay, who was a high-profile confidant of then president-elect George W. Bush. The company was leveraging its expertise in energy trading to other market opportunities, including trading in paper, metals, water, and telecommunication capacity (or broadband). Enron believed that it could exploit the power of the Internet to create online markets in almost anything. The media loved the company. In 2000, *Fortune* magazine voted Enron "the most innovative company of the year." The *Economist* wrote that Enron "has created what may be the most successful Internet venture of any company in any industry anywhere."

A few months after these words were written, Enron had ceased to exist as a functioning entity. On its last trading day, the stock stood at 61 cents per share, down from a high of $90 just a year earlier. Numbered among the stockholders who had seen their Enron holdings implode in value were many Enron employees, who had been obliged by company policies to hold Enron stock in their retirement accounts.

What made the collapse of Enron so disturbing was not just the size of the failure, but the manner in which the company unraveled. What brought Enron down so rapidly was an accumulation of more than $27 billion in

off-balance-sheet debt held by partnerships hidden from the view of most investors, employees, and regulators. These partnerships were set up to exploit Enron's forays into ever more exotic online trading ventures, such as water and bandwidth trading. The partnerships were controlled by Enron managers but not owned by Enron, so the debt did not appear on Enron's balance sheets and thus did not affect the company's credit rating and borrowing costs. The partnerships were financed with debt raised from institutional investors. Using the company's high-flying stock as collateral, Enron guaranteed that debt. It often transferred its own assets to the partnerships, registering the transfer as revenues.

The partnerships were the brainchild of Enron's chief financial officer, Andrew Fastow, who used them as a way of making Enron's balance sheet and earnings look stronger than they really were. Fastow also personally profited from the partnerships, many of which he controlled, reportedly making over $30 million from them. The partnership strategy, however, was very risky. If the aggressive investments the partnerships were making did not pan out, Enron, as the guarantor of partnership debt, would be on the hook. Moreover, if Enron's stock fell too far, guarantees backed by stock would have to be replaced by cash, which would require Enron to raise more debt.

The first cracks in Enron's facade started to appear in August 2001 when the CEO, Jeffrey Skilling, suddenly and unexpectedly resigned, citing "personal reasons." Skilling had sold some $17.5 million of Enron stock in the months before he quit. Chairman Kenneth Lay, himself the former

CEO, stepped back into the CEO position and reassured investors, who were spooked by Skilling's sudden departure. Then, in October 2001, Enron recorded a third-quarter loss of $618 million and announced that it was reducing shareholder equity by $1.2 billion, primarily because of losses accumulated at partnerships. Enron's stock, which had lost half its value since December 2000, suddenly plummeted. This created a death spiral in which Enron had to raise debt to guarantee debt accumulated at partnerships, a spiral that quickly led to bankruptcy.

When the existence of the partnerships was revealed, the financial community was stunned: there had been scarcely a reference to any of them in Enron's audited financial statements. By implication, investors were ignorant of the tremendous risks associated with the partnership strategy. It was difficult to escape the conclusion that Enron's management had deliberately played down the existence of the partnerships in order to mislead the financial markets about the true state of the company. Questions were also asked about Enron's auditor, Arthur Andersen. Why had it not drawn attention to the partnerships? Surely, as auditor, it must have known about them. Why had Andersen apparently agreed with the tactic of keeping these partnerships hidden from public view? Was it to protect a lucrative financial relationship with an important client? Enron paid Andersen some $52 million in 2000—$25 million for auditing services and $27 million for consulting services. The questions about Andersen's role became even sharper when it was revealed that the Andersen partner responsible for the Enron audit had instructed his staff to shred documents relating to the audit. Was Andersen trying to hide what it had known about the true financial state of the company?

The voices of critics grew louder when it was discovered that, in August 2001, a midlevel Enron official, Sherron Watkins, had sent a memo to Kenneth Lay outlining the risks associated with the partnership strategy. Watkins warned Lay that Enron could implode in a wave of accounting scandals. Lay apparently expressed concern but continued to present a bullish face to the outside world and appears to have done nothing to rein in the CFO, Fastow. Lay moved to replace Fastow only on October 24, two days after the Securities and Exchange Commission announced that it had started an investigation into Enron's accounting practices. Worse still, throughout 2001, Enron's senior managers continued to sell millions of dollars of their own holdings in Enron's stock, while many employees were limited or prohibited from selling the Enron stock they held in their retirement accounts.

Did the managers know something that they kept hidden from their own employees?

A 2002 exposé of Enron by author Robert Bryce added interesting details to the Enron story. Bryce painted a picture of widespread self-dealing and fraud at Enron. According to Bryce, top managers systematically enriched themselves and their own families at shareholders' expense. Bryce tells how former Enron CEO Kenneth Lay made sure that his own family benefited handsomely from Enron. Much of Enron's corporate travel business was handled by a travel agency partly owned by Lay's sister. When an internal auditor recommended that the company could do better by using another travel agency, he soon found himself out of a job. In 1997 Enron acquired a company owed by Kenneth Lay's son, Mark Lay, which was trying to establish a business trading paper and pulp products. At the time Mark Lay and another company he controlled were targets of a federal criminal investigation of bankruptcy fraud and embezzlement. As part of the deal, Enron hired Mark Lay as an executive with a three-year contract that guaranteed him at least $1 million in pay over that period, plus options to purchase about 20,000 shares of Enron. Bryce also details how Lay's grown daughter used an Enron jet to transport her king-sized bed to France.

Bryce also discussed how Lay's successor as CEO at Enron, Jeff Skilling, put a performance evaluation system in place that weeded out 15 percent of underperformers every six months. According to Bryce, this created a pressure cooker culture with a myopic focus on short-run performance. Some executives and energy traders responded to that pressure by falsifying their performance, such as by inflating the value of trades, to make it look as if they were doing better than was actually the case.

In the aftermath of Enron's collapse, the U.S. Congress announced that it would investigate allegations of financial misdealing at the company. Called before a House Committee, Lay and Fastow took the Fifth, while Skilling claimed ignorance of the details of the partnership dealings. Was the law broken? It would seem so. By late 2004 several former Enron executives were in jail for fraud, including CFO Fastow, who was serving a ten-year jail sentence for fraud, while others, including Lay and Skilling, had been indicted by prosecutors and were scheduled to stand trial. For his part, Lay has acknowledged that there was wrongdoing at Enron, but he claims that he did not know about it. Lay has blamed Enron's troubles on Fastow, who he says "betrayed" his position of trust in the company.[34]

Case Discussion Questions

1. In whose best interests were Fastow, Lay, and Skilling acting? Do you think what happened at Enron is an example of the agency problem?

2. Do you think the Enron board exercised its fiduciary duty during the late 1990s? To what extent might the effectiveness of the board have been limited by the fact that Kenneth Lay, the former CEO, was chairman? What does this tell you about how boards can work?

3. How might the culture of the company under the leadership of Lay and Skilling have contributed to Enron's ethical problems?

4. Do you think Lay is himself a victim of an agency problem, as he seems to claim? Does he bear any responsibility, legal or otherwise, for the demise of Enron?

5. Did Arthur Andersen behave ethically? If not, why not?

Chapter 12

Implementing Strategy in Companies That Compete in a Single Industry

Opening Case

Nokia's New Product Structure

Nokia is the world's largest cellular or mobile phone maker in the world, with sales of over $40 billion in 2004. The company was a pioneer of cell phone technology, and throughout the 1990s its sales surged every year; however, business has not been as good in the 2000s. Like Motorola, another cell phone pioneer, Nokia's profits have fallen because it has run into tough competition from companies like Samsung, Sony, and hand-held makers like Palm that have been rushing to offer their customers new and improved varieties of hand-held devices or smart phones. In the *Opening Case* to Chapter 5, we saw how Samsung was the first company to realize that customers wanted a color screen so that they could play games on their phones, as well as one of the first to realize the potential of integrating digital cameras into phones. The market is growing for game-playing phones, Internet-connected phones, and smart phones that include functions such as an MP3 player, record-keeping software, and applications software for PowerPoint presentations and word processing. Also growing rapidly is the market for wireless technology that can securely link smart phones used in the field to the company's central databases and the PCs in employees' offices or homes, especially now that broadband communication is becoming the norm.

Analysts claim that Nokia was slow to sense these emerging trends partly because of its organizational structure and culture. Nokia's way of operating was to push down or decentralize decision making to lower levels where teams of employees were made responsible for developing innovative new cell phone software and hardware. Bureaucracy was kept to a minimum, and team members normally discussed product development in informal meetings. In addition, Nokia's culture was based on Finnish values and norms that emphasized democratic, shared, and informal work relationships rather than the use of formal authority.

This way of implementing strategy had led to superior innovation and a successful business model, but as Nokia grew bigger, problems emerged. While the cell phone market was changing rapidly, Nokia's team structure was still resulting in slow decision making. It was taking more and more time for Nokia to innovate new products and bring them to the market. Higher-level managers had to wait longer to find out what the teams below them were doing, and then top managers from all parts of the organization had to meet in "company committees" to decide which products should be given most funding and priority. Another problem was that Nokia's top managers, headquartered in Espoo, Finland, were remote from global customers, and its marketing and engineering managers were slow to pick up on developing wireless trends, such as customers' desire for digital cameras. In particular, they did not appreciate how fast the global market was fragmenting into customers in rich countries like Japan and the United States who wanted sophisticated, broadband-capable smart phones and were prepared to pay high prices for them, and customers in developing countries such as South America, China, and India who needed an inexpensive cell phone infrastructure and service, as well as inexpensive cell phones.[1]

In the early 2000s, when the company's sales started to fall as its Japanese competitors took the lead, Nokia's managers realized they needed to change the way the company operated to quicken Nokia's response to the changing marketplace. Nokia's CEO, Jorma Ollila, announced that in 2004 Nokia would split up its activities into four separate product divisions, each of which would focus on developing cell phone software and hardware for a particular market segment. Three of these were new divisions: (1) the *mobile phone* division, which would primarily design and sell low-cost/low-priced handsets primarily for voice calls; (2) the *multimedia* division, which would design and sell advanced smart phones with features such as gaming and picture taking and which would pursue differentiation and, hopefully, premium pricing; and (3) the *networks* division, which would sell the technology necessary to build mobile phone networks and create wireless infrastructure in regions and countries around the globe. Finally, Nokia announced it would greatly expand the activities of its *enterprise solutions* division, which was responsible for developing hardware and software products for corporate customers in search of a wireless corporate intranet. Here, it was competing directly against companies like Microsoft, IBM, and Hewlett-Packard.

The plan is that each product division will be under the control of its own team of top executives and each team will build the business model necessary to compete successfully in its market segment.[2] By decentralizing control to each division, Nokia hopes to speed up team decision making, reasoning that managers will be in much closer contract with these teams and can intervene quickly as the need arises. Nokia hopes the new structure will allow it to innovate new models of cell phones at a faster rate and lower cost and so combat the threat from Samsung. In addition, to get closer to its customers, Nokia announced that it would expand its overseas operations—for example, by outsourcing more manufacturing to Asia and establishing more local sales offices. It would also create a U.S. headquarters for its new enterprise solutions division, and it hired a former HP executive, Mary McDowell, to head the division and spearhead its push into this large and profitable corporate networking market. Only time will tell if Nokia's new structure will be successful, but the company announced that many new products would be introduced in 2005 and beyond and that its sales were once again on the upward path.[3]

Overview

As the story of Nokia suggests, organizational structure and culture can have a direct bearing on a company's profits. This chapter examines how managers can best implement their strategies through their organization's structure and culture to achieve a competitive advantage and superior performance. A well-thought-out business model becomes profitable only if it can be implemented successfully. In practice, however, implementing strategy through structure and culture is a difficult, challenging, and never-ending task. Managers cannot just create an organizing framework for a company's value-chain activities and then assume it will keep working efficiently and effectively over time, just as they cannot select strategies and assume that these strategies will still work in the future when the competitive environment is changing.

We begin by discussing the main elements of organizational design and the way they work together to create an organizing framework that allows a company to implement its strategy. We also discuss how strategic managers can use structure, control, and culture to pursue functional-level strategies that create and build distinctive competencies. The analysis then moves to the industry level and the issues facing managers in a single industry. The next chapter takes up where this one leaves off and examines strategy implementation across industries and countries—that is, corporate and global strategy. By the end of this chapter and the next, you will understand why the fortunes of a company often rest on its managers' ability to design and manage its structure, control systems, and culture to best implement its business model.

Implementing Strategy Through Organizational Design

Strategy implementation involves the use of **organizational design,** the process of deciding how a company should create, use, and combine organizational structure, control systems, and culture to pursue a business model successfully. **Organizational structure** assigns employees to specific value creation tasks and roles and specifies how these tasks and roles are to be linked together in a way that increases efficiency, quality, innovation, and responsiveness to customers—the distinctive competencies that build competitive advantage. The purpose of organizational structure is to *coordinate and integrate* the efforts of employees at all levels—corporate, business, and functional—and across a company's functions and business units so that they work together in the way that will allow it to achieve the specific set of strategies in its business model.

Organizational structure does not by itself provide the set of incentives through which people can be *motivated* to make it work. Hence, there is a need for control systems. The purpose of a **control system** is to provide managers with (1) a set of incentives to motivate employees to work toward increasing efficiency, quality, innovation, and responsiveness to customers and (2) specific feedback on how well an organization and its members are performing and building competitive advantage so that managers can constantly take action to strengthen a company's business model. Structure provides an organization with a skeleton; control gives it the muscles, sinews, nerves, and sensations that allow managers to regulate and govern its activities.

Organizational culture, the third element of organizational design, is the specific collection of values, norms, beliefs, and attitudes that are shared by people and groups in an organization and that control the way they interact with each other and with stakeholders outside the organization.[4] Organizational culture is a company's "way of doing something": it describes the characteristic ways in which members of an organization "get the job done," such as the way Nokia uses teams to speed innovation. As we discuss in detail below, top managers, because they can influence which kinds of beliefs and values develop in an organization, are an important determinant of how organizational members will work toward achieving organizational goals.[5]

Figure 12.1 sums up the discussion so far. Organizational structure, control, and culture are the means by which an organization motivates and coordinates its members to work toward achieving the building blocks of competitive advantage.

FIGURE 12.1

Implementing Strategy Through Organizational Design

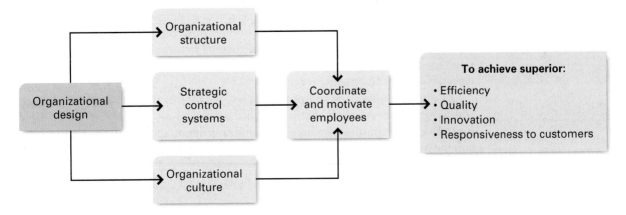

Top managers who wish to find out why it takes a long time for people to make decisions in a company, why there is a lack of cooperation between sales and manufacturing, or why product innovations are few and far between need to understand how the design of a company's structure and control system and the values and norms in its culture affect employee motivation and behavior. *Organizational structure, control, and culture shape people's behaviors, values, and attitudes and determine how they will implement an organization's business model and strategies.*[6] On the basis of such an analysis, top managers can devise a plan to restructure or change their company's structure, control systems, and culture to improve coordination and motivation. Effective organizational design allows a company to obtain a competitive advantage and achieve above-average profitability.

Building Blocks of Organizational Structure

After formulating a company's business model and strategies, managers must make designing an organizational structure their next priority. The value creation activities of organizational members are meaningless unless some type of structure is used to assign people to tasks and connect the activities of different people and functions.[7] Managers must make three basic choices:

1. How best to group tasks into functions and to group functions into business units or divisions to create distinctive competencies and pursue a particular strategy

2. How to allocate authority and responsibility to these functions and divisions

3. How to increase the level of coordination or integration between functions and divisions as a structure evolves and becomes more complex

We first discuss basic issues and then revisit them when considering appropriate choices of structure at different levels of strategy.

■ Grouping Tasks, Functions, and Divisions

Because, to a large degree, an organization's tasks are a function of its strategy, the dominant view is that companies choose a form of structure to match their organizational strategy. Perhaps the first person to address this issue formally was the Harvard business historian Alfred D. Chandler.[8] After studying the organizational problems experienced in large U.S. corporations such as DuPont and GM as they grew in the early decades of the twentieth century, Chandler reached two conclusions: (1) that, in principle, organizational structure follows the range and variety of tasks that the organization chooses to pursue; and (2) that U.S. companies' structures change as their strategy changes in a predictable way over time.[9] In general, this means that most companies first group people and tasks into functions, and then functions into divisions.[10]

As we discuss earlier, a *function* is a collection of people who work together and perform the same types of tasks or hold similar positions in an organization.[11] For example, the salespeople in a car dealership belong to the sales function. Together, car sales, car repair, car parts, and accounting are the set of functions that allow a car dealership to sell and maintain cars.

As organizations grow and produce a wider range of products, the amount and complexity of the *handoffs*, that is the work exchanges or transfers between people, functions, and subunits, increase. The communications and measurement problems and the managerial inefficiencies surrounding these transfers or handoffs are a major source of *bureaucratic costs*, the costs of monitoring and managing the exchanges necessary to add value to a product as it flows along a company's value chain to the final customer.[12]

We discuss why bureaucratic costs increase as companies pursue more complex strategies later in the chapter. For now, it is important to note that managers group tasks into functions and, when necessary, group functions into business units or divisions to reduce bureaucratic costs. For example, as Nokia started to produce a wide range of different mobile phones for different kinds of customers, it created separate product divisions. A *division* is a way of grouping functions to allow an organization to better produce and dispose of its goods and services to customers. In developing an organizational structure, managers must decide how to group an organization's activities by function and division in a way that achieves organizational goals effectively, such as happened at Nokia.[13]

Top managers can choose from among many kinds of structure to group their activities. The choice is made on the basis of the structure's ability to implement the company's business models and strategies successfully.

■ **Allocating Authority and Responsibility**

As organizations grow and produce a wider range of goods and services, the size and number of their functions and divisions increase. The number of handoffs or transfers between employees also increases, and to economize on bureaucratic costs and effectively coordinate the activities of people, functions, and divisions, managers must develop a clear and unambiguous **hierarchy of authority**, or chain of command, that defines each manager's relative authority, from the CEO down through the middle managers and first-line managers, to the nonmanagerial employees who actually make goods or provide services.[14] Every manager, at every level of the hierarchy, supervises one or more subordinates. The term **span of control** refers to the number of subordinates who report directly to a manager. When managers know exactly what their authority and responsibility are, information distortion problems that promote managerial inefficiencies are kept to a minimum, and handoffs or transfers can be negotiated and monitored to economize on bureaucratic costs. For example, managers are less likely to risk invading another manager's turf and thus can avoid the costly fights and conflicts that inevitably result from such encroachments.

■ **Tall and Flat Organizations** Companies choose the number of hierarchical levels they need on the basis of their strategy and the functional tasks necessary to create distinctive competencies.[15] As an organization grows in size or complexity (measured by the number of its employees, functions, and divisions), its hierarchy of authority normally lengthens, making the organizational structure taller. A **tall structure** has many levels of authority relative to company size; a **flat structure** has fewer levels relative to company size (see Figure 12.2). As the hierarchy becomes taller, problems that make the organization's structure less flexible and slow managers' response to changes in the competitive environment may result. It is vital that managers understand how these problems arise so they know how to change a company's structure to respond to them.

First, communication problems may arise. When an organization has many levels in the hierarchy, it can take a long time for the decisions and orders of top managers to reach managers further down in the hierarchy, and it can take a long time for top managers to learn how well their decisions worked out. Feeling out of touch, top managers may want to verify that lower-level managers are following orders and may require written confirmation from them. Lower-level managers, who know they will be held strictly accountable for their actions, start devoting more time to the process of making decisions in order to improve their chances of being right. They might even try to avoid responsibility by making top managers decide what actions to take.

FIGURE 12.2

Tall and Flat Structures

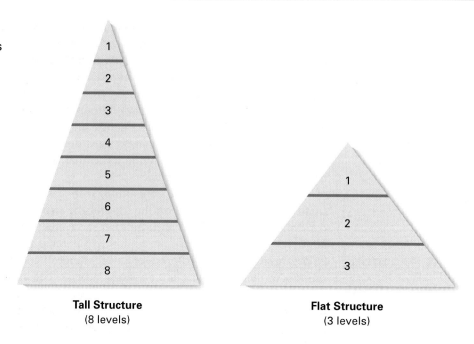

Tall Structure
(8 levels)

Flat Structure
(3 levels)

A second communication problem that can result is the distortion of commands and orders as they are transmitted up and down the hierarchy, which causes managers at different levels to interpret what is happening differently. Accidental distortion of orders and messages occurs when different managers interpret messages from their own narrow functional perspectives. Intentional distortion can occur because managers lower in the hierarchy decide to interpret information to increase their own personal advantage.

A third problem with tall hierarchies is that they usually indicate that an organization is employing *too many* managers, and managers are expensive. Managerial salaries, benefits, offices, and secretaries are a huge expense for organizations. Large companies such as IBM, General Motors, and Nokia pay their managers billions of dollars a year. In the 2000s, hundreds of thousands of middle managers were laid off as dot-coms collapsed and high-tech companies like Hewlett-Packard and Lucent attempted to reduce costs by restructuring and downsizing their work forces.

■ **The Minimum Chain of Command** To ward off the problems that result when an organization becomes too tall and employs too many managers, top managers need to ascertain whether they are employing the right number of top, middle, and first-line managers and see whether they can redesign their hierarchies to reduce the number of managers. Top managers might well follow a basic organizing principle: the **principle of the minimum chain of command**, which states that a company should choose the hierarchy with the *fewest* levels of authority necessary to use organizational resources efficiently and effectively.

Effective managers constantly scrutinize their hierarchies to see whether the number of levels can be reduced—for example, by eliminating one level and giving the responsibilities of managers at that level to managers above and empowering employees below. This practice has become increasingly common as companies battle with low-cost overseas competitors and search for ways to reduce costs. One manager who is constantly trying to empower employees and keep the hierarchy flat is Colleen C. Barrett, the number-two executive of Southwest Airlines.[16] Barrett, the highest-ranking woman in the airline industry, is well known for continually reaffirming Southwest's message that employees should feel free to go above and beyond their prescribed roles to provide better customer service. Her central message is that Southwest values and trusts its employees, who are empowered to take responsibility. Southwest employees are encouraged not to look to their superiors for guidance but rather to take responsibility to find ways to do the job better themselves. As a result, Southwest keeps the number of its middle managers to a minimum.

When companies become too tall and the chain of command too long, strategic managers tend to lose control over the hierarchy, which means that they lose control over their strategies. Disaster often follows because a tall organizational structure decreases, rather than promotes, motivation and coordination between employees and functions, and bureaucratic costs escalate as a result. One important way to overcome such problems, at least partially, and to lessen bureaucratic costs is to decentralize authority—that is, vest authority in the hierarchy's lower levels as well as at the top.

■ **Centralization or Decentralization?** Authority is centralized when managers at the upper levels of a company's hierarchy retain the authority to make the most important decisions. When authority is decentralized, it is delegated to divisions, functions, and employees at lower levels in the company. By delegating authority in this fashion, managers can economize on bureaucratic costs and avoid communication and coordination problems because information does not have to be constantly sent to the top of the organization for decisions to be made. There are three advantages to decentralization.

First, when top managers delegate operational decision-making responsibility to middle- and first-level managers, they reduce information overload and so are able to spend more time on positioning the company competitively and strengthening its business model. Second, when managers in the bottom layers of the company become responsible for implementing strategies to suit local conditions, their motivation and accountability increase. The result is that decentralization promotes flexibility and reduces bureaucratic costs because lower-level managers are authorized to make on-the-spot decisions; handoffs are not needed. The third advantage is that when lower-level employees are given the right to make important decisions, fewer managers are needed to oversee their activities and tell them what to do—a company can flatten its hierarchy. Strategy in Action 12.1 shows how Union Pacific experienced some of these advantages after it decentralized its operations.

If decentralization is so effective, why don't all companies decentralize decision making and avoid the problems of tall hierarchies? The answer is that centralization has its advantages too. Centralized decision making allows for easier coordination of the organizational activities needed to pursue a company's strategy. If managers at all levels can make their own decisions, overall planning becomes extremely difficult, and the company may lose control of its decision making.

Centralization also means that decisions fit broad organization objectives. When its branch operations were getting out of hand, for example, Merrill Lynch increased centralization by installing more information systems to give corporate managers greater control over branch activities. Similarly, Hewlett-Packard centralized R&D responsibility at the corporate level to provide a more directed corporate strategy.

Strategy in Action 12.1

Union Pacific Decentralizes to Increase Customer Responsiveness

Union Pacific, one of the biggest rail freight carriers in the United States, was experiencing a crisis in the late 1990s. The U.S. economic boom was causing a record increase in the amount of freight that the railroad had to transport, but at the same time, the railroad was experiencing record delays in moving the freight. Union Pacific's customers were irate and complaining bitterly about the problem, and the delays were costing the company millions of dollars in penalty payments—$150 million annually.

The problem stemmed from Union Pacific's very centralized management approach, devised in its attempt to cut costs. All scheduling and route planning were handled centrally at its headquarters office in an attempt to promote operating efficiency. The job of regional managers was largely to ensure the smooth flow of freight through their regions. Now, recognizing that efficiency had to be balanced by the need to be responsive to customers,

Union Pacific's CEO, Dick Davidson, announced a sweeping reorganization to the company's customers. Henceforth, regional managers were to be given the authority to make operational decisions at the level at which they were most important: field operations. Regional managers could now alter scheduling and routing to accommodate customer requests even if this raised costs. The goal of the organization was to "return to excellent performance by simplifying our processes and becoming easier to deal with." In making this decision, the company was following the lead of its competitors, most of which had already moved to decentralize their operations. Union Pacific has continued its decentralization approach in the 2000s. In its recent announcement that it was adding a new region, it stated that "the new four-region system will continue the effort to decentralize decision-making into the field, while fostering improved customer responsiveness, operational excellence, and personal accountability."[a]

Furthermore, in times of crisis, centralization of authority permits strong leadership because authority is focused on one person or group. This focus allows for speedy decision making and a concerted response by the whole organization. How to choose the right level of centralization for a particular strategy is discussed later.

■ **Integration and Integrating Mechanisms**

Much coordination takes place among people, functions, and divisions through the hierarchy of authority. Often, however, as a structure becomes complex, this is not enough, and top managers need to use various **integrating mechanisms** to increase communication and coordination among functions and divisions. The greater the complexity of an organization's structure, the greater is the need for coordination among people, functions, and divisions to make the organizational structure work efficiently.[17] We discuss three kinds of integrating mechanisms that illustrate the kinds of issues involved.[18] Once again, these mechanisms are employed to economize on the information distortion problems that commonly arise when managing the handoffs or transfers among the ideas and activities of different people, functions, and divisions.

■ **Direct Contact** Direct contact among managers creates a context within which managers from different functions or divisions can work together to solve mutual problems. However, several problems are associated with establishing this contact. Managers from different functions may have different views about what must be done to achieve organizational goals. But if the managers have equal authority (as functional managers typically do), the only manager who can tell them what to do is the CEO. If functional managers cannot reach agreement, no mechanism exists to resolve the conflict apart from the authority of the boss. In fact, one sign of a poorly performing organizational structure is the number of problems sent up the hierarchy for top managers to solve. The need to solve everyday conflicts and solve handoff or transfer problems raises bureaucratic costs. To reduce such conflicts and solve transfer problems, top managers use more complex integrating mechanisms to increase coordination among functions and divisions.

■ **Liaison Roles** Managers can increase coordination among functions and divisions by establishing liaison roles. When the volume of contacts between two functions increases, one way to improve coordination is to give one manager in each function or division the responsibility for coordinating with the other. These managers may meet daily, weekly, monthly, or as needed to solve handoff issues and transfer problems. The responsibility for coordination is part of the liaison's full-time job, and usually an informal relationship forms between the people involved, greatly easing strains between functions. Furthermore, liaison roles provide a way of transmitting information across an organization, which is important in large organizations where employees may know no one outside their immediate function or division.

■ **Teams** When more than two functions or divisions share many common problems, direct contact and liaison roles may not provide sufficient coordination. In these cases, a more complex integrating mechanism, the **team**, may be appropriate. One manager from each relevant function or division is assigned to a team that meets to solve a specific mutual problem; members are responsible for reporting back to their subunits on the issues addressed and the solutions recommended. Teams are increasingly being used at all organizational levels.

Strategic Control Systems

Strategic managers choose the organizational strategies and structure they hope will allow the organization to use its resources most effectively to pursue its business model and create value and profit. Then they create **strategic control systems**, tools that allow them to monitor and evaluate whether, in fact, their strategy and structure are working as intended, how they could be improved, and how they should be changed if they are not working.

Strategic control is not just about monitoring how well an organization and its members are performing currently or about how well the firm is using its existing resources. It is also about how to create the incentives to keep employees motivated and focused on the important problems that may confront an organization in the future so that they work together to find solutions that can help an organization perform better over time.[19] To understand the vital importance of strategic control, consider how it helps managers to obtain superior efficiency, quality, innovation, and responsiveness to customers, the four basic building blocks of competitive advantage:

■ *Control and efficiency.* To determine how *efficiently* they are using organizational resources, managers must be able to measure accurately how many units of inputs (raw materials, human resources, and so on) are being used to produce a unit of output. They must also be able to measure the number of units of outputs (goods and services) they produce. A control system contains the measures or yardsticks that allow managers to assess how efficiently they are producing goods and services. Moreover, if managers experiment to find a more efficient way to produce goods and services, these measures tell managers how successful they have been. Without a control system in place, managers have no idea how well their organizations are performing and how they can make it perform better, something that is becoming increasingly important in today's highly competitive environment.[20]

■ *Control and quality.* Today, competition often revolves around increasing the *quality* of goods and services. In the car industry, for example, within each price range, cars compete against one another in terms of their features, design, and reliability. So whether a customer buys a Ford Taurus, a GM Cavalier, a Chrysler Intrepid, a Toyota Camry, or a Honda Accord depends significantly on the quality of each company's product. Strategic control is important in determining the quality of goods and services because it gives managers feedback on product quality. If managers consistently measure the number of customers' complaints and the number of new cars returned for repairs, they have a good indication of how much quality they have built into their product.

■ *Control and innovation.* Strategic control can help to raise the level of *innovation* in an organization. Successful innovation takes place when managers create an organizational setting in which employees feel empowered to be creative and authority is decentralized to employees so that they feel free to experiment and take risks, such as at Nokia. Deciding on the appropriate control systems to encourage risk taking is an important management challenge, and, as discussed later in the chapter, an organization's culture becomes important in this regard.

■ *Control and responsiveness to customers.* Finally, strategic managers can help make their organizations more *responsive to customers* if they develop a control system that allows them to evaluate how well employees with customer contact are performing their jobs. Monitoring employees' behavior can help managers find ways to help increase employees' performance level, perhaps by revealing areas in which skills training can help employees or by finding new procedures that allow employees to perform their jobs better. When employees know their behaviors are being monitored, they may have more incentive to be helpful and consistent in the way they act toward customers.

Strategic control systems are the formal target-setting, measurement, and feedback systems that allow strategic managers to evaluate whether a company is achieving superior efficiency, quality, innovation, and customer responsiveness and implementing its strategy successfully. An effective control system should have three characteristics. It should be *flexible* enough to allow managers to respond as necessary to unexpected events; it should provide *accurate information*, giving a true picture of organizational performance; and it should supply managers with the information in a *timely manner* because making decisions on the basis of outdated information is a recipe for failure.[21] As Figure 12.3 shows, designing an effective strategic control system requires four steps: establishing standards and targets, creating measuring and monitoring systems, comparing performance against targets, and evaluating the result.

■ **Levels of Strategic Control**

Strategic control systems are developed to measure performance at four levels in a company: corporate, divisional, functional, and individual. Managers at all levels must develop the most appropriate set of measures to evaluate corporate-, business-, and functional-level performance. As the balanced scorecard approach discussed in Chapter 11 suggests, these measures should be tied as closely as possibly to the goals of developing distinctive competencies in efficiency, quality, innovativeness, and

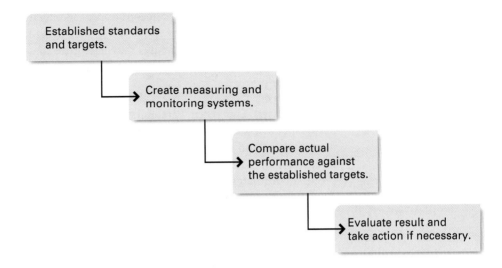

responsiveness to customers. Care must be taken, however, to ensure that the standards used at each level do not cause problems at the other levels—for example, that a division's attempts to improve its performance does not conflict with corporate performance. Furthermore, controls at each level should provide the basis on which managers at lower levels design their control systems. Figure 12.4 illustrates these links.

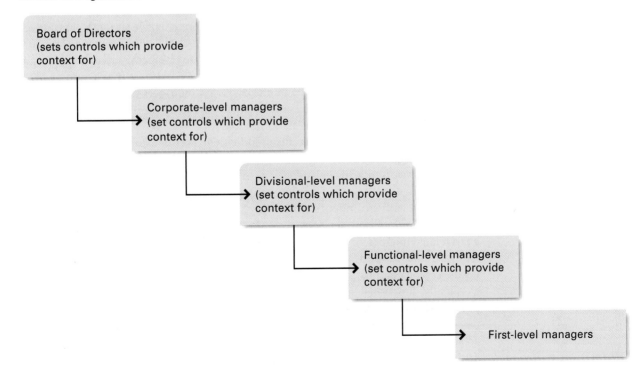

■ Types of Strategic Control Systems

In Chapter 11, the balanced scorecard approach was discussed as a way to ensure that managers complement the use of ROIC with other kinds of strategic controls to ensure they are pursuing strategies that maximize long-run profitability. Here we consider three more types of control systems: *personal control, output control,* and *behavior control.*

■ Personal Control

Personal control is the desire to shape and influence the behavior of a person in a *face-to-face interaction* in the pursuit of a company's goals. The most obvious kind of personal control is direct supervision from a manager further up in the hierarchy. The personal approach is useful because managers can question and probe subordinates about problems or new issues they are facing to get a better understanding of the situation, as well as to ensure that subordinates are performing their work effectively and not hiding any information that could cause problems down the line. Personal control also can come from a group of peers, such as occurs when people work in teams. Once again, personal control at the group level means that there is more possibility for learning to occur and competencies to develop, as well as greater opportunities to prevent free-riding or shirking.

■ Output Control

Output control is a system in which strategic managers estimate or forecast appropriate performance goals for each division, department, and employee and then measure actual performance relative to these goals. Often a company's reward system is linked to performance on these goals, so output control also provides an incentive structure for motivating employees at all levels in the organization. Goals keep managers informed about how well their strategies are creating a competitive advantage and building the distinctive competencies that lead to future success. Goals exist at all levels in an organization.

Divisional goals state corporate managers' expectations for each division concerning performance on such dimensions as efficiency, quality, innovation, and responsiveness to customers. Generally, corporate managers set challenging divisional goals to encourage divisional managers to create more effective strategies and structures in the future. At Nokia, for example, each product division now has a clear performance goal to achieve, and divisional managers are given considerable autonomy in formulating the strategies necessary to achieve their business model and to meet this goal. For example, the mobile phone division's managers must decide how best to pursue a cost-leadership model and the smart phone division's managers must decide how best to pursue a differentiation model.

Output control at the functional and individual levels is a continuation of control at the divisional level. Divisional managers set goals for functional managers that will allow the division to achieve its goals. As at the divisional level, functional goals are established to encourage the development of the generic competencies that provide the company with a competitive advantage, and functional performance is evaluated by how well a function develops a competency. In the sales function, for example, goals related to efficiency (such as cost of sales), quality (such as number of returns), and customer responsiveness (such as the time needed to respond to customer needs) can be established for the whole function.

Finally, functional managers establish goals that individual employees are expected to achieve to allow the function to achieve its goals. Sales personnel, for example, can be given specific goals (related to functional goals) that they are required to achieve. Functions and individuals are then evaluated on the basis of achieving or not achieving their goals, and in sales, compensation is commonly pegged to achievement.

The achievement of these goals is a sign that the company's strategy is working and meeting organizational objectives.

The inappropriate use of output control can promote conflict among divisions. In general, setting across-the-board output targets, such as ROIC targets, for divisions can lead to destructive results if divisions single-mindedly try to maximize divisional ROIC at the expense of corporate ROIC. Moreover, to reach output targets, divisions may start to distort the numbers and engage in strategic manipulation of the figures to make their divisions look good—which increases bureaucratic costs.[22]

■ **Behavior Control** **Behavior control** is control through the establishment of a comprehensive system of rules and procedures to direct the actions or behavior of divisions, functions, and individuals.[23] The intent of behavior controls is not to specify the g*oals* but to standardize the *way or means* of reaching them. Rules standardize behavior and make outcomes predictable. If employees follow the rules, then actions are performed and decisions handled the same way time and time again. The result is predictability and accuracy, the aim of all control systems. The main kinds of behavior controls are operating budgets, standardization, and rules and procedures.

Once managers at each level have been given a goal to achieve, they establish operating budgets that regulate how managers and workers are to attain those goals. An **operating budget** is a blueprint that states how managers intend to use organizational resources to achieve organizational goals most efficiently. Most commonly, managers at one level allocate to managers at a lower level a specific amount of resources to use to produce goods and services. Once they have been given a budget, these lower-level managers must decide how they will allocate certain amounts of money for different organizational activities. They are then evaluated on the basis of their ability to stay inside the budget and make the best use of it. For example, managers at GE's washing machine division might have a budget of $50 million to develop and sell a new line of washing machines; they have to decide how much money to allocate to R&D, engineering, sales, and so on so that the division generates the most revenue and hence makes the biggest profit. Most commonly, large companies treat each division as a stand-alone profit center, and corporate managers evaluate each division's performance by its relative contribution to corporate profitability, something discussed in detail in the next chapter.

Standardization refers to the degree to which a company specifies how decisions are to be made so that employees' behavior becomes predictable.[24] In practice, there are three things an organization can standardize: *inputs, conversion activities,* and *outputs.*

When managers standardize, they screen *inputs* according to preestablished criteria or standards that determine which inputs to allow into the organization. If employees are the input in question, for example, then one way of standardizing them is to specify which qualities and skills they must possess and then to select only applicants who possess them. If the inputs in question are raw materials or component parts, the same considerations apply. The Japanese are renowned for the high quality and precise tolerances they demand from component parts to minimize problems with the product at the manufacturing stage. Just-in-time inventory systems also help standardize the flow of inputs.

The aim of standardizing *conversion activities* is to program work activities so that they are done the same way time and time again. The goal is predictability. Behavior controls, such as rules and procedures, are among the chief means by which companies can standardize throughputs. Fast-food restaurants such as McDonald's and

Burger King standardize all aspects of their restaurant operations; the result is consistent fast food.

The goal of standardizing *outputs* is to specify what the performance characteristics of the final product or service should be—the dimensions or tolerances the product should conform to, for example. To ensure that their products are standardized, companies apply quality control and use various criteria to measure this standardization. One criterion might be the number of goods returned from customers or the number of customers' complaints. On production lines, periodic sampling of products can indicate whether they are meeting performance characteristics.

As with other kinds of controls, the use of behavior control is accompanied by potential pitfalls that must be managed if the organization is to avoid strategic problems. Top management must be careful to monitor and evaluate the usefulness of behavior controls over time. Rules constrain people and lead to standardized, predictable behavior. However, rules are always easier to establish than to get rid of, and over time the number of rules an organization uses tends to increase. As new developments lead to additional rules, often the old rules are not discarded, and the company becomes overly bureaucratized. Consequently, the organization and the people in it become inflexible and are slow to react to changing or unusual circumstances. Such inflexibility can reduce a company's competitive advantage by lowering the pace of innovation and reducing its responsiveness to customers.

■ Using Information Technology

Information technology is playing an increasing role in strategy implementation at all organizational levels. In fact, it is making it much easier for organizations to cost-effectively develop output and behavior controls that give strategic managers much more and much better information to monitor the many aspects of their strategies and to respond appropriately. IT, which provides a way of standardizing behavior through the use of a consistent, often cross-functional software platform, is a form of behavior control. IT is also a form of output control because when all employees or functions use the same software platform to provide up-to-date information on their activities, this codifies and standardizes organizational knowledge and makes it easier to monitor progress toward strategic objectives. IT is also a kind of integrating mechanism because it provides people at all levels in the hierarchy and across all functions with more of the information and knowledge they need to perform their roles effectively. For example, today functional-level employees are able to access information easily from other functions using cross-functional software systems that keep them all informed about changes in product design, engineering, manufacturing schedules, and marketing plans that will have an impact on their activities. In this sense, IT overlays the structure of tasks and roles that is normally regarded as the "real" organizational structure. The many ways in which IT affects strategy implementation is discussed in different sections of this and the next chapter. Strategy in Action 12.2 illustrates one way in which IT can help managers monitor and coordinate the effectiveness with which their strategies are being put into action.

■ Strategic Reward Systems

Organizations strive to control employees' behavior by linking reward systems to their control systems.[25] Based on the company's strategy (cost leadership or differentiation, for example), strategic managers must decide which behaviors to reward. They then create a control system to measure these behaviors and link the reward structure to them. Determining how to relate rewards to performance is a crucial strategic decision because it determines the incentive structure that affects the way managers and employees at all levels in the organization behave. As Chapter 11 points out, top managers

Strategy in Action   12.2

Control at Cypress Semiconductor

In the fast-moving semiconductor business, a premium is placed on organizational adaptability. At Cypress Semiconductor, CEO T. J. Rodgers was facing a problem: how to control his growing 1,500-employee organization without developing a bureaucratic management hierarchy. Rodgers believed that a tall hierarchy hinders the ability of an organization to adapt to changing conditions. He was committed to maintaining a flat and decentralized organizational structure with a minimum of management layers. At the same time, he needed to control his employees to ensure that they performed in a manner consistent with company goals. The solution that Rodgers adopted was to implement a computer-based information system through which he can manage what every employee and team is doing in the decentralized organization. Each employee maintains a list

of ten to fifteen goals, such as "Meet with marketing for new product launch" or "Make sure to check with customer X." Noted next to each goal is when it was agreed on, when it is due to be finished, and whether it has been finished. All of this information is stored on a central computer. Rodgers claims that he can review the goals of all 1,500 employees in about four hours, and he does so each week. He can do this because he manages by exception, looking only for employees who are falling behind. He then calls them—not to scold but to ask whether there is anything he can do to help them get the job done. It takes only about half an hour each week for employees to review and update their lists. This system allows Rodgers to exercise control over his organization without resorting to the expensive layers of a management hierarchy.[b]

can be encouraged to work in shareholders' interests by being rewarded with stock options linked to a company's long-term performance. Furthermore, companies such as Kodak and GM require managers to buy company stock, and when managers become shareholders they are more motivated to pursue long-term rather than short-term goals. Similarly, in designing a pay system for salespeople, the choice is whether to motivate them through straight salary or salary plus a bonus based on how much they sell. Neiman Marcus, the luxury retailer, pays employees a straight salary because it wants to encourage high-quality service but discourage a hard-sell approach. Thus, there are no incentives based on quantity sold. On the other hand, the pay system for rewarding car salespeople encourages high-pressure selling; it typically contains a large bonus based on the number and price of cars sold.

Organizational Culture

The third element that goes into successful strategy implementation is managing *organizational culture*, the specific collection of values and norms shared by people and groups in an organization.[26] Organizational values are beliefs and ideas about what kinds of goals members of an organization *should* pursue and about the appropriate kinds or standards of behavior organizational members *should* use to achieve these goals. Bill Gates is famous for the set of organizational values that he emphasizes: entrepreneurship, ownership, creativity, honesty, frankness, and open communication. By stressing entrepreneurship and ownership, he strives to get his employees to feel that Microsoft is not one "big bureaucracy" but a collection of smaller and very adaptive companies run by their members. Gates emphasizes giving lower-level managers autonomy and encourages them to take risks—to act like entrepreneurs, not corporate bureaucrats.[27]

From organizational values develop organizational norms, guidelines, or expectations that *prescribe* appropriate kinds of behavior by employees in particular situations and control the behavior of organizational members toward one another. The norms of behavior for software programmers at Microsoft include working long hours and weekends, wearing whatever clothing is comfortable (but never a suit and tie), consuming junk food, and communicating with other employees by e-mail and the company's state-of-the-art intranet.

Organizational culture functions as a kind of control in that strategic managers can influence the kind of values and norms that develop in an organization—values and norms that specify appropriate and inappropriate behaviors and that shape and influence the way its members behave.[28] Strategic managers such as Gates deliberately cultivate values that tell their subordinates how they should perform their roles; in Microsoft and Nokia, innovation and creativity are stressed. These companies establish and support norms that tell employees they should be innovative and entrepreneurial and should experiment even if there is a significant chance of failure.

Other managers might cultivate values that tell employees they should always be conservative and cautious in their dealings with others, consult with their superiors before they make important decisions, and record their actions in writing so they can be held accountable for what happens. Managers of organizations such as chemical and oil companies, financial institutions, and insurance companies—any organization in which great caution is needed—may encourage a conservative, vigilant approach to making decisions.[29] In a bank or mutual fund, for example, the risk of losing investors' money makes a cautious approach to investing highly appropriate. Thus, we might expect that managers of different kinds of organizations will deliberately try to cultivate and develop the organizational values and norms that are best suited to their strategy and structure.

Organizational socialization is the term used to describe how people learn organizational culture. Through socialization, people internalize and learn the norms and values of the culture so that they *become* organizational members.[30] Control through culture is so powerful that once these values have been internalized, they become part of the individual's values, and the individual follows organizational values without thinking about them.[31] Often the values and norms of an organization's culture are transmitted to its members through the stories, myths, and language that people in the organization use, as well as by other means.

■ **Culture and Strategic Leadership**

Organizational culture is created by the strategic leadership provided by an organization's founder and top managers. The organization's founder is particularly important in determining culture because the founder imprints his or her values and management style on the organization. Walt Disney's conservative influence on the company he established continued until well after his death. Managers were afraid to experiment with new forms of entertainment because they were afraid "Walt Disney wouldn't like it." It took the installation of a new management team under Michael Eisner to turn around the company's fortunes and allow it to deal with the realities of the new entertainment industry.

The leadership style established by the founder is transmitted to the company's managers, and as the company grows, it typically attracts new managers and employees who share the same values. Moreover, members of the organization typically recruit and select only those who share their values. Thus, a company's culture becomes more and more distinct as its members become more similar. The virtue of these shared values and common culture is that it *increases integration and improves coordination among organizational members.* For example, the common language that typically emerges in an organization because people share the same beliefs and values facilitates cooperation among managers. Similarly, rules and procedures and direct supervision are less important when shared norms and values control behavior and motivate employees. When organizational members buy into cultural norms and values, they feel bonded to the organization and are more committed to finding new ways to help it succeed. Strategy in Action 12.3 profiles how Ray Kroc built a strong culture at McDonald's.

Strategic leadership also affects organizational culture through the way managers design organizational structure, that is, the way they delegate authority and divide up task relationships. Thus, the way an organization designs its structure affects the cultural norms and values that develop within the organization. Managers need to be aware of this fact when implementing their strategies. Nokia changed its structure to change its cultural values and norms. Its emphasis on innovation is no longer sufficient to give the company a competitive advantage; today it also needs to emphasize responsiveness to customers to succeed in the cell phone business.

Strategy in Action 12.3

How Ray Kroc Established McDonald's Culture

In the restaurant business, maintaining product quality is all-important because the quality of the food and the service varies with the chefs and waiters as they come and go. If a customer gets a bad meal, poor service, or dirty silverware, that customer may not come back, and other potential customers may stay away as negative comments travel by word of mouth. This was the problem that Ray Kroc, the man who pioneered McDonald's growth, faced when McDonald's franchises began to open by the thousands throughout the United States. Kroc solved his problem by developing a sophisticated control system that specified every detail of how each McDonald's restaurant was to be operated and managed. This control system also created a distinct organizational culture.

First, Kroc developed a comprehensive system of rules and procedures for franchise owners and employees to follow in running each restaurant. The most effective way to perform tasks, from cooking burgers to cleaning tables, was worked out in advance, written down in rule books, and then taught to each McDonald's manager and employee through a formal training process. Prospective franchise owners had to attend "Hamburger University," the company's training center in Chicago, where in an intensive, month-long program they learned all aspects of a McDonald's operation. They were then expected to train their work force and make sure that employees thoroughly understood operating procedures. Kroc's goal in establishing this system of rules and procedures was to build a common culture so that customers would always find the

same level of quality in food and service. If customers always get what they expect from a restaurant, the restaurant has developed superior customer responsiveness.

Kroc also developed the McDonald's franchise system to help the company control its structure as it grew. He believed that a manager who is also a franchise owner (and thus receives a large share of the profits) is more motivated to buy into a company's culture than a manager paid on a straight salary. Thus, the McDonald's reward and incentive system allowed it to keep control over its operating structure as it expanded. Moreover, McDonald's was very selective in selling to its franchisees; they had to be people with the skills and capabilities that Kroc believed McDonald's managers should have.

Within each restaurant, franchise owners were instructed to pay particular attention to training their employees and instilling in them McDonald's concepts of efficiency, quality, and customer service. Shared norms, values, and an organizational culture also helped McDonald's standardize employees' behavior so that customers would know how they would be treated in a McDonald's restaurant. Moreover, McDonald's includes customers in its culture: it asks customers to bus their own tables, and it also shows concern for customers' needs by building playgrounds, offering Happy Meals, and organizing birthday parties for children. In creating its family-oriented culture, McDonald's ensures future customer loyalty because satisfied children are likely to become loyal adult customers.

■ **Traits of Strong and Adaptive Corporate Cultures**

Few environments are stable for any prolonged period of time. If an organization is to survive, managers must take actions that enable it to adapt to environmental changes. If they do not take such action, they may find themselves faced with declining demand for their products.

Managers can try to create an **adaptive culture**, one that is innovative and that encourages and rewards middle - and lower-level managers for taking the initiative.[32] Managers in organizations with adaptive cultures are able to introduce changes in the way the organization operates, including changes in its strategy and structure that allow it to adapt to changes in the external environment. Organizations with adaptive cultures are more likely to survive in a changing environment and indeed should have higher performance than organizations with inert cultures.

Several scholars in the field have tried to uncover the common traits that strong and adaptive corporate cultures share and to find out whether there is a particular set of values that dominates adaptive cultures that is missing from weak or inert ones. An early but still influential attempt is T. J. Peters and R. H. Waterman's account of the values and norms characteristic of successful organizations and their cultures.[33] They argue that adaptive organizations show three common value sets. First, successful companies have values promoting a *bias for action*. The emphasis is on autonomy and entrepreneurship, and employees are encouraged to take risks—for example, to create new products—even though there is no assurance that these products will be winners. Managers are closely involved in the day-to-day operations of the company and do not simply make strategic decisions isolated in some ivory tower, and employees have a hands-on, value-driven approach.

The second set of values stems from the *nature of the organization's mission*. The company must stick with what it does best and develop a business model focused on its mission. A company can easily get sidetracked into pursuing activities outside its area of expertise just because they seem to promise a quick return. Management should cultivate values so that a company sticks to its knitting, which means strengthening its business model. A company must also establish close relationships with customers as a way of improving its competitive position. After all, who knows more about a company's performance than those who use its products or services? By emphasizing customer-oriented values, organizations are able to learn customers' needs and improve their ability to develop products and services that customers desire. All of these management values are strongly represented in companies such as McDonald's, Wal-Mart, and Toyota, which are sure of their mission and continually take steps to maintain it.

The third set of values bears on *how to operate the organization*. A company should try to establish an organizational design that will motivate employees to do their best. Inherent in this set of values is the belief that productivity is obtained through people and that respect for the individual is the primary means by which a company can create the right atmosphere for productive behavior. An emphasis on entrepreneurship and respect for the employee leads to the establishment of a structure that gives employees the latitude to make decisions and motivates them to succeed. Because a simple structure and a lean staff best fit this situation, the organization should be designed with only the number of managers and hierarchical levels that are necessary to get the job done. The organization should also be sufficiently decentralized to permit employees' participation but centralized enough for management to make sure that the company pursues its strategic mission and that cultural values are followed.

In summary, these three main sets of values are at the heart of an organization's culture, and management transmits and maintains them through strategic leadership.

Strategy implementation continues as managers build strategic control systems that help perpetuate a strong adaptive culture, further the development of distinctive competencies, and provide employees with the incentive to build a company's competitive advantage. Finally, organizational structure contributes to the implementation process by providing the framework of tasks and roles that reduces transaction difficulties and allows employees to think and behave in ways that enable a company to achieve superior performance. The *Running Case* describes the way in which the frugal Sam Walton (he used to drive a thirty-year-old pickup truck and lived in a very modest home) used all the kinds of control systems discussed here to implement Wal-Mart's cost-leadership business model.

Building Distinctive Competencies at the Functional Level

In this section we turn to the issue of creating specific kinds of structure, control systems, and culture to implement a company's business model. The first level of strategy to examine is the functional level because, as Chapters 3 and 4 discuss, a company's business model is implemented through the functional strategies managers adopt to develop the distinctive competencies that allow it to pursue a particular business model.[34] What is the best kind of structure to use to group people and tasks to build competencies? The answer for most companies is to group them by function and create a functional structure.

■ Functional Structure: Grouping by Function

In the quest to deliver a final product to the customer, two related value-chain management problems increase. First, the range of value-chain activities that must be performed expands, and it quickly becomes clear that a company lacks the expertise needed to perform them effectively. For example, in a new company it quickly becomes apparent that the services of a professional accountant, a production manager, or a marketing expert are needed to take control of specialized tasks as sales increase. Second, it also becomes clear that no one person can successfully perform more than one value-chain activity without becoming overloaded. The new company's founder, for instance, who may have been performing many value-chain activities, realizes that he or she can no longer simultaneously make and sell the product. As most entrepreneurs discover, they have to decide how to group new employees to perform the various value-chain activities most efficiently. Most choose the functional structure.

Functional structures group people on the basis of their common expertise and experience or because they use the same resources.[35] For example, engineers are grouped in a function because they perform the same tasks and use the same skills or equipment. Figure 12.5 shows a typical functional structure. Each of the rectangles

FIGURE 12.5

Functional Structure

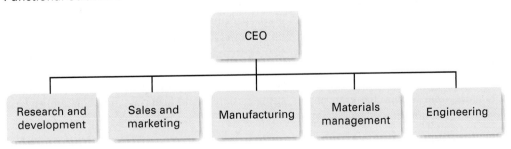

Running Case

Sam Walton's Approach to Implementing Wal-Mart's Strategy

Wal-Mart, headquartered in Bentonville, Arkansas, is the largest retailer in the world, with sales of over $80 billion in 2004. Its success rests on the way that its founder, the late Sam Walton, decided to implement the company's business model. Walton wanted all his managers and workers to have a hands-on approach to their jobs and to be totally committed to Wal-Mart's main goal, which he defined as total customer satisfaction. To motivate his employees, Walton created a sophisticated control system and a culture that gave employees at all levels continuous feedback about their own and the company's performance.

First, Walton developed a financial control system that provided managers with day-to-day feedback about the performance of all aspects of the business. Through a sophisticated companywide satellite system, corporate managers at its Bentonville headquarters can evaluate the performance of each store, and even of each department in each store. Information about store profits and the rate of turnover of goods is provided to store managers daily, and store managers in turn communicate this information to Wal-Mart's 625,000 employees (who are called associates). Through such information sharing, Walton's method encourages all associates to learn the fundamentals of the retailing business so they can work to improve it.

If any store seems to be underperforming, managers and associates meet to probe the reasons and to find solutions to help raise performance. Wal-Mart's top managers routinely visit stores that are having problems to lend their expertise, and each month top managers use the company's aircraft to fly to various Wal-Mart stores so they can keep their fingers on the pulse of the business. It is also customary for Wal-Mart's top managers to spend their Saturdays meeting together to discuss the week's financial results and their implications for the future.

Walton insisted on linking performance to rewards. Each manager's individual performance, measured by his or her ability to meet specific goals or output targets, is reflected in pay raises and chances for promotion (promotion to bigger stores in the company's 3,000-store empire and even to corporate headquarters, because Wal-Mart routinely promotes from within the company rather than hires managers from other companies). Top

managers receive large stock options linked to the company's performance targets and stock price, and even ordinary associates receive stock in the company. An associate who started with Walton in the 1970s would by now have accumulated more than $250,000 in stock because of the appreciation of Wal-Mart's stock over time.

Walton instituted an elaborate system of controls, such as rules and budgets, to shape employees' behavior. Each store performs the same activities in the same way, and all employees receive the same kind of training so they know how to behave toward customers. In this way, Wal-Mart is able to standardize its operations, which leads to major cost savings and allows managers to make storewide changes easily.

Finally, Walton was not content just to use output and behavior controls and monetary rewards to motivate his associates. To involve associates in the business and encourage them to develop work behaviors focused on providing quality customer service, he established strong cultural values and norms for his company. Some norms that associates are expected to follow include the *ten-foot attitude*, which developed when Walton, during his visits to the stores, encouraged associates to "promise that whenever you come within 10 feet of a customer you will look him in the eye, greet him, and ask him if you can help him"; the *sundown rule*, which states that employees should strive to answer customers' requests by sundown on the day they receive them; and the Wal-Mart cheer ("Give me a W, give me an A," and so on), which is used in all its stores.

The strong customer-oriented values that Walton created are exemplified in the stories its members tell one another about the company's concern for its customers. They include stories such as the one about Sheila, who risked her own safety when she jumped in front of a car to prevent a little boy from being struck; about Phyllis, who administered CPR to a customer who had suffered a heart attack in her store; and about Annette, who gave up the Power Ranger she had on layaway for her own son so a customer's son could have his birthday wish. The strong Wal-Mart culture also helps to control and motivate its employees and helps associates to achieve the stringent output and financial targets the company has set for itself.[c]

represents a different functional specialization—R&D, sales and marketing, manufacturing, and so on—and each function concentrates on its own specialized task.[36]

Functional structures have several advantages. First, if people who perform similar tasks are grouped together, they can learn from one another and become more specialized and productive at what they do. This can create capabilities and competencies in each function. Second, they can monitor each other to make sure that all are performing their tasks effectively and not shirking their responsibilities. As a result, the work process becomes more efficient, reducing manufacturing costs and increasing operational flexibility. A third important advantage of functional structures is that they give managers greater control of organizational activities. As already noted, many difficulties arise when the number of levels in the hierarchy increases. If people are grouped into different functions, each with their own managers, then *several different hierarchies are created*, and the company can avoid becoming too tall. There will be one hierarchy in manufacturing, for example, and another in accounting and finance. Managing the business is much easier when different groups specialize in different organizational tasks and are managed separately.

■ **The Role of Strategic Control**   An important element of strategic control is to design a system that sets ambitious goals and targets for all managers and employees and then develops performance measures that *stretch and encourage managers and employees* to excel in their quest to raise performance. A functional structure promotes this goal because it increases the ability of managers and employees to monitor and make constant improvements to operating procedures. The structure also encourages organizational learning because managers, working closely with subordinates, can mentor them and help develop their technical skills.

Grouping by function also makes it easier to apply output control. Measurement criteria can be developed to suit the needs of each function to encourage members to stretch themselves. Each function knows how well it is contributing to overall performance, and indeed the part it plays in reducing the cost of goods sold or the gross margin. Managers can look closely to see if they are following the principle of the minimum chain of command and whether they need several levels of middle managers. Perhaps, instead of using middle managers, they could practice **management by objectives**, a system in which employees are encouraged to help set their own goals so that managers, like Cypress's Rodgers, *manage by exception*, intervening only when they sense something is not going right. Given this increase in control, a functional structure also makes it possible to institute an effective strategic reward system in which pay can be closely linked to performance and managers can accurately assess the value of each person's contributions.

■ **Developing Culture at the Functional Level**   Often functional structures offer the easiest way for managers to build a strong, cohesive culture. We discussed earlier how both Ray Kroc and Sam Walton, both of whom first developed a functional structure to implement their cost-leadership business models, worked hard to create values and norms that were shared by the members of all a company's different functions. To see how structure, control, and culture help create distinctive competencies, we consider how they affect the way three functions—manufacturing, R&D, and sales—operate.

■ **Manufacturing**   In manufacturing, functional strategy usually centers on improving efficiency and quality. A company must create an organizational setting in which managers can learn how to economize on costs and lower the cost structure. Many companies today follow the lead of Japanese companies such as Toyota and Honda, which developed strong capabilities in manufacturing by operating total quality management (TQM) and flexible manufacturing systems (see Chapter 4).

With TQM, the inputs and involvement of all employees in the decision-making process are necessary to improve production efficiency and quality. Thus, it becomes necessary to decentralize authority to motivate employees to improve the production process. In TQM, work teams are created, and workers are given the responsibility and authority to discover and implement improved work procedures. Managers assume the role of coach and facilitator, and team members jointly take on the supervisory burdens. Work teams are often given the responsibility to control and discipline their own members and even to decide who should work in their team. Frequently, work teams develop strong norms and values, and work group culture becomes an important means of control; this type of control matches the new decentralized team approach. Quality control circles are created to exchange information and suggestions about problems and work procedures. A bonus system or employee stock ownership plan (ESOP) is frequently established to motivate workers and to allow them to share in the increased value that TQM often produces.

Nevertheless, to move down the experience curve quickly, most companies still exercise tight control over work activities and create behavior and output controls that standardize the manufacturing process. For example, human inputs are standardized through the recruitment and training of skilled personnel, the work process is programmed, often by computers, and quality control is used to make sure that outputs are being produced correctly. In addition, managers use output controls such as operating budgets to continuously monitor costs and quality. The extensive use of output controls and the continuous measurement of efficiency and quality ensure that the work team's activities meet the goals set for the function by management. Efficiency and quality increase as new and improved work rules and procedures are developed to raise the level of standardization. The aim is to find the match between structure and control and a TQM approach so that manufacturing develops the distinctive competency that leads to superior efficiency and quality.

R&D The functional strategy for an R&D department is to develop distinctive competencies in innovation and quality as excellence that result in products that fit customers' needs. Consequently, the R&D department's structure, control, and culture should provide the coordination necessary for scientists and engineers to bring high-quality products quickly to market. Moreover, these systems should motivate R&D scientists to develop innovative products.

In practice, R&D departments typically have a flat, decentralized structure that gives their members the freedom and autonomy to experiment and be innovative. Scientists and engineers are also grouped into teams because their performance can typically be judged only over the long term (it may take several years for a project to be completed). Consequently, extensive supervision by managers and the use of behavior control are a waste of managerial time and effort.[37] By letting teams manage their own transfer and handoff issues rather than using managers and the hierarchy of authority to coordinate work activities, managers avoid the information distortion problems that cause bureaucratic costs. Strategic managers take advantage of scientists' ability to work jointly to solve problems and to enhance each other's performance. In small teams, too, the professional values and norms that highly trained employees bring to the situation promote coordination. A culture for innovation frequently emerges to control employees' behavior, as at Nokia, Intel, and Microsoft, where the race to be first energizes the R&D teams. To create an innovative culture and speed product development, Intel uses a team structure in its R&D function. Intel has many work teams that operate side by side to develop the next generation of chips. So, when it makes mistakes, as it has recently, it can act quickly to join each team's innovations together to make a state-of-the-art chip that does meet customer needs, such as for multimedia chips. At the same time, to sustain its leading-edge technology, the company creates healthy competition between teams to encourage its scientists and engineers to champion new product innovations that will allow Intel to control the technology of tomorrow.[38]

To spur teams to work effectively, the reward system should be linked to the performance of the team and company. If scientists, individually or in a team, do not share in the profits a company obtains from its new products, they may have little motivation to contribute wholeheartedly to the team. To prevent the departure of their key employees and encourage high motivation, companies such as Merck, Intel, and Microsoft give their researchers stock options, stock, and other rewards that are tied to their individual performance, their team performance, and the company's performance.

■ **Sales** Salespeople work directly with customers, and when they are dispersed in the field, these employees are especially difficult to monitor. The cost-effective way to monitor their behavior and encourage high responsiveness to customers is usually to develop sophisticated output and behavior controls. Output controls, such as specific sales goals or goals for increasing responsiveness to customers, can be easily established and monitored by sales managers. Then, these controls can be linked to a bonus reward system to motivate salespeople. Behavior controls, such as detailed reports that salespeople file describing their interactions with customers, can also be used to standardize salespeople's behavior and make it easier for supervisors to review their performance.[39]

Usually, few managers are needed to monitor salespeople's activities, and a sales director and regional sales managers can oversee even large sales forces because outputs and behavior controls are employed. Frequently, however, and especially when salespeople deal with complex products such as pharmaceutical drugs or even luxury clothing, it becomes important to develop shared employee values and norms about the importance of patient safety or high-quality customer service, and managers spend considerable time training and educating employees to create such norms.

Similar considerations apply to the other functions, such as accounting, finance, engineering, and human resource management. Managers must implement functional strategy through the combination of structure, control, and culture to allow each function to create the competencies that lead to superior efficiency, quality, innovation, and responsiveness to customers. Strategic managers must also develop the incentive systems that motivate and align employees' interests with those of their companies.

■ **Functional Structure and Bureaucratic Costs**

No matter how complex their strategies become, most companies always retain a functional orientation because of its many advantages. Whenever different functions work together, however, bureaucratic costs inevitably arise because of information distortions that lead to the communications and measurement problems discussed in Chapter 10. Often these problems arise from the transfers or handoffs across different functions that are necessary to deliver the final product to the customer.[40]

Indeed, it is the need to economize on the bureaucratic costs of solving such problems that leads managers to adopt new organizational arrangements that reduce the scope of information distortions. Most commonly, companies divide their activities according to a more complex plan to match their business model and strategy in a discriminating way. These more complex structures are discussed later in the chapter. First, we review five areas in which information distortions can arise—communications, measurement, customers, location, and strategy.

■ **Communication Problems** As separate functional hierarchies evolve, functions can grow more remote from one another, and it becomes increasingly difficult to communicate across functions and to coordinate their activities. This communication problem stems from *differences in goal orientations*: the various functions develop distinct outlooks or understandings of the strategic issues facing a company.[41] For example, often the pursuit of different competencies can lead to different time or goal orientations. Some functions, such as manufacturing, have a short time frame and concentrate on achieving short-run goals, such as reducing manufacturing costs. Others, such as R&D, have a long-term point of view; their product development goals may have a time horizon of several years. These factors may cause each function to develop a different view of the strategic issues facing the company. Manufacturing, for example, may see the strategic issue as the need to reduce costs, sales may see it as the need to increase customer responsiveness, and R&D may see it as the need to create new products. These communication and coordination problems between functions increase bureaucratic costs.

■ **Measurement Problems** Often a company's product range widens as it develops new competencies and enters new market segments, as happened to Nokia. When this happens, a company may find it difficult to gauge or measure the contribution of a product or a group of products to its overall profitability—as noted in Chapter 10. Consequently, the company may turn out some unprofitable products without realizing it and may also make poor decisions about resource allocation. This means that the company's measurement systems are not complex enough to serve its needs. Dell Computer's explosive growth in the early 1990s, for example, caused it to lose control of its inventory management systems; hence, it could not accurately project supply and demand for the components that go into its personal computers. Problems with its organizational structure plagued Dell, reducing efficiency and quality. As one manager commented, designing its structure to keep pace with its growth was like "building a high-performance car while going around the race track."[42] However, Dell succeeded and today enjoys a 10 to 20 percent cost advantage over competitors like Gateway and Hewlett-Packard.

■ **Customer Problems** As the range and quality of an organization's goods and services increase, often more, and different kinds of, customers are attracted to its products. Servicing the needs of more customer groups and tailoring products to suit new kinds of customers result in increasing handoff problems between functions. It becomes increasingly difficult to coordinate the activities of value-chain functions across the growing product range. Also, functions like production, marketing, and sales have little opportunity to differentiate products and increase value for customers by specializing in the needs of particular customer groups. Instead, they are responsible for servicing the complete product range. Thus, the ability to identify and satisfy customer needs may fall short in a functional structure.

■ **Location Problems** Location factors may hamper coordination and control. If a growing company begins producing or selling in many different regional areas, then a functional structure may not be able to provide the flexibility needed for managers to respond to the different customer needs or preferences in the various regions. A functional structure is simply not the right way to handle regional diversity.

■ **Strategic Problems** Sometimes the combined effect of all these factors is that long-term strategic considerations are ignored because managers are preoccupied with solving communication and coordination problems. As a result, a company may lose direction and fail to take advantage of new opportunities while bureaucratic costs escalate.

Experiencing one or more of these problems is a sign that bureaucratic costs are increasing and that managers must change and adapt their organization's structure, control systems, and culture to economize on bureaucratic costs, build new distinctive competencies, and strengthen its business model. These problems indicate that the company has outgrown its structure and that managers need to develop a more complex structure that can meet the needs of their competitive strategy. An alternative, however, is to reduce these problems by adopting the outsourcing option.

■ **The Outsourcing Option** Rather than move to a more complex, expensive structure, increasingly companies are turning to the outsourcing option (discussed in Chapter 9) and solving the organizational design problem by contracting with other companies to perform specific functional tasks. Obviously it does not make sense to outsource activities in which a company has a distinctive competency, because this would lessen its competitive advantage. But it does make sense to outsource and contract with companies to perform particular value-chain activities in which they specialize and therefore have a competitive advantage.

Thus, one way of avoiding the kinds of communication and measurement problems that arise when a company's product line becomes complex is to reduce the number of functional value-chain activities it performs. This allows a company to focus on those competencies that are at the heart of its competitive advantage and to economize on bureaucratic costs. Today, responsibility for activities such as a company's marketing, pension and health benefits, materials management, and information systems is being increasingly outsourced to companies that often specialize in the needs of a company in a particular industry. More outsourcing options, such as using a global network structure, are considered in Chapter 13.

Implementing Strategy in a Single Industry

Building capabilities in organizational design that allow a company to develop a competitive advantage starts at the functional level. However, to pursue its business model successfully, managers must find the right combination of structure, control, and culture that *links and combines* the competencies in a company's value-chain functions in a way that enhances its ability to differentiate products or lower the cost structure. Therefore, it is important to coordinate and integrate across functions and business units or divisions. In organizational design, there are two important issues that managers must take into consideration: one concerns the revenue side of the profit equation and the other the cost side, as Figure 12.6 illustrates.

First, effective organizational design improves the way in which people and groups choose the business-level strategies that lead to increasing differentiation, more value

FIGURE 12.6

How Organizational
Design Increases
Profitability

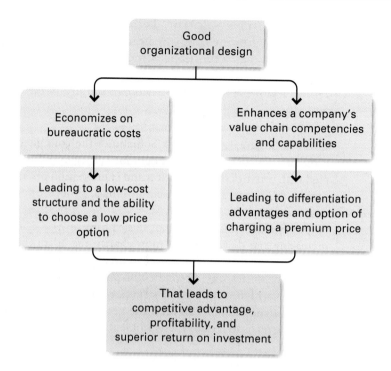

for customers, and the opportunity to charge a premium price. For example, capabilities in managing its structure and culture allow a company to more rapidly and effectively combine its distinctive competencies or transfer or leverage competencies across business units to create new and improved differentiated products.

Second, effective organizational design reduces the bureaucratic costs associated with solving the measurement and communications problems that derive from such things as transferring a product in progress between functions or a lack of cooperation between marketing and manufacturing or between business units. A poorly designed or inappropriate choice of structure or control system or a slow-moving bureaucratic culture (for example, a structure that is too centralized, an incentive system that causes functions to compete and not to cooperate, or a culture whose value and norms have little impact on employees) can cause the motivation, communication, measurement, and coordination problems that lead to high bureaucratic costs.

Effective organizational design often means moving to a more complex structure that economizes on bureaucratic costs. A more complex structure will cost more to operate because additional, experienced, and more highly paid managers will be needed, a more expensive IT system will be required, there may be a need for extra offices and buildings, and so on. However, these are simply costs of doing business, and a company will happily bear this extra expense provided its new structure leads to increased revenues from product differentiation and/or new ways to lower its *overall* cost structure by obtaining economies of scale or scope from its expanded operations.

In the following sections, we first examine the implementation and organizational design issues involved in pursuing a cost-leadership or differentiation business model. Then we describe different kinds of organizational structures that allow companies to pursue business models oriented at (1) managing a wide range of products; (2) being responsive to customers; (3) expanding nationally; (4) competing in a fast-changing high-tech environment; and (5) focusing on a narrow product line.

■ Implementing Cost Leadership

The aim of a company pursuing cost leadership is to become the lowest-cost producer in the industry, and this involves reducing costs across *all* functions in the organization, including R&D and sales and marketing.[43] If a company is pursuing a cost-leadership strategy, its R&D efforts probably focus on product and process development rather than on the more expensive product innovation, which carries no guarantee of success. In other words, the company stresses competencies that improve product characteristics or lower the cost of making existing products. Similarly, a company tries to decrease the cost of sales and marketing by offering a standard product to a mass market rather than different products aimed at different market segments, which is also more expensive.[44]

To implement cost leadership, a company chooses a combination of structure, control, and culture compatible with lowering its cost structure while preserving its ability to attract customers. In practice, the functional structure is the most suitable provided that care is taken to select integrating mechanisms that will reduce communication and measurement problems. For example, a TQM program can be effectively implemented when a functional structure is overlaid with cross-functional teams, for now team members can search for ways to improve operating rules and procedures that lower the cost structure or standardize and raise product quality.[45]

Cost leadership also requires that managers continuously monitor their structures and control systems to find ways to restructure or streamline them so that they operate more effectively. For example, managers need to be alert to ways to use IT to standardize operations and lower costs. To reduce costs further, cost leaders use the cheapest and easiest forms of control available: output controls. For each function, a cost leader adopts output controls that allow it to closely monitor and evaluate functional performance. In the manufacturing function, for example, the company imposes tight controls and stresses meeting budgets based on production, cost, or quality targets.[46] In R&D, too, the emphasis falls on the bottom line, and to demonstrate their contribution to cost savings, R&D teams focus on improving process technology. Cost leaders are likely to reward employees through generous incentive and bonus plans to encourage high performance. Often their culture is based on values that emphasize the bottom line, such as those of Wal-Mart, Dell, and McDonald's.

■ Implementing Differentiation

Effective strategy implementation can improve a company's ability to add value and to differentiate its products. To make its product unique in the eyes of the customer, for example, a differentiated company must design its structure, control, and culture around the *particular source* of its competitive advantage.[47] Specifically, differentiators need to design their structures around the source of their distinctive competencies, the differentiated qualities of their product, and the customer groups they serve. Commonly, in pursuing differentiation, a company starts to produce a wider range of products to serve more market segments, which means it has to customize its products for different groups of customers. These factors make it more difficult to standardize activities and usually increase the bureaucratic costs associated with managing the handoffs or transfers between functions. Integration becomes much more of a problem; communications, measurement, location, and strategic problems increasingly arise; and the demands on functional managers increase.

To respond to these problems, strategic managers develop more sophisticated control systems, increasingly make use of IT, and focus on developing cultural norms and values that overcome problems associated with differences in functional orientations and focus on cross-functional objectives. The control systems used to match the structure are geared to a company's distinctive competencies. For successful differentiation, it is important that the various functions do not pull in different directions; indeed, cooperation among the functions is vital for cross-functional integration. However, when functions work together, output controls become much harder to use. In general, it is much more difficult to measure the performance of people in different functions when they are engaged in cooperative efforts. Consequently, a differentiator must rely more on behavior controls and shared norms and values.

That is why companies pursuing differentiation often have a markedly different kind of culture from those pursuing cost leadership. Because human resources—good scientists, designers, or marketing people—are often the source of differentiation, these organizations have a culture based on professionalism or collegiality, one that emphasizes the distinctiveness of the human resource rather than the high pressure of the bottom line.[48] Hewlett-Packard, Motorola, and Coca-Cola, all of which emphasize some kind of distinctive competency, exemplify companies with professional cultures.

In practice, the implementation decisions that confront managers who must simultaneously strive for differentiation and a low cost structure are dealt with together as strategic managers move to implement new, more complex kinds of organizational structure. As a company's business model and strategies evolve, strategic managers usually start to *superimpose* a more complex divisional grouping of activities on its functional structure to better coordinate value-chain activities. This is especially true of those companies that are seeking to become *broad differentiators*, the companies that have the ability to both increase differentiation and lower their cost structures. These, the most profitable companies in their industry, have to be especially adept at organizational design, for this is a major source of a differentiation and cost advantage (see Figure 12.6). No matter what their business model, however, although more complex structures cost more to operate than a simple functional structure, managers are willing to bear this extra cost so long as the new structure makes better use of functional competencies, increases revenues, and lowers the overall cost structure.

■ Product Structure: Implementing a Wide Product Line

The structure that organizations most commonly adopt to solve the control problems that result from producing many different kinds of products for many different market segments is the *product structure*. The intent is to break up a company's growing product line into a number of smaller, more manageable subunits to reduce bureaucratic costs due to communication, measurement, and other problems. This was the problem facing Nokia in the *Opening Case*, and, as we discussed, Nokia moved to a product structure.

An organization that chooses a product structure first divides its overall product line into product groups or categories (see Figure 12.7). Each product group focuses on satisfying the needs of a particular customer group and is managed by its own team of managers. Second, to keep costs as low as possible, value-chain support functions such as basic R&D, marketing, materials, and finance are centralized at the top

FIGURE 12.7

Nokia's Product Structure

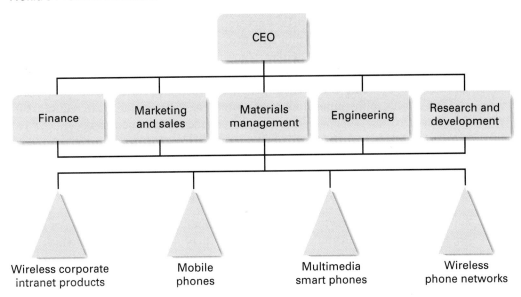

of the organization, and the different product groups share their services. Each support function, in turn, is divided into product-oriented teams of functional specialists who focus on the needs of one particular product group. This arrangement allows each team to specialize and become expert in managing the needs of its product group. However, because all of the R&D teams belong to the same centralized function, they can share knowledge and information with each other and so can build their competence over time.

Strategic control systems can now be developed to measure the performance of each product group separately from the others. Thus, the performance of each product group is easy to monitor and evaluate, and corporate managers at the center can move more quickly to intervene if necessary. Also, the strategic reward system can be more closely linked to the performance of each product group, although top managers can still decide to make rewards based on corporate performance an important part of the incentive system. Doing so will encourage the different product groups to share ideas and knowledge and promote the development of a corporate culture, as well as the product group culture that naturally develops inside each product group. A product structure is commonly used by food processors, furniture makers, personal and health products companies, and large electronics companies like Nokia.

■ **Market Structure: Increasing Responsiveness to Customer Groups**

Suppose the source of competitive advantage in an industry depends on the ability to meet the needs of distinct and important sets of customers or different customer groups. What is the best way of implementing strategy now? Many companies develop a **market structure** that is conceptually quite similar to the product structure except that the focus is on customer groups instead of product groups.

For a company pursuing a strategy based on increasing responsiveness to customers, it is vital that the nature and needs of each different customer group be identified. Then people and functions are grouped by customer or market segment, and a different set of managers becomes responsible for developing the products that each group of customers wants and tailoring or customizing products to the needs of each particular customer group. In other words, to promote superior responsiveness to customers, companies design a structure around their customers and a market structure is adopted. A typical market structure is shown in Figure 12.8.

A market structure brings customer group managers and employees closer to specific groups of customers. These people can then take their detailed knowledge and feed it back to the support functions, which are kept centralized to reduce costs. For example, information about changes in customers' preferences can be quickly fed back to R&D and product design so that a company can protect its competitive advantage by supplying a constant stream of improved products for its installed customer base. This is especially important when a company serves well-identified customer groups such as *Fortune 500* companies or small businesses.

■ **Geographic Structure: Expanding Nationally**

Suppose a company starts to expand nationally through internal expansion or by engaging in horizontal integration and merging with other companies to expand its geographical reach. A company pursuing this competitive approach frequently moves to a **geographic structure** in which geographic regions become the basis for the grouping of organizational activities (see Figure 12.9). A company may divide its manufacturing operations and establish manufacturing plants in different regions of the country, for example. This allows it to be responsive to the needs of regional customers and reduces transportation costs. Similarly, as a service organization such as a store chain or bank expands beyond one geographic area, it may begin to organize sales and marketing activities on a regional level to better serve the needs of customers in different regions.

A geographic structure provides more coordination and control than a functional structure because several regional hierarchies are created to take over the work, just as in a product structure several product group hierarchies are created. A company such as FedEx clearly needs to operate a geographic structure to fulfill its corporate goal: next-day delivery. Large merchandising organizations, such as Neiman Marcus, Dillard's Department Stores, and Wal-Mart, also moved to a geographic structure as they started building stores across the country. With this type of struc-

FIGURE 12.8

Market Structure

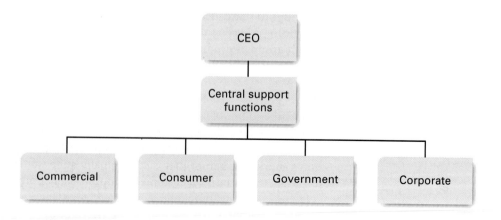

FIGURE 12.9

Geographic Structure

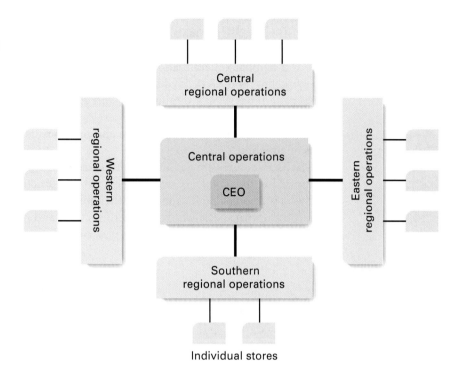

Individual stores

ture, different regional clothing needs (for example, sunwear in the South, down coats in the Midwest) can be handled as required. At the same time, because the information systems, purchasing, distribution, and marketing functions remain centralized, they can leverage their skills across all the regions. Thus, in using a geographic structure, a company can achieve economies of scale in buying, distributing, and selling and lower its cost structure while at the same time being more responsive (differentiated) to customer needs.

Neiman Marcus developed a geographic structure similar to the one shown in Figure 12.9 to manage its nationwide chain of stores. In each region, it established a team of regional buyers to respond to the needs of customers in each geographic area, for example, the western, central, eastern, and southern regions. The regional buyers then fed their information to the central buyers at corporate headquarters, who coordinated their demands to obtain purchasing economies and to ensure that Neiman Marcus's high-quality standards, on which its differentiation advantage depends, were maintained nationally.

■ **Matrix and Product-Team Structures: Competing in Fast-Changing, High-Tech Environments**

The communication and measurement problems that lead to bureaucratic costs escalate quickly when technology is rapidly changing and industry boundaries are blurring. Frequently, competitive success depends on fast mobilization of a company's skills and resources, and managers face complex strategy implementation issues. A new grouping of people and resources becomes necessary, often one that is based on fostering a company's distinctive competencies in R&D, and managers need to make structure, control, and culture choices around the R&D function. At the same time, they need to ensure that implementation will result in new products that meet customer needs and in a way that is cost-effective and will not result in high-priced products that are so expensive customers will not wish to buy them.

■ **Matrix Structure** To address these problems many companies choose a matrix structure.[49] In a **matrix structure**, value-chain activities are grouped in two ways (see Figure 12.10). First, activities are grouped vertically by *function*, so that there is a familiar differentiation of tasks into functions such as engineering, sales and marketing, and R&D. In addition, superimposed on this vertical pattern is a horizontal pattern based on grouping by *product or project* in which people and resources are grouped to meet ongoing product development needs. The resulting network of reporting relationships among projects and functions is designed to make R&D the focus of attention.

Matrix structures are flat and decentralized, and employees inside a matrix have two bosses: a *functional boss*, who is the head of a function, and a *product or project boss*, who is responsible for managing the individual projects. Employees work on a project team with specialists from other functions and report to the project boss on

FIGURE 12.10

Matrix Structure

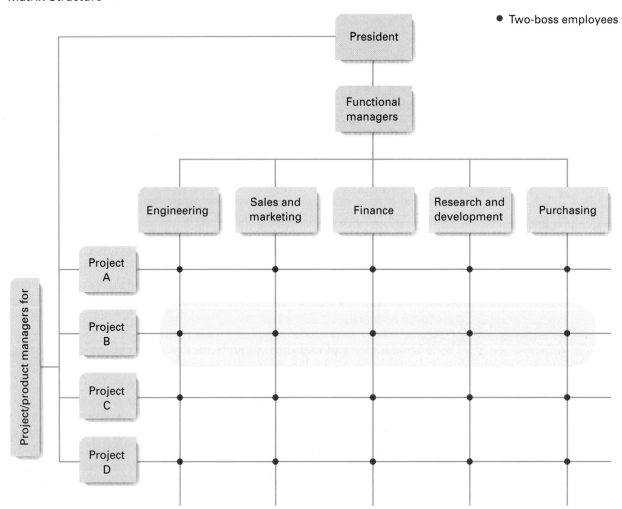

project matters and the functional boss on matters relating to functional issues. All employees who work in a project team are called **two-boss employees** and are responsible for managing coordination and communication among the functions and projects.

Implementing a matrix structure promotes innovation and speeds product development, for this type of structure permits intensive cross-functional integration. Integrating mechanisms such as teams help transfer knowledge among functions and are designed around the R&D function. Sales, marketing, and production targets are geared to R&D goals, marketing devises advertise programs that focus on technological possibilities, and salespeople are evaluated on their understanding of new-product characteristics and their ability to inform potential customers about them.

Matrix structures were first developed by companies in high-technology industries such as aerospace and electronics, for example, TRW and Hughes. These companies were developing radically new products in uncertain, competitive environments, and speed of product development was the crucial consideration. They needed a structure that could respond to this need, but the functional structure was too inflexible to allow the complex role and task interactions necessary to meet new-product development requirements. Moreover, employees in these companies tend to be highly qualified and professional and perform best in autonomous, flexible working conditions. The matrix structure provides such conditions.

This structure requires a minimum of direct hierarchical control by supervisors. Team members control their own behavior, and participation in project teams allows them to monitor other team members and learn from each other. Furthermore, as the project goes through its different phases, different specialists from various functions are required. For example, at the first stage, the services of R&D specialists may be called for, and then at the next stage, engineers and marketing specialists may be needed to make cost and marketing projections. As the demand for the type of specialist changes, team members can be moved to other projects that require their services. Thus, the matrix structure can make maximum use of employees' skills as existing projects are completed and new ones come into existence. The freedom given by the matrix not only provides the autonomy to motivate employees but also leaves top management free to concentrate on strategic issues, since they do not have to become involved in operating matters. On all these counts, the matrix is an excellent tool for creating the flexibility necessary for quick reactions to competitive conditions.

In terms of strategic control and culture, the development of norms and values based on innovation and product excellence is vital if a matrix structure is to work effectively.[50] The constant movement of employees around the matrix means that time and money are spent establishing new team relationships and getting the project off the ground. The two-boss employee's role, balancing as it does the interests of the project with the function, means that cooperation between people is problematic and conflict between different functions and between functions and projects is possible and must be managed. Furthermore, the changing composition of product teams, the ambiguity arising from having two bosses, and the greater difficulty of monitoring and evaluating the work of teams increase the problems of coordinating task activities. A strong and cohesive culture with unifying norms and values can mitigate these problems, as can a strategic reward system based on a group- and organizational-level reward system.

■ **Product-Team Structure** A major structural innovation in recent years has been the **product-team structure**. Its advantages are similar to those of a matrix structure, but it is much easier and far less costly to operate because of the way people are organized into permanent cross-functional teams, as Figure 12.11 illustrates. In the product-team structure, as in the matrix structure, tasks are divided along product or project lines. However, instead of being assigned only *temporarily* to different projects, as in the matrix structure, functional specialists become part of a *permanent* cross-functional team that focuses on the development of one particular range of products such as luxury cars or computer workstations. As a result, the problems associated with coordinating cross-functional transfers or handoffs are much lower than in a matrix structure, in which tasks and reporting relationships change rapidly. Moreover, cross-functional teams are formed at the beginning of the product development process so that any difficulties that arise can be ironed out early, before they lead to major redesign problems. When all functions have direct input from the beginning, design costs and subsequent manufacturing costs can be kept low. Moreover, the use of cross-functional teams speeds innovation and customer responsiveness because when authority is decentralized, team decisions can be made more quickly.

A product-team structure groups tasks by product, and each product group is managed by a cross-functional product team that has all the support services necessary to bring the product to market. This is why it is different from the product structure, where support functions remain centralized. The role of the product team is to protect and enhance a company's differentiation advantage and at the same time coordinate with manufacturing to lower costs.

■ **Focusing on a Narrow Product Line** As Chapter 5 discusses, a focused company concentrates on developing a narrow range of products aimed at one or two market segments, which may be defined by type of customer or location. As a result, a focuser tends to have a higher cost structure than a cost leader or differentiator because output levels are lower, making it harder to obtain substantial scale economies. For this reason, a focused company

Product-Team Structure

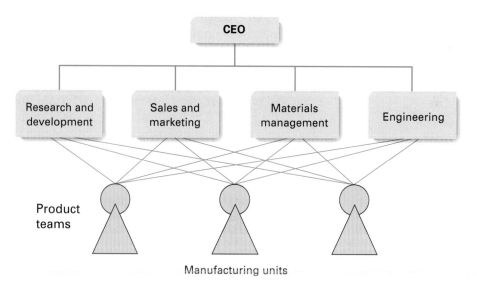

must exercise cost control. On the other hand, some attribute of its product gives the focuser its distinctive competency—possibly its ability to provide customers with high-quality, personalized service. For both reasons, the structure and control system adopted by a focused company has to be inexpensive to operate but flexible enough to allow a distinctive competency to emerge.

A company using a focus strategy normally adopts a functional structure to meet these needs. This structure is appropriate because it is complex enough to manage the activities necessary to make and sell a narrow range of products for one or a few market segments. At the same time, the handoff problems are likely to be relatively easy to solve because a focuser remains small and specialized. Thus, a functional structure can provide all the integration necessary, provided that the focused firm has a strong, adaptive culture, which is vital to the development of some kind of distinctive competency.[51] Additionally, because such a company's competitive advantage is often based on personalized service, the flexibility of this kind of structure lets the company respond quickly to customers' needs and change its products in response to customers' requests. The way in which Lexmark reorganized itself to focus on the production of office printers, examined in Strategy in Action 12.4, illustrates many of the issues in implementing a focus strategy.

Strategy in Action   12.4

Restructuring at Lexmark

Lexmark, a printer and typewriter manufacturer, was one of IBM's many divisions, but IBM sold it after years of losses brought on by high operating costs and an inability to produce new printers that could compete with those made by Hewlett-Packard and Canon. Marvin Mann, an ex-IBM executive, was given the task of finding a way to restructure the company and turn it around. Mann realized at once that the company had to focus on producing a particular kind of printer to lower its out-of-control cost structure.

One of the biggest contributors to its high cost structure was Lexmark's structure and control system, so Mann decided to transform it. Then, he believed, he could begin to focus the company on producing a line of state-of-the-art laser and ink jet office printers. Like the rest of IBM at that time, Lexmark had developed a tall, centralized structure, and all important decision making was made by top managers. This slowed decision making and made it very difficult to communicate across functions because so many managers at different levels and in different functions had to approve new plans. Moving quickly to change this system, Mann streamlined the company's hierarchy, which meant terminating 50 percent of its managers. This action cut out three levels in the hierarchy. He then decentralized authority to the managers

of each of the company's four product lines and told them to develop their own plans and goals. In addition, to continue the process of decentralization, product managers were instructed to develop cross-functional teams comprising employees from all functions, with the goal of finding new and improved ways of organizing task activities to reduce costs. The teams were to use competitive benchmarking and evaluate their competitors' products in order to establish new performance standards to guide their activities. Finally, as an incentive for employees to work hard at increasing efficiency, innovation, and quality, Mann established a company stock ownership scheme to reward employees for their efforts.

Mann's strategy of restructuring Lexmark to focus on a narrow range of printers was successful. Within two years, the cost of launching new products went down by 50 percent and its new-product development cycle speeded up by 30 percent. Focusing on a narrow range of products also improved Lexmark's R&D competence. Lexmark is a technology leader in the laser and ink jet industry and makes the printers sold by Dell—showing that it is a focused cost leader in the printer market. Its stock has performed well as a result, and the company is enjoying considerable success against HP and Japanese competitors.

The message of the preceding sections is clear. Strategic managers must continually monitor the performance of their organization as measured by its ability to increase differentiation, lower costs, and increase profitability. When managers sense declining performance or sense ways to increase performance, they must move quickly to change the way people and activities are organized and controlled. Organizational design, the process of combining and harmonizing structure, control, and culture, is a demanding and difficult task but one that is crucial to promoting and sustaining competitive advantage.

Restructuring and Reengineering

To improve performance a single business company often employs restructuring and reengineering. **Restructuring** a company involves two steps: (1) streamlining the hierarchy of authority and reducing the number of levels in the hierarchy to a minimum, and then (2) reducing the number of employees to lower operating costs. When Jack Smith took over as head of General Motors, for example, GM had more than twenty-two levels in the hierarchy and more than 20,000 corporate managers. Describing his organization as a top-heavy bureaucracy, Smith quickly moved to slash costs and restructure the company. Today, GM has only twelve levels in the hierarchy and half as many corporate managers. In 2004, Kodak announced it would lay off 20 percent of its work force over a three-year period to reduce costs.

Restructuring and downsizing become necessary for many reasons.[52] Sometimes a change in the business environment occurs that could not have been foreseen; perhaps a shift in technology made the company's products obsolete, as happened to Kodak as the use of digital cameras exploded. Sometimes an organization has excess capacity because customers no longer want the goods and services it provides, perhaps because they are outdated or offer poor value for the money—as happened to Nokia when it was slow to catch up with changing customer needs. Sometimes organizations downsize because they have grown too tall and inflexible and bureaucratic costs have become much too high—as happened to IBM. Sometimes they restructure even when they are in a strong position simply to build and improve their competitive advantage and stay on top—which Dell and Microsoft frequently do.

All too often, however, companies are forced to downsize and lay off employees because they fail to monitor and control their basic business operations and have not made the incremental changes to their strategies and structures over time that allow them to adjust to changing conditions. Advances in management, such as the development of new models for organizing work activities, or advances in information technology offer strategic managers the opportunity to implement their strategies in more effective ways.

One way of helping a company operate more effectively is to use **reengineering**, which involves the "fundamental rethinking and radical redesign of business processes to achieve dramatic improvements in critical, contemporary measures of performance such as cost, quality, service, and speed."[53] As this definition suggests, strategic managers who use reengineering must completely rethink how they organize their value-chain activities. Instead of focusing on how a company's *functions* operate, strategic managers make business *processes* the focus of attention.

A **business process** is any activity that is vital to delivering goods and services to customers quickly or that promotes high quality or low costs (such as IT, materials management, or product development) and that is not the responsibility of any *one* function but *cuts across functions*. Because reengineering focuses on business processes and not on functions, a company that reengineers always has to adopt a different approach to organizing its activities. Companies that take up reengineering deliberately ignore the existing arrangement of tasks, roles, and work activities. They start the reengineering process with the customer (not the product or service) and ask, "How can we reorganize the way we do our work, our business processes, to provide the best quality and the lowest-cost goods and services to the customer?"

Frequently, when companies ask this question, they realize that there are more effective ways to organize their value-chain activities. For example, a business process that encompasses members of ten different functions working sequentially to provide goods and services might be performed by one person or a few people at a fraction of the cost. Often individual jobs become increasingly complex, and people are grouped into cross-functional teams as business processes are reengineered to reduce costs and increase quality.

Hallmark Cards, for example, reengineered its card design process with great success. Before the reengineering effort, artists, writers, and editors worked separately in different functions to produce all kinds of cards. After reengineering, these same artists, writers, and editors were put in cross-functional teams, each of which now works on a specific type of card, such as birthday, Christmas, or Mother's Day. The result is that the time it took to bring a new card to market dropped from years to months, and Hallmark's performance increased dramatically.

Reengineering and total quality management (TQM), discussed in Chapter 4, are highly interrelated and complementary. After reengineering has taken place and value-chain activities have been altered to speed the product to the final customer, TQM takes over, with its focus on how to continue to improve and refine the new process and find better ways of managing task and role relationships. Successful organizations examine both questions simultaneously and continuously attempt to identify new and better processes for meeting the goals of increased efficiency, quality, and customer responsiveness. Thus, they are always seeking to improve their visions of their desired future state.

Another example of reengineering is the change program that took place at IBM Credit, a wholly owned division of IBM that manages the financing and leasing of IBM computers, particularly mainframes, to IBM's customers. Before reengineering took place, when a financing request arrived at the division's headquarters in Old Greenwich, Connecticut, it went through a five-step approval process that involved the activities of five different functions. First, the IBM salesperson called the credit department, which logged the request and took details about the potential customer. Second, this information was taken to the credit-checking department, where a credit check on the potential customer was made. Third, when the credit check was complete, the request was taken to the contracts department, which wrote the contract. Fourth, from there it went to the pricing department, which determined the actual financial details of the loan, such as the interest rate and the term of the loan. Finally, the whole package of information was assembled by the dispatching department and delivered to the sales representative, who gave it to the customer.

This series of cross-functional activities took an average of seven days to complete, and sales representatives constantly complained that this delay resulted in a low level of customer responsiveness that reduced customer satisfaction. Also, potential customers were tempted to shop around for financing and even to look at competitors' machines. The delay in closing the deal caused uncertainty for all concerned.

The change process began when two senior IBM credit managers reviewed the finance approval process. They found that the time spent by different specialists in the different functions actually processing a loan application was only ninety minutes. The seven-day approval process was caused because of the delay in transmitting information and requests between departments. The managers also came to understand that the activities taking place in each department were not complex; each department had its own computer system containing its own work procedures, but the work done in each department was pretty routine.

Armed with this information, IBM managers realized that the approval process could be reengineered into one overarching process handled by one person with a computer system containing all the necessary information and work procedures to perform the five loan-processing activities. If the application were complex, a team of experts stood ready to help process it, but IBM found that after the reengineering effort a typical application could be done in four hours rather than the previous seven days. A sales representative could go back to the customer the same day to close the deal, and all the uncertainty surrounding the transaction was removed.

As reengineering consultants Hammer and Champy note, this dramatic performance increase was brought about by a radical change to the process as a whole. Change through reengineering requires managers to go back to the basics and pull apart each step in the work process to identify a better way to coordinate and integrate the activities necessary to provide customers with goods and services. As this example makes clear, the introduction of new IT is an integral aspect of reengineering. IT also allows a company to restructure its hierarchy because it provides more and better-quality information. IT today is an integral part of the strategy implementation process.

Summary of Chapter

1. Implementing a company's business model and strategies successfully depends on organizational design, the process of selecting the right combination of organizational structure, control systems, and culture. Companies need to monitor and oversee the organizational design process to achieve superior profitability.

2. Effective organizational design can increase profitability in two ways. First, it economizes on bureaucratic costs and helps a company lower its cost structure. Second, it enhances the ability of a company's value creation functions to achieve superior efficiency, quality, innovativeness, and customer responsiveness and to obtain the advantages of differentiation.

3. The main issues in designing organizational structure are how to group tasks, functions, and divisions; how to allocate authority and responsibility (whether to have a tall or flat organization, or to have a centralized or decentralized structure); and how to use integrating mechanisms to improve coordination between functions (such as direct contacts, liaison roles, and teams).

4. Strategic control provides the monitoring and incentive systems necessary to make an organizational structure work as intended and extends corporate governance down to all levels inside the company. The main kinds of strategic control systems are personal control, output control, and behavior control. Information technology is an aid to output and behavior control, and reward systems are linked to every control system.

5. Organizational culture is the set of values, norms, beliefs, and attitudes that help to energize and motivate employees and control their behavior. Culture is a way of doing something, and a company's founder and top managers help determine which kinds of values emerge in an organization.

6. At the functional level, each function requires a different combination of structure and control system to achieve its functional objectives.

7. To successfully implement a company's business model, structure, control, and culture must be combined in ways that increase the relationships among all functions to build distinctive competencies.

8. Cost leadership and differentiation each require a structure and control system that strengthens the business model that is the source of their competitive advantage. Managers have to use organizational design in a way that balances pressures to increase differentiation against pressures to lower the cost structure.

9. Other specialized kinds of structures include the product, market, geographic, matrix, and product-team structures. Each has a specialized use and is implemented as a company's strategy warrants.
10. Restructuring and reengineering are two ways of implementing a company's business model more effectively.

Discussion Questions

1. What is the relationship of organizational structure, control, and culture? Give some examples of when and under what conditions a mismatch between these components might arise.

2. What kind of structure best describes the way your (a) business school and (b) university operate? Why is the structure appropriate? Would another structure fit better?
3. When would a company choose a matrix structure? What are the problems associated with managing this structure, and why might a product-team structure be preferable?
4. For each of the structures discussed in the chapter, outline the most suitable control systems.
5. What kind of structure, controls, and culture would you be likely to find in (a) a small manufacturing company, (b) a chain store, (c) a high-tech company, and (d) a Big Four accounting firm?

Practicing Strategic Management

SMALL-GROUP EXERCISE
Deciding on an Organizational Structure

Break up into groups of three to five people, and discuss the following scenario. You are a group of managers of a major soft drink company that is going head-to-head with Coca-Cola to increase market share. Your business model is based on increasing your product range to offer a soft drink in every segment of the market to attract customers. Currently you have a functional structure. What you are trying to work out now is how best to implement your business model in order to launch your new products. Should you move to a more complex kind of product structure, and, if so, which one? Alternatively, should you establish new-venture divisions, and spin off each kind of new soft drink into its own company so that it can focus its resources on its market niche? Thinking strategically, debate the pros and cons of the possible organizational structures, and decide which structure you will implement.

ARTICLE FILE 12
Find an example of a company that competes in one industry and that has recently changed the way it implements its business model and strategies. What changes did it make? Why did it make these changes? What effect did these changes have on the behavior of people and functions?

STRATEGIC MANAGEMENT PROJECT
Module 12

This module asks you to identify how your company implements its business model and strategy. For this part of your project, you need to obtain information about your company's structure, control systems, and culture. This information may be hard to obtain unless you can interview managers directly. But you can make many inferences about the company's structure from the nature of its activities, and if you write to the company, it may provide you with an organizational chart and other information. Also, published information, such as compensation for top management, is available in the company's annual reports or 10-K reports. If your company is well known, magazines such as *Fortune* and *Business Week* frequently report on corporate culture or control issues. Nevertheless, you may be forced to make some bold assumptions to complete this part of the project.

1. How large is the company as measured by the number of its employees? How many levels in the hierarchy does it have from the top to the bottom? Based on these two measures and any other information you may have, would you say your company operates with a relatively tall or flat structure? Does your company have a centralized or decentralized approach to decision making?

2. What changes (if any) would you make to the way the company allocates authority and responsibility?

3. Draw an organizational chart showing the main way in which your company groups its activities. Based on this chart, decide what kind of structure (functional, product, or divisional) your company operates with.

4. Why did your company choose this structure? In what ways is it appropriate for its business model? In what ways is it not?

5. What kind of integration or integration mechanisms does your company use?

6. What are the main kinds of control systems your company is using? What kinds of behaviors is the organization trying to (a) shape and (b) motivate through the use of these control systems?

7. What role does the top management team play in creating the culture of your organization? Can you identify the characteristic norms and values that describe the way people behave in your organization? How does the design of the organization's structure affect its culture?

8. What are the sources of your company's distinctive competencies? Which functions are most important to it? How does your company design its structure, control, and culture to enhance its (a) efficiency, (b) quality, (c) innovativeness, and (d) responsiveness to customers?

9. How does it design its structure and control systems to strengthen its business model? For example, what steps does it take to further cross-functional integration? Does it have a functional, product, or matrix structure?

10. How does your company's culture support its business model? Can you determine any ways in which its top management team influences its culture?

11. Based on this analysis, would you say your company is coordinating and motivating its people and subunits effectively? Why or why not? What changes (if any) would you make to the way your company's structure operates? What use could it make of restructuring or reengineering?

▉ EXPLORING THE WEB
Visiting Home Depot

Go to **www.homedepot.com**, and examine corporate information such as the company overview, history, and press releases. Based on this information, what kind of structure, control systems, and culture do you think Home Depot has in place to implement its business model and strategies?

General Task   Search the Web for an example of a company that has been changing the way it implements its business model. What were its problems? How did it use structure, control, and culture to improve the way it operates?

Closing Case

Strategy Implementation at Dell Computer

Dell Computer was one of the fastest-growing companies of the 1990s, and its stock price increased at the rate of 100 percent a year, delighting its stockholders. Achieving this high return has been a constant challenge for Michael Dell, and one of his biggest battles has been to manage and change Dell's organizational structure, control systems, and culture as his company grows.

Dell was nineteen when, in 1984, he took $1,000 and spent it on the computer parts he assembled himself into PCs that he then sold over the phone. Increasing demand for his PCs meant that within a few weeks he needed to hire people to help him, and soon he found himself supervising three employees who worked together around a six-foot table to assemble computers while two more employees took orders over the phone.

By 1993, Dell employed 4,500 workers and was hiring over 100 new workers each week just to keep pace with the demand for the computers. When he found himself working eighteen-hour days managing the company, he realized that he could not lead the company single-handedly. The company's growth had to be managed, and he knew that he had to recruit and hire strategic managers who had experience in managing different functional areas, such as marketing, finance, and manufacturing. He recruited executives from IBM and Compaq and with their help created a functional structure, one in which employees are grouped by the common skills they have or tasks they perform, such as sales or manufacturing, to organize the value-chain activities necessary to deliver his PCs to customers. As a part of this organizing process, Dell's structure also became taller, with more levels in the management hierarchy, to ensure that he and his managers had sufficient control over the different activities of his growing business. Dell delegated authority to control Dell's functional value-chain activities to his managers, which gave him the time he needed to perform his entrepreneurial task of finding new opportunities for the company.

Dell's functional structure worked well, and under its new management team, the company's growth continued to soar. By 1993, the company had sales of over $2 billion, twice as much as in 1992. Moreover, Dell's new structure had given functional managers the control they needed to squeeze out costs, and Dell had become the lowest-cost PC maker. Analysts also reported that Dell had developed a lean organizational culture, meaning that employees had developed norms and values that emphasized the importance of working hard to help each other find innovative new ways of making products to keep costs low and increase their reliability. Indeed, with the fewest customer complaints, Dell rose to the top of the customer satisfaction rankings for PC makers; its employees became known for the excellent customer service they gave to PC buyers who were experiencing problems with setting up their computers.

However, Michael Dell realized that new and different kinds of problems were arising. Dell was now selling huge numbers of computers to different kinds of customers, for example, home, business, and educational customers and the different branches of government. Because customers now demanded computers with very different features or different amounts of computing power, the company's product line broadened rapidly. It started to become more difficult for employees to meet the needs of these different kinds of customers efficiently because each employee needed information about all product features or all of Dell's thousands of different sales offers across its product range.

In 1995, Dell moved to change his company to a market structure and created separate divisions, each geared to the needs of a different group of customers: a consumer division, a business division, and so on. In each division, teams of employees specialize in servicing the needs of one of these customer groups. This move to a more complex structure also allowed each division to develop a unique subculture that suited its tasks, and employees were able to obtain in-depth knowledge about the needs of their market that helped them to respond better to their customers' needs. So successful was this change in structure and culture that by 1999 Dell's revenues were over $30 billion and its profits were in excess of $2.5 billion, a staggering increase from 1984.

Dell has continued to alter his company's structure to respond to changing customer needs and to the company's increase in distinctive competencies. For example, Dell realized he could leverage his company's strengths in materials management, manufacturing, and Internet sales over a wider range of computer hardware products. So he decided to begin assembling servers, workstations, and storage devices to compete with IBM, Sun, and Compaq. The increasing importance of the Internet led him to split the market divisions into thirty-five smaller subunits that focus on more specialized groups of customers, and they all conduct the majority of their business over the Internet. Today, for example, Dell can offer large and small companies and private buyers a complete range of computers, workstations, and storage devices that can be customized to their needs.

To help coordinate its growing activities, Dell is increasingly making use of its corporate intranet and using information technology (IT) to standardize activities across divisions so as to integrate across functions. Dell's hierarchy is shrinking as managers are increasingly delegating everyday decision making to employees who have access, through IT, to the information they need to provide excellent customer service. To help reduce costs, Dell has also outsourced some of its customer service activities. As a result of these moves, Dell's work force has become even more committed to sustaining its low-cost advantage, and its cost-conscious culture has become an important source of competitive advantage that is the envy of its competitors.[54]

Case Discussion Questions

1. How has Dell redesigned its structure over time to better implement its cost-leadership model?

2. What organizational design lessons could other companies learn from Dell's example?

Chapter 13

Implementing Strategy in Companies That Compete Across Industries and Countries

Opening Case

GM Searches for the Right Global Structure

In the past, GM, like the other major U.S. carmakers, decentralized control of its overseas car operations to the managers who controlled its global car divisions in countries such as the United Kingdom, Germany, Australia, and Sweden. Each of GM's global car divisions was responsible for designing cars that suited local customer tastes, and each global division had its own design, component parts, manufacturing, and sales functions. Today, GM has to rethink the way its global structure operates. Although it is the world's biggest carmaker in terms of volume of sales, it is one of the least profitable. GM currently only makes about 1 percent profit margin on the cars it sells in the United States, and it loses money on its sales overseas. The problem facing GM is to find ways to make its global structure operate more efficiently and effectively to implement its global business model.

The major reason for GM's low profit margins is its high cost structure, which is largely due to the way it has allowed its global divisions to operate autonomously in a decentralized fashion. Over time, this mode of operating led its divisions to become fiercely independent to protect their own interests, and this independence resulted in a massive duplication of functional activities. For example, when GM asked its Saab division to work on building a small car based on the Vectra platform developed by its German division as a way to share resources, Saab managers proceeded to give the car a whole new electrical system and engine mounting, expensive modifications that eroded all the potential cost savings from sharing resources.

To reduce its global cost structure, GM decided to place all authority over important car design and production decisions with top managers at its U.S. corporate headquarters. Now its top executives tell its global divisions what they must do to keep costs down, such as which global component suppliers to buy from. As an example of how this can reduce costs, in the past GM's global divisions bought 270 different kinds of radios from global suppliers, and if GM can achieve its goal of reducing this number to 50 by 2006, it will slash 40 percent off the cost of its global radio purchases.

Another goal of GM's policy of recentralizing control of decision making is to better coordinate the activities of its global engineering and design groups to speed the development of new car models. GM now tells its global divisions how they should work together and share their expertise to design cars that can be sold anywhere in the world. It currently takes GM about five years to design a new model, whereas it takes Toyota only three—a tremendous advantage. Now a global council in Detroit makes the key model development decisions. Although this activity involves a $7 billion yearly investment in new car design, it also prevents global car divisions from pursuing their own goals. In fact, after the Saab debacle GM basically took away all authority from Saab's engineering department and its engineers now work according to GM's master plan. Similarly, GM's Daewoo division in Korea decided it didn't want to use an existing GM SUV platform and modify it to fit the Korean market, but instead to create a new one from scratch. GM squashed the resistance and took the steps necessary to make its division toe the line. Although GM wants cars to be customized to the needs of each market, CEO Rich Waggoner says he wants "all these variations to be 'plug and play,'" meaning they do not involve costly redesigns that can adds hundreds of millions of dollars to the new car design budget.

Despite its cost problems, GM, like other U.S. carmakers, has been rapidly catching up with the quality of Japanese carmakers and has closed the gap substantially. So, on the differentiation side of the equation, it must facilitate communication between its global car divisions to take advantage of the enormous pool of talent that it has throughout the world. If it can use its new more centralized global product-group structure to design cars that better satisfy customer needs more quickly, it will be able to compete effectively against companies such as Toyota and Honda in the future.

Overview

The story of GM's efforts to develop a competitive global business model to compete effectively in car markets around the world suggests how complex strategic thinking can become at the corporate level. Companies have to continually examine how to improve the way they implement their business and multibusiness models to increase their long-run profitability and grow their profits. This chapter takes off where the last one ends and examines how to implement strategy when a company decides to enter and compete in new industries, or in new countries when it expands globally, and when it chooses strategies such as merger or outsourcing to strengthen its business model. The strategy implementation issue remains the same: how to use organizational design and combine organizational structure, control, and culture to allow a company to pursue its business model and strategies successfully. Once a company decides to compete across industries and countries, however, it confronts a new set of problems, some of them continuations of problems discussed in Chapter 12 and some of them a direct consequence of its decision to enter and compete in overseas markets and new industries. As a result, it has to make a new series of organizational design decisions to successful implement its new global and multibusiness model.

By the end of the chapter, you will appreciate the many complex issues and choices confronting managers of multibusiness and global companies and the reasons that strategy implementation is an integral part of achieving superior performance.

Managing Corporate Strategy Through the Multidivisional Structure

As Chapter 10 discusses, there are many ways in which corporate-level strategies such as vertical integration or diversification can be used to strengthen a company's business model to improve its competitive position. However, substantial implementation problems arise as well, many of them due to the increasing bureaucratic costs associated with managing a larger collection of companies that operate in different industries. These costs are especially high when a company is seeking to gain the differentiation and low-cost advantages of transferring, sharing, or leveraging its distinctive competencies across its business units in different industries. For companies pursuing a multibusiness model, the problems and costs of managing the handoffs or transfers between value-chain functions across industries to obtain these benefits rise sharply. It is the need to economize on these costs that propels strategic managers to search for improved ways of implementing the corporate-level strategies necessary to pursue a multibusiness model.

As a company begins to enter new industries and produce completely different kinds of products such as cars, fast food, and computers, the structures described in Chapter 12, such as the functional and product structures, are not up to the task. They cannot provide sufficient coordination between functions and motivation to employees that implementing a multibusiness model requires. As a result, the control problems that give rise to bureaucratic costs, such as those related to measurement, customers, location, or strategy, escalate. Experiencing these problems is a sign that the company has outgrown its structure. Strategic managers need to invest more resources to develop a more complex structure—one that can meet the needs of its multibusiness model and strategies. The answer for most large, complex companies is to move to a multidivisional structure, design a cross-industry control system, and fashion a corporate culture to reduce these problems and economize on bureaucratic costs.

The multidivisional structure possesses two main innovations over a functional or product structure that allow a company to grow and diversify while reducing the coordination and control problems inherent in entering and competing in new industries. First, in each industry in which a company operates, strategic managers organize its business units or companies in that industry into one or more *divisions*. Sometimes each division contains a full set of all the value-chain functions it needs to pursue its business model; in this case, it is called a *self-contained division*. For example, GE competes in over 150 different industries, and in each industry, all of its divisions are self-sufficient and perform all the value creation functions. Sometimes, however, divisions in *different* industries *share* value-chain functions to obtain cost savings and to benefit from leveraging competencies across divisions, as discussed in detail below. For example, PepsiCo has two major divisions in the soft drink and snack foods industries; each has its own R&D and manufacturing functions, but they share the marketing and distribution functions to lower operating costs and achieve the gains from differentiation.

Second, the office of *corporate headquarters staff* is created to monitor divisional activities and to exercise financial control over each of the divisions.[1] This staff contains the corporate-level managers who oversee the activities of divisional managers. Hence, the organizational hierarchy is taller in a multidivisional structure than in a product or functional structure. The role of the new level of corporate management is to develop strategic control systems that lower a company's overall cost structure, including finding ways to economize on the costs of controlling the handoffs and transfers between divisions. The extra cost of these corporate managers is more than justified if their actions can lower the cost structure of the operating divisions or increase divisions' ability to differentiate their product—both of which boost a company's return on invested capital (ROIC).

In the multidivisional structure, day-to-day operations of each division are the responsibility of divisional management; that is, divisional management has *operating responsibility*. The corporate headquarters, which includes top executives as well as their support staff, is responsible for overseeing the company's long-term multibusiness model and for providing guidance for interdivisional projects. These executives

FIGURE 13.1

Multidivisional Structure

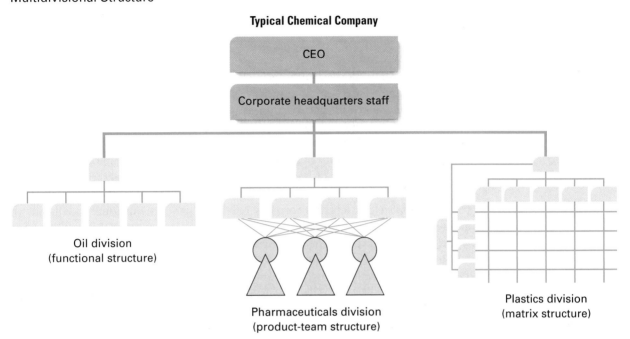

have *strategic responsibility.* Such a combination of self-contained divisions with a centralized corporate management provides the extra coordination and control necessary to manage entry into new industries.

Figure 13.1 illustrates a typical multidivisional structure found in a large chemical company such as DuPont. Although this company might easily have twenty different divisions, only three—the oil, pharmaceuticals, and plastics divisions—are represented here. Each division possesses some combination of the value-chain functions it needs to pursue its own business model. Each is also normally treated by the corporate center as a profit center, and strategic control measures such as ROIC are used to monitor and evaluate each division's performance.[2] The use of this kind of output control makes it easier for corporate managers to identify high-performing and underperforming divisions and to take corrective action as necessary.

Because they have been separated into subunits by industry, each division is also able to develop the structure and culture that best suit its particular business model, for example, a product, matrix, or market structure. As a result, implementing a multidivisional structure allows a multibusiness company to take into account the need for each separate division to adopt the structure and control systems necessary to implement its business model and strategies effectively.

Figure 13.1 shows that the oil division has a functional structure because it is pursuing cost leadership. The pharmaceuticals division has a product-team structure to encourage speedy development of new drugs, and the plastics division has a matrix structure to allow it to quickly develop new kinds of customized plastic products to suit the changing needs of its customers—these divisions are pursuing differentiation based on a distinctive competence in innovation. Sometimes the size of its operations alone is enough to compel a company to use a multidivisional structure.

For example, inside one industry, the car industry, GM operates the whole corporation through a multidivisional structure, and each of its main car brands—Cadillac, Buick, and so on—is organized as a separate division. In addition, as we discuss in the *Opening Case*, GM has an overseas division in each country abroad in which it assembles cars. A former GM CEO, Alfred Sloan, implemented its multidivisional structure in 1921, noting that GM "needs to find a principle for coordination without losing the advantages of decentralization."

Each of GM's different car brands was placed in a self-contained division with support services like sales, production, engineering, and finance. Each division became a profit center and was evaluated on its return on investment. Sloan was quite clear about the main advantage of linking decentralization to return on investment: it raised the visibility of each division's performance. And, Sloan observed, it (1) "increases the morale of the organization by placing each operation on its own foundation,…assuming its own responsibility and contributing its share to the final result"; (2) "develops statistics correctly reflecting…the true measure of efficiency"; and (3) "enables the corporation to direct the placing of additional capital where it will result in the greatest benefit to the corporation as a whole."[3]

Sloan recommended that exchanges or handoffs between divisions be set by a *transfer-pricing scheme* based on cost plus some predetermined rate of return. However, to avoid protecting a high-cost internal supplier, he also recommended a number of steps involving analysis of the operations of outside competitors to determine the fair price. Sloan established a strong, professional, centralized headquarters management staff to perform such calculations. Corporate management's primary role was to audit divisional performance and plan strategy for the total organization. Divisional managers were to be responsible for all product-related decisions.

As the *Opening Case* relates, fierce competition from efficient Japanese competitors resulted in GM reassessing the way its multidivisional structure was operating. The duplication of R&D and engineering between divisions at home and abroad, and the purchasing of components by each division independently, was costing the company billions of extra dollars. Globally, GM has reduced the number of cars in its product range and the number of different platforms used to make cars. It has also vertically disintegrated by spinning off high-cost internal suppliers and has recentralized the purchasing of component parts using the car industry's sophisticated B2B network, Covisint, to outsource more of its components. As GM's experience suggests, operating a multidivisional structure is a *continuing* challenge for managers. Because the multidivisional structure is so widely used, it is necessary to look closely at its advantages and disadvantages.

■ Advantages of a Multidivisional Structure

When managed effectively at both the corporate and the divisional levels, a multidivisional structure offers several advantages. Together, they can raise corporate profitability to a new peak because they allow a company to more effectively implement its multibusiness model and strategies at all levels.

■ Enhanced Corporate Financial Control

The profitability of different business divisions is clearly visible in the multidivisional structure.[4] Because each division is its own profit center, financial controls can be applied to each business on the basis of profitability criteria such as ROIC. Typically, these controls cover establishing targets, monitoring performance on a regular basis, and selectively intervening when problems arise. Corporate headquarters is also in a better position to allocate corporate financial resources among competing divisions. The visibility of divisional performance means that corporate headquarters can identify the divisions in which investment of funds will yield the greatest long-term ROIC. In a sense, the corporate office is in a position to act as the investor or banker in an internal capital market, channeling funds to high-yield uses.

■ **Enhanced Strategic Control** The multidivisional structure frees corporate managers from business-level responsibilities. Corporate managers have the time and scope for contemplating wider strategic issues and for developing responses to environmental changes, such as quickly changing industry boundaries. The multidivisional structure also enables corporate headquarters to obtain the proper information to perform long-run strategic and scenario planning for the entire corporation, including decisions about which businesses to expand and which to exit from.

■ **Growth** The multidivisional structure lets the company overcome an organizational limit to its growth. Because information overload at the center is reduced, corporate managers can consider emerging opportunities for further growth and diversification. Communication problems are reduced because the same set of standardized accounting and financial output controls can be used for all divisions. Also, from a behavior control perspective, corporate managers are able to implement a policy of management by exception, which means that they intervene only when problems arise.

■ **Stronger Pursuit of Internal Efficiency** As a company grows, it often becomes difficult for managers to accurately assess the profit contribution of each functional activity because their activities are so interdependent. This means that it is often more difficult for top managers to evaluate how well their company is performing relative to others in its industry. As a result, inside one company considerable degrees of organizational slack—that is, the unproductive use of functional resources—can go undetected. For example, the head of the finance function might employ a larger staff than required for efficiency to reduce work pressures inside the department and to bring the manager higher status. In a multidivisional structure, however, corporate managers can compare the performance of one division against another in terms of its cost structure or the profit it generates. The corporate office is thus in a better position to identify the managerial inefficiencies that result in bureaucratic costs, and divisional managers can have no alibis for poor performance.

■ **Problems in Implementing a Multidivisional Structure**

Although research suggests that large companies that adopt a multidivisional structure outperform those that retain the functional structure, this structure has its disadvantages as well.[5] Good management can eliminate some of them, but others are inherent in the way the structure operates and require constant managerial attention, as GM's problems suggest.

■ **Establishing the Divisional-Corporate Authority Relationship** The authority relationship between corporate headquarters and the divisions must be correctly established. The multidivisional structure introduces a new level in the hierarchy: the corporate level. The problem lies in deciding how much authority and control to delegate to the operating divisions and how much authority to retain at corporate headquarters to increase long-run profitability. This was the problem Sloan encountered when he implemented GM's multidivisional structure.[6] What Sloan found was that when headquarters retained too much power and authority, the operating divisions lacked sufficient autonomy to develop the business model and strategies that best met their needs. On the other hand, when too much power was delegated to the divisions, they pursued divisional objectives, with little heed to the needs of the whole corporation. As a result, not all the potential gains from using this structure could be achieved.

Thus, the central issue in managing the multidivisional structure is how much authority should be *centralized* at corporate headquarters and how much should be *decentralized* to the divisions. This issue must be decided by each company in reference to the nature of its business- and corporate-level strategies. There are no easy answers, and as the environment changes or the company alters its multibusiness model strategies over time, the balance between corporate and divisional control will also change, as Strategy in Action 13.1 suggests.

Strategy in Action 13.1

Amoco, ARCO, and Burmah Castrol Become Part of BP

As with most other global oil companies, Amoco was engaged in three major activities: oil exploration, refining, and chemicals manufacturing. To manage these activities, it used a three-legged structure and created three independent operating *subsidiaries* to manage each of its three main activities. Each subsidiary had its own set of managers responsible for overseeing all the many different *divisions* inside each subsidiary; thus, there was an extra level of control: the subsidiary level. The managers of all three subsidiaries then reported to Amoco's corporate-level managers, who oversaw their activities and made the final decision on what each subsidiary should be doing. Because all important decision making at Amoco was centralized at the top, it often took a long time to make decisions because of the many managerial layers between Amoco's corporate managers and its divisional managers. The slow decision-making process hampered divisional managers' attempts to build a competitive advantage, but this situation was left unattended too during the prosperous oil industry of the 1980s.

By the 1990s, Amoco, like other global oil companies such as Exxon, British Petroleum, and Mobil, had experienced intense pressure to reduce costs because of flat gas prices. To try to boost profits, Amoco laid off more than one-quarter of its work force, but this did not work. Amoco's managers then took a close look at its structure to see whether there was a way to increase its performance.

Amoco's CEO, H. Laurence Fuller, decided that a massive reorganization of Amoco's structure was necessary. Fuller eliminated Amoco's three-legged structure completely and removed all the managers at the subsidiary level. The three subsidiaries were divided into seventeen independent divisions according to their industry, and Amoco changed to a multidivisional structure. Henceforth, strategic responsibilities were decentralized to the managers of each division, who were free to pursue the most effective business model. Each division was evaluated on the basis of its ability to reach certain ROIC targets set by corporate managers, but their own managers determined the way they achieved those targets.

By 1996, it was clear that Fuller's move to a multidivisional structure had worked. Managers were acting more entrepreneurially, and the company was operating more efficiently. However, in the late 1990s, oil industry companies began to consolidate further to make better use of their resources and lower their cost structure. Fuller agreed to merge Amoco with British Petroleum (BP).[7] Because many of both companies' divisions were competing in the same industries, their functional activities overlapped and duplicated one another, so BP developed a value creation grid and then merged Amoco's seventeen divisions with its own thirty-three divisions. In 2001, BP acquired ARCO for its extensive gas reserves and Burmah Castrol, the well-known fuel oil maker. Once again, it integrated these companies into its existing operations, and from these mergers it strengthened its differentiated position in its major sectors of oil, gas, chemicals, and downstream activities such as retailing. BP also announced that it expected to achieve $5.9 billion in cost savings from these moves. BP has continued to make new acquisitions or form joint ventures around the world to strengthen its position in many emerging markets. For example, it took a 20 percent stake in China's biggest gas refiner and gas station chain to leverage the use of its resources into this fast-growing market.[a]

■ **Distortion of Information** If corporate headquarters places too much emphasis on each division's individual profitability—for instance, by setting very high and stringent ROIC targets—divisional managers may choose to distort the information they supply top management and paint a rosy picture of it at the expense of future profitability. Bureaucratic costs now increase as divisions may attempt to make ROIC look better by cutting product development or new investments or marketing expenditures. Although such actions might boost short-run ROIC, they do so at the cost of cutting back on investments and expenditures necessary to maintain the long-term profitability of the company. The problem stems from too tight financial control. GM suffered from this problem in recent years as declining performance prompted divisional managers to try to make their divisions look good to corporate headquarters to secure greater funds for future investment. Managing the corporate-divisional interface requires coping with subtle power issues.

■ **Competition for Resources** The third problem of managing a multi-divisional structure is that the divisions themselves may compete for resources and this rivalry can make it difficult or impossible to obtain the gains from transferring, sharing, or leveraging distinctive competencies across business units. For example, the amount of capital for investment that corporate managers have to distribute to the divisions is fixed. Generally, the divisions that can demonstrate the highest ROIC get the lion's share of the money. Because that large share strengthens them in the next time period, the strong divisions grow stronger. Consequently, divisions may actively compete for resources and thereby reduce interdivisional coordination. As a result, the potential gains from pursuing a multibusiness model will be lost.

■ **Transfer Pricing** Divisional competition may lead to battles over **transfer pricing,** that is, conflicts over establishing the fair or "competitive" price of a resource or skill developed in one division that is to be transferred and sold to other divisions that require it. As we discuss in Chapter 9, one of the origins of the problems of handoffs or transfers between divisions, and thus a major source of bureaucratic costs, is the problem of setting prices for resource transfers to obtain the benefits of the multibusiness models when pursuing a vertical integration or related diversification strategy.

Rivalry among divisions is common in the transfer pricing process because each supplying division has the incentive to set the highest price for its resources or skills to maximize its own revenues and profits. However, purchasing divisions view attempts to charge high prices as undermining their own profitability—hence the problem. Such competition can completely undermine the corporate culture and make a company a battleground. If such battles go unresolved, the benefits of the multibusiness model will not be achieved. Hence, there is a need for the sensitive design of incentive and control systems to make the multidivisional structure work.

■ **Short-Term R&D Focus** If corporate headquarters sets extremely high and rigid ROIC targets, there is a danger that the divisions will cut back on R&D expenditures to improve their financial performance. Although this inflates divisional performance in the short term, it undermines a division's ability to develop new products and leads to a fall in the stream of long-term profits. Hence, corporate headquarters personnel must carefully control their interactions with the divisions to ensure that both the short- and long-term goals of the business are being achieved.

■ **Duplication of Functional Resources** Because each division often possesses its own set of value-chain functions, multidivisional structures are expensive to run and manage. R&D is an especially costly activity, and so some companies centralize such functions at the corporate level to serve all divisions. The duplication of specialist services is not a problem if the cost and differentiation gains from having separate specialist functions are substantial, however. Corporate managers decide whether duplication is financially justified and, if so, which functions to centralize or decentralize to optimize short- and long-run profitability.

In sum, the advantages of divisional structures must be balanced against problems of implementing them, but an observant, professional management team that is aware of the issues involved can manage these problems. The increasing use of information technology is also making implementation easier. We discuss information technology after we describe the use of structure, control, and culture for different kinds of multibusiness models.

■ **Structure, Control, Culture, and Corporate-Level Strategy**

Once strategic managers select a multidivisional structure, they must then make choices about what kind of integrating mechanisms and control systems to use to make the structure work efficiently. Such choices depend on whether a company chooses to pursue a multibusiness model based on a strategy of unrelated diversification, vertical integration, or related diversification.

As discussed in Chapter 9, many possible differentiation and cost advantages derive from vertical integration. A company can coordinate resource-scheduling decisions among divisions operating in adjacent industries to reduce manufacturing costs and improve quality, for example.[8] This might mean locating a rolling mill next to a steel furnace to save the costs of reheating steel ingots and make it easier to control the quality of the final product.

The principal benefits from related diversification also come from transferring, sharing, or leveraging functional resources or skills across divisions, such as sharing distribution and sales networks to increase differentiation or lower the overall cost structure. With both strategies, the benefits to the company come from some *exchange of distinctive competencies* among divisions. To secure these benefits, the company must coordinate activities among divisions. Consequently, structure and control must be designed to handle the handoffs or transfers among divisions.

In the case of unrelated diversification, the multibusiness model is based on using general managerial capabilities in entrepreneurship, organizational design, or strategy—for example, through top managers' ability to create a culture that supports entrepreneurial behavior that leads to rapid product development; or from restructuring an underperforming company and establishing an efficient internal capital market that allows corporate managers to make superior capital allocation decisions than would be possible using the external capital market. With this strategy, there are no exchanges among divisions, each operates separately and independently, and the exchanges that need to be coordinated take place between divisions and corporate headquarters. Structure and control must therefore be designed to allow each division to operate independently while giving corporate managers easy ability to monitor and to intervene if necessary.

The choice of structure and control mechanisms depends on the degree to which a company using a multidivisional structure needs to control the handoffs and interactions among divisions. The more interdependent the divisions—that is, the more they depend on each other for skills, resources, and competencies—the greater are the

TABLE 13.1

Corporate Strategy and Structure and Control

Corporate Strategy	Appropriate Structure	Need for Integration	Type of Control		
			Financial Control	Behavior Control	Organizational Culture
Unrelated Diversification	Multidivisional	Low (no exchanges between divisions)	Great use (e.g., ROIC)	Some use (e.g., budgets)	Little use
Vertical Integration	Multidivisional	Medium (scheduling resource transfers)	Great use (e.g., ROIC, transfer pricing)	Great use (e.g., standardization, budgets)	Some use (e.g., shared norms and values)
Related Diversification	Multidivisional	High (achieving synergies between divisions by integrating roles)	Little use	Great use (e.g., rules, budgets)	Great use (e.g., norms, values, common language)

bureaucratic costs associated with obtaining the potential benefits from a particular strategy.[9] Table 13.1 indicates what forms of structure and control companies should adopt to economize on the bureaucratic costs associated with the three corporate strategies of unrelated diversification, vertical integration, and related diversification.[10] We examine these strategies in detail in the next sections.

■ **Unrelated Diversification** Because there are *no exchanges or linkages* among divisions, unrelated diversification is the easiest and cheapest strategy to manage; it is associated with the lowest level of bureaucratic costs. The main requirement of the structure and control system is that it allows corporate managers to evaluate divisional performance easily and accurately. Thus, companies use a multidivisional structure, and each division is evaluated by output controls such as return on invested capital. A company also applies sophisticated accounting controls to obtain information quickly from the divisions so that corporate managers can readily compare divisions on several dimensions. Textron and Dover are good examples of companies that use sophisticated computer networks and accounting controls to manage their structures, which allow them almost daily access to divisional performance.

Divisions usually have considerable autonomy *unless* they fail to reach their ROIC goals. Generally, corporate headquarters will not intervene in the operations of a division unless there are problems. If problems arise, corporate headquarters may step in to take corrective action, perhaps replacing managers or providing additional financial resources, depending on the reason for the problem. If they see no possibility of a turnaround, they may decide to divest the division. The multidivisional structure allows the unrelated company to operate its businesses as a portfolio of investments that can be bought and sold as business conditions change. Often managers in the various divisions do not know one another; they may not even know what other companies are in the corporate portfolio. Hence, the idea of a corporate culture is meaningless.

The use of financial controls to manage a company means that no integration among divisions is necessary. This is why the bureaucratic costs of managing an unrelated company are low. The biggest problem facing corporate personnel is determining capital allocations to the various divisions so that the overall profitability of the portfolio is maximized. They also have to oversee divisional managers and make sure that divisions are achieving ROIC targets.

Alco Standard, based in Valley Forge, Pennsylvania, demonstrates how to operate a successful strategy of unrelated diversification. Alco is one of the largest office supply companies in the United States, distributing office and paper supplies and materials through a nationwide network of wholly owned distribution companies. The policy of Alco's top management is that authority and control should be completely decentralized to the managers in each of the company's fifty divisions. Each division is left alone to make its own manufacturing or purchasing decisions even though some potential benefits, in the form of corporate-wide purchasing or marketing, are being lost. Top management pursues this nonintervention policy because it believes that the gains from allowing its managers to act as independent entrepreneurs exceed any potential cost savings that might result from coordinating interdivisional activities. It believes that a decentralized operating system allows a big company to act in a way that is similar to a small company, avoiding the problem of growing bureaucracy and organizational inertia.

At Alco, top management interprets its role as relieving the divisions of administrative chores, such as bookkeeping and accounting, and collecting market information on competitive pricing and products, which allows divisional managers to improve their business-level strategy. Centralizing these information activities reduces each division's cost structure and provides the standardization that lets top management make better decisions about resource allocation. Alco's division heads are regarded as partners in the corporate enterprise and are rewarded through stock options linked to the performance of their divisions. So far, Alco has been very successful with its decentralized operating structure and has achieved a compound growth rate of 19 percent a year.

■ **Vertical Integration** Vertical integration is a more expensive strategy to manage than unrelated diversification because *sequential resource flows* from one division to the next must be coordinated. Once again, the multidivisional structure economizes on the bureaucratic costs associated with achieving such coordination. This structure provides the centralized control necessary for the vertically integrated company to achieve benefits from the control of resource transfers. Corporate personnel assume the responsibility for devising financial output and behavior controls that solve the problems of transferring resources among divisions; for example, they are involved in solving transfer pricing problems. Also, complex rules and procedures are instituted that specify how exchanges are to be made to solve potential transaction problems. As previously noted, complex resource exchanges can lead to conflict among divisions, and corporate managers must try to minimize divisional conflicts.

Centralizing authority at corporate headquarters must be done with care in vertically related companies. It carries the risk of involving corporate managers in operating issues at the business level to the point at which the divisions lose their autonomy and motivation. These companies must strike the right balance of centralized control at corporate headquarters and decentralized control at the divisional level if they are to implement this strategy successfully.

Because their interests are at stake, divisions need to have input into scheduling and decisions regarding resource transfer. For example, the plastics division in a chemical company has a vital interest in the activities of the oil division, for the quality of the products it gets from the oil division determines the quality of its own products. Divisional integrating mechanisms can bring about direct coordination and information transfers among divisions.[11] To handle communication among divisions, a company sets up teams for that purpose; it can also use **integrating roles,** whereby an experienced senior manager assumes responsibility for managing complex transfers between two or more divisions. The use of integrating roles to coordinate divisions is common in high-tech and chemical companies, for example.

Thus, a strategy of vertical integration is managed through a combination of corporate and divisional controls. As a result, the organizational structure and control systems used for managing this strategy to economize on bureaucratic costs are more complex and more difficult to implement than those used for unrelated diversification. However, as long as the benefits that derive from vertical integration are realized, the extra expense in implementing this strategy can be justified.

■ **Related Diversification** In the case of related diversification, the gains from pursuing this multibusiness model derive from the transfer, sharing, or leveraging of R&D knowledge, industry information, customer bases, and so on across divisions. Also, with this structure, the high level of resource sharing and joint production by divisions makes it hard for corporate managers to measure the performance of each individual division.[12] Thus, bureaucratic costs are substantial. The multidivisional structure helps to economize on these costs because it provides some of the extra coordination and control that is required. However, if a related company is to obtain the potential benefits from using its competencies efficiently and effectively, it has to adopt more complicated forms of integration and control at the divisional level to make the structure work.

First, output control is difficult to use because divisions share resources, so it is not easy to measure the performance of an individual division. Therefore, a company needs to develop a corporate culture that stresses cooperation among divisions and corporate rather than purely divisional goals. Second, corporate managers must establish sophisticated integrating devices to ensure coordination among divisions. Integrating roles and even integrating teams of managers are often essential because they provide the context in which managers from different divisions can meet and develop a common vision of corporate goals. HP, for instance, created a high-level integrating team composed of scores of managers to coordinate the merger process with Compaq.[13]

An organization with a multidivisional structure must have the right mix of incentives and rewards for cooperation if it is to achieve gains from sharing skills and resources among divisions.[14] With unrelated diversification, divisions operate autonomously, and the company can quite easily reward managers on their division's individual performance. With related diversification, however, rewarding divisions is more difficult because they are engaged in so many shared activities, and strategic managers must be sensitive and alert to achieve equity in rewards among divisions. The aim always is to design structure and control systems so that they can maximize the benefits from pursuing the strategy while economizing on bureaucratic costs.

The Role of Information Technology

The expanding use of IT is increasing the advantages and reducing the problems associated with implementing a multibusiness model effectively. IT does this because it facilitates output control, behavior control, and integration between divisions and between divisions and corporate headquarters.

On the advantage side, IT provides a common software platform that can make it much less problematic for divisions to share information and knowledge and obtain the benefits from leveraging their competencies. IT also facilitates output and financial control, making it easier for corporate headquarters to monitor divisional performance and decide when to intervene selectively. It also helps corporate managers better use their strategic and implementation skills because they can react more quickly given that they possess higher-quality, more timely information from the use of a sophisticated cross-organizational IT infrastructure.

In a similar fashion, IT makes it easier to manage the problems that occur when implementing a multidivisional structure. Because it provides both corporate and divisional managers with more and better information, it makes it easier for corporate managers to decentralize control to divisional managers and yet react quickly if the need arises. IT can also make it more difficult to distort information and hide bad news because divisional managers must provide standardized information that can be compared across divisions. Finally, IT eases the transfer pricing problem because divisional managers have access to detailed up-to-date information about how much a certain resource or skill would cost to buy in the external marketplace. Thus, a fair transfer price is easier to determine. The way in which SAP's enterprise resources planning software helps to integrate the activities of divisions in a multidivisional structure is discussed in Strategy in Action 13.2.

Implementing Strategy Across Countries

Global strategy can play a crucial role in strengthening the business model of both single-business and multibusiness companies. Indeed, few large companies that have expanded into new industries have not already expanded globally and replicated their business model in new countries to grow their profits. Companies can use four basic strategies as they begin to market their products and establish production facilities abroad:

- A *localization strategy* is oriented toward local responsiveness, and a company decentralizes control to subsidiaries and divisions in each country in which it operates to produce and customize products to local markets.

- An *international strategy* is based on R&D and marketing being centralized at home and all the other value creation functions being decentralized to national units.

- A *global standardization strategy* is oriented toward cost reduction, with all the principal value creation functions centralized at the optimal global location.

- A *transnational strategy* is focused so that it can achieve local responsiveness and cost reduction. Some functions are centralized and others decentralized at the global location best suited to achieving these objectives.

The need to coordinate and integrate global value-chain activities increases as a company moves from a localization to an international to a global standardization and then to a transnational strategy. To obtain the benefits of pursuing a transnational strategy, a company must transfer its distinctive competencies to the global location where they can create the most value and establish a global network to coordinate its divisions at home and abroad. The objective of such coordination is to obtain the benefits from transferring or leveraging competencies across a company's

Strategy in Action

SAP's ERP Systems

13.2

SAP is the world's leading supplier of enterprise resources planning (ERP) software; it introduced the world's first ERP system in 1973. So great was the demand for its software that it had to train thousands of IT consultants from companies like IBM, HP, Accenture, and Cap Gemini to install and customize its software to meet the needs of companies around the globe. SAP's ERP system is popular because it manages functional activities at all stages of a company's value chain, as well as resource transfers between a company's different divisions.

First, SAP's software has modules specifically designed to manage each core functional activity. Each module contains the set of best practices that SAP's IT engineers have found works best to build competencies in efficiency, quality, innovation, and responsiveness to customers. Each function inputs its data into its functional module in the way specified by SAP. For example, sales inputs all the information about customer needs required by SAP's sales module, and materials management inputs information about the product specifications it requires from suppliers into SAP's materials-management module. Each SAP module functions as an *expert system* that can reason through the information that functional managers put into it. It then provides managers with real-time feedback about the current state of vital functional operations—and gives recommendations that allow managers to improve them. However, the magic of ERP does not stop there. SAP's ERP software then connects across functions inside each division. This means that managers in all functions of a division have access to other functions' expert systems, and SAP's software is designed to alert managers when their functional operations are affected by changes taking place in another function. *Thus, SAP's ERP allows managers across a division to better coordinate their activities*, which is a major source of competitive advantage.

Moreover, SAP software, running on corporate mainframe computers, takes the information from all the different expert systems in the divisions and creates a companywide ERP system that provides corporate managers with an overview of the operations of all a company's divisions. In essence, SAP's ERP system creates a sophisticated corporate-level expert system that can reason through the huge volume of information being provided by all its divisions and functions. The ERP system can then recognize and diagnose common issues and problems and recommend organization-wide solutions, such as by suggesting new ways to leverage, transfer, and share competencies and resources. Top managers, armed with the knowledge their ERP provides, can also use it to adjust their business model with the changing environment. The result, SAP claims, is that when a multidivisional company implements its corporatewide ERP software, it can achieve productivity gains of 30 to 50 percent, which amounts to billions of dollars of savings for large multinational companies like Nestlé and Exxon.

global business units. Thus, the bureaucratic costs associated with solving the communication and measurement problems that arise in managing handoffs or transfers across countries are much higher for companies pursuing a transnational strategy than for those pursuing the other strategies. The localization strategy does not require coordinating activities on a global level because value creation activities are handled locally, by country or world region. The international and global standardization strategies fit between the other two strategies: although products have to be sold and marketed globally, and hence global product transfers must be managed, there is less need to coordinate skill and resource transfers than for a transnational strategy.

The implication is that as companies change from a localization to an international, global standardization, or transnational strategy, they require a more complex structure, control system, and culture to coordinate the value creation activities associated with implementing that strategy. More complex structures economize on

TABLE 13.2

Global Strategy/Structure Relationships

	Localization Strategy	International Strategy	Global Standardization Strategy	Transnational Strategy
	Low ←——————— Need for Coordination ———————→ High			
	Low ←——————— Bureaucratic Costs ———————→ High			
Centralization of Authority	Decentralized to national unit	Core competencies centralized, others decentralized to national units	Centralized at optimal global location	Simultaneously centralized and decentralized
Horizontal Differentiation	Global-area structure	Global-division structure	Global product-group structure	Global-matrix structure, matrix-in-the-mind
Need for Complex Integrating Mechanisms	Low	Medium	High	Very high
Organizational Culture	Not important	Quite important	Important	Very important

bureaucratic costs. In general, the choice of structure and control systems for managing a global business is a function of three factors:

1. The decision on how to distribute and allocate responsibility and authority between managers at home and abroad so that effective control over a company's global operations is maintained

2. The selection of the organizational structure that groups divisions both at home and abroad in a way that allows the best use of resources and serves the needs of foreign customers most effectively

3. The selection of the right kinds of integration and control mechanisms and organizational culture to make the overall global structure function effectively

Table 13.2 summarizes the appropriate design choices for companies pursuing each of these strategies.

■ **Implementing a Localization Strategy**

When a company pursues a localization strategy, it generally operates with a global-area structure (see Figure 13.2). When using this structure, a company duplicates all value creation activities and establishes an overseas division in every country or world area in which it operates. Authority is decentralized to managers in each overseas division, who devise the appropriate strategy for responding to the needs of the local environment. Managers at global headquarters use market and output controls, such as ROIC, growth in market share, and operation costs, to evaluate the performance of overseas divisions. On the basis of such global comparisons, they can make decisions about capital allocation and orchestrate the transfer of new knowledge among divisions.

FIGURE 13.2

Global-Area Structure

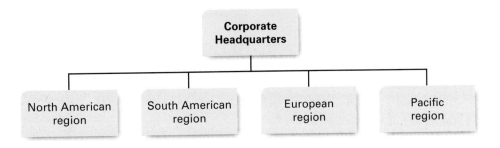

A company that makes and sells the same products in many different countries often groups its overseas divisions into world regions to simplify the coordination of products across countries. Europe might be one region, the Pacific Rim another, and the Middle East a third. Grouping allows the same set of output and behavior controls to be applied across all divisions inside a region. Thus, global companies can reduce communications and transfer problems because information can be transmitted more easily across countries with broadly similar cultures. For example, consumers' preferences regarding product design and marketing are likely to be more similar among countries in one world region than among countries in different world regions.

Because the overseas divisions themselves have little or no contact with others in different regions, no integrating mechanisms are needed. Nor does a global organizational culture develop because there are no transfers of skills or resources or transfer of personnel among managers from the various world regions. Historically, car companies such as DaimlerChrysler, GM, and Ford used global-area structures to manage their overseas operations. Ford of Europe, for example, had little or no contact with its U.S. parent; capital was the principal resource exchanged.

One problem with a global-area structure and a localization strategy is that the duplication of specialist activities across countries raises a company's overall cost structure. Moreover, the company is not taking advantage of opportunities to transfer, share, or leverage its competencies and capabilities on a global basis; for example, it cannot apply the low-cost manufacturing expertise that has developed in one world region in another. Thus, localization companies lose the many benefits of operating globally. As Chapter 8 discusses, the popularity of this strategic orientation has decreased.

■ **Implementing an International Strategy**

A company pursuing an international strategy adopts a different route to global expansion. Normally, the company shifts to this strategy when it decides to sell domestically made products in markets abroad. Until the 1990s, for example, companies such as Mercedes-Benz and Jaguar made no attempt to produce in a foreign market; instead, they distributed and sold their domestically produced cars internationally. Such companies usually just add a *foreign sales organization* to their existing structure and continue to use the same control system. If a company is using a functional structure, this department has to coordinate manufacturing, sales, and R&D activities with the needs of the foreign market. Efforts at customization are minimal. In overseas countries, a company usually establishes a subsidiary to handle local sales and distribution. For example, the Mercedes-Benz overseas subsidiaries allocate dealerships, organize supplies of spare parts, and, of course, sell cars. A system of behavior controls is then established to keep the home office informed of changes in sales, spare parts requirements, and so on.

FIGURE 13.3

Global Division
Structure

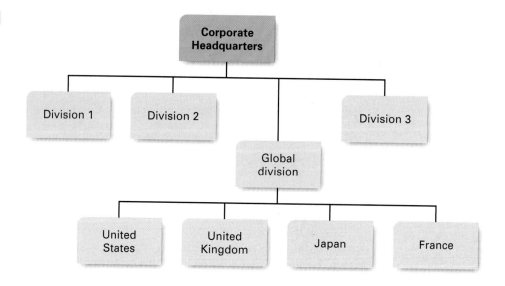

A company with many different products or businesses operating from a multidivisional structure has the challenging problem of coordinating the flow of different products across different countries. To manage these transfers, many companies create a *global division,* which they add to their existing divisional structure (see Figure 13.3).[15] Global operations are managed as a separate divisional business, with managers given the authority and responsibility for coordinating domestic product divisions with overseas markets. The global division also monitors and controls the overseas subsidiaries that market the products and decides how much authority to delegate to managers in these countries.

This arrangement of tasks and roles reduces the transaction of managing handoffs across countries and world regions. However, managers abroad are essentially under the control of managers in the global division, and if domestic and overseas managers compete for control of strategy making, conflict and lack of cooperation may result. Many companies such as IBM, Citibank, and DaimlerChrysler have experienced this problem. Very often, significant strategic control has been decentralized to overseas divisions. When cost pressures force corporate managers to reassess their strategy and they decide to intervene, this frequently provokes resistance, much of it due to differences in culture—not just corporate but also country differences.

■ **Implementing
a Global
Standardization
Strategy**

When a company embarks on a global standardization strategy today, it locates its manufacturing and other value-chain activities at the global location that will allow it to increase efficiency, quality, and innovation. In doing so, it has to solve the problems of coordinating and integrating its global value-chain activities. It has to find a structure that lowers the bureaucratic costs associated with resource transfers between corporate headquarters and its overseas divisions and provides the centralized control that a global standardization strategy requires. The answer for many companies is a *global product-group structure* (see Figure 13.4).

In this structure, a product-group headquarters is created to coordinate the activities of its home and overseas operations. The managers at each product group's headquarters decide where to locate the different functions at the optimal global location for performing that activity. For example, Phillips has one product group responsible for global R&D, manufacturing, marketing, and sales of its light bulbs, another for

FIGURE 13.4

Global Product-Group
Structure

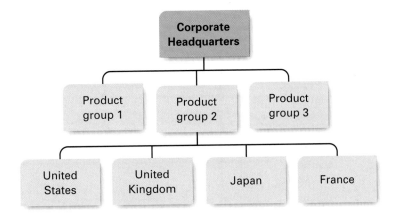

medical equipment, and so on. The headquarters of the medical division and its R&D is located in Bothell, Washington, manufacturing is done in Taiwan, and the products are sold by sales subsidiaries in each local market.

The product-group structure allows managers to decide how best to pursue a global standardization strategy—for example, to decide which value-chain activities, such as manufacturing or product design, should be performed in which country to increase efficiency. Increasingly, U.S. and Japanese companies are moving manufacturing to low-cost countries such as China but establishing product design centers in Europe or the United States to take advantage of foreign skills and capabilities to obtain the benefits from this strategy.

■ **Implementing a Transnational Strategy**

The main failing of the global product-group structure is that although it allows a company to achieve superior efficiency and quality, it is weak when it comes to responsiveness to customers because the focus is still on centralized control to reduce costs. Moreover, this structure makes it difficult for the *different product divisions* to trade information and knowledge and to obtain the benefits from transferring, sharing, and leveraging their competencies. Sometimes the potential gains from sharing product, marketing, or R&D knowledge between product groups are high, but so too are the bureaucratic costs associated with achieving these gains. Is there a structure that can simultaneously economize on these costs and provide the coordination necessary to obtain these benefits?

In the 1990s, many companies implemented a *global-matrix structure* to simultaneously lower their global cost structures *and* differentiate their activities through superior innovation and responsiveness to customers globally. Figure 13.5 shows such a structure that might be used by a company such as HP, SAP, or Nestlé. On the vertical axis, instead of functions, there are the company's product *groups,* which provide specialist services such as R&D, product design, and marketing information to its overseas divisions, which are often grouped by world region. These might be the petroleum, plastics, pharmaceuticals, or fertilizer product groups. On the horizontal axis are the company's *overseas divisions* in the various countries or world regions in which it operates. Managers at the regional or country level control local operations. Through a system of output and behavior controls, they then report to managers in product-group headquarters in the United States and ultimately to the CEO. Managers for world regions or countries are also responsible for working with U.S. product-group managers to develop the control and reward systems that will promote transfer, sharing, or leveraging of competencies.

FIGURE 13.5

Global-Matrix
Structure

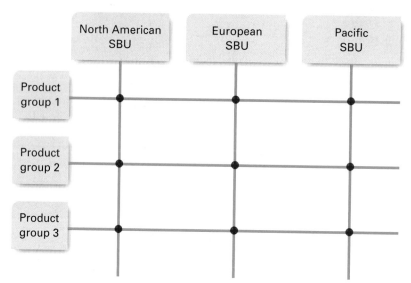

Implementing a matrix structure thus decentralizes control to overseas managers and provides them with considerable flexibility for managing local issues, but it can still give product-group and top corporate executives in the United States the centralized control they need to coordinate company activities on a global level. The matrix structure can allow knowledge and experience to be transferred among divisions in both product groups and geographic regions because it offers many opportunities for face-to-face contact between managers at home and abroad. The matrix also facilitates the transmission of a company's norms and values and, hence, the development of a global corporate culture. This is especially important for a company with far-flung global operations for which lines of communication are longer. Club Med, for instance, uses a matrix to standardize high-quality customer service across its global vacation villages. Nestlé's experience with the global-matrix structure is profiled in Strategy in Action 13.3.

Nestlé is not the only company to find the task of integrating and controlling a global-matrix structure a difficult task. Some, like ABB, Ford, and Motorola, have dismantled their matrix structures and moved to a simplified global product-group approach using IT to integrate across countries. If a matrix is chosen, however, other possible ways of making it work effectively include developing a strong cross-country organizational culture to facilitate communication and coordination among managers. For example, many companies are increasingly transferring managers between their domestic and overseas operations so they can implant the domestic culture in the new location and also learn by studying how their structure and systems work in the foreign country.

Toyota has made great efforts to understand how to manage car plants in overseas locations and how to transplant its culture into those plants. When it decided to enter and make cars in the United States, it first formed a joint venture with GM, and the companies combined their expertise in this car-making venture, which was known as NUMMI. Toyota was responsible for implanting its knowledge of lean production in this plant; all the workers were cross-trained and taught how to monitor and benchmark their own performance and how to work in quality teams to improve it.

Strategy in Action   13.3

Using IT to Make Nestlé's Global Structure Work

Nestlé, based in Vevey, Switzerland, is the world's biggest food company, with global sales in excess of $65 billion in 2004. The company has been pursuing an ambitious program of global expansion by acquiring many famous companies—for instance, Perrier, the French mineral water producer, and Rowntree, the British candy maker. In the United States, Nestlé bought the giant Carnation Company, Stouffer Foods, Contadina, Ralston Purina, and Dreyer's Grand Ice Cream.

Traditionally, Nestlé pursued a localization strategy and managed its operating companies through a global-area structure. In each country, each individual division (such as its Carnation division) was responsible for managing all aspects of its business-level strategy: in other words, companies were free to control their own product development and marketing and to manage all local operations. Nestlé's corporate executives decided acquisitions, expansions, and corporate resource decisions such as capital investment at the Vevey headquarters. Because all important decisions were made centrally, the size of the corporate staff increased dramatically. In the 1990s, Nestlé realized it had major problems.

Corporate managers had become remote from the difficulties experienced by the individual operating divisions or companies, and the centralized structure slowed decision making and made it difficult for Nestlé to respond quickly to the changing environment. Moreover, the company was forfeiting all the possible benefits from sharing and leveraging its distinctive competencies in food product development and marketing, both between divisions in a product group and between product groups and world regions. Because each product group operated separately, corporate executives could not integrate product-group activities around the world. To raise corporate performance, Nestlé's managers sought to find a new way of organizing its activities.

Its CEO at the time, Helmut Maucher, started restructuring Nestlé from the top down. He stripped away the power of corporate managers by decentralizing authority to the managers of seven global product groups that he created to oversee the company's major product lines (for example, coffee, milk, and candy). Each global product group was to integrate the activities of all the operating divisions in its group to transfer and leverage distinctive competencies to create value. After the change,

managers in the candy product group, for instance, began orchestrating the marketing and sale of Rowntree candy products such as After Eight Mints and Smarties throughout Europe and the United States, and sales climbed by 60 percent.

Maucher then grouped all divisions within a country or world region into one national or regional strategic business unit (SBU) and created a team of SBU managers to link, coordinate, and oversee their activities. When the different divisions started to share joint purchasing, marketing, and sales activities, major cost savings resulted. In the United States, the SBU management team reduced the number of sales officers nationwide from 115 to 22 and decreased the number of suppliers of packaging from 43 to 3.

Finally, Maucher decided to use a matrix structure to integrate the activities of the seven global-product groups with the operations of Nestlé's country-based SBUs. The goal of this matrix structure is to have the company pursue a transnational strategy that allows it to obtain the gains from both differentiation through global learning and cost reduction. For example, regional SBU managers now spend considerable time in Vevey with product-group executives discussing ways of exploiting and sharing the resources of the company on a global basis.

Although the new decentralized matrix structure improved Nestlé's ability to coordinate its structure, by 1998 it was clear that it still was not providing enough integration and coordination. Although more coordination was taking place between product groups *inside* a region such as the United States, little coordination was taking place across world regions. Nestlé's top managers searched for ways to improve integration on a global scale. Their conclusion was that more output and behavior control was needed so that different product groups and regional SBUs could learn from and understand what everyone else was doing—for example, what their product development plans were or how each product group handled its global supply chain.

Nestlé's solution was to sign a $300 million contract with SAP in 2002 to install and maintain a companywide ERP system to integrate across *all* its global operations. Top managers hoped this system would give them the information they needed to exert centralized control over operations, which the matrix structure apparently did not provide. In essence, Nestlé began to use SAP's value-chain management software as a *substitute* for the matrix structure. With this IT, they would no longer need to rely on divisional managers to transfer information but henceforth could obtain it from their ERP system. They would then be able to intervene at a global level as necessary.

Nestlé's "Globe Project" to create uniform business processes and computer systems around the world has led to major successes. Nestlé was able to shut down 15 percent of its global operating structure by 2005, which has saved billions of dollars and lowered its cost structure. At the

same time, it has been able to leverage the competencies of its product groups around the world by creating new kinds of food and candy products. However, its ROIC is still significantly lower than that of competitors like Hershey and Cadbury Schweppes because, some analysts claim, the company's global food empire is simply too big to manage—no global structure can make it operate profitably. What Nestlé should do is sell off many of its businesses, reduce the number of its product groups, exit countries where its profits are marginal, and in this way shrink until it can increase its ROIC and profits to match those of its competitors.[b]

Toyota then took all its learning from this venture and transferred it to its wholly owned car plant in Georgetown, Kentucky, where it turns out cars with as good a reliability record as those produced in its Japanese plants.

Every Toyota plant is under the control of Japanese managers, however, and managers from Toyota's Japanese headquarters are constantly monitoring its plant's performance and transferring and implanting Toyota's R&D innovations into its next car models. Toyota used a similar implementation strategy when it established car component and assembly operations in south Wales to serve the European Union market. Indeed, it chose south Wales and Virginia as locations for its plants because both regions have a strong local culture based on family and tradition that closely parallels Japan's culture. Toyota's managers felt that a similar local culture would enable them to better implement Toyota's highly efficient work processes and procedures.

As the example of Toyota suggests, forming global networks of managers who can move to and work in other countries so they can turn to each other for help is an important aspect of helping a company realize the benefits from its global operations. When managers can hold a "*matrix-in-the-mind*"—that is, learn to think about how they could transfer competencies around the company to create value—they can work to develop an information network that lets a company capitalize globally on the skills and capabilities of its employees.[16] To foster the development of the matrix-in-the-mind concept and promote cooperation, companies are increasingly making use of IT's integrating capability by using online teleconferencing, e-mail, and global intranets among the parts of their global operations. For example, Hitachi coordinates its nineteen Japanese laboratories by means of an online teleconferencing system. Both Microsoft and HP make extensive use of global intranets to integrate their activities, and Nestlé still hopes its Globe Project will accomplish the same goal.

Entry Mode and Implementation

As we discuss in Chapter 10, today many organizations are altering their business models and strategies and restructuring their organizations to find new ways to use their resources and capabilities to create value. This section focuses on the implementation issues that arise when companies use the three different modes of entry into new industries: internal new venturing, joint ventures, and mergers and acquisitions.

Internal New Venturing

Chapter 10 discusses how companies can enter new industries by using internal new venturing and by transferring and leveraging their existing resources to create the set of value-chain activities necessary to compete effectively in a new industry. How can managers create a setting in which employees are to be encouraged to act in ways that allow them to see how their functional competencies or products can be used in other industries? Specifically, how can structure, control, and culture be used to increase the success of the new-venturing process?

At the heart of the issue is that corporate managers must treat the internal new-venturing process as a form of entrepreneurship and the people who are to pioneer and lead new ventures as **intrapreneurs**, or inside or internal entrepreneurs. This means that organizational structure, control, and culture must be designed to encourage creativity and give new-venture managers autonomy and freedom to develop and champion new products. At the same time, corporate managers want to make sure that the investment in new markets will be profitable and that a fit does exist between the new industry and the old one so that benefits can in fact be leveraged.[17] As we discuss in Chapter 10, 3M is one company that carefully uses structure, control, and culture to create a formal organization-wide new-venturing process that is one of the best known for promoting product innovation. 3M's goal is that at least 30 percent of its growth in sales each year should be attributed to new products developed within the past five years. To achieve this challenging goal, 3M has developed an implementation formula to ensure that its employees are provided with the freedom and motivation to experiment and take risks.

On the structure side, 3M recognized early on the increasing importance of linking and coordinating the efforts of people in different functions to speed product development. As noted in the previous chapter, people in different functions tend to develop different subunit orientations and to focus their efforts on their own tasks to the exclusion of the needs of other functions. The danger of such tendencies is that each function will develop norms and values that suit its own needs but do little to promote organizational coordination and integration.

To avoid this problem, 3M established a system of cross-functional teams composed of members of product development, process development, marketing, manufacturing, packaging, and other functions to create organization-wide norms and values of innovation. So that all groups have a common focus, the teams work closely with customers; customers' needs become the platform on which the different functions can then apply their skills and capabilities.[18] For example, one of 3M's cross-functional teams worked closely with disposable diaper manufacturers to develop the right kind of sticky tape for their needs. To promote integration in the team and foster cooperative norms and values, each team is headed by a "product champion" who takes the responsibility for building cohesive team relationships and developing a team culture. In addition, one of 3M's senior managers becomes a "management sponsor" whose job is to help the team get resources and provide support when the going gets tough. After all, product development is a highly risky process; many projects do not succeed.

3M is also careful to use integrating mechanisms such as high-level product development committees to screen new ideas. Proven entrepreneurs and experienced managers from the other divisions and from R&D, marketing, sales, and manufacturing serve on this committee to screen the new ideas. New-product champions defend their products and projects before this committee to secure the resources for developing them. (Chapter 4 describes this development funnel.) On the control side,

3M copied HP and developed a companywide norm that researchers should use 15 percent of their time on their own projects, which helps create new products such as Post-it Notes. In addition, 3M is careful to establish career ladders for its scientists in order to gain their long-term commitment, and it rewards successful product innovators. For example, it established the "Golden Step" program that gives employees substantial monetary bonuses to honor and reward the launch of successful new products and to develop norms and values that support and reward the sharing of information among scientists and people in different functions.

3M's structure and control systems have created an atmosphere in which employees know it is better to take a chance and risk making a mistake than to do nothing at all. Managers understand that their job is to encourage creativity in their employees and teams and to foster a culture of innovation. However, the regular work of the organization goes on side by side with all this intrapreneurial activity.

The other main approach to internal new venturing has been championed by those who believe that the best way to encourage new-product development is to separate this effort from the rest of the organization. To provide new-venture managers with the autonomy to experiment and take risks, the company sets up a **new-venture division**, separate and independent from its other divisions, for the development of a new product. The logic behind this is that if a new-product team works from within a company's existing structure, its members will never have the freedom or autonomy to pursue radical new-product ideas. Away from the day-to-day scrutiny of top managers, new-venture managers will be able to pursue the creation of a new product and develop a new business model as though they were external entrepreneurs.

The new-venture division is controlled in a way that reinforces the entrepreneurial spirit. Thus, strict output controls are regarded as inappropriate because they can promote short-term thinking and inhibit risk taking. Instead, stock options are often used to reinforce a culture for entrepreneurship. Another issue with output controls is to keep top managers at bay. The thinking is that the up-front R&D costs of new venturing are high and its success uncertain. After spending millions of dollars, corporate managers might become concerned about the new-venture division's performance and might try to introduce tight output controls or strong budgets to increase accountability, measures that hurt the entrepreneurial culture.[19] Corporate managers may believe it is important to institute behavior and output controls that put some limits on freedom of action; otherwise, costly mistakes may be made and resources wasted on frivolous ideas.

Recently, there have been some indications that 3M's internal approach may be superior to the use of external new-venture divisions. It appears that many new-venture divisions have failed to get successful new products to market. And even if they do, usually the new-venture division eventually begins to operate like any other division, and a company's cost structure rises because of the duplication of value-chain activities.

Another issue is that scientists are often not the best people to develop successful business models because they lack formal training. Just as many medical doctors are earning MBAs today to understand the many strategic issues confronting their profession, so scientists need to be able to think strategically, and these skills may be lacking in a new-venture division.

HP illustrates many of these issues. Early in its history, HP used the new-venturing approach. As soon as a new self-supporting product was developed in one of HP's operating divisions, a new-venture division was spun off to develop and market the product. In this fashion, HP's goal was to keep its divisions small and entrepreneurial. Soon HP had over twenty-eight different divisions, each with its own value-chain functions. At first, the value these divisions created exceeded their operating costs, but then problems emerged because of changing technological conditions. Because they were operated separately, the divisions could not learn from each other, and because they all had separate R&D departments, sales forces, and so on, they began to compete for resources. For example, when one HP scientist pioneered what was to become biotechnology, the managers of other divisions could not see how it related to HP's existing activities and would not fund it. HP became saddled with high operating costs and missed-product opportunities. To solve the problem, it merged some divisions and brought their technologies and product lines together. It also sold off divisions to other companies to focus its activities and thus make it easier to transfer resources between its divisions.

■ **Joint Venturing**

Internal new venturing is one important way in which large, established companies can maintain their momentum and grow from within.[20] One alternative is for two companies to establish a joint venture and to collaborate on the development of a new business model to compete in a new market or industry. Often in joint venturing, two or more companies agree to pool specific resources and capabilities that they believe will create more value for both companies, and they appoint managers from both companies to oversee the new operation. In this case, no separate entity is set up. Sometimes companies do establish a separate company and agree to share ownership of the new company, often 50/50 ownership, but sometimes one company insists on having a 51 percent or more stake to give it the controlling interest. The companies then transfer to the new company whatever resources and capabilities they have agreed on to help it pursue the business model that will promote both companies' interests. From an implementation perspective, important issues concern the way the venture is structured and controlled and the problems that frequently emerge in managing differences between the cultures of companies in a joint venture.

Allocating authority and responsibility is the first major implementation issue companies have to decide on. Both companies need to be able to monitor the progress of the joint venture so that they can learn from what goes on and benefit from their investment in it. Some companies prefer to establish a new company and obtain a 51 percent ownership of it because then they can solve the problem of which company will have the ultimate authority and control over the new venture. As discussed in Chapter 8, a company also risks losing control of its core technology or competence when it enters into a strategic alliance. Because the future is unknown, it is unclear which company will benefit the most from whatever innovations the new company might develop.[21] A joint venture can also be dangerous not only because the partners may take their learning and then go it alone but also because the other party might be *acquired by a competitor*. For example, Compaq shared its technical knowledge with a company in the computer storage industry to promote joint product development, only to watch helplessly as that company was acquired by Sun Microsystems, which consequently obtained Compaq's knowledge.

The implementation issues are strongly dependent on whether the purpose of the joint venture is to share and develop technology, to jointly distribute and market products and brands, or to share access to customers. Sometimes companies can simply realize the joint benefits from collaboration without having to form a new company.

For example, in 2001, Nestlé and Coca-Cola announced a ten-year joint venture, to be called Beverage Partners Worldwide, through which Coca-Cola will distribute and sell Nestlé's Nestea iced tea, Nescafe, and other brands throughout the globe.[22] Similarly, Starbuck's Frappuccino is distributed by Pepsi. In this kind of joint venture, both companies can gain from sharing and pooling different competencies so that both realize value that would not otherwise be possible. In these cases, issues of ownership are less important, although the issue of allocating responsibility and monitoring performance remains.

Once the ownership issue has been settled, one company appoints the CEO, who is responsible for creating a cohesive top management team from the ranks of managers who have been transferred from the parent companies. The job of the top management team is to develop a successful business model. These managers then need to choose an organizational structure, such as the functional or product team, that will make the best use of the resources and skills transferred from the parent. The need to provide a framework that combines their activities and integrates across people and functions is of paramount importance. So is the need to build a new company culture that can unite the members of the hitherto different cultures. In essence, top managers need to solve all the implementation problems discussed in the previous chapter.

Because solving these issues is expensive and time-consuming, it is not surprising that if there is a lot at stake and the future possibilities are unknown, many companies decide that they would be better off by acquiring the other company and integrating it into their operations. This has been Microsoft's favored strategy in recent years as it enters new industries in the computer sector. Normally, it takes a 51 percent stake in an emerging company that gives it the right to buy out the company and integrate it into Microsoft should it have technology that proves vital to Microsoft's future interests. Then, Microsoft shares its resources and expertise with the new company to spur its research and development. If the stakes are less, however, and the future easier to forecast, as in the venture between Coca-Cola and Nestlé, then it makes sense to establish a new entity that can manage the transfers of complementary resources and skills between companies.

Mergers and Acquisitions

Mergers and acquisitions are the third, and most widely used, vehicle that companies can use to enter new industries or countries.[23] How to implement structure, control systems, and culture to manage a new acquisition is important because many acquisitions are unsuccessful. And one of the main reasons acquisitions perform poorly is that many companies do not anticipate the difficulties associated with merging or integrating new companies into their existing operations.[24]

At the level of structure, managers of both the acquiring and acquired companies have to confront the problem of how to establish new lines of authority and responsibility that will allow them to make the best use of both companies' competencies. The merger between HP and Compaq illustrates the issues (see the *Closing Case*). Before the merger the top management teams of both companies spent thousands of hours analyzing the range of both companies' activities and performing a value-chain analysis to determine how cost and differentiation advantages might be achieved. Based on this analysis, they merged all of both company's divisions into four main product groups.

Imagine the problems in deciding who would control which group and which operating division and to whom these managers would report! To counter fears that infighting would prevent the benefits of the merger from being realized, in press releases the companies' top executives were careful to announce that the process of merging divisions was going smoothly and that battles over responsibilities and control of resources were being resolved. One problem with a mishandled merger is that skilled managers who feel they have been demoted will leave the company, and if many do leave, this also may prevent its benefits from being realized.

Once the issue of lines of authority has been addressed, the merged companies must decide how to coordinate and streamline operations to reduce costs and leverage competencies. For large companies, the answer, as for HP, is the multidivisional structure, but important control issues have to be resolved. In general, the more similar or related are the acquired companies' products and markets (if a company has made a related acquisition, as in the HP case), the easier it is to integrate their operations. Providing the acquiring company has an efficient control system, it can be adapted to the new company to standardize the way its activities are monitored and measured. Or managers can work hard to combine the best elements of each company's control systems and cultures or introduce a new IT system.

If managers make unrelated acquisitions, however, and then try to interfere with a company's strategy in an industry they know little about or apply inappropriate structure and controls to manage the new business, then major strategy implementation problems can arise. For example, if managers try to integrate unrelated companies with related ones in the search for some elusive benefits, apply the wrong kinds of controls at the divisional level, or interfere in business-level strategy, corporate performance can suffer as bureaucratic costs skyrocket. These mistakes explain why related acquisitions are sometimes more successful than unrelated ones.[25]

Even in the case of related diversification, the business processes of each company frequently are different, and their computer systems may be incompatible, as in the Nestlé case. The issue facing the merged company is how to use output and behavior controls to standardize business processes and reduce the cost of handing off and transferring resources. While installing the SAP software, for example, managers in charge of the U.S. effort discovered that each of Nestlé's 150 different U.S. divisions was buying its own supply of the flavoring vanilla from the same set of suppliers. However, the divisions were not sharing information about how they were doing this, and vanilla suppliers, dealing with each Nestlé division separately, tried to charge each division as much as they could, with the result that each division paid a different price for the same input![26] How could this happen? Each division used a different code for its independent purchase, and managers at U.S. headquarters did not have the information to discover this. SAP's software provides such information.

Finally, even when acquiring a company in a closely related industry, managers must realize that each company has a unique culture, or way of doing things. Such idiosyncrasies must be understood in order to manage the merged company effectively. Indeed, such idiosyncrasies are likely to be especially important when companies from different countries merge. Over time, top managers can change the culture and alter the internal workings of the company, but this is a difficult implementation task. The differences between HP and Compaq are a case in point. HP has a research-oriented culture and prizes its technology and the people who create it. Compaq was a marketing-driven organization and prized a hands-on, value-driven approach. By 2004, after the departure of most top Compaq managers, it was clear that HP's culture would remain research oriented; however, the new HP has a very different culture than the old HP, which prided itself on a policy of no layoffs. To compete against Dell, HP was forced to lay off thousands of employees and shut down duplicate facilities.

Compaq's marketing skills have been a valuable addition, but unfortunately it did not acquire Dell's low-cost skills.

In sum, managers' capabilities in organizational design are vital to ensure the success of a merger or acquisition. Their ability to integrate and connect divisions to leverage competencies ultimately determines how well the new merged company will perform.[27] The path to merger and acquisition is fraught with dangers, which is why some companies claim that internal new venturing is the safest path and that it is best to grow organically from within. Yet with industry boundaries blurring and new global competitors emerging, companies often do not have the time or resources to go it alone. How to enter a new industry or country is a complex implementation issue that requires thorough strategic analysis.

Information Technology, the Internet, and Outsourcing

The many ways in which advances in IT impact strategy implementation is an important issue today. Evidence that managerial capabilities in managing IT can be a source of competitive advantage is growing; companies that do not adopt leading-edge information systems are likely to be at a competitive disadvantage. IT includes the many different varieties of computer software platforms and databases and the computer hardware on which they run, such as mainframes and servers. IT also encompasses a broad array of communication media and devices that link people, including voice-mail, e-mail, voice conferencing, videoconferencing, the Internet, groupware and corporate intranets, cell phones, fax machines, personal digital assistants (PDAs), smart phones, and so on.[28]

■ Information Technology and Strategy Implementation

At the level of organizational structure, control, and culture, IT has given strategic managers many new options in implementing their strategies. IT is instrumental in both shaping and integrating resources and capabilities—capabilities that can be difficult to imitate since they are often embedded in firm-specific IT skills. Wal-Mart, for example, legally protected what it regards as a core competency in IT by blocking the movement of some of its key programmers to dot-coms like amazon.com. A company's ability to pursue a cost-leadership or differentiation business model depends on its possession of distinctive competencies in efficiency, quality, innovation, and customer responsiveness, and IT has a major impact on these sources of competitive advantage.[29]

Information technology enables companies to integrate knowledge and expertise across functional groups so that they can deliver new differentiated goods and services to customers. The way in which Citibank implemented an organization-wide IT to increase responsiveness to customers is instructive. In 2000, Citibank set as its goal to be the premier global international financial company. After studying its business model, managers found that the main customer complaint was the amount of time customers had to wait for a response to their request, so it set out to solve this problem. Teams of managers examined the way Citibank's current IT worked and then redesigned it to empower employees and reduce the handoffs between people and functions. Employees were then given extensive training in operating the new IT system. Citibank has been able to document significant time and cost savings, as well as an increase in the level of personalized service it is able to offer its clients, which has led to a significant increase in the number of global customers.[30]

Indeed, IT has important effects on a company's ability to innovate. It improves the base of knowledge that employees draw on when they engage in problem solving and decision making and provides a mechanism for promoting collaboration and information sharing both inside and across functions and business units. However, knowledge or information availability alone will not lead to innovation; it is the ability to use knowledge creatively that is the key to promoting innovation and creating competitive advantage. One argument is that it is not the absolute level of knowledge a firm possesses that leads to competitive advantage, but the speed or velocity with which it is circulated in the firm.[31] IT transfers knowledge where it can add the highest value to the organization.

The project-based work characteristic of matrix structures provides a vivid example of this process. As a project progresses, the need for particular team members waxes and wanes. Some employees will be part of a project from beginning to end, and others will be asked to participate only at key times when their expertise is required. IT provides managers with the real-time capability to monitor project progress and needs and to allocate resources accordingly to increase the value added of each employee. Traditionally, product design has involved sequential processing across functions, with handoffs as each stage of the process is completed (see Chapter 4). This linear process is being replaced by parallel, concurrent engineering made possible through the application of IT that allows employees to work simultaneously with continual interaction through electronic communication. All of this can promote innovation.

IT has major effects on other aspects of a company's structure and control systems. The increasing use of IT has been associated with a flattening of the organizational hierarchy and a move toward greater decentralization and increased integration within organizations. By electronically providing managers with high-quality, timely, and relatively complete information, IT has reduced the need for a management hierarchy to coordinate organizational activities. E-mail systems and the development of organization-wide corporate intranets are breaking down the barriers that have traditionally separated departments, and the result has been improved performance.[32] To facilitate the use of IT and to make organizational structure work, however, a company must create a control and incentive structure to motivate people and subunits, as Strategy in Action 13.4 suggests.

Some companies are taking full advantage of IT's ability to help them integrate their activities to respond better to customer needs. These companies make the most cost-effective use of their employees' skills by using a virtual organizational structure. The **virtual organization** is composed of people who are linked by computers, faxes, computer-aided design systems, and video teleconferencing and who may rarely, if ever, see one another face to face. People come and go as their services are needed, much as in a matrix structure.

Accenture, the global management consulting company, is becoming just such a virtual organization. Consultants are connected by laptops to an organization's **knowledge management system**, its company-specific information system that systematizes the knowledge of its employees and provides them with access to other employees who have the expertise to solve the problems that they encounter as they perform their jobs. The consultants pool their knowledge in a massive internal database they can easily access through computer and the company's intranet. The company's 40,000 consultants often work from their homes, traveling to meet the company's clients throughout the world and only rarely stopping in at one of Accenture's branch offices to meet their superiors and colleagues. CEO George Shaheen says the company's headquarters are wherever he happens to be at the time. (He spends 80 percent of his time traveling.)[33]

Strategy in Action   13.4

Oracle's New Approach to Control

Oracle is the second largest independent software company after Microsoft. Like Bill Gates, Microsoft's chairman, Oracle's cofounder and chairman, Larry Ellison, recognized in 1999 that his company had a major problem: it was not using the software it had developed to control its own activities, even though its customers were! As a result, Oracle was having a difficult time understanding its customers' needs, and internally it was not experiencing the cost savings that could result from implementing its own database and financial control software. Ellison moved quickly to change Oracle's control systems so that they were Internet based.

One of the main advantages of Internet-based control software is that it permits the centralized management of a company's widespread operations. Corporate managers can easily compare and contrast the performance of different divisions spread throughout the globe in real time and can quickly identify problems and take corrective action. However, to his embarrassment, Ellison discovered that Oracle's financial and human resource information was located on over seventy different computing systems across the world. It took a lot of time and effort to track such basic things as the size of the company's work force and the sales of its leading products. As a result, it took a long time to take corrective action, and many opportunities were being missed.

Recognizing the irony of the situation, Ellison ordered his managers to change the way the company controlled—that is, monitored and evaluated—its activities and to implement its new Internet-based control systems as quickly as possible. His goal was to have all of Oracle's sales, cost, profit, and human resource information systems consolidated in two locations and to make this information available to managers throughout the company with one click of a mouse. In addition, he instructed managers to investigate which kinds of activities were being monitored and controlled by people and, wherever possible, to substitute Internet-based control. For example, previously Oracle had over three hundred people responsible for monitoring and managing such tasks as paper-based travel planning and expense report systems. These tasks were automated into software systems and put online, and employees were made responsible for filing their own reports. These three hundred people were then transferred into sales and consulting positions. The savings was over $1 billion a year.

By using Internet software-based control systems, Oracle's managers are also able to get closer to their customers. In 1999, Oracle gave all its salespeople new customer relationship management software and instructed them to enter into the system detailed information about customers' purchases, future plans, Web orders, and service requests. As a result, headquarters managers can now track sales orders easily, and if they see problems such as lost sales or multiple service requests, they can quickly contact customers to solve those problems. This speed builds better customer relations.

So amazed has Ellison been at the result of implementing Internet software systems that he has radically rethought Oracle's control systems. He now believes that because of the advances of modern computer information systems, Oracle's employees should be doing only one of three things: building its products, servicing its products, or selling its products. All other activities should be automated by developing new information control systems, and it should be the manager's job to use control only to facilitate one of these three front-line activities.

■ **Strategic Outsourcing and Network Structure**

Information technology has also affected a company's ability to pursue strategic outsourcing to strengthen its business model. As Chapter 9 discusses, the use of strategic outsourcing is increasing rapidly as organizations recognize the many opportunities it offers to promote differentiation, reduce costs, and increase flexibility. Recall that outsourcing occurs as companies use short- and long-term contracts, joint ventures, and strategic alliances to form relationships with other companies. IT increases the efficiency of such relationships. For example, it allows for the more efficient movement of raw materials and component parts between a company and its suppliers and distributors. It also promotes the transfer, sharing, and leveraging of competencies between companies, which can lead to design and engineering improvements that increase differentiation and lower costs.

As a consequence, there has been growing interest in electronic **business-to-business (B2B)** networks in which most or all of the companies in an industry (for example, carmakers) use the same software platform to link to each other and establish industry specifications and standards. Then these companies jointly list the quantity and specifications of the inputs they require and invite bids from the thousands of potential suppliers around the world. Since suppliers also use the same software platform, electronic bidding, auctions, and transactions are possible between buyers and sellers around the world. The idea is that high-volume standardized transactions can help drive down costs and raise quality at the industry level. The role Li & Fung plays in managing the global supply chain for companies in Southeast Asia is instructive in this regard, as Strategy in Action 13.5 shows.

Cross-company global electronic networks reduce the costs associated with finding and monitoring competing suppliers and make global strategic alliances and joint ventures more attractive than vertical integration. In addition, companies that use electronic networks not only reduce costs because they increase the pool of potential

Strategy in Action   13.5

Li & Fung's Global Supply-Chain Management

Finding the overseas suppliers that offer the lowest-priced and highest-quality products is an important task facing the managers of global organizations. These suppliers are located in thousands of cities in many countries around the world, so finding them is difficult. Often global companies use the services of foreign intermediaries or brokers, located near these suppliers, to find the one that best meets their input requirements. Li & Fung, now run by brothers Victor and William Fung, is one of these brokers that have helped hundreds of global companies to locate suitable foreign suppliers, especially suppliers in mainland China.

In the 2000s, managing global companies' supply chains became an even more complicated task because overseas suppliers were increasingly specializing in just one part of the task of producing a product in their search for ways to reduce costs. For example, in the past, a company such as Target might have negotiated with a supplier to manufacture 1 million units of a shirt at a certain cost per unit. But with specialization, Target might find it can reduce the costs of producing the shirt even further by splitting the operations involved in producing the shirt and having different suppliers, often in different countries, perform each operation. For example, to get the lowest cost per unit, Target might first negotiate with

a yarn manufacturer in Vietnam to make the yarn; then ship the yarn to a Chinese supplier to weave it into cloth; and then to several different factories in Malaysia and the Philippines to cut the cloth and sew the shirts. Another company might take responsibility for packaging and shipping the shirts to wherever in the world they are required. Since a company like Target has thousands of different clothing products under production and these change all the time, the problems of managing such a supply chain to get the full cost savings from global expansion are clear.

This is the opportunity that Li & Fung has capitalized on. Realizing that many global companies do not have the time or expertise to find such specialized low-price suppliers, they moved quickly to provide such a service. Li & Fung employs 3,600 agents who travel across thirty-seven countries to find new suppliers and inspect existing suppliers to find new ways to help their clients, global companies, get lower prices or higher-quality products. Global companies are happy to outsource their supply-chain management to Li & Fung because they realize significant cost savings. And although they pay a hefty fee to Li & Fung, they avoid the costs of employing their own agents. As the complexity of supply-chain management continues to increase, more and more companies like Li & Fung are appearing.

suppliers, but they also reduce the bargaining power of suppliers. Similarly, beyond using IT to link backward with suppliers, companies can use IT to link forward in the value chain to connect its operations with those of customers, something that reduces their costs and creates a disincentive for customers to seek other suppliers.

To implement outsourcing effectively, strategic managers must decide what organizational arrangements to adopt. Increasingly, a **network structure**—the set of strategic alliances that an organization creates with suppliers, manufacturers, and distributors to produce and market a product—is becoming the structure of choice to implement outsourcing. An example of a network structure is the series of strategic alliances that Japanese carmakers such as Toyota and Honda formed with their suppliers of inputs, such as car axles, gearboxes, and air-conditioning systems. Members of the network work together on a long-term basis to find new ways to reduce costs and increase the quality of their products. Moreover, developing a network structure allows an organization to avoid the high bureaucratic costs of operating a complex organizational structure. Finally, a network structure allows a company to form strategic alliances with foreign suppliers, which gives managers access to low-cost foreign sources of inputs. The way Nike uses a global network structure to produce and market its sports, casual, and dress shoes is instructive.

Nike, located in Beaverton, Oregon, is the largest and most profitable sports shoe manufacturer in the world. The key to Nike's success is the network structure that Philip Knight, its founder and CEO, created to allow his company to produce and market shoes. The most successful companies today simultaneously pursue a low-cost and a differentiation strategy. Knight realized this early on and created an organizational structure to allow his company to achieve this goal.

By far, the largest function at Nike's headquarters in Beaverton is the design function, staffed by talented designers who pioneer innovations in sports shoe design such as the air pump and Air Jordans that Nike introduced so successfully. Designers use computer-aided design (CAD) to design their shoes, and all new-product information, including manufacturing instructions, is stored electronically. When the designers have done their work, they relay the blueprints for the new products electronically to a network of suppliers and manufacturers throughout Southeast Asia with which Nike has formed strategic alliances. Instructions for the design of a new sole, for example, may be sent to a supplier in Taiwan, and instructions for the leather uppers to a supplier in Malaysia. These suppliers produce the shoe parts, which are then sent for final assembly to a manufacturer in China with which Nike has established an alliance. From China, these shoes are shipped to distributors throughout the world. Of the 99 million pairs of shoes Nike makes each year, 99 percent are made in Southeast Asia.

There are three main advantages to this network structure for Nike. First, Nike can lower its cost structure because wages in Southeast Asia are a fraction of what they are in the United States. Second, Nike is able to respond to changes in sports shoe fashion very quickly. Using its global computer system, it can, literally overnight, change the instructions it gives to each of its suppliers so that, within a few weeks, its foreign manufacturers are producing new kinds of shoes. Any alliance partners that fail to perform up to Nike's standards are replaced with new partners, so Nike has great control over its network structure. In fact, the company works closely with its suppliers to take advantage of any new developments in technology that can help it reduce costs and increase quality. Third, the ability to outsource all its manufacturing abroad allows Nike to keep its U.S. structure fluid and flexible. Nike uses a functional structure to organize its activities and decentralizes control of the design process to teams that are assigned to develop each of the new kinds of sports shoes for which Nike is known.

In conclusion, the implications of IT for strategy implementation are still evolving and will continue to do so as new software and hardware reshape a company's business model and its strategies. IT is changing the nature of value-chain activities both inside and between organizations, affecting all four building blocks of competitive advantage. For the multibusiness company as for the single-business company, the need to be alert to such changes to strengthen its position in its core business has become a vital matter, and the success of companies like Dell and Wal-Mart compared to the failure of others like Gateway and Kmart can be traced, in part, to their success in developing the IT capabilities that lead to sustained competitive advantage.

Summary of Chapter

1. A company uses organizational design to combine structure, control systems, and culture in ways that allow it to implement its multibusiness model successfully.

2. As a company grows and diversifies, it adopts a multidivisional structure. Although this structure costs more to operate than a functional or product structure, it economizes on the bureaucratic costs associated with operating through a functional structure and enables a company to handle its value creation activities more effectively.

3. As companies change their corporate strategies over time, they must change their structures because different strategies are managed in different ways. In particular, the move from unrelated diversification to vertical integration to related diversification increases the bureaucratic costs associated with managing a multibusiness model. Each requires a different combination on structure, control, and culture to economize on those costs.

4. As a company moves from a localization to an international, global standardization, and transnational strategy, it also needs to switch to a more complex structure that allows it to coordinate increasingly complex resource transfers. Similarly, it needs to adopt a more complex integration and control system that facilitates resource sharing and the leverage of competencies around the globe. When the gains are substantial, companies frequently adopt a global-matrix structure to share knowledge and expertise or to implement their control systems and culture.

5. To encourage internal new venturing, companies must design an internal venturing process that gives new-venture managers the autonomy they need to develop new products. Corporate managers need to provide the oversight that keeps new-venture managers motivated and on track.

6. The profitability of mergers and acquisitions depends on the structure and control systems that companies adopt to manage them and the way a company integrates them into its existing businesses.

7. IT is having increasingly important effects on the way multibusiness companies implement their strategies. Not only does IT help improve the efficiency with which the multidivisional structure operates, but it also allows for the better control of complex value-chain activities. The growth of outsourcing has also been promoted by IT, and some companies have developed network structures to coordinate their global value-chain activities.

Discussion Questions

1. When would a company decide to change from a functional to a multidivisional structure?

2. If a related company begins to buy unrelated businesses, in what ways should it change its structure or control mechanisms to manage the acquisitions?

3. What prompts a company to change from a global standardization to a transnational strategy, and what new implementation problems arise as it does so?

4. How would you design a structure and control system to encourage entrepreneurship in a large, established corporation?

5. What are the problems associated with implementing a strategy of related diversification through acquisitions?

Practicing Strategic Management

■ SMALL-GROUP EXERCISE
Deciding on an Organizational Structure (Continued)

Break into the same groups used for the Chapter 12 Small-Group Exercise. Reread the scenario in the Chapter 12 exercise, and recall your group's debate about the appropriate organizational structure for your soft drink company. Because it is your intention to compete with Coca-Cola for market share worldwide, there should also be a global dimension to your strategy, and you must consider what is the best structure globally as well as domestically. Debate the pros and cons of the types of global structures, and decide which is most appropriate and will best fit with your domestic structure.

■ ARTICLE FILE 13

Find an example of a company pursuing a multibusiness model that has changed its structure and control systems to manage its strategy better. What were the problems with the way it formerly implemented its strategy? What changes did it make to its structure and control systems? What effects does it expect these changes to have on performance?

■ STRATEGIC MANAGEMENT PROJECT
Module 13

Take the information you collected in the Chapter 12 Strategic Management Project on strategy implementation, and link it to the multibusiness model. You should collect information to determine if your company competes across industries or countries and also to see what role IT plays in allowing it to implement its business model. If your company does operate across countries or industries:

1. Does your company use a multidivisional structure? Why or why not? What crucial implementation problems must your company manage to implement its strategy effectively? For example, what kind of integration mechanisms does it employ?

2. What are your company's corporate-level strategies? How do they affect the way it uses organizational structure, control, and culture?

3. What kind of international strategy does your company pursue? How does it control its global activities? What kind of structure does it use? Why?

4. Can you suggest ways of altering the company's structure or control systems to strengthen its business model? Would this change increase or decrease bureaucratic costs?

5. Does your company have a particular entry mode that it has used to implement its strategy?

6. In what ways does your company use IT to coordinate its value-chain activities?

7. Assess how well you think your company has implemented its multibusiness (or business) model.

■ EXPLORING THE WEB
Visiting Sears

Go to **www.sears.com** and **www.kmart.com**, and locate information for investors. Study the information and press releases about the merger of these two companies. How has the merger strengthened the business model of the new company? What kinds of changes in structure, control systems, and culture have occurred as a result of the merger?

General Task   Search the Web for a multibusiness company that is in the process of modifying or changing the way it implements its business model and strategy. What changes is it making to its structure or control systems? Does IT have a role in the changes? What structure is it moving toward? Why is this structure more appropriate than the old one?

Closing Case

The New HP Gets Up to Speed

Between 2002 and 2004 Hewlett-Packard and Compaq moved steadily forward to combine their skills and resources to strengthen their competitive advantage. The new HP is a leading global multibusiness IT-infrastructure provider, selling a complete range of computer hardware, software and solutions, information services, and imaging and printing products. The task facing HP's managers was how to position the company to compete across industries against competitors like IBM, also a multibusiness IT-infrastructure provider, and Dell, the leader in the fiercely competitive PC industry.

The justification for the merger was that the new company would have cross-industry product lines that would allow it to reap the benefits of both cost savings and differentiation. Joining both companies' product lines would allow the new company to eliminate the duplication of costly functional activities and so achieve billions in cost savings. Combining joint operations would also allow both companies to transfer, share, and leverage competencies and achieve the value-creating benefits of increased product differentiation. Importantly, as a result of the merger HP will be able to use product bundling to provide customers with a *complete range* of totally compatible computing and IT products backed by a service group that will be able to provide software and expertise to customize these products to the needs of customers. As a result, HP claims its products will provide better flexibility, better interoperability, and the lowest cost of ownership of any company in the industry.

To achieve these benefits, the two companies' many business units have been integrated and reorganized into four major product divisions using a multidivisional structure: hardware, software, services, and imaging and printing. Each division is an independent profit center, and the divisions must work together to coordinate their new products and activities to make sure they are in keeping with its corporate strategy.

The task facing Carly Fiorina, HP's CEO, is to find ways to strengthen the company's multibusiness model and to forecast how changes in IT might shift industry boundaries and affect the company in the future. Formulating HP's global multibusiness strategy will also be one of her major concerns, for the complexity of HP's global operations is staggering. The need to customize products to the needs of different world regions and to work out where to make them to lower HP's cost structure and increase the appeal of its products are major questions confronting all of HP's top management.

Case Discussion Questions

1. What kind of multibusiness model is HP pursuing?

2. What kind of global strategy is most appropriate for the company in the future?

3. What kind of global structure will allow it to most effectively coordinate the production and sale of its products around the world?

Notes

Chapter 1

1. *Sources:* "How Big Can It Grow?" *Economist,* April 17, 2004, pp. 74–78; "Trial by Checkout," *Economist,* June 26, 2004, pp. 74–76; Wal-Mart 10-K, 2000; information at Wal-Mart's website (**www.walmartstores.com**); Robert Slater, *The Wal-Mart Triumph* (Portfolio Trade Books, 2004).

2. There are several different ratios for measuring profitability, such as return on invested capital, return on assets, and return on equity. Although these different measures are highly correlated with each other, finance theorists argue that the return on invested capital is the most accurate measure of profitability. See Tom Copeland, Tim Koller, and Jack Murrin, *Valuation: Measuring and Managing the Value of Companies* (New York: Wiley, 1996).

3. Trying to estimate the relative importance of industry effects and firm strategy on firm profitability has been one of the most important areas of research in the strategy literature during the past decade. See Y. E. Spanos and S. Lioukas, "An Examination of the Causal Logic of Rent Generation," *Strategic Management Journal* 22:10 (October 2001): 907–934; and R. P. Rumelt, "How Much Does Industry Matter?" *Strategic Management Journal* 12 (1991): 167–185. See also A. J. Mauri and M. P. Michaels, "Firm and Industry Effects Within Strategic Management: An Empirical Examination," *Strategic Management Journal* 19 (1998): 211–219.

4. This view is known as "agency theory." See M. C. Jensen and W. H. Meckling, "Theory of the Firm: Managerial Behavior, Agency Costs and Ownership Structure," *Journal of Financial Economics* 3 (1976): 305–360; and E. F. Fama, "Agency Problems and the Theory of the Firm," *Journal of Political Economy* 88 (1980): 375–390.

5. K. R. Andrews, *The Concept of Corporate Strategy* (Homewood, Ill.: Dow Jones Irwin, 1971); H. I. Ansoff, *Corporate Strategy* (New York: McGraw-Hill, 1965); C. W. Hofer and D. Schendel, *Strategy Formulation: Analytical Concepts* (St. Paul, Minn.: West, 1978). See also P. J. Brews and M. R. Hunt, "Learning to Plan and Planning to Learn," *Strategic Management Journal* 20 (1999): 889–913; and

R. W. Grant, "Planning in a Turbulent Environment," *Strategic Management Journal* 24 (2003): 491–517.

6. **www.kodak.com/US/en/corp/careers/why/ valuesmission.jhtml**.

7. **www.ford.com/en/company/about/overview.htm**.

8. These three questions were first proposed by P. F. Drucker, *Management—Tasks, Responsibilities, Practices* (New York: Harper & Row, 1974), pp. 74–94.

9. Derek F. Abell, *Defining the Business: The Starting Point of Strategic Planning* (Englewood Cliffs, N.J.: Prentice-Hall, 1980).

10. P. A. Kidwell and P. E.Ceruzzi, *Landmarks in Digital Computing* (Washington, D.C.: Smithsonian Institute, 1994).

11. See G. Hamel and C. K. Prahalad, "Strategic Intent," *Harvard Business Review* (May–June 1989): 64.

12. J. C. Collins and J. I. Porras, "Building Your Company's Vision," *Harvard Business Review* (September–October 1996): 65–77.

13. **www.nucor.com/**. Reprinted courtesy of Nucor.

14. See J. P. Kotter and J. L. Heskett, *Corporate Culture and Performance* (New York: Free Press, 1992). For similar work, see Collins and Porras, "Building Your Company's Vision."

15. E. Freeman, *Strategic Management: A Stakeholder Approach* (Boston: Pitman Press, 1984).

16. M. D. Richards, *Setting Strategic Goals and Objectives* (St. Paul, Minn.: West, 1986).

17. E. A. Locke, G. P. Latham, and M. Erez, "The Determinants of Goal Commitment," *Academy of Management Review* 13 (1988): 23–39.

18. R. E. Hoskisson, M. A. Hitt, and C. W. L. Hill, "Managerial Incentives and Investment in R&D in Large Multiproduct Firms," *Organization Science* 3 (1993): 325–341.

19. Robert H. Hayes and William J. Abernathy, "Managing Our Way to Economic Decline," *Harvard Business Review* (July–August 1980): 67–77.

20. Andrews, *Concept of Corporate Strategy;* Ansoff, *Corporate Strategy;* Hofer and Schendel, *Strategy Formulation.*

21. For details, see R. A. Burgelman, "Intraorganizational Ecology of Strategy Making and Organiza-

tional Adaptation: Theory and Field Research," *Organization Science* 2 (1991): 239–262; H. Mintzberg, "Patterns in Strategy Formulation," *Management Science* 24 (1978): 934–948; S. L. Hart, "An Integrative Framework for Strategy Making Processes," *Academy of Management Review* 17 (1992): 327–351; G. Hamel, "Strategy as Revolution," *Harvard Business Review* 74 (July–August 1996): 69–83; and R. W. Grant, "Planning in a Turbulent Environment," *Strategic Management Journal* 24 (2003): 491–517.

22. This is the premise of those who advocate that complexity and chaos theory should be applied to strategic management. See S. Brown and K. M. Eisenhardt, "The Art of Continuous Change: Linking Complexity Theory and Time Based Evolution in Relentlessly Shifting Organizations," *Administrative Science Quarterly* 29 (1997): 1–34; and R. Stacey and D. Parker, *Chaos, Management and Economics* (London: Institute for Economic Affairs, 1994). See also H. Courtney, J. Kirkland, and P. Viguerie, "Strategy Under Uncertainty," *Harvard Business Review* 75 (November–December 1997): 66–79.

23. Hart, "Integrative Framework"; Hamel, "Strategy as Revolution."

24. See Burgelman, "Intraorganizational Ecology," and Mintzberg, "Patterns in Strategy Formulation."

25. R. A. Burgelman and A. S. Grove, "Strategic Dissonance," *California Management Review* (Winter 1996): 8–28.

26. C. W. L. Hill and F. T. Rothaermel, "The Performance of Incumbent Firms in the Face of Radical Technological Innovation," *Academy of Management Review* 28 (2003): 257–274.

27. This story was related to the author by George Rathmann, who at one time was head of 3M's research activities.

28. Richard T. Pascale, "Perspectives on Strategy: The Real Story Behind Honda's Success," *California Management Review* 26 (1984): 47–72.

29. This viewpoint is strongly emphasized by Burgelman and Grove, "Strategic Dissonance."

30. C. C. Miller and L. B. Cardinal, "Strategic Planning and Firm Performance: A Synthesis of More than Two Decades of Research," *Academy of Management Journal* 37 (1994): 1649–1665. Also see P. R. Rogers, A. Miller, and W. Q. Judge, "Using Information Processing Theory to Understand Planning/Performance Relationships in the Context of Strategy," *Strategic Management Journal* 20 (1999): 567–577.

31. P. J. Brews and M. R. Hunt, "Learning to Plan and Planning to Learn," *Strategic Management Journal* (1999) 20: 889–913.

32. Courtney, Kirkland, and Viguerie, "Strategy Under Uncertainty."

33. P. J. H. Schoemaker, "Multiple Scenario Development: Its Conceptual and Behavioral Foundation," *Strategic Management Journal* 14 (1993): 193–213.

34. C. Kim and R. Mauborgne, "Procedural Justice, Strategic Decision Making, and the Knowledge Economy," *Strategic Management Journal* 19 (1998): 323–338; W. C. Kim and R. Mauborgne, "Fair Process: Managing in the Knowledge Economy," *Harvard Business Review* 75 (July–August 1997): 65–76.

35. G. Hamel and C. K. Prahalad, *Competing for the Future* (New York: Free Press, 1994).

36. See G. Hamel and C. K. Prahalad, "Strategic Intent," *Harvard Business Review* (May–June 1989): 64.

37. See C. R. Schwenk, "Cognitive Simplification Processes in Strategic Decision Making," *Strategic Management Journal* 5 (1984): 111–128; and K. M. Eisenhardt and M. Zbaracki, "Strategic Decision Making," *Strategic Management Journal* 13 (Special Issue, 1992): 17–37.

38. H. Simon, *Administrative Behavior* (New York: McGraw-Hill, 1957).

39. The original statement of this phenomenon was made by A. Tversky and D. Kahneman, "Judgment Under Uncertainty: Heuristics and Biases," *Science* 185 (1974): 1124–1131. See also D. Lovallo and D. Kahneman, "Delusions of Success: How Optimism Undermines Executives' Decisions," *Harvard Business Review* 81 (July 2003): 56–67; and J. S. Hammond, R. L. Keeny, and H. Raiffa, "The Hidden Traps in Decision Making," *Harvard Business Review* 76 (September–October 1998): 25–34.

40. Schwenk, "Cognitive Simplification Processes," pp. 111–128.

41. B. M. Staw, "The Escalation of Commitment to a Course of Action," *Academy of Management Review* 6 (1981): 577–587.

42. R. Roll, "The Hubris Hypotheses of Corporate Takeovers," *Journal of Business* 59 (1986): 197–216.

43. Irvin L. Janis, *Victims of Groupthink*, 2nd ed. (Boston: Houghton Mifflin, 1982). For an alternative view, see S. R. Fuller and R. J. Aldag, "Organizational Tonypandy: Lessons from a Quarter Century of the Groupthink Phenomenon," *Organizational Behavior and Human Decision Processes* 73 (1998): 163–184.

44. See R. O. Mason, "A Dialectic Approach to Strategic Planning," *Management Science* 13 (1969): 403–414; R. A. Cosier and J. C. Aplin, "A Critical View of Dialectic Inquiry in Strategic Planning," *Strategic Management Journal* 1 (1980): 343–356; and I. I. Mintroff and R. O. Mason, "Structuring III—Structured Policy Issues: Further Explorations in a Methodology for Messy Problems," *Strategic Management Journal* 1 (1980): 331–342.

45. Mason, "A Dialectic Approach," pp. 403–414.

46. Lovallo and Kahneman, "Delusions of Success."

47. For a summary of research on strategic leadership, see D. C. Hambrick, "Putting Top Managers Back into the Picture," *Strategic Management Journal* 10 (Special Issue, 1989): 5–15. See also D. Goldman, "What Makes a Leader?" *Harvard Business Review* (November–December 1998): 92–105; H. Mintzberg, "Covert Leadership," *Harvard Business Review* (November–December 1998): 140–148; and R. S. Tedlow, "What Titans Can Teach Us," *Harvard Business Review* (December 2001): 70–79.

48. N. M. Tichy and D. O. Ulrich, "The Leadership Challenge: A Call for the Transformational Leader," *Sloan Management Review* (Fall 1984): 59–68; F. Westley and H. Mintzberg, "Visionary Leadership and Strategic Management," *Strategic Management Journal* 10 (Special Issue, 1989): 17–32.

49. E. Wrapp, "Good Managers Don't Make Policy Decisions," *Harvard Business Review* (September–October 1967): 91–99.

50. J. Pfeffer, *Managing with Power* (Boston: Harvard Business School Press, 1992).

51. D. Goldman, "What Makes a Leader?" *Harvard Business Review* (November–December 1998): 92–105.

52. *Sources*: Y. J. Dreazn, "Behind the Fiber Glut," *Wall Street Journal*, September 26, 2002, p. B1; R. Blumenstein, "Overbuilt Web: How the Fiber Barons Plunged the Nation into a Telecom Glut," *Wall Street Journal*, June 18, 2001, p. A1; D. K. Berman, "Level 3 Finds a Way to Fight Telecom Crash," *Wall Street Journal*, November 19, 2002, p. C1; Level 3 10-K Reports, 2002 and 2003.

53. *Sources*: C. Y. Baldwin, *Fundamental Enterprise Valuation: Return on Invested Capital*, Harvard Business School Note 9-801-125, July 3, 2004; T. Copeland et al., *Valuation: Measuring and Managing the Value of Companies* (New York: Wiley, 2000).

Chapter 2

1. *Sources:* Staff Reporter, "Pharm Exec 50," *Pharmaceutical Executive*, May 2004, pp. 61–68; J. A. DiMasi, R. W. Hansen, and H. G. Grabowski, "The Price of Innovation: New Estimates of Drug Development Costs," *Journal of Health Economics* 22 (March 2003): 151–170; Staff Reporter, "Where the Money Is: The Drug Industry," *Economist*, April 26, 2003, pp. 64–65; Value Line Investment Survey, various issues.

2. M. E. Porter, *Competitive Strategy* (New York: Free Press, 1980).

3. J. E. Bain, *Barriers to New Competition* (Cambridge, Mass.: Harvard University Press, 1956). For a review of the modern literature on barriers to entry, see R. J. Gilbert, "Mobility Barriers and the Value of Incumbency," in R. Schmalensee and R. D. Willig (eds.), *Handbook of Industrial Organization*, vol. 1 (Amsterdam: North-Holland, 1989). See also R. P. McAfee, H. M. Mialon, and M. A. Williams, "What Is a Barrier to Entry?" *American Economic Review* 94 (May 2004): 461–468.

4. A detailed discussion of switching costs and lock in can be found in C. Shapiro and H. R. Varian, *Information Rules: A Strategic Guide to the Network Economy* (Boston: Harvard Business School Press, 1999).

5. Most of this information on barriers to entry can be found in the industrial organization economics literature. See especially the following works: Bain, *Barriers to New Competition*; M. Mann, "Seller Concentration, Barriers to Entry and Rates of Return in 30 Industries," *Review of Economics and Statistics* 48 (1966): 296–307; W. S. Comanor and T. A. Wilson, "Advertising, Market Structure and Performance," *Review of Economics and Statistics* 49 (1967): 423–440; Gilbert, "Mobility Barriers"; and K. Cool, L.-H. Roller, and B. Leleux, "The Relative Impact of Actual and Potential Rivalry on Firm Profitability in the Pharmaceutical Industry," *Strategic Management Journal* 20 (1999): 1–14.

6. For a discussion of tacit agreements, see T. C. Schelling, *The Strategy of Conflict* (Cambridge, Mass.: Harvard University Press, 1960).

7. M. Busse, "Firm Financial Condition and Airline Price Wars," *Rand Journal of Economics* 33 (2002): 298–318.

8. For a review, see F. Karakaya, "Market Exit and Barriers to Exit: Theory and Practice," *Psychology and Marketing* 17 (2000): 651–668.

9. P. Ghemawat, *Commitment: The Dynamics of Strategy* (Boston: Harvard Business School Press, 1991).

10. A. S. Grove, *Only the Paranoid Survive* (New York: Doubleday, 1996).

11. In standard microeconomic theory, the concept used for assessing the strength of substitutes and complements is the cross elasticity of demand.

12. For details and further references, see Charles W. L. Hill, "Establishing a Standard: Competitive Strategy and Technology Standards in Winner Take All Industries," *Academy of Management Executive* 11 (1997): 7–25; and Shapiro and Varian, *Information Rules*.

13. The development of strategic group theory has been a strong theme in the strategy literature. Important contributions include the following: R. E. Caves and Michael E. Porter, "From Entry Barriers to Mobility Barriers," *Quarterly Journal of Economics* (May 1977): 241–262; K. R. Harrigan, "An Application of Clustering for Strategic Group Analysis," *Strategic Management Journal* 6 (1985): 55–73; K. J. Hatten and D. E. Schendel, "Heterogeneity Within an Industry: Firm Conduct in the U.S. Brewing Industry, 1952–71," *Journal of Industrial Economics* 26 (1977): 97–113; Michael E. Porter, "The Structure Within Industries and Companies' Performance," *Review of Economics and Statistics* 61 (1979): 214–227. See also K. Cool and D. Schendel, "Performance Differences Among Strategic Group Members," *Strategic Management Journal* 9 (1988): 207–233; A. Nair and S. Kotha, "Does Group Membership Matter? Evidence from the Japanese Steel Industry," *Strategic Management Journal* (2001): 221–235; and G. McNamara, D. L. Deephouse, and R. A. Luce, "Competitive Positioning Within and Across a Strategic Group Structure," *Strategic Management Journal* (2003): 161–180.

14. For details on the strategic group structure in the pharmaceutical industry, see K. Cool and I. Dierickx, "Rivalry, Strategic Groups, and Firm Profitability," *Strategic Management Journal* 14 (1993): 47–59.

15. Charles W. Hofer argued that life cycle considerations may be the most important contingency when formulating business strategy. See Hofer, "Towards a Contingency Theory of Business Strategy," *Academy of Management Journal* 18 (1975): 784–810. There is empirical evidence to support this view. See C. R. Anderson and C. P. Zeithaml, "Stages of the Product Life Cycle, Business Strategy, and Business Performance," *Academy of Management Journal* 27 (1984): 5–24; and D. C. Hambrick and D. Lei, "Towards an Empirical Prioritization of Contingency Variables for Business Strategy," *Academy of Management Journal* 28 (1985): 763–788. See also G. Miles, C. C. Snow, and M. P. Sharfman, "Industry Variety and Performance," *Strategic Management Journal* 14 (1993): 163–177; G. K. Deans, F. Kroeger, and S. Zeisel, "The Consolidation Curve," *Harvard Business Review* 80 (December 2002): 2–3.

16. The characteristics of declining industries have been summarized by K. R. Harrigan, "Strategy Formulation in Declining Industries," *Academy of Management Review* 5 (1980): 599–604. See also J. Anand and H. Singh, "Asset Redeployment, Acquisitions and Corporate Strategy in Declining Industries," *Strategic Management Journal* 18 (1997): 99–118.

17. This perspective is associated with the Austrian school of economics, which goes back to Schumpeter. For a summary of this school and its implications for strategy, see R. Jacobson, "The Austrian School of Strategy," *Academy of Management Review* 17 (1992): 782–807; and C. W. L. Hill and D. Deeds, "The Importance of Industry Structure for the Determination of Industry Profitability: A Neo-Austrian Approach," *Journal of Management Studies* 33 (1996): 429–451.

18. "A Tricky Business," *Economist*, June 30, 2001, pp. 55–56.

19. D. F. Barnett and R. W. Crandall, *Up from the Ashes* (Washington, D.C.: Brookings Institution, 1986).

20. M. E. Porter, *The Competitive Advantage of Nations* (New York: Free Press, 1990).

21. The term *punctuated equilibrium* is borrowed from evolutionary biology. For a detailed explanation of the concept, see M. L. Tushman, W. H. Newman, and E. Romanelli, "Convergence and Upheaval: Managing the Unsteady Pace of Organizational Evolution," *California Management Review* 29:1 (1985): 29–44; C. J. G. Gersick, "Revolutionary Change Theories: A Multilevel Exploration of the Punctuated Equilibrium Paradigm," *Academy of Management Review* 16 (1991): 10–36; and R. Adner and D. A. Levinthal, "The Emergence of Emerging Technologies," *California Management Review* 45 (Fall 2002): 50–65.

22. A. J. Slywotzky, *Value Migration: How to Think Several Moves Ahead of the Competition* (Boston: Harvard Business School Press, 1996).

23. R. D'Aveni, *Hypercompetition* (New York: Free Press, 1994).

24. G. McNamara, P. M. Vaaler, and C. Devers, "Same as It Ever Was: The Search for Evidence of Increasing Hypercompetition," *Strategic Management Journal* 24 (2003): 261–278.

25. Hill and Deeds, "Importance of Industry Structure."

26. R. P. Rumelt, "How Much Does Industry Matter?" *Strategic Management Journal* 12 (1991): 167–185. See also A. J. Mauri and M. P. Michaels, "Firm and Industry Effects Within Strategic Management: An Empirical Examination," *Strategic Management Journal* 19 (1998): 211–219.

27. See R. Schmalensee, "Inter-Industry Studies of Structure and Performance," in Schmalensee and Willig (eds.), *Handbook of Industrial Organization*. Similar results were found by A. N. McGahan and M. E. Porter, "How Much Does Industry Matter, Really?" *Strategic Management Journal* 18 (1997): 15–30.

28. For example, see K. Cool and D. Schendel, "Strategic Group Formation and Performance: The Case of the U.S. Pharmaceutical Industry, 1932–1992," *Management Science* (September 1987): 1102–1124.

29. See M. Gort and J. Klepper, "Time Paths in the Diffusion of Product Innovations," *Economic Journal* (September 1982): 630–653. Looking at the history of forty-six products, Gort and Klepper found that the length of time before other companies entered the markets created by a few inventive companies declined from an average of 14.4 years for products introduced before 1930 to 4.9 years for those introduced after 1949.

30. The phrase was originally coined by J. Schumpeter, *Capitalism, Socialism and Democracy* (London: Macmillan, 1950), p. 68.

31. M. E. Porter, "Strategy and the Internet," *Harvard Business Review* (March 2001): 62–79.

32. U.S. Dept. of Labor, Bureau of Labor Statistics.

33. *Economist, The Economist Book of Vital World Statistics* (New York: Random House, 1990).

34. For a detailed discussion of the importance of the structure of law as a factor explaining economic change and growth, see D. C. North, *Institutions, Institutional Change, and Economic Performance* (Cambridge: Cambridge University Press, 1990).

35. K. Fiewege, "Wall Street Hot on Airlines Despite 4th-Qtr Losses," Reuters Wire Report, January 15, 2002.

36. *Sources*: "Turbulent Skies: Low Cost Airlines," *Economist*, July 10, 2004, pp. 68–72; "Silver Linings, Darkening Clouds," *Economist*, March 27, 2004, pp. 90–92; W. Zellner and M. Arndt, "Big Airlines: Not Much Runway Left," *Business Week*, July 5, 2004, p. 50; S. McCartney, "Coast to Coast Fares Drop to New Low," *Wall Street Journal*, May 12, 2004, p. D4; H. W. Jenkins, "Let Failure Be an Option," *Wall Street Journal*, June 23, 2004, p. A17.

Chapter 3

1. *Sources:* D. Hunter, "How Dell Keeps from Stumbling," *Business Week,* May 14, 2001, pp. 38–40; "Enter the Eco-System: From Supply Chain to Network," *Economist,* November 11, 2000; "Dell's Direct Initiative," *Country Monitor,* June 7, 2000, p. 5; D. G. Jacobs, "Anatomy of a Supply Chain," *Transportation and Distribution,* June 2003, pp. 60–61; S. Scherreik, "How Efficient Is That Company," *Business Week,* December 23, 2003, pp. 94–95; *Dell Computer Corporation 10K,* January 2004; Staff Reporter, "Dell Is Market Leader on Strong Shipments," *Wall Street Journal,* April 16, 2004, p. A1.

2. M. Cusumano, *The Japanese Automobile Industry* (Cambridge, Mass.: Harvard University Press, 1989); S. Spear and H. K. Bowen, "Decoding the DNA of the Toyota Production System," *Harvard Business Review* (September–October 1999): 96–108.

3. The material in this section relies on the resource-based view of the company. For summaries of this perspective, see J. B. Barney, "Company Resources and Sustained Competitive Advantage," *Journal of Management* 17 (1991): 99–120; J. T. Mahoney and J. R. Pandian, "The Resource-Based View Within the Conversation of Strategic Management," *Strategic Management Journal* 13 (1992): 63–380; R. Amit and P. J. H. Schoemaker, "Strategic Assets and Organizational Rent," *Strategic Management Journal* 14 (1993): 33–46; M. A. Peteraf, "The Cornerstones of Competitive Advantage: A Resource-Based View," *Strategic Management Journal* 14 (1993): 179–191; B. Wernerfelt, "A Resource Based View of the Company," *Strategic Management Journal* 15 (1994): 171–180; and K. M. Eisenhardt and J. A. Martin, "Dynamic Capabilities: What Are They?" *Strategic Management Journal* 21 (2000): 1105–1121.

4. For a discussion of organizational capabilities, see R. R. Nelson and S. Winter, *An Evolutionary Theory of Economic Change* (Cambridge, Mass.: Belknap Press, 1982).

5. W. Chan Kim and R. Mauborgne, "Value Innovation: The Strategic Logic of High Growth," *Harvard Business Review* (January–February 1997): 102–115.

6. The concept of consumer surplus is an important one in economics. For a more detailed exposition, see D. Besanko, D. Dranove, and M. Shanley, *Economics of Strategy* (New York: Wiley, 1996).

7. However, $P = U$ only in the special case when the company has a perfect monopoly and it can charge each customer a unique price that reflects the utility of the product to that customer (i.e., where perfect price discrimination is possible). More generally, except in the limiting case of perfect price discrimination, even a monopolist will see most customers capture some of the utility of a product in the form of a consumer surplus.

8. This point is central to the work of Michael Porter. See M. E. Porter, *Competitive Advantage* (New York: Free Press, 1985). See also P. Ghemawat, *Commitment: The Dynamic of Strategy* (New York: Free Press, 1991), chap. 4.

9. L. Hawkins, "US Auto Makers Get Better Grades for Productivity," *Wall Street Journal*, June 11, 2004, p. A3.

10. Porter, *Competitive Advantage*.

11. Ibid.

12. This approach goes back to the pioneering work by K. Lancaster: *Consumer Demand, a New Approach* (New York: Columbia University Press 1971).

13. D. Garvin, "Competing on the Eight Dimensions of Quality," *Harvard Business Review* (November–December 1987): 101–119; P. Kotler, *Marketing Management* (Millennium ed.) (Upper Saddle River, N.J.: Prentice-Hall, 2000).

14. "Proton Bomb," *Economist*, May 8, 2004, p. 77.

15. C. K. Prahalad and M. S. Krishnan, "The New Meaning of Quality in the Information Age," *Harvard Business Review* (September–October 1999): 109–118.

16. See D. Garvin, "What Does Product Quality Really Mean," *Sloan Management Review* 26 (Fall 1984): 25–44; P. B. Crosby, *Quality Is Free* (New York: Mentor, 1980); and A. Gabor, *The Man Who Discovered Quality* (New York: Times Books, 1990).

17. M. Cusumano, *The Japanese Automobile Industry* (Cambridge, Mass.: Harvard University Press, 1989);

S. Spear and H. K. Bowen, "Decoding the DNA of the Toyota Production System," *Harvard Business Review* (September–October 1999): 96–108.

18. Kim and Mauborgne, "Value Innovation."

19. G. Stalk and T. M. Hout, *Competing Against Time* (New York: Free Press, 1990).

20. Ibid.

21. Tom Copeland, Tim Koller, and Jack Murrin, *Valuation: Measuring and Managing the Value of Companies* (New York: Wiley, 1996). See also S. F. Jablonsky and N. P. Barsky, *The Manager's Guide to Financial Statement Analysis* (New York: Wiley, 2001).

22. Copeland, Koller, and Murrin, *Valuation*.

23. This is done as follows. Signifying net profit by π, invested capital by K, and revenues by R, then $ROIC = \pi/K$. If we multiply through by revenues, R, this becomes $R \times (\pi/K) = (\pi \times R)/(K \times R)$, which can be rearranged as $\pi/R \times R/K$. π/R is the return on sales and R/K capital turnover.

24. Note that Figure 3.9 is a simplification and ignores some other important items that enter the calculation, such as depreciation/sales (a determinant of ROS) and other assets/sales (a determinant of capital turnover).

25. This is the nature of the competitive process. For more detail, see C. W. L. Hill and D. Deeds, "The Importance of Industry Structure for the Determination of Company Profitability: A Neo-Austrian Perspective," *Journal of Management Studies*, 33 (1996): 429–451.

26. As with resources and capabilities, so the concept of barriers to imitation is also grounded in the resource-based view of the company. For details, see R. Reed and R. J. DeFillippi, "Causal Ambiguity, Barriers to Imitation, and Sustainable Competitive Advantage," *Academy of Management Review* 15 (1990): 88–102.

27. E. Mansfield, "How Economists See R&D," *Harvard Business Review* (November–December 1981): 98–106.

28. S. L. Berman, J. Down, and C. W. L. Hill, "Tacit Knowledge as a Source of Competitive Advantage in the National Basketball Association," *Academy of Management Journal* (2002): 13–33.

29. P. Ghemawat, *Commitment: The Dynamic of Strategy* (New York: Free Press, 1991).

30. W. M. Cohen and D. A. Levinthal, "Absorptive Capacity: A New Perspective on Learning and Innovation," *Administrative Science Quarterly* 35 (1990): 128–152.

31. M. T. Hannah and J. Freeman, "Structural Inertia and Organizational Change," *American Sociological Review* 49 (1984): 149–164.

32. See "IBM Corporation," Harvard Business School Case #180-034.

33. Ghemawat, *Commitment*.

34. D. Miller, *The Icarus Paradox* (New York: Harper-Business, 1990).

35. P. M. Senge, *The Fifth Discipline: The Art and Practice of the Learning Organization* (New York: Doubleday, 1990).

36. D. Kearns, "Leadership Through Quality," *Academy of Management Executive* 4 (1990): 86–89.

37. The classic statement of this position was made by A. A. Alchain, "Uncertainty, Evolution, and Economic Theory," *Journal of Political Economy* 84 (1950): 488–500.

38. *Sources:* Google Form S1, filed with the SEC; "Spiders in the Web," *Economist*, May 15, 2004, pp. 14–16; "The Weakness of Google," *Economist*, May 1, 2004, pp. 67–68; B. Elgin, "Google's Success Is Spurring Competitors to Take Search Technology to the Next Level," *Business Week*, May 17, 2004, pp. 46–47.

Chapter 4

1. *Sources:* A. Latour and C. Nuzum, "Verizon Profit Soars Fivefold on Wireless Growth," *Wall Street Journal*, July 28, 2004, p. A3; S. Woolley, "Do You Fear Me Know?" *Forbes*, November 10, 2003, pp. 78–80; A. Z. Cuneo, "Call Verizon Victorious," *Advertising Age*, March 2004, pp. 3–5.

2. G. J. Miller, *Managerial Dilemmas: The Political Economy of Hierarchy* (Cambridge: Cambridge University Press, 1992).

3. H. Luft, J. Bunker, and A. Enthoven, "Should Operations Be Regionalized?" *New England Journal of Medicine* 301 (1979): 1364–1369.

4. S. Chambers and R. Johnston, "Experience Curves in Services," *International Journal of Operations and Production Management* 20 (2000): 842–860.

5. G. Hall and S. Howell, "The Experience Curve from an Economist's Perspective," *Strategic Management Journal* 6 (1985): 197–212; M. Lieberman, "The Learning Curve and Pricing in the Chemical Processing Industries," *RAND Journal of Economics* 15 (1984): 213–228; R. A. Thornton and P. Thompson, "Learning from Experience and Learning from Others," *American Economic Review* 91 (2001): 1350–1369.

6. Boston Consulting Group, *Perspectives on Experience* (Boston: Boston Consulting Group, 1972); Hall and Howell, "The Experience Curve," pp. 197–212; W. B. Hirschmann, "Profit from the Learning Curve," *Harvard Business Review* (January–February 1964): 125–139.

7. A. A. Alchian, "Reliability of Progress Curves in Airframe Production," *Econometrica* 31 (1963): 679–693.

8. M. Borrus, L. A. Tyson, and J. Zysman, "Creating Advantage: How Government Policies Create Trade in the Semi-Conductor Industry," in P. R. Krugman (ed.), *Strategic Trade Policy and the New International Economics* (Cambridge, Mass.: MIT Press, 1986); S. Ghoshal and C. A. Bartlett, "Matsushita Electrical Industrial (MEI) in 1987," Harvard Business School Case #388-144 (1988).

9. Abernathy and Wayne, "Limits of the Learning Curve," pp. 109–119.

10. D. F. Barnett and R. W. Crandall, *Up from the Ashes: The Rise of the Steel Minimill in the United States* (Washington, D.C.: Brookings Institution, 1986).

11. See P. Nemetz and L. Fry, "Flexible Manufacturing Organizations: Implications for Strategy Formulation," *Academy of Management Review* 13 (1988): 627–638; N. Greenwood, *Implementing Flexible Manufacturing Systems* (New York: Halstead Press, 1986); J. P. Womack, D. T. Jones, and D. Roos, *The Machine That Changed the World* (New York: Rawson Associates, 1990); and R. Parthasarthy and S. P. Seith, "The Impact of Flexible Automation on Business Strategy and Organizational Structure," *Academy of Management Review* 17 (1992): 86–111.

12. B. J. Pine, *Mass Customization: The New Frontier in Business Competition* (Boston: Harvard Business School Press, 1993); S. Kotha, "Mass Customization: Implementing the Emerging Paradigm for Competitive Advantage," *Strategic Management Journal* 16 (1995): 21–42; J. H. Gilmore and B. J. Pine II, "The Four Faces of Mass Customization," *Harvard Business Review* (January–February 1997): 91–101.

13. P. Waurzyniak, "Ford's Flexible Push," *Manufacturing Engineering*, September 2003.

14. F. F. Reichheld and W. E. Sasser, "Zero Defections: Quality Comes to Service," *Harvard Business Review* (September–October 1990): 105–111.

15. The example comes from ibid.

16. Ibid.

17. R. Narasimhan and J. R. Carter, "Organization, Communication and Coordination of International Sourcing," *International Marketing Review* 7 (1990): 6–20.

18. H. F. Busch, "Integrated Materials Management," *IJDP & MM* 18 (1990): 28–39.

19. G. Stalk and T. M. Hout, *Competing Against Time* (New York: Free Press, 1990).

20. See Peter Bamberger and Ilan Meshoulam, *Human Resource Strategy: Formulation, Implementation, and Impact* (Thousand Oaks, Calif.: Sage, 2000); P. M. Wright and S. Snell, "Towards a Unifying Framework for Exploring Fit and Flexibility in Human Resource Management," *Academy of Management Review* 23 (October 1998): 756–772.

21. A. Sorge and M. Warner, "Manpower Training, Manufacturing Organization, and Work Place Relations in Great Britain and West Germany," *British Journal of Industrial Relations* 18 (1980): 318–333; R. Jaikumar, "Postindustrial Manufacturing," *Harvard Business Review* (November–December 1986): 72–83.

22. J. Hoerr, "The Payoff from Teamwork," *Business Week*, July 10, 1989, pp. 56–62.

23. "The Trouble with Teams," *Economist*, January 14, 1995, p. 61.

24. T. C. Powell and A. Dent-Micallef, "Information Technology as Competitive Advantage: The Role of Human, Business, and Technology Resource," *Strategic Management Journal* 18 (1997): 375–405; B. Gates, *Business @ the Speed of Thought* (New York: Warner Books, 1999).

25. "Cisco@speed," *Economist*, June 26, 1999, p. 12; S. Tully, "How Cisco Mastered the Net," *Fortune*, August 17, 1997, pp. 207–210; C. Kano, "The Real King of the Internet," *Fortune*, September 7, 1998, pp. 82–93.

26. Gates, *Business @ the Speed of Thought*.

27. See the articles published in the special issue of the *Academy of Management Review on Total Quality Management* 19:3 (1994). The following article provides a good overview of many of the issues involved from an academic perspective: J. W. Dean and D. E. Bowen, "Management Theory and Total Quality," *Academy of Management Review* 19 (1994): 392–418. See also T. C. Powell, "Total Quality Management as Competitive Advantage," *Strategic Management Journal* 16 (1995): 15–37.

28. For general background information, see "How to Build Quality," *Economist*, September 23, 1989,

pp. 91–92; A. Gabor, *The Man Who Discovered Quality* (New York: Penguin, 1990); and P. B. Crosby, *Quality Is Free* (New York: Mentor, 1980).

29. W. E. Deming, "Improvement of Quality and Productivity Through Action by Management," *National Productivity Review* 1 (Winter 1981–1982): 12–22.

30. J. Bowles, "Is American Management Really Committed to Quality?" *Management Review* (April 1992): 42–46.

31. O. Port and G. Smith, "Quality," *Business Week*, November 30, 1992, pp. 66–75. See also "The Straining of Quality," *Economist*, January 14, 1995, pp. 55–56.

32. Bowles, "Is American Management Really Committed to Quality?" pp. 42–46; "The Straining of Quality," pp. 55–56.

33. Gabor, *The Man Who Discovered Quality*.

34. W. E. Deming, *Out of the Crisis* (Cambridge, Mass.: MIT Center for Advanced Engineering Study, 1986).

35. Deming, "Improvement of Quality and Productivity," pp. 12–22.

36. A. Ries and J. Trout, *Positioning: The Battle for Your Mind* (New York: Warner Books, 1982).

37. R. G. Cooper, *Product Leadership* (Reading, Mass.: Perseus Books, 1999).

38. E. Mansfield, "How Economists See R&D," *Harvard Business Review* (November–December 1981): 98–106.

39. Ibid.

40. G. A. Stevens and J. Burley, "Piloting the Rocket of Radical Innovation," *Research Technology Management* 46 (2003): 16–26.

41. Ibid.; see also S. L. Brown and K. M. Eisenhardt, "Product Development: Past Research, Present Findings, and Future Directions," *Academy of Management Review* 20 (1995): 343–378; M. B. Lieberman and D. B. Montgomery, "First Mover Advantages," *Strategic Management Journal* 9 (Special Issue, Summer 1988): 41–58; D. J. Teece, "Profiting from Technological Innovation: Implications for Integration, Collaboration, Licensing and Public Policy," *Research Policy* 15 (1987): 285–305; and G. J. Tellis and P. N. Golder, "First to Market, First to Fail?" *Sloan Management Review* (Winter 1996): 65–75.

42. Stalk and Hout, *Competing Against Time*.

43. K. B. Clark and S. C. Wheelwright, *Managing New Product and Process Development* (New York: Free Press, 1993); M. A. Schilling and C. W. L. Hill,

"Managing the New Product Development Process," *Academy of Management Executive* 12:3 (August 1998): 67–81.

44. Clark and Wheelwright, *Managing New Product and Process Development*.

45. P. Sellers, "Getting Customers to Love You," *Fortune*, March 13, 1989, pp. 38–42.

46. O. Port, "Moving Past the Assembly Line," *Business Week* (Special Issue, Reinventing America, 1992): 177–180.

47. G. P. Pisano and S. C. Wheelwright, "The New Logic of High Tech R&D," *Harvard Business Review* (September–October 1995): 93–105.

48. K. B. Clark and T. Fujimoto, "The Power of Product Integrity," *Harvard Business Review* (November–December 1990): 107–118; Clark and Wheelwright, *Managing New Product and Process Development*; Brown and Eisenhardt, "Product Development"; Stalk and Hout, *Competing Against Time*.

49. C. Christensen, "Quantum Corporation-Business and Product Teams," Harvard Business School Case #9-692-023.

50. S. Caminiti, "A Mail Order Romance: Lands' End Courts Unseen Customers," *Fortune*, March 13, 1989, pp. 43–44.

51. Sellers, "Getting Customers to Love You."

52. Caminiti, "A Mail Order Romance," pp. 43–44.

53. Stalk and Hout, *Competing Against Time*.

54. *Sources:* D. Welch and K. Kerwin, "Detroit Tries It the Japanese Way," *Business Week*, January 26, 2004, p. 76; A. Taylor, "Detroit Buffs Up," *Fortune*, February 9, 2004, pp. 90–94; J. Muller, "The Little Car That Could," Forbes, December 8, 2003, p. 82; "The Year of the Car," *Economist*, January 3, 2004, p. 47.

Chapter 5

1. **www.samsung.com** (2004).

2. R. Foroohar and J. Lee, "Masters of the Digital Age," *Newsweek*, October 18, 2004, pp. E10–E13.

3. **www.samsung.com** (2004).

4. Derek F. Abell, *Defining the Business: The Starting Point of Strategic Planning* (Englewood Cliffs, N.J.: Prentice-Hall, 1980), p. 169.

5. R. Kotler, *Marketing Management*, 5th ed. (Englewood Cliffs, N.J.: Prentice-Hall, 1984); M. R. Darby and E. Karni, "Free Competition and the Optimal Amount of Fraud," *Journal of Law and Economics* 16 (1973): 67–86.

6. Abell, *Defining the Business*, p. 8.

7. Some of the theoretical underpinnings for this approach can be found in G. R. Jones and J. Butler, "Costs, Revenues, and Business Level Strategy," *Academy of Management Review* 13 (1988): 202–213; and C. W. L. Hill, "Differentiation Versus Low Cost or Differentiation and Low Cost: A Contingency Framework," *Academy of Management Review* 13 (1988): 401–412.

8. This section, and material on the business model, draw heavily on C. W. L. Hill and G. R. Jones, "The Dynamics of Business-Level Strategy" (unpublished paper, 2002).

9. Many authors have discussed cost leadership and differentiation as basic competitive approaches—for example, F. Scherer, *Industrial Market Structure and Economic Performance*, 10th ed. (Boston: Houghton Mifflin, 2000). The basic cost-leadership/differentiation dimension has received substantial empirical support; see, for example, D. C. Hambrick, "High Profit Strategies in Mature Capital Goods Industries: A Contingency Approach," *Academy of Management Journal* 26 (1983): 687–707.

10. Michael E. Porter, *Competitive Advantage: Creating and Sustaining Superior Performance* (New York: Free Press, 1985), p. 37.

11. Ibid., pp. 13–14.

12. **www.walmart.com** (2002).

13. D. Miller, "Configurations of Strategy and Structure: Towards a Synthesis," *Strategic Management Journal* 7 (1986): 217–231.

14. J. Guyon, "Can the Savoy Cut Costs and Be the Savoy?" *Wall Street Journal*, October 25, 1994, p. B1.

15. Michael E. Porter, *Competitive Strategy: Techniques for Analyzing Industries and Competitors* (New York: Free Press, 1980), p. 46.

16. Peter F. Drucker, *The Practice of Management* (New York: Harper, 1954).

17. Charles W. Hofer and D. Schendel, *Strategy Formulation: Analytical Concepts* (St. Paul, Minn.: West, 1978).

18. W. K. Hall, "Survival Strategies in a Hostile Environment," *Harvard Business Review* 58 (1980): 75–85; Hambrick, "High Profit Strategies," pp. 687–707.

19. J. Guyon, "Can the Savoy Cut Costs and Be the Savoy?" *Wall Street Journal*, October 25, 1994, p. B1.

20. The development of strategic-group theory has been a strong theme in the strategy literature. Important contributions include R. E. Caves and Michael Porter, "From Entry Barriers to Mobility

Barriers," *Quarterly Journal of Economics* (May 1977): 241–262; K. R. Harrigan, "An Application of Clustering for Strategic Group Analysis," *Strategic Management Journal* 6 (1985): 55–73; K. J. Hatten and D. E. Schendel, "Heterogeneity Within an Industry: Company Conduct in the U.S. Brewing Industry, 1952–1971," *Journal of Industrial Economics* 26, pp. 97–113; and Michael E. Porter, "The Structure Within Industries and Companies Performance," *Review of Economics and Statistics* 61 (1979): 214–227.

21. G. Hamel and C. K. Prahalad, *Competing for the Future* (Boston: Harvard Business School

22. *Sources:* www.E*trade.com (2004); www.E*trade.com, press releases (1999, 2001, 2004).

Chapter 6

1. www.nike.com (2004), press release.

2. "The New Nike," yahoo.com (2004), September 12.

3. www.nike.com (2004).

4. A. Wong, "Nike: Just Don't Do It," *Newsweek*, November 1, 2004, p. 84.

5. M. Porter, *Competitive Strategy: Techniques for Analyzing Industries and Competitors* (New York: Free Press, 1980), pp. 191–200.

6. S. A. Shane, "Hybrid Organizational Arrangements and Their Implications for Firm Growth and Survival: A Study of New Franchisors," *Academy of Management Journal* 1 (1996): 216–234.

7. Microsoft is often accused of not being an innovator, but the fact is that Gates and Allen wrote the first commercial software program for the first commercially available personal computer. Microsoft was the first mover in their industry. See P. Freiberger and M. Swaine, *Fire in the Valley* (New York: McGraw-Hill, 2000).

8. J. M. Utterback, *Mastering the Dynamics of Innovation* (Boston: Harvard Business School Press, 1994).

9. See Freiberger and Swaine, *Fire in the Valley*.

10. G. A. Moore, *Crossing the Chasm* (New York: HarperCollins, 1991).

11. Utterback, *Mastering the Dynamics of Innovation*.

12. Everett Rogers, *Diffusion of Innovations* (New York: Free Press, 1995).

13. Charles W. Hofer and D. Schendel, *Strategy Formulation: Analytical Concepts* (St. Paul, Minn.: West, 1978).

14. Ibid.

15. Ibid.

16. Ibid.

17. J. Brander and J. Eaton, "Product Line Rivalry," *American Economic Review* 74 (1985): 323–334.

18. Ibid.

19. Porter, *Competitive Strategy*, pp. 76–86.

20. O. Heil and T. S. Robertson, "Towards a Theory of Competitive Market Signaling: A Research Agenda," *Strategic Management Journal* 12 (1991): 403–418.

21. Robert Axelrod, *The Evolution of Cooperation* (New York: Basic Books, 1984).

22. F. Scherer, *Industrial Market Structure and Economic Performance*, 10th ed. (Boston: Houghton Mifflin, 2000), chap. 8.

23. The model differs from Ansoff's model for this reason.

24. H. Igor Ansoff, *Corporate Strategy* (London: Penguin Books, 1984), pp. 97–100.

25. Robert D. Buzzell, Bradley T. Gale, and Ralph G. M. Sultan, "Market Share—A Key to Profitability," *Harvard Business Review* (January–February 1975): 97–103; Robert Jacobson and David A. Aaker, "Is Market Share All That It's Cracked Up to Be?" *Journal of Marketing* 49 (1985): 11–22.

26. Ansoff, *Corporate Strategy*, pp. 98–99.

27. Figure copyright © Gareth R. Jones, 2004.

28. The next section draws heavily on Marvin B. Lieberman, "Strategies for Capacity Expansion," *Sloan Management Review* 8 (1987): 19–27; and Porter, *Competitive Strategy*, pp. 324–338.

29. For a basic introduction to game theory, see A. K. Dixit and B. J. Nalebuff, *Thinking Strategically* (London: W.W. Norton, 1991). See also A. M. Brandenburger and B. J. Nalebuff, "The Right Game: Using Game Theory to Shape Strategy," *Harvard Business Review* (July–August 1995): 59–71; and D. M. Kreps, *Game Theory and Economic Modeling* (Oxford: Oxford University Press, 1990).

30. www.zara.com (2004); www.gucci.com (2004); C. Vitzthum, "Just-in-Time-Fashion," *Wall Street Journal*, May 18, 2001, pp. B1, B4.

Chapter 7

1. *Sources:* D. Pringle, "Symbian Grabs Bigger Market Share," *Wall Street Journal*, August 3, 2004, p. B2; B. McDonough, "Microsoft Jostles for Mobile Market Position," **Wireless.Newsfactor.com**, February 19, 2002; A. Reinhardt, "Cell Phones:

Don't Count Linux Out," *Business Week*, September 6, 2003, p. 66.

2. Bureau of Economic Analysis, *Survey of United States Current Business*, 2001.

3. P. Woodall, "Survey: The New Economy: Untangling Economics," *Economist*, September 23, 2000, pp. S5–S7.

4. J. M. Utterback, *Mastering the Dynamics of Innovation* (Boston: Harvard Business School Press, 1994). C. Shapiro and H. R. Varian, *Information Rules: A Strategic Guide to the Network Economy* (Boston: Harvard Business School Press, 1999).

5. The layout is not universal, although it is widespread. The French, for example, use a different layout.

6. M. Craig, "Dueling DVD Recorder Formats," *Seattle Times*, January 9, 2002, p. C3.

7. For details, see Charles W. L. Hill, "Establishing a Standard: Competitive Strategy and Technology Standards in Winner Take All Industries," *Academy of Management Executive* 11 (1997): 7–25; Shapiro and Varian, *Information Rules*; B. Arthur, "Increasing Returns and the New World of Business," *Harvard Business Review* (July-August 1996): 100–109; G. Gowrisankaran and J. Stavins, "Network Externalities and Technology Adoption: Lessons from Electronic Payments," *Rand Journal of Economics* 35 (2004): 260–277; and V. Shankar and B. L. Bayus, "Network Effects and Competition: An Empirical Analysis of the Home Video Game Industry," *Strategic Management Journal* 24 (2003): 375–394.

8. See Shapiro and Varian, *Information Rules*; Hill, "Establishing a Standard"; and M. A. Shilling, "Technological Lockout: An Integrative Model of the Economic and Strategic Factors Driving Technology Success and Failure," *Academy of Management Review* 23:2 (1998): 267–285.

9. Microsoft does not disclose the per unit licensing fee that it gets from original equipment manufacturers.

10. P. M. Romer, "The Origins of Endogenous Growth," *Journal of Economic Perspectives* 8:1 (1994): 3–22.

11. Data from **www.btechnews.com**.

12. Shapiro and Varian, *Information Rules*.

13. International Federation of the Phonographic Industry, *Fighting Piracy*, 2003. Available from **www.ifpi.org**.

14. Business Software Alliance, *Seventh Annual BSA Global Software Piracy Study*, June 2003. Available from **www.bsa.org**.

15. Ibid.

16. N. Ridgeway, "Let Them Burn," *Forbes*, March 4, 2002, p. 88.

17. Much of this section is based on Charles W. L. Hill, Michael Heeley, and Jane Sakson, "Strategies for Profiting from Innovation," in *Advances in Global High Technology Management* (Greenwich, Conn.: JAI Press, 1993) 3: 79–95.

18. M. Lieberman and D. Montgomery, "First Mover Advantages," *Strategic Management Journal* 9 (Special Issue, Summer 1988): 41–58.

19. W. Boulding and M. Christen, "Sustainable Pioneering Advantage? Profit Implications of Market Entry Order?" *Marketing Science* 22 (2003): 371–386; C. Markides and P. Geroski, "Teaching Elephants to Dance and Other Silly Ideas," *Business Strategy Review* 13 (2003): 49–61.

20. J. Borzo, "Aging Gracefully," *Wall Street Journal*, October 15, 2001, p. R22.

21. The importance of complementary assets was first noted by D. J. Teece. See D. J. Teece, "Profiting from Technological Innovation," in D. J. Teece (ed.), *The Competitive Challenge* (New York: Harper & Row, 1986), pp. 26–54.

22. M. J. Chen and D. C. Hambrick, "Speed, Stealth, and Selective Attack: How Small Firms Differ from Large Firms in Competitive Behavior," *Academy of Management Journal* 38 (1995): 453–482.

23. E. Mansfield, M. Schwartz, and S. Wagner, "Imitation Costs and Patents: An Empirical Study," *Economic Journal* 91 (1981): 907–918.

24. E. Mansfield, "How Rapidly Does New Industrial Technology Leak Out?" *Journal of Industrial Economics* 34 (1985): 217–223.

25. This argument has been made in the game theory literature. See R. Caves, H. Cookell, and P. J. Killing, "The Imperfect Market for Technology Licenses," *Oxford Bulletin of Economics and Statistics* 45 (1983): 249–267; N. T. Gallini, "Deterrence by Market Sharing: A Strategic Incentive for Licensing," *American Economic Review* 74 (1984): 931–941; and C. Shapiro, "Patent Licensing and R&D Rivalry," *American Economic Review* 75 (1985): 25–30.

26. M. Christensen, *The Innovator's Dilemma* (Boston: Harvard Business School Press, 1997). R. N. Foster, *Innovation: The Attacker's Advantage* (New York: Summit Books, 1986).

27. Foster, *Innovation*.

28. Ray Kurzweil, *The Age of the Spiritual Machines* (New York: Penguin Books, 1999).

29. See Christensen, *The Innovator's Dilemma*; and C. M. Christensen and M. Overdorf, "Meeting the Challenge of Disruptive Change," *Harvard Business Review* (March–April 2000): 66–77.

30. Charles W. L. Hill and Frank T. Rothaermel, "The Performance of Incumbent Firms in the Face of Radical Technological Innovation," *Academy of Management Review* 28 (2003): 257–274.

31. *Sources:* S. Yoon, "The Mod Squad," *East Asian Economic Review*, November 7, 2002, pp. 34–36; R. Cunningham, "Controversy as Sony Loses Mod-Chip Verdict," *Managing Intellectual Property*, September 2002, pp. 15–18; A. Pham, "Video Game Losses Nearly $2 Billion," *Los Angeles Times*, February 18, 2002, p. C8; Andy Holloway, "License to Plunder," *Canadian Business*, November 10, 2003, p. 95.

Chapter 8

1. *Sources:* J. Neff, "P&G Outpacing Unilever in Five Year Battle," *Advertising Age*, November 3, 2003, pp. 1–3; G. Strauss, "Firm Restructuring into Truly Global Company," *USA Today*, September 10, 1999, p. B2; Procter & Gamble *10K Report, 2004*; M. Kolbasuk McGee, "P&G Jump-Starts Corporate Change," *Information Week*, November 1, 1999, pp. 30–34.

2. World Trade Organization, *International Trade Trends and Statistics, 2003* (Geneva: WTO, 2003). WTO press release, "World Trade for 2003: Prospects for 2004," April 4, 2004. Available at **www.wto.org**.

3. World Trade Organization, *International Trade Statistics, 2003* (Geneva: WTO, 2003), and United Nations, *World Investment Report, 2003*.

4. P. Dicken, *Global Shift* (New York: Guilford Press, 1992).

5. I. Metthee, "Playing a Large Part," *Seattle Post-Intelligencer*, April 9, 1994, p. 13.

6. T. Levitt, "The Globalization of Markets," *Harvard Business Review* (May–June 1983): 92–102.

7. M. E. Porter, *The Competitive Advantage of Nations* (New York: Free Press, 1990). See also R. Grant, "Porter's Competitive Advantage of Nations: An Assessment," *Strategic Management Journal* 7 (1991): 535–548.

8. Porter, *Competitive Advantage of Nations*.

9. Example is disguised. Comes from interviews by Charles Hill.

10. See J. Birkinshaw and N. Hood, "Multinational Subsidiary Evolution: Capability and Charter Change in Foreign Owned Subsidiary Companies," *Academy of Management Review* 23 (October 1998), pp. 773–795; A. K. Gupta and V. J. Govindarajan, "Knowledge Flows Within Multinational Corporations," *Strategic Management Journal* 21 (2000), pp. 473–496; V. J. Govindarajan and A. K. Gupta, *The Quest for Global Dominance* (San Francisco: Jossey-Bass, 2001); T. S. Frost, J. M. Birkinshaw, and P. C. Ensign, "Centers of Excellence in Multinational Corporations," *Strategic Management Journal* 23 (2002), pp. 997–1018; and U. Andersson, M. Forsgren, and U. Holm, "The Strategic Impact of External Networks," *Strategic Management Journal* 23 (2002), pp. 979–996.

11. S. Leung, "Armchairs, TVs and Espresso: Is It McDonald's?" *Wall Street Journal*, August 30, 2002, pp. A1, A6.

12. C. K. Prahalad and Yves L. Doz, *The Multinational Mission: Balancing Local Demands and Global Vision* (New York: Free Press, 1987). See also J. Birkinshaw, A. Morrison, and J. Hulland, "Structural and Competitive Determinants of a Global Integration Strategy," *Strategic Management Journal* 16 (1995): 637–655.

13. J. E. Garten, "Wal-Mart Gives Globalization a Bad Name," *Business Week*, March 8, 2004, p. 24.

14. Prahalad and Doz, *Multinational Mission*. Prahalad and Doz actually talk about local responsiveness rather than local customization.

15. Levitt, "Globalization of Markets."

16. C. A. Bartlett and S. Ghoshal, *Managing Across Borders* (Boston: Harvard Business School Press, 1989).

17. C. J. Chipello, "Local Presence Is Key to European Deals," *Wall Street Journal*, June 30, 1998, p. A15.

18. Bartlett and Ghoshal, *Managing Across Borders*.

19. Ibid.

20. T. Hout, M. E. Porter, and E. Rudden, "How Global Companies Win Out," *Harvard Business Review* (September–October 1982): 98–108.

21. See Charles W. L. Hill, *International Business: Competing in the Global Marketplace* (New York: McGraw-Hill, 2000).

22. This can be reconceptualized as the resource base of the entrant, relative to indigenous competitors. For work that focuses on this issue, see W. C. Bogenr, H. Thomas, and J. McGee, "A Longitudinal Study of the Competitive Positions and Entry Paths of European Firms in the U.S. Pharmaceutical

Market," *Strategic Management Journal* 17 (1996): 85–107; D. Collis, "A Resource Based Analysis of Global Competition," *Strategic Management Journal* 12 (1991): 49–68; and S. Tallman, "Strategic Management Models and Resource Based Strategies Among MNE's in a Host Market," *Strategic Management Journal* 12 (1991): 69–82.

23. For a discussion of first-mover advantages, see M. Liberman and D. Montgomery, "First Mover Advantages," *Strategic Management Journal* 9 (Special Issue, Summer 1988): 41–58.

24. J. M. Shaver, W. Mitchell, and B. Yeung, "The Effect of Own Company and Other Company Experience on Foreign Direct Investment Survival in the U.S., 1987–92," *Strategic Management Journal* 18 (1997): 811–824.

25. S. Zaheer and E. Mosakowski, "The Dynamics of the Liability of Foreignness: A Global Study of Survival in the Financial Services Industry," *Strategic Management Journal* 18 (1997): 439–464.

26. Shaver, Mitchell, and Yeung, "The Effect of Own Company and Other Company Experience."

27. P. Ghemawat, *Commitment: The Dynamics of Strategy* (New York: Free Press, 1991).

28. This section draws on several studies, including C. W. L. Hill, P. Hwang, and W. C. Kim, "An Eclectic Theory of the Choice of International Entry Mode," *Strategic Management Journal* 11 (1990): 117–128; C. W. L. Hill and W. C. Kim, "Searching for a Dynamic Theory of the Multinational Company: A Transaction Cost Model," *Strategic Management Journal* 9 (Special Issue on Strategy Content, 1988): 93–104; E. Anderson and H. Gatignon, "Modes of Foreign Entry: A Transaction Cost Analysis and Propositions," *Journal of International Business Studies* 17 (1986): 1–26; F. R. Root, *Entry Strategies for International Markets* (Lexington, Mass.: D. C. Heath, 1980); and A. Madhok, "Cost, Value and Foreign Market Entry: The Transaction and the Company," *Strategic Management Journal* 18 (1997): 39–61.

29. F. J. Contractor, "The Role of Licensing in International Strategy," *Columbia Journal of World Business* (Winter 1982): 73–83.

30. O. E. Williamson, *The Economic Institutions of Capitalism* (New York: Free Press, 1985).

31. Andrew E. Serwer, "McDonald's Conquers the World," *Fortune*, October 17, 1994, pp. 103–116.

32. B. Kogut, "Joint Ventures: Theoretical and Empirical Perspectives," *Strategic Management Journal* 9 (1988): 319–332.

33. D. G. Bradley, "Managing Against Expropriation," *Harvard Business Review* (July–August 1977): 78–90.

34. C. W. L. Hill, "Strategies for Exploiting Technological Innovations," *Organization Science* 3 (1992): 428–441.

35. See K. Ohmae, "The Global Logic of Strategic Alliances," *Harvard Business Review* (March–April 1989): 143–154; G. Hamel, Y. L. Doz, and C. K. Prahalad, "Collaborate with Your Competitors and Win!" *Harvard Business Review* (January–February 1989): 133–139; W. Burgers, C. W. L. Hill, and W. C. Kim, "Alliances in the Global Auto Industry," *Strategic Management Journal* 14 (1993): 419–432; and P. Kale, H. Singh, and H. Perlmutter, "Learning and Protection of Proprietary Assets in Strategic Alliances: Building Relational Capital," *Strategic Management Journal* 21 (2000): 217–237.

36. "Asia Beckons," *Economist*, May 30, 1992, pp. 63–64.

37. C. Souza, "Microsoft Teams with MIPS, Toshiba," *EBN*, February 10, 2003, p. 4.

38. M. Frankel, "Now Sony Is Giving Palm a Hand," *Business Week*, November 29, 2000, p. 50.

39. Kale, Singh, and Perlmutter, "Learning and Protection of Proprietary Assets."

40. R. B. Reich and E. D. Mankin, "Joint Ventures with Japan Give Away Our Future," *Harvard Business Review*, March–April 1986, pp. 78–90.

41. J. Bleeke and D. Ernst, "The Way to Win in Cross-Border Alliances," *Harvard Business Review* (November–December 1991): 127–135.

42. E. Booker and C. Krol, "IBM Finds Strength in Alliances," *B to B*, February 10, 2003, pp. 3, 27.

43. W. Roehl and J. F. Truitt, "Stormy Open Marriages Are Better," *Columbia Journal of World Business* (Summer 1987): 87–95.

44. K. McQuade and B. Gomes-Casseres, "Xerox and Fuji-Xerox," Harvard Business School Case #9–391–156.

45. See T. Khanna, R. Gulati, and N. Nohria, "The Dynamics of Learning Alliances: Competition, Cooperation, and Relative Scope," *Strategic Management Journal* 19 (1998), pp. 193–210; and Kale, Singh, and Perlmutter, "Learning and Protection of Proprietary Assets."

46. Kale, Singh, and Perlmutter, "Learning and Protection of Proprietary Assets."

47. Hamel, Doz, and Prahalad, "Collaborate with Your Competitors and Win!"

48. B. Wysocki, "Cross Border Alliances Become Favorite Way to Crack New Markets," *Wall Street Journal*, March 4, 1990, p. A1.

49. *Sources:* Starbucks 10-K, various years; C. McLean, "Starbucks Set to Invade Coffee-Loving Continent," *Seattle Times*, October 4, 2000, p. E1; J. Ordonez, "Starbucks to Start Major Expansion in Overseas Market," *Wall Street Journal*, October 27, 2000, p. B10; S. Homes and D. Bennett, "Planet Starbucks," *Business Week*, September 9, 2002, pp. 99–110; J. Batsell, "A Bean Counters Dream," *Seattle Times*, March 28, 2004, p. E1; Staff Reporter, "Boss Talk: It's a Grande Latte World," *Wall Street Journal*, December 15, 2003, p. B1.

Chapter 9

1. Y. J. Dreazen, G. Ip, and N. Kulish, "Why the Sudden Rise in the Urge to Merge and Create Oligopolies?" *Wall Street Journal*, February 25, 2002, p. A1; L. Kowalczyk, "A Matter of Style," *Boston Globe*, February 22, 2002, p. C1.

2. United Nations, *World Investment Report 2001* (New York: United Nations, November 2001).

3. Dreazen, Ip, and Kulish, "Why the Sudden Rise?"

4. For evidence on acquisitions and performance, see R. E. Caves, "Mergers, Takeovers, and Economic Efficiency," *International Journal of Industrial Organization* 7 (1989): 151–174; M. C. Jensen and R. S. Ruback, "The Market for Corporate Control: The Scientific Evidence," *Journal of Financial Economics* 11 (1983): 5–50; R. Roll, "Empirical Evidence on Takeover Activity and Shareholder Wealth," in J. C. Coffee, L. Lowenstein, and S. Rose (eds.), *Knights, Raiders and Targets* (Oxford: Oxford University Press, 1989); A. Schleifer and R. W. Vishny, "Takeovers in the 60s and 80s: Evidence and Implications," *Strategic Management Journal* 12 (Special Issue, Winter 1991): 51–60; and T. H. Brush, "Predicted Changes in Operational Synergy and Post Acquisition Performance of Acquired Businesses," *Strategic Management Journal* 17 (1996): 1–24.

5. "Few Takeovers Pay Off for Big Buyers," *Investors Business Daily*, May 25, 2001, p. 1.

6. K. R. Harrian, "Formulating Vertical Integration Strategies," *Academy of Management Review* 9 (1984): 638–652.

7. This is the essence of Chandler's argument. See Alfred D. Chandler, *Strategy and Structure* (Cambridge, Mass.: MIT Press, 1962). The same argument is also made by Jeffrey Pfeffer and Gerald R. Salancik, *The External Control of Organizations* (New York: Harper & Row, 1978). See also K. R. Harrigan, *Strategic Flexibility* (Lexington, Mass.: Lexington Books, 1985); K. R. Harrigan, "Vertical Integration and Corporate Strategy," *Academy of Management Journal* 28 (1985): 397–425; and F. M. Scherer, *Industrial Market Structure and Economic Performance* (Chicago: Rand McNally, 1981).

8. Oliver E. Williamson, *The Economic Institutions of Capitalism*. For recent empirical work that uses this framework, see L. Poppo and T. Zenger, "Testing Alternative Theories of the Firm: Transaction Cost, Knowledge Based, and Measurement Explanations for Make or Buy Decisions in Information Services," *Strategic Management Journal* 19 (1998): 853–878.

9. Williamson, *Economic Institutions of Capitalism*.

10. A. D. Chandler, *The Visible Hand* (Cambridge, Mass.: Harvard University Press, 1977).

11. Julia Pitta, "Score One for Vertical Integration," *Forbes,* January 18, 1993, pp. 88–89.

12. Joseph White and Neal Templin, "Harsh Regimen: A Swollen GM Finds It Hard to Stick with Its Crash Diet," *Wall Street Journal*, September 9, 1992, p. A1.

13. Harrigan, *Strategic Flexibility,* pp. 67–87. See also Allan Afuah, "Dynamic Boundaries of the Firm: Are Firms Better Off Being Vertically Integrated in the Face of a Technological Change?" *Academy of Management Journal* 44 (2001): 1121–1228.

14. Kevin Kelly, Zachary Schiller, and James Treece, "Cut Costs or Else," *Business Week,* March 22, 1993, pp. 28–29.

15. X. Martin, W. Mitchell, and A. Swaminathan, "Recreating and Extending Japanese Automobile Buyer-Supplier Links in North America," *Strategic Management Journal* 16 (1995): 589–619; C. W. L. Hill, "National Institutional Structures, Transaction Cost Economizing, and Competitive Advantage," *Organization Science* 6 (1995): 119–131.

16. Standard & Poor's Industry Survey, Autos—Auto Parts, June 24, 1993.

17. See James Womack, Daniel Jones, and Daniel Roos, *The Machine That Changed the World* (New York: Rawson Associates, 1990); and James Richardson, "Parallel Sourcing and Supplier Performance in the Japanese Automobile Industry," *Strategic Management Journal* 14 (1993): 339–350.

18. R. Mudambi and S. Helper, "The Close but Adversarial Model of Supplier Relations in the U.S. Auto Industry," *Strategic Management Journal* 19 (1998): 775–792.

19. Williamson, *Economic Institutions of Capitalism.* See also J. H. Dyer, "Effective Inter-Firm Collaboration: How Firms Minimize Transaction Costs and Maximize Transaction Value," *Strategic Management Journal* 18 (1997): 535–556.

20. Richardson, "Parallel Sourcing."

21. W. H. Davidow and M. S. Malone, *The Virtual Corporation* (New York: Harper & Row, 1992).

22. A. M. Porter, "Outsourcing Gains Popularity," *Purchasing*, March 11, 1999, pp. 22–24.

23. D. Garr, "Inside Outsourcing," *Fortune* 142:1 (2001): 85–92.

24. J. Krane, "American Express Hires IBM for $4 billion," *Columbian*, February 26, 2002, p. E2.

25. J. Vijayan, "The Outsourcing Boom," *Computerworld*, March 18, 2002, pp. 42–43.

26. Davidow and Malone, *The Virtual Corporation.*

27. Ibid; H. W. Chesbrough and D. J. Teece, "When Is Virtual Virtuous? Organizing for Innovation," *Harvard Business Review* (January–February 1996): 65–74; J. B. Quinn, "Strategic Outsourcing: Leveraging Knowledge Capabilities," *Sloan Management Review* (Summer 1999): 9–21.

28. *Sources:* S. N. Mehta, "Can Bernie Bounce Back?" *Fortune*, January 22, 2001; S. N. Mehta, "WorldCom's Bad Trip," *Fortune*, March 4, 2002; R. Blumenstein, J. R. Wilke, N. Harris, and D. Solomon, "Called Off?" *Wall Street Journal*, June 28, 2000, p. A1.

Chapter 10

1. G. Hamel and C. K. Prahalad, *Competing for the Future* (Boston: Harvard Business School Press, 1994).

2. Ibid.

3. D. Leonard Barton and G. Pisano, "Monsanto's March into Biotechnology," Harvard Business School Case #690-009 (1990). See Monsanto's homepage for details about its genetically engineered seed products (**http://www.monsanto.com**).

4. This resource-based view of diversification can be traced to Edith Penrose's seminal book, *The Theory of the Growth of the Firm* (Oxford: Oxford University Press, 1959).

5. D. J. Teece, "Economies of Scope and the Scope of the Enterprise," *Journal of Economic Behavior and Organization* 3 (1980): 223–247. For recent empirical work on this topic, see C. H. St. John and J. S. Harrison, "Manufacturing Based Relatedness, Synergy and Coordination," *Strategic Management Journal* 20 (1999): 129–145.

6. Teece, "Economies of Scope." For recent empirical work on this topic, see St. John and Harrison, "Manufacturing Based Relatedness, Synergy and Coordination."

7. For a detailed discussion, see C. W. L. Hill and R. E. Hoskisson, "Strategy and Structure in the Multiproduct Firm," *Academy of Management Review* 12 (1987): 331–341.

8. See, for example, G. R. Jones and C. W. L. Hill, "A Transaction Cost Analysis of Strategy Structure Choice," *Strategic Management Journal* (1988): 159–172; and Oliver E. Williamson, *Markets and Hierarchies, Analysis and Antitrust Implications* (New York: Free Press, 1975), pp. 132–175.

9. R. Buderi, *Engines of Tomorrow* (New York: Simon & Schuster, 2000).

10. C. W. L. Hill, "The Role of Headquarters in the Multidivisional Firm," in R. Rumelt, D. J. Teece, and D. Schendel (eds.), *Fundamental Issues in Strategy Research* (Cambridge, Mass.: Harvard Business School Press, 1994), pp. 297–321.

11. See, for example, Jones and Hill, "A Transaction Cost Analysis"; Williamson, *Markets and Hierarchies;* and Hill, "The Role of Headquarters in the Multidivisional Firm."

12. The distinction goes back to R. P. Rumelt, *Strategy, Structure and Economic Performance* (Cambridge, Mass.: Harvard Business School Press, 1974).

13. For evidence, see C. W. L. Hill, "Conglomerate Performance over the Economic Cycle," *Journal of Industrial Economics* 32 (1983): 197–212; and D. T. C. Mueller, "The Effects of Conglomerate Mergers," *Journal of Banking and Finance* 1 (1977): 315–347.

14. For reviews of the evidence, see V. Ramanujam and P. Varadarajan, "Research on Corporate Diversification: A Synthesis," *Strategic Management Journal* 10 (1989): 523–551; G. Dess, J. F. Hennart, C. W. L. Hill, and A. Gupta, "Research Issues in Strategic Management," *Journal of Management* 21 (1995): 357–392; and David C. Hyland and J. David Diltz, "Why Companies Diversify: An Empirical Examination," *Financial Management* 31 (Spring 2002): 51–81.

15. M. E. Porter, "From Competitive Advantage to Corporate Strategy," *Harvard Business Review* (May–June 1987): 43–59.

16. For reviews of the evidence, see Ramanujam and Varadarajan, "Research on Corporate Diversification"; Dess, Hennart, Hill, and Gupta, "Research Issues in Strategic Management"; and Hyland and Diltz, "Why Companies Diversify."

17. C. R. Christensen et al., *Business Policy Text and Cases* (Homewood, Ill.: Irwin, 1987), p. 778.

18. See Booz, Allen, and Hamilton, *New Products Management for the 1980's* (privately published, 1982); A. L. Page, "PDMA's New Product Development Practices Survey: Performance and Best Practices" (presented at the PDMA Fifteenth Annual International Conference, Boston, October 16, 1991); and E. Mansfield, "How Economists See R&D," *Harvard Business Review* (November–December 1981): 98–106.

19. See R. Biggadike, "The Risky Business of Diversification," *Harvard Business Review* (May–June 1979): 103–111; R. A. Burgelman, "A Process Model of Internal Corporate Venturing in the Diversified Major Firm," *Administrative Science Quarterly* 28 (1983): 223–244; and Z. Block and I. C. MacMillan, *Corporate Venturing* (Boston: Harvard Business School Press, 1993).

20. Biggadike, "The Risky Business of Diversification"; Block and Macmillan, *Corporate Venturing.*

21. Buderi, *Engines of Tomorrow.*

22. I. C. MacMillan and R. George, "Corporate Venturing: Challenges for Senior Managers," *Journal of Business Strategy* 5 (1985): 34–43.

23. See R. A. Burgelman, M. M. Maidique, and S. C. Wheelwright, *Strategic Management of Technology and Innovation* (Chicago: Irwin, 1996), pp. 493–507. Also see Buderi, *Engines of Tomorrow.*

24. Buderi, *Engines of Tomorrow.*

25. See Block and Macmillan, *Corporate Venturing;* and Burgelman, Maidique, and Wheelwright, *Strategic Management of Technology and Innovation.*

26. J. Warner, J. Templeman, and R. Horn, "The Case Against Mergers," *Business Week,* October 30, 1995, pp. 122–134.

27. "Few Takeovers Pay Off for Big Buyers," *Investors Business Daily,* May 25, 2001, p. 1.

28. For evidence on acquisitions and performance, see R. E. Caves, "Mergers, Takeovers, and Economic Efficiency," *International Journal of Industrial Organization* 7 (1989): 151–174; M. C. Jensen and R.

S. Ruback, "The Market for Corporate Control: The Scientific Evidence," *Journal of Financial Economics* 11 (1983): 5–50; R. Roll, "Empirical Evidence on Takeover Activity and Shareholder Wealth," in J. C. Coffee, L. Lowenstein, and S. Rose (eds.), *Knights, Raiders and Targets* (Oxford: Oxford University Press, 1989); A. Schleifer and R. W. Vishny, "Takeovers in the 60s and 80s: Evidence and Implications," *Strategic Management Journal* 12 (Special Issue, Winter 1991): 51–60; T. H. Brush, "Predicted Changes in Operational Synergy and Post Acquisition Performance of Acquired Businesses," *Strategic Management Journal* 17 (1996): 1–24; and T. Loughran and A. M. Vijh, "Do Long Term Shareholders Benefit from Corporate Acquisitions?" *Journal of Finance* 5 (1997): 1765–1787.

29. D. J. Ravenscraft and F. M. Scherer, *Mergers, Sell-offs, and Economic Efficiency* (Washington, D.C.: Brookings Institution, 1987).

30. See J. P. Walsh, "Top Management Turnover Following Mergers and Acquisitions," *Strategic Management Journal* 9 (1988): 173–183.

31. See A. A. Cannella and D. C. Hambrick, "Executive Departure and Acquisition Performance," *Strategic Management Journal* 14 (1993): 137–152.

32. R. Roll, "The Hubris Hypothesis of Corporate Takeovers," *Journal of Business* 59 (1986): 197–216.

33. "Coca-Cola: A Sobering Lesson from Its Journey into Wine," *Business Week,* June 3, 1985, pp. 96–98.

34. P. Haspeslagh and D. Jemison, *Managing Acquisitions* (New York: Free Press, 1991).

35. For views on this issue, see L. L. Fray, D. H. Gaylin, and J. W. Down, "Successful Acquisition Planning," *Journal of Business Strategy* 5 (1984): 46–55; C. W. L. Hill, "Profile of a Conglomerate Takeover: BTR and Thomas Tilling," *Journal of General Management* 10 (1984): 34–50; D. R. Willensky, "Making It Happen: How to Execute an Acquisition," *Business Horizons* (March–April 1985): 38–45; Haspeslagh and Jemison, *Managing Acquisitions;* and P. L. Anslinger and T. E. Copeland, "Growth Through Acquisition: A Fresh Look," *Harvard Business Review* (January–February 1996): 126–135.

36. M. L. A. Hayward, "When Do Firms Learn from Their Acquisition Experience? Evidence from 1990–1995," *Strategic Management Journal* 23 (2002): 21–39; K. G. Ahuja, "Technological Acquisitions and the Innovation Performance of Acquiring Firms: A Longitudinal Study," *Strategic*

Management Journal 23 (2001): 197–220; H. G. Barkema and F. Vermeulen, "International Expansion Through Startup or Acquisition," *Academy of Management Journal* 41 (1998): 7–26.

37. Hayward, "When Do Firms Learn from Their Acquisition Experience?"

38. For a review of the evidence and some contrary empirical evidence, see D. E. Hatfield, J. P. Liebskind, and T. C. Opler, "The Effects of Corporate Restructuring on Aggregate Industry Specialization," *Strategic Management Journal* 17 (1996): 55–72.

39. A. Lamont and C. Polk, "The Diversification Discount: Cash Flows Versus Returns," *Journal of Finance* 56 (October 2001): 1693–1721; R. Raju, H. Servaes, and L. Zingales, "The Cost of Diversity: The Diversification Discount and Inefficient Investment," *Journal of Finance* 55 (February 2000): 35–80.

40. For example, see Schleifer and Vishny, "Takeovers in the 60s and 80s."

41. *Sources:* J. R. Laing, "Tyco's Titan," *Barron's*, April 12, 1999, pp. 27–32; M. Maremont, "How Is Tyco Accounting for Cash Flow?" *Wall Street Journal*, March 5, 2002, p. C1; J. R. Laing, "Doubting Tyco," *Barron's*, January 28, 2002, pp. 19–20; Staff Reporter, "Tyco's Troubles," *Economist*, June 8th, 2002, p. 71.

Chapter 11

1. *Sources:* "Boycott Nike," CBS News *48 Hours,* October 17, 1996; D. Jones, "Critics Tie Sweatshop Sneakers to 'Air Jordan,'" *USA Today,* June 6, 1996, p. 1B; "Global Exchange Special Report: Nile Just Don't Do It," available at **http://www.globalexchange.org/education/ publications/newsltr6.97p2.html#nike;** S. Greenhouse, "Nike Shoeplant in Vietnam Is Called Unsafe for Workers," *New York Times,* November 8, 1997; V. Dobnik, "Chinese Workers Abused Making Nikes, Reeboks," *Seattle Times,* September 21, 1997, p. A4.

2. E. Freeman, *Strategic Management: A Stakeholder Approach* (Boston: Pitman Press, 1984).

3. C. W. L. Hill and T. M. Jones, "Stakeholder-Agency Theory," *Journal of Management Studies* 29 (1992): 131–154; J. G. March and H. A. Simon, *Organizations* (New York: Wiley, 1958).

4. Hill and Jones, "Stakeholder-Agency Theory."

5. I. C. Macmillan and P. E. Jones, *Strategy Formulation: Power and Politics* (St. Paul, Minn.: West, 1986).

6. Tom Copeland, Tim Koller, and Jack Murrin, *Valuation: Measuring and Managing the Value of Companies* (New York: Wiley, 1996).

7. R. S. Kaplan and D. P. Norton, *Strategy Maps* (Boston: Harvard Business School Press, 2004).

8. A. L. Velocci, D. A. Fulghum, and R. Wall, "Damage Control," *Aviation Week*, December 1, 2003, pp. 26–27.

9. M. C. Jensen and W. H. Meckling, "Theory of the Firm: Managerial Behavior, Agency Costs and Ownership Structure," *Journal of Financial Economics* 3 (1976): 305–360; E. F. Fama, "Agency Problems and the Theory of the Firm," *Journal of Political Economy* 88 (1980): 375–390.

10. Hill and Jones, "Stakeholder-Agency Theory."

11. For example, see R. Marris, *The Economic Theory of Managerial Capitalism* (London: Macmillan, 1964); and J. K. Galbraith, *The New Industrial State* (Boston: Houghton Mifflin, 1970).

12. Fama, "Agency Problems and the Theory of the Firm."

13. A. Rappaport, "New Thinking on How to Link Executive Pay with Performance," *Harvard Business Review* (March–April 1999): 91–105.

14. L. Lavelle, J. Hempel, and D. Brady, "Executive Pay," *Business Week,* April 19, 2004, pp. 106–112.

15. John Byrne et al., "How to Fix Corporate Governance," *Business Week,* May 6, 2002, pp. 69–78; Lavelle, Hempel, and Brady, "Executive Pay."

16. For academic studies that look at the determinants of CEO pay, see M. C. Jensen and K. J. Murphy, "Performance Pay and Top Management Incentives," *Journal of Political Economy* 98 (1990): 225–264; Charles W. L. Hill and Phillip Phan, "CEO Tenure as a Determinant of CEO Pay," *Academy of Management Journal* 34 (1991): 707–717; H. L. Tosi and L. R. Gomez-Mejia, "CEO Compensation Monitoring and Firm Performance," *Academy of Management Journal* 37 (1994): 1002–1016; and Joseph F. Porac, James B. Wade, and Timothy G. Pollock, "Industry Categories and the Politics of the Comparable Firm in CEO Compensation," *Administrative Science Quarterly* 44 (1999): 112–144.

17. Ellen Goodman, "CEO Pay Cap: Why Not Try It for Size?" *Houston Chronicle*, April 18, 1999, p. 6.

18. For recent research on this issue, see Peter J. Lane, A. A. Cannella, and M. H. Lubatkin, "Agency Problems as Antecedents to Unrelated Mergers and Diversification: Amihud and Lev Reconsidered," *Strategic Management Journal* 19 (1998): 555–578.

19. E. T. Penrose, *The Theory of the Growth of the Firm* (London: Macmillan, 1958).

20. "Money Well Spent: Corporate Parties," *Economist*, November 1, 2003, p. 79.

21. G. Edmondson and L. Cohn, "How Parmalat Went Sour," *Business Week*, January 12, 2004, pp. 46–50. "Another Enron? Royal Dutch Shell," *Economist*, March 13, 2004, p. 71.

22. O. E. Williamson, *The Economic Institutions of Capitalism* (New York: Free Press, 1985).

23. Fama, "Agency Problems and the Theory of the Firm."

24. S. Finkelstein and R. D'Aveni, "CEO Duality as a Double Edged Sword," *Academy of Management Journal* 37 (1994): 1079–1108; B. Ram Baliga and R. C. Moyer, "CEO Duality and Firm Performance," *Strategic Management Journal* 17 (1996): 41–53; M. L. Mace, *Directors: Myth and Reality* (Cambridge, Mass.: Harvard University Press, 1971); S. C. Vance, *Corporate Leadership: Boards of Directors and Strategy* (New York: McGraw-Hill, 1983).

25. W. G. Lewellen, C. Eoderer, and A. Rosenfeld, "Merger Decisions and Executive Stock Ownership in Acquiring Firms," *Journal of Accounting and Economics* 7 (1985): 209–231.

26. C. W. L. Hill and S. A. Snell, "External Control, Corporate Strategy, and Firm Performance," *Strategic Management Journal* 9 (1988): 577–590.

27. Quoted in G. Morgenson, "Stock Options Are Not a Free Lunch," *Forbes*, May 18, 1998, pp. 212–217.

28. D. Henry and M. Conlin, "Too Much of a Good Incentive?" *Business Week*, March 4, 2002, pp. 38–39.

29. J. P. Walsh and R. D. Kosnik, "Corporate Raiders and Their Disciplinary Role in the Market for Corporate Control," *Academy of Management Journal* 36 (1993): 671–700.

30. R. S. Kaplan and D. P. Norton, "The Balanced Scorecard—Measures That Drive Performance," *Harvard Business Review* (January–February 1992): 71–79; Kaplan and Norton, *Strategy Maps*.

31. R. S. Kaplan and D. P. Norton, "Using the Balanced Scorecard as a Strategic Management System," *Harvard Business Review* (January–February 1996): 75–85; Kaplan and Norton, *Strategy Maps*.

32. R. S. Kaplan and D. P. Norton, "Putting the Balanced Scorecard to Work," *Harvard Business Review* (September–October 1993): 134–147; Kaplan and Norton, *Strategy Maps*.

33. Kaplan and Norton, "The Balanced Scorecard," p. 72.

34. *Sources:* "Why Honesty Is the Best Policy," *Economist*, March 9, 2002; "The Amazing Disintegrating Firm—Enron," *Economist*, December 8, 2001; Wendy Zellner et al., "The Fall of Enron," *Business Week*, December 17, 2001, pp. 30–40; Ken Brown et al., "Paper Trail: Andersen Fires Partner It Says Led Shredding of Enron Documents," *Wall Street Journal*, January 16, 2002, p. A1; Johnathan Weil, "Justice Department Finds Building a Case Against Lay Tough," *Wall Street Journal*, August 26, 2002, p. A3; Robert Bryce, *Pipe Dreams: Greed, Ego, and the Death of Enron* (New York: Public Affairs, 2002); J. R. Emshwiller et al., "Lay Strikes Back as Indictment Cites Narrow Role in Enron Fraud," *Wall Street Journal*, July 9, 2004, p. A1.

Chapter 12

1. A. Reinhardt, "Can Nokia Capture Mobile Workers?" *Business Week*, February 9, 2004, p.80.

2. D. Pringle, "Nokia Unveils a Major Shake-Up," *Wall Street Journal*, September 29, 2003, p. B6.

3. **www.nokia.com** (2004, 2005).

4. L. Smircich, "Concepts of Culture and Organizational Analysis," *Administrative Science Quarterly* 28 (1983): 339–358.

5. G. R. Jones and J. M. George, "The Experience and Evolution of Trust: Implications for Cooperation and Teamwork," *Academy of Management Review* 3 (1998): 531–546.

6. Ibid.

7. J. R. Galbraith, *Designing Complex Organizations* (Reading, Mass.: Addison-Wesley, 1973).

8. Alfred D. Chandler, *Strategy and Structure* (Cambridge, Mass.: MIT Press, 1962).

9. The discussion draws heavily on ibid. and B. R. Scott, *Stages of Corporate Development* (Cambridge, Mass.: Intercollegiate Clearing House, Harvard Business School, 1971).

10. R. L. Daft, *Organizational Theory and Design*, 3rd ed. (St. Paul, Minn.: West, 1986), p. 215.

11. Child, *Organization*, pp. 52–70

12. G. R. Jones and J. Butler, "Costs, Revenues, and Business Level Strategy," *Academy of Management Review* 13 (1988): 202–213; G. R. Jones and C. W. L. Hill, "Transaction Cost Analysis of Strategy-Structure Choice," *Strategic Management Journal* 9 1988): 159–172.

13. G. R. Jones, *Organizational Theory: Text and Cases* (Englewood Cliffs, N.J.: Prentice-Hall, 2000).

14. P. Blau, "A Formal Theory of Differentiation in Organizations," *American Sociological Review* 35 (1970): 684–695.

15. G. R. Jones, "Organization-Client Transactions and Organizational Governance Structures," *Academy of Management Journal* 30 (1987): 197–218.

16. S. McCartney, "Airline Industry's Top-Ranked Woman Keeps Southwest's Small-Fry Spirit Alive," *Wall Street Journal,* November 30, 1995, p. B1; **www.southwest.com**, 2005.

17. P. R. Lawrence and J. Lorsch, *Organization and Environment* (Boston: Division of Research, Harvard Business School, 1967), pp. 50–55.

18. Galbraith, *Designing Complex Organizations,* chap. 1; J. R. Galbraith and R. K. Kazanjian, *Strategy Implementation: Structure System and Process,* 2nd ed. (St. Paul, Minn.: West, 1986), chap. 7.

19. R. Simmons, "Strategic Orientation and Top Management Attention to Control Systems," *Strategic Management Journal* 12 (1991): 49–62.

20. R. Simmons, "How New Top Managers Use Control Systems as Levers of Strategic Renewal," *Strategic Management Journal* 15 (1994): 169–189.

21. W. G. Ouchi, "The Transmission of Control Through Organizational Hierarchy," *Academy of Management Journal* 21 (1978): 173–192; and W. H. Newman, *Constructive Control* (Englewood Cliffs, N.J.: Prentice-Hall, 1975).

22. E. Flamholtz, "Organizational Control Systems as a Managerial Tool," *California Management Review* (Winter 1979): 50–58.

23. O. E. Williamson, *Markets and Hierarchies: Analysis and Antitrust Implications* (New York: Free Press, 1975); and W. G. Ouchi, "Markets, Bureaucracies, and Clans," *Administrative Science Quarterly* 25 (1980): 129–141.

24. H. Mintzberg, *The Structuring of Organizations* (Englewood Cliffs, N.J.: Prentice-Hall, 1979), pp. 5–9.

25. E. E. Lawler III, *Motivation in Work Organizations* (Monterey, Calif.: Brooks/Cole, 1973); and Galbraith and Kazanjian, *Strategy Implementation,* chap. 6.

26. Smircich, "Concepts of Culture and Organizational Analysis."

27. General Electric, Harvard Business School Case #9-385-315 (1984).

28. Ouchi, "Markets, Bureaucracies, and Clans," p. 130.

29. Jones, *Organizational Theory.*

30. J. Van Maanen and E. H. Schein, "Towards a Theory of Organizational Socialization," in B. M. Staw (ed.), *Research in Organizational Behavior* (Greenwich, Conn.: JAI Press, 1979), pp. 1, 209–264.

31. G. R. Jones, "Socialization Tactics, Self-Efficacy, and Newcomers' Adjustments to Organizations," *Academy of Management Journal* 29 (1986): 262–279.

32. J. P. Kotter and J. L. Heskett, *Corporate Culture and Performance.*

33. T. J. Peters and R. H. Waterman, *In Search of Excellence: Lessons from America's Best-Run Companies* (New York: Harper & Row, 1982).

34. G. Hamel and C. K. Prahalad, "Strategic Intent," *Harvard Business Review* (May–June 1989): 64.

35. Galbraith and Kazanjian, *Strategy Implementation;* Child, *Organization;* R. Duncan, "What Is the Right Organization Structure?" *Organizational Dynamics* (Winter 1979): 59–80.

36. J. Pettet, "Wal-Mart Yesterday and Today," *Discount Merchandiser* (December 1995): 66–67; M. Reid, "Stores of Value," *Economist,* March 4, 1995, pp. ss5–ss7; M. Troy, "The Culture Remains the Constant," *Discount Store News,* June 8, 1998, pp. 95–98; **www.walmart.com.id.**, p. 39.

37. W. G. Ouchi, "The Relationship Between Organizational Structure and Organizational Control," *Administrative Science Quarterly* 22 (1977): 95–113.

38. R. Bunderi, "Intel Researchers Aim to Think Big While Staying Close to Development," *Research-Technology Management* (March–April 1998): 3–4.

39. K. M. Eisenhardt, "Control: Organizational and Economic Approaches," *Management Science* 16 (1985): 134–148.

40. Williamson, *Markets and Hierarchies.*

41. Lawrence and Lorsch, *Organization and Environment.*

42. K. Pope, "Dell Refocuses on Groundwork to Cope with Rocketing Sales," *Wall Street Journal,* June 18, 1987, 7–32.

43. Michael E. Porter, *Competitive Strategy: Techniques for Analyzing Industries and Competitors* (New York: Free Press, 1980); D. Miller, "Configurations of Strategy and Structure," *Strategic Management Journal* 7 (1986): 233–249.

44. D. Miller and P. H. Freisen, *Organizations: A Quantum View* (Englewood Cliffs, N.J.: Prentice-Hall, 1984).

45. J. Woodward, *Industrial Organization: Theory and Practice* (London: Oxford University Press, 1965); Lawrence and Lorsch, *Organization and Environment.*

46. R. E. White, "Generic Business Strategies, Organizational Context and Performance: An Empirical Investigation," *Strategic Management Journal* 7 (1986): 217–231.

47. Porter, *Competitive Strategy*; Miller, "Configurations of Strategy and Structure."

48. E. Deal and A. A. Kennedy, *Corporate Cultures* (Reading, Mass.: Addison-Wesley, 1985); "Corporate Culture," *Business Week*, October 27, 1980, pp. 148–160.

49. S. M. Davis and R. R. Lawrence, *Matrix* (Reading, Mass.:Addison-Wesley, 1977); J. R. Galbraith, "Matrix Organization Designs: How to Combine Functional and Project Forms," *Business Horizons* 14 (1971): 29–40.

50. Duncan, "What Is the Right Organizational Structure?"; Davis and Lawrence, *Matrix*.

51. D. Miller, "Configurations of Strategy and Structure," in R. E. Miles and C. C. Snow (eds.), *Organizational Strategy, Structure, and Process* (New York: McGraw-Hill, 1978).

52. G. D. Bruton, J. K. Keels, and C. L. Shook, "Downsizing the Firm: Answering the Strategic Questions," *Academy of Management Executive* (May 1996): 38–45.

53. M. Hammer and J. Champy, *Reengineering the Corporation* (New York: HarperCollins, 1993).

54. *Sources:* G. McWilliams, "Dell Looks for Ways to Rekindle the Fire It Had as an Upstart," *Wall Street Journal*, August 31, 2000, pp. A.1, A.8; "Dell Hopes to Lead Firm out of Desert," *Houston Chronicle*, September, 3, 2000, p. 4D; www.dell.com (2004, 2005).

Chapter 13

1. Alfred D. Chandler, *Strategy and Structure* (Cambridge, Mass.: MIT Press, 1962); O. E. Williamson, *Markets and Hierarchies* (New York: Free Press, 1975); L. Wrigley, "Divisional Autonomy and Diversification" (Ph.D. diss., Harvard Business School, 1970).

2. R. P. Rumelt, *Strategy, Structure, and Economic Performance* (Boston: Division of Research, Harvard Business School, 1974); B. R. Scott, *Stages of Corporate Development* (Cambridge, Mass.: Intercollegiate Clearing House, Harvard Business School, 1971); Williamson, *Markets and Hierarchies.*

3. A. P. Sloan, *My Years at General Motors* (Garden City, N.Y.: Doubleday, 1946); A. Taylor III, "Can GM Remodel Itself?" *Fortune*, January 13, 1992, pp. 26–34; W. Hampton and J. Norman, "General Motors: What Went Wrong?" *Business Week*, March 16, 1987, pp. 102–110; www.gm.com (2002). The quotations are on pp. 46 and 50 in Sloan, *My Years at General Motors.*

4. The discussion draws on each of the sources cited in endnotes 20–27 and on G. R. Jones and C. W. L. Hill, "Transaction Cost Analysis of Strategy-Structure Choice," *Strategic Management Journal* 9 (1988): 159–172.

5. H. O. Armour and D. J. Teece, "Organizational Structure and Economic Performance: A Test of the Multidivisional Hypothesis," *Bell Journal of Economics* 9 (1978): 106–122.

6. Sloan, *My Years at General Motors.*

7. C. Soloman, "Amoco to Cut More Jobs and Radically Alter Its Structure," *Wall Street Journal*, July 22, 1995, p. B4; "Shell Reorganizes for Speed and Profit," *Oil and Gas Journal*, December 21, 1998, p. 31.

8. Jones and Hill, "Transaction Cost Analysis of Strategy-Structure Choice." *Strategic Management Journal* 9 (1988): 159–172.

9. Ibid.

10. R. A. D'Aveni and D. J. Ravenscraft, "Economies of Integration Versus Bureaucracy Costs: Does Vertical Integration Improve Performance?" *Academy of Management Journal* 5 (1994): 1167–1206.

11. P. R. Lawrence and J. Lorsch, *Organization and Environment* (Boston: Division of Research, Harvard Business School, 1967); J. R. Galbraith, *Designing Complex Organizations* (Reading, Mass.: Addison-Wesley, 1973); Michael Porter, *Competitive Advantage: Creating and Sustaining Superior Performance* (New York: Free Press, 1985).

12. P. R. Nayyar, "Performance Effects of Information Asymmetry and Economies of Scope in Diversified Service Firm," *Academy of Management Journal* 36 (1993): 28–57.

13. www.hp.com (2002).

14. L. R. Gomez-Mejia, "Structure and Process of Diversification, Compensation Strategy, and Performance," *Strategic Management Journal* 13 (1992): 381–397.

15. J. Stopford and L. Wells, *Managing the Multinational Enterprise* (London: Longman, 1972).

16. C. A. Bartlett and S. Ghoshal, *Managing Across Borders: The Transnational Solution* (Cambridge, Mass.: Harvard Business School, 1991).

17. R. A. Burgelman, "Managing the New Venture Division: Research Findings and the Implications for Strategic Management," *Strategic Management Journal* 6 (1985): 39–54.

18. G. Imperato, "3M Expert Tells How to Run Meetings That Really Work," *Fast Company,* May 23, 1999, p. 18.

19. Burgelman, "Managing the New Venture Division."

20. R. A. Burgelman, "Corporate Entrepreneurship and Strategic Management: Insights from a Process Study," *Management Science* 29 (1983): 1349–1364.

21. R. Jones, "Towards a Positive Interpretation of Transaction Cost Theory: The Central Role of Entrepreneurship and Trust," in M. Hitt, R. E. Freeman, and J. S. Harrison (eds.), *Handbook of Strategic Management* (London: Blackwell, 2001), pp. 208–228.

22. M. Prendergast, "Is Coke Turning into a Mickey Mouse Outfit?" *Wall Street Journal,* March 5, 2001, p. A.22.

23. M. S. Salter and W. A. Weinhold, *Diversification Through Acquisition* (New York: Free Press, 1979).

24. F. T. Paine and D. J. Power, "Merger Strategy: An Examination of Drucker's Five Rules for Successful Acquisitions," *Strategic Management Journal* 5 (1984): 99–110.

25. H. Singh and C. A. Montgomery, "Corporate Acquisitions and Economic Performance," unpublished manuscript, 1984.

26. B. Worthen, "Nestlé's ERP Odyssey," *CIO,* May 15, 2002, pp. 1–5.

27. G. D. Bruton, B. M. Oviatt, and M. A. White, "Performance of Acquisitions of Distressed Firms," *Academy of Management Journal* 4 (1994): 972–989.

28. T. Dewett and G. R. Jones, "The Role of Information Technology in the Organization: A Review, Model, and Assessment," *Journal of Management* 27 (2001): 313–346.

29. M. E. Porter, *Competitive Strategy* (New York: Free Press, 1980).

30. Rucker, 2000.

31. Hamel and Prahalad, "Strategic Intent."

32. Ibid.

33. "Andersen's Androids," *Economist,* May 4, 1996, p. 72.

34. Fulk and DeSanctis, 1995.

35. G. S. Capowski, "Designing a Corporate Identity," *Management Review* (June 1993): 37–38.

36. J. Marcia, "Just Doing It," *Distribution* (January 1995): 36–40.

37. *Sources:* M. Hays, "Compaq Maps Future," *Informationweek,* June 17, 1998, p. 14; A. Taylor III, "Compaq Looks Inside for Salvation," *Fortune,* August 16, pp. 124–128; www.compaq.com, press release (September 1999); www.hp.com (2002).

Box Source Notes

Chapter 1

a. *Sources:* Interviews by Charles Hill; R. J. Herbold, "Inside Microsoft: Balancing Creativity and Discipline," *Harvard Business Review* (January 2002), Vol 80, Number 1: 72–79.

b. *Source:* Interviews by Charles Hill.

c. *Source:* M. Dickson, "Back to the Future," *Financial Times,* May 30, 1994, p. 7. **www.3m.com/profile/looking/mcknight.jhtml.**

d. *Sources:* D. Priest and D. Linzer, "Panel Condemns Iraq Prewar Intelligence," *Washington Post,* July 10, 2004, p. A1; D. Jehl, "Senators Assail CIA Judgments of Iraq's Arms as Deeply Flawed," *New York Times,* July 10, 2004, p. A1; M. Isikoff, "The Dots Never Existed," *Newsweek,* July 19, 2004, pp. 36–40.

Chapter 2

a. *Sources:* A. Kaplan, "Cott Corporation," *Beverage World,* June 15, 2004, p. 32; J. Popp, "2004 Soft Drink Report," *Beverage Industry,* March 2004, Vol 95, Issue 3: pp. 13–18; L. Sparks, "From Coca-Colonization to Copy Catting: The Cott Corporation and Retailers Brand Soft Drinks in the UK and US," *Agribusiness,* March 1997, Vol 13, Issue 2: pp. 153–127; E. Cherney, "After Flat Sales, Cott Challenges Pepsi, Coca-Cola," *Wall Street Journal,* January 8, 2003, pp. B1, B8.

b. *Sources:* G. Morgenson, "Denial in Battle Creek," *Forbes,* October 7, 1996, p. 44; J. Muller, "Thinking out of the Cereal Box," *Business Week,* January 15, 2001, p. 54; A. Merrill, "General Mills Increases Prices," *Star Tribune,* June 5, 2001, p. 1D; S. Reyes, "Big G, Kellogg Attempt to Berry Each Other," *Brandweek,* October 7, 2002, p. 8.

c. *Sources:* "How Big Can it Grow—Wal-Mart," *Economist,* April 17, 2004, pp. 74–76; H. Gilman, "The Most Underrated CEO Ever," *Fortune,* April 5, 2004, pp. 242–247; K. Schaffner, "Psst! Want to Sell to Wal-Mart?" *Apparel Industry Magazine,* August 1996, pp. 18–20.

Chapter 3

a. *Sources:* R. Langreth, "High Anxiety: Rivals Threaten Prozac's Reign," *Wall Street Journal,* May 9, 1996, pp. B1–B2; G. Harris, "Drug Prices—Why They Keep Soaring," *Wall Street Journal,* April 18, 2002, p. A1; Pfizer 10-K report.

b. *Sources:* M. Troy, "Logistics Still the Corner Stone of Competitive Advantage," *DSN Retailing Today,* June 9, 2003, pp. 109–110; "How Big Can it Grow?" *Economist,* April 17, 2004, pp. 74–78; "Trial by Checkout," *Economist,* June 26, 2004, pp. 74–76; company 10-K reports.

c. *Sources:* M. Brelis, "Simple Strategy Makes Southwest a Model for Success," *Boston Globe,* November 5, 2000, p. F1; M. Trottman, "At Southwest, New CEO Sits in the Hot Seat," *Wall Street Journal,* July 19, 2004, p. B1; J. Helyar, "Southwest Finds Trouble in the Air," *Fortune,* August 9, 2004, p. 38; Southwest Airlines 10-K 2001.

d. *Sources:* D. Miller, *The Icarus Paradox* (New York: HarperBusiness, 1990); P. D. Llosa, "We Must Know What We Are Doing," *Fortune,* November 14, 1994, p. 68.

e. *Source:* Stephen Manes and Paul Andrews, *Gates* (New York: Simon & Schuster, 1993).

Chapter 4

a. *Sources:* G. Stalk and T. M. Hout, *Competing Against Time* (New York: Free Press, 1990); D. Miller, *The Icarus Paradox* (New York: HarperBusiness, 1990).

b. *Sources:* M. A. Cusumano, *The Japanese Automobile Industry* (Cambridge, Mass.: Harvard University Press, 1989); Ohno Taiichi, *Toyota Production System* (Cambridge, Mass.: Productivity Press, 1990); J. P. Womack, D. T. Jones, and D. Roos, *The Machine That Changed the World* (New York: Rawson Associates, 1990).

c. *Sources:* M. Prior, "Major Office Suppliers Hone Supply Chain Efficiencies," *DSN Retailing,* November 5, 2001, pp. 27–31; B. Albright, "Office

Depot Consolidates Supply Chain Operations," *Frontline Solutions,* March 2004, Volume 5, Issue 4: pp. 38–40.

d. *Sources:* Sam Walton, *Made in America* (Sam Walton, 1992); S. Maich, "Wal-Mart's Mid Life Crisis," *Maclean's,* August 23, 2004, p. 45; "The People Make It All Happen," *Chain Store Age,* October 1999, Vol 75, Issue 13: pp. 103–106; **www.walmartstores.com.**

e. *Sources:* C. H. Deutsch, "Six-Sigma Enlightenment," *New York Times,* December 7, 1998, p. 1; J. J. Barshay, "The Six-Sigma Story," *Star Tribune,* June 14, 1999, p. 1; D. D. Bak, "Rethinking Industrial Drives," *Electrical/Electronics Technology,* November 30, 1998, p. 58.

f. *Sources:* I. R. Lazarus and K. Butler, "The Promise of Six-Sigma," *Managed Healthcare Executive* (October 2001): 22–26; D. Scalise, "Six-Sigma, the Quest for Quality," *Hospitals and Health Networks* (December 2001): 41–44; S. F. Gale, "Building Frameworks for Six Sigma Success," *Workforce* (May 2003), Vol 82, Issue 5: 64–69.

Chapter 5

a. *Sources:* D. McGinn, "Is This Any Way to Run an Airline?" *Newsweek,* October 4, 2004, pp. E14–E19; E. Torbenson, "Budget Carriers Rule the European Skies," *Dallas Morning News,* September 22, 2004, p. D1; **www.ryanair.com** (2004).

b. *Sources:* **www.llbean.com** (2004); D. McGinn, "Swimming Upstream," *Newsweek,* October 1, 2004, pp. E10–E12.

c. *Source:* **www.toyotausa.com** (2004).

d. *Sources:* "The Holiday Inns Trip: A Breeze for Decades, Bumpy Ride in the 1980s," *Wall Street Journal,* February 11, 1987, p. 1; Holiday Inns, Annual Report (1985); U.S. Bureau of Labor Statistics, *U.S. Industrial Output* (Washington, D.C.: U.S. Government Printing Office, 1986); Mark Gleason and Alan Salomon, "Fallon's Challenge: Make Holiday Inn More 'In,'" *Advertising Age,* September 2, 1996, p. 14; Julie Miller, "Amenities Range from Snacks to Technology," *Hotel and Motel Management,* July 3, 1996, pp. 38–40; **www.sixcontinenthotels.com** (2005).

Chapter 6

a. *Sources:* **www.clearchannel.com** (2004); A. W. Mathews, "From a Distance: A Giant Chain Is Per-

fecting the Art of Seeing Local," *Wall Street Journal,* February 25, 2002, pp. A1, A4.

b. *Sources:* **www.AOLTimeWarner.com** (2002, 2004); Kara Swisher, *aol.com* (New York: Random House, 1998).

c. *Sources:* **www.toysrus.com** (2002, 2004); M. Maremont and G. Bowens, "Brawls in Toyland," *Business Week,* December 21, 1992, pp. 36–37; S. Eads, "The Toys 'R' Us Empire Strikes Back," *Business Week,* June 7, 1999, pp. 55–59; **amazon.com** (2002).

d. *Sources:* **www.cocacola.com** (2004); **www.pepsico.com** (2004).

e. *Sources:* P. Haynes, "Western Electric Redux," *Forbes,* January 26, 1998, pp. 46–47.

Chapter 7

a. *Sources:* E. Ramstad, "DVD Makers Battle over Tech Standard," *Wall Street Journal,* November 9, 2000, p. B6; B. Dudley, "Dueling DVD-Recorder Formats Make Playing Discs a Challenge," *Seattle Times,* January 9, 2002, p. C3; K. Hun, "Consumers Early Casualties of the DVD Recorder Wars," *Chicago Tribune,* March 28, 2004, p. 2; H. Bray, "Stage Is Set for Another Format Fight," *Boston Globe,* March 22, 2004, p. D4.

b. *Sources:* M. Snider, "Ray Dolby, Audio Inventor," *USA Today,* December 28, 2000, p. D3; D. Dritas, "Dealerscope Hall of Fame: Ray Dolby," *Dealerscope* (January 2002): 74–76; J. Pinkerton, "At Dolby Laboratories: A Clean Audio Pipe," *Dealerscope* (December 2000): 33–34; Company history archived at **www.dolby.com**; L. Himelstein, "Dolby Gets Ready to Make a Big Noise," *Business Week,* February 9, 2004, p. 78.

c. *Sources:* Interviews by Charles W. L. Hill; SonoSite 10-K for 2003.

d. *Source:* M. Christensen, *The Innovator's Dilemma* (Boston: Harvard Business School Press, 1997).

Chapter 8

a. *Sources:* "Lessons from the Frozen North," *Economist,* October 8, 1994, pp. 76–77; G. Edmondson, "Grabbing Markets from the Giants," *Business Week* (Special Issue: 21st Century Capitalism, 1995), p. 156; Q. Hardy, "Bypassing the Bells—A Wireless World," *Wall Street Journal,* September 21, 1998, p. R16; Q. Hardy and G. Naik, "Nokia Takes the Lead as Wireless Makers Sell 162.9 Million Phones in 1998," *Wall Street Journal,* February 8, 1999, p. A1; "A Finnish Fable," *Economist,* October

14, 2000; M. Newman, "The U.S. Starts to Catch Up," *Wall Street Journal,* September 23, 2002, p. R6; D. Pringle, "How Nokia Thrives by Breaking the Rules," *Wall Street Journal,* January 3, 2003, p. A7; and Nokia website at **www.nokia.com.**

b. *Sources:* A. Lillo, "Wal-Mart Says Global Going Good," *Home Textiles Today,* September 15, 2003, pp. 12–13; A. de Rocha and L. A. Dib, "The Entry of Wal-Mart into Brazil," *International Journal of Retail and Distribution Management* 30 (2002): 61–73; Anonymous, "Wal-Mart: Mexico's Biggest Retailer," *Chain Store Age,* June 2001, pp. 52–54; M. N. Hamilton, "Global Food Fight," *Washington Post,* November 19, 2000, p. H1; "Global Strategy—Why Tesco Will Beat Carrefour," *Retail Week,* April 6, 2001, p. 14; "Shopping All Over the World," *Economist,* June 19, 1999, pp. 59–61; M. Flagg, "In Asia, Going to the Grocery Increasingly Means Heading for a European Retail Chain," *Wall Street Journal,* April 24, 2001, p. A21; and Wal-Mart website.

c. *Sources:* M. Gunther, "MTV's Passage to India," *Fortune,* August 9, 2004, pp. 117–122; B. Pulley and A. Tanzer, "Sumner's Gemstone," *Forbes,* February 21, 2000, pp. 107–111; K. Hoffman, "Youth TV's Old Hand Prepares for the Digital Challenge," *Financial Times,* February 18, 2000, p. 8; presentation by Sumner M. Redstone, chairman and CEO, Viacom Inc., delivered to Salomon Smith Barney 11th Annual Global Entertainment Media, Telecommunications Conference, Scottsdale, AZ, January 8, 2001, archived at **www.viacom.com**; Viacom 10-K Statement, 2003.

d. *Sources:* "Japan's Big Bang. Enter Merrill," *Economist,* January 3, 1998, p. 72; J. P. Donlon, "Merrill Cinch," *Chief Executive* (March 1998): 28–32; D. Holley, "Merrill Lynch to Open 31 Offices Throughout Japan," *Los Angeles Times,* February 13, 1998, p. D1; A. Rowley, "Merrill Thunders into Japan," *Banker* (March 1998): 6; Staff Reporter, "Hard Times: Foreign Brokers in Japan," *Economist,* February 23, 2002, pp. 78–79; and Merrill Lynch's website, **www.ml.com.**

Chapter 9

a. *Sources:* **www.hp.com** (2004); **www.dell.com** (2004); P. Burrows and A. Park, "Compaq and HP: What's an Investor to Do?" *Business Week,* March 18, 2002, pp. 62–64; "Carly v Walter," *Economist,* January 26, 2002; "Sheltering from the Storm," *Economist,* September 8, 2001.

b. *Sources:* Y. J. Dreazen, G. Ip, and N. Kulish, "Why the Sudden Rise in the Urge to Merge and Create Oligopolies?" *Wall Street Journal,* February 25, 2002, p. A1; L. Kowalczyk, "A Matter of Style," *Boston Globe,* February 22, 2002, p. C1.

c. *Source:* J-F. Hennart, "Upstream Vertical Integration in the Aluminum and Tin Industries," *Journal of Economic Behavior and Organization* 9 (1988): 281–299.

d. *Source:* J. H. Dyer, "How Chrysler Created an American Keiretsu," *Harvard Business Review* (July–August 1996): 42–56.

e. *Sources:* S. N. Mehta, "Cisco Fractures Its Own Fairy Tale," *Fortune,* May 14, 2001, pp. 104–112; P. Kaihla, "Inside Cisco's $2 Billion Blunder," *Business 2.0* (March 2002), available at **www.business2.com**.

Chapter 10

a. *Sources:* W. E. Coyne, "How 3M Innovates for Long-Term Growth," *Research Technology Management* (March–April 2001): 21–24; 3M's 2004 10-K form.

b. *Source:* R. Arensman, "Intel's Second Try," *Electronic Business* (March 2001): 62–70; Intel 10-K Report, 2001.

c. *Sources:* M. Murray and J. Rebelled, "Mellon Bank Corp: One Big Unhappy Family," *Wall Street Journal,* April 28, 1995, pp. B1, B4; K. Holland, "A Bank Eat Bank World—with Indigestion," *Business Week,* October 30, 1995, p. 130.

Chapter 11

a. *Sources:* J. E. Rigdon and J. S. Lubin, "Why Morrison Board Fired Agee," *Wall Street Journal,* February 13, 1995, p. B1; C. McCoy, "Worst Five and One Year Performer: Morrison Knudson," *Wall Street Journal,* February 29, 1996, p. R2; "Morrison Knudson Settles Most Shareholder Lawsuits," *Wall Street Journal,* September 21, 1995, p. B8; J. E. Rigdon, "William Agee to Leave Morrison Knudson," *Wall Street Journal,* February 2, 1995, p. B1.

b. *Sources:* S. Tully, "A House Divided," *Fortune,* December 18, 2000, pp. 264–275; J. Chaffin, "Sotheby's Ex CEO Spared Jail Sentence," *Financial Times,* April 30, 2002, p. 10; T. Thorncroft, "A Courtroom Battle of the Vanities," *Financial Times,* November 3, 2001, p. 3.

c. *Sources:* J. Guidera, "Probe of Computer Associates Centers on Firm's Revenues," *Wall Street Journal,* May 20, 2002,
pp. A3, 15; Ronna Abramson, "Computer Associates Probe Focus on 1998, 1999 Revenue," *The Street.Com,* May 20, 2002; C. Forelle, M. Maremont, and G. Fields, "U.S. Indicts Sanjay Kumar for Fraud, Lies," *Wall Street Journal,* September 23, 2004, p. A1.

d. *Sources:* S. Holt, "Wal-Mart Workers Suit Wins Class Action Status," *Seattle Times,* October 9, 2004, pp. E1, E4; C. Daniels, "Women v Wal-Mart," *Fortune,* July 21, 2003, pp. 79–82; C. R. Gentry, "Off the Clock," *Chain Store Age,* February 2003, pp. 33–36; M. Grimm, "Wal-Mart Uber Alles," *American Demographic,* October 2003, pp. 38–42.

Chapter 12

a. **www.unionpacific.com** (2005). 95, p. B.1.

b. **www.cypress.com,** press release, 1998; B. Dumaine, "The Bureaucracy Busters," *Fortune,* June 17, 1991, p. 46, pp. 5–9.

c. J. Pettet, "Wal-Mart Yesterday and Today," *Discount Merchandiser* (December 1995): 66–67; M. Reed, "Stories of Value" *Economist,* March 4, 1995, pp. ss5–ss7; M. Troy, "The Culture Remains the Constant," *Discount Store News,* June 8, 1998, pp. 95–98; **www.walmart.com.**

Chapter 13

a. *Source:* **www.bp.com** (2004).

b. *Sources:* A. Edgecliffe-Johnson, "Nestlé and Pillsbury Forge Ice Cream Alliance in U.S.," *Financial Times,* August 20, 1999, p. 2; B. Worthen, "Nestlé's ERP Odyssey," *CIO,* May 15, 2002, pp. 1–5.

c. *Source:* M. Moeller, "Oracle: Practicing What It Preaches," *Business Week,* August 16, 1999, pp. 1–5.

d. *Source:* "Business Link in the Global Chain," *Economist,* June 2, 2001, pp. 62–63.

Introduction:
Analyzing a Case Study and
Writing a Case Study Analysis

What Is Case Study Analysis?

Case study analysis is an integral part of a course in strategic management. The purpose of a case study is to provide students with experience of the strategic management problems that actual organizations face. A case study presents an account of what happened to a business or industry over a number of years. It chronicles the events that managers had to deal with, such as changes in the competitive environment, and charts the managers' response, which usually involved changing the business- or corporate-level strategy. The cases in this book cover a wide range of issues and problems that managers have had to confront. Some cases are about finding the right business-level strategy to compete in changing conditions. Some are about companies that grew by acquisition, with little concern for the rationale behind their growth, and how growth by acquisition affected their future profitability. Each case is different because each organization is different. The underlying thread in all cases, however, is the use of strategic management techniques to solve business problems.

Cases prove valuable in a strategic management course for several reasons. First, cases provide you, the student, with experience of organizational problems that you probably have not had the opportunity to experience firsthand. In a relatively short period of time, you will have the chance to appreciate and analyze the problems faced by many different companies and to understand how managers tried to deal with them.

Second, cases illustrate the theory and content of strategic management. The meaning and implications of this information are made clearer when they are applied to case studies. The theory and concepts help reveal what is going on in the companies studied and allow you to evaluate the solutions that specific companies adopted to deal with their problems. Consequently, when you analyze cases, you will be like a detective who, with a set of conceptual tools, probes what happened and what or who was responsible and then marshals the evidence that provides the solution. Top managers enjoy the thrill of testing their problem-solving abilities in the real world. It is important to remember that no one knows what the right answer is. All that managers can do is to make the best guess. In fact, managers say repeatedly that they are happy if they are right only half the time in solving strategic problems. Strategic management is an uncertain game, and using cases to see how theory can be put into practice is one way of improving your skills of diagnostic investigation.

Third, case studies provide you with the opportunity to participate in class and to gain experience in presenting your ideas to others. Instructors may sometimes call on students as a group to identify what is going on in a case, and through classroom discussion the issues in and solutions to the case problem will reveal themselves. In such a situation, you will have to organize your views and conclusions so that you can present them to the class. Your classmates may have analyzed the issues differently from you, and they will want you to argue your points before they will accept your conclusions, so be prepared for debate. This mode of discussion is an example of the dialectical approach to decision making. This is how decisions are made in the actual business world.

Instructors also may assign an individual, but more commonly a group, to analyze the case before the whole class. The individual or group probably will be responsible for a thirty- to forty-minute presentation of the case to the class. That presentation must cover the issues posed, the problems facing the company, and a series of recommendations for resolving the problems. The discussion then will be thrown open to the class, and you will have to defend your ideas. Through such discussions and presentations, you will experience how to convey your ideas effectively to others. Remember that a great deal of managers' time is spent in these kinds of situations: presenting their ideas and engaging in discussion with other managers who have their own views about what is going on. Thus, you will experience in the classroom the actual process of strategic management, and this will serve you well in your future career.

If you work in groups to analyze case studies, you also will learn about the group process involved in working as a team. When people work in groups, it is often difficult to schedule time and allocate responsibility for the case analysis. There are always group members who shirk their responsibilities and group members who are so sure of their own ideas that they try to dominate the group's analysis. Most of the strategic management takes place in groups, however, and it is best if you learn about these problems now.

Analyzing a Case Study

The purpose of the case study is to let you apply the concepts of strategic management when you analyze the issues facing a specific company. To analyze a case study, therefore, you must examine closely the issues confronting the company. Most often you will need to read the case several times—once to grasp the overall picture of what is happening to the company and then several times more to discover and grasp the specific problems.

Generally, detailed analysis of a case study should include eight areas:

1. The history, development, and growth of the company over time

2. The identification of the company's internal strengths and weaknesses

3. The nature of the external environment surrounding the company

4. A SWOT analysis

5. The kind of corporate-level strategy that the company is pursuing

6. The nature of the company's business-level strategy

7. The company's structure and control systems and how they match its strategy

8. Recommendations

To analyze a case, you need to apply the concepts taught in this course to each of these areas. To help you further, we next offer a summary of the steps you can take to analyze the case material for each of the eight points we just noted:

1. *Analyze the company's history, development, and growth.* A convenient way to investigate how a company's past strategy and structure affect it in the present is to chart the critical incidents in its history—that is, the events that were the most unusual or the most essential for its development into the company it is today. Some of the events have to do with its founding, its initial products, how it makes new-product market decisions, and how it developed and chose functional competencies to pursue. Its entry into new businesses and shifts in its main lines of business are also important milestones to consider.

2. *Identify the company's internal strengths and weaknesses.* Once the historical profile is completed, you can begin the SWOT analysis. Use all the incidents you have charted to develop an account of the company's strengths and weaknesses as they have emerged historically. Examine each of the value creation functions of the company, and identify the functions in which the company is currently strong and currently weak. Some companies might be weak in marketing; some might be strong in research and development. Make lists of these strengths and weaknesses. The SWOT Checklist (Table 1) gives examples of what might go in these lists.

3. *Analyze the external environment.* To identify environmental opportunities and threats, apply all the concepts on industry and macroenvironments to analyze the environment the company is confronting. Of particular importance at the industry level are Porter's five forces model and the stage of the life cycle model. Which factors in the macroenvironment will appear salient depends on the specific company being analyzed. Use each factor in turn (for instance, demographic factors) to see whether it is relevant for the company in question.

   Having done this analysis, you will have generated both an analysis of the company's environment and a list of opportunities and threats. The SWOT Checklist table also lists some common environmental opportunities and threats that you may look for, but the list you generate will be specific to your company.

4. *Evaluate the SWOT analysis.* Having identified the company's external opportunities and threats as well as its internal strengths and weaknesses, consider what your findings mean. You need to balance strengths and weaknesses against opportunities and threats. Is the company in an overall strong competitive position? Can it continue to pursue its current business- or corporate-level strategy profitably? What can the company do to turn weaknesses into strengths and threats into opportunities? Can it develop new functional, business, or corporate strategies to accomplish this change? *Never merely generate the SWOT analysis and then put it aside.* Because it provides a succinct summary of the company's condition, a good SWOT analysis is the key to all the analyses that follow.

5. *Analyze corporate-level strategy.* To analyze corporate-level strategy, you first need to define the company's mission and goals. Sometimes the mission and goals are stated explicitly in the case; at other times, you will have to infer them from available information. The information you need to collect to find out the company's corporate strategy includes such factors as its lines of business and the nature of its subsidiaries and acquisitions. It is important to analyze the relationship among the company's businesses. Do they trade or exchange resources? Are there gains to be achieved from synergy? Alternatively, is the company just running a portfolio of investments? This analysis should enable you to define the corporate strategy that the company is pursuing (for example, related or unrelated diversification, or a

TABLE 1

A SWOT Checklist

Potential internal strengths	Potential internal weaknesses
Many product lines?	Obsolete, narrow product lines?
Broad market coverage?	Rising manufacturing costs?
Manufacturing competence?	Decline in R&D innovations?
Good marketing skills?	Poor marketing plan?
Good materials management systems?	Poor material management systems?
R&D skills and leadership?	Loss of customer good will?
Information system competencies?	Inadequate human resources?
Human resource competencies?	Inadequate information systems?
Brand name reputation?	Loss of brand name capital?
Portfolio management skills?	Growth without direction?
Cost of differentiation advantage?	Bad portfolio management?
New-venture management expertise?	Loss of corporate direction?
Appropriate management style?	Infighting among divisions?
Appropriate organizational structure?	Loss of corporate control?
Appropriate control systems?	Inappropriate organizational
Ability to manage strategic change?	structure and control systems?
Well-developed corporate strategy?	High conflict and politics?
Good financial management?	Poor financial management?
Others?	Others?
Potential environmental opportunities	Potential environmental threats
Expand core business(es)?	Attacks on core business(es)?
Exploit new market segments?	Increases in domestic competition?
Widen product range?	Increase in foreign competition?
Extend cost or differentiation advantage?	Change in consumer tastes?
Diversify into new growth businesses?	Fall in barriers to entry?
Expand into foreign markets?	Rise in new or substitute products?
Apply R&D skills in new areas?	Increase in industry rivalry?
Enter new related businesses?	New forms of industry competition?
Vertically integrate forward?	Potential for takeover?
Vertically integrate backward?	Existence of corporate raiders?
Enlarge corporate portfolio?	Increase in regional competition?
Overcome barriers to entry?	Changes in demographic factors?
Reduce rivalry among competitors?	Changes in economic factors?
Make profitable new acquisitions?	Downturn in economy?
Apply brand name capital in new areas?	Rising labor costs?
Seek fast market growth?	Slower market growth?
Others?	Others?

combination of both) and to conclude whether the company operates in just one core business. Then, using your SWOT analysis, debate the merits of this strategy. Is it appropriate given the environment the company is in? Could a change in corporate strategy provide the company with new opportunities or transform a weakness into a strength? For example, should the company diversify from its core business into new businesses?

Other issues should be considered as well. How and why has the company's strategy changed over time? What is the claimed rationale for any changes? Often, it is a good idea to analyze the company's businesses or products to assess its situation and identify which divisions contribute the most to or detract from its competitive advantage. It is also useful to explore how the company has built its portfolio over time. Did it acquire new businesses, or did it internally venture its own? All of these factors provide clues about the company and indicate ways of improving its future performance.

6. *Analyze business-level strategy.* Once you know the company's corporate-level strategy and have done the SWOT analysis, the next step is to identify the company's business-level strategy. If the company is a single-business company, its business-level strategy is identical to its corporate-level strategy. If the company is in many businesses, each business will have its own business-level strategy. You will need to identify the company's generic competitive strategy—differentiation, low cost, or focus—and its investment strategy, given its relative competitive position and the stage of the life cycle. The company also may market different products using different business-level strategies. For example, it may offer a low-cost product range and a line of differentiated products. Be sure to give a full account of a company's business-level strategy to show how it competes.

    Identifying the functional strategies that a company pursues to build competitive advantage through superior efficiency, quality, innovation, and customer responsiveness and to achieve its business-level strategy is very important. The SWOT analysis will have provided you with information on the company's functional competencies. You should investigate its production, marketing, or research and development strategy further to gain a picture of where the company is going. For example, pursuing a low-cost or a differentiation strategy successfully requires very different sets of competencies. Has the company developed the right ones? If it has, how can it exploit them further? Can it pursue both a low-cost and a differentiation strategy simultaneously?

    The SWOT analysis is especially important at this point if the industry analysis, particularly Porter's model, has revealed threats to the company from the environment. Can the company deal with these threats? How should it change its business-level strategy to counter them? To evaluate the potential of a company's business-level strategy, you must first perform a thorough SWOT analysis that captures the essence of its problems.

    Once you complete this analysis, you will have a full picture of the way the company is operating and be in a position to evaluate the potential of its strategy. Thus, you will be able to make recommendations concerning the pattern of its future actions. However, first you need to consider strategy implementation, or the way the company tries to achieve its strategy.

7. *Analyze structure and control systems.* The aim of this analysis is to identify what structure and control systems the company is using to implement its strategy and to evaluate whether that structure is the appropriate one for the company. Different corporate and business strategies require different structures. You need to determine the *degree of fit between the company's strategy and structure.* For example, does the company have the right level of vertical differentiation (e.g., does it have the appropriate number of levels in the hierarchy or decentralized control?) or horizontal differentiation (does it use a functional structure when it should be using a product structure?)? Similarly, is the company using the right integration or control systems to manage its operations? Are managers being appropriately rewarded? Are the right rewards in place for encouraging cooperation among divisions? These are all issues to consider.

In some cases, there will be little information on these issues, whereas in others there will be a lot. In analyzing each case, you should gear the analysis toward its most salient issues. For example, organizational conflict, power, and politics will be important issues for some companies. Try to analyze why problems in these areas are occurring. Do they occur because of bad strategy formulation or because of bad strategy implementation?

Organizational change is an issue in many cases because the companies are attempting to alter their strategies or structures to solve strategic problems. Thus, as part of the analysis, you might suggest an action plan that the company in question could use to achieve its goals. For example, you might list in a logical sequence the steps the company would need to follow to alter its business-level strategy from differentiation to focus.

8. *Make recommendations.* The quality of your recommendations is a direct result of the thoroughness with which you prepared the case analysis. Recommendations are directed at solving whatever strategic problem the company is facing and increasing its future profitability. Your recommendations should be in line with your analysis; that is, they should follow logically from the previous discussion. For example, your recommendation generally will center on the specific ways of changing functional, business, and corporate strategies and organizational structure and control to improve business performance. The set of recommendations will be specific to each case, and so it is difficult to discuss these recommendations here. Such recommendations might include an increase in spending on specific research and development projects, the divesting of certain businesses, a change from a strategy of unrelated to related diversification, an increase in the level of integration among divisions by using task forces and teams, or a move to a different kind of structure to implement a new business-level strategy. Make sure your recommendations are mutually consistent and written in the form of an action plan. The plan might contain a timetable that sequences the actions for changing the company's strategy and a description of how changes at the corporate level will necessitate changes at the business level and subsequently at the functional level.

After following all these stages, you will have performed a thorough analysis of the case and will be in a position to join in class discussion or present your ideas to the class, depending on the format used by your professor. Remember that you must tailor your analysis to suit the specific issue discussed in your case. In some cases, you might completely omit one of the steps in the analysis because it is not relevant to the situation you are considering. You must be sensitive to the needs of the case and not apply the framework we have discussed in this section blindly. The framework is meant only as a guide, not as an outline.

Writing a Case Study Analysis

Often, as part of your course requirements, you will need to present a written case analysis. This may be an individual or a group report. Whatever the situation, there are certain guidelines to follow in writing a case analysis that will improve the evaluation your work will receive from your instructor. Before we discuss these guidelines and before you use them, make sure that they do not conflict with any directions your instructor has given you.

The structure of your written report is critical. Generally, if you follow the steps for analysis discussed in the previous section, *you already will have a good structure for your written discussion.* All reports begin with an *introduction* to the case. In it, outline briefly what the company does, how it developed historically, what problems it is experiencing, and how you are going to approach the issues in the case write-up. Do this sequentially by writing, for example, "First, we discuss the environment of Company X. . . . Third, we discuss Company X's business-level strategy. . . . Last, we provide recommendations for turning around Company X's business."

In the second part of the case write-up, the *strategic analysis* section, do the SWOT analysis, analyze and discuss the nature and problems of the company's business-level and corporate strategies, and then analyze its structure and control systems. Make sure you use plenty of headings and subheadings to structure your analysis. For example, have separate sections on any important conceptual tool you use. Thus, you might have a section on Porter's five forces model as part of your analysis of the environment. You might offer a separate section on portfolio techniques when analyzing a company's corporate strategy. Tailor the sections and subsections to the specific issues of importance in the case.

In the third part of the case write-up, present your *solutions and recommendations.* Be comprehensive, and make sure they are in line with the previous analysis so that the recommendations fit together and move logically from one to the next. The recommendations section is very revealing because your instructor will have a good idea of how much work you put into the case from the quality of your recommendations.

Following this framework will provide a good structure for most written reports, though it must be shaped to fit the individual case being considered. Some cases are about excellent companies experiencing no problems. In such instances, it is hard to write recommendations. Instead, you can focus on analyzing why the company is doing so well, using that analysis to structure the discussion. Following are some minor suggestions that can help make a good analysis even better:

1. Do not repeat in summary form large pieces of factual information from the case. The instructor has read the case and knows what is going on. Rather, use the information in the case to illustrate your statements, defend your arguments, or make salient points. Beyond the brief introduction to the company, you must avoid being *descriptive*; instead, you must be *analytical.*

2. Make sure the sections and subsections of your discussion flow logically and smoothly from one to the next. That is, try to build on what has gone before so that the analysis of the case study moves toward a climax. This is particularly important for group analysis, because there is a tendency for people in a group to split up the work and say, "I'll do the beginning, you take the middle, and I'll do the end." The result is a choppy, stilted analysis; the parts do not flow from one to the next, and it is obvious to the instructor that no real group work has been done.

3. Avoid grammatical and spelling errors. They make your work look sloppy.

4. In some instances, cases dealing with well-known companies end in 1998 or 1999 because no later information was available when the case was written. If possible, do a search for more information on what has happened to the company in subsequent years.

Many libraries now have comprehensive web-based electronic data search facilities that offer such sources as *ABI/Inform, The Wall Street Journal Index,* the *F&S Index,* and the *Nexis-Lexis* databases. These enable you to identify any article that has been written in the business press on the company of your choice within the past few years. A number of nonelectronic data sources are also useful. For example, *F&S Predicasts* publishes an annual list of articles relating to major companies that appeared in the national and international business press. *S&P Industry Surveys* is a great source for basic industry data, and *Value Line Ratings and Reports* can contain good summaries of a firm's financial position and future prospects. You will also want to collect full financial information on the company. Again, this can be accessed from web-based electronic databases such as the Edgar database, which archives all forms that publicly quoted companies have to file with the Securities and Exchange Commission (SEC; e.g., 10-K filings can be accessed from the SEC's Edgar database). Most SEC forms for public companies can now be accessed from Internet-based financial sites, such as Yahoo's finance site (**http://finance.yahoo.com/**).

5. Sometimes instructors hand out questions for each case to help you in your analysis. Use these as a guide for writing the case analysis. They often illuminate the important issues that have to be covered in the discussion.

If you follow the guidelines in this section, you should be able to write a thorough and effective evaluation.

The Role of Financial Analysis in Case Study Analysis

An important aspect of analyzing a case study and writing a case study analysis is the role and use of financial information. A careful analysis of the company's financial condition immensely improves a case write-up. After all, financial data represent the concrete results of the company's strategy and structure. Although analyzing financial statements can be quite complex, a general idea of a company's financial position can be determined through the use of ratio analysis. Financial performance ratios can be calculated from the balance sheet and income statement. These ratios can be classified into five subgroups: profit ratios, liquidity ratios, activity ratios, leverage ratios, and shareholder-return ratios. These ratios should be compared with the industry average or the company's prior years of performance. It should be noted, however, that deviation from the average is not necessarily bad; it simply warrants further investigation. For example, young companies will have purchased assets at a different price and will likely have a different capital structure than older companies do. In addition to ratio analysis, a company's cash flow position is of critical importance and should be assessed. Cash flow shows how much actual cash a company possesses.

■ Profit Ratios

Profit ratios measure the efficiency with which the company uses its resources. The more efficient the company, the greater is its profitability. It is useful to compare a company's profitability against that of its major competitors in its industry to determine whether the company is operating more or less efficiently than its rivals. In addition, the change in a company's profit ratios over time tells whether its performance is improving or declining.

A number of different profit ratios can be used, and each of them measures a different aspect of a company's performance. Here, we look at the most commonly used profit ratios.

■ Return on Invested Capital

This ratio measures the profit earned on the capital invested in the company. It is defined as follows:

$$\text{Return on invested capital (ROIC)} = \frac{\text{Net profit}}{\text{Invested capital}}$$

Net profit is calculated by subtracting the total costs of operating the company away from its total revenues (total revenues − total costs). Total costs are the (1) costs of goods sold, (2) sales, general, and administrative expenses, (3) R&D expenses, and

(4) other expenses. Net profit can be calculated before or after taxes, although many financial analysts prefer the before-tax figure. Invested capital is the amount that is invested in the operations of a company—that is, in property, plant, equipment, inventories, and other assets. Invested capital comes from two main sources: interest-bearing debt and shareholders' equity. Interest-bearing debt is money the company borrows from banks and from those who purchase its bonds. Shareholders' equity is the money raised from selling shares to the public, *plus* earnings that have been retained by the company in prior years and are available to fund current investments. ROIC measures the effectiveness with which a company is using the capital funds that it has available for investment. As such, it is recognized to be an excellent measure of the value a company is creating.[1] Remember that a company's ROIC can be decomposed into its constituent parts.

■ **Return on Total Assets (ROA)** This ratio measures the profit earned on the employment of assets. It is defined as follows:

$$\text{Return on total assests} = \frac{\text{Net profit}}{\text{Total assets}}$$

■ **Return on Stockholders' Equity (ROE)** This ratio measures the percentage of profit earned on common stockholders' investment in the company. It is defined as follows:

$$\text{Return on stockholders' equity} = \frac{\text{Net profit}}{\text{Stockholders' equity}}$$

If a company has no debt, this will be the same as ROIC.

■ **Liquidity Ratios** A company's liquidity is a measure of its ability to meet short-term obligations. An asset is deemed liquid if it can be readily converted into cash. Liquid assets are current assets such as cash, marketable securities, accounts receivable, and so on. Two liquidity ratios are commonly used.

■ **Current Ratio** The current ratio measures the extent to which the claims of short-term creditors are covered by assets that can be quickly converted into cash. Most companies should have a ratio of at least 1, because failure to meet these commitments can lead to bankruptcy. The ratio is defined as follows:

$$\text{Current ratio} = \frac{\text{Current assets}}{\text{Current liabilities}}$$

■ **Quick Ratio** The quick ratio measures a company's ability to pay off the claims of short-term creditors without relying on selling its inventories. This is a valuable measure since in practice the sale of inventories is often difficult. It is defined as follows:

$$\text{Quick ratio} = \frac{\text{Current assets} - \text{inventory}}{\text{Current liabilities}}$$

[1] Tom Copeland, Tim Koller, and Jack Murrin, *Valuation: Measuring and Managing the Value of Companies* (New York: Wiley, 1996).

■ **Activity Ratios**   Activity ratios indicate how effectively a company is managing its assets. Two ratios are particularly useful.

■ **Inventory Turnover** This measures the number of times inventory is turned over. It is useful in determining whether a firm is carrying excess stock in inventory. It is defined as follows:

$$\text{Inventory turnover} = \frac{\text{Cost of goods sold}}{\text{Inventory}}$$

Cost of goods sold is a better measure of turnover than sales because it is the cost of the inventory items. Inventory is taken at the balance sheet date. Some companies choose to compute an average inventory, beginning inventory, and ending inventory, but for simplicity, use the inventory at the balance sheet date.

■ **Days Sales Outstanding (DSO) or Average Collection Period** This ratio is the average time a company has to wait to receive its cash after making a sale. It measures how effective the company's credit, billing, and collection procedures are. It is defined as follows:

$$\text{DSO} = \frac{\text{Accounts receivable}}{\text{Total sales}/360}$$

Accounts receivable is divided by average daily sales. The use of 360 is the standard number of days for most financial analysis.

■ **Leverage Ratios**   A company is said to be highly leveraged if it uses more debt than equity, including stock and retained earnings. The balance between debt and equity is called the *capital structure*. The optimal capital structure is determined by the individual company. Debt has a lower cost because creditors take less risk; they know they will get their interest and principal. However, debt can be risky to the firm because if enough profit is not made to cover the interest and principal payments, bankruptcy can result. Three leverage ratios are commonly used.

■ **Debt-to-Assets Ratio** The debt-to-assets ratio is the most direct measure of the extent to which borrowed funds have been used to finance a company's investments. It is defined as follows:

$$\text{Debt-to-assets ratio} = \frac{\text{Total debt}}{\text{Total assets}}$$

Total debt is the sum of a company's current liabilities and its long-term debt, and total assets are the sum of fixed assets and current assets.

■ **Debt-to-Equity Ratio** The debt-to-equity ratio indicates the balance between debt and equity in a company's capital structure. This is perhaps the most widely used measure of a company's leverage. It is defined as follows:

$$\text{Debt-to-equity ratio} = \frac{\text{Total debt}}{\text{Total equity}}$$

■ **Times-Covered Ratio** The times-covered ratio measures the extent to which a company's gross profit covers its annual interest payments. If this ratio declines to less than 1, the company is unable to meet its interest costs and is technically insolvent. The ratio is defined as follows:

$$\text{Times-covered ratio} = \frac{\text{Profit before interest and tax}}{\text{Total interest charges}}$$

■ **Shareholder-Return Ratios**

Shareholder-return ratios measure the return that shareholders earn from holding stock in the company. Given the goal of maximizing stockholders' wealth, providing shareholders with an adequate rate of return is a primary objective of most companies. As with profit ratios, it can be helpful to compare a company's shareholder returns against those of similar companies as a yardstick for determining how well the company is satisfying the demands of this particularly important group of organizational constituents. Four ratios are commonly used.

■ **Total Shareholder Returns** Total shareholder returns measure the returns earned by time $t + 1$ on an investment in a company's stock made at time t. (Time t is the time at which the initial investment is made.) Total shareholder returns include both dividend payments and appreciation in the value of the stock (adjusted for stock splits) and are defined as follows:

$$\text{Total shareholder returns} = \frac{\text{Stock price } (t+1) - \text{stock price } (t) + \text{sum of annual dividends per share}}{\text{Stock price } (t)}$$

If a shareholder invests $2 at time t and at time $t + 1$ the share is worth $3, while the sum of annual dividends for the period t to $t + 1$ has amounted to $0.20, total shareholder returns are equal to $(3 - 2 + 0.2)/2 = 0.6$, which is a 60 percent return on an initial investment of $2 made at time t.

■ **Price-Earnings Ratio** The price-earnings ratio measures the amount investors are willing to pay per dollar of profit. It is defined as follows:

$$\text{Price-earnings ratio} = \frac{\text{Market price per share}}{\text{Earnings per share}}$$

■ **Market-to-Book Value** Market-to-book value measures a company's expected future growth prospects. It is defined as follows:

$$\text{Market-to-book value} = \frac{\text{Market price per share}}{\text{Earnings per share}}$$

■ **Dividend Yield** The dividend yield measures the return to shareholders received in the form of dividends. It is defined as follows:

$$\text{Dividend yield} = \frac{\text{Dividend per share}}{\text{Market price per share}}$$

Market price per share can be calculated for the first of the year, in which case the dividend yield refers to the return on an investment made at the beginning of the year. Alternatively, the average share price over the year may be used. A company must decide how much of its profits to pay to stockholders and how much to reinvest in the company. Companies with strong growth prospects should have a lower dividend payout ratio than mature companies. The rationale is that shareholders can invest the money elsewhere if the company is not growing. The optimal ratio depends on the individual firm, but the key decider is whether the company can produce better returns than the investor can earn elsewhere.

■ **Cash Flow**   Cash flow position is cash received minus cash distributed. The net cash flow can be taken from a company's statement of cash flows. Cash flow is important for what it reveals about a company's financing needs. A strong positive cash flow enables a company to fund future investments without having to borrow money from bankers or investors. This is desirable because the company avoids paying out interest or dividends. A weak or negative cash flow means that a company has to turn to external sources to fund future investments. Generally, companies in strong-growth industries often find themselves in a poor cash flow position (because their investment needs are substantial), whereas successful companies based in mature industries generally find themselves in a strong cash flow position.

A company's internally generated cash flow is calculated by adding back its depreciation provision to profits after interest, taxes, and dividend payments. If this figure is insufficient to cover proposed new investments, the company has little choice but to borrow funds to make up the shortfall or to curtail investments. If this figure exceeds proposed new investments, the company can use the excess to build up its liquidity (that is, through investments in financial assets) or repay existing loans ahead of schedule.

Conclusion

When evaluating a case, it is important to be *systematic*. Analyze the case in a logical fashion, beginning with the identification of operating and financial strengths and weaknesses and environmental opportunities and threats. Move on to assess the value of a company's current strategies only when you are fully conversant with the SWOT analysis of the company. Ask yourself whether the company's current strategies make sense given its SWOT analysis. If they do not, what changes need to be made? What are your recommendations? Above all, link any strategic recommendations you may make to the SWOT analysis. State explicitly how the strategies you identify take advantage of the company's strengths to exploit environmental opportunities, how they rectify the company's weaknesses, and how they counter environmental threats. Also, do not forget to outline what needs to be done to implement your recommendations.

Case 1

Brown-Forman Wine Estates

This case was prepared by Armand Gilinsky Jr., Professor of Business at Sonoma State University; Sally Baack, Assistant Professor of Business at San Francisco State University; Murray Silverman, Professor of Business at San Francisco State University; and Lew Brown, Associate Professor of Business at the University of North Carolina, Greensboro.

Steve Dorfman flicked his turn signal and edged his BMW to the left, merging in the congested flow of traffic onto the south entrance to the Golden Gate Bridge. As traffic crept along, Steve had the chance to glance across the Bay and enjoy a clear view of downtown San Francisco.

Dorfman's cell phone rang, and he answered, "Hello."

"Steve?"

Recognizing Keith LaVine's voice, he responded, "Yes, Keith, what's going on?"

"Where are you?"

"Just crossing the Golden Gate, headed back to the office."

"Well, sorry to bother you, but I thought you'd want to know I just learned that Tom Burnet has announced his resignation. He's going to become the

Copyright © 2004 by Armand Gilinsky Jr., Sally Baack, Murray Silverman, and Lew Brown. This case was prepared by Armand Gilinsky Jr., Sally Baack, Murray Silverman, and Lew Brown as the basis for class discussion rather than to illustrate either effective or ineffective handling of an administrative situation. Reprinted by permission of Armand Gilinsky Jr., Sally Baack, Murray Silverman, and Lew Brown. All rights reserved. This case was originally presented at the 2002 North American Case Research Association conference in Banff, Canada. The authors gratefully acknowledge a Business and International Education (BIE) grant from the U.S. Department of Education and a matching grant from the College of Business at San Francisco State University in support of this research. We also gratefully acknowledge the contributions of student researchers Scott Sissom and Kimberly Stark, whose work was underwritten by a case writing grant from the Wine Business Program at Sonoma State University. For the most recent financial results of the company discussed in this case, go to http://finance.yahoo.com, input the company's stock symbol, and download the latest company report from its homepage.

president and CEO of Southcorp, the Australian Winery," said LaVine, Dorfman's senior vice president for sales.

"That's interesting," Dorfman continued after a pause. "I'm sure he'll do a good job there, and it's a good move for him. But it sure raises some interesting questions for us. Look, I'd better keep my eyes on all this traffic. I'll stop by your office when I get back. Thanks for the call."

Dorfman served as managing director of Brown-Forman's Wine Estates (WE) division. WE was headquartered in Healdsburg, California, sixty miles north of the Golden Gate Bridge in the heart of the world-renowned Napa, Mendocino, and Sonoma wine-growing regions. WE marketed premium and ultra-premium branded wines.

One year earlier, in late July 2001, Brown-Forman Corporation (BFC), headquartered in Louisville, Kentucky, had created WE as a corporate venture group to house its portfolio of small, upscale brands, and appointed Dorfman to head the division. WE's brands included California wines from Bonterra, Bel Arbor, Jekel, Mariah, and Sonoma-Cutrer, and Australian wines from Chateau Tahbilk, Geoff Merrill Reserve, and Owen's Estate.

At the time of WE's creation, BFC had decided to keep its older wine brands, Bolla, Fetzer, Fontana Candida, Korbel, MacPherson, and Michel Picard, within its established Wine Division (WD). Thomas Burnet, as WD's president, had championed the idea of setting WE up as a separate division.

Since WE's creation, however, its sales had been flat relative to the premium wine segment's double-digit growth rates, and Dorfman felt the pressure to improve results. He knew that some of BFC's executives questioned the decision to make WE a separate division. They wanted more centralized control over all the wine brands and the implied ability to cut costs and reduce duplication. However, other executives believed that keeping the premium brands separate was important to maintaining their images and positioning and preserving the entrepreneurial spirit behind those brands.

Dorfman knew that there had been growing tension within the organization over this issue and that he needed to justify WE's existence as an entity distinct from BFC's Wine Division. Now, with Burnet's departure, he also knew that the tension would escalate.

As Dorfman turned into his parking place, he realized that he had been lost in thought, and the sixty miles since the Golden Gate seemed to have vanished. He parked and headed for Lavine's office.

Dorfman knocked on LaVine's office door, and he looked up from his work.

"Hi, Steve. Did you have a good trip?"

"Well, I was lost in thought after your call, Keith. You know I hate to see Tom leave, but his timing may be good for us. It's August now and we have the annual planning meetings coming up next month. That's when we have to present our marketing strategy for 2003–2004. I know that we're going to get pressure to justify our continued existence as a separate unit. So, obviously, even more than normal, we have to show a plan to improve the division's performance. But, and this is the interesting thought, maybe we also need to revisit the idea of BFC's having all its wine brands in one division. Could be those executives pushing for this are correct. Either way, we need to be prepared to present and defend our strategy recommendations. And looking at both sides of the argument will help us prepare and strengthen our position. Let's get to work."

Recent Trends in the U.S. Wine Industry

The U.S. wine industry was composed of approximately 1,500 wineries. However, it was highly concentrated. The top 10 wineries accounted for 70 percent (by volume) of U.S. production, according to the 1999 *Adams Wine Handbook*. California dominated the U.S. wine industry with over 800 wineries, which accounted

for more than 90 percent of the wine produced in and exported by the United States. Washington, Oregon, and Idaho had attracted approximately 200 wineries and were developing an export presence and a reputation for quality wines.

During the late 1990s three significant trends had emerged in the U.S. wine industry. These trends were (1) consolidation of the industry's "three-tier" distribution network (winery-wholesaler/distributor-retailer); (2) market segmentation due to consumers' "trading up" from inexpensive jug wines to premium-priced varietals, such as Chardonnay, Merlot, and Cabernet Sauvignon; and (3) the emergence of global markets for wines.

Distribution Channels

Wine was sold through a three-tier distribution system. Wineries (the first tier) or importers sold wine to wholesalers (the second tier), who provided legal fulfillment of wine products to local retail businesses (the third tier) within a certain state. Wine was a controlled substance, and laws in each state differed regarding how wine could be sold. Typically, wine passed through each tier of the distribution system, making direct shipping to retailers or selling wine through the Internet difficult or impossible in most states.

The third tier of the distribution system consisted of retail and nonretail outlets. Off-premises sales via supermarkets, convenience stores, club stores, mail order and Internet retailers, specialty stores, and wine clubs accounted for 78 percent of total sales volume. Supermarkets alone accounted for 52 percent of retail wine sales and were dominant in food and drink retailing, having made one-stop shopping an appealing concept for consumers. Supermarkets had therefore developed considerable bargaining leverage with wholesalers. Conversely, the role of specialty stores in wine distribution had diminished due to the increasing power of supermarkets. Specialty stores' share of retail wine sales shrank to about 30 percent by 1998. However, specialty stores were not likely to disappear soon because they provided superior customer service and extensive knowledge of wines. Specialty stores also carried specialty brands and limited production labels, attracting wine connoisseurs and enthusiasts. On-premises sales via nonretail outlets such as restaurants, hotels, and airlines accounted for the remaining 22 percent of wine volume in the United States, according to *Adams*.

Market Segmentation

"Table" wines were those with 7 to 14 percent alcohol content by volume and were traditionally consumed with food. This was in contrast to other wine products such as sparkling wines (champagnes if from France), wine coolers, and fortified wines, which were typically consumed as stand-alone beverages. Table wines that retailed at less than $3 per 750-milliliter bottle were generally considered to be "economy" or "jug" wines, whereas those selling for more than $3 per bottle were considered "premium" wines.

Premium wines generally had a vintage date on their labels. This meant that the product was made with at least 95 percent of grapes harvested, crushed, and fermented in the calendar year shown on the label and used grapes from an appellation of origin (e.g., Napa Valley, Sonoma Valley, Central Coast, etc.). Within the premium table wine category, a number of market segments emerged, based on retail price points. Subpremium wines generally fell into the $3 to $7 per bottle range, while premium wines retailed for $7 to $10 per bottle. The super premium category sold for $10 to $14 per bottle. Any retail price above $14 per bottle was considered deluxe premium.

U.S. wine market retail sales reached about $15 billion in 2002 (Exhibit 1). In retail sales, the U.S. wine market was ranked third in the world behind France and Italy, but only twelfth in the world in per capita consumption (Exhibit 2). The greatest concentration of core U.S. wine consumers was in the forty to forty-nine age bracket (Exhibit 3). About the same proportion of men and women consumed wine. While all income levels consumed wine, higher income was associated with greater wine consumption. By 1998, adults in families earning over $75,000 annually represented 18.7 percent of the population and 31.4 percent of the domestic table wine consumption

EXHIBIT 1

U.S. Table Wine Retail Sales, by Price Segment: 2001 and 2002 (Estimated)

		Retail Sales ($ millions)		
		2001	2002e	% Change
Total Economy (under $3.00)		$1,448	$1,518	4.8%
	Domestic	1,442	1,512	4.9
	Imported	6	6	—
Total Sub-Premium ($3.00–$6.99)		4,790	5,328	11.2
	Domestic	3,310	3,562	7.6
	Imported	1,480	1,766	19.3
Total Premium ($7.00–$9.99)		3,553	3,691	3.9
	Domestic	1,975	1,989	0.7
	Imported	1,578	1,702	7.9
Total Super-Premium ($10.00–$13.99)		2,956	3,399	15.0
	Domestic	2,148	2,395	11.5
	Imported	808	1,004	24.3
Total Deluxe ($14.00 and over)		1,312	1,416	7.9
	Domestic	1,018	1,073	5.4
	Imported	294	343	16.7
Total Table Wine		$14,059	$15,352	9.2
	Domestic	9,893	10,531	6.4
	Imported	4,166	4,821	15.7

Source: Data compiled from IMPACT Databank Review and Forecast, *The U.S. Wine Market,* 2003 edition, p. 360.

EXHIBIT 2

Per-Capita Wine Consumption in the United States: 1990, 1995, and 2000–2002 (Estimated)

Country	Population Year 2000	Liters Per Capita[1]					Average Annual Compound Growth Rate		Percent Change[2]		Volume Rank
		1990	1995	2000	2001	2002e	1990–1995	1995–2000	2000–2001	2001–2002e	
France	59,329,691	72.56	62.94	55.54	56.68	55.05	−2.8%	−2.5%	2.1%	−2.9%	1
Portugal	10,048,232	50.73	60.51	50.12	49.79	49.22	3.6	−3.7	−0.7	−1.1	10
Italy	57,634,691	62.07	62.13	49.89	48.87	48.16	0.0	−4.3	−2.0	−1.5	2
Spain	39,996,671	42.08	38.76	36.33	35.07	35.07	−1.6	−1.3	−3.5	0.0	5
Argentina	36,955,182	54.46	38.81	33.73	32.11	31.60	−6.6	−2.8	−4.8	−1.6	7
Germany[3]	82,797,408	20.53	22.75	23.85	23.97	23.87	2.1	0.9	0.5	−0.4	4
Australia	19,357,594	18.06	18.25	20.32	20.48	21.19	0.2	2.2	0.8	3.5	12
Romania	22,411,121	25.77	29.11	23.24	21.00	21.16	2.5	−4.4	−9.6	0.8	11
United Kingdom	59,508,382	10.95	12.38	16.32	17.36	20.87	2.5	5.7	6.4	20.2	6
Netherlands	15,892,237	16.08	14.01	19.38	19.46	19.67	−2.7	6.7	0.4	1.1	15
South Africa	43,421,021	9.93	10.31	8.99	9.03	8.79	0.8	−2.7	0.4	−2.7	13
United States	275,562,673	6.26	6.40	7.25	7.28	7.64	0.4	2.5	0.4	4.9	3
Russia[4]	146,001,176	13.53	4.22	3.99	4.01	4.04	−20.8	−1.1	0.5	0.7	9
Brazil	172,860,370	1.95	1.94	1.95	2.09	2.06	−0.1	0.1	7.2	−1.4	14
China	1,261,832,482	0.03	0.32	0.43	0.45	0.49	60.5	6.1	4.7	8.9	8
Average - Top 15		27.00	25.52	23.42	23.18	23.26	−1.1	−1.7	−1.0	0.4	
Rest of World	3,784,338,702	1.23	1.22	1.20	1.19	1.16	−0.2	−0.3	−0.8	−2.5	
World Average		4.39	3.90	3.61	3.58	3.57	−2.3	−1.5	−0.8	−0.3	

[1] Based on total population.
[2] Based on unrounded data.
[3] 1990 includes West Germany only.
[4] 1990 includes the entire (former) Soviet Union.

Source: Impact Databank, 2003. New York: M. Shanken Publications, p. 504.

according to the *Adams Wine Handbook*. Still, barely more than 10 percent of the adults in the United States consumed 86 percent of all wine sold according to the Wine Market Council.

EXHIBIT 3

Wine Consumer: Age Segmentation, Percent

Ages	50–59	40–49	30–39	21–29
Core Wine Consumers	23	40	21	16
Marginal Consumers	19	26	33	22
Non-Wine Drinkers	11	27	31	31

Source: Wine Market Council.

Emergence of Global Markets

By 2000, the United States had become the second largest market for exported wine and the fourth leading producer of wine in the world. In 2000, U.S. wine exports to 164 countries totaled $560 million, more than 90 percent of which came from California. Wine was produced commercially in over 60 countries with 23 percent (by volume) of the wine produced exported to international markets according to *Wines & Vines*. Leading wine producers included the "Old World" wineries in France, Italy, and Spain, which were also the leading exporters. So-called "New World" producers, such as the United States, Australia, Chile, Argentina, and South Africa, had been making both production and export inroads globally over the past few decades. Although France, Italy, and

Spain all exported more than 25 percent of the wine they produced, Australia exported over 40 percent of its production and Chile over 80 percent. Many observers attributed these higher export numbers to the small size of the respective home markets.

Until the mid-1990s, the U.S. wine market had remained largely a domestic industry, with some imports from France, Italy, and Spain competing with U.S. wineries. By 1999, however, imports had risen to 20 percent of the U.S. market, seven percentage points above 1995, according to *Wine Business Monthly.* Australian and Chilean wines had become increasingly dominant in the U.S. market: From 1995 to 1999, Australia increased the value of its exports to the United States by 243 percent and Chile by 152 percent. Since 1995, the unfavorable balance of trade for wine in the United States had increased by 78 percent. Tariffs and trade barriers, meanwhile, continued to play a pivotal role in obstructing U.S. wineries' access to export markets.

Owing to the globalization of markets and the creation of the European Union, trade barriers were beginning to fall worldwide. The worldwide consolidation trend accelerated among wineries and distributors. For example, Allied Domecq (United Kingdom), Constellation Brands (United States), Diageo PLC (United Kingdom), and BFC all courted larger premium wineries around the world. In the largest deal to date, Foster's Group of Australia had completed its friendly $1.5 billion merger with Beringer Wine Estates of California in October 2000.[1] Southcorp (Australia) and Kendall-Jackson (California) were most often rumored as takeover targets. Wine industry analysts expected further consolidation in the wine industry. Industry observers expected that large wine and alcoholic beverage companies would acquire smaller winery operations across national borders, in order to gain access to premium and ultra-premium brands, as well as access to the growing markets for those brands.

BFC's Main Competitors in the Wine Industry

The premium segment was highly fragmented, composed of hundreds of individual, small to large

wine-producing operations that were all competing to produce the most acclaimed wines each year. Although larger producers held advantages in scale and capital, smaller "boutique" wineries were able to compete by consistently producing high-quality wines in limited quantities that gained critical acclaim by wine enthusiasts. Smaller wine producers, however, were at a disadvantage in the competition for grape sources. Larger better-financed competitors, such as Constellation Brands's Canandaigua division, Diageo PLC's Chateau & Estates division, E & J Gallo, Foster's Group's Beringer Blass Wine Estates division, Kendall-Jackson, and Robert Mondavi Corporation, all had extensive vineyard holdings in different wine-growing regions around the world. Larger rivals could therefore develop portfolios of brands and offer wines of many varietal types across the price spectrum of the premium, super-premium, and deluxe premium market segments.

BFC competed with two major types of large wine businesses: stand-alone wineries and conglomerates. BFC's primary stand-alone winery competitors in the United States included publicly traded Robert Mondavi and Chalone and the privately held Kendall-Jackson, E&J Gallo, and a host of medium-size wineries primarily based in Northern California, such as Sebastiani and Bonnie Doon. Selected financial data for BFC's publicly traded competitors are shown in Exhibit 4 and Exhibit 5.

BFC's major privately held competitor, E&J Gallo (Modesto, California), had been dominant in the U.S. wine industry since the end of Prohibition in 1933. E&J Gallo had been, until January 2003, the single largest wine producer in the world. E&J Gallo had a market share comprising approximately 45 percent of California wine sales. In recent years E&J Gallo, like many other jug wine producers, sought to enter the premium wine market, choosing to develop and launch new E&J Gallo brands from twenty-three hundred acres of prime vineyards in Sonoma County, acreage acquired to supply the development of new premium and ultra-premium brands. Gallo had also purchased Louis M. Martini, a premium winery based in Napa, California, in the summer of 2002.

Large conglomerate competitors included Allied Domecq, Constellation, Diageo, Fortune Brands, Foster's Group, Louis Vuitton Möet Hennesey (LVMH), and UST (formerly known as US Tobacco). These conglomerates expanded their wine portfolios through acquisitions of independent wineries and purchases of and majority interests in the beverage divisions of

[1]Constellation subsequently announced its $1.4 billion purchase of BRL Hardy, an Australian wine producer, in the second week of January 2003. This deal was expected to make Constellation the largest wine producer in the world, overtaking the previous industry leader, E&J Gallo.

EXHIBIT 4

Selected Financial and Operating Highlights of Publicly Traded Wine Businesses, October 2002

Company	Ticker Symbol	Recent Stock Price	P/E Ratio (x)	12 mo. Trail EPS	30 Day Price Change (%)	1 Year Price Change (%)	Beta	Yield (%)	Stk. Mkt. Capitaliz. ($ millions)	Return on Equity (%)	Pretax Margin (%)	LTD to Capital (%)
Brown-Forman Corp.	BF.B	$75.00	23x	$3.29	13%	23%	0.44	1.9	$2,963	18.3%	17.8%	2.8%
Chalone Wine Group	CHLN	8.65	62	0.14	8	−10	0.25	Nil	104	2.8	6.5	38.6
Constellation Brands	STZ	25.50	14	1.82	0	19	0.30	Nil	1,994	17.5	8.2	53.6
Diageo plc*ADS	DEO	46.14	15	2.98	−8	15	0.39	3.1	39,346	24.8	13.4	40.5
Robert Mondavi Corp.	MOND	31.86	14	2.21	6	−1	0.82	Nil	305	6.1	9.3	41.0

Source: Richard Joy, *Standard & Poor's Rankings,* through October 3, 2002.

other conglomerates (e.g., Diageo's late 2000 takeover of Seagram's drink business). In 2000 and 2001, conglomerates began divesting those satellite businesses that diverted resources from their core beverage businesses, including Allied Domecq's sale of the majority of its food operations and Diageo's sale of its Pillsbury Unit to General Mills in a $10.5 billion deal. Exhibit 6 presents a comparison of portfolios and recent strategic

EXHIBIT 5

Selected Financial and Operating Highlights of Global Alcohol and Beverage Conglomerates: 1999–2001

Company	HQ Location	Sales ($ millions)			Net Income ($ millions)			ROE (%)		ROA (%)	
		2001	2000	1999	2001	2000	1999	2001	2000	2001	2000
Allied-Domecq[1]	Bristol, England	$4,318	$6,154	$3,948	$516	$476	$114	117.7%	N/A	12.7%	N/A
Brown-Forman	Louisville, KY	2,180	2,009	2,134	233	202	218	19.6	20.8	19.3	19.3
Constellation Brands, Inc.	Fairport, NY	3,154	2,340	1,497	136	97	77	14.4	15.8	3.9	3.3
Diageo plc[1]	London, England	12,933	18,716	29,229	1,848	1,593	1,630	25.6	25.1	9.1	8.0
Fortune Brands	Lincolnshire, IL	5,678	5,579	5,844	385	(891)	(138)	18.9	−6.2	7.5	−2.3
Foster's Group[2]	Australia	2,244	1,874	1,656	256	236	203	12.2	18.5	9.0	12.8
Louis Vuitton Moet Hennessy (LVMH)[3]	Paris, France	1,168	8,589	10,909	10	696	680	0.2	10.3	2.0	8.4
Southcorp[2]	Australia	1,375	1,441	1,554	118	168	11	15.2	N/A	N/A	N/A
UST	Greenwich, CT	1,670	1,548	1,512	492	442	469	84.6	163.3	24.4	26.8

N/A = Not Available.
[1]Converted from British £ sterling to U.S. dollars at a rate of £1 = $1.50 U.S
[2]Converted from Australian dollars to U.S. dollars at a rate of $1 Australian = $0.55 U.S.
[3]Converted from Euros to U.S. dollars at a rate of 1€ = $0.95 U.S.

Source: Company reports, *Value Line,* and **WSRN.com**, accessed October 25, 2002.

EXHIBIT 6

Profiles of Brown-Forman's Major Wine Business Competitors: Brand Portfolios and Recent Strategic Moves

Company	Portfolio Brands—Wine	Other Portfolio Brands	Annual Wine Production	Recent Strategic Moves
Allied Domecq	Clos du Bois, Callaway Coastal, Atlas Peak, William Hill, Bodegas Balbi, Graffigna & Ste Sylvie, Montana, Marques de Arienzo, Harveys, Cockburn's, La Ina, Mumm and Perrier-Jouet.	*Spirits:* Ballantine's, Beefeater, Kahlua, Sauza, Stolichnaya, Tia Maria, Maker's Mark, Courvoisier Canadian Club *Fast-food:* Dunkin' Donuts, Baskin-Robbins and Togo's	Atlas Peak: 40,000 cases; 500 acres owned Callaway: 340,000 cases; 40 acres owned, 605 leased or controlled Clos du Bois: 1.4 million cases; 640 owned, 160 leased or controlled	Unsuccessfully bid to acquire Seagram's drinks businesses' assets in 2001.
Constellation (Canandigua)	Almaden, Arbor Mist, Franciscan Oakville Estate, Ravenswood, Simi, Estancia, Talus, Taylor, Vendange	*Spirits:* Paul Masson brandy, Corona Extra, Modelo Especial, St. Pauli Girl, Alice White, Black Velvet, Fleischmann's, Schenley, Ten High, Stowells of Chelsea,	30 million cases; 765 acres owned, 2,600 leased or controlled	Acquired Ravenswood Estates (Sonoma. CA) for $148 million in cash and assumed debt in July 2001. Announced $1.4 bill. purchase of Australia's BRL Hardy in January 2003.
Diageo (UDV Guinness NA)	Sterling Vineyards, Beaulieu Vineyards, Glen Ellen, M.G. Vallejo, Blossom Hill	*Spirits:* Captain Morgan, Crown Royal, and VO Canadian whiskeys, Guinness Stout, Harp Lager, Johnnie Walker Scotch, Tanqueray gin, Smirnoff vodka	6 million cases; 2,000 acres	Sold Pillsbury unit to General Mills for $20.5 billion in 2001; sold Guinness Book of World Records unit for $63 million in July 2001; completed spin-off of Burger King unit in 2002.
E & J Gallo	E & J Gallo (Modesto, CA): Gallo, Thunderbird, Carol Rossi, Bartles & Jaymes Gallo of Sonoma: E&J Gallo Estate, Gallo of Sonoma, Anapamu, Marcelina, Rancho Zabacho, Indigo Hills, Louis M. Martini	None	E & J Gallo (Modesto, CA): 90 million cases (est.) Gallo of Sonoma (Healdsburg, CA): 1 million cases (est.); 3,000 acres	Is world's largest wine producer and leading U.S. wine exporter, selling in 85 countries; wines also account for over 25% of all U.S. wine sales; exports one million bottles annually to the French market; plans to create first-mover advantage in the Indian wine market.
Kendall-Jackson	Kendall-Jackson, Pepi, La Crema, Edmeades Estate, Camelot, Tapiz, Villa Arceno, Calina	None	4 million cases; 12, 000 acres	Launched new Australian line, Yangarra Park in 2001; in May 2001, rejected several rumored takeover bids, including one by BFC; also lost five-year battle with Gallo over alleged theft of trade secrets.
Robert Mondavi	Robert Mondavi Winery, Robert Mondavi Coastal, Woodbridge, La Famiglia de Robert Mondavi, Byron, Arrowood, Vichon Mediterranean, Opus One, Caliterra, Luce	None	Unknown; 7,730 acres	Joint ventures with producers in France, Chile, and Italy; created a $10 million wine country attraction in 2001 at Disney's California Adventure theme park; began shift from vineyard development to production; internal grape supply expected to rise from 7% to 20% by 2004.

Source: Dow Jones Interactive on-line, Wines and Vines's *2002 Annual Buyers' Guide.*

moves by some of BFC's major publicly and privately held competitors.

BFC's History

George Brown and John Forman opened the BFC Distillery in Louisville, Kentucky, in 1870 to produce Old Forester–brand bourbon. Old Forester sold well through the end of the century, in part because of the company's innovative packaging (safety seals and quality guarantees on the bottles). When Forman died in 1901, Brown bought his interest in the company. Old Forester continued to be successful under the Brown family. BFC obtained government approval to produce alcohol for medicinal purposes during Prohibition. In 1923, it made its first acquisition, Early Times, and then went public in 1933. In the year after the repeal of Prohibition, Old Forester was reintroduced as an alcoholic beverage. During World War II, the U.S. government had greatly curtailed alcoholic beverage production, because alcohol was needed for the war effort. BFC compensated by providing alcohol for wartime rubber and gunpowder production.

In 1956, BFC purchased Lynchburg, Tennessee, based Jack Daniel's (sour-mash whiskey). The company retained the simple, black Jack Daniel's label and promoted the image of a small Tennessee distillery for the brand. BFC achieved global success by introducing Jack Daniels into new markets overseas, becoming the second largest brand of premium whiskey sold worldwide.

Subsequent to the Jack Daniels purchase, BFC continued to expand its spirits line, developing marketing relationships with Quality Importers (Ambassador Scotch, Ambassador Gin, and Old Bushmills' Irish Whisky, 1967), and Canadian Mist (blended whiskey, 1971). In 1979, BFC purchased a top-selling liqueur, Southern Comfort. BFC launched Gentleman Jack Rare Tennessee Whiskey in 1988, the first new whiskey from its Jack Daniels distillery in more than one hundred years. In 1999, BFC purchased a 33 percent interest in Tequila Orendain de Jalisco, S.A. de C.V., and 67 percent in a new company that was expected to develop Tequila Orendain products for markets outside Mexico. BFC then purchased a 45 percent stake in Tuoni & Canepa SpA of Italy, and became the exclusive marketer for that company's Tuaca liqueur. In 2000, the company bought 45 percent of Finlandia Vodka Worldwide for $83 million.

BFC also diversified into luxury consumer durables, purchasing well-known global brands. Its nonbeverage acquisitions included Lenox, a leading American maker of fine china, crystal, and gifts, in 1983; Hartmann, luggage, in 1983; Kirk Stieff, silver and pewter, in 1990; Dansk International Designs, china, crystal, and silver, in 1991; and the high-quality Gorham silver and crystal lines, in 1991. By 2002, BFC's subsidiary locations and manufacturing branches included seven production facilities in the United States, two in Italy, and one each in the U.S. Virgin Islands and Canada. Its Consumer Durables segment owned production facilities in New Jersey, North Carolina, Pennsylvania, Rhode Island, and Tennessee.

BFC's fiscal year 2002 net sales were $2.2 billion, rising 1 percent from the previous year. By contrast, in the fiscal year ending April 2001, BFC's net sales had grown 6 percent over fiscal year 2000. Operating and net incomes for 2002 were flat, dropping by 6 percent to $353 million and 2 percent to $228 million, respectively. Wine and Spirits segment sales had grown by 6 percent. Sales of the WD's Fetzer, Bolla, and Korbel brands had increased 6 percent, 3 percent, and 3 percent, respectively. Sales of the WE's brands increased 7.5 percent in fiscal 2002, after a decline of 4.6 percent the previous year. Exhibits 7–9 present company historical income statements, balance sheets, and cash flow statements, from 1998–2002. Exhibits 10 and 11 present BFC wine brand sales in 1995 and 2000–2002.

BFC's Organization

Headquartered in Louisville, Kentucky, BFC was publicly owned, though descendants of the cofounding Brown family remained in control. In 1993, Owsley Brown II succeeded his brother, Lee, as CEO. In 1999, BFC appointed the first woman, Dace Brown Stubbs, to serve on its board of directors. By 2002, members of the fifth generation of the Brown family were working in the organization, in such areas as corporate development, the spirits division, U.S. sales, international sales, and in the WE division.

BFC employed seventy-four hundred people worldwide, and 19 percent of BFC's workforce (fourteen hundred) was employed on a part-time or temporary/seasonal basis. The average age of BFC's top executives was fifty-five years. Most of its senior management had spent over thirteen years with the

EXHIBIT 7

Brown-Forman Corporation, Consolidated Income Statements
(Years ended April 30; $ millions, except share and per share amounts)

	2002	2001	2000	1999	1998
Net sales	$2,208	$2,180	$2,134	$2,009	$1,924
Excise taxes	250	256	257	254	255
Cost of sales	825	771	774	736	690
Gross profit	1,133	1,153	1,103	1,019	979
Advertising expenses	299	295	281	263	260
Selling, general, and administrative expenses	481	484	474	434	412
Operating income	353	374	348	322	307
Interest income	3	8	10	6	3
Interest expense	8	16	15	10	14
Income before income taxes	348	366	343	318	296
Taxes on income	120	133	125	116	111
Net income after tax	$228	$233	$218	$202	$185
Earnings per share:					
Basic	$3.33	$3.40	$3.18	$2.93	$2.67
Diluted	$3.33	$3.40	$3.18	$2.93	$2.67
Weighted average shares used to calculate earnings per share:					
Basic	68.3	68.5	68.5	68.6	68.9
Diluted	68.5	68.6	68.6	68.7	69.0

Source: Company reports.

company. (See Exhibit 12 for BFC's and WE's organization charts.)

BFC divided its operations into two major segments: Wine and Spirits, and Consumer Durables. The Wine and Spirits segment included the operations, manufacturing, bottling, importing, exporting, and marketing of all alcoholic beverages (whiskey, champagne, and wine). BFC distributed products in this segment domestically through state agencies or wholesale distributors. It used contracts with authorized dealers for international distributions. Consumer Durables included the manufacturing and marketing of fine china, silver, luggage, giftware, leather, and collectibles. Items within this segment were sold and distributed through retail chains, department stores, mail order, catalogs, and via the Internet.

Development of BFC's Wine Portfolio

In 1965, BFC entered the wine business through multiple marketing and distribution arrangements with Korbel champagne and brandies in California. A similar relationship with the Bolla family winery in Italy, begun in 1968, eventually led to full ownership. BFC acquired Jekel Vineyards in 1991 and Fetzer Vineyards in 1992. In 1999, BFC added four new wine brands to its portfolio. It bought an 80 percent stake in Sonoma-Cutrer Vineyards of California

EXHIBIT 8

Brown-Forman Corporation, Consolidated Balance Sheets
(Years ended April 30; $ millions, except share and per share amounts)

	2002	2001	2000	1999	1998
Assets					
Cash and cash equivalents	$116	$86	$180	$171	$78
Accounts receivable, less allowance for doubtful accounts of $10 in 1997, $11 in 1998, and $11 in 1999	280	303	294	274	265
Inventories:					
Barreled whiskey	219	219	202	191	187
Finished goods	183	216	184	189	179
Work in process	118	93	80	89	88
Raw materials and supplies	58	49	48	56	48
Total inventories	578	577	514	525	502
Current portion of deferred income taxes					
Prepaid income taxes	31	—	—	—	—
Other current assets	24	28	32	29	24
Total Current Assets	1,029	994	1,020	999	869
Investment in affiliates	127	—	—	—	—
Property, plant, and equipment, net	437	424	376	348	281
Intangible assets, less accumulated amortization of $130 in 1998 and $135 in 1999	246	263	270	264	250
Other assets	177	258	136	124	94
Total Assets	**$2,016**	**$1,939**	**$1,802**	**$1,735**	**$1,494**
Liabilities					
Commercial paper	$167	$204	$220	$226	$107
Accounts payable and accrued expenses	296	281	271	235	233
Current portion of long-term debt	—	—	6	18	7
Accrued taxes on income	32	45	1	0	8
Deferred income taxes	—	8	15	31	27
Total Current Liabilities	495	538	513	510	382
Long-term debt	40	40	41	53	50
Deferred income taxes	58	62	95	137	150
Accrued postretirement benefits	60	59	58	57	55
Other liabilities and deferred income	52	53	47	61	40
Total Liabilities	705	752	754	818	677
Stockholders' Equity					
Capital Stock:					
Preferred $0.40 cumulative, $10 par value; 1,177,948 authorized & outstanding shares redeemed in 1999 at $10.25 per share plus unpaid accrued dividends.	—	—	—	—	12

EXHIBIT 8

(Continued) Brown-Forman Corporation, Consolidated Balance Sheets
(Years ended April 30; $ millions, except share and per share amounts)

	2002	2001	2000	1999	1998
Class A common stock, voting, $0.15 par value; authorized shares, 30,000,000; issued shares, 28,988,091	4	4	4	4	4
Class B common stock, nonvoting, $0.15 par value; authorized shares, 60,000,000; issued shares, 40,008,147	6	6	6	6	6
Retained Earnings	1,360	1,226	1,080	945	821
Cumulative translation adjustment	(15)	(17)	(12)	(8)	(9)
Treasury stock, at cost (310,000 and 490,000 Class B common shares in 1998 and 1999, respectively)	(40)	(32)	(30)	(30)	(17)
Pension liability adjustment	(3)	—	—	—	—
Unrealized loss on cash flow hedge contracts	(1)	—	—	—	—
Common Stockholders' Equity	1,311	1,187	1,048	917	805
Total Stockholders' Equity	1,311	1,187	1,048	917	817
Total Liabilities and Stockholders' Equity	$2,016	$1,939	$1,802	$1,735	$1,494

Source: Company reports.

(superpremium Chardonnay); introduced two new Australian wines, McPherson Wines and Owen's Estates Wines; and purchased Mariah Wines of California. (See Exhibit 13 for a timeline of events in the creation of BFC's wine portfolio.)

Preceding the formation of the WE group was BFC's Beverages Wine Division (WD). Established in 1991, the WD was emblematic of the parent organization's new commitment to building premium wine brands. The WD's brands are listed in Exhibit 14. Since its acquisition by BFC in 1992, Fetzer had been considered to be the WD's flagship brand in the crowded popular-priced premium wine category. A good deal of the WD's reputation and clout in the wine industry had been built around Fetzer over the years, particularly in terms of relationships with its distributors.

Fetzer Vineyards

BFC acquired its second winery Fetzer Vineyards, Hopland (Mendocino County), California, in 1992. Fezer was well known in the industry for being a certified organic grower of grapes. Since 1993, its recycling and waste diversion programs reduced the amount of material hauled to landfills by 93 percent. Fetzer led the industry in organic wine best practices. Paul Dolan, president of Fetzer Vineyards, had joined the winery in 1977 as a head winemaker. Dolan came from a generation of family winemakers, and he became president in 1992. The winery employed about 325 people.

Although Fetzer continued to be headquartered in Hopland, the California Central Coast region, which had contributed about one-third of Fetzer's cabernet sauvignon grapes in the past, was rapidly becoming its major locus of wine-growing operations. In San Luis Obispo County, Fetzer was building a 200,000-square-foot winery on North River Road, across from the San Miguel Mission. The first phase of the plant construction cost more than $7 million. Construction was expected to continue through 2004. The winery would by then employ a staff of 30 to 50, in addition to seasonal help. Fetzer was also building a 20,000-ton capacity winery, on 630 acres, to grow red grapes

EXHIBIT 9

Brown-Forman Corporation, Consolidated Statements of Cash Flow
(Years ended April 30 in $ millions)

	2002	2001	2000	1999	1998
Cash Flows from Operating Activities:					
Net income	$228	$233	$218	$202	$185
Adjustments to reconcile net income to net cash provided by (used for) operations:					
Depreciation	55	53	52	46	42
Amortization	—	11	10	9	9
Deferred income taxes	(43)	(40)	(51)	(25)	19
Other	(22)	(20)	(14)	(5)	(14)
Change in assets and liabilities, excluding the effects of business acquired or sold:					
Accounts receivable	23	(9)	(20)	(5)	(2)
Inventories	5	(63)	8	(8)	(52)
Other current assets	5	3	(3)	2	7
Accounts payable and accrued expenses	15	10	36	8	24
Accrued taxes on income	(13)	44	1	(8)	2
Accrued postretirement benefits	1	1	1	2	1
Other liabilities and deferred income	(4)	8	3	(5)	(1)
Cash provided by operating activities	$250	$231	$241	$213	$220
Cash Flows from Investing Activities:					
Additions to property, plant, and equipment	(71)	(96)	(78)	(46)	(44)
Disposals of property, plant, and equipment	—	—	—	—	13
Acquisitions of business, net of cash acquired		(114)	(27)	(54)	—
Other	(5)	(2)	(14)	(17)	(15)
Cash (used for) investing activities	$(76)	$(212)	$(119)	$(117)	$(46)
Cash Flows from Financing Activities:					
Net change in commercial paper	(37)	(16)	(6)	119	(48)
Proceeds from long-term debt	—	—	—	—	1
Reduction of long-term debt		(7)	(24)	(18)	(14)
Dividends paid	(94)	(87)	(83)	(79)	(76)
Acquisition of treasury stock	(13)	(3)		(13)	(17)
Redemption of preferred stock	—	—	—	(12)	—
Cash (used for) financing activities	(144)	(113)	(113)	(3)	(154)
Net increase in cash and cash equivalents	30	(94)	9	93	20
Cash and cash equivalents, beginning of year	86	180	171	78	58
Cash and cash equivalents, end of year	$116	$86	$180	$171	$78

Source: Company reports.

EXHIBIT 10

Brown-Forman Corporation Wine Brands, Sales by Brand, and Estimated Market Share: 1990, 1995, and 2001–2002 (Estimated)

Brand	Thousands of Nine-Liter Cases					Domestic Share, %		
	1990	1995	2000	2001	2002e	2000	2001	2002e
Bel Arbor	—	—	—	—	—	—	—	—
Bolla	925	955	1,095	1,180	1,215	7.1%	6.7%	6.2%
Bonterra	—	—	90	95	105	0.1	0.1	0.1
Chateau Tahbilk	—	—	—	—	—	—	—	—
Fetzer	1,380	1,875	2,310	2,225	2,350	1.6	1.6	1.6
Fontana Candida	285	200	205	225	235	1.3	1.3	1.2
Geoff Merrill Res.	—	—	—	—	—	—	—	—
Jekel	—	60	115	105	120	0.1	0.1	0.1
Korbel*	1,105	1,050	925	1,015	1,090	11.1	12.7	13.5
Mariah	—	—	—	—	—	—	—	—
McPherson	—	—	105	140	175	1.7	1.9	1.7
Owen's Estate	—	—	15	15	20	0.2	0.3	0.2
Picard	—	—	65	60	65	0.7	0.6	0.7
Sonoma-Cutrer	—	—	155	140	150	0.1	0.1	0.1

*Sparkling wine.

Source: Data compiled from IMPACT Databank Review and Forecast, *The U.S. Wine Market,* 2003 edition, pp. 261–301.

organically. The winery was expected to process and age red varietals grown locally. Ninety percent of these grapes were cabernet sauvignon and merlot. Once aged, the wine would be sent to the company's headquarters in Hopland for blending. Fetzer had 12,000 acres on long-term contracts with grape growers in the Paso Robles appellation. Fetzer grew 100 acres of Chardonnay grapes in the Paso Robles area that was sent to Greenfield, California, for processing by Jekel Vineyards.

The most popular Fetzer brands included Sundial Chardonnay, Valley Oaks Cabernet Sauvignon, Eagle Peak Merlot, and home Ranch Zinfandel. Fetzer also produced superpremium reserve wines such as Cabernet Sauvignon, Merlot, Pinot Noir, Chardonnay, and Zinfandel. Fetzer's critically acclaimed classic varietals included Johannisberg Riesling, Gewürztraminer, and White Zinfandel. The majority of Fetzer's sales, however, came from wines in the $6 to $7 per bottle range.

Michel Picard

Michel Picard was the second largest wine producer and the third largest vineyard (227 acres) in Burgundy. BFC entered into a joint venture with Picard *Père et Fils* in 1997 to market and sell their wines in North America and the West Indies. Among other varietals and blends, Michel Picard produced Syrah, Chardonnay, Cabernet Sauvignon, Chablis, Pouilly-Fuisse, and Chateauneuf-du-Pâpe, as well as other brands.

Thomas Burnet became the WD's group president in 1999 and chairman in 2000. Burnet had previously been involved in the start-up of the very successful NutraSweet Company and worked for it from its founding in 1981. He had served in various capacities at NutraSweet, including chief financial officer (CFO), general manager of its international business, and director of the company's new product development activities. Burnet had joined BFC as the CFO of Brown-Forman Beverage Company in 1990. In 1994, he became CFO of Brown-Forman Beverages Worldwide,

Sales of Brown-Forman Corporation's Leading Wine Brands: 1995 and 2000–2002 (Estimated)

Brand	Type of Wine	Thousands of Nine-Liter Cases				Growth Rate[1]	Percent Change[2]		Share of Company Portfolio[2]			
		1995	2000	2001	2002e	1995– 2000	2000– 2001	2001– 2002e	1995	2000	2001	2002e
Fetzer	California table	1,875	2,310	2,225	2,350	4.3%	−3.7%	5.6%	39.7%	42.7%	40.3%	40.2%
Bolla	Italian table	955	1,095	1,180	1,215	2.8	7.8	3.0	20.2	20.3	21.4	20.8
Korbel	California sparkling	1,050	925	1,015	1,090	−2.5	9.7	7.4	22.2	17.1	18.4	18.6
Fontana Candida	Italian table	200	205	225	235	0.5	9.8	4.4	4.2	3.8	4.1	4.0
McPherson	Australian table	—	105	140	175	N/A	33.3	25.0	—	1.9	2.5	3.0
Total Top 5		4,080	4,640	4,785	5,065	2.6	3.1	5.9	86.4	85.8	86.8	86.6
Other brands		640	765	730	785	3.6	−4.6	7.5	13.6	14.2	13.2	13.4
Total Brown-Forman Wine[3]		4,720	5,405	5,515	5,850	2.7%	2.0%	6.1%	100.0%	100.0%	100.0%	100.0%

[1] Average annual compound growth rate.
[2] Based on unrounded data.
[3] Addition of columns may not agree due to rounding.

Source: Data compiled from IMPACT Databank Review and Forecast, *The U.S. Wine Market,* 2003 edition, p. 258.

then a newly formed global division of BFC. In the following year, Burnet accepted additional corporate financial responsibilities and was subsequently named president of the Advancing Markets Group in 1997. Burnet's major responsibility was to oversee the evolution of a loosely organized portfolio of wine brands into a more tightly knit group.

On July 20, 2001, BFC announced the formation of WE, a corporate venture that would be responsible for vineyards, production, sales, and marketing for the company's finest high-end wine brands. In a company press release, Burnet said,

> This is the natural next step in the development of our fine wine business. For the past two years, we've run our Estates Group and Sonoma-Cutrer as separate organizations. We can take better advantage of the strengths of both organizations by combining them. The goal of WE is to build our fine-wine business to be the best in the industry, and we believe that merging these two outstanding organizations will help us accomplish that mission.

Based on Fetzer's established strengths in the distribution and retail channels, Burnet hoped that WE's recently acquired brands, primarily sold to on-premises accounts such as restaurants and hotels, could be leveraged onto off-premises accounts, such as distributors and retailers.

Burnet promoted Steve Dorfman, formerly vice president of Winery Operations at BFC, to serve as managing director of WE. Dorfman, forty-one, and a native of New Jersey, graduated from the University of California at Davis, earning a bachelor's degree in winemaking, and from St. Mary's College, where he earned an MBA. Dorfman had joined Fetzer in 1983 as a winemaker, and over the next seventeen years, he had held positions of increasing responsibility. Dorfman had been involved in grower relations, vineyard management, vineyard acquisitions, and business development. Since BFC's initial purchase of Sonoma-Cutrer in 1999, Dorfman had served as the liaison between BFC and the Sonoma-Cutrer organization. Dorfman felt the key to the Sonoma-Cutrer deal was

EXHIBIT 12

Brown-Forman Corporation's Organization Chart, 2001

Source: Steve Dorfman and Brown-Forman Corporation *Annual Report, 2001.*

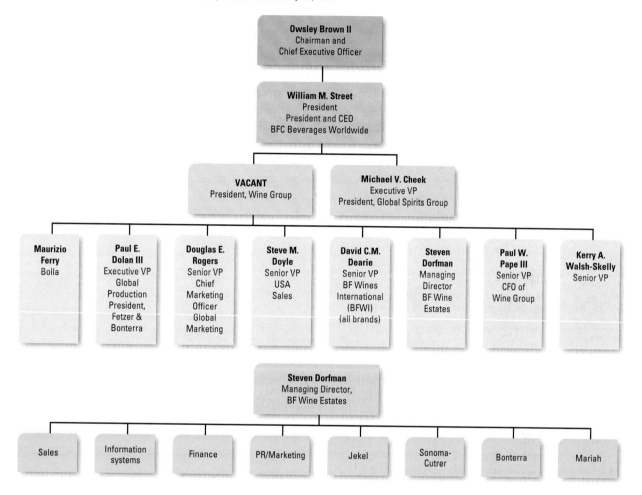

Sonoma-Cutrer sold 97 percent of its wine to on-premise accounts, such as restaurants. This was important to BFC because we didn't have much of a presence in on-premise wine sales. Also, Sonoma Cutrer had an incredible tracking system that enabled management to know where every one of its bottles was sold for the past 10 years. It was basically a sophisticated contact management system with 25,000 accounts and hundreds of thousands of contact transactions over 10+ years, an account history that potentially provides the Estates group the opportunity to penetrate sales of our other brands to Sonoma-Cutrer's accounts. We plan to incorporate that account management system into our other brands. There are also opportunities to expand this system, in order to obtain better knowledge of accounts than our distributors have. This should increase our power over distributors, given that they don't want to lose Sonoma-Cutrer and our other brands.

At the time of Dorfman's promotion, BFC announced that Brice Cutrer Jones, sixty-one, was leaving Sonoma-Cutrer, which he had founded in 1970, over policy disagreements regarding the decision to merge the Sonoma-Cutrer and WE organizations. After Jones departed, a senior BFC executive warned Dorfman, "We know that wine has a low ROA [return on assets], Steve. Don't screw with a tried and true system! Especially when you're just making peanuts vis-à-vis Jack Daniels!" Dorfman felt that if top executives at BFC

EXHIBIT 13

How Brown-Forman Corporation Built Its Wine Portfolio

1965	The company acquired exclusive distribution rights to Korbel's California Champagnes and Brandies.
1968	Bolla Italian Wines added to the company's portfolio.
1987	Distribution rights for Fontana Candida Italian Wines obtained.
1990	Brolio Wines, Italy, exclusive U.S. sales and marketing rights obtained.
1991	BFC Beverages Wine Division established. Jekel Vineyards's super-premium wines added to the portfolio.
1992	Fetzer of Mendocino County purchased.
1994	BFC Beverages Worldwide (BFBW) created. The new wine division was renamed BFC Beverages Worldwide Wine Group (BFBWWG).
1996	John Ash, Fetzer's culinary director, won the Julia Child Best Cookbook of the Year Award for *From the Earth to the Table*.
1997	The Wine Group entered into a joint venture with Michel Picard et Fils, to market French wines in North America and the West Indies.
	Korbel Champagne designated the "Official Champagne of the Millennium" for ten consecutive years, to serve as the exclusive champagne for all New Year's Eve Times Square celebrations until 2007.
1999	Four new brands added: Sonoma-Cutrer Chardonnay, Owen's Estates Wines, McPherson Wines, Mariah Wines.
2000	Thomas P. Burnet named president of the Wine Group, succeeding David Higgins, who retired after forty years with BFC in February 2000.
2001	Steven P. Dorfman named managing director of Brown-Forman Wine Estates (WE), a new group within BFC comprising its super-premium and ultra-premium California and Australian wine brands.
2002	Thomas P. Burnet departs to become president and CEO of Southcorp Wines (Australia).

Source: Company press releases.

really believed that brand power was all that mattered, then they should let WE build brands and do what it needed to do with a minimum of interference. In early January 2002, Dorfman recalled why he had taken the position:

> Becoming Managing Director was the third leg on my stool. For the first time, I had the abilities *and* experience to do everything on my own. I started out in the wine industry as a vintner and grower, and was now comfortable to do something on my own, because I knew the growers, sales, marketing, and distribution channels.

WE's brands are listed in Exhibit 15. Each is discussed in more detail below:

Bonterra Bonterra was, along with Bel Arbor, created as a second label of Fetzer's. Bonterra grew Chardonnay, Merlot, Cabernet Sauvignon, and Petite Syrah on 133 acres. Bonterra also purchased the historic 378-acre organic McNab Ranch. Paul Dolan, president of Fetzer, also performed those duties for Bonterra Vineyards.

Jekel Vineyards This winery was founded by Bill Jekel in Greenfield, California, in 1972. It was located along the ancient bed of the Arroyo Seco River. The winery produces estate-bottled wines in the superpremium category. Among them are Cabernet Sauvignon, Pinot Noir, Syrah, and Riesling in the $11 to $30 prices range. Furthermore, Chardonnay—grown on one hundred acres by Fetzer in the Paso Robles area—was being sent for processing to Jekel Vineyards. Jekel Vineyards was acquired by BFC in 1991.

EXHIBIT 14

Brown-Forman Corporation: Wine Division Portfolio Brands

Brand	Price Segment	Location	Vineyard Holdings	Facilities	Other Information
Bolla	Premium	Verona, Italy	Grower based	Bolla Verona Bolla Soave	
Fetzer	Premium Super-Premium Ultra-Premium	Mendocino County, CA	1,000 acres	Fetzer Mendocino Fetzer Paso Robles	Recognized industry leader in environmental best practices.
Fontana Candida	Premium	Italy	Grower based	Fontana Candida	
Korbel	Premium	Sonoma County, CA	Agency brand	Sonoma County	
McPherson	Ultra-Premium	McLaren Vale, Australia	Grower based	Del Farras	
Picard	Premium	Chany, France	Grower based	Chany Montpelier	2nd largest wine producer and 3rd largest vineyard (227 acres) in Burgundy.

Source: Based on personal correspondence with Steve Dorfman.

EXHIBIT 15

Brown-Forman Wine Estates: Portfolio of Brands

Brand	Price Segment	Location	Vineyard Holdings	Facilities	Other Information
Bonterra	Premium	Mendocino County, CA	325 acres	Fetzer Mendocino	Started as second label of Fetzer; certified organic.
Bel Arbor	Bulk	Mendocino County, CA	Bulk Wines	Fetzer Mendocino	Second label of Fetzer.
Ch. Tahbilk	Ultra-Premium	Golburn Valley, Australia	Agency brand	Ch, Tahbilk	
Geoff Merril Reserve	Ultra-Premium	McLaren Vale, Australia	JV trademark	Geoff Merrill Wines	
Jekel	Super-Premium Ultra-Premium	Monterey County, CA	310 acres	Jekel Monterey	Estate-bottled wines in $11–$30 per bottle range.
Mariah	Ultra-Premium	Mendocino County, CA	27 acres	Fetzer Mendocino	Produces 2,000 cases/yr of reserve Zinfandel for on-premise sales.
Owen's Estate	Ultra-Premium	McLaren Vale, Australia	Agency brand	Geoff Merrill Wines	
Sonoma-Cutrer	Ultra-Premium Luxury Premium	Sonoma County, CA	1125 acres	Sonoma-Cutrer	Mostly on-premises sales of premium Chardonnays.

Source: Based on personal correspondence with Steve Dorfman.

Mariah Wines   Acquired by BFC in 1999, Mariah produced wines in the Mendocino Ridge (Mendocino County) appellation in the ultra-premium price range. This winery produced 250 cases of Reserve Zinfandel a year from 24 acres of plantings. It sold high-end Zinfandel on-premise (restaurant) only.

Owen's Estate, Geoff Merrill Reserve, and Chateau Tahbilk   Due to deregulation in the 1990s, the Australian wine industry experienced unprecedented boom-times and record harvests, which brought about an oversupply of good quality grapes. Australia was by 2001 the fourth largest exporter of wine to the United States, following Italy, France, and Chile. BFC entered into joint ventures with these three Australian estate wineries to market their high-quality wines worldwide.

Sonoma-Cutrer Winery   Founded by Brice Jones in 1970, Sonoma-Cutrer was located in California's Sonoma Coast region. Sonoma-Cutrer used modern technology combined with Burgundian traditions (i.e., extended underground aging in proprietary French oak barrels). To obtain the best French oak possible, Sonoma-Cutrer went into the forestry

business in 1994. They grew, cut, and aged the wood (for three years) in France. Barrel coopering was done locally in France. The winery used traditional cave or underground cellars with earthen floors, in order to provide natural humidity (over 90 percent) and constant cool, ambient air (at 58°F) that prevented oxidation and evaporation. Sonoma-Cutrer owned and farmed its own vineyards and did not purchase fruit from outside sources. Sonoma-Cutrer was well known in the high-end restaurant trade for its ultra-premium Chardonnay wines. Its luxury premium products, Les Pierres, The Cutrer, and The Russian River Ranches, were estate-bottled Chardonnays sold on an allocation basis to select on-premises accounts.

Given BFC's historical emphasis on achieving ROA targets in excess of 19 percent, the past year had been a disappointment. Dorfman was mindful that any projected sales of WE's brands would have to show how his group could contribute to meeting BFC's corporate targeted ROA for 2003 and beyond. Past results and internal financial projections for 2002–2004 by wine brand are shown in Exhibits

EXHIBIT 16

Brown-Forman Corporation, Actual and Projected Sales by Brand, 1998–2004 ($000s)

	Actual Sales				Projected Sales		
	1998	1999	2000	2001	2002	2003	2004
Brown-Forman Wine Estates' U.S. Brands							
Sonoma-Cutrer	$—	$—	$17,078	$18,136	$18,798	$21,302	$24,246
Bonterra—International	6,913	8,016	11,633	12,368	15,504	18,668	21,119
Bonterra—U.S.	5,503	5,823	7,885	9,006	9,779	11,740	13,329
Jekel	7,229	7,788	9,995	9,997	11,809	14,193	16,515
Mariah	—	99	405	293	414	986	1,116
Brown-Forman Wine Estates' Australian Brands							
Owen's Estates	—	—	1,364	1,699	2,514	3,119	3,849
Geoff Merrill Reserve	—	—	53	197	217	217	224
Tahbilk	—	—	60	297	790	945	1,100
Consolidated Wine Group Brands							
Fetzer—Worldwide	$156,518	$176,620	$185,744	$187,815	$224,414	$235,704	$249,541
Fetzer—U.S.	105,609	115,212	123,342	127,717	144,656	145,378	148,321
Bolla—International	26,857	49,367	46,056	43,481	56,158	62,439	67,176
Bolla—U.S.	44,119	44,949	50,399	55,358	62,438	64,583	69,530
Korbel	83,177	101,486	120,587	82,425	96,354	107,682	110,932

Source: Prepared by case writers from personal correspondence with Steve Dorfman.

EXHIBIT 17

Brown-Forman Wine Estates, Actual and Projected Brand Profit per Case, 1998–2004

	Actual Per Case				Projected Per Case		
	1998	1999	2000	2001	2002	2003	2004
Brown-Forman Wine Estates' U.S. Brands							
Sonoma-Cutrer	$—	$—	$11.64	$14.14	$14.64	$19.01	$24.41
Bonterra—International	9.04	1.35	12.53	11.47	13.04	16.94	19.05
Bonterra—U.S.	5.44	(4.67)	10.95	14.91	13.62	17.49	20.89
Jekel	22.86	16.36	15.52	9.30	13.90	16.89	17.69
Mariah	—	(21.13)	1.84	4.54	21.51	57.59	59.58
Australian Brands							
Owen's Estates	—	—	(7.29)	(2.75)	2.45	3.85	6.11
Geoff Merrill Reserve	—	—	8.85	18.19	13.67	31.91	32.69
Tahbilk	—	—	(13.08)	5.32	12.23	12.23	11.56
Consolidated Wine Group Brands							
Fetzer—Worldwide	$5.77	$4.97	$6.29	$7.97	$7.84	$8.07	$8.58
Fetzer—U.S.	6.75	5.64	7.79	9.99	9.84	9.62	9.70
Bolla—International	3.56	5.82	4.32	4.08	3.56	3.99	4.43
Bolla—U.S.	5.28	5.83	5.72	7.68	8.43	8.53	9.46
Korbel	2.99	6.29	4.28	1.23	6.60	5.78	5.33

Source: Prepared by case writers from personal correspondence with Steve Dorfman.

16–18. These projections include brand sales in dollars, per case income, and incremental ROAs for selected super- and ultra-premium labels.

Exhibit 19 provides BFC's internal projections out to the year 2020, showing the respective shares of its wine and spirits segments in its drinks portfolio. These projections were based on internal estimates that the growth rate in wine sales would be nearly seven times as fast as the growth rate in sales of spirits.

BFC also maintained a significant presence in export markets via its international division. In the past, this division had been primarily responsible for selling Fetzer wines into export markets. BFC's Wines International Division, headed by David Dearie, marketed Fetzer and twenty-five other brands in seventy-five countries and was expanding rapidly. Prior to assuming his position as managing director of Wines International, Dearie had worked for four years in BFC's international spirits division. BFC executives hoped that Dearie's International Division could sell WE's super- and ultra-premium wine portfolio brands into export markets. Exhibit 20 illustrates BFC's current estimated share of California wine exports based on volume of cases sold, using 1999 shipments as a base.

BFC's Future Prospects

Over the previous ten years, sales of wine in the premium and ultra-premium segments had enjoyed double-digit growth rates. However, in summer 2002 news coming from the California wine industry indicated that growth was slowing. After modest declines in sales immediately following the September 11, 2001, terrorist attacks in New York and Washington, D.C., California wines had continued to experience a "difficult year" thus far in 2002. The U.S. wine industry as a whole was undergoing increasing consolidation as the rapid growth of the 1990s—which had enticed numerous new entrants into the wine industry—gave way to overproduction, oversupply of grapes, and inadequate growth in demand to keep up with the increasing supply. The "Two Buck Chuck" phenomenon was also contributing to lackluster growth in premium wine sales. Franzia's Charles Shaw wines (nicknamed "Two Buck Chuck") had been the greatest

EXHIBIT 18

Brown-Forman Corporation, Actual and Projected Returns on Assets (ROA) by Brand, 1998–2004

	Actual Incremental ROA				Projected Incremental ROA		
	1998	1999	2000	2001	2002	2003	2004
U.S. Brands							
Sonoma-Cutrer	—	—	5.3%	5.0%	4.4%	4.4%	4.7%
Bonterra—International	N/A	6.9	14.7	12.1	13.4	16.6	17.4
Bonterra—U.S.	8.9	6.4	18.6	19.3	17.5	22.1	24.1
Jekel	10.6	11.4	16.5	9.4	13.4	14.9	15.0
Mariah	0.0	−1.0	5.0	3.4	17.2	39.1	38.9
Australia							
Owen's Estates	—	—	−0.7	7.8	20.6	22.3	27.1
Geoff Merrill Reserve	—	—	11.2	16.7	25.1	49.8	52.6
Tahbilk	—	—	−5.1	−13.0	35.2	35.5	35.3
Consolidated Wine Group							
Fetzer—Worldwide	19.5	19.1	23.3	22.6	21.2	20.6	20.3
Fetzer —U.S.	26.8	26.0	35.0	30.9	28.8	27.4	26.3
Bolla—International	4.8	10.1	6.4	6.1	5.9	6.3	7.1
Bolla—U.S.	81.2	24.2	23.8	48.3	56.2	43.7	47.7
Korbel	78.2	96.4	107.0	84.6	172.5	164.2	153.8

Source: Prepared by case writers from personal correspondence with Steve Dorfman.

EXHIBIT 19

Projected Share of Total U.S. Wine and Spirits Revenue
for Brown-Forman Corporation

Source: Brown-Forman Wine Estates.

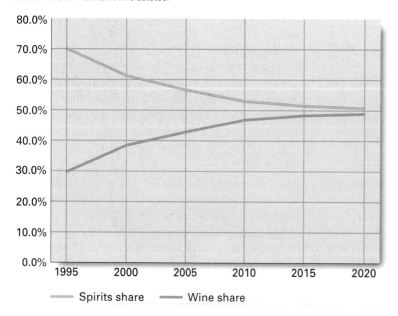

Spirits share   Wine share

EXHIBIT 20

Brown-Forman Wine Segment: Estimated Export Volume
as a Percentage of California Exports

Key Markets	BFC Volume (000 cases)	Total California Exports (000 cases)	BFC's Share of Total California Exports
United Kingdom	222	7,069	3%
Japan	160	5,742	3%
Canada	107	5,054	2%
Netherlands	8	2,126	—
Switzerland	41	1,290	3%
Germany	42	1,040	4%
Denmark	3	566	<1%

Source: Brown-Forman Wine Estates' estimates.

success story in the wine industry in the first half of 2002, retailing for $24 per case of twelve bottles at Trader Joe's Markets.

In this uncertain sales environment and with his champion Burnet now heading up a rival firm in Australia, Dorfman was preparing for a presentation of his annual plan back at BFC's headquarters in Kentucky. Dorfman felt sure that his preferred strategy, retaining WE as a separate "intrapreneurial" venture within the WD, would be met with skepticism. Still, WE might be spared if he were to identify how to re-structure its portfolio of wine businesses, selling off poorly performing or noncore brands, as well as how to implement cost reductions across the remaining brands. However, throughout its long history BFC had never divested a business it had previously pur-chased. Dorfman felt that bowing to the inevitable pressure to fold the WE group back in with the WD could reduce costs but likely result in his own job as managing director being redefined or possibly elimi-nated entirely.

Upon his return to Healdsburg, Dorfman asked for Keith LaVine's counsel. After a long career in hotel beverages purchasing and wholesale distribu-tion of wine, LaVine had become Sonoma-Cutrer's regional manager for the Southeast United States, just two years prior to its purchase by BFC in 1999. Since then, LaVine had been promoted to national sales manager and moved to California, becoming WE's senior vice president of sales in late July 2001.

LaVine began the meeting by saying flatly that,

It is time for us to become more flexible, Steve. Corporate is streamlining, 'trimming the fat.' This includes layoffs and spin-offs. I believe that we can meet any future challenge, but the bad news is that the wine industry isn't going to get better for the next few years. We need to be as productive as in the past, just with fewer personnel. Does keeping the our division the way it is make any sense now or should we just fold it in with the WD's brands and have a 'monster' wine division?

Dorfman reminded LaVine of the potential syn-ergies among WE's and the WD's brands.

Well, there is going to have to be some more in-teraction in the future, Keith. Sales, marketing, and finance are probably where any future combina-tions will occur in order to avoid duplication of ef-fort. Corporate will look for cost advantages such as vineyard purchasing, grape purchasing, glass pro-curement, and other things where buying in larger quantity or centralized negotiations gives us a leg up.

LaVine mentioned several rumors that had been circulating around the WD.

Steve, I hear that corporate might decide to inte-grate some of the high-end spirits into our division. The advantage to our division the way it is today is that we can focus more on fewer brands, which gar-ners more attention for those brands. What do the spirits salespeople know about selling wine?

Dorfman agreed to some extent.

Keith, there is *some* potential for synergy between wines and spirits, since spirits, like wines, are sold through similar distribution channels, *if* the goal is to grow price by entering premium segments. Look, the major benefit of having BFC as our parent organization is that it provides access to capital and talent. Corporate is akin to a mutual fund or investment bank first; a marketer, second. Whatever happens, we need to maintain a symbiotic relationship with BFC. That's how we were able to hire our new CFO—we hired her from Fetzer. Corporate formerly ran Sonoma-Cutrer like a mutual fund—one organization didn't bother the other—yet this had some negative effects in that some BFC salespeople didn't know what Sonoma-Cutrer was or how to sell or position its wine. Also, corporate views distributors as its customers while Sonoma-Cutrer views each account as a customer and distributors as a necessary evil.

LaVine wasn't sure that corporate executives at BFC held all the cards.

Okay, Steve, but there is also a 'halo effect' created by small wineries such as Mariah to help consumers look at Brown-Forman as a diversified company instead of just being a 'Bourbon house.' We are in a unique position, really, because we have a parent who is cash rich. We also have an opportunity to take advantage of someone else's misfortune during the coming hard times in the wine industry and perhaps purchase new smaller wineries.

Dorfman ended the meeting with LaVine and sat down to prepare his presentation for the upcoming Beverages Division meeting in Louisville. In addition to choosing a course of action, Dorfman faced the challenge of identifying what managerial components WE needed to correct in order to implement any changes that he (with BFC approval) might want to make. He reflected on his dilemma:

Before I went into the wine industry, I wish I had known how complex this business was. You have to be able to make wine, sell it, and market it. Marketing is very difficult, and it is very competitive on the sales side. It seems to me that the cost savings of combining all wines into a centralized organization are outweighed by the differentiation in production that results from separation. This can carry through to sales and marketing,

because the decisions that each production unit [winery] makes every day allows for a unique sales story to be told out in the marketplace.

Mindful that selection of either strategic option would require BFC's approval, Dorfman decided to sit down and rethink what role his group of brands should play within BFC's conglomerate portfolio and how he would implement this role.

REFERENCES

Adams (1999). *Adams Wine Handbook*, Adams Business Media, New York.

Anonymous (1999). And Now the Numbers, *Wine & Vines,* July.

Anonymous (2001). Gallo "Expansion Project Slowed." [Online]. **www.kj.com/.**

Anonymous (2001). "Lew Platt Was Out at KJ." *Wines and Vines,* June.

Appel, T. (1995). "Deal Closed for Top Wineries Sale, Include Beringer, a Record." *Santa Rosa Press Democrat,* November 22, p. E1.

Brown-Forman Corporation (2000, 2001). *Annual Reports.*

California Wine Export Program (2000). *World Vineyard, Grape, and Wine Report, 2000,* July, 425 Market Street, Suite 1000, San Francisco, California 94105.

Correspondence to the case writers with Steve Dorfman (2001). May 8.

De Luca, J. (2002). "The Outlook for the California Wine Industry in 2002," Presentation to the North Bay Economic Outlook Conference, Rohnert Park. California, February.

Echikson, W. et al. (2001). "Wine War," *Business Week,* September 3, pp. 54–60.

Gomberg-Fredrikson (1999). *1999 Annual Wine Industry Review,* Gomberg, Fredrikson & Associates, 703 Market Street, Suite 1602, San Francisco, California 94103.

Gould, L. E. (2001). "A Golden Opportunity," Advantstar Communications.

IMPACT Databank Review and Forecast (2003). *The U.S. Wine Market,* 2003 edition. New York: M. Shanken Publications.

Interviews with Steve Dorfman, April 2001, January 2002, and April 2003.

Interviews with Keith LaVine, March and October 2003.

Love, J. M. (2000). "United States Wine Producers Face Increasing Competition." *Wine Business Monthly,* June, p. 1.

Moran, T. (2001). "California Wineries Quietly End Legal Battle." *Modesto Bee,* March 31, p. C1.

Motto Kryla Fisher. (2002). "High-end California Wine Sales Increase 10% in 2001." Unified Grape Symposium, Sacramento, California, January.

Mutual Acceptance Agreement on Oenological Practices, 2001. April 9.

Nation's Restaurant News, 35(10), March 5, 2001.

www.hoovers.com/. Hoovers Online Capsule: Diageo PLC, 2001.

www.napanews.com/. Saturday, March 10, 2001.

www.hoovers.com. Hoovers Online Capsule: Robert Mondavi Corporation, 2001.

Peterson, T. (2001). "For the Mondavis, It's a Long Way from Muscatel." *Business Week,* June 15.

Sinton, P. (1999). "California Wines Quenching the World." *San Francisco Chronicle,* January 23, p. D1.

Tagliabue, J. (2001). "Trying to Make the Wine List." *New York Times,* April 11.

U.S. Department of Commerce (2000). *2000 National Trade Data Bank.*

Wine Institute (2000). Wine Institute, 425 Market Street, Suite 1000, San Francisco, California 94105, www.wineinstitute.org.

Wines & Vines (2001). *Directory and Buyer's Guide,* vol. 81, p. 12-A (December 31, 2000), The Hiaring Company, San Rafael, California.

Case 2

Welch Foods, Inc.

This case was prepared by Vincent Amanor-Boadu, Michael Boland, and David Barton, Kansas State University.

W elch Foods Inc. (Welch's) is a wholly owned subsidiary of the National Grape Cooperative Association, Inc. (National Grape). Welch's president and CEO, Dan Dillon, says his company faces an increasingly strong challenge to remain relevant to customers and consumers. He put it this way: "At our current size, are we going to be able to remain on the radar screen of companies such as Wal-Mart? Will they want to see us if we request a meeting?" Additionally, says Dillon, it is critical for Welch's that its consumers associate grape juice with the distinctive characteristics of Concord and Niagara grapes. This question of competitive relevance and scale is critical to all food companies in the rapidly consolidating marketplace. But perhaps more important to the viability and survival of a cooperative-owned food processing company such as Welch's is its organizational system. The unique structure of the two-board of directors has to support the strategies that Welch's needs to remain relevant.

Dillon has made it his mission to maintain Welch's relevancy by strengthening relationships with key customers and suppliers, as well as providing consumers with the products they want at a price point they believe is competitive. The question of relevance was not new at Welch's or to Dillon. When a consultant advised Welch's to move away from dark juices in the early 1980s, Dillon, then a young Welch's executive,

responded sharply that that view was unacceptable. He proceeded to embark on a mission to prove that "the purple grape juice" was not only a successful product with a future but also capable of leading the entire juice category. By 2002, Welch's purple grape juice and other products claimed number one or number two spots among all noncitrus multiserve manufacturers.

Origin of National Grape Cooperative and Welch Foods

Jack Kaplan, an entrepreneur, purchased a small grape processing facility in 1933 from some investment bankers in Brocton, New York, and called his new company National Grape Corporation. To control inflation during World War II, the U.S. government instituted price control policies for most industries but exempted farmer cooperatives, allowing them to pass through their prices to the market. Kaplan decided to take advantage of this legislation by selling his company to the growers supplying grapes to his plant on the condition they formed a cooperative. The growers accepted and National Grape was born in 1945. Its membership has grown to encompass the majority of the Concord and Niagara grape growers in Michigan, New York, Ohio, Pennsylvania, Washington, and Ontario, Canada.

In 1869, Dr. Thomas Welch and his son Charles applied Louis Pasteur's theory to the processing of Concord grapes, succeeding in producing an unfermented wine for use at church services. Charles took over the business in the 1870s, producing "Dr. Welch's Unfermented Wine" on a part-time basis while running his dentistry practice. He changed the brand name to "Dr. Welch's Grape Juice" in 1890, and after a

Copyright © 2004 by Vincent Amanor-Boadu, Michael Boland, and David Barton. This case was prepared by Vincent Amanor-Boadu, Michael Boland, and David Barton, Kansas State University, as the basis for class discussion rather than to illustrate either effective or ineffective handling of an administration situation. Reprinted by permission of Michael Boland. All rights reserved.

C35

successful exhibition of the product at the Chicago World Fair in 1893, dropped the "Dr." from the label. This success at the World Fair also caused the younger Dr. Welch to quit his dentistry practice and devote his attention to the company full time, significantly growing the business and the brand. Charles successfully ran the company until his death in 1926 and the company was sold to a group of private investors from Tennessee shortly thereafter.

Welch's came up for sale in 1945, and Kaplan purchased it and became its president. Kaplan set in motion for National Grape to purchase Welch's during the early 1950s, with the objective of giving growers "complete control of their destiny, from raw fruit to finished product." But since the growers did not have the money to pay outright, Kaplan offered them a "mortgage" that allowed him to specify how the processing company was governed. In 1956, the directors of National Grape Cooperative voted to purchase Welch's stock and paid off the mortgage on the company in three years.

Over time, National Grape Cooperative Association set the vision "to be the best choice of present and future members to market their grape production." Its mission focused on being "dedicated to providing the most profitable long-term market for all of its members' quality Concord and Niagara grapes." Its ownership of Welch Foods, Inc., provided it with a vehicle to achieve the vision and accomplish the mission.

The Governance System in National Grape and Welch Foods

National Grape and Welch's each has its own board of directors, a stipulation put in place by Kaplan when he sold his processing company to the growers. Aware of the failure rate of farmer cooperatives attempting to undertake consumer products manufacturing and marketing, Kaplan stipulated a two-board system to allow the growers to govern the cooperative and a mix of growers and people knowledgeable in the packaged goods industry to govern Welch's. The two-board system turned out to provide the appropriate checks and balances required to manage the complex business of growing, processing, and marketing consumer packaged goods. "What you have is an arrangement that carefully balances the needs and concerns of the growers with the needs of the business," explained Dillon. "You have this stable system in place that care-

fully analyzes and weighs the costs and benefits of every key decision that needs to be made," Dillon continued about the two-board system.

In 2003, National Grape's governance was based on the traditional one-member, one-vote principle of cooperative representation. The key Concord and Niagara grape growing areas for National Grape were Yakima Valley in Washington State, southwestern Michigan and northern Ohio, the Lake Erie area of New York and Pennsylvania, and the Finger Lakes in New York and Ontario, Canada. These four key areas were divided into thirteen production districts and 103 geographic sections.

National Grape's board of directors was comprised of thirteen members elected from each of the production areas and was responsible for establishing policies regarding member needs and raw grape production. The board elected the officers of National Grape annually and appointed a general manager to implement board policy and oversee operations. The distribution of directors in the different areas is based on the number of grower members in the area. Areas I, II, and III each has three directors while Area IV has four directors. Because the directors are elected by area, it is possible for more than one director to come from a particular district. Each director is elected to a three-year term, and director terms are staggered into three classes, each class representing a particular year on the board. There are no term limits on directors as long as they are willing to serve and are elected by members in their area.

In addition to the board, National Grape's members annually elected thirteen delegates to represent them in each of the organization's thirteen production districts. Their responsibilities included acting as a critical communications link between members, the board, and management and chairing their district's membership meetings. Finally, the advisory committees, 103 members, are elected from the geographic sections to provide direct feedback on issues to the board and to management and to provide a gauge on the pulse of the general membership. Advisory committee members meet at the local level about four to six times per year.

There are 10 people on Welch's board; 4 representatives from the National Grape board, 4 outside directors, and 2 representatives of Welch's management, including the company's CEO (Figure 1). The 4 representatives from National Grape include the

FIGURE 1

National Grape and Welch's Two-Board System

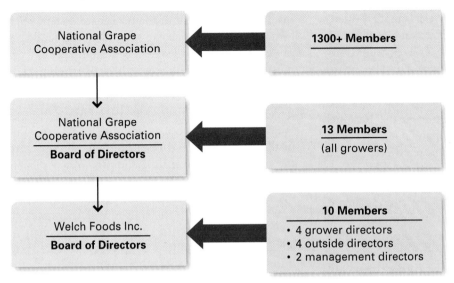

chair of National Grape's board and 3 others elected by National Grape's board. The outside directors are appointed from a slate of candidates, and the management representatives are submitted by the nominating committee of Welch's board to the National Grape board. Membership of the Welch's board is for one year. "The fact that there are four outside directors and four growers provides the balance that has contributed to the effectiveness of this model," Dillon observed.

Dillon was very clear in his perception about the relationship between the two companies. "We look at the members of National Grape as our stockholders and we think about the National Grape board in the same way General Motors thinks about its investment bankers," he explained. "We provide them with all the information they need, but we do not ask them for a vote."

When there are major issues that could affect growers—acquisitions, divestitures, plant closings, etc.—Welch's discussed those issues with the National Grape board to ensure that there was enhanced understanding of the possible ramifications. Welch's also negotiated grape quality specifications with National Grape to ensure that Welch's products remained competitive in the consumer marketplace in terms of its value proposition and that growers received competitive compensation for their products. Once these

specifications are decided, neither Welch's nor National Grape can change them without the other's consent. This arrangement has worked very well for both companies, given that the National Grape board has all the relevant information motivating decisions at Welch's.

The two-board system demanded significant effort from all concerned to work effectively. For example, Welch's staff devoted a lot of time educating new National Grape and Welch's directors to create a "common language" and facilitate communication. A. B. (Trey) Wright, Welch's CFO, explained it this way: "Outside board members have to learn the difference between proceeds and profits, and the grower-members, who tend to talk and think in terms of crop year results, have to learn to convert to fiscal year results because Welch's is run on a fiscal year basis."

The representatives of National Grape's board on Welch's board have changed more frequently than the outside directors. Consequently, they needed more training to ensure that the "common language" was maintained among Welch's board members. For example, Welch's people noted that they often have to explain to new growers on Welch's board the importance of financing assets with sufficient equity because there is a belief that since Welch's can borrow at better interest rates than producers, it should distribute all proceeds and borrow or leverage with debt to finance capital improvements. This education was not limited to just National Grape's representatives on Welch's board. Welch's made presentations to the National Grape board at almost every National Grape board meeting and answered any questions that allowed National Grape's board members to increase their understanding of the packaged goods business and industry. Welch's also provided all necessary information to the National Grape board, as any public company does. "We have to do this. It helps us operate more efficiently and create the value that is our primary objective," Dillon pointed out.

There was significant collegiality among board members, despite their different backgrounds. "The outside directors respect the growers because of their extensive agricultural knowledge and the owners respect the outside directors for their commitment and valuable input," noted Wright about the relationship among Welch's board members. "In twenty-two years of going to six board meetings a year, I can count on one hand the number of times we have ever had a vote that wasn't unanimous," Dillon added. Thus, the system works because people learn quickly to appreciate the challenges confronting the packaged goods company and their responsibilities in addressing these challenges. "Even those who get elected to the board on the promise of changing the system change their opinions once they come on the board and recognize the effort everyone is putting in to addressing the issues confronting us," Dillon noted.

Welch's board structured its management compensation incentives to be aligned with the grower-owners' rewards. For example, management was rewarded on items such as net proceeds per ton of grapes received and not on profit per case of grape juice sold. "This ties it all together," Wright pointed out. "Even though we are separate companies and we focus on the different segments of the business, the reward systems are the same and they tie the two companies together."

The governance structure at National Grape and Welch's offered two critical advantages: (1) it allowed National Grape to focus on its core functions—such as cooperative and ownership issues and the production and delivery of quality grapes; and (2) it allowed Welch's to focus on the job of product development, manufacturing, marketing, and sale of packaged goods. Since the issues facing grape producers and the packaged goods company were different, the governance system ensured that the critical issues in each facet were not overlooked or underemphasized. Dillon recognized this important benefit of the two-board system when he noted that "we are able to succeed at what we do because of the two-board system which insulates us from most of the issues occurring at the production level."

The Business of Welch Foods

Welch's saw its purpose as building long-term value in the cooperative and releasing that value back to the grower-owner over time and providing a reliable market for their grapes through excellence in product quality, customer service, market responsiveness, and consumer satisfaction. Welch's processed 50 percent of Concord grapes and 80 percent of Niagara grapes produced in the United States into juices, jellies, jams, and other products. It was the leading marketer of Concord and Niagara grape-based products in the world. The company produced a variety of other fruit-based products, including 100 percent juices and juice cocktails. The company owned the Welch's and BAMA brand names, using the latter in the marketing of its jams, jellies, and preserves in the South. Its products were available in bottled, refrigerated, single-serve, and frozen and shelf-stable formats. Additionally, it served the industrial market, supplying concentrates to further processors and other manufacturers (Figure 2).

Marketing and Promotion

Welch's was one of the first food companies to take advantage of radio and television to market products. In 1934, it began an eleven-year sponsorship of the Irene Rich radio show. It became one of television's first corporate sponsors when it found a fit between its products and its image and *The Howdy Doody Show* in 1951. Its "Memories" advertising campaign, which features young spokeschildren, enters its tenth year in 2004. Since the early days with Charles Welch, the company focused on innovative marketing and sales approaches—magazines, radio, television, the sides of trolley cars—to reach customers and consumers. For example, it advertised in magazines to explain to its customers why there were shortages of Welch's products during World War II. Welch's also introduced the long-running jelly glasses in 1953, featuring Howdy Doody as the first "star."

FIGURE 2

Product Categories at Welch Foods, Inc.

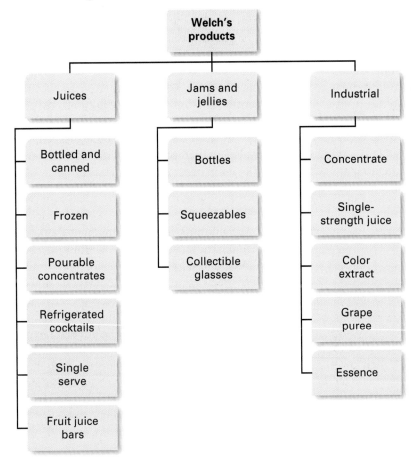

Since then the campaign has featured kids' favorite movie and cartoon characters such as Simba's Pride, Winnie the Pooh, Tom and Jerry, Looney Tunes characters, the Flintstones, Jimmy Neutron, and Dragon Tales characters.

Welch's always looked for ways to extend its strong brand image. One such opportunity was the 1999 licensing agreement with C. H. Robinson, which allowed Welch's to enter the fresh produce aisle with branded fresh grapes. The program had been very successful, generating sales of more than 16 million packages of Welch's Fresh Grapes to consumers and involving more than thirty grocery chains across the country in its first year.

Welch's was very aggressive in the increasingly competitive fruit juice market, using new product launchings, well-crafted and targeted consumer promotions and advertising, and enhanced consumer communication in various media, including via the Internet. The company recently established a loyalty program with Upromise, whereby money is contributed to a child's college education fund when a consumer (with a Upromise account) purchases Welch's jelly products. The company has also collaborated with **ValuPage.com** to offer consumers the opportunity to select particular promotional products online and print associated coupons to be used in participating stores for discounts on its products.

International Activities

By 2003, Welch's was marketing its products in forty international markets, but the company's principal export markets were Canada, Japan, South Korea, and the Latin America–Caribbean area. Through an alliance arrangement, the company processed and distributed a variety of shelf-stable products in the United Kingdom, introducing seven new products in 2002 and launching an approximately $8 million marketing campaign (television ads, a public relations campaign championing the health benefits of its products, and a tactical sampling program encompassing radio promotions) to support them. The company also signed a distribution agreement with Nong Shim, a South Korean consumer products company, to improve its penetration into the Southeast Asian market. Welch's had used a similar strategic alliances approach when it entered Japan, reducing new market entry costs and enhancing its competitive advantage. Total international sales in 2003 reached $120 million compared with $100 million in 2002.

Innovations in Products and Packaging

From its early days, Welch's had continuously looked to product and packaging innovation as a competitive strategy (Figure 3). For example, it introduced the squeezable containers for jelly and jams in 1985 to improve the feasibility of kids preparing their own sandwiches and launched the shatterproof jelly jar in 1999 to minimize accidents when kids took the initiative to "take care of themselves." Welch's also focused on innovation in convenience, such as the introduction of shelf-stable juice concentrates in 1996 which allowed juice to be mixed without waiting for it to thaw. In 2003, the company introduced three new 100 percent white grape blends into the market.

A principal driver in these efforts is the objective to have 25 percent of the company's sales come from new products (products that have been introduced within the past five years). This objective was considered essential not only in extending and growing Welch's brand, but also in answering the demands of consumers as their tastes and needs evolved. "In other words," emphasizes Dillon, "it's what the company has to do in order to remain relevant."

Research and Development

In 1997, Welch's built a new Technology Center in Billerica, Massachusetts, a short drive from the company's Concord headquarters. The forty-thousand-square-foot facility, one of the largest among cooperative organizations, employed about fifty quality control, engineering, and research and development professionals. Prior to building the Technology Center, Welch's research and development, engineering, and quality control professionals were located three hundred fifty miles away in Westfield, New York, away from the marketing, market research, and operations people with whom they needed to interact frequently. It was hoped that by bringing the marketing and

FIGURE 3

FIGURE 3

Innovation at Welch's Through the Years

Source: Developed from information on Welch Foods Inc.'s website (**www.welchs.com**).

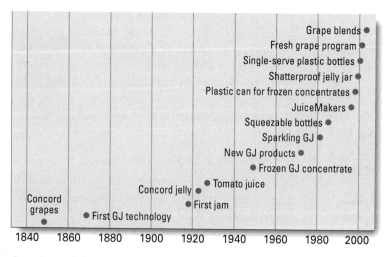

GJ = Grape juice

market research group together with the engineering, quality control, and research and development group in the same facility, ideas would flow more easily and the enhanced communication would engender more new products. It did—in the generation of both products and intellectual property. Dillon explained it this way: "In the first fifty years of the company's existence, we received two patents; in the last five years, we have filed for fourteen patents and to date have received patent awards on nine of those. It tells you what sort of company we are today compared to what we have been."

Welch's has driven its product development objective with its own internal effort as well as through collaboration with other organizations and researchers. For example, the company has contributed to funding research exploring the health benefits of grape juice made from Concord and Niagara grapes. A USDA study found that Welch's Purple 100 percent grape juice had three times more antioxidant power than other popular juices such as grapefruit, orange, tomato, and apple, and more antioxidant power than forty two other tested fruits and vegetables.[1] Other preliminary studies have suggested that the antioxidant activity of Concord grape juice may be similar to that of red wine. In 1999, *Circulation*, the journal of the American Heart Association, published a report by researchers from the University of Wisconsin Medical School indicating that the elasticity of blood vessels increased significantly and the rate at which their LDL ("bad") cholesterol oxidized decreased significantly when their subjects drank purple grape juice for two weeks.[2] Similarly, in 2002, researchers at the University of Illinois Urbana–Champaign indicated that purple grape juice fed to laboratory animals led to significant reductions in both mammary tumor mass and the number of tumors per animal.[3] In another study, researchers at University of California, Davis Medical Center, also found that

Concord grape juice flavonoids are potent antioxidants that may protect against oxidative stress and reduce the risk of free radical damage and chronic diseases.[4]

Not one to miss opportunities, Welch's recruited such celebrity personalities as Larry King and Paul Harvey to extol the health benefits of Welch's products to consumers. The company also communicated directly with medical practitioners and attended the relevant medical conventions to educate and exhibit to the professionals the role of its products in human health.

Technology and Quality

Welch's had an intense focus on protecting its brand image while listening and responding to the needs of consumers. The company's reputation for quality has been earned through sustained dedication to uniform standards. Welch's excellent quality control enabled the company to offer premium products consistently and continuously. The company also introduced new technologies, such as its three-time pasteurization process (once after harvest, once after filtering, and a final pasteurization after the bottle is filled), which, according to company reports, has increased first-pass inspection from approximately 70 percent to over 90 percent.

The company installed a web-based information system to provide up-to-date information on prices, promotion, and category information in 1998. Company officials note that not only did this improve information flow and support efficient customer service, but also it allowed Welch's to respond faster to market conditions. Although retailers were not tied into Welch's extranet information system directly, the system allowed sales representatives to get more accurate and timely information. To improve its merchandising performance, Welch's also installed software in partnership with a software development company to create orders and manage the inventories of its retail customers. This technology allowed some retailers to double the number of times they turned Welch's products. These efforts at improving efficiency of customers through effective use of information technology matched Welch's desire to strengthen customer relationships.

[1]H. Wang, C. Guohua, R. L. Prior, "Total Antioxidant Capacity of Fruits," *Journal of Agricultural and Food Chemistry* 44 (1996): 701–703.

[2]J. H. Stein, J. G. Keevil, D. A. Wiebe, S. Aeschlimann, and J. D. Folts, "Purple Grape Juice Improves Endothelial Function and Reduces the Susceptibility of LDL Cholesterol to Oxidation in Patients with Coronary Artery Disease," *Circulation* 100 (1999): 1050–1055.

[3]K. W. Singletary, M. J. Stansbury, M. Giusti, R. B. van Breemen, M. Wallig, and A. Rimando, "Inhibition of Rat Mammary Tumorigenesis by Concord Grape Juice Constituents," *Journal of Agricultural and Food Chemistry* 51 (2003): 7280–7286.

[4]D. J. O'Byrne, S. Devaraj, S. M. Grundy, and I. Jialal, "Comparison of the Antioxidant Effects of Concord Grape Juice Flavonoids and Alpha-Tocopherol on Markers of Oxidative Stress in Healthy Adults," *American Journal of Clinical Nutrition* 76 (2002): 1367–1374.

TABLE 1

Summary of Financial Indicators for Welch Foods, 1998 to 2002

(In Thousands) Operations	1998	1999	2000	2001	2002
Net Sales	509,331	526,454	550,275	535,027	553,476
Cost of Sales	319,835	327,485	350,126	347,390	346,051
Patron Cash Distribution	55,723	57,621	60,608	51,314	56,358
Patron Equity Investment	16,645	17,211	18,103	15,327	14,982
Net Proceeds	69,807	70,532	78,084	67,367	65,056
Financial Position					
Working Capital	66,173	147,025	158,008	150,063	130,602
Net Property, Plant and Equipment	08,919	111,241	118,134	119,648	122,073
Total Assets	66,841	351,269	383,155	352,647	330,472
Current Liabilities	07,641	101,472	119,205	93,783	106,580
Non-Current Liabilities	167,381	157,151	165,795	155,603	128,730
Owners' Equity	91,819	92,646	98,155	103,261	95,162

Source: National Grape Cooperative Association Inc. and Welch Foods Inc. Annual Report, various years.

Financial Performance

Common profitability measures, such as return on equity or investment, cannot be calculated and compared in the usual way to other food processing companies because net proceeds in Welch's are not equivalent to net income. Welch's operates on a pool basis, and, hence, its cost of sales does not include the cost of purchasing grapes from members. Members are not paid a market price for their grapes but receive net proceeds which include the purchase value of their grapes. The net sales and case sold equivalent data indicated that the company experienced slightly higher average unit prices for its products in 2002 compared with the two previous years (Figure 4).

Patron Financial Performance

The members of the cooperative are the residual recipients of the company's financial performance, and their payment is referred to as patronage distribution or refund. The patronage distribution or refund received by a member depended on the volume of business the member did with the cooperative. Patron proceeds have varied widely over the five years, 1998–2002. They ranged from a high of $78.7 million in 2000 to a low of $66.6 million in 2001. Although most members consider proceeds received per acre as

the most important measure of their profitability, the fact that some of their acreage is nonbearing can confuse this measure. However, since proceeds per ton were based primarily on members' patronage in the particular year, it provided a good indicator of their performance, reflecting the impact of weather and other conditions in the industry. Proceeds per ton have varied from $255 in 2000 to $208 in 2002, and paralleled the average price per case even as total tons sold by members varied between about 239,529 tons in 2002 and 309,218 tons in 2000 (Figure 5).

Challenges and Options

The future presented some interesting challenges for Welch's and National Grape because of changes in the market and industry. Dillon believed that because his company offered growers premium prices and a secure market for their grapes provided quality specifications were met, National Grape's share of good Concord and Niagara grape growers would continue to increase. But access to high-quality grapes is only one side of the equation; the other side is for Welch's to remain relevant by living its ethos, by strengthening the brand, and by responding to customer needs. "If we continue to be innovative, then we can remain relevant in the marketplace," Dillon emphasized.

FIGURE 4

Case Equivalent Sales and Average Price per Case Sold (1998–2002)

Source: National Grape Cooperative Association Inc. and Welch Foods Inc. Annual Report, various years.

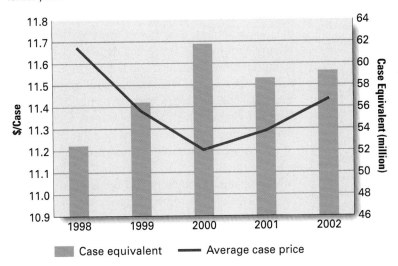

Case equivalent   Average case price

The challenges presented by well-financed competitors and private label products continued to put pressure on the cooperative. Chicago-based Information Resources Inc. reported that total category sales for bottled grape juice was $221.4 million in the 52 weeks ending December 29, 2002 and private labels accounted for almost 24 percent. However, while private label grape juice dollar sales increased by 3.6 percent compared with the year before, the total grape juice category declined by 1.7 percent. Overall, 7 of the top 14 bottled shelf-stable juice subcategories posted gains in market share, and 9 of these outperformed the subcategory as a whole in the 52 weeks ending December 29, 2002. The challenge posed by store brands was that they often offered lower prices and, when bundled with the same or higher quality and

FIGURE 5

Total Patron Tonnage Sold and Patronage per Ton (1998–2002)

Source: National Grape Cooperative Association Inc. and Welch Foods Inc. Annual Report, various years.

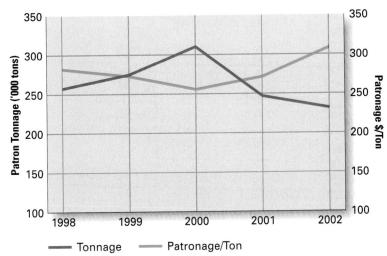

Tonnage   Patronage/Ton

packaging presentation, they successfully seized market share away from national branded products. Other competitors to Welch's were SoBe's new Long John Lizard's Grape Grog which, although it contained only 5 percent real grape fruit, had grape seed extract and vitamin C added and was marketed to a different market segment—young and active—with an intense aggressiveness akin to the marketing strategies of its parent company, PepsiCo.

Grape juice was in direct competition with other fruit juices, especially apple juice. New research results showed the nutraceutical qualities of grape juice and other fruit juices such as cranberries, and the companies are using these results to differentiate themselves in the face of increasing competition among processors and marketers. For this reason, government regulations that provided inequitable distribution of advantages in the manufacturing process could adversely affect grape juice's competitiveness. A case in point was the changes in labeling regulations imposed by the Food and Drug Administration (FDA), which required that grape juice manufacturers who declared "grape juice" or "from grape concentrate" on their retail product labels cannot dilute those products below 16.0° brix. Processors used to dilute some grape juice products to 14.3° brix. On the other hand, apple and pear concentrates can be diluted to 11.2° brix and still qualify in labeling their products "juice" or "from concentrate." Since higher brix implied lower volume, this meant that grape manufacturers processed a lower volume of juice from the same quantity of concentrate than their apple or pear competitors. For example, a gallon of grape juice concentrate yields 5.4 gallons of reconstituted juice while a gallon of apple juice concentrate yields 8.1 gallons of reconstituted juice. While these regulations may help producers sell more grapes for processing, they do impose significant pressure on processors who are confronted with competition from other juices and beverages in the marketplace.

Finally, there were numerous mergers and consolidations in the beverage products and inputs industries leading to increased concentration. Larger companies had larger product lines to offer wholesalers and distributors who were looking to minimize their operating costs. Larger companies also tended to have lower technology costs and were more able to adopt technologies that offered supply chain benefits. Smaller companies that were unable to meet the service needs of larger customers and provide economies of size benefits to their suppliers face an increasing threat of becoming less relevant in their markets. Welch's is a unique company with control over a unique input—Concord and Niagara grapes.

Conclusion

Welch's and National Grape had done well when most producer-owned packaged goods companies and agricultural cooperatives were facing significant performance challenges. Welch's and its owner-cooperative, National Grape, have successfully used a two-board system to ensure that there is an equitable balance between the needs of growers and the needs of the packaged products company. This structure allowed the two companies to identify and focus on the critical components of their respective but related businesses.

However, the market landscape was changing rapidly, and Welch's board needed to continuously explore ways to maintain and improve the company's relevancy with its consumers, its customers, and its suppliers. For example, to expand its product portfolio, Welch's may have to adopt the traditional mergers and acquisition approach that many in the industry are using to increase market share and gain economies of size, or it may also embark on building larger strategic alliances. Either of these options may require significant capital outlay. One way to achieve the required investment is to reduce cash patronage payments and cash equity redemptions, increasing the equity investment of patrons. Dillon and Welch's need to assess the two-board system, which has worked well over the last half-century for Welch's and National Grape, will support the different strategies that they need to pursue to maintain Welch's relevance in the changing marketplace.

REFERENCES

Gale Group, Inc. "Drink up! The Shelf Stable Juice Segment Proves Fruitful for Private Label, Though Opportunities Remain in Single-Serves and Isotonics." *Private Label Buyer,* 17, no. 3 (March 2003): 31.

National Grape Cooperative. Annual reports, 1998–2002.

Welch Foods. Annual Reports, 1998–2003.

Appendix A: The U.S. Grape Juice Industry

The United States has the third largest grape output after Italy and France and the fifth largest acreage after Spain, France, Italy, and Turkey. Its acreage and production shares have averaged about 5 percent and about 10 percent, respectively, over the past four years (FAO, 2002). The USDA (2002) reported that the U.S. grape industry has consistently been, over more than a decade, the most valuable crop among nuts, fruits, and vegetables, ahead of oranges, apples, and strawberries.

Total U.S. utilized grape production, divided between processing and table grapes, increased by 52.5 percent, from 4.3 million short tons to about 6.6 million short tons between 1977 and 2001. This increase resulted from acreage increases and improved varieties. Between 1991 and 2001, processing grapes' share of total utilized grapes averaged about 86.5 percent of annual production. Table grapes' share of total U.S. grape production has declined due to imports from countries such as Chile, which accounted for about 78 percent of total U.S. imports in 2001.

These improvements in production have been accompanied by strengthening average prices in the grape production industry (Exhibit A1). The average price per ton of table grapes increased by 57 percent compared with a 151 percent increase in the average price per ton of processing grapes between 1977 and 2001. The average annual growth rate in processing grape prices was 3.8 percent over that period compared with 2 percent for table grapes.

U.S. grape production is concentrated in California, which accounts for about 90 percent of total processing grape production and utilization. New York and Washington each account for about 3 percent of total domestic grape production. Weather and soil conditions support the distribution of grape varieties because the vinifera varieties are primarily grown in California while the juice grape varieties of Concord and Niagara are primarily grown in New York and Washington.

Processed grape products are divided into four main categories: juice, canned, raisins, and alcoholic beverages (mainly wine). Wine and raisins account for about 60 percent and 30 percent, respectively, of total processing grape production in the United States. Less than 1 percent of total processing grape production goes to canned, and the remaining 9 percent is allocated to juice. Although there are eight thousand varieties of grapes, the largest proportion of juice grape acreage in the United States is planted to the native Concord and Niagara varieties.

These varieties are also the most common varieties used in juice production and are primarily produced in four states: Michigan, New York, Pennsylvania, and Washington (Exhibit A2). Total juice grape production increased from 353,250 tons in 1998 to almost 418,000 tons in 2002, an increase of about 18 percent. This was a result of both acreage and yield improvement in the industry.

There were also some significant shifts in the distribution of juice grape production within that period.

EXHIBIT A1

Nominal Price of U.S. Table and Processing Grapes in Current Dollars, 1977–2001

Source: NASS/USDA.

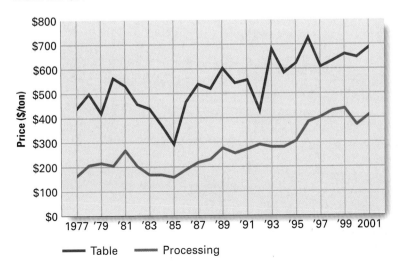

EXHIBIT A2

EXHIBIT A2

Production of Juice Grapes by State, 1998–2002

State	1998	1999	2000	2001	2002
			Quantity (Tons)		
Michigan	67,500	71,500	83,600	26,000	29,200
New York	87,000	152,000	111,000	107,000	109,000
Ohio	5,000	7,500	6,400	4,700	4,500
Pennsylvania	41,500	74,000	46,000	48,500	45,900
Washington	152,000	195,000	175,000	183,000	217,000
Others	250	2,050	2,250	650	2,200
U.S. Total	353,250	502,050	424,250	369,850	417,800

For example, Washington's share of juice production increased from 43 percent in 1998 to 52 percent in 2002 while Michigan's share decreased from 19 percent to 11 percent over the same period. There was little change in New York and Pennsylvania. A similar trend was observed for Niagara production. It is important to recognize the increasing production in Ontario, Canada, which is being shipped to the United States for processing and production and is not reflected in Exhibit A2.

Concord grapes are native to North America and grow well only in certain geographic regions. In New York, Pennsylvania, and Ohio, Concord grapes grow along a narrow stretch of no more than 6 miles in its widest points along a 90-mile stretch of Lake Erie, Lake Ontario, and the Finger Lakes in northwest New York. Michigan's production all occurs in a 40-mile stretch in the southwestern region of the state. Washington's Concord grape production is primarily located in the semidesert region of lower Yakima Valley, east of the Cascade Mountains, and is irrigated with water from the Cascades. The higher temperature and water availability are the major advantages that Washington has in Concord grape production.

Concord grapes have higher yields, higher sugar-acid ratios, and milder labrusca flavors than other

EXHIBIT A3

Juice Grape Demand, 1990–2001

Source: Economic Research Service/U.S. Department of Agriculture, 2002.

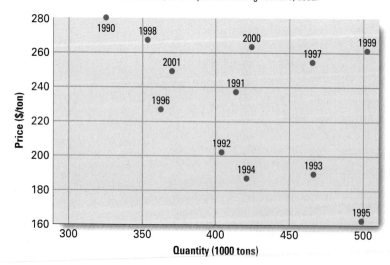

EXHIBIT A4

Grape Product Prices, 1990–2001

Source: Economic Research Service/U.S. Department of Agriculture, 2002.

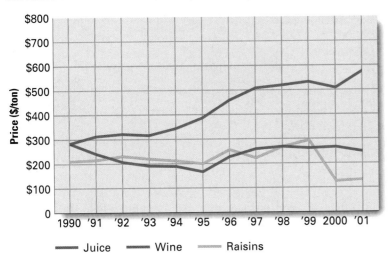

grape varieties. Europe, for example, uses vinifera or wine grape strains to make grape juice, giving it a lower sugar-acid ratio, as well as a less sweet taste than the juice made from Concord and Niagara grape production. These natural production advantages allow the industry to have better control over its marketplace in comparison to other agricultural commodities. That notwithstanding, the juice grape market is subject to price volatility because of supply fluctuations due to weather and other factors, including competition among the different uses and the substitutability among different varieties.

When both quantity and price increase over time, it is indicative of product demand increasing faster than its supply. However, juice grape demand has been variable over the past ten years (Exhibit A3).

The average price per ton of wine and juice grapes was about $280 in 1990. However, the average price of wine grapes by 2001 was about twice that of juice grapes at $250 per ton (Exhibit A4). The growth of the wine industry in the last decade likely explains a significant component of the price trend for wine grapes during the same time period. The industry has seen enhanced competitiveness against traditional French and Italian products arising from increased varieties, technology, and education. The price of raisin grapes has fallen significantly over the same period, reaching about $130 per ton in 2001. The trend in juice grape prices, however, indicates

that prices have been strengthening since the mid-1990s after consistently falling between 1990 and 1995.

Appendix B: Processing Grape Juice Industry

Grape Juice processors obtain 185 to 190 gallons of single strength juice from a ton of grapes, regardless of the variety.[1] However, depending on the brix (or sugar solids) strength of the single strength juice, a ton of Concord grapes yields only 34 gallons of 68° brix concentrate. The higher the brix of the juice, the higher the volume of concentrate it produces. In general, the soil and water conditions in Washington give its Concord grapes a higher brix than Concord grapes produced in Michigan, New York, and Pennsylvania. This implies that in general Washington Concord grapes yield higher volumes of concentrate than Eastern Concord grapes. In contrast, Eastern Concord grapes have higher acids and deeper color allowing them to be blended with concentrates fr_ cheaper viniferous varieties without losing ' taste. Processors who purchase the concentra_ water to reconstitute the original single st_ some other strength juice.

[1]Single strength means straight juice that is neith_ centrated. Concentrates are produced from sin_ evaporating water from the juice using heat a_

EXHIBIT B1

A Simplified Overview of the Grape Processing Process

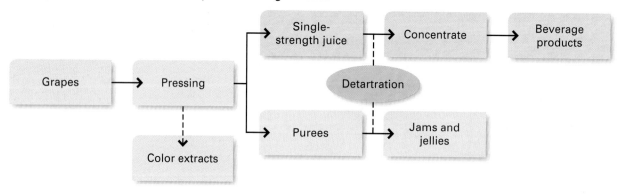

Grape juice production is different from other fruit juices because it is the only fruit juice that cannot be concentrated immediately after pressing because of the presence of potassium salts, commonly called tartrates, in the juice that cannot be filtered or centrifuged out. They have to be detartrated by gravity, a process that usually takes about six weeks. Juice grapes such as Concord and Niagara are used in the manufacture of jelly, jam, straight or sparkling juice, drinks diluted 50 percent or more with water, ades diluted with up to 98 percent water and added sugar, drink bases, carbonated beverages, frozen and shelf stable concentrates that may be diluted with water, frozen bars and slush, ice cream topping, yogurt base, pie mix, powders, and crystals (Exhibit B1).

The total value of shipments for frozen fruits, juices, drinks, and cocktails was about $2.86 billion in 1997. The total value of shipments for companies producing grape juice concentrates was almost $58 million in 1997 compared with $74.2 million in 1992. This implies that the grape juice industry is a relatively small component of the fruit juice industry, and it is accounted for by very few companies. In fact, there were only seventeen companies in 1997,

EXHIBIT B2

Number of Firms, Shipment Quantity, and Value for Frozen Grape Juice Concentrate Manufacturers

Product Types	1997			1992		
	No. of Companies ($100K + Shipments)	Quantity of Shipments	Value of Shipments ($1,000)	No. of Companies ($100K + Shipments)	Quantity of Shipments	Value of Shipments ($1,000)
Frozen Concentrate grape juice (4.1 oz–7 oz), 1,000 cases of 48	4	1770.1	18057	5	1745.6	17750
Frozen Concentrate grape juice (10.1 oz–13 oz), 1,000 cases of 24	6	1994.6	24643	5	2709.1	31300
Frozen Concentrate grape juice (other sizes), 1,000# solid	7	16.9	15290	10	28.9	25150

Source: Frozen Fruit, Juice, and Vegetable Manufacturing, 1997 Manufacturing Industry Census, Washington, D.C.: U.S. Census Bureau, November 1999, p. 10.

EXHIBIT B3

Per Capita Consumption of Selected Fruit Juices (Gallons per Year Single Strength Equivalent)

Season	Apple	Grape	Pineapple	Cranberry	Prune	Total Noncitrus	Total Citrus	Total Fruit Juice
1990/91	1.72	0.28	0.50	0.14	0.04	2.68	5.21	7.89
1991/92	1.51	0.36	0.50	0.17	0.03	2.57	4.82	7.39
1992/93	1.56	0.38	0.47	0.16	0.04	2.61	5.96	8.57
1993/94	1.78	0.35	0.41	0.15	0.04	2.73	5.79	8.52
1994/95	1.77	0.29	0.35	0.19	0.04	2.64	6.16	8.80
1995/96	1.57	0.45	0.38	0.16	0.03	2.59	6.14	8.73
1996/97	1.69	0.38	0.38	0.17	0.03	2.65	6.18	8.83
1997/98	1.54	0.41	0.34	0.20	0.03	2.52	6.29	8.81
1998/99	1.79	0.27	0.29	0.21	0.03	2.59	6.00	8.59
1999/00	1.78	0.44	0.32	0.23	0.02	2.79	6.66	9.46
2000/01	1.80	0.34	0.30	0.20	0.02	2.66	5.95	8.61
2001/02	1.76	0.33	0.31	0.17	0.03	2.60	5.81	8.41

Source: Economic Research Service/U.S. Department of Agriculture, 2002.

down from twenty in 1992 (Exhibit B2).[2] It is important to note that these data do not present the whole picture of the grape juice processing industry because, as shown in Exhibit B1, there are other products being supplied by the industry besides frozen concentrates. It does, however, illuminate the challenge in the industry with respect to the general trends of consolidations and rationalization of products toward retail packs.

Grape Juice Consumption

Per capita consumption of grape juice has exhibited an upward trend since 1977, growing at about 2.2 percent per annum. It increased from 0.28 gallons per capita per annum in 1990/91 to 0.33 gallons per person per year in 2001/02 (Exhibit B3). Citrus is the only fruit increasing its share of fruit juice consumption in the United States. Between 1990/91 and 2001/02, it was estimated that citrus share of the per capita

consumption of fruit juices increased at an average annual rate of 0.45 percent. This contrasts with −0.4 percent for grape juice, −0.13 percent for apple juice, and −6.0 percent for pineapple.

Citrus was by far the fruit juice of choice in the United States, accounting for almost 70 percent of the total fruit juice consumed on a per capita basis in 2001/02. Apple juice was the second largest with a share of almost 21 percent in the same year. The remaining 9 percent is distributed among the rest of the fruit juices, with grapes and pineapple accounting for 3.9 percent and 3.7 percent, respectively, and cranberry accounting for 2 percent. The year-to-year change in per capita consumption of total fruit juice consumed has been most unstable for grape juice. For example, between 1996/97 and 1997/98, the per capita consumption of grape juice increased by 8 percent, decreased by about 34 percent the following period, and increased by 63 percent thereafter. This pattern is likely due to data collection methods, inventory, and promotional activities carried out by processors.

These appendices were written using public data from USDA and National Grape's annual reports.

[2]Companies in the census are defined as businesses with value of shipments in excess of $100,000.

The Global Automobile Industry in 2004

This case was prepared by Charles W. L. Hill, the University of Washington.

Some fifty years ago renowned management author Peter Drucker called the automobile industry the "industry of industries." In many respects his characterization is still true today. The industry makes some 60 million cars and trucks a year, employs millions of people in factories scattered around the globe, and accounts for about 10 percent of the gross domestic product in rich countries. The top ten global producers collectively sold $1.1 trillion worth of vehicles in 2003. The industry consumes nearly half the world's output of rubber, 25 percent of its glass and 15 percent of its steel.[1] Its products are responsible for almost half of the world's oil consumption and are a major source of rising carbon dioxide levels in the atmosphere, the greenhouse gas implicated in global warming. Modern cities with their attendant suburban sprawl have been designed around the automobile. The automobile has shaped our landscape, changed our atmosphere, and exerted a profound influence on the global economy. It is indeed, still the industry of industries—and today the industry of industries is going through wrenching changes.

Background

The emergence of the modern industry can be dated back to 1913 and Henry Ford's first implementation of the production technology that would revolutionize so much of industrial capitalism over the next few

decades, the continuously moving assembly line. Ford quickly became the master of mass production, churning out thousands of black Model T Fords from his Highland Park plant in Michigan. Mass production dramatically lowered the costs of building cars and paved the way for the emergence of a mass consumer market. It was not Ford, however, but Alfred Sloan, the CEO of General Motors, who in the mid-1920s realized that the key to success in the industry was serving the customer by offering them "a car for every purse and purpose."[2] Under Sloan, GM segmented the market, producing a differentiate range of models to consumers. In doing so, the company seized market leadership from Ford and has not relinquished it since.

By the 1960s, General Motors, Ford, and Chrysler dominated the U.S. market; then by far the world's largest. GM at one point made over 60 percent of all automobile sales in the United States, and collectively the three companies accounted for over 90 percent of sales. Moreover, the companies were now multinationals with significant operations outside of North America, and particularly in Europe, the world's second biggest car market. This, however, was all about to change. Riding the wave of economic disruption caused by the OPEC oil price hikes of the 1970s, foreign manufacturers of fuel efficient cars began to invade the U.S. market. First there was Volkswagen, with its revolutionary VW Beatle, and then a slew of Japanese manufacturers including, most notably, Honda, Nissan, and Toyota.

It was one of these foreign invaders, Toyota, that was to usher in the next revolution in car making.

Faced with a small and intensely competitive home market, and constrained by a lack of capital, Toyota started to tweak the mass production system first developed by Ford. Engineers tried to find ways to build cars efficiently in smaller volumes and with less capital. After years of experimentation, by the 1970s a new production system was emerging at Toyota. Later dubbed "lean production," it was based upon innovations that reduced setup times for machinery and made shorter production runs economical. When coupled with the introduction of just-in-time inventory systems, flexible work practices, an organization-wide focus on quality, and the practice of stopping the assembly line to fix defects (which was the antithesis of Ford's continually moving assembly line), the lean production system yielded significant gains in productivity and product quality. In turn, this lowered costs, improved brand equity, and gave Toyota a competitive advantage.

As was the case with mass production, Toyota's innovation of lean production was imitated, with varying degrees of success, by other volume car makers. Japanese competitors were the first to try and adopt Toyota's innovation. During the 1990s the American volume car makers jumped on the bandwagon. Despite this, Toyota still enjoys a competitive advantage in the automobile industry that is based upon production excellence. Just as significantly, the sluggish American response to Japanese and European invasions of their home market allowed the foreigners to capture ever more market share.

By the early years of the new century, America's big three (now often referred to as the Detroit Three) were rapidly losing their grip on their domestic market. Collectively, GM, Ford, and Chrysler (now part of the German-owned Daimler Chrysler Corporation) accounted for just 47.1 percent of passenger car sales in 2003. The other 52.9 percent of sales were attributed to foreign producers, up from 34 percent in 1988.[3] Moreover, in stark contrast to the situation in the 1980s when most foreign cars were imported into the United States, by 2003 most foreign nameplates were built in "transplant" factories located in North America.

What saved the Detroit Three during the 1990s were robust sales of light trucks, and particularly sports utility vehicles (SUVs). Foreign manufacturers had been caught off-guard by the American appetite for SUVs, which surged as oil prices remained low and the economy boomed. In 2003, GM, Ford, and Chrysler still accounted for 74 percent of light truck sales. This pumped up their overall market share of U.S. light vehicles to 61.8 percent in 2003. But here, too, market share was eroding (it had fallen from 66.8 percent in 2000) due to gains made by Japanese and European SUV models.[4] Making matters worse, rapidly rising oil prices during 2004 hinted at an end to the decade long boom in SUV sales. With competition in the passenger car segment intensifying, the outlook for the Detroit Three looked increasingly grim.

Competition in the U.S. Market, 2004

Demand and Supply

Total sales of passenger cars and light trucks in the United States peaked in 2000 at 17.35 million units before declining for three consecutive years to 16.64 million units in 2003 (see Exhibit 1). In total, U.S. dealers sold some $400 billion worth of vehicles in 2003. The decline between 2000 and 2003 was pronounced in the passenger car segment, where volume fell from 8.85 million units in 2000 to 7.61 million in 2003. Light truck sales, however, continued to expand from 8.5 million units to 9 million units between 2000 and 2003, driven in large part by America's continuing love affair with SUVs.[5]

The decline in overall vehicle sales was a product of the economic slowdown following the long boom of the 1990s and September 11, 2001. The sales decline has left the American industry with too much productive capacity. Estimates suggest that in 2003, the industry had the capacity to build some 18 million cars and light trucks in the United States, but actually only made 13.33 million units (the balance of sales was accounted for by imports).[6]

In large part, the excess capacity situation has been created by foreign car makers, who have made significant investments in the United States over the last twenty years. Japanese investments began in the early 1980s as a response to the threat of import controls on exports from Japan. By the early 2000s, foreign owned producers had the capacity to build some 3 million automobiles in the United States, up from zero in 1981.[7] (The figure excludes the Chrysler division of Daimler Chrysler, which is counted as one of the Detroit Three, even though it is now owned by a German firm).

The foreign investment shows no sign of slowing down. Hyundai will open its first U.S. factory in

EXHIBIT 1

Sales of Cars and Light Trucks, 1992–2003 (000s)

Source: Standard & Poor's.

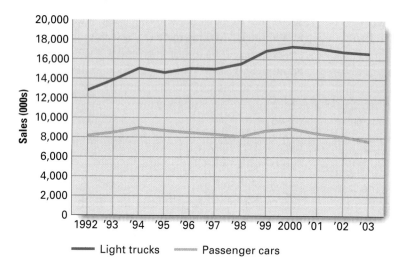

Montgomery, Alabama, in 2005, making it the first Korean car company to build in North America. Meanwhile, Toyota will open its sixth North American factory in San Antonio, Texas, in 2006. Collectively, foreign-owned auto factories accounted for 26 percent of U.S. automobile production in 2003, and that percentage seems set to rise.

Many states offered financial incentives such as tax breaks in an effort to attract inward investment by foreign producers, and the associated jobs. Estimates suggest that by 2003 the cumulative value of incentives given to attract new factories amounted to between $1.2 billion and $2 billion, which translates into an investment incentive of $1,000 for every car built by a foreign-owned factory.[8]

Price Competition

In the aftermath of September 11, 2001, sales slumped at American car dealers. Faced with excess capacity, high fixed costs, and an inability to quickly shutter capacity due to commitments made to labor unions, General Motors responded with aggressive sales incentives. These included 0 percent financing deals and cash back rebates on certain vehicles that reached as high as $3,000. Very quickly its rivals were forced to respond, and incentives became the industry norm. The size of incentives, however, varied from producers to producer. While the Detroit Three have been offering incentive packages that have

exceeded $4,000 per vehicle, the big Japanese producers, Honda, Nissan, and Toyota, have been less aggressive. Toyota, for example, offered incentives of just over $2,000 per vehicle in 2003, compared with GM's average incentive package of $4,300 a vehicle.[9]

The incentives have had the effect of making cars more affordable. In 1973, the average U.S. citizen needed 17.5 weeks of annual family earnings to purchase an average priced car. By 1994, that figure had risen to 24 weeks, but by 2003, it had declined to 20.7 weeks. The signs are that the downtrend continued in 2004.[10]

In late 2003, GM tried to cut back on incentives, only to find that sales declined as consumers bought cars from those who kept incentives in place. In part, GM noted, two years of incentives had conditioned consumers to expect them, and breaking that habit was proving difficult. By February 2004, GM had gone back to offering a full range of sales incentives—indeed, it had even boosted them slightly in an effort to shift unsold inventory that was starting to accumulate of dealers lots.[11]

One effect of sales incentives has been to get consumers to sell their used vehicles at a higher rate than would otherwise have been the case. This has hurt the price of used cars. An index of used car prices, for example, fell from 115 in 2002 to 102.4 by April 2003.[12] Ironically, falling used car prices can hurt demand for new cars as more consumers purchase

EXHIBIT 2A

Market Share of U.S. Dealer Passenger Cars (%)

Manufacturer	2000	2001	2002	2003
General Motors	28.6	27	25.5	25.7
Ford	19.1	17.8	16.4	15.4
Daimler Chrysler	7.3	6.6	6.5	6.0
Toyota	11.0	11.3	12.2	13.1
Honda	10.0	10.7	10.3	10.8
Nissan	4.8	4.9	6.1	6.6
Volkswagen	4.9	5.1	5.1	4.8

EXHIBIT 2B

Market Share of U.S. Dealer Light Trucks (%)

Manufacturer	2000	2001	2002	2003
General Motors	28.0	29.7	31.5	30.5
Ford	28.9	27.8	25.8	25.1
Daimler Chrysler	22.0	19.7	19.3	18.5
Toyota	7.6	9.0	8.8	9.6
Honda	3.3	3.5	4.7	5.9
Nissan	3.9	3.3	2.9	3.2

Source: Standard & Poor's.

used cars, trapping the car producers in something of a vicious cycle. Moreover, the fall in used car prices is of direct concern to the automobile companies, who have expanded their leasing programs in the last decade. Ford in particular took a financial hit in 2001 when it found that vehicles coming off lease were worth less than originally projected.

Market Share

The launching of incentives by GM was not sufficient to stem market share losses during the early 2000s (see Exhibit 2). Between 2000 and 2003, GM saw its share of passenger cars fall from 28.6 percent to 25.7 percent. Ford and Chrysler also experienced significant declines in passenger car share, while Toyota, Nissan, and BMW made significant gains. Toyota, in particular, captured 13.1 percent of U.S. passenger car sales in 2003, more than twice as much as Chrysler.

While GM was able to offset losses in the passenger car segment by gains in the light truck segment where it held 30.5 percent of the market in 2003, Ford and Chrysler experienced market share declines here, too. Toyota and Honda were the largest gainers. Both companies introduced new SUVs in this time period and were reaping the gains. In 2003, Toyota held a 9.6 percent share of the U.S. light truck market, up from 7.6 percent in 2000.

Quality seems to be an important factor explaining market share changes in the industry. J.D. Power Associates produces quality rankings for automobiles sold in the U.S. market. According to these rankings, Toyota and Honda consistently have the best quality rankings in the industry. In 2004, J.D. Power's Vehicle Dependability Study, which measures quality after cars have been on the market for three years, ranked Toyota and Honda one and two, with 207 and 210 problems reported per 100 vehicles respectively, compared to an industry average of 269 (see Exhibit 3). J.D. Power's Initial Quality Study, which measures problems reported in the first 90 days after sale, similarly ranked Toyota and Honda one and two in terms of quality, with scores of 101 and 102 against an industry average of 119. GM came out best of the Detroit Three on both surveys.[13]

However, tracking of quality improvements since 1998 suggests that the Detroit Three are closing the quality gap between themselves and foreign producers and may ultimately achieve parity (see Exhibit 4). If the trend continues, differentiation on factors other than quality—such as styling, design, and technology—will come to the fore. Also of major note in Exhibit 4 are the poor performance of Korean manufacturers in 1998 and their rapid improvement over the next six years.

Profitability and Labor Productivity

The combination of falling demand, excess capacity, and incentives hurt profits, particularly for the Detroit Three, all of whom saw their profits slump in 2001, and despite a recovery, have seen their profits remain below through to 2004 (see Exhibit 5). Toyota, on the other hand, made record profits in 2003 and 2004. Indeed, in both years it made more than the Detroit Three combined.

What is not evident from Exhibit 5 is that Toyota's earnings were held back by weak conditions in Japan. In the United States, the company has been very successful in recent years. According to a 2004 study by

EXHIBIT 3

J.D. Power 2004 Vehicle Dependability Study

Source: J.D. Power Associates.

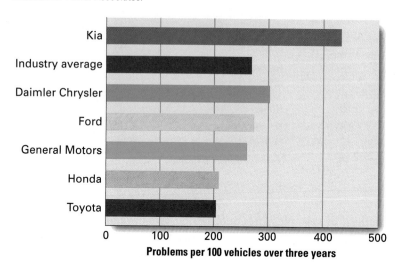

Problems per 100 vehicles over three years

Harbour & Associates, in 2003 Toyota made $1,742 in profit on every vehicle it manufactured in North America. Nissan did even better, making $2,402 on every car sold in North America, while Honda made $1,488. General Motors, in contrast, made only $178 profit per vehicle, Ford lost $48 and Daimler Chrysler lost $496 per vehicle (Ford was profitable in 2003 only due to the success of its foreign operations).[14]

As noted earlier, Toyota has the best reputation for quality in the industry. The higher quality translates into a higher value and allows Toyota to charge 5 to 10 percent higher prices than General Motors for equivalent cars. Historically, Toyota and other Japanese manufacturers also benefited from superior labor productivity in their North American plants, but according to the Harbour Report, the labor productivity gap in North American plants has narrowed significantly in recent years. In 2002, the last year for which full data are available, Nissan was the productivity leader in U.S. assembly operations,

EXHIBIT 4

J.D. Power Initial Quality Study, Trends in Quality 1998–2004

Source: J.D. Power Associates.

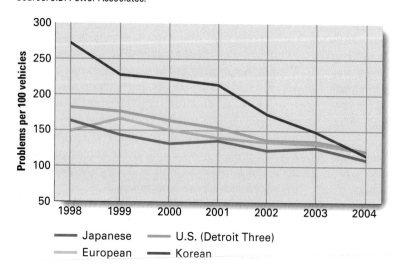

EXHIBIT 5

Net Income 2000–2004 (Millions)

Company	2000	2001	2002	2003	2004
General Motors	$4452	$601	$1736	$2862	$3990
Ford	$4823	–$5443	$284	$921	$4000
Daimler Chrysler	$3338	–$589	$5114	–$526	$2945
Toyota	$5447	$4177	$6247	$10995	$11800

taking just 17.92 employee hours to build a car. Honda took 19.78 hours, Toyota 22.53, General Motors 26.10, Ford 26.87, and Daimler Chrysler 30.82 hours.[15]

The 2004 report revealed that improvements continued across the board. Nissan's assembly plant in Tennessee led the way, building a car in 15.33 hours of labor. The most improved automaker was Daimler Chrysler, which increased labor productivity at its assembly plants by 7.8 percent over the prior year. General Motors also registered improvement in its assembly operations, and on average took 23.61 hours to build a car, down from 26.10 in 2002.[16] Since neither Honda nor Toyota fully participated in the 2004 study, data for them are no longer available. Still, the author of the Harbour Report, Ron Harbour, has noted that over the 1999–2004 period productivity gains at Japanese plants in North America have been relatively modest, and lagged the gains made by the Detroit Three. The problem for the Detroit Three, according to Harbour, is that the variance of productivity across their plants is much greater than at Japanese manufacturers.[17]

For their part, American manufacturers argue that their profitability has been hurt by huge pension burdens. General Motors, for example, has 2.4 pensioners for every current employee. The more that these companies lay off older workers, the more they add to their burden of pensions and health care costs. The collapse of the stock market in 2000–2001 didn't help matters either, since it reduced the value of company pension funds. Both Ford and GM had to issue bonds worth billions of dollars just to plug the holes in their pension funds. GM now has to pay out $1 billion a year in interest payments just to service these bonds. Moreover, the company has to pay out some $3 billion a year to cover health care costs for retirees. Just as troubling, GM may have to increase funds going into its pension plan if the fund does not earn a long-term return of 9 percent per annum.[18]

Industry Trends

In an effort to cope with the tough competitive conditions in the North American market and elsewhere, automobile companies are looking hard at additional ways to take costs out of their system or to capture more of the available demand. Among the most notable initiatives underway have been an industrywide attempt to streamline product development, offer a wider range of niche cars, work more closely with suppliers, develop systems for building cars to order, and introduce a new breed of hybrid cars.

Market Fragmentation and Product Development

Historically it took four years and cost as much as $1 billion to develop a new car model and prepare a factory for its production. To recoup those fixed costs, automobile companies needed high-volume sales, which required selling the car without a major update for four years and sometimes as long as seven years. To attain maximum economies of scale, automobile companies tried to run their plants at full capacity, producing 240,000 units a year. The ideal was to have each plant produce just one model.

In recent years the automobile market has become increasingly fragmented. Models are now updated more frequently to keep pace with changing consumer tastes and competitive pressures, shortening product life cycles. Customers have demanded more variety, and automobile companies have been willing to give it to them, bringing a wider variety of niche cars to the market. The Ford Taurus, for example, was once the best-selling passenger car in America with annual sales of around 500,000 (equivalent to two plants running at full capacity). As sales have slipped, Ford has decided to kill the Taurus, and replace it with two models, one smaller than the Taurus and one bigger.

To recoup the costs of such offerings, development and manufacturing costs have to be reduced. Automobile companies are trying to do this by using a common platform and parts in a wider range of cars. An example of the industry's new philosophy is GM's 2005 roadster, the Pontiac Solstice. Under the old economics, the Solstice would never have made it off the drawing board. The car is forecasted to sell only 25,000 units a year. With a projected sticker price of $20,000 the volume was insufficient under the old paradigm to recoup costs. To make the car economically, GM has had to revolutionize its product design philosophy. By digitalizing much of the design of the car and tools, GM was able to cut $50 million out of design costs. It used to take 12 design engineers 3 months to produce a clay model, an essential step in the design process. Now a single designer can take an idea on a computer screen to an animated video of a vehicle in three weeks. GM saved another $80 million by designing the car so that it could use existing tools at its factory. More money was saved by a decision to base the car on a common platform architecture called Kappa, which will be used for other small rear drive cars. According to GM Design Chief Bob Lutz, GM can make an almost unlimited number of bodies on the Kappa architecture, and each vehicle will be profitable with a volume of 20,000 to 25,000 a year.[19]

Using the same platform across a wide model range is fast becoming industry standard practice. As with so many other industry trends, the Japanese pioneered the practice. Honda, for example, builds its Odyssey minivan, and Pilot and Acura MDX SUVs on the same platform, and has added a pickup truck to the mix. Currently Chrysler bases its vehicle fleet on thirteen distinct platforms. The company is trying to bring this down to just four platforms, in the process reducing the product development budget from $42 billion to $30 billion. Ford and General Motors have similar aims. The Kappa platform for GM's Pontiac Solstice will also be used for its new Saturn coupe and at least one more GM car. As GM develops its next generation Chevy Silverado and GMC Sierra pickups, it plans to reuse much of the existing platform, cutting development costs in half to nearly $3 billion. Over the next eight years, Ford plans to use its Mazda 6 sedan

platform (Ford owns Mazda) as the basis for ten new vehicles. The idea, according to Ford's head of operations, is to engineer it once, use it often.[20]

Another design goal is to try and use the same parts in a wider variety of car models and where appropriate use parts from old models in new cars. Detroit auto designers used to boast that new models were completely redesigned from the floor up with all new parts. Now that is seen as costly and time consuming. At General Motors the current goal is to reuse 40–60 percent of parts from one car generation to the next, thereby reducing design time and tooling costs. At Ford, the number of parts has been slashed. For example, Ford engineers now choose from just four steering wheels, instead of contemplating fourteen different designs.

As a result of all these changes, the costs and time for bringing new cars to market is shrinking. Most of GM's new development projects are now on 24-month schedules—a far cry from the late 1980s when GM engineers celebrated because they were able to bring out the Chevrolet Corsica in *just* 45 months![21] Ford has reduced its product development time by 25 percent since the late 1990s, and is still getting better by 10 percent per year.

Flexible Factories

Hand in hand with changes in design philosophy, automobile companies are retooling their factories to reduce costs and make them capable of producing several car models from the same line. By doing so, they hope to be able to reduce the break-even point for a new car model. With the Solstice, for example, GM cut design costs by using a common platform and parts. It has cut tooling and production costs by investing in flexible manufacturing technologies that can be used to produce multiple designs based on the Kappa platform from the same basic line. GM has also worked hard to get unions to agree to changes in inflexible work rules. Assembly line workers now perform several different jobs, which reduces waste and boosts productivity.

Ford hopes to have 75 percent of its production built on flexible assembly lines by 2010. If successful, its investments in flexible factories could reduce annual costs by some $2 billion a year.[22] Ford spent $400 million modernizing an eighty-year-old assembly plant in Chicago. This plant is now capable of making eight models from two different chassis.

Reengineering their plants to accommodate a wider range of models is not cheap. In 2003, GM spent some $7.3 billion on capital improvements at its automobile plants, up from an average of $5.4 billion in the early 1990s. A In the early 1990s, Ford spent some $3.5 billion annually on capital improvements. More recently its capital spending has been running at a $7.5–$8 billion annual rate. Chrysler, too, has increased its spending, while Toyota planned to spend some $9 billion upgrading its factories in 2004.[23]

Supplier Relations

At one time the American automobile companies were highly vertically integrated, producing as much as 70 percent of their component parts in-house. Those parts that were not made in-house were often purchased using an annual competitive bidding process. The last decade has seen enormous changes here. Both Ford and GM have sold off a major chunk of their in-house suppliers. GM spun out its in-house suppliers in 1999 as Delphi Automotive. Delphi took some 200,000 former GM employees with it, about one-third of the total, many of who were union members. Ford spun out its in-house suppliers the following year as Visteon Corporation. Delphi and Visteon are now the number one and two auto parts suppliers in the United States. In an effort to assert their independence, both companies are moving rapidly to build a more diverse set of customers.

The Detroit Three have also been reconfiguring their relationships with independent suppliers. The automobile companies are now expecting their Tier 1 or major suppliers to produce modules—larger vehicle parts that comprise several components such as fully assembled chassis, finished interiors, and "ready for the road" exterior trim. These modules are then bolted and welded together to make finished vehicles, rather like toy models being snapped together. For such an approach to work, the suppliers have to get involved earlier in the process of designing and developing new models and engineering assembly tools. To create an incentive for them to do so, the automobile manufacturers have been entering into longer term contracts with their Tier 1 suppliers. At the same time, Tier 1 suppliers face intense price pressures and requirements for quality improvements. If they don't meet these, the automobile companies have shown a willingness to walk away from long-term deals. In 2003,

for example, Daimler Chrysler pulled a $90 million contract from a supplier of interior products, Collins & Aikman, because of poor product quality.[24]

Another trend has been to encourage major suppliers to locate new facilities next to assembly plants. Ford's refurbished plant in Chicago has a supplier park located next door. The idea is to get suppliers to deliver inventory to the assembly line on a just-in-time basis. At the Chicago plant, the average component now needs to travel only half a mile, as opposed to 450 miles in the past. The proximity has saved suppliers transportation costs, which are passed onto Ford in the form of lower prices. In addition, Ford has reduced inventory on hand at its Chicago plant from two to three days' worth to just eight hours' worth.[25]

Dealer and Customer Relations

Once a car is built, it spends between forty and eighty days sitting in factory lots, distribution centers, and dealers' forecourts before it is actually sold. This represents a huge amount of working capital that is tied up in inventory. To make matters worse, one of the biggest problems in the automobile industry is predicting what demand will be. To a large extent, repeated rounds of price cutting (disguised as incentives) in the American automobile industry have been initiated in an attempt to move slow selling inventory sitting on dealers' lots. If automobile companies could predict demand more accurately, they might be able to reduce the mismatch between inventories and demand—and hence the need to resort to incentives.

In an effort to improve this end of the value chain, the automobile companies have been trying to reduce the time between ordering and delivery. The ultimate goal is to have cars built to order, with cars being assembled and shipped to a dealer within days of a customer placing an order. This is similar in conception to the way that Dell sells computers, with customers ordering a computer, and paying for it, online, while the machine is shipped out within days. Nissan has calculated that if it could move to a build-to-order system with a short cycle time, it could reduce costs by as much as $3,600 a vehicle.[26]

Achieving this goal, however, is easier in theory than in practice. One obvious problem is that if the flow of orders is lumpy or seasonal, so will be the output of a factory, which might result in periods where capacity is not being fully utilized. Another problem involves changing buyer behavior. In America, at least, many consumers look for instant gratification and expect to be able to purchase a car when they walk onto a dealer's lot, which is the antithesis of a build-to-order system. Still, there are some signs of a shift away from this mentality. Honda, for example, has been building its best-selling MDX SUV to order—although the delivery time is more like two months than two days. In Germany, BMW now builds some 60 percent of its cars to order, but once again the delivery time can be as long as two months. Toyota, too, is trying to build more cars to order. In late 2004, the automaker claimed that it was building about 11 percent of the cars it sold in the United States to order, with a build time of just fourteen days.[27]

New Technologies

For years automobile companies have experimented with alternative power sources, most notably fuel cells. These investments have been driven by national and local government demands for lower emissions of carbon dioxide, carbon monoxide, and nitrogen oxides. Of particular concern has been the global buildup of carbon dioxide, the greenhouse gas implicated in global warming. In Europe, the European Commission has persuaded car makers to agree to a voluntary deal to cut overall emissions across their car fleet by 25 percent by 2008, or face the imposition of strict emission rules on specific models. In California, draft regulations may require car manufacturers to reduce emissions of carbon dioxide by 30 percent, starting in 2009. In addition, California already has regulations in place that require 2 percent of a car maker's fleet to be zero emission vehicles (ZEV) by 2005 (although this requirement is proving to be a "soft" one).

The only conceivable ZEV at this juncture is a car powered by an electric motor that runs on a fuel cell. A fuel cell combines hydrogen with oxygen from the air to produce water. The process generates an electric current strong enough to power a car. For all of their promise, however, fuel cells have drawbacks. It costs about ten times more to produce a fuel cell than an internal combustion engine, the range of cars using fuel cells is still too limited for most customers, and replenishing hydrogen will require a network of hydrogen filling stations, which is currently not available.

Automakers have also been experimenting with modified internal combustion engines that use hydrogen rather than gasoline as a fuel. Here too, however, progress has been held back by the total absence of a network of hydrogen filling stations and serious technical problems associated with storing liquid hydrogen (which requires very cold temperatures).

More promising in the short to medium term are hybrid cars. In hybrid cars, at low speed the power comes from an electric motor which gets electricity from an onboard battery. At higher speed, the internal combustion engine kicks in and provides power, while simultaneously recharging the battery through a generator. When braking, energy from the slowing wheels is sent back through the electric motor to charge the batteries. The result can be substantial savings in fuel consumption, with little in the way of a performance penalty. Toyota's Prius hybrid can go from standstill to 60 mph in 10 seconds, averages 60 mpg in the city, and 51 mpg highway driving. This makes the Prius an ideal commuting car. The big drawback is that the hybrid propulsion system adds about $3,000 to $5,000 to a vehicle's sticker price, and the battery has to be replaced about every 100,000 miles at a cost of around $2,000. At an average gas price of $2 a gallon, it takes some five years for a hybrid to repay the additional investment.

Introduced in 1997, Toyota had sold some 200,000 Prius cars by mid-2004. Sales started to increase rapidly in 2003 and 2004 as higher fuel prices made consumers more concerned about fuel economy. In 2004, sales in the United States were limited only by supply constraints to 47,000 units. For 2005, Toyota is planning to sell 100,000 Prius cars in the United States and some 300,000 units worldwide. The company will introduce hybrid versions of its Lexus SUV, Highlander SUV, and Camry sedan in 2005. In addition to Toyota, Honda also had a hybrid on the market in 2002, its Honda Civic hybrid, which was expected to sell over 40,000 units in 2004. Ford introduced a hybrid version of its Escape SUV in late 2004. Priced at $27,000, the hybrid version of the Escape costs $6,000 more than the regular version. GM and Daimler Chrysler also have plans to introduce hybrids in 2006 and 2007.

J.D. Power has estimated that the U.S. market for hybrids could reach 500,000 units by 2008. A more aggressive forecast from Booze, Allen, and Hamilton suggests that hybrids could capture some 20 percent of the U.S. automobile market by 2010 (assuming that gasoline prices stay high), which would represent unit sales of about 3.4 million.[28]

International Developments

Over 80 percent of the world's cars and light trucks are sold in just three markets—North America, Europe, and Japan. Europe is a close second to North America in terms of size, with total sales estimated to be around 16 million units in 2004. The two largest automobile companies in Europe are Volkswagen and PSA Peugeot Citroen with 17.5 percent and 14.4 percent of the market, respectively, in the first half of 2004. Ford had 11.5 percent, Renault 10.4 percent, GM 9.7 percent, and Fiat 9.7 percent. Collectively the Japanese companies held 13.4 percent of the European market in the first half of 2004 (Toyota had a 5.1 percent share).[29]

In some respects, these figures understate the degree of market concentration in Europe. GM, for example, owns 20 percent of Fiat, and Renault owns some 44 percent of Nissan. The Renault/Nissan alliance is particularly close. Renault took its stake in Nissan in the late 1990s when the Japanese company was in deep financial trouble. For Renault, the move was designed to give it access to the large American market where Nissan has a significant presence. For Nissan, it was a matter of survival. Renault invested some $5 billion in Nissan, effectively stabilizing the Japanese company's balance sheet and helping to engineer a turnaround. Although the two companies are continuing to keep their separate identities, their plans call for them to share common car platforms across both companies and to reduce the number of platforms from 40 in 2000 to 10 by 2010, saving some $500 million in costs.

The competitive picture in Europe is not that different from the picture in North America. A combination of inward investment and market share gains by Japanese automakers, and slowing export sales to North America due to the strong euro, have hurt demand and helped to create an excess capacity situation. As in the United States, automakers have responded by introducing sales incentives to try and shift inventory. Consequently, profits are down across the board.

Globally, the big story has been the continued rise of Toyota, which in 2003 passed Ford to become the world's second largest automobile company after GM (see Exhibit 6). With Ford now firmly in the rear view mirror, Toyota is setting its sights on GM. Toyota's plans call for the company to capture 15 percent of the global market for automobiles in 2010, up

EXHIBIT 6

Global Sales in 2003

Company	Vehicle Units Sold (millions)
GM	8.59
Toyota	6.78
Ford	6.54
Volkswagen	5.02
Daimler Chrysler	4.36
PSA Peugeot Citroen	3.29
Hyundai	3.05
Nissan	2.97
Honda	2.91
Renault	2.39

Source: Company Reports, Automotive News.

from 10 percent in 2003. If that goal is attained, Toyota will surpass GM to become the world's largest auto company (it is already the world's most profitable auto company—see Exhibit 5).

The most rapidly growing automobile market in the world is China. Production and sales of cars in China have soared since the country joined the World Trade Organization in 2001. Some 4.1 million cars and light trucks were sold in China in 2003, a 37 percent rise over the prior year, and China seems set to surpass Japan as the world's third largest automobile market in 2004.[30] With just 8 vehicles per 1,000 residents in 2003, versus 940 in the United States and 584 in Europe, many think that China is set to continue growing for years to come, and could potentially become the world's largest automobile market by 2020.[31]

The majority of these vehicles were made locally, often by joint ventures between foreign automobile companies and Chinese enterprises. Collectively, foreign automobile companies invested some $19 billion in China between 1994 and 2003. In 2004, General Motors, Ford, Volkswagen, and Toyota all announced plans to invest in new factories in China, with some $13 billion of investment planned for 2005–2010. The largest foreign player in China in 2003 was Volkswagen. Volkswagen was the first foreign manufacturer to set up operations in China, and has reaped the benefits of its early investments. Its two joint ventures with Chinese companies accounted for about 35 percent of total sales in 2003. GM and its local joint venture partner, SAIC, were second with about 11 percent of the total market.

Investments by foreign companies should increase production capacity in China to some 5.4 million units by 2006. If the demand continues to grow at its torrid pace, this will not be enough to serve local demand—but if local demand softens, the result could be excess capacity. Some think in such circumstances, China might start to become an export base for car makers.

ENDNOTES

1. The *Economist*, A Survey of the Car Industry, "Perpetual Motion," September 4, 2004, pages 3–4.
2. The phrase first appeared in GM's 1924 Annual Report to Shareholders, and more than anything else, it captured the essence of Sloan's revolutionary marketing philosophy. For details visit GM's website at **http://www.gm.com/company/corp_info/history/index.html.**
3. Figures from Standard & Poor's, *Industry Survey: Autos & Auto Parts*, June 24, 2004.
4. Figures from Standard & Poor's, *Industry Survey: Autos & Auto Parts*, June 24, 2004.
5. Figures from Standard & Poor's, *Industry Survey: Autos & Auto Parts*, June 24, 2004.
6. The *Economist*, A Survey of the Car Industry, "Detroit's Nine Lives," September 4, 2004, pages 6–9.
7. The *Economist*, A Survey of the Car Industry, "Detroit's Nine Lives," September 4, 2004, pages 6–9.
8. The *Economist*, A Survey of the Car Industry, "Detroit's Nine Lives," September 4, 2004, pages 6–9.
9. D. Welch, "Price Breaks Are Here to Stay," *Business Week*, February 16, 2004, page 39.
10. Figures from Standard & Poor's, *Industry Survey: Autos & Auto Parts*, June 24, 2004.
11. D. Welch, "Price Breaks Are Here to Stay," *Business Week*, February 16, 2004, page 39.
12. Figures from Standard & Poor's, *Industry Survey: Autos & Auto Parts*, June 24, 2004.
13. J.D. Power Press Release, April 28, 2004, "Korean Branded Vehicles Overtake Europeans and Domestics in Initial Quality," J.D. Press Release, June 29, 2004, "Toyota Motor Sales Capture Top Corporate Rankings in Vehicle Dependability."
14. L. Hawkins, "US Auto Makers Get Better Grades for Productivity," *Wall Street Journal*, June 11, 2004, page A3.
15. D. Winter, "Efficiency Scoreboard," *Ward's Auto World*, July 2002, page 53.
16. Harbor Consulting, "New Benchmarks Set in 2004," Harbour Report, Press Release, June 10, 2004. Available at **http://www.harbourinc.com/.**
17. L. Hawkins, "US Auto Makers Get Better Grades for Productivity," *Wall Street Journal*, June 11, 2004, page A3.
18. D. Welch, "Has GM Outrun Its Pension Problems?" *Business Week*, January 19, 2004, page 70.
19. M. Phelan, "GM Predicts Sporty Profits Even From Fewer Sales," *Knight Ridder Tribune Business News*, March 13, 2004, page 1.
20. D. Welch and K. Kerwin, "Detroit Tries It the Japanese Way," *Business Week*, January 26, 2004, page 76; A. Taylor, "Detroit Buffs Up," *Fortune*, February 9, 2004, pages 90–94.
21. D. Winter, "Shrinking Product Development Time," *Ward's Auto World*, June 2003, pages 36–40.
22. J. Muller, "The Little Car That Could," *Forbes*, December 8, 2003, page 82; The *Economist*, "The Year of the Car," January 3, 2004, page 47.
23. Standard & Poor's, *Industry Survey: Autos & Auto Parts*, June 24, 2004.
24. Standard & Poor's, *Industry Survey: Autos & Auto Parts*, June 24, 2004.
25. K. Kerwin, "Ford to Suppliers: Let's Get Cozier," *Business Week*, September 20, 2004, page 8.
26. The *Economist*, A Survey of the Car Industry, "Fighting Back," September 4, 2004, pages 14–16.
27. R. Rosmarin, "Your Custom Car Is Ready at Toyota," *Business*, 2 (October 2004): 150–151.
28. S.S. Carty, "Hybrids Could Hitt 20 Percent of Car Market by 2010," *Wall Street Journal*, October 14, 2002, page D3.
29. The *Economist*, A Survey of the Car Industry, "The New European Order," September 4, 2004, pages 9–11.
30. Standard & Poor's, *Industry Survey: Autos & Auto Parts*, June 24, 2004.
31. D. Welch, D. Roberts, and G. Edmondson, "GM: Gunning It in China," *Business Week*, June 21, 2004, pages 112–114.

Case 4

Toyota: Origins, Evolution, and Current Prospects

This case was prepared by Charles W. L. Hill, the University of Washington.

The growth of Toyota has been one of the great success stories of Japanese industry during the last half century. In 1947, the company was a little-known domestic manufacturer producing around 100,000 vehicles a year. As 2004 drew to a close, Toyota stated that the company and its affiliates would produce a record 7.84 million vehicles in 2004, placing it comfortably ahead of Ford and second only to General Motors in the global industry. Moreover, the company raised its production targets for 2006 to 8.5 million vehicles following better than expected sales in both North America and Asia. If Toyota meets this goal, it could surpass GM to become the world's largest automobile company. It would also put the company ahead of schedule to achieve its stated goal of gaining a 15 percent share of the global automobile market by 2010.[1]

This case describes the rise of Toyota from an obscure Japanese automobile company into the giant of today. It explains how the revolutionary production system developed at Toyota during the quarter of a century after 1950 paved the way for the company's current success. The case closes with a look at the challenges and opportunities Toyota now faces.

The Origins of Toyota

The original idea behind the founding of the Toyota Motor Company came from the fertile mind of Toyoda Sakichi.[2] The son of a carpenter, Sakichi was an entrepreneur and inventor whose primary interest lay in the textile industry, but he had been intrigued by automobiles since a visit to the United States in 1910. Sakichi's principal achievement was the invention of an automatic loom that held out the promise of being able to lower the costs of weaving high-quality cloth. In 1926, Sakichi set up Toyoda Automatic Loom to manufacture this product. In 1930, Sakichi sold the patent rights to a British textile concern, Platt Brothers, for about 1 million yen, a considerable sum in those days. Sakichi urged his son, Toyoda Kiichiro, to use this money to study the possibility of manufacturing automobiles in Japan. A mechanical engineer with a degree from the University of Tokyo, in 1930 Kiichiro became managing director of loom production at Toyoda Automatic Loom.

Kiichiro was at first reluctant to invest in automobile production. The Japanese market was at that time dominated by Ford and General Motors, both of which imported knock-down car kits from the United States and assembled them in Japan. Given this, the board of Toyoda Automatic Loom, including Kiichiro's brother-in-law and the company's president, Kodama Risaburo, opposed the investment on the grounds that it was too risky. Kiichiro probably would not have pursued the issue further had not his father made a deathbed request in 1930 that Kiichiro explore the possibilities of automobile production. Kiichiro had to push, but in 1933, he was able to get

C61

permission to set up an automobile department within Toyoda Automatic Loom.

Kiichiro's belief was that he would be able to figure out how to manufacture automobiles by taking apart U.S.-made vehicles and examining them piece by piece. He also felt that it should be possible to adapt U.S. mass-production technology to manufacture cost efficiently at lower volumes. His confidence was based in large part upon the already considerable engineering skills and capabilities at his disposal through Toyoda Automatic Loom. Many of the precision engineering and manufacturing skills needed in automobile production were similar to the skills required to manufacture looms.

Kiichiro produced his first 20 vehicles in 1935, and in 1936, the automobile department produced 1,142 vehicles—910 trucks, 100 cars, and 132 buses. At this time, however, the production system was essentially craft-based rather than a modern assembly line. Despite some progress, the struggle might still have been uphill had not fate intervened in the form of the Japanese military. Japan had invaded Manchuria in 1931 and quickly found American-made trucks useful for moving men and equipment. As a result, the military felt that it was strategically important for Japan to have its own automobile industry. The result was the passage of an automobile manufacturing law in 1936 which required companies producing more than 3,000 vehicles per year in Japan to get a license from the government. Moreover, to get a license over 50 percent of the stock had to be owned by Japanese investors. The law also placed a duty on imported cars, including the knock-down kits that Ford and GM brought into Japan. As a direct result of this legislation, both GM and Ford exited from the Japanese market in 1939.

Once the Japanese government passed this law, Kodama Risaburo decided that the automobile venture could be profitable and switched from opposing to proactively supporting Kiichiro (in fact, Risaburo's wife, who was Kiichiro's elder sister, had been urging him to take this step for some time). The first priority was to attract the funds necessary to build a mass-production facility. In 1937, Risaburo and Kiichiro decided to incorporate the automobile department as a separate company in order to attract outside investors—which they were successful in doing. Kiichiro Toyoda was appointed president of the new company. The company was named the Toyota Motor Company. (The founding family's name, "Toyoda," means "abundant rice field" in Japanese. The new name had no meaning in Japanese.)

Upon incorporation, Risaburo and Kiichiro's vision was that Toyota should expand its passenger car production as quickly as possible. However, once again fate intervened in the form of the Japanese military. Toyota had barely begun passenger car production when war broke out; in 1939, the Japanese government, on advice from the military, prohibited passenger car production and demanded that the company specialize in the production of military trucks.

The Evolution of Toyota

After the end of World War II, Kiichiro was determined that Toyota should reestablish itself as a manufacturer of automobiles.[3] Toyota, however, faced a number of problems in doing this:

1. The Japanese domestic market was too small to support efficient-scale mass-production facilities such as those common in America by that time.

2. The Japanese economy was starved of capital, which made it difficult to raise funds to finance new investments.

3. New labor laws introduced by the American occupiers increased the bargaining power of labor and made it difficult for companies to lay off workers.

4. North America and Western Europe were full of large auto manufacturers eager to establish operations in Japan.

In response to the last point, in 1950 the new Japanese government prohibited direct foreign investment in the automobile industry and imposed high tariffs on the importation of foreign cars. This protection, however, did little to solve the other problems facing the company at this time.

Limitations of Mass Production

At this juncture a remarkable mechanical engineer entered the scene: Ohno Taiichi. More than anyone else, it was Ohno who was to work out a response to the above problems. Ohno had joined Toyoda Spinning and Weaving in 1932 as a production engineer in cotton thread manufacture and entered Toyota when the former company was absorbed into the latter in 1943. Ohno worked in auto production for two years, was promoted, and managed auto assembly and machine shops between 1945 and 1953, and in 1954, he was appointed a company director.

When Ohno Taiichi joined Toyota, the mass-production methods pioneered by Ford had become the accepted method of manufacturing automobiles. The basic philosophy behind mass production was to produce a limited product line in massive quantities to gain maximum economies of scale. The economies came from spreading the fixed costs involved in setting up the specialized equipment required to stamp body parts and manufacture components over as large a production run as possible. Since setting up much of the equipment could take a full day or more, the economies involved in long production runs were reckoned to be considerable. Thus, for example, Ford would stamp 500,000 right-hand door panels in a single production run and then store the parts in warehouses until they were needed in the assembly plant, rather than stamp just those door panels that were needed immediately and then change the settings and stamp out left-hand door panels or other body parts.

A second feature of mass production was that each assembly worker should perform only a single task, rather than a variety of tasks. The idea here was that as the worker became completely familiar with a single task, he could perform it much faster, thereby increasing labor productivity. Assembly line workers were overseen by a foreman who did not perform any assembly tasks personally, but instead ensured that the workers followed orders. In addition, a number of specialists were employed to perform nonassembly operations such as tool repair, die changes, quality inspection, and general "housecleaning."

After working in Toyota for five years and visiting Ford's U.S. plants, Ohno became convinced that the basic mass-production philosophy was flawed. He saw five problems with the mass-production system:

1. Long production runs created massive inventories that had to be stored in large warehouses. This was expensive both because of the cost of warehousing and because inventories tied up capital in unproductive uses.

2. If the initial machine settings were wrong, long production runs resulted in the production of a large number of defects.

3. The sheer monotony of assigning assembly line workers to a single task generated defects, since workers became lax about quality control. In addition, since assembly line workers were not responsible for quality control, they had little incentive to minimize defects.

4. The extreme division of labor resulted in the employment of specialists such as foremen, quality inspectors, and tooling specialists, whose jobs logically could be performed by assembly line workers.

5. The mass-production system was unable to accommodate consumer preferences for product diversity.

In addition to these flaws, Ohno knew that the small domestic market in Japan and the lack of capital for investing in mass-production facilities made the American model unsuitable for Toyota.

Reducing Setup Times

Given these flaws and the constraints that Toyota faced, Ohno decided to take a fresh look at the techniques used for automobile production. His first goal was to try to make it economical to manufacture auto body parts in small batches. To do this, he needed to reduce the time it took to set up the machines for stamping out body parts. Ohno and his engineers began to experiment with a number of techniques to speed up the time it took to change the dies in stamping equipment. This included using rollers to move dies in and out of position along with a number of simple mechanized adjustment mechanisms to fine-tune the settings. These techniques were relatively simple to master, so Ohno directed production workers to perform the die changes themselves. This in itself reduced the need for specialists and eliminated the idle time that workers previously had enjoyed while waiting for the dies to be changed.

Through a process of trial and error, Ohno succeeded in reducing the time required to change dies on stamping equipment from a full day to 15 minutes by 1962, and to as little as 3 minutes by 1971. By comparison, even in the early 1980s many American and European plants required anywhere between 2 and 6 hours to change dies on stamping equipment. As a consequence, American and European plants found it economical to manufacture in lots equivalent to 10 to 30 days' supply and to reset equipment only every other day. In contrast, since Toyota could change the dies on stamping equipment in a matter of minutes, it manufactured in lots equivalent to just one day's supply, while resetting equipment three times per day.

Not only did these innovations make small production runs economical, but they also had the added benefit of reducing inventories and improving product quality. Making small batches eliminated the need to hold large inventories, thereby reducing warehousing costs and freeing up scarce capital for investment elsewhere. Small production runs and the lack of inventory also meant that defective parts were produced only in small numbers and entered the assembly process almost immediately. This had the added effect of making those in the stamping shops far more concerned about quality. In addition, once it became economical to manufacture small batches of components, much greater variety could be included into the final product at little or no cost penalty.

Organization of the Workplace

One of Ohno's first innovations was to group the work force into teams. Each team was given a set of assembly tasks to perform, and team members were trained to perform each task that the team was responsible for. Each team had a leader who was himself an assembly line worker. In addition to coordinating the team, the team leader was expected to perform basic assembly line tasks and to fill in for any absent worker. The teams were given the job of housecleaning, minor tool repair, and quality inspection (along with the training required to perform these tasks). Time was also set aside for team members to discuss ways to improve the production process (the practice now referred to as "quality circles").

The immediate effect of this approach was to reduce the need for specialists in the workplace and to create a more flexible work force in which individual assembly line workers were not treated simply as human machines. All this resulted in increased worker productivity.

None of this would have been possible, however, had it not been for an agreement reached between management and labor after a 1950 strike. The strike was brought on by management's attempt to cut the work force by 25 percent (in response to a recession in Japan). After lengthy negotiations, Toyota and the union worked out a compromise. The work force was cut by 25 percent as originally proposed, but the remaining employees were given two guarantees, one for lifetime employment and the other for pay graded by seniority and tied to company profitability through bonus payments. In exchange for these guarantees, the employees agreed to be flexible in work assignments. In turn, this allowed for the introduction of the team concept.

Improving Quality

One of the standard practices in the mass-production automobile assembly plants was to fix any errors that occurred during assembly in a rework area at the end of the assembly line. Errors routinely occurred in most assembly plants either because bad parts were installed or because good parts were installed incorrectly. The belief was that stopping an assembly line to fix such errors would cause enormous bottlenecks in the production system. Thus it was thought to be more efficient to correct errors at the end of the line.

Ohno viewed this system as wasteful for three reasons: (1) since workers understood that any errors would be fixed at the end of the line, they had little incentive to correct errors themselves; (2) once a defective part had been embedded in a complex vehicle, an enormous amount of rework might be required to fix it; and (3) since defective parts were often not discovered until the end of the line when the finished cars were tested, a large number of cars containing the same defect may have been built before the problem was found.

In an attempt to get away from this practice, Ohno decided to look for ways to reduce the amount of rework at the end of the line. His approach involved two elements. First, he placed a cord above every workstation and instructed workers to stop the assembly line if a problem emerged that could not be fixed. It then became the responsibility of the whole team to come over and work on the problem. Second, team members were taught to trace every defect back to its ultimate cause and then to ensure that the problem was fixed so that it would not reoccur.

Initially, this system produced enormous disruption. The production line was stopping all the time, and workers became discouraged. However, as team members began to gain experience in identifying problems and tracing them back to their root cause, the number of errors began to drop dramatically and stops in the line became much rarer, so that today in most Toyota plants the line virtually never stops.

Developing the Kanban System

Once reduced setup times had made small production runs economical, Ohno began to look for ways to coordinate the flow of production within the Toyota manufacturing system so that the amount of inventory in the system could be reduced to a minimum. Toyota produced about 25 percent of its major components in-house (the rest were contracted out to independent suppliers). Ohno's initial goal was to arrange for components and/or subassemblies manufactured in-house to be delivered to the assembly floor only when they were needed, and not before (this goal was later extended to include independent suppliers).

To achieve this, in 1953 Ohno began experimenting with what came to be known as the kanban system. Under the kanban system, component parts are delivered to the assembly line in containers. As each container is emptied, it is sent back to the previous step in the manufacturing process. This then becomes the signal to make more parts. The system minimizes work in progress by increasing inventory turnover. The elimination of buffer inventories also means that defective components show up immediately in the next process. This speeds up the processes of tracing defects back to their source and facilitates correction of the problem before too many defects are made. Moreover, the elimination of buffer stocks, by removing all safety nets, makes it imperative that problems be solved before they become serious enough to jam up the production process, thereby creating a strong incentive for workers to ensure that errors are corrected as quickly as possible. In addition, by decentralizing responsibility for coordinating the manufacturing process to lower-level employees, the kanban system does away with the need for extensive centralized management to coordinate the flow of parts between the various stages of production.

After perfecting the kanban system in one of Toyota's machine shops, Ohno had a chance to apply the system broadly in 1960 when he was made general manager of the Motomachi assembly plant. Ohno already had converted the machining, body stamping, and body shops to the kanban system, but since many parts came from shops that had yet to adopt

the system, or from outside suppliers, the impact on inventories was initially minimal. However, by 1962 he had extended the kanban to forging and casting, and between 1962 and 1965, he began to bring independent suppliers into the system.

Organizing Suppliers

Assembly of components into a final vehicle accounts for only about 15 percent of the total manufacturing process in automobile manufacture. The remaining 85 percent of the process involves manufacturing more than ten thousand individual parts and assembling them into about one hundred major components, such as engines, suspension systems, transaxles, and so on. Coordinating this process so that everything comes together at the right time has always been a problem for auto manufacturers. Historically, the response at Ford and GM to this problem was massive vertical integration. The belief was that control over the supply chain would allow management to coordinate the flow of component parts into the final assembly plant. In addition, American firms held the view that vertical integration made them more efficient by reducing their dependence on other firms for materials and components and by limiting their vulnerability to opportunistic overcharging.

As a consequence of this philosophy, even as late as the mid-1990s General Motors made 68 percent of its own components in-house, while Ford made 50 percent (in the late 1990s both GM and Ford deintegrated, spinning out much of their in-house supply operations as independent enterprises). When they didn't vertically integrate, U.S. auto companies historically tried to reduce the procurement costs that remain through competitive bidding—asking a number of companies to submit contracts and giving orders to suppliers offering the lowest price.

Under the leadership of Kiichiro Toyoda during the 1930s and 1940s, Toyota followed the American model and pursued extensive vertical integration into the manufacture of component parts. In fact, Toyota had little choice in this matter, since only a handful of Japanese companies were able to make the necessary components. However, the low volume of production during this period meant that the scale of integration was relatively small. In the 1950s, however, the volume of auto production began to increase dramatically. This presented Toyota with a dilemma: Should the company increase its capacity to manufacture components in-house in line with the growth in production of autos, or should the company contract out?

In contrast to American practice, the company decided that while it should increase in-house capacity for essential subassemblies and bodies, it would do better to contract out for most components. Four reasons seemed to bolster this decision:

1. Toyota wanted to avoid the capital expenditures required to expand capacity to manufacture a wide variety of components.

2. Toyota wanted to reduce risk by maintaining a low factory capacity in case factory sales slumped.

3. Toyota wanted to take advantage of the lower wage scales in smaller firms.

4. Toyota managers realized that in-house manufacturing offered few benefits if it was possible to find stable, high-quality, and low-cost external sources of component supply.

At the same time, Toyota managers felt that the American practice of inviting competitive bids from suppliers was self-defeating. While competitive bidding might achieve the lowest short-run costs, the practice of playing suppliers off against each other did not guarantee stable supplies, high quality, or cooperation beyond existing contracts to solve design or engineering problems. Ohno and other Toyota managers believed that real efficiencies could be achieved if the company entered into long-term relationships with major suppliers. This would allow them to introduce the kanban system, thereby further reducing inventory holding costs and realizing the same kind of quality benefits that Toyota was already beginning to encounter with its in-house supply operations. In addition, Ohno wanted to bring suppliers into the design process since he believed that suppliers might be able to suggest ways of improving the design of component parts based upon their own manufacturing experience.

As it evolved during the 1950s and 1960s, Toyota's strategy toward its suppliers had several elements. The company spun off some of its own in-house supply operations into quasi-independent entities in which it took a minority stake, typically holding between 20 percent and 40 percent of the stock. It then recruited a number of independent companies with a view to establishing a long-term relationship with them for the supply of critical components. Sometimes, but not always, Toyota took a minority stake in these companies as well. All these companies were designated as "first-tier suppliers." First-tier suppliers were responsible for working with Toyota as an integral part of the new product development team. Each first tier was responsible for the formation of a "second tier" of suppliers under its direction. Companies in the second tier were given the job of fabricating individual parts. Both first- and second-tier suppliers were formed into supplier associations.

By 1986 Toyota had three regional supply organizations in Japan with 62, 135, and 25 first-tier suppliers. A major function of the supplier associations was to share information regarding new manufacturing, design, or materials management techniques among themselves. Concepts such as statistical process control, total quality control, and computer-aided design were rapidly diffused among suppliers by this means.

Toyota also worked closely with its suppliers, providing them with management expertise, engineering expertise, and sometimes capital to finance new investments. A critical feature of this relationship was the incentives that Toyota established to encourage its suppliers to focus on realizing continuous process improvements. The basic contract for a component would be for four to five years, with the price being agreed in advance. If by joint efforts the supplier and Toyota succeeded in reducing the costs of manufacturing the components, then the additional profit would be shared between the two. If the supplier by its own efforts came up with an innovation that reduced costs, the supplier would keep the additional profit that the innovation generated for the lifetime of the contract.

As a consequence of this strategy, Toyota outsourced more production than almost any other major auto manufacturer. By the late 1980s Toyota was responsible for only about 27 percent of the value going into a finished automobile, with the remainder coming from outside suppliers. In contrast, at the time General Motors was responsible for about 70 percent of the value going into a finished automobile. Other consequences included long-term improvements in productivity and quality among Toyota's suppliers that were comparable to the improvements achieved by Toyota itself. In particular, the extension of the kanban system to include suppliers, by eliminating buffer inventory stocks, in essence forced suppliers to focus more explicitly on the quality of their product.

Consequences

The consequences of Toyota's production system included a surge in labor productivity and a decline in the number of defects per car. Exhibit 1 compares the number of vehicles produced per worker at General Motors, Ford, Nissan, and Toyota between 1965 and 1983.

These figures are adjusted for the degree of vertical integration pursued by each company. As can be seen, in 1960 productivity at Toyota already outstripped that of Ford, General Motors, and its main Japanese competitor, Nissan. As Toyota refined its production system over the next eighteen years, productivity doubled. In comparison, productivity essentially stood still at General Motors and Ford during the same period (see Exhibit 2).

Exhibit 2 provides another way to assess the superiority of Toyota's production system. Here the performance of Toyota's Takaoka plant is compared with that of General Motors's Framingham plant in 1987. As can be seen, the Toyota plant was more productive, produced far fewer defects per one hundred cars, and kept far less inventory on hand.

A further aspect of Toyota's production system is that the short setup times made it economical to manufacture a much wider range of models than is feasible at a traditional mass-production assembly plant. In essence, Toyota soon found that it could supply much greater product variety than its competitors with little in the way of a cost penalty. In 1990 Toyota was offering consumers around the world roughly as

EXHIBIT 1

Vehicles Produced per Worker (Adjusted for Vertical Integration), 1965–1983

Year	General Motors	Ford	Nissan	Toyota
1965	5.0	4.4	4.3	8.0
1970	3.7	4.3	8.8	13.4
1975	4.4	4.0	9.0	15.1
1979	4.5	4.2	11.1	18.4
1980	4.1	3.7	12.2	17.8
1983	4.8	4.7	11.0	15.0

Source: M. A. Cusumano, *The Japanese Automobile Industry* (Cambridge, Mass.: Harvard University Press, 1989), Table 48, p. 197.

EXHIBIT 2

General Motors's Framingham Plant Versus Toyota's Takaoka Plant, 1987

	GM Framingham	Toyota Takaoka
Assembly Hours per Car	31	16
Assembly Defects per 100 Cars	135	45
Inventory of Parts	2 weeks	2 hours

Source: J. P. Womack, D. T. Jones, and D. Roos, *The Machines That Changed the World* (New York: Macmillan, 1990), Figure 4.2, p. 83.

many products as General Motors (about 150), even though Toyota was still only half GM's size. Moreover, it could do this at a lower cost than GM.

Distribution and Customer Relations

Toyota's approach to its distributors and customers as it evolved during the 1950s and 1960s was in many ways just as radical as its approach toward suppliers. In 1950, Toyota formed a subsidiary, Toyota Motor Sales, to handle distribution and sales. The new subsidiary was headed by Kaymiya Shotaro from its inception until 1975. Kaymiya's philosophy was that dealers should be treated as "equal partners" in the Toyota family. To back this up, he had Toyota Motor Sales provide a wide range of sales training and service training for dealership personnel.

Kaymiya then used the dealers to build long-term ties with Toyota's customers. The ultimate aim was to bring customers into the Toyota design and production process. To this end, through its dealers, Toyota Motor Sales assembled a huge database on customer preferences. Much of these data came from monthly or semiannual surveys conducted by dealers. These asked Toyota customers their preferences for styling, model types, colors, prices, and other features. Toyota also used these surveys to estimate the potential demand for new models. This information was then fed directly into the design process.

Kaymiya began this process in 1952 when the company was redesigning its Toyopet model. The Toyopet was primarily used by urban taxi drivers. Toyota Motor Sales surveyed taxi drivers to try to find out what type of vehicle they preferred. They wanted something reliable, inexpensive, and with good city fuel mileage—which Toyota engineers then set about designing. In 1956, Kaymiya formalized this process when he created a unified department for planning and market research whose function was to coordinate the marketing strategies developed by researchers at Toyota Motor Sales with product planning by Toyota's design engineers. From this time on, marketing information played a critical role in the design of Toyota's cars and in the company's strategy. In particular, it was the research department at Toyota Motor Sales that provided the initial stimulus for Toyota to start exporting during the late 1960s after predicting, correctly, that growth in domestic sales would slow down considerably during the 1970s.

Expanding Internationally

Large-scale overseas expansion did not become feasible at Toyota until the late 1960s for one principal reason: despite the rapid improvement in productivity, Japanese cars were still not competitive.[4] In 1957, for example, the Toyota Corona sold in Japan for the equivalent of $1,694. At the same time the Volkswagen Beetle sold for $1,111 in West Germany, while Britain's Austin company was selling its basic model for the equivalent of $1,389 in Britain. Foreign companies were effectively kept out of the Japanese market, however, by a 40 percent value-added tax and shipping costs.

Despite these disadvantages, Toyota tried to enter the U.S. market in the late 1950s. The company set up a U.S. subsidiary in California in October 1957 and began to sell cars in early 1958, hoping to capture the American small car market (which at that time was poorly served by the U.S. automobile companies). The result was a disaster. Toyota's cars performed poorly in road tests on U.S. highways. The basic problem was that the engines of Toyota's cars were too small for prolonged high-speed driving and tended to overheat and burn oil, while the poorly designed chassis resulted in excessive vibration. Sales were slow, and in 1964, Toyota closed down its U.S. subsidiary and withdrew from the market.

The company was determined to learn from its U.S. experience and quickly redesigned several of its models based on feedback from American consumer surveys and U.S. road tests. As a result, by 1967 the picture had changed considerably. The quality of Toyota's cars was now sufficient to make an impact in the U.S. market, while production costs and retail prices had continued to fall and were now comparable with international competitors in the small car market.

In the late 1960s, Toyota reentered the U.S. market. Although sales were initially slow, they increased steadily. Then the OPEC-engineered fourfold increase in oil prices that followed the 1973 Israeli/Arab conflict gave Toyota an unexpected boost. U.S. consumers began to turn to small fuel-efficient cars in droves, and Toyota was one of the main beneficiaries. Driven primarily by a surge in U.S. demand, worldwide exports of Toyota cars increased from 157,882 units in 1967 to 856,352 units by 1974 and 1,800,923 units by 1984. Put another way, in 1967 exports accounted for 19 percent of Toyota's total output. By 1984, they accounted for 52.5 percent.

Success brought its own problems. By the early 1980s, political pressures and talk of local content regulations in the United States and Europe were forcing an initially reluctant Toyota to rethink its exporting strategy. Toyota already had agreed to "voluntary" import quotas with the United States in 1981. The consequence for Toyota was stagnant export growth between 1981 and 1984. Against this background, in the early 1980s Toyota began to think seriously about setting up manufacturing operations overseas.

Transplant Operations

Toyota's first overseas operation was a 50/50 joint venture with General Motors established in February 1983 under the name New United Motor Manufacturing, Inc. (NUMMI). NUMMI, which is based in Fremont, California, began producing Chevrolet Nova cars for GM in December 1984.[5] The maximum capacity of the Fremont plant is about 250,000 cars per year.

For Toyota, the joint venture provided a chance to find out whether it could build quality cars in the United States using American workers and American suppliers. It also provided Toyota with experience dealing with an American union (the United Auto Workers Union) and with a means of circumventing "voluntary" import restrictions. For General Motors, the venture provided an opportunity to observe in full detail the Japanese approach to manufacturing. While General Motors's role was marketing and distributing the plant's output, Toyota designed the product and designed, equipped, and operated the plant. At the venture's start, thirty-four executives were loaned to NUMMI by Toyota and sixteen by General Motors. The chief executive and chief operating officer were both Toyota personnel.

By the fall of 1986, the NUMMI plant was running at full capacity, and the early indications were that the NUMMI plant was achieving productivity and quality levels close to those achieved at Toyota's major Takaoka plant in Japan. For example, in 1987 it took the NUMMI plant nineteen assembly hours to build a car, compared with sixteen hours at Takaoka, while the number of defects per one hundred cars was the same at NUMMI as at Takaoka—forty-five.[6]

Encouraged by its success at NUMMI, in December 1985 Toyota announced that it would build an automobile manufacturing plant in Georgetown, Kentucky. The plant, which came on stream in May 1988, officially had the capacity to produce 200,000 Toyota Camrys a year. Such was the success of this plant, however, that by early 1990 it was producing the equivalent of 220,000 cars per year. This success was followed by an announcement in December 1990 that Toyota would build a second plant in Georgetown with a capacity to produce a further 200,000 vehicles per year.[7]

By 2001, Toyota had four vehicle assembly plants in North America with a total capacity to produce over 1 million vehicles per year. In addition, the company had two engine plants, an aluminum wheel plant, an aluminum casting plant, special parts and body parts plants, and an automatic transmission plant. In total, these factories employed more than 123,000 Americans, more than Coca-Cola, Microsoft, and Oracle combined. Some 60 percent of all Toyota vehicles sold in the United States were now locally produced, and the company had announced plans to add another U.S. plant capable of turning out an additional 250,000 vehicles a year by 2005.[8]

In addition to its North American transplant operations, Toyota moved to set up production in Europe in anticipation of the 1992 lowering of trade barriers among the twelve members of the European Economic Community. In 1989, the company announced that it would build a plant in England with the capacity to manufacture 200,000 cars per year by 1997.

In 2001, Toyota opened a second European plant in France, raising its total production capacity within the European Union to 370,000. Toyota's goal was to sell 800,000 cars a year in the EU by 2005, which would give the company a 5 percent share of the EU market.[9]

Despite Toyota's apparent commitment to expand U.S.- and European-based assembly operations, it was not all smooth sailing. One problem was building an overseas supplier network comparable to Toyota's Japanese network. For example, in a 1990 meeting of Toyota's North American supplier's association, Toyota executives informed their North American suppliers that the defect ratio for parts produced by 75 North American and European suppliers was 100 times greater than the defect ratio for parts supplied by 147 Japanese suppliers—1,000 defects per million parts versus 10 defects per million among Toyota's Japanese suppliers. Moreover, Toyota executives pointed out that parts manufactured by North American and European suppliers tend to be significantly more expensive than comparable parts manufactured in Japan.

Because of these problems, Toyota had to import many parts from Japan for its U.S. assembly operations. However, for political reasons Toyota was being pushed to increase the local content of cars assembled in North America. The company's plan was for 50 percent of the value of Toyota cars assembled in the United States to be locally produced by January 1991. By the early 2000s, the local content of cars produced in North America was over 70 percent. To improve the efficiency of its U.S.-based suppliers, Toyota embarked upon an aggressive supplier education process. In 1992, it established the Toyota Supplier Support Center to teach its suppliers the basics of the Toyota production system. By 2001, eighty-nine supplier companies had been through the center. Many have reportedly seen double- and triple-digit productivity growth as a result, as well as dramatic reductions in inventory levels.[10]

Product Strategy

Toyota's initial production was aimed at the small car/basic transportation end of the automobile market. This was true both in Japan and of its export sales to North America and Europe. During the 1980s, however, Toyota progressively moved up market and abandoned much of the lower end of the market to new entrants such as the South Koreans. Thus, the company's Camry and Corolla models, which initially were positioned toward the bottom of the market, have been constantly upgraded and now are aimed at the middle-income segments of the market. This upgrading reflects two factors: (1) the rising level of incomes in Japan and the commensurate increase in the ability of Japanese consumers to purchase midrange and luxury cars and (2) a desire to hold onto its U.S. consumers, many of whom initially purchased inexpensive Toyotas in their early twenties and who have since traded up to more expensive models.

The constant upgrading of Toyota's models reached a logical conclusion in September 1989 when the company's Lexus division began marketing luxury cars to compete with Jaguars, BMWs, and the like. Although the Lexus brand initially got off to a slow start—in large part due to an economic recession—by 2001 Toyota was selling over 200,000 Lexus models a year in the United States, making it the best-selling luxury brand in the country.

Another addition to Toyota's product range in the late 1980s was a minivan. This vehicle was aimed at the North American market, where the minivan segment had grown rapidly. Toyota first introduced a minivan in 1986, but it flopped. The company dispatched product planners and design engineers to showrooms to find out why. Among the problems they identified were that the minivans lacked an aisle down the center, the short wheelbase gave them a pitchy ride, and the engine was not easy to service. Based on this feedback, Toyota designers completely redesigned the vehicle and reintroduced it in April 1990 as the Previa minivan; sales soon exceeded expectations.[11]

Toyota in 2004

As 2004 drew to a close, Toyota was enjoying one of its best years ever. The company had overtaken Ford to become the second largest automobile company in the world, and it had its sights firmly set on General Motors. Its goal of attaining a 15 percent share of the global market seemed attainable. Toyota was now a truly international company. Its overseas operations had grown from 11 production facilities in 9 countries in 1980 to 42 production facilities in 24 countries around the world by 2004.[12] In the all important U.S. market, the world's largest, Toyota held a 13.1 percent share of passenger car sales in 2003 and a 9.6 percent share of light truck sales, up from 11 percent and 7.6 percent, respectively, in 2000.[13]

The company was very profitable. In the financial year ending March 2004, it earned $11 billion net profits on sales of $163 billion. It had more profits than General Motors, Ford, and Daimler Chrysler combined and ended the year with some $30 billion in cash and short-term investments.

According to data from J.D. Power, Toyota was still the quality leader in the U.S. market. For cars that had been on the market for over three years, Toyota led the pack with 207 problems per 100 vehicles, compared with an industry average of 269 problems per 100 vehicles. Toyota also had the best record in the industry when measured by problems reported in the first 90 days after a sale—101 problems per 100 cars versus an industry average of 119 problems per 100 cars.[14]

J.D. Power also found that Toyota led the market in Japan. An April 2004 survey found that for vehicles purchased in 2002, Toyota had 89 problems per 100 vehicles compared with an industry average of 104. Honda was next with 91 problems per 100 vehicles, followed by Nissan with 108 problems per 100 vehicles.[15]

Furthermore, Toyota seemed to be maintaining a high level of productivity. In its American assembly operations, Toyota took 20.6 employee hours to build a car in 2004. This compares with 23.6 hours at General Motors, 25.4 hours at Ford, and 26.0 hours at Daimler Chrysler. However, both Nissan and Honda had more productive factories in the United States. Indeed, Nissan took 17.32 employee hours to build a car at its North American factories.[16] On the other hand, according to J.D. Power, Toyota has the three most efficient assembly plants in the world, all of which are located in Japan.

Toyota's ability to stay on top of productivity and quality rankings can be attributed to a company-wide obsession with continuing to improve the efficiency and effectiveness of its manufacturing operations. The latest round of these was initiated in 2000 by Toyota President, Fujio Cho. Cho, who worked for a while under Toyota's legendary engineer, Taichi Ohno, introduced an initiative known as "Construction of Cost Competitiveness for the 21st Century" or CCC21. The initiative has as a goal slashing component part costs by 30 percent on all new models. Attaining this goal necessitated Toyota working closely with suppliers—something it has long done.

According to news reports, by 2004 Toyota was close to attaining its CCC21 goal. In implementing CCC21, no detail has been too small. For example, Toyota took a close look at the grip handles mounted above the doors inside most cars. By working closely with suppliers, they managed to reduce the number of parts in these handles from 34 to 5, which cut procurement costs by 40 percent and reduced the time needed for installation from 12 seconds to 3 seconds.[17]

More generally, Toyota continues to refine its lean production system. For example, in die making, by 2004 Toyota had reduced the lead time to engineer and manufacture die sets for large body panels to 1.7 months, down from 3 months in 2002. By reducing lead time, Toyota reduces the startup costs associated with producing a new model, and the development time.[18]

In welding, Toyota has developed and installed a simplified assembly process known as the "global body line" or GBL. First developed in a low-volume Vietnamese assembly plant in 1996, and introduced into its first Japanese plant in 1998, by 2004 the GBL was operating in some 20 of the company's 50 assembly plants and was scheduled to be found in all 50 by 2007. The GBL system replaced Toyota's flexible body line assembly philosophy that has been in place since 1985. The GBL system is based upon a series of programmable robotic welding tools. Under the old FBL system, each car required three pallets to hold body parts in place during the welding process, each gripping either a major body side assembly or the roof assembly. The GBL system replaces these three pallets with a single pallet that holds all three major body panels in place from the inside as welding proceeds.[19]

According to Toyota, the GLB system has the following consequences:

- 30 percent reduction in the time a vehicle spends in the body shop

- 70 percent reduction in the time required to complete a major body change

- 50 percent cut in the cost to add or switch models

- 50 percent reduction in the investment to set up a line for a new model

- 50 percent reduction in assembly line footprint

The floor space freed up by the GLB allows two assembly lines to be placed in the space traditionally required for one, effectively doubling plant capacity. Moreover, using GLB technology as many as eight different models can be produced on a single assembly line. To achieve this, Toyota has pushed for consistency in design across model ranges, particularly with regard to the "hard points" that are grasped by the single master pallet.

Meanwhile, Toyota has also been accelerating the process of moving toward fewer vehicle platforms, the goal being to build a wide range of models on a limited range of platforms that use many of the same component parts or modules. The company is reportedly working toward a goal of having just ten platforms, down from over twenty in 2000.[20]

While Toyota is undoubtedly making progress refining its manufacturing efficiency, the fact remains that the productivity and quality gap between Toyota and its global competitors has narrowed. General Motors and Ford have both made significant strides in improving their quality and productivity in recent years. Moreover, in the American market at least, Toyota has suffered from the perception that its product offerings lack design flair and are not always as well attuned to consumer tastes as they might be. Here, too, however, there are signs that Toyota is improving matters, interestingly enough, by listening more to its American designers and engineers.

A pivotal event in the changing relationship between Toyota and its American designers occurred in the late 1990s. Japanese managers had resisted their U.S. colleagues' idea that the company should produce a V8 pickup truck for the American market. To change their minds, the U.S. executives flew their Japanese counterparts over from Japan and took them to a Dallas Cowboys football game—with a pit stop in the Texas Stadium parking lot. There the Japanese saw row upon row of full-size pickups. Finally, it dawned on them that Americans see the pickup as more than a commercial vehicle, considering it primary transportation. The result of this was Toyota's best-selling V8 pickup truck, the Toyota Tundra.[21]

American designers also pushed Toyota to redesign the Prius, its hybrid car first introduced in Japan in 1997. The Americans wanted a futuristic design change so that people would notice the technology. The result, the new Prius has become a surprise hit with Toyota, forecasting global sales of 300,000 units in 2005.[22]

Toyota's Americanization runs deeper than just product design issues. On the sales front, the company now sells more cars and trucks in North America than it does in Japan, and 70–80 percent of Toyota's global profits come from North America. On the personnel front, President Cho himself made his reputation by opening Toyota's first U.S. production plant in Georgetown, Kentucky, in 1988. His likely successor, Yoshi Inaba, spent eight years in the United States and has an MBA from Northwestern University. Americans are also starting to make their way into Toyota's top ranks. Two Americans from Toyota's U.S. subsidiary now rank among Toyota's top forty-two executives, and each spends from one to two weeks a month in Japan.[23]

Another concern of Toyota has been the aging of its customer base. According to J.D. Power, the average Toyota customer is 44 years old, compared with 38 for Volkswagen and 41 for Honda. Concerned that it was loosing its cache with the younger generation, some 60 million of whom will reach driving age over the next few years, Toyota introduced a new car brand, the Scion, into America in June 2004. Currently the brand has three models, all priced in the $13,000–$17,000 range. The cars are targeted at young entry level buyers and can be purchased over the web in addition to buying through traditional Toyota dealers. Early sales results suggest that the brand is doing well. Toyota's initial sales goals for the brand were 100,000 cars in 2005, but in October 2004, it raised that target to 170,000. The average buyer in the months following launch was 31 years old.[24]

As Toyota entered 2005, the key question facing management was whether the company was doing enough to attain its goal of capturing 15 percent of the global marketplace, particularly given the renewed efforts by its global rivals to close the quality and productivity gap between themselves and Toyota.

ENDNOTES

1. J. Sapsford, "Toyota Aims to Rival GM in Production," *Wall Street Journal*, November 2, 2004, page A3.
2. This section is based primarily on the account given in M. A. Cusumano, *The Japanese Automobile Industry* (Cambridge, Mass.: Harvard University Press, 1989).
3. The material in this section is drawn from three main sources: M. A. Cusumano, *The Japanese Automobile Industry*; Ohno Taiichi, *Toyota Production System* (Cambridge, Mass.: Productivity Press, 1990; Japanese edition, 1978); J. P. Womack, D. T. Jones, and D. Roos, *The Machine That Changed the World* (New York: Macmillan, 1990).
4. The material in this section is based on M. A. Cusumano, *The Japanese Automobile Industry*.
5. Niland Powell, "U.S.-Japanese Joint Venture: New United Motor Manufacturing, Inc.," *Planning Review*, January–February 1989, pp. 40–45.
6. From J. P. Womack, D. T. Jones, and D. Roos, *The Machine That Changed the World*.
7. J. B. Treece, "Just What Detroit Needs: 200,000 More Toyotas a Year," *Business Week*, December 10, 1990, page 29.
8. C. Dawson and L. Armstrong, "The Americanization of Toyota," *Business Week*, April 15, 2002, pages 52–54.
9. W. Kimberley, "Toyota Is Building in France," *Automotive Manufacturing and Production*, December 1999, p. 38.
10. P. Strozniak, "Toyota Alters the Face of Production," *Industry Week*, August 13, 2001, pages 46–48.
11. J. Flint, "The New Number Three?" *Forbes*, June 11, 1990, pages 136–140.
12. J. Sapsford, "Toyota Aims to Rival GM Production," *Wall Street Journal*, November 2, 2004, page A3.
13. Standard & Poor's Industry Surveys, *Auto and Auto Parts*, June 24, 2004.
14. J.D. Power Press Releases, April 28, 2004, "Korean Branded Vehicles Overtake Europeans and Domestics in Initial Quality"; June 29, 2004, "Toyota Motor Sales Capture Top Corporate Rankings in Vehicle Dependability."
15. J.D. Power Press Releases, "Toyota Ranks Highest in Japan's First Long Term Vehicle Dependability Study," September 2, 2004.
16. Data reported in J. Palmer, "Can Anyone Stop Toyota?" *Barron's*, September 13, 2004, pages 25–29.
17. B. Bremner and C. Dawson, "Can Anything Stop Toyota?" *Business Week*, November 17, 2003, pages 114–117.
18. M. Hara, "Moving Target," *Automotive Industries*, June 2004, pp. 26–29.
19. B. Visnic, "Toyota Adopts New Flexible Assembly Process," *Ward's Auto World*, November 2002, pages 30–31; M. Bursa, "A Review of Flexible Automotive Manufacturing," *Just Auto*, May 2004, page 15.
20. M. Hara, "Moving Target," *Automotive Industries*, June 2004, pages 26–29.
21. C. Dawson and L. Armstrong, "The Americanization of Toyota," *Business Week*, April 15, 2002, pages 52–54.
22. A. Taylor, "Toyota's Secret Weapon," *Fortune*, August 23, 2004, pages 66–65.
23. A. Taylor, "The Americanization of Toyota," *Fortune*, December 8, 2004, page 165.
24. N. Shirouzu, "Scion Plays Hip-Hop Impresario to Impress Young Drivers," *Wall Street Journal*, October 5, 2004, page B1.

Case 5

General Motors in 2005

This case was prepared by Gareth R. Jones, Texas A&M University.

General Motors (GM) is one of the largest industrial corporations in the world. In 2005, GM employed over 325,000 people globally, down from over 700,000 in 1995. Its manufacturing operations were in 32 countries, producing 9 million vehicles that are sold in 200 countries. But despite its size, GM is one of the least profitable global carmakers; its return on invested capital is a measly 1% compared with Toyota's 6%. To understand why it had performed so poorly over the last few decades, it is necessary to examine the history of the company and the car industry.

GM's Origins

The company was founded on September 16, 1908, when William C. Durant formed the General Motors Company by bringing twenty-five independent car companies, including Buick and Cadillac, together. At the beginning each company retained its own individual identity, and GM was simply a holding company, that is, a central office surrounded by its twenty-five satellites. Hundreds of models of cars were produced, principally targeted at wealthy customers who were the only individuals who could afford them at the time because the costs of manufacturing cars was so high.

GM's principal competitor at this time was the Ford Motor Car Company, and in 1908, Henry Ford announced the development of the Model T car which was to be produced by a revolutionary method—mass

production. Ford's new mass production technology was based on moving conveyor belts; the belt brought the car to be assembled by unskilled workers rather than having skilled workers work in small teams to make a car. Ford also pioneered the use of standardized auto parts that could be easily fitted together to make assembly easier and less costly. As a result of his efforts, the costs of manufacturing cars plummeted, and Ford created a mass market for the Model T. Ford became the industry leader, and GM was suddenly in a losing situation due to its production of a wide variety of expensive cars for a very small market (as opposed to Ford's single, inexpensive product targeted at the middle of the market). Ford grew rich during the period 1910–1920 while GM struggled to keep its head above water.

In 1920, Alfred P. Sloan took control of GM as chief executive officer, and he saw that major changes were necessary if GM was to be able to compete effectively with Ford. It was clear to Sloan that operating twenty-five different car companies that produced hundreds of different models was very inefficient compared with Ford's strategy of producing one model of car in large quantities. Moreover, GM's high cost–high priced cars were competing against one another for the same set of wealthy customers. In addition, GM's car companies were not learning anything from one another; they were all purchasing or making their own sets of auto components, so that economies of scale in parts manufacturing or auto assembly were not being obtained. Sloan saw that GM's very survival was at stake.

GM's New Structure

Sloan searched for a new way to organize and manage GM's different car companies to increase their competitive advantage. While he realized the need to reduce costs and increase efficiency, Sloan also saw that Ford's strategy to produce only one model of car for the whole market meant that Ford ignored the needs of other market segments—such as the luxury end that GM served. Moreover, he also realized that customers in the middle of the market might want a superior product to the standard Ford Model T and that there were a lot of opportunities to produce cars for market segments between those served by the standardized Model T or the expensive GM models.

The problem Sloan faced was how to organize GM's twenty-five different car divisions to achieve both superior efficiency and customer responsiveness. The solution he hit upon was to group the twenty-five different companies into five major self-contained operating divisions: Chevrolet, Pontiac, Oldsmobile, Buick, and Cadillac.

Each of the different divisions was given its own support services like sales, production, engineering, and finance, and each became responsible for producing a range of cars that was aimed at a specific socio-economic market segment. Sloan's plan was that GM's divisions would market five lines of cars to customers in five different socioeconomic segments. Chevrolet, for example, would manufacture inexpensive cars for customers at the entry level of the market. Pontiac, Oldsmobile, and Buick would produce cars for progressively more prosperous market segments while Cadillac would specialize in the high-price, luxury end of the market. Sloan's goal was to be responsive to each segment of the car market by producing a car to meet each segment's specific needs. He hoped that customers would move up to the next most expensive line of GM car as they prospered, and GM carefully priced the cars of the different divisions to entice customers to move up, for example, from an Oldsmobile to a Buick, or from a Buick to a Cadillac. Realizing that customers might be confused about the number of GM models they would be choosing from, he was insistent that each division develop a range of cars that had a unique image so that the cars of the different divisions would be clearly differentiated. Thus, for example, Cadillac customers needed to believe that the Cadillac they were buying was a product that was clearly superior to a Buick, not just a more expensive car with a different name.[1]

Sloan's goal in reorganizing GM into five different car divisions was also to increase operating efficiency and car design. His plan was for each division to operate as an independent profit center that would be evaluated on its return on investment. Decision making would be decentralized to the divisions, and each division would be in control of its own strategy. Managers would be responsible for bottom line results. Sloan's idea was that this new way of organizing GM's activities would create competition between divisions that would lead them to improve their efficiency in order to receive more capital for future investment. As Sloan wrote in his autobiography, he thought the creation of independent operating divisions would "(1) increase the morale of the organization by placing each operation on its own foundation . . . assuming its own responsibility and contributing its share to the final result, (2) develop statistics correctly reflecting . . . the true measure of efficiency, (3) and enable the corporation to direct the placing of additional capital where it will result in the greatest benefit to the corporation as a whole."[2]

Sloan also recommended that interdivisional transactions of auto parts, technology, and so on should be set by a transfer pricing scheme based on cost plus some predetermined rate of return. To avoid protecting a high-cost internal supplier, however, he also recommended a number of steps involving analysis of the parts and assembly operations of outside competitors to determine the fair price. In this way he hoped to keep down the cost of GM's inputs. Sloan established a strong, professional centralized headquarters staff to determine the fair price of inputs and to establish transfer prices between divisions. The staff's primary role would be to audit divisional performance and to plan strategy for the total organization. The divisions were responsible for all product-related decisions.

The results of this change in GM's business model and strategies were dramatic. By 1925, GM became the dominant U.S. car company as it took a large share of the market from Ford which saw the demand for its Model T plummet as customers switched to GM's upscale cars. Ford was soon forced to close down his factory for seven months in order to retool the production line to imitate GM and produce new models of cars targeted at different kinds of customers.

[1]A.P. Sloan, *My Years at General Motors*. Garden City, New York, Doubleday, 1964.

[2]A.P. Sloan, *My Years at...* p. 50.

Demand for the Model T plummeted because customers could get an affordable, better equipped, more prestigious, or more luxurious GM car.

With its new strategy and structure in place, GM took the lead in the U.S. car market and has enjoyed the largest market share of any car manufacturer since. From 1925–1975, it embarked on a continuous program to expand its product range to include all kinds of models of cars, full-size trucks, lightweight trucks, and various forms of specialized vehicles such as vans and ambulances. As time went on, GM also began to take over its suppliers and became highly vertically integrated. For example, GM took over Fisher Body Co., which made the car bodies for GM cars. GM also internally developed many of its own car parts' manufacturing operations, such as its Delco Division which still supplies GM with most of its electrical and electronic components (it was spun off in the 2000s as discussed later). From 1925–1975, GM dominated the U.S. car market, controlling over 65 percent of domestic sales. Together, GM, Ford, and Chrysler (now DaimlerChrysler), the Big Three carmakers, controlled over 90 percent of the U.S. vehicle market.

1970s: Big Changes in the Global Car Industry

GM's preeminent position in the U.S. car market was broken in the 1970s by a combination of two factors that altered the nature of competition in the car industry forever: the oil crisis and the emergence of low-cost Japanese competition. The oil embargo of 1973 revealed the inefficiency of U.S. "gas guzzler" cars that frequently only obtained six to nine miles per gallon. U.S. customers began to demand smaller, more fuel-efficient vehicles, which the Big Three were not equipped to build. The Japanese, however, were competent in the production of small, fuel-efficient cars, and customers began to switch to their vehicles. Moreover, as U.S. customers began buying inexpensive Japanese cars, such as the Honda Accord and the Toyota Celica, they began to realize that these cars were not only inexpensive but also they were reliable. One major survey, for example, reported that while Japanese cars averaged 1.3 flaws per vehicle, Ford averaged 2, GM had 2.5, and Chrysler had almost 3.

The combination of the switch in customer demand to small, reliable cars and the ability of the Japanese to serve the small car niche precipitated a crisis for GM. Demand for its large sedans plummeted, and divisions like Buick and Cadillac began to lay off thousands of employees because of their inability to satisfy customers' needs for smaller, more fuel-efficient cars. Moreover, growing customer awareness that the quality problems that plagued GM's cars were not present in those of Japanese carmakers helped contribute to GM's declining market share. The problem lay not in the car but the company that made the car.

GM's operating philosophy that large cars meant large profits was revealed as false as Japanese carmakers, which had been developing efficient, quality-enhancing "lean production" techniques to reduce manufacturing costs, began to make enormous profits selling their economy cars to U.S. customers. Customers flocked to the rapidly expanding Japanese car dealerships that were spreading over the United States during the 1970s. Within the space of five years, 1973–1978, not only was it revealed that the Big Three were high-cost carmakers, it was also revealed that they were low-quality car makers. In particular, GM's extensive range of large, luxurious, boxy car models had began to compare unfavorably either with the inexpensive (and boxy) Japanese models or with the sleek European luxury cars like Jaguar, Mercedes, and BMW, which also began to rapidly steal away GM's share of the luxury car market by the late 1970s. GM was being attacked both at the inexpensive and the luxury ends of the market, and its profits fell drastically as the sales of its large cars slowed to a trickle.

GM Fights Back

Reeling from the onslaught of the new competition, GM began to use its huge resources (e.g., in 1978 despite its problems GM still earned $3.5 billion on $63 billion in sales) to try to restore its competitive advantage. Under the control of a new CEO, Roger Smith, who took over in 1980, GM began several major programs to reduce costs and improve quality; by 1990 these programs had cost the company over $100 billion—enough money, analysts pointed out, to have bought Toyota and Honda given their market value at that time.

New Technology

To enhance its competitive position in cars and trucks, GM invested over $50 billion to improve and update its technology and to gain expertise in the Japanese lean-manufacturing techniques. Beginning in the early 1980s, Roger Smith started to champion the development of automated factories and robots as a way of reducing costs and raising productivity. Under his leadership, plants, such as GM's Saginaw Vanguard plant in Michigan, became heavily automated. As in Japanese factories, GM used automated equipment mold parts, robots to assemble car components, and automated vehicles to pick up and distribute parts to the robots on the assembly line. While these automated factories were impressive, they proved very expensive to operate. For example, axles made in the new factories cost twice as much as ones produced conventionally. Moreover, they were subject to frequent downtime as robots broke down and stopped the production line. By some estimates, GM's new automated factories were no more productive than those that operated conventionally. GM seemed to lack the Japanese know-how to operate automated factories successfully.

Saturn Project

A major experiment that GM began in 1982 to develop new skills in manufacturing low-cost, quality cars was the Saturn Project. Smith created a new GM division called Saturn, which was given the task of creating a Japanese-like manufacturing unit that could produce a small car at the same cost as Japanese small cars. The division was deliberately kept separate from GM's other divisions so that new skills could be developed from scratch. GM chose Spring Hill, Tennessee, as the location for the new plant. In 1987, the board approved $1.9 billion for the new factory, equipment, and tooling. Saturn became the biggest construction undertaking in GM's history. In 1990, the plant moved into full production, and Saturn cars went on sale in 1991 priced from $10,000 to $12,000 to compete with the Honda Civic and Toyota Corolla. By 1991, Saturn had built just 50,000 cars, short of its 240,000 capacity. Saturn lost $800 million in 1991.

By 1992, Saturn was selling well, and its cars were ranked in the top ten list of customer satisfaction. However, it still lost $700 million, and the skills that GM developed in lean manufacturing through its Saturn Project did not spread widely through the company as GM had hoped. Moreover, GM realized that Saturn never could match the low costs of Japanese manufacturers. The division built a high-quality product, but it never had the sales success that GM had hoped for in competing with Japanese carmakers.

Strategic Alliances

In another venture to learn Japanese techniques in lean manufacturing, in 1983 GM created a joint venture with Toyota called New United Motor Manufacturing, Inc. (NUMMI) to produce Chevrolet Novas in GM's Freemont, California, plant, which had closed in 1982 because of poor quality and bad labor-management relations. Through the venture Toyota would get the chance to see if it could make high-quality cars in the United States with American workers and suppliers, while GM would gain intimate knowledge and access to Toyota's lean manufacturing techniques. In 1984, NUMMI reopened under the control of Japanese management. By 1986, its productivity was higher than any other GM factory, and it was operating at twice the old level under GM management.

One of the primary reasons for its success was the use of flexible work teams. At the NUMMI factory, Toyota divided the work force into 350 flexible work teams consisting of 5 to 7 people plus a team leader. Each worker was trained to perform the jobs of other workers, and they all regularly rotated jobs . In addition, all workers were taught the procedures for analyzing jobs to improve work procedures. Team members designed all the team's jobs, timed each other using stopwatches, and continually attempted to find better ways to perform tasks. GM previously had employed eighty managers to perform this analysis; now not only did flexible work teams do it but also they were responsible for monitoring product quality. The role of managers in the new factory was to provide shop-floor workers with support, not to monitor or supervise their activities. From this venture GM finally learned how Toyota's lean production system worked and that work relationships are at least as important as automated factories in increasing productivity and reducing costs. From this point on, it began to implement the new system across all its hundreds of manufacturing plants although this was a slow process.

From its investment in new automated technology, its Saturn Project, and by learning Japanese lean-manufacturing techniques from its joint ventures with Toyota and other companies, by 1990 GM had been able to reduce the number of defects per car, raise quality, and reduce costs. However, Ford and Chrysler had learned the new manufacturing methods *better* than GM. For most of the 1980s and 1990s, their quality ratings were higher and their market share rose while GM's continued to fall. For example, in 1987 Ford earned higher profits than GM for the first time since 1924 because of its $3 billion investment in developing a new line of higher quality cars at lower costs. One reason for Ford's success was that it was highly centralized, which made it easier for its top managers to pursue new quality initiatives quickly. GM, with its hundreds of divisions, found it much more difficult to transfer new information and knowledge between them, and top management orders were often lost in the bureaucracy.

In sum, although GM was successful in reducing its operating costs and increasing quality during the 1980s, its competitors were more successful, and it failed to obtain a competitive edge over them. GM was still at a major disadvantage compared with its Japanese competitors, which, in the 1990s, began to open their own plants inside the United States at an accelerating pace. Toyota and Honda led the quality ranking of U.S. made cars, and by 1995 manufactured over 1.5 million cars a year in the United States.

Changing Its Structure

In the 1980s, fierce competition from the Japanese forced GM to take a hard look at its multidivisional structure and the way it impacted the company's competitive advantage. Compared with Ford, Chrysler, and Japanese companies that operated with flat, streamlined structures, GM, with its hundreds of divisions, an extensive array of internal suppliers, and a corporate headquarters with thirty thousand managers, had become a huge lumbering bureaucracy. Roger Smith and his top management team, prompted by outside critics, realized that GM's structure had reduced its competitive advantage in several ways.

First, each division performed its own research and development and engineering, and the duplication of value creation activities across divisions was costing the company billions of extra dollars. Each division also purchased its inputs independently of other divisions so that economies of purchasing and distribution were being lost, which raised costs. Moreover, as discussed earlier, divisions were not sharing their knowledge about new, more efficient methods of design and manufacturing so that quality was slow to increase.

Second, each division produced cars in its own traditional way using its own set of platforms—the basic design behind which cars are assembled and made. Each division used several different platforms,

which is very expensive because each platform requires different inputs and its own method of manufacturing, and a specific platform could not be used to produce other models of cars. Chrysler, for example, decided to use only one platform in the 1990s, the K-Platform, to build all its cars; this led to substantial savings in manufacturing costs. Another problem for GM was the sheer cost of its huge staff of corporate executives, a cost that many analysts calculated to be several billions of dollars.

Beyond reduced efficiency, GM's tall, overly bureaucratic structure also slowed innovation because it took the organization a long time to adopt new technological advances and reduced GM's ability to recognize and respond to changing customer demands. As mentioned earlier, GM was slow to see the move toward small, more nimble, fuel-efficient, high-reliability cars from the long, boxy, chrome-laden, heavyweight vehicles that had become the principal offerings of the Big Three.

On all fronts, GM's organizational structure reduced its competitive advantage. For example, whereas Toyota only had seven levels in the hierarchy in the early 1980s, there were twenty-one levels in GM's hierarchy. One consequence was that while it took GM five to six years to bring a new car to market, it took Toyota only thirty-six months—a major source of competitive advantage.

The 1984 Reorganization

To try to solve many of these problems and increase its competitiveness, in 1984 GM consolidated its five powerful, autonomous vehicle divisions into two business groups. The operations of Chevy and Pontiac would be managed together, and these divisions would concentrate on smaller cars. Buick, Oldsmobile, and Cadillac (BOC) divisions would be managed together and would focus on bigger, luxury cars. The goal behind the change was to reduce costs by centralizing R&D, engineering, and purchasing activities at the level of the business group. Also GM hoped that this reorganization would speed product development.

The 1984 reorganization added yet another layer of GM bureaucracy: In addition to corporate management and individual divisional managers, there was now the level of group manager (e.g., BOC group manager). Divisions inside a group would produce car models from a limited number of platforms, and each model would be assembled from a limited number of inputs to reduce costs. Each division would then customize its models for specific groups of customers.

The reorganization was a disaster. The result of centralizing decision making at the group level and standardizing the activities of the divisions inside a group was that by 1987 all the cars produced by a group began to look alike. Cadillac buyers did not know why they paid more for a car that looked like other less expensive GM models such as Buicks, and sales of Cadillacs plummeted. Eighty percent of Buicks, Olds, and Pontiacs only differed slightly in price and engineering, and due to the lack of a unique image, sales of those three divisions fell sharply because their cars were basically similar. Divisions had become just marketing organizations.

The basic problem was that key decisions were made by central engineering and manufacturing staffs instead of by the five divisions. Moreover, the central engineering design staff reported to top management only two layers below the CEO and not to the heads of the car divisions. Consequently, division managers had to bargain with the design staff to get the desired car styling for its unit! This new structure prevented GM from launching a range of successful new models, as Ford and the Japanese were doing, and costs were still not falling by as much as had been hoped. Even though design time had been reduced, the result was poorer, not better, customer responsiveness as GM's new models failed to attract buyers.

As Roger Smith recognized, GM's problem was that it needed to centralize many of its activities to achieve economies of scale and reduce costs, but only decentralization can provide the flexibility needed to react to changes quickly and to allow divisions to design and develop products to meet the needs of their customers. Realizing their mistake GM's top management made some moves to give control of engineering and design back to the divisions. However, the benefits of centralizing R&D and purchasing were realized, and these activities became increasingly controlled at the group level.

The 1988 Reorganization

The Cadillac division benefited the most from the new policy of decentralization. Due to centralized engineering at the group level, Cadillac's image had became tainted, and its sales had fallen. For example, due to an anticipated energy crisis in 1986, GM decided that the Cadillac Eldorado and Seville should be made smaller but increased their price. GM tried to target these cars at import buyers as well as traditional buyers, which were the over fifty age group. However, traditional customers did not like these models because the cars were built on a common platform, which made them look similar to cheaper cars; for example, the new Cadillacs looked like Buicks. As a result, 1986 sales were 51 percent less than 1985 sales which was a severe blow to GM since profit margins on luxury cars were some of the highest.

To turn around the division, Cadillac was granted its own engineering team in 1988, and they moved quickly to forge a new identity for the division. Once again in control of its decision making, Cadillac managers lengthened the cars two inches, restyled them, increased advertising, and promoted test drives of the cars through direct mail. By 1990, Cadillac had gross margins of 40 to 45 percent compared with 30 percent for the rest of GM's divisions. Cadillac had become very successful, launching redesigned models in 1991, 1992, and 1993, and their sales rose steadily over time. GM's other car divisions experienced mixed fortunes during the 1990s. In its small car business group, GM implemented a major plan to reduce the number of car platforms and to centralize purchasing of inputs to reduce costs through its GM10 program. The GM10 program was created to replace all of GM's midsize cars such as the Chevy Celebrity, Pontiac 6000, Buick Century, and Olds Cutlass Supreme. Each of these four divisions would get a coupe and a sedan. At a cost of $7 billion, GM10 was the largest new model program ever created, indicating GM's interest in obtaining economies of scale from its reorganized car operations. However, design errors resulting from its centralized design operations led to failure. None of these cars became a major seller of the order of a Ford Taurus, Honda Accord, or Toyota Camry because GM still didn't understand what customers wanted.

For example, sales in its Buick division declined from 1984 to 1988, but then Edward Mertz, who took over the division in 1986, established a major program to increase quality and began to listen to dealers, customers, and employees. Mertz insisted that Buick should be given its own engineering team to respond to its customers' needs and to listen to dealer and customer complaints. This engineering team communicated directly with plant engineers who were instructed to work with manufacturing to build quality into its cars. With its revised lineup of cars, Buick began doing fairly well in the midsize car segment.

By 1991, sales of Buick's 1991 models increased 6.6 percent at a time when total U.S. car sales decreased 8.2 percent, and its cars were recognized as among the most reliable.

The upturn in Buick's fortunes came at the expense of Oldsmobile, however. Oldsmobile's cars were similar to Buick's and targeted the same customer segment. Sales declined from 1.1 million cars in 1986 to about 560,000 cars in 1990 because of declining quality and because they lacked a distinct image. By 1992, with falling sales the future of the Oldsmobile Division was called into question; however, it was not until 2001 that GM finally announced it would close down this division's operations. Finally, even Chevrolet suffered from GM's flawed design process during the 1980s and by 1990 was desperately in need of new models.

The result was that throughout the 1980s Japanese carmakers continuously gained market share, mainly by stealing sales from GM. In 1978, American automakers had an 84 percent market share compared with 68 percent in 1989. From 1985 to 1989, GM's market share declined from about 44 percent to about 33 percent while Japan's share increased from 19 percent to 26 percent.

By the early 1990s, more changes were occurring in the global car environment. Japanese companies, which now dominated the small- to medium-size car market, decided to compete in the luxury segment. Toyota established its Lexus division, Nissan its Infinity, and Honda its Acura to compete with Cadillac and upscale European makers for luxury sales. Japan also decided to enter the profitable large truck segment dominated by Chevrolet. Of all vehicles sold in the United States, trucks are the most profitable. To fight back GM introduced sixteen new vehicles; for example, the 1992 Cadillac Seville STS was successfully launched to compete with Toyota's Lexus and Germany's Mercedes, and it redesigned its large trucks.

Diversification at GM

During the 1980s, to help reduce costs and improve quality and customer responsiveness GM also began a program of diversification and acquisition. To help its core automotive business it bought Electronic Data Systems (EDS) and Hughes Aircraft. In 1984, GM was the largest user of computers in the world. Each of its divisions used different computer systems or programs, however, so that the corporation lacked an integrated computer network. Moreover, GM saw

that many of the problems it had experienced with its advanced factories and robotically controlled manufacturing were due to its lack of programming ability in computer aided manufacturing (CAM). To quickly develop a competence in CAM that would allow it to operate its new manufacturing systems effectively, in 1984 it acquired EDS for $2.5 billion.

GM's goal was that EDS would program its manufacturing operations and integrate its computers into one network. As it turned out, however, EDS had little experience in CAM; its strengths were in data processing. EDS helps customers develop and customize computer hardware and software systems to match their needs, which is called systems integration. EDS was the leader in this field and in information technology (IT) outsourcing, which entails maintaining and upgrading a company's IT in return for a fee. Thus, while EDS was able to help GM integrate its incompatible system of computers and automated machines, it could not help it to improve its CAM skills. Many analysts wondered why GM bought EDS, rather than simply buying its skills like other companies, and thought the money could have been spent better in developing GM's core skills in car making. However, fortuitously for GM, it had bought a rising star whose revenues increased throughout the 1990s.

In 1985, GM acquired Hughes Aircraft, a large defense contractor, for $5.2 billion. GM Hughes operated in four business segments: 32 percent automotive, 18 percent telecommunications, 44 percent defense, and 6 percent commercial. GM bought Hughes to create synergies with its vehicle-making operations by using Hughes's radar and satellite technology to develop advanced electronics, such as guidance systems for future cars. However, once again analysts wondered why GM would spend so much money on such a risky venture, one in which returns were far into the future.

A New Management Team Takes Over

In 1990, GM's board chose Robert Stempel, Roger Smith's hand-picked successor, to succeed Smith on his retirement. Stempel, who had been head of the BOC group, focused on manufacturing and engineering; however, like Smith he moved slowly to downsize the corporation and was reluctant to make the huge cuts in its work force that analysts thought imperative to turn around the company. For example, even though GM's market share had declined rapidly (GM's market share declined from 50 percent in 1978 to 35 percent in 1992) it had not reduced the number of its manufacturing plants or downsized its work force in any significant way. The downsizing process was slow because Smith insisted that GM would reach a 50 percent market share again. Everyone but GM's top executives recognized that the company had at least 100,000 white-collar workers and an even larger excess of production employees, but top managers would not make drastic cuts.

In 1991, John Smale, an outside director, began looking for ways to stop GM's losses. In April 1992, the board finally took action. Robert Stempel was removed from his position as chairman of the GM board's executive committee and replaced by Smale who was a former CEO of Procter & Gamble. Stempel remained CEO and a board member. Jack Smith, the former head of GM's European operations, took over the president's position from one of Stempel's followers. Finally, by 2002 GM announced that it would lay off 80,000 workers and close 10 U.S. assembly plants by 1995; 4 engine factories and 11 parts plants would also be closed. About 54,000 of GM's 304,000 blue-collar workers would be cut through attrition, early retirement, and layoffs. A total of 26,000 white-collar workers would also be axed, and the corporate staff was to be reduced from 13,500 people to around 2,300 people.

GM's board had watched Jack Smith cut white-collar staff, freeze salaries, reduce health care benefits, and put some noncore businesses up for sale. The board decided to replace Stempel with Smith in late 1992 and also promoted younger GM executives into top positions—defying the GM tradition of top executives being in their midfifties and sixties. New CEO Jack Smith soon defined GM's future strategies to become profitable: an aggressive focus of reducing costs and improving quality, an aggressive marketing of redesigned vehicles to better satisfy customers' needs, and a new, more flexible decentralized organizational structure.

New Production Manufacturing Initiatives

Smith, who had been in charge of GM's European operations and responsible for implementing new lean production techniques there, had a clear vision of what GM needed to do to reduce its cost structure. First,

GM has learned from its failures over the last ten years, especially the importance of dropping unsuccessful products and trimming its product line to reduce costs. By 1993, GM reduced the number of models in production from 85 to 65 while introducing over 20 new cars and trucks. To do this cost-effectively, GM imitated other carmakers by reducing the number of its basic platforms from 14 to 6 by the late 1990s, such as platforms for small, medium, large cars, and trucks, and then making each different division produce similar-sized vehicles using the same basic platform but with parts customized to their individual design.

Beginning in the mid 1990s, GM began a program to improve the technology built into its cars and to reduce the cost of developing it. For example, GM formed a new powertrain division by integrating two independent divisions to cut costs. Also to implement common systems and processes and use best industry practices throughout its North American Operations, GM created a centralized vehicle launch center. Now engineers from each of the car and truck divisions work with engineers from the centralized vehicle launch center and with manufacturing to speed product development. This program was so successful that in 2000 GM announced that its North American car and truck operating groups would be consolidated into one new manufacturing group.

A major part of GM's new efficiency program was to build new state-of-the-art assembly plants and close down old, inefficient ones. In 2000, GM started to build a $1 billion new vehicle manufacturing plant in Lansing, Michigan, that utilizes the most advanced flexible manufacturing configurations and technologies to help GM raise its quality nearer to that of its Japanese competitors. The new plant consists of three buildings, covering 2.4 million square feet, and vehicle production began in 2005. GM also finally closed its Oldsmobile division in 2004.

The result of all these efforts was that GM improved its productivity more than any of its other U.S. competitors in 1991 and surpassed DaimlerChrysler's productivity in North America. GM claims that once its new plants and technology come online, it will equal both Japanese productivity and quality by 2010.

New Supply Chain

Finding more cost-effective ways to manage its supply chain has also been a major part of GM's strategy in the last decade. In developing its unsuccessful line of new models in the 1980s, GM learned the need to standardize components across models and to reduce the number of parts needed to produce a car, thereby reducing costs and speeding product development. Smith directed GM's engineers to work to reduce the number of parts used to make a car's basic metal frame by one-third, something that customers would not see.

However, GM also began to change the way it managed relationships with suppliers. In 1992, GM obtained 57 percent of its parts from its own component divisions, compared with Chrysler's 30 percent and Toyota's 5 percent. GM's car assembly divisions were locked into own "allied plant" suppliers such as Central Foundry for casting, Delco for brakes, and so on. In 1993, GM introduced a new strategy so that its in-house parts operations would no longer be protected from efficient outside suppliers.

To help suppliers reduce costs, GM followed Toyota and implemented a Purchased Input Concept Optimization with Suppliers (PICOS) strategy, where teams of GM engineers visit supplier plants and work with suppliers to reduce costs. However, with the program up and running GM, unlike Toyota, began to bargain hard with its suppliers to get lower component prices. It started to give one supplier's plans to other suppliers to get lower prices from them, essentially trading off one against the other, and made them rebid contracts year by year to try to get them to lower their bids. This angered outside suppliers, who advised GM that if it bought mainly on price they would not invest money to improve the components that GM wanted them to make and would move their business to Ford, Chrysler, and Japanese companies operating inside the United States. As a result, GM had to rethink its aggressive strategy.

GM also extended its supply chain management program globally and began to develop hundreds of alliances with overseas parts manufacturers to produce components that could be used in its cars assembled around the world. For example, GM formed a joint venture with a Hungarian company to build axles and diesel engines for assembly in cars sold under the Opel name throughout Western Europe. The next major development in the supply chain management process took place in 2000 when GM, Ford, and Daimler-Chrysler announced they would form an organization called Covisint to coordinate their purchase of standardized car components through the Internet. Billed as the world's largest virtual marketplace, Covisint

gives large carmakers considerable power over global suppliers, which essentially are forced to compete to obtain the Big Three's business. However, at the same time this presents the opportunity to create economies of scale in producing many kinds of components.

At the same time, however, Japanese carmakers established many factories inside the United States, and they also created networks of efficient high-quality component suppliers that have allowed them to maintain high productivity and quality. U.S. carmakers are still in a "catch up" position. Toyota, for example, was the first to launch a joint program with its suppliers to radically reduce the number of steps needed to make components and car parts; it saw costs fall by $2.6 billion. Toyota also created an integrated, flexible, global manufacturing system based on assembly plants from Indonesia to Argentina, which are designed both to customize cars for local markets and to shift production to quickly satisfy any increases in demand in any market worldwide. This also is a way Toyota can keep costs low because this avoids the need to build more plants—which cost over $1 billion to build today. (Recall how GM's new plants each cost over $1 billion.)

In the 2000s, GM introduced a new initiative to reduce costs, its Global Manufacturing System (GMS), which is being implemented across all GM facilities worldwide to standardize its approach to making cars. To implement its new system, GM drastically changed its hundreds of old IT legacy systems and chose a standardized platform that links all its car plants directly to its chain of global suppliers to improve the efficiency of its global supply chain management. This was one of the major reasons for the jump in its productivity in North America. Also, it explains why in 2001–2002 GM became the best-performing domestic manufacturer in initial quality by J.D. Power Associates. GM had fourteen top three performing vehicles, including three that were ranked first in their market segments.

With IT continually advancing, it is necessary for carmakers to keep up with their suppliers in the design and manufacture of car parts. The current trend in the car industry is to develop strong relationships with Tier One parts suppliers, which are able to collaborate and improve the quality and lower the cost of vehicle components or modules that are assembled into the final vehicle. As carmakers seek to lower costs and increase quantity, they are increasingly requiring their primary or first-tier suppliers to take on the cost of creating the car modules that otherwise carmakers would have to do themselves. For example, after GM spun off its auto-parts division, Delphi, to reduce costs, it outsourced assembly of car modules to suppliers like Delphi because they have the ability to make these modules cheaper than GM. If this trend of outsourcing component and module development to suppliers continues, barriers to entry will shrink as carmakers become more like car designers, and component suppliers become more and more like car manufacturers.

Structural Changes

Side-by-side with changes to its production and supply chain operations, GM also radically altered its corporate structure. Starting in 1990, GM realized the need to streamline its operations and to decentralize decision making and to integrate its design and manufacturing operations. In 1992, it consolidated its 9 engine groups into 5 and brought together its divisional engineering and manufacturing units to eliminate redundancy. Also, 5 different design and technical departments at GM's Technical Center were combined into 3 to speed product development. GM also created a new product design system to provide strong single point management of a vehicle program and to accelerate the vehicle development process. GM's goal was to achieve economies of scale through integrating and coordinating its functional activities in product development, engineering, manufacturing, and marketing around the world. In this way it could avoid unnecessary duplication of activities between divisions and facilitate the sharing and learning about cost-saving processes and quality innovations across divisions and countries. Restructuring has led to more flexible decision making, better use of resources, an increase in management accountability, and an improved ability to serve its customers.

Promoting innovation is also a key element of GM's strategy, in particular the need to improve vehicle design and engineering, develop new models to target profitable market segments, and to provide high-margin add-on vehicle accessories, such as its OnStar service, to increase the profit made on each car sale. Cooperation between the United States and Europe became vital to achieve these goals in the 1990s because GM's engineers must share resources and best practices to develop a wide range of vehicles in order to suit many different customer needs

from the six vehicle platforms GM now has. Fewer platforms significantly reduce costs as discussed earlier. In addition, the industry average development time for new cars has gone down from five years in 1990 to three years by the late 1990s, and today some companies like Toyota are able to develop a new car within eighteen months—a major competitive advantage that GM is striving to copy.

To permit such integration, GM changed its global organizational structure and adopted the global matrix structure shown in Exhibit 1. The vertical axis consists of GM's five main business units and the four world regions in which GM operates, that is, North America, Europe, Asia-Pacific, and Latin America, Africa, and the Middle East. The fifth business unit is GM's Financial Services Division which is responsible for financing the sale of GM's cars throughout the world.

On the horizontal axis are the main value chain activities required to efficiently orchestrate the global production of its cars: supply chain management, product development, production, customer experience or marketing, and business services. Where the axes intersect are found the hundreds of assembly plants and engineering facilities that belong to a specific GM car division such as Cadillac, Buick, and so on, but while each car division operates as an independent entity, at the same time it is embedded in the global value-chain organization GM needs to compete against its highly efficient global rivals.

For example, GM created a new Vehicle Engineering Center at its Warren, Michigan, Technical Center campus to harmonize product engineering across all its car divisions. The 2.2-million square foot facility houses eight thousand employees and further enhances the collaboration between the engineering, design, and manufacturing groups as they work with the car divisions and managers in its global business units to create the cars that customers want.

The Role of IT

IT plays a vital part in helping GM implement its new global organizational structure. IT provides the integration necessary to manage the enormously complex transactions required to operate global assembly and value chain activities using a matrix structure. Using software and consultancy services from IBM, GM has harmonized all its IT systems across the company. All its divisions and business activities are now seamlessly

EXHIBIT 1

GM's Global Matrix Structure

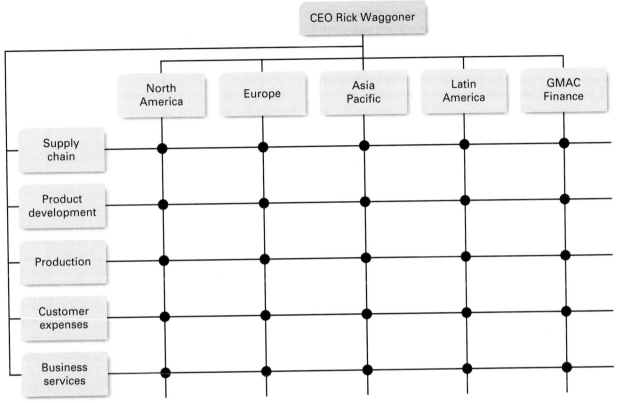

● GM assembly, design, and operating units located in countries around the world.

interconnected, and no conversion work has to be done to transmit information from one GM facility to another anywhere in the world.

IT has helped GM better implement its business model in many ways. First, it has permitted fast global coordination in design and engineering development. Engineers can share information globally real-time, and this has reduced costs and lessened the duplication of work by engineers in different research areas. Second, it has increased the efficiency of GM's supply chain operations, for example, in 2004 GM was able to cut its material costs by 3 percent in North America and by 3.5 percent in Europe. Third, GM's new Internet-enabled IT has helped it lower the costs of value creation in many ways. For example, using the new IT, GM reduced the costs associated with communicating with its thousands of U.S. car dealers by $25 million in 2000. In another initiative GM created **GMsupplypower.com** in 2001 which gives suppliers an online window into GM's future production plans and allows them to better manage inventory, overtime, and freight costs.

GM Exits Many Businesses

As discussed earlier GM bought several large companies in the 1980s to promote its efficiency and effectiveness. GM did receive some benefits from this; for example, in 1994 its Hughes Electronics Division developed the OnStar technology that has helped GM differentiate its cars, a system that today it also licenses to other carmakers. The OnStar system is an in-vehicle safety, security, and information system that provides automatic notifications of airbag releases, stolen vehicles, assistance and access to emergency service providers, and remote entry. Hughes also introduced DIRECTV—the first high-quality direct satellite TV distribution system in the United States.

However, GM recognized that it was not obtaining the synergies it had expected, and it was fortunate in that EDS and Hughes, as a result of the escalation in stock prices during the 1990s, were worth many times what it had paid for them. Consequently it began the process of selling off the companies. In 1996, EDS was officially split off from GM and later divested. In 2004, GM sold its Hughes DIRECTV operations to News Corp., the entertainment and media company. GM used the proceeds from both sales to fund its company pension plan and to invest in its new global vehicles.

During the 1990s, GM also began to sell off some of its vehicle-building assets. In 1998, signaling its intention to vertically disintegrate, GM announced that it would spin off its Delphi electronics unit through an initial public offering of Delphi stock, and the company was spun off in 1999. In 1999, GM sold its defense unit, which built light armored vehicles (LAVs) to General Dynamics Corporation. On the other hand, in 2001 GM announced it was entering the collision repair business with the introduction of the Goodwrench auto body center program, and it established a nationwide chain of body shops to take advantage of the high-profit margin repair business.

Global Expansion

In the 1990s, watching the Japanese carmakers expand into Europe and North America, GM realized it needed to take steps to bolster its global presence. Recall that GM had early expanded into Europe, Canada, and Australia to take advantage of these large markets. As discussed earlier, GM now had the goal of learning Japanese lean-manufacturing techniques. In 1996, GM formed joint ventures with Japanese companies Isuzu Motors and Suzuki to learn Japanese lean-manufacturing techniques and to establish jointly owned facilities to make specialized kinds of vehicle engines and transmissions for specific market segments, such as the European diesel engine market. GM also took a minority equity stake in these ventures. In 2000, GM also acquired a 20 percent equity stake in Fuji, the manufacturer of Subaru brand vehicles. A strategic alliance with Honda was also established.

While Japan was an important market, GM also realized the need to strengthen its presence in the rapidly developing Chinese and Eastern European markets. In 2002, GM formed an alliance with a Russian company to produce a line of low-cost Chevrolets

tailored to the needs of customers in Eastern Europe. After several years of cooperation with Chinese companies, in 2001 GM's new assembly plant in Shanghai, China, began production of the Regal economy car for the Chinese market. All global makers were rushing to seize a share of this market that they hoped would prove profitable in the future.

In Europe, too, GM took steps to compete against DaimlerChrysler, BMW, and Ford which had acquired the U.K. carmaker Jaguar and Sweden's Volvo after a bidding war with GM. In 2000, GM acquired Saab, and it also bought a 20 percent stake in Fiat and an option to buy the whole company later. The Fiat alliance was ill-fated, however, because in 2005 GM had to pay $2 billion to terminate its option to buy the troubled company. Its Saab operation also proved to be an expensive acquisition and lost hundreds of millions of dollars. In the meantime, GM's established European Brands like Opel, its German subsidiary, and Vauxhall, its British unit, were also struggling to compete effectively against Ford, the largest European manufacturer; Japanese companies that now had established operations within the European Union; and Renault, which had bought a controlling interest in struggling Japanese company Nissan in 2000. However, after installing a star Renault manager to head its Japanese subsidiary, Nissan's performance soared, and the company became a major competitor in all global markets.

Watching its competitors enter China, potentially the largest market in the world, in 2000 GM also decided to acquire the car operations of Korean conglomerate Daewoo to help it enter the Asian and Chinese markets. It also opened a new car assembly complex in Brazil, utilizing state-of-the-art modular assembly techniques to produce cars for the rapidly growing South American market. Similar assembly plants were opened in Thailand and in Germany as part of its program to extend the learning it was gaining from its global matrix operations. Meanwhile, the joint venture between GM and Shanghai Automotive Industry Corporation led to its launch of the Buick Sail, the first modern family car built in China. Also, the Chevrolet Cruze developed by GM and its alliance partner Suzuki, the first GM vehicle to be built in Japan since the 1930s, was launched in 2001.

To build competitive advantage in Europe, GM built a new facility at Russelsheim, Germany, which allows its Opel division to assemble up to four different vehicle models on a three-shift, flexible line system with a total capacity of 270,000 vehicles a year. In Mexico GM's new plants led to record sales of 230,636 vehicles in 2002. Holden, GM's Australian automotive division, also announced vehicle sales in 2002 that reached an all-time record. Holden was the Australian industry's sales leader for the second straight year.

Although GM has been strengthening its global operations in these many ways, its problem is that it still has had to meet the challenge of its global competitors, and it has had mixed success. In Europe, for example, the new vehicles made by its Vauxhall and Opel divisions have had mixed success against Ford and Volkswagen's new vehicles and against upscale sedan makers such as BMW, Volvo, and Mercedes. GM has no luxury sedan to compete in this important upscale market. All global carmakers have been working to improve their efficiency and design profitable niche models, and even in China competition is intense as all major global carmakers are competing head to head, which lowers profit margins.

Brands and Marketing

Finding the right way to brand and market its cars has been one of GM's biggest problems in the last decade as global competition increased. Its problems with its Cadillac and Oldsmobile divisions were discussed earlier. Since 2000, GM has moved to focus its resources on new models of cars and trucks, and each of its car and truck divisions, including Saturn and GMC Truck, have a separate marketing strategy to differentiate its vehicles.

GM's Chevrolet division became a keystone of its plan to increase its truck sales around the world, and GM is investing hundreds of millions to promote its brand name since the cost of developing a new brand from scratch today would cost billions. The Chevrolet name has equity in many parts of the world, and GM began a big push in the 1990s to develop the trucks and SUVs that are the mainstay of Chevrolet's reputation. Today, however, these market segments are saturated and so GM plans to spend its resources producing new sedans and niche vehicles targeted toward more specific market segments.

As a part of this push, in 1999 GM signed an agreement to acquire exclusive rights to the Hummer automotive brand from AM General Corp. It also entered an agreement with XM Satellite Radio to introduce its services into its vehicles and package it

with its OnStar service, which is now standard on most GM models. OnStar had over 1 million subscribers by 2003. In 2000, GM also created a new diversity marketing and sales organization to focus on the women's market and the growing markets of African-American, Hispanic-American, and Asian-American customers in the United States to meet the needs of these niche markets.

As noted earlier, in the beginning of the 1990s GM decentralized control of product design to its Cadillac division and instructed it to reestablish its place as a luxury brand. The Cadillac division developed a bold exterior and interior Cadillac design, the CTS, a radical departure from traditional Cadillac styling, and has since introduced a series of vehicles that all possess this new style, the latest being its convertible sports car introduced in 2004. These moves have helped Cadillac become GM's most profitable car division in North America, and its sales are currently the highest they have been for a decade. However, other GM brands have not fared so well. Oldsmobile is gone. The Saturn division experienced declining sales in the 1990s because its models were aging, and the success of its new ones remains to be seen. In 2002, GM announced it would end production of its Chevrolet Camaro and Pontiac Firebird and discontinue the Camaro and Firebird models because of the loss of this market niche to competitors such as Ford, Nissan, and Toyota. In 2003, GM announced that its entire midsize car portfolio in North America would be revamped over the next three years, focusing on fewer yet stronger "nameplates" or on its premium brands. GM's strategy was to introduce ten new or restyled midsize vehicles between 2003 and 2006 to strengthen its product line. To support its efforts, GM spent $2.4 billion on intensive marketing campaigns in national media outlets in 2003 and has spent the same or more in each year since.

GM also began a major customer relations management program that led to 1.5 million more vehicles being sold in 2004 than in 2003. This program was designed to show U.S. customers cars made inside the United States are equal in quality to those that are imported, and in fact, three of its new midsize and full-size cars received top quality ratings. GM's goal was to encourage people to try out their cars, for example, by allowing them to take home one of its cars for the weekend and test drive it to experience its superior quality.

New Leadership but Same Old Problems

In 2000, GM also went through a change in leadership when Rick Wagoner became its new CEO with Jack Smith remaining as chairman of the board. Also, Gary L. Cowger was elected group vice president and president, GM North America, and he assumed control of GM's North American vehicle operations. A thirty-six-year veteran of GM, Cowger's previous assignments include president, GM de Mexico; group vice president in charge of global manufacturing; and CEO of GM's Opel division. In 2003, Rick Wagoner became chairman and CEO following the retirement of Chairman Jack Smith, and Cowger is next in line to assume control of the company.

Its new leaders all have an extensive background in global operations that has helped promote GM's rapid global revival. However, they still have to deal with GM's huge problems because of the legacies of its past. During the 1960s and 1970s, GM's high profitability and dominance of the U.S. car market meant that the company had little incentive to resist its trade unions' demands for ever higher pay and benefits. Shareholders, managers, and workers were all enjoying rising prosperity. When the Japanese put an end to this fortunate situation, GM, like Ford and Chrysler, found itself saddled with strict union rules that prevented it from laying off employees or closing down facilities quickly, as well as huge health care and pension liabilities to its former and current employees—something that has been estimated at over $45 billion. GM also pays its current work force much more than its competitors. In benefits, for example, GM pays an average of $35 for each employee's pension and medical costs compared with the $11 Toyota pays for the same benefits.

It has been estimated that the costs of paying these pensions and benefits gives Toyota and Honda, which have no such problems, a cost advantage of about $1,500 a car. However, GM cannot charge a $1,500 premium for its cars and, indeed, has to charge less than its stronger competitors, so its profit margins are extremely low, and it sells many of its vehicles at a loss. In 2004, GM's return on sales was 1.5 percent, which was considerably less than Toyota's 6.8 percent. Although Toyota's revenues are 33 percent lower than GM's, its net earnings are 60 percent higher. Toyota's ROIC was almost 6 percent in 2004, while GM's was 1 percent, Ford's .6 percent, and DaimlerChrysler was a negative .5 percent.

The principal reason why GM makes any ROIC is because of the profitability of its financing division, GMAC, which has earned the company billions and allowed it to remain profitable even though its *total* vehicle operations have been making a loss. GM makes most of its profit on financing the sale of its vehicles to customers, rather than on actually making the vehicle itself. And intense competition and the recession of the early 1990s led GM to begin its zero-percent financing program and to offer rebates to undercut competitors. However, GM's strategic move to gain market share resulted in a price war when other car companies, such as Ford and Honda, also began price discounting and special offers to match GM. Similarly, GM is in a discounting war with Volkswagen in Germany.

GM was forced into its discounting strategy because it has considerable excess capacity and makes many more cars than it can profitably sell. Indeed, it has been estimated that there is 20 percent overcapacity in the car industry as a whole, which makes price wars more likely. In order to get its cars off the lot and protect its market share, GM must discount its cars. Although the profitability of each car sale is low, GM claims that 67 percent of its customers return and buy a second GM vehicle, which is the highest loyalty rate in the industry. Therefore, if overcapacity falls and prices rise in the next decade as carmakers continue to prune and simplify their global operations this will help GM's bottom line considerably. No carmaker boasts such a large installed base of customers. GM sells 9 million vehicles annually, and each of these new vehicles represents a potential opportunity to generate future profits from maintaining customer relationships, from its OnStar system or Goodwrench repair centers.

In the 2000s, however, the bad news for GM has been that Japanese automakers have been rapidly introducing new and improved SUVs and trucks, and GM is having to fight back to maintain its sales in this area. Since this also threatens Ford, price wars may develop in this market segment, too, which would be a severe blow to GM. GM also needs to look closely at the need to introduce hybrid and fuel-efficient cars to maintain its market share and profitability given that many hybrid SUVs, sedans, and even trucks were being introduced in the mid 2000s. GM placed its bet on hydrogen fuel-cell technology, but this technology is far from practical. In the meantime, Toyota's gas/electric hybrid technology has become the industry standard, and Toyota licenses this technology to other carmakers. For example, Ford introduced vehicles using this system in 2005. This segment will only become more important in the future if the high oil prices of the mid 2000s continue.

Thus, GM's fight continues, and global carmakers are all locked in a battle to develop the right kinds of vehicles to meet changing customer needs all around the globe. U.S. carmakers are catching up, but the question is can they catch up with Japanese carmakers that have so far maintained their first mover advantage by striving to be one step ahead of their competitors.

Case 6

The Comeback of Caterpillar, 1985–2002

This case was prepared by Isaac Cohen, San Jose State University.

For three consecutive years, 1982, 1983, and 1984, the Caterpillar Company lost $1 million a day. Caterpillar's major competitor was a formidable Japanese company called Komatsu. Facing a tough global challenge, the collapse of its international markets, and an overvalued dollar, Caterpillar had no choice. It had to reinvent itself, or die.

Caterpillar managed to come back as a high-tech, globally competitive, growth company. Over a period of fifteen years, and throughout the tenure of two CEOs—George Schaefer (1985–1990) and Donald Fites (1990–1999)—Caterpillar had transformed itself. George Schaefer introduced cost-cutting measures and employee involvement programs; outsourced machines, parts, and components; and began modernizing Caterpillar's plants. Donald Fites diversified Caterpillar's product line and reorganized the company structurally. He also completed Caterpillar's plant modernization program, revitalized Caterpillar's dealership network, and altered radically Caterpillar's approach to labor relations.

As Donald Fites retired in February 1999, Glen Barton was elected CEO. Barton was in an enviable position. The world's largest manufacturer of construction and mining equipment, and a Fortune 100 company, Caterpillar generated $21 billion in revenues in 1998,

the sixth consecutive record year. Leading its industry while competing globally, Caterpillar recorded a $1.5 billion profit in 1998, the second best ever.[1]

Notwithstanding Caterpillar's dramatic comeback, Barton could not count on the continual prosperity of the company because the U.S. construction industry was moving into a grinding economic downturn. At the time Barton completed his first year as CEO, on February 1, 2000, the company announced its 1999 result: sales declined by 6 percent and earnings by 37 percent. In March 2000, Caterpillar share price was trading close to its fifty-two-week low ($36 against a high of $66), and one industry analyst declared, "The stock for the foreseeable future is dead money."[2]

What should Barton do? Should Barton follow the strategies implemented by Schaefer and Fites to enhance Caterpillar's competitive position relative to its principal rivals, Komatsu, John Deere, and CNH Global? (CNH was the product of a 2000 merger between the Case Corp. and New Holland.) Should he, instead, reverse some of the policies introduced by his predecessors? Or should he, rather, undertake whole new strategies altogether?

To assess Barton's strategic choices in improving Caterpillar's results, the case looks back at the experience of his two predecessors. How precisely did both Schaefer and Fites manage to turn Caterpillar around?

This case was presented at the October 2001 meeting of the North American Case Research Association (NACRA) at Sedona, AZ. Copyright © 2001 by Isaac Cohen and NACRA. Reprinted by permission. All rights reserved. For the most recent financial results of the company discussed in this case, go to **http://finance.yahoo.com,** input the company's stock symbol, and download the latest company report from its homepage.

The Heavy Construction Equipment Industry

The heavy construction equipment industry supplied engineering firms, construction companies, and mine operators. The industry's typical product line included

EXHIBIT 1

Global Demand of Heavy Construction Equipment
by Major Categories, 1985–2005

Item	1985	1994	2000	2005*
Earthmoving Equipment	50%	49%	49%	49%
Off Highway Trucks	8%	7%	7%	7%
Construction Cranes	9%	11%	10%	10%
Mixers, Pavers, and Related Equipment	6%	6%	7%	7%
Parts and Attachments	27%	27%	27%	26%
	—	—	—	—
Total Demand (billions)	$38	$56	$72	$90

Source: Andrew Gross and David Weiss, "Industry Corner: The Global Demand for Heavy Construction Equipment," *Business Economics,* July 1996, p. 56.

*Percentages do not add up to 100 because of rounding.

earthmovers (bulldozers, loaders, and excavators), road building machines (pavers, motor graders, and mixers), mining related equipment (off-highway trucks, mining shovels), and large cranes. Most machines were offered in a broad range of sizes, and a few were available with a choice of wheels or crawler tracks. Most were used for the construction of buildings, power plants, manufacturing plants, and infra-structure projects such as roads, airports, bridges, tunnels, dams, sewage systems, and water lines. On a global basis, earthmoving equipment accounted for about half of the industry's total sales in the 1990s (Exhibit 1). Among earthmovers, hydraulic excavators accounted for 45 percent of the sales. Excavators were more productive, more versatile, and easier to use in tight spaces than either bulldozers or loaders. Off-highway trucks that hauled minerals, rocks, and dirt were another category of fast-selling equipment.[3]

Global demand for heavy construction machinery grew at a steady rate of 4.5 percent in the 1990s. The rate of growth, however, was faster among the developing nations of Asia, Africa, and Latin America than among the developed nations. In the early 2000s, North America and Europe were each expected to account for 25 percent of the industry's sales, Japan for 20 percent, and the developing nations for the remaining 30 percent.[4]

The distinction between original equipment and replacement parts was an essential feature of the industry. Replacement parts and "attachments" (work tools) made up together over a quarter of the total revenues of the heavy construction equipment industry (Exhibit 1), but accounted for a substantially larger share of the industry's earnings for two reasons: First, the sale of replacement parts was more profitable than that of whole machines; and second, the market for replacement parts was less cyclical than that for original equipment.[5] As a rule of thumb, the economic life of a heavy construction machine was 10 to 12 years, but in many cases, especially in developing countries, equipment users kept their machines in service much longer, perhaps 20 to 30 years, thus creating an ongoing stream of revenues for parts, components, and related services.[6]

Another characteristic of the industry was the need to achieve economies of scale. According to industry observers, the optimal scale of operation was about 90,000 units annually, in other words, up to a production level of 90,000 units a year. Average equipment unit cost declined as output increased, and therefore capturing a large market share was critical for benefiting from economies of scale.[7] The relatively low volume of global sales—200,000 to 300,000 earthmoving equipment units per year (1996)[8]—further intensified competition over market share among the industry's leading firms.

Successful marketing also played an important role in gaining competitive advantage. A widespread distribution and service network had always been essential for competing in the heavy construction equipment industry because "downtime" resulting from the inability to operate the equipment at a construction site was very costly. Typically, manufacturers used a worldwide network of dealerships to sell machines, provide support, and offer after-sales service. Dealerships were independent, company owned, or both, and were normally organized on an exclusive territorial basis. Since heavy construction machines operated in a tough and inhospitable environment, equipment wore out and broke down frequently, parts needed to be rebuilt or replaced often, and therefore manufacturers placed dealers in close proximity to equipment users, building a global service network that spread all over the world.

Manufacturers built alliances as well. Intense competition over market share drove the industry's top firms to form three types of cooperative agreements. The first were full-scale joint ventures to share production. Caterpillar's joint venture with Mitsubishi Heavy Industries was a notable case in point. The second were technology sharing agreements between equipment manufacturers and engine makers to ensure access to the latest engine technology. The joint venture between Komatsu and Cummins Engine, on the one hand, and the Case Corporation and Cummins, on the other, provided two examples. The third type of agreements were technology sharing alliances between major global firms and local manufacturers whereby the former gained access to new markets, and in return, supplied the latter with advanced technology. Caterpillar utilized such an arrangement with Shanghai Diesel in China, and Komatsu did so with the BEML Company in India.[9]

History of Caterpillar

At the turn of the century, farmers in California faced a serious problem. Using steam tractors to plow the fine delta land of the San Joaquin valley, California farmers fitted their tractors with large drive wheels to provide support on the moist soil; nevertheless, despite their efforts, the steamer's huge wheels—measuring up to 9 feet high—sank deeply into the soil. In 1904, Benjamin Holt, a combine maker from Stockton, California, solved the problem by replacing the wheels with a track, thereby distributing the tractor's weight on a broader surface. Holt, in addition, replaced the heavy steam engine with a gasoline engine, thus improving the tractor's mobility further by reducing its weight (a steam tractor weighed up to

20 tons). He nicknamed the tractor "Caterpillar," acquired the Caterpillar trademark, and applied it to several crawler-type machines that his company manufactured and sold. By 1915, Holt tractors were sold in twenty countries.[10]

Outside agriculture, crawler tractors were first used by the military. In 1915, the British military invented the armor tank, modeling it after Holt's machine, and during World War I, the United States and its allies in Europe utilized Holt's track-type tractors to haul artillery and supply wagons. In 1925, the Holt Company merged with another California firm, the Best Tractor Company, to form Caterpillar (Cat). Shortly thereafter, Caterpillar moved its corporate headquarters and manufacturing plants to Peoria, Illinois. The first company to introduce a diesel engine on a moving vehicle (1931), Caterpillar discontinued its combine manufacturing during the 1930s and focused instead on the production of road-building, construction, logging, and pipe laying equipment. During World War II, Caterpillar served as the primary supplier of bulldozers to the U.S. Army; its sales volume more than tripled between 1941 and 1944 to include motor graders, diesel engines, and electric generators, apart from tractors and wagons.[11]

Demand for Caterpillar products exploded in the early post war years. Cat's equipment was used to reconstruct Europe, build the U.S. interstate highway system, erect the giant dams of the Third World, and lay out the major airports of the world. The company managed to differentiate itself from its competitors by producing reliable, durable, and high-quality equipment, offering a quick after-sales service, and providing a speedy delivery of replacement parts. As a result, during the 1950s and 1960s, Caterpillar had emerged as the uncontested leader of the heavy construction equipment industry, far ahead of any rival. By 1965, Caterpillar had established foreign manufacturing subsidiaries—either wholly owned or joint ventures—in Britain, Canada, Australia, Brazil, France, Mexico, Belgium, India, and Japan. Caterpillar's fifty/fifty joint venture with Mitsubishi in Japan, established in 1963, had become one of the most successful, stable, and enduring alliances among all American-Japanese joint ventures.[12]

Caterpillar's distribution and dealership network also contributed to the company's worldwide success. From the outset, the company's marketing organization rested on a dense network of independent dealers who sold and serviced Cat equipment. Strategically located throughout the world, these dealers were self-sustaining entrepreneurs who invested their own capital in their business, derived close to 100 percent of their revenues from selling and supporting Cat equipment, and cultivated close relationships with Caterpillar customers. On average, a Caterpillar dealership had remained in the hands of the same family—or company—for over fifty years. Indeed, some dealerships, including several located overseas, predated the 1925 merger that gave birth to Caterpillar.[13] In 1981, on the eve of the impending crisis, the combined net worth of Cat dealers equaled that of the company itself, and the total number of employees working for Cat dealers was slightly lower than the company's own workforce.[14]

The Crisis of the Early 1980s

Facing weak competition both at home and abroad, Caterpillar charged premium prices for its high-quality products, paid its production workers union-scale wages, offered its shareholders high rates of return on their equity, and enjoyed superior profits. Then, in 1982, following a record year of sales and profits, Caterpillar suddenly plunged into three successive years of rising losses totaling nearly $1 billion. "Quite frankly, our long years of success made us complacent, even arrogant,"[15] Pierre Guerindon, an executive vice president at Cat conceded.

The crisis of 1982–1984 stemmed from three sources: a global recession, a costly strike, and unfavorable currency exchange rates. First, the steady growth in demand for construction machinery, dating back to 1945, came to an end in 1980, as highway construction in the United States slowed down to a halt while declining oil prices depressed the worldwide market for mining, logging, and pipe laying equipment. Second, Caterpillar's efforts to freeze wages and reduce overall labor cost triggered a seven-month strike (1982–1983) among its U.S. employees. Led by the United Auto Workers (UAW) union, the strike accounted for a sizable portion of the company's three-year loss. The third element in Caterpillar's crisis was a steep rise in the value of the dollar (relative to the Yen and other currencies) that made U.S. exports more expensive abroad and U.S. imports (shipped by Caterpillar's competitors) cheaper at home. "The strong dollar is a prime factor in Caterpillar's reduced sales and earning ... [and]

is undermining manufacturing industries in the United States,"[16] said Cat's annual reports for 1982 and 1984.

Taking advantage of the expensive dollar, Komatsu Limited had emerged as Caterpillar's principal rival. Komatsu ("little pine tree" in Japanese) had initially produced construction machinery for the Japanese and Asian markets, then sought to challenge Caterpillar's dominance in the markets of Latin America and Europe, and eventually penetrated the United States to rival Caterpillar in its domestic market. Attacking Caterpillar head-on, Komatsu issued a battle cry, *Maru C*, meaning "encircle Cat." Launching a massive drive to improve quality while reducing costs, Komatsu achieved a 50 percent labor productivity advantage over Caterpillar, and, in turn, underpriced Caterpillar's products by as much 30 percent. The outcome was a dramatic change in market share. Between 1979 and 1984, Komatsu global market share more than doubled to 25 percent while Caterpillar's fell by almost a quarter to 43 percent.[17]

Turnaround: George Schaefer's Caterpillar, 1985–1990

Competition with Komatsu and the crisis of 1982–1984 forced Caterpillar to reexamine its past activities. Caterpillar's new CEO (1985), George Schaefer, was a congenial manager who encouraged Cat executives to openly admit the company's past mistakes. "We have experienced a fundamental change in our business—it will never again be what it was," Schaefer said as he became CEO. "We have no choice but to respond, and respond vigorously, to the new world in which we find ourselves."[18] Under Schaefer's direction, Caterpillar devised and implemented a series of strategies that touched upon every important function of the company, including purchasing, manufacturing, marketing, personnel, and labor relations.

Global Outsourcing

Traditionally, Caterpillar functioned as a vertically integrated company that relied heavily on in-house production. To ensure product quality as well as an uninterrupted supply of parts, Cat self-produced two-thirds of its parts and components, and assembled practically all of its finished machines. Under the new policy of "shopping around the world," Caterpillar sought to purchase parts and components from low-cost suppliers who maintained high quality standards. Working closely with its suppliers, Caterpillar moved toward the goal of outsourcing 80 percent of its parts and components.[19]

An additional goal of the policy was branding, that is, the purchase of final products for resale. Through its branding program, Caterpillar sold out-sourced machines under its own brand name, taking advantage of its superior marketing organization and keeping production costs down. Beginning in the mid 1980s, Cat contracted to buy lift trucks from a Norwegian company, hydraulic excavators from a West German manufacturer, paving machines from an Oklahoma corporation, off-highway trucks from a British firm, and logging equipment from a Canadian company, and resell them all under the Cat nameplate. Ordinarily, Caterpillar outsourced product manufacturing but not product design. By keeping control over the design of many of its outsourced products, Caterpillar managed to retain in-house design capability, and ensure quality control.[20]

Broader Product Line

For nearly a decade, the DC10 bulldozer had served as Caterpillar's signature item. It stood 15 feet tall, weighed 73 tons, and sold for more than $500,000 (1988). It had no competitors. But as demand for highway construction projects dwindled, Caterpillar needed to reevaluate its product mix because heavy equipment was no longer selling well. Sales of light construction equipment, on the other hand, were fast increasing. Between 1984 and 1987, accordingly, Caterpillar doubled its product line from 150 to 300 models of equipment, introducing many small machines that ranged from farm tractors to backhoe loaders (multipurpose light bulldozers), and diversified its customer base. Rather than focusing solely on large clients, that is, multinational engineering and construction firms like the Bechtel corporation—a typical user of heavy bulldozers—Cat began marketing its lightweight machines to a new category of customers: small-scale owner operators and emerging contractors. Still, the shift in Cat's product mix had a clear impact on the company's bottom line. Unlike the heavy equipment market where profit margins were wide, intense competition in the market for light products kept margins slim and pitted Caterpillar against John Deere and the Case corporation, the light equipment market leaders.[21]

Labor Relations

To compete successfully, Caterpillar also needed to repair its relationship with the union. In 1979, following the expiration of its collective bargaining agreement, Caterpillar experienced an eighty-day strike, and three years later, in 1982, contract negotiations erupted in a 205-day strike, the longest company-wide work stoppage in the UAW history.[22] Named CEO in 1985, George Schaefer led the next two rounds of contract negotiations.

Schaefer's leadership style was consensual. By contrast to the autocratic style of his predecessors, Schaefer advocated the free flow of ideas between officers, managers, and production workers, and he promoted open communication at all levels of the company. A low-key CEO who often answered his own phone, Schaefer possessed exceptional people skills. Asked to evaluate Schaefer's performance, John Stark, editor of *Off Highway Ledger*, a trade journal, said, "Schaefer is probably the best manager the construction machinery industry has ever had."[23]

Schaefer's social skills led to a significant improvement in Cat's relations with the UAW. Not a single strike broke out over contract negotiations during Schaefer's tenure; on the contrary, each cycle of bargaining was settled peacefully. Under Schaefer's direction, furthermore, the union agreed to reduce the number of labor grades and job classifications and to streamline seniority provisions—a move that enhanced management flexibility in job assignment and facilitated the cross utilization of employees.[24] More important, improved labor relations contributed to the success of two programs that played a critical role in Caterpillar's turnaround strategy, namely, an employee involvement plan based on teamwork and a reengineering effort of plant modernization and automation.

Employee Involvement

An industrywide union famous for its cooperative labor-management efforts at the Saturn corporation, the NUMMI plant (a GM-Toyota joint-venture in Fremont, California), and elsewhere, the UAW lent its support to Caterpillar's employee involvement program. Called the Employee Satisfaction Process (ESP), and launched by Schaefer in 1986, the program was voluntary. ESP members were organized in work teams, met weekly with management, and offered suggestions that pertained to many critical aspects of the manufacturing process, including production management, workplace layout, and quality enhancement. Implemented in a growing number of U.S. plants, the program resulted (1990) in productivity gains, quality improvements, and increased employee satisfaction. At the Cat plant in Aurora, Illinois, for example, the local ESP chairman recalled that the ESP program "changed everything: the worker had some say over his job … [and t]op management was very receptive. We zeroed in on quality, anything to make the customer happy." Management credited the ESP teams at Aurora with a steep fall in the rate of absenteeism, a sharp decline in the number of union grievances filed, and cost savings totaling $10 million.[25] At another ESP plant, a Cat assembly-line worker told a *Fortune* reporter in 1988: "Five years ago the foreman wouldn't even listen to you, never mind the general foreman or plant supervisor. . . . Now everyone will listen." Caterpillar applied the ESP program to outside suppliers as well. Typically, ESP teams made up of Caterpillar machinists visited suppliers' plants to check and certify equipment quality. The certified vendors received preferential treatment, mostly in the form of reduced inspection, counting, and other controls. Only 0.6 percent of the parts delivered by certified suppliers were rejected by Caterpillar compared with a reject rate of 2.8 percent for noncertified suppliers.[26]

Plant with a Future

Caterpillar's employee involvement plan went hand in hand with a $1.8 billion plant modernization program launched by Schaefer in 1986.[27] Dubbed "Plant with a Future" (PWAF), the modernization program combined just-in-time inventory techniques, a factory automation scheme, a network of computerized machine tools, and a flexible manufacturing system. Several of these innovations were pioneered by Komatsu late in the 1970s. The industry's technological leader, Komatsu had been the first construction equipment manufacturer to introduce both the just-in-time inventory system and the "quick changeover tooling" technique, a flexible tooling method designed to produce a large variety of equipment models in a single plant.[28]

To challenge Komatsu, top executives at Caterpillar did not seek to merely imitate the Japanese. This was not enough. They studied, instead, the modernization efforts of several manufacturing companies, and arrived at two important conclusions: It was necessary (1) to change the layout of an entire plant, not just selected departments within a plant; and (2) to implement the program companywide, that is, on a global basis both at home and abroad. Implementing such a comprehensive program took longer than expected, however, lasting seven years: four under Schaefer's direction and three more under the direction of his successor, Donald Fites.[29]

The traditional manufacturing process at Caterpillar, known as "batch" production, was common among U.S. assembly plants in a number of industries. Under batch production, subassembly lines produced components (radiators, hydraulic tanks, etc.) in small lots. Final assembly lines put together complete models, and the entire production system required large inventories of parts and components owing to the high level of "work in process" (models being built at any one time). Under batch production, furthermore, assembly tasks were highly specialized, work was monotonous and dull, and workers grew lax and made mistakes. Correcting assembly mistakes, it should be noted, took more time than the assembly process itself because workers needed to disassemble components in order to access problem areas. Parts delivery was also problematic. Occasionally, delays in delivery of parts to the assembly areas forced workers to leave the line in order to locate a missing part. Occasionally, the early arrival of parts before they were needed created its own inefficiencies.[30]

To solve these problems, Caterpillar reconfigured the layout of its manufacturing plants into flexible work "cells." Grouped in cells, workers used computerized machine tools to perform several manufacturing steps in sequence, processing components from start to finish and sending them "just-in-time" to an assembly area, as the following example suggests. To manufacture steel tractor-tread under the batch production layout, Cat workers were required to cut, drill, and heat-treat steel beams on three distinct assembly lines. Under cellular manufacturing, by contrast, all three operations were carried out automatically in single tractor-tread cells linked together by computers.[31]

Caterpillar, in addition, reduced material handling by means of an automated electrified monorail which delivered parts to storage and assembly areas, traveling on a long aluminum track throughout the modernized plant. When parts arrived at the delivery point, a flash light alerted the assembly line workers, semiautomatic gates (operated by infrared remote

EXHIBIT 2

George Schaefer's Caterpillar: Highlights of
Financial Data, Caterpillar Versus Komatsu

	Cat		Komatsu	
	Sales ($ billion)	Income as % of Sales	Sales ($ billion)	Income as % of Sales
1985	$6.7	2.9%	*	1.8%
1986	$7.3	1.0%	*	2.8%
1987	$8.2	3.9%	$5.1	1.3%
1988	$10.4	5.9%	$6.2	0.4%
1989	$11.1	4.5%	$6.0	2.6%

Source: For Caterpillar, *Hoover's Handbook of American Business, 1995*, p. 329; for Komatsu, *Hoover's Handbook of World Business, 1995–96*, p. 291.

*Sales are available only in Yen: 1985, 796 billion Yen; 1986, 789 billion Yen.

control) opened, and a lift lowered the components directly onto an assembly line. Don Western, a manufacturing manager at the Cat Aurora plant, observed, "Materials now [1990] arrive at the assembly point only when required—and in the order required. At most, we hold about a 4 hour supply of large parts and components on the line."[32]

Caterpillar, finally, improved product quality. Formerly, components moved down the assembly line continuously, not intermittently, and therefore workers were unable to respond quickly to quality problems. Managers alone controlled the speed of the line. Under the new assembly plan, on the other hand, components moved automatically between work areas and remained stationary during the actual assembly operation. More important, under the PWAF plan, managers empowered production workers to change the speed of the assembly line at will, granting them the flexibility necessary to resolve quality and safety problems.[33]

The PWAF program resulted in productivity and quality gains across the board in many of Caterpillar plants. At the Aurora plant in Illinois, for instance, factory workers managed to reduce the assembly process time fourfold, building and shipping a customer order in 4 rather than 16 days, and cutting product defects by one-half in 4 years (1986–1990).[34] At the Cat plant in Grenoble, France, to mention another case, workers slashed the time it took to assemble machinery parts from 20 to 8 days in 3 years

(1986–1989). Companywide changes were equally impressive: collectively, Caterpillar's 30 worldwide plants cut inventory levels by 50 percent and manufacturing space by 21 percent in 3 years.[35]

Looking back at Schaefer's five year-long tenure, Caterpillar had reemerged as a globally competitive company, lean, flexible, and technologically advanced. Caterpillar's world market share rebounded from 43 percent to 50 percent (1984–1990),[36] revenues increased by 66 percent (1985–1989), and the company was profitable once again. As Caterpillar prospered, Komatsu was retrenching. In 1989, Caterpillar's sales totaled over $11 billion or nearly twice the sales reported by Komatsu, Caterpillar's profit margins exceeded Komatsu's, and the gap between the two companies—in terms of both market share and income on sales—was growing (Exhibit 2).

The Transformation Continued: Donald Fites's Caterpillar, 1990–1999

Notwithstanding Schaefer's achievements, the transformation of Caterpillar was far from over. For one thing, the company stock lagged far behind its earnings; Cat shares underperformed the S&P 500 index by over 50 percent for five years (1987–1992).[37] For another, Caterpillar was facing an industrywide downturn in both its domestic and international markets. Partly as a result of the cyclical nature of the construction equipment industry, and also as a result of an increase in the value of the dollar (a weak dollar in the late 1980s helped Caterpillar's foreign sales), Caterpillar revenues and profits fell. During the two years following Schaefer's retirement, the company actually lost money (see Exhibit 3).

Replacing Schaefer in the winter of 1990, Donald Fites viewed Caterpillar's financial troubles as an opportunity to introduce change: "I certainly didn't count on ... [a] recession ... but [the recession] made it easier to accept the fact that we needed to change."[38] "It's hard to change an organization when you're making record profits."[39]

Leadership

Fites's leadership style stood in stark contrast to Schaefer's. "George was ... a consensus builder" while "[Don] expects people to challenge him forcefully,"[40] one Cat executive said, and another (former Cat CEO Lee Morgan) described Fites as "one of the most determined men I've ever met."[41] Fites was a hard-line executive, feared by his subordinates, respected by his peers, and cheered by Wall Street. An imposing man standing 6 feet 5 inches, Fites led by explicit command rather than persuasion, asserted the company's "right to manage" in face of mounting union opposition, and did not hesitate to cut thousands of management and production jobs at a stroke.

The son of a subsistence corn farmer, Fites had joined Caterpillar in 1956, rising through the ranks, and spending sixteen years overseas. A career marketeer, he worked for Cat in South Africa, Germany, Switzerland, Brazil, Japan, and other countries. In 1971, Fites had earned an MBA from MIT, writing a thesis titled "Japan Inc.: Can U.S. Industry Compete?" and soon thereafter, he received an assignment in Japan, serving nearly five years as the marketing director of the Caterpillar-Mitsubishi joint venture. Fites's Japanese experience resonated throughout the remainder of his career. He was impressed, first of all, by the ways in which the Japanese trained their managers, rotating executives through functional departments in order to educate them in all aspects of the business. Returning from Japan to Peoria in the mid 1970s, Fites revamped Cat's product development process, utilizing an integrated approach based on Japanese-style functional teams. He also admired Japanese labor relations. Historically, American unions had been organized on an industrywide basis, and therefore labor relations in the United States were often adversarial. Trade unions in Japan, by contrast, were company-based organizations, loyal, cooperative, and, in Fites's words, "deeply dedicated to the success of the [firm]."[42] Leading Caterpillar in the 1990s, Fites sought to bring Caterpillar's labor relations closer to the Japanese model.

Reorganization

A marketing manager, Fites was convinced that Caterpillar did not pay sufficient attention to customer needs because global pricing decisions were made at the company's headquarters in Peoria with little knowledge of the local market conditions around the world. In 1985, as he took charge of Cat's worldwide marketing organization, Fites delegated district offices the authority to set prices, thereby pushing responsibility down the chain of command to the lowest possible level. Promoted to president in 1989, Fites applied the same principle to Caterpillar's entire structure, developing a companywide reorganization plan under Schaefer's direction.[43]

Caterpillar's organizational structure was archaic. It was a functional structure suitable for a small company that operated just a few plants, all located within the United States. A centralized body with only four primary functions—engineering, manufacturing, marketing, and finance—the old structure served Caterpillar well until World War II, but as the company expanded globally in subsequent decades, the limitations of such a structure had become apparent. First, decisions were made at the top of each functional unit, and executives were reluctant to delegate authority to mid- or low-level managers. Second, each functional unit tended to focus on its own goal rather than the enterprise's objectives (marketing was preoccupied with market share, engineering with product safety, manufacturing with assembly problems, etc.), making it difficult for top management to coordinate functional goals.[44] And third, the bureaucratization of the decision-making process impaired effective communication. Under the old structure, Fites recalled, the flow of information upward was "so filtered with various prejudices—particularly functional prejudice[s]—that you didn't know whether you were really looking at the facts or looking at someone's opinion."[45]

To equip Caterpillar with the flexibility, speed, and agility necessary to operate in the global economy, Fites broke the company into 17 semiautonomous divisions or "profit centers"; 13 were responsible for products (tractors, engines, etc.) and 4 for services.[46]

EXHIBIT 3

Donald Fites's Caterpillar:
Employment and Sales

Year	Number of Employees	Sales ($ billion)
1990	60,000	11.4
1991	56,000	10.2
1992	52,000	10.2
1993	50,000	11.6
1994	54,000	14.3
1995	54,000	16.1
1996	57,000	16.5
1997	60,000	18.9
1998	64,000	21.0

Source: For 1990–1997: *Hoover's Handbook of American Business, 1999*, p. 329; for 1998, Caterpillar Inc. 1999 Annual Report, p. 1.

He then required each division to post a 15 percent rate of return on assets, and threatened to penalize any division that fell behind. He stood by his words. When Caterpillar's forklift division failed to improve its return on assets in 1992, Fites transferred it into an 80 percent to 20 percent joint venture controlled by Mitsubishi.[47]

Caterpillar's new divisional structure facilitated downsizing. Under the new structure, Caterpillar cut 10,000 jobs in three years, 1990–1993 (Exhibit 3). Of the 7,500 employees who lost their jobs between January 1990 and August 1992, 2,000 were salaried managers and 5,500 hourly workers.[48] As Caterpillar's sales grew from $10 billion to $15 billion in the first half of the 1990s, the number of managers employed by the company fell by 20 percent.[49] In addition, the move from a functional into a divisional structure, coupled with the drive for profit making, brought about a change in the methods of managerial compensation. Traditionally, Cat managers were paid in proportion to the size of the budget they controlled or the number of employees they supervised. Under the new plan, Caterpillar based all its incentive compensation schemes on return on assets.[50] Lastly, Caterpillar decentralized its research and development activities. With each division controlling its own product development programs and funding, R&D activities under the new plan were more customer driven than at any other period in the past.[51]

Marketing and Dealerships

Caterpillar's reorganization plan affected the company's distribution network as well. Under the new structure, dealers seeking assistance could contact any of the seventeen product and service profit centers directly, saving time and money; they no longer needed to call the General Office in their search for assistance within the company.[52] The new structure also facilitated a more frequent interaction between Caterpillar's managers and dealers, a development that resulted in "virtually everyone from the youngest design engineer to the CEO" having "contact with somebody in [a] dealer organization" (wrote Fites). Ordinarily, low-level managers at Caterpillar communicated daily with their counterparts at Cat dealerships and senior corporate executives, several times a week.[53]

Caterpillar's network of dealerships was extensive. In 1999, 207 independent dealers served Caterpillar: 63 were stationed in the United States and 144 abroad. The number of employees working for Cat dealers exceeded the company's own workforce (67,000) by nearly one-third; the combined net worth of Cat dealers surpassed Caterpillar's stockholders' equity ($5.5 billion)[54] by nearly one-quarter (Exhibit 4). Many of Caterpillar's dealerships were privately owned; a few were public companies. On average, the annual sales of a Caterpillar dealership amounted to $150 million (1996); several of the large dealerships, however, generated annual revenues of up to $1 billion.

To Caterpillar, the informal relationships between the company and its dealers were far more important than the formal contractual relations. Dealership

EXHIBIT 4

Caterpillar Dealerships, 1999

	Inside U.S.	Outside U.S.	Worldwide
Dealers	63	144	207
Branch Stores	382	1,122	1,504
Employees	34,338	54,370	88,708
Service Bays	6,638	5,529	12,167
Estimated Net Worth	$3.22 bil.	$3.54 bil.	$6.77 bil.

Source: Caterpillar Inc. 1999 Annual Report, p. 43.

agreements ran only a few pages, had no expiration date, and allowed each party to terminate the contract at will, following ninety-days' notice. Notwithstanding the open-ended nature of the contract, turnover among Cat dealerships was extremely low. Caterpillar actively encouraged its dealers to keep the business in their families, running seminars on tax issues and succession plans for dealers, holding regular conferences in Peoria for the sons and daughters of "dealer Principals" (dealership owners), and taking concrete steps to encourage a proper succession from one generation to another.[55]

While Caterpillar had always protected its dealers against failure, under Fites's direction, Caterpillar did so more aggressively than before, assisting individual dealers who were subjected to intense price competition by rival manufacturers. To help a dealer, Caterpillar sometimes offered discounted prices, sometimes helped reduce the dealer's costs, and occasionally launched a promotion campaign in the dealer's service territory, emphasizing the lower lifetime cost of a Cat machine relative to a competitor's. Caterpillar also protected dealers during recessions. Despite the company's loses during the industry slump of 1991–1992, Fites's Caterpillar helped vulnerable Cat dealers survive the downturn, stay in the business, and order equipment in advance of the 1993 upturn. Caterpillar's competitors, in contrast, saw several of their dealers go out of business during the recession.[56]

Fites's Caterpillar cooperated with dealers in other ways. During the 1990s, Caterpillar worked together with its dealers to conduct surveys among customers in order to improve customer service and parts delivery. Sending out ninety thousand survey forms annually, Cat received a response rate of nearly 40 percent. Through its "Partners in Quality" program, Caterpillar involved dealers in quality control discussions, linking personnel at Cat plants and dealerships, and sponsoring quarterly meetings. Periodically, Caterpillar invited its entire body of independent dealers to a week-long conference in Peoria to review corporate strategy, manufacturing plants, and marketing policies. A firm believer in strong personal business ties, Fites explained

> Dealers can call me or any senior corporate officer at any time, and they do. Virtually any dealer in the world is free to walk in my door. I'll know how much money he made last year and his market position. And I'll know what is happening in his family. I consider the majority of dealers personal friends. Of course, one reason I know the dealers so well is that I rose through our distribution organization.[57]

Caterpillar's worldwide distribution system, according to Fites, was the company's single greatest advantage over its competitors. It was a strategic asset whose importance was expected to grow in the future: "Until about 2010," Fites predicted, "distribution"— that is, after-sales support, product application, and service information—" will be what separates the winners from the losers in the global economy."[58] Contrasting American and Japanese manufacturing firms, Fites elaborated

> Although many Japanese companies had the early advantage in manufacturing excellence, U.S. companies may have the edge this time around. . . . they know more about distribution than anyone else. . . . Quite frankly, distribution traditionally has not been a strength of Japanese companies. Marketing people and salespeople historically have been looked down upon in Japanese society.[59]

Information Technology

Fites's Caterpillar invested generously in expanding and upgrading Caterpillar's worldwide computer network—a system linking together factories, distribution centers, dealers, and large customers. By 1996, the network connected 1,000 locations in 160 countries across 23 time zones, providing Caterpillar with the most comprehensive and fastest part delivery system in the industry. Although Caterpillar had long guaranteed a 48-hour delivery of parts anywhere in the world, by 1996, Cat dealers supplied 80 percent of the parts a customer needed at once; the remaining 20 percent—not stocked by the dealers—were shipped by the company on the same day the parts were ordered. With 22 distribution centers spread all around the world, Caterpillar serviced a total of 500,000 different parts, keeping over 300,000 in stock, and manufacturing the remainder on demand.[60]

A critical element in Caterpillar's drive for technological leadership was an electronic alert information system the company was developing under Fites. The new system was designed to monitor machines remotely, identify parts that needed to be replaced, and replace them before they failed. Once fully operational in the mid 2000's, the new IT system was expected first to help dealers repair machines before they broke down, thereby reducing machine down-time, on the one hand, and saving repair costs, on the other; and second to provide Caterpillar and its dealers with the opportunity to slash their inventory costs. In 1995, the value of the combined inventories held by Caterpillar and its dealers amounted to $2 billion worth of parts.[61]

Diversification

Fites's Caterpillar expanded its sales into farm equipment, forest products, and compact construction machines, introducing new lines of products, one at a time. Between 1991 and 1999, Caterpillar entered a total of thirty-eight mergers and joint venture agreements, many of which contributed to the company's efforts to diversify.[62]

The growth in Caterpillar's engine sales was the company's largest. Caterpillar had traditionally produced engines for internal use only, installing them on Cat machines, but beginning in the mid 1980s, as the company was recovering from its most severe crisis, Cat embarked on a strategy of producing engines for sale to other companies. In 1999, engine sales accounted for 35 percent of Cat's revenues, up from 21 percent in 1990, and Cat engines powered about one-third of the big trucks in the United States. Apart from trucking companies, Caterpillar produced engines for a variety of other customers, including petroleum firms, electric utility companies, and shipbuilding concerns (see Exhibit 6). Only 10 percent of the diesel engines manufactured by Caterpillar in 1999 were installed on the company's own equipment.[63]

Two important acquisitions by Caterpillar helped the company compete in the engine market. In 1996, Donald Fites purchased the MaK Company—a German maker of engines for power generation. Partly because governments of developing countries were reluctant to build large power plants, and partly because the utility industry in the United States deregulated and new electrical suppliers entered the market, worldwide demand for generators was fast increasing. The rise in demand helped Caterpillar increase its sales of power generators by 20 percent annually between 1995 and 1999.[64]

Similarly, in 1998, Fites bought Britain's Perkins Engines, a manufacturer of engines for compact construction machinery, for $1.3 billion. The new acquisition contributed to Caterpillar's efforts to increase its share in the small equipment market which was growing at a rate of 10 percent a year. Perkins's best-selling engine powered the skid steer loader. A compact wheel tractor operated by one person and capable of maneuvering in tight spaces, the skid dug ditches, moved dirt, broke up asphalt, and performed a wide variety of other tasks.[65]

Labor Relations

Perhaps no other areas of management had received more attention than Caterpillar's labor relations under Fites. For nearly seven years, 1991–1998, Fites fought the UAW in what had become the longest U.S. labor dispute in the 1990s. On the one side, a union official described the UAW relationship with Fites as "the single most contentious … in the history of the union"; on the other, a Wall Street analyst called Fites "the guy who broke the union, pure and simple."[66]

In part, Fites's opposition to the UAW was ideological: It "is not so much a battle about economics as it is a battle about who's going to run the company."[67] Yet economics did matter, and Fites was determined to ensure Caterpillar's global competitiveness by cutting the company's labor cost. His principal target was a UAW "pattern" agreement, a collective bargaining contract modeled on agreements signed by the UAW and Caterpillar's domestic competitors, John Deere, the Case Corporation, and others (a pattern agreement tied separate labor contracts together so that changes in one led to similar changes in others within the same industry). Fites rejected pattern bargaining because Caterpillar was heavily dependent on the export of domestically manufactured products, selling over 50 percent of its American-made equipment in foreign markets, and thus competing head-to-head with foreign-based, global companies like Komatsu. Cat's U.S.-based competitors, by contract, exported a far smaller proportion of their domestically made goods. Because Cat's global competitors paid lower wages overseas than the wages paid by Cat's American-based competitors at home, Fites argued, Caterpillar could not afford paying the UAW pattern of wages.[68]

The first Caterpillar strike erupted in 1991, at a time when Caterpillar's 17,000 unionized employees were working under a contract. The contract was set to expire on September 30, and Fites was prepared. He had built up enough inventory to supply customers for six months, giving Cat dealers special incentives to buy and stock parts and equipment in case a strike shut down the company's U.S. plants. Caterpillar's contract offer included three principal demands: no pattern on wages, flexible work schedules, and a two-tier wage system. The union rejected the offer outright and staged a strike. About 50 percent of the strikers were within six years of retirement, and as the strike prolonged, 30 percent of the strikers crossed the picket line. Five months into the strike, Fites threatened to replace the strikers permanently if they did not return to work within a week. Shortly thereafter, the union called off the strike, the strikers went back to work "unconditionally," and Cat's unionized employees continued working without a contract under the terms of the rejected offer.[69]

One casualty of the 1991–1992 strike was Caterpillar's Employee Satisfaction Process. The strike effectively put an end to Cat's ESP program which George Schaefer had launched in 1986 and strove so painstakingly to perverse. As the climate of labor relations at Caterpillar deteriorated, the number of unresolved grievances increased. At the Aurora plant at Illinois, the number of grievances at the final stage before arbitration rose from less than twenty prior to the strike to over three hundred in the year following the end of the strike. When Cat employees began wearing their own ESP buttons to read "Employee Stop Participating," Caterpillar terminated the program altogether.[70]

During 1992–1994, Caterpillar's unionized employees continued to resist Fites's hard-line stand against the UAW. They organized shop floor disruptions ("informational picketing"), slowdowns ("work to rule"), wildcat strikes in selected plants, and picket lines at Cat's dealerships.[71] Fites, in the meantime, trained managers and office workers to operate factory machinery and reassigned many of them to the shop floor of plants undergoing short-term work stoppages. Once again, he was fully prepared for a long strike. The 1994–1995 strike broke out in June 1994, lasted seventeen months, was bitterly fought by the striking unionists, and came to an abrupt end when the UAW ordered its members to return to work "immediately and unconditionally" in order to save their jobs.[72] During the strike, Caterpillar supplemented its workforce with 5,000 reassigned white collar employees, 3,700 full-time and part-time new hires, 4,000 union members who crossed the picket line, and skilled workers borrowed from its dealerships. The company, furthermore, shifted work to nonunion plants in the South. Additionally, Caterpillar supplied the U.S. market with equipment imported from its plants in Europe, Japan, and Brazil.[73] Operating effectively all through the strike, Caterpillar avoided massive customer defection, and managed to keep up production, expand sales, increase profits, and drive up the company stock price. In 1995, the company earned record profits for the second year in a row (see Exhibit 5). During the two years following the end of the strike, the shop floor struggle between Cat management and the union resumed. Caterpillar issued strict rules of workplace conduct, limiting employees' behavior as well as speech.

EXHIBIT 5

Caterpillar's Financial Results
During the Labor Disputes of the 1990s

	Sales ($ Mil.)	Net Income ($Mil.)	Income as % of Sales	Stock Price FY Close
1991	10,182	(404)	—	10.97
1992	10.194	(2,435)	—	13.41
1993	11,615	652	5.6%	22.25
1994	14.328	955	6.7%	27.56
1995	16.072	1,136	7.1%	29.38
1996	16,522	1,361	8.2%	37.63
1997	18,925	1,665	8.8%	48.50

Source: Hoover's Handbook for American Business, 1999, p. 329.

Union activists, in response, launched a work-to-rule campaign in Cat's unionized plants. The UAW, in addition, filed numerous charges with the National Labor Relations Board (NLRB), alleging that the company committed unfair labor practices. Accepting many of these charges, the NLRB issued formal complaints.[74] Meanwhile, in 1997, Caterpillar racked up record profits for the fourth year in a row (Exhibit 5).

In February 1998, at long last Caterpillar and the union reached an agreement. The terms of the 1998 agreement clearly favored Caterpillar. First and most important, the contract allowed Caterpillar to break away from the long-standing practice of pattern bargaining. Second, the contract allowed Caterpillar to introduce a two-tier wage system and pay new employees 70 percent of the starting union scale. A third clause of the contract provided for a more flexible work schedule, allowing management to keep employees on the job longer than eight hours a day and during weekends (without paying overtime). The contract also granted management the right to hire temporary employees at certain plants without the union's approval, and reduce the number of union jobs below a certain level. Running for six years rather than the typical three years, the contract was expected to secure Caterpillar with a relatively long period of industrial peace.[75]

Several provisions of the contract were favorable to the union. The contract's key economic provisions included an immediate wage increase of 2 to 4 percent and future increases of 3 percent in 1999, 2001, and 2003; cost of living allowances; and substantial gains in pension benefits (the average tenure of the 1994–1995 strikers was twenty-four years). Another provision favorable to the UAW was a moratorium on most plant closings. But perhaps the most significant union gain was simply achieving a contract, as AFL-CIO Secretary Treasurer Rich Trumka observed: "The message to corporate America is this: Here's one of the biggest companies, and they couldn't walk away from the union."[76]

Why, then, was Fites willing to sign a contract? Why did a company that operated profitably year after year without a contract, and operated effectively during strikes, suddenly seek to reach an agreement with the UAW?

Fites's decision was influenced by two developments. First, Caterpillar's record revenues and profits during 1993–1997 came to an end in 1998–1999,

as the industry was sliding into a recession. Revenues and profits were declining as a result of a strong dollar coupled with a weak demand for Cat products. Caterpillar, therefore, needed a flexible wage agreement, stable employment relations, and a more cooperative workforce in order to smooth its ride during the impending downturn. Another reason why Fites sought accommodation with the union was the need to settle some four hundred unfair labor practice charges filed by the NLRB against the company during the dispute. These charges were not only costly to adjudicate but also could have resulted in huge penalties that the company had to pay in cases where the NLRB ruled in favor of the UAW. One of Caterpillar's principal demands in the 1998 settlement— to which the UAW agreed—was dropping these unfair labor practice charges.[77]

The Future: Glen Barton's Caterpillar, 1999–

As Fites retired in February 1999, Glen Barton, a thirty-nine-year Cat veteran, assumed the company's leadership. During his first year in office, Barton lost two potential allies on the Cat Board of Directors, Glen Schaefer and Donald Fites. In January 2000, Caterpillar's Board of Directors revised the company's corporate governance guidelines to prohibit retired Cat employees from sitting on the board. The move was intended to safeguard the interests of stockholders and prevent the company's inside directors from opposing swift actions proposed by the board's outside members.[78]

Barton faced other difficulties. In 1999, Caterpillar's profits fell 37 percent to $946 million, the worst results since 1993, and its North American market, which accounted for half of Cat's sales and nearly two-thirds of its profits, was in a slump.[79]

Barton believed that the downturn in the U.S. construction market could be offset by an upturn in the international market. He thought that Caterpillar could take advantage of its global positioning to cushion the U.S. decline by increasing sales in Asia and Latin America where economies were rebounding. But being cautious, Barton also realized that he needed to ensure the future of Caterpillar in the long run. He, therefore, embarked on four growth strategies: expansion into new markets, diversification, the development of a new distribution channel, and the buildup of alliances with global competitors.

New Markets

In 1999, 80 percent of the world's population lived in developing countries, and Caterpillar's sales to developing nations accounted for only 23 percent of the total company's sales. Developing countries had limited access to water, electricity, and transportation, and therefore needed to invest in building highways, bridges, dams, and waterways. Under Barton's leadership, increased sales of Caterpillar's equipment to the developing nations of Asia, Latin America, Eastern Europe, and the Commonwealth of Independent States (the former Soviet Union) was a top strategic priority.[80]

Diversification

Just as globalization protected Caterpillar from the cyclical movements of boom and bust, so did diversification. Cat's expansion into the engine business is a case in point. In 1999, Caterpillar's overall sales fell by 6 percent, yet its engine sales rose by 5 percent. Cat's engine business itself was further diversified, with truck-engine sales making up just over one-third of all Cat's engine sales in 1999 (Exhibit 6).

Such a diversification, according to Barton, ensured the company that any future decline in truck engine sales could be offset, at least in part, by an increase in sales of non-truck engines. By 2010, Caterpillar's total engine sales were expected to double to nearly $14 billion.[81]

Of all Cat engine sales, the growth in sales of electric diesel generators—20 percent a year since 1996—had been the fastest (Exhibit 7). Caterpillar's energy business clearly benefited from the energy crisis. Large corporations, manufacturing facilities, Internet

EXHIBIT 7

Caterpillar's Sales of Power Generators

	Power Generator Sales (Billions)	Power Generator Sales as % of Total Revenues
1996	$1.2	7.3%
1997	$1.3	6.9%
1998	$1.6	7.6%
2000	$1.8	9.1%
2001	$2.3	11.4%

Source: David Barboza, "Cashing in on the World's Energy Hunger," *New York Times*, May 22, 2001.

server centers, and utility companies had installed backup diesel generators for standby or emergency use; in the nine months ending May 2001, Cat sales of mobile power modules (trailer equipped with a generator) quadrupled.[82]

The world's largest manufacturer of diesel generators, Caterpillar nevertheless faced a serious challenge in its efforts to transform itself into an ET (energy technology) company: diesel generators produced far more pollution than other sources of power. To address this problem, Barton's Caterpillar accelerated its shift toward cleaner micropower. In 2001, only 10 percent of Caterpillar's generators were powered by natural gas; in 2011, the corresponding figure was expected to climb to 50 percent.[83]

To diversify the company in still another way, Barton planned to double its farm equipment sales in five years (1999–2004).[84] In the agricultural equipment market, Caterpillar needed to compete head-to-head with the John Deere Co. and the CNH Corporation (former Case Corp. and New Holland), the leading U.S. manufacturers.

A New Distribution Channel

Under Barton's direction, Caterpillar expanded its rental equipment business, reaching a new category of customers both at home and abroad. Formerly, Caterpillar sold or rented equipment to rental centers, and these centers, in turn, rerented the equipment to end users. Rarely did Caterpillar rent directly to customers. Now Barton was making aggressive efforts to help Cat dealers diversify into rentals. Nearly half of all Cat's machines sold in North America in 2000 entered the market through the rental distribution channel, and

EXHIBIT 6

Cat Engine Sales to End Users, 1999, 2000

	1999	2000
Trucks	34%	27%
Electric Power Generators	26%	33%
Oil Drilling Equipment	20%	19%
Industrial Equipment	11%	13%
Ships and Boats	9%	8%

Source: Caterpillar Inc. 1999 Annual Report, p. 24; and 2000 Annual Report.

the fastest growing segment of the business was short-term rentals. Implemented by Barton in 1999–2000, the Cat Rental Store Program was designed to assist dealers in operating a one-stop rental shop that offered a complete line of rental equipment from heavy bulldozers and tractors, to light towers, work platforms, and hydraulic tools.[85]

Joint Ventures

Increasingly, Caterpillar had used joint ventures to expand into new markets and diversify into new products. In November 2000, Barton's Caterpillar announced a plan to form two joint ventures with DaimlerChrysler, the world's leading manufacturer of commercial vehicles. One was for building medium-duty engines; the other was for manufacturing fuel systems. The combined share of the two companies in the medium-duty engine market was only 10 percent, yet the medium-duty engine market generated worldwide sales of $10 billion annually. The sales of fuel systems were even more promising. Fuel systems were designed to increase the efficiency of diesel engines and thereby reduce diesel emissions. Participating in the two joint ventures were Cat and DaimlerChrysler plants in four U.S. states (South Carolina, Georgia, Illinois, and Michigan) and at least five other countries.[86]

EXHIBIT 8

Caterpillar: Five-Year Financial Summary

(Dollars in million except per share data)	2001	2000	1999	1998	1997
Sales and Revenues	$20,450	$20,175	19,702	20,977	18,925
Profits	$805	1,053	946	1,513	1,665
As % of Sales & Revenue	3.9%	5.2%	4.8%	7.2%	8.8%
Profits per Share	$2.35	3.04	2.66	4.17	4.44
Dividends per Share	$1,390	1.345	1,275	1.150	0.950
Return on Equity	14.4%	19.0%	17.9%	30.9%	37.9%
R&D Expenses	$898	854	814	838	700
As % of Sales & Revenue	4.4%	4.2%	4.1%	4.0%	3.7%
Wages, Salaries, & Employee Benefits	$4,272	4,029	4,044	4,146	3,773
Number of Employees	70,678	67,200	66,225	64,441	58,366
December 31					
Total assets					
Consolidated	$30,657	28,464	26,711	25,128	20,756
Machinery & Engines	$17,275	16,554	16,158	15,619	14,188
Financial Products	$15,895	14,618	12,951	11,648	7,806
Long-term debt					
Consolidated	$11,291	11,334	9,928	9,404	6,942
Machinery & Engines	$3,492	2,854	3,099	2,993	2,367
Financial Products	$7.799	8,480	6,829	6,411	4,575
Total debt					
Consolidated	$16,602	15,067	13,802	12,452	8,568
Machinery & Engines	$3,784	3,427	3,317	3,102	2,474
Financial Products	$13.021	11,957	10,796	9,562	6,338

Source: Caterpillar Inc. 2000 and 2001 Annual Reports (2000, p. 39, 2001, p. 25.)

Future Prospects

Notwithstanding their initial prospects, Barton's strategic initiatives failed to address adequately two major concerns that could have affected the company's future. One had to do with the state of labor relations, particularly Cat's employee satisfaction program, which Schaefer had introduced and Fites terminated. Implemented effectively by Schaefer, the ESP program, we have seen, contributed to increased labor productivity, improved product quality, enhanced employee satisfaction, and reduced employee absenteeism. Should Barton, then, reintroduce Cat's employee satisfaction program and thereby improve the climate of labor relations at the company's U.S. plants? Would Barton be able to cooperate closely with the local union leadership to persuade shop floor employees to join the program?

Another challenge Barton faced pertained to the impact of E-commerce. How could Caterpillar take advantage of the opportunities offered by E-commerce without undermining its distribution system? How, in other words, could Caterpillar benefit from utilizing the Internet for the marketing, distribution, and service of its products without weakening its strong dealers' networks?

ENDNOTES

1. The Caterpillar Company 1999 Annual Report, p. 39
2. Michael Arndt, "This Cat Isn't So Nimble," *Business Week*, February 21, 2000, p. 148; online, Lexis-Nexis Academic Universe; Mark Tatge, "Caterpillar's Truck-Engine Sales May Hit Some Breaking," *Wall Street Journal*, March 13, 2000.
3. Andrew Gross and David Weiss, "Industry Corner: The Global Demand for Heavy Construction Equipment," *Business Economics*, 31 no. 3 (July 1996), pp. 54–55.
4. Ibid., p. 54.
5. Ibid., p. 55.
6. Donald Fites, "Making Your Dealers Your Partners," *Harvard Business Review*, March–April 1996, p. 85.
7. U. Srinivasa Rangan, "Caterpillar Tractor Co.," in Christopher Bartlett and Sumantra Ghoshal, eds., *Transatlantic Management: Text, Cases, and Readings in Cross Border Management* (Homewood, IL.: Irwin, 1992), p. 296.
8. Fites, "Making Your Dealers Your Partners," p. 85.
9. Gross and Weiss, "Industry Corner," p. 58.
10. William L. Naumann, *The Story of Caterpillar Tractor Co.* (New York: Newcomen Society, 1977), pp. 7–9.
11. "Caterpillar Inc.," *Hoover's Handbook of American Business* 1999 (Austin: Hoover Business Press, 1999), p. 328; "The Story of Caterpillar," online, **Caterpillar.com**, accessed March 9, 2000.
12. Michael Yoshino and U. Srinivasa Rangan, *Strategic Alliances: An Entrepreneurial Approach to Globalization* (Boston: Harvard Business School Press, 1995), p. 93; Naumann, *Story of Caterpillar*, pp. 12–14; William Haycraft, *Yellow Power: The story of the Earthmoving Equipment Industry* (Urbana: University of Illinois Press, 2000), pp. 118–122, 159–167, 196–203.
13. Fites, "Making Your Dealers Your Partners," p. 94.
14. Rangan, "Caterpillar Tractor Co.," p. 304; James Risen, "Caterpillar: A Test of U.S. Trade Policy," *Los Angeles Times*, June 8, 1986, online, Lexis-Nexis, Academic Universe.
15. Cited in Kathleen Deveny, "For Caterpillar, the Metamorphosis Isn't Over," *Business Week*, August 31, 1987, p. 72.
16. Cited in Dexter Hutchins, "Caterpillar's Triple Whammy," *Fortune*, October 27, 1986, p. 91. See also Robert Eckley, "Caterpillar's Ordeal: Foreign Competition in Capital Goods," *Business Horizons*, March-April 1989, pp. 81–83.
17. James Abegglen and George Stalk, *Kaisha, the Japanese Corporation* (New York: Basic Books, 1985), pp. 62, 117–118; Yoshino and Rangan, *Strategic Alliances*, pp. 94–95; "Komatsu Ltd.," *Hoover's Handbook of World Business*, 1999, p. 320.
18. Quoted in Yoshino and Rangan, *Strategic Alliances*, p. 96.
19. Ibid., p. 97; Eckley, "Caterpillar's Ordeal," p. 84.
20. Eckley, "Caterpillar's Ordeal," p. 84; *Business Week*, August 31, 1987, p. 73; Yoshino and Rangan, *Strategic Alliances*, p. 97.
21. Ronald Henkoff, "This Cat Is Acting Like a Tiger," *Fortune*, December 19, 1988, pp. 67, 72, 76; *Business Week*, August 31, 1987, p. 73.
22. Eckley, "Caterpillar Ordeal," pp. 81, 83.
23. Quoted in *Fortune*, December 19, 1988, p. 76.
24. Eckley, "Caterpillar Ordeal," p. 84; *Fortune*, December 19, 1988, p. 76; Alex Kotlowitz, "Caterpillar Faces Shutdown with UAW," *Wall Street Journal*, March 5, 1986. Online. ABI database.
25. Barry Bearak, "The Inside Strategy: Less Work and More Play at Cat," *Los Angeles Times*, May 16, 1995. Online. Lexis-Nexis. Academic Universe.
26. *Fortune*, December 19, 1988, p. 76.
27. Brian Bremner, "Can Caterpillar Inch Its Way Back to Heftier Profits?" *Business Week*, September 25, 1989, p. 75.
28. Abegglen and Stalk, *Kaisha*, p. 118.
29. *Fortune*, December 19, 1988, pp. 72, 74; *Business Week*, September 25, 1989, p. 75.
30. Karen Auguston, "Caterpillar Slashes Lead Times from Weeks to Days," *Modern Materials Handling*, February 1990, p. 49.
31. Barbara Dutton, "Cat Climbs High with FMS," *Manufacturing Systems*, November 1989, pp. 16–22; *Business Week*, August 31, 1987, p. 73; September 25, 1989, p. 75.
32. Quoted in Auguston, "Caterpillar Slashes Lead Times," p. 49.
33. Auguston, "Caterpillar Slashes Lead Times," pp. 50–51.
34. Ibid.," pp. 49, 51.
35. *Business Week*, September 25, 1989, p. 75.
36. Yoshino and Rangan, *Strategic Alliances*, p. 98.
37. Jennifer Reingold, "CEO of the Year," *Financial World*, March 28, 1995, p. 68.
38. Quoted in "An Interview with Caterpillar Inc. Chairman and CEO Donald V. Fites," *Inter-Business Issues*, December 1992, p. 32.
39. Quoted in Tracy Benson, "Caterpillar Wakes Up," *Industry Week*, May 20, 1991, p. 36.
40. Quoted in Reingold, "CEO of the Year," p. 74.
41. Quoted in Kevin Kelly, "Caterpillar's Don Fites: Why He Didn't Blink," *Business Week*, August 10, 1992, p. 56.
42. Quoted in *Business Week*, August 10, 1992, pp. 56–57.
43. *Business Week*, August 10, 1992, p. 57.
44. Quoted in Benson, "Caterpillar Wakes Up," p. 32.
45. "An Interview with Fites," *Inter Business Issues*, p. 32.
46. Benson, "Caterpillar Wakes Up," p. 33.
47. *Business Week*, August 10, 1992, p. 56.
48. J. P. Donlon, "Heavy Metal," *Chief Executive*, September 1995, p. 50.
49. Andrew Zadoks, "Managing Technology at Caterpillar," *Research Technology Management*, January 1997, pp. 49–51. Online. Lexis-Nexis. Academic Universe.
50. *Business Week*, August 10, 1992, p. 56.

51. Donlon, "Heavy Metal," p. 50.
52. Benson, "Caterpillar Wakes Up," p. 36.
53. Fites, "Make Your Dealers Your Partners," p. 93.
54. Caterpillar Inc. 1999 Annual Report, p. 34.
55. Fites, "Make Your Dealers Your Partners." pp. 89, 91–92, 94.
56. Fites, "Make Your Dealers Your Partners," pp. 92–93.
57. Quoted in Fites, "Make Your Dealers Your Partners," p. 94, but see also pp. 90, 93.
58. Quoted in Donlon. "Heavy Metals," p. 50.
59. Quoted in Fites, "Make Your Dealers You Partners," p. 86.
60. Myron Magnet, "The Productivity Payoff Arrives," *Fortune*, June 27, 1994, pp. 82–83; Benson, "Caterpillar Wakes Up," p. 36; Fites, "Making Your Dealers Your Partners," pp. 88–89.
61. Quoted in Steven Prokesch, "Making Global Connections in Caterpillar," *Harvard Business Review*, March-April 1996, p. 89, but see also p. 88; and Donlon, "Heavy Metals," p. 50.
62. "Caterpillar's Growth Strategies," Copyright 1999. Online. **Caterpillar.com.**
63. *Wall Street Journal*, March 13, 2000; David Barboza, "Aiming for Greener Pastures," *New York Times*, August 4, 1999.
64. De'Ann Weimer, "A New Cat on the Hot Seat," *Business Week*, March 9, 1998, p. 61; *Wall Street Journal*, March 13, 2000.
65. *Business Week*, March 9, 1998; *Wall Street Journal*, March 13, 2000.
66. The quotations, in order, are from Reingold, "CEO of the Year," p. 72; Carl Quintanilla, "Caterpillar Chairman Fites to Retire," *Wall Street Journal*, October 15, 1998. Online. ABI database.
67. Quoted in Reingold, "CEO of the Year," p. 72.
68. "An Interview with Fites," *Inter Business Issues*, pp. 34–35; "What's Good for Caterpillar," *Forbes*, December 7, 1992. Online. ABI database.
69. Michael Cimini, "Caterpillar's Prolonged Dispute Ends," *Compensation and Working Conditions*, Fall 1998, pp. 5–6; Kevin Kelly, "Cat May Be Trying to Bulldoze the Immovable," *Business Week*, December 2, 1991, p. 116, "Cat vs. Labor: Hardhats, Anyone?" *Business Week*, August 26, 1991, p. 48. Lexis-Nexis. Academic Universe.
70. Michael Verespej, "Bulldozing Labor Peace at Caterpillar," *Industry Week*, February 15, 1993, p. 19. Online. ABI database.
71. "Caterpillar: Union Bull," *Economist*, January 9, 1993, p. 61. Online. Lexis-Nexis. Academic Universe; Cimini "Caterpillar's Prolonged Dispute Ends," pp. 7–9.
72. Cimini, "Caterpillar's Prolonged Dispute Ends," p. 9; Robert Rose, "Caterpillar Contract with UAW May Be Tough to Sell to Workers," *Wall Street Journal*, February 17, 1998. Online. ABI database; Reingold, "CEO of the Year," p. 72.
73. Cimini, "Caterpillar's Prolonged Dispute Ends," pp. 8–9.
74. Ibid., pp. 9–10.
75. Carl Quintanilla, "Caterpillar Touts Its Gains as UAW Battle Ends," *Wall Street Journal*, March 24, 1998; Dirk Johnson, "Auto Union Backs Tentative Accord with Caterpillar," *New York Times*, February 14, 1998.
76. Quoted in Philip Dine, "Gulf Remains Wide in Caterpillar's Home," *St. Louis Post Dispatch*, March 29, 1998. Online. Lexis-Nexis. Academic Universe. See also Cimini, "Caterpillar's Prolonged Dispute Ends," p. 11.
77. "The Caterpillar Strike: Not Over Till Its Over," *Economist*, February 28, 1998.
78. *Business Week*, February 21, 2000, p. 148.
79. *Business Week*, February 21, 2000, p. 148.
80. "Growth Strategies." www.caterpillar.com, p. 2.
81. *Wall Street Journal*, March 13, 2000.
82. David Barboza, "Cashing in on the World's Energy Hunger," *New York Times*, May 22, 2001.
83. Ibid.; "Energy Technology: Beyond the Bubble," *Economist*, April 21, 2001.
84. Heather Landy, "Putting More Cats Down on the Farm," *Chicago Sun Times*, March 28, 1999. Online. Lexis-Nexis. Academic Universe.
85. Michael Roth, "Seeing the Light," *Rental Equipment Register*, January 2000. Online. Lexis-Nexis. Academic Universe; Nikki Tait, "Cat Sharpens Claws to Pounce Again," *Financial Times*, November 8, 2000. Online. Lexis-Nexis. Academic Universe.
86. Joseph Hallinan, "Caterpillar, DaimlerChrysler Team Up," *Wall Street Journal*, November 23, 2000.

Huawei Technologies Co., Ltd.

This case was prepared by Jie Xu and Robert H. Girling, Sonoma State University.

Until quite recently, China was regarded exclusively as a world factory for inexpensive products. Its inexpensive exports, such as textiles, toys, and plastic merchandise, have occupied the majority of discount store shelves worldwide. As symbols of low price and durability, these "Made-in-China" products have also carried connotations of being low-tech.

But this is not the whole picture. As a result of China's recent rapid technological development, low-tech products are no longer the totality of this world factory. An avalanche of high-tech "Made-in-China" products, especially those in the information technology (IT) industry such as semiconductors and telecommunication equipment, have increasingly flooded into the world market and caught the world's eyes. These products, which boast not only Chinese-made but also Chinese-designed traits, have bit by bit seized market shares, which used to be monopolized by the top-tier firms in the developed countries.

Recently, noticing these products, the world began to pay attention to their creators: numerous Chinese high-tech companies. Just how were these companies able to take business from well-known multinational giants in the tough world market? This case study examines the emergence of one such example, a Chinese telecommunication company.

Huawei Technologies Co., Ltd. is China's biggest telecommunication equipment manufacturer and one of the fastest developing firms in China. Unlike most large companies in China, Huawei was never a state-owned enterprise, and unlike most Chinese high-tech firms, it was never a result of a joint-venture with a foreign multinational. It grew from a simple imported-product vendor, which just had about US$ 3,000[1] capital at the beginning. Now it is a leading international provider offering almost the full range of telecommunication equipment and network solutions. In 2003, Huawei earned an annual revenue of US$ 3.83 billion.

While multinational companies clamor for a share of the Chinese market, Huawei strives to "step out of China" and conquer overseas markets. It is getting the upper hand over its rivals not only by its low price but also by its innovation ("High-tech firms sharpen edge," 2004). Cisco Systems, the leading manufacturer of telecommunication equipment, has had to put Huawei's name on its competitors' list and has had to seriously concern itself with Huawei's market strategy (Angell, 2003). Other multinational giants such as IBM, 3Com, and Siemens have built partnerships with Huawei. Last year, it reaped US$ 1.05 billion from markets in more than forty countries, an evident growth of 90 percent over the previous year.

China's Telecommunication Industry Background

China's telecommunication industry lagged far behind the world during the central planning period (1949–1978). During that period, as an autarkic country, China seldom accepted foreign investments and concepts. In 1978, its telephone penetration rate was just thirty for every thousand people, less than

---

[1]The numerical value in this paper is based on the exchange rate of 1 USD = CYN 8.27.

one-tenth of the world average, and its number of telephone subscribers equaled that of the United States at the beginning of the twentieth century (Liu, 2001). Meanwhile, China's telecommunication equipment was made solely by the state-owned enterprises, which were directly under the monopoly of the government. In that uncontested position, the government designated the production plan and directed purchases and sales, while at the same time, the restricted development of technology caused China's telecommunication products to fall behind those of the rest of the world. In the 1970s, China was barely skilled at analog technology and transmission technology, whereas the world's advanced countries were already using digital communication products, such as switching and optical products.

Beginning in 1978 with the "Open Door Policy," China started an economic reform process. The telecommunication industry, as one of the country's most important basic industries, experienced a huge change and became a notable contributor to the nation's economy. Beginning in 1995, the industry grew at three times the growth rate of the GDP ("Comprehensive overview of China's IT industry in the past 13 years," 2002). The development of the industry within this quarter century can be broken into three periods: (1) a period of preparation, (2) a period of high-speed development, and (3) a period of globalization.

Preparation Period

This first stage began in 1978 and lasted until 1989. At the beginning of China's economic reform, inefficient telecommunication restricted the development of China's economy. For example, in 1978, even in Beijing, the capital of the country, an estimated 20 percent of long-distance phone calls could not be connected, and another 15 percent were connected only after a one-hour wait ("Shi jie dian xin fa zhan shi," 2004). To break this bottleneck, the central government decided to modernize the industry by making policies to streamline it as the first priority.

To raise capital, which would assist the improvement of the inadequate telecommunication infrastructure, a policy of collecting telephone installation fees was initiated in 1979. This policy was a critical contributor to further development of industry. Between 1979 and 1995, one-third of the investment (US$ 33 billion) in the development of infrastructure came from the collection of this installation fee (Li, 2001).

In order to rapidly close the gap with the rest of world, the government decided to introduce advanced foreign equipment and technologies. In 1982, China imported its first digitally programmed switch. Two years later, a state-owned enterprise, under the Ministry of Post and Telecommunication (MPT), working with Belgium Bell Telephone Co., founded Shanghai Bell Telephone Equipment Manufacturing Co., Ltd., the first joint venture telecommunication company to research and develop the Chinese digitally programmed switches. Subsequently, to encourage the introduction of advanced equipment, the government in 1986 reduced by half the import tariff for telecommunication products ("Wo guo tong xin ling yu gai ge fa zhan da shi ji," 2001). During the same period, domestic small private telecommunication companies began to enter the industry by importing telecommunication products and serving as dealers to telecommunication companies abroad. These changes furthered preparation of the infrastructure for the next stage.

High-Speed Development Period

During the second stage, from 1990 to 2000, the central government continued a series of reform measures to speed up the development of the infrastructure, including accelerating depreciation of equipment, increasing capital input, and reorganizing the industry's management structure. Meanwhile, a sharply increased demand pushed the industry into a leapfrogging growth.

In one of its reports to the APEC (Asian-Pacific Economic Cooperation) Information and Telecommunication Work Group at the end of the 1990s, China presented the following information:

> Qualitative changes have taken place in network technology and service level, as represented by the transition from manual to automatic operation, analog to digital technology, small to large capacity and mono- to multi-service. Optical cable, digital microwave, satellite, stored and programmed control, mobile communication, data and multimedia and other advanced technologies have been widely used on telecommunication network. Long distance communication, telephone switching and mobile communication have been digitalized. Telecommunication network is migrating to a new generation of broadband multimedia information network and overall network capability and technological level are in the front rank in the world. ("Rapidly developing China's telecommunication industry")

China set up its first long distance optical cable in 1990. In 1998, it completed the "Eight Vertical, Eight Horizontal" grillwork optical backbone project, thereby shaping its own long-distance telecommunication backbone network. By 2000, the length of nationwide optical cable reached 1.25 million km, with 286,000 km of domestic long-distance cable. During this period, China also built international optical cables with Japan and America and merged its international optical network ("Wo guo tong xin ling yu gai ge fa zhan da shi ji," 2001).

In the telecommunication service area, the central government was cognizant of the disadvantages of the old structure and worked to change this position. In 1993, to break China Telecom Corporation's (China Telecom) monopoly in the service area, the government set up another state-owned telecommunication enterprise, China United Telecommunications Corporation (China Unicom), to provide telecommunication service. In the following years, China's government strengthened the force of previous reforms by separating enterprises from the government and restructuring service sectors. The purpose of service carriers was changed from merely obeying central directives to responding to customers and seeking to satisfy the continuously increasing demands for high-quality services. In 1997 and 2000, China Unicom and China Telecom went public sequentially to improve their capital structure, thereby improving their competitive

abilities and visibility to prepare for contending with international rivals in the future. At the end of 2000, China reduced the telecommunication service fees in order to stimulate demand. Meanwhile, the first joint venture telecommunication carrier, Shanghai Xintian Telecom Co., Ltd., was established. It indicated that China's telecommunication service had begun to accept foreign rivals and become more competitive.

The huge transformation built China's position in the world's telecommunication industry. The number of fixed-line telephone subscribers became the world's second largest in 1997 and in 2000 reached 200 million with a penetration rate of about 20 per hundred (see Exhibits 1 and 2). In 1994, China began to develop GSM mobile telecommunication, and at the end of 2000, the number of mobile phone subscribers grew to become the world's second largest. Also by 2000 China had over 16 million Internet users since its introduction in 1994 (Ministry of Information Industry [MII], 2001).

Telecommunication equipment manufacturing also experienced a rapid development. Numerous foreign manufacturers have come into the Chinese market. Besides introducing advanced products and setting up joint venture companies, they poured technology and advanced management skills into launching R&D centers in China. In 1994, the Chinese R&D Center of North Telecommunications, the first foreign R&D institute in China, was established (Jiang, 2004).

EXHIBIT 1

Number of China's Telephone Subscribers 1991–2004
(Unit: Thousands)

Source: 1998–2002 telecommunication industry annual report, 2003–2004 telecommunication industry monthly report from Ministry of Information Industry (MII). **www.mii.gov.cn.** Organized by Jie Xu.

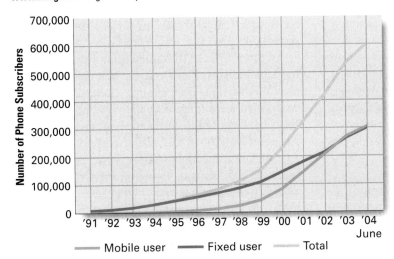

EXHIBIT 2

Telephone Penetration Rate in China from 1995–2004 June (Per hundred people)

Source: 1998–2002 telecommunication industry annual report, 2003–2004 telecommunication industry monthly report from Ministry of Information Industry (MII). **www.mii.gov.cn.** Organized by Jie Xu.

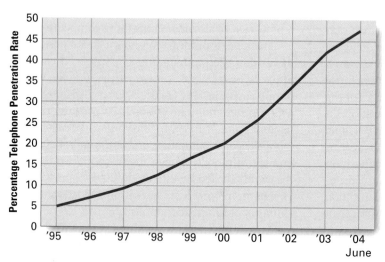

The nation's telecommunication manufacturers rapidly grew up after the first independently developed HJD-04 digitally programmed switch came out in 1991. During a short period, these manufacturers had the abilities to develop and manufacture most of the products in all telecommunication sectors, including digitally programmed switching equipment, optical cable, and mobile networks. The interaction among (a) the direct introduction of foreign telecommunication equipment and technology, (b) establishment of joint venture enterprises, and (c) the development of independent developing domestic telecommunication products catapulted China's telecommunication industry. With the maturation of domestic manufacturers, the government discontinued preferential tariffs to telecommunication equipment imports and began to encourage purchasing from domestic companies in 1996 ("Wo guo tong xin ling yu gai ge fa zhan da shi ji," 2001), which resulted in the end of China's status as an importer in the industry and gradually exportation of the equipment abroad.

Globalization Period

From 2001 to the present, China's telecommunication industry has exhibited rapid development. On December 11, 2001, China entered the WTO (World Trade Organization). According to its commitment to related WTO regulations, China has gradually opened its telecommunication provider market to other WTO members. This has included eliminating tariffs on computers, computer equipment, telecommunication equipment, semiconductors, and other high-tech products before 2005 ("WTO and opening up China's telecommunications market," 2000). To complete its legal frame for ensuring its WTO accession, in 2001, it enacted two important regulations: (1) the People's Republic of China Telecommunications Regulations and (2) the Regulations on Foreign Investment in Telecom Enterprises. It also set up provincial telecommunications administrations (PTAs) to complete its nationwide regulatory system ("The U.S. commercial service promotes U.S. exports to China," 2002).

In order to meet the competition from strong international firms, China restructured its telecommunications market. Even though China Unicom was established for a long time, the monopoly of China Telecom was not really dismantled. China Unicom's assets were just 1/260 of that of China Telecom (Li, 2001). To bring in competition in all the service segments and break the company's monopoly, the government separated China Telecom into four companies. Now, China has seven basic telecommunication carriers to carry basic telecommunication services and at least two carriers in every segment. Through optimizing the network structure and supplying all the telecommunication services, carriers have satisfied and stimulated the demands in different levels of society. As a result of these efforts, in 2001 China had the world's largest number of mobile phone users, and mobile phone users exceeded the number of fixed-line users in 2003 ("Zhong guo yi dong yong hu ju shi jie di yi," 2001). The number of Internet users in China grew to the second largest in the world (see Exhibit 3). China's telecommunications network grew to become the world's largest in 2002, and as of June 2004 had over 600 million users with a penetration rate of 47.4 percent (see Exhibits 1 and 2).

Like telecommunication service, telecommunication equipment manufacturing has also experienced an explosive development. Multinationals have adjusted their investment strategies to compete with the Chinese rivals, using methods such as acquisition and creating partnerships with indigenous companies. The domestic Chinese manufacturers have broadly introduced advanced management methods and pushed forward international cooperation, while independently developing their own products. They have strived not only to satisfy the indigenous markets but also to extend the overseas market. By the end of 2003, ten Chinese manufacturers were exporting products abroad. The total exports of digitally programmed

switches reached US$ 450 million, an increase of 81.8 percent compared with the previous year. The value of handsets exports increased to US$ 738 million, 39.4 percent more than in the previous year (MII, 2004). China's telecommunication products have won a reputation of high quality and low prices in the international market and have spread to more than forty countries and regions worldwide ("Wo guo xin xi chan yie shi xian li shi xing kua yue," 2002).

Huawei Technologies Co., Ltd. Background

At the end of the 1980s, following the period of economic reform, the Chinese government encouraged the introduction of advanced foreign telecommunication equipment to change the lagging position of its telecommunication industry. An estimated 90 percent of the equipment used in Chinese telecommunication networks came from foreign companies (Angell, 2003). Huawei Technologies Co., Ltd. was founded in Shenzhen, China's first Special Economic Zone (SEZ), in 1988. During this time, with fourteen employees and about US$ 3,000 capital, it was a vendor of imported PABX (Private Automatic Branch Exchange) systems.

EXHIBIT 3

Top Ten Countries with Highest Number of Internet Users

	Country or Region	Internet Users Latest Data	% of World Usage/Users
1	United States	201,661,159	24.80%
2	China	87,000,000	10.70%
3	Japan	66,763,838	8.20%
4	Germany	47,182,668	5.80%
5	United Kingdom	34,874,469	4.30%
6	South Korea	30,670,000	3.80%
7	Italy	28,610,000	3.50%
8	France	24,352,522	3.00%
9	Canada	20,450,000	2.50%
10	Brazil	19,311,854	2.40%
	Top Ten Countries	560,876,470	69.00%
	Rest of the World	252,055,122	31.00%
	Totals	812,931,592	100.00%

Source: Internet Usage Statistics (2004). **http://www.internetworldstats.com/ top10.htm.**

By the end of 1992, responding to the growing Chinese telecommunication market, Huawei's sales revenue had grown to US$ 12 million with profits of more than US$ 1.2 million. At this juncture, Ren Zhengfei, the founder and president of Huawei, decided to reinvest all the profits into research and development for Huawei's own digitally programmed switch. It was an unusual decision. The telecommunication equipment manufacturing required a huge capital and technological input with high risk; companies seldom wanted to take this chance. But Ren Zhengfei believed this field had a potential opportunity. Through the experience of selling imported products for several years, he noticed that, due to the scarcity of telecommunication equipment in China, the imported products sold at very high prices and earned attractive margins. If Huawei could manufacture its own products, even if they were sold cheaper than imported products, it still could gain considerable profits.

In 1993, imitating international advanced technology, Huawei released its first digitally programmed switch—2,000 ports of C&C08 switch—which could provide the basic voice switching functions. It was successfully put into commercial use in a rural county of Zhejiang province. This success transformed Huawei from a vendor of imported equipment into an independent manufacturer. Subsequently, the company continued to develop the C&C08 switching system and made it its pillar product.

In the beginning years, Huawei's product was only used in the poor, rural regions of China. Its product was not yet mature, and the capacity of the product was not adequate to meet the demands of urban telecommunication carriers. Likewise, multinational companies, which had first-mover advantage in China, had already penetrated the urban markets; the good performance and stability of their products made the telecommunication carriers unable to make the switch from imported to domestic products easily. Even so, Huawei didn't give up. It adopted the suggestion from the telecommunication carriers and experts, thereby continuously developing the C&C08 switch with a view to China's particular needs. For example, due to China's vast territory, it is important that telecommunication equipment in some remote rural villages—many of which have atrocious weather and difficult geography—should have anti-lightning and power reduction functions. Huawei worked out a solution that used fiber as a connecting method. Compared with the conventional international method,

which used cable as a connecting tool, this solution greatly reduced the cost and was applicable in the country's vast rural telecommunication markets.

In the middle of the 1990s, because of the rapid development of the industry, the urban carriers needed to extend the capacity of the telecommunication network to meet increasing demands of telephone users. They were attracted by C&C08's gradually matured performance—which had gotten the praise of its rural users—and its low price—which was just 80 percent of those of imported products—and finally chose it as the cost-effective alternative to those of multinational rivals. Therefore, Huawei's products at last entered into the profitable urban markets.

C&C08's national success was a good start. Huawei gradually extended its product lines from telephone exchange equipment to the other key telecommunication technology fields, including fiber optic networks, mobile telephone technologies, data routing systems, intelligent networks, routers, and videoconferencing, and set up sales distribution in almost every province. However, Ren Zhengfei realized that as the home market grew, it would also increasingly become tougher to compete: Cheaper domestic rivals would rapidly blossom and more foreign competitors would continue to step in. Therefore, the competition would decrease profit margins. If Huawei wanted to achieve long-term success, it should turn its eyes to the global market.

In 1996, Huawei signed its first overseas sales contract with Hutchison Global Communications Limited, Hong Kong's telecommunication carrier, consequently beginning its overseas entry.[2] Its high-quality product and service received Hutchison's praise and laid the foundation for future global exploit. But the road to conquest abroad was bumpy. Because of Huawei's obscurity in the telecommunication industry, it was hard to compete with the veteran global telecommunication giants. Ren Zhengfei realized that if Huawei were to win in the global market, it must become a multinational company first, with distinctive products and an effective management structure. Understanding this, Huawei undertook a full-range reform in 1997. Domestic and international think tanks were invited to design a highly effective organizational structure. Huawei built a market-driven R&D model

[2]Although Hong Kong returned to China on July 1, 1997, trade between Hong Kong and mainland China is still treated as international business. Investments from Hong Kong are still looked as foreign investments. Based on this designation, in this thesis, the Hong Kong market is categorized as an international market.

EXHIBIT 4

Huawei's R&D Centers Worldwide

Source: Huawei Company Profile 2004.

Research Institutes = ■ (The Silicon Valley, Dallas, Stockholm, Moscow, Bangalore, Beijing, Shanghai, Nanjing, Xi'an, Chengdu, Hangzhou)

Headquarters = ▲ (Shenzhen)

for developing customized products. In order to better understand customer demands and respond more quickly, it set up 40 branch offices, 8 regional headquarters, 4 R&D centers, and many customer support and training centers outside of China (see Exhibits 4 and 5). It also built joint laboratories with leading players, such as IBM, Intel, Motorola, and Texas Instruments (TI). In order to hasten the process to enter the developed markets, such as those in the United States, in 2003, Huawei joined with 3Com and incorporated a joint venture company: Huawei-3Com.

At the end of 2003, Huawei had 22,000 employees and was one of the world's major vendors with full-range telecommunication product manufacturing capability. It had a 40 percent share in the fixed-line switch market, as well as 55 percent of transmission equipment in the domestic market (Buckley, 2003). From 2001 to 2003, its sales of C&C08 remained first in the world switch market. In 2003, its broadband and optic network products ranked second in their respective markets ("Huawei's overseas strategy starts to pay off," 2004); more than 120 telecommunication carriers used its products worldwide ("Huawei undergoes international tests," 2004); and its sales revenue reached US$ 3.83 billion (see Exhibit 6), including US$ 1.05 billion from international markets that year.

Huawei's International Strategy

Huawei's development can be categorized in three stages. The first stage was from 1988 to 1992. During this time, as an imported telecommunication products vendor, Huawei gained a lot of experience: learning the advantages of foreign products and the Chinese market demands and also accumulating capital for a future changeover to make its own products.

The second stage was from 1993 to 1996. In this stage, Huawei imitated and followed world advanced technology to manufacture its own products. At the same time as being accepted by the domestic telecommunication carriers, it set the goal to go abroad. In 1996, it successfully entered the Hong Kong market.

EXHIBIT 5

Huawei's Overseas Branch Offices

Source: Huawei Company Profile 2004.

Headquarters = ▲ (Shenzhen)

The third stage was the global phase, beginning in 1997. While introducing the advanced management methods to restructure its internal process, Huawei had pushed its global strategy by establishing overseas R&D centers and branch offices. It also cooperated with leading industrial players by building joint laboratories and joint-venture companies to create a win-win situation. Its global process can be explained by Yip's (1990) "total global strategy" (see Exhibit 7). Huawei developed its core strategy by first opening home markets from the rural areas to urban areas. Then it extended this strategy to the international markets by opening the markets from the developing countries to developed countries. Finally it built its market-driven R&D model to integrate the strategy across countries. Its efforts to provide customers with high-quality products, sound service, and cost-effective solutions built its international reputation.

Since 1996, when it first stepped out of China, via the spread of its products worldwide, Huawei gradually became a major provider of telecommunication equipment in the industry. Its customers included AT&T, Brazil Telecom, British Telecom, Hutchison Telecom (Hong Kong), French Telecom, Rostelecom (Russia), Telefonica, and so on. Its international sales revenue increased from US$ 50 million in 1999 to US$ 128 million in 2000 and to US$ 1.05 billion in 2003.

Huawei thrives because of its high price-performance ratio, customized products, sound service, and unswerving tenacity in the international market, including these markets described below.

Hong Kong Market

Hong Kong, China's Special Administrative Region (SAR), is an important international financial center in the world. Because of its special history, as a

EXHIBIT 6

Huawei's Sales Revenue 1998–2003 (Based on
Annual Signed Contract Value)

Source: Huawei Company Profile 2004.

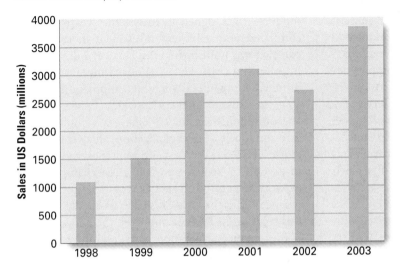

colony of the United Kingdom, this Asian city has its unique capacity for merging Eastern and Western factors. Most Mainland Chinese companies choose Hong Kong as their bridge to enter into the world market, and Huawei was no exception.

In the middle of the 1990s, as the important tool of external trade, Hong Kong's telecommunication service level and network facilities were already advanced. World famous telecommunication giants looked to Hong Kong as an important telecommunication market, and sold their latest switching products there. Telecommunication carriers competed to use the new technology, which could provide new services to attract customers.

Hutchison Global Communications Limited was a late entrant to the competitive Hong Kong telecommunication market. In 1996, it was looking for a reliable manufacturer to provide cost-effective advanced telecommunication equipment to meet its

EXHIBIT 7

Total Global Strategy

Source: Yip, G.S. (1995), *Total Global Strategy*, p. 4.

1. Develop core
   business strategy

2. Internationalize
   the strategy

3. Globalize
   the strategy

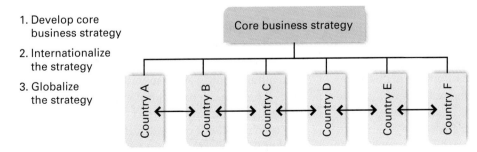

licensing requirement. After carefully comparing the numerous providers and products, it chose Huawei as its partner.

Huawei could outperform its international rivals because it not only had the ability to supply advanced cost-effective products and flexible technical support, but it also promised to support a specific workforce to provide a tailor-made solution in only half a year, which others could not. It established a technical support department in Hong Kong to respond to its customers' need and get timely feedback. To improve its service development ability, it set up a test platform there. Huawei strived to work out a solution that could help Hutchison gain the advantage in a competitive environment. After signing the contract on June 5, 1996, the first batch of equipment was delivered to Hong Kong on October 28. Two months later—on December 28—the C&C08 Switching System was applied and interconnected with the Hong Kong telecommunication network ("C&C08 EV in Hutchison IP business network," 2002).

Huawei's outstanding products made Hutchison able to support low-cost, diversified services to its customers, thereby increasing Hutchison's competitive ability and enabling it to recover its investment in only one year. Since then, Hutchison and Huawei have built a strategic partner relationship. Through several years' cooperation, Hutchison's fixed network has gradually become Hong Kong's second largest fixed network, and all the switching equipment on its network comes from Huawei ("Successful cooperation between Hutchison and Huawei," 2002). This first overseas success also built a stable foundation for further products of Huawei, such as transmission, data communication, NGN, and multimedia products, which have entered into wider telecommunication areas in Hong Kong. In 2003, the sales revenue in Hong Kong reached over US$ 56 million.

Russian Market

After successfully gaining the first foothold in Hong Kong, Huawei focused on its next target, Russia's huge potential telecommunication market. However, before the entry of Huawei, multinational giants, such as Alcatel, Lucent, and Siemens, dominated this lucrative market. At the time, the unfamiliarity of Russia to the Chinese high-tech products made Huawei's entry more difficult. When Huawei's salesmen first visited Russian telecommunication carriers, they even didn't believe China could produce switching equipment, and rejected cooperation with Huawei.

In 1997 Huawei decided to use a new method to enter the Russian market. It set up its first joint venture, Beto-Huawei, in Russia to manufacture C&C08 switches and used this joint venture (JV) platform to exploit the market. The first sales contract—US$12 million— was signed in Russia that year; however, compared with Huawei's investment in its JV, this contract was uninspiring. But Huawei didn't give up. In following years, Huawei noticed there were many different companies' switching equipment that operated in Russia's network, which made Russia's telecommunication network have a complex structure and low level of digitalization. Huawei proposed to use a LCMS (Low Cost and Multi Service) solution in its C&C08 switches to help carriers improve the network structure and get O&M (Operation & Maintenance) efficiency. Russia's carriers finally accepted this solution in 1999. It improved the network capabilities, reduced operation costs, and increased network profit. Huawei's endeavor got recognition; by 2002, the LCMS solution was used in over twenty-two administrative regions ("Network optimization application in Russia," 2002).

Coupled with rapid economic development, Russia's telecommunication industry grew quickly, thereby requiring more new services. Based on C&C08's outstanding performance, Huawei's other products were rapidly accepted by Russia's carriers and finally helped in constructing a high-end optical national "backbone." On the last day of 2002, Huawei and Rostelecom, the largest national long-haul carrier in Russia, signed a final engineering acceptance test report for the national optical "backbone" project. This project, from Moscow to Samara, had a transmission distance of up to 1021 km. It was the first time that Huawei applied its high-end optical equipment in Russia. In 2003, Huawei earned more than US$ 300 million sales revenue there ("Huawei helps Rostelecom to complete Russia's national backbone," 2003.)

West European Market

In contrast with Russia, West Europe has mature telecommunication markets. These markets have solid infrastructures and a sophisticated service structure. When the information and communication technology industry blossomed, the telecommunication carriers did not care much about costs and chose most of the products from the top telecommunication manufacturers (Bolande & Hutzler, 2002). However, at the turn of the century, the dotcom bubble collapse spread to the whole IT industry and made the industry decline. The telecommunication carriers had to be more rational and cautious when they made investments.

Besides facing the decline of the IT industry, the fixed carriers also experienced more serious tribulation than other carriers. Due to mobile communication's fast development, the number of mobile subscribers gradually exceeded that of fixed users. The decrease of fixed traffic volume resulted in a decline of revenues. The European fixed carriers, which faced the challenge of expensive operation costs and poor earnings, had to constrain their spending and needed to rebuild an effective new fixed network to cut down costs, promote broadband services, and provide customized services ("Huawei demonstrating its brand-new overall fixed network solution throughout Europe," 2004).

Emerging as a lower-cost rival to giant companies, such as Cisco System and Lucent, Huawei engaged the attention of European carriers. It responded to such changes in customers' demands rapidly and presented its SOFTX3000 IP softswitch and media gateway management systems—"21CN Fixed Line architecture." In this brand-new fixed network solution, it incorporated its latest fixed network solution, including softswitch (NGN), data communication, next generation access network (NG-AN), and IP telecommunication network. One of the big advantages of this solution was that it's a win-win strategy, not only between the telecommunication provider and carrier but also between the carrier and its customers. It lowered the operation costs, supported the full range of next-generation protocols, and formed the flexible networks, which let the customers of the carriers get cost-savings and huge capacity ("Huawei U-SYS next generation network entering into the U.K. telecommunication markets," 2004).

EEscape, one of Europe's largest telecommunication carriers and UK's first IP Network carrier, introduced this solution and used Huawei's equipment to provide the integrated voice-data-video services to its corporate and small/medium business customers in April 2004. It greatly reduces complexity and cost of operation by using MPLS (Multi Protocol Label Switching), the original infrastructure, to provide clients new voice services. Mark Lower, CEO of EEscape, claimed the cooperation with Huawei "will see new price, service and quality benchmarks for multi-sited business customers in the UK" ("EEscape deploys Huawei VOIP kit," 2004).

Huawei's International Marketing Strategy

Similar to its domestic market strategy, which occupied markets from the outlying rural areas to the central cities, Huawei's overseas market strategy was to open markets from the developing countries to the developed countries. This process also facilitated brand recognition.

Entry Strategy

Huawei first focused on entering the Asia-Pacific, Africa, East Europe, and Latin American markets. These rising markets, which had lower telephone penetration rates and lagging telecommunication infrastructure, were similar to the initial development stage of China's telecommunication industry and presented huge market potential. Huawei hoped to use its abundant experience, which it gained from China's market, to open these markets.

Although it had ambition, Huawei experienced its hardest time during the initial several years of its overseas campaign. The biggest disadvantage was that the world market knew nothing about Huawei at that time. Since a telecommunication project is an investment-style project, which involves huge capital and technology outlays, carriers could not take a risk by choosing an unknown company as a partner. Building its name recognition became a pressing affair to transform this disadvantage.

The first step was to let customers know Huawei's name. At the beginning, Huawei entered numerous international bids, even though it knew that it had no chance to get the bids. The purpose of this action was to just let the telecommunication carriers know that this Chinese company had the ability to manufacture advanced telecommunication products. Huawei's constant presence gradually got the customers' notice. But soon after connecting with customers, Huawei found another problem. The impression of China in customers' minds, which came from literature and movies, stopped several decades before, or even earlier. They thought China was still very backward in its standard of living and level of technologies. Under these conditions, it was hard to imagine that they would order several million dollars of high-tech equipment from a company from China. To change their notions, Huawei published an elaborate brochure named "Huawei in China"—a collection of China's natural scenes and modern buildings—to present China's huge transformation during economic reform. In this volume, Huawei cleverly interjected the application of its equipment in China, thereby representing its important position in China's telecommunication industry. This method renovated customers' out-of-date impressions of China and compelled them to put Huawei's name in their list of choices.

The next step was to get customers to believe Huawei's high-quality products can compete with those of the famous brands. Since 1996, Huawei began to attend international exhibitions with a high frequency. Through presenting its products with the multinationals in the same arena, Huawei let customers know about its products' advantages. Customers, who always looked down upon China's products, were astounded by Huawei's products. Those products, which used all self-designed chips, were able to carry out the similar functions to those of Western companies but were 20 to 40 percent cheaper. More important was that Huawei offered better customized solutions for its customers. Huawei's higher margins were in part attributed to its lower engineering labor cost—where one-fifth were those paid by American companies—and effective sales teams, which set up branch offices and recruited local employees worldwide. As its name became well-known, Huawei was able to enter the overseas market. In 1997, it penetrated the Russian market. In 1998, it went into the Indian market, and in 2000, it stepped into the Middle East and African markets.

Win-Win Strategy

America, dominated by the world's newer technologies, was the toughest market. Many tier-one companies, such as Cisco Systems, started up there and have absolute control there. They use enormous protocols to set a high-priced gate to enter, thereby blocking out newcomers. Ren Zhengfei realized if Huawei just depended on its own force to enter, it would be costly and problematic. A better way for Huawei would be to cooperate with an established company in possession of an established position in America and to rely on its distribution channels and well-known brand name. Thinking of this plan, Huawei attempted to form a joint venture with somebody. At the same time, 3Com, the tier-one voice and data products provider in the industry, was looking for a strategic partner that could help it complement its product lines and consolidate its position in the Asian—especially Chinese—market. These matched objectives finally let Huawei and 3Com join hands. On November 7, 2003, Huawei-3Com Co., Ltd., a joint venture of developing and manufacturing

enterprise-class networking equipment, was established in Hangzhou, China. The press release from 3Com said

> Huawei-3Com Co., Ltd., will deliver enterprise networking solutions including routers and LAN switches. 3Com has the rights to market and support the Huawei-3Com products under the 3Com brand in all countries except China and Japan. In China and Japan, Huawei-3Com will sell products sourced internally as well as from 3Com....

> Huawei is contributing to Huawei-3Com its enterprise networking business assets, including LAN switches and routers, engineering and sales/marketing resources and personnel, and licenses to its related intellectual property. 3Com is contributing $160 million in cash, assets related to its operations in China and Japan, and licenses to certain intellectual property. In two years, 3Com has the right to acquire a majority ownership interest in Huawei-3Com. (Huawei-3Com Joint Venture Begins Operations)

This cooperation was a win-win situation. It let 3Com extend its product range by adding Huawei's enterprise-class equipment in and securing its position in China and Japan; on the other hand, it let Huawei's products be branded 3Com, and through 3Com's formidable distribution network—comprising 41,000 distribution partners in areas outside China and Japan—it sped up its entry in world markets, especially those of North America ("Step to world: Huawei-3Com established," 2003). The complementary businesses have very little overlaps in product lines and regional sales channels, thereby saving the costs of new product research and market development for both companies ("3Com, Huawei join hands behind Cisco's back," 2003).

Huawei's R&D Strategy

Admittedly, having outstanding products is an extremely important factor to achieve overseas success. To a company looking for long-term development, the most important factor is whether this company can continuously invent outstanding products to meet the customers' increasing demands. Imitators can only share and occupy the existent profit space—the more imitators, the less profit to share; only the innovator can build a new profit space center and gain huge returns from it. Ren Zhengfei realized this and set a goal to make Huawei an innovator in the industry. He believed that if Huawei were to get a high return, it should have a formidable R&D capability first, because in the telecommunication industry, the advanced level of technology decides the competition's victory or defeat.

Based on this viewpoint, Huawei spent no less than 10 percent of its sales revenue on its R&D every year to specialize in designing silicon chips and developing new products. Huawei is one of the few companies in China that can design its own chip. All of its products are based on one common platform, which is supported by its own ASIC (Application Specific Integrated Circuits) chips. This core strength allowed Huawei to lower its costs dramatically: A chip bought from the West costs more than US$ 100, but a similar one designed by Huawei and produced by an American company costs less than US$ 15. In a year, Huawei uses several million self-designed chips, which means it can save more than US$ 100 million per year ("Huawei quan mian xi hua," 2004). Also, its independence ensures that Huawei can freely pursue its own research (see Exhibit 8).

To attract the cream of the employee crop and chase the latest industry trends, Huawei created thirteen R&D centers worldwide. Seven domestic centers are scattered in Shenzhen (headquarters), Beijing, Shanghai, Nanjing, Xi'an, Hangzhou, and Chengdu to gain access to their university graduates and their established economic positions in China. Meanwhile Huawei set up four overseas centers and recruited local employees. Because of America's leading position as disseminator of first-class IT technologies, Huawei set up a center in Dallas, Texas, to do the chip design. India's reputation as "the software hothouse of Asia" encouraged Huawei to set up a software center in Bangalore. Likewise, considering that Sweden is the front end of mobile technology development and Russia is the top player in the RF (Radio Frequency) area, Huawei also built centers in Stockholm and Moscow. Now Huawei has over ten thousand employees working in R&D domestically and worldwide, which is 46 percent of its

EXHIBIT 8

Huawei's Products

Source: Huawei Company Profile 2004.

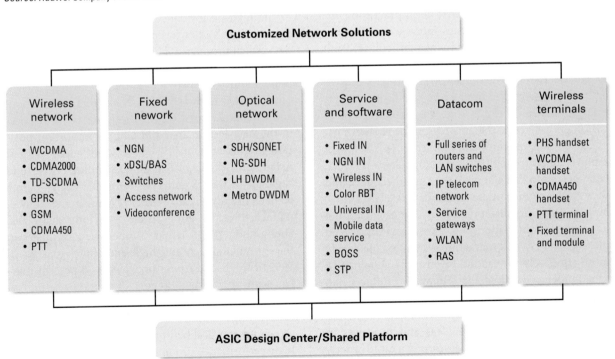

- Products are based on shared platform of technologies and self-designed ASIC chips.
- All products are TL 9000, ISO 14001 compliant as certified by DNV.

EXHIBIT 9

Huawei's Human Resources

Source: Huawei Company Profile 2004.

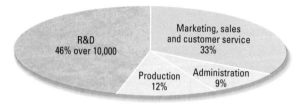

R&D
46% over 10,000

Marketing, sales
and customer service
33%

Production
12%

Administration
9%

total employees (see Exhibit 9). These employees, who are part of Huawei's fortune, are not just bright and well educated but extremely curious. Their hard work guarantees the high reliability and low cost of Huawei's products.

The high capital and work force input in R&D can produce tangible profits only when directed by the correct R&D orientation. While some of the high-tech companies concentrated too much on developing tech-savvy products, Huawei drew its product roadmap based on customer needs. It believed that the direction of innovation should be market oriented; the objective of innovation should be to forecast the market, guide consumption, and satisfy the customers' demands. Otherwise an impracticable innovation is lifeless and wastes money, even causing the company to experience finance difficulties. With this realization, Huawei builds its mission statement as "Huawei is in pursuit of realizing customers' dreams in the IT sector, and becoming a business with sustainable growth" and believes that "the enhancement of customers' interest is the only reason for Huawei's existence" ("Huawei company profile," 2004). Before it explores a new technology or develops a new product, Huawei tries to find out what the customers need and then strives to meet these needs. In 2003, Huawei rebuilt its R&D organization by turning each product line into a profit center. This transformation forced the R&D system and marketing system to collaborate more effectively to respond to customers' demands. This guideline ensured that Huawei's products had the ideal functions and price-performance ratio.

As an aggressive firm, Huawei attaches importance to learning advanced ideas and processes in order to make its own R&D develop in a more orderly and active fashion. To enhance the capability in some research areas, it has partnered with Texas Instruments, Motorola, Microsoft, Intel, Sun Micro Systems, and so on to build joint laboratories. Through cooperation, Huawei and its partner can license and cross-license their respective patents to each other.

Competitor Analysis

Cisco Systems

Cisco Systems, Inc., the worldwide leader of developing and manufacturing telecommunication and networking equipment, was established in 1984 in California. In 1990, it went public. During its peak time, the stock price reached US$ 82 per share after many splits. In its 2003 fiscal year, it had 34,466 employees and obtained a sales revenue of US$ 18.878 billion. Cisco made its first acquisition in 1993. As of July 2004, its total acquisitions numbered eighty-four companies. Through these acquisitions, Cisco Systems not only controlled numerous newer technologies and products, but also eliminated the threat that those small companies would be acquired by rivals or grow up to be rivals, thereby maintaining its dominant position. Its products, as a key factor of Internet infrastructure, have provided a broad range of solutions and have been used in corporations, public institutions, telecommunication companies, commercial businesses, and personal residences. It has a reputation for its high-performance products. Seventy-five percent of Cisco's sales revenues came from routers and data switch products ("Huawei ban dao si ke," 2004).

In 1994, Cisco Systems set up its first China branch office in Beijing. In the following years, it opened other branch offices in Shanghai, Guangzhou, and Chengdu. Based on the extension of its business in the Asia-Pacific area and China's important position in this area, in 1998 it established the largest Asian network lab in Beijing. Depending on its solid capability, Cisco Systems has been able to maintain a 50 percent growth rate of sales revenue in the Chinese market ("Na xie gong si she xian long duan zhai zhong guo," 2004). It has competitive advantages in the Ethernet switch and high-end router market. In 1999, its high-end router occupied a 78 percent market share in China ("Report of market research of network equipment in China," 2000). In recent years, even though China's domestic manufacturers have grown up and grabbed back some of the markets, its high-performance products still maintain a dominant position in China. In 2002, it owned a 60 percent share in China's data networking market (Angell, 2003). Although its router products' market share fell to 41.6 percent that year, it was still far more than the

EXHIBIT 10

Router Product Brand Distribution in China's Telecommunication Market (2003)

Source: CCID Telecommunication Market Report, February, 2004.

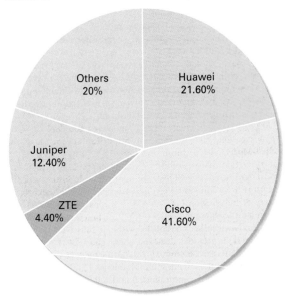

nearest Chinese rival—Huawei—which had just a 21.6 percent share (see Exhibit 10).

Zhongxing Telecom Equipment Corporation (ZTE)

ZTE Corporation was founded in 1985. Initially, it was a state-owned company and sponsored by NO. 591 Factory under former Ministry of Aerospace Industry, Changcheng Industrial Co., Ltd. and Yunxing Electronic Trading Co., Ltd. In 1997, ZTE went public. Now it is one of China's largest telecommunication equipment providers, with 17,000 employees. In 2003, its sales revenue got US$ 1.9 billion. Its products have been distributed in over forty countries, including the United States, Russia, and Zambia.

As a full-scale telecommunication equipment provider, it provides equipment for fixed, mobile, data, intelligent, optical, and next-generation networks. The main product lines include switch, access, transmission, mobile communications, PHS (Personal Handy-phone System) networks and terminals, videoconferencing, data communications, and mobile handset.

ZTE has several competitive advantages. It was the first individual manufacturer member of 3rd Generation Partnership 2 (3GPP2) in China and was an International Telecommunication Union (ITU) member ("ZTE profile," 2004). It is also a strong player in PHS.

The company seized the opportunity to develop this cheap, low-tech service's local mobile-telephone network and has become not only the leading supplier of PHS equipment, but also the big seller of PHS handsets, which sold 2.6 million in 2003 and held about 30 percent of the PHS market in China. Huawei's misstep was that it spurned involvement in this area, lost this market, and let its rivals such as ZTE get the best opportunity easily. Finally ZTE attained a sizable market share of the CDMA (Code Division Multiple Access) mobile communication system products during the past several years, as well as the reputation of "Top Chinese CDMA Brand."

The Future

Huawei has succeeded in entering into the global market as one of the world's major telecommunication manufacturers. Currently, Huawei is still developing rapidly by improving its reputation and consolidating its presence in the global market.

It is striking that Huawei never relied on the capital market. As a private company fully owned by its employees, it collected capital from issuing internal stock and getting bank loans. Its financial performance looks healthy (see Exhibit 11). However, coupled with Huawei's global extension, which continuously demands huge investments in R&D and marketing, it is important to reserve capital for potential needs. Solely depending on internal capital sources cannot satisfy these future demands. To keep its growth trend healthy for the long term, Huawei will need to raise substantial funds from an initial public offering (IPO) in the capital market. Currently, Huawei is preparing for the possibility to go public in mid-2005 ("Huawei to capitalize on international capital market," 2004).

EXHIBIT 11

Huawei's Financial Performance (2000–2003)

Year ended December 31	2000	2001	2002	2003
	(USD in millions)			
Revenue	1933	2290	2128	2694
Net Income	345	258	108	384
Cash Flow from Operations	255	204	311	385
Operating Ratio	24%	17%	10%	19%
Return on Net Assets	36%	16%	7%	20%

Source: Huawei Company Profile 2004.

To pave the way for its listing, Huawei will need to consider reorganization. Huawei may need to divide itself into several companies based on specialization. In the past sixteen years, the company grew quickly, and because of the huge structure, the company will find it difficult to respond rapidly to the dynamic market. Huawei will need to continue to offer better services to its customers to maintain its competitiveness.

Ten years ago, none of its earnings came from the overseas market. In 2003, one-third of its income was gained from the international market. By 2008, Huawei hopes to earn two-thirds of its annual revenue from the rest of the world. As the company regroups for the future, Huawei's management is considering what they would need to do to gain the confidence of foreign investors.

REFERENCES

A comprehensive overview of China's IT industry in the past 13 years. (2002, October 15). Available at: **http://web.syr.edu/~ztan/China-tel.html** (in Chinese).

Angell, M. (2003, January 29). Cisco hopes to block knock-offs produced by Chinese firm. *Investor's Business Daily,* p. A5.

Bolande, H. A., and Hutzler, C. (2002, September 24). Huawei's cost advantage spurs sales amid the telecom slump. *Wall Street Journal,* p. B7.

Buckley, C. (2003, October 6). Rapid growth of China's Huawei has its high-tech rivals on guard. *The New York Times,* p. 1.

C&C08 EV in Hutchison IP Business Network. (2002). Available at **http://www.huawei.com/products/infodetail.jsp?type=1&id=231.**

EEscape deploys Huawei VOIP kit. (2003, December 12). Available at **http://www.lightreading.com/document.asp?doc_id=44816.**

High-tech firms sharpen edge. (2004, April 14). Available at **http://0-web.lexis-nexis.com.iii1.sonoma.edu/universe/document?_m=5c101c46a289fd515636fa62624c3d8b&_docnum=2&wchp=dGLbVtz-zSkVb&_md5=4d165db124ec23379c21495343cc4cba.**

Huawei ban dao si ke. (2004). Available at **http://www.ce.cn/cysc/telecom/xwzx/gndt/200407/30/t20040730_1364341.shtml.**

Huawei C&C08 fa zhan li cheng.(2004, May 20). Available at **http://www.huawei.com/news/media/1804.shtml.**

Huawei corporate profile. (2004). Available at **http://www.huawei.com/about/Corporate/Corp-Profile/index.shtml.**

Huawei demonstrating its brand-new overall fixed network solution throughout Europe. (2004, May 17). Available at **http://www.huawei.com/about/News-Events/News-Center/947.shtml.**

Huawei helps Rostelecom to complete Russia's national backbone. (2003). Available at **http://www.huawei.com/about/News-Events/News-Center/848.shtml.**

Huawei quan mian xi hua. (2004, September 13). Available at **http://telecom.chinabyte.com/NetCom/218425681439096832/20040913/1853003_1.shtml.**

Huawei's overseas strategy starts to pay off. (2004, April 29). Available at **http://0-web.lexis-nexis.com.iii1.sonoma.edu/universe/document?_m=93d92bb6ad1ab73e42ff5d039859357a&_docnum=1&wchp=dGLbVlz-zSkVb&_md5=97ab1a985227f53c0da4bbd8b809a215.**

Huawei to capitalize on international capital market. (2004, July 27). *China Internet Weekly,* p. 1.

Huawei undergoes international tests. (2004, August 17). *The Economic Observer,* p. 1.

Huawei U-SYS next generation network entering into the U.K. telecom markets. (2003). Available at **http://www.huawei.com.cn/news/newscenter/1637.shtml.**

Huawei-3Com joint venture begins operations. (2003). Available at **http://www.3com.com/corpinfo/en_US/pressbox/press_release.jsp?INFO_ID=170570.**

Jiang, J. (2004). FDI and technology transfer in China. Available at **http://www.hhs.se/NR/rdonlyres/ezbze2zdp4jsfu7d4pbvv7keslkmhvanrcpqosyrqfiiup23kn3jlyc56o766y6lr2h24hfahbypif.**

Li, J. (2001). China's telecom industry reform. Available at **http://tech.sina.com.cn/it/t/2001-12-11/95470.shtml.**

Liu, X. (2001). Dian hua chu zhuang wei zhong guo dian xin li xia han ma gong lao. Available at **http://it.sohu.com/20010714/file/0000,643,100002.html.**

Ministry of Information Industry (MII) (China). (2001). 2000 Annual statistic report of Ministry of Information Industry. Available at **http://www.mii.gov.cn/mii/hyzw/tongji/gongbao2000.htm.**

Ministry of Information Industry (MII) (China). (2004). 2003 Annual statistic report of Ministry of Information Industry. Available at **http://www.mii.gov.cn/mii/hyzw/tongji/2004-040501.htm.**

Na xie gong si she xian long duan zhai zhong guo. (2004). Available at **http://info.news.hc360.com/HTML/001/002/009/004/47794.htm.**

Network optimization application in Russia. (2002). Available at **http://www.huawei.com/products/infodetail.jsp?type=1&id=229.**

Rapidly developing China's telecommunication industry. (2000). Available at **http://www.apectelwg.org/apecdata/telwg/24tel/plenary/12POLICY%20AND%20REGULATORY%20UPDATE%20CHINA.htm.**

Report of market research of network equipment in China. (2000). Available at **http://www.china-asean.net/china_biz/marketing_report/china_report_network.html.**

Shi jie dian xin fa zhan shi. (2004, June 30). Available at **http://news.chinabyte.com/busnews/216456456113750016/20040630/1825874.shtml.**

Step to world: Huawei-3Com established. (2003). Available at **http://industry.ccidnet.com/pub/disp/Article?articleID=41242&columnID=32.**

Successful cooperation between Hutchison and Huawei. (2002). *C&C08 and HONET in Hong Kong.* Shenzhen: Huawei.

The U.S. commercial service promotes U.S. exports to China. (2002). Available at **http://www.buyusa.gov/china/en/telecommunications.html.**

Wo guo tong xin ling yu gai ge fa zhan da shi ji. (2001). Available at **http://ydqy.cnii.com.cn/20020203/ca30945.htm.**

Wo guo xin xi chan yie shi xian li shi xing kua yue. (2002, October 16). Available at **http://news.xinhuanet.com/zhengfu/2002-10/16/content_598059.htm.**

WTO and opening up China's telecommunications market. (2000). Available at **http://www.prcinvestment.com/dtt/wto.php?id=7230.**

Yip, G.S. (1995). *Total global strategy.* New Jersey: Prentice Hall.

Zhong guo yi dong yong hu ju shi jie di yi. (2001, June 21). Available at **http://www.zaobao.com/special/newspapers/2001/06/jjckb210601.html.**

ZTE portfolio. (2004) Available at **http://www.zte.com.cn/English/01about/index.jsp.**

3Com, Huawei join hands behind Cisco's back. (2003). Available at **http://siliconvalley.internet.com/news/article.php/2119621.**

Case 8

The Home Video Game Industry: From Pong to Halo 2

This case was prepared by Charles W. L. Hill, the University of Washington.

Introduction: November 2004

On November 9, 2004, Microsoft released Halo 2, the second version of its bestselling science fiction video game for the company's Xbox console. Orders for Halo 2 were closely watched in the industry. The original Halo was the game that more than any other attracted millions of users to Microsoft's Xbox. Launched in November 2001, some 18 months after rival Sony launched PlayStation 2 (PS2), Microsoft's Xbox has trailed PlayStation 2 by a wide margin. As of mid 2004, Sony had sold some 70 million PS2 consoles worldwide, compared with 14 million Xbox consoles, and 13 million units of Nintendo's Game Cub, which was also launched in 2001. Had Microsoft not had Halo, it might well have been a distant third to Nintendo.

Could Halo 2 help close the gap between Xbox and PS2? Might Microsoft be able to ride Halo 2 into a leadership position in the industry, particularly given that all participants in the industry were busy developing a new generation of super powerful video game consoles? Dramatic leadership changes had happened before in the industry. The industry was once dominated by Atari, and then by Nintendo, which in turn lost its lead to Sega, which was subsequently overtaken by Sony with its original PlayStation console. Might Microsoft be able to seize industry leadership with the next generation gaming machine?

As first day sales for Halo 2 were totaled up, executives at Sony had to be worried. Microsoft announced that Halo 2 had sales of $125 million in its first 24 hours on the market in the United States and Canada. These figures represented sales of 2.38 million units, and put Halo 2 firmly on track to be one of the biggest video games ever with a shot at surpassing Nintendo's Super Mario 64, which had sold $308 million in the United States since its September 1996 debut.

An Industry Is Born

In 1968, Nolan Bushnell, the twenty-four-year-old son of a Utah cement contractor, graduated from the University of Utah with a degree in engineering.[1] Bushnell then moved to California, where he worked briefly in the computer graphics division of Ampex. At home, Bushnell turned his daughter's bedroom into a laboratory. There, he created a simpler version of Space War, a computer game that had been invented in 1962 by an MIT graduate student, Steve Russell. Bushnell's version of Russell's game, which he called Computer Space, was made of integrated circuits connected to a nineteen-inch black-and-white television screen. Unlike a computer, Bushnell's invention could do nothing but play the game, which meant that, unlike a computer, it could be produced cheaply.

Bushnell envisioned video games like his standing next to pinball machines in arcades. With hopes of having his invention put into production, Bushnell left Ampex to work for a small pinball company that manufactured fifteen hundred copies of his video game. The game never sold, primarily because the player had to read a full page of directions before he or she could play the game—way too complex for an arcade game. Bushnell left the pinball company, and with a friend, Ted Dabney, put up $500 to start a company that would develop a simpler video game. They wanted to call the company Syzygy, but the name was already taken, so they settled on Atari, a Japanese word that was the equivalent of "*check* in the *go*."

In his home laboratory, Bushnell built the simplest game he could think of. People knew the rules immediately, and it could be played with one hand. The game was modeled on table tennis, and players batted a ball back and forth with paddles that could be moved up and down sides of a court by twisting knobs. He named the game "Pong" after the sonarlike sound that was emitted every time the ball connected with a paddle.

In the fall of 1972, Bushnell installed his prototype for Pong in Andy Capp's tavern in Sunnyvale, California. The only instructions were "avoid missing the ball for a high score." In the first week, 1,200 quarters were deposited in the casserole dish that served for a coin box in Bushnell's prototype. Bushnell was ecstatic; his simple game had brought in $300 in a week. The pinball machine that stood next to it averaged $35 a week.

Lacking the capital to mass-produce the game, Bushnell approached established amusement game companies, only to be repeatedly shown the door. Down but hardly out, Bushnell cut his hair, put on a suit, and talked his way into a $50,000 line of credit from a local bank. He set up a production line in an abandoned roller skating rink, and he hired people to assemble machines while Led Zeppelin and the Rolling Stones were played at full volume over the speaker system of the rink. Among his first batch of employees was a skinny seventeen-year-old named Steve Jobs, who would later found a few companies of his own, including Apple Computer, NeXT, and Pixar. Like others, Jobs had been attracted by a classified ad that read "Have Fun and Make Money."

In no time at all, Bushnell was selling all the machines that his small staff could make—about ten per day—but to grow, he needed additional capital.

While the ambience at the rink, with its mix of rock music and marijuana fumes, put off most potential investors, Don Valentine, one of the country's most astute and credible venture capitalists, was impressed with the growth story. Armed with Valentine's money, Atari began to increase production and expand their range of games. New games included Tank and Breakout; the latter was designed by Jobs and a friend of his, Steve Wozniak, who had left Hewlett-Packard to work at Atari.

By 1974, 100,000 Ponglike games were sold worldwide. Although Atari manufactured only 10 percent of the games, the company still made $3.2 million that year. With the Pong clones coming on strong, Bushnell decided to make a Pong system for the home. In fact, Magnavox had been marketing a similar game for the home since 1972, although sales had been modest.[2] Bushnell's team managed to compress Atari's coin-operated Pong game down to a few inexpensive circuits that were contained in the game console. Atari's Pong had a sharper picture and more sensitive controllers than Magnavox's machine. It also cost less. Bushnell then went on a road show, demonstrating Pong to toy buyers, but he received an indifferent response and no sales. A dejected Bushnell returned to Atari with no idea of what to do next. Then the buyer for the sporting goods department at Sears came to see Bushnell, reviewed the machine, and offered to buy every home Pong game Atari could make. With Sears's backing, Bushnell boosted production. Sears ran a major television ad campaign to sell home Pong, and Atari's sales soared, hitting $450 million in 1975. The home video game had arrived.

Boom and Bust

Nothing attracts competitors like success, and by 1976, about twenty different companies were crowding into the home video game market, including National Semiconductor, RCA, Coleco, and Fairchild. Recognizing the limitations of existing home video game designs, Fairchild came out in 1976 with a home video game system capable of playing multiple games. The Fairchild system consisted of three components—a console, controllers, and cartridges. The console was a small computer optimized for graphics processing capabilities. It was designed to receive information from the controllers, process it, and send signals to a television monitor. The controllers were handheld devices used to direct on-screen action. The cartridges contained chips encoding the instructions for a game. The cartridges were designed to be inserted into the console.

In 1976, Bushnell sold Atari to Warner Communications for $28 million. Bushnell stayed on to run Atari. Backed by Warner's capital, in 1977 Atari developed and bought out its own cartridge-based system, the Atari 2600. The 2600 system was sold for $200, and associated cartridges retailed for $25 to $30. Sales surged during the 1977 Christmas season. However, a lack of manufacturing capacity on the part of market leader Atari and a very cautious approach to inventory by Fairchild led to shortages and kept sales significantly below what they could have been. Fairchild's cautious approach was the result of prior experience in consumer electronics. A year earlier it had increased demand for its digital watches, only to accumulate a buildup of excess inventory that had caused the company to take a $24.5 million write-off.[3]

After the 1977 Christmas season, Atari claimed to have sold about 400,000 units of the 2600 VCA, about 50 percent of all cartridge-based systems in American homes. Atari had also earned more than $100 million in sales of game cartridges. By this point, second-place Fairchild sold around 250,000 units of its system. Cartridge sales for the year totaled about 1.2 million units, with an average selling price of around $20. Fresh from this success and fortified by market forecasts predicting sales of 33 million cartridges and an installed base of 16 million machines by 1980, Bushnell committed Atari to manufacturing 1 million units of the 2600 for the 1978 Christmas season. Atari estimated that total demand would reach 2 million units. Bushnell was also encouraged by signals from Fairchild that it would again be limiting production to around 200,000 units. At this point, Atari had a library of nine games. Fairchild had seventeen.[4]

Atari was not the only company to be excited by the growth forecasts. In 1978, a host of other companies, including Coleco, National Semiconductor, Magnavox, General Instrument, and a dozen other companies, entered the market with incompatible cartridge-based home systems. The multitude of choices did not seem to entice consumers, however, and the 1978 Christmas season brought unexpectedly low sales. Only Atari and Coleco survived an industry shakeout. Atari lost Bushnell, who was ousted by Warner executives. (Bushnell went on to start Chuck E. Cheese Pizza Time Theater, a restaurant chain that had 278 outlets by 1981.) Bushnell later stated that part of the problem was a disagreement over strategy. Bushnell wanted Atari to price the 2600 at cost and make money on sales of software; Warner wanted to continue making profits on hardware sales.[5]

Several important developments occurred in 1979. First, several game producers and programmers defected from Atari to set up their own firm, Activision, and to make games compatible with the Atari 2600. Their success encouraged others to follow suit. Second, Coleco developed an expansion module that allowed its machine to play Atari games. Atari and Mattel (which entered the market in 1979) did likewise. Third, the year 1979 saw the introduction of three new games to the home market—Space Invaders, Asteroids, and Pac Man. All three were adapted from popular arcade games and all three helped drive demand for players.

Demand recovered strongly in late 1979 and kept growing for the next three years. In 1981, U.S. sales of home video games and cartridges hit $1 billion. In 1982, they surged to $3 billion, with Atari accounting for half of this amount. It seemed as if Atari could do no wrong; the 2600 was everywhere. About 20 million units were sold, and by late 1982, a large number of independent companies, including Activision, Imagic, and Epyx, were now producing hundreds of games for the 2600. Second-place Coleco was also doing well, partly because of a popular arcade game, Donkey Kong, which it had licensed from a Japanese company called Nintendo.

Atari was also in contact with Nintendo. In 1982, the company very nearly licensed the rights to Nintendo's Famicom, a cartridge-based video game system machine that was a big hit in Japan. Atari's successor to the 2600, the 5200, was not selling well, and the Famicom seemed like a good substitute. The negotiations broke down, however, when Atari discovered that Nintendo had extended its Donkey Kong license to Coleco. This allowed Coleco to port a version of the game to its home computer, which was a direct competitor to Atari's 800 home computer.[6]

After a strong 1982 season, the industry hoped for continued growth in 1983. Then the bottom dropped out of the market. Sales of home video games plunged to $100 million. Atari lost $500 million in the first nine months of the year, causing the stock of parent company Warner Communications to drop by half. Part of the blame for the collapse was laid at the feet of an enormous inventory overhang of unsold games. About 15 to 20 million surplus game cartridges were left over from the 1982 Christmas season (in 1981, there were none). On top of this, around 500 new games hit the market in 1993. The average price of a cartridge plunged from $30 in 1979 to $16 in 1982, and then to $4 in 1983. As sales slowed, retailers cut back on the shelf space allocated to video games. It proved difficult for new games to make a splash in a crowded market. Atari had to dispose of 6 million ET: The Extraterrestrial games. Meanwhile, big hits from previous years, such as Pac Man, were bundled with game players and given away free to try to encourage system sales.[7]

Surveying the rubble, commentators claimed that the video game industry was dead. The era of dedicated game machines was over, they claimed. Personal computers were taking their place.[8] It seemed to be true. Mattel sold off its game business, Fairchild moved on to other things, Coleco folded, and Warner decided to break up Atari and sell its constituent pieces—at least, those pieces for which it could find a buyer. No one in America seemed to want to have anything to do with the home video game business—no one, that is, except for Minoru Arakawa, the head of Nintendo's U.S. subsidiary, Nintendo of America (NOA). Picking through the rubble of the industry, Arakawa noticed that there were people who still packed video arcades, bringing in $7 billion a year, more money than the entire movie industry. Perhaps it was not a lack of interest in home video games that had killed the industry. Perhaps it was bad business practice.

The Nintendo Monopoly

Nintendo was a century-old Japanese company that had built up a profitable business making playing cards before diversifying into the video game business. Based in Kyoto and still run by the founding Yamauchi family, the company started to diversify into the video game business in the late 1970s. The first step was to license video game technology from Magnavox. In 1977, Nintendo introduced a home video game system in Japan based on this technology that played a variation of Pong. In 1978, the company began to sell coin-operated video games. It had its first hit with Donkey Kong, designed by Sigeru Miyamoto.

The Famicom

In the early 1980s, the company's boss, Hiroshi Yamauchi, decided that Nintendo had to develop its own video game machine. He pushed the company's engineers to develop a machine that combined superior graphics-processing capabilities and low cost. Yamauchi wanted a machine that could sell for $75, less than half the price of competing machines at the time. He dubbed the machine the Family Computer, or Famicom. The machine that his engineers designed was based on the controller, console, and plug in the cartridge format pioneered by Fairchild. It contained two custom chips—an 8-bit central processing unit and a graphics-processing unit. Both chips had been scaled down to perform only essential functions. A 16-bit processor was available at the time, but to keep costs down, Yamauchi refused to use it.

Nintendo approached Ricoh, the electronics giant, which had spare semiconductor capacity. Employees at Ricoh said that the chips had to cost no more that 2,000 yen. Ricoh thought that the 2,000-yen price point was absurd. Yamauchi's response was to guarantee Ricoh a 3 million chip order within two years. Since the leading companies in Japan were selling, at most, 30,000 video games per year at the time, many within the company viewed this as an outrageous commitment, but Ricoh went for it.[9] Another feature of the machine was its memory—2,000 bytes of random access memory (RAM), compared with the 256 bytes of RAM in the Atari machine. The result was a machine with superior graphics-processing capabilities and faster action that could handle far more complex games than Atari games. Nintendo's engineers also built a new set of chips into the game cartridges. In addition to chips that held the game program, Nintendo developed memory map controller (MMC) chips that took over some of the graphics-processing work from the chips in the console and enabled the system to handle more complex games. With the addition of the MMC chips, the potential for more sophisticated and complex games had arrived. Over time, Nintendo's engineers developed more powerful MMC chips, enabling the basic 8-bit system to do things that originally seemed out of reach. The engineers also figured out a way to include a battery backup system in cartridges that allowed some games to store information independently—to keep track of where a player had left off or to track high scores.

The Games

Yamauchi recognized that great hardware would not sell itself. The key to the market, he reasoned, was great games. Yamauchi had instructed the engineers, when they were developing the hardware, to make sure that "it was appreciated by software engineers." Nintendo decided that it would become a haven for game designers. "An ordinary man," Yamauchi said, "cannot develop good games no matter how hard he tries. A handful of people in this world can develop games that everyone wants. Those are the people we want at Nintendo."[10]

Yamauchi had an advantage in the person of Sigeru Miyamoto. Miyamoto had joined Nintendo at the age of twenty-four. Yamauchi had hired Miyamoto, a graduate of Kanazawa Munici College of Industrial Arts, as a favor to his father and an old friend, although he had little idea what he would do with an artist. For three years, Miyamoto worked as Nintendo's staff artist. Then in 1980, Yamauchi called Miyamoto into his office. Nintendo had started selling coin-operated video games, but one of the new games, Radarscope, was a disaster. Could Miyamoto come up with a new game? Miyamoto was delighted. He had always spent a lot of time drawing cartoons, and as a student, he had played video games constantly. Miyamoto believed that video games could be used to bring cartoons to life.[11]

The game Miyamoto developed was nothing short of a revelation. At a time when most coin-operated video games lacked characters or depth, Miyamoto created a game around a story that had both. Most games involved battles with space invaders or heroes shooting lasers at aliens; Miyamoto's game did neither. Based loosely on *Beauty and the Beast* and *King Kong*, Miyamoto's game involved a pet ape who runs off with his master's beautiful girlfriend. His master is an ordinary carpenter called Mario, who has a bulbous nose, a bushy mustache, a pair of large pathetic eyes, and a red cap (which Miyamoto added because he was not good at hairstyles). He does not carry a laser gun. The ape runs off with the girlfriend to get back at his master, who was not especially nice to the beast. The man, of course, has to get his girlfriend back by running up ramps, climbing ladders, jumping off elevators, and the like, while the ape throws objects at the hapless carpenter. Since the main character is an ape, Miyamoto called him Kong; because the main

character is as stubborn as a donkey, he called the game Donkey Kong.

Released in 1981, Donkey Kong was a sensation in the world of coin-operated video arcades and a smash hit for Nintendo. In 1984, Yamauchi again summoned Miyamoto to his office. He needed more games, this time for Famicom. Miyamoto was made the head of a new research and development (R&D) group and told to come up with the most imaginative video games ever.

Miyamoto began with Mario from Donkey Kong. A colleague had told him that Mario looked more like a plumber than a carpenter, so a plumber he became. Miyamoto gave Mario a brother, Luigi, who was as tall and thin as Mario was short and fat. They became the Super Mario Brothers. Since plumbers spend their time working on pipes, large green sewer pipes became obstacles and doorways into secret worlds. Mario and Luigi's task was to search for the captive Princess Toadstool. Mario and Luigi are endearing bumblers, unequal to their tasks yet surviving. They shoot, squash, or evade their enemies—a potpourri of inventions that include flying turtles and stinging fish, man-eating flowers and fire-breathing dragons—while they collect gold coins, blow air bubbles, and climb vines into smiling clouds.[12]

Super Mario Brothers was introduced in 1985. For Miyamoto, this was just the beginning. Between 1985 and 1991, Miyamoto produced eight Mario games. About 60 to 70 million were sold worldwide, making Miyamoto the most successful game designer in the world. After adapting Donkey Kong for Famicom, he also went on to create other top-selling games, including another classic, The Legend of Zelda. While Miyamoto drew freely from folklore, literature, and pop culture, the main source for his ideas was his own experience. The memory of being lost among a maze of sliding doors in his family's home was re-created in the labyrinths of the Zelda games. The dog that attacked him when he was a child attacks Mario in Super Mario. As a child, Miyamoto had once climbed a tree to catch a view of far-off mountains and had become stuck. Mario gets himself in a similar fix. Once Miyamoto went hiking without a map and was surprised to stumble across a lake. In the Legend of Zelda, part of the adventure is in walking into new places without a map and being confronted by surprises.

Nintendo in Japan

Nintendo introduced Famicom into the Japanese market in May 1983. Famicom was priced at $100, more than Yamauchi wanted, but significantly less than the products of competitors. When he introduced the machine, Yamauchi urged retailers to forgo profits on the hardware because it was just a tool to sell software, and that is where they would make their money. Backed by an extensive advertising campaign, 500,000 units of Famicom were sold in the first two months. Within a year, the figure stood at 1 million, and sales were still expanding rapidly. With the hardware quickly finding its way into Japanese homes, Nintendo was besieged with calls from desperate retailers frantically demanding more games.

At this point Yamauchi told Miyamoto to come up with the most imaginative games ever. However, Yamauchi also realized that Nintendo alone could not satisfy the growing thirst for new games, so he initiated a licensing program. To become a Nintendo licensee, companies had to agree to an unprecedented series of restrictions. Licensees could issue only five Nintendo games per year, and they could not write those titles for other platforms. The licensing fee was set at 20 percent of the wholesale price of each cartridge sold (game cartridges wholesaled for around $30). It typically cost $500,000 to develop a game and took around six months. Nintendo insisted that games not contain any excessively violent or sexually suggestive material and that they review every game before allowing it to be produced.[13]

Despite these restrictions, six companies (Bandai, Capcom, Konami, Namco, Taito, and Hudson) agreed to become Nintendo licensees, not least because millions of customers were now clamoring for games. Bandai was Japan's largest toy company. The others already made either coin-operated video games or computer software games. Because of these licensing agreements, they saw their sales and earnings surge. For example, Konami's earnings went from $10 million in 1987 to $300 million in 1991.

After the six licensees began selling games, reports of defective games began to reach Yamauchi. The original six licensees were allowed to manufacture their own game cartridges. Realizing that he had given away the ability to control the quality of the cartridges, Yamauchi decided to change the contract for future licensees. Future licensees were required to submit all manufacturing orders for cartridges to Nintendo. Nintendo charged licensees $14 per cartridge, required that they place a minimum order for 10,000 units (later the minimum order was raised to 30,000), and insisted on cash payment in full when the order was placed. Nintendo outsourced all manufacturing to other companies, using the volume of its orders to get rock bottom prices. The cartridges were estimated to cost Nintendo between $6 and $8 each. The licensees then picked up the cartridges from Nintendo's loading dock and were responsible for distribution. In 1985, there were seventeen licensees. By 1987, there were fifty. By this point, 90 percent of the home video game systems sold in Japan were Nintendo systems.

Nintendo in America

In 1980, Nintendo established a subsidiary in America to sell its coin-operated video games. Yamauchi's American-educated son-in-law, Minoru Arakawa, headed the subsidiary. All of the other essential employees were Americans, including Ron Judy and Al Stone. For its first two years, Nintendo of America (NOA), based originally in Seattle, struggled to sell second-rate games such as Radarscope. The subsidiary seemed on the brink of closing. NOA could not even make the rent payment on the warehouse. Then they received a large shipment from Japan: 2,000 units of a new coin-operated video game. Opening the box, they discovered Donkey Kong. After playing the game briefly, Judy proclaimed it a disaster. Stone walked out of the building, declaring that "it's over."[14] The managers were appalled. They could not imagine a game less likely to sell in video arcades. The only promising sign was that a twenty-year employee, Howard Philips, rapidly became enthralled with the machine.

Arakawa, however, knew he had little choice but to try to sell the machine. Judy persuaded the owner of the Spot Tavern near Nintendo's office to take one of the machines on a trial basis. After one night, Judy discovered $30 in the coin box, a phenomenal amount. The next night there was $35, and $36 the night after that. NOA had a hit on its hands.

By the end of 1982, NOA had sold over 60,000 copies of Donkey Kong and had booked sales in excess of $100 million. The subsidiary had outgrown its Seattle location. They moved to a new site in Redmond, a Seattle suburb, where they located next to a small but fast-growing software company run by an old school acquaintance of Howard Philips, Bill Gates.

By 1984, NOA was riding a wave of success in the coin-operated video game market. Arakawa, however, was interested in the possibilities of selling Nintendo's new Famicom system in the United States. Throughout 1984, Arakawa, Judy, and Stone met with numerous toy and department store representatives to discuss the possibilities, only to be repeatedly rebuffed. Still smarting from the 1983 debacle, the representatives wanted nothing to do with the home video game business. They also met with former managers from Atari and Caloco to gain their insights. The most common response they received was that the market collapsed because the last generation of games was awful.

Arakawa and his team decided that if they were going to sell Famicom in the United States, they would have to find a new distribution channel. The obvious choice was consumer electronics stores. Thus, Arakawa asked the R&D team in Kyoto to redesign Famicom for the U.S. market so that it looked less like a toy (Famicom was encased in red and white plastic), and more like a consumer electronics device. The redesigned machine was renamed the Nintendo Entertainment System (NES).

Arakawa's big fear was that illegal, low-quality Taiwanese games would flood the U.S. market if NES was successful. To stop counterfeit games being played on NES, Arakawa asked Nintendo's Japanese engineers to design a security system into the U.S. version of Famicom so that only Nintendo-approved games could be played on NES. The Japanese engineers responded by designing a security chip to be embedded in the game cartridges. NES would not work unless the security chips in the cartridges unlocked, or shook hands with, a chip in NES. Since the code embedded in the security chip was proprietary, the implication of this system was that no one could manufacture games for NES without Nintendo's specific approval.

To overcome the skepticism and reluctance of retailers to stock a home video game system, Arakawa decided in late 1985 to make an extraordinary commitment. Nintendo would stock stores and set up displays and windows. Retailers would not have to pay for anything they stocked for ninety days. After that, retailers could pay Nintendo for what they sold and return the rest. NES was bundled with Nintendo's best-selling game in Japan, Super Mario Brothers. It was essentially a risk-free proposition for retailers, but even with this, most were skeptical. Ultimately, thirty Nintendo personnel descended on the New York area. Referred to as the Nintendo SWAT team, they persuaded some stores to stock NES after an extraordinary blitz that involved eighteen-hour days. To support the New York product launch, Nintendo also committed itself to a $5 million advertising campaign aimed at the seven- to fourteen-year-old boys who seemed to be Nintendo's likely core audience.

By December 1985, between 500 and 600 stores in the New York area stocked Nintendo systems. Sales were moderate, about half of the 100,000 NES machines shipped from Japan were sold, but it was enough to justify going forward. The SWAT team then moved first to Los Angeles, then to Chicago, then to Dallas. As in New York, sales started at a moderate pace, but by late 1986, they started to accelerate rapidly, and Nintendo went national with NES.

In 1986, around 1 million NES units were sold in the United States. In 1987, the figure increased to 3 million. In 1988, it jumped to over 7 million. In the same year, 33 million game cartridges were sold. Nintendo mania had arrived in the United States. To expand the supply of games, Nintendo licensed the rights to produce up to five games per year to thirty-one American software companies. Nintendo continued to use a restrictive licensing agreement that gave it exclusive rights to any games, required licensees to place their orders through Nintendo, and insisted on a 30,000-unit minimum order.[15]

By 1990, the home video game market was worth $5 billion worldwide. Nintendo dominated the industry, with a 90 percent share of the market for game equipment. The parent company was, by some measures, now the most profitable company in Japan. By 1992, it was netting over $1 billion in gross profit annually, or more than $1.5 million for each employee in Japan. The company's stock market value exceeded that of Sony, Japan's premier consumer electronics firm. Indeed, the company's net profit exceeded that of all the American movie studios combined. Nintendo games, it seemed, were bigger than the movies.

As of 1991, there were over 100 licensees for Nintendo, and over 450 titles were available for NES. In the United States, Nintendo products were distributed through toy stores (30 percent of volume), mass merchandisers (40 percent of volume), and department stores (10 percent of volume). Nintendo tightly controlled the number of game titles and games that could be sold, quickly withdrawing titles as soon as interest appeared to decline. In 1988, retailers requested 110 million cartridges from Nintendo. Market surveys suggested that perhaps 45 million could have been sold, but Nintendo allowed only 33 million to be shipped.[16] Nintendo claimed that the shortage of games was in part due to a worldwide shortage of semiconductor chips.

Several companies had tried to reverse-engineer the code embedded in Nintendo's security chip, which competitors characterized as a lockout chip. Nintendo successfully sued them. The most notable was Atari Games, one of the successors of the original Atari, which in 1987 sued Nintendo of America for anticompetitive behavior. Atari claimed that the purpose of the security chip was to monopolize the market. At the same time, Atari announced that it had found a way around Nintendo's security chip and would begin to sell unlicensed games.[17] NOA responded with a countersuit. In a March 1991 ruling, Atari was found to have obtained Nintendo's security code illegally and was ordered to stop selling NES-compatible games. However, Nintendo did not always have it all its own way. In 1990, under pressure from Congress, the Department of Justice, and several lawsuits, Nintendo rescinded its exclusivity requirements, freeing up developers to write games for other platforms. However, developers faced a real problem: what platform could they write for?

Sega's Sonic Boom

Back in 1954, David Rosen, a twenty-year-old American, left the U.S. Air Force after a tour of duty in Tokyo.[18] Rosen had noticed that Japanese people needed lots of photographs for ID cards, but that local photo studios were slow and expensive. He formed a company, Rosen Enterprises, and went into the photo-booth business, which was a big success. By 1957, Rosen had established a successful nationwide chain. At this point, the Japanese economy was booming, so Rosen decided it was time to get into another business—entertainment. As his vehicle, he chose arcade games, which were unknown in Japan at the time. He picked up used games on the cheap from America and set up arcades in the same Japanese

department stores and theaters that typically housed his photo booths. Within a few years, Rosen had 200 arcades nationwide. His only competition came from another American-owned firm, Service Games (SeGa), whose original business was jukeboxes and fruit machines.

By the early 1960s, the Japanese arcade market had caught up with the U.S. market. The problem was that game makers had run out of exciting new games to offer. Rosen decided that he would have to get into the business of designing and manufacturing games, but to do that he needed manufacturing facilities. SeGa manufactured its own games, so in 1965, Rosen approached the company and suggested a merger. The result was Sega Enterprise, a Japanese company with Rosen as its CEO.

Rosen himself designed Sega's first game, Periscope, in which the objective was to sink chain-mounted cardboard ships by firing torpedoes, represented by lines of colored lights. Periscope was a big success not only in Japan, but also in the United States and Europe, and it allowed Sega to build up a respectable export business. Over the years, the company continued to invest heavily in game development, always using the latest electronic technology.

Gulf and Western (G&W), a U.S. conglomerate, acquired Sega in 1969, with Rosen running the subsidiary. In 1975, G&W took Sega public in the United States, but left Sega Japan as a G&W subsidiary. Hayao Nakayama, a former Sega distributor, was drafted as president. In the early 1980s, Nakayama pushed G&W to invest more in Sega Japan so that the company could enter the then-booming home video game market. When G&W refused, Nakayama suggested a management buyout. G&W agreed, and in 1984, for the price of just $38 million, Sega became a Japanese company once more. (Sega's Japanese revenues were around $700 million, but by now the company was barely profitable.)

Sega was caught off guard by the huge success of Nintendo's Famicom. Although it released its own 8-bit system in 1986, the machine never commanded more than 5 percent of the Japanese market. Nakayama, however, was not about to give up. From years in the arcade business, he understood that great games drove sales. Nevertheless, he also understood that more powerful technology gave game developers the tools to develop more appealing games. This philosophy underlay Nakayama's decision to develop a 16-bit game system, Genesis.

Sega took the design of its 16-bit arcade machine and adapted it for Genesis. Compared with Nintendo's 8-bit machine, the 16-bit machine featured an array of superior technological features, including high-definition graphics and animation, a full spectrum of colors, two independent scrolling backgrounds that created an impressive depth of field, and near CD quality sound. The design strategy also made it easy to port Sega's catalog of arcade hits to Genesis.

Genesis was launched in Japan in 1989 and in the United States in 1990. In the United States, the machine was priced at $199. The company hoped that sales would be boosted by the popularity of its arcade games, such as the graphically violent Altered Beast. Sega also licensed other companies to develop games for the Genesis platform. In an effort to recruit licensees, Sega asked for lower royalty rates than Nintendo, and it gave licensees the right to manufacture their own cartridges. Independent game developers were slow to climb on board, however, and the $200 price tag for the player held back sales.

One of the first independent game developers to sign up with Sega was Electronic Arts. Established by Trip Hawkins, Electronic Arts had focused on designing games for personal computers and consequently had missed the Nintendo 8-bit era. Now Hawkins was determined to get a presence in the home video game market, and aligning his company's wagon with Sega seemed to be the best option. The Nintendo playing field was already crowded, and Sega offered a far less restrictive licensing deal than Nintendo. Electronic Arts subsequently wrote several popular games for Genesis, including John Madden football and several gory combat games.[19]

Nintendo had not been ignoring the potential of the 16-bit system. Nintendo's own 16-bit system, Super NES, was ready for market introduction in 1989—at the same time as Sega's Genesis. Nintendo introduced Super NES in Japan in 1990, where it quickly established a strong market presence and beat Sega's Genesis. In the United States, however, the company decided to hold back longer to reap the full benefits of the dominance it enjoyed with the 8-bit NES system. Yamauchi was also worried about the lack of backward compatibility between Nintendo's 8-bit and 16-bit systems. (The company had tried to make the 16-bit system so that it could play 8-bit games but concluded that the cost of doing so was prohibitive.) These concerns may have led the company to delay market introduction until the 8-bit market was saturated.

Meanwhile, in the United States, the Sega bandwagon was beginning to gain momentum. One development that gave Genesis a push was the introduction of a new Sega game, Sonic the Hedgehog. Developed by an independent team that was contracted to Sega, the game featured a cute hedgehog that impatiently tapped his paw when the player took too long to act. Impatience was Sonic's central feature—he had places to go, and quickly. He zipped along, collecting brass rings when he could find them, before rolling into a ball and flying down slides with loops and underground tunnels. Sonic was Sega's Mario.

In mid 1991, in an attempt to jump-start slow sales, Tom Kalinske, head of Sega's American subsidiary, decided to bundle Sonic the Hedgehog with the game player. He also reduced the price for the bundled unit to $150, and he relaunched the system with an aggressive advertising campaign aimed at teenagers. The campaign was built around the slogan "Genesis does what Nintendon't." The shift in strategy worked, and sales accelerated sharply.

Sega's success prompted Nintendo to launch its own 16-bit system. Nintendo's Super NES was introduced at $200. However, Sega now had a two-year head start in games. By the end of 1991, about 125 game titles were available for Genesis, compared with twenty-five for Super NES. In May 1992, Nintendo reduced the price of Super NES to $150. At this time Sega was claiming a 63 percent share of the 16-bit market in the United States, and Nintendo claimed a 60 percent share. By now, Sega was cool. It began to take more chances with mass media–defined morality. When Acclaim Entertainment released its bloody Mortal Kombat game in September 1992, the Sega version let players rip off heads and tear out hearts. Reflecting Nintendo's image of their core market, its version was sanitized. The Sega version outsold Nintendo's two to one.[20] Therefore, the momentum continued to run in Sega's favor. By January 1993, there were 320 titles available for Sega Genesis and 130 for Super NES. In early 1994, independent estimates suggested that Sega had 60 percent of the U.S. market and Nintendo had 40 percent, figures Nintendo disputed.

3DO

Trip Hawkins, whose first big success was Electronic Arts, founded 3DO in 1991.[21] Hawkins's vision for 3DO was to shift the home video game business away from the existing cartridge-based format and toward a CD-ROM-based platform. The original partners in 3DO were Electronic Arts, Matsushita, Time Warner, AT&T, and the venture capital firm Kleiner Perkins. Collectively they invested over $17 million in 3DO, making it the richest start-up in the history of the home video game industry. 3DO went public in May 1993 at $15 per share. By October of that year, the stock had risen to $48 per share, making 3DO worth $1 billion—not bad for a company that had yet to generate a single dollar in revenues.

The basis for 3DO's $1 billion market cap was patented computer system architecture and a copyrighted operating system that allowed for much richer graphics and audio capabilities. The system was built around a 32-bit RISC microprocessor and proprietary graphics processor chips. Instead of a cartridge, the 3DO system stored games on a CD-ROM that was capable of holding up to 600 megabytes of content, sharply up from the 10 megabytes of content found in the typical game cartridge of the time. The slower access time of a CD-ROM compared with a cartridge was alleviated somewhat by the use of a double-speed CD-ROM drive.[22]

The belief at 3DO—a belief apparently shared by many investors—was that the superior storage and graphics-processing capabilities of the 3DO system would prove very attractive to game developers, allowing them to be far more creative. In turn, better games would attract customers away from Nintendo and Sega. Developing games that used the capabilities of a CD-ROM system altered the economics of game development. Estimates suggested that it would cost approximately $2 million to produce a game for the 3DO system and could take as long as twenty-four months to develop. However, at $2 per disc, a CD-ROM cost substantially less to produce than a cartridge.

The centerpiece of 3DO's strategy was to license its hardware technology for free. Game developers paid a royalty of $3 per disc for access to the 3DO operating code. Discs typically retailed for $40 each.

Matsushita introduced the first 3DO machine into the U.S. market in October 1993. Priced at $700, the machine was sold through electronic retailers that carried Panasonic high-end electronics products. Sega's Tom Kalinsky noted, "It's a noble effort. Some people will buy 3DO, and they'll have a wonderful experience. It's impressive, but it's a niche. We've done the research. It does not become a large market until you go below $500. At $300, it starts to get interesting. We make no money on hardware. It's a cutthroat business. I hope Matsushita understands that."[23] CD-ROM discs for the 3DO machine retailed for around $75. The machine came bundled with Crash n Burn, a high-speed combat racing game. However, only eighteen 3DO titles were available by the crucial Christmas period, although reports suggested that 150 titles were under development.[24]

Sales of the hardware were slow, reaching only 30,000 by January 1994.[25] In the same month, AT&T and Sanyo both announced that they would begin to manufacture the 3DO machine. In March, faced with continuing sluggish sales, 3DO announced that it would give hardware manufacturers two shares of 3DO stock for every unit sold at or below a certain retail price. Matsushita dropped the price of its machine to $500. About the same time, Toshiba, LG, and Samsung all announced that they would start to produce 3DO machines.

By June 1994, cumulative sales of 3DO machines in the United States stood at 40,000 units. Matsushita announced plans to expand distribution beyond the current 3,500 outlets to include the toy and mass merchandise channels. Hawkins and his partners announced that they would invest another $37 million in 3DO. By July, there were 750 3DO software licensees, but only forty titles were available for the format. Despite these moves, sales continued at a very sluggish pace, and the supply of new software titles started to dry up.[26]

In September 1996, 3DO announced that it would either sell its hardware system business or move it into a joint venture.[27] The company announced that about 150 people, one-third of the workforce, would probably lose their jobs in the restructuring. According to Trip Hawkins, 3DO would now focus on developing software for online gaming. Hawkins stated that the Internet and Internet entertainment constituted a huge opportunity for 3DO. The stock dropped $1.375 to $6.75.

Sega's Saturn

3DO was not alone in moving to a CD-ROM-based format. Both Sega and Sony also introduced CD-ROM-based systems in the mid 1990s. Sega had in fact beaten 3DO to the market with its November 1992 introduction of the Sega CD, a $300 CD-ROM add-on for the 16-bit Genesis. Sega sold 100,000 units in its first month alone. Sales then slowed down, however, and by December 1993 were standing at just 250,000 units. One reason for the slowdown, according to critics, was a lack of strong games. Sega was also working on a 32-bit CD-ROM system, Saturn, which was targeted for a mid 1995 introduction in the United States. In January 1994, Sega announced that Microsoft would supply the operating system for Saturn.[28]

In March 1994, Sega announced the Genesis Super 32X, a $150 add-on cartridge designed to increase the performance of Genesis cartridge and CD-ROM games. The 32X contained the 32-bit Hitachi microprocessor that was to be used in Saturn. Sega called the 32X "the poor man's 32-bit machine" because it sold for a mere $149. Introduced in the fall of 1994, the 32X never lived up to its expectations. Most users appeared willing to wait for the real thing, Sega Saturn, promised for release the following year.

In early 1995, Sega informed the press and retailers that it would release Saturn on "Sega Saturn Saturday, Sept 2nd," but Sega released the 32-bit Saturn in May 1995. It was priced at $400 per unit and accompanied by the introduction of just ten games. Sega apparently believed that the world would be delighted by the May release of the Saturn. However, Saturn was released without the industry fanfare that normally greets a new game machine. Only four retail chains received the Saturn in May, while the rest were told they would have to wait until September. This move alienated retailers, who responded by dropping Sega products from their stores.[29] Sega appeared to have made a marketing blunder.[30]

Sony's PlayStation

In the fall of 1995, Sony entered the fray with the introduction of the Sony PlayStation.[31] PlayStation used a 32-bit RISC microprocessor running at 33 MHz and using a double-speed CD-ROM drive. PlayStation cost an estimated $500 million to develop. The machine had actually been under development since 1991, when Sony decided that the home video game industry was getting too big to ignore. Initially, Sony was in an alliance with Nintendo to develop the machine. Nintendo walked away from the alliance in 1992, however, after a disagreement over who owned the rights to any future CD-ROM games. Sony went alone.[32]

From the start, Sony felt that it could leverage its presence in the film and music business to build a strong position in the home video game industry. A consumer electronics giant with a position in the Hollywood movie business and the music industry (Sony owned Columbia Pictures and the Columbia record label), Sony believed that it had access to significant intellectual property that could form the basis of many popular games.

In 1991, Sony established a division in New York: Sony Electronic Publishing. The division was to serve as an umbrella organization for Sony's multimedia offerings. Headed by Iceland native Olaf Olafsson, then just twenty-eight years old, this organization ultimately took the lead role in both the market launch of PlayStation and in developing game titles.[33] In 1993, as part of this effort, Sony purchased a well-respected British game developer, Psygnosis. By the fall of 1995, this unit had twenty games ready to complement PlayStation: The Haldeman Diaries, Mickey Mania (developed in collaboration with Disney), and Johnny Mnemonic, based on the William Gibson short story. To entice independent game developers such as Electronic Arts, Namco, and Acclaim Entertainment, Olafsson used the promise of low royalty rates. The standard royalty rate was set at $9 per disc, although developers that signed on early enough were given a lower royalty rate. Sony also provided approximately four thousand game development tools to licensees in an effort to help them speed games to market.[34]

To distribute PlayStation, Sony set up a retail channel separate from Sony's consumer electronics sales force. It marketed the PlayStation as a hip and powerful alternative to the outdated Nintendo and Sega cartridge-based systems. Sony worked closely with retailers before the launch to find out how it could help them sell the PlayStation. To jump-start demand, Sony set up in-store displays to allow potential consumers to try the equipment. Just before the launch, Sony had lined up an impressive 12,000 retail outlets in the United States.[35]

Sony targeted its advertising for PlayStation at males in the eighteen- to thirty-five-year age range. The targeting was evident in the content of many of the games. One of the big hits for PlayStation was Tomb Raider, whose central character, Lara Croft, combined sex appeal with savviness and helped to recruit an older generation to PlayStation.[36] PlayStation was initially priced at $299, and games retailed for as much as $60. Sony's Tokyo-based executives had reportedly been insisting on a $350 to $400 price for PlayStation, but Olafsson pushed hard for the lower price. Because of the fallout from this internal battle, in January 1996, Olafsson resigned from Sony. By then, however, Sony was following Olafsson's script.[37]

Sony's prelaunch work was rewarded with strong early sales. By January 1996, more than 800,000 PlayStations had been sold in the United States, plus another 4 million games. In May 1996, with 1.2 million PlayStations shipped, Sony reduced the price of PlayStation to $199. Sega responded with a similar price cut for its Saturn. The prices on some of Sony's initial games were also reduced to $29.99. The weekend after the price cuts, retailers reported that PlayStation sales were up by between 350 percent and 1,000 percent over the prior week.[38] The sales surge continued through 1996. By the end of the year, sales of PlayStation and associated software amounted to $1.3 billion, out of a total for U.S. sales at $2.2 billion for all video game hardware and software. In March 1997, Sony cut the price of PlayStation again, this time to $149. It also reduced its suggested retail price for games by $10 to $49.99. By this point, Sony had sold 3.4 million units of PlayStation in the United States, compared with Saturn's 1.6 million units.[39] Worldwide, PlayStation had outsold Saturn by 13 million to 7.8 million units, and Saturn sales were slowing.[40] The momentum was clearly running in Sony's favor, but the company now had a new challenge to deal with: Nintendo's latest generation game machine, the N64.

Nintendo Strikes Back

In July 1996, Nintendo launched Nintendo 64 (N64) in the Japanese market. This release was followed by a late fall introduction in the United States. N64 is a 64-bit machine developed in conjunction with Silicon Graphics. Originally targeted for introduction a year earlier, N64 had been under development since 1993. The machine used a plug-in cartridge format rather than a CD-ROM drive. According to Nintendo, cartridges allow for faster access time and are far more durable than CD-ROMs (an important consideration with children).[41]

The most-striking feature of the N64 machine, however, was its 3D graphics capability. N64 provides fully rounded figures that can turn on their heels and rotate through 180 degrees. Advanced ray tracing techniques borrowed from military simulators and engineering workstations added to the sense of realism by providing proper highlighting, reflections, and shadows.

N64 was targeted at children and young teenagers. It was priced at $200 and launched with just four games. Despite the lack of games, initial sales were very strong. Indeed, 1997 turned out to be a banner year for both Sony and Nintendo. The overall U.S. market was strong, with sales of hardware and software combined reaching a record $5.5 billion. Estimates suggest that PlayStation accounted for 49 percent of machines and games by value. N64 captured a 41 percent share, leaving Sega trailing badly with less than 10 percent of the market. During the year, the average price for game machines had fallen to $150. By year-end there were 300 titles available for PlayStation, compared with forty for N64. Games for PlayStation retailed for $40, on average, compared with over $60 for N64.[42]

By late 1998, PlayStation was widening its lead over N64. In the crucial North American market, PlayStation was reported to be outselling N64 by a two-to-one margin, although Nintendo retained a lead in the under-twelve category. At this point, there were 115 games available for N64 versus 431 for PlayStation.[43] Worldwide, Sony had now sold close to 55 million PlayStations. The success of PlayStation had a major impact on Sony's bottom line. In fiscal 1998, PlayStation business generated revenues of $5.5 billion for Sony, 10 percent of its worldwide revenues, but accounted for $886 million, or 22.5 percent, of the company's operating income.[44]

The 128-Bit Era

When Nintendo launched its 64-bit machine in 1996, Sony and Sega didn't follow, preferring instead to focus on the development of even more powerful 128-bit machines.

Sega was the first to market a 128-bit video game console, which it launched in Japan in late 1998 and in the United States in late 1999. The Dreamcast came equipped with a 56-kilobit modem to allow for online gaming over the Internet. By late 2000, Sega had sold around 6 million Dreamcasts worldwide, accounting for about 15 percent of console sales since its launch. Sega nurtured Dreamcast sales by courting outside software developers who helped develop new games, including Crazy Taxi, Resident Evil, and Quake III Arena. The company had a goal of shipping 10 million units by March 2001, a goal it never reached.[45]

Despite its position as first mover with a 128-bit machine, and despite solid technical reviews, by late 2000, the company was struggling. Sega was handicapped first by product shortages due to constraints on the supply of component parts and then by a lack of demand as consumers waited to see whether Sony's 128-bit offering, the much anticipated PlayStation 2 (PS2), would be a more attractive machine. In September 2000, Sega responded to the impending U.S. launch of Sony's PS2 by cutting the price for its console from $199 to $149. Then in late October, Sega announced that, due to this price cut, it would probably lose over $200 million for the fiscal year ending March 2001.[46]

Sony's PlayStation 2

PlayStation 2 was launched in Japan in mid 2000 and in the United States at the end of October 2000. Initially priced at $299, PlayStation 2 is a powerful machine. At its core is a 300-megahertz graphics processing chip that was jointly developed with Toshiba and consumed about $1.3 billion in R&D. Referred to as the Emotion Engine processor, the chip allows the machine to display stunning graphic images previously found only on supercomputers. The chip made the PlayStation 2 the most powerful video game machine yet.

The machine is set up to play different CD and DVD formats, as well as proprietary game titles. As is true with the original PlayStation, PlayStation 2 can play audio CDs. The system is also compatible with the original PlayStation: any PlayStation title can be played on the PlayStation 2. To help justify the initial price tag, the unit doubled as a DVD player with picture quality as good as current players. The PlayStation 2 did not come equipped with a modem, but it did have networking capabilities and a modem could be attached using one of two USB ports.[47]

Nintendo's GameCube

Nintendo had garnered a solid position in the industry with its N64 machine by focusing on its core demographic, seven- to twelve-year-olds. In 1999, Nintendo took 33 percent of the hardware market and 28 percent of the game market. Nintendo's next generation video game machine, GameCube, packed a modem and a powerful 400-megahertz, 128-bit processor made by IBM into a compact cube. GameCube marked a shift away from Nintendo's traditional approach of using proprietary cartridges to hold game software. Instead, software for the new player came on 8-centimeter compact disks, which are smaller than music compact disks. The disks hold 1.5 gigabytes of data each, far greater storage capacity than the old game cartridges. Players could control GameCube using wireless controllers.[48]

Nintendo tried to make the GameCube easy for developers to work with rather than focusing on raw peak performance. While developers no doubt appreciated this, by the time GameCube hit store shelves in late 2001, PlayStation 2 had been on the market for eighteen months and boasted a solid library of games. Despite its strong brand and instantly recognized intellectual property, which included Donkey Kong, Super Mario Brothers, and the Pokemon characters, Nintendo was playing catch up to Sony. Moreover, another new entrant into the industry launched its 128-bit offering at around the same time: Microsoft.

Microsoft's Xbox

Microsoft was first rumored to be developing a video game console in late 1999. In March 2000, Bill Gates made it official when he announced that Microsoft would enter the home video game market in fall 2001 with a console code named Xbox. In terms of sheer computing power, the 128-bit Xbox had the edge over competitors. Xbox has a 733-megahertz Pentium III processor, a high-powered graphics chip from Nvidia Corp, a built-in broadband cable modem to allow for online game playing and high-speed Internet browsing, 64 megabytes of memory, CD and DVD drives, and an internal hard disk drive. The operating system was a stripped-down version of its popular Windows system optimized for graphics-processing capabilities. Microsoft claimed that because the Xbox was based on familiar PC technology, it would be much easier for software developers to write games for, and it would be relatively easy to convert games from the PC to run on the Xbox.[49]

Although Microsoft was a new entrant to the video game industry, it was no stranger to games. Microsoft had long participated in the PC gaming industry and was one of the largest publishers of PC games, with hits such as Microsoft Flight Simulator and Age of Empires I and II to its credit. Sales of

Microsoft's PC games have increased 50 percent annually between 1998 and 2001, and the company now controls about 10 percent of the PC game market in 2001. Microsoft had also offered online gaming for some time, including its popular MSN Gaming Zone site. Started in 1996, by 2001 the website had become the largest online PC gaming hub on the Internet with nearly 12 million subscribers paying $9.95 a month to play premium games such as Asheron's Call or Fighter Ace. Nor is Microsoft new to hardware; its joysticks and game pads outsell all other brands and it has an important mouse business.

To build the Xbox, Microsoft chose Flextronics, a contract manufacturer that already made computer mice for Microsoft. Realizing that it would probably have to cut Xbox prices over time, Microsoft guaranteed Flextronics a profit margin, effectively agreeing to subsidize Flextronics if selling prices fell below a specified amount. By 2003, Microsoft was thought to be losing $100 on every Xbox sold. To make that back and turn a profit, Microsoft reportedly had to sell between six and nine video games per Xbox.[50]

Analysts speculated that Microsoft's entry into the home video game market was a response to a potential threat from Sony. Microsoft was worried that Internet-ready consoles like PlayStation 2 might take over many web-browsing functions from the personal computer. Some in the company described Internet-enabled video game terminals as Trojan horses in the living room. In Microsoft's calculation, it made sense to get in the market to try and keep Sony and others in check. With annual revenues in excess of $20 billion worldwide, the home video game market is huge and an important source of potential growth for Microsoft. Still, by moving away from its core market, Microsoft was taking a huge risk, particularly given the scale of investments required to develop the Xbox, reported to run as high as $1.5 billion.

Mortal Combat: Microsoft Versus Sony

The launch of Xbox and GameCube helped propel sales of video game hardware and software to a record $9.4 billion in 2001, up from $6.58 billion in 2000. Although both Xbox and Nintendo initially racked up strong sales, the momentum started to slow significantly in 2002. Microsoft in particular found it very difficult to penetrate the Japanese market. By September 2002, Sony had sold 11.2 million units of PS2 in the United States, versus 2.2 million units of Xbox and 2.7 million units of Nintendo's GameCube. Unable to hold onto market share in the wake of the new competition, Sega withdrew from the console market, announcing that henceforth it would focus just on developing games for other platforms.

In June 2002, Sony responded to the new entry by cutting the price for PS2 from $299 to $199. Microsoft quickly followed, cutting the price for Xbox from $299 to $199, while Nintendo cut its price from $299 to $149.[51] A year later, Sony cut prices again, this time to $179 a console. Again, Microsoft followed with a similar price cut, and in March 2004, it took the lead, cutting Xbox prices to $149. Snoy followed suit two months later.[52]

Microsoft's strategy, however, involved far more than just cutting prices. In November 2002, Microsoft announced that it would introduce a new service for gamers, Xbox Live. For $50 a year, Xbox Live subscribers with broadband connections would be able to play online enabled versions of Xbox games with other online subscribers. To support Xbox Live, Microsoft invested some $500 million in its own data centers to host online game playing.

Online game playing was clearly a strategic priority from the outset. Unlike the PS2 and GameCube, Xbox came with a built in broadband capability. The decision to make the Xbox broadband capable was made back in 1999 when less than 5 percent of U.S. homes were linked to the Internet with a broadband connection. Explaining the decision to build broadband capabilities into the Xbox at a time when rivals lacked them, the head of Xbox, Jay Allard, noted that "my attitude has always been to bet on the future, not against it."[53] While Sony's PS2 can be hooked up to the Internet via a broadband connection, doing so requires purchase of a special network adapter for $40.

By mid 2003, Xbox Live had some 500,000 subscribers, versus 80,000 who had registered to play PlayStation 2 games online. By this point in time there were 28 online games for Xbox, and 18 for PS2. By January 2004, the comparative figures stood at 50 for Microsoft and 32 for Sony. By mid 2004, Xbox Live reportedly had over 1 million subscribers, with Sony claiming a similar number of online players.[54] In May 2004, Microsoft struck a deal with Electronic Arts, the world's largest video game publisher, to bring EA games, including its bestselling Madden Football, to the Xbox Live platform. Until this point, EA had only produced live games for Sony's platform.

In spite of all these strategic moves, by late 2004 Xbox was still a distant second of PS2 in the video game market, having sold 14 million consoles against Sony's 70 million. While Sony was making good money from the business, Microsoft was registering significant losses. In fiscal 2004, Microsoft's home and entertainment division, of which Xbox is the major component, registered $2.45 billion in revenues but lost $1.135 billion. By way of contrast, Sony's game division had $7.5 billion of sales in fiscal 2004 and generated operating profits of $640 million.

Microsoft, however, indicated that it was in the business for the long term. The remarkable early success of Halo 2 suggested that the company was continuing to attract a strong following for its platform. More important perhaps, Microsoft was rumored to be ahead of Sony by as much as a year to bring the next generation video game console to market. Current reports suggest that Xbox 2, which is code named Xenon, will be on the market in time for the 2005 Christmas season, probably a full year ahead of Sony's PlayStation 3. Sony is rumored to be running into technical problems as it tries to develop PlayStation 3. To date the specifications for Xbox 2 have been kept under tight wraps.[55]

Microsoft is also trying to make it easier for developers to write games for Xbox and Xbox 2 by investing programming tools that automate many of the key software tasks. Currently it costs $5 to $10 million to develop a game, and this may double or even triple with the next round of games. Back in the early 1990s, Microsoft gained an edge over rival computer operating systems such as Apple's Macintosh and IBM's OS/2 because it developed its Visual Basic Programming Language that made it easier for developers to write applications for Windows. The increased supply of applications helped to secure a market leadership role for Windows. Now Microsoft is hoping that it can do the same in the video game industry by helping to reduce the costs of developing games for Xbox 2.[56]

ENDNOTES

1. A good account of the early history of Bushnell and Atari can be found in S. Cohen, *Zap! The Rise and Fall of Atari* (New York: McGraw-Hill, 1984).
2. Isaacs, R., "Video Games Race to Catch a Changing Market," *Business Week*, December 26, 1977, p. 44B.
3. Pagnano, P., "Atari's Game Plan to Overwhelm Its Competitors," *Business Week*, May 8, 1978, p. 50F.
4. Isaacs, R., "Video Games Race to Catch a Changing Market," *Business Week*, December 26, 1977, p. 44B.
5. Pagnano, P., "Atari's Game Plan to Overwhelm Its Competitors," *Business Week*, May 8, 1978, p. 50F; and Sheff, D., *Game Over* (New York: Random House, 1993).
6. Cohen, S., *Zap! The Rise and Fall of Atari* (New York: McGraw-Hill, 1984).
7. Kehoe, L., "Atari Seeks Way Out of Video Game Woes," *Financial Times*, December 14, 1983, p. 23.
8. Schrage, M., "The High Tech Dinosaurs: Video Games, Once Ascendant, Are Making Way," *Washington Post*, July 31, 1983, p. F1.
9. Sheff, D., *Game Over* (New York: Random House, 1993).
10. Quoted in Sheff, D., *Game Over* (New York: Random House, 1993), p. 38.
11. Sheff, D., *Game Over* (New York: Random House, 1993).
12. Golden, D., "In Search of Princess Toadstool," *Boston Globe*, November 20, 1988, p. 18.
13. Gross, N., and Lewis, G., "Here Come the Super Mario Bros.," *Business Week*, November 9, 1987, p. 138.
14. Sheff, D., *Game Over* (New York: Random House, 1993).
15. Golden, D., "In Search of Princess Toadstool," *Boston Globe*, November 20, 1988, p. 18.
16. Staff Reporter, "Marketer of the Year," *Adweek*, November 27, 1989, p. 15.
17. Lazzareschi, C., "No Mere Child's Play," *Los Angeles Times*, December 16, 1988, p. 1.
18. For a good summary of the early history of Sega, see Battle, J. and Johnstone, B., "The Next Level: Sega's Plans for World Domination," *Wired*, release 1.06, December 1993.
19. Sheff, D., *Game Over* (New York: Random House, 1993).
20. Battle, J., and Johnstone, B., "The Next Level: Sega's Plans for World Domination," *Wired*, release 1.06, December 1993.
21. For background details, see Flower, J., "3DO: Hip or Hype?" *Wired*, release 1.02, May/June 1993.
22. Brandt, R., "3DO's New Game Player: Awesome or Another Betamax?" *Business Week*, January 11, 1993, p. 38.
23. Flower, J., "3DO: Hip or Hype?" *Wired*, release 1.02, May/June 1993.
24. Jacobs, S., "Third Time's a Charm (They Hope)," *Wired*, release 2.01, January 1994.
25. Dunkin, A., "Video Games: The Next Generation," *Business Week*, January 31, 1994, p. 80.
26. Greenstein, J., "No Clear Winners, Though Some Losers; the Video Game Industry in 1995," *Business Week*, December 22, 1995, p. 42.
27. Staff Reporter, "3DO Says 'I Do' on Major Shift of Its Game Strategy," *Los Angeles Times*, September 17, 1996, p. 2.
28. Battle, J., and Johnstone, B., "The Next Level: Sega's Plans for World Domination," *Wired*, release 1.06, December 1993.
29. Greenstein, J., "No Clear Winners, Though Some Losers: The Video Game Industry in 1995," *Business Week*, December 22, 1995, p. 42.
30. Hamilton, D. P., "Sega Suddenly Finds Itself Embattled," *Wall Street Journal*, March 31, 1997, p. A10.
31. Taves, S., "Meet Your New Playmate," *Wired*, release 3.09, September 1995.
32. Kunni, I., "The Games Sony Plays," *Business Week*, June 15, 1998, p. 128.
33. Platt, C., "WordNerd," *Wired*, release 3.10, October 1995.
34. Kunni, I., "The Games Sony Plays," *Business Week*, June 15, 1998, p. 128.
35. Trachtenberg, J. A., "Race Quits Sony Just Before U.S. Rollout of Its PlayStation Video-Game System," *Wall Street Journal*, August 8, 1995, p. B3.
36. Beenstock, S., "Market Raider: How Sony Won the Console Game," *Marketing*, September 10, 1998, p. 26.

37. Trachtenberg, J. A., "Olafsson Calls It Quits as Chairman of Sony's Technology Strategy Group," *Wall Street Journal*, January 23, 1996, p. B6.

38. Greenstein, J., "Price Cuts Boost Saturn, PlayStation Hardware Sales," *Video Business*, May 31, 1996, p. 1.

39. Greenstein, J., "Sony Cuts Prices of PlayStation Hardware," *Video Business*, March 10, 1997, p. 1.

40. Hamilton, D., "Sega Suddenly Finds Itself Embattled," *Wall Street Journal*, March 31, 1997, p. A10.

41. Staff Reporter, "Nintendo Wakes Up," *The Economist*, August 3, 1996, pp. 55–56.

42. Takahashi, D., "Game Plan: Video Game Makers See Soaring Sales Now—And Lots of Trouble Ahead," *Wall Street Journal*, June 15, 1998, p. R10.

43. Takahashi, D., "Sony and Nintendo Battle for Kids Under 13," *Wall Street Journal*, September 24, 1998, p. B4.

44. Kunni, I., "The Games Sony Plays," *Business Week*, June 15, 1998, p. 128.

45. Guth, R. A., "Sega Cites Dreamcast Price Cuts for Loss Amid Crucial Time for Survival of Firm," *Wall Street Journal*, October 30, 2000, p. A22.

46. Guth, R. A., "Sega Cites Dreamcast Price Cuts for Loss Amid Crucial Time for Survival of Firm," *Wall Street Journal*, October 30, 2000, p. A22.

47. Oxford, T., and Steinberg, S. "Ultimate Game Machine Sony's PlayStation 2 Is Due on Shelves Oct. 26. It Brims with Potential—But at This Point Sega's Dreamcast Appears a Tough Competitor," *Atlanta Journal/Atlanta Constitution*, October 1, 2000, p. P1.

48. Guth, R. A., "New Players From Nintendo Will Link to Web," *Wall Street Journal*, August 25, 2000, p. B1.

49. Takahashi, D., "Microsoft's X-Box Impresses Game Developers," *Wall Street Journal*, March 13, 2000, p. B12.

50. Powers, K., "Showdown", *Forbes*, August 11, 2003, pp. 86–87.

51. *The Economist*, "Console Wars," June 22, 2002, p. 71.

52. Guth, R. A., "Game Gambit: Microsoft to Cut Xbox Price," *Wall Street Journal*, March 19, 2004, p. B1.

53. Powers, K., "Showdown", *Forbes*, August 11, 2003, pp. 86–87.

54. Taub, E., "No Longer a Solitary Pursuit: Video Games Move Online," *New York Times*, July 5, 2004, p. C4.

55. Greene, J., and Edwards, C., "Microsoft Plays Video Leapfrog," *Business Week*, May 10, 2004, pp. 44–45.

56. Guth. R. A., "Microsoft Bets Software Tools Will Spur Xbox," *Wall Street Journal*, March 24, 2004, p. B1.

Case 9

Satellite Radio: XM Versus Sirius

This case was prepared by Charles W. L. Hill, the University of Washington.

The Birth of a Market

More than anyone else, Canadian-born David Margolese was the key player in the creation of the satellite radio business. In 1978, at the tender age of twenty, Margolese dropped out of college to create a Vancouver-based paging company. He soon turned his attention to the nascent cellular telephone business. When he tried to obtain funding to establish a cellular telephone business in Canada, he was initially rebuffed by venture capitalists who told him that the industry would never amount to much. At best, they said, cellular phones would only be used by a few CEOs and diplomats. Undeterred, Margolese persisted in his fund-raising efforts. In 1980, when cellular was still little more than a dream, he convinced Ameritech to invest in his company, Cantel.

Using these funds he acquired licenses to cellular phone rights in Canada. Along the way, he joined forces with others, including Ted Rodgers of Rodgers Communications, to create what became Rogers Wireless, which by 2001 was Canada's largest cellular telephone company. In the late 1980s, while he was still just thirty-one, Margolese sold his stake for $2 billion in cash and set himself up as a venture capitalist.

It was in that capacity that Margolese met Robert Briskman, a former NASA engineer and the operations chief at Geostar, a satellite messaging company that went bankrupt in 1991. Briskman had designed the core technology for satellite radio,

called the unified S-band. He and other former Geostar employees had established a company named Satellite Radio CD to commercialize the technology, but they were without funding and needed to overcome numerous regulatory hurdles.

Initially Margolese invested just $1 million in the business, whose name was changed to CD Radio, but he soon decided that this was the best business he had ever seen. What attracted Margolese was the fact that radio programs beamed from satellite, using the unified S-band technology and digital signals, could deliver nationwide coverage and CD quality sound. Established radio was local, the quality of the analog signal was often poor, and it faded quickly outside of the local area. Moreover, the local markets served by established radio businesses were too small to support niche programming, such as stations devoted to jazz, classical music, or Reggae, but this might not be the case for a radio company that could serve a nationwide market.

However, numerous hurdles stood in the way of establishing a viable satellite radio business. It would be very expensive to put satellites into space, easily several hundred million dollars. The Federal Communication Commission (FCC) had to be persuaded to allocate radio spectrum to satellite radio. Receiving the radio signal from space would require special radios, and how could potential customers be persuaded to purchase these when they already had radios in their cars and at home? Moreover, it would be difficult to get advertisers to support a service that initially had no listeners—a classic chicken and egg problem—and without the advertisers, how would the service generate revenues?

By 1994, Margolese was estimating that satellite radio would be operational by 1997 and cost some $500 million, but CD Radio faced substantial roadblocks.

Despite lobbying from Margolese, the FCC had not yet decided if it would license radio spectrum for satellite radio. Fierce opposition from the National Association of Broadcasters (NAB), which represented existing radio stations, was slowing things down. Among other things, NAB filings with the FCC argued that satellite radio would lead to the demise of local radio service, hundreds of which would close, to the detriment of local communities that relied on AM and FM radio for important local news.

It wasn't until 1997 that the FCC finally auctioned off the spectrum for satellite radio. There were four bidders for the spectrum. The FCC decided to license two providers, creating a duopoly. CD Radio and XM Radio won the auction, paying $83.3 million and $89.8 million, respectively. Established in 1992, XM Radio was a development stage company backed by American Mobile Satellite Corp, which was itself owned by Hughes Electronics (then a subsidiary of General Motors) and McCaw Cellular. With spectrum in hand, CD Radio, which in 1999 changed its name to Sirius, and XM Radio now had to deliver on their promise to establish a nationwide satellite radio service. If they did not, the FCC would not renew the licenses when they came up for review in 2007. If not renewed, the licenses would expire on February 14, 2010.

The Radio Industry

The radio industry dates back to 1921 when the first radio station was licensed. Radio involves the transmission of sound waves, which are sent from amplitude modulated (AM) or frequency modulated (FM) stations. AM radio operates on relatively low frequencies and was the earliest broadcast service. FM radio, which was first patented in 1933, operates at much higher frequencies, but was very slow to catch on because of heavy investment by stations and listeners in AM equipment.

Radios are ubiquitous, and can be found in 99 out of 100 American households. The average number of radios per household is 5.6, including radios in cars (there are approximately 150 million radios in vehicles). Some 95.4 percent of radio owners listen to the radio during any given week. The typical adult listener tunes in for 3 hours and 12 minutes every weekday, and 5 hours 30 minutes on weekends. On a typical weekday the average person of 12 years or older spends 41.7 percent of radio listening time in a car or truck, 37.3 percent while at home, and

21 percent at work or other places. On weekends car listening jumps to 47.3 percent, home listening to 40.5 percent, and listening elsewhere falls to 12.1 percent. On average, some 13 to 17 percent of airtime every hour is devoted to advertising on FM/AM radio stations.[1]

Encouraged by broadcast deregulation, the number of radio stations in the United States increased from 10,500 in 1985 to roughly 13,000 by the end of 2001.[2] In 1996, the Telecommunications Act removed limits on the number of radio stations that a company could own in a given market (a "market" is generally defined as a discrete geographic area, such as a city or county). Prior to 1996, a company could only own 2 FM and 2 AM stations in any one market, no matter how populated that market. Under the new regulations, a company may own or operate up to 8 stations in any one market, with up to 5 in one service (AM or FM). These new rules have facilitated consolidation in the industry and led to the growth of large radio broadcasting companies that own many stations. The leader among these, Clear Channel Communications, owned 1,182 U.S. radio stations at the end of 2003, reached an audience of 180 million, and generated $3.70 billion in revenues from radio advertising.[3] The next largest radio broadcasting company in terms of revenues, Infinity Broadcasting, owned 180 radio stations, which were concentrated in the most populated markets in the United States. By 2002, the ten largest broadcasters owned about 17 percent of all U.S. stations, and accounted for over 40 percent of radio industry advertising revenues (the largest broadcasters are focused on the largest markets where advertising revenues are greater). Most analysts believe that the industry will continue to consolidate over the next few years.

Due to the limited range of their signal, radio stations focus on the market in which they are located. Radio stations earn their revenues from advertising. Advertising rates are a function of a station's ability to attract an audience that has certain demographic characteristics. Stations offer programs of a specific format in order to attract the demographic that advertisers are interested in. Popular formats include news/talk radio, rock, oldies, sports, country, or jazz. The ability of radio to offer different programs that target different demographics is a big selling point, attracting advertisers pursuing narrowly defined audiences. Also important are the number of other stations and advertising media competing

EXHIBIT 1

Radio Advertising Spending ($ billion)

Source: Standard & Poor's Industry Survey, Broadcasting and Cable Industry, July 2002.

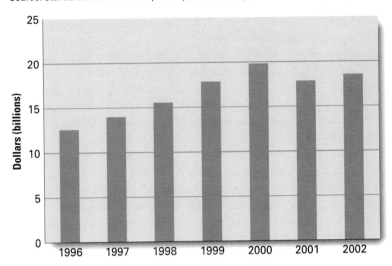

in that market. Advertising rates are normally highest during morning and evening drive-time hours.

In 2002, advertising revenues for radio stations was $18.6 billion, an increase from $12.41 billion in 1996 (see Exhibit 1). Advertising revenues dropped by almost $2 billion in 2001 compared with 2000 due to a weak national economy and the impact of September 11, 2001. The cost structure of radio broadcasters is largely fixed, making the profitability of radio stations sensitive to the overall level of advertising revenues.

The Business Plan for Satellite Radio

The Business Case

The business case for Sirius and XM was based on the argument that the number of radio stations in local markets is limited, most of these stations focus on the same five formats, and the geographic range of service is also limited with the signal fading outside of the market area. According to market data, over 48 percent of all commercial radio stations use one of only three general programming formats— country, news/talk/sports, and adult contemporary— and over 71 percent of all commercial radio stations use one of only five general formats—the same three, plus oldies and religion.[4] The small number of available

programming choices means that artists representing other niche music formats are likely to receive little or no airtime in many markets. Radio stations prefer featuring artists they believe appeal to the broadest market. Meanwhile, according to the Recording Industry Association of America, recorded music sales of niche music formats such as classical, jazz, movie and Broadway soundtracks, religious programming, new age, children's programming, and others comprised up to 27 percent of total recorded music sales in 2001.

Both Sirius and XM planned to offer around 100 channels. Sirius planned to keep 50 channels of music commercial free, while selling advertising spots on the remaining news, sports, and information channels. XM planned to have 15 to 20 channels commercial free, while limiting advertising sports to just seven minutes an hour on other channels. The channels would focus on a wide range of different music formats and news/information/talk formats. For example, XM planned to offer music channels focusing on each decade from the 1940s to the 1990s, plus contemporary music channels, several different country formats (e.g., bluegrass, Nashville), Christian rock channels, numerous news formats, information formats, and so on. Both Sirius and XM also planned to enter into agreements with established broadcasters to offer satellite radio formats of their services. These formats included MTV, VH1, CNN, the BBC, ESPN, Court TV, C-Span, and Playboy. XM also partnered with Clear Channel Communications, the largest owner of FM and AM stations in the nation, to offer Clear Channel program formats, such as the KISS pop music station, over XM Satellite radio.

To generate revenues, in addition to advertising fees both Sirius and XM decided to charge a subscription-based fee for their services that would run at around $10 to $12 per month. When it was pointed out that existing radio is offered for free to consumers, executives at Sirius and XM noted that the same is true for traditional broadcast TV, but, nevertheless, consumers have been more than willing to pay a monthly subscription fee for cable TV service and satellite TV service. Penetration data relating to cable, satellite television, and premium movie channels suggest that consumers are willing to pay for services that expand programming choice or enhance quality. There were more than 22.9 million digital cable subscribers and 22.3 million satellite television subscribers in early 2004. As of 2004, some 69 percent of TV households subscribed to basic cable television, and 20 percent of TV households subscribed to satellite television.[5]

Infrastructure

Although the technology used by Sirius and XM Radio differs in important ways, both companies followed the same basic business plan. Sirius and XM decided to place satellites in orbit to serve the United States. Sirius planned to put three satellites in elliptical orbits 23,000 miles above the earth, while XM planned to put a pair of more powerful satellites in geostationary orbits at 22,300 miles. The satellites were expected to have a useful life of up to fifteen years. Both Sirius and XM planned to keep a spare satellite in storage that could be launched quickly in the event of failure of one of their satellites. If an orbiting satellite were to fail, it would take approximately six months to get a replacement satellite into space. Service would be partially interrupted during this time. Initial plans called for Sirius to launch its satellites in 1999 and XM in 2000, with service starting soon thereafter.

The satellites broadcast a digital signal that can be converted into CD quality sound by radios fitted with the appropriate chip set and receivers that decode, decompress, and output digital signals from a satellite. The S-band signal used by both companies can be picked up by moving vehicles and will not be "weathered out" by dense cloud cover. The radios were expected to cost between $200 and $400. Since the digital signal cannot be picked up by a standard radio, this required the customer to invest in new radio equipment.

At least initially, a radio with a Sirius receiver would not pick up XM Radio, and vice versa. On February 16, 2000, XM and Sirius signed an agreement to develop a unified standard for satellite radios, enabling consumers to purchase one radio capable of receiving both Sirius and XM services. The technology relating to this unified standard was jointly developed and funded by the two companies that share ownership. The unified standard was mandated by the FCC, which required interoperability with both licensed satellite radio systems. Radios based on the unified standard started to become available at the end of 2004.

To offer truly seamless nationwide coverage, satellites alone would not be enough. To receive a satellite signal, a clear line of sight is needed. In tunnels, buildings, and the urban canyons of American cities, a clear line of sight is not available. To solve this problem, both companies had plans to build a nationwide network of terrestrial repeaters. Sirius initially planned to put up 105 repeaters in 42 cities, and XM some 1,700 repeaters in about 70 cities. Sirius could get away with fewer repeaters because the orbits of its satellites allowed for a better coverage of the United States—but to get that Sirius had to put three satellites in space, not two, placing them in figure 8 orbits that have 2 of the 3 satellites high in the sky over North America at any time during the day. In contrast, XM Radio's two satellites are in geostationary orbits. The chipsets required to pick up Sirius signals are more expensive than those for XM Radio.

In addition to satellites and repeaters, the third infrastructure element required to offer the service is recording studios. XM established three recording studios, one in Washington, D.C., one in New York City, and one in Nashville. Taken together, the three studios comprise an all digital radio complex that is one of the largest in the world with over eighty soundproof studios of different configurations. Sirius built a single studio complex in New York City.

By mid 2000, Sirius was expecting to spend $1.2 billion and XM Radio $1.1 billion to develop this infrastructure. These estimates had increased considerably from the initial estimates made in the mid 1990s, which were around $500 million. Given the infrastructure, operational, and advertising costs, the companies estimated that they needed to have 2 to 3 million subscribers each to make a profit. In 2000, forecasts by market research agencies and securities analysts suggested that in total, satellite radio could have as many as 15 million subscribers by 2006, 36 million by 2010, and around 50 million by 2014.[6]

Distribution

Both Sirius and XM believe that installation in cars and trucks was likely to drive early growth for satellite radio. In the early 2000s, 17 to 18 million new cars and light trucks were sold in the United States each year. Some 30 million car radios were sold, either embedded in new cars or in the aftermarket. In total there were over 210 million vehicles on American roads. Both companies made deals with major automobile manufacturers to have satellite radios installed in new cars as optional—and ultimately standard—equipment. The price of the radio is embedded in the price of the car, with the customer signing up for service at the time of purchase. XM has an exclusive deal with General Motors and Honda, and Sirius with Ford and DaimlerChrysler. Both companies have now entered into an agreement with the FCC under which they have agreed to refrain from making any more exclusive deals. Plans called for satellite radio to be offered as an option on certain models, with the offering to be increased to more models over time.

The exclusive deals with automobile companies do not come cheap. As part of its deal with Daimler-Chrysler, Sirius reimbursed DaimlerChrysler for some advertising expenses and hardware costs, and issued to DaimlerChrysler Corporation a warrant to purchase 4 million shares of Sirius common stock at an exercise price of $3 per share. The deal with Ford was very similar. The deal between Sirius and Daimler-Chrysler expires in October 2007, while the Ford deal expires May 2007.

The agreement between XM and General Motors requires XM to guarantee annual, fixed payment obligations to GM. However, the agreement is subject to renegotiation if General Motors does not achieve and maintain specified installation levels, starting with 1,240,000 by November 2005 and installations of 600,000 per year thereafter. The GM agreement expires September 2013. For its part, Honda has committed to shipping 400,000 cars with XM Radios in 2005.

The companies also lined up manufacturers of aftermarket car receivers and signed retail arrangements with the Best Buy and Circuit City chains to distribute them.

Capital Requirements and Investors

Financing these two ventures was not trivial. XM Radio raised some $2.6 billion equity and debt proceeds through January 2004 from investors and strategic partners to fund its infrastructure build out and operations. The strategic investors in XM Radio included General Motors, Hughes Electronics/DIRECTV, Clear Channel Communications, American Honda, and Hearst Communications. Financial investors in XM included Columbia Capital, Madison Dearborn Partners, AEA Investors, BayStar Capital, and Eastbourne Capital. XM Radio went public in late 1999. Honda and General Motors are major investors in XM Radio, with stakes of 13 percent and 8.6 percent, respectively, in late 2004.[7] Similarly, Sirius, which went public in 1995, had raised around $2.5 billion by 2004.

Much of the funds raised went into building out the infrastructure. At the end of 2003, XM Radio reported that it had spent $470 million to put its two satellites in orbit and purchase a spare satellite, $267 million to set up a system of ground repeaters covering 60 cities, and $130 million on satellite control facilities and studios. Sirius is believed to have spent similar amounts.

Competition

Satellite radio faces competition from three main sources. Traditional AM/FM radio stations are obvious competitors. The big advantage of AM/FM radio is its local content, such as local news, sports, and weather, which listeners do want. Although AM/FM radio is predominantly local, the emergence of consolidators such as Clear Channel Communications is beginning to change this. Clear Channel has made an effort to realize scale economies by developing a nationwide branded format for radio shows, most notably its pop format that goes under the KISS brand. KISS offers standard programming developed in a national studio. Local content such as news, weather, sports, and some dialogue is spliced into KISS programming to make it seem as if the broadcast is local.[8] There are also signs that traditional AM/FM radio will ultimately move toward digital broadcasting, although doing so will require that consumers purchase radios capable of receiving a digital signal.

Internet radio is a second potential competitor. A number of FM and AM radio stations are now broadcasting digital signals over the Internet that can be accessed anywhere in the world for users with the appropriate equipment (a computer, Internet connection, and media player).

A third competitor comes in the form of satellite TV and cable TV systems. Both satellite and cable TV providers are offering digital radio services as part of a package of digital services, with the radio being bundled with TV service, typically at no additional cost to the consumer.

Launching the Services

Initially Sirius was thought to have the lead over XM Radio, but this changed when technical problems with the chip sets to go in the radio receivers delayed the launch of Sirius's service for two years (the receivers, which were built by Lucent, did a poor job of picking up the digital signal and had to be redesigned).

XM Radio also had some delays due to problems with the Boeing rockets that were to launch its satellites, but was able to launch its two satellites—named "Rock" and "Roll" in early 2001, more than a year behind its initial schedule. XM started offering national service in November 2001 for a monthly fee of $9.95. XM Radio's launch was supported by an advertising campaign that was in excess of $100 million.

Beset by technical problems, Sirius did not launch its final satellite until early 2002 and did not start offering service until July 2002. Sirius charged $12.95 a month, justifying its price premium over XM by the fact that all of Sirius's 60 music channels run without commercials. XM has limited commercials of about two minutes per hour on 35 of its 70 music channels (see Exhibit 2 for a comparison between XM and Sirius). Sirius has stated that it will depend upon subscriptions for about 85 percent of its revenue. XM initially expected to rely somewhat more on advertising revenues.

By the end of 2003, Sirius had 133 terrestrial repeaters in 92 urban markets where high buildings interfere with line of sight. XM had some 800 repeaters in 60 markets.

The nine-month lead that XM gained as a result of Sirius's technical problems proved to be invaluable. By the end of 2002, XM had 347,000 subscribers, while Sirius had just 30,000. XM passed the 500,000 subscriber milestone in April 2003 and was projecting that it would end 2003 with over 1 million subscribers. This rapid subscriber accrual helped XM Radio sell faster than CD and DVD players did in their first year on the market.[9] Sirius, meanwhile, was aiming to end 2003 with some 300,000 subscribers and had just over 100,000 by midyear. Both companies were now estimating that they needed 2 to 3 million subscribers to break even, with XM predicting that it would be cash flow positive by late 2004.

In addition to XM's nine-month lead in the market, analysts attribute much of the company's early gains to an aggressive push by General Motors. GM rolled out XM's satellite radio as optional factory-installed equipment in 25 of its 57 car, light truck, and sport's utility models, including the entire Cadillac line. GM planned to increase that figure to 44 models for the 2004 model year, and the company expected to sell some 800,000 cars autos with XM's radio installed during 2004, and 1.1 million during 2005. The GM-installed radio, which is built by GM supplier Delphi, costs $325 and is bundled into the price of the vehicle. In addition to being a shareholder of XM, GM is believed to get about $100 from XM for every radio it installs.

In early 2003, Honda stated that it planned to include XM radios as standard equipment in the 2004 Acura RL, and as factory-installed options in the 2004 Accord. In September 2003, Honda announced that XM radios would be installed as standard equipment in certain Honda Accord models. An XM Satellite Radio spokesman said that between the Accord, Pilot, and S2000 models, Honda will release about 200,000 automobiles that have the XM radio as a factory-installed feature during the 2004 model year and 400,000 during the 2005 model year.[10] In addition to GM and Honda, XM radios are now available as dealer-installed options on certain offerings from Toyota, Volkswagen, and Audi, among others.

In contrast, Sirius's main partners are not as far along putting Sirius radios into their vehicles. Daimler and BMW offer Sirius radios as a dealer-installed option, as opposed to factory installed, meaning that a buyer has to request that the dealer install the equipment. In 2004, Daimler committed to factory install 550,000 radios by mid 2007. Ford reportedly planned to offer factory-installed radios in select models for the 2004 model year, but that did

EXHIBIT 2

XM Versus Sirius in 2003

	XM Satellite	Sirius
Monthly Cost	$9.99	$12.95
Radio Cost	$325 factory installed radio, $400–$500 for dealer installed $200–$299 for home radio	$400–$500 for dealer installed radio No home radio
Programming	101 channels 70 music 30 talk, sports, news 1 premium channel (Playboy)	100 channels 60 music 40 sports, talk, news
Commercials	None on 35 music channels Limited commercials on rest (about 2 minutes per hour)	None on music channels
Key Formats	Classic (3 channels) Pop (10 channels) Jazz/Blues (7 channels) Country (6 channels) Rock (12 channels) Latin (5 channels) Frank's Place The Joint (Reggae) Broadway Old Time Radio Classics	Classic (3 channels) Pop (9 channels) Jazz/standards (5 channels) Hip Hop (5 channels) Country (5 channels) Dance (6 channels) R&B (4 channels) Rock (13 channels) Broadway Radio Classics
News	Fox, CNN, CNBC, ESPN, Others	Fox, CNN, CNBC, ESPN, Others
Automotive Partners	GM, Honda	Ford, DaimlerChrysler, BMW
Subscribers as of Mid 2003	692,253	105,186

not transpire. Now Ford has announced that it will begin factory installing Sirius radios in the 2006 model year, and will be factory installing Sirius radios in twenty of its twenty-one car lines by 2007.[11]

The wild card in the industry may be Toyota, which had not aligned itself with either XM or Sirius by late 2004, although Toyota did offer XM Radio as a dealer-installed option on some models. Nissan, too, has not aligned itself with either company, but the company again offers either XM or Sirius radios as a dealer-installed option.

Both XM and Sirius are also starting to offer an array of satellite radios for home use. The best selling of these in 2002 and 2003 was the Delphi XM SkyFi

radio, which is made by Delphi for XM and sold through major consumer electronics chains for between $199 and $230 a unit. By mid 2003, some 80,000 Delphi XM SkyFi units had been sold, and Wal-Mart, the nation's largest retailer, now stocked the item. The SkyFi radio could be used both at home, where it slots into an audio player, and adapted to fit into a car (see Exhibit 3). In late 2004, XM Radio and Delphi announced that they would start selling a handheld portable radio, the Delphi MyFi, in December 2004.

Early surveys suggest high customer satisfaction with satellite radio. Surveys carried out by GM reported a 90 percent satisfaction rate among customers

EXHIBIT 3

Delphi XM SkiFi Radio Receiver in a Car[12]

Source: Reprinted courtesy of XM Satellite Radio, Inc.

who chose satellite radio as an option, with 70 to 75 percent saying that they are likely to order satellite radio for their next vehicle.[13] Several consumer products reporters have also given satellite strong reviews although some have complained that the sound quality is not quite CD quality.[14]

Sirius's late entry into the market and relatively low traction has left it in a very shaky financial condition (see Exhibit 4 for Sirius's financial data). In October 2001, CEO David Margolese abruptly resigned, presumably a casualty of the company's failure to launch its service on time. Margolese continues as non–executive chairman of Sirius. The delay in the launch of its service resulted in Sirius running down its cash reserves, and by mid 2002, it looked almost certain that the company would default on debt payments and have to file for chapter 11 bankruptcy protection. However, at the last minute in October 2002 Sirius was able to pull off something of a coup, converting $700 million in debt and $525 million in preferred stock into common equity. In addition, three of the original investors in Sirius agreed to supply the company with another $200 million in cash. As a result of the recapitalization plan, the existing holders of the company's common stock ended up owning just 8 percent of the recapi-

talized company. It remains to be seen whether these funds will be sufficient to see the company through to profitability.

XM Radio also returned to the capital markets in early 2003, lining up an additional $475 million in funding (see Exhibit 5 for financial data from XM). Of the $475 million, $225 million came from new investors, and the remainder from General Motors in the form of deferred payments and credit facilities. Critical to the deal's success was the agreement by more than 90 percent of the holders of $325 million in XM bonds to swap them for newly issued debt that pays no interest until 2006.

Although XM did launch on schedule, it, too, has experienced some technological problems that do represent a potential cloud on the horizon. XM's two satellites, "Rock" and "Roll," are experiencing unexpected degradation of their solar power panels. The degradation has prompted XM to cut their useful life to 2008 from 2015. However, XM believes that it will be able to launch additional satellites by the time the degradation impacts signal strength. XM believes that its current insurance policies cover this problem and that it will be able to claim sufficient funds from insurance to be able to launch additional satellites.

EXHIBIT 4

Selected Consolidated Financial Data for Sirius[15]

Sirius Satellite Radio Inc. and Subsidiary
Consolidated Statements of Operations (in Thousands, Except per Share Amounts)

	For the Years Ended December 31,		
	2003	2002	2001
Revenue:			
Subscriber revenue, including effects of mail-in rebates	$12,615	$623	$
Advertising revenue, net of agency fees	116	146	—
Equipment revenue	61	—	—
Other revenue	80	36	—
Total Revenue	12,872	805	—
Operating Expenses:			
Cost of services (excludes depreciation expense shown separately below):			
Satellite and transmission	32,604	39,308	31,056
Programming and content	30,398	22,728	9,836
Customer service and billing	23,657	7,862	6,572
Cost of equipment	115	—	—
Sales and marketing	121,216	87,347	21,566
Subscriber acquisition costs	74,860	21,038	—
General and administrative	36,211	30,682	28,536
Research and development	24,534	30,087	47,794
Depreciation expense	95,353	82,747	9,052
Non-cash stock compensation expense (benefit) (1)	11,454	(7,867)	14,044
Total Operating Expenses:	450,402	313,932	168,456
Loss from operations	(437,530)	(313,127)	(168,456)
Other Income (Expense):			
Debt restructuring	256,538	(8,448)	—
Gain on extinguishment of debt	—	—	5,313
Interest and investment income	5,287	5,257	17,066
Interest expense, net of amounts capitalized	(50,510)	(106,163)	(89,686)
Total Other Income (Expense):	211,315	(109,354)	(67,307)
Net loss	(226,215)	(422,481)	(235,763)
Preferred Stock Dividends	(8,574)	(45,300)	(41,476)
Preferred Stock Deemed Dividends	(79,634)	(685)	(680)
Net Loss Applicable to Common Stockholders	$(314,423)	$(468,466)	$(277,919)
Net Loss per Share Applicable to Common Stockholders (Basic and Diluted)	$ (0.38)	$ (6.13)	$ (5.30)
Weighted Average Common Shares Outstanding (Basic and Diluted)	827,186	76,394	52,427

(continued)

EXHIBIT 4 (*continued*)

Sirius Satellite Radio Inc. and Subsidiary

Consolidated Balance Sheets (in Thousands, Except Share and per Share Amounts)

Period Ending	31-Dec-03	31-Dec-02	31-Dec-01
Assets			
Current Assets			
Cash and Cash Equivalents	520,979	18,375	4,726
Short Term Investments	30,901	155,327	326,216
Net Receivables	—	—	—
Inventory	—	—	—
Other Current Assets	27,784	25,907	12,303
Total Current Assets	**579,664**	**199,609**	**343,245**
Long-Term Investments	6,750	7,200	—
Property Plant and Equipment	941,052	1,032,874	1,082,915
Goodwill	—	—	—
Intangible Assets	83,654	83,654	83,654
Accumulated Amortization	—	—	—
Other Assets	493	17,603	17,791
Deferred Long Term Asset Charges	5,704	—	—
Total Assets	**1,617,317**	**1,340,940**	**1,527,605**
Liabilities			
Current Liabilities			
Accounts Payable	67,268	48,320	45,313
Short/Current Long-Term Debt	—	—	15,000
Other Current Liabilities	14,735	—	—
Total Current Liabilities	**82,003**	**48,320**	**60,313**
Long-Term Debt	194,803	670,357	589,990
Other Liabilities	11,593	54,264	47
Deferred Long-Term Liability Charges	3,724	—	69,438
Minority Interest	—	—	—
Negative Goodwill	—	—	—
Total Liabilities	**292,123**	**1,304,094**	**1,204,956**
Stockholders' Equity			
Misc. Stock Options Warrants	—	531,153	485,168
Redeemable Preferred Stock	—	—	—
Preferred Stock	—	—	—
Common Stock	1,138	77	57
Retained Earnings	(1,153,694)	(927,479)	(504,998)
Treasury Stock	—	—	—
Capital Surplus	2,525,135	963,335	827,590
Other Stockholder Equity	(47,385)	913	—
Total Stockholder Equity	**1,325,194**	**36,846**	**322,649**
Net Tangible Assets	**$1,241,540**	**($46,808)**	**$238,995**

EXHIBIT 5

Selected Financial Data for XM Radio[16]

XM Satellite Radio Holdings Inc. and Subsidiaries
Consolidated Statements of Operations Years Ended December 31, 2003, 2002, and 2001

	2003	2002	2001
	(in thousands except share amounts)		
Revenue:			
Subscription revenue	$78,275	$ 16,344	$ 238
Activation revenue	1,868	484	8
Equipment revenue	6,692	757	—
Net ad sales revenue	4,065	2,333	251
Other	881	263	36
Total revenue	91,781	20,181	533
Operating Expenses:			
Cost of revenue (excludes depreciation & amortization, shown below):			
Revenue share & royalties	26,440	12,790	1,739
Customer care & billing	25,945	16,069	5,724
Cost of equipment	9,797	1,679	—
Ad sales	3,257	1,870	2,243
Satellite & terrestrial	39,692	44,818	62,641
Broadcast & operations	19,712	19,851	21,960
Programming & content	23,109	25,379	17,649
Total cost of revenue	147,952	122,456	111,956
Research & development (excludes depreciation and amortization, shown below)	12,285	10,843	13,689
General & administrative (excludes depreciation and amortization, shown below)	27,418	26,448	20,250
Marketing (excludes depreciation and amortization, shown below)	200,267	169,165	93,584
Impairment of goodwill	—	11,461	—
Depreciation & amortization	158,317	118,588	42,660
Total operating expenses	546,239	458,961	282,139
Operating Loss	(454,458)	(438,780)	(281,606)
Other Income (Expense):			
Interest income	3,066	5,111	15,198
Interest expense	(110,349)	(63,573)	(18,131)
Other income (expense)	(22,794)	2,230	160
Net loss	(584,535)	(495,012)	(284,379)
8.25% Series B Preferred Stock Dividend Requirement	(2,471)	(3,766)	(3,766)
8.25% Series B Preferred Stock Retirement Gain	8,761	—	—
8.25% Series C Preferred Stock Dividend Requirement	(15,098)	(17,093)	(19,387)
8.25% Series C Preferred Stock Retirement Loss	(11,537)	—	—
Net loss attributable to common stockholders	$ (604,880)	$ (515,871)	$ (307,532)
Net Loss Per Share:			
Basic and diluted	$ (4.83)	$ (5.95)	$ (5.13)
Weighted Average Shares Used in Computing Net Loss per Share-Basic and Diluted	125,176,320	86,735,257	59,920,196

(*continued*)

EXHIBIT 5 (*continued*)

XM Satellite Radio Holdings Inc. and Subsidiaries
Consolidated Balance Sheets December 31, 2003 and 2002

ASSETS	2003	2002
	(in thousands except share data)	
Current Assets:		
Cash and cash equivalents	$418,307	$32,818
Short-term investments	—	9,997
Restricted investments	116	25,014
Accounts receivable, net of allowance for doubtful accounts of $796 and $241	13,160	3,756
Due from related parties	5,176	1,478
Related party prepaid expenses	22,261	—
Prepaid and other current assets	19,542	10,362
Total current assets	478,562	83,425
Restricted investments, net of current portion	4,035	4,728
System under construction	92,577	55,016
Property and equipment, net of accumulated depreciation and amortization of $315,063 and $158,266	709,501	847,936
DARS license	141,200	144,042
Intangibles, net of accumulated amortization of $4,433 and $3,172	8,429	9,690
Deferred financing fees, net of accumulated amortization of $10,561 and $3,898	43,999	13,276
Related party prepaid expenses, net of current portion	44,521	—
Prepaid and other assets, net of current portion	3,958	2,167
Total assets	$1,526,782	$1,160,280
Liabilities and Stockholders' Equity		
Current Liabilities:		
Accounts payable	$35,773	$40,006
Accrued expenses	57,293	46,924
Accrued network optimization expenses	4,136	2,201
Current portion of long-term debt	38,686	3,845
Due to related parties	2,103	13,410
Accrued interest	5,427	16,651
Deferred revenue	39,722	9,925
Total current liabilities	183,140	132,962
Related party long-term debt, net of current portion	141,891	—
Long-term debt, net of current portion	601,363	412,540
Due to related parties, net of current portion	23,921	10,618
Deferred revenue, net of current portion	14,162	2,372
Other non-current liabilities	29,417	9,477
Total liabilities	993,894	567,969

(*continued*)

EXHIBIT 5 (*continued*)

XM Satellite Radio Holdings Inc. and Subsidiaries
Consolidated balance sheets December 31, 2003 and 2002

ASSETS	2003	2002
	(in thousands except share data)	
Stockholders' Equity:		
Series A convertible preferred stock, par value $0.01 (liquidation preference of $102,739 at December 31, 2003, and December 31, 2002); 15,000,000 shares authorized, 10,786,504 shares issued and outstanding at December 31, 2003 and December 31, 2002	108	108
Series B convertible redeemable preferred stock, par value $0.01 (liquidation preference of $23,714 and $43,364 at December 31, 2003 and December 31, 2002, respectively); 3,000,000 shares authorized, 474,289 and 867,289 shares issued and outstanding at December 31, 2003 and December 31, 2002, respectively	5	9
Series C convertible redeemable preferred stock, par value $0.01 (liquidation preference of $153,605 and $239,508 at December 31, 2003, and December 31, 2002, respectively); 250,000 shares authorized, 120,000 and 200,000 shares issued and outstanding at December 31, 2003 and December 31, 2002, respectively	1	2
Series D convertible redeemable preferred stock, par value $0.01 (liquidation preference of $0 at December 31, 2003 and December 31, 2002); 250,000 authorized; no shares issued and outstanding at December 31, 2003 and December 31, 2002, respectively	—	—
Class A common stock, par value $0.01; 600,000,000 and 225,000,000 shares authorized, 160,665,194 and 91,706,056 shares issued and outstanding at December 31, 2003 and December 31, 2002, respectively	1,607	917
Class C common stock, par value $0.01; 15,000,000 shares authorized, no shares issued and outstanding at December 31, 2003 and December 31, 2002, respectively	—	—
Additional paid-in capital	2,001,688	1,477,261
Accumulated deficit	(1,470,521)	(885,986)
Total stockholders' equity	532,888	592,311
Commitments and contingencies		
Total liabilities and stockholders' equity	$1,526,782	$1,160,280

By mid 2003, some analysts remained very bullish about the potential of XM Radio, although the future of Sirius was somewhat hazy. A May 2002 study by the Yankee Group projected satellite radio would achieve 15 million subscribers by 2006. Other market studies conducted for XM Radio project that as many as 50 million people may subscribe to satellite radio by 2012. More conservative investment analysts were suggesting that satellite radio might garner 4 to 5 million subscribers by mid-decade, and that the ultimate total may be closer to 40 to 50 million. According to some projections made in early 2003, if XM hits 10 million subscribers in 2007 it could earn $500 million, or $1.50 a share. If XM Radio were ultimately to garner 30 million subscribers, it could earn $7 or more a share.[17]

EXHIBIT 6

Forecasted Subscriber Growth (millions)

Source: Salmon Smith Barney Estimates. 2003 figures are actual figures.

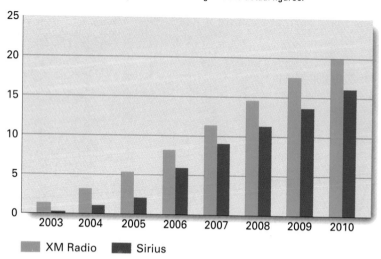

Significant Developments in 2004

As 2004 drew to a close, subscription data suggested that XM Radio was continuing to capitalize on its early lead over Sirius in the industry. Analysts were now expecting XM to end 2004 with 3.11 million subscribers versus around 1 million for Sirius (see Exhibit 6). During 2004, XM Radio's net subscriber additions (gross additions less cancellations) were 1.75 million, versus 0.76 million for Sirius. XM was forecasted to have 5.31 million subscribers in 2005, versus 2.14 million for Sirius.

Sirius had tried to differentiate itself by aggressively signing valuable branded content. In December 2003, Sirius signed a seven-year exclusive deal with the NFL to broadcast football games, beginning with the 2005–2006 season. The deal cost Sirius $188 million in cash over the course of the contract, plus $32 million in warrants. In early October 2004, Sirius signed up "shock jock" Howard Stern to an exclusive five-year deal for $500 million, which would start to air on January 1, 2006. The branded content was used by Sirius to justify the premium subscription price of its service.

XM Radio has responded to these moves with deals of its own. In October 2004, XM signed an eleven-year $650 million deal with Major League Baseball (MBL), giving XM exclusive rights to the satellite broadcast of MLB games beginning in 2005, including the World Series. Also in October 2004, XM launched a premium channel dedicated to shock jocks Opie and Anthony, who had previously been removed from the air due to profanity. The Opie and Anthony channel will cost subscribers an additional $1.99 a month.

By late 2004, the business models at XM Radio and Sirius were starting to crystallize. It was now clear that earlier statements regarding breakeven subscription levels were too low. A detailed research report on XM Radio by Salmon Smith Barney suggested that the company would not start to generate positive earnings before interest, tax, depreciation and amortization (EBITDA) until 2007, when the subscriber base was forecasted to be around 11 million (see Exhibit 7).[18] On the same basis, Sirius was not expected to start generating a positive EBITDA until 2008.

The key variables in analysts' estimation of breakeven volume were subscription revenues, fixed costs, variable costs, customer acquisition costs, and customer churn rates. For 2004, Smith Barney estimated that XM Radio would have revenues of $243 million, with only $6 million of those being attributed to advertising revenues. Fixed costs—which included costs related to equipment, broadcasting,

EXHIBIT 7

Financial Performance and Forecasts for XM Radio

$(million)	2003	2004E	2005E	2006E	2007E
Revenue	$91.8	$243.5	$469.7	$790	$1,183.2
Variable Costs	($52.4)	($96.5)	($150.9)	($231.5)	($324.3)
Fixed Costs	($143.1)	($175.9)	($248.7)	($281.1)	($299.6)
Customer Acquisition Costs	($192.4)	($279.9)	($347.4)	($412.5)	($508.1)
EBITDA	($296.1)	($308.8)	($277.2)	($135.7)	$51.1

Source: Company Reports and Salmon Smith Barney.

programming and content, and customer support—were estimated to be around $175 million. Variable costs—including revenue sharing with partners such as GM, royalties paid for the right to broadcast songs, and customer care costs—amounted to $96.5 million. The average cost of acquiring a customer—including advertising, marketing, and subsidies given to equipment suppliers—was pegged at $130 per customer, and forecasted to hit $279.9 million in 2004. In its 2003 10K, XM Radio estimated that 1.3 percent of its paying customers left the service every month. However, if nonpaying customers who get the service on a trial basis through automobile companies are counted in, the churn rate rises to 3.5 percent a month.

Sirius had a similar revenue and cost structure to XM Radio, although accounting differences make a direct comparison difficult (see Exhibit 8). The largest difference was that Sirius still charged a premium price for subscriptions, but was also committed to paying higher fees for content on an annualized basis. In 2006, for example, forecasts suggest that programming costs per subscriber will be $3.88 at Sirius and $1.31 at XM Radio.[19] Sirius also had a larger customer churn rate than XM Radio in 2004, around 1.7 percent a month, and larger customer acquisitions costs, which were forecasted to be around $247 a customer in 2005. The higher customer acquisition costs, relative to XM Radio, were because Sirius paid a larger subsidy to equipment manufacturers, and it had a small base over which to spread its marketing costs. In Exhibit 8, customer acquisition costs are bundled in with marketing expenses.

EXHIBIT 8

Financial Performance and Forecasts for Sirius

$(million)	2003	2004	2005	2006	2007
Revenue	$12.9	$68.2	$186.7	$520.7	$1383.4
Non-Marketing Operating Expense	($160.9)	($224.7)	($258.3)	($469.6)	($614.4)
Marketing Expenses	($194.1)	($294.4)	($339.8)	($542.5)	($489.5)
EBITDA	($342.2)	($450.9)	($411.3)	($513.7)	$154.2

Source: Company Reports and Salmon Smith Barney.

REFERENCES

K. Bachman. "The next wave." *Mediaweek*, April 12, 1999, pages 26–31.

K. Bachman. "Reaching for the stars." *Mediaweek*, March 25, 2002, pages 22–28.

A. Barry. "A sound idea." *Barrons*, February 17, 2003, pages 17–19.

A. Barry. "Interference." *Barrons*, April 21, 2003, pages 13–14.

A. Cosper. "Sirius competition." *Satellite Broadband*, March 2002, pages 24–29.

P. Lewis. "Satellite Radio." *Fortune*, October 15, 2001, pages 253–256.

P. Lewis. "Sirius competition." *Fortune*, June 23, 2003, pages 130–132.

A. W. Mathews. "From a distance." *Wall Street Journal*, February 25, 2002, page A1.

B. McLean. "Satellite killed the radio star." *Fortune*, January 22, 2001, pages 94–99.

E. Rathbun. "Radio flyer." *Broadcasting & Cable*, June 5, 2000, pages 18–23.

A. Rodgers. "A little space music." *Newsweek*, November 12, 2001, pages 67–69.

Salmon Smith Barney. XM Satellite Radio Holdings. October 26, 2004.

Sirius Radio 2002 and 2003 10K Form.

Standard & Poor's *Industry Survey*. Broadcasting and Cable, July 25, 2002.

XM Radio 2002 and 2003 10K Form.

ENDNOTES

1. Statistics from Standard & Poor's *Industry Survey*, Broadcasting and Cable, July 25, 2002.

2. Standard & Poor's *Industry Survey*, Broadcasting and Cable, July 25, 2002.

3. Clear Channel Communications 2002 10K Form.

4. XM Radio 2003 10K Form.

5. National Cable Television Association website and **skyreport.com** website.

6. XM Radio 2002 10K Form. Smith Barney, *XM Satellite Radio Holdings*, October 26, 2004.

7. Smith Barney, *XM Satellite Radio Holdings*, October 26, 2004.

8. A. W. Mathews, "From a distance," *Wall Street Journal*, February 25, 2002, page A1.

9. Anonymous, "Outstanding subscriber growth for XM," *Dealerscope*, June 2003, page 5.

10. Anonymous, "XM Satellite Radio to be standard equipment on Honda Accord models," Dow Jones News Wire, September 9, 2003.

11. Smith Barney, *XM Satellite Radio Holdings*, October 26, 2004.

12. Image Gallery XM radio at **http://www.xmradio.com/newsroom/photo_gallery_sub.jsp?cat=Facilities**.

13. A. Barry. "A sound idea," *Barrons*, February 17, 2003, pages 17–19.

14. K. Bachman, "Reaching for the stars," *Mediaweek*, March 25, 2003, pages 22–30.

15. Sirius Satellite Radio 2003 10K Form.

16. XM Radio 2003 10K Form.

17. A. Barry, "A sound idea," *Barrons*, February 17, 2003, pages 17–19.

18. Smith Barney, *XM Satellite Radio Holdings*, October 26, 2004.

19. Smith Barney, *Sirius Satellite Radio*, October 26, 2004.

Case 10

Strategic Inflection: TiVo in 2003

This case was prepared by Professors David Yoffie and Pai-Ling Yin, and
Christina Darwall of the HBS California Research Center.

Mike Ramsay, chief executive officer of TiVo Inc., looked out at the Santa Cruz Mountains, not far from the company's headquarters in San Jose, California. Midway through 2003, he felt buoyed by TiVo's strong first-quarter increase in subscribers and steadily rising stock price, but he was pensive about the company's next steps.

TiVo was a leading provider of digital video recorder (DVR) technology and services, selling directly to consumers as well as through original equipment manufacturers (OEMs) and licensees. (See Exhibit 1.) DVRs—an emerging consumer electronics (CE) category—were similar to videocassette recorders (VCRs) except that TV recordings were made to hard disks rather than to cassette tapes. Also referred to as personal video recorders (PVRs), DVRs could change the way consumers experienced television. A user could pause live TV, fast-forward through commercials, and run instant replay during his or her favorite sporting event. Along with many other features, TiVo would even suggest and record programs that the consumer might like.

Despite having the strongest brand, the most differentiated product in terms of features, and one of the largest installed bases, TiVo would be at an inflection point in 2003, Ramsay knew. TiVo's competition had increased from just one competitor in 1998 to more than a dozen. Moreover, the cable TV industry was in the midst of a massive transition from analog to digital set-top boxes. If TiVo did not participate during this transition, it would become much more difficult to enter the market. At the same time, TiVo had suffered $500 million in operating losses since it was founded, and the company was just turning the financial corner. Ramsay had to balance long-term strategy with the company's short-term finances. While financial discipline had been relatively less important in the early days of the Internet bubble, Ramsay and his management team knew that the future of the company depended on avoiding the excesses of the past. As Ramsay told the casewriters:

> From day one, I've had a strong conviction that we're going to change the way people relate to home entertainment. Starting with DVR isn't bad—in fact it's a killer app. Our users tell us, "TiVo's changed my life," so we can see that the service is important to them. But in the long run we want TiVo to be the portal to entertainment services in the home. People think our competitors are other DVR manufacturers, but we aren't really in the "DVR" business—we're in the user interface and entertainment services business.

Glossary of Terms

CPU	The central processing unit was the "brains" of a computer.
DVD	DVD stood for digital video disc or digital versatile disc and was a type of optical disc-storage medium that could store a full-length feature film.
DVD-DVR	DVD-DVR was a consumer electronics device that combined a digital video disc player with a digital video recorder.
DVR	DVR stood for digital video recorder. A DVR was similar to a VCR (video cassette recorder) except that it recorded digitally onto a hard drive instead of onto video-cassette tape. This meant that it could store dozens of hours of programming and perform many functions that a VCR could not, such as pausing and rewinding live TV. DVRs were sometimes referred to as PVRs (see below).
EPG	EPGs, or electronic programming guides, were available on most cable and satellite services as well as most DVRs. EPGs allowed consumers to see from three to 14 days of programming in advance and, in the case of DVRs, to click on a show to record it or double click to record it every time the show was shown. Stand-alone DVRs required a connection to a phone line to download the EPG each evening. EPGs were also referred to as IPGs (see below).
GB	Gigabyte was a unit used to measure the capacity of hard drives.
IPG	IPG was an abbreviation for interactive programming guide. (See EPG above.) IPGs could have more advanced features than EPGs.
IR Blaster	A feature of most DVRs but usually lacking in DVD-DVRs, an IR (infrared) blaster was a small bulb on a wire that acted like a remote control to change channels on cable or satellite set-top boxes. Without an IR blaster, consumers had to set the recording device to the correct channel before recording.
MPEG	MPEG, a digital compression standard, stood for motion picture experts group.
MSO	MSO, an abbreviation for multiple services operator—meaning a cable operator with more than one network—was a term commonly used for all cable operators.
PVR	PVR stood for personal video recorder. Also referred to as DVR (see above).
STB	STB was an abbreviation for set-top box, which meant any piece of hardware (generally in the shape of a VCR) that was placed on top of (or beside or beneath) the television.
SVOD	SVOD stood for subscription video on demand, which provided consumers with continuous access to certain content (e.g., HBO shows) for a monthly fee.
VOD	VOD stood for video on demand, a service that allowed consumers to pay for a movie or other content and watch it on their cable or satellite TV at their convenience.

Source: Casewriter research, adapted from Webopedia web site, **<http://www.webopedia.com>**, and The Online ITV Dictionary, **<http://itvdictionary.com/broadband.html>**, accessed May 7, 2003.

The big issue we are facing today is whether, given our long-term goals, we should go all out to "mass market" TiVo and speed consumer adoption, or whether we should strive for increased levels of innovation and differentiation to maintain the substantial distance between ourselves and the increasing number of knockoffs.

What Is TiVo?

Former Silicon Graphics, Inc. executives Ramsay and Jim Barton—who had been working on a joint venture with Time Warner to create the first large-scale interactive TV system—founded TiVo in 1997. At its simplest, the TiVo product was a hard disk-based replacement for the VCR.[1] TiVo enabled consumers to

[1]There were over 500 million VCRs in the world in 2003. While introduced to allow consumers to watch TV shows they had previously recorded, the worldwide installed base of VCRs grew from fewer than 10 million in 1980 to over 200 million in 1990 as consumers began using their VCRs to watch prerecorded movies—with adult movies the first killer app. Jimmy Schaeffler, "Ten Trends in Consumer Electronics," *Satellite News*, Vol. 26, No. 13, March 31, 2003; David Backus and Luis Cabral, "Betamax and VHS," NYU Stern School Case, November 26, 2001, p. 2; and Peter Sealey, Ph.D., "Commercial Television: Rest in Peace," speech to the 2003 Association of National Advertisers, March 13, 2003.

record and play back TV shows, to pause "live" TV, to record shows based on general preferences (by using TiVo's WishList feature to input a favorite actor, director, sport, hobby, or whatever), and to "time-shift" their television viewing watching shows whenever they wanted. In fact, many users preferred to watch prerecorded shows even if they were home when the show was shown live. It was easier for a TiVo user to control the viewing experience, and users could fast-forward through the commercials. TiVo users could access two weeks' worth of electronic program guide (EPG) information, recording shows the "old-fashioned way"—by noting the date and time of the show they wanted to record—or simply by telling the TiVo device to record an entire season's worth of a favorite show (TiVo's "Season Pass" feature). The TiVo product even had a suggestion engine, similar to the technology found on Amazon.com. Based on consumers' viewing habits and their ability to give shows a positive or negative rating, TiVo would record programs that might be enjoyed by the consumer.

TiVo helped the consumer solve two problems. One was that, due to conflicts, consumers were sometimes unable to watch their favorite TV shows when they were broadcast. TiVo, as well as other DVRs, allowed users to record shows when they were broadcast, storing them for playback in the future. The other problem was that—with the advent of cable and satellite TV—sifting through hundreds of channels to find the most interesting shows had become a daunting task.

After purchasing a TiVo machine with 40 to 80 hours of recording time for between $249 and $349, the consumer had to install the machine and activate the service, which cost $12.95 per month or a one-time up-front fee of $299. Installing the TiVo was not as easy as plugging in an appliance and turning it on. The TiVo not only needed to connect to the TV but also to a phone jack or the Internet.[2] There were up to six cables that needed to be connected,[3] and most users needed help from the customer service desk during installation.[4] However, once the TiVo unit

had been set up and activated, it was very easy to operate, generally getting high marks from consumers for its user interface and ease of use. (See Exhibit 2.)

In early 2002, TiVo launched its second-generation product, the TiVo Series2, which featured a more robust processor and increased memory, creating an opportunity to offer new premium services such as digital music and broadband VOD (video on demand). TiVo and DirecTV—the largest U.S. satellite TV operator—then launched an integrated DirecTV/DVR set-top box based on TiVo's Series2 technology and announced that DirecTV would both market to and service the accounts.[5] (TiVo would have no ongoing costs associated with DirecTV subscribers.) DirecTV offered a DVR subscription price of $4.95 per month with free service to subscribers to DirecTV's premium package; the hardware was priced at $199.[6] DirecTV paid a monthly fee per household to TiVo. The average monthly fee to TiVo was $3 in mid-2003, but TiVo expected a lower average fee in the future.

In the spring of 2003, TiVo shipped its first premium service application—the Home Media Option (HMO)—which enabled users to view digital photos, listen to and catalog digital music, and schedule programs to be recorded. TiVo Series2 subscribers could purchase HMO for a one-time fee of $99, with an additional $49 fee for each additional machine. Once the HMO software was downloaded via broadband or telephone line and activated at the TiVo web site, the TiVo DVR was capable of linking over wired or wireless (802.11b) networks with either Apple or Windows PCs. Users with HMO could do remote scheduling over the Internet and use their TVs to view digital photos or listen to digital music. In addition, households with more than one TiVo unit could record programs on one TiVo and then transfer the programs to another for viewing. In theory, HMO also created an opportunity for new services such as broadband VOD, where content could be streamed directly to TVs. Broadband to the home was growing more rapidly than pay television services, either

---

[2]Almost all DVRs included automatic access to an EPG; in order to update the EPG daily, DVRs either had an internal modem that allowed them to dial out on a phone line or used an Internet, cable, or satellite connection to access the EPG.

[3]Dawn C. Chmielewski, "The Number of Cables Needed for TiVo Should Have Been a Clue," *The San Jose Mercury News*, June 19, 2003, p. 1E.

[4]TiVo outsourced call center operations to be a big call center operator. Customer service costs varied, primarily with new subscribers.

[5]iVo had had a partnership with DirecTV since 1999, and under terms of the earlier agreement, TiVo had shouldered most of the marketing and operations costs and received a high proportion of the monthly subscriber fees generated.

[6]Richard Shim, "DirecTV Cuts Fee for TiVo Service," CNET News.com Web site, September 3, 2002 <**http://news.com.com/2100-1040-956384.html**>, accessed July 2, 2003.

EXHIBIT 2

TiVo Subscriber History

For Quarter Ended	Net New Additions			Total Cumulative Subscriptions			Percent of TiVo Service Cumulative Subscriptions Paying Recurring Fees
	TiVo Svc	DirecTV	Total	TiVo Svc	DirecTV	Total	
1999 June			1,000			1,000	
1999 September			1,500			2,500	
1999 December			15,500			18,000	
2000 March			14,000			32,000	
2000 June			16,000			48,000	
2000 September			25,000			73,000	
2000 December			63,000			136,000	
2001 January			18,000			154,000	
2001 April	22,000	13,000	35,000	160,000	29,000	189,000	36
2001 July	22,000	18,000	40,000	182,000	47,000	229,000	37
2001 October	24,000	27,000	51,000	206,000	74,000	280,000	39
2002 January	40,000	60,000	100,000	246,000	134,000	380,000	41
2002 April	24,000	18,000	42,000	270,000	152,000	422,000	34
2002 July	21,000	21,000	42,000	291,000	173,000	464,000	33
2002 October	30,000	16,000	46,000	321,000	189,000	510,000	34
2003 January	74,000	40,000	114,000	396,000	228,000	624,000	34
2003 April	37,000	42,000	79,000	433,000	270,000	703,000	34
2003 July	34,000	56,000	90,000	467,000	326,000	793,000	34
2003 October	59,000	150,000	209,000	526,000	476,000	1,002,000	35

Note 1: The "Percent of TiVo Service Cumulative Subscriptions Paying Recurring Fees" excludes DirecTV subscribers.

Note 2: TiVo changed its fiscal year-end from December 31 to January 31 to better capture the holiday sales season in its fourth quarter. Due to this change, the month ending January 31, 2001 was accounted for separately and not in conjunction with any fiscal year.

Note 3: By mid-2003, approximately 45% of new subscribers were choosing to pay the up-front lifetime fee, whereas 55% were opting to pay the monthly fee.

Source: Casewriter research, adapted from company reports and press releases, TiVo Web site, **<http://www.tivo.com>**, accessed February, 2004.

digital cable or satellite, with multiple services operator (MSO, i.e., cable company) broadband providers enjoying greater growth and a larger share than digital-subscriber line (DSL) broadband providers. Estimated at more than 2 million at the end of 2002, the number of home-based wireless networks was projected to grow to nearly 20 million by the end of 2006.[7] However, an obstacle to streaming content was obtaining the digital rights from content providers.

TiVo also sold services to advertisers and networks. TiVo's "Showcases" were long-form (four to six minutes) commercials that were designed to be very entertaining, as TiVo subscribers had to choose to "opt in" to watch them. TiVo helped advertisers develop interactive ads which would allow viewers to solicit more information on a product or record a pilot program by responding to a prompt during a commercial for a new show. TiVo's audience-measurement services allowed buyers to analyze viewer behavior, for example, whether commercials or shows did

[7]Marc van Impe, "20 Million U.S. Households to Go 802.11 by 2006," Nordic Wireless Watch Web site, July 13, 2002, <http://www.nordicwirelesswatch.com/wireless/story.html?story_id= 1939>, accessed July 7, 2003.

better at certain times or in certain markets. TiVo's deal with DirecTV allowed TiVo to collect and share data on audience viewing habits, and if TiVo sold advertising to DirecTV customers, it also shared those revenues.

TiVo Technology

The TiVo DVR was essentially a computer with a large hard disk, read-write MPEG digital video chips for encoding and decoding, a modem, and other components. The product was designed to keep costs low and manufacturing relatively easy since the unit was outsourced. The biggest portion of the bill of materials was the hard disk at 33%, with the MPEG components also expensive. The TiVo DVR ran on an MIPS CPU core with the Linux operating system.

TiVo took security and privacy very seriously. The TiVo DVR's microprocessor, containing cryptography software, was soldered into the box. This made TiVo very difficult to hack. The DVRs would call in—usually through the public switched telephone network—for EPG information and/or any software updates. Although TiVo was able to download data to the DVRs, TiVo was not able to upload all data residing on the DVR. In effect, every night TiVo would upload anonymous batch files that would be aggregated across the TiVo user base, allowing the company to analyze viewing habits at a very granular level. Showcases were distributed to the TiVo DVRs via broadcast whenever possible. Each night TiVo bought 30 minutes of very early morning broadcast time on the Discovery Channel. TiVos that had access to the Discovery Channel would automatically record any Showcases, giving TiVo an inexpensive method for transferring large files to the DVRs.

David Courtney, TiVo's CFO and executive vice president for operations and administration, explained that broadcast center costs "scaled with subscriber volume fairly logarithmically" and in 2003 "cost pennies per day per subscriber." Broadcast center costs consisted primarily of annual fees for program guide content (less than 10 cents per subscriber per month), local Internet access service charges (about 15 to 20 cents per month per subscriber), and the capital and maintenance costs of maintaining big server farms. Ultimately, TiVo could scale to 100 million users without changing the underlying infrastructure.

TiVo management believed strongly that TiVo should be a platform technology where third parties could add value. At the same time, TiVo would never operate like a PC, where software providers would write software directly to TiVo's operating system. Barton, a company cofounder whose role was chief technical officer and senior vice president of research and development, elaborated, "Our future lies not with APIs [application program interfaces] but with protocols. For example, we now have a music protocol that allows TiVo to play digital music on your television. In the future, other services will interact with, but not sit on top of, the DVR." One of the company's bigger challenges with regard to its technology platform was that TiVo was not originally built to be an extensible system that could be easily adapted to different hardware and software environments. In mid-2003, the TiVo platform could only handle the English language, which ultimately limited the number of subscribers. In addition, TiVo was not modular; additional engineering work and therefore significant costs were required whenever TiVo wanted to extend its technology to a new OEM or CE device.

Having filed for patents early in the company's life, TiVo management received three major patents in 2001: one for personal video recording software and hardware design, and two for core DVR functions and home networking capabilities. Several aspects of TiVo's system were patent protected including the scheduling and optimization of disk space—for example, what was recorded when—and resolving recording conflicts—for example, when a subscriber wanted to tape two shows whose broadcast times overlapped, the TiVo DVR "knew" that there was a conflict and tried to resolve it by finding another time when one of the shows would be broadcast. In 2003, TiVo sued a major competitor (EchoStar) for the first time for violating one of its approximately 50 patents.

TiVo Manufacturing and Licensees

Initially, TiVo management decided to focus on software. In order to entice brand-name CE firms to manufacture and distribute the TiVo DVR, the company had to subsidize CE manufacturers up to $200 per TiVo unit shipped. After TiVo discontinued CE subsidies in 2002 in an effort to conserve cash, management discovered that there was not enough profit in the TiVo Series2 box for CE manufacturers to make their required margins. As one TiVo executive commented, "We had a difficult time in 2002—we had no manufacturers, and therefore no retail relationships, and not much money." To correct the situation, TiVo management set out to produce the product more cheaply than the CE firms had done. By reducing the number of parts and outsourcing to a very efficient contracting firm, TiVo was indeed able to lower the cost of the box. In TiVo's fiscal year ending January 2003, TiVo manufactured 55% of all TiVo-enabled DVRs.[8] The great majority of the TiVo-manufactured DVRs (81%) were sold through national CE retailers such as Best Buy and Circuit City, major regional retailers such as The Good Guys, and online retailer Amazon.com, with about one-fifth sold directly to consumers through TiVo's own Web site. TiVo's agreement with Best Buy stipulated that TiVo would share a portion of the TiVo service revenue generated from the TiVo-manufactured DVRs sold by Best Buy. CE retailers such as Best Buy had product margins ranging from 15% to 30%, with those margins tending toward the lower end during recessions.[9]

In mid-2003, TiVo signed up two new Japan-based brand-name licensees (Toshiba and Pioneer) with TiVo's new "basic service" option. The basic service option allowed licensees to include "entry-level" DVR functionality—with no monthly fee—in high-end integrated CE devices such as a combination DVD player with a built-in DVR. This version of the TiVo service used the TiVo interface and allowed consumers to pause live TV and record from the three days of EPG or manually using date and time, but it would not have access to popular TiVo features such as WishList and Season Pass. TiVo planned to offer consumers a 45-day free trial for the full service at the time of installation, hoping to spur adoption of TiVo's $12.95 monthly service. When a company licensed TiVo's DVR technology, it generally paid an up-front license fee of several million dollars, with annual maintenance fees set at about 15% to 20% of the up-front license fee. TiVo devoted engineering resources to then make TiVo's technology compatible with the CE company's product.

Buy TiVo!

End Users: Consumers

The market for TVs, TV-related devices, and TV services in the United States was a large one, with around 105 million households owning a TV in 2003. While cable and satellite services and devices such as VCRs and DVD players had made significant inroads into most households, DVR penetration remained low, around 2% to 4% (See Exhibit 3.) Some industry observers believed that the price of DVR devices needed to fall below $200 before growth would accelerate, citing adoption patterns for consumer devices such as DVD players.[10] (See Exhibits 4 and 5.)

To build awareness of the TiVo brand and educate consumers about TiVo's "personal TV service" during calendar years 2000 and 2001, TiVo spent over $250 million on sales and marketing, including advertising campaigns.[11] (See Exhibit 6.) The company initially tried to enumerate all of TiVo's features and benefits in one 30-second ad, which proved difficult to do; eventually the ads focused on how TiVo could help consumers overcome a specific TV-related problem.[12] Despite a big spike in brand recognition following the advertising, TiVo management found that consumers were still confused about what a DVR did and did not do—and in particular, what the TiVo product could and could not do. Even the name of the device was not settled—half the manufacturers and market analysts used "PVR" for "personal video recorder," while the other half used "DVR." TiVo had done research that showed that the term "personal video recorder" caused consumers to conjure up images of a small, personal electronic device rather than the actual set-top box product. In addition, TiVo had found that consumers were still somewhat confused about the fact that they first had to purchase the product in a retail store and then subsequently pay a monthly service fee.

Although the average consumer was not yet clear about the DVR concept, TiVo users were rabid fans. Almost all (97%) TiVo users were very satisfied—saying

---

[8]Half of TiVo's 248 employees were in engineering, with one-fourth in general and administrative and the remainder split about evenly between service operations and sales and marketing. About 10% worked on hardware design and management.

[9]Joseph Palenchar, "Microsoft: See SPOT Run Despite Past Wristwatch-Pager Failures," TWICE Web site, March 10, 2003, <http://www.twice.com>, accessed April 30, 2003.

[10]David Farina, Mary O'Toole, and Ralph Schackart, "TiVo Inc.," William Blair & Company, March 17, 2003, p. 10.

[11]Through its IPO, the sale of convertible preferred stock, and subsequent stock offerings, TiVo raised approximately $280 million in capital during the 1999 to 2000 time frame.

[12]Om Malik, "Ta-Ta TiVo," Red Herring Web site, January 29, 2003, <http://www.redherring.com/investor/2003/01/tivo012903.html>, accessed June 16, 2003.

EXHIBIT 3

Projected DVR Demand by Type of DVR (households, millions)

	Actual 2000	Actual 2001	Estimated 2002	Forecast 2003	Forecast 2004	Forecast 2005
Satellite DVR/STB	0.1	0.7	1.36	2.4	4.2	6.4
Satellite gateway	0	0	0	0.1	0.2	1.1
Satellite stand-alone	0.09	0.1	0.26	0.6	0.9	1.2
Cable DVR/STB	0	0	0.05	0.3	0.8	1.3
Cable gateway	0	0	0.02	0.1	0.5	1.9
Cable stand-alone	0.05	0.08	0.21	0.7	2.7	5.6
Other stand-alone	0.01	0.02	0.05	0.1	0.1	0.2
Total DVR	**0.25**	**0.9**	**1.95**	**4.3**	**9.6**	**17.8**
Stand-alone DVRs	0.15	0.2	0.52	1.4	3.7	7.0
DVRs sold through satellite companies	0.1	0.7	1.36	2.5	4.4	7.5
DVRs sold through cable companies	0	0	0.07	0.4	1.3	3.2

Note: A "gateway" is a node on a network that acts as the entrance to another network. In homes, the Internet service provider (ISP) was traditionally considered the gateway since it connected the consumer to the Internet. "Gateway" or "media gateway" eventually came to refer to a means to connect multiple media paths and to traverse a converged network. A home media gateway could connect several different sorts of networks from the public switched telephone network to an Internet protocol (IP) network.

Source: Casewriter research, adapted from Josh Bernoff, "Will Ad-Skipping Kill Television?" Forrester Research, Inc., November 2002.

they would recommend TiVo to a friend—and many spoke gushingly about how TiVo had changed their life. Numerous celebrities sang the praises of TiVo, including Oprah Winfrey—who often spoke about "TiVo-ing" a favorite show—and Michael Powell, head of the Federal Communications Commission, who called TiVo "God's machine." TiVo had found

EXHIBIT 4

Example of CE Device Adoption Rates

CE Device	Number of Years to Reach Adoption by 30% of U.S. Households
Color TV	17
VCR	13
Cell phone	12
Personal computer	10
CD player	8
DVD	5

Source: Casewriter research, adapted from David Farina, Mary O'Toole, and Ralph Schackart, "TiVo Inc.," William Blair & Company, March 17, 2003.

that its core consumer segment was "discriminating enthusiasts," people comfortable with technology, but not necessarily "techies," whose lives revolved around their passions. The typical discriminating enthusiast was married, between 25 and 45 years old, and had a household income of $70,000–$100,000. Families with young children were particularly found of TiVo, not only because of its "TV on demand" aspect but the parental controls as well. Susan Cashen, TiVo's vice president of marketing, spoke about other consumer research findings:

We're a bit nervous about saying "you can love your TV," but over three-fourths of our subscribers agree that "TiVo has made my life better." When we ask what that means, they say, "We don't fight with our kids, we have dinner as a family, I can go out with my husband in the evening and then he can watch the game when we get home."

Among nonusers, TiVo is viewed differently. Somebody else has it and loves it, but they're not sure why. Cable customers with some DVR capability say, "It's free and it gets me into digital recording, but it's not TiVo and my friends love TiVo." This is because when you buy a DVR it allows you to pause live TV and time-shift what

EXHIBIT 5

Price and Units Shipped for DVDs and DVRs (1998–2002)

	DVD Players		DVRs				
Year	Average Price/Unit ($)	Units Shipped (millions)	Average Price/Unit ($)	Average Monthly Charge ($)	Lifetime Subscription Fee	Units Shipped (millions)
1998	504	0.9	N/A	N/A	N/A	N/A
1999	353	3.6	499	10	199	0.04
2000	247	9.9	311	10	199	0.25
2001	173	16.7	300	7	199	0.90
2002	129	25.1	250	9	250	1.95

Note 1: Not all DVRs had a monthly subscription fee. The average monthly subscription fee for DVRs that charged a fee is TiVo's fee in 1999 and 2000 and casewriter's estimate for 2001–2002.
Note 2: The 1999 DVR price per unit reflects TiVo's pricing, whereas the 2000–2002 price per unit indicates the average price per unit for all units shipped.

Source: Casewriter research, adapted from David Farina, Mary O'Toole, and Ralph Schackart, "TiVo Inc.," William Blair & Company, March 17, 2003; and Greg Tori, "'02 Digital Gains to Offset Analog Video Sales Declines," This Week in Consumer Electronics Web site, January, 28, 2002, **<http://www.twice.com/ index.asp?layout=story_stocks & articleid=CA193456>**, accessed June 13, 2003.

you watch—but ultimately, you *love* it for other reasons. Systems such as EchoStar's and Time Warner's provide the basic DVR functions, but they don't have the features that make users passionate about the product and service. One of the things that will help us the most is getting the cost of our product low enough that we can sell the product for $199.

We like to think of ourselves as the Google of TV. As more and more people get premium TV programming, we can help people manage their TV better—and with HMO [Home Media Option], we can take it beyond that to managing all the digital content in the home. With HMO, we're targeting TiVo users who have home networks and broadband.

Market research on consumer willingness to pay a monthly fee for DVR devices was conflicting. On the one hand, one study showed that while one-fourth of consumers were interested in getting television programs whenever they wanted them, just 5% said they were willing to pay a monthly fee for a DVR product.[13] On the other hand, another study showed that consumers were willing to pay cable operators between $5 and $10 a month for DVR service and that there was high satisfaction with the service.[14] Once consumers subscribed to TiVo, they seemed to believe the service was worth continuing. TiVo's churn rate—the rate at which customers gave up their subscriptions—was extremely low. At less than 1% per month and about 10% per year, it was lower than churn rates for other subscription services such as cell phone service (about 33% per year), cable TV service (about 30% per year), and DirecTV (about 18% per year).[15]

The confusion about what drove consumer purchases and the differences between TiVo fanatics and uninformed potential DVR customers made it hard to position TiVo clearly in the market. Management was clearly comforted by the uptick in consumer adoption in 2003 and the projected growth in DirectV subscribers, but TiVo was still not exploding. If TiVo was going to reach its full potential, Ramsay and the management team had to find additional ways to increase TiVo subscribers and/or sell additional services.

[14]David Farina, Mary O'Toole, and Ralph Schackart, "TiVo Inc.," William Blair & Company, March 17, 2003, p. 13.
[15]Ibid., p. 25; and Bob Parks, "Where the Customer Service Rep Is King," *Business 2.0*, June 2003, <http://www.business2.com/articles/ mag/print/0,1643,49462,00.html>, accessed July 1, 2003.

[13]"Research Notes 3Q 2002," Leichtman Research Group, Inc., p. 1.

EXHIBIT 6

TiVo Income Statements and Selected Balance Sheet Items ($000s)

	Year Ended 12/31/1999	Year Ended 12/31/2000	1 Mo. Ended 1/31/2001	Year Ended 1/31/2002	Year Ended 1/31/2003	9 Mos. Ended 10/31/2002	9 Mos. Ended 10/31/2003
Revenues							
Service revenues	223	3,782	989	19,297	39,261	27,911	42,477
Technology revenues	0	0	0	100	20,909	18,544	13,671
Hardware revenues	0	0	0	0	45,620	31,109	47,345
Rebates and other payments to channel	−667	−5,029	−630	0	−9,780	−4,568	−5,045
Net Revenues	−444	−1,247	359	19,397	96,010	72,996	98,448
Costs and Expenses							
Cost of service revenues	4,183	18,734	1,719	19,825	17,119	12,399	12,453
Cost of technology revenues	0	0	0	62	8,033	5,924	11,113
Cost of hardware revenues	0	0	0	0	44,647	30,599	48,149
Research and development	10,158	25,070	2,544	27,205	20,714	14,395	16,693
Sales and marketing	39,183	151,658	13,946	104,897	48,117	44,152	14,205
General and administrative	7,834	15,537	1,395	18,875	14,465	11,100	11,788
Other operating expense, net	7,210	0	0	0	0	0	0
Loss from operations	−69,012	−212,246	19,245	−151,494	−57,085	−45,573	−15,953
Interest income/expense and other	2,447	7,406	655	−5,211	−23,086	−2,232	−3,552
Provision for income taxes	0	0	0	−1,000	−425	−261	−152
Net loss	−66,565	−204,840	−18,590	−157,705	−80,596	−48,066	−19,657
Net loss after Series A expenses	−66,565	−206,354	−19,013	−160,723	82,261	−49,731	−19,657
Net cash on hand (unrestricted)	139,687	106,096	124,474	52,327	44,201	40,593	61,807
Current assets	148,781	214,646	189,619	124,391	63,811	66,324	97,371
Long-term assets	4,061	21,672	21,924	22,543	18,509	21,474	14,546
Current liabilities	18,454	91,673	100,783	77,007	62,676	60,716	72,913
Long-term liabilities	1,141	12,806	13,868	56,316	44,341	46,784	47,613
Accumulated shareholders' deficit	−76,881	−283,235	−302,248	−462,971	−545,232	−512,702	−564,889
Total shareholders' deficit	133,247	34,849	50,337	−29,944	−24,697	−19,702	−8,609

Note 1: TiVo changed its fiscal year-end from December 31 to January 31 to better capture the holiday sales season in its fourth quarter. Due to this change the month ending January 31, 2001 was accounted for separately and not in conjunction with any fiscal year.

Note 2: Service revenues include customer subscription fees, showcases, and audience-measurement revenues; technology revenues include license fees and engineering service fees. Technology revenues were particularly high in FY 2003 due to a one-time payment from Sony of approximately $10 million as part of the sale of TiVo source code to Sony for use in Japan.

Source: Casewriter research, adapted from TiVo Inc. 10-K for the year ended January 31, 2003, published April 2003; and TiVo financial press releases, 2000–2003.

Advertisers

Although advertising had been in a lull given the U.S. economic recession, TV advertising remained significant, with advertising expenditures for broadcast and cable TV totaling over $57 billion in 2002 and total advertising in the United States representing 2% of the gross domestic product.[16] TV advertising was relatively much more important for broadcast networks than for cable operators because TV stations typically received about 90% of their revenues from advertising, while cable system operators received from 65% to 70% of their revenues from subscriber fees.[17] In addition, cable operators generated revenue from such things as installation charges and sales of VOD movies and events. About one-third of cable advertising revenues went to the cable operators and two-thirds to the cable networks, content generators such as Nickelodeon.

Some analysts believed that advertising was shifting away from traditional 30-second commercials and away from broadcast TV as the anchor medium. Advertising was instead moving toward such things as 1) "minimovies," which were in essence very entertaining commercials, often shown on the advertiser's (e.g., Anheuser Busch's) Web site; 2) creating TV series where product placement was integral (e.g., the reality TV series "Survivor" and MTV's "Surf Girl" series for young girls, which featured Roxy clothing); 3) commercial-free programming (the WB network was in the process of developing such a show, which would have two paid sponsors mentioned briefly at the beginning and end of the show); and 4) reallocation of some advertising dollars from TV to the Internet.[18] (In 2003, approximately $6 billion in advertising was spent on the Internet.) Overall, the trends signaled a move to more "opt-in" advertising, where the consumer chose which commercials he or she wanted to view.

TiVo's "Showcase" service, dubbed "advertainment" by some, fit in with this trend. Showcases provided specialized digital content meant to entertain subscribers while promoting an advertiser's product, such as a new movie or automobile. Subscribers could choose whether to "opt in" and could be given other choices

as well, for example, to enter a contest or receive a free product or brochure. These types of interactive features had to be written specifically for the TiVo platform. TiVo frequently sold Showcases in combination with another service aimed at networks and advertisers, TiVo's audience-measurement service. This service allowed second-by-second analysis of viewing patterns within TV programs or ads. Networks and advertisers could analyze such things as what percentage of viewers opted to watch a Showcase and how many times they watched it. Courtney explained, "TiVo charges a few hundred thousand dollars to place content over three to six months, although we're moving towards charging a cost per viewer fee so that revenues would reflect the size of the subscriber base." Showcase and audience-research revenues were relatively small, although Showcase revenues were projected to reach several million dollars in fiscal-year 2004. (See Exhibit 7.)

TiVo's Ecosystem

TiVo operated in a complex ecosystem, which required the company to manage a wide array of potential competitors, partners, and complementors. (See Exhibit 8.) The most important players for TiVo included content aggregators, such as the major networks, content providers, including the big entertainment companies, advertisers, consumer electronics companies, and content distributors, especially the MSOs (cable companies) and satellite operators.

Content Aggregators and Distributors

The three major types of TV distributors were the terrestrial TV stations, the cable operators, and the satellite companies. The Big Three broadcasters' (ABC, CBS, and NBC) share of the prime-time television audience had declined for several decades. Cable had grown to have the lion's share of U.S. TV households, while satellite's share was the fastest growing. The cable operators and the satellite companies were both potential DVR customers and potential DVR competitors.

Believing that it was important to have the blessing of at least some of the major TV networks and cable operators, TiVo management had pursued the networks and MSOs when searching for major equity investors early in the company's life. One-fourth of the company was owned by industry-related firms such as AOL Time Warner (10%), DirecTV (6%),

[16]"Industry Survey: Broadcasting and Cable," Standard & Poor's report, July 25, 2002, p. 1.

[17]Ibid., p. 12.

[18]Dr. Peter Sealey, "Commercial Television: Rest in Peace," speech to the 2003 Meeting of the Association of National Advertisers, March 13, 2003.

EXHIBIT 7

Types of Revenue Generated by TiVo's Lines of Business

Product or Service	Customer	Types of Revenue Generated
TiVo DVR	Consumers	*Hardware revenues* *Services revenues* (either a lifetime fee amortized over 48 months or a recurring monthly fee)
Showcases (advertising services)	Networks/studios/advertisers	*Services revenues* (the company intended to use a CPM-like model to charge for advertising services revenues)
Audience research services	Networks/advertisers	*Services revenues* (research services)
DVR technology	OEMs and CE manufacturer licensees	*Technology revenues,* which included 1) license fees—both up-front fees, which ranged from several million dollars for object code and up to $10 million for source code; 2) per unit license fees; and 3) engineering service fees, which were charged by the man-hour for the engineering services necessary to help OEMs and licensees adapt the TiVo technology to the licensees/OEMs' hardware. *Service revenues,* whenever TiVo received a percentage of the monthly fees paid by consumers to the CE or OEM; e.g., DirecTV paid TiVo a monthly per subscriber fee for each of DirecTV's DVR subscribers.

Source: TiVo Inc.

EXHIBIT 8

Home Entertainment Ecosystem

Source: Casewriters.

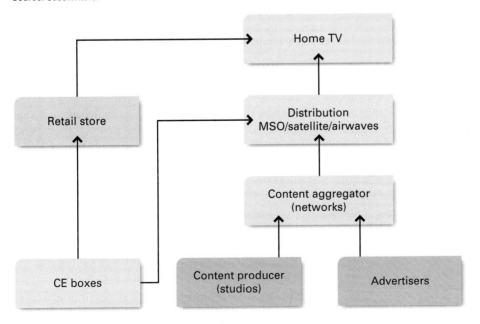

EXHIBIT 9

U.S. Satellite, Cable, and Broadband Subscribers and Monthly Revenue
(Q1 2003)

Company	Number of Subscribers	Net Adds, Q1 2003	Average Revenue per Customer per Month	Churn
DirecTV—satellite	11,420,000	245,000	$59.00	1.60%
EchoStar—satellite	8,530,000	350,000	$51.48	
Total Satellite	19,950,000	595,000		
Digital Cable subscribers	21,500,000	691,000	$60.00	
Analog (Basic) Cable subscribers	46,500,000	44,000	$40.57	2.50%
Broadband Internet—Top MSOs	12,304,779	1,250,831		
Broadband Internet—Top DSL Providers	6,806,000	651,918		
Total Broadband Internet	19,110,779	1,902,749	~$42	

Note 1: "Churn" is defined as the average monthly rate of loss of subscribers. Net new subscriber additions take churn into account.

Note 2: The top 10 MSOs represent approximately 90% of all cable subscribers.

Note 3: "Top MSOs" and "Top DSL Providers" represent approximately 98% of all broadband Internet subscribers.

Source: Casewriter research, adapted from TiVo financial statements; "US Premium Cable Subscription Market, 2002–2007," *eMarketer* report, May 1, 2003, Chase Carey (News Corp. board member), "Keynote speech at 2003 Spring SkyFORUM," May 20, 2003, <http://www.newscorp.com/news>, accessed July 3, 2003; David Lieberman, "Tolls Stack Up On Info Superhighway," *USA Today,* June 2, 2002, <http://www.usatoday.com/tech/news>, accessed July 3, 2003; "Research Notes 1Q 2003," Leichtman Research Group, Inc. report, p. 1; "Research Notes 2Q 2003," Leichtman Research Group, Inc. report, p. 9; David Farina, Mary O'Toole, and Ralph Schackart, "TiVo Inc.," William Blair & Company Research report, March 17, 2003, p. 25; Jed Kolko, with James L. McQuivey, Jennifer Gordon, and Charles Q. Strohm, "The Big Picture: Today's Consumer Approaches Technology with a Purpose," Forrester Research report, June 2003, p. 40.

Sony (5%), General Electric and its NBC subsidiary (4% combined), and Discovery Communications (1%). The chairman and CEO of Discovery, the president of NBC Cable, and the president of DirecTV Global Digital Media joined TiVo's board of directors.

The battle between cable and satellite had, important implications for TiVo. The MSOs were at a critical juncture in their history. In 2002, basic cable had lost subscribers, while satellite gained several million new customers.[19] The MSOs had spent billions of dollars in the past decade upgrading their systems to carry digital signals. Over the next several years, the cable industry was projected to go through a massive change, as millions of subscribers switched their analog set-top boxes for new digital boxes. Cable operators averaged around $40 per analog subscriber per month and $60 per digital subscriber, providing a big incentive for using consumers to make the switch. (See Exhibit 9.)

The MSOs had been very slow to adopt DVRs, with some, such as Comcast, urging the cable industry to adopt VOD instead of DVR. (See Exhibit 10.) Taken to an extreme, if all content were available "on demand," consumers would have no need for DVR products. AOL Time Warner was developing a large VOD system set to debut in mid-2005. Dubbed "Mystro TV," the system would store programming

[19]Chase Carey (News Corp. board member and industry consultant), "Keynote Speech at 2003 Spring SkyFORUM," May 20, 2003, <http://www.newscorp.com/news/news_191.html>, accessed July 2, 2003.

EXHIBIT 10

Cable Operators' VOD and DVR Activity (mid-2003)

Cable Operator	Millions of Subscribers		Current VOD Activity			Current DVR Activity			Comments
	Basic/Digital	Broadband	Deployment	Tests	Pricing	Deployment	Tests	Pricing	
Comcast/AT&T	21.3/6.8	3.3	30 markets (movie-based VOD) 2 markets (3-pronged VOD—see Note 2)	N/A	$3.95 for new releases $2.95 for library titles	None	2 markets Plan trials in 2003 with Ucentric and with Motorola DCT 6000 DVR-enabled set-top boxes	N/A	"Most bullish on VOD" (EVP, Marketing) 5%–6% VOD usage overall 25% usage in one market with 3-pronged VOD offered
Time Warner Cable	11.0/3.9	2.3	33 markets	N/A	N/A	14 markets (more than 100,000 in the field)	Plan trial in one market with Microsoft's DVR-capable IPG software	$4.95–$9.95 per month	"SVOD substantially reduces churn" by as much as 40% (EVP, Marketing)
Charter Communications	6.7/2.7	1.1	18 markets	SVOD being tested in 2 markets	$3.99 for new releases $2.99 for library titles	None	1 market Have ordered 100,000 DVR-enabled set-top boxes	N/A	"Not sure DVR and VOD need to coexist" (VP, Marketing)
Cox	6.3/2.7	1.3	4 markets	2 markets	$3.95 for most movies. Some content is free SVOD pricing will be $6.95 a month for HBO, Showtime, etc.	2 markets	None	$9.95 per month for 80GB storage plus set-top lease fee	"We're very encouraged by what we see with DVR" (VP, video product management)
Adelphia (in bankruptcy)	5.3/1.7	0.6	2 limited deployments	None	$3.99 for new releases $2.99 for library titles SVOD will be $5.95 per month for HBO, Showtime	None	None	N/A	
Cablevision	2.9/0.4	0.7	3 markets	None	$4.95 for new releases $2.95 for library titles $8.95 for adult titles	None	None	N/A	

Note 1: SVOD refers to subscription video on demand, which provided consumers with continuous access to certain content for a monthly fee.

Note 2: Comcast was experimenting with three types of VOD: (1) movie based; (2) an SVOD offering that provided access to Showtime content anytime; and (3) free VOD, which offered about 750 hours of a month of programming that could be accessed anytime, free of charge.

Source: "US Cable Subscriber Statistics," *eMarketer* report, April 1, 2003; "Deploy and Conquer," *Cable World*, April 7, 2003, **<http://www.seachangeinternational.com/news-events/articles/ 2003/Cable_World_April_7_2003.pdf>**, accessed July 23, 2003; Shirley Brady, "Mystro Wants to Play," *Cable World*, July 2, 2003, **<http://cableworld.com/microsites>**, accessed July 23, 2003; and "4Q 2002 Research Notes," Leichtman Research Group, Inc. report, p. 5.

C165

in the central "hubs" of cable networks, allowing the networks to control the features (e.g., there would be no ability to skip ads). The two largest roadblocks to developing the service were that cable hubs would need significant centralized storage capacity—compared to the TiVo system, where capacity was decentralized—and licensing agreements with studios and networks would be necessary.

The cable industry was highly fragmented, and cable set-top boxes could vary slightly from locale to locale. Most MSOs sold their DVR-capable set-top boxes directly through their local subsidiary. Both the Time Warner and Cox cable operations had begun using Scientific Atlanta's Explorer 8000—the first integrated set-top box for the cable industry—in local market experiments. Some of these experiments were proving very successful. The Time Warner cable operator in Rochester, New York, for example, had more than 12% of its subscribers sign up in the first six months.[20] TiVo management estimated that Time Warner had 100,000 DVR-capable boxes in place. Those cable companies offering DVR-capable receivers generally did not charge for the receiver/DVR set-top box (or charged a nominal monthly lease fee of $5), but they did charge a DVR subscription fee ranging from $5 to $10 a month. DVR was viewed by some as having the potential to help push consumers from analog cable to digital cable—or to satellite TV. One consulting firm's report highlighted DVR as one of two features that cable companies should use to gain and keep subscribers, recommending that MSOs offer DVR as a subscription-based service integrated with the cable EPG, with the DVR service priced at $4.99 per month to maximize revenue.[21]

Both U.S. satellite operators provided DVR capabilities. DirecTV utilized TiVo's DVR technology, and EchoStar offered DVR capability based on OpenTV's technology. Both satellite providers had been experiencing healthy growth rates. EchoStar's Dish Network was estimated to be one of the leading providers of DVR devices, with approximately 550,000 subscribers.[22] EchoStar initially offered DVRs for $100 with no service fee, but in the spring of 2003 it announced that new DVR customers would be charged a monthly fee of $9.99 per month for "Top 100" subscribers, $4.98 per month for "Top 150" subscribers, and no fee for premium-package subscribers.[23] However, EchoStar once again introduced an aggressive offer in the summer of 2003 when it began promoting "free DVR" for new customers who purchased the "Top 50" programming package (a $24.99 monthly fee) for a minimum of 12 months.

DirecTV had become a very successful channel for TiVo. However, the future of the DirecTV relationship was murky in 2003. In the late 1990s, TiVo had sold its first-generation product to BSkyB, a satellite operator in the United Kingdom. Rupert Murdoch, the CEO of News Corp. and the majority owner of BSkyB, discontinued TiVo, replacing it with a DVR product developed in-house using another technology. Because it had acquired Hughes Electronics, News Corp. was scheduled to take control of DirecTV in 2003—and given Murdoch's mercurial reputation, no one was certain about his plans for his new satellite company. Nonetheless, 200 man-years of engineering time had been dedicated by TiVo and DirecTV to make the integrated set-top box a success. Moreover, DirecTV announced publicly that it expected more than three-quarters of a million customers with integrated TiVo boxes in their homes by the end of 2003.

Relative to satellite and cable offerings, TiVo remained a highly differentiated product. The cable and satellite DVR products lacked the features that TiVo fans valued most (e.g., WishList, Season Pass, the ability to handle programming conflicts intelligently, and the suggestion engine), but MSO products as well as the EchoStar (Dish Network) DVRs were lower priced, with the hardware sometimes "leased" for free, and the service price ranging from free to $9.98 a month. In addition, DVR solutions that featured an integrated receiver/DVR set-top box helped ensure DVR accuracy and quality. A common problem for TiVo and other stand-alone DVRs was that they controlled nonintegrated set-top boxes indirectly via an infrared "blaster." Since the set-top box manufacturers had no incentives to help TiVo or other stand-alone DVRs interconnect with their products, such DVRs might fail to tune to the correct channel. Finally, when using an integrated

[20]Lance Williams, "Time Warner Launches DVR Service," *The Business Courier*, April 14, 2003 <http://boston.bizjournals.com/cincinnati/stories/2003/04/14/story4.html>, accessed July 15, 2003.
[21]Leszek Izdebski, "Path to Profitability: How Cable Companies Can Achieve Attractive Returns from iTV Services," an Accenture report, 2001, p. 6.
[22]"EchoStar/DISH US Subscriber Statistics, Q1 2003," *eMarketer*, April 1, 2003.
[23]Ellen Cheng, "EchoStar to Charge for Digital Video Recorder Functions," *Dow Jones Newswire*, July 30, 2003.

receiver/DVR set-top box, consumers did not have to have an extra set-top box on top of their television.

Content Providers

Filmed-entertainment content providers had become more concentrated following several acquisitions and mergers in the late 1990s and early 2000s. The industry's top nine companies owned a variety of entertainment assets ranging from Hollywood studios to television networks to theme parks. The four major U.S. TV broadcast networks, which attracted about 40% of prime-time viewers, were each owned by one of these top entertainment companies. Seven of the top nine companies also owned cable TV operations.

The TV and movie content providers were somewhat conflicted regarding DVR technology. On the one hand, several Hollywood studios sued TiVo competitor ReplayTV over its "send show" feature, which allowed consumers to record and then send shows to others, and its "commercial advance" feature, which allowed consumers to skip commercials with the push of a button. On the other hand, several large players had significant ownership positions in DVR companies—for example, AOL retained a large share of TiVo's equity; News Corp., which sold its own DVR product in the United Kingdom, was acquiring a controlling interest in Hughes Electronics, which owned DirecTV with its TiVo-powered DVR offering; and Sony manufactured and sold DVRs in Japan and in the United States. Some smaller players such as Liberty Media, which had a controlling interest of OpenTV, were also involved with DVR technologies.

In 2003, filmed-entertainment content providers were concerned about preserving their rights and not falling into the trap that music producers had fallen into when MP3 technology appeared. The widespread downloading of music over the Internet—without compensation—struck the music industry like a tidal wave, and although some players (such as Apple Computer) had introduced mechanisms to enable consumers to pay for downloads, the long-term outcome for the music industry was still unclear.

Equipment and Technology Competitors

In addition to cable and satellite DVR offerings, there were several other types of DVR competitors. (See Exhibits 11 and 12.) These included stand-alone DVR providers, technology-component (e.g., software and chips) suppliers, and PC manufacturers. ReplayTV was the only major competitor in the stand-alone DVR product category. Founded at about the same time as TiVo, ReplayTV sold the DVRs most often compared with TiVo's, with some reviewers preferring TiVo's features and some preferring ReplayTV's. However, ReplayTV, unlike TiVo, antagonized the TV and movie industry with some of its operational features and had not enjoyed the relative success of TiVo.

Initially ReplayTV did not charge a monthly service fee, instead charging more for the DVR unit, which included lifetime service. In 2002 Replay began charging a monthly service fee—$9.95—for the first time. Management said that although they and consumers believed that paying one price for the hardware and the service up front was much simpler, CE retailers wanted the DVR unit priced lower, and the only way to do that was to charge a separate service fee.

In part because the DVR was more like a computer than the typical CE device, there were several DVR component suppliers, with some selling to CE manufacturers and PC makers and others selling to consumers. Scientific Atlanta's combination cable receiver/DVR set-top boxes were powered by MetaByte Networks software and Keen Personal Media software. Keen received 80 cents per DVR. OpenTV's middleware platform was used by dozens of large and small set-top box manufacturers. Consumers could purchase one of several DVR hardware components or software packages, but these were for the more adventurous, as generally several components—costing several hundred dollars—were needed to make the PC a functional DVR. Some software packages required a monthly subscription fee of about $5 a month in order to receive an EPG, while in other cases, programming guide information was included for free. Almost all DVR component companies were experiencing financial difficulties, losing money and/or suffering a decline in revenues.

Consumers could also purchase PCs that included DVR technology. PCs that used Microsoft's Windows XP Media Center were the best example. HP and Gateway made such Media Center PCs, priced from about $1,400 to $2,000. The Sony Vaio also included DVR capability.

The Debate Over Future Strategies

The DVR industry was in a rapid state of change; each month brought an announcement of a new product or approach. TiVo management knew that

EXHIBIT 11

DVR Competitors (excludes pure DVR technology providers, as of June 2003)

Product	Company	Parent Company	DVR Technology Used	Box Manufacturer	Hard-Drive Capacity	Comments on Features	Price of Hardware	Subscription Fee	Total Estimated DVR Units Sold to Date
Stand-alone DVRs									
TiVo Series2	TiVo	N/A	TiVo	TiVo (contract mfr.) Sony	40GB–80GB 80GB		$249–$349 $449 (80GB)	$12.95 or $299 lifetime	433,000 (plus 270,000 DirecTV, see below)
ReplayTV	ReplayTV	D&M Holdings	ReplayTV	Various	40GB		$249 (40GB)	$9.95 or $250 lifetime	~120,000 (Replay TV '02 revenue was about $22mm)
Stand-alone DVD-DVRs									
DMR-HS2 (DVD-R-DVR)	Panasonic	Matsushita	N/A	Self	40GB	No EPG; no IR blaster	$999	None	
Scenium DRS7000ON (DVD-DVR)	RCA	N/A	N/A	Thomson	40GB	Only 2½ days of EPG; no IR blaster	$599	None	
Satellite and Cable Integrated Set-top Boxes									
HDVR2	DirecTV (satellite)	Hughes Electronics	TiVo	Hughes, Samsung, RCA, Philips	40GB		$199	$4.95; free to premium subscribers	270,000
DishPVR508 and 721	Dish Network (satellite)	EchoStar Communications	OpenTV	N/A	40GB–120GB		$199 to $549 with rebate	$4.98–$9.99; free to premium subscribers	550,000+
Digital Video Recorder	Time Warner Cable	AOL Time Warner	Scientific Atlanta 8000 with Keen and MetaByte Networks technology	Scientific Atlanta	40GB–80GB (2 tuners)		$650 list (free to digital subscribers)	$10	100,000+
PCs w/DRV software									
Media Center PC	Microsoft	N/A	Microsoft (Ultimate TV)	Various (e.g., Hewlett Packard)	30GB–90GB (75% of total storage)		$1,399–$1,999	None	300,000+ (~180,000 used as DVRs)

Source: Casewriter research, adapted from company Web sites (<http://www.tivo.com>, <http://www.digitalnetworksna.com/replaytv>, <http://www.rca.com>, <http://www.panasonic.com>, <http://www.directv.com>, <http://www.dishnetwork.com>, <http://www.timewarnercable.com>, <http://www.microsoft.com>), accessed July 14, 2003; "Interdependence Day," a CED In-depth report, July 2002; David Farina, Mary O'Toole, and Ralph Schackart, "TiVo Inc.," William Blair & Company, March 17, 2003, p. 13; "WinHec 2003 New Orleans," Jon Peddie research, May 9, 2003, <http://www.jonpeddie.com/dispatches/WinHec2003>, accessed August 6, 2003.

EXHIBIT 12

Product Features of Selected DVR Products

	TiVo Basic	TiVo Series2	TiVo S2 with Home Media	ReplayTV 4000	ReplayTV 5000	DirecTV with TiVo	EchoStar's Dish PVR 508	EchoStar's Dish PVR 721	Example Cable: Time Warner Scientific Atlanta 8000	Example DVD/DVR: Panasonic
Pricing—Hardware	Varies by CE manufacturer, but integrated DVD/DVRs will cost ~$500–$600	$249–40GB $349–80GB	N/A	$249	$349–$449 after rebate	$199	$199 with rebate	Bundled with a premium set-top box	Equipment leased free of charge (cost to cable company $300)	$500+
Pricing—Service	None	$12.95/mo. or $299 lifetime	$99 one-time fee per box to upgrade	$9.95/mo. $250 lifetime	$9.95/mo. or $250 lifetime	$4.95/mo. Free to premium subscribers	$4.98–$9.99/mo. Free to premium subscribers	$4.98–$9.99/mo. Free to premium subscribers	$9.95/mo.	None
Hard-disk recording, VCR style (e.g., by date, time)	x	x	x	x	x	x	x	x	x	x
Record from EPG	x	x	x	x	x	x	x	x	x	No
Amount of program guide data	3 days	14 days	14 days	12 days	12 days	14 days	7 days	7 days	7 days	N/A
Skip forward 30 seconds	x	x	x	x	x	x	x	x	x	x
Two tuners	No	No	N/A	No	No	x	No	x	x	No
Storage capacity (GB)	Varies	40–80	N/A	Up to 320	Up to 160	Up to 35	Up to 60	Up to 90	80	80
Ability to "suggest" shows to user based on user's viewing habits	No	x	x	No	No	x	No	No	No	No
Ability to let DVR know the types of shows the user is interested in by theme or person (e.g., gardening)	No	x	x	x (personal channels)	x (personal channels)	x	x (themes list)	x (themes list)	No	No
DVR is integrated into cable or satellite receiver	No	No	N/A	No	No	x	x	x	x	No
Ability to display digital photos	No	No	x	x	x	x	No	No	x	No
Ability to play digital music (MP3 files)	No	No	x	No	x	No	No	No	No	No
Source of DVR technology	TiVo	TiVo	TiVo	ReplayTV	ReplayTV	TiVo	OpenTV	OpenTV	MetaByte Networks & Keen Personal Media DVR software	

Note: Two tuners enabled a user to record two live programs at once, record live while watching live, or record two programs live while watching one prerecorded.

Source: Casewriter research, adapted from "Dish Network PVR Brochures," Dish Network Web site, **<http://www.pvrcmpare.com/featurechart.html>**, accessed July 9, 2003; TiVo Web site, **<http://www.tivo.com/2.0asp>**, accessed July 7, 2003; TiVo Inc. Form 10-K for years ended January 31, 2003, May 1, 2003, pp. 11–12.

the industry was likely to remain unsettled for the foreseeable future, making it even harder to predict which strategy had the best odds of succeeding. In mid-2003 TiVo management was debating many possible strategic options.

One option being debated was the possibility of **manufacturing and selling a TiVo Basic DVR** that would have no monthly fee. This was seen as having more upside and more risk than licensing CE manufacturers to include TiVo Basic functionality in high-end CE devices. On the upside, TiVo could sell a TiVo Basic DVR at a price point lower than bundled units offering basic functionality, plus engineering resources could be conserved. On the other hand, TiVo would receive no monthly revenues until buyers began upgrading to the full TiVo service, yet the company would incur some monthly costs for EPG content and transmission. Edward Lichty, TiVo's vice president of business development, pointed out that the cost to build a TiVo Basic DVR would not differ significantly from the cost to build a regular DVR given that the product needed to be automatically capable of being upgraded. "The two main issues we have to grapple with are how much we would cannibalize our current revenue stream, and whether the buyers of the TiVo basic product would upgrade," commented Lichty. Added Stuart West, the vice president of finance:

> There's a tension between making the TiVo Basic service good enough to sell a machine, but not so good that consumers won't want to upgrade to the full service. The key is how many customers will convert. Somewhere around 20% the model doesn't work, but at 50 to 60% or higher, it's fantastic. Predicting how many would convert is critical—but obviously not possible. We have to be comfortable with uncertainty to take that step.

Another more radical option was **manufacturing and selling a DVR "white box" to CE retailers,** allowing the retailers to sell their own branded DVR device. Jeff Klugman, the vice president of the licensing group, believed that most CE companies had relatively high cost structures, in part because they had been slow to move their manufacturing operations offshore and in part because they had to amortize large R&D budgets. "One example of a company that used offshore manufacturing to their big advantage is Apex, who went from number ten to number one in DVD market share in a very short time," explained

Klugman. Apex sourced its products from multiple Chinese manufacturers and had a three- to six-month design cycle, compared with the Japanese DVD manufacturers' two-year cycle.[24] Many TiVo executives were uncomfortable with the "white box" option. Echoing the thoughts of others, Klugman commented, "We don't want to be Lexus, and it's OK to be Toyota, but we don't want to be Hyundai."

Another option being debated was exploring ways to lower the price of TiVo-enabled units at retail. Cashen believed this was important because there were certain market segments that were very interested in purchasing TiVo but could not quite afford it. One way in which this could be done was by **lowering the license fee TiVo charged CE manufacturers.** Lowering the per unit license fee by $1.00 decreased the retail price by $1.50, to $1.75, and lowering the up-front license fee lowered the amount of amortized license fee per unit sold. This was one way in which TiVo could help reduce the retail price of its CE licensees' products, thus helping spur demand. In addition, this might help TiVo expand its pool of CE partners. Klugman explained, "We want consumers to see TiVo associated with many different brands at retail—and I think that DVD-Rs [units that could record as well as play DVDs] will be the driving force that pulls DVR." The obvious downside to lowering fees associated with licensing was that the company was on the cusp of breaking even, a goal viewed as very important to investors.

Given the large number of cable TV households and the shift from analog to digital cable boxes under way, TiVo management often discussed **entering into a major partnership with a cable company.** Clearly, the biggest upside in terms of TV homes lay in the cable market. Klugman emphasized the need to move quickly in the DVR market, saying, "We need to swing for the fences. Losing a cable household today to a digital cable/DVR box means you lose them for at least five years." And several executives believed that TiVo had a compelling story for the cable operators, whose promises to Wall Street about VOD generating large profits had not yet materialized. Marty Yudkovitz,

---

[24]Russ Arensman, "Watch Out Sony: Apex Is Taking Aim at TVs," *Electronic Business,* May 1, 2002, <**http://www.e-insite.net/eb-mag**>, accessed July 20, 2003.

TiVo's president, believed that TiVo could make an appealing offer:

> We can offer cable—and satellite—a stream of enhanced advertising revenue and other premium-service revenue that they hadn't planned on if they use TiVo's Showcases. Since this additional revenue would come without additional capital investment, or operational headache or risk, it would be a great demonstration to Wall Street of the leverage the MSO can get from having built the new digital plant. And we've found from our satellite and stand-alone business that TiVo subscribers use their DVRs far more than any other DVR service, an issue of importance to cable and satellite distributors. The technology is great, but the economic impact of TiVo is what can really make a difference to distributors.

Despite the importance of the cable market, entering into a substantive partnership with a cable company presented several challenges. West elaborated, "One obvious challenge is whether the cable companies will settle on a 'good enough' solution from their current set-top box suppliers—Scientific Atlanta and Motorola—or whether they will want to go with a new provider that can offer a better product and enhanced revenue potential." The second challenge was whether, given the market-by-market monopsony into which cable market suppliers sold, TiVo would be able to build a profitable business in the cable market. One of the major economic negotiating points for TiVo management was the company's goal of receiving recurring fees, as was the case with TiVo's DirecTV partnership in the satellite industry. The goal of receiving ongoing fees conflicted with the cable industry's custom of paying up-front fees for hardware (set-top boxes) and not sharing any of the ongoing subscriber revenues. TiVo management was well aware of the many cable industry suppliers that had been very successful in terms of volumes of units sold to the industry—but very unsuccessful in terms of making a profit. Yet another challenge was that TiVo would probably have to integrate into one of the standard industry set-top boxes. TiVo could become a software application that operated on a Scientific Atlanta or Motorola box. Despite these challenges, the possibility of a major cable partnership remained a widely discussed alternative.

Some executives argued that, while continuing to push for mass deployment in the DVR market was important, **expanding efforts to grow TiVo's services for advertisers** was equally important. The advertising market was enormous, and the TV audience-measurement research market was also large, with Nielsen—the largest supplier in the audience-research market—having an estimated $800 million in revenues. In addition, although Nielsen measured TV program ratings, no one currently measured the ratings of ads.

Yudkovitz believed strongly that TiVo should be a television services company. Prior to joining TiVo in the spring of 2003, he had been an executive at NBC, where for 20 years he was involved with most of NBC's new business initiatives—including programming, cable, and Internet. He shared his point of view:

> Our customers will be media companies—programmers, broadcasters, networks, satellite and cable distributors, and advertisers—as well as consumers for consumer-facing services. We can deepen the media companies' connection with the customer, allow the consumer to interact and become more involved with the advertising and programming, and measure all of it in a way that no other service does. This is exactly what interactive TV tried to do for so long without success—the difference is that we've actually done it in the marketplace. Two-thirds of our viewers opt in to one of our Showcases each month and spend an average of four minutes viewing it.
>
> For an advertiser to be able to enhance their ads with interaction and measurement is key. To track the effectiveness of ad viewing in various programming in various parts of the country is a major step forward for advertisers. The fact that we can offer a better financial proposition—for example, offering ad enhancement and other premium services that drive revenue up, and costs and churn down—is what will make the difference. We can change the way that advertising is bought and sold on television, and in the war between the networks and advertisers, I want to be the arms dealer.

Cashen agreed and shared her belief that the company had proven that Showcases could work well for advertisers:

> Our Showcases are very compelling. Even our worst performing Showcase attracted 35% of our subscribers for about two to three minutes. Our most successful Showcase attracted over two-thirds of our subscribers for an average of four to six minutes each, with many subscribers watching that Showcase—which featured Mike Myers talking about the movie *Austin Powers in Goldmember*—multiple times.

The last major strategic option being discussed was **focusing resources on developing new DVR and home entertainment capabilities.** Several executives believed that pursuing this option was important to the company's future. Barton expanded on the dilemma faced by engineering:

> Our engineering work for OEMs and licensees provides us with revenues and some margin, and we use the opportunity to enhance aspects of our system architecture. Nevertheless, there are some costs, as we're not able to work as much on other projects. The types of things we would spend more time on if we could include software portability, improving Showcase authoring capabilities to make Showcases more dynamic, developing the ability to work with another EPG supplier, and continuing to upgrade the user interface. Our next big development opportunities are making the platform more advertiser friendly and continuing to make the TiVo DVR cheaper.

Lichty believed that DVR technology was fast becoming a commodity and that therefore TiVo needed to become a platform for delivering distinctive value-added services such as the HMO. "The only way to keep your pricing up is to have unique offerings," he said. Brodie Keast, TiVo's senior vice president and general manager of TiVo service, agreed, adding that, along with developing new not-yet-announced services for the TiVo platform, the company should develop tiered pricing for different levels and types of service.

The View from TiVo

Ramsay worried that if the consumer adoption rate remained relatively slow, it would give competitors time to catch up. This meant that TiVo was truly at an inflection point. Should the company aggressively pursue mass deployment? Or should the company focus its limited resources on product development and differentiation? Ramsay understood that it was in TiVo's best interest for both the industry and TiVo to grow rapidly. The fact that millions of households still had analog cable service convinced him that there was still much room to maneuver—but again, TiVo had to move quickly to convert these consumers to TiVo users before the cable operators upgraded the consumers to new digital receivers using another company's DVR technology. Yudkovitz believed that there were no longer any obstacles to mass deployment, sharing that "it's now obvious that DVRs will be mass deployed, and even the cable and media folks accept that." Yet Ramsay also believed that DVR providers that did not charge a monthly service fee would eventually see the error of their ways. "My prediction is that people who give it away will realize that it's expensive to do—and they will eventually go back and do it right," he said. And finally, he was convinced that TiVo needed to maintain its position as the value-added DVR leader able to charge premium pricing if the company was to keep from falling into the trap that so many DVR providers had—charging very little for their products and hoping to "make it up in volume." Given TiVo management's emphasis on cash flow break-even, he knew that the company would have to focus primarily on just one of the many options being debated. The company simply did not have the luxury of pursuing them all.

The Music Industry in the Age of the Internet: From Napster to Apple's iPod

This case was prepared by Charles W. L. Hill, the University of Washington.

Sometime in the fall of 1998, an indifferent eighteen-year-old student at Northeastern University in Boston had an epiphany. Wouldn't it be great, he thought, if people could share their music with each other over the Internet.[1] The student's name was Shawn Fanning, and the service that grew out of his epiphany, Napster, would shake the very foundations of the music recording industry. By 2000, Napster had taken center stage in a pivotal struggle for the future of the industry. On one side was the Recording Industry Association of America (RIAA), the big five music recording labels, and several high-profile recording artists, all of whom argued that Napster was violating copyright laws, facilitating the illegal copying and distribution of copyrighted music, and should be shut down. On the other was a small company with less than fifty employees and limited funds, but which had 30 million users. In the middle was the U.S. judicial system.

By 2001, the RIAA had won the first round of the struggle. Napster had been effectively put out of business by judicial decree. But the genie that Napster sprung out of the Internet bottle would not go back in.

New file sharing technologies based on peer-to-peer computing such as Kazaa had sprung up and were diffusing rapidly through the Internet. Unlike Napster, these new technologies were proving to be more difficult to stop. To complicate matters further, the music recording labels knew that even if they could shut down Kazaa and its ilk for copyright violations, the digital distribution of music over the Internet was here to stay and might potentially revolutionize the industry value chain. Consequently, in the wake of Napster's decline they decided to set up their own Internet-based distribution services. But demand for these services was slow to develop, and they were soon eclipsed by the rapid rise of Apple's iPod digital music player and iTunes online music service. From a standing start in 2001, Apple generated over $1 billion in sales from the iPod and iTunes service in 2004. In 2000, industry observers were fretting over the possibility that Napster might revolutionize the music industry—now it looked as if Apple was doing just that.

The Music Recording Industry

The music recording industry grew at a robust rate throughout the 1990s, registering global sales of $38.5 billion in 1999. The largest markets were the United States (37 percent), Japan (16.7 percent), the United Kingdom (7.6 percent), Germany (7.4 percent), France (5.2 percent), and Canada (2.3 percent). The growth was helped by the introduction of a new technology in the late 1980s, CDs, and significant replacement demand as consumers replaced their favorite vinyl records with CDs. By 2003, CD sales dominated the U.S. market for record sales, accounting for $11.2 billion out of an $11.85 billion total. Cassette tapes accounted for $108 million in sales, and vinyl records just $21 million. A relatively new product category, DVD videos, accounted for some $369 million of sales in 2003, up from $80 million in 2000.[2]

The years of strong growth came to an end in 2000, when global sales fell 5 percent. They fell for the next three years, hitting a low of $32 billion in 2003. Despite the fall in sales, the International Federation of the Phonographic Industry (IFPI) claimed that demand for music was higher than ever, but that the decline in sales reflected the fact that "the commercial value of music is being widely devalued by mass copying and piracy."[3] According to the IFPI, 40 percent of all CDs and cassettes around the globe were illegally produced and sold in 2003, suggesting that piracy cost the industry over $12 billion per annum.[4] Although historically illegal plants in Asia have been the source of many pirated CDs and tapes, by the early 2000s the IFPI was increasingly concerned about consumers "burning" songs downloaded over the Internet onto CDs. In Germany, 18 percent of 10,000 consumers surveyed in 2001 said burning CDs resulted in them buying less music. In the United States in 2001, nearly 70 percent of people who downloaded music burned the songs onto a CD-R disc, while 35 percent of people downloading more than twenty songs per month said they purchased less music as a result.[5]

Industry Structure

In 2003, the industry was dominated by five large recording companies that collectively accounted for around 75 percent of global recorded music sales (see Exhibit 1 for market share figures). The five were Sony Music, Universal Music Group (which was owned by Vivendi, a French media conglomerate), EMI, Warner Music Group, and Bertelsmann Music Group or BMG (owned by Bertelsmann, a large German media conglomerate). The industry concentration was due in large part to mergers between majors and acquisitions of independent record labels by the majors during the 1990s.

The last big merger between majors occurred in the late 1990s, when Universal acquired PolyGram NV for $10.5 billion. In 2000, Warner Music Group and EMI had attempted to merge their activities, but were prohibited from doing so by antitrust authorities in the European Union (EU), who believed that the merger would put too much market power in the hands of a small number of recording labels. At the time, Warner was owned by the media conglomerate AOL Time Warner. Having failed in their attempt to merge with EMI, Time Warner subsequently spun off Warner to a group of independent investors led by Edgar Bronfman for $2.6 billion. Bronfman was at one time CEO of Seagram, which owned Universal Music. Bronfman had sold Seagram to Vivendi for $30 billion in 2000. In explaining his reentry into the industry, Bronfman argued that despite several years of declining revenues, demand could improve in the future as illegal Internet-based distribution services were replaced with legal services such as Apple's iTunes.[6]

In 2004, Sony made a bid to acquire BMG. Many thought that once again, the EU antitrust authorities would stand in the way of a deal. But in a closed door session before the EU's competition commission, the companies argued that the rise of Internet-based music distribution services were hurting the big labels, and the merger was necessary to reduce costs and respond to this new competitive threat. This time the EU bought the argument, and the merger was cleared both by EU regulators, and then by regulators in the United States. In August 2004, the deal was completed. The new

EXHIBIT 1

Global Market Share Figures, 2002 and 2003

Year	BMG	EMI	Sony	Universal	Warner	Independents
2002	9.6%	12.2%	13.8%	25.4%	11.8%	27.1%
2003	11.9%	13.4%	13.2%	23.5%	12.7%	25.3%

Source: IFPI, "IFPI publishes global market shares." IFPI Press Release, June 16, 2004.

company, known as Sony BMG Music Entertainment, rivaled Universal in market share. After the merger, Sony BMG stated that it would lay off 20 percent of the combined workforce as part of a plan to achieve annual cost savings of $350 million.[7]

The Hit Making Machine

Music recording companies sign artists in return for royalties on units sold, which generally run between 12 percent and 16 percent of net revenues. The typical contract specifies that in return for royalties on future sales, the copyright of the artists' creations become the property of the music company. Most contracts also bind recording artists to multi-album deals with the recording company—a constraint that many successful artists try to break (the artist formally known as Prince being a prime example).

The music company bears the costs of recording and producing the music, pressing the CDs, marketing, and distribution. Production costs for a typical album are around $125,000, but they can reach $1 million. Marketing expenses range from $100,000 to over $500,000 per album for a major artist. Music videos are now an essential additional marketing tool for many artists, and production costs for those can run anywhere from $100,000 to $250,000. Thus, it can cost from $350,000 to $2 million to launch an artist.[8] Under standard royalty contracts, these upfront costs are normally deducted from the artists' royalties. Moreover, under an industry practice know as cross-collateralization, if an artist does not cover product and marketing costs on their first album, the deficit is then applied to the second album, and so on, making it very difficult for some artists to ever make a return from their work.

The hit rate in the music business is very low. Although there are rare cases of instant hits where an album will sell over a million copies, the vast majority of new CDs are never profitable. Each year the major music recording companies issue about 7,000 new CDs (and minor "independent" labels issue another 20,000). Most never recover the upfront recording and marketing costs. In the end, less than 10 percent are profitable. Music recording companies make most of their returns from a handful of "gold" albums that sell over 500,000 copies a year. In 2001, of some 6,455 new albums released by major labels, only 112 sold at least that many.[9]

A *Wall Street Journal* article reported one example of how difficult it is to produce a hit album. In 2001, MCA, which is part of the Universal Music Group, spent some $2.2 million to produce and promote an eighteen-year-old artist from Ireland, Carly Hennessy. MCA hoped that Hennessy would be the next teen diva. She had a very strong singing voice, good looks, and stage presence. Her album, *Ultimate High*, was produced by Gregg Alexander, who had produced albums for The Spice Girls. The single from the album, "I'm Going to Blow Your Mind," was accompanied by a video that cost $250,000 to make. The reviews were solid. Carly Hennessy went on a four-week promotional tour, which cost a further $150,000, and involved Hennessy singing at malls and radio-sponsored concerts. MCA also spent some $200,000 to hire independent promoters, who visited radio producers to try and secure airplay. It was all to no avail. Three months after the release of the album, it had sold just 378 copies, generating $4,900 in revenues, and Ms. Hennessy disappeared from public view.[10]

Record industry executives claim that producing a new hit album has become ever harder due to industry trends. Most new acts first get heard on radio, but deregulation of the radio industry in 1996 ushered in a wave of consolidation, with companies like Clear Channel Communications purchasing rival radio stations. Under increased pressures to maximize audience ratings, radio stations now quickly pull songs that are not instant nationwide hits. The growing importance of music videos also makes it more difficult to succeed, since there are only a limited number of TV stations that play music videos, such as MTV and VH1, and they, too, quickly pull videos that are not instant hits.

In the 1950s and 1960s, the industry would pay radio station deejays to play records. The practice, know as "payola," caused a major scandal when it was exposed in the 1960s, and is now illegal. Under current law, broadcasters are prohibited from taking cash or anything of value in return for playing a specific song, unless they disclose the transaction to listeners. But in a practice that is common in the industry, major record labels hire independent promoters, who in turn pay radio stations annual fees, which range from $20,000 to $300,000, not to play specific records, but to get advanced access to a stations' play lists. The promoters then bill the record labels for each new song that is played. In echoes of the 1960s payola scandals, in late 2004, New York Attorney General Elliot Spitzer announced his intention to investigate the practice of using independent promoters for possible antitrust violations. For their part, radio stations argue that the use of independent promoters hasn't affected their airplay decisions. In 2003, in an attempt to avoid the appearance of pay for play, Clear Channel Communications, the nation's largest radio chain, ended its deals with promoters.[11]

Distribution

Historically, the other big players in the music industry have been retailers. In 2003, 86 percent of sales of recorded music in the United States were still made through retail stores. However, the nature of distribution was changing, with discount stores such as Wal-Mart beginning to account for a larger proportion of total CD sales as opposed to traditional music retailers. In 1994, traditional music stores accounted for 53.3 percent of record sales, but only 33.2 percent in 2003. Sales over the Internet were still small in 2003, amounting to just 5 percent of the total, but they had grown from just 1 percent in 1998.[12] Amazon.com, in particular, was emerging as an important distributor of CDs over the Internet, while Apple's iTunes business accounted for around 1 percent of total sales in 2003, but it was growing very fast. In addition, experiments by the big five music companies in the online distribution of music were causing tensions with retailers, who started to fear that they might be cut out of the equation.

Industry Pricing Trends

Since CDs were first introduced in 1983, their average price in real terms has fallen significantly. Between 1983 and 1996, the average price of a CD fell by more than 40 percent, while the consumer price index rose by nearly 60 percent. Despite the price fall, antitrust authorities on both sides of the Atlantic have investigated the music recording industry for alleged price fixing. In May 2000, the big five companies settled a suit with the United States Federal Trade Commission, agreeing to end a requirement that retail stores adhere to minimum prices in advertisements.[13] The agreement was expected to open the way for more price discounting of CDs in retail stores.[14] In August 2001, the EU ended a similar investigation after three major recording companies agreed to end minimum price requirements.

In September 2003, Universal rocked the music industry when it announced its intention to significantly cut prices for CDs. The company stated that it would drop its wholesale price by just over $3 from

$12.12 to $9.09, and lower the suggested retail price by $6 from $18.98 to $12.98. In addition, Universal said that it would end cooperative advertising payments, discounting programs, and other mechanisms that gave retailers an incentive to sell CDs at a lower price. None of Universal's major rivals followed suit.[15]

For this initiative to work, Universal reportedly had to see sales volume rise by 21 percent to offset the lower wholesale price. However, in the first nine months of the initiative the company reportedly only saw volume increases in the 8 percent to 13 percent range. In part, this was because discount retailers such as Wal-Mart and Best Buy were already offering CDs at a low price to drive traffic into their stores. As for traditional music retailers, such as Tower Records, many of them simply refused to follow the suggested retail price. Indeed, they stated that if Universal placed a sticker with the recommended retail price on a CD, which was the company's original plan, they would cover it up with a sticker of their own charging a higher price. By late 2004, it appeared as if Universal was retreating from its price initiative, and was nudging wholesale prices back up.[16]

Intellectual Property Rights, Technology, and Piracy

Music recordings are copyrighted material. In the United States, the rights given to copyright holders are based on the Copyright Act on 1976 (similar legislation exists in other nations, and intellectual property is protected under World Trade Organization agreements, which over 120 countries have signed). Under the 1976 act, copyright holders have the exclusive right to control the reproduction, modification, distribution, public performance, and public displays of their copyrighted material. This set of rights can be violated in three ways:[17]

1. **Direct copyright infringement:** The direct infringer violated any of the copyright holder's exclusive rights. For example, producing and selling a CD without obtaining permission from the copyright holder.

2. **Vicarious copyright infringement:** The vicarious infringer had the right and ability to control the direct infringer's actions and reaped financial benefits from those actions. For example, the courts have held that swap meet organizers vicariously infringed if they knowingly created and administered a market in which bootleg music is bought and sold and are paid a fee for admission.

3. **Contributory copyright infringement:** The infringer knowingly induced or caused the directly infringing conduct. For example, an electronic bulletin board service was found liable when it encouraged subscribers to upload *Playboy* pictures so that other subscribers could download them.

Historically the music industry had always been concerned about the potential for piracy of copyrighted material. New technology has often facilitated the low-cost copying and distribution of music. In the 1960s and 1970s, the advent of the audio cassette tape led to widespread illegal copying and distribution of music. In the early 1990s, the industry was deeply concerned about attempts by Sony to commercialize its digital audio tape (DAT) technology, which they felt would facilitate high fidelity copying of recorded music and thus lead to greater piracy. Although the RIAA initially opposed Sony, they switched to supporting the technology once Sony agreed to incorporate software that would make it difficult to use DAT technology to make multiple copies of a music recording. In addition, in 1992 the Audio Home Recording Act required DAT manufacturers to pay a royalty on each blank tape they sold to compensate music companies for the piracy that would take place through DAT. In any event, DAT technology was not accepted by consumers, but it was clear the underlying copyright issues would not go away.

Another technology that raised the specter of copyright infringement was MP3. Originally developed in the 1980s, MP3 is a software technology for creating compressed digital music files which could be downloaded for free from the Internet. MP3 music files were created through a process knowing as "ripping," in which computer owners copy a CD into MP3's digital format that is about one-twelfth the size of the original file. This compression was achieved by eliminating overlapping sound waves and digital audio signals that fell outside of human hearing range. The great virtue of compressed MP3 files is that they take up less space on a hard drive, and can be transferred more easily over the Internet. Until the late 1990s, however, the speed of most Internet connections was so slow that there was little online demand for MP3 music files. Three things changed that: the emergence of high-speed Internet connections, especially on college campuses; the growth of websites such as MP3.com, which

archived MP3 files; and the introduction of portable MP3 players.

In November 1997, MP3.com launched its site. MP3.com had purchased thousands of CDs and converted their contents into MP3 files which were stored on its web servers, where subscribers to MP3.com's service could access and download them. In an attempt to protect itself from legal problems, MP3.com required users to demonstrate that they owned the CD for which they were downloading MP3 files by inserting a copy of the CD into their computer's CD-ROM drive for a few seconds, where it could be detected by software MP3.com used. In the same year, Diamond Multimedia introduced the Rio, a small portable device that could play up to two hours of MP3s.

The music industry immediately saw the threat—consumers could use high-speed Internet connections to download MP3 files over the Internet and store them on their Rios, circumventing copyright in the process. The RIAA filed a temporary restraining order against Diamond in October 1998, but the U.S. Court of Appeals ruled that converting the digital content of a CD to other formats for personal use was protected by the so called *fair use* doctrine contained in the 1976 Copyright Act (the fair use doctrine allows individuals to make copies from copyrighted material they have purchased for their personal use—i.e., not for resale or distribution).

Having failed to halt the sale of the Rio, Universal Music Group (UMG) immediately went after websites from which MP3 files could be downloaded. MP3.com was the obvious first target. In May 2000, the U.S. District Court ruled that MP3.com had directly infringed on music companies' copyrights, noting that in actuality MP3.com was "replaying for the subscribers converted versions of the recordings it copied, without authorization, from plaintiffs' copyrighted CDs."[18] On September 6, Judge Jed Rakoff delivered his ruling that MP3.com would have to pay the music companies $25,000 for each of the CDs it had copied to stream to consumers who also owned those discs. It looked as if MP3.com would have to pay UMG between $118 million and $250 million. In making his judgment, Rakoff stated that "some companies operating in the area of the Internet seemed to believe that because their technology is somewhat novel, they are somehow immune from the ordinary application of the law."[19] Around the same time, the

RIAA was also trying to shut down another Internet music service, Napster.

In addition to seeking legal recourse against copyright violators, the music industry also tried to develop technology that would protect digital audio recordings from piracy and counterfeiting. The RIAA recruited Leonard Chiariglione, inventor of the MP3 format, to head up the effort. Chiariglione pulled together a consortium of 180 firms, including record companies and consumer electronics and software firms, in an attempt to create the Security Digital Music Initiative (SDMI), a set of technological guidelines that was intended to reduce the risk of copyright infringements of digital audio media. The SDMI tried to develop guidelines for two types of security measures: (1) digital watermarks would be embedded in digital music, which then could only be played on SDMI compliant music players, and (2) digital rights management technology would embed digital music within an encrypted digital package that would limit the number of times a CD could be copied. Unfortunately, the SDMI made little progress, reportedly because there were too many competing voices, all with veto power. Apparently, different sides in the industry kept vetoing each other's schemes for copyright protection.[20]

Blindsided: The Rise of Napster

While the music industry was struggling with the SDMI, Shawn Fanning was giving birth to its biggest challenge yet, Napster. There was nothing remarkable about Fanning that would lead one to believe that he would spawn a potentially world-shattering idea.[21] One of five children, he grew up in Brockton, Massachusetts, a small town some twenty miles south of Boston. His family was solidly working class with one exception, his uncle, John Fanning, was a computer industry entrepreneur who ran a company called NetGames. During summers at high school, Shawn worked at John's company where he picked up programming skills from other interns who were studying computer science at Carnegie Mellon. It was at this time that he also became a regular visitor to Internet chat rooms, and particularly Internet Rely Chat, or IRC, which had become a de facto meeting place in cyberspace for hackers, traders of copied software and music, and so on. To enter IRC rooms, Fanning had to give a user name, so he chose his nickname from high school, Napster.

Although Fanning tried to get into Carnegie Mellon, he had to settle for Northeastern. As luck would have it, one of Fanning's roommates was obsessed with MP3 technology, which he used to download music from Internet sites and play on his computer. What caught Fanning's interest was not so much the ability to trade music files over the Internet using MP3 technology, as his roommate's constant complaints about the process. Internet music sites were not always easy to find, they were unreliable, the links were often broken, and the indices listing music on a site were more often than not out of date. At the time, Fanning was disenchanted with his courses at Northeastern, which he found to be pretty basic, and was looking around for something to do. Solving his roommate's problems seemed to fit the bill.

As it developed, Fanning's approach to fixing this problem was relatively straightforward. He envisioned an index managed by a central server that would list all of the MP3 music files that people had on their hard drives and were willing to share, along with the embedded web addresses of their location. The list could be created if people downloaded a piece of "client" software onto their PCs. This software would update the central list every time someone logged onto the Internet, or logged off. The MP3 files themselves would continue to reside on the hard drives of individual PCs. To download a file, a user simply had to click on the title of the song, and so long as the PC where the title was located was logged on, the file would be transferred from one PC to the other over the Internet.

In essence, Fanning was proposing to create a peer-to-peer network of personal computers, coordinated by a central server that managed the index of MP3 files. First of all, however, Fanning had to get the program written, and he needed some help. Fanning roped in two friends, Jordan Ritter and Sean Parker, that he had met through an online hacker group called w00w00. Together they would develop the core of Napster. As Ritter later commented, "At that stage, Napster was really just Shawn and a bunch of friends trying to help out. There were no venture capitalists, no uncles on the scene and no shady hangers on."[22] What drove Fanning on, according to another friend, was that people kept telling him it wouldn't work. They said that people would not be willing to share their music files. According to this friend, Fanning was "driven more by the desire to prove to everyone that he was right than he was by any realization or recognition of a potential revolution."[23]

By early 1999, Shawn Fanning had dropped out of Northeastern and was working around the clock writing code for the server and client. To prove his doubters wrong, he decided to try out an early version of his software, which he had christened Napster, giving out the client software to around thirty friends. He asked them not to pass it on, an instruction that several ignored, and within a few days, the software had been downloaded by about three to four thousand people. Many of these early adopters proved to be an invaluable resource, providing feedback that helped Fanning to improve the software.

It was around this time that Shawn Fanning told his uncle, thirty-six-year-old John Fanning, what he was up to. John quickly saw the commercial potential of Napster. In May 1999, he incorporated Napster as a company and went looking for investors. According to *Business Week*, when the company was incorporated John took 70 percent of the equity and Shawn 30 percent.[24] One insider reportedly commented that "I am told that this was done without Shawn Fanning's immediate knowledge or involvement. Newspapers have accurately reported the morally deplorable distribution of equity."[25]

Digital Boom

The embryonic company clearly had a number of problems to solve. First, it needed capital; second, it had to develop a business model that would enable it to profit from the service; and third, it needed to prepare itself for the inevitable challenge from the RIAA. Early on, John Fanning began to explore the legal ramifications of Napster's business. Among others, he consulted with the law firm of Wilson, Sonsini, Goodrich & Rosati, which had successfully defended Diamond Multimedia against the RIAA. The conversations reportedly gave John the confidence to push the business forward, and the belief that if Napster were sued, the company would have a good shot of winning in court.[26] John seemed to think that because Napster did not actually copy and distribute MP3 files, but simply put people who wanted to swap files in touch with each other, it was not breaking the law.

In the summer of 1999, John Fanning started to get initial funding for Napster. His first calls were to high–net worth individuals whom he knew personally. A friend, Yosi Amram, kicked in $250,000, and another added $100,000. By the end of the summer,

John had raised enough capital to keep Napster going through to year end. Napster moved to Silicon Valley in the fall of 1999, primarily on John's suggestion that being in the Valley would help in the quest to raise more capital. Shawn and his friends (now all Napster employees) were working long stints writing code—sixteen- to twenty-hour days—while John was out looking for more venture capital.

In September, realizing that the company needed a CEO who could develop a business model, Eileen Richardson, who had ten years' experience in the venture capital world—but had never run a company—was hired. Richardson's main claim to fame was that she had led an investment in Firefly, an Internet service that recommends music that was subsequently purchased by Microsoft. Her task was to help secure additional funding, develop a business model, and then hand off the job to her replacement. In October 1999, Napster had raised $2 million in series B venture capital funding from a number of wealthy Silicon Valley executives, including Angel Investors founding partner, Ron Conway, and Joe Kraus, founder of *Excite@Home*. What helped to secure the funds for the fledgling company was the extraordinary growth of Napster over the previous few months.

Formally launched in June 1999, the program spread with unprecedented speed. There was no marketing or advertising to sell the service, which was given away for free. The service spread through word of mouth. The early adopters were students on university campuses with access to personal computers and high bandwidth Internet connections. In the fall of 1999, there was a feature on Napster on the website download.com. This helped to raise the service to new heights. In July 1999, the Napster community was estimated at 4.9 million. By October 2000, it was 32 million, and the site was growing by a million users a week, with some 800,000 logged on at any one time.

Among the first to take notice were the administrators of university computing and communications resources. The utilization of their networks was skyrocketing as students used them to transfer MP3 files. By October 1999, Napster was already occupying 10 percent of the Internet bandwidth capacity at Oregon State University, which became the first to ban the service. At Florida State University Napster was taking up 20 to 30 percent of bandwidth, and at the University of Illinois, the figures at times soared to seventy-five to eighty percent. Soon, university after university banned Napster. In almost all cases, the primary motive was not the protection of copyright, but a desire to protect scarce computing resources from being soaked up by Napster. By February 2000, for example, the popularity of Napster had pushed network utilization at New York University to 98 percent, slowing down access and impeding its value as an academic tool. Once Napster was banned, network utilization dropped immediately to 60 percent of capacity.[27] Not all universities banned Napster, however. Several Ivy League universities, including MIT and Harvard, continued to allow students to use the service, citing their commitment to providing Internet access for all of their community, and noting that they did not regulate or monitor a user's choice of sites to visit. Moreover, in many universities that did ban Napster, students fought back using 1960s style rhetoric to claim that a ban on Napster amounted to "censorship" and a violation of free speech.

Why was Napster so attractive? The obvious appeal was that users could download music for free. Why pay $17.95 for a CD that contained ten tracks—only three of which you wanted—when you could download the best three from the Internet for free and leave out the junk? Others cited the immediacy of the technology. To get new music, you didn't have to go down to a music store. You just booted up your computer, logged onto the service, and quickly downloaded what you wanted. Many also found it interesting to browse through the play lists of other users, finding music that they would not otherwise listen to. And you could find music on Napster that you could not find in a retail store: old music recordings, esoteric music, unpopular noncommercial music, and so on. Napster also seemed to go hand in hand with two other developments: the spread of portable MP3 players and new technology that allowed PC users to burn or create customized CDs. In both cases, users could create personal collections or play lists of music tracks from Napster downloads.

According to an RIAA survey of 1,015 music consumers on the attractions of peer to peer file sharing services, having access to a large selection and variety of artists ranked highest (87 percent), followed by the capability to download files quickly (84 percent), the ability to download individual songs (83 percent), a convenient search feature (81 percent), and the ability to get music for free (79 percent). Ability to access songs not commercially available ranked lowest (64 percent).[28]

Collision Course

It was soon apparent that Napster was on a collision course with the music industry. The core of the problem, according to the RIAA, was that Napster's service was violating copyright, facilitating massive piracy of intellectual property, and consequently stealing. The RIAA, along with executives from several music companies, started informal discussions with Napster during the late summer of 1999. Record industry executives insist that the talks were a sincere attempt to find some common ground. One idea being floated at the time was to sell a minority stake in Napster to the record companies, and allow Napster to license a host of content. On the other hand, many Napster insiders believed that the record industry executives were never serious about negotiating a deal, and they were just biding time. Whatever the truth, many observers do agree that Napster's new CEO, Eileen Richardson, did nothing to help matters. By all reports, Richardson had an abrasive and combative manner in her dealings with the record companies and RIAA, which only served to distance the two sides.[29] For example, the following exchange apparently occurred in a CNN online chat room:

> *RIAA*: While there are many legitimate uses of MP3s, don't you feel that your service will be primarily used by music pirates?
> *Eileen Richardson*: We are about enabling amateur and unknown artists to share their music on this new medium. Our job is not to stop pirating, that is your job.[30]

According to other sources, Eileen Richardson was once heard yelling on the phone to Frank Creighton, the head of the RIAA's antipiracy group. Richardson also had face-to-face meetings with Hilary Rosen, the RIAA's president, that apparently did not go too well. One observer noted that "Eileen got into fights with Hilary. . . . Eileen was fairly arrogant and thought what they were doing was right."[31]

Whatever the truth, on December 7, 1999, with talks between Napster and the RIAA at an impasse, the RIAA filed suit against Napster on behalf of eighteen record companies, citing copyright infringement. Several songwriters filed suit a few days later, and others were to follow. The RIAA alleged that Napster was vicariously infringing copyright and that it contributed to the direct infringement of copyright held by members of the music industry. The RIAA claimed damages of $100,000 for each copyrighted musical work that was copied as a result of Napster's software. For its part, Napster contended that its users did not infringe copyright because they only made personal copies and used the service in a way that amounted to sampling. The "fair use" section of the 1976 Copyright Protection Act stated, "The fair use of a copyrighted work, including such use by reproduction in copies or phonorecords or by any other means specified by that section, for purposes such as criticism, comment, news reporting, teaching (including multiple copies for class room use), scholarship, or research, is not an infringement of copyright."[32]

One of the most high-profile suits filed by songwriters was by the music group Metallica. Metallica had protested that Napster's users were engaged in the unauthorized copying and distribution of copyrighted material. Napster responded that if Metallicca could identify users that were violating copyright law, it would remove them from the service. In April 2000, the band's attorney, Howard King, filed suit against Napster and several universities that allowed the service to continue, alleging that Napster and the universities were violating the Racketeering Influenced and Corrupt Organizations Act, legislation that was originally aimed at organized crime. King and the band's drummer, Lars Ulrich, also turned up at Napster's headquarters with thirteen boxes of computer printouts that contained the names of 335,435 Napster users who had swapped Metallica MP3 files and asked Napster to take them off the service. According to Ulrich, their complaint was that "Napster hijacked our music without asking . . . my band authored the music which is Napster's lifeblood. We should decide what happens to it, not Napster—a company with no rights in our recordings, which has never invested a penny in Metallica's music or had anything to do with its creation."[33] Shawn Fanning, a Metallica fan himself, was somewhat disturbed at the criticism made by one of his heroes. Thereafter, he would frequently appear in public wearing a Metallica T-shirt, most notably, at the MTV Music Awards, where Ulrich sat in the audience.

One of the defenses of Napster often voiced at this time was that far from hurting CD sales, Napster actually encouraged them. The basic argument was that Napster was dispensing free samples. When something was appealing enough as a sound file on a

home computer, people would go out to a record store and buy the entire CD, just as they would if they had heard the song on the radio.[41] In early 2000, N Sync, Britney Spears, and Eminem each had huge hits. In the weeks before their records came out, these were the three most heavily trafficked artists on Napster's services, causing some to wonder if marketing departments at their respective labels had seeded Napster with prerelease copies of their music as a promotional tool.[42] In contrast to Metallica, some musicians also supported Napster. Smashing Pumpkins broke with its label, Virgin, and gave away the group's final album for free via Napster, a move that met with a massive response. Even some senior record industry executives seemed to exhibit a degree of schizophrenia. Thomas Middelhoff, the CEO of Bertelsmann, owner of BMG, noted, "Let's be honest, despite all the dangers, Napster is pretty cool." He thought that file sharing as a system was a great idea, but that Fanning's mistake was "not having developed a complementary system for the protection of intellectual property rights and combining the two."[43]

Roadblock

By late spring Napster had its back against the wall. Not only was the company the object of several lawsuits, but it was also fast running out of cash. Into the breach stepped Hummer Winblad, a high-profile Silicon Valley venture capital firm. On May 21, Hummer Winblad announced that it would invest $15 million in Napster. A Hummer Winblad partner, Hank Barry, was brought in as CEO, replacing Richardson, while Hummer cofounder, John Hummer, joined Napster's board. Hank Barry was an interesting choice for CEO. A former lawyer with a strong background in intellectual property law, he promised to build a working business model for the company and to solve its legal problems. One of Barry's first actions was to bring in David Boies, who had led the Justice Department to victory in the Microsoft antitrust case, to defend Napster against the RIAA. He also hired two seasoned record industry executives to round out the senior management team.

However, Barry had little breathing room. The pace of the legal assault against Napster was quickening. On June 12, 2000, the RIAA filed for a preliminary injunction that would shut down Napster pending trial, citing ongoing and widespread copyright infringement that was causing the industry great harm. On July 26, 2000, Napster had its day in court. Inside Napster, there seemed to be a strong belief that the company would triumph. John Fanning sent around an internal e-mail stating, "If the motion is granted, the order will be stayed pending appeal to the Ninth Circuit, where the motion will be decided . . . and if they rule against us, which I view as a 10% chance, we would be appealing to the Supreme Court, where the future of the world will be hanging in the balance."[44] It was not to be. After a two-hour hearing and a brief fifteen-minute recess, the presiding judge dismissed virtually every argument that Boies could muster for Napster, and granted the injunction. In making her ruling, Judge Marilyn Patel noted that there was a big

difference between making copies for friends, which might be protected by the fair use section of the 1976 act, and making copies available via Napster, where a music file could be downloaded by millions of anonymous users.[45]

With the injunction granted, and the service shut down, Barry scrambled to develop a business model that would make sense and would facilitate an alliance with Napster's opponents, the music labels. With the cash burn rate running in excess of $500,000 a month, Barry realized that he needed to move as expeditiously as possible. One idea floated was for the music labels to take a minority stake in Napster, and split subscription, sponsorship, and advertising revenues. The economics seemed compelling; if 20 million users (half of Napster's total in mid 2000) paid $100 a year for subscriptions that would allow for unlimited downloads, that would be $2 billion a year for Napster and the record labels. One survey found that 68 percent of Napster users would be prepared to pay a $15 monthly subscription for the service. Barry himself was reportedly contemplating a subscription of $4.95 a month.[46]

In the interim, Napster continued to hope that it would ultimately win out in court but that hope was dashed when on February 12, 2001, a three-judge panel from the Ninth Circuit Court of Appeals issued its ruling. The Appeals Court upheld Patel's injunction and determined that Napster should be held liable for copyright infringement. The judges stated that using Napster to "get something for free they would ordinarily have to buy" was a commercial use, and thus copyright infringement. Although the Appeals Court did send the injunction back to Patel for clarification, it was clear that Napster would get little relief from the courts. The service stayed shut.

BMG Attempts a Rescue

While the court drama was unfolding, on October 31, 2000, Bertelsmann (owner of BMG) broke ranks with the other major labels and announced that it was forming an alliance with Napster to develop a subscription based music distribution service based on Napster's peer-to-peer technology. As part of the alliance, Bertelsmann provided Napster with a $60 million loan, buying the service much needed time. In explaining the decision, Bertelsmann's CEO Thomas Middelhoff indicated that the genie was already out of the bottle with file swapping technology. Indeed, with two other Napster alternatives, Gnutella and FreeNet, already making an appearance, Middelhoff suggested that the industry needed to embrace the technology, not rail against it in the courts.

Middelhoff's goal was that BMG and Napster would introduce a paid subscription service by mid 2001. However, progress was slow. In November 2001, with no subscription service in sight, and Napster's service now shut down, Bertelsmann kicked in an additional $25 million loan to help the company. By early 2002, Bertelsmann was contemplating a bid to buyout Napster for $15 million.[47] However, the bid was derailed by internal strife at Napster. On March 25, board member John Fanning filed a lawsuit against two fellow directors, John Hummer and Hank Barry, claiming that the two venture capitalists were no longer directors because they were voted out on March 24, 2002. Napster's new CEO, the third, Konrad Hilbers, issued a statement calling the lawsuit "legally groundless." Observers speculated that the reason for the lawsuit was that Napster was running out of cash, and might have to file for bankruptcy, leaving John Fanning (and very possibly Shawn Fanning) with no return from Napster. On April 12, Napster announced that it would lay off 30 percent of its workforce, and this followed a 10 percent reduction in the previous month.[48]

In mid May, CEO Hilbers resigned after Napster's board formally rejected a buyout offer from BMG. Most of the management team resigned at the same time, including company cofounder Shawn Fanning. With no service to offer, no business model, and no cash in hand, it was only a matter of time. On September 4, 2002, Napster announced its liquidation.

The Revolution Continues

With Napster on a death watch, the major record labels continued to push ahead with plans to introduce their own online music service. In early 2002, the big five companies launched two services. Both services sold monthly subscriptions that allow users to listen to songs without downloading by using streaming audio technology. Alternatively, subscribers could download versions of songs that in most cases could not be burned onto a CD or transferred to a portable device. Each service only offered songs from certain labels.

MusicNet, which offered songs from Warner Music, BMG, and EMI, had one subscription plan—$9.85 a month for 100 streams and 100 downloads. After 30 days, downloads expired and couldn't be played.

Pressplay, which offered music from Sony, Universal, and EMI, had 4 subscription plans, from $9.95 to $24.95 a month, for up to 1,000 streams and 100 downloads. The higher subscription fee service from Pressplay let users burn up to 20 songs a month onto CDs that would not expire, but no more than two songs could be burned from any one artist.[49]

Second Generation Peer to Peer Networks

The introduction of legal services for downloading music over the Internet did little to stop online piracy. In very short order after Napster's service was shut down, a number of new file sharing services started to rapidly gain users. Foremost among these were Kazaa, Grokster, and Morpheus. By mid 2002, these three networks had some 70 million active users between them, more than twice the users Napster had at its peak.[50] These services were all peer to peer networks, but, unlike Napster, they did not rely upon a central registry or central server to track and control the transfer of files between users. These second generation networks were truly distributed and decentralized. All one needed to do was download the software from a central site, and you were ready to go. The software would reach out over the net and link up with other users of that software, scanning their play lists to find the song you were looking for. No central institution mediated, controlled, or tracked the transfer of a file from one computer to another. They were true peer to peer networks.

The music industry responded as it had with Napster, filing lawsuits in an attempt to shut down the services for copyright violation. But in this case it was more difficult to prove infringement. The software had legal uses, too—for example, file sharing within an organization—and its makers claimed that they could not control how it was used. The music industry filed its first suit against several second generation peer to peer networks in October 2001. In April 2003, the court ruled that the creators of Internet file sharing software should be allowed to stay in business, despite piracy by users of their programs. According to the court, the makers of such software were not violating copyright by simply making software available that allows users to trade files. The industry immediately appealed, and the case wound up at the Ninth Circuit Court of Appeals in San Francisco—the very same court that had shut down Napster. The appeal was to no avail, however, for in August 2004 the higher court upheld the lower court's ruling.

The Big Chill

By this juncture, however, the industry had decided on a different approach to the copyright problem—to go after users. In 2003, the industry won a landmark case against Verizon, which runs a broadband Internet service, forcing the company to release the names of subscribers who were believed to be infringing copyright. The RIAA then sent subpoenas to Internet Service Providers, seeking to have them identify and contact customers who were potential copyright infringers. Armed with names, between September and December 2003 the RIAA sued some 382 individuals for copyright infringement. All of these individuals had made over 1,000 unique copyrighted files available for distribution to millions of other users of peer to peer networks. The law allowed the RIAA to collect up to $150,000 per violation. Many of those identified quickly settled out-of-court, reportedly for amounts ranging from $2,500 to $10,000, although some individuals elected to fight in court, arguing that their privacy rights had been invaded.[51]

According to comScore Media Matrix, an online tracking service, the effect was immediate. In the four months following the RIAA announcement that it would sue individuals for copyright violation, the percentage of Americans who downloaded music over the Internet dropped by half from 29 percent of Internet users to just 18 percent. Moreover, on an average day during early 2003, some 4 percent of Internet users surveyed said they downloaded music files. The same survey in late 2003 found that only 1 percent admitted to downloading music files. comScore also found that the user base for peer-to-peer applications fell between 9 percent and 59 percent from November 2002 to November 2003 depending on the network. Mirroring this decline was a rapid rise in usage of legal online music services, such as Apple's iTunes.[52]

In a spring 2004 survey, comScore found that the number of people actively running second generation peer to peer networks continued to decline, with 5 million fewer people running the largest network, which is based on software from Kazaa. Moreover, the same data indicated that in March more than 11 million U.S. Internet users visited six major paid online music services.[53]

Throughout 2004, the RIAA kept up its legal assault against people who use peer to peer networks to illegally download music. In the first three months of 2004 alone, it filed almost 1,600 lawsuits, roughly 530 a month. Those targeted were sharing an average of 837 songs. In March the RIAA targeted users at twenty-one universities around the country. The RIAA also sent letters to several universities detailing massive illegal uploading of digital music files through their networks. The universities responded by taking steps to stop downloading. Virginia State University put in firewalls that block known sites for illegal music, and updated the firewalls as new sites emerged. Columbia University placed limits on outgoing bandwidth usage, and simultaneously disseminated material to students informing them that it is illegal to share copyrighted material over the Internet. The University of Florida developed its own software to detect illegal downloading from peer to peer networks. Students who do so are cut off from the Internet—fifteen minutes for the first offense and five days for the second offense. To regain access they have to read a presentation about copyright law. Third time offenders are cut off for 30 days and a notice is placed in their academic files. In the first 10 months of operation, the University caught 4,000 first time violators, 400 second time violators, and just 7 third time violators. There have been no fourth time violators.[54]

Apple's iTunes and iPod

Apple's entry into the music downloading business was born out of an oversight—in the late 1990s, when students were starting to burn their favorite CDs, Macs did not have a CD burner or software to manage their digital music collections. Realizing the mistake, CEO Steven Jobs ordered Apple's software developers to create the iTunes program to help Mac users manage their growing digital music collections. The first iTunes program led to the concept of the iPod. If people were going to maintain the bulk of their music collection on a computer, they needed a portable device to take music with them—a Sony Walkman for the digital age. While there were such devices on the market already, they could only hold a few dozen songs each.

To run the iPod, Apple licensed software from PortalPlayer. Apple also learnt that Toshiba was building a tiny 1.8 inch hard drive that could hold over one thousand songs. Apple quickly cut a deal with Toshiba, giving it exclusive rights to the drive for eighteen months. Meanwhile, Apple's engineers focused on designing the user interface, the exterior styling, and the synchronization software to make it work with the Mac.

The iPod was unveiled in October 2001 to mixed reviews. The price of $399 was significantly above that of competing devices, and since the iPod only worked with Apple computers, it seemed destined to be a niche product. However, initial sales were strong. It turned out that consumers were willing to pay a premium price for the iPod's huge storage capacity. Moreover, Jobs made the call to develop a version of the iPod that would be compatible with Windows. After it was introduced in mid 2002, sales surged.

By this times Jobs was dealing with a bigger strategic issue—how to persuade the music companies to make their music available for legal downloads. By all accounts, it was here that Steve Job's legendary selling ability came into play. With a prototype for an online iTunes store in hand, Jobs met with executives from the major labels. He persuaded them that it was in their best interest to support a legal music download business. People would pay to download music over the Internet, he argued. Although all of the labels were setting up their own online businesses, Jobs felt that since they were limited to selling music owned by the parent companies, demand would be limited too. What was needed was a reputable, independent online music retailer, and Apple fit the bill. If it was going to work, however, all of the labels needed to get on board. Under Jobs's scheme, iTunes files would be downloaded for 99 cents each. The only portable digital player that the files could be stored and played on was an iPod. Jobs's pitch was that this closed world made it easier to protect copyrighted material from unauthorized distribution.

Jobs also met with twenty of the world's top recording artists, including U2's Bono, Sheryl Crow, and Mick Jagger. His pitch to them—digital distribution is going to happen, and the best way to protect your interests is to support a legal online music distribution business. Wooed by Jobs, these powerful stakeholders encouraged the music recording companies to take Apple's proposal seriously.

By early 2003, Jobs had all of the major labels onboard. Launched in April 2003, within days it was clear that Apple had a major hit on its hands. A million songs were sold in the first week. In mid 2004, iTunes passed the 100 million download mark and sales kept accelerating, hitting the 150 million download market in October 2004. At that point, customers were downloading over 4 million songs per week, which represented a run rate of more than 200 million a year. However, Jobs has admitted that Apple does not make much money from iTune downloads, probably only 10 cents a song, but it does make good margins on

sales of the iPod—and sales of the iPod ballooned in late 2004. By September 2004, Apple had sold 5.7 million iPods, some 2 million in the third quarter alone, netting over $500 million in revenues. iTunes revenues for the third quarter were close to $100 million. Apple had 61 percent of the total digital audio player market at that point and more than 90 percent of the market for high-capacity players.[55]

As 2004 drew to a close, the pace of expansion in Apple's legal digital music business did not seem to be slowing down. In mid 2004, Apple inked a deal with Hewlett Packard under which HP would install iTunes software on its PCs and sell iPods under its brand name. In October 2004, Apple opened iTunes stores to serve Europe and Canada, and Japan was reportedly next in line.

The Emerging Competitive Battle

As 2004 drew to a close, there were signs that the competitive battle to dominate the legal music download business was heating up. A host of other device makers were offering powerful portable digital audio players, although none worked with iTunes. RealNetworks had entered the online music business in 2002 and now had some 1 million subscribers who paid $9.95 a month to listen to music streamed to their PC through Real Player. They could choose from a playlist that included some 700,000 titles. Although the streamed media could not be downloaded onto PCs or portable devices, Real had also set up a Real Player online music store. This sold downloads that could be played on a wide range of portable devices, including the iPod. In August 2004, Real started to sell music downloads at 49 cents each—far below the 89 cents Real had to pay the music companies for the titles. The sales promotion was scheduled to last for just three weeks, but some observers wondered if it was the first shot in a price war.[56] Wal-Mart was also offering music downloads from its website at 89 cents each.

In the fall of 2004, Microsoft entered the fray. The company announced that the new version of Windows Media Player would synchronize with legal online music stores and with a wide range of mobile devices. Using Media Player, users could browse different stores, download music onto their PC, and transfer it onto a portable device, all while staying with Media Player.

Napster also resurfaced in 2003, this time as a legal streaming media and music downloading service owned by Roxio, which made its name selling CD burning software. Roxio had purchased the rights to the defunct company's brand name for $6.1 million in November 2002. The company then purchased PressPlay from Sony and Universal in March 2003 for some $39 million. Roxio also persuaded Samsung to create a portable music player designed to work with the new service. Launched in October 2003, the service, dubbed Napster 2.0, offers downloads for 99 cents each and the ability to stream songs to a PC for $9.95 a month. In September 2004, Napster raised the competitive stakes when it introduced a service, called Napster to Go, which enables consumers to download an unlimited number of songs for a subscription price of just $14.95 a month.[57]

Yahoo also entered the market in late 2004 when it purchased Musicmatch, a software company whose jukebox software to digitalize CDs had been preinstalled on Dell PCs for several years. Musicmatch had set up an online store for downloading music that by late 2004 was selling 1.5 to 2 million downloads per month, roughly similar to estimates of the monthly download rate at Napster and Real Networks. Apple, in contrast, was estimated to be selling some 16 million downloads per month.[58]

ENDNOTES

1. Trevor Merriden, *Irresistible Forces* (Oxford, UK: Capstone Books, 2001).
2. Recording Industry Association of America, 2003 Year End Statistics, archived at **www.riaa.com**.
3. IFPI news release, "Global Music Sales Down 5% in 2001," **www.ifpi.org**.
4. International Federation of the Phonographic Industry, Commercial Piracy Report 2004, **www.ifpi.org**.
5. IFPI News release, "Global Music Sales Down 5% in 2001," **www.ifpi.org**.
6. J.R. Laing, "Bronfman's Return," *Barron's*, December 1, 2003, page 13.
7. B. Mitchener, "Sony, Bertelsmann Deal Defended," *Wall Street Journal*, June 10, 2004, page B4.
8. RIAA, "How Much Does It Cost to Make a CD?" **www.riaa.org**.
9. J. Ordonez, "Behind the Music," *Wall Street Journal*, February 26, 2002, page A1.
10. Ibid.
11. E. Smith, "Spitzer Probes How Music Labels Get Radio Airplay," *Wall Street Journal*, October 22, 2004, page A2.
12. Recording Industry Association of America, 2003 Consumer Profile, at **www.riaa.com**.
13. J.R. Wilke, "Music Firms, U.S. Hold Settlement Talks." *Wall Street Journal*, December 16, 1999, page A3.
14. J.R. Wilke, "FTC Move Expected to Bring Lower CD Prices," *Wall Street Journal*, May 10, 2000, page A3.
15. E. Smith, "Universal's CD Price Cuts Will Squeeze Music Retailers," *Wall Street Journal*, September 18, 2003, page B1.
16. E. Smith, "Harsh Feedback," *Wall Street Journal*, June 4, 2004, page A1.
17. D. Kiron, C.E. Bagley, and M.J. Roberts, Napster, Harvard Business School Case # 801-219, March 29, 2001.
18. UMG Recordings v MP3.com Inc., 92 F. Supp. 2d 349 (S.D.N.Y. 2000).
19. John Alderman, *Sonic Boom* (Cambridge, MA: Perseus Publishing, 2001), page 143.
20. Ibid., page 91.
21. Ibid.
22. Merriden, *Irresistible Forces*, page 6.
23. Ibid., page 7.
24. S.P. Ante, S.V. Brull., D.K. Berman, and M. France, "How the Music Sharing Phenomenon Began, Where It Went Wrong, and What Happens Next," *Business Week*, August 14, 2000, pages 112–120.
25. Merriden, *Irresistible Forces*, page 9.
26. Ante, Brull, Berman, and France, "How the Music Sharing Phenomenon Began," pages 112–120.
27. Ibid.
28. RIAA, Market Data, **www.riaa.org**.
29. Ante, Brull, Berman, and France, "How the Music Sharing Phenomenon Began," pages 112–120.
30. Cited in D. Kiron, C.E. Bagley, and M.J. Roberts, Napster, Harvard Business School Case # 801-219, March 29, 2001.
31. Ante, Brull, Berman, and France, "How the Music Sharing Phenomenon Began," pages 112–120.
32. Section 107 on the Copyright Act of 1976.
33. **Salon.com** magazine, May 1, 2000.
34. Merriden, *Irresistible Forces*, page 45.
35. Ibid.
36. Alderman, *Sonic Boom*, page 114.
37. Ibid., page 116.
38. Ibid., page 10.
39. Merriden, *Irresistible Forces*, page 26.
40. Ante, Brull, Berman, and France, "How the Music Sharing Phenomenon Began," page 114.
41. J. Selvin, "Did Napster Help Boost Record Sales?" *San Francisco Chronicle*, August 5, 2001.
42. Alderman, *Sonic Boom*, page 117.
43. Ibid., page 116.
44. Quoted in Ante, Brull., Berman and France, "How the Music Sharing Phenomenon Began," pages 112–120.
45. Anonymous, "Rewired for Sound," *The Economist*, August 5, 2000, pages 59–60.
46. S. Ante, "Napster: Tune In, Turn on, Pay Up," *Business Week*, November 13, 2000, page 52.
47. L. Himelstein and T. Lowry, "The Sound at Napster: Tick, Tick, Tick," *Business Week*, April 8, 2002, page 73.
48. N. Wingfield, "Napster Lays Off 30% of Workers," *Wall Street Journal*, April 12, 2002, page A 16.
49. W.S. Mossberg, "Record Labels Launch Two Feeble Services to Replace Napster," *Wall Street Journal*, February 7, 2002, page B1.
50. M. Warner, "The New Napsters," *Fortune*, August 12, 2002, pages 115–117.
51. N. Wingfield and S. McBride, "Green Light for Grokster," *Wall Street Journal*, August 20, 2004, page B1.
52. comScore Matrix, "Sharp Decline in Music File Swapping," Press Release, January 4, 2004, archived at **comscore.com**.
53. comScore Matrix, "One in Seven Internet Users Say They No Longer Download Music Files," Press Release, April 26, 2004, archived at **comscore.com**.
54. S. McBride, "Stop the Music!" *Wall Street Journal*, August 23, 2004, page B1.
55. N. Wingfield and E. Smith, "U2's Gig: Help Apple Sell iPods," *Wall Street Journal*, October 20, 2004, page D5; Apple Computer Press Release, "iTunes Music Store Downloads Top 150 Million Songs," October 14, 2004.
56. N. Wingfield, "Price War in Online Music," *Wall Street Journal*, August 17, 2004, page D1.
57. P. Burrows, "Napster Lives Again," *Business Week*, October 20, 2003, page 66; "Napster to Go," *Wall Street Journal*, September 2, page 1.
58. K.J. Delaney, "Yahoo Agrees to Buy Musicmatch," *Wall Street Journal*, September 15, 2004, page B10.

Staples

This case was prepared by Charles W. L. Hill, the University of Washington.

Introduction

It was 1985, and a thirty-six-year-old retailer called Tom Stemberg was being interviewed by the CEO of the Dutch-based warehouse club, Makro, for the top job at Makro's nascent U.S. operation. Stemberg didn't think Makro's concept would work in the United States, but he was struck by one thing as he toured Makro's first U.S. store in Langhorne, Pennsylvania: office supplies were flying off the shelves. "It was obvious that this merchandise was moving very fast," he later recalled. "That aisle (where the office supplies were located) was just devastated."[1] Stemberg began to wonder whether an office supplies supermarket would be a viable concept. He thought it might be possible that a supermarket selling just office supplies could do to the office supplies business what Toys "R" Us had done to the fragmented toy retailing industry; that is, consolidate it and create enormous economic value in the process.

Within a year Stemberg had founded Staples, the first office supplies supermarket. Less than two decades later, Staples was a leading retailer in the office supplies business with 1,088 stores in the United States, 212 in Canada, and 188 in Europe. Its revenues for 2003 exceeded $13 billion, net profit was over $540 million, and the company had earned a return on invested capital of between 12.5 percent and 14 percent for the last six years, which was considered high for retailing.[2]

Tom Stemberg

Despite his young age, by 1985 Stemberg had assembled an impressive resume in retailing. Stemberg had been born in Los Angeles but spent much of his teens in Austria, where his parents were originally from. He moved back to the United States to enter Harvard University, ultimately graduating with an MBA from Harvard Business School in 1973. Stemberg was hired out of Harvard by the Jewel Corporation, which put him to work at Star Market, the company's supermarket grocery division in the Boston area.

Henry Nasella, Stemberg's first boss at Jewel, who would later work for Stemberg at Staples, remembers meeting Stemberg on his first day at Jewel: "He came in 15 minutes late, his hair too long, his tie over his shoulder, his shirt hanging out over the back of his pants. I thought, what in the world do I have here?"[3] (Stemberg is still known for his disheveled appearance.) What he had was a man who started out on the store floor, bagging groceries, stocking the aisle, and ringing up sales at the checkout counter. Stemberg rose rapidly, however, and by the time he was twenty-eight, he had been named vice president of sales and marketing at Star Market, the youngest vice president in the history of the Jewel Corporation.

At Jewel, Stemberg became known as an aggressive marketer, competing vigorously on price and introducing generic brands (Stemberg developed and launched the first line of "generic" foods sold in the country).[4] According to Stemberg, "It was a nutso thing we were trying to do, and the fact that it worked out well was a miracle. We opened all these big stores, and we were trying to take market share away from people who were much better financed than we were. They retaliated and lowered prices. . . . I learnt to experience the challenges of rapid growth. There was no better experience to have been through. It taught me the necessity of having infrastructure and putting it in place."[5]

One of the supermarkets that Stemberg found himself battling with was Heartland Food Warehouse, the first successful deep discount warehouse supermarket in the country. Heartland was run by Leo Kahn, one of the country's leading supermarket retailers. Kahn had started the Purity Supreme supermarket chain in the late 1940s, making him one of the founding fathers of the supermarket business. Stemberg and Kahn fought relentless marketing battles with each other. In a typical example of their tussles, at one point Kahn ran ads guaranteeing that his customers would get the best price on Thanksgiving turkeys. Stemberg responded with his own ads promising that Star would match the lowest advertised price on turkeys. Technically that made Kahn's claim incorrect, a point that Stemberg made to the Massachusetts attorney general's office, who told Kahn to pull his ad.

In 1982, Stemberg left Jewel to run the grocery division of another retailer, First National Supermarkets Inc. To build market share, he decided to take the company into the warehouse food business, imitating Leo Kahn's Heartland chain. Stemberg soon came into conflict with the CEO at First National. As he later admitted, "I probably didn't do a very good job, in a corporate political sense, of making sure he understood the risks in what we were trying to do. The situation was very stressful."[6] In January 1985, things came to a head and Stemberg was fired. It was probably the best thing that ever happened to him.

When Kahn heard that Stemberg had been fired, he quickly got in touch with him. Kahn had just sold his own business for $80 million, and he was looking for investment opportunities. He had developed a great respect for his old adversary, and wanted to back him in a new retailing venture. As Stemberg paraphrases it, Kahn said "I want to back you in a business kid, what have you got in mind?"[7] Kahn agreed to put up $500,000 in seed money to help Stemberg develop a new venture opportunity. He also took on the role of mentor, evaluating Stemberg's ideas.

Initially Kahn and Stemberg looked at the business they both knew best, supermarket grocery retailing.

But they were put off by the intense competition now raging in the business, and the high price they would have to pay for properties. At this juncture, Bob Nakasone, then president of Toys "R" Us, stepped into the picture. Nakasone had worked at Jewel alongside Stemberg before moving to Toys "R" Us. It was Nakasone who urged Stemberg to "think outside of the food box." Nakasone told Stemberg that there were more similarities than differences across product categories, and that profit margins were much better outside of the grocery business.

While mulling over possible entrepreneurial opportunities, Stemberg continued to explore other options, including working for an established retailer. It was this parallel search that took him down to Makro for a job interview, and it was there that he suddenly realized there was a possible opportunity to be had in starting the Toys "R" Us of office supplies.

The Founding of Staples

Hot on the heels of his trip to Makro, Stemberg started to think about his idea. The first thing was to get a handle on the nature of the market. Stemberg started by asking people if they knew how much they spent on office supplies. In his words:

> "There was this lawyer I knew in Hartford, which is where I lived then. If ever there was a cheap bastard in this world, he was a cheap bastard. And I said, 'Gee, how much do you spend on office supplies?' He said, "Oh I don't know, I guess about a couple of hundred bucks a person, 40 people in the office, I bet you we spend ten grand.' I said, 'Do me a favor will you? You've got good records. Go through your records and tell me exactly how much you spend': he calls me up the next day. 'Son of a bitch, I spend $1,000 apiece! But I'm getting a discount, I'm paying 10% off list': I said, 'Toys "R" Us' is paying 60% off list': He says, 'Are you kidding me? You mean I could save like half? I could save like twelve grand?' In his mind, this is the payment on his new Jaguar."[8]

Stemberg began to think that this idea had some potential. He reasoned that people want to save money, and in this case the money they could save might be substantial, but they didn't even know they were paying too much. Small businesses in particular, he thought, might be a viable target market. While working on the idea, the printer ribbon on his printer ran out. It was a weekend. He drove down to the local office supply store in Hartford, and it was closed. Went to another, but that was also closed. He ended up going to BJ's Wholesale Club, a deep discount warehouse club. BJ's was open, they sold office supplies at low prices, but the selection was limited and they didn't carry the type of ribbon Stemberg wanted. Stemberg immediately saw the opportunity.

Around the same time, Stemberg went to see another mentor of his, Walter Salmon, who taught retailing at Harvard Business School. Over lunch they discussed the supermarket business and Stemberg's quest. Salmon asked Stemberg if he had thought of applying his retailing skills to a product category that was growing faster than the grocery business and was not well served by modern retailers. Stemberg replied that he had been thinking about office supplies. Salmon's response, "Gee, this is a really big idea."

Scoping Out the Opportunity

Stemberg ended up hiring a former teaching assistant of Salmon's for $20,000 to do some basic market research on the industry and validate the market. As he tells the story: "I never forget the night I went to her house and we went through the slide deck. I always want to jump ahead. And she puts her hand on my hand and says, 'Wait, we will walk though it.' She's teasing us! Finally she said it was a $45 billion market growing at 15% per year. And it turns out she was lying. That was actually at the manufacturer level. It was actually more than $100 billion already if you looked at retail. She confirmed that the pricing umbrellas were as big as we thought they were, and that small businesses were getting raped the way we had said they were. I was pretty damn excited during the long drive home."[9]

The market growth, it turned out, was being driven by some favorable demographic trends. The U.S. economy was recovering from the recessions of the late 1970s and early 1980s, and underlying economic growth was strong. A wave of new technology was finding its way into American businesses, including personal computers, printers, faxes, and small copiers, and this was driving demand for office supplies including basic equipment along with consumables from paper and printer ink to diskettes and copy toner.

The wave of downsizing that had swept corporate America in the early 1980s also had a beneficial side effect—unemployed people were starting their own businesses. The rate of new business formation was the highest in years. There were 11 million small businesses in the country—Stemberg's proposed target market, the vast majority of which had less than twenty employees. This sector was the engine of job growth in the economy—between 1980 and 1986, small enterprises had been responsible for a net increase of 10.5 million jobs. Many of these new jobs were in the service sector, which was a big consumer of office supplies. Each new white-collar job meant another $1,000 a year in office supplies.

Stemberg's research started to uncover an industry that was highly fragmented at the retail level, but had some huge participants. Upstream in the value chain were the manufacturers. This was a very diverse collection of companies including paper manufacturers such as Boise Cascade; office furniture makers; manufacturers of pencils, pens, and markers such as the Bic Corporation; companies like 3M that supplied Post-it Notes, and a whole lot more besides, such as office equipment companies from Xerox and Canon (manufacturers of copiers and consumables) to manufacturers of personal computers, printers, and faxes such as Apple, Compaq, and Hewlett Packard.

Then there were the wholesalers, some of which were very large such as United Stationers and McKesson. The wholesalers bought in bulk and sold to business clients and smaller retail establishments, either directly or through a network of dealers. The dealers often visited businesses to collect orders and arrange for delivery. The dealers themselves ranged in scale from small one person enterprises to large firms that sold through central warehouses. Some dealers also had a retail presence, while others did not. Manufacturers and wholesalers would also sell directly to large businesses through catalogs or a direct sales presence.

The retailers fell into two main categories. There were the local office supply retailers, generally small businesses themselves, and there were the general merchandise discounters, such as BJ's Wholesale and Wal-Mart. The smaller retailers had an intrinsically high-cost structure. They were full service retailers who purchased in small lots and delivered in trucks or sold out of the store. The general merchandise discounters purchased from wholesalers, or direct from manufacturers, and their prices were much lower, but they did not carry a wide range of product.

On the consumer side, most large businesses had dedicated personnel for purchasing office supplies. They either bought from dealers, who purchased directly from manufacturers or through wholesalers, or bought direct from the manufacturer themselves. Large firms were able to negotiate on price and received discounts that could be as large as 80 percent of the list price on some items. Businesses of fewer than one hundred people did not generally have someone dedicated to managing office supplies, and they tended to rely primarily on dealers. For these companies, product availability, not price, was viewed as key. In even smaller firms, it was the convenience of being able to get office supplies that seemed to matter more than anything else.

Consistent with his initial insight, Stemberg found that smaller firms were ignored by the big dealers. To verify this he called Boise Cascade, which operated as both a dealer and a manufacturer, to see what service they might offer. First he called on behalf of Ivy Satellite Network, a small company that Stemberg owned that broadcast events of Ivy League schools to alumni around the world. Boise couldn't even be bothered to send a catalog to this company. Then he called Boise back, this time representing the one hundred–person office of a friend of his who was a food broker. This time Boise was happy to send a representative to the food broker. The representative offered the broker deep discounts. A Bic pen from Boise that cost Ivy $3.68 from the local stationary store was offered for just 85 cents. More generally, Stemberg found that while an office manager in a company with more than one thousand employees could often obtain discounts averaging 50 percent from dealers, small businesses with fewer than twenty employees were lucky to get a 10 percent discount, and often had to pay full price.[10]

Stemberg also found a study produced by researchers at the Wharton School that seemed to confirm his suspicions. "Essentially they first asked dealers. 'What does the customer want?' Ninety percent of the dealers said, 'Better service' and 10% said, 'other.' Then they asked customers, and 90% of the customers said what they really wanted was lower prices. Ha! The dealers were totally out of touch. They were making 40% to 50%, the wholesalers were making 30%, and the manufacturers were making huge margins. Everybody's rich, fat, and happy, and they're all going what's wrong with this?"[11]

Creating the Company

Stemberg knew from experience that for Staples to succeed it would have to execute well, and to do that, it needed experienced management. Stemberg turned to people he knew, managers who like him had risen quickly through the ranks at the Jewel Corporation or other Boston area retailers. From Jewel came Myra Hart, who was to become the Staples group vice president for growth and development; Todd Krasnow, who became vice president for marketing; Paul Korian, the Staples vice president of merchandising; and Henry Nasella, Stemberg's mentor at Star market who subsequently became president of Staples. The CFO was Bob Leombruno, who had bought Mammoth Mart, a failed retail operation, out of bankruptcy for a group of investors. Stemberg took on the CEO role, while Kahn became chairman. Most of these people started working full time on January 1, 1986. They gave up secure jobs, high salaries, and annual bonuses for a salary cut, loss of bonuses, and fourteen-hour days.

According to Stemberg, the pitch to prospective managers was this: "I'm going to give you a big chunk of stock in this thing. This is your chance. We're all going to work our tails off. We're going to work crazy hours. But here you'll be part of a retailing revolution. If you own 2% of the company and it gets to be worth $100 million, you're going to make $2 million."[12] In the end, each member of the top management team got a 2.5 percent stake in the company.

By now Stemberg had a name for this nascent company, Staples. Reflecting on how it came about years later, he noted that "I'm driving between Hartford and Boston. I'm thinking about names. Pencils? Pens? 8 1/2 by 11? Staples? Staples! Staples the Office Superstore. That was it. The bad thing about the name was that when we started out, we had to explain to everybody what it was. Office Depot basically copied Home Depot and put the 'office' in front. It was Home Depot for the office, and it lived off the Home Depot name. Office Club was a Price Club for the office. It lived off the Price Club name. In the early days ours was actually a problem. But those other names aren't a brand. Ours is a brand."[13]

With the management team in place, the next steps were to refine the concept and raise capital. The concept itself was relatively straightforward, implementing it would not be. The plan was to offer a wide selection of merchandise in a warehouse type setting with prices deeply discounted from those found in mom-and-pop retailers. Because it was to be a supermarket, the idea was to move from full-service to a self-service format. At the same time, the management team recognized the staff would need to be trained in office supplies so that they could provide advice when asked.

To make the concept viable, a number of issues had to be dealt with. They had to decide where to locate the stores. How big a population base would be needed to support a store? What kind of selection was required? How many stock keeping units (SKUs) should the store offer? There was the problem of educating the customer. If potential customers currently didn't know that they were paying excessive prices for office supplies, and consistently underestimated how much they spent on the category, what could Staples do to change this?

To get low prices, Staples would need to cut costs to the bone and be managed very efficiently. They would have to get manufacturers or wholesalers to deliver directly to Staples. How could this be done? Wouldn't wholesalers and manufacturers create channel conflict with dealers and established retailers by delivering straight to Staples? How was this to be resolved? Staples also needed to minimize its inventory, thereby reducing its working capital needs. Management knew that if they could turn inventory over twelve times a year, and delay payment to vendors for thirty days, then vendors would essentially finance Staples's inventory. Pulling that off would require state-of-the-art information systems, and the state of the art at the time in office supplies did not include bar coding on individual items. How was Staples to deal with this?

There was also the potential competition to worry about. Stemberg was sure that once Staples unveiled its concept, others would follow quickly. To preempt competitors, the plan called for rapid rollout of the concept, with sales ramping up from nothing to $42 million after three years. This would require a lot of capital. It also required that the concept be very easy to replicate so that once the first store was opened, others could be opened in quick succession. This meant that the systems that were put in place for the first store had to be the right ones, and able to support rapid expansion. There wasn't much room for error here.

As the management team refined the concept, they came to the realization that the information systems were one of the keys to the entire venture. With the right information systems in place, Staples could track sales and inventory closely at the level of individual items and figure out its gross profit on each item sold, adjusting its merchandising mix accordingly. This would be a departure from existing retailers, the majority of whom lacked the ability to calculate profit on each item sold, and could only calculate the average gross profit across a range of items. The right information systems could also be used to collect data on customers at the point of sales, and this would assist greatly in market research and direct marketing to customers.

On the other hand, raising capital proved to be easier than they thought. Stemberg valued Staples, which was still little more than a concept, a management team, and a business plan full of unanswered questions, at $8 million. He went looking for $4 million, which he would exchange for 50 percent of the company. The venture capitalists were initially reluctant. They seemed to hold back, waiting to see who would commit first. They also valued Staples at $6 million, and wanted a 67 percent stake for the $4 million in first round financing. Stemberg balked at that, and instead focused his efforts on one firm that seemed more willing to break away from the pack. The firm was Bain Venture Capital, whose managing general partner, Matt Romney, later observed, "A lot of retailing startups come by, but a lot of them are a twist on an old theme, or a better presentation. . . . Stemberg wasn't proposing just a chain of stores, but an entirely new retailing category. That really captures your attention. It slaps you in the face with the idea that this could be big."[14]

To validate the business concept, Romney's firm surveyed one hundred small businesses after being urged to do so by Stemberg. Auditing invoices from these companies for office supplies, Romney discovered what Stemberg already knew—the companies were spending about twice what they estimated. Romney then ran the numbers on his own company and found that his firm would save $117,000 a year by purchasing supplies at the discount that Stemberg promised. That was enough for Romney, and he committed to investing. Others followed, and Staples raised $4.5 million in its first round of financing, which closed on January 23, 1986. This gave the company enough capital to go ahead with the first store. In return for the financing, Staples had to give the VCs a 54 percent stake in the company. To get the money, however, Staples had to commit to opening its first store on May 1, 1986, and to meet a plan for rolling out additional stores as quickly as possible.

The First Store

With just four months to open their first store, the management team went into overdrive. They would meet every morning at about seven A.M. in a session that could run from thirty minutes to two hours. Someone would rush out to get sandwiches for lunch, and they would keep working. The workday came to a close at nine or ten P.M. Not only was there no template for what they were doing, but also they knew they had to put a system in place that would allow them to quickly roll out additional stores.

One of the most difficult tasks fell on the shoulders of Leombruno, the CFO. In addition to setting up an accounting system, he was put in charge of installing the entire information system for Staples. The system had to be able to track customer purchases so that Staples could reorder products. The cash registers, which were to be connected individually to the system, had to be easy to operate so that there would be no congestion at the checkout stands. Stemberg himself was adamant that the register receipts indicate the list price of each item, as well as a much lower Staples price, and an even lower price for customers who became Staples members. He also wanted the system to collect detailed demographics on each customer.

Leombruno insisted that the system be able to do two things: First, calculate the gross profit margin Staples made on each item sold. Most retailers at the time could only calculate the average profit margin across the mix of inventory. Second, Leombruno wanted to make sure that inventory turned over at least twelve times a year, and good information systems were the key to that. With most vendors requiring payment in thirty days, an inventory turnover of greater than twelve would allow Staples to cut its working capital requirements.

As the wish list for the information systems grew, it soon became apparent that it would not be possible to do everything in the allotted time span. No existing software package did what the management team wanted, and they had to hire consultants to customize existing packages. In the end, several proposed features were dropped. However, at Stemberg's insistence the three-way price requirements remained. To track sales and inventory levels, Staples assigned a six-digit look up code for each item. While entering the codes was a slower process than scanning items, most manufacturers in the office supplies business were still not marking their products with bar codes, which meant scanning was not feasible.

Another problem was to get suppliers to ship products to the first Staples store. The company was asking suppliers to bypass the existing distribution system, and risk alienating long-time customers in the established channel of distribution. To get suppliers on board, Staples used a number of tactics. One was a visionary pitch. The company told suppliers that they were out to revolutionize the retail end of the industry. Staples would be very big, they said, and it was in the best interests of the suppliers to back the startup. Stemberg's punch line was simple: "I'm going to be very loyal to those who stick their necks out for us. But it's going to cost you a lot more to get in later."[15] Connections also helped to get suppliers to deliver to Staples. One of the VC backers of Staples, Bessemer Venture Partners, also owned a paper manufacturer, Ampad. Bessemer told Ampad to start selling to Staples, which they did, even though existing distributors complained bitterly about the arrangement.

Finding real estate also presented a problem. As an enterprise with no proven track record, Staples found it difficult to rent decent real estate large enough to stock and display the five thousand SKUs that it was planning for its first store, and to do so at a decent price. Most landlords wanted sky high rent from Staples. In the end, the best that Staples could do was a site in Brighton, Massachusetts, that was within site of a housing project and had failed as a site for several different retailers. There was one redeeming feature of the site—it was smack in the middle of a high concentration of small businesses.

Despite all of the problems, Staples was able to open its first store on May 1, 1986. The opening day was busy, but only because everybody who worked at Staples had invited everybody they knew. On the second day just sixteen people came through the store. On the third day, it was the same number. A few weeks of this, and Staples would have to shut its doors. Desperate, Krasnow decided to bribe customers to get them into the store. The company sent $25 to each of thirty-five office managers, inviting them to shop in the store and pass along their reactions. According to Krasnow, "A week later we called them back. They had all taken the money, but none of them had come into the store. I was apoplectic."[16] In the end, nine of them finally came in, and they gave Staples rave reviews. Slowly the momentum started to build, and by August lines were starting to form at the cash registers at lunch time.

The 1990s: Growth, Competition, and Consolidation

Growth

Staples had set of target of $4 million in first year sales from its Brighton Store, but within a few months, the numbers were tracking up toward a $6 million annual run rate. The concept was starting to work. The number of customers coming through the door every month was growing, but it was not only customers that were coming. One day Joe Antonini, the CEO of Kmart, was spotted walking around the Staples store. Around the same time, Stemberg heard from contacts that Staples had been mentioned at a Wal-Mart board meeting. He realized that if other discount retailers were noticing Staples when it had just one store, competition could not be far behind.

Within five months of the opening of the first Staples store, a clone had appeared in the Southeast: Office Depot. Needing money fast to fund expansion and lock in Staples territory, Stemberg went back to the venture capitalists. While the initial backers were only willing to value Staples at $15 million, Stemberg held out for and got a valuation of $22 million, raising another $14 million. He pulled off this trick by finding institutional investors who were willing to invest on a valuation of $22 million. He then went back to the original VCs and told them that the deal was closing fast, which persuaded them to commit.

By May 1987, Staples had 3 stores open and planned to increase the number to 20 by the end of 1988 (in the event it opened 22). Sales were running at anywhere from $300 to $800 per square foot. In contrast, high-volume discount stores were lucky to get $300 per square foot. By mid 1989, three years after its first store opened, Staples had 27 stores open in the northeast and an annual sales run rate of $120 million, way above the original three-year target of $42 million. The stores now average 15,000 square feet and stocked 5,000 items.

Explaining the success, Stemberg noted, "From a value perspective, I think there is no question that we have been a friend to the entrepreneur. If you look at the average small town merchant, we've lowered the costs of his office products—where he was once paying say $4,000 to $5,000 a year, now he's paying $2,000 or $3,000. We've made him more efficient."[17]

Helping to drive sales growth was the development of a direct marketing pitch. Every time Staples opened a store, it purchased a list of small businesses within fifteen minutes' driving distance. Then a group of telemarketers would go to work calling up the buyer of office supplies at the businesses. The telemarketers would tell them Staples was opening up a store like Toys "R" Us for office supplies, ask them how much they spent on office supplies every year (often they did not know), cite typical cost savings at small businesses, and sent them a coupon for a free item such as copy paper. At first the customers would come in slowly, but momentum would build up as customers realized the scale of the savings they were getting.

Every time a customer redeemed a coupon at a store, they were given a free Staples Card. This "membership" card entitled cardholders to even deeper discounts on select items. The card quickly became the lynchpin of Staples's direct marketing effort. From the card application, Staples gathered information about the customer—what type of business they were in, how many employees they had, where they were located. This information was entered into a customer database, and every time a card member used that card, the card number and purchases were logged into the database via the cash register. This gave Staples up-to-date information about what was being purchased and by whom. This information then allowed Staples to target promotions at certain customer groups—for example, card members who were not making purchases. The goal was to get existing customers to spend more at Staples, a goal that over time was attained.

Because Staples started to reach so many of its customers through direct marketing (about 80 percent of its sales were made to cardholders), it was able to spend less on media ads—in some areas it dropped media advertising altogether, saving on costs. This was an important source of cost savings in the Northeast where the media is expensive.

A problem that continued to bedevil Staples as it expanded was the shortage of good real estate locations that could be rented at a reasonable price, particularly in the Northeast. Finding a good site in the early days required flexibility; at various times Staples converted anything and everything from restaurants to massage parlors into Staples stores. As the company grew, its real estate strategy started to take a defensive aspect, with Staples bidding for prime sites in order to preempt competitors.

The high cost of real estate in the Northeast led Staples to establish its first distribution center in 1987.

This decision was hotly debated within the company and opposed by some of the investors who thought that the capital should be used to build more stores, but Stemberg prevailed. The distribution center was located off an interstate highway in an area of rural Connecticut where land was cheap. The facility cost $6 million to build, and tied up a total of $10 million in working capital, almost 29 cents out of every dollar that the company had raised to that point. But Stemberg saw this as a necessary step. The inventory storage capacity at the distribution center enabled the company to operate with smaller stores than many of its rivals, but still offer the same variety of goods. By 1989, the average Staples store was 35 percent smaller than the Office Depot outlets that were then opening up all over the Southeast, saving on real estate costs. The distribution center also helped save labor costs, since wages are lower in rural areas. Equally important, inventory storage at the distribution centers allowed the stores to remain fully stocked. A Stemberg noted, "In competition with the clones, it will come down to who has the lowest costs and the best in stock position."[18]

The expansion strategy at Staples was very methodical. Stores were clustered together in a region, even to the extent that they cannibalized each other on the margin, so that Staples could become the dominant supplier in that market. The early focus was on major metropolitan areas such as Boston, New York, Philadelphia, and Los Angeles. Although high real estate and labor costs in these areas were a disadvantage, strong demand from local businesses helped compensate, as did the distribution centers. In 1990, Staples open its second distribution center in California to support expansion there.

The expansion at Staples was fueled by the proceeds from a 1989 Initial Public Offering, which raised $61.7 million of capital—enough for Staples to accelerate its store openings. By mid 1991, Staples store count passed over one hundred.

Competition

A rash of imitators to Staples soon appeared on the market. The first of these was Office Depot, which was focused on the Southeast. By the end of 1988, Office Depot had 26 stores, Office Club had opened 15, Biz Mart had established 10, and Office Max around a dozen. More than a dozen other office supplies superstores had sprung up. Some of these businesses were financed by venture capitalists looking to

repeat the success with Staples, others were financed by established retailers, or even started by them. For example, Ben Franklin started Office Station in 1987, but shut it down in 1989 as it failed to gain traction.

Initially, most of the competitors focused in unique regions—Office Depot on the Southeast, Office Club on California, Office Max on the Midwest, BizMart on the Southwest—but as the number of entrants increased, head-to-head competition started to become more frequent. Stemberg's belief had always been that competition was inevitable, and that the winners in the competitive race would not necessarily be those that grew the fastest but those that executed best. It was this philosophy that underpinned Stemberg's insistence that the company should grow by focusing on key urban areas and achieving a critical mass of stores served by a central distribution system.

Not everyone agreed with this recipe for success. Office Depot did the opposite—the company grew as fast as possible, entering towns quickly to preempt competitors. Office Depot lacked the centralized distribution systems, but made up for that by locating in less expensive areas than Staples, persuading suppliers to ship directly to stores and keeping more backup inventory on the premises. Although this meant larger stores, the lower rental costs in Office Depot's markets offset this.

What soon became apparent is that the rash of entrants included a number of companies that simply could not execute. Very quickly a handful of competitors emerged in the forefront of the industry—Staples, Office Depot, Office Max, and Office Club. As the market leaders grew, they increasingly came into contact with each other. The result was price wars. These first broke out in California. Staples entered the market in 1990 and initially focused on pricing not against Office Club, but against Price Club. Although Price Club was a warehouse store selling food and general merchandise, it still had the largest share of the office supplies market in California. Staples positioned itself as having the same low prices as Price Club, but a wider selection of office supplies and no membership fee.

Todd Krasnow, the executive vice president of marketing at Staples, describes what happened next: "What we failed to realize was that Price Club was very worried about Office Club—and was pricing against Office Club. So when we went and matched Price Club, we were matching Office Club. And Office Club was saying: 'We are not going to let anybody have the same prices as us.'"[19] Office Club lowered its prices, causing Price Club to lower prices, and Staples followed. Not willing to be beat, Office Club cut prices again, and so they continued the spiral down. The price war drove profit margins down by as much as 8 percent.

Ultimately Krasnow noted, "We realized that by engaging in this price war, we were focusing on our competitors, not our customers. Our customers weren't paying attention to this spat. So we raised our prices a little. You feel like you're just doing absolutely the wrong thing, because your whole position is: We have the lowest price."[20] Be that as it may, Office Club and Price Club followed suit, and prices started to rise again. Ultimately the three companies carved out different price niches, each unwilling to be undercut on about twenty or so top-selling items, but in general, they were not the same items.

What happened in California also occurred elsewhere. When Office Max entered the Boston market in 1992, for example, a price war broke out again. There was an unanticipated effect this time because the price cuts apparently broadened the market by making buying from Staples attractive to customers with between twenty-five and one hundred employees, who previously bought directly from mail order and retail stationers.[21]

Ultimately Krasnow noted that price wars such as those that started to break out in California and Boston started to moderate. "We finally realized that it's not in any company's self-interest to have a price war because you can get lots of market share without having a price war. And having a price war among low priced competitors doesn't get you more market share. It doesn't serve any purpose."[22] Other factors that may have contributed toward more rational pricing behavior in the market were the strong economy of the 1990s and industry consolidation.

Industry Consolidation

At its peak in 1991, there were twenty-five chains in the office supply industry.[23] Industry consolidation started when some of the clones began to fall by the wayside, filing for bankruptcy. U.S. Office Supply, itself the result of a merger between two office supplies chains, filed for bankruptcy in 1991, as did Office Stop. Consolidation was also hastened by acquisitions. In 1991, Office Depot acquired Office Club, giving the primary rival of Staples more than twice the number of stores. For its part, Staples acquired

HQ Office Supplies Warehouse in 1991, and in 1992, it purchased another smaller chain, Workplace.[24]

As these trends continued, by the mid 1990s it was apparent that three players were rising to dominance in the industry: Office Depot, Staples, and Office Max. By mid 1996, Office Depot led the industry with 539 stores, followed by Staples with 517 and Office Max with around 500 stores. In terms of revenues, Office Depot had a clear lead with $5.3 billion in 1996, Staples was second with $3.07 billion, and Office Max third with $2.6 billion. Staples remained concentrated in the Northeast and California, with a large number of stores in dense urban areas. Office Depot's stores were concentrated in the South, and the company continued to stay clear of congested cities. Office Max was still strongest in the Midwest.[25]

The consolidation phase peaked in September 1996 when Staples announced an agreement to purchase its larger rival, Office Depot, for $3.36 billion. The executives of the two companies had apparently been talking about merger possibilities for years, while continuing to pursue their own independent-growth strategies. If the merger went through, Tom Stemberg would step into the CEO role. The two companies sold the merger to the investment community on the basis of cost savings. The combined firm would have almost eleven hundred stores and revenues of $8.5 billion. The combination, Stemberg argued, would attain terrific economies of scale that would allow it to significantly lower costs, saving an estimated $4.9 billion over five years, including $2.2 billion in product cost savings.

In a move to preempt a possible investigation by the Federal Trade Commission (FTC), the companies claimed that since their stores focused on different territories, the combination would not reduce competition. They also noted that Staples still faced intense competition not only from Office Max, but also from the likes of Wal-Mart, Circuit City, and mail order outlets. Indeed, Stemberg claimed that the combined company would still only account for 5 percent of the total sales of office supplies in the United States.[26]

The FTC didn't buy the arguments, quickly started an investigation, and in May 1997 sought an injunction to block the deal. The FTC claimed that the deal would stifle competition and raise prices for office supplies, especially in those markets where the two firms competed head to head. To buttress its case, the FTC released a report of pricing data that showed that nondurable office supplies such as paper were 10 percent to 15 percent higher in markets where Staples faced no direct rivals. Staples claimed that the FTC's pricing surveys were done selectively and were biased.

In July 1997, a federal judge granted the FTC's request for an injunction to halt the merger. Staples realized that it was in a losing fight, and pulled its bid for Office Depot. But the failure had a silver lining—not anticipating much interference from the FTC, Office Depot had put most of its expansion plans on hold, opening just two stores in eight months. In comparison, Staples opened forty-three, allowing the company to close the gap between itself and its larger rival.

Staples's Evolving Strategy

Moving Into Small Towns

Stemberg has described Staples's initial strategy to deal with the high costs of doing business in the Northeast as follows: "Establish superstores that were smaller than most, save on rent and operating costs, cluster them in densely populated areas to justify paying for expensive advertisements, and stock the stores from a distribution center."[27] The drawback with this strategy, in retrospect, was that Staples ignored a lot of potentially lucrative markets in smaller towns. While Office Depot was barnstorming into towns with populations of just seventy-five thousand, Staples could not see how they made it pay. Surely towns of that size were just too small to support an office supplies superstore?

As it turned out, they were not. The mistake Staples made was to assume that a store would serve customers within a ten- to fifteen-minute drive. But in smaller cities, customers would drive much farther to get good prices. The revelation did not hit home until Staples opened its first store in Portland, Maine. With a population of two hundred thousand, the town was smaller than most areas focused on by Staples, but within a few months, the store was doing very well. To test the hypothesis, in 1992 and 1993 Staples opened stores in a number of smaller towns. The results were surprising. Many of the stores actually generated higher sales per square foot that those located in large cities. Sales were helped by the fact that in many of these small towns the only competitors were small "mom and pop" stationers, and that many small towns also lacked supermarket electronic retailers, such as Circuit City, selling low priced office equipment, allowing Staples to pick up a much larger

share of that business. Moreover, the lower rent, labor costs, advertising costs, and shrinkage made these stores significantly more profitable.

From that point on, Staples moved into small towns and suburban locations, where the same economics apply. Stemberg has described not moving into small towns earlier as "one of the dumbest mistakes I made." In 1994, some 10 percent of Staples stores were in small towns; by 1998, that figure had risen to 28 percent, and some of the most profitable stores in the Staples network were located in small towns.[28]

Selling Direct

Established as a retailer, Staples initially turned its back on customer requests for delivery and mail or telephone order service. The reason for doing this was simple: Staples saw itself as a low cost retailer, and a delivery service would probably raise costs. However, Staples competitors started to offer mail order and delivery service, and customers continued to ask for the service, so in 1988, Staples began to experiment with this.

Initially the experimentation was halfhearted. Store managers were not enthusiastic about supporting a delivery service that they believed decreased store sales, and Staples discouraged delivery by tacking a 5 percent delivery charge onto the order price. Moreover, the company questioned whether it could generate the volume of business to cover the costs of a delivery service and make a decent return on capital.

What changed this was a study undertaken for Staples by a management consulting firm. The study found that the customers who purchased via a catalog and required delivery were not always the same ones who brought directly from the store. While there was a lot of cross shopping, the mail order customers tended to be bigger and somewhat more interested in service, whereas those buying from the store were often buying for home offices. Staples also could not help but notice that its major rivals were offering a delivery service, and that business seemed to be thriving.

In 1991, Staples set up an independent business unit within the company to handle the mail/telephone order and delivery service, known as Contract and Commercial. The guts of this business unit was a division know as Staples Direct (it is now called Staples Business Delivery). The man put in charge of this business, Ronald Sargent, would ultimately replace Stemberg as CEO of Staples in 2003.

One issue that had to be dealt with was the potential conflict between Staples Direct and the stores. The stores didn't want to push business the way of Staples Direct because they would not get credit for the sale. As Sargent commented later, "We were like the bad guys inside Staples, because the feeling was that if customers got products delivered they wouldn't shop inside our stores."[29] To align incentives, Staples changed the compensation systems so that (a) the store would get credit if a delivery order was placed through the store, and (b) the annual bonus of store employees was partly based on how well they meet goals for generating delivery sales.

As Staples Direct started to grow, the company also discovered that the delivery infra-structure they put in place could be used to serve clients in addition to the company's established small business customers, which typically had less than 50 employees. Increasingly, medium-sized business (with 50 to 100 employees) and larger businesses with more than 100 employees started to utilize Staples Direct. To support this new business, Staples started to grow by acquisition, purchasing a number of regional stationary companies with established customers and delivery systems. Typically Staples kept the owners of these businesses on as Staples employees, often because they had long-established relationships with key accounts in large organizations such as Xerox, Ford, and Pepsi Cola. Staples, however, established a consistent product line, brand image, and computer and accounting systems across all of the acquisitions.

Between 1991 and 1996, Staples Direct grew from a $30 million business to almost $1 billion. As sales volume ramped up, Staples was able to get greater efficiencies out of its distribution network, which helped to drive down the costs of doing business through this channel. Staples used a network of regional distribution centers to hold an inventory of some 15,000 SKUs for delivery, compared with 8,000 SKUs in a typical store. In 1998, a web-based element was added to Staples Direct, Staples.com. Through the web or a catalog, Staples customers could get access to some 130,000 SKUs, many of which were shipped directly from manufacturers with Staples acting as an intermediary and consolidator.

To continue building the direct business, in 1988, Staples acquired Quill Corporation for $685 million in Staples stock. Established in 1956, Quill is a direct mail catalog business with a targeted approach to servicing the business products needs of around a million small- and medium-sized businesses in the United States. Quill differentiated itself through excellent customer service. Staples decided to let Quill keep its own organization, setting it up as a separate division within the Contract and Commercial business unit, but integrated Quill's purchasing with those of the rest of Staples to gain economies of the input side. Quill now operates under two brands— Staples National Advantage, which focuses on large multiregional businesses, and Staples Business advantage, which focuses on large- and medium-sized regional companies, and has the flexibility to handle smaller accounts (although these are mostly handled via Staples Direct). In justifying the acquisition of Quill, Stemberg noted that the direct business amounted to a $60 billion a year industry, but it was highly fragmented with the top eight players accounting for less than 20 percent of the market.[30]

By 2002, the combined delivery business had grown to become a $3.4 billion enterprise in its own right.

Going International

Staples's first foray into international markets occurred in the early 1990s when the company was approached by a Canadian retailer, Jack Bingleman, who wanted to start a Staples type chain north of the border. Bingleman also approached Office Depot and Office Max, but had a preference for Staples because of the close geographic proximity. Board members at Staples initially opposed any expansion into Canada, arguing that scarce resources should be dedicated toward growth in the much larger United States, but Stemberg liked Bingleman's vision, and pushed the idea. Ultimately, in 1991 Staples agreed to invest $2 million in Bingleman's startup for a 16 percent equity stake.

Known as Business Depot, the Canadian venture expanded rapidly, modeling itself after Staples. Between 1991 and 1994, the number of Canadian Business Depot stores expanded to 30 stores, and the enterprise turned profitable in 1993. In 1994, Staples announced an agreement to purchase Business Depot outright for $32 million.[31] By 2003, there were 215 stores in Canada.

The Canadian venture was soon followed by investments in Europe. Staples entered the U.K. market in 1992, partnering with Kingfisher PLC, a large U.K. retailer that operated home improvement and consumer electronics stores among other things. The Canadian venture had taught Staples that a local partner was extremely valuable. As one Staples executive noted later: "You absolutely cannot do it yourself. There are too many cultural impediments for you to know where the booby traps lie. In a retail startup, the most important task is to generate locations. There's no way a U.S. national can go into any country and generate the real estate it needs. That person will be chasing his tail for a long time."[32]

On the heels of entry into the United Kingdom, Staples purchased MAXI-Papier, a German company that was attempting to copy what Staples had done in the United States. This was followed by entry into the Netherlands and Portugal. By early 2003, Staples had 188 stores in Europe, 83 in the United Kingdom, 56 in Germany, 37 in the Netherlands, and 12 in Portugal. By 2002, the European operations were generating over a billion dollars in revenues, primarily through retail sales. In late 2002, Staples purchased the mail order business of a French company, Guilbert, for nearly $800 million, which boosted delivery sales in Europe from $50 million a year to $450 million a year almost overnight.[33]

Staples in 2003

In February 2002, Tom Stemberg announced that he was stepping down as CEO, and passing the baton on to Ron Sargent. Stemberg would remain on as chairman. Upon taking over as CEO, Sargent put the breaks on store expansion, declaring that Staples would open no more than 75 new stores a year, down from over 130 in 2000. He used the slowdown to refocus attention upon internal operating efficiencies. The product line within stores was rationalized, with Staples cutting back on the stocking of low margin items such as personal computers. He also set up a task force to look for ways to take every excess cent out of the cost structure. As a result, operating margins at Staples stores came in at 5.9 percent of sales in 2002, the best in the industry, and up from 4.5 percent in 2000.

Going forward, Sargent's task is to grow the top line. With the retail market for office supplies superstores now approaching saturation in the United States, Sargent has turned his attention to the business where he made his name, the direct delivery business. He points out that although the number of independent office supplies dealers is down to 6,000 from 15,000 a decade ago, the delivery market is still highly fragmented and very large. Ultimately Sargent believes that direct delivery from warehouses can be as big a business as Staples office supplies stores. He also sees huge potential for growth in Europe, which is the second largest office supplies market in the world and still years behind the United States in terms of consolidation.

At the same time, Staples continues to face strategic challenges. The retail market in the United States is now consolidated, and additional expansion by Staples is likely to bring it increasingly into head-to-head contact with Office Depot or Office Max. To compound matters, in mid 2003 Boise Cascade, the large wood and paper products company which has long had its own direct delivery business, purchased Office Max for $1.2 billion. Prior to the purchase, Office Max had 2002 sales of $4.8 billion against Staples's sales of $11.6 billion, and Office Depot's sales of $11.4 billion. The merger boosts the combined office supplies sales of the new company to $8.3 billion.

ENDNOTES

1. Stephen D. Solomon, "Born to Be Big," *Inc.* (June 1989): 94.
2. Value Line. Value Line Investment Survey, Staples, October 17, 2003.
3. Solomon, "Born to Be Big", page 96.
4. Tom Stemberg, *Staples for Success* (Santa Monica, CA: Knowledge Exchange, 1996).
5. Michael Barrier, "Tom Stemberg Calls the Office," *Nation's Business* (July 1990): 42.
6. Ibid., page 44.
7. Ibid., page 44.
8. Tom Stemberg and David Whiteford, "Putting a Stop to Mom and Pop," *Fortune Small Business* (October 2002): 39.
9. Ibid., page 40.
10. Stemberg, *Staples for Success.*
11. Stemberg and Whiteford, "Putting a Stop to Mom and Pop," page 40.
12. Stemberg, *Staples for Success*, page 17.
13. Stemberg and Whiteford, "Putting a Stop to Mom and Pop," page 41.
14. Solomon, "Born to Be Big," pages 94 and 95.
15. Stemberg, *Staples for Success*, page 24.
16. Ibid., page 27.
17. Stemberg and Whiteford, "Putting a Stop to Mom and Pop," page 40.
18. Solomon, "Born to Be Big," page 100.
19. Stemberg, *Staples for Success*, page 97.
20. Ibid.
21. Norm Alster, "Penney Wise," *Forbes*, February 1, 1993, pages 48–51.
22. Stemberg, *Staples for Success*, page 97.
23. Renee Covion Rouland, "And Then There Were Three," *Discount Merchandiser* (December 1994): 27.

24. Leland Montgomery. "Staples: Buy the Laggard," *Financial World*, November 9, 1993, page 22; Anonymous, "The New Plateau in Office Supplies," *Discount Merchandiser* (November 1991): 50–54.

25. James S. Hirsch and Eleena de Lisser, "Staples to Acquire Archrival Office Depot," *Wall Street Journal*, September 5, 1996, page A3.

26. Joseph Pereira and John Wilke, "Staples Faces FTC in Antitrust Showdown on Merger," *Wall Street Journal*, May 19, 1997, page B4.

27. Stemberg, *Staples for Success*, page 128.

28. William M. Bulkeley, "Office Supplies Superstores Find Bounty in the Boonies," *Wall Street Journal*, September 1, 1998, page B1.

29. William C. Symonds, "Thinking Outside the Big Box," *Business Week*, August 11, 2003, page 62.

30. William M. Bulkeley, "Staples, Moving Beyond Superstores, Will Buy Quill for $685 Million in Stock," *Wall Street Journal*, April 8, 1998, page A1.

31. Steff Gelston, "Staples Goes on Buying Spree to Acquire Business Depot, National Office Supply Company," *Boston Herald*, January 25, 1994, page 24.

32. Stemberg, *Staples for Success*, page 90.

33. Symonds, "Thinking Outside the Big Box," pages 62–64.

Case 13

Gap International: A Specialty Apparel Retailer

This case was prepared by Robert J. Mockler, St. John's University.

Introduction

On September 26, 2002, Gap Inc. announced that Paul Pressler, fifteen-year veteran of The Walt Disney Company and chairman of its global theme park and resorts division, had been named president and chief executive officer of the company. Pressler succeeded outgoing CEO Millard Drexler, who had announced in May his plans to retire as soon as his replacement was hired [Kaiser, 2002]. Earlier that month, Gary Muto, former president of Banana Republic division, was appointed the new president of the Gap division of Gap Inc. They were both faced with the inevitable task of developing an effective differentiating enterprise-wide strategy if Gap was to survive and prosper against aggressive competition over the intermediate and long-term future.

Gap Inc. sold its private label clothing in its own retail stores only and to no other retailer, wholesaler, or independent distributor. The three main brands/divisions were Banana Republic, Gap, and Old Navy, as shown in Figure 1.

The three divisions had a presence in Japan, United Kingdom, France, Canada, and Germany, but the majority of the stores were based in the United States. Each brand targeted a different type of customer with

varying income level and lifestyle. Each division was an independent strategic business unit. Gap Inc. had had major problems for more than two years after an ill-fated foray into trendy clothes in early 2000 that had alienated its traditional customers. In September 2002, it reported its twenty-eighth straight month of declines in sales at stores open at least one year. The company's problems were reflected in its stock price. The stock reached its highest price of $51.68 on February 4, 2000. On October 8, 2002, the stock closed at $9.59, as shown in Figure 2.

All three divisions were having problems, but the Gap division was in the worst condition. For the past two years, since 2000, it had been struggling with problems resulting from overexpansion and mis-judgment of fashion trends. The Gap division's stores went from casual to trendy, with bold colors, low-cut jeans, and teeny tops. New product lines were no longer appealing to regular customers, and they did not attract new ones. Overexpansion added to the "wrong-merchandise problem" by creating the effect of cannibalism of sales; individual stores sold less and less with operating costs going up.

Gap was no exception in its industry. According to the U.S. Department of Commerce, sales at specialty apparel stores rose only 0.7 percent in 2001. Family clothing stores had the best performance, with sales up 1.6 percent. Sales at women's apparel stores fell 2.5 percent, and those at men's stores declined 1.8 percent [Standard & Poor's, 2002A].

In light of all the problems, Muto and Pressler had to come up with a future strategy for the Gap division, including especially decisions in the areas of product

FIGURE 1

Brands/Divisions of Gap Inc.

mix, including colors, fabrics, fashions, and quality. Gap also had to identify its customer base. For example, decisions such as staying with the same customer base or expanding to the plus sizes or extended plus-sizes market had to be made. The main question to be resolved was how to differentiate Gap from its competition and to achieve a winning edge over competitors within intensely competitive, rapidly changing immediate, intermediate, and long-term time frames.

Industry and Competitive Market: Retail

Retailing includes all business activities that involve the sale of goods and services to consumers for personal, family, or household use. It is largely a high-volume, low-margin business. It can be divided into two main categories: general retail and specialty retail, as shown in Figure 3. General retail includes department stores and general merchandisers, and specialty retail includes home furnishing stores, building supplies stores, office supplies stores, consumer electronics stores, miscellaneous goods stores, and apparel stores.

The year 2001 was challenging for retailers. The difficulties had their roots in the confluence of three trends. First, U.S. consumers had a wide choice of stores competing for their business, so the industry remained highly competitive. Second, consumer spending was growing slowly due to the economic slowdown. Consumers were able to choose among

FIGURE 2

Gap Inc.'s Five-Year Stock History

Source: CBS Market Watch (2002), [Online], **http://cbs.marketwatch.com/tools/quotes/intchart.asp?symb=gps&siteid=mktw&dist=mktwqn**, accessed October 9.

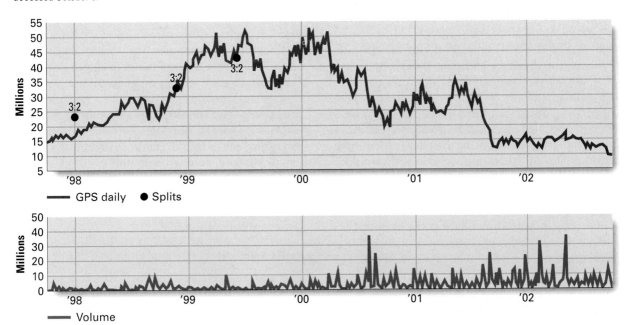

FIGURE 3

The Retail Industry

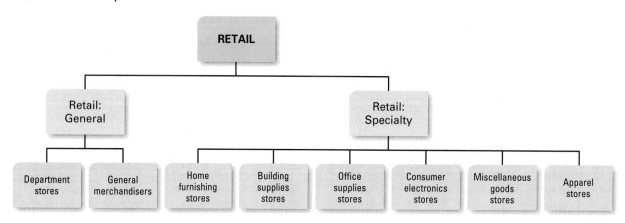

more places to shop than ever before, but at the same time had less interest in shopping. Finally, value had become crucial. Consumers moved to shopping at lower-priced, value-driven retailers, which resulted in most department store chains suffering [Standard & Poor's, 2002A].

Retail: General

General retailers included department stores and general merchandisers.

Department Stores The U.S. government defines department stores as establishments selling the following lines of merchandise: furniture, home furnishings, appliances, and radio and television sets; a general line of apparel for the family; and household linens and dry goods [Standard & Poor's, 2002A]. Most department stores, however, stopped offering certain categories of merchandise, including major appliances, electronics, toys, sporting goods, furniture, and photographic supplies, as margins on those lines had declined. In addition, such items took up large amounts of floor space, tied up capital in inventory costs, or required more aggressive pricing than department store retailing allowed. Meanwhile, selections of women's apparel, accessories, cosmetics, and fragrances, which typically generate higher margins and have a more up-scale image, have been greatly expanded.

General merchandisers have taken over the department store's old role as purveyors of everything. Department stores' market share continued to erode as consumers shopped more at discount stores (general merchandisers). According to the Department of Commerce, in 1992, department stores accounted for 50 percent of general merchandise, apparel, and furniture sales. By 2001, department stores' share of those sales had fallen to 37 percent, while general merchandise stores share reached 32 percent, up from 25 percent in 1992 [Standard & Poor's, 2002A]. Department stores learned their lesson. Inventory levels were being reduced and expenses were being cut. Managers were examining the business with a more careful eye toward demographic changes and remerchandising departments accordingly, appealing to a young customer and focusing on the fast growing junior market. Major department stores included Macy's (Federated Department Stores), J.C. Penney (Penney Co.), Sears, and Nordstrom.

General Merchandisers The term "general merchandiser" applies to stores carrying a much broader assortment of merchandise than most department stores. They strive to be all things to all people by carrying broad assortments of merchandise, catering to a value-conscious consumer who demands low prices every day. The term applies mainly to discounters such as Target, Wal-Mart, or Kmart. In times of recession, such as in 2002, many customers were willing to sacrifice brand names and even quality for lower prices. As value became increasingly important for many customers, discounters became competition for department stores and specialty retailers [Standard & Poor's, 2002A].

Retail: Specialty

The specialty retailing industry was comprised of merchants that sold a single category of merchandise, as well as those carrying a few closely related categories of products. Retail specialty stores included home furnishing stores, building supplies stores, office supplies stores, electronics stores, miscellaneous goods stores (including sporting goods, pets, books, and toys), and apparel stores.

Home Furnishing Stores Retail home furnishing stores were divided into two categories: large-sized superstores and small specialty stores. Superstores carried a broad assortment of merchandise for living rooms, bedrooms, dining rooms, kitchens, and bathrooms. The main competitors included Bed Bath and Beyond, Linens and Things, Pier 1 Imports, and IKEA. Smaller specialty stores carried a limited assortment of goods within a specified niche, and were usually more expensive than the big competitors. This segment of the market was highly influenced by the housing market and interest rates. In a low interest–rate environment, consumers were more likely to buy new homes and spend money on furniture, new appliances, and home improvement.

Building Supplies Stores The building supply segment was dominated by a few large warehouse stores that allowed customers to buy products for their homes at a discount from the prices found at traditional hardware stores. Two main competitors in this segment were Home Depot and Lowes.

Office Supplies Stores Office supplies stores consisted of stores that sold office supplies and equipment that served the needs of businesses and individuals. Main competitors in this segment included Staples and Office Depot.

Consumer Electronics Stores Consumer electronic stores sold home electronic goods such as televisions, stereos, or videocassette recorders. The market was becoming saturated. In 2001, the popularity of digital videodisk (DVD) players, digital cameras, and home theater systems were boosting the sales of those stores. Main competitors included Best Buy, Circuit City, and Radio Shack.

Miscellaneous Goods Stores Miscellaneous stores included toy stores, sporting goods stores, pet stores, and bookstores.

Toy Stores Toy stores included Toys "R" Us, K-B Toys, and FAO Schwarz. The market for toys has been gradually changing. Specialty stores have been losing their market shares to discounters such as Target or Wal-Mart that offered a wide assortment of toys at highly competitive prices.

Sporting Goods Stores Sporting goods stores consisted of stores that sold products to amateur athletes. The assortment of goods included football, baseball, golf, tennis, ski, fishing, and camping equipment. The main competitors included The Sports Authority and Dick's Sporting Goods. As with toy stores, sporting goods have also been facing increasing competition from the discount stores.

Pet Stores Pet stores sold not only pets, but also food and other supplies for pets. PETsMART and Petco Animal Supplies dominated this segment. Both chains also offered services, such as training programs or veterinary services. As the pet population was increasing, both chains were adding more stores.

Bookstores Bookstores were being heavily influenced by e-commerce. The main competitors included Barnes & Noble and Borders Group. They faced strong competition not only from Internet retailers such as Amazon, but also from discounters such as Target or Wal-Mart.

Apparel Stores Apparel stores included retailers that sold clothing and accessories. The main competitors included Gap Inc., Limited Brands, Abercrombie and Fitch Co., Hennes & Mauritz (H&M), and American Eagle Outfitters. Besides competing against each other, they also faced competition from department stores and general merchandise discounters.

Apparel specialty retailers are the focus of this study, and are discussed in detail in the following sections.

Industry and Competitive Market: Specialty Apparel Retail

For specialty apparel retailers, the beginning of the twenty-first century was a difficult time. According to the Department of Commerce, sales rose only 0.7 percent in 2001. Although consumers bought more of their apparel from specialty stores (23 percent of annual spending on clothes) than from any other type of retail establishment (18 percent department stores, and 14 percent for general merchandisers), their sales were still rather weak. Apparel purchases accounted for almost 3.2 percent of disposable income in 2001, down from 3.5 percent in 1991, and

3.7 percent in 1981. In addition, prices had fallen in each of the prior three years. Therefore, stores had to sell more items just to stay even with the total sales dollars of the prior year. Many retailers suffered from overexpansion and misjudgment of fashion trends. Throughout the segment the same-store sales and margins were declining [Standard & Poor's, 2002B].

How the Industry Segment Works:
The Essence of the Business Process

The industry under study sells a variety of clothing, accessories, and body care products to individual customers of all genders, ages, sizes, and income levels, as shown in Figure 4. Their decisions to buy are influenced by a number of different factors such as price, style, quality of the fabric, and color.

Products are sold through retail stores, catalogs, and companies' websites. All customer groups have different preferences as to where they like to buy. A number of factors influence that decision. For some, convenience or speed may be important; others like to spend time doing their shopping and enjoy the experience.

Retailers have a choice of manufacturing their goods in-house or outsourcing the production to outside vendors. All firms in the segment use a number of ways of advertising their products, from TV and radio commercials, to outdoor billboards, newspapers and magazines, to advertisements on the Internet. The industry takes advantage of the available technology in different ways both to reach the consumer and to improve operating efficiency. This is a fiercely competitive market domestically as well as internationally.

According to a recent study by the America's Research Group of South Carolina, about 73 percent of consumers surveyed said they believed that stores within the same retail category tend to look alike. In addition, the product mix from store to store was virtually identical [Standards & Poor's, 2002B]. As a result most simple expansion strategies, such as adding new store locations, could no longer guarantee sustainable revenue growth for a company. Rather, sales growth has become contingent upon connecting with target customers and building a distinct image. Specialty retailers that built strong brand names—such as Gap, Limited Brands Inc., or Abercrombie & Fitch—were likely to take away market share from those that did not. Those that concentrated on strong brand management were also likely to reap the rewards of increased customer loyalty, thus improving long-term growth prospects. If a company was able to build its retail store name into a brand, it would also usually be able to leverage that name into other categories. Gap and Limited were good examples.

The participants in the industry included specialty retailers, such as Gap, Limited, H&M, American Eagle Outfitters, and Abercrombie and Fitch. They compete not only with each other but also with department stores, such as Macy's and J.C. Penney, and general merchandise discounters, such as Target and Wal-Mart.

Products

Specialty apparel retailers sold a wide variety of clothing, accessories, and body care products.

Clothing Clothing sold at specialty stores included loungewear, sleepwear, underwear, activewear, jeans, dressy wear, and casual wear.

Loungewear and sleepwear. Loungewear and sleepwear included pajamas, robes, pants, hooded sweatshirts, and T-shirts.

FIGURE 4

Specialty Apparel Retail Segment Business Model

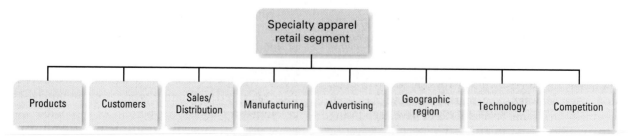

Underwear. Underwear included tank tops, t-shirts, briefs, boxers, panties, and bras.

Activewear. Activewear included jackets, hooded sweatshirts, sweatshirts, sweatpants, t-shirts, and tank tops.

Jeans. Jeans were available in many styles and colors.

Dressy wear. Dressy wear included coats, jackets, blazers, pants, dresses, shirts, blouses, and skirts.

Casual wear. Casual wear, or weekend wear as some sources referred to it, included shirts, pants, blouses, sweaters, jackets, skirts, capri pants, and skirts.

Accessories Accessories included shoes, socks, bags, handbags, backpacks, belts, wallets, jewelry, hats, scarves, gloves, and mittens.

Body Care Products Many apparel retailers added body care products to their product mix. They included lotions, body mists, fragrances, soaps, shower gels, and makeup lines, to name few.

In addition to having a strong brand image, having "the right merchandise, in the right place, at the right time" was a major success factor. It meant not only right fashions but also right colors, high quality, and durable fabrics. Although buildings, property, and equipment usually exceeded inventory value in dollar terms, merchandise inventories were a retailer's most important asset. Inventory generated sales were the key determinant of a retailer's success or failure, profitability, or loss. Although consumer buying decisions were influenced by a variety of retailing variables, such as price, location, and service, it's primarily the merchandise in the store that drove consumers to shop there and that built customer loyalty over time.

Companies needed to keep adequate inventories of merchandise. When a retailer correctly anticipated the next hot fashion trend, the merchandise sold quickly. It was very important that a store had enough of the popular product. When "wrong" merchandise, which did not appeal to customers, occupied shelf space, sales plummeted. In that case the retailer had to mark its price down to make room for new— and hopefully more salable—items. Low-turnover products could not occupy the valuable shelf space for too long. Merchants always planned for some sales, but excess markdowns eroded profitability.

It was also important for the companies to have good customer service via more appealing product displays, improved customer-friendly, understandable signage, and highly trained employees able to provide any requested information regarding the products sold in the stores.

Customers

Specialty apparel retailers catered to women and men of all ages, sizes, and income levels. For specialty retailers, as noted earlier, stores had to be stocked with goods that appealed to those customers. To build an appropriate business strategy, retailers had to anticipate changes in customers' needs and desires over time. Even more important than the number of people was the composition of that population—especially for specialty retailers, which often targeted a specific age group for their products.

Gender Apparel retailers catered to both women and men.

Women. Women accounted for 80 percent of household spending and 83 percent of all purchases [Reyes, 2002]. Approximately 72 percent of American women worked full time, which for apparel retailers was good news because it meant more income at the disposal of the most important customer [Stein, 2000]. It also meant that they needed to buy a new wardrobe suitable for their work. Women bought not only clothes for themselves, but also for their kids. In addition, they had a great influence on what their husbands were buying. Quality and affordability were important. Also women were driving the Internet sales. In 1999, the percentage of online shoppers who were women had jumped to 38 percent from 29 percent, and was continually rising [Tedeschi, 1999].

Men. Men were increasingly purchasing casual clothes. They were spending a growing percentage of their apparel money on casual wear, because of the changes in the dressing codes for many white-collar workers. For men the important issues were quality and durability of the products, as well as reliable customer service and product information. Return policies of the stores were also very important, a success factor in dealing with all types of customers.

Age For analysis purposes, customers can be divided into five major age groups: seniors, the baby boomers, Generation X, Generation Y, and little emperors [Standard & Poor's, 2002B].

Seniors. Seniors were comprised of individuals sixty-five-years old and older. They accounted for more than 12 percent of the U.S. population. When the baby boomers would begin turning sixty-five, the number of senior citizens was expected to swell, and was assumed to comprise nearly 15 percent of the U.S. population by 2015, as shown in Figure 5. Companies had to take the aging of the population into consideration. Successful store designs had to include features that catered to the demands and needs of an aging population, such as brighter lighting, larger letters on labels and signs, and better security. Loungewear, sleepwear, underwear, activewear, and casual wear were popular with seniors. They also bought accessories and body care products.

Baby Boomers. The baby boom generation, comprising individuals born between 1946 and 1964, constituted some 77 million Americans. They accounted for about 23 percent of the population. As the baby boomers moved into adulthood and formed households, they fueled much of the boom in retail sales in the 1970s and 1980s. Over

time, their spending habits have affected various retail categories. The boomers were in their forties and fifties in the early 2000s. Their priorities have shifted to tuition payments for children, saving for retirement, and caring for elderly parents. Although people in this age group continued to spend on furnishings and accessories for their homes, fashion had become less important. Baby boomers spent money on loungewear, sleepwear, underwear, activewear, dressy wear, casual wear, accessories, and body care products.

Generation X was comprised of approximately 45 million people born between 1965 and 1976. They accounted for about 15 percent of the U.S. population. These individuals began reaching adulthood in the mid 1980s. Although they have remained single longer than previous generations, they were beginning to form families. Home improvement and home furnishing retailers were likely to target this group. Members of this generation bought sleepwear, underwear, activewear, dressy wear, casual wear, jeans, accessories, and body care products.

FIGURE 5

U.S. Population Projections

Age Group	2002 Number (Thous.)	2002 % of Total	2010 Number (Thous.)	2010 % of Total	2015 Number (Thous.)	2015 % of Total
Under 5 yrs.	18,944	6.8	20,099	6.7	21,179	6.8
5 to 14 yrs.	39,938	14.2	39,345	13.1	40,549	13.0
15 to 19 yrs.	20,163	7.2	21,668	7.2	20,892	6.7
20 to 24 yrs.	19,438	6.9	21,151	7.1	21,748	7.0
25 to 29 yrs.	17,386	6.2	19,849	6.6	20,765	6.6
30 to 34 yrs.	19,536	7.0	19,002	6.3	20,484	6.6
35 to 39 yrs.	21,236	7.6	19,039	6.3	19,442	6.2
40 to 44 yrs.	22,988	8.2	20,404	6.8	19,346	6.2
45 to 49 yrs.	21,021	7.5	22,227	7.4	20,057	6.4
50 to 54 yrs.	18,240	6.5	21,934	7.3	21,929	7.0
55 to 64 yrs.	26,113	9.3	35,429	11.8	39,919	12.8
65 yrs. & over	35,303	12.6	39,715	13.2	45,959	14.7
All ages	280,306	100.0	299,862	100.0	312,268	100.0

Source: Standard & Poor's (2002A), "Retailing: General," [Online], **http://www.netadvantage.standardpoor.com/**, accessed September 26.

Generation Y. According to the Census Bureau, about 72 million Americans were born between 1977 and 1994, representing about 25 percent of the population. Members of this group were becoming young adults and teenagers. This group is known as Generation Y. Their numbers were good news for retailers. Teenagers typically did much of the household shopping and had influence on spending by their parents. Teens decided for themselves where to spend their money. Much of their spending, over $200 billion in 2001, went toward clothing items, such as jeans, activewear, dressy wear, casual wear, and accessories. They also bought body care products [Standard & Poor's, 2002B].

For a retailer to be successful with members of Generation X and Generation Y, it had to adopt the changes in fashion trends quickly.

Little Emperors. According to the Census Bureau, the population of children younger than five years of age reached 18.9 million in 2001, up from 16.3 million in 1980, and was expected to keep climbing over the next decade. To tap into this growing customer base, well-known specialty retailers have extended their product lines into infant and children's clothing. For example, Gap sold to these markets via its GapKids and BabyGap outlets; the Talbots Inc. operated Talbots Kids and added infants' clothing as well [Standard & Poor's, 2002B].

Size The customers in the specialty apparel market were divided into three main groups. Sizes 0 to 14, sizes 16 to 26, also called plus sizes, and sizes 28 to 34, called extended plus sizes. The first section of the market was already highly saturated, but plus sizes and extended plus sizes presented an opportunity for the competitors in that segment. Customers were looking for comfortable, stylish, and durable clothes. No successful company could afford to miss that opportunity. Even as concerns were growing about the health consequences of rising obesity in the United States, it still was a very large and potentially highly lucrative market [Ellison, 2002].

Income Specialty apparel stores targeted all income levels. Consumers were divided into three groups: high income, middle income, and lower income [DeNavas-Walt, 2002].

High-income. Twenty percent of all households that had the highest income of at least $83,500 during 2001 tended to be family households that included two or more earners, lived in the suburbs of a large city, and had a working householder between 35 and 54 years old [DeNavas-Walt, 2002]. For those consumers quality, brand name, customer service, and convenience of shopping mattered the most. Since most of those customers worked full time, time was also personally important. Consumers seemed more strapped for time than ever, and shopping became less of a fun pastime than it was in the 1980s. Research indicated that consumers were attempting to limit the time they spent shopping and looked to buy what they needed as quickly as possible, rather than scanning the mall in search of the perfect item. To satisfy consumer demand for convenience, retailers had to provide a full range of merchandise, speedy checkout, and generally good customer service which included sufficient number of sales representatives being able to answer questions about product selection, quality, prices, and availability. For specially retailers, the upside of this trend was that shoppers were spending more money per visit to the store, as their time constraints made their shopping ventures more purposeful. This was, however, true for all income levels.

Middle-income. Sixty percent of American households belonged to the middle-income group. Most of them lived in metropolitan areas; more than 70 percent were family households with either one or two earners [DeNavas-Walt, 2002]. High quality and affordability were the most important for these customers. In addition, the keys to success mentioned in the high-income customers' section applied to middle-income customers as well.

Lower-income. Twenty percent of all households had the lowest income of around $18,000 during 2001, and tended to be living in a city. Many included an elderly householder who lived alone and did not work [DeNavas-Walt, 2002]. These consumers were extremely price conscious. Sales and seasonal price reductions were important to them.

A successful company in this retail segment had to offer competitive prices. "Value," a subjective term that often connoted low prices, became increasingly important. This was distinctly different from the attitudes of the 1980s when high prices seemed synonymous with high quality. In the twenty-first century, the shopper who bought expensive jewelry at Tiffany & Co. was just as likely to purchase commodity goods at a BJ's Wholesale Club. This change in spending habits appeared to be a permanent shift in behavior. Another change was that more consumers tended to wait for sales before making their purchases [Standard & Poor's, 2002A].

Another very important trend for the specialty retailers was the increasing popularity of store credit cards. The ease of obtaining credit was driving sales for most retailers. In addition, many retailers offered their own credit cards. Consumer debt levels had continued to rise. According to the Federal Reserve, U.S. household debt at the end of the fourth quarter of 2001 represented 14.3 percent of disposable personal income, including 7.93 percent in consumer loans and 6.37 percent in mortgage payments, as shown in Figure 6. Successful companies had to take advantage of this trend by providing valuable customers with store credit cards.

Consumers were spending a growing percentage of their apparel money on casual wear, particularly in the United States where more than half of the country's white-collar workers were wearing casual clothing to work on a daily basis. While this trend has been troublesome for department stores and men's specialty stores, which have watched their sales of men's suits plummet, it has been a boon of sorts for casual-apparel specialty outlets such as The Gap, Abercrombie & Fitch, and American Eagle Outfitters.

Sales/Distribution

Specialty apparel retailers sold their products through retail stores, catalogs, and websites.

Retail Stores The ability to obtain prime store locations was key to any specialty retailer's success. Retailers had two choices: lease stores (as most did) or opt to own the real estate. The decision about whether to buy or lease was made only after a careful financial analysis of all the options. When a company bought real estate, it had to have the capital to pay the purchase price. Such purchases were financed either by obtaining a loan or by using currently available funds. In the case of leasing, the retailer paid a yearly rental fee. Both leasing and ownership had their pros and cons. Leasing could be restrictive in regard to subleases, store expansion, and the ability to close unprofitable stores. On the plus side, leases eventually expired and thus gave retailers the flexibility to relocate or close units. To finance a real estate purchase, a company had to be in good financial

FIGURE 6

Household Debt

Source: Board of Governors of the Federal Reserve System (2002), "Monetary Policy Report to the Congress," July 16, [Online], **http://www.federalreserve.gov/boarddocs/ hh/2002/July/FullReport.pfd/**, accessed October 8.

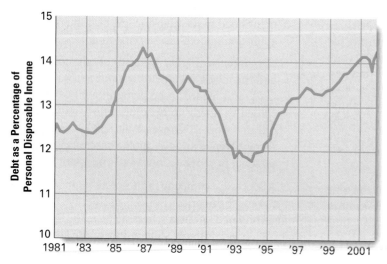

shape, with cash on its balance sheet and ample borrowing power.

Specialty retailers used both stand-alone stores and shopping mall locations. According to a recent study by *Management Horizons*, the number of trips to the mall has decreased 50 percent since the early 1990s. In 1980, mall visits were 4.6 per month, but dropped to 1.6 per month as early as 1995. The number of stores visited per trip had dropped from seven to three. According to Kurt Salmon Associates, more than half of consumers surveyed said that they shop less often and that shopping is a "hassle." One of the main reasons for this decline was the time pressure faced by Americans. Americans were going to the mall less. When they shopped, they were generally looking for a specific item [Barta et al., 1999].

Successful specialty retailers used information about customer shopping habits to improve store layout and design, even to the point of "market basket analysis," which involved identifying product pairs or groups that tend to be purchased together, and then stocking those items next to each other in the store. Goods displays and use of mannequins to provide the customers with inspiration about how they could match and combine available products was also important.

Merchandise shipping and receiving were a crucial part of the retail industry's operations. Carefully managing the way inventory was ordered, transported, received, distributed, reordered—and generally monitored—was a driving factor in lowering costs. Retailers generally operated one or more distribution centers that served stores in a particular region. Localization of the centers was very important. As a retailer expanded into new regions, additional distribution facilities were needed. In efficient distribution centers, merchandise was scanned via bar coding equipment; this process was almost totally automated. Throughout the distribution center, automated conveyance systems allowed for the flow of merchandise. Merchandise was stored until it was picked up for distribution and sent to stores. This automation helped to minimize the retailer's overall inventory levels while maintaining optimal in-stock positions at the store level.

Customer service was very important for specialty retailers. As a result, all competitors paid considerable attention to the training of their store employees. Sales representatives were trained not only in how to assist customers, but they also had to learn everything there was to know about the products. They learned about the selection, the quality, the fabrics, the availability of items, the sizes available, and the like. They were trained to talk to the customers in a way that would help them get to know the customer, so they could offer him/her the right product.

Catalogs Many specialty retailers used catalogs to sell their products. The key here was to get to know the customers through the data gathering, so the catalogs were sent to those customers likely to make a purchase. It was also important that the process of ordering the products was simple. Speedy delivery of the products was also important. Another crucial factor was low shipping and handling fees. Many customers got discouraged by high costs of shipping and handling and ended up not buying the products for that reason. This was also true for online shoppers.

Websites Due to the Internet, the majority of specialty retailers were able to make their products available to a wider range of customers 24/7. Websites were not only another way for the consumers to make a purchase. It was also a way for the company to get to know the customer. Safety and simplicity of online shopping were very important. Many companies allowed their customers to return the items ordered online in their retail stores. The option of picking up items ordered online in the stores was, however, not frequent.

A study by the National Retail Federation found that 68 percent of any particular company's catalog shoppers had also shopped at the company's stores. Among a retailer's online shoppers, 59 percent had also made purchases in the store, and 43 percent shopped from the retailer's catalog [Lipke, 2000]. Successful specialty retailers transformed themselves into multichannel retailers. It was very important that the customers felt that the three channels were part of one big entity [Hansell, 2002]. The information about the customers gathered in any of those channels should be used wherever the customer was making a purchase. Integrated data-collection efforts were a key. New analytic systems, such as CustomerCentric from SPSS Inc. or MerchantReach from IBM, made the integration possible. Using a process called ETLM (Extract, Transport, Load, Manage), which extracted, transported, loaded, and managed company's existing data stores into a single, comprehensive data warehouse, these systems provided a full view of a customer. When a customer's credit card was run through the system, their past purchases from the store, the website, or company's catalog were analyzed, and a sales suggestion would appear on the register's screen [Lipke, 2000].

Manufacturing

Retailers could choose between manufacturing the products they sold or outsourcing the production to vendors.

In-House Due to the high cost of manufacturing in-house, virtually all specialty retailers outsourced the production of their products. In most cases, the retailers provided the designs for the products themselves.

Outsourcing Due to the high costs of manufacturing in-house, most retailers outsourced the production of their products.

Retailers were dependent on suppliers to provide a steady and reliable supply of product. Disruptions in supply, including those due to manufacturers' product quality, which could differ from the quality agreed on when the retailer was ordering the items, or any other issues, could have a disastrous effect on the retailers' sales. Higher than expected demand could also place a strain on retailers. It was crucial for a retailer to have established high standards when selecting vendors. Close and continuous monitoring of vendors was also very important. Most retailers had a separate department within the company that dealt with vendors. Employees of the retailer would evaluate and monitor vendors' facilities on a daily basis. They conducted health and safety inspections, checked sewing machines for required features and safety guards, reviewed payroll records, and interviewed workers.

Advertising/Promotion

Specialty retailers have been using all means of advertising their products to reach the customers. Companies have used television, print, outdoor, and the Internet.

Television Most specialty retailers advertised on television. It was a very important channel of promotion because for many people it was the main, if not only, source of information. Through television ads retailers not only promoted their products but also built their brand names. Selection of highly watched net-

work channels was important. Also crucial was the time that the commercial would appear and the type of show during which it would be shown. The financial situation of a retailer was a key to success here since this was the most expensive channel of advertising.

Print Specialty retailers used a number of magazines to advertise their brands in. Depending on what type of customer they wanted to reach, they would turn to the type of magazine the target customers would typically read. Retailers also advertised in daily newspapers, but those ads were used more to inform about sales and other events than to help build the brand name.

Outdoor Outdoor posters and billboards were used by many specialty retailers to promote sales and new products, announce new store locations, or help build a strong brand name. Location was a key. To be effective, billboards were located in areas of high traffic or close to the new store location announced by the billboard.

Internet As the Internet became more popular, the need to use it as a means of advertising became clear. Internet ads were used to promote new products or to announce a sale or other event. The main use of the Internet for the specialty retailers was, however, branding. It was achieved through a variety of means, such as banners or pop-up ads. People browsing the Internet often stared at a screen for several seconds while a page downloaded, so an ad that appeared at the top of the page, or in a window covering the page, could have had a significant impact on a viewer [Murray, 2001]. The key was to select the right web pages to advertise on. Getting to know the potential customer and that customer's interests was also a key success factor.

Successful specialty retailers realized how information about their customers could be used to compete. Establishing one-to-one relationships with customers so a retailer was able to cater to their needs and desires and thus build customer loyalty was very important. Customer-driven marketing initiatives, or data-mining efforts, served to boost customer loyalty in the tightening retail market. Retailers gathered information about their customers in different ways, varying from data collection at the cash register to development of customer-loyalty programs that tracked spending habits through the use of sign-in forms on their e-commerce sites. Credit cards, warranty registrations, or gift registries were also an opportunity to collect customer data. Website users were asked about their age, gender, household income, hobbies, names of stores they liked to shop in, marital status, and other demographic information. The information gathered was used in a variety of ways. As specialty retailers gained a clearer understanding of their customers' needs, they were able to avoid development of low-demand products and step up production and orders for items that held better promise. It was, however, very important to effectively utilize the information and feedback from the customers.

Regardless of the channel used, one of the most important tasks that retailers were facing when advertising was communicating a clear message. Advertisements needed to be clear and understandable, so that the message they conveyed would not confuse customers in any way.

Strong brand was very important for specialty retailers. According to Richard S. Tedlow, a professor of business administration at the Harvard Business School, brand is a "promise" of a relationship between the product and the user [Hazel, 1999]. A strong brand promised that customers would be happy with the product they bought. As a result, high quality of product was essential. Unique design of the stores was also very important. Many companies improved their image, and built their brand names through charitable activities. By doing so, they made the customers familiar with the brand names. Competitors were sponsoring cultural and sports events. They were also helping to fund many organizations committed to different issues, such as the environment, education, health, and helping underprivileged kids.

Geographic Region

Specialty apparel retailers operated in domestic and international markets. Most large competitors had some kind of presence abroad.

Domestic Domestically, specialty retailers have to be present in major U.S. cities. Overexpansion, however, had to be avoided, because as the experience of Limited or Gap showed it could lead to cannibalism of sales. It was also important for the retailers to be present in densely populated suburbs, where the potential shopping traffic was high. It was, however,

crucial for any specialty retailer to carefully select malls in which to locate their outlets. Presence in a poor quality mall could damage the brand name of a retailer.

International In light of the mature and oversaturated markets in the most developed countries of the world and the accompanying competitive pressures, the majority of specialty retailers operating in more saturated markets such as the United States, Canada, Europe, and Japan were pursuing expansion in faster-growing international markets. Expanding information technologies enabled retailers to manage globally. Improved economic efficiency, increased competition, economic growth, and increased consumer purchasing power have made emerging markets such as China, Latin America, or Central Europe attractive for the retailers. International expansion allowed specialty retailers to reduce their dependency on regional economies by spreading risks across economic areas, and further provided specialized products and targeted untapped niche markets throughout the world.

Global expansion was not possible without significant investment; therefore, a solid financial situation and ability to attract investors were crucial.

Problems associated with entering new markets included the potential for misunderstanding local consumers, their tastes and needs as far as service and quality were concerned, having to compete against unfamiliar companies, and dealing with the different labor laws and work ethics of different countries. Specialty retailer The Home Depot, for example, which has been expanding quickly in Latin American and South American countries, has run into serious challenges in promoting its customer-service culture among local workers, who are not accustomed to the level of service that their employers were demanding from them. Thorough research of any potential market was unavoidable. Potential customers and their tastes, potential and existing competitors, the economic situation, and the legal environment had to be analyzed and incorporated in all planning and operations.

Even expanding from the United States to the European Union or other developed markets could pose challenges for a retailer. A U.S.-based retailer might find it difficult to export its domestic retail concept to other markets and might have to purchase a local retailer who was more attuned to local preferences and tastes to make inroads into the market.

Technology

Technology used by specialty apparel retailers included e-tailing, interactive kiosks, bar coding, and electronic data interchange.

E-tailing E-commerce offered many opportunities to specialty retailers worldwide. In addition to allowing them to target customers in previously untapped markets—without building new stores—it also removed physical barriers that were present in brick-and-mortar retailing. Small and regional businesses could immediately become global players through e-commerce. Online retailers have struggled with a variety of challenges, including orders' fulfillment, heavy competition, underdeveloped business plans, and slowing demand. These difficulties have been particularly hard-hitting for pure Internet companies, which have struggled with capital shortages. With years of retail experience, the traditional outlets had numerous advantages over the pure e-tailers, including brand-name recognition, preexisting supply chain and system infrastructure, economies of scale, and experience in dealing with seasonal peaks.

Internet usage continued to gain consumers' confidence. E-commerce sales in 2001 totaled U.S.$ 32.6 billion, up 19.3 percent from 2000, which was well above the 3.4 percent gain in overall retail sales in 2001 [Standard & Poor's, 2002A]. Increasingly, the traditional retailers were capturing a larger and larger share of these online sales. Virtually all major retailers have developed e-commerce strategies, and retailers with international operations were also developing separate websites for the global customers.

For the bricks-and-clicks operations to be successful, a retailer had to have brand recognition. Customers bought a product online if they were familiar with the company and brand name. Selection and convenience were very important. Clear and easy return policies, for example, the possibility of returning an item bought online in a physical retail store, were also crucial. As far as the website itself was concerned, content, reliability, and accurate and speedy delivery were crucial success factors. The success of companies that used the Internet for sales was highly dependent on order fulfillment. The time it took to receive orders after they had been placed was critical. It also was crucial to ensure consumers that the transaction they made over the Internet was secure.

Interactive Kiosks A growing number of specialty retailers were placing interactive kiosks in their stores to attract traffic to their retail outlets and their websites and to offer other services or information. Kiosks were used to tie retailers' stores to their Internet strategies in an effort to develop true "clicks-and-bricks" operations. Kiosks offered information about retailers' products and store availability—and even offered recommendations, in some cases. Consumers could also walk over to a kiosk and order an item online that was out of stock. Some apparel retailers, such as Gap Inc., had pulled the kiosks out of their stores because customers did not want to spend time online when they were in a store and were able to touch and feel the clothes. Even if that was the case, kiosks could still have been useful. Instead of making customers use them by themselves, sales representatives could use them while helping customers pick the right product, order an item not available in the store, or locate a store carrying a certain item.

Bar Coding and Electronic Data Interchange Among the more ubiquitous technologies for inventory management by specialty retailers worldwide was the practice of bar coding via universal product codes, or UPCs. The bar code provided a universal language, with an alphabet composed of alternating black and white parallel lines, which encoded product information and was read by laser scanners. Having this efficient system in place was very important. Bar codes conveyed a great deal of useful information for retailers, including the identities of items sold, their sizes and colors, and their manufacturers. When retailers received products, they would feed bar-code data into their databases, which also held detailed information about price and inventory count. This system allowed companies to change prices more efficiently via computers versus manually marking down price tags on individual products. Another significant use of that technology was in the point-of-sale (POS) systems. POS scanning equipment at the checkout counter, which was linked to a computer, was able to read the universal product code (UPC) labels on products, instantly providing the retailer with detailed sales data. This allowed the retailer to follow customers' demands, gauge emerging merchandise trends, and meet inventory replenishment requirements. POS scanners also reduced labor costs, by eliminating the need to mark items individually, and enhanced price accuracy. From the customer's perspective, scanners reduced checkout time and generated a receipt that detailed the type and price of each item purchased.

Given the need to maximize efficiency in distribution and turnover, retailers had embraced electronic data interchange (EDI) as a source for quick and accurate transactions. EDI helped companies manage inventories during slower or quicker sales cycles. It was based upon direct, electronic communication with suppliers and distributors. EDI technology had been around, in one form or another, for at least three decades, and new forms were constantly emerging. One recent development to influence EDI was satellite technology. Retailers used EDI to transmit information on a timely basis from stores to headquarters or other central locations. Successful specialty retailers demanded sophisticated planning and technology so that decisions could be made on the basis of information rather than intuition. Those systems helped maintain lean inventories and avoid overstocking, while ensuring that retailers have on hand the merchandise that customers want to buy when they want to buy it. Under this program, retailer and manufacturers were linked via EDI, which allowed the transfer of information from one computer to another. By notifying vendors immediately when new merchandise had to be ordered, EDI made quicker replenishment cycles possible. As packages were received and their bar code labels were scanned, the system knew exactly which store to route it to. The merchandise spent only a few hours at the warehouse, instead of a few days.

As the age of technology offered opportunities for cost savings in the supply chain, retailers were increasingly teaming up to maximize efficiencies in merchandise ordering and delivery. In an evolving practice known as business-to-business (B2B) e-commerce, companies were transacting sales between themselves via the Internet. B2B provided a communication medium for retailers to view products, share information, and place orders across multiple manufacturers' product lines. B2B gave rise to an improved purchasing process that could minimize inventory, reduce delivery cycle times, and increase productivity. It also gave firms the ability to connect internationally without major infrastructure investments. More important, it was expected to level the playing field for smaller retailers, who could consolidate orders with other retailers to obtain discounts from manufacturers. One of the B2Bs serving specialty retailers, DirectSource.com (a product of DirectSource Global Purchasing) focused on serving small- and medium-sized retailers looking to import products from Asia by giving them access to online catalogs of goods. Larger retailers could make online purchases directly from about five thousand suppliers in Hong Kong, Taiwan, China, and other Asian countries.

The potential of other technologies being developed was also expected to have a major impact in retailing. For example, Wal-Mart, working with MIT, was in October 2001 testing a new wireless tool (initially called "Radio Frequency ID Tags") that could be printed or painted onto or attached to individual products (and/or by extension clothing or even skin) which would enable tracking the location and usage of a product through this radio/wireless device and which could be directly linked to a computer. For instance, it would substantially reduce in-store theft, enable producers to know just how long an individual consumer took to use a product, such as a tube of toothpaste, an item of clothing, and generally produce a wide range of detailed market information [Downes, 2001; Rendon, 2002]. The tests were begun when the cost of this technology was predicted to drop to only one cent per individual product. The implications of this technology were enormous, extending beyond business to finding lost or stolen autos or helicopter parts (the government is developing a radio frequency system for this), tracking the location of children and other people, and the like. At the same time, all of this potential also raised many questions about invasion of privacy [Konicki, 2001].

Competition

Retailing was a fiercely competitive industry. Besides competing with each other, specialty retailers also faced competition from department stores and discount stores (general merchandisers).

Specialty Retailers Limited Brands, Abercrombie and Fitch (A&F), and Hennes & Mauritz (H&M) were the main competition in the Gap market. They offered high-quality products, which in most cases appealed to the customers. Most stores offered an alternative way of shopping, some through the Internet, some through catalogs. Specialty stores had a good and reliable customer service. The store personnel were trained to answer customers' questions regarding product mix. In most cases seasonal price reductions and sales were offered. All the stores outsourced the manufacturing of their products. One of the main strengths of those stores was the ability to establish one-on-one relationships with the customer.

Stores gathered the information about their customers and studied their spending habits. Most of those retailers was available in major U.S. cities and densely populated suburbs. Specialty retailers did not offer products in plus or extended plus sizes. Most of them did not offer an extensive product line that went beyond clothing. One of the most important weaknesses, however, was the inability to remove the low-turnover products from the stores. These products occupied the shelves for too long, costing those retailers money, and even more importantly customers.

Limited Brands After a disagreement with his father in 1963 over the operation of the family store (Leslie's), Leslie Wexner, then twenty-six, opened the first Limited store in Columbus, Ohio. When The Limited went public in 1969, it had only five stores, but the rapid development of large, covered malls spurred growth to one hundred stores by 1976. Two years later The Limited acquired Mast Industries, an international apparel purchasing and importing company. The company opened Express in 1980 to serve the teen market.

The Limited grew with acquisitions, including the 1982 purchases of Lane Bryant (large sizes) and Victoria's Secret (lingerie). That year it formed the Brylane fashion catalog division and acquired Roaman's, a bricks-and-mortar and catalog merchandiser. Wexner bought The Lerner Stores (budget women's apparel) and Henri Bendel (high fashion) in 1985, sportswear retailer Abercrombie & Fitch (A&F) in 1988, and London-based perfumer Penhaligon's in 1990 (sold in 1997). The Limited introduced several in-store shops, including Cacique (French lingerie) in 1988 and Limited Too (girls' fashions), which were expanded into stand-alone stores. It also launched Structure (men's sportswear) in 1989 and Bath & Body Works shops in 1990. All of these stores were in malls, often strategically clustered together.

The Limited in 1993 closed many of The Limited and Lerner stores and sold 60 percent of its Brylane catalog unit to Freeman Spogli (taking it public in 1997). It opened four Bath & Body Works stores in the United Kingdom (its first non-U.S. stores) to compete with British rival The Body Shop. In 1994, The Limited bought Galyan's Trading Co., a chain of sporting goods superstores.

The company began spinning off its businesses while keeping controlling stakes; it spun off Intimate Brands (Victoria's Secret, Cacique, and Bath & Body Works) in 1995 and A&F in 1996. The Limited sold its remaining 84 percent in A&F in 1998. In 1997, the company closed more than one hundred of its women's apparel stores; the next year it closed nearly three hundred more companywide (excluding the Intimate Brands chains) and all but one of its Henri Bendel stores. Also in 1997, Intimate Brands closed the Cacique chain. In 1998, White Barn Candle Co. (candle and home fragrance stores) was launched. The following year the company spun off Limited Too, its most successful chain, as Too, Inc., and reduced its interest in Galyan's to 40 percent. Galyan's management and the buyout firm Freeman Spogli owned 60 percent of the sporting goods chain. The Limited (as well as Intimate Brands) declared a two-for-one stock split in 2000.

To boost profits, in 2001 The Limited folded the Structure brand into the Express unit and spun off its Galyan's and Alliance Data Systems subsidiaries, retaining 22 percent and 20 percent, respectively. The Limited sold its Lane Bryant unit to Charming Shoppers for $335 million that year.

The Columbus, Ohio, based retailer operated about forty-six hundred U.S. stores that sold a variety of apparel and personal care products in late 2002. Its apparel store names included The Limited, Express, Lerner New York, Henri Bendel, and Structure (which the company was rebranding as Express Men's). Its stores under its Intimate Brands subsidiary included Victoria's Secret, Bath & Body Works, and White Barn Candle Co. [Hoover's Online, 2002].

Limited Brands offered its products through fully owned retail stores. It did not, however, sell its products through the Internet (except for Victoria's Secret). Although Limited once owned a brand selling large sizes (Lane Bryant), it was sold on August 16, 2001. Since then the company did not offer plus or extended plus-sizes. Limited Brands' products were high quality. All brands allowed the customers to make returns easily. Stores often offered seasonal price reduction. The layout and design of the stores was strategic. Products often bought together were placed close to each other. Stores were frequently using mannequins to inspire customers. Limited outsourced its manufacturing. Like other specialty retailers, Limited had problems with inventory management. In many cases unpopular, low-turnover products occupied shelf space for too long.

Abercrombie and Fitch (A&F) Scotsman David Abercrombie began selling camping equipment in lower Manhattan in 1892. Joined by lawyer Ezra Fitch, Abercrombie & Fitch (A&F) soon established itself as the purveyor of outdoors equipment for the very rich. A&F supplied Theodore Roosevelt and Ernest Hemingway for safaris and provided gear for polar explorer Richard Byrd.

A&F thrived through the 1960s. However, by the 1970s the number of A&F's core customers was falling. Hunting was no longer popular and the company struggled to find new markets. In 1977, A&F filed for bankruptcy. A year later sports retailer Oshman's bought the company and expanded the number of stores while providing an eclectic assortment of goods. In 1988, clothing retailer The Limited bought A&F, then with about twenty-five stores, and shifted the company's emphasis to apparel. Michael Jeffries took over in 1992 and transformed the unprofitable chain into an outfitter for college students. In 1995, A&F returned to profitability. The company went public in 1996 with more than 110 stores. In 1998, The Limited spun off its remaining 84 percent stake. Also that year A&F sued rival American Eagle Outfitters, claiming it illegally copied A&F's clothing (the suit was dismissed in 1999). In 1999, the SEC launched an investigation after A&F leaked sales figures to an analyst before they were made available to the public. In 2000, A&F launched its new teen store concept called Hollister Co.

Through about 490 stores nationwide (mostly in malls), New Albany, Ohio, based A&F sold upscale, casual apparel for men, women, and kids. Its clothing included shirts, khakis, jeans, underwear, and outerwear. Most items were emblazoned with the A&F logo. The company also sold merchandise through its subscription catalog, A&F Quarterly, and its website.

Though college students were the company's main target market, A&F sold its products to adults, teens, and kids as well. Its children's stores were called Abercrombie, and the teen stores concept was called Hollister Co. The company's carefully selected college-age sales staff and photos of twenty-something models adorning the walls imbued its main stores with an upscale fraternity house feel.

A&F was no stranger to controversy. In the last four years, various marketing techniques and product choices (including sexually suggestive ads and children's thong underwear) have drawn complaints and criticism from conservative politicians, family advocacy groups, cultural groups, Mothers Against Drunk Driving and other women's groups [Hoover's Online, 2002].

The company offered products of good quality, which appealed to its target market. A&F sold its goods in retail stores, through catalogs, and through the Internet. As other specialty apparel retailers, the company had problems with removing low turnover products from shelf space to make space for new product lines. Compared with other retailers A&F's products were also quite pricey. Like the majority of competitors A&F did not offer their products in plus and extended plus-sizes. Stores allowed their customers to return the products. It was also possible to return an item bought online into a physical retail store. One of the weaknesses of A&F when compared with other specialty retailers was the store layout. Stores rarely used mannequins, and the display of the products needed improvement.

Hennes and Mauritz (H&M) In 1947, Erling Persson opened his first Hennes (Swedish for "hers," because it only sold women's apparel) store in Västerås, Sweden. The company expanded, opening its first foreign stores in Norway in 1964 and Denmark in 1967. As it grew and increased volume, the retailer was able to offer lower prices. The company bought hunting and men's clothing shop Mauritz Widforss in 1968 and began offering men's clothing in Mauritz stores.

In 1974, the company went public. H&M Hennes & Mauritz introduced cosmetics in 1975 and began opening stores in London the following year. Also in 1976, the company introduced its teenage clothing stores under the Impulse banner. By the end of the 1970s, the company had moved into Switzerland (1978) and Germany (1980) and introduced baby clothes. In 1980, H&M also purchased mail-order company Rowell.

Stefan Persson took over as CEO from his father, Erling, in 1982. He expanded throughout northern Europe, and H&M boasted two hundred stores in 1985. By 1988, the company was experiencing annual sales growth rates of 25 to 30 percent. The firm's European expansion continued, and by 1998, H&M had entered six more countries, including France, Austria, Finland, and the Benelux countries. By this time the company had also consolidated its men's, women's, children's, and teens' stores under the H&M

banner. Stefan gave up his CEO position and became executive chairman of the board in 1998. The company's purchasing director, Fabian Månsson, succeeded him as CEO. In 1998 and 1999, H&M began selling online, first in Sweden, then in Denmark and Finland.

The company moved into the United States and Spain in 2000. The openings, considered a success by H&M, put a strain on earnings, which sent the stock into a dive. In a move the company said was unrelated, Månsson resigned and was replaced by Danish subsidiary CEO Rolf Eriksen.

H&M designed cheap but chic clothing, mainly for men and women ages eighteen to forty-five, children's apparel, and its own brands of cosmetics. H&M operated some eight hundred stores in fourteen countries with direct sales operations in selected areas. Half of its clothing was made in Europe, the rest mostly in Asia.

More than 85 percent of sales come from outside of H&M's home country, and the company was continuing to expand, planning to open nearly one hundred stores per year, including in new markets in Europe and the United States. H&M has slowed its plans to have up to eighty-five stores in the United States by 2003. Women's clothing accounted for 60 percent of sales; private-label brands included Hennes, L.O.G.G. (Label of Graded Goods), and BiB (Big is Beautiful).

H&M was controlled by the family of Chairman Stefan Persson (the son of founder Erling Persson); they owned about 33 percent of the company's stock [Hoover's Online, 2002].

H&M's most important strength and advantage over competitors was its competitive pricing. Stores were strategically designed. Mannequins were often used, and products were attractively displayed. Items often purchased together were placed close to each other. The quality of the products, although still good, was lower than of other specialty apparel retailer's products. The company was fairly new on the U.S. market. It was not yet present in major U.S. cities or in suburbs. H&M did not offer its products through catalogs or the Internet in the United States, although it planned to in the future. The company did not offer store credit cards for its customers.

Department Stores Specialty retailers also competed with department stores. The main competitors included Macy's and J.C. Penney. Department stores offered extensive product lines of good quality. They attracted customers with seasonal price reductions and sales, and most of them offered store credit cards. Their strengths also included a wide domestic presence, both in major U.S. cities and in densely populated suburbs. They offered clothes in sizes 1 through 14, and limited selections of clothes in plus sizes. The main weakness of those stores was a lack of strong customer service. Although trained staff was present, in most department stores it was hard to find the right person able to provide the information about offered products. Another problem in department stores was long checkout time, at times long enough for customers to feel discouraged and leave the store without making a purchase.

General Merchandisers In times when consumers became increasingly price conscious, discounters such as Wal-Mart, Kmart, or Target were posing a huge threat to both specialty retailers and department stores. The ability to price products competitively and a wide product line were the main strengths of those merchandisers. Those stores also targeted the market for plus, and extended plus sizes, which was ignored by department stores and most specialty retailers. The weakness of those stores was in customer service and product quality areas. Although the product line was extensive, many products were of poor quality. The styles, colors, and fabrics of clothes often did not appeal to customers. Although returns were possible, the staff often lacked information about the products that were offered in the store. These stores did not try to establish more personal relationships with the customers. Unlike most specialty retailers, the majority of discounters did not work on building their own brands.

The Company

History

Donald Fisher and his wife, Doris, opened a small store in 1969 near what is now San Francisco State University. The couple named their store The Gap (after "the generation gap") and concentrated on selling Levi's jeans. The couple opened a second store in San Jose, California, eight months later, and by the end of 1970, there were six Gap stores. The Gap went public six years later.

In the beginning, the Fishers catered almost exclusively to teenagers, but in the 1970s, they expanded into active wear that would appeal to a larger spectrum of customers. Nevertheless, by the early 1980s The Gap—which had grown to about five hundred stores—was still dependent on its large teenage customer base. However, it was less dependent on Levi's (about 35 percent of sales), due to its growing private labels.

In a 1983 effort to revamp the company's image, Fisher hired Mickey Drexler, a former president of AnnTaylor with a very successful apparel industry track record, as The Gap's new president. Drexler immediately overhauled the motley clothing lines to concentrate on sturdy, brightly colored cotton clothing. He also consolidated the stores' many private clothing labels into the Gap brand. As a final touch, Drexler replaced circular clothing racks with white shelving so that clothes could be neatly stacked and displayed. Also in 1983, The Gap bought Banana Republic, a unique chain of jungle-themed stores that sold safari clothing. The company expanded the chain, which enjoyed tremendous success in the mid 1980s but slumped after the novelty of the stores wore off late in the decade. In response, Drexler introduced a broader range of clothes (including higher-priced leather items) and dumped the safari lines in 1988. By 1990, Banana Republic was again profitable, and in 1995, it opened its first two stores outside the United States, both in Canada.

The first GapKids store opened in 1985 after Drexler couldn't find clothing that he liked for his son. In 1990, Gap Inc. introduced babyGap in twenty-five GapKids stores, featuring miniature versions of its GapKids line. The Gap announced in 1991 that it would no longer sell Levi's (which had fallen to less than 2 percent of total sales) and would sell nothing but private-label items.

In 1994, The Old Navy Clothing Co. was launched, named after a bar Drexler saw in Paris.

Robert Fisher (the founders' son) became the president of the Gap division (including babyGap and GapKids) in 1997 and was charged with reversing the segment's sales decline. The company refocused its Gap chain on basics (jeans, T-shirts, and khakis) and helped boost its performance with a high-profile advertising campaign focusing on those wares. Later in 1997, the Gap opened an online Gap store. In 1998, the retailer opened its first GapBody stores and introduced its only catalog (for Banana Republic). In late 1999, amid sluggish Gap division sales, Robert resigned, and CEO Drexler took over his duties. Beginning in 2000, Gap Inc. started to report its store count based on the number of concepts for Gap brand. This meant that any Gap Adult, GapKids, babyGap, or GapBody meeting a certain square footage threshold was counted as a separate store even when residing within a single physical location. GapMaternity was a part of babyGap, but it did not have separate stores. Gap concepts are shown in Figure 7.

In 2000, Gap misjudged fashion trends, which resulted in disappointing earnings. In May 2002, Drexler announced that he wanted to retire, and that he would do so as soon as a replacement was found. On September 26, 2002, Paul Pressler was named president and chief executive officer of Gap Inc. In September 2002, the company reported its twenty-eighth straight month of declines in sales at stores open at least one year [Gap Inc. Company Website, 2002].

The focus of this case study is on one of the three divisions of Gap Inc., namely, The Gap.

FIGURE 7

Gap Store Concepts

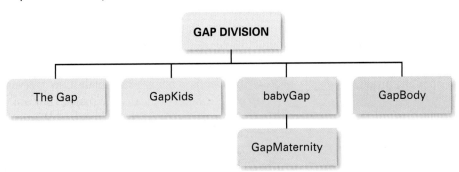

FIGURE 8

The Gap Division of Gap, Inc.

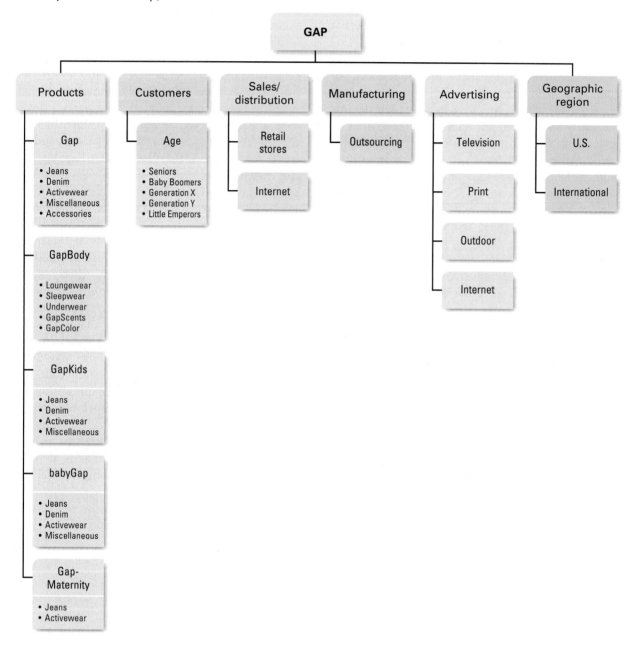

Products

The Gap brand name can be divided into five concepts. Each of them offered different products for different customers.

The Gap The Gap, or Gap Adult as some sources referred to it, offered activewear, denim products, accessories, jeans, and miscellaneous products to both men and women. They all came in a variety of fits, colors and washes, and fabrics.

Jeans and Pants. This is what made Gap famous. Gap offers a variety of jeans and pants. They came in a variety of styles, fabrics, and colors. Women's jeans included boot cut, long and lean, low-rise boot cut, flare, modern boot cut, classic, loose fit, square pocket, utility, sidewinder, carpenter, and patch pocket. They were available in dark faded, light faded, stretch brown tinted, stretch faded, stretch black, stretch rinsed, stretch sandblasted, sandblasted, stonewashed, khaki, dark khaki, dark cement, and black. The men's selection included boot fit, easy fit, standard fit, relaxed fit, loose fit, wide leg, carpenter, worker, and straight fit. They came in vintage, faded, antiqued, brown tinted, rustic, black tinted, stonewashed, rinsed, black, dark blasted, black blasted, dark sandblasted, tinted rinsed, and black.

Denim. Denim products included shirts, blouses, jackets, skirts, dresses, accessories, and shoes.

Activewear. Activewear included sweatshirts, hooded sweatshirts, fleece sweatshirts, sweatpants, T-shirts, and tops.

Miscellaneous. Miscellaneous products included sweaters, turtlenecks, vee-necks, blouses, shirts, dresses, jackets, coats, pea coats, trench coats, vests, tops, T-shirts, and polos.

Accessories. Accessories included bags, handbags, backpacks, tote bags, belts, hats, scarves, gloves, mittens, socks, shoes, flip-flops, and slides.

GapBody With a focus on everyday essentials, GapBody offered loungewear, sleepwear, underwear, GapScents, and Gap Color.

Loungewear, Sleepwear, and Underwear. GapBody offered loungewear, sleepwear, women's bras and panties, and men's underwear. One of the most popular products was the GapBody Seamless style, T-shirts, tanks, and camisoles with no seams or bulky edges. They were created on a cylinder, which made it possible to eliminate side seams.

GapScents. Body lotions, body mists, and eau de toilette were available in "So Pink," "Dream," and "Heaven" fragrances. Gap also introduced "G," a men's fragrance composed of crisp white cotton, juniper, and musk. There were "G" eau de toilette, aftershave balm, hair and body wash, body lotion, soap on a rope, and gift sets available. Gap also introduced "Simply White," a new women's fragrance with floral top notes of honeysuckle and jasmine and warm, woodsy bottom notes. There were eau de toilette, shower gel, moisturizing soap, body mist, body lotion, intensified fragrance lotion, shimmer lotion, and gift sets available in this fragrance line.

GapColor. GapBody introduced GapColor, a new line of wearable, high-quality cosmetics that were offered in a range of versatile colors for lips, eyes, face, and nails. Some of the products included lip glaze, lip gloss in 10 shades, lip color in 25 shades, lipstick in 10 shades, lip care in 4 shades, lip liners in 5 shades, nail color in 12 shades, eye color in 20 shades, face powder in 8 shades, and 5 kinds of brushes.

GapKids GapKids's products included activewear styles, jackets, sweaters, pants, and jeans. As always, the emphasis on quality was shown in the details: from embellished denim for girls and knit tops for boys, to expanded washes in jeans and bright, simple colors across the assortment. Highlights for girls included flare, bootcut, and classic jeans; embellished jeans were also available—glitter flares, glitter patch pocket, charm and heart styles. Other offerings included polos, cotton cardigans, yoga pants, zip hoodies, velour or tricot track suits, boots, clogs, and slip-ons. Some highlights for boys included jeans (basic five-pocket jeans, carpenter, cargo, all in stonewash blast, antique blast, dark sandblast, and whisker antique), basic tops, polos, Oxford shirts, tracksuits, hooded sweatshirts, sneakers, and slip-ons. GapKids also offered bags, small backpacks for younger kids, premier backpacks for older students, and messenger-style bags.

babyGap babyGap offered products for the little kids, from newborns up to age five. Products included bodysuits, playwear, overalls, tops, cardigans, sweaters, socks, and shoes, all in denim and cozy fabrics.

GapMaternity GapMaternity did not have its own separate stores. It was a section of babyGap stores. The products for moms-to-be included jeans and activewear. According to Rachel DiCarlo, vice president of fashion public relations for Gap, "These are the same jeans women wear when they're not pregnant" [Gap Inc. Company's Website, 2002]. The favorite items from Gap were translated into maternity wear so women could maintain their sense of style throughout their pregnancy. A wide range of fits and washes was available; maternity jeans took on a modern look in different styles. Jeans included stretch patch pocket, a worker-inspired jean with front patch pockets, the sandblasted stretch long and lean that fits slim through the leg and has a demi-belly panel that sits slightly lower at the waist, and stretch boot cut. The stretch fabric in all of the jeans styles improved fit, maximized comfort, and provided ease of movement. GapMaternity also offered activewear, which included stretch hoods, pants, and jackets. Stores carried sizes from XS to XL. Styles have been designed for comfort throughout the pregnancy, with stretch fabrics and special features such as four comfortable belly panels (the new demi-panel, no panel, side panel, and full panel) to ensure that jeans fit perfectly at every stage.

Overall, Gap had a strong brand name. Its products were high quality. The fashions and colors appealed to the customers. Products were attractively displayed on white shelving. Products' labels were clear and understandable and they provided sufficient product information. Gap often marked down the prices of different products. The company had some problems with inventory management, low-turnover products occupied shelf space for too long, and there were cases of inadequate inventory of high turnover items.

Customers

Gap catered to women and men of almost all ages. Different Gap brands targeted different age groups. Gap paid close attention to the age distribution and priorities of potential customers in its markets.

Gap targeted women and men through all its store concepts. *Women* accounted for 80 percent of household spending and 83 percent of all purchases [Reyes, 2002]. Most women worked full time, which for apparel retailers such as Gap was good news because it meant not only more income at the disposal of the most important customer, but also a need to buy a new wardrobe suitable for their work. Women bought not only clothes for themselves, but also for their kids. In addition, they had a great influence on what their husbands were buying. *Men* were spending a growing percentage of their apparel money on casual wear, because of the changes in the dressing codes for many white-collar workers. This was a good change for specialty retailers such as Gap that specialized in casual clothing.

Seniors Seniors are comprised of individuals sixty-five years old and older. They accounted for more than 12 percent of the U.S. population. By 2015, they are expected to comprise nearly 15 percent of the U.S. population. Gap and GapBody targeted seniors.

Baby Boomers The baby boom generation, comprising individuals born between 1946 and 1964, constituted some 77 million Americans. The boomers were then in their forties and fifties. Gap and GapBody targeted those consumers.

Generation X Generation X was comprised of approximately 45 million people born between 1965 and 1976. These individuals had reached adulthood in the mid 1980s, and were then in their twenties and thirties. Products from Gap, GapBody, and GapMaternity were targeting this group.

Generation Y The Generation Y group included individuals born between 1977 and 1994, representing about 25 percent of the population. Gap, GapBody, and GapKids targeted this segment.

The Little Emperors The little emperors included a population of children younger than five years of age. Gap sold to these markets via its GapKids and babyGap outlets.

Gap sold high-quality products at competitive price levels. Consumers were able to shop whenever it was convenient for them, by either going to a physical store or to the Gap websites. It also offered a store credit card for its customers. Gap offered products in sizes 0 to 14, a limited selection of products in plus-sizes, but no extended plus-sizes. Another important strength of Gap was the customer service the company provided. Company stores had bright lighting, and products were attractively displayed on shelves. A sufficient number of cash registers provided speedy checkout for the customers. Sales associates and other store personnel were trained to answer customers' questions about fabric, fit, and fashion, and to help them select merchandise that would be perfect for them.

Sales and Distribution

Gap was headquartered in the San Francisco Bay Area, its product development offices were in New York City, and distribution operations and offices coordinating sourcing activities were located around the globe. Third-party manufacturers shipped merchandise to distribution centers, which sorted and redistributed it to the stores. Strategically placed throughout the United States, Canada, the United Kingdom, the Netherlands, and Japan, the distribution centers were the backbone of Gap Inc.'s worldwide operations. The company used bar coding and electronic data interchange systems in inventory management. The company operated all its stores, it did not franchise or enter into joint ventures, and it did not wholesale its products or serve as a supplier to other companies.

Retail Stores Gap's retail stores were attractively located. Gap used stand-alone stores and mall locations. Gap leased most of its store premises. Store layout and design were strategic, and products often bought together were placed in close proximity. Products were attractively displayed on white shelving, and mannequins provided ideas and inspiration for customers. Sales associates and other store personnel were trained to answer customers' questions about fabric, fit, and fashion, and to help them select merchandise that would be perfect for them.

Internet Gap products were available through the website that included gap.com, gapbody.com, gapkids.com, and babygap.com. Shopping on those websites was safe, quick, and simple. Customers were able to return products bought online to the company's retail stores. Ordered products were sent to the customer directly from one of the distribution centers. However, customers were not able to pick up their online orders in retail stores.

Manufacturing

Gap Inc.'s goods were produced in approximately thirty-six hundred factories in more than fifty countries. It did not manufacture any of the goods itself; it neither owned nor operated any garment factories. Instead, it was almost always one of a manufacturer's many customers. Gap was a designer and marketer.

Gap Inc. developed a set of principles and operating standards for garment manufacturers that reflected its values, beliefs, and business ethics. These standards were set out in its Code of Vendor Conduct, which was first written in the early 1990s and updated in 1996. The Code focused on compliance with local labor laws, working conditions, and the natural environment. It also spelled out to vendors Gap's expectations regarding wages, child labor, health, and safety issues, respecting the right of workers to unionize and much more. It was written in order to help vendors understand and apply these standards to their day-to-day operations, and adopt

them as "company policy." Few factories, if any, in the United States or anywhere else were in total compliance all of the time.

Gap Inc.'s Global Compliance department was comprised of over ninety full-time employees dedicated exclusively to working with potential and current vendors to help them understand and achieve compliance with the Code. Before Gap approved or placed an order with a vendor, the Global Compliance team was involved. First, before any orders were placed, a manufacturer and the factories it intended to use were subjected to a comprehensive approval process to make sure they could operate under the Code of Vendor Conduct. Second, if a garment factory was eventually approved, the Compliance team monitored compliance on an ongoing basis. In addition, other Gap employees visited factories—from quality assurance and production experts to employees who determined if a vendor was capable of producing a specific kind of garment.

Advertising/Promotion

Gap advertised its products in a number of ways. Each of the three main brands, including Gap, has its own marketing team headquartered in the San Francisco Bay Area. In-house marketing teams created everything from hangtags and in-store posters to billboards and TV commercials. A more recent campaign was titled "For Every Generation." The global campaign was comprised of television, print, outdoor, and online initiatives.

Television Gap TV spots were aired in the United States, United Kingdom, Canada, and Japan. TV spots in the United States were shown during prime-time programs, including *Friends, Will & Grace, West Wing, Law & Order, Ed, Scrubs,* and *ER* on NBC; *Alias, The Practice* and *My Wife & Kids* on ABC; *CSI* and *Survivor* on CBS; and *Malcolm in the Middle* and *Boston Public* on Fox [Howard, 2002A]. In those TV spots, Gap has turned to celebrities such as Lauren Hutton or Bridget Hall for help [Brown, 2002].

Print Print ads appeared in more than forty international magazines, which included *Vogue, Harper's Bazaar, Marie Claire, InStyle, Details, Vanity Fair, W, ESPN, GQ, Spin, Sports Illustrated, Rolling Stone,* and *Interview.* They also appeared in major newspapers.

Outdoor Major market outdoor billboards were used by Gap. Billboards, walls, and transit posters appeared in high-visibility markets throughout the United States, Canada, Europe, and Japan.

Internet Gap pop-up ads and banners appeared on various popular web pages, such as aol.com or yahoo.com. Those ads were used not only to promote Gap brand name but also to announce new product lines and sales.

Although Gap took advantage of various channels of promotion, some customers complained that the message of the advertisements was sometimes unclear and confusing. This highlighted another problem in the company; it took a long time for Gap to react to the negative feedback and reaction of the customers.

Gap worked hard to earn a good reputation and establish a strong brand name. To enhance and exceed the expectations of every customer, Gap store designers were constantly evolving everything that touches the customers—from store signage and merchandise displays, to dressing rooms and inventory systems. Their goal was to create a relaxed shopping environment that intensifies Gap's bold brand expression and enhances the sales associates' ability to provide outstanding service. Going forward, these design changes were originated to help support Gap's growth and future vision, and make the customers' experiences the best of any retailer. Gap wanted its customers to know that when they visited one of their stores, they're not just walking into a store, they're walking into a brand.

High-quality products, good customer service, and a distinct shopping environment ensure a good reputation, but it often is not enough. In 1977, Gap Inc. established its charitable arm—Gap Foundation. In order to make a name for itself Gap, through Gap Foundation, engaged in a number of partnerships. It funded two national organizations that share the commitment to helping underserved youth. Boys & Girls Clubs of America and the Lorraine Monroe Leadership Institute aimed to help students develop self-esteem, stay in school, and succeed academically so they can lead more rewarding and fulfilling lives. To help teens make sound educational decisions, explore career opportunities, and prepare for the workforce, Gap was funding a career exploration and mentoring program for more than twenty-six hundred Boys & Girls Clubs nationwide. Gap Inc. employees were also in charge of workshops, conducted Career Day sessions at their local Boys & Girls Clubs, and provided job-shadowing opportunities for youth at headquarters and store locations. Dr. Lorraine Monroe acknowledges the challenges of education in underserved urban areas. By embracing these challenges—adding a mix of first-rate teachers, a creative but disciplined environment, and the expectation of perfection—Dr. Monroe has helped transform the future of public urban education. This is the premise of the Lorraine Monroe Leadership Institute, which is focused on developing leaders for public schools who are committed to educating underserved youth. Through funding from Gap Foundation, the Institute created Demonstration Schools to train teachers and administrators in Dr. Monroe's extraordinary leadership principles. In addition to the major partnerships with Boys & Girls Clubs of America and the Lorraine Monroe Leadership Institute, Gap Inc. supported nonprofit organizations serving kids in local communities around the world. Although it focused primarily on education and youth development, Gap, Banana Republic and Old Navy supported many other organizations in areas such as health and human services, civics and arts, and the environment [Gap Inc. Company Website, 2002].

Geographic Region

Gap stores were located in five countries outside the United States—the United Kingdom, Canada, France, Japan, and Germany, as shown in Figure 9. The company was successful in expanding into international markets. It was not present in any emerging markets, such as Eastern and Central Europe, as well as Asian or South American countries.

Because it was a sole owner of all its subsidiaries, and it operated its stores by itself, it was able to avoid any problems associated with loss of control. Because it did not enter into joint ventures or franchises, the expansion was slower than it could have been.

Gap operated 2,323 store concepts domestically, 235 in the United Kingdom, 192 in Canada, 155 in Japan, 54 in France, and 20 in Germany, as shown in Figure 9. The actual number of stores was less because in some instances "concepts" were located in a single store.

FIGURE 9

Gap Division Stores in Operation as of August 3, 2002.*

Gap Domestic	**2,323**
Gap Adult	1,024
GapKids	819
babyGap	193
GapBody	154
Gap Outlet	133
Gap International	**656**
Canada	192
United Kingdom	235
France	54
Japan	155
Germany	20
Total	**2,979**

*For the past two years, Gap Inc. has reported store count based on the number of concepts for Gap brand. This means that any Gap Adult, GapKids, babyGap or GapBody meeting a certain square footage threshold is counted as a separate store even when residing within a single physical location.

Source: Gap Inc. Company Website (2002), [Online], **http://www.gapinc.com**, accessed September 26.

Although Gap was present in all states of the United States, it concentrated mostly on highly populated areas, such as in California, Florida, New York, and Texas, as shown in Figure 10.

Financials

Gap Inc. was in a reasonably good financial condition. In 2001, because of its decreased current liabilities, liquidity of the company had increased. However, as a result of various problems in the company, as well as decreasing sales, Gap Inc. was forced to increase its long-term debts, as shown in Figure 11. The debt to equity ratio grew from 1.32 in 2000 to 1.52 in 2002.

Due to misjudgment of fashion trends in 2000 and 2001, Gap's revenue grew slower than the cost of goods sold, as shown in Figure 12. Between January 2001 and January 2002, revenues grew less than 2 percent. At the same time, costs of goods sold grew more than 10 percent. As a result gross profit margin fell from

more than 41 percent to 35.8 percent, as shown in Figure 12.

Comparable store sales by division for the second quarter of 2002 were as follows: Gap Domestic reported negative 13 percent versus a negative 8 percent in 2001; Gap International reported negative 12 percent versus a negative 6 percent in 2001.

Total sales by division for the second quarter of 2002 were as follows: Gap Domestic reported $1.1 billion versus $1.2 billion in 2001, Gap International reported $374 million versus $388 million in 2001.

Comparable store sales by division for year-to-date were as follows: Gap Domestic reported negative 17 percent versus a negative 6 percent in 2001, Gap International reported negative 15 percent versus a negative 7 percent in 2001.

Total sales by division for the year-to-date (2002) were as follows: Gap Domestic reported $2.1 billion versus $2.4 billion last year, Gap International reported $692 million versus $765 million last year, as shown in Figure 13.

Comprehensive earnings included net earnings and other comprehensive earnings (losses). Other comprehensive earnings (losses) included foreign currency translation adjustments and fluctuations in the fair market value of certain derivative financial instruments. Figure 14 presents comprehensive earnings for the thirteen and twenty-six weeks ended August 3, 2002, and August 4, 2001, respectively.

Although Gap was still able to raise capital, the worsening situation has made it more expensive. On February 14, 2002, Moody's reduced Gap's long- and short-term senior unsecured credit ratings from Baa3 to Ba2 and from Prime-3 to Not Prime, respectively, with a negative outlook on long-term ratings. Standard & Poor's reduced the long- and short-term credit ratings from BBB+ to BB+ and from A-2 to B, respectively, with a stable outlook on long-term ratings. On February 27, 2002, Moody's reduced the long-term senior unsecured credit ratings from Ba2 to Ba3 and stated that its outlook on the long-term ratings was stable. On May 9, 2002, and May 24, 2002, the outlook on Gap's credit ratings was changed from stable to negative by Standard & Poor's and Moody's, respectively.

As a result of the downgrades in the long-term credit ratings, effective June 15, 2002, the interest rates payable by Gap on $700 million of outstanding notes increased by 175 basis points to 9.9 percent per

FIGURE 10

Gap Division U.S. Store Concepts in Operation as of August 3, 2002

State	Number of Concepts	State	Number of Concepts	State	Number of Concepts
Alaska	29	Louisiana	35	Ohio	89
Arkansas	20	Massachusetts	105	Oklahoma	27
Arizona	35	Maryland	39	Oregon	27
California	235	Maine	12	Pennsylvania	132
Colorado	36	Michigan	51	Puerto Rico	12
Connecticut	50	Minnesota	39	Rhode Island	18
District of Columbia	5	Missouri	37	South Carolina	25
		Mississippi	14	South Dakota	5
Delaware	8	Montana	6	Tennessee	38
Florida	145	North Carolina	51	Texas	179
Georgia	61	North Dakota	4	Utah	31
Hawaii	16	Nebraska	11	Virginia	47
Iowa	31	New Hampshire	17	Vermont	6
Idaho	8	New Jersey	86	Washington	40
Illinois	97	New Mexico	14	Wisconsin	31
Indiana	34	Nevada	19	West Virginia	10
Kansas	23	New York	212	Wyoming	1
Kentucky	20				
Total of 2,323					

Source: Gap Inc. Company Website (2002), [Online], **http://www.gapinc.com**, accessed September 26.

annum on $200 million of outstanding notes due in 2005, and to 10.55 percent per annum on $500 million of outstanding notes due in 2008. The interest rates payable on these notes would be decreased only upon upgrades of long-term credit ratings by these rating agencies. Any further downgrades of those ratings by these rating agencies would result in further increases in the interest rates payable on the notes.

As a result of the downgrades in the short-term credit ratings, Gap Inc. no longer had meaningful access to the commercial paper market. In addition, it was expected that both the recent, and any future, lowering of the ratings on Gap Inc.'s debt would result in reduced access to the capital markets and higher interest costs on future financing. The increase in interest expense in the second quarter and first half of fiscal 2002 as compared with the same periods in fiscal 2001 was primarily due to an increase

in long-term borrowings and higher interest rates on new debt issuance. Long-term debt (in $000) as of August 3, 2002, was equal to 2,873,132, up 126 percent from 1,961,397 on August 4, 2001 [Gap Inc., 2002].

Management and Strategy

Gap Inc.'s management has demonstrated that they are very proactive, especially when it comes to looking for opportunities for growth. For example, in 1983 the company seemed to have become stagnant so Mickey Drexler was brought in as president. Since then Gap Inc. has grown tremendously, the store's image has been changed, and new store concepts have been started, such as GapKids, babyGap, and Old Navy. The firm also expanded with the acquisition of Banana Republic in 1983.

Gap Inc. opened 663 new stores between October 1999 and October 2000 but had slowed new-store openings in 2001 and 2002, as it continued to be

FIGURE 11

Gap Inc. Balance Sheet

Balance Sheet	Jan 02	Jan 01	Jan 00
Cash	1,035.7	408.8	450.4
Net Receivables	0.0	0.0	0.0
Inventories	1,677.1	1,904.2	1,462.0
Other Current Assets	331.7	335.1	285.4
Total Current Assets	3,044.6	2,648.1	2,197.8
Net Fixed Assets	4,161.3	4,007.7	2,715.3
Other Noncurrent Assets	385.5	357.2	275.7
Total Assets	**7,591.3**	**7,012.9**	**5,188.8**
Accounts Payable	1,105.1	1,067.2	805.9
Short-term Debt	41.9	1,029.9	169.0
Other Current Liabilities	909.2	702.0	778.0
Total Current Liabilities	2,056.2	2,799.1	1,752.9
Long-term Debt	1,961.4	780.2	784.9
Other Noncurrent Liabilities	564.1	505.3	417.9
Total Liabilities	4,581.7	4,084.6	2,955.7
Preferred Stock Equity	0.0	0.0	0.0
Common Stock Equity	3,009.6	2,928.2	2,233.0
Shares Outstanding (mil.)	865.7	854.0	850.5
Total Equity	3,009.6	2,928.2	2,233.0
Total Liabilities and Shareholders' Equity	**7,591.3**	**7,012.9**	**5,188.8**

Source: Gap Inc. (2001). Annual Report.

plagued by the merchandising, marketing, and logistical problems that have wreaked havoc since spring 2000. Long accustomed to spectacular growth and flashy television advertising, Gap Inc. revamped its strategies in 2001, as competition in the apparel industry continued to increase, and the absence of new merchandise offerings and new trends turned up the heat even more.

Gap Inc. pursued a hybrid strategy containing elements of both cost leadership and differentiation, as defined by Porter. It relied on strong brand differentiation and had made considerable investment in brand image, as well as customer service. At the same time, the strategy also contained several characteristics affiliated with the cost leadership approach, including economies of scale and scope, simple product designs, and low-cost distribution.

Because of all the problems, which referred mainly to the Gap division, changes in management have been made. On August 8, 2002, Gap Inc. announced that Gary Muto, President, Banana Republic, had been named president of Gap U.S. On September 26, 2002, it was announced that Paul Pressler had been named president and chief executive officer of Gap Inc., effective immediately [Day, 2002].

Looking Toward the Future

Although Gap had strong and well-established brand recognition in the specialty apparel retailers market, the mistakes that were made within the company, the increasing competition, and changing consumer groups and tastes all added pressure on this division to reevaluate its strategies in order to

FIGURE 12

Gap Inc. Income Statement

Income Statement All amounts in millions of U.S. dollars except per share amounts.	Jan 02	Jan 01	Jan 00
Revenue	13,847.9	13,673.5	11,635.4
Cost of Goods Sold	8,893.9	8,009.1	6,339.1
Gross Profit	4,954.0	5,664.4	5,296.3
Gross Profit Margin	35.8%	41.4%	45.5%
SG&A Expense*	3,806.0	3,629.3	3,043.4
Depreciation & Amortization	810.5	590.4	436.2
Operating Income	337.5	1,444.7	1,816.7
Operating Margin	2.4%	10.6%	15.6%
Nonoperating Income	13.3	12.0	0.0
Nonoperating Expenses	109.2	74.9	31.8
Income Before Taxes	241.6	1,381.8	1,784.9
Income Taxes	249.4	504.4	657.9
Net Income After Taxes	(7.8)	877.4	1,127.0
Net Profit Margin	—	6.4%	9.7%
Diluted Net Earnings (loss) Per Share	(0.01)	1.00	1.26
Dividends per Share	0.09	0.09	0.09

*Selling, General, and Administrative Expenses include all salaries, indirect production, marketing, and general corporate expenses.

Source: Gap Inc. (2001). Annual Report.

FIGURE 13

Store Sales for Gap Domestic and Gap International

	Gap Domestic	Gap International
Comparable Store Sales for Second Quarter of 2002 (Second Quarter of 2001)	−13% (−8%)	−12% (−6%)
Total Sales for Second Quarter of 2002 (2001)	$1.1 billion ($1.2 billion)	$347 million ($388 million)
Comparable Store Sales for Year-to-Date for 2002 (2001)	−17% (−6%)	−15% (−7%)
Total Sales for Year-to-Date for 2002 (2001)	$2.1 billion ($2.4 billion)	$692 million ($765 million)

Source: Gap Inc. (2002). Form 10-Q.

FIGURE 14

Gap Inc.'s Comprehensive Earnings

($000)	Thirteen Weeks Ended		Twenty-six Weeks Ended	
	August 3, 2002	August 4, 2001	August 3, 2002	August 4, 2001
Net earnings	56,780	89,751	93,458	205,231
Other comprehensive earnings (losses)	18,664	(7,488)	25,433	(19,647)
Comprehensive earnings	75,444	82,263	118,891	185,584

Source: Gap Inc. (2002). Form 10-Q.

remain competitive. The new CEO of Gap Inc., Paul Pressler, and the new president of Gap U.S., Gary Muto, were faced with various alternatives in order to put the company ahead of competition. Both alternatives focused on customers and the mix of products offered to them. Both maintained that changes were needed. Each one, however, had a different view on what exactly needed to be done.

The first alternative considered was to extend the customer base. It proposed that Gap would target the plus sizes (sizes 16 to 26) and extended plus sizes (sizes 28 to 34) markets. In a sense Gap would offer the same mix of products, such as clothing, accessories, and body care products, to an expanded customer base.

The *benefit* of this alternative was that Gap would get into major unsaturated markets with substantial growth opportunities.

The alternative was *feasible* because of the brand recognition Gap had in the market, which could be extended into new customer groups. It was also feasible because of the widely recognized high quality of Gap products.

This alternative could *win against competition*, because Gap had good relationships with its vendors, and would be able to produce the goods in the new sizes, which would not differ from existing ones as far as quality and the fabrics of the products were concerned. Gap monitored its vendors closely, and had high standards when choosing new ones. This could also be a winning strategy for Gap because the competition present in that market, including H&M, some discounters, such as Wal-Mart or Target, and department stores, such as Macy's, offered only a limited selection of those products, often of poor quality and styles, while Gap was known for classic and comfortable styles and high-quality, durable fabrics. Gap was also better than the competition because among those offering plus sizes it was the only one having a widely recognized, strong brand name, while others were either just beginning to build a brand name, such as H&M, or did not sell products under private labels, such as department stores or discounters.

The *drawback* within this alternative was that creating clothes in extended plus sizes was difficult. The same trajectory of sizing up could not be continued; it required drawing new patterns, because necks, for example, don't get larger above a certain weight, but backs, thighs, or tummies do.

A way around this drawback was to utilize the good relationships with the vendors and pay extra attention to the new designs by hiring designers with experience in this area. With good designs prepared by Gap employees, and close monitoring by the Compliance Department, the quality could be achieved.

The second alternative was to maintain the same customer base and to extend the product line offered to them. Besides jeans, casual wear, activewear, loungewear, sleepwear, underwear, accessories, and body care products, Gap would also offer various home goods, such as picture frames, throw rugs, pillows, sheets, pillowcases, comforters, and towels.

The *benefit* of this alternative was that Gap would be stretching the brand that was widely known and identified with quality.

This alternative is *feasible* because Gap could use the experiences of its sister division Banana Republic to better plan and execute this strategy. It was also feasible because through Banana Republic, Gap would also have access to already tested and reliable vendors that were selected using high standards, and then monitored by the Compliance Department.

Gap would be able to *win against the competition* because the company would be able to offer a broader range of products than most of its competitors. The only competitors that offered a substantially wider product range were discounters and department stores. The goods offered by discounters, such as Target or Wal-Mart, often lacked the quality that Gap was able to provide. Gap was also better than most department stores, such as J.C. Penney or Macy's, because through extensive data gathering it was able to establish a one-to-one relationship with its customers and offer them reliable customer service and product information. Through their efforts to get to know their customers, Gap was able to develop customer loyalty, which would help persuade the customers that the new product lines offered by Gap were as good as the ones they already were used to and trusted. Gap would also be using a recognized brand name and image to market the products, while competitors, such as H&M, were only beginning to build their brand names.

The *drawback* of this alternative was the fact that creating a new product line could stretch the brand too much and diminish the quality brand image that Gap had worked hard to create. It also might use valuable store space now given to apparel. Or the store size needed to be expanded, something that is not always possible.

The way around this drawback was to continue using the highest quality materials and designs, using the same high standards when choosing the vendors, as with other Gap products, and using close monitoring by the Compliance Department.

Both alternatives seemed to make sense. They both seemed to have advantages and disadvantages. Both presented views about how to achieve the same results of maintaining and increasing the market share and getting ahead of the competitors. Muto and Pressler decided to study both alternatives further, especially within present financial situations, as well as other alternatives in other strategic areas, in order to decide which would be most appropriate. The only sure thing at this point in time was that if Gap was to stay competitive, immediate action needed to be taken.

REFERENCES

Barta, S., Jason, M., Frye, J., and Woods, M. (1999). "Trends in Retail Trade." Oklahoma State University, November. [Online], http://www.agweb.okstate.edu/pearl/agecon/resource/wf-565.pdf, accessed December 2, 2002.

Board of Governors of the Federal Reserve System (2002). "Monetary Policy Report to the Congress." July 16. [Online], http://www.federalreserve.gov/boarddocs/hh/2002/July/FullReport.pfd/, accessed October 8.

Brown, S. (2002). "Gap Customers Get Reassurance; Ads Emphasize Store's Classic Style." *Denver Post*, August 22, p. F01.

Day, S. (2002). "The Gap Chooses Next Chief." *New York Times*, September 27.

DeNavas-Walt, C. and R. Cleveland (2002). "Money Income in the United States: 2001." *Current Population Reports, U.S. Census Bureau*, September.

Downes, L. (2001). "Perpetual Strategy: Building an Information Supply Chain." *Presentation, Foresight on the Future: An Executive Form*, New York: Business Objects and IBM DB2, October 3.

Ellison, S. (2002). "Obese America: Retailer Bets Super-Size Women Will Buy Clothes That Fit—Catherine's Expands Plus Line for Those Who Need a 28 or 34; Studying How Body Gets Larger." *Wall Street Journal*, June 21, p. B1.

Gap Inc. (2000). Annual Report.

Gap Inc. (2001). Annual Report.

Gap Inc. (2002). Form 10-Q.

Gap Inc. Company Website (2002). [Online], http://www.gapinc.com/, accessed September 26.

Hansell, S. (2002). "A Retailing Mix: On Internet, in Paint and in Store." *New York Times*, December 14, p. C1.

Hazel, D. (1999). "Is Branding Working? Developers Hope the Name Game Will Pay Off." *Shopping Centers Today*, September 1. [Online], http://www.icsc.org/srch/sct/current/sct9909/02.html, accessed October 20.

Hoover's Online (2002). "Company Profiles." [Online], http://hoovers.com/, accessed October 20.

Howard, T. (2002A). "Gap Counts on Known, New Stars; Chain Puts Fresh Face on Classic Clothing." *USA Today*, August 8, p. B02.

Howard, T. (2002B). "Gap Goes Back to Basics; Turnaround Plan Is About a Lot More Than Fashion." *USA Today*, August 8, p. B01.

Huff, L. (2002). "Apparel Specialty Stores: A Year to Forget." *Chain Store Age*, 78 no. 8 (August): A14–A15.

Kaiser, E. (2002). "Interview—New Gap CEO Starting at the Bottom." *CBS Market Watch*. [Online], http://cbs.marketwatch.com/, accessed September 26.

Konicki, S. (2001). "Sophisticated Supply." *InformationWeek*, December 10.

Lee, L. (2002). "Buried Alive in Khakis." *Business Week*, 3747 no. 40, (July 9): 40.

Lipke, D. (2000). "Mystery Shoppers." *American Demographics*, December, pp. 41–43.

Murray, S. (2001). "The Second Coming." *American Demographics*, April, pp. 28–30.

Rendon, J. (2002). "The Supply Chain's RFID Gambit." *Mbusiness*, March.

Reyes, S. (2002). "Tapping Girl Power." *Brandweek*, 43 no. 16 (April 22): 26–30.

Standard & Poor's (2002A). "Retailing: General." [Online], **http://www.netadvantage.standardpoor.com/**, accessed September 26.

Standard & Poor's (2002B). "Retailing: Specialty." [Online], **http://www.netadvantage.standardpoor.com/**, accessed September 26.

Stein, A. (2000). "The Money in the Middle: Step Right Up to the Roaring 2000s." *American Demographics*, April 01.

Strasburg, J. (2002). "Gap Gets Ready to Try on a New Leadership Style." *San Francisco Chronicle*, August 11, p. G1.

Tedeschi, B. (1999). "As Women Start to Use Internet More for Shopping, the Prospects Sharply Improve for On-line Retailers." *New York Times*, July 12, p. 4.

Valkin, V. (2002). "Gap Taps Ex-Disney Executive as CEO." *Financial Times*, September 26.

Waters, J. (2002). "Gap Finds a New Leader From Disney." *CBS MarketWatch*. [Online], **http://cbs.marketwatch.com/**, accessed September 26.

Charles Schwab

This case was prepared by Charles W. L. Hill, the University of Washington.

Introduction

In 1971, Charles Schwab, who was thirty-two years old at the time, set up his own stock brokerage concern, First Commander. Later he would change the name to Charles Schwab & Company, Inc. In 1975, when the Securities and Exchange Commission abolished mandatory fixed commissions on stock trades, Schwab moved rapidly into the discount brokerage business, offering rates that were as much as 60 percent below those offered by full commission brokers. Over the next twenty-five years, the company experienced strong growth, fueled by a customer-centric focus, savvy investments in information technology, and a number of product innovations, including a bold move into online trading in 1996.

By 2000, the company was widely regarded as one of the great success stories of the era. Revenues had grown to $5.7 billion and net income to $718 million, up from $1.1 billion and $124 million, respectively, in 1993. Online trading had grown to account for 84 percent of all stock trades made through Schwab, up from nothing in 1995. The company's stock price had appreciated by more than that of Microsoft over the prior ten years. In 1999, the market value of Schwab eclipsed that of Merrill Lynch, the country's largest full service broker, despite Schwab's revenues being more than 60% lower.

However, 2000 proved to be a high-water mark. Between March 2000 and mid 2003, share prices in the United States tumbled, with the technology heavy NASDAQ index losing 80 percent of its value from peak to trough. The volume of online trading at Schwab slumped from an average of 204,000 trades a day in 2000 to 112,000 trades a day in 2002. Revenues fell to $4.14 billion, net income to $109 million, and the stock price fell from a high of $51.70 a share in 1999 to a low of $6.30 in early 2003. By mid 2003, the key question facing Charles Schwab and his co-CEO David Pottruck was how to reverse the decline, revitalize growth, and attain the company's goal of 20 percent a year revenue growth and a profit margin greater than 12 percent?

The Securities Brokerage Industry[1]

A security refers to financial instruments, such as stocks, bonds, commodity contracts, stock option contracts, and foreign exchange contracts. The securities brokerage industry is concerned with the issuance and trading of financial securities, as well as a number of related activities. A broker's clients may be individuals, corporations, or government bodies. Brokers undertake one or more of the following functions: assist corporations to raise capital by offering stocks and bonds, help governments raise capital through bond issues, give advice to businesses on their foreign currency needs, assist corporations with mergers and acquisitions, help individuals plan their financial future and trade financial securities, and provide detailed investment research to individuals and institutions so that they can make more informed investment decisions.

Industry Background

In 2002, there were more than 8,000 broker-dealers registered in the United States, down from 9,515 in 1987. The industry is highly concentrated with some 261 firms that are members of the New York Stock Exchange (NYSE) accounting for 81 percent of the assets of all broker-dealers, and 70 percent of the revenue and capital. The ten largest NYSE firms accounted for 59 percent of the gross revenue in the industry in 2001, up from 48 percent in 1998. The consolidation of the industry has been driven in part by deregulation, which is discussed in more detail below.

Broker-dealers make their money in a number of ways. They earn *commissions* (or fees) for executing a customer's order to buy or sell a given security (stocks, bonds, option contracts, etc). They earn *trading income*, which is the realized and unrealized gains and losses on securities held and traded by the brokerage firm. They earn money from *underwriting fees*, which are the fees charged to corporate and government clients for managing an issue of stocks or bonds on their behalf. They earn *asset management fees*, which represent income from the sale of mutual fund securities, from account supervision fees, or from investment advisory or administrative service fees. They earn *margin interest*, which is the interest that customers pay to the brokerage when they borrow against the value of their securities to finance purchases. They earn *other securities related revenue* which comes from subscription fees for research services, charges for advisory work on proposed mergers and acquisitions, and so on. Finally, many brokerages earn *non-securities revenue* from other financial services, such as credit card operations or mortgage services. Exhibit 1 illustrates the breakdown between the various income sources for brokers in 2002.

Industry Groups

Brokerage firms can be segmented into five groups. First, there are *national full line firms*, which are the largest full-service brokers with extensive branch systems. They provide virtually every financial service and product that a brokerage can offer to both households (retail customers) and institutions (corporations, governments, and other nonprofit organizations such as universities). Examples of such firms include Merrill Lynch, Salmon Smith Barney, and A.G. Edwards. Most of these firms are headquartered in New York. For retail customers, national full line firms provide access to a personal financial consultant, traditional brokerage services, securities research reports, asset management services, financial planning advice, and a range of other services such as margin loans, mortgage loans, and credit cards. For institutional clients, these firms will also arrange and underwrite the issuance of financial securities, manage their financial assets, provide advice on mergers and acquisitions, and provide more detailed research reports than those normally provided to retail customers, often for a fee.

Large investment banks are a second group. This group includes Bear Stearns, Goldman Sachs, and Morgan Stanley. These banks have a limited branch network and focus primarily on institutional clients, although they also may have a retail business focused on high net worth individuals (typically individuals with more than $1 million to invest).

A third group are *regional brokers*, which are full service brokerage operations with a branch network in certain regions of the country. Regional brokers typically focus on retail customers, although some have an institutional presence.

Fourth, there are a number of *New York City–based* brokers, who conduct a broad array of financial services, including brokerage, investment banking, traditional money management, and so on.

Finally, there are the *discounters*, who are primarily involved in the discount brokerage business and focus on executing orders to buy and sell stocks for retail customers. Commissions are their main source of business revenue. They charge lower commissions than full service brokers, but do not offer the same infrastructure such as personal financial consultants and detailed research reports. The discounters provide trading and execution services at deep discounts

EXHIBIT 1

Brokers' Line of Business, as a Percentage of Revenues, 2002

Source: Securities Industry Association.

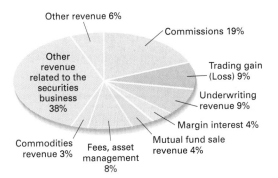

online via the Web. Many discounters, such as Ameritrade and E*Trade, do not maintain branch offices. Schwab, which was one of the first discounters, and remains the largest, has a network of brick and mortar offices, as well as a leading online presence.

Earnings Trends

Industry revenues and earnings are volatile, being driven by variations in the volume of trading activity (and commissions), underwriting, and merger and acquisition activity. All of these tend to be highly correlated with changes in the value of interest rates and the stock market. In general, when interest rates fall, the cost of borrowing declines so corporations and governments tend to issue more securities, which increases underwriting income. Also, low interest rates tend to stimulate economic growth which leads to higher corporate profits, and thus higher stock values. When interest rates decline, individuals typically move some of their money out of low interest bearing cash accounts or low yielding bonds, and into stocks, in an attempt to earn higher returns. This drives up trading volume and hence commissions. Low interest rates, by reducing the cost of borrowing, can also increase merger and acquisition activity. Moreover, in a rising stock market, corporations often use their stock as currency with which to make acquisitions of other companies. This drives up merger and acquisition activity, and the fees brokerages earn from such activity.

The 1990s was characterized by one of the strongest stock market advances in history (see Exhibit 2, which shows the value of the Standard & Poor's 500 stock market index between January 1990 and October 2003). This was driven by a favorable economic environment, including falling interest rates, new information technology, productivity gains in American industry, and steady economic expansion, all of which translated into growing corporate profits and rising stock prices.

Also feeding the stock market's advance were favorable demographic trends. During the 1990s American baby boomers started to save for retirement, pumping significant assets into equity funds. In 1989, some 32.5 percent of U.S. households owned equities. By 2002, the figure had risen to 49.5 percent. In 1975, some 45 percent of the liquid financial assets of American households were in financial securities, including stocks, bonds, mutual funds, and money market funds. By 2002, this figure had increased to 75 percent. The total value of household liquid financial assets increased from $1.7 trillion to $15 trillion over the same period.[2] Adding fuel to the fire, by the late 1990s stock market mania had taken hold. Stock prices rose to speculative highs rarely seen before as "irrationally exuberant" retail investors who seemed to believe that stock prices could only go up made increasingly risky and speculative "investments" in richly valued equities.[3]

The long stock market boom drove an expansion of industry revenues, which, for brokerages that were members of the NYSE, grew from $54 billion in 1990

EXHIBIT 2

The S&P 500 Index, January 1990 to October 2003

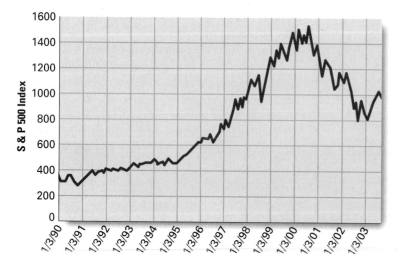

EXHIBIT 3

Total Revenue for the Brokerage Industry, 1990–2002

Source: Securities Industry Association.

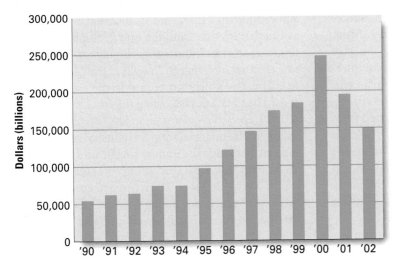

to $245 billion in 2000 (see Exhibit 3). As the bubble burst and the stock market slumped in 2001 and 2002, so brokerage revenues plummeted to $149 billion, forcing brokerages to cut expenses.

The expense structure of the brokerage industry is dominated by two big items—interest expenses and compensation expenses (see Exhibit 4), which together account for about three-quarters of industry expenses. Interest expenses reflect the interest rate paid on cash deposits at brokerages, and rise or fall with the size of deposits and interest rates. As such, they are generally not regarded as a controllable expense (since the interest rate is ultimately set by the U.S. Federal Reserve and market forces).

Compensation expenses reflect both employee headcount and bonuses. For some brokerage firms, particularly those dealing with institutional clients, bonuses can be enormous, with multimillion dollar

EXHIBIT 4

Expense Structure of Brokerages, 1990–2002

Source: Securities Industry Association.

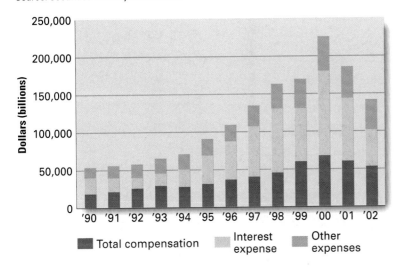

bonuses being awarded to productive employees. Compensation expenses and employee headcount tend to grow during bull markets, only to be rapidly curtailed once a bear market sets in.

The bursting of the 1990s stock market bubble brought a fall in profitability for brokerage firms. However, the fall was not as bad as many expected because it was accompanied by a sharp drop in interest rates to historic lows, by quick reductions in employee headcounts, and by a drop in bonuses. Pretax profit margins for the NYSE members dropped from 15.6 percent in 1999 to 6.9 percent in 2002. The drop was most significant among discounters, who saw their pretax profit margin fall from 20.1 percent in 2000 to 1.5 percent in 2001. By comparison, the pretax profit margin of national full line brokers fell from 14.1 percent in 2000 to 6.1 percent in 2001.

Exhibit 5 provides more detail on industry profitability, comparing the profitability, measured by return on invested capital, of five firms for 1993–2002. These firms were the national full line firms Merrill Lynch and A.G. Edwards, the investment banks Bears Stearns and Legg Mason, and the largest discounter, Charles Schwab. The exhibit shows Schwab's premier performance during the 1990s, but also shows that Schwab suffered a rapid decline in profitability during 2000–2002. Significantly though, Schwab still outperformed all but Legg Mason in 2002.

Deregulation

The industry has been progressively deregulated since May 1, 1975, when a fixed commission structure on securities trades was dismantled. This development allowed for the emergence of discount brokers such as Charles Schwab. Until the mid 1980s, however, the financial services industry was highly segmented due to a 1933 act of Congress known as the Glass-Steagall Act. This act, which was passed in the wake of widespread bank failures following the stock market crash of 1929, erected regulatory barriers between different sectors of the financial services industry, such as commercial banking, insurance, saving and loans, and investment services (including brokerages). Most significantly, Section 20 of the act erected a wall between commercial banking and investment services, barring commercial banks from investing in shares of stocks, limiting them to buying and selling securities as an agent, prohibiting them from underwriting and dealing in securities, and from being affiliated with any organization that did so.

In 1987, Section 20 was relaxed to allow banks to earn up to 5 percent of their revenue from securities underwriting. The limit was raised to 10 percent in 1989 and 25 percent in 1996. In 1999, the Gramm-Leach-Bliley (GLB) Act was past, which finalized the repeal of the Glass-Steagall Act. By removing the walls between commercial banks, broker-dealers, and

EXHIBIT 5

Return on Invested Capital (%), 1993–2002

Source: Value Line Investment Survey.

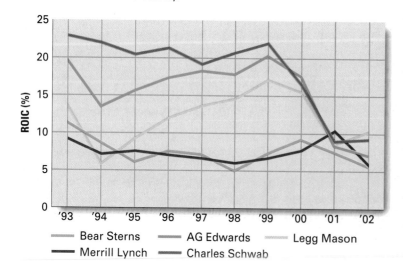

insurance companies, many predicted that the GLB Act would lead to massive industry consolidation, with commercial banks purchasing brokers and insurance companies. The rationale was that such diversified financial services firms would become one-stop financial supermarkets, cross-selling products to their expanded client base. For example, a financial supermarket might sell insurance to brokerage customers, or brokerage services to commercial bank customers. The leader in this process was Citigroup, which was formed in 1998 by a merger between Citicorp, a commercial bank, and Traveler's, an insurance company. Since Traveler's had already acquired Salmon Smith Barney, a major brokerage firm, the new Citigroup seemed to signal a new wave of consolidation in the industry. The passage of the GLB Act allowed Citigroup to start cross-selling products.

However, industry reports suggest that cross-selling is easier in theory than practice, in part because customers were not ready for the development.[4] In an apparent admission that this was the case, in 2002 Citigroup announced that it would spin off Traveler's Insurance as a separate company. At the same time, the fact remains that the GLB Act has made it easier for commercial banks to get into the brokerage business, and there have been several acquisitions to this effect. The most significant entry by commercial banks so far has been into the securities underwriting business.

The Growth of Schwab

The son of an assistant district attorney in California, Charles Schwab started to exhibit an entrepreneurial streak from an early age. As a boy he picked walnuts and bagged them for $5 per 100-pound sack. He raised chickens in his backyard, sold the eggs door to door, killed and plucked the fryers for market, and peddled the manure as fertilizer. Schwab called it "my first fully integrated businesses."[5]

As a child, Schwab had to struggle with a severe case of dyslexia, a disorder that makes it difficult to process written information. To keep up with his classes, he had to resort to Cliffs Notes and Classics Illustrated comic books. Schwab believes, however, that his dyslexia was ultimately a motivator, spurring him on to overcome the disability and excel. Schwab excelled enough to gain admission to Stanford, where he received a degree in economics, which was followed by an MBA from Stanford Business School.

Fresh out of Stanford in the 1960s, Schwab embarked upon his first entrepreneurial effort, an investment advisory newsletter, which grew to include a mutual fund with $20 million under management. However, after the stock market fell sharply in 1969, the State of Texas ordered Schwab to stop accepting investments through the mail from its citizens because the fund was not registered to do business in the state. Schwab went to court and lost. Ultimately, he had to close his business, leaving him with $100,000 in debt and a marriage that had collapsed under the emotional strain.

The Early Days

Schwab soon bounced back. Capitalized by $100,000 that he borrowed from his uncle Bill, who had a successful industrial company of his own called Commander Corp, in 1971 Schwab started a new company, First Commander. Based in San Francisco, a world away from Wall Street, First Commander was a conventional brokerage that charged clients fixed commissions for securities trades. The name was changed to Charles Schwab the following year.

In 1974, at the suggestion of a friend, Schwab joined a pilot test of discount brokerage being conducted by the Securities and Exchange Commission. The discount brokerage idea instantly appealed to Schwab. He personally hated selling, particularly cold calling, the constant calling on actual or prospective customers to encourage them to make a stock trade. Moreover, Schwab was deeply disturbed by the conflict of interest that seemed everywhere in the brokerage world, with stock brokers encouraging customers to make questionable trades in order to boost commissions. Schwab also questioned the worth of the investment advice brokers gave clients, feeling that it reflected the inherent conflict of interest in the brokerage business and did not empower customers.

Schwab used the pilot test to finetune his model for a discount brokerage. When the SEC abolished mandatory fixed commission the following year, Schwab quickly moved into the business. His basic thrust was to empower investors by giving them the information and tools required to make their own decisions about securities investments, while keeping Schwab's costs low so that this service could be offered at a deep discount to the commissions charged by full-service brokers. Driving down costs meant that unlike full-service brokers, Schwab did not employ financial analysts and researchers who developed proprietary investment research for the firm's clients. Instead, Schwab focused on providing clients with third-party investment research. These "reports" evolved to include a company's financial history, a smatter of comments from securities analysts at other brokerage firms that had appeared in the news, and a tabulation of buy and sell recommendations from full commission brokerage houses. The reports were sold to Schwab's customers at cost (in 1992, this was $9.50 for each report plus $4.75 for each additional report).[6]

A founding principle of the company was a desire to be the most useful and ethical provider of financial services. Underpinning this move was Schwab's own belief in the inherent conflict of interest between brokers at full-service firms and their clients. The desire to avoid a conflict of interest caused Schwab to rethink the traditional commission-based pay structure. As an alternative to commission-based pay, Schwab paid all of its employees, including its brokers, a salary plus a bonus that was tied to attracting and satisfying customers and achieving productivity and efficiency targets. Commissions were taken out of the compensation equation.

The chief promoter of Schwab's approach to business, and marker of the Schwab brand, was none other than Charles Schwab himself. In 1977, Schwab started to use pictures of Charles Schwab in its advertisements, a practice it still follows today.

The customer centric focus of the company led Schwab to think of ways to make the company accessible to customers. In 1975, Schwab became the first discount broker to open a branch office and to offer access twenty-four hours a day seven days a week. Interestingly, however, the decision to open a branch was not something that Charles Schwab initially embraced. He wanted to keep costs low and thought it would be better if everything could be managed by way of a telephone. However, Charles Schwab was forced to ask his uncle Bill for more capital to get his nascent discount brokerage off the ground. Uncle Bill agreed to invest $300,000 in the company, but on one condition: He insisted that Schwab open a branch office in Sacramento and employee uncle Bill's son-in-law as manager![7] Reluctantly Charles Schwab agreed to Uncle Bill's demand for a show of nepotism, hoping that the branch would not be too much of a drain on the company's business.

What happened next was a surprise; there was an immediate and dramatic increase in activity at Schwab, most of it from Sacramento. Customer inquiries, the number of trades per day, and the number of new accounts, all spiked upward. Yet there was also a puzzle here, for the increase was not linked to an increase in foot traffic in the branch. Intrigued, Schwab opened several more branches over the next year, and each time noticed the same pattern. For example, when Schwab opened its first branch in Denver it had three hundred customers. It added another seventeen hundred new accounts in the months following the opening of the branch, and yet there was not a big spike up in foot traffic at the Denver branch.

What Schwab began to realize is that the branches served a powerful psychological purpose—they gave customers a sense of security that Schwab was a real company. Customers were reassured by seeing a branch with people in it. In practice, many clients would rarely visit a branch. They would open an account, and execute trades over the telephone (or later, via the Internet). But the branch helped them to make that first commitment. Far from being a drain, Schwab realized that the branches were a marketing tool. People wanted to be "perceptually close to their money," and the branches satisfied that deep psychological need. From one branch in 1975, Schwab grew to have 52 branches in 1982, 175 by 1992, and 430 in 2002.

By the mid 1980s, customers could access Schwab in person at a branch during office hours, by phone day or night, by a telephone voice recognition quote and trading service known as TeleBroker, and by an innovative proprietary online network. To encourage customers to use TeleBroker or its online trading network, Schwab reduced commissions on transactions executed this way by 10 percent, but it saved much more than that because doing business via computers was cheaper. By 1995, Telebroker was handling 80 million calls and 10 million trades a year, 75 percent of Schwab's annual volume. To service this system, in the mid 1980s Schwab invested $20 million in four regional customer call centers, routing all calls to them rather than branches. Today these call centers have four thousand employees.

Schwab was the first to establish a PC-based online trading system in 1986, with the introduction of its Equalizer service. The system had 15,000 customers in 1987, and 30,000 by the end of 1988. The online system, which required a PC with a modem, allowed investors to check current stock prices, place orders, and check their portfolios. In addition, an "offline" program for PCs enabled investors to do fundamental and technical analysis on securities. To encourage customers to start using the system, there was no additional charge for using the online system after a $99 sign-up fee. In contrast, other discount brokers with PC-based online systems, such as Quick and Riley's (which had a service known as "Quick Way") or Fidelity's (whose service was called "Fidelity Express") charged users between 10 cents and 44 cents a minute for online access depending on the time of day.[8]

Schwab's pioneering move into online trading was in many ways just an evolution of the company's early utilization of technology. In 1979, Schwab spent $2 million, an amount equivalent to the company's entire net worth at the time, to purchase a used IBM System 360 computer, plus software, that was leftover from CBS's 1976 election coverage. At the time, brokerages generated and had to process massive amounts of paper to execute buy and sell orders. The computer gave Schwab a capability that no other brokerage had at the time: take a buy or sell order that came in over the phone, edit it on a computer screen, and then submit the order for processing without generating paper. Not only did the software provide for instant execution of orders, but it also offered what were then sophisticated quality controls, checking a customer's account to see if funds were available before executing a transaction. As a result of this system Schwab's costs plummeted as it took paper out of the system. Moreover, the cancel and rebill rate—a measure of the accuracy of trade executions—dropped from an average of 4 percent to 0.1 percent.[9] Schwab soon found it could handle twice the transaction volume of other brokers, at less cost, and with much greater accuracy. Within two years, every other broker in the nation had developed similar systems, but Schwab's early investment had given it an edge and underpinned the company's belief in the value of technology to reduce costs and empower customers.

By 1982, the technology at Schwab was well ahead of that used by most full-service brokers. It was this commitment to technology that allowed Schwab to offer a product that was similar in conception to Merrill Lynch's revolutionary Cash Management Account (CMA), which was introduced in 1980. The CMA account automatically sweeps idle cash into money market funds and allows customers to draw on their money by check or credit card. Schwab's system, know as the Schwab One Account, was introduced in 1982. It went beyond Merrill's in that it allowed brokers to execute orders instantly through Schwab's computer link to the exchange floor.

In 1984, Schwab moved into the mutual fund business, not by offering its own mutual funds, but by launching a mutual fund marketplace, which allowed customers to invest in some 140 no-load mutual funds (a "no-load" fund has no sales commission). By 1990, the number of funds in the market place was four hundred, and the total assets involved exceeded $2 billion. For the mutual fund companies, the mutual fund marketplace offered distribution to Schwab's growing customer base. For its part, Schwab kept a small portion of the revenue stream that flowed to the fund companies from Schwab clients.

In 1986, Schwab made a gutsy move to eliminate the fees for managing individual retirement accounts (IRAs). IRAs allow customers to deposit money in an account where it accumulates interest tax free until withdrawal at retirement. The legislation establishing IRAs had been passed by Congress in 1982. At the time, estimates suggest that IRA accounts could attract as much as $50 billion in assets within ten years. In actual fact, the figure turned out to be $725 billion!

Initially Schwab followed industry practice and collected a small fee for each IRA. By 1986, the fees amounted to $9 million a year, not a trivial amount for Schwab in those days. After looking at the issue, Charles Schwab himself made the call to scrap the fee, commenting, "It's a nuisance, and we'll get it back."[10] He was right; Schwab's No-Annual Fee IRA immediately exceeded the company's most optimistic projections.

Despite technological and product innovations, by 1983 Schwab was scrapped for capital to fund expansion. To raise funds, he sold the company to Bank of America for $55 million in stock and a seat on the bank's board of directors. The marriage did not last long. By 1987, the bank was reeling under loan losses, and the entrepreneurially minded Schwab was frustrated by banking regulations that inhibited his desire to introduce new products. Using a mixture of loans, his own money, and contributions from other managers, friends, and family, Schwab led a management buyout of the company for $324 million in cash and securities.

Six months later on September 22, 1987, Schwab went public with an IPO that raised some $440 million, enabling the company to pay down debt and leaving it with capital to fund an aggressive expansion. At the time, Schwab had 1.6 million customers, revenues of $308 million, and a pretax profit margin of 21 percent. Schwab announced plans to increase its branch network by 30 percent to around 120 offices over the next year. Then on Monday, October 19, 1987, the U.S. stock market crashed, dropping over 22 percent, the biggest one-day decline in history.

October 1987–1995

After a strong run up over the year, on Friday, October 16, the stock market dropped 4.6 percent. During the weekend, nervous investors jammed the call centers and branch offices, not just at Schwab, but at many other brokerages, as they tried to place sell orders. At Schwab, 99 percent of the orders taken over the weekend for Monday morning were sell orders. As the market opened on Monday morning, it went into free fall. At Schwab, the computers were overwhelmed by eight A.M. The toll free number to the call centers was also totally overwhelmed. All the customers got when they called were busy signals. When the dust had settled, Schwab announced that it had lost $22 million in the fourth quarter of 1987, $15 million of which came from a single customer who had been unable to meet margin calls.

The loss, which amounted to 13 percent of the company's capital, effectively wiped out the company's profit for the year. Moreover, the inability of customers to execute trades during the crash damaged Schwab's hard-earned reputation for customer service. Schwab responded by posting a two-page ad in the *Wall Street Journal* on October 28, 1987. On one page there was a message from Charles Schwab thanking customers for their patience, on the other an ad thanking employees for their dedication.

In the aftermath of the October 1987 crash, trading volume fell by 15 percent as customers, spooked by the volatility of the market, sat on cash balances. The slowdown prompted Schwab to cut back on its expansion plans. Ironically, however, Schwab added a significant number of new accounts in the aftermath of the crash as people looked for cheaper ways to invest.[11]

Beset by weak trading volume through the next eighteen months and reluctant to lay off employees, Schwab sought ways to boost activity. One strategy started out as a compliance issue within Schwab. A compliance officer in the company noticed a disturbing pattern: A number of people had given other people limited power of attorney over their accounts. This in itself was not unusual—for example, the middle-aged children of an elderly individual might have power of attorney over their account—but what the Schwab officer noticed was that some individuals had power of attorney over dozens, if not hundreds, of accounts.

Further investigation turned up the reason—Schwab had been serving an entirely unknown set of customers, independent financial advisors who were managing the financial assets of their clients using Schwab accounts. In early 1989, there were some five hundred financial advisors who managed assets totaling $1.5 billion at Schwab, about 8 percent of all assets at Schwab.

The advisors were attracted to Schwab for a number of reasons, including cost and the company's commitment not to give advice, which was the business of the advisors. When Charles Schwab heard about this, he immediately saw an opportunity. Financial advisors, he reasoned, represented a powerful way to acquire customers. In 1989, the company rolled out a program to aggressively court this group. Schwab hired a marketing team and told them to focus explicitly on financial planners, set apart a dedicated trading desk for them, and gave discounts of as much as 15 percent on commissions to financial planners with significant assets under management at Schwab accounts. Schwab also established a Financial Advisors Service, which provided its clients with a list of financial planners who were willing to work solely for a fee, and had no incentive to push the products of a particular client. At the same time, the company stated that it wasn't endorsing the planners' advice, which would run contrary to the company's commitment to offer no advice. Within a year, financial advisors had some $3 billion of clients' assets under management at Schwab.

Schwab also continued to expand its branch network during this period, at a time while many brokerages, still stunned by the October 1987 debacle, were retrenching. Between 1987 and 1989, Schwab's branch network increased by just five, from 106 to 111, but in 1990, it opened up an additional 29 branches and another 28 in 1991.

By the 1990s, Schwab's positioning in the industry had become clear. Although a discounter, Schwab was by no means the lowest price discount broker in

EXHIBIT 6

Commission Structure in 1990

Type of Broker	Average Commission Price on 20 Trades Averaging $8,975 Each
Deep Discount Brokers	$54
Average Discounters	$73
Banks	$88
Schwab, Fidelity, and Quick & Reilly	$92
Full Service Brokers	$206

Source: E. C. Gottschalk, "Schwab Forges Ahead as Other Brokers Hesitate," *Wall Street Journal*, May 11, 1990, page C1.

the country. Its average commission structure was similar to that of Fidelity, the Boston-based mutual fund company that had moved into the discount brokerage business, and Quick & Reilly, a major national competitor (see Exhibit 6). While significantly below that of full-service brokers, the fee structure was also above that of deep discount brokers. Schwab differentiated itself from the deep discount brokers, however, by its branch network, technology, and the information (not advice) that it gave to investors.

In 1992, Schwab rolled out another strategy aimed at acquiring assets—OneSource, the first mutual fund "supermarket." OneSource was created to take advantage of America's growing appetite for mutual funds. By the early 1990s, there were more mutual funds than individual equities. On some days Fidelity, the largest mutual fund company, accounted for 10 percent of the trading volume on the New York Stock Exchange. As American baby boomers aged, they seemed to have an insatiable appetite for mutual funds. But the process of buying and selling mutual finds had never been easy. As Charles Schwab explained in 1996:

> In the days before the supermarkets, to buy a mutual fund you had to write or call the fund distributor. On Day Six, you'd get a prospectus. On Day Seven or Eight you call up and they say you've got to put your money in. If you're lucky, by Day Ten you've bought it. . . . It was even more cumbersome when you redeemed. You had to send a notarized redemption form.[12]

OneSource took the hassle out of owning funds. With a single visit to a branch office, telephone call, or PC-based computer transaction, a Schwab client could buy and sell mutual funds. Schwab imposed no fee at all on investors for the service. Rather, in return for shelf space in Schwab's distribution channel and access to the more than 2 million accounts at Schwab, Schwab charged the fund companies a fee amounting to 0.35 percent of the assets under management. By inserting itself between the fund managers and customers, Schwab changed the balance of power in the mutual fund industry. When Schwab sold a fund through OneSource, it passed along the assets to the fund managers, but not the customers' names. Many fund managers did not like this, because it limited their ability to build a direct relationship with customers, but they had little choice if they wanted access to Schwab's customer base.

OneSource quickly propelled Schwab to the number three position in direct mutual fund distribution, behind the fund companies Fidelity and Vanguard. By 1997, Schwab customers could choose from nearly fourteen hundred funds offered by two hundred different fund families, and Schwab customers had nearly $56 billion in assets invested through OneSource.

1996–2000: eSchwab

In 1994, as access to the World Wide Web began to diffuse rapidly throughout America, a two-year-old start-up run by Bill Porter, a physicist and inventor, launched its first dedicated website for online trading. The company's name was E*Trade. E*Trade announced a flat $14.95 commission on stock trades, significantly below Schwab's average commission, which at the time was $65. It was clear from the outset that E*Trade and other online brokers, such as Ameritrade, offered a direct threat to Schwab. Not only were their commission rates considerably below those of Schwab, but also the ease, speed, and flexibility of trading stocks over the Web suddenly made Schwab's proprietary online trading software, Street Smart, seem limited. (Street Smart was the Windows-based successor to Schwab's DOS-based Equalizer program.) To compound matters, talented people started to leave Schwab for E*Trade and its brethren, which they saw as the wave of the future.

At the time, deep within Schwab, William Pearson, a young software specialist who had worked on the development of Street Smart, quickly saw the transformational power of the Web and believed that it would make proprietary systems like Street Smart obsolete. Pearson believed that Schwab needed to develop its own Web-based software, and quickly. Try as he might, though, Pearson could not get the attention of his supervisor. He tried a number of other executives, but found support hard to come by. Eventually he approached Anne Hennegar, a former Schwab manager that he knew who now worked as a consultant to the company. Hennegar suggested that Pearson meet with Tom Seip, an executive vice president at Schwab who was known for his ability to think outside of the box. Hennegar approached Seip on Pearson's behalf, and Seip responded positively, asking her to set up a meeting. Hennegar and Pearson turned up expecting to meet just Seip, but to their surprise in walked Charles Schwab; his chief operating officer, David Pottruck; and the vice presidents in charge of strategic planning and the electronic brokerage arena.

As the group watched Pearson's demo of how a Web-based system would look and work, they became increasingly excited. It was clear to those in the room that a Web-based system based on real-time information, personalization, customization, and interactivity all advanced Schwab's commitment to empowering customers. By the end of the meeting, Pearson had received a green light to start work on the project.

It soon transpired that several other groups within Schwab had been working on projects that were similar to Pearson's. These were all pulled together under the control of Dawn Lepore, Schwab's chief information officer, who headed up the effort to develop the Web-based service that would ultimately become eSchwab. Meanwhile, significant strategic issues were now beginning to preoccupy Charles Schwab and David Pottruck. They realized that Schwab's established brokerage and a Web-based brokerage business were based on very different revenue and cost models. The Web-based business would probably cannibalize business from Schwab's established brokerage operations, and that might lead people in Schwab to slow down or even derail the Web-based initiative. As Pottruck later put it:

> The new enterprise was going to use a different model for making money than our traditional business, and we didn't want the comparisons to form the basis for a measurement of success or failure. For example, eSchwab's per trade revenue would be less than half that of the mainstream of the company, and that could be seen as a drain on resources rather than a response to what customers would be using in the future.[13]

Pottruck and Schwab understood that unless eSchwab was placed in its own organization, isolated and protected from the established business, it might never get off the ground. They also knew that if they did not cannibalize their own business with eSchwab, someone would do it for them. Thus they decided to set up a separate organization to develop eSchwab. The unit was headed up by Beth Sawi, a highly regarded marketing manager at Schwab who had very good relations with other managers in the company. Sawi set up the development center in a unit physically separated from other Schwab facilities.

eSchwab was launched in May 1996, but without the normal publicity that accompanied most new products at Schwab. Schwab abandoned its sliding scale commission for a flat rate commission of $39 (which was quickly dropped to $29.95) for any stock trade up to 1,000 shares. Within two weeks, 25,000 people had opened eSchwab accounts. By the end of 1997, the figure would soar to 1.2 million, bringing in assets of about $81 billion, or ten times the assets of E*Trade.

Schwab initially kept the two businesses segmented. Schwab's traditional customers were still paying an average of $65 a trade while eSchwab customers were paying $29.95. While Schwab's traditional customers could make toll-free calls to Schwab brokers, eSchwab clients could not. Moreover, Schwab's regular customers couldn't access eSchwab at all. The segmentation soon gave rise to problems. Schwab's branch employees were placed in the uncomfortable position of telling customers that they couldn't set up eSchwab accounts. Some eSchwab customers started to set up traditional Schwab accounts with small sums of money so that they could access Schwab's brokers and Schwab's information services, while continuing to trade via eSchwab. Clearly the segmentation was not sustainable.

Schwab began to analyze the situation. The company's leaders realized that the cleanest way to deal with the problem would be to give every Schwab customer online access, adopt a commission of $29.95 on trading across all channels, and maintain existing levels of customer service at the branch level, and on the phone. However, internal estimates suggested that the cut in commission rates would reduce revenues by $125 million, which would hit Schwab's stock. The problem was compounded by two factors: First, employees owned 40 percent of Schwab's stock, so they would be hurt by any fall in stock price, and second, employees were worried that going to the Web would result in a decline in business at the branch level, and hence a loss of jobs there.

An internal debate ranged within the company for much of 1997, a year when Schwab's revenues surged 24 percent to $2.3 billion. The online trading business grew by more than 90 percent during the year, with online trades accounting for 37 percent of all Schwab trades during 1997, and the trend was up throughout the year.

Looking at these figures, Pottruck, the COO, knew that Schwab had to bite the bullet and give all Schwab customers access to eSchwab (Pottruck was now running the day-to-day operations of Schwab, leaving Charles Schwab to focus on his corporate marketing and PR role). His first task was to enroll the support of the company's largest shareholder, Charles Schwab. With 52 million shares, Charles Schwab would take the biggest hit from any share price decline. According to a *Fortune* article, the conversation between Schwab and Pottruck went something like this:[14]

> *Pottruck*: We don't know exactly what will happen. The budget is shaky. We'll be winging it.
> *Schwab*: We can always adjust our costs.
> *Pottruck*: Yes, but we don't have to do this now. The whole year could be lousy. And the stock!
> *Schwab*: This isn't that hard a decision, because we really have no choice. It's just a question of when, and it will be harder later.

Having secured the agreement of Schwab's founder, Pottruck formed a task force to look at how best to implement the decision. The plan that emerged was to merge all of the company's electronic services into Schwab.com, which would then coordinate Schwab's online and off line business. The base commission rate would be $29.95 whatever channel was used to make a trade—online, branch, or the telephone. The role of the branches would change, and they would start to focus more on customer support. This required a change in incentive systems. Branch employees had been paid bonuses on the basis of the assets they accrued to their branches, but now they would be paid bonuses on assets that came in via the branch or the Web. They would be rewarded for directing clients to the Web.

Schwab implemented the change of strategy on January 15, 1998. Revenues dropped 3 percent in the first quarter as the average commission declined from $63 to $57. Earnings also came in short of expectations

by some $6 million. The company's stock had lost 20 percent of its value by August 1998. However, over much of 1998 new money poured into Schwab. Total accounts surged, with Schwab gaining a million new customers in 1998, a 20 percent increase, while assets grew by 32 percent. As the year progressed, trading volume grew, doubling by year end. By the third quarter, Schwab's revenues and earnings were surging past analysts' expectations. The company ultimately achieved record revenues and earnings in 1998. Net income ended up 29 percent over the prior year, despite falling commission rates, aided by surging trading volume and the lower cost of executing trades over the Web. By the end of the year, 61 percent of all trades at Schwab were made over the Web. After its summer lows, the stock price recovered, ending the year up 130 percent, pushing Schwab's market capitalization past that of Merrill Lynch.[15]

2000–2003: After the Boom

The end of the long stock market boom of the 1990s hit Schwab hard (see Exhibit 7 for selected financial and operating data) as the average number of trades made per day through Schwab fell from 300 million to 190 million between 2000 and 2002. Reflecting this, revenues slumped from $5.79 billion to $4.14 billion and net income from $718 million to $109 million. To cope with the decline, Schwab was forced to cut back on its employee headcount, which fell from a peak of nearly 26,000 employees in 2000 to just over 16,000 in late 2003.

Schwab's strategic reaction to the sea change in market conditions was already taking form as the market implosion began. In January 2000, Schwab acquired U.S. Trust for $2.7 billion. U.S. Trust is a 149-year-old investment advisement business that manages money for high–net worth individuals whose invested assets exceed $2 million. When acquired, U.S. Trust had 7,000 customers and assets of $84 billion, compared with 6.4 million customers and assets of $725 billion at Schwab.[16]

Schwab made the acquisition because it discovered that high–net worth individuals were starting to defect from Schwab for money managers like U.S. Trust. The main reason was that as Schwab's clients got older and richer they started to need institutions that specialized in services that Schwab didn't offer, including personal trusts, estate planning, tax services, and private banking. With baby boomers starting to enter middle to late middle age, and their average net worth projected

EXHIBIT 7

Selected Financial and Operating Data (in Millions, Except per Share Amounts, Ratios, Number of Offices, Average Revenue per Revenue Trade, and as Noted)

| | Growth Rates | | | | | | |
	Compounded 5-Year 1997–2002	Annual 1-Year 2001–2002	2002	2001	2000	1999	1998
Operating Results							
Revenues	9%	(5%)	$4,135	$4,353	$5,788	$4,486	$3,178
Expenses excluding interest	13%	(6%)	$3,967	$4,218	$4,557	$3,387	$2,500
Net income	(19%)	(45%)	$109	$199	$718	$666	$410
Basic earnings per share[1]	(20%)	(43%)	$.08	$.14	$.53	$.51	$.32
Diluted earnings per share[1]	(20%)	(43%)	$.08	$.14	$.51	$.49	$.31
Adjusted operating income[2]	3%	(3%)	$396	$407	$849	$666	$410
Dividends declared per common share[3]	7%		$.0440	$.0440	$.0407	$.0373	$.0360
Weighted-average common shares outstanding—diluted			1,375	1,399	1,404	1,373	1,343
Non-trading revenues as a percentage of revenues[4]			66%	63%	51%	47%	49%
Trading revenues as a percentage of revenues[4]			34%	37%	49%	53%	51%
Effective income tax rate			42.6%	44.1%	41.7%	39.4%	39.5%
Capital expenditures—cash purchases of equipment, office facilities, property, and internal-use software development costs, net	1%	(47%)	$160	$301	$705	$370	$199
Capital expenditures as a percentage of revenues			3.9%	6.9%	12.2%	8.3%	6.3%
Performance Measures							
Revenue growth (decline)			(5%)	(25%)	29%	41%	19%
Pre-tax profit margin—reported			4.6%	8.2%	21.3%	24.5%	21.3%
After-tax profit margin—reported			2.6%	4.6%	12.4%	14.9%	12.9%
After-tax profit margin—operating[2]			9.6%	9.4%	14.7%	14.9%	12.9%
Return on stockholders' equity			3%	5%	21%	31%	27%
Financial Condition (at year end)							
Total assets	14%	(2%)	$39,705	$40,464	$38,154	$34,322	$26,407
Long-term debt	8%	(12%)	$642	$730	$770	$518	$419
Stockholders' equity	24%	(4%)	$4,011	$4,163	$4,230	$2,576	$1,673
Assets to stockholders' equity ratio			10	10	9	13	16
Long-term debt to total financial capital (long-term debt plus stockholders' equity)			14%	15%	15%	17%	20%
Client Information (at year end)							
Active client accounts[5]	11%	3%	8.0	7.8	7.5	6.6	5.6
Client assets (in billions)	12%	(10%)	$764.8	$845.9	$871.7	$846.0	$594.3

EXHIBIT 7   (*continued*)

Selected Financial and Operating Data (in Millions, Except per Share Amounts, Ratios, Number of Offices, Average Revenue per Revenue Trade, and as Noted)

| | Growth Rates | | | | | | |
	Compounded 5-Year 1997–2002	Annual 1-Year 2001–2002	2002	2001	2000	1999	1998
Total mutual fund assets (in billions)	14%	(6%)	$323.8	$342.8	$330.3	$294.0	$218.1
Active independent investment advisors (in thousands)	2%	2%	5.9	5.8	5.7	5.8	5.4
Independent investment advisor client accounts (in thousands)	17%	9%	1,182.4	1,081.7	986.5	848.3	689.9
Independent investment advisor client assets (in billions)	16%	(5%)	$222.4	$235.0	$231.3	$213.1	$146.4
Number of Schwab domestic branch offices	7%	(2%)	388	395	384	340	291
Number of U.S. Trust offices	12%		34	34	31	28	24
Employee Information							
Full-time equivalent employees (at year end, in thousands)	3%	(15%)	16.7	19.6	26.3	20.1	15.1
Revenues per average full-time equivalent employee (in thousands)	2%	15%	$220	$192	$239	$249	$214
Compensation and benefits expense as a percentage of revenues			44.8%	43.1%	41.7%	42.1%	43.3%
Clients' Daily Average Trading Volume (in thousands)							
Daily average revenue trades	13%	(16%)	134.1	159.7	242.0	163.1	97.2
Mutual Fund OneSource and other asset-based trades	10%	4%	56.1	54.0	58.1	45.6	40.3
Daily average trades	12%	(11%)	190.2	213.7	300.1	208.7	137.5
Average Revenue per Revenue Trade	(10%)	8%	$37.78	$35.02	$37.38	$45.55	$53.44

[1]Both basic and diluted earnings per share include an extraordinary gain of $.01 per share in 2002 and $.08 per share in 2001.
[2]Represents a non-GAAP income measure, which in 2002 excludes an extraordinary gain, restructuring charges, goodwill and other impairment charges, and merger- and acquisition-related costs totaling $287 million after-tax. In 2001, excludes an extraordinary gain, non-operating revenue (which primarily consists of a gain on the sale of an investment), restructuring and other charges, and merger- and acquisition-related costs totaling $208 million after-tax. In 2000, excludes merger- and acquisition-related costs totaling $131 million after-tax.
[3]Dividends declared per common share do not include dividends declared by USTC prior to the completion of the merger in 2000.
[4]Non-trading revenues include asset management and administration fees, net interest revenue, and other revenues. Trading revenues include commission and principal transaction revenues.
[5]Effective in 1998, active accounts are defined as accounts with balances or activity within the preceding eight months instead of twelve months as previously defined. This change in definition had the effect of decreasing the number of active accounts in 1998 by approximately 200,000.

to rise, Schwab decided that it needed to get into this business or lose high–net worth clients.

The decision, though, started to bring Schwab into conflict with the network of six thousand or so independent financial advisors that the company had long fostered through the Schwab Advisers Network, and who funneled customers and assets into Schwab accounts. Some advisors felt that Schwab was starting to move in on their turf, and they were not too happy about it.

In May 2002, Schwab made another move in this direction when it announced that it would launch a new service targeted at clients with more than $500,000 in assets. Known as Schwab Private Client, and developed with the help of U.S. Trust employees, for a fee of 0.6 percent of assets Private Client customers can meet face to face with a financial consultant to work out an investment plan and return to the same consultant for further advice. Schwab stressed that the consultant would not tell clients what to buy and sell—that is still left to the client. Nor will clients get the legal, tax, and estate planning advice offered by U.S. Trust and independent financial advisors. Rather, they get a financial plan and consultation regarding industry and market conditions.[17]

To add power to this strategy, Schwab also announced that it would start a new stock rating system. The stock rating system is not the result of the work of financial analysts. Rather, it is the product of a computer model, developed at Schwab, that analyzes more than 3,000 stocks on twenty-four basic measures, such as free cash flow, sales growth, insider trades, and so on, and then assigns grades. The top 10 percent get an A, the next 20 percent a B, the middle 40 percent a C, the next 20 percent a D, and the lowest 10 percent an F. Schwab claims that the new system is "a systematic approach with nothing but objectivity, not influenced by corporate relationships, investment banking, or any of the above."[18]

Critics of this strategy were quick to point out that many of Schwab's branch employees lacked the qualifications and expertise to give financial advice. At the time the service was announced, Schwab had some 150 qualified financial advisors in place, and planned to have 300 by early 2003. These elite employees will of course demand a higher salary than the traditional Schwab branch employees, who in many respects were little more than order takers and providers of prepackaged information.

The Schwab Private Client service also caused further grumbling among the private financial advisors affiliated with Schwab. In 2002, there were 5,900 of these. In total their clients amounted to $222 billion of Schwab's $765 billion in client assets. Several stated that they would no longer keep clients' money at Schwab. However, Schwab stated that it would use the Private Client Service as a device for referring people who wanted more sophisticated advice than Schwab

could offer to its network of registered financial advisors, and particularly an inner circle of 330 advisors who have an average of $500 million in assets under management and seventeen years of experience.[19] According to one member of this group, "Schwab is not a threat to us. Most people realize the hand holding it takes to do that kind of work and Schwab wants us to do it. There's just more money behind the Schwab Advisors Network. The dead wood is gone, and firms like ours stand to benefit from even more additional leads."[20]

Also in May 2002, Schwab announced that it would be raising commission rates for broker assisted trades from $39 to $54.95 on June 1, 2002. The fee for trading via the automated telephone service went from $29.95 to $49.95, and a $3 "handling fee" was tacked onto the basic $29.95 online commission rate.

ENDNOTES

1. Material for this section is drawn from two main sources: (a) *Securities Industry 2002 Fact Book*, Securities Industry Association, New York, 2002; and (b) *Standard & Poor's Industry Survey*, Investment Services, May 1, 2003.
2. Securities Industry Association, *Key Trends in the Securities Industry*, November 7, 2002.
3. Robert E. Shiller, *Irrational Exuberance* (Princeton, NJ: Princeton University Press, 2002).
4. Anthony O'Donnell, "New Thinking on Convergence," *Wall Street & Technology*, May 2002, pages 16–18.
5. Terence P. Pare, "How Schwab Wins Investors," *Fortune*, June 1, 1992, pages 52–59.
6. Ibid.
7. John Kador, *Charles Schwab: How One Company Beat Wall Street and Reinvented the Brokerage Industry* (New York: John Wiley & Sons, 2002).
8. Earl C. Gottschalk, "Computerized Investment Systems Thrive as People Seek Control over Portfolios," *Wall Street Journal*, September 27, 1988, page 1.
9. Kador, *Charles Schwab*.
10. Ibid., page 73.
11. G. C. Hill, "Schwab to Curb Expansion, Tighten Belt Because of Post Crash Trading Decline," *Wall Street Journal*, December 7, 1987, page 1.
12. Kador, *Charles Schwab*, page 185.
13. Ibid., page 217.
14. Erick Schonfeld, "Schwab Puts It All Online," *Fortune*, December 7, 1998, pages 94–99.
15. Anonymous, "Schwab's e-Gambit," *Business Week*, January 11, 1999, page 61.
16. Amy Kover, "Schwab Makes a Grand Play for the Rich," *Fortune*, February 7, 2000, page 32.
17. Louise Lee and Emily Thornton, "Schwab v Wall Street," *Business Week*, June 3, 2002, pages 64–70.
18. Quoted in Lee and Thornton, "Schwab v Wall Street," pages 64–70.
19. Erin E. Arvedlund, "Schwab Trades Up," *Barron's*, May 27, 2002, pages 19–20.
20. Ibid., page 20.

Li & Fung—The Global Value Chain Configurator

This case was prepared by S.S. George, ICFAI Center for Management Research.

In an age when the Internet is supposedly going to eliminate the middleman, here's a middleman, an old Asian trading company that has made itself indispensable.[1]

—An Article in Forbes

We deliver a new type of value added, truly global product that has never been seen before. We're pulling apart the value chain and optimising each step—and we're doing it globally.[2]

—Victor Fung, Chairman, Li & Fung, in June 2000

Strengthening Its Fort

In January 2004, Li & Fung Limited (Li & Fung), a Hong Kong–based global consumer goods trading giant, announced that Li & Fung Trading (Shanghai), its wholly owned subsidiary, had been granted an export company license by the Ministry of Commerce of the People's Republic of China (China). After receiving the license, Li & Fung Trading (Shanghai) became the first wholly owned foreign trading company to be offered direct export rights in China. The company was authorized to export China-sourced goods directly to customers worldwide and import raw materials for manufacturing in China. Li & Fung was until then dependent on its Chinese partners for exporting from China.

According to William Fung (William), managing director, Li & Fung, the license freed the group companies (see Exhibit 1) from the many trading restrictions in China. It would enhance the company's competitiveness and increase its share in the global market. William said, "With the ability to directly export products from China to our customers worldwide, Li & Fung is now able to offer an even more complete supply chain service."[3]

After China joined the World Trade Organization (WTO) in 2001, it emerged as the world's largest exporter of textile and clothing. The country also consolidated its position as one of the world's largest and fastest growing manufacturing economies. According to the U.S. International Textiles Association, export of textiles and clothing from China to the United States

---

[1]"Stitches in Time," www.forbes.com, June 9, 1999.
[2]"Winning at a Global Game: Part Five of an Eleven Part Series," www.asiabusinesstoday.org, June 10, 2000.
[3]"First Hong Kong Trading Firm to Gain China Licence," www.hktrader.net, February 2004.

EXHIBIT 1

Li & Fung's Major Subsidiaries and Associated Companies

Held Directly	Place of Incorporation and Operation	Issued and Fully Paid Share Capital	Principal Activities
Li & Fung (B.V.I.) Limited	British Virgin Islands	US$ 400,010	Marketing services and investment holding
Basic & More Fashion Limited	Hong Kong	HK$ 1,000,000	Export trading
Black Cat Fireworks Limited	England	GBP 1,200,000	Wholesaling
Camberley Enterprises Limited	Hong Kong	HK$ 250,000	Apparel exporting
Civati Limited	Hong Kong	US$ 450,000	Export trading
Colby International Limited	Hong Kong	HK$ 1,500,000	Exporting of garments and sundry goods
Colby Tekstil ve Dis Ticaret Limited Sirketi	Turkey	TL 50,000,000,000	Export trading
CS International Limited	Hong Kong	HK$ 1,000,000	Provision of export assistance service
Dodwell (Mauritius) Limited	Hong Kong	HK$ 500,000	Export trading
Golden Gate Fireworks Inc.	U.S.A.	US$ 600,000	Commission agent and investment holding
GSCM (HK) Limited	Hong Kong	HK$ 140,000	Export trading
Hillung Enterprises Limited	Hong Kong	HK$ 300,000	Export trading
International Sourcing Group, LLC	U.S.A.	US$ 300,000	Trading of apparel
Janco Overseas Limited	Hong Kong	HK$ 760,000	Buying agent
Kariya Industries Limited	Hong Kong	HK$ 1,000,000	Manufacturing and trading
LF Maclaine (Thailand) Limited	Thailand	Baht 4,000,000	Export trading
Li & Fung Agencia De Compras em Portugal, Limitada	Portugal	PTE 20,000,000	Export trading
Li & Fung (Exports) Limited	Hong Kong	HK$ 8,610,000	Export trading
Li & Fung (Fashion Accessories) Limited	Hong Kong	HK$ 600,000	Export trading
Li & Fung (India)	India	Rupees 64,000,200	Export trading
Li & Fung (Italia) S.r.l.	Italy	Lire 90,000,000	Export trading
Li & Fung (Korea) Limited	Korea	Won 200,000,000	Export trading
Li & Fung (Korea) Limited	Mauritius	Rupees 1,250,000	Export trading
Li & Fung Mumes sillik, Pazarlama Limited	Turkey	TL 25,000,000,000	Export trading
Li & Fung (Phillippines) Inc.	The Philippines	Peso 500,000	Export trading
Li & Fung (Properties) Limited	Hong Kong	HK$ 1,000,000	Property investment
Li & Fung Taiwan Holdings Limited	Taiwan	NT$ 287,996,000	Investment holding
Li & Fung Taiwan Investments Limited	British Virgin Islands	US$ 4,912,180	Investment holding
Li & Fung (Taiwan) Limited	Taiwan	NT$ 63,000,000	Export trading
Li & Fung (Thailand) Limited	Thailand	Baht 6,000,000	Export trading

EXHIBIT 1   *(continued)*
Li & Fung's Major Subsidiaries and Associated Companies

Held Directly	Place of Incorporation and Operation	Issued and Fully Paid Share Capital	Principal Activities
Li & Fung (Trading) Limited	Hong Kong	HK$ 10,000,200	Export trading and investment holding
Li & Fung Trading (Shanghai) Limited	The People's Republic of China	RMB 50,000,000	Export trading
Li & Fung (Zhanjiang) Limited	The People's Republic of China	US$ 1,999,055	Packaging
Livring Limited	Mauritius	Rs 250,000	Export trading
Lloyd Textile Trading Limited	Hong Kong	HK$ 1,000,000	Export trading
Maclaine Limited	Hong Kong	HK$ 5,570,150	Export trading
Perfect Trading Inc.	Egypt	LE 2,480,000	Export trading
Shiu Fung Fireworks Company Limited	Hong Kong	HK$ 1,200,000	Export trading
The Millwork Trading Co., Ltd	U.S.A.	US$ 1,331,000	Distribution and wholesaling
Toy Island Manufacturing Company Limited	Hong Kong	HK$ 62,000,000	Design and marketing
Verity Enterprises Limited	Hong Kong	HK$ 2,000,000	Export trading
W S Trading Limited	Hong Kong	HK$ 1,000,000	Export trading

Notes:
(1) Li & Fung (B.V.I.) Limited provides the subsidiaries with promotional and marketing services outside Hong Kong.
(2) Subsidiaries not audited by PricewaterhouseCoopers, Hong Kong. The aggregate net assets of subsidiaries not audited by PricewaterhouseCoopers, Hong Kong amounted to approximately 5 percent of the Group's total net assets.

Exhibit 1 lists out the principal subsidiaries of the company as of December 31, 2003, which, in the opinion of the directors, principally affected the results for the year or form a substantial portion of the net assets of the Group. To give details of other subsidiaries would, in the opinion of the directors, result in particulars of excessive length.

Source: Li & Fung Annual Report, 2003.

doubled from US$ 6.5 billion in 2001 to US$ 11.6 bn in 2003. With export quotas among WTO members proposed to be eliminated from January 2005, China would be free of restrictions on quantity of exports to the United States, enabling further growth.

In this light, analysts felt Li & Fung stood to benefit significantly from its new license as it was one of the world's leading textile export traders, and the largest to the United States. The company was well placed to leverage China's leadership position in textile manufacturing and exports, as that country was the company's largest manufacturing hub, from where it sourced over US$ 2 bn worth of products annually. Li & Fung had sixteen offices in China, which it planned to take to thirty-six by 2007. The downside was that in early 2004, Li & Fung faced

many challenges such as a slowdown in its overall revenues and net profit growth, overdependence on the U.S. market, declining share of revenues from the European market, and negligible growth in revenues from the rapidly growing Asian markets.

Background Note

The history of Li & Fung goes back to the early 1900s, making it the oldest trading company in Hong Kong. The company was founded in 1906 by Fung Pak-Liu (Pak-Liu) and Li To-ming (To-ming) in Guangzhou (South China) and was one of the first Chinese-owned export companies. Trade in China at that time was controlled by foreign commercial houses. Li & Fung began operations by exporting porcelain and silk, mainly to the United States. It later expanded its product portfolio to include bamboo, jade, ivory, rattan ware, fireworks, and handicrafts.

During the early 1900s, since U.S. buyers did not know Chinese and Chinese sellers did not know English, traders who could speak both languages became essential mediators between buyers and sellers. Therefore, Li & Fung prospered, earning commissions as high as 15 percent on each export deal. Li & Fung was formally established in Hong Kong as a limited company in 1937.

World War II disrupted trading in the early 1940s, forcing Li & Fung to cease trading for some years. In 1943, Pak-Liu passed away. Shortly after the end of the war, To-ming, who had been a silent partner, retired and sold his stake to Pak-Liu's family. With this, the Fung family became the sole owners of Li & Fung.

In 1949, Pak-Liu's son, Fung Hon-chu (Hon-chu), restarted trading operations in Hong Kong, which had come under British control. Hon-chu was instrumental in leading Li & Fung into the new era. The trading business picked up momentum in Hong Kong during the mid 1900s, driven by the influx of refugees, which transformed China into a manufacturing economy that exported labor intensive consumer products. Li & Fung began exporting consumer products such as garments, electronics, plastic flowers, and toys and was soon Hong Kong's biggest exporter.

By the early 1970s, the trading business in Hong Kong began to struggle owing to stiff competition from other manufacturing economies in Asia such as Taiwan and Singapore. Trading margins also went down significantly to 3 percent, as buyers and sellers became comfortable dealing directly with each other, doing away with intermediaries.

Under these circumstances, Hon-chu called his sons—William and Victor Fung (Victor)—back home from the United States. Victor was teaching at the Harvard Business School, and William had just finished his MBA from the same business school. Despite their friends' warning that trading would die out in a decade, the two brothers returned to Hong Kong to join their family firm.

Victor and William worked hard to modernize and rebuild Li & Fung into a well-structured organization, professionally managed at all levels. In 1973, the company went public and was listed on the Hong Kong Stock Exchange. Li & Fung's initial public offering was oversubscribed 113 times—a record that stood for fourteen years.

With the opening up of the Chinese economy in 1979, many manufacturers in Hong Kong relocated their factories to southern China, which was more cost effective thanks to low labor costs. The rapid industrialization of underdeveloped Asian countries widened the choice of supply sources. Li & Fung realized that there was a huge potential for the trading business. To benefit, the company established a regional network of sourcing offices in Asian countries such as Taiwan, Singapore, and Korea in the 1980s. It emerged as a major regional trading company in Asia.

In 1989, with trading margins decreasing further, Victor and William realized the need for drastic changes to safeguard the company's business. As a result, in that year, Li & Fung was again made a private company, in one of the first management buyouts in Hong Kong. The company was then restructured into a diversified group with export trading and retail as its core businesses. In 1992, the firm's export trading business, Li & Fung (Trading) Pvt. Limited., was relisted on the Hong Kong Stock Exchange.

As Li & Fung expanded its business, it understood that sourcing could no longer be restricted to a few countries but a vast network of sourcing offices to sustain trading business was required. Thus, the company established sourcing offices across the world, mainly around its major markets, the United States and Europe. Li & Fung also went in for acquisitions to strengthen its sourcing and distribution networks and expand its product lines and customer networks. It pursued an active information technology (IT) and Internet strategy to enhance the efficiency and effectiveness of its internal and external communications.

By the turn of the twentieth century, Li & Fung was a premier global trading company, with more than 95 percent of its revenues coming from North America and Europe. East Asia and the South Hemisphere accounted for the rest. In the fiscal year 2002, North America and Europe accounted for 76 percent and 19 percent of the group's total revenues, while East Asia and the South Hemisphere were placed at 3 percent and 2 percent, respectively (see Table 1 for Li & Fung's revenues by geographic segments in percentage terms).

The group's major product segments were both soft and hard goods. While soft goods included garments, hard goods constituted product lines such as fashion accessories, footwear, gifts, and furnishings (see Table 2 for Li & Fung's major product lines). Soft

TABLE 1

Revenues by Geographic Segments (1999–2003) (in percentage terms)

Geographic Regions	1999	2000	2001	2002	2003
North America	69%	70%	75%	76%	75%
Europe	27%	26%	21%	19%	19%
East Asia	1%	1%	1%	3%	3%
South Hemisphere	3%	3%	3%	2%	2%
Total (%)	100%	100%	100%	100%	100%
Total Revenues (in HK$ bn)	16.298	24.992	32.941	37.281	42.631

Source: Li & Fung Annual Report 2003.

goods contributed to a majority of the group's revenues. In 2002, this segment accounted for 68 percent of Li & Fung's total revenues, while hard goods generated the remaining 32 percent (see Table 3 for Li & Fung's revenues by product segments in percentage terms).

In 2002, export trading remained Li & Fung's major business, but it also actively operated in the retailing and distribution business through its privately held companies. The retailing business was confined to China and the Asian market, where it operated as a regional license holder for Toys "R" Us, the biggest US toy products chain and was the franchisee for the

TABLE 2

Li & Fung's Product Lines

Soft Goods	Hard Goods
Garments	Fashion Accessories
	Footwear
	Furnishings
	Gifts
	Handicrafts
	Home Products
	Promotional Merchandise
	Toys
	Stationery
	Sporting Goods
	Travel Goods

Source: **www.lifung.com**.

Hong Kong–based Circle K convenience store chain. The distribution business, too, was confined to China and the Asian region. Li & Fung was also involved in other businesses such as venture capital, investment holding, and property investment.

In the fiscal 2002, Li & Fung registered revenues of HK$ 37.3 bn, a 13 percent increase over HK$ 32.94 bn revenues in 2001. The company recorded a net profit of HK$ 1.08 bn in 2002, an increase of 38 percent over the figure of HK$ 782 mn in 2001. The company's largest customer in the United States was Kohl's Department Store Chain, accounting for nearly 13 percent of Li & Fung's total revenues in 2002. Other major clients included Abercrombie & Fitch, Ann Taylor, Disney, American Eagle Outfitters, Guess, Laura Ashley Jeans, Levi Strauss & Company (Levi's), Reebok, The Limited Inc., and Warner Brothers.

By this time, Li & Fung had successfully positioned itself as a cutting edge sourcing company in the world, with a well-established sourcing network of 68 offices across 40 countries and over 4,500 employees. In 2002, Li & Fung was reportedly one of the best professionally run companies in Hong Kong. The company's commitment to excellence and high standards in corporate governance practices earned it many awards and recognitions. Li & Fung was named one of Hong Kong's best companies, by *Euromoney* magazine, in the category "Asia's Best Company 2002." The same year, Li & Fung was named the "Best Managed Company 2002" and "Company Most Committed to Corporate Governance" by *Finance Asia* magazine (see Figure 1 for the corporate governance structure of Li & Fung).

TABLE 3

Revenues by Product Segments (1999–2003) (in percentage terms)

Product Segments	1999	2000	2001	2002	2003
Soft Goods	75%	78%	72%	68%	67%
Hard Goods	25%	22%	28%	32%	33%
Total (%)	100%	100%	100%	100%	100%
Total Revenues (in HK$ bn)	16.298	24.992	32.941	37.281	42.631

Source: Li & Fung Annual Report 2003.

Analysts credited the growth and success of Li & Fung to the visionary leadership and managerial capabilities of Victor and William. Since the early 1970s, the duo had led Li & Fung through a series of transformations in line with changes in the external environment. The major factors that helped Li & Fung evolve into a major global export trading company were the focus on efficiently managing the supply chain of its clients, a unique customer-centric organizational structure, leveraging IT and the Internet and global expansion strategies.

Managing the Global Supply Chain

Li & Fung's evolution into a supply chain manager took place in three stages, driven by significant changes in the global retailing industry, customer and retailer preferences, and economic trends across Asia through the early 1970s.

In the first stage (during the 1970–1978 period), Li & Fung acted as a regional sourcing agent. The company extended its geographic reach by establishing sourcing offices in Singapore, Korea, and Taiwan. Li & Fung's knowledge and reach in the Asian region held value for customers. This was because many big buyers could manage their own sourcing if they needed to deal only in Hong Kong. Dealing with the whole region was far more complex, and buyers did not have the necessary resources. Commenting on the complexity of sourcing from the region, in an interview to *Harvard Business Review*, Victor said that as quotas governed world trade in the textiles industry, knowledge on which quotas had been used up in Hong Kong and which was the next best place to source textiles from, where quotas had not been

FIGURE 1

Li & Fung's Corporate Governance Structure

Source: Li & Fung Annual Report, 2003.

exhausted, enabled Li & Fung to provide customers with a complete product package.

In the second stage (1979–1982), Li & Fung evolved from a sourcing agent into a manager and deliverer of production programs. When a customer came up with an idea of a product and gave specifications such as look, color, and quality, the company developed a detailed manufacturing program for that product. In other words, the firm created an entire manufacturing program for its customers for a particular fashion season. The program involved all tasks from specifying the product mix to scheduling the manufacturing process and delivery time. Li & Fung worked with factories to plan and monitor the manufacturing process and to ensure quality and on-time delivery.

This strategy worked well for Li & Fung. Yet, the 1980s brought a new challenge. This led to its third stage of evolution (1983 to the present period). Other countries in Asia such as Korea, Taiwan, and Thailand had by then emerged as labor-intensive manufacturing hubs, while Hong Kong had become an expensive and noncompetitive place to manufacture. The Chinese economy was being liberalized, and the company soon took the advantage by moving the labor-intensive portion of production to southern China.

Dispersed Manufacturing

Li & Fung broke the value chain into parts that it called "dispersed manufacturing." Under this, the company performed all high-end value-added activities such as design and quality control in Hong Kong and outsourced low-end activities like manufacturing to the best possible locations across the world. For every order, the company aimed at customizing the supply chain to meet the client's specific requirements. For example, when Li & Fung got an order for transistor radios, it created little kits (plastic bags) filled with all the components necessary to build a radio and shipped the kits to China, where they were assembled. The assembled radios were then shipped back to Hong Kong, where they underwent final testing and inspection.

Similarly, to fulfill an order for baby dolls, Li & Fung designed them in Hong Kong, produced molds for the dolls using sophisticated machinery, and then shipped the molds to China, where plastic was injected into the molds, the dolls were assembled, their fingers were painted, and their clothes were tailored. After the completion of such labor-intensive work in

China, the dolls were shipped back to Hong Kong for final testing, inspection, packaging, transportation and distribution. So, while the front and back ends of the value chain were taken care of in Hong Kong, the middle portion was performed in China.

Once Li & Fung understood the benefits of dispersed manufacturing and gained expertise in it, the company extended its network beyond southern China. It moved into the inner parts of China, where wages were even lower. Li & Fung also began searching for other labor-intensive and potential sources of supply outside China and established a strong global network of suppliers by the late 1990s. Soon, the concept of dispersed manufacturing spread to other industries in Hong Kong, which led to the transformation of Hong Kong from a manufacturing economy into a service economy. By 1997, 84 percent of Hong Kong's gross domestic product[4] came from services (see Exhibits 2 and 3).

Meanwhile, owing to maturing markets, intense competition and changing consumer trends, many companies in the Western countries were compelled to outsource not only their manufacturing but also the entire supply chain management (SCM) to reap time and cost benefits. Li & Fung, with its extensive sourcing depth and network, grew from a deliverer of production programs into a potential manager of supply chains for companies looking for optimum SCM.

Li & Fung described SCM as "tackling the soft $3" in the structure—that is, if the price of a consumer product when it leaves a factory in China was $1, it would end up on retail shelves at $4. The company felt there was very little companies could do to further reduce production costs, as they had already exhausted all possible ways. It would be easier to cut on costs that were spread across distribution channels—that is, the $3 (difference between the product price on retail shelves and price when it left the factory).

Li & Fung took its dispersed manufacturing technique further, dissecting the entire value chain and optimizing every step of the chain, from product design and development, raw material sourcing, production planning, conducting quality assurance and factory inspections, managing production and logistics of

---

[4]GDP is used to measure the growth and health of an economy and is defined as the total market value of all final goods and services produced in a country in a given year, equal to total customer, investment, and government spending, plus the value of the total exports, minus the value of total imports.

EXHIBIT 2

Exports and Imports of Services in Hong Kong (2000–2002)

| Major Service Group | Year | Exports of Services | | | Imports of Services | | | Net Exports of Services |
		HK$ mn	Share (%)	Year-on-Year % Change	HK$ mn	Share (%)	Year-on-Year % Change	HK$ mn
Transportation	2000	99,513	33.0	11.5	48,628	25.4	23.9	50,885
	2001	93,675	30.4	−5.9	50,916	26.5	4.7	42,759
	2002	103,751	30.9	10.8	48,518	24.3	−4.7	55,233
Travel	2000	46,019	15.2	7.4	97,402	50.9	−4.4	−51,383
	2001	46,362	15.1	0.7	96,057	49.9	−1.4	−49,695
	2002	58,855	17.5	26.9	96,846	48.5	0.8	−37,991
Insurance services	2000	3,452	1.1	12.6	4,111	2.1	−17.4	−659
	2001	3,556	1.2	3.0	4,028	2.1	−2.0	−472
	2002	3,421	1.0	−3.8	4,618	2.3	14.6	−1,197
Financial services	2000	20,859	6.9	8.6	5,536	2.9	−3.4	15,323
	2001	21,823	7.1	4.6	5,242	2.7	−5.3	16,581
	2002	19,564	5.8	−10.4	4,876	2.4	−7.0	14,688
Merchanting and other trade-related services	2000	97,616	32.3	19.7	11,170	5.8	6.3	86,446
	2001	106,447	34,6	9.0	11,802	6.1	5.7	94,645
	2002	115,996	34.6	9.0	14,660	7.3	24.2	101,336
Other services	2000	34,355	11.4	15.8	24,695	12.9	13.7	9,660
	2001	35,794	11.6	4.2	24,408	12.7	−1.2	11,386
	2002	33,826	10.1	−5.5	30,158	15.1	23.6	101,336
All services	2000	301,813	100.0	13.7	191,543	100.0	4.1	110,270
	2001	307,657	100.0	1.9	192,453	100.0	0.5	115,204
	2002	335,412	100.0	9.0	199,676	100.0	3.8	135,736

Notes:
(1) Figures for exports of travel services have incorporated the new data released by the Hong Kong Tourism Board in November 2003 on destination consumption expenditure of incoming visitors and travelers. For details, please refer to the feature article "Statistics on Inbound Tourism" in the December 2003 issue of the *Hong Kong Monthly Digest of Statistics*.
(2) The sum of individual items and the corresponding total shown in the table may not tally because of rounding.

Source: **www.info.gov.hk.**

exporting, timely delivery, and complying with import and export quota restrictions, imposed by the buyer and seller countries, respectively. The company became a much broader intermediary by connecting and coordinating many links in the supply chain. It made its services more valuable by delivering a better product, which translated into better price and margins for customers (see Exhibit 4).

Global Supplier Network

When Li & Fung got an order from a customer, it sifted through its global supplier network (see Exhibit 5) to find the right manufacturer for the specific product and the most attractive combination of cost and quality. The company broke up its supply chain to disperse different production processes to manufacturers in various countries, based on factors

EXHIBIT 3

Hong Kong's External Trade Performance

	2003 (HK$ Mn)	2004 Jan–May (HK$ Mn)	% Change 03/02	% Change J–M 04/03
Overall				
- Domestic Exports	121,687	44,668	−7	1
- Re-exports	1,620,749	713,531	13	16
- Imports	1,805,770	816,918	12	19
- Total Trade	3,548,206	1,575,117	12	17
Balance	−63,334	−58,719	8	99
Total Exports—Major Markets				
All Markets	1,742,436	758,199	12	15
- China	742,544	334,450	21	18
- U.S.A.	324,215	122,950	−3	5
- E.U.	231,033	98,469	12	13
- Japan	94,003	41,241	12	13
- Singapore	35,704	16,866	13	27
- Taiwan	42,269	20,334	22	23
- Rep. of Korea	35,526	18,054	17	29
Total Exports—Major Products				
All Products	1,742,436	758,199	12	15
- Electronics #	732,653	332,023	20	23
- Clothing	180,357	65,408	3	5
- Electrical Products #	192,485	88,524	13	21
- Textile Yarn & Fabrics	101,923	45,067	5	9
- Toys & Games	75,008	22,538	1	−3
- Footwear	44,755	17,874	−1	−3
- Watches and Clocks	41,903	17,237	9	8
- Travel Goods & Handbags	32,070	14,333	*	12
- Plastic Articles	23,872	9,309	−8	−6
- Food	15,404	5,597	−8	−7
- Jewelry	22,231	9,794	17	21
Re-exports—with China				
Total Re-exports	1,620,749	713,531	13	16
- To China	705,787	321,126	23	19
- Of China Origin	967,104	418,816	12	16
Imports—End-use Categories				
Total Imports	1,805,770	816,918	12	19
- Foodstuffs	53,439	22,747	−3	8
- Consumer Goods	573,926	235,109	5	9
- Raw Materials	654,452	319,439	17	27
- Fuels	35,398	18,026	13	28
- Capital Goods	481,081	218,494	12	18

Overlap with other products

*Insignificant

Source: **http://stat.tdctrade.com**.

EXHIBIT 4

Li & Fung's Supply Chain

Source: Li & Fung Annual Report, 2003.

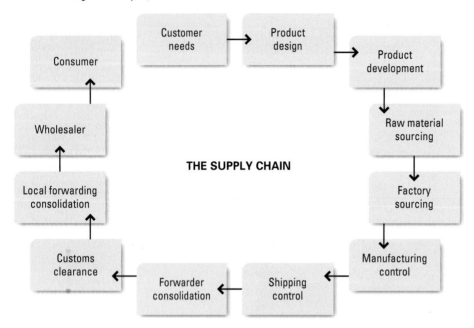

such as labor costs, quality, trade barriers, transportation costs, and so on. The company coordinated all processes in the value chain, managing the logistics and arranging the shipment of the finished order to the client. Li & Fung also ensured that suppliers complied with rules and regulations pertaining to environmental standards, child labor, and so on in the importing countries (see Exhibit 6).

For instance, when Li & Fung got an order from Levi's, a leading retail clothes chain in the United States, with garment designs for the next fashion season, the company took the basic product concepts and researched the market to find the right kind of raw materials such as yarn, dye, and buttons. The company then assembled the raw materials to create a prototype, which was sent to Levi's for inspection. Once the prototype was approved, Levi's placed an order for the garments with Li & Fung, asking for delivery within six weeks.

Li & Fung immediately went to work; it distributed various tasks of the overall manufacturing process to different producers based on their capabilities and costs. It decided to purchase yarn from a Korean supplier but have it woven and dyed in Taiwan. The yarn was picked up from Korea and

shipped to Taiwan. As the Japanese offered best quality zippers and buttons, which they got manufactured in China, Li & Fung approached the leading zipper manufacturer in Japan to order the right zippers from Chinese factories. Li & Fung decided to manufacture the final garments in Thailand, based on factors like quota availability and favorable labor conditions. It moved all the materials to Thailand. Since the order had to be fulfilled within six weeks, the order was divided across five factories in Thailand. Li & Fung ensured that within the scheduled date of delivery, the finished products, all looking as if they came from one factory, arrived at Levi's retail stores.

Efficient SCM also addressed the problem of obsolete inventory, a major area of concern for fast-moving consumer goods (FMCG) companies, which were consumer driven. FMCG companies preferred buying closer to the market as it shortened the buying cycle and gave them more time to get a better sense of the changing needs and preferences of consumers. Such quick changes led to shorter product cycles, and the problem of obsolete inventories went up significantly. This was where Li & Fung's global SCM expertise was useful, as it aimed at buying the right things at the right place, at the right cost and quality.

EXHIBIT 5

EXHIBIT 5

Li & Fung's Global Sourcing Network

EUROPE & THE MEDITERRANEAN	THE AMERICAS	NORTH ASIA
Amsterdam	Boston	Beijing
Bucharest	Guadalajara	Dalian
Cairo	Guatemala City	Dongguan
Denizli	Managua	Guangzhou
Florence	Mexico City	Hepu
Huddersfield	New York City	Hong Kong
Istanbul	San Francisco	Huizhu
Izmir	San Pedro Sula	Liuyang
London	Santo Domingo	Longhua
Oporto	**SOUTHEAST ASIA**	Macau
Tunis	Bangkok	Nanjing
Turin	Hanoi	Ningbo
SOUTH ASIA	Ho Chi Minh City	Qingdao
Amman	Jakarta	Seoul
Bahrain	Makati	Shanghai
Bangalore	Phnom Penh	Shantou
Chennai	Saipan	Shenzhen
Colombo	Shan Alam	Taipei
Delhi	Singapore	Tokyo
Dhaka	**SOUTH AFRICA**	Zhanjiang
Karachi	Durban	Zhongshan
Lahore	Madagascar	
Mumbai	Mauritius	
Sharjah		

Source: Li & Fung Annual Report, 2003.

The SCM Strategy

To ensure shorter product delivery cycles, Li & Fung managed the whole supply chain of its customers. To shrink the delivery cycle, the company reached upstream to organize production and ensure small production runs, which resulted in improved response time for retailers, enabling them to alter production in tandem with market trends. For instance, Li & Fung got to know that Levi's would order 1 million pieces of garments, but did not have specific details of style or colors. This would be disclosed only four weeks before delivery was due. Under these circumstances, based on trust and its strong relationship with suppliers, Li & Fung reserved undyed yarn and locked up capacity at mills for weaving and dying. It told suppliers that they would receive an order for a specific size and colors six days before delivery. Then the company contacted the factory owners, stating that it did not know product specifications yet, but it had organized the colors, fabric, and trim for them, and they should deliver the order on a specific date, say two weeks from the arrival of raw materials at their factories.

Having a vast network of suppliers enabled Li & Fung to configure activities as if they were modules in a process. For instance, a South Korean yarn

EXHIBIT 6

Li & Fung's Code of Conduct for Suppliers

Li & Fung (Trading) Limited Code of Conduct ("Code of Conduct") outlines the basic requirements on working conditions that must be satisfied by all vendors ("Vendors") to principals of Li & Fung (Trading) Limited ("Li & Fung"). Li & Fung and its principals can supplement these requirements at any time.

Child Labour: Vendors shall not use child labour. A "Child" is defined as a person who is not older than the local age for completing compulsory education, but in no event is less than 15 years old. Vendors must verify the age of their workers and maintain copies of proof of age. Vendors must follow all applicable laws and regulations regarding working hours and conditions for minors.

Involuntary Labour: Vendor shall not use involuntary labour. "Involuntary Labour" is defined as work or service extracted from any person under threat or penalty for its non-performance, and for which the worker does not offer himself or herself voluntarily. It includes prison, bonded, indentured and forced labour.

Disciplinary Practices: Vendors shall not use corporal punishment, any form of physical or psychological coercion or intimidation against workers.

Non-discrimination: Vendors shall employ workers solely on the basis of their ability to do the job. They shall not discriminate on the basis of age, gender, racial characteristics, maternity or marital status, nationality or cultural, religious or personal beliefs in relation to hiring, wages, benefits, termination or retirement.

Health and Safety: Vendors shall maintain a clean, safe and healthy workplace in compliance with applicable laws and regulations. They shall ensure that workers have access to clean drinking water, sanitary washing facilities and adequate number of toilets, fire-extinguishers and fire exits. Workplaces should provide adequate lighting and ventilation. Vendors shall ensure that these standards are also met in any canteen and/or dormitory provided for workers.

Environmental Protection: Vendors shall comply with all applicable laws and regulations to protect the environment and maintain procedures for notifying the local authorities in the event of an environmental accident resulting from the vendors' operations.

Wages and Benefits: Vendors shall provide wages and benefits that comply with all applicable laws and regulations or match prevailing local manufacturing or industry rates, whichever is higher. Overtime pay shall be calculated at the legally required rate, regardless of whether workers are compensated hourly or by piece rate.

Working Hours: Vendors shall not require workers to work, including overtime, more than 60 hours per week or more than the maximum number of hours per week set by applicable laws and regulations, whichever is less. Vendors shall guarantee that workers receive at least one day off during each seven-day period.

Freedom of Association: Vendors shall respect the right of workers to associate, organize and bargain collectively in a legal and peaceful manner.

Familiarization and Display of this Code of Conduct: Vendors shall familiarize workers with this Code of Conduct and display it, translated in the local language, at each of their facilities in a place readily visible and accessible to workers.

Legal Requirements: Vendors shall comply with all legal requirements applicable to the conduct of their businesses, including those set out above.

Contractors and Suppliers: Vendors shall ensure that their contractors and suppliers adhere to this Code of Conduct.

Monitoring of Compliance: Vendors authorize Li & Fung and its principals to conduct scheduled and unscheduled inspections of vendors' facilities for ensuring compliance with the Code of Conduct. During these inspections, Li & Fung and its principals have the right to review all employee-related books and records maintained by vendors and to interview workers.

Corrective Action: When violations are found, Li & Fung and the vendor concerned will agree on a corrective action plan that eliminates the problem in a timely manner. If it is determined that a vendor is knowingly and/or repeatedly in violation of this Code of Conduct, Li & Fung and its principals shall take appropriate corrective action. This may include cancellation of orders and/or termination of business with that vendor.

Source: **www.lifung.com**.

provider might be appropriate for a product line, but an Indonesian supplier who used different raw materials and production technology might be a better choice for the needs and preferences of a specific customer. Li & Fung assembled the right modules for each job, customizing value chain solutions for its clients. Such flexible modules also meant that the company could quickly change its plans if there were unforeseen problems at the manufacturing site. The company could tap its worldwide network and send the order to another company to avoid delays in order fulfillment. For example, Li & Fung quickly shifted production from high-risk countries to lower risk countries following the September 11, 2001, terrorist attacks in the United States.

A major supplier management strategy of Li & Fung was to utilize anywhere from 30 percent to 70 percent of factory capacity of suppliers, ensuring that at such a capacity, the company would be one of their important customers. Most times, Li & Fung would be their largest customer. Li & Fung also ensured that it did not use up the entire capacity of any manufacturer to give itself flexibility. It did not want manufacturers to be completely dependent on the company. This strategy also enabled the company to gain exposure to new suppliers.

To improve suppliers' performance, Li & Fung managers, based on their interactions with them, provided a detailed performance feedback to each supplier, mentioning strengths and weaknesses. Faltering suppliers were dropped from a project or from the company's network if they failed to improve. According to analysts, as Li & Fung offered many economic incentives to suppliers, they willingly customized their own operations to fit Li & Fung's supply chain strategy. The major benefits to suppliers were substantial and steady business from Li & Fung and the opportunity to improve their performance, as the company set detailed benchmarks across its entire process network and gave all partners valuable insights into their specific strengths and weaknesses. It also helped them address performance gaps.

To further strengthen its supplier network, Li & Fung constantly looked out for new suppliers. The company evaluated the experience and skills of each prospect to determine whether its operational standards could be met. By the early 2000s, Li & Fung had an extensive network of over seventy-five hundred regular suppliers; each on an average had about two hundred employees. Li & Fung described itself as

a smokeless factory. Though it did not own any manufacturing concern, it was involved in various functions that qualified it as a manufacturer.

Customer-Centric Organizational Structure

Li & Fung had an organizational structure that masked its size. In line with the transformation of the company's business strategy during the 1980s, Li & Fung revamped its organizational structure to manage its global sourcing network better and meet customer needs. The company discarded its traditional structure of geographic division as it found inefficiencies in this. During this period, all large trading companies in the world with vast supplier networks were organized geographically with country units as profit centers. Such a structure made it tough for the companies to optimize the value chains for their customers, as the country units competed against each other for business. The lack of cooperation and coordination among country units also resulted in loss of customers, affecting a company's business.

To eliminate this, Li & Fung adopted a new customer-centric structure, where it organized itself into various small customer-centric divisions.[5] Under the new structure, an entire division focused on serving a big customer such as The Limited, Levi's, Kohl's, and Abercrombie & Fitch. A single division aimed at fulfilling the needs of a group of smaller customers, with similar needs. For example, the company's theme-store division served a group of customers like Warner Brothers stores chain and Rainforest Café. According to company sources, this new model assisted them in creating a customized value chain for each customer order.

As part of its customer-centric strategy, Li & Fung created small divisions dedicated to serving one customer, and a person managing the unit as if it was his/her own company. Li & Fung hired people who were entrepreneurial in nature and whose ultimate aim was to run their own business. Thus, each division was run by a lead entrepreneur, designated as division manager, who was responsible for understanding customers' needs and fulfilling them by mobilizing resources from the group's sourcing and process network. For instance, the Gymboree division, which served

---

[5]In 2002, Li & Fung had about 120 business divisions across forty countries.

Gymboree, a leading U.S.-based clothing store, was headquartered in a separate office within the Li & Fung building in Hong Kong. It had forty plus employees focused on meeting Gymboree's needs. The division was further broken up into specialized teams in areas such as technical support, raw material purchase, quality assurance, merchandising, and shipping. Apart from the employees at its head office, the division also had dedicated sourcing teams across the branch offices of Li & Fung in China, Indonesia, and Philippines, the countries from where the division purchased in high volumes.

These divisions also promoted knowledge sharing during their interactions with customers, which benefited customers. Commenting on this, Frank Leong (Leong), CFO and head of the Operation Support Group (OSG), Li & Fung, said, "Our people sit down to share with them the latest information from the production side—what sort of material is hot, what new colours are available, where a product can be produced."[6] Such discussions not only expanded the fashion retailers' knowledge, but also gave them scope for more creativity and financial liberty in designing garments for a season. If required, the divisions also offered trade financing services to customers, through Letters of Credit (L/C).[7]

To preserve the entrepreneurial spirit, Li & Fung kept each division relatively small, with average revenues ranging between HK$ 30 million and HK$ 50 million. The company allowed each division to act as an independent unit with its own customers and profit and loss accounts. Li & Fung gave considerable freedom to division managers to run their divisions, as it believed that autonomy would encourage a free spirit. To further ensure the commitment of division managers, Li & Fung tied up their compensation to their division's bottom line. To motivate them to achieve their division's targets, the company gave out substantial financial incentives. Reportedly, Li & Fung did not fix any ceilings on bonuses. The company followed the same policy of performance

based compensation and incentives for other employees, too.

Li & Fung provided the divisions with all necessary financial resources and administrative support, mainly through the OSG, which provided back-end support to the entire group operations. The OSG supplied all divisions with personal computers and network connections, at a charge per PC, which covered the entire network, including order processing, production tracking, and e-mail communication. These charges were paid from the division's revenues.

The OSG also acted as an in-house HR provider, as it supplied recruitment services by internally matching staff from across various divisions, to meet some specific requirements of clients, and training them. It also acted as the divisions' chief banker as all divisional revenues finally went to the OSG. According to company sources, the divisions could take loans from the OSG at an interest rate cheaper than the market rate.

The OSG's performance was measured against its profit and loss account as was the case of any other division in the group. According to Leong, such a performance measurement strategy ensured that the OSG provided advanced high-quality services to its customers (other divisions) and at the same time optimized its costs.

The logic behind such an organizational structure was to allow each division to function like an independent company without worrying about back-end needs. Such a model provided the group with the flexibility of a small company, while having the strengths of a large, global company. As Leong said, "We're marrying the strength of being small and big together. Big companies tend to get bureaucratic, while small companies can do specialized products. Our small business units act extremely fast, but at the back-end, they get the level of service of a huge company."[8]

However, while Li & Fung believed in flexibility in some things, the company was highly conservative when it came to financial control and operating procedures. These were centralized and tightly managed. Li & Fung also maintained tight control over its working capital. All cash flows were centrally managed through headquarters in Hong Kong. For instance, L/Cs from all divisions came to headquarters for approval and were then reissued. The company

---

[6]"Asset Lite," www.cfoasia.com, April 2002.
[7]A document, consisting of specific instructions by the buyer of goods, that is issued by a bank to the seller who is authorized to draw a specified sum of money under certain conditions, that is, the receipt by the bank of certain documents within a given time. A confirmed L/C is one issued by a foreign bank, which is validated or guaranteed by a Hong Kong bank for a Hong Kong exporter in the case of default by the foreign buyer or bank.

[8]"Asset Lite," www.cfoasia.com, April 2002.

also had a standardized and fully computerized order executing and tracking system used by all divisions.

Leveraging IT and the Internet

To leverage the potential of IT, Li & Fung took many initiatives through the mid 1990s. It tied up its global network of offices with intranet[9] since 1995, to enable free information flow. In 1998, the company began creating dedicated extranet[10] sites for major customers. These sites enabled the company to interact with customers, track their orders, help in product development, and perform many other tasks in a cost-efficient manner. The extranet also enabled customers to track their orders and gain access to related information through Li & Fung's Electronic Trading System, known as XTS, which was linked to Li & Fung's global network of offices.

The major benefits of a dedicated extranet site can be understood from the following example. In the late 1990s, Coca-Cola, the leading soft drinks company, and many of its independent bottlers worldwide, largely relied on merchandize tied to sporting events to promote the company's core brand, Coca-Cola. As Coca-Cola was mainly a beverage company, with no exposure to manufacturing, the company found managing the manufacturing activity (for its merchandise) expensive and outside its area of core expertise. The company also feared that its manufacturing process might be too slow to respond to sporting and entertainment events. As a result, in March 2001, the company turned to Li & Fung for managing its manufacturing activities. Li & Fung designed and built an extranet site, called Kodimsum.com (KO for Coke's stock symbol, and dimsum for a Hong Kong food delicacy), enabling Coca-Cola's executives and bottlers to place online orders. The extranet also allowed bottlers to check orders placed by other bottlers of the company, enabling them to place a similar order if they found that the product would be useful in their own markets.

[9]An intranet is a restricted-access network that works like the Internet. Usually owned and managed by a corporation, an intranet enables an organization to provide content and services to its employees across its various divisions, without allowing external people to view it.
[10]An extranet is an Internet site that is offered to a select group of people such as customers, suppliers, and business partners, usually to provide or share nonpublic information.

With the emergence of the Internet as a major communication medium, industry observers felt it would make trading companies like Li & Fung redundant. Li & Fung opposed this view, stating that the key to its business was not hardware but information and its application to the management of client supply chains. The company believed that instead of being a threat, the Internet and e-commerce would offer more opportunities by helping it drive supply chain costs down and integrating management of supply chain via IT. Analysts, too, felt that this was true. They said that the real value of Li & Fung's business model lay not just in its ability to link suppliers and buyers, but in its power to influence suppliers and manufacturers, with whom the company had a strong relationship of trust.

Thus, Li & Fung used the Internet as a tool to make supply chains more transparent. When Li & Fung received an order from a customer, it used extranet sites and the Internet to fine-tune specifications. It then took instructions from the customer and fed the information on to its intranet to find the right raw material suppliers and right factory or factories to assemble the product. The Web also aided customers in quickly assessing shifting consumer demands. Thus, as an order moved through different phases of production, customers could make last-minute changes through Li and Fung's website, which hosted real-time information on the entire production process.

This real-time tracking by customers was not possible until the mid-1990s, when Li & Fung began using phone and fax. For instance, when a customer ordered 50,000 khaki cargo pants, the company delivered the pants five months later, leaving the customer with little chance of altering their orders in line with changing market trends. By the early 2000s, once the Web-based communication system was established, customers could cancel their order until the time the material was woven, change the color until the fabric was dyed, and alter design or size until the fabric was cut.

In March 2000, Li & Fung announced its Internet strategy to enter the e-commerce market, through its Business-to-Business (B2B) initiatives. Li & Fung aimed at creating economies of scale and scope for small- and medium-sized enterprises by bundling their orders for the same products and then customizing the mass-produced product to meet the requirements of each customer.

Commenting on this, William said

Li & Fung has done private-label manufacturing for a long time. We can only do this if the customers are very large and they have the scale, since you need intensive interaction when you do private-label work. To capture economies of scale, we need large customers, not small ones.... What the Internet does is allow us to reach the small and midsize guys we could never reach before. What do they want? What the big guys have—a private label, their own differentiated line, and at the same price as the big guys.... The Internet allows us to reach those people—without intensive interaction—and to aggregate their orders. We can allow you different styles, limited customisation using American yarn, knitted in China, assembled in Bangladesh. And we can allow you to put in your own label, embroidery, colours, packages, boxes. We can reap the economics of mass production, but with enough customisation.[11]

As part of Li & Fung's Internet strategy, StudioDirect Inc. was formed in April 2000 as an e-commerce subsidiary of the company (57 percent controlling stake) with an investment of US$19 million. StudioDirect's website, www.studiodirect.com, launched in March 2001, allowed placement of highly individualized orders from small- and medium-sized retailers, enabling them to choose from a wide variety of fabrics, colors, and accessories such as cuffs, pockets, buttons, and embroidery. According to Li & Fung sources, StudioDirect had customization options that could satisfy 90 percent of the smaller retailers.

StudioDirect aggregated all orders placed on its website and put them on to Li & Fung's manufacturers, resulting in a series of private-label lines ready for delivery. To handle the logistics needed to deliver finished goods to retailers across the world, StudioDirect tied up with Danzas AEI Intercontinental, a business division of the Danzas Group, which specialized in logistics services and had already worked with Li & Fung.

StudioDirect was reportedly capable of beginning production within six hours of receiving an order from a client over the Internet. For marketing its B2B initiative, the company chose the strategy of direct mailing. Through this, the company aimed at reaching about one thousand small- and medium-sized retailers in the first year and expected to do business

of $2 million with each of them, in the next five years. The initiative was launched in the United States in early 2001.

Analysts felt that Li & Fung, with its sound global sourcing network and strong financials (US$ 270 million in cash reserves) was poised to establish itself as a strong player in the B2B market place. Commenting on what Li & Fung could provide small- and medium-sized customers with, Barnett, a Goldman Sachs's analyst, said, "A large company that uses Li & Fung typically pays 4% to 12% of the value of the order [because of economies of scale]. It's about 30% for a small company. Those costs come down to 4% to 12% if clients use the studiodirect.com Internet site."[12]

In the early 2000s, Li & Fung maintained Internet-based communication with all its major customers worldwide. About 75 percent of them were large retailers in the United States, who reaped significant benefits from the transparent SCM attained due to the use of IT and the Internet.[13] Laurence H. Alberts, managing partner, Mercer Management Consulting (Asia), said, "They [Li and Fung] are the leaders in Asia in providing this full solution of sourcing and supply-chain management. They've built up a very considerable barrier to anyone else trying to replicate it."[14]

Global Expansion

During the late 1990s, with the growing popularity of private label brands, shortening product life cycles, and acute competition in the retailing industry, companies had to focus on their supply chain processes. As many companies did not have expertise in SCM and outsourcing was a cost-efficient alternative, the demand for companies that offered SCM services increased. Li & Fung, which already had an impressive sourcing network and SCM expertise, increased efforts to position itself as a global consumer goods trading company. The company devised an acquisition strategy to strengthen its position in the global trading market. The strategy aimed at expanding the sourcing network, product lines, and customer base.

---

[11]"A Different Kind of B2B Play in China?" www.businessweek.com, May 8, 2000.

[12]"Picking Asian Winners in the Internet Age," www.asiaweek.com, 2000.

[13]However, in countries such as China, Bangladesh, Philippines, Africa, and the Caribbean, where communication systems are still underdeveloped, Li & Fung relied on personal visits, phones, faxes, and couriers to communicate information and manage operations.

[14]"Middleman Becomes Master," www.chiefexecutive.net, October 2002.

In 1995, Li & Fung acquired Inchcape Buying Services (also known as Dodwell) from Inchcape Pacific, a leading British trading conglomerate. That company had an established network of offices in South Asia, the Mediterranean, and Caribbean regions, where Li & Fung had little or no presence. The acquisition nearly doubled the size and geographic reach of Li & Fung and brought with it a vast European customer base that complemented Li & Fung's strength in North America. The acquisition also contributed significantly to the company's success in achieving its three-year plan (1995–1998) target of doubling its profits from HK$ 225 million in 1995 to HK$ 455 million in 1998.

As a part of its proximity strategy, which aimed at producing products closer to the customer market (North America and Europe), Li & Fung began establishing and expanding its sourcing networks in regions such as the Mediterranean, Eastern Europe, North Africa, South Africa, and Central America in the late 1990s.

In December 1999, Li & Fung acquired Swire & Maclaine and Camberley Enterprises, the trading businesses of the Hong Kong–based group, Swire Pacific, for HK$ 450 million. While Swire & Maclaine was a major provider of product sourcing and quality assurance services in Hong Kong, Camberley Enterprises made high-quality ladies sportswear, ready-to-wear garments, and home accessories. These acquisitions offered Li & Fung design process expertise and helped it further strengthen its customer base in the United States and Europe, by adding some major customers such as Laura Ashley and Ann Taylor. As Swire & Maclaine had been a major competitor of Li & Fung in Hong Kong, its acquisition helped Li & Fung further consolidate its business in Hong Kong and strengthened its position as one of the world's leading sourcing and supply chain management companies.

In November 2000, Li & Fung announced the acquisition of Colby Group Holdings Limited; a Hong Kong–based leading consumer goods trading company, for HK$ 2.2 billion to consolidate its global competitive position further and helped it emerge as the largest consumer goods export trading groups in Hong Kong. Commenting on the rationale behind the acquisition, William said, "Colby has strong brand recognition, especially among US department stores. Its seasoned staff and diversified sourcing capabilities will complement our existing business. With this acquisition, we will be able to expand our customer base and further penetrate what is an important new market segment."[15] Even after the acquisition, Colby continued to operate under its own company name as a subsidiary of Li & Fung.

In the early 2000s, Li & Fung focused its acquisition strategy on hard goods companies. In mid 2002, Li & Fung acquired Janco Overseas, a Hong Kong–based buying agent, specializing in hard goods, for HK$ 249.6 million. According to company sources, the acquisition was expected to increase Li & Fung's turnover by HK$ 1.4 billion. Reportedly, Janco's strengths in the hard goods segment and focus on large food retailers, who were rapidly expanding their nonfood offerings, was expected to strengthen Li & Fung's position in the hard goods segment. It was also expected to open up new customer segments and opportunities on account of expansion in its hard goods product portfolio.

In the fiscal year 2002, the hard goods segment accounted for 32 percent of Li & Fung's revenues compared with 28 percent in 2001. The segment registered a 29 percent increase in revenues and 70 percent in operating profits over 2001. Li & Fung sources said the acquisition of Janco was a major factor that contributed to such a significant growth in its hard goods business.

In August 2003, Li & Fung announced plans to purchase the remaining one-third stake in the group's New York–based garment importer unit, International Sourcing Group (ISG), for US$ 5.22 million, from ISG's chief executive, Alan Chartash, who owned that stake. The acquisition was expected to increase Li & Fung's profitability. Victor said, "By further leveraging the group's financial resources, management strength and entrepreneurial corporate culture, it is envisaged that a more comprehensive service will be provided to ISG's customers."[16]

During the early 2000s, Li & Fung focused on expanding its customer base in non-U.S. markets to balance the group's overall revenue portfolio, which was highly skewed toward the United States. It concentrated on the fast developing economies in Asia and the Southern Hemisphere, where more and more companies were outsourcing manufacturing and SCM on account of increasing globalization and resulting competitive pressures that were forcing companies to optimize resources.

[15]"Li & Fung to Acquire Colby," www.irasia.com, November 9, 2000.
[16]"Li & Fung to Buy Out Last Stake of US Unit," Hong Kong iMail (China), August 20, 2003.

EXHIBIT 7

Li & Fung's Five-Year Stock Price Chart (August 1999–July 2004)
(Price in HK$, Volume in mns)

Source: **www.prophet.net**.

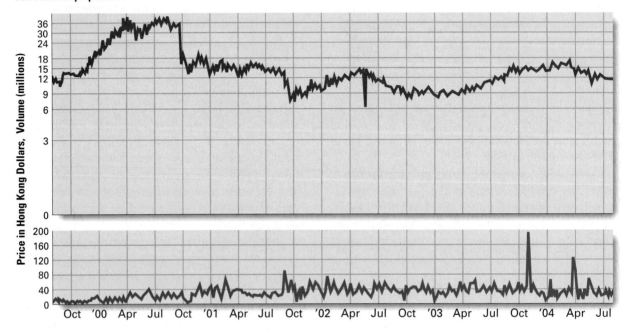

Li & Fung identified Japan as a potential market, where the fashion retailing business was booming. In October 2003, Li & Fung entered into an alliance with Nichimen Corporation (Nichimen), a leading general trading firm in Japan, to offer higher value for Japanese retailers. This was possible due to the integration of Li & Fung's global sourcing network with Nichimen's customer servicing capabilities.

In December 2003, Li & Fung acquired the sourcing business of the Hong Kong–based Firstworld Garments Limited and the U.S.-based International Porcelain Inc. for US$ 27 million. These two companies would together operate under the name "International Sources." They were expected to strengthen Li & Fung's presence in the hard goods business and enable it to reach out to Mexico.

The Challenges

By the end of 2003, Li & Fung emerged as one of the few global consumer goods trading companies with geographic flexibility and depth of expertise required for success in the fiercely competitive business environment of the early twenty-first century. In the fiscal year ending December 31, 2003, the group's revenues amounted to HK$ 42.6 billion, a 14.3 percent

rise over HK$ 37.3 billion in 2002. Net profits amounted to HK$ 1.22 billion in fiscal 2003, a 13.2 percent increase over the HK$ 1.08 billion in fiscal 2002. In December 2003, the share price of Li & Fung was quoting around HK$ 13 (see Exhibit 7).

However, according to company sources, revenues and profits were below expectations. The Iraq War,[17] the SARS epidemic,[18] and poor business

[17]The U.S. government believed that the Osama Bin Laden led terrorist organization, Al-Qaida, which was responsible for the September 11, 2001, terrorist attacks on the World Trade Center in the United States, may obtain weapons of mass destruction (WMD) from Iraq. As Iraq was ruled by Saddam Hussein (Hussein), who was openly hostile to the United States, the U.S. officials considered it a severe threat to the country's security, and felt the need for preemptive war against Iraq to prevent further damage from occurring in the United States. In March 2003, the United States declared war against Iraq (the second war, the first being in January 1991), called "Operation Iraqi Freedom." In May 2003, the U.S. Army captured Tikrit, the birthplace of Saddam Hussein. Saddam himself was captured in December 2003.
[18]According to **www.cdc.gov**, Severe Acute Respiratory Syndrome (SARS) is a viral respiratory illness caused by a corona virus called the SARS associated corona virus (SARS–CoV). The first case of SARS was reported in Asia in February 2003. Within a few months, the illness spread to more than twenty-four countries throughout the world. The outbreak of SARS in the Asian region severely damaged its economic performance—the hardest-hit business was the region's tourism industry.

performance in the holiday season of some major customers were cited as reasons. The drop in the group's nontrading income also had an unfavorable effect on overall financial results. Reportedly, the net loss from Li & Fung's venture capital business amounted to HK$ 8 million in the fiscal 2003.

That year, the soft goods segment accounted for 67 percent of Li & Fung's total revenues, while hard goods accounted for the remaining 33 percent. Geographically, North America continued to be the company's largest export market, accounting for 75 percent of its total revenues. It was followed by Europe (19 percent), East Asia (3 percent), and the Southern Hemisphere (3 percent). As part of achieving its three-year plan (2001–2004) goal of doubling profits by the fiscal 2004, Li & Fung announced that it would continue its aggressive acquisition drive, focused at non-U.S. companies, and new product lines that could open up more revenue opportunities.

In August 2003, Li & Fung finalized a licensing agreement with Levi's, under which the former would design, manufacture, and market clothing under the latter's Levi Strauss Signature label. According to company sources, these products would be marketed in the United States by late 2004. In early 2004, Li & Fung also signed similar licensing deals with Official Pillowtex LLC, a U.S.-based company that owned the Royal Velvet linen brand. Commenting on these deals, William said, "Leveraging our strong position in the supply chain, we are building a higher-margin business model of licensing well-known brand names. This new business model will augment our core sourcing business and will be an important growth driver for the group in our next three-year plan for 2005–2007."[19]

By mid 2004, Li & Fung had an extensive network of over 65 offices in 40 countries worldwide, managed by a dedicated employee base of over 6,000. Reportedly, the company faced very little competition, which analysts attributed to its unique positioning as a supply chain manager for its clients and its focused acquisition strategy. William E. Connor & Associates (WEC&A), an American-owned, Hong Kong–based trading company, was the closest competitor to Li & Fung in Hong Kong as textiles was WEC&A's major product line. But, as WEC&A focused on large department store customers and Li & Fung concentrated on specialty store chains, analysts felt that competition between them was not intense (see Exhibit 8).

While Li & Fung's business model might seem error free and its future bright, analysts were quick to point out that every business had its negative side, and Li & Fung also had made miscalculations. They said the company's much hyped B2B initiative "StudioDirect," had failed to get the expected response, forcing Li & Fung to restructure its operations. In 2002, Li & Fung converted StudioDirect from a full-service e-commerce company into a private label golf-wear specialist, offering services to customers through the Internet. The company also reduced its stake in StudioDirect from 57 percent to 15 percent. Li & Fung attributed this restructuring to changes in market conditions in the United States, which were not conducive to the growth of StudioDirect's business. It stated that it was still committed to e-commerce, and its aim was to reach smaller and midsized retailers. However, even by early 2004, StudioDirect had failed to make major progress on this front.

The continuous fall in the annual growth of revenues and profitability through the early 2000s was also perceived as an area of concern by many analysts (see Exhibit 9). While Li & Fung registered a high growth in revenues and profit after taxation of 53.35 percent and 49 percent, respectively, for the fiscal year ending December 31, 2000, the growth in revenues and profit after taxation came down to 14.35 percent and 12.06 percent, respectively, by the fiscal 2003. Analysts felt that the sharp decline in the share of overall revenues derived from European markets, during the early 2000s, was not a good sign for the company. They felt the company had failed to come up with effective strategies to increase revenue share from the European market, which, next to the United States, had immense potential for fashion goods, especially garments, Li & Fung's major business. They criticized Li & Fung for failing to build on the opportunities provided by its acquisition of Inchcape Buying Services, which had a strong presence in Europe.

Analysts also felt that Li & Fung's high dependence on large retailers, especially in the United States and Europe, might prove a threat for the company in the long run, given the uncertainties in the retailing industry. They pointed out that a major consolidation in the North American retailing industry, Li & Fung's largest export market, might severely affect the company's business. For instance, if a retailing giant such as Wal-Mart,

---

[19]"Hong Kong Li & Fung Posts 13% Net Profit Rise on Sales Growth," **www.prophet.net**, March 24, 2004.

EXHIBIT 8

A Note on Hong Kong's Export Trade Industry

The Export Trade Industry:

Hong Kong has always been one of the world's major export trade centres. Until the 1970s, Hong Kong was a manufacturing economy, supplying the world with textiles, handbags, toys, plastic flowers, watches and footwear. Most of its exports were to the US and Europe. After the Chinese economy was liberalized in 1979 (initially only some coastal regions were opened up for foreign investors) many companies across all the major industrial segments and trading companies in Hong Kong moved the labour-intensive part of manufacturing to China.

The rapid industrialization of Asian countries from the 1980s resulted in expansion of production capabilities in the manufacturing sector and related supporting services especially in other low cost countries like Taiwan and Korea. This in turn led to trading companies expanding their sourcing reach beyond China to optimise sourcing costs for their clients. By the late 1990s, Hong-Kong emerged as a service economy with 84% of GDP derived from services. According to a survey by the Hong Kong Trade Development Council (TDC) in 1998, 64% of international buyers sourced China-made products through trading companies in Hong Kong. The country's strategic location, good physical infrastructure, expertise in international trade and well-established legal framework made trading reliable, simple and convenient. By the turn of the 20th century, Hong Kong became one of the world's largest export trade countries.

In 2001, Hong Kong earned HK$ 106 bn from exporting trade-related services, accounting for 32.7% of total services exports. In 2002, one in five employed persons in Hong Kong were engaged in the import-export trade. The sector produced a net output of HK$ 249 bn and accounted for 21% of Hong Kong's GDP. In 2002, there were more than 1,133 companies involved in the wholesale, retail and import and export trade businesses.

In the early 2000s, off shore export trading was increasing rapidly on account of many factors. The use of advanced technology, sophisticated production processes and on-site inspections by trading firms eliminated the need for further processing of products like final assembly, packaging and imposing quality control procedures. At the same time, the increased availability of cost-effective and reliable transport services contributed to the rise in off shore export trade. Some expected changes in the regional trade regimes including the China-ASEAN Free Trade Agreement and the Closer Economic Partnership Arrangement (CEPA) between Hong Kong and mainland China were expected to further boost the trading industry in Hong Kong.

In 2003, Hong Kong was the world's freest and 10th largest trading economy. It was a major trading centre with total merchandise trade amounting to US$ 457 bn, equivalent to 289% of GDP for that year. Major exports included clothing, electrical machinery, apparatus, textiles, jewelry, insurance services, financial services, transportation and travel services. In 2003, Hong Kong earned US$ 287.9 bn from exporting goods and services. Major export trading partners included mainland China (39.3%), US (21.3%), Japan (5.4%) and the UK (3.5%). With trading volumes of such magnitude, Hong Kong became a leading sourcing hub in the Asia-Pacific region in the early 21st century.

Export Trading Firms in Hong Kong:

Export trading firms in Hong Kong can be divided into three categories:

Left hand–right hand traders: Traditional trading firms that matched sellers and buyers but did not add significant value. These firms identified goods produced in Hong Kong or neighbouring countries and shipped them to their customers.

Traders with some value-added services: These firms, apart from sourcing raw material for their customers, offered some additional value such as providing trade finance and freight forwarding services.

Traders with sophisticated value-added services: These exporting firms went beyond traditional trading services. Additional services included product designing and development, manufacturing prototypes, offering supply chain management services, undertaking distribution and delivery of finished goods.

Hong Kong's export trading firms source garments, toys, electronic items and other manufactured goods. The sourcing activities are of three types:

- Sourcing goods produced in Hong Kong.
- Sourcing goods from the Asian region for re-export from Hong Kong.
- Sourcing goods from one country for direct shipping to another country, without touching Hong Kong. This is called offshore trade.

Trading firms in Hong Kong usually specialize in one product. In most cases, they offer shipping services to customers and manage their own warehousing facilities. Such facilities enable exporters of durable goods to offer better customer service, as a certain quantity of stock is always readily available for shipment. For goods like textiles, trading firms use temporary storage, with emphasis placed on prompt dispatch for shipping.

EXHIBIT 8 (*continued*)

A Note on Hong Kong's Export Trade Industry

Most export trading firms in Hong Kong are closely involved in manufacturing activities, though indirectly, as actual production is usually sub-contracted. Short production cycles, a preference for smaller quantities of more product lines and keeping tight deadlines ensured that companies met customer needs. They provided supplier factories with advanced production techniques and know-how and helped solve production bottlenecks.

Profile of William E. Conner & Associates (Li & Fung's Major Competitor):
William E. Conner & Associates (WEC&A) was founded in 1949 in Tokyo and moved to Hong Kong in 1985. It is one of the major export trade companies in Hong Kong in the early 21st century and the closest competitor to the market leader, Li & Fung, in the consumer goods trading market. WEC&A optimised the supply chain for its clients by managing every aspect of sourcing, right from product design & development to distribution and delivery of the finished product. The company's products included apparel, fabrics, fashion accessories, footwear, decorative accessories, textiles, housewares, furniture, lighting, office products, stationery and fashion-related products.

In the early 2000s, WEC&A had a global network of 35 offices in 20 countries. With an employee base of over 1,400, the company fulfilled the requirements of over 70 customers, which included leading department stores, specialty stores, catalogue companies, e-commerce retailers and importers, mainly in North America, Australia, Europe, Latin America and Japan. In 2002, WEC&A's net worth amounted to US$ 850 mn.

Sources: **www.tdc.trade.com** and **www.weconnor.com**.

EXHIBIT 9

Li & Fung—Consolidated Statements of Income (1997–2003)

Year Ending December 31	2003 HK$'000	2002 HK$'000	2001 HK$'000	2000 HK$'000	1999 HK$'000	1998 HK$'000	1997 HK$'000
Continuing operations	42,630,510	37,281,360	32,941,392	24,992,227	16,297,501	14,312,618	13,345,722
Discontinued operations	—	—	87,183	791	—	—	—
Total Turnover	**42,630,510**	**37,281,360**	**33,028,575**	**24,993,018**	**16,297,501**	**14,312,618**	**13,345,772**
Counting operations	1,285,952	1,134,605	904,520	830,223	592,885	469,501	361,289
Discontinued operations	—	—	(237,955)	(39,375)	—	—	—
Gross Profit	**1,285,952**	**1,134,605**	**666,565**	**790,848**	**592,885**	**469,501**	**361,289**
Interest income	38,373	49,581	112,837	140,330	43,830	56,093	37,772
Interest expenses	(9,813)	(8,987)	(12,464)	(20,585)	(32,243)	(61,346)	(6,270)
Share of profit less losses of associated companies	2,015	393	1,443	13,677	9,389	6,850	6,666
Profit before taxation	1,316,527	1,175,592	768,381	924,270	613,861	471,098	399,457
Taxation	(105,513)	(94,896)	(55,637)	(64,178)	(36,638)	(16,425)	(25,326)
Profit after taxation	1,211,014	1,080,696	712,744	860,092	577,223	454,673	374,131
Minority interests	12,104	(228)	69,567	10,296	(2,585)	495	974
Continuing operations	1,223,118	1,080,468	951,307	893,118	574,638	455,168	375,105
Discontinued operations	—	—	(168,996)	(22,730)	—	—	—
Net Profit	**1,223,118**	**1,080,468**	**782,311**	**870,388**	**574,638**	**455,168**	**375,105**

Source: Li & Fung Annual Report, 2003.

which rarely outsourced its manufacturing activities, acquired other major American retailers, or put them out of business, it could lead to an 8 percent to 10 percent cut in margins for Li & Fung. Such consolidation might also result in only a few large retailing giants surviving (with other companies either having been acquired or forced to quit) in the market, which might also have severe implications on Li & Fung's revenues. This was because the company mainly derived its revenues from a large base of companies in the United States, with revenues of over US$ 100 million.

Analysts further added that Li & Fung's hopes of benefiting from increased manufacturing activity in China to strengthen its competitive position in the United States, after the removal of the quota system in January 2005, might fail. They were of the view that according to WTO rules, the United States and Europe were entitled to impose "antisurge" quotas until the end of 2008, in case they felt any threat to domestic industry from exports. Antisurge quotas restricted annual growth of imports from a country to 7.5 percent per product category. Analysts also said that it was very likely that the antisurge quotas would come into existence in 2005.

Despite these challenges, industry observers felt that with Li & Fung focusing on expanding its customer base outside the United States, especially in Asia, in the years to come the company could reduce its dependence on the United States, its largest market. Meanwhile, Li & Fung had already achieved considerable success in lessening its dependence on soft goods over the years, reducing some risks in its business.

Media reports expressed optimism for Li & Fung's future. They wrote that the company, powered by its depth of sourcing knowledge and positioning as an efficient manager of global supply chains, was well poised for growth, in the light of increasing globalization. An *Economist* article had quoted in 2001, "Li & Fung appears to have as bright a future as globalisation itself."[20]

[20]"Li & Fung: Optimising Supply Chain for Other Companies," *The Economist*, May 31, 2001.

Case 16

Starbucks Corporation: Competing in a Global Market

This case was prepared by Suresh Kotha and Debra Glassman, the University of Washington.

Starbucks Corporation is a Seattle, Washington, based coffee company. It buys, roasts, and sells whole bean specialty coffees and coffee drinks through an international chain of retail outlets. From its beginnings as a seller of packaged, premium specialty coffees, Starbucks has evolved into a firm known for its coffeehouses, where people can purchase beverages and food items as well as packaged whole bean and ground coffee. Starbucks is credited with changing the way Americans—and people around the world—view and consume coffee, and its success has attracted global attention.

Starbucks has consistently been one of the fastest growing companies in the United States. Over a ten-year period starting in 1992, the company's net revenues increased at a compounded annual growth rate of 20 percent to $3.3 billion in fiscal 2002. Net earnings have grown at an annual compounded growth rate of 30 percent to $218 million in fiscal 2002, which is the highest reported net earnings figure in the company's history (see Exhibit 1). As *Business Week* tells it:

On Wall Street, Starbucks is the last great growth story. Its stock, including four splits, has soared more than 2,200% over the past decade, surpassing Wal-Mart, General Electric, PepsiCo, Coca-Cola, Microsoft, and IBM in total return. Now at $21 [September 2002], it is hovering near its all-time high of $23 in July [2002], before the overall market drop.[1]

To continue this rapid pace of growth, the firm's senior executives are looking to expand internationally. Specifically, they are interested in further expansion in Europe (including the Middle East), Asia Pacific (including Australia and New Zealand), and Latin America. Expanding in these three continents represents both a challenge and an opportunity to Starbucks. While the opportunity of increased revenues from further expansion is readily apparent to the company's top management, what is not clear is how to deal with growing "antiglobalization" sentiment around the world.

This case looks at issues that are arising as Starbucks seeks to dominate specialty coffee markets around the world and explores what changes in strategy might be required.

Background

In 1971, three Seattle entrepreneurs—Jerry Baldwin, Zev Siegl, and Gordon Bowker—started selling whole-bean coffee in Seattle's Pike Place Market. They named

[1]Planet Starbucks, *Business Week*, September 9, 2002, pp. 100–110.

EXHIBIT 1

Selected Financial and Store Data
(in Thousands, Except Earnings per Share and Store Operating Data)

As of and for the Fiscal Year Ended (1)	Sept 29, 2002 (52 Wks)	Sept 30, 2001 (52 Wks)	Oct 1, 2000 (52 Wks)	Oct 3, 1999 (53 Wks)	Sept 27, 1998 (52 Wks)
Results of Operations Data					
Net revenues:					
Retail	$2,792,904	$2,229,594	$1,823,607	$1,423,389	$1,102,574
Specialty	496,004	419,386	354,007	263,439	206,128
Total net revenues	3,288,908	2,648,980	2,177,614	1,686,828	1,308,702
Merger expenses (2)	—	—	—	—	8,930
Operating income	318,725	281,094	212,252	156,711	109,216
Internet-related investment losses	—	2,940	58,792	—	—
Gain on sale of investment	13,361	—	—	—	—
Net earnings	$215,073	$181,210	$94,564	$101,693	$68,372
Net earnings per common share—diluted	$0.54	$0.46	$0.24	$0.27	$0.19
Balance Sheet Data					
Working capital	$310,048	$148,661	$146,568	$135,303	$157,805
Total assets	2,292,736	1,846,519	1,491,546	1,252,514	992,755
Long-term debt (including current portion)	5,786	6,483	7,168	7,691	1,803
Shareholders' equity	1,726,638	1,375,927	1,148,399	961,013	794,297
Store Operating Data					
Percentage change in comparable store sales (3)					
North America	7%	5%	9%	6%	5%
International	(3)%	2%	23%	20%	28%
Consolidated	6%	5%	9%	6%	5%
Systemwide retail store sales (4)	$3,796,000	$2,950,000	$2,250,000	$1,633,000	$1,190,000
Systemwide stores opened during the year: (5)	1,177	1,208	1,003	612	474
Systemwide stores open at year end:					
Continental North America					
Company-operated stores	3,496	2,971	2,446	2,038	1,622
Licensed stores	1,078	809	530	179	133
International					
Company-operated stores	384	295	173	97	66
Licensed stores	928	634	352	184	65
Total	5,886	4,709	3,501	2,498	1,886

(1) The company's fiscal year ends on the Sunday closest to September 30. All fiscal years presented include 52 weeks, except fiscal 1999, which includes 53 weeks.
(2) Merger expenses relate to the business combination with Seattle Coffee Holdings Limited.
(3) Includes only company-operated stores open 13 months or longer.
(4) Systemwide retail store sales include sales at company-operated and licensed stores and are believed by management to measure global penetration of Starbucks retail stores.
(5) Systemwide store openings are reported net of closures.

their store Starbucks, after the first mate in *Moby Dick*.[2] By 1982, the business had grown to five stores, a small roasting facility, and a wholesale business selling coffee to local restaurants. At the same time, Howard Schultz had been working as Vice President of U.S. operations for Hammarplast, a Swedish house wares company in New York, marketing coffee makers to a number of retailers, including Starbucks. Through selling to Starbucks, Schultz was introduced to the three founders, who then recruited him to bring marketing savvy to their company. Schultz, twenty-nine and recently married, was eager to leave New York. He joined Starbucks as manager of retail sales and marketing.

A year later, Schultz visited Italy for the first time on a buying trip. He noticed that coffee is an integral part of the culture in Italy; Italians start their day at an espresso bar and later in the day return with their friends. There are 200,000 coffee bars in Italy, and about 1,500 in Milan alone. Schultz believed that, given the chance, Americans would pay good money for a premium cup of coffee and a stylish place to enjoy it. Enthusiastic about his idea, Schultz returned to tell Starbucks's owners of his plan for a national chain of cafés styled on the Italian coffee bar. The owners, however, did not want to be in the restaurant business. Undaunted, Schultz wrote a business plan and began looking for investors. By April 1985, he had opened his first coffee bar, Il Giornale (named after the Italian newspaper), where he served Starbucks coffee. Following Il Giornale's immediate success, he expanded to three stores. In 1987, the owners of Starbucks agreed to sell the firm to Schultz for $4 million. The Il Giornale coffee bars took on the name of Starbucks.

Convinced that Starbucks would one day be in every neighborhood in America, Schultz focused on growth. At first, the company's losses almost doubled (to $1.2 million in fiscal 1990), as overhead and operating expenses ballooned with the expansion. Starbucks lost money for three years running, and the stress was hard on Schultz, but he stuck to his

conviction not to "sacrifice long-term integrity and values for short-term profit."[3] In 1991, sales shot up 84 percent, and the company turned profitable. In 1992, Schultz took the firm public at $17 a share.

Believing that market share and name recognition are critical to the company's success, Schultz continued to expand the business aggressively. Schultz observes, "There is no secret sauce here. Anyone can do it." From the beginning, Schultz has professed a strict growth policy. Although many other coffeehouses or espresso bars are franchised, Starbucks owns all of its North American stores outright, with the exception of license agreements in airports. Further, rather than trying to capture all the potential markets as soon as possible, Starbucks goes into a geographic market and tries to completely dominate it before setting its sights on further expansion. Using this strategy, Starbucks has grown from 17 coffee shops in 1987 to 5,688 outlets in 28 countries by the end of fiscal 2002 (see Exhibit 2). It also employed over 60,000 individuals, including approximately 50,000 in retail stores at the end of 2002.

Starbucks Corporation is organized into two business units that correspond to the company's operating segments: North American and International. In 1995, Starbucks Coffee International, a wholly owned subsidiary of Starbucks Coffee Company, was set up to build Starbucks's businesses outside North America, including opening company-owned, licensed, and joint-venture-based retail stores worldwide.

A recent article in *Business Week* notes:

Starbucks also has a well-seasoned management team. Schultz, 49, stepped down as chief executive in 2000 to become chairman and chief global strategist. Orin Smith, 60, the company's numbers-cruncher, is now CEO and in charge of day-to-day operations. The head of North American operations is Howard Behar, 57, a retailing expert who returned last September, two years after retiring. The management trio is known as H2O, for Howard, Howard, and Orin.[4]

Exhibit 3 provides a partial list of Starbucks top management, and Appendix A provides a timeline and history of Starbucks.

[2]According to *Business Week* (September 9, 2002, p. 103), "The name came about when the original owners looked to Seattle history for inspiration and chose the moniker of an old mining camp: Starbo. Further refinement led to Starbucks, after the first mate in *Moby Dick*, which they felt evoked the seafaring romance of the early coffee traders (hence the mermaid logo).

[3]*Success*, April 1993.
[4]Planet Starbucks, *Business Week*, September 9, 2002, pp. 100–110.

EXHIBIT 2

Starbucks Store Locations (as of November 2002)

Source: Starbucks Corporation.

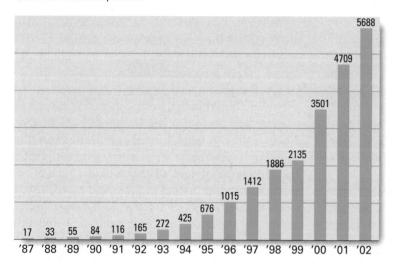

The Starbucks Model

Howard Schultz's goal is to: "Establish Starbucks as the premier purveyor of the finest coffee in the world while maintaining uncompromising principles as we grow." The company's twenty-five-year goal is to "become an enduring, great company with the most recognized and respected brand in the world, known for inspiring and nurturing the human spirit." The company's mission statement articulates several guiding principles to measure the appropriateness of the firm's decisions (see Exhibit 4). In describing Starbucks's unique approach to competition, *Fortune* notes

> The strategy is simple: Blanket an area completely, even if the stores cannibalize one another's business. A new store will often capture about 30% of the sales of a nearby Starbucks, but the company considers that a good thing: The Starbucks-everywhere approach cuts down on delivery and management costs, shortens customer lines at individual stores, and increases foot traffic for all the stores in an area. Last week 20 million people bought a cup of coffee at a Starbucks. A typical customer stops by 18 times a month; no American retailer has a higher frequency of customer visits. Sales have climbed an average of 20% a year since the company went public. Even in a down economy, when other retailers have taken a beating, Starbucks store traffic has risen between 6% and 8% a year. Perhaps

even more notable is the fact that Starbucks has managed to generate those kinds of numbers with virtually no marketing, spending just 1% of its annual revenues on advertising. (Retailers usually spend 10% or so of revenues on ads.)[5]

Business Week adds

> Clustering stores increases total revenue and market share, [CEO] Orin Smith argues, even when individual stores poach on each other's sales. The strategy works, he says, because of Starbucks size. It is large enough to absorb losses at existing stores as new ones open up, and soon overall sales grow beyond what they would have with just one store. Meanwhile, it's cheaper to deliver to and manage stores located close together. And by clustering, Starbucks can quickly dominate a local market.[6]

And Schultz points out:

> The market is much larger than we originally thought. . . . In most cases local competitors benefit from our arrival because of the expansion of the marketplace. Our strategy is never to eliminate or hurt the competition. We never underprice our coffee and it's clear that we position ourselves so as not to undercut the pricing structure in the marketplace.

[5]Mr. Coffee. *Fortune*, March 30, 2003.
[6]Planet Starbucks, *Business Week*, September 9, 2002, p. 103.

EXHIBIT 3

Starbucks Top Management Team

Howard Schultz is the founder of the company and has been chairman of the board since its inception in 1985. Mr. Schultz served as chief executive officer from 1985 until June 2000, when he transitioned into the role of chief global strategist. From 1985 to June 1994, Mr. Schultz was also the company's president. From September 1982 to December 1985, Mr. Schultz was the director of Retail Operations and Marketing for Starbucks Coffee Company, a predecessor to the company; and from January 1986 to July 1987, he was the chairman of the board, chief executive officer and president of Il Giornale Coffee Company, a predecessor to the company.

Orin C. Smith joined Starbucks Corporation in 1990 and has served as president and chief executive officer of the company since June 2000. From June 1994 to June 2000, Mr. Smith served as the company's president and chief operating officer. Prior to June 1994, Mr. Smith served as the company's vice president and chief financial officer and later, as its executive vice president and chief financial officer.

Peter Maslen joined Starbucks in August 1999 as president, Starbucks Coffee International, Inc. Prior to joining Starbucks, Mr. Maslen served in various executive positions within Asia Pacific and Europe with Mars Inc., PepsiCo, Inc. and Tricon Global Restaurants. From 1992 to 1999, as senior vice president with Tricon, he served as president of its German, Swiss, Austrian and Central Europe divisions.

Jim Donald joined Starbucks in November 2002 as president, Starbucks North America. He is responsible for managing Starbucks North America company-owned and licensed stores, business alliances (food service, grocery, club channels of distribution, joint venture partnerships with Pepsi-Cola Company and Dreyer's Grand Ice Cream)—in the United States and Canada, store development, retail systems, administration and retail partner resources. Jim brings 32 years of experience in the retail and food industry. Prior to joining Starbucks, he was chairman, president and chief executive officer at Pathmark Stores, Inc. since 1996. In addition, he has held several senior leadership positions at top-tier retail companies including Safeway, Wal-Mart and Albertson's.

Michael Casey joined Starbucks in August 1995 as senior vice president and chief financial officer and was promoted to executive vice president, chief financial officer and chief administrative officer in September 1997. Prior to joining Starbucks, Mr. Casey served as executive vice president and chief financial officer of Family Restaurants, Inc. from its inception in 1986. During his tenure there, he also served as a director from 1986 to 1993, and as president and chief executive officer of its El Torito Restaurants, Inc. subsidiary from 1988 to 1993.

Eduardo R. (Ted) Garcia joined Starbucks in April 1995 as senior vice president, Supply Chain Operations and was promoted to executive vice president, Supply Chain and Coffee Operations in September 1997. From May 1993 to April 1995, Mr. Garcia was an executive for Gemini Consulting. From January 1990 until May 1993, he was the vice president of Operations Strategy for Grand Metropolitan PLC, Food Sector.

Source: Starbucks Corporation, November 2002.

Schultz observes that the company is still in its early days of growth worldwide. "We are opening three or four stores every day," he notes. "We feel strongly that the driver of the equity of the brand is directly linked to the retail experience we create in our stores. Our commitment to the growth of the company is significant and will continue to be based on the long-term growth potential of our retail format."

Securing the Finest Raw Materials

Starbucks's coffee quality begins with the purchase of high-quality *arabica* coffee beans. Although many Americans were raised on a commodity-like coffee made from lower quality *robusta* beans (or arabica beans mixed with less-expensive filler beans), Starbucks

coffee is strictly *arabica*, and the company ensures that only the highest quality beans are used. Dave Olsen, the company's then senior vice president and then chief coffee procurer, scoured mountain trails in Indonesia, Kenya, Guatemala, and elsewhere in search of Starbucks's premium bean. His standards were demanding, and he conducted exacting experiments in order to get the proper balance of flavor, body, and acidity.

From the company's inception, it has worked on developing relationships with the countries from which it buys coffee beans. Traditionally, Europeans and Japanese bought most of the premium coffee beans. Olsen sometimes had to convince coffee growers to sell to Starbucks—especially since American

EXHIBIT 4

Starbucks Mission Statements and Guiding Principles

Mission Statement

Establish Starbucks as the premier purveyor of the finest coffee in the world while maintaining our uncompromising principles while we grow.

The following six guiding principles will help us measure the appropriateness of our decisions:

- Provide a great work environment and treat each other with respect and dignity.
- Embrace diversity as an essential component in the way we do business.
- Apply the highest standards of excellence to the purchasing, roasting and fresh delivery of our coffee.
- Develop enthusiastically satisfied customers all of the time.
- Contribute positively to our communities and our environment.
- Recognize that profitability is essential to our future success.

Environmental Mission Statement

Starbucks is committed to a role of environmental leadership in all facets of our business.

We fulfill this mission by a commitment to:

- Understanding of environmental issues and sharing information with our partners.
- Developing innovative and flexible solutions to bring about change.
- Striving to buy, sell and use environmentally friendly products.
- Recognizing that fiscal responsibility is essential to our environmental future.
- Instilling environmental responsibility as a corporate value.
- Measuring and monitoring our progress for each project.
- Encouraging all partners to share in our mission.

coffee buyers are notorious purchasers of the "dregs" of the coffee beans. In 1992, Starbucks set a new precedent by outbidding European buyers for the exclusive Narino Supremo Bean crop.[7] Starbucks collaborated with a mill in the tiny town of Pasto, located on the side of the Volcano Galero. There they set up a special operation to single out the particular Narino Supremo bean, and Starbucks guaranteed to purchase the entire yield. This enabled Starbucks to be the exclusive purveyor of Narino Supremo, purportedly one of the best coffees in the world.[8]

Vertical Integration

Roasting the coffee bean is close to an art form at Starbucks. Starbucks currently operates multiple roasting and distribution facilities. Roasters are promoted from within the company and trained for over a year, and it is considered quite an honor to be chosen. The coffee is roasted in a powerful gas-fired drum roaster for twelve to fifteen minutes while roasters use sight, smell, hearing, and computers to judge when beans are perfectly done. The color of the beans is even tested in an Agtron blood-cell analyzer, with the whole batch being discarded if the sample is not deemed perfect.

---

[7]This Colombian coffee bean crop is very small and grows only in the high regions of the Cordillera mountain range. For years, the Narino beans were guarded zealously by Western Europeans, who prized their colorful and complex flavor. It was usually used for upgrading blends. Starbucks was determined to make them available for the first time as a pure varietal. This required breaking Western Europe's monopoly over the beans by convincing the Colombian growers that it intended to use "the best beans for a higher purpose."

[8]The *Canada Newswire*, March 1, 1993.

The Starbucks Experience

According to Schultz, "We're not just selling a cup of coffee, we are providing an experience." In order to create American coffee enthusiasts with the dedication of their Italian counterparts, Starbucks provides a seductive atmosphere in which to imbibe. Its stores are distinctive and sleek, yet comfortable. Though the sizes of the stores and their formats vary, most are modeled after the Italian coffee bars where regulars sit and drink espresso with their friends.

Starbucks stores tend to be located in high-traffic locations such as malls, busy street corners, and even grocery stores. They are well lighted and feature plenty of light cherry wood and artwork. The people who prepare the coffee are referred to as "baristas," Italian for bartender. Jazz or opera music plays softly in the background. The stores range from 200 to 4,000 square feet, with new units tending to range from 1,500 to 1,700 square feet. In 2003, the average cost of opening a new store (including equipment, inventory and leasehold improvements) is in the neighborhood of $350,000; a "flagship" store costs much more.

Building a Unique Culture

While Starbucks enforces almost fanatical standards about coffee quality and service, the policy at Starbucks toward employees is laid back and supportive. They are encouraged to think of themselves as partners in the business. Schultz believes that happy employees are the key to competitiveness and growth.

> We can't achieve our strategic objectives without a work force of people who are immersed in the same commitment as management. Our only sustainable advantage is the quality of our work force. We're building a national retail company by creating pride in—and stake in—the outcome of our labor.[9]

On a practical level, Starbucks promotes an empowered employee culture through generous benefits programs, an employee stock ownership plan, and thorough employee training. Each employee must have at least twenty-four hours of training. Classes cover everything from coffee history to a seven-hour workshop called "Brewing the Perfect Cup at Home." This workshop is one of five classes that all employees must complete during their first six weeks with the company. Reports *Fortune*:

> It's silly, soft-headed stuff, though basically, of course, it's true. Maybe some of it sinks in. Starbucks is a smashing success, thanks in large part to the people who come out of these therapy-like training programs. Annual barista turnover at the company is 60% compared with 140% for hourly workers in the fast-food business.[10]

Starbucks offers its benefits package to both part-time and full-time employees. The package includes medical, dental, vision, and short-term disability insurance, as well as paid vacation, paid holidays, mental health/chemical dependency benefits, an employee assistance program, a 401k savings plan, and a stock option plan. They also offer dependent coverage that includes same-sex partners.[11] Schultz believes that without these benefits, people do not feel financially or spiritually tied to their jobs. He argues that stock options and the complete benefits package increase employee loyalty and encourage attentive service to the customer.[12]

Employee turnover is also discouraged by Starbucks's stock option plan known as the Bean Stock Plan. Implemented in August 1991, the plan made Starbucks the only private company to offer stock options unilaterally to all employees.

Starbucks's concern for employee welfare extends beyond its retail outlets to coffee producers. The company's guidelines call for overseas suppliers to pay wages and benefits that "address the basic needs of workers and their families" and to allow child labor only when it does not interrupt required education.[13] This move has set a precedent for other importers of agricultural commodities.

---

[9] *Inc.*, January 1993.

[10] *Fortune*, December 9, 1996.

[11] The decision to offer benefits even to part-time employees (who represent roughly two-thirds of Starbucks's 10,000 employees) has gained a great deal of attention in the press. According to a Hewitt Associates L.L.C. survey of more than 500 employers, only 25 percent of employers offer medical coverage to employees working less than 20 hours a week. It was difficult to get insurers to sign Starbucks up since they did not understand why Starbucks would want to cover part-timers.

[12] *Inc.*, January, 1993.

[13] *Wall Street Journal*, October 23, 1995.

Leveraging the Brand

Multiple Channels of Distribution Besides its stand-alone stores, Starbucks has set up cafés and carts in hospitals, banks, office buildings, supermarkets, and shopping centers. Other distribution agreements have included office coffee suppliers, hotels, and airlines. Office coffee is a large segment of the coffee market. Associated Services (an office coffee supplier) provides Starbucks coffee exclusively to thousands of businesses around the United States. Starbucks has deals with airlines, such as an agreement with United Airlines to provide Starbucks coffee to United's nearly 75 million passengers a year. Starbucks, through a licensing agreement with Kraft Foods Inc., offers its coffee in grocery stores across the United States.

Brand Extensions In 1995, Starbucks launched a line of packaged and prepared teas in response to growing demand for teahouses and packaged tea. Tea is a highly profitable beverage for restaurants to sell, costing only 2 cents to 4 cents a cup to produce.[14] As its tea line became increasingly popular, in January 1999 it acquired Tazo, a Portland, Oregon, based tea company.

Starbucks coffee is also making its way onto grocery shelves via a carefully planned series of joint ventures.[15] An agreement with PepsiCo Inc. brought a bottled version of Starbucks Frappuccino (a cold, sweetened coffee drink) to store shelves in August 1996. In another fifty-fifty partnership, Dreyers' Grand Ice Cream Inc. distributes seven quart-products and two bar-products of Starbucks coffee ice cream.

Other partnerships by the company are designed to form new product associations with coffee. For instance, the company's music subsidiary, Hear Music, regularly releases CDs, some in collaboration with major record labels, that are then sold through Starbucks retail stores.

While Starbucks is the largest and best known of the coffeehouse chains and its presence is very apparent in metropolitan areas, the firm's estimates indicate that only a small percentage (about 7 percent) of the U.S. population has tried its products. Through distribution agreements and the new product partnerships, Starbucks hopes to capture more of the U.S. market.

International Expansion

For many years analysts have observed that the U.S. coffee-bar market may be reaching saturation. They point to market consolidation, as bigger players snap up some of the smaller coffee bar competitors.[16] Further, they note that Starbucks's store base is also maturing, leading to a slowdown in the growth of unit volume and firm profitability. In response, some argue, Starbucks has turned its attention to foreign markets for continued growth. For instance *Business Week* notes

> To duplicate the staggering returns of its first decade, Starbucks has no choice but to export its concept aggressively. Indeed, some analysts give Starbucks only two years at most before it saturates the U.S. market. The chain now [in August 2002] operates 1,200 international outlets, from Beijing to Bristol. That leaves plenty of room to grow. Indeed, about 400 of its planned 1,200 new stores this year will be built overseas, representing a 35% increase in its foreign base. Starbucks expects to double the number of its stores worldwide, to 10,000 in three years.[17]

However, of the predicted three or four stores that will open each day, the majority will continue to be in the United States.

Early Expansion

In 1995, the firm established a subsidiary called Starbucks Coffee International Inc. At that time, the subsidiary consisted of twelve managers located in Seattle. Today this subsidiary is led by Australian expatriate Peter Maslen and is staffed with about one hundred eighty experienced multinational and

---

[14]*Nations Restaurant News*, July 10, 1995.
[15]The Specialty Coffee Association of America notes that supermarkets account for over 60 percent of all coffee sold in America, followed by gourmet stores (14 percent), mass market (11 percent), mail order (8 percent), and other.

[16]The *Washington Post*, August 1, 1995.
[17]Planet Starbucks, *Business Week*, September 9, 2002, p. 102. However, Schultz firmly believes that Starbucks growth is far from saturation both in the United States and overseas: "We have less than 7% of the coffee-consuming opportunities in North America. People are still drinking bad coffee."

multilingual managers located in Seattle and three regional offices around the world. This group is responsible for all Starbucks business development outside North America, including developing new businesses, financing and planning stores, managing operations and logistics, merchandising, and training and developing Starbucks's international managers.

Starbucks's first non–North American store was opened in 1996 in Tokyo. In reflecting on this early step in internationalizing the chain, Schultz notes

> Two years prior to opening up in Japan, we hired this blue-chip consulting firm to guide us to succeed here. Basically, they said we would not succeed in Japan. There were a number of things they told us to change. [They said] we had to have smoking, but that was a non-starter for us. They also said no Japanese would ever lose face by drinking from a cup in the street. And third, they said that given the [high] rent, stores couldn't be larger than 500 square feet.... Well, our no smoking policy made us an oasis in Japan. As for our to-go business, you can't walk down a street in Tokyo today and not see someone holding a cup of Starbucks coffee. And our store size in Japan is identical to our store size in the U.S., about 1,200 to 1,500 square feet. It just shows the power of believing in what you do. And also that Starbucks is as relevant in Tokyo, Madrid, or Berlin as it is in Seattle.[18]

The Starbucks Way

According to *US News and World Report*:

> When venturing overseas, there is a Starbucks way. The company finds local business partners in most foreign markets.... It tests each country with a handful of stores in trendy districts, using experienced Starbucks managers. It sends local baristas to Seattle for 13 weeks of training. Then it starts opening stores by the dozen. Its coffee lineup doesn't vary, but Starbucks does adapt its food to local tastes. In Britain, it won an award for its mince pie. In Asia, Starbucks offers curry puffs and meat buns. The company also fits its interior

décor to the local architecture, especially in historic buildings. "We don't stamp these things out cookie-cutter style," says Peter Maslen, president of Starbucks Coffee International.[19]

Although Starbucks is committed to owning its North American stores, it has sought partners for much of its overseas expansion. As Kathy Lindemann, senior vice president of operations for Starbucks International, describes it:

> Our approach to international expansion is to focus on the *partnership first, country second*. We rely on the local connection to get everything up and working. The key is finding the right local partners to negotiate local regulations and other issues. We look for partners who share our values, culture, and goals about community development. We are primarily interested in partners who can guide us through the process of starting up in a foreign location. We look for firms with: (1) similar philosophy to ours in terms of shared values, corporate citizenship, and commitment to be in the business for the long haul, (2) multi-unit restaurant experience, (3) financial resources to expand the Starbucks concept rapidly to prevent imitators, (4) strong real-estate experience with knowledge about how to pick prime real estate locations, (5) knowledge of the retail market, and (6) the availability of the people to commit to our project.

In an international joint venture, it is the partner that chooses store sites. These are submitted for approval to Starbucks, but the partner does all the preparatory and selection work. Cydnie Horwat, vice president for international assets development systems and infrastructure, explains how a Starbucks market entry plan starts with brand building, which then facilitates rapid further expansion in a country:

> When first entering a market, we're looking for different things in the first one to three years than later on. During these early years, we're building our brand. Our stores are the biggest source of advertising, since we do not do a lot of separate advertising. So we have a higher investment in stores in the first three years. About 60–70% of stores opened in these first three years are our high brand-builders.

[18]Online Extra: Q&A with Starbucks' Howard Schultz, *Business Week*, September 9, 2002.

[19]*US World and News Report*, February 19, 2001.

Adds Horwat:

> First, we look for extremely visible sites in well-trafficked areas and focus on three major factors: demographics, branding potential, and financials. Second, we categorize sites on an A to D scale. "A" sites are "signature" sites that are qualitatively superior to all other sites within the trade area [an area within which Starbucks chooses to locate one store]. We rarely take a "C" or "D" store.[20] Third, we ask our international market business unit[21] (MBU) to send in the "site" submittal package with quantitative and qualitative measures, such as how the site meets Starbucks' established criteria and the partner's agreed-upon criteria. This package is reviewed by a number of functional units—operations, finance, and real estate—within the International Group. Fourth, we move into the design phase, which is done in Seattle using information provided by the partner. Next we negotiate the lease with landlord and initiate the construction when the appropriate permits are obtained. Finally, we turn over the store to operations. The whole process takes about 13–16 weeks from start to finish.

Establishing Starbucks as a Global Brand

Based on the success in Japan and other locations, Schultz's goal is for Starbucks to have a ubiquitous image as one of the most respected brands in the world. He notes

> Whenever we see the reception we're getting in markets in places such as China, the Philippines, Malaysia, the U.K., and most recently Spain and Germany, we recognize that the growth potential for the company [overseas] is very significant. We want to accelerate that growth, maintain our

leadership position, and, ultimately, become one of the most respected brands in the world.[22]

Since its early foray into the Japanese market, the pace of international expansion has picked up significantly. In 1998, Starbucks acquired Seattle Coffee Company in the United Kingdom, a chain with more than thirty-eight retail locations. That same year, it opened stores in Taiwan, Thailand, New Zealand, and Malaysia. In 1999, Starbucks opened in China (Beijing), Kuwait, South Korea, and Lebanon. In 2000, it entered another seven markets (China—Hong Kong and Shanghai, Dubai, Australia, Qatar, Saudi Arabia, and Bahrain). It added three markets in 2001 (Switzerland, Israel, and Austria). Last year, another nine markets were opened (Oman, Spain, Indonesia, Germany, Southern China—Macau and Shenzhen, Mexico, Puerto Rico, and Greece). Exhibit 5 highlights the growth of international stores, and Exhibit 6 provides the list of countries where Starbucks has a presence.

Schultz says that this expansion is only beginning and confidently predicts more to come:

> Ten years ago, we had 125 stores and 2000 employees. Today we have 62,000 people working in 30 countries outside of North America, serving approximately 22 million customers a week. Our core customer is coming in about 18 times a month. With the majority of adults around the world drinking two cups of coffee a day and with Starbucks having less than 7% share of total coffee consumption in the U.S. and less than 1% worldwide, these are the early days for the growth and development of the company. We've got a model that has been well tested from market to market.

Starbucks is well on its way to becoming a global brand. According to *Business Week*:

> The Starbucks name and image connect with millions of consumers around the globe. It was one of the fastest-growing brands in a *Business Week* survey of the top 100 global brands published August 5 [2002]. At a time when one corporate star after another has crashed to earth, brought down by revelations of earnings

[20]The difference between an "A" store and a "D" store can be substantial. A "D" store is expected to have about 50–60 percent lower sales. Starbucks classifies a store as "A" if the store location is the focal point of the area, has great visibility, has readily available parking, has excellent access to and from the site, cannot be out-positioned by competitors, and fits with Starbucks's desire to build a distinctive image.
[21]Starbucks's international businesses are typically joint ventures in which Starbucks holds various levels of equity (ranging from 5 percent to 100 percent). These ventures are referred to as market business units (MBUs). Regardless of the level of equity Starbucks holds, it supports all of its MBUs in an "ownership blind" manner by providing all MBUs with the same level of support.

[22]Online Extra: Q&A with Starbucks' Howard Schultz, *Business Week*, September 9, 2002.

EXHIBIT 5

Growth of International Stores 1996–2002

Source: Starbucks International Group.

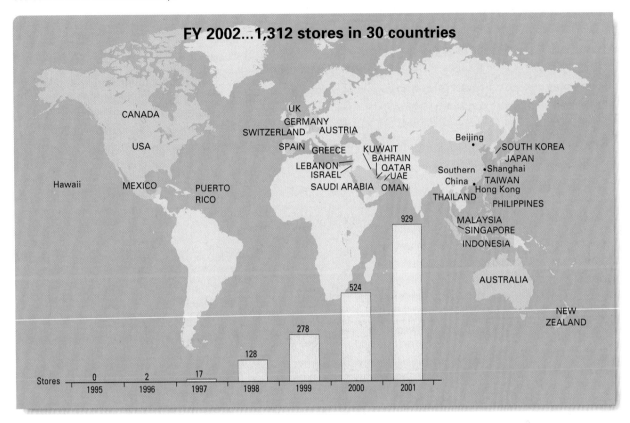

FY 2002...1,312 stores in 30 countries

Perils of Globalization

As Starbucks establishes a global presence, its growing ubiquity has not gone unnoticed by antiglobalization activists. A clear manifestation of this came in November 1999, as tens of thousands of protesters took to the streets of downtown Seattle when the World Trade Organization (WTO) held its third ministerial conference there. Although non-governmental organizations (NGOs) and activists had gathered to oppose the WTO, some activists deliberately targeted multinationals like Starbucks, Nike, and McDonald's.[25]

misstatements, executive greed, or worse, Starbucks hasn't faltered.[23]

But becoming a global company is not without risks. As *Business Week* points out:

> Global expansion poses huge risks for Starbucks. For one thing, it makes less money on each overseas store because most of them are operated with local partners. While that makes it easier to start up on foreign turf, it reduces the company's share of the profits to only 20% to 50%.[24]

In addition, the firm is becoming a target for antiglobalization activists around the world.

[25]The protesters claim that international organizations like the WTO and International Monetary Fund (IMF) are tools of multinational corporations. Since Seattle, violent protests have been the norm at events such as the annual meetings of the IMF and World Bank, G-8 summits, and the World Economic Forum.

[23] *Business Week*, "Planet Starbucks," September 9, 2002, p. 102
[24] Ibid.

EXHIBIT 6

Licensed Starbucks International Stores (as of September 2002)

Asia-Pacific		Europe/Middle East/Africa		Latin America	
Japan	397	United Arab Emirates	23	Hawaii	30
Taiwan	99	Saudi Arabia	22	Mexico	1
China	88	Kuwait	16	Puerto Rico	1
South Korea	53	Switzerland	12		
Philippines	49	Lebanon	11		
New Zealand	34	Israel	6		
Singapore	32	Austria	5		
Malaysia	26	Spain	5		
Indonesia	5	Germany	4		
		Qatar	3		
		Bahrain	2		
		Greece	2		
		Oman	2		
Total	783		113		32

Product sales to, and royalty and license fee revenues from, licensed international retail stores accounted for approximately 17 percent of specialty revenues in fiscal 2002. *These figures do not include company operated stores.*

Source: Starbucks 10-K report.

A small, but vocal, percentage of these protestors garnered international press coverage by committing acts of vandalism against carefully chosen targets. As a report in *Business Week* recalls

> Protesters flooded Seattle's streets, and among their targets was Starbucks, a symbol, to them, of free-market capitalism run amok, another multinational out to blanket the earth. Amid the crowds of protesters and riot police were black-masked anarchists who trashed the store, leaving its windows smashed and its tasteful green-and-white decor smelling of tear gas instead of espresso.[26]

Recalling this incident against his firm Schultz says: "It's hurtful. I think people are ill-informed. It's very difficult to protest against a can of Coke, a bottle of Pepsi, or a can of Folgers. Starbucks is both a ubiquitous brand and a place where you can go and break a window. You can't break a can of Coke."

Antiglobalization protesters target recognizable global brands because they are convenient symbols. The following excerpt from "The Ruckus Society's Action Planning Manual and Media Manual"[27] illustrates the close ties between global brands and the principles of direct action against them:

> First, [we] use direct action to reduce the issues to symbols. These symbols must be carefully chosen for their utility in illustrating a conflict: an oil company vs. an indigenous community, a government policy vs. the public interest. Then we work to place these symbols in the public eye, in order to identify the evildoer, detail the wrongdoing and, if possible, point to a more responsible option.

[26] *Business Week*, "Planet Starbucks," September 9, 2002.

[27] The Ruckus Society website, **http://ruckus.org/man/action_planning.html** (site visited 3/14/03).

The message that activists want to communicate focuses on the overseas activities of corporations. They accuse multinationals of paying less than a living wage to workers in the Third World, of engaging in labor and environmental practices that would be outlawed in their home countries, of driving local competitors out of business, and of furthering "cultural imperialism." As one Global Trade Watch field organizer describes it:

> The rules by which trade is governed need to have more to do with the interests of citizens than with the back pockets and cash wads of a couple corporate CEOs. And we want to make sure that there is a balance consideration. Obviously people are always going to be concerned with their profits—it's business, we understand that, we accept that. But we think that needs to be balanced with concern for the rights of workers, basic human rights, [and] protecting the environment.[28]

Critics further accuse international organizations such as the WTO, World Bank, and IMF of promoting corporate globalization by supporting trade liberalization, by promoting export-based economic development, and by facilitating foreign direct investment. According to an organization that bills itself as Mobilization for Global Justice:

> Most of the world's most impoverished countries have suffered under IMF/World Bank programs for two decades: they've seen debt levels rise, unemployment skyrocket, poverty increase, and environments devastated. Urged to export, they focus on cash crops like coffee instead of food for their own people, and allow foreign governments to build sweatshops—which also puts pressure on jobs in the US.[29]

When Starbucks opened its first store in Mexico in September 2002, it chose a site in the Sheraton Hotel on Reforma Boulevard in Mexico City. This was Starbucks's first store in Latin America and its first in an "origin country," that is, a coffee-producing country. An article on the Organic Consumers Association website describes Starbucks' Mexican flagship store:

> The new Starbucks on Reforma features soft lighting and an aromatic ambiance.... Behind the counter, well-groomed employees whip out the signature Frappuccinos and lattes. Indeed, the only jarring note is the 36 pesos ($3.60) the young woman at the register wants for a double latte, 10 times the price Indian farmers are getting for a pound of their product in Chiapas, Oaxaca, and other coffee-rich states of southern Mexico.... There is no starker contrast in the economics of coffee these days than between the cushy comforts and gourmet blends of the Starbucks "Experiencia" and the grim, daily existence of 360,000 mostly Indian coffee farmers who work small plots carved from the jungle mountains of southern Mexico.[30]

Multinational corporations and their supporters respond that the effects of—and solutions for—globalization are more complicated than the critics contend. They note that multinationals create jobs, pay better prices and wages than domestic firms, and conform to *local* labor and environmental regulations.

> The skeptics are right to be disturbed by sweatshops, child labour, bonded labour and the other gross abuses that go on in many poor countries (and in the darkest corners of rich ones, too). But what makes people vulnerable to these practices is poverty. . . . The more thoroughly these companies [multinationals] penetrate the markets of the third world, the faster they introduce their capital and working practices, the sooner poverty will retreat and the harder it will be for such abuses to persist.[31]

Moreover, multinationals argue, they have responded to the criticism of profit-driven behavior by developing corporate codes of conduct, corporate social responsibility programs, and partnerships with nongovernmental organizations.[32] They point out, however, that

[28]Interview with Alesha Daughtrey, Global Trade Watch field organizer, August 17, 2000; archived in the WTO History Project, University of Washington Center for Labor Studies, **http://depts.washington.edu/ wtohist/Interviews/Interviews.htm**.
[29]From the website of Mobilization for Global Justice, **http://sept .globalizethis.org** (site visited 3/14/03).
[30]John Ross, "The Unloving Cup," December 12, 2002, Organic Consumers Association website, **www.organicconsumers.org/starbucks**.
[31]"Grinding the Poor," *The Economist*, November 6, 1997.
[32]For example, Starbucks's *Commitment to Origins*™ is a four-part Corporate Social Responsibility Program that includes offering Fair Trade certified coffee, organic certified coffee, Farm Direct (single-origin coffees purchased directly from the farmer), and Conservation coffees (emphasizing shade-grown in partnership with the NGO Conservation International). See **www.starbucks.com/aboutus/ cto_coffees.asp**.

they are in a no-win situation vis-à-vis their critics, because they can always be criticized for not doing enough.

Starbucks has found that global concerns often get mixed up with and intertwined with local issues. Even the mere act of opening a Starbucks retail store in a neighborhood can result in local activism and community "push-back" against the Starbucks brand. For example, when Starbucks opened a store in Cambridge, Massachusetts, in 1998, picketers carrying signs that read "Don't Let Corporate Greed Destroy Our Neighborhood" greeted it. A lawyer who helps communities keep national chains out, says, "It's part of the growing tension in the world between the mass-market economy and people's desire to retain self-control and some local culture. . . . If you've got a beef with Starbucks, you've got a beef with capitalism."[33]

Starbucks has faced a variety of "community push back" situations around the world. Soon Beng Yeap, one of Starbucks's International brand reputation managers, notes, "This [community push-back] is a live issue and Starbucks manages each push-back incident case-by-case. In some markets [we] have gone in and in some [we] have pulled out." He cites two recent examples, one in London, where Starbucks decided to withdraw its efforts to open a store after local activists actively campaigned against the firm, and the other in Beijing, where the firm opened a store in an historic district, and, following subsequent and significant adverse comment reported in local and international media, decided to stay put.

Primrose Hill and Starbucks's Decision to Withdraw

In 2002, Starbucks made plans to open a store in Primrose Hill, a London suburb. Located in North West London, Primrose Hill is a well-known historical and picturesque area comprised of a public park, a shopping "village" area, and attractive Victorian residential housing. Residents of Primrose Hill—many of whom are writers, photographers, actors, and musicians—take great pride in the area and are protective of their local environment, acting to ensure that no chain stores operate in the area.[34]

In early 2002, Starbucks selected Primrose Hill as a potential site for a store, and in April 2002 submitted an application to the local council. When this information was published in the local papers, it received considerable negative feedback from the residents, in particular from the Primrose Hill Conservation Area Advisory Committee. This committee claimed that litter, noise, and disruption from deliveries to a Starbucks store in Primrose Hill would ruin the village ambience and contribute to the "homogenization of the high street." The opposition surprised Starbucks because Primrose Hill residents, associations (including the Primrose Hill Conservation Area Advisory Committee), and businesses had been contacted as part of the consultation period for the potential site. Although the objections to Starbucks's entry focused on local planning issues, there was an antiglobalization element as well. One critic was quoted as saying that Starbucks was "renowned for not paying proper money to coffee growers."[35]

In response to the critics, Starbucks offered to arrange meetings between the planning committee, local councilors, and its representatives to discuss the issue and hear their concerns. Despite Starbucks's efforts, no meeting offers were accepted, and minimal responses were received.

In the meantime, the Primrose Hill Conservation Area Advisory Committee began to campaign strongly against Starbucks. They collected more than one thousand three hundred letters of objection, which they then presented to the local council. Many celebrities, such as the actor Jude Law, National Theater Director Nicholas Hytner, broadcaster Joan Bakewell, singer Neneh Cherry, author Jeanette Winterson, and artist Patrick Caufield, lent their support by opposing the Starbucks application. Media coverage that was initially local became national when celebrities became involved. According to Horwat:

---

[33]Edward McMahon, quoted in "Brewing a Tempest in a Coffee Cup," *Christian Science Monitor*, February 25, 1998.

[34]This desire for protection dates back to 1841 when the residents actively campaigned against the area being opened up to the general public. Such actions discouraged further building developments, thus enabling the residents to retain the look and feel of their neighborhood.

[35]From "Stars v Starbucks: Not a Bean for the Coffee Shop Giant," *Independent on Sunday* (London), June 2, 2002.

Primrose Hill was an "A" site. A very affluent neighborhood, little or no competition and we knew it would be a winner. Everyone [at Starbucks International] loved it. The real estate people, the finance people and others signed off on the deal. Opposition came only when city council was about to approve [our application]. The opposition claimed that our entry would raise rents in the community. So we went back to city council to argue our case. But activists brought in movie stars and got local and national media attention.

In early June 2002, when it was apparent that Starbucks was not welcome in Primrose Hill, the company decided against opening the store. Reflecting on their decision to withdraw, Horwat explained

We care about the views of the communities of which we are a part. We try to have our stores be part of a community. We had hoped to make a positive contribution for people to get together in Primrose Hill. If the community does not welcome us, it's not someplace we want to be.

Adds Soon Beng Yeap:

You have to understand the bigger picture in the UK to appreciate what was going on locally at that time—Starbucks was seen as an American chain coming into the British market and the British media tend to be very cynical. The specialty coffee market was becoming crowded and extremely competitive with several other chains such as Café Nero, Coffee Republic and Costa Coffee making a strong push for market share. The Starbucks team reviewed all the factors involved as well as listened carefully to the community concerns. At the end of the day, we decided to withdraw our application.

Beijing and Starbucks's Decision to Stay

Starbucks opened its first outlet in Beijing in January 1999 and has over one hundred stores in the country today. However, Starbucks touched a nationalist nerve in 2000 when it opened a small coffee shop in Beijing's Forbidden City.[36] In highlighting this particular store, the *New York Times* noted

If ever there was an emblem of the extremes to which globalization has reached, this is it: mass-market American coffee culture in China's most hallowed historic place. Even a McDonald's in the Kremlin would not come as close. Starbucks opened its Forbidden City shop a month ago [September 2000] with a signature menu board advertising the usual Americano and decaf latte coffee and a glass display case filled with fresh glazed donuts, cinnamon rings and banana walnut muffins.

Starbucks, for its part, had taken extraordinary care to ensure that its presence was unobtrusive. To avoid ruining the atmosphere of the Forbidden City, the signs and brand images were placed inside for this store. This small store (barely a closet according to some reports) had only two small tables and few chairs. It was located on the edge of the Forbidden City, among fifty other retailers, including some selling souvenirs and trinkets. Despite such a low-key presence, this store ignited controversy. Dozens of Chinese newspapers reported on reactions to the shop. According to one such report in the *People's Daily*:

The reason for the uproar is due to the café's location: the Forbidden City, the world's largest imperial palace.... First constructed in 1406, the Forbidden City is China's best-preserved ancient architecture encircled by a rampart of three kilometers. The cafe, named Starbucks, is situated in the southeastern corner of the Hall of Preserving Harmony (Baohedian), one of the three most impressive buildings on the palace ground. The hall used to be the venue to hold feasts by emperors and nobles of ethnic groups on New Year's Eve of China's lunar calendar.... Debates over the mini-cafe took place first on the web. A survey by Sina.com showed that over 70 percent of nearly 60,000 people surveyed were opposed to the cafe's entry into the Forbidden City, the main reason being the damaging effects to Chinese cultural heritage and its atmosphere.[37]

The administrators of the Forbidden Palace and other government officials took note of the controversy but were supportive of Starbucks. Chen, a spokesperson for the Forbidden City Museum, maintained that

---

[36] *The Economist*, "Coffee With Your Tea?" October 4, 2001.

[37] "Starbucks Cafe in Forbidden City Under Fire," *People's Daily*, November 24, 2000.

allowing Starbucks into the Forbidden City was part of their efforts to improve services in the area. Moreover, Chen added, "The reaction has been very intense. Some people say this is a gem of Chinese culture and that foreign brands should not be allowed in.... We can't give up eating for the fear of choking."[38]

According to Horwat:

> The Forbidden City location was a "C" site at best. But definitely not a "D" site, because there was still the benefit of brand presence. But the government said, "We think you should come in," and it was difficult to say no. There was no local community, only tourists.

Following the flurry of articles in the Chinese media, CNN began to run news clips of this story in the United States. Watching this unfold in the U.S. media, some senior managers at Starbucks became alarmed at the negative publicity. According to Soon Beng Yeap:

> The immediate reaction was to "close the store!" due to the relentless negative coverage generated by the international media. After serious discussion among the senior executives, we felt as guests in a foreign country, we should be respectful of our hosts—the Forbidden City officials—who invited us to be there in the first place. We decided to not pull out because it was the international media that stirred up the whole controversy. Unlike the Primrose Hill case, there was no real local community "push-back." It was all media-driven. A few reporters got hold of the story and ran with it, all citing the same survey by Sina.com. We were very disappointed by the negative media coverage, which created a false sense of "cultural imperialism" about our intentions in opening the store, especially when we worked very hard to be culturally sensitive and listen to the local community.

The controversy has since died down, as a recent report (February 2003) in *The Straits Times* (Singapore) indicates: "[Today] if anything, the tourists were more upset than the Beijing residents about the presence of Starbucks in the Forbidden City, complaining that it was out of place in a historical site.... Asked what were the hottest issues of the day for or-

dinary citizens, taxi driver Liu Zhiming said: 'Cars, apartments and making money. What else?'"[39]

Entering Rio de Janeiro, Brazil

Peter Maslen, president of Starbucks International, hurriedly convened a meeting of his key executives in Starbucks International, including Julio Gutierrez, his president for Latin America. Starbucks's entry into Brazil was in jeopardy, because certain activists opposing Starbucks's presence in the country were gaining momentum.

Brazil is the largest coffee-producing country in the world, and this was Starbucks's second foray into Latin America (after Mexico). The company chose not to seek a joint venture partner to enter Brazil. Since many copycat chains had sprung up in Rio de Janeiro, some imitating Starbucks to the last detail, Peter felt that his team had to move quickly before any particular group established itself as the premier chain. After several years of work by Julio's Latin America team, no suitable joint venture partner had been identified, and Peter was considering establishing a 100 percent Starbucks-owned MBU (as it had already done in the United Kingdom, Australia, and Thailand).

The business development group, with Julio's team, had picked a site in the Ipanema area of Rio de Janeiro. They proposed that a flagship store be opened on this neighborhood's main commercial street—Rua Visconde de Pirajá (see Figure 1). Many of Rio's most traditional boutiques started in Ipanema, later to be exported to the malls and other parts of town. Many world-renowned brands such as Cartier, Louis Vuitton, and Polo Ralph Lauren had stores on the Rua Visconde de Pirajá. It is often said that news in Ipanema makes headlines all over Brazil.

Starbucks had also chosen other sites, four to be specific, where the company could open stores immediately following the opening of the flagship Ipanema store. One of these stores was to be located in the posh neighborhood of Barra de Tijuca; another was slated for Leblon, and two others for shopping malls located in affluent residential neighborhoods in the city. The real estate group was ready to sign the lease with the agents of the Ipanema property owner,

---

[38]Quoted in "Globalization Puts a Starbucks into the Forbidden City in Beijing," *New York Times*, November 25, 2000.

[39]"Capitalism Runs Amok," *The Straits Times*, February 16, 2003.

FIGURE 1

Map of the Ipanema Area, Rio de Janeiro, Brazil

Source: **www.ipanema.com**

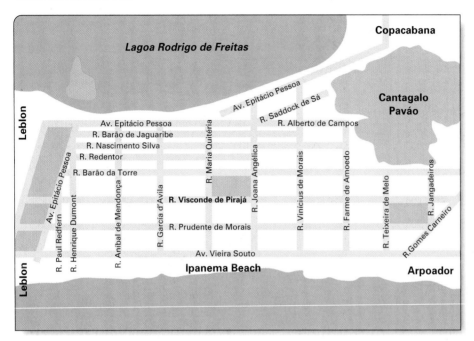

but was awaiting a formal response from the city council members.

The business development group, let by Troy Alstead, senior vice president of finance and business development at Starbucks International, was confident that the Ipanema location was an "A" category site. "The demographics of this area are just right for a flagship store. They are affluent, young and love American brands." The business development group's financial projections indicated that the Ipanema Starbucks store would be profitable in a short time, and Alstead believed that this was a conservative figure. Further, he pointed out:

> Based on the company's experiences of opening flagship stores in similar, high traffic posh neighborhoods in other cites around the world—our store in Ginza, Japan comes to mind—we believe the Ipanema store would be viable for Starbucks. We estimate meeting store level ROI targets in aggregate for the first five stores within two years.

Exhibit 7 provides the finance group's forecast for the Ipanema and the other four stores in Brazil for the first five years of operations.

But Peter had some concerns. He was troubled by reports of rising levels of violence and street crime in Rio and São Paulo. In response to this growing violence, some of the most fashionable retailers were relocating themselves in shopping malls. He also questioned whether the timing for Starbucks was off. Current world events had generated anti-American feeling in many countries.

Following the standard practice, Starbucks had been working with the local chamber of commerce since January 2003, and with the local city council for the required permits. The members of the city council and local chamber of commerce were positive about granting Starbucks permission to begin construction. While the formal voting had yet to be undertaken, it looked certain that, barring anything unusual, permission would be granted.

But nongovernmental organizations like the Organic Consumers Association and Global Exchange were mobilizing faster than expected to oppose Starbucks's entry into Brazil. They found out about Starbucks's intent to enter Brazil when the Ipanema district chamber of commerce newsletter proudly

EXHIBIT 7

Financial Analysis for the First 5 Brazilian Stores

Projected P&L for Ipanema Store (US $)					
	Year 1	Year 2	Year 3	Year 4	Year 5
Net Sales (1)	$1,000,000	$1,100,000	$1,210,000	1,270,500	1,334,025
Cost of Goods Sold (2)	$350,000	$330,000	$326,700	$343,035	$360,187
Gross Profit	$650,000	$770,000	$883,300	$927,465	$973,838
Staff Costs	$200,000	$225,000	$250,000	250,000	250,000
Marketing (3)	$75,000	$50,000	$50,000	50,000	50,000
Other Costs	$75,000	$100,000	$125,000	125,000	125,000
Occupancy Costs	$175,000	$175,000	$175,000	175,000	175,000
Total Costs	$525,000	$550,000	$600,000	$600,000	$600,000
Operating Cash Flow	$125,000	$220,000	$283,300	$327,465	$373,838
Depreciation (4)	$54,200	$54,200	$54,200	$54,200	$54,200
Store Pretax Profit	$70,800	$165,800	$229,100	$273,265	$319,638
Construction Costs (5)	$400,000				
Key Money (6)	$1,000,000				

Projected P&L for a "Typical" Store in Locations Outside the Ipanema Area (US $)*					
	Year 1	Year 2	Year 3	Year 4	Year 5
Net Sales (1)	$625,000	$650,000	$700,000	$735,000	$771,750
Cost of Goods Sold (2)	$218,750	$195,000	$189,000	$198,450	$208,373
Gross Profit	$406,250	$455,000	$511,000	$536,550	$563,378
Staff Costs	$100,000	$115,000	$135,000	$135,000	$135,000
Marketing (3)	$45,000	$30,000	$30,000	$30,000	$30,000
Other Costs	$60,000	$75,000	$75,000	$75,000	$75,000
Occupancy Costs	$70,000	$70,000	$70,000	$70,000	$70,000
Operating Cash Flow	$131,250	$165,000	$201,000	$226,550	$253,378
Depreciation (4)	$25,000	$25,000	$25,000	$25,000	$25,000
Store Pretax Profit	$106,250	$140,000	$176,000	$201,550	$228,378
Construction Costs (5)	$215,000				
Key Money (6)	$400,000				

*Starbucks intends to open four such stores in Rio, in addition to the one in Ipanema.

Notes:
(1) Net sales are projected to grow at 10 percent for years 1 and 2, and at 5 percent thereafter.
(2) Due to increases in efficiency, the cost of goods sold are estimated at 35 percent for year 1, 30 percent for year 2, and 27 percent thereafter.
(3) Marketing costs are higher for year 1.
(4) Straight-line ten-year depreciation for construction and equipment costs.
(5) These represent initial design and construction costs.
(6) Monies paid to the landlord to secure the site.

announced "We are extremely pleased to welcome Starbucks into the fashionable district of Ipanema. By opening a store in our neighborhood, they will join other global brands and help enhance further our district's image as *the* place to be in Rio."

The NGOs were recruiting local activists and had informed Starbucks that they would oppose its entry into Brazil by petitioning the local council to reject its application. They also threatened to start picketing in front of the store once construction was initiated. The "brand" group at Starbucks was concerned about the turn of events. Soon Beng elaborated:

> People in Latin America know the brand because of their proximity to the US. Potential partners are always contacting us about coming in. Before we go into a place like Brazil, what is the due diligence we have to do? It's an origin country for us [i.e., coffee producing country]. It's a very vocal place, and there is a love-hate relationship with the United States. Finance people always want to say yes to a store when the numbers look good. Today some in Starbucks, at least in our group, say that maintaining and protecting our strong "brand" reputation is equally important. Others counter: if our brand is strong then why worry about it? This is a discussion we have here every day in the company. While the "push-back" is not totally unexpected, it is hard to gauge to the severity of the situation and its likely impact on our brand.

Peter asked Troy's business development group to work with Julio's Latin American team to estimate how the picketing in front of the store might impact the financial projections his group had prepared. Their answer:

> Our financial estimates for the Ipanema store are based on comparables from other flagship stores in locations similar to Rio in other parts of the world. Our financial models are sensitive to the demographics of the area. We project that demand could fall from 5 to 25%, because of people picketing in front of the store. We acknowledge it is much harder to guess what the impact on our entire system in Brazil might be as we open new stores. It all depends upon the type of media coverage the activists are able to muster and the issues the media choose to highlight.

Volunteered Soon Beng:

> The tide of public opinion is unpredictable. We review each "push–back" incident the best we can, and we have a reasonable track record of predicting outcomes. But, every time we walk into a potential site somewhere in the world, we potentially face this ['push-back']. It would be great to have a foolproof tool or system to help us evaluate these sorts of issues and make the appropriate decisions.

Peter had to leave Seattle to attend an important meeting in Europe the following day. He called together his key managers and said

> Look, we've experienced a variety of "push-backs" and protests before. What lessons have we learned? We've been deciding whether to go into sites or pull out on a case-by-case basis. If we're going to grow to 25,000 stores, we cannot keep taking an ad-hoc approach. We need a systematic method to respond to push-back—to decide whether we stay with a site or pull out. I want you to come up with a way to help me decide whether to go into Rio at all. And it's got to be a system or decision process that would work equally well in London or Beijing or anyplace else that we want to open. Let's meet again when I get back to town in a couple days.

The managers of Starbucks International had their work cut out for them. But they looked forward to tackling the issues raised by Peter.

APPENDIX A

Starbucks Timeline and History

1971

Starbucks opens its first location in Seattle's Pike Place Market.

1982

Howard Schultz joins Starbucks as director of retail operations and marketing. Starbucks begins providing coffee to fine restaurants and espresso bars.

1983

Schultz travels to Italy, where he's impressed with the popularity of espresso bars in Milan. He sees the potential in Seattle to develop a similar coffee bar culture.

1984

Schultz convinces the founders of Starbucks to test the coffee bar concept in a new location in downtown Seattle. This successful experiment is the genesis for a company that Schultz founds in 1985.

1985

Schultz founds Il Giornale, offering brewed coffee and espresso beverages made from Starbucks coffee beans.

1987

With the backing of local investors, Il Giornale acquires Starbucks assets and changes its name to Starbucks Corporation.

Opens in Chicago and Vancouver, B.C.

Starbucks location total = 17

1988

Starbucks introduces mail order catalog with service to all fifty states.

Starbucks location total = 33

1989

Opens in Portland, Oregon.

Starbucks location total = 55

1990

Starbucks expands headquarters in Seattle and builds a new roasting point.

Starbucks location total = 84

1991

Establishes a relationship with CARE, the international relief and development organization, and introduces the CARE coffee sampler.

Becomes the first U.S. privately owned company to offer a stock option program that includes part-time employees.

Opens first licensed airport location with HMS Host at Sea-Tac International Airport.

Opens in Los Angeles.

Starbucks location total = 116

1992

Completes initial public offering with Common Stock being traded on the Nasdaq National Market under the trading symbol "SBUX."

Opens in San Francisco; San Diego; Orange County, California; and Denver.

Starbucks location total = 165

1993

Begins Barnes & Noble, Inc. relationship.

Opens in Washington, D.C.

Starbucks location total = 272

1994

Awarded ITT/Sheraton (now Starwood Hotel) account.

Opens in Minneapolis; Boston; New York; Atlanta; Dallas; and Houston.

Starbucks location total = 425

1995

Based on an extremely popular in-house music program, Starbucks begins selling compact discs.

Awarded United Airlines account.

Begins serving Frappuccino® blended beverages, a line of low-fat, creamy, iced coffee beverages.

Forms alliance with Canadian bookstore Chapters Inc.

Starbucks Coffee International forms joint venture with SAZABY Inc., to develop Starbucks coffeehouses in Japan.

Opens in Philadelphia; Pittsburgh; Las Vegas; Cincinnati; Baltimore; San Antonio; and Austin, Texas.

Starbucks location total = 676

1996

Starbucks Coffee International opens locations in Japan, Hawaii, and Singapore.

Awarded Westin (now Starwood Hotel) account.

Starbucks and Dreyer's Grand Ice Cream, Inc. introduce Starbucks® Ice Cream and Starbucks Ice Cream bars. Starbucks Ice Cream quickly becomes the number one brand of coffee ice cream in the United States.

North American Coffee Partnership (Starbucks and Pepsi-Cola Company business venture) begins selling a bottled version of Starbucks Frappuccino® blended beverage.

Opens in Rhode Island; Idaho; North Carolina; Arizona; Utah; and Ontario, Canada.

Starbucks location total = 1,015

1997

Starbucks Coffee International opens locations in the Philippines.

Awarded Canadian Airlines account.

Forms alliance with eight companies to enable the gift of more than 320,000 new books for children through the All Books for Children first annual book drive.

Establishes the Starbucks Foundation, benefiting local literacy programs in communities where Starbucks has coffeehouses.

Opens in Florida, Michigan, and Wisconsin.

Starbucks location total = 1,412

1998

Starbucks Coffee International opens locations in Taiwan, Thailand, New Zealand, and Malaysia.

Introduces Tiazzi® blended juice tea, a refreshing mixture of tea, fruit juice, and ice.

Acquires Seattle Coffee Company in the United Kingdom with more than sixty retail locations.

Acquires Pasqua Inc., a San Francisco–based coffee retailer.

Forms Urban Coffee Opportunities, a joint venture with Earvin "Magic" Johnson's Johnson Development Corp., to develop Starbucks Coffee locations in underserved, urban neighborhoods throughout the United States.

Signs a licensing agreement with Kraft Foods Inc. to extend the Starbucks brand into grocery channels across the United States.

Launches Starbucks.com.

Opens two new coffeehouse concepts, Cafe Starbucks in Seattle and Circadia® Coffee House in San Francisco.

Opens in New Orleans; St. Louis; Kansas City, Missouri; and Portland, Maine.

Starbucks location total = 1,886

1999

Starbucks Coffee International opens locations in China, Kuwait, Korea, and Lebanon.

Acquires Tazo®, a Portland, Oregon, based tea company.

Partners with Conservation International to promote environmentally sound methods of growing coffee.

Introduces Shade Grown Mexico Coffee.

Acquires Hear Music, a San Francisco–based music company.

Enters agreement with Albertson's, Inc. to open more than one hundred Starbucks locations in their supermarkets in the year 2000.

Opens in Memphis and Nashville, Tennessee; and Saskatchewan, Canada.

Starbucks location total = 2,135

2000

Enters into licensing agreement with TransFair USA to market and sell Fair Trade Certified^{SM} coffee.

Introduces a Commitment to Origin™ coffee category that includes shade grown, organic, and Fair Trade Certified selections.

Expands contribution to Conservation International to establish conservation efforts in five new sites.

Enters agreement with Host Marriott International to open locations in select properties. Starbucks Coffee International opens in Dubai, Hong Kong, Shanghai, Qatar, Bahrain, Saudi Arabia, and Australia.

Starbucks location total = 3,501

2001

Introduces coffee sourcing guidelines developed in partnership with the Center for Environmental Leadership in Business, a division of Conservation International.

Commits to the purchase of 1 million pounds of Fair Trade Certified^{SM} coffee.

Offers $1 million in financial support to coffee farmers through Calvert Community Investments.

Begins to offer high-speed wireless Internet access in stores.

The Starbucks Foundation awards more than 450 grants totaling $4.2 million to literacy, schools, and community-based organizations across North America.

Begins offering the Starbucks Card, a stored value card for customers to use and reload.

Enters agreement with Hyatt Hotels Corp.

Starbucks Coffee Japan introduces a stock option program for eligible full- and part-time partners and successfully implements IPO.

Starbucks and international business partners seed Starbucks Cares Fund with $1.2 million contribution to benefit September 11th Fund. Customers and partners contribute more than $1.4 million to Starbucks Cares.

Starbucks opens 300th location in Japan and celebrates fifth year of business in Japan.

Starbucks Coffee International opens in Switzerland, Israel, and Austria.

Starbucks location total = 4,709

2002

Signs memorandum of understanding with Fair Trade Labelling Organizations International (FLO) that enables the company to enter into licensing agreements with national Fair Trade organizations to sell Fair Trade certified coffee in the countries where Starbucks does business.

Publishes its first Corporate Social Responsibility Annual Report.

Celebrates ten-year anniversary of Starbucks IPO.

Introduces Starbucks DoubleShot™ to the ready-to-drink coffee category.

Signs licensing agreement with TransFair Canada to bring Fair Trade Certified℠ coffee to more than 270 retail locations in Canada.

Starbucks Coffee International opens in Oman, Indonesia, Germany, and Spain.

Current location total = 5,688

Case 17

Kentucky Fried Chicken and the Global Fast-Food Industry

This case was prepared by Jeffrey A. Krug, Appalachian State University.

Kentucky Fried Chicken Corporation (KFC) was the world's largest chicken restaurant chain and third largest fast-food chain in 2004. It held more than 51 percent of the U.S. market in terms of sales and operated more than 12,200 restaurants in 99 countries. KFC was one of the first fast-food chains to go international in the late 1950s and is one of the world's most recognizable brands. KFC's early international strategy was to grow its company and franchise restaurant base throughout the world. By early 2004, however, KFC had refocused its international strategy on several high growth markets that included China, Canada, the United Kingdom, Australia, South Africa, Malaysia, Thailand, Mexico, Korea, and Indonesia. KFC planned to base much of its growth in these markets on company-owned restaurants, which gave KFC greater control over product quality, service, and restaurant cleanliness. In other international markets, KFC planned to grow primarily through franchises, which were operated by local business people who understood the local market better than KFC. Franchises

enabled KFC to more rapidly expand into smaller countries that could only support a small number of restaurants. KFC planned to more aggressively expand its company-owned restaurants into other major international markets in Europe and Latin America in the future. Latin America was an appealing area for investment because of the size of its markets and geographic proximity to the United States. Mexico was of particular interest because of the North American Free Trade Agreement (NAFTA), a free trade zone between Canada, the United States, and Mexico that went into effect in 1994. McDonald's, Burger King, and Wendy's, however, were rapidly expanding into other countries in Latin America such as Argentina, Chile, Brazil, and Venezuela. KFC's task in Latin America was to develop an effective strategy for further penetrating the Latin American market.

Company History

Fast-food franchising was still in its infancy in 1952 when Harland Sanders began his travels across the United States to speak with prospective franchisees about his "Colonel Sanders Recipe Kentucky Fried Chicken." By 1960, "Colonel" Sanders had granted KFC franchises to more than two hundred take-home retail outlets and restaurants across the United States. He had also established a number of franchises in Canada. By 1963, the number of KFC franchises had risen to more than three hundred and revenues topped $500 million. The Colonel celebrated his seventy-fourth birthday the following year and was eager to lessen the load of running the day-to-day operations of his business. He sold his business to two Louisville businessmen—Jack Massey and John Young Brown Jr.—for $2 million. The Colonel stayed on as a public relations man and goodwill ambassador for the company. During the next five years, Massey and Brown concentrated on growing KFC's franchise system across the United States. In 1966, they took KFC public, and the company was listed on the New York Stock Exchange. By the late 1960s, a strong foothold had been established in the United States. Massey and Brown then turned their attention to international markets. In 1969, a joint venture was signed with Mitsuoishi Shoji Kaisha, Ltd. in Japan, and the rights to operate franchises in England were acquired. Subsidiaries were later established in Hong Kong, South Africa, Australia, New Zealand, and Mexico. By 1971, KFC had established 2,450 franchises and 600 company-owned restaurants in 48 countries.

Heublein, Inc

In 1971, KFC entered into negotiations with Heublein, Inc. to discuss a possible merger. The decision to pursue a merger was partially driven by Brown's desire to pursue other interests that included a political career (Brown was elected governor of Kentucky in 1977). Several months later, Heublein acquired KFC. Heublein was in the business of producing vodka, mixed cocktails, dry gin, cordials, beer, and other alcoholic beverages. It had little experience, however, in the restaurant business. Conflicts quickly erupted between Colonel Sanders and Heublein management. In particular, Colonel Sanders was distraught over poor quality control and restaurant cleanliness. By 1977, new restaurant openings had slowed to only twenty a year. Few restaurants were being remodeled, and service quality had declined. To combat these problems, Heublein sent in a new management team to redirect KFC's strategy. A "back-to-the-basics" strategy was implemented, and new restaurant construction was halted until existing restaurants could be upgraded and operating problems eliminated. A program for remodeling existing restaurants was implemented, an emphasis was placed on cleanliness and service, marginal products were eliminated, and product consistency was reestablished. This strategy enabled KFC to gain better control of

its operations, and it was soon again aggressively building new restaurants.

R.J. Reynolds Industries, Inc.

In 1982, R.J. Reynolds Industries, Inc. (RJR) acquired Heublein and merged it into a wholly owned subsidiary. The acquisition of Heublein was part of RJR's corporate strategy of diversifying into unrelated businesses such as energy, transportation, food, and restaurants to reduce its dependence on the tobacco industry. Tobacco had driven RJR's sales since its founding in North Carolina in 1875. Sales of cigarettes and tobacco products, however, while profitable, were declining as consumption continued to fall in the United States. Reduced consumption was largely the result of increased awareness among Americans of the negative health consequences of smoking.

RJR, however, had a little more experience in the restaurant business than did Heublein when it acquired KFC eleven years earlier. In contrast to Heublein, which tried to actively manage KFC using its own managers, RJR allowed KFC to operate autonomously. RJR believed that KFC's executives were better qualified to operate the business than its own managers; therefore, KFC's top management team was left largely intact. In doing so, RJR avoided many of the operating problems that plagued Heublein during its ownership of KFC. In 1985, RJR acquired Nabisco Corporation for $4.9 billion. The acquisition of Nabisco was an attempt to redefine RJR as a world leader in the consumer foods industry. Nabisco sold a variety of well-known food products such as Oreo cookies, Ritz crackers, Planters peanuts, Lifesavers, and Milk-Bone dog biscuits. RJR subsequently divested many of its nonconsumer food businesses. It sold KFC to PepsiCo, Inc. one year later.

PepsiCo, Inc.

PepsiCo, Inc. was formed in 1965 with the merger of the Pepsi-Cola Co. and Frito-Lay Inc. The merger created one of the largest consumer products companies in the United States. Pepsi-Cola's traditional business was the sale of soft drink concentrates to licensed independent and company-owned bottlers that manufactured, sold, and distributed Pepsi-Cola soft drinks. Pepsi-Cola's best known trademarks were Pepsi-Cola, Diet Pepsi, and Mountain Dew. Frito-Lay manufactured and sold a variety of leading snack foods such as Lay's Potato Chips, Doritos Tortilla Chips, Tostitos Tortilla Chips, and Ruffles Potato Chips.

PepsiCo believed the restaurant business complemented its consumer product orientation. The marketing of fast-food followed many of the same patterns as soft drinks and snack foods. Pepsi-Cola and Lay's Potato Chips, for example, could be marketed in the same television and radio segments, which provided higher returns for each advertising dollar. Restaurant chains also provided an additional outlet for the sale of Pepsi soft drinks. PepsiCo believed it could take advantage of numerous synergies by operating the three businesses under the same corporate umbrella. PepsiCo also believed that its management skills could be transferred among the three businesses. This practice was compatible with PepsiCo's policy of frequently moving managers among its business units as a means of developing future executives. PepsiCo's acquisition of KFC in 1986 followed earlier acquisitions of Pizza Hut and Taco Bell. The three restaurant chains were the market leaders in the chicken, pizza, and Mexican categories.

Following the acquisition of KFC, PepsiCo initiated sweeping changes. It announced that the franchise contract would be changed to give PepsiCo greater control over KFC franchisees and to make it easier to close poorly performing restaurants. Staff at KFC was reduced to cut costs, and many KFC managers were replaced with PepsiCo managers. Soon after the acquisition, KFC's new personnel manager, who had just relocated from PepsiCo's New York headquarters, was overheard in the KFC cafeteria saying, "There will be no more home grown tomatoes in this organization." Rumors spread quickly among KFC employees about their opportunities for advancement within KFC and PepsiCo. Harsh comments by PepsiCo managers about KFC, its people, and its traditions; several restructurings that led to layoffs throughout KFC; the replacement of KFC managers with PepsiCo managers; and conflicts between KFC and PepsiCo's corporate cultures created a morale problem within KFC. KFC's culture was built largely on Colonel Sanders' laid-back approach to management. Employees enjoyed good job security and stability. A strong loyalty had been created over the years as a result of the Colonel's efforts to provide for his employees' benefits, pension, and other nonincome needs. In addition, the Southern environment in Louisville resulted in a friendly, relaxed atmosphere at KFC's corporate offices.

PepsiCo's culture, in contrast, was characterized by a strong emphasis on performance. Top performers expected to move up through the ranks quickly. PepsiCo used its KFC, Pizza Hut, Taco Bell, Frito Lay, and Pepsi-Cola divisions as training grounds for its executives, rotating its best managers through the five divisions on average every two years. This practice created pressure on managers to demonstrate their management skills within short periods to maximize their potential for promotion. This practice reinforced feelings among KFC managers that they had few opportunities for advancement within the new company. One PepsiCo manager commented, "You may have performed well last year, but if you don't perform well this year, you're gone, and there are 100 ambitious guys with Ivy League MBAs at PepsiCo's headquarters in New York who would love to have your job." An unwanted effect of this performance driven culture was that employee loyalty was lost, and turnover was higher than in other companies.

Kyle Craig, president of KFC's U.S. operations, commented on PepsiCo's relationship with KFC:

> The KFC culture is an interesting one because it was dominated by a lot of KFC folks, many who have been around since the days of the Colonel. Many of those people were very intimidated by the PepsiCo culture, which is a very high performance, high accountability, highly driven culture. People were concerned about whether they would succeed in the new culture. Like many companies, we have had a couple of downsizings which further made people nervous. Today, there are fewer old KFC people around and I think to some degree people have seen that the PepsiCo culture can drive some pretty positive results. I also think the PepsiCo people who have worked with KFC have modified their cultural values somewhat and they can see that there were a lot of benefits in the old KFC culture.

> PepsiCo pushes their companies to perform strongly, but whenever there is a slip in performance, it increases the culture gap between PepsiCo and KFC. I have been involved in two downsizings over which I have been the chief architect. They have been probably the two most gut-wrenching experiences of my career. Because you know you're dealing with peoples' lives and their families, these changes can be emotional if you care about the people in your organization. However, I do fundamentally believe that your first obligation is to the entire organization.

A second problem for PepsiCo was its poor relationship with KFC franchisees. A month after becoming president and chief executive officer in 1989, John Cranor addressed KFC's franchisees in Louisville to explain the details of the new franchise contract. This was the first contract change in thirteen years. It gave PepsiCo greater power to take over weak franchises, relocate restaurants, and make changes in existing restaurants. In addition, restaurants would no longer be protected from competition from new KFC units, and PepsiCo would have the right to raise royalty fees on existing restaurants as contracts came up for renewal. After Cranor finished his address, there was an uproar among the attending franchisees, who jumped to their feet to protest the changes. KFC's franchise association later sued PepsiCo over the new contract. The contract remained unresolved until 1996, when the most objectionable parts of the contract were removed by KFC's new president and CEO, David Novak. A new contract was ratified by KFC's franchisees in 1997.

PepsiCo's divestiture of KFC, Pizza Hut, and Taco Bell PepsiCo's strategy of diversifying into three distinct but related markets—soft drinks, snack foods, and fast-food restaurants—created one of the world's largest food companies and a portfolio of some of the world's most recognizable brands. Between 1990 and 1996, PepsiCo's sales grew at an annual rate of more than 10 percent, surpassing $31 billion in 1996. PepsiCo's growth, however, masked troubles in its fast-food businesses. Operating margins (profit after tax as a percent of sales) at Pepsi-Cola and Frito Lay averaged 12 and 17 percent, respectively. During the same period, margins at KFC, Pizza Hut, and Taco Bell fell from an average of more than 8 percent in 1990 to a little more than 4 percent in 1996. Declining margins in the fast-food chains reflected increasing maturity in the U.S. fast-food industry, intense competition, and the aging of KFC and Pizza Hut's restaurant bases. As a result, PepsiCo's restaurant chains absorbed nearly one-half of PepsiCo's annual capital spending during the 1990s but generated less than one-third of PepsiCo's cash flows. This meant that cash had to be diverted from PepsiCo's soft drink and snack food businesses to its restaurant businesses. This reduced PepsiCo's corporate return on assets, made it more difficult to compete effectively with Coca-Cola, and hurt its stock price. In 1997, PepsiCo decided to spin off its restaurant businesses into a new company called Tricon Global Restaurants, Inc.

The new company was based in KFC's headquarters in Louisville, Kentucky.

PepsiCo's objective was to reposition itself as a beverage and snack food company, strengthen its balance sheet, and create more consistent earning growth. PepsiCo received a one-time distribution from Tricon of $4.7 billion, $3.7 billion of which was used to pay off short-term debt. The balance was earmarked for stock repurchases. In 1998, PepsiCo acquired Tropicana Products, which controlled more than 40 percent of the U.S. chilled orange juice market. Because of the divestiture of KFC, Pizza Hut, and Taco Bell, PepsiCo sales fell by $11.3 billion, and assets fell by $7.0 billion. Profitability, however, soared. Operating margins rose from 11 percent in 1997 to 14 percent in 1999, and ROA rose from 11 percent in 1997 to 16 percent in 1999. By focusing on high cash flow market leaders, PepsiCo raised profitability while decreasing its asset base. In 2001, PepsiCo acquired The Quaker Oats Company, which included Gatorade. Gatorade and Tropicana were moved into a separate division to increase efficiencies. By 2003, PepsiCo sales exceeded $25 billion annually.

Yum! Brands, Inc.

The spin-off created a new, independent, publicly held company called Tricon Global Restaurants, Inc. The new company managed the KFC, Pizza Hut, and Taco Bell franchise systems. David Novak became Tricon's new CEO and moved quickly to create a new culture within the company. One of his primary objectives was to reverse the long-standing friction between management and franchisees that was created under PepsiCo ownership. Novak announced that PepsiCo's top-down management system would be replaced by a new management emphasis on providing support to the firm's franchise base. Franchises would have greater independence, resources, and technical support. Novak symbolically changed the name on the corporate headquarters' building in Louisville to "KFC Support Center" to drive home his new philosophy.

In 2002, Tricon announced the acquisition of Long John Silver's and A&W All-American Food Restaurants. The acquisition increased Tricon's worldwide system to 32,500 restaurants. The acquisition signaled Tricon's decision to aggressively promote a multibranding strategy that combined two brands in one restaurant and attracted a larger consumer base by offering them a broader menu selection in one location. One week after it announced the acquisition, shareholders approved a

EXHIBIT 1

Yum! Brands, Inc. Organizational Chart (2004)

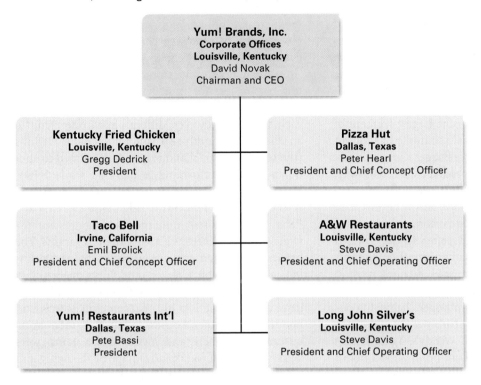

corporate name change to Yum! Brands, Inc. The new name reflected the company's expanding portfolio of fast-food brands (see Exhibit 1). In 2003, Novak announced the acquisition of Pasta Bravo, a made-to-order pasta and salad concept based in California. The acquisition followed several months of test marketing of the multibranding of Pasta Bravo and Pizza Hut.

Novak also initiated a plan to reduce the company-owned restaurant base by either closing poorly performing restaurants or selling company restaurants to individual franchisees. In 1997, 38 percent of the restaurant base (KFC, Pizza Hut, and Taco Bell) was company owned. By early 2004, company-owned restaurants had declined to 23 percent of the total. The long-term goal was to reduce the company base to 20 percent. The firm's new emphasis on supporting individual franchisees had an immediate effect on morale. In 1997, the year of the divestiture, the company recorded a loss of $111 million in net income. In 2003, net income was estimated at $585 million on estimated sales of $8.3 billion, a return on sales of about 7.0 percent.

Fast-Food Industry

The National Restaurant Association (NRA) estimated that U.S. food service sales increased by 4.3 percent to $408 billion in 2002. More than 858,000 restaurants made up the U.S. restaurant industry and employed almost 12 million people. Sales were highest in the full-service, sit-down sector, which grew 4.5 percent to $147 billion. Fast-food sales grew at a slower rate, rising about 3.7 percent to $115 billion. The fast-food sector was increasingly viewed as a mature market. As U.S. incomes rose during the late 1990s and early 2000s, more consumers frequented sit-down restaurants that offered better service and a more comfortable dining experience. Together, the full-service and fast-food segments made up about 64 percent of all U.S. food service sales.

Major Fast-Food Segments

Eight major segments made up the fast-food segment of the restaurant industry: sandwich chains, pizza chains, family restaurants, grill buffet chains, dinner houses, chicken chains, non-dinner concepts, and other chains. Sales data for the leading restaurant chains in each segment are shown in Exhibit 2. Most striking is the dominance of McDonald's, which had sales of more than $20 billion in 2002. McDonald's accounted for 13 percent of the sales of the top 100 chains. To put McDonald's dominance in perspective, the second largest chain—Burger King—held less than 6 percent of the market.

Sandwich chains made up the largest segment of the fast-food market. McDonald's controlled 33 percent of the sandwich segment, while Burger King ran a distant second with a 14 percent market share. Sandwich chains, however, were struggling because of continued price discounting that lowered profits. The threat of obesity lawsuits and increased customer demand for more healthy food items and better service lowered demand for the traditional hamburger, fries, and soft drink combinations. Per store sales declined most at Hardee's, Carl's Jr., McDonald's, and Jack in the Box, the segment's best-known hamburger chains. In contrast, per store sales increased sharply at Quiznos, Taco Bell, Schlotsky's, Subway, and Wendy's. These chains made in-roads by offering more healthy food items. Wendy's promoted its leadership in gourmet salads, while Subway heavily advertised its low-fat sandwiches. Taco Bell rolled out a new "fresco" menu that replaced cheese and sour cream on most menu items with fat-free salsa. To meet health trends, McDonald's introduced premium salads, and Burger King introduced a new line of low-fat, grilled chicken sandwiches. In contrast, Hardee's introduced a new "Thickburger" menu that included 1/3-, 1/2-, and 2/3-pound Angus burgers in an attempt to distinguish itself from other hamburger chains.

Dinner houses made up the second largest and fastest growing fast-food segment. Sales in the dinner house segment increased by more than 9 percent in 2002, surpassing the average increase of 4 percent among other segments. Much of the growth in dinner houses came from new unit construction, a marked contrast with the other fast-food segments, which have slowed U.S. construction because of market saturation. Much of the new unit construction took place in new suburban markets and small towns. Applebee's, Red Lobster, Outback Steakhouse, and Chili's Grill & Bar dominated the dinner house segment. Each chain generated sales of more than $2 billion in 2002. The fastest growing dinner houses, however, were chains generating less than $600 million in sales, such as

Texas Road House, P.F. Chang's China Bistro, and The Cheesecake Factory. Each of these chains increased sales by more than 20 percent.

Increased growth among dinner houses came at the expense of sandwich chains, pizza and chicken chains, grilled buffet chains, and family restaurants. "Too many restaurants chasing the same customers" was responsible for much of the slower growth in these other fast-food categories. Sales growth within each segment, however, differed from one chain to another. In the family segment, for example, Denny's (the segment leader) and Shoney's continued to shut down poorly performing restaurants while IHOP, Bob Evans, and Cracker Barrel expanded their bases. In the pizza segment, Pizza Hut, Little Caesars, and Papa John's closed underperforming restaurants while Chuck E. Cheese's added more restaurants. The hardest hit segment was grilled buffet chains. Declining sales caused both Sizzlin' and Western Sizzlin' to drop out of the list of Top 100 chains, leaving only three chains in the Top 100 (Golden Grill, Ryan's, and Ponderosa). Dinner houses, because of their more upscale atmosphere and higher ticket items, were better positioned to take advantage of the aging and wealthier U.S. population. Even dinner houses, however, faced the prospect of market saturation and increased competition in the near future.

Chicken Segment

KFC continued to dominate the chicken segment with sales of $4.8 billion in 2002 and estimated sales of $5.0 billion in 2003 (see Exhibit 3). Its nearest competitor, Chick-fil-A, ran a distant second with sales of $1.4 billion. KFC's leadership in the U.S. market was so extensive that it had fewer opportunities to expand its U.S. restaurant base, which was only growing at about one percent per year. Despite its dominance, KFC was slowly losing market share as other chicken chains increased sales at a faster rate. KFC's share of chicken segment sales fell from 64 percent in 1993 to less than 51 percent in 2003, a ten-year drop of 14 percent (see Exhibit 4). During the same period, Chick-fil-A and Boston Market increased their combined market share by 11 percent. In the 1990s, many industry analysts predicted that Boston Market would challenge KFC for market leadership. Boston Market was a new chain that emphasized roasted rather than fried chicken. It successfully created the image of an upscale deli offering healthy, "home-style" alternatives to fried chicken.

EXHIBIT 2

Top U.S. Fast-Food Restaurants (Ranked by 2002 Sales, $ 000s)

Rank	Sandwich Chains	Sales	Share	Rank	Dinner Houses	Sales	Share
1	McDonald's	20,306	33.3%	9	Applebee's	3,183	15.2%
2	Burger King	8,350	13.7	14	Red Lobster	2,360	11.3
3	Wendy's	6,953	11.4	15	Outback Steakhouse	2,271	10.9
5	Subway	5,230	8.6	16	Chili's Grill & Bar	2,240	10.7
6	Taco Bell	5,200	8.5	21	Olive Garden	1,940	9.3
12	Arby's	2,695	4.4	23	T.G.I. Friday's	1,746	8.3
17	Jack in the Box	2,240	3.7	33	Ruby Tuesday	1,255	6.0
18	Sonic Drive-In	2,205	3.6	55	Bennigan's	681	3.3
19	Dairy Queen	2,190	3.6	62	Romano's Mac. Grill	639	3.1
24	Hardee's	1,700	2.8	63	Hooters	629	3.0
	Other Chains	3,980	6.5		Other Chains	3,985	19.0
	Total Segment	61,049	100.0%		Total Segment	20,928	100.0%

Rank	Pizza Chains	Sales	Share	Rank	Chicken Chains	Sales	Share
7	Pizza Hut	5,100	43.4%	8	KFC	4,800	50.7%
10	Domino's	2,927	24.9	31	Chick-fil-A	1,373	14.5
22	Papa John's	1,749	14.9	34	Popeyes	1,215	12.8
37	Little Caesars	1,150	9.8	51	Church's	720	7.6
80	Chuck E. Cheese's	460	3.9	61	Boston Market	641	6.8
95	Round Table Pizza	374	3.2	97	El Pollo Loco	364	3.8
	Total Segment	11,761	100.0%	99	Bojangles'	347	3.7
					Total Segment	9,460	100.0%

Rank	Family Restaurants	Sales	Share	Rank	Other Dinner Chains	Sales	Share
20	Denny's	2,120	22.2%	49	Long John Silver's	756	23.5%
27	IHOP	1,461	15.3	52	Disney Theme Parks	705	21.9
29	Cracker Barrel	1,406	14.7	54	Panera Bread Co.	688	21.4
43	Bob Evans	876	9.2	67	Old Country Buffet	574	17.8
46	Perkins	798	8.3	74	Captain D's Seafood	497	15.4
48	Waffle House	768	8.0		Total Segment	3,219	100.0%
	Other Chains	2,133	22.3	Rank	Non-Dinner Concepts	Sales	Share
	Total Segment	9,561	100.0%	11	Dunkin' Donuts	2,700	34.6%

Rank	Grill Buffet Chains	Sales	Share	Rank	Non-Dinner Concepts	Sales	Share
36	Golden Coral	1,157	46.3%	13	Starbuck's	2,478	31.7
44	Ryan's	812	32.5	32	7-Eleven	1,335	17.1
71	Ponderosa	532	21.3	47	Krispy Kreme	772	9.9
	Total Segment	2,501	100.0%	72	Baskin-Robbins	523	6.7
					Total Segment	7,808	100.0%

Source: Nation's Restaurant News. Sales rankings for contract and hotel chains not included.

To distinguish itself from more traditional fast-food, it refused to construct drive-thrus and established most of its units outside of shopping malls rather than at major city intersections.

On the surface, it appeared that Boston Market and Chick-fil-A's market share gains were achieved by taking customers away from KFC. Another look at the data, however, reveals that KFC's sales have grown at a

EXHIBIT 3

Top Chicken Chains

	1997	1998	1999	2000	2001	2002	Growth Rate
Sales ($ Millions)							
KFC	4,000	4,200	4,300	4,400	4,700	4,800	4%
Chick-fil-A	643	764	943	1,082	1,242	1,373	16%
Popeyes	720	843	986	1,077	1,179	1,215	11%
Church's	574	620	705	699	721	720	5%
Boston Market	1,197	929	855	685	640	641	−12%
El Pollo Loco	235	245	275	305	339	364	9%
Bojangles'	229	250	270	298	333	347	9%
Total	7,598	7,851	8,334	8,546	9,154	9,460	5%
U.S. Restaurants							
KFC	5,092	5,105	5,231	5,364	5,399	5,472	1%
Chick-fil-A	749	812	897	958	1,014	1,074	8%
Popeyes	945	1,066	1,165	1,248	1,327	1,380	8%
Church's	1,070	1,105	1,178	1,217	1,242	1,232	3%
Boston Market	1,166	889	858	712	657	653	−11%
El Pollo Loco	243	261	270	279	293	306	5%
Bojangles'	258	255	265	278	280	292	3%
Total	9,551	9,493	9,864	10,056	10.212	10.409	2%
Sales per Unit ($ 000s)							
KFC	781	823	822	820	871	877	2%
Chick-fil-A	859	941	1,051	1,130	1,225	1,278	8%
Popeyes	762	790	847	863	889	880	3%
Church's	536	561	598	574	581	584	2%
Boston Market	1,027	1,045	997	962	974	982	−1%
El Pollo Loco	967	939	1,019	1,094	1,157	1,190	4%
Bojangles'	888	980	1,020	1,072	1,189	1,188	6%
Total	796	827	845	850	896	909	3%

Source: Nation's Restaurant News.

stable rate during the last ten years. Boston Market, rather than drawing customers away from KFC, appealed to new consumers who did not regularly frequent KFC and wanted non–fried chicken alternatives. Boston Market was able to expand the chicken segment beyond its traditional emphasis on fried chicken by offering non–fried chicken products that appealed to this new consumer group. After aggressively growing its restaurant base through 1997, however, Boston Market fell on hard times as it was unable to handle mounting debt problems. It soon entered bankruptcy proceedings. McDonald's acquired Boston Market in 2000. The acquisition followed earlier acquisitions of Donatos Pizza in 1999 and Chipotle Mexican Grill in 1998. McDonald's hoped the acquisitions would help it expand its U.S. restaurant base as there were few opportunities to expand the McDonald's concept. Chick-fil-A's early strategy was to establish sit-down restaurants in shopping malls. As more malls added food courts, however, malls became less enthusiastic about allocating separate store space to restaurants. As a result, Chick-fil-A began to open smaller units

EXHIBIT 4

Top Chicken Chains—Market Share (%, Based on Annual Sales)

	KFC	Chick-fil-A	Popeyes	Church's	Market	Loco	Bojangles'	Total
1993	64.2	7.5	10.7	8.3	2.9	3.2	3.2	100.0
1994	60.7	7.8	10.6	8.0	6.6	3.1	3.2	100.0
1995	56.6	7.7	10.1	7.7	11.6	3.0	3.3	100.0
1996	54.2	7.9	9.3	7.3	15.3	3.0	3.0	100.0
1997	52.5	8.5	9.5	7.6	15.8	3.1	3.0	100.0
1998	53.4	9.7	10.7	7.9	11.8	3.1	3.2	100.0
1999	51.6	11.3	11.8	8.5	10.3	3.3	3.2	100.0
2000	51.4	12.7	12.6	8.2	8.0	3.6	3.5	100.0
2001	51.3	13.6	12.9	7.9	7.0	3.7	3.6	100.0
2002	50.8	14.5	12.8	7.6	6.8	3.8	3.7	100.0
10-Year Change (%)								
	−13.4	7.0	2.1	−0.7	3.9	0.6	0.5	0.0
5-Year Compounded Annual Growth Rate (CAGR %)								
	−2.6	7.6	2.1	−1.0	10.0	2.1	1.5	0.0

in shopping mall food courts and to build free-standing restaurants that competed head-to-head with existing chicken chains. Despite market share gains by Boston Market and Chick-fil-A, however, KFC's customer base has remained loyal to the KFC brand because of its unique taste.

The maturation of the U.S. fast-food industry increased the intensity of competition within the chicken segment. While Chick-fil-A and Popeyes continued to grow new restaurants at a fast pace, other chains focused their strategies on new product introductions, product launches beyond fried chicken, and intensive marketing campaigns. All chains attempted to differentiate themselves based on unique product and customer characteristics. KFC used animated images of the "Colonel" to drive home its home-style image. Recent product introductions included popcorn chicken, honey BBQ chicken, and spicy BBQ wings. Popeyes continued to reimage its restaurants with its "Heritage" design which included a balcony over the drive-thru, Cajun-style murals, and new signage. It recently introduced a Chicken Strip Po' Boy sandwich to expand its New Orleans–style menu of spicy chicken, jambalaya, etouffée, and gumbo. Bojangles' also promoted a Cajun décor but focused more heavily on core chicken products such as its Cajun fried chicken, Cajun filet sandwich, and Buffalo bites.

El Pollo Loco served marinated, flame-broiled chicken and other Mexican food entrees such as chicken burritos, tostada salads, and chicken nachos. Church's emphasized its "made-from-scratch," Southern-style fried chicken and side dishes such as corn-on-the-cob, fried okra, and macaroni and cheese. It was testing new products such as batter-fried fish, fried thigh filets, and fried fruit pies that would be introduced later in 2004. Chick-fil-A continued to focus on its pressure-cooked and char-grilled skinless chicken breast sandwiches. It focused on introducing salads and more portable menu items such as the recently introduced Cool Wrap Chicken Sandwich.

Trends in the Restaurant Industry

A number of demographic and societal trends influenced the demand for food eaten outside of the home. During the last two decades, rising incomes, greater affluence among a greater percentage of American households, higher divorce rates, and the fact that people married later in life contributed to the rising number of single households and the demand for fast-food. More than 50 percent of women worked outside of the home, a dramatic increase since 1970. This number was expected to rise to 65 percent by 2010. Double-income households contributed to rising household incomes and increased the number of times families ate out. Less time to prepare meals inside the home added to this trend. Countering these trends, however, was a slower growth rate of the U.S. population and an overpopulation of fast-food chains that increased consumer alternatives and intensified competition.

Baby Boomers 35 to 50 years of age constituted the largest consumer group for fast-food restaurants. Generation X'ers (ages 25 to 34) and the "Mature" category (ages 51 to 64) made up the second and third largest groups. As consumers aged, they became less enamored with fast-food and were more likely to trade up to more expensive restaurants such as dinner houses and full-service restaurants. Sales of many Mexican restaurants, which were extremely popular during the 1980s, began to slow as Japanese, Indian, and Vietnamese restaurants became more fashionable. Ethnic foods were rising in popularity as U.S. immigrants, who constituted 13 percent of the U.S. population in early 2004, looked for establishments that sold their native foods.

Labor was the top operational challenge of U.S. restaurant chains. Restaurants relied heavily on teenagers and college age workers. Twenty percent of all employed teenagers worked in food service, compared with only 4 percent of all employed men over the age of eighteen and 6 percent of all employed women. As the U.S. population aged, fewer young workers were available to fill food service jobs. The short supply of high school and college students also meant they had greater opportunities outside of food service. Turnover rates were notoriously high. The National Restaurant Association estimated that about 96 percent of all fast-food workers quit within a year, compared with about 84 percent of employees in full-service restaurants.

Labor costs made up about 30 percent of the fast-food chain's total costs, second only to food and beverage costs. To deal with the decreased supply of employees in the sixteen to twenty-four age category, many restaurants were forced to hire lower quality workers, which affected service and restaurant cleanliness. To improve quality and service, restaurants increasingly hired elderly employees who were interested in returning to the work force. To attract more workers, especially the elderly, restaurants offered health insurance, noncontributory pension plans, and profit-sharing benefits that were generally not given only ten years before. To combat high turnover rates, restaurants also turned to better training

programs and mentoring systems, which paired new employees with more experienced ones. Mentoring systems were particularly helpful in increasing the learning curve of new workers and providing better camaraderie among employees.

Intense competition in the mature restaurant industry made it difficult for restaurants to increase prices sufficiently to cover the increased cost of labor. Consumers made decisions about where to eat partially based on price. As a result, profit margins were squeezed. To reduce costs, restaurants eliminated low-margin food items, increased portion sizes, and improved product value to offset price increases. Restaurants also attempted to increase consumer traffic through discounting, by accepting coupons from competitors, by offering two-for-one specials, and by making limited-time offerings.

Technology was increasingly used to lower costs and improve efficiencies. According to the National Restaurant Association, restaurant operators viewed computers as their number one tool for improving efficiency. Computers were used to improve labor scheduling, accounting, payroll, sales analysis, and inventory control. Most restaurant chains also used point-of-sale systems that recorded the selected menu items and gave the cashier a breakdown of food items and the ticket price. These systems reduced serving times and cashier accuracy. Other chains like McDonald's and Carl's Jr. converted to new food preparation systems that allowed them to prepare food more accurately and a variety of sandwiches using the same process.

Higher costs and poor availability of prime real estate was another trend that negatively affected profitability. A plot of land suitable for a freestanding restaurant cost between $1.5 and $2.5 million. Leasing was a less costly alternative to buying. Nevertheless, market saturation decreased per store sales as newer units cannibalized sales from existing units. As a result, most food chains began to expand their U.S. restaurant bases into alternative distribution channels in hospitals, airports, colleges, highway rest areas, gas stations, shopping mall food courts, and large retail stores or by dual branding with other fast-food concepts.

The Global Fast-Food Industry

As the U.S. market matured, more restaurants turned to international markets to expand sales. Foreign markets were attractive because of their large customer bases and comparatively little competition. McDonald's, for example, operated 46 restaurants for every 1 million U.S. residents. Outside of the United States, it operated only one restaurant for every 3 million residents. McDonald's, KFC, Burger King, and Pizza Hut were the earliest and most aggressive chains to expand abroad beginning in the 1960s. By early 2004, at least 35 chains had expanded into a least one foreign country. McDonald's operated more than 13,000 U.S. units and 17,000 foreign units in the 119 countries. With the acquisition of A&W and Long John Silver's, however, Yum! Brands became the world's largest restaurant chain in 2003. It operated more than 21,000 U.S. and close to 33,000 non-U.S. KFC, Pizza Hut, Taco Bell, A&W, and Long John Silver's restaurants in 88 countries. Because of their early expansion abroad, McDonald's, KFC, Burger King, and Pizza Hut had all developed strong brand names and managerial expertise operating in international markets. This made them formidable competitors for fast-food chains investing abroad for the first time. Subway, TCBY, and Domino's were more recent global competitors but were expanding more aggressively than McDonald's or KFC. By 2003, each was operating in more than 65 countries.

Exhibit 5 lists the world's thirty-five largest restaurant chains. The global fast-food industry had a distinctly American flavor. Twenty-eight chains (80 percent of the total) were headquartered in the United States. U.S. chains had the advantage of a large domestic market and ready acceptance by the American consumer. European firms had less success developing the fast-food concept because Europeans were more inclined to frequent midscale restaurants, where they spent several hours enjoying multicourse meals in a formal setting. KFC had trouble breaking into the German market during the 1970s and 1980s because Germans were not accustomed to buying take-out or ordering food over the counter. McDonald's had greater success penetrating the German market because it made a number of changes to its menu and operating procedures to appeal to German tastes. German beer, for example, was served in all of McDonald's restaurants in Germany. In France, McDonald's used a different sauce on its Big Mac sandwich that appealed to the French palate. KFC had more success in Asia and Latin America, where chicken was a traditional dish.

Aside from cultural factors, international business carried risks not present in the domestic market. Long distances between headquarters and foreign franchises made it more difficult to control the quality of individual restaurants. Large distances also caused servicing and support problems. Transportation and other resource costs were higher than in the domestic market. In addition, time, cultural, and language differences increased communication and operational problems. As a result, most restaurant chains limited expansion to their domestic market as long as they were able to meet profit and growth objectives. As companies gained greater expertise abroad, they turned to profitable international markets as a means of expanding restaurant bases and increasing sales, profits, and market share. Worldwide demand for fast-food was expected to grow rapidly during the next two decades as rising per capita incomes worldwide made eating out more affordable for greater numbers of consumers. In addition, the development of the Internet was quickly breaking down communication and language barriers. Greater numbers of children were growing up with computers in their homes and schools. As a result, teenagers in Germany, Brazil, Japan, and the United States were equally likely to be able to converse about the Internet. The Internet also exposed more teenagers to the same companies and products, which enabled firms to quickly develop global brands and a worldwide consumer base.

Kentucky Fried Chicken Corporation

Marketing Strategy

Many of KFC's problems during the 1980s and 1990s surrounded its limited menu and inability to quickly bring new products to market. The popularity of its Original Recipe Chicken allowed KFC to expand through the 1980s without significant competition from other chicken chains. As a result, new product introductions were not a critical part of KFC's business strategy. KFC suffered one of its most serious setbacks in 1989 as it prepared to introduce a chicken sandwich to its menu. KFC was still experimenting with the chicken sandwich concept when McDonald's rolled out its McChicken sandwich. By beating KFC to the market, McDonald's developed strong consumer awareness for its sandwich. This significantly increased KFC's cost of developing awareness for its own sandwich,

EXHIBIT 5

The World's 35 Largest Fast-Food Chains in 2004[1]

	Franchise	Corporate Headquarters	Home Country	Countries
1.	McDonald's	Oakbrook, Illinois	U.S.A.	121
2.	KFC	Louisville, Kentucky	U.S.A.	99
3.	Pizza Hut	Dallas, Texas	U.S.A.	92
4.	Subway Sandwiches	Milford, Connecticut	U.S.A.	74
5.	TCBY	Little Rock, Arkansas	U.S.A.	67
6.	Domino's Pizza	Ann Arbor, Michigan	U.S.A.	65
7.	Burger King	Miami, Florida	U.S.A.	58
8.	T.G.I. Friday's	Dallas, Texas	U.S.A.	53
9.	Baskin Robbins	Glendale, California	U.S.A.	52
10.	Dunkin' Donuts	Randolph, Massachusetts	U.S.A.	40
11.	Wendy's	Dublin, Ohio	U.S.A.	34
12.	Chili's Grill & Bar	Dallas, Texas	U.S.A.	22
13.	Dairy Queen	Edina, Michigan	U.S.A.	22
14.	Little Caesar's Pizza	Detroit, Michigan	U.S.A.	22
15.	Popeyes	Atlanta, Georgia	U.S.A.	22
16.	Outback Steakhouse	Tampa, Florida	U.S.A.	20
17.	A&W Restaurants	Lexington, Kentucky	U.S.A.	17
18.	PizzaExpress	London, England	U.K.	16
19.	Carl's Jr.	Anaheim, California	U.S.A.	14
20.	Church's Chicken	Atlanta, Georgia	U.S.A.	12
21.	Taco Bell	Irvine, California	U.S.A.	12
22.	Hardee's	Rocky Mt., North Carolina	U.S.A.	11
23.	Applebee's	Overland Park, Kansas	U.S.A.	9
24.	Sizzler	Los Angeles, California	U.S.A.	9
25.	Arby's	Ft. Lauderdale, Florida	U.S.A.	7
26.	Denny's	Spartanburg, South Carolina	U.S.A.	7
27.	Skylark	Tokyo	Japan	7
28.	Lotteria	Seoul	Korea	5
29.	Taco Time	Eugene, Oregon	U.S.A.	5
30.	Mos Burger	Tokyo	Japan	4
31.	Orange Julius	Edina, Minnesota	U.S.A.	4
32.	Yoshinoya	Tokyo	Japan	4
33.	IHOP	Glendale, California	U.S.A.	3
34.	Quick Restaurants	Brussels	Belgium	3
35.	Red Lobster	Orlando, Florida	U.S.A.	3

[1]Case writer research.

which KFC introduced several months later. KFC eventually withdrew the sandwich because of low sales. Today, about 95 percent of chicken sandwiches are sold through traditional hamburger chains.

KFC's focus on fried chicken ("chicken-on-the-bone") became a serious problem by the 1990s as the U.S. fast-food industry matured. In order to expand sales, restaurant chains began to diversify their menus to include non-core products, thereby cutting into the business of other fast-food segments. For example, hamburger and pizza chains, family restaurants, and dinner houses all introduced a variety of chicken items such as chicken sandwiches and chicken wings to expand their consumer base. This made it difficult for KFC to increase per-unit sales. By 2003, McDonald's boasted a menu that included hamburgers, chicken sandwiches, fish sandwiches, burritos, a full line of breakfast items, ice cream, and milkshakes. By diversifying its menu, McDonald's was able to raise annual sales to $1.5 million per restaurant. This compared with KFC's average restaurant sales of $883,000. In 2003, Yum! Brands conducted market research showing that customers preferred multiple menu offerings over single-concept menus like chicken or pizza by a six-to-one margin.

KFC's short-term strategy was to diversify its menu. It rolled out a buffet that included over thirty dinner, salad, and dessert items. The buffet was most successful in rural locations and suburbs but less successful in urban areas where restaurant space was limited. It then introduced Colonel's Crispy Strips and a line of chicken sandwiches that complimented its core fried chicken products. More recent product innovations include popcorn chicken, chunky chicken pot pie, and twisters (a flour tortilla filled with chunks of chicken). To increase brand awareness for these new products, KFC introduced a new television campaign featuring a cartoon caricature of Colonel Sanders stating "I'm a Chicken Genius!" It also featured Jason Alexander from the television sitcom *Seinfeld* promoting popcorn chicken using the slogan "There's fast food, then there's KFC." Sandwiches and other non-core items, however, cannibalized sales of KFC's core chicken products. Most important, it did little to address the consumer's desire for greater menu variety beyond chicken.

Multibrand Strategy

By 2000, the company began to open "2-in-1" units that sold both KFC and Taco Bell or KFC and Pizza Hut in the same location. Most of KFC's sales (64 percent) and Pizza Hut's sales (61 percent) were driven by dinner, while most of Taco Bell's sales (50 percent) were driven by lunch (50 percent). The combination of KFC and Taco Bell was a natural success because it increased per unit sales simply by filling up counter space left empty by KFC at lunch or Taco Bell at dinner. It became increasingly apparent, however, that the real value of combining restaurant concepts was in attracting greater numbers of consumers who wanted more menu variety. The acquisition of A&W and Long John Silver's in 2002 provided additional opportunities to create a variety of combinations of five highly differentiated fast-food category leaders. By 2003, Yum! Brands had opened 1,975 multibrand restaurants worldwide that included KFC/Taco Bell, KFC/A&W, Taco Bell/Pizza Hut, and A&W/Long John Silver's. The company believed there was potential for opening thirteen thousand multibrand restaurants in the United States alone. The increase in per unit sales that resulted from multibranding meant that new restaurants could be opened in more expensive locations and lower population areas than were profitable with stand-alone restaurants.

International Operations

KFC's early experience operating abroad put it in a strong position to take advantage of the growing trend toward global expansion. By early 2004, 56 percent of KFC's restaurants were located outside of the United States. KFC was the most global of the five brands managed by Yum! Brands, Inc. The other brands had a significantly smaller percentage of their restaurant base outside of the United States—Pizza Hut (37 percent), Taco Bell (4 percent), Long John Silver's (2 percent), and A&W (22 percent). Historically, franchises made up a large portion of KFC's international restaurant base because franchises were owned and operated by local entrepreneurs who had a deeper understanding of local language, culture, customs, law, financial markets, and marketing characteristics. Franchising was also a good strategy for establishing a presence in smaller countries such as Grenada, Bermuda, and Suriname, whose small populations could only support a single restaurant. The costs of operating company-owned restaurants were prohibitively high in these smaller markets. Of the seven thousand KFC restaurants located outside of the United States, 77 percent were franchises, licensed restaurants, or joint ventures. In larger markets such as Mexico, China, Canada, Australia, Puerto Rico, Korea, Thailand, and the United Kingdom, there was a stronger emphasis on building company-owned restaurants. By coordinating purchasing, recruiting, training, financing, and advertising in these larger markets, fixed costs could be spread over a larger restaurant base. KFC could also maintain tighter control over product quality and customer service.

Latin American Strategy

KFC operated 650 restaurants in Latin America in 2003 (Exhibit 6). Its primary presence was in Mexico, Puerto Rico, and the Caribbean. KFC established subsidiaries in Mexico and Puerto Rico in the late 1960s and expanded through company-owned restaurants. Franchises were used to penetrate countries in the Caribbean whose market size prevented KFC from profitably operating company-owned restaurants.

Subsidiaries were later established in the Virgin Islands, Venezuela, and Brazil. KFC had planned to expand into these regions using company-owned restaurants. The Venezuelan subsidiary, however, was later closed because of the high costs of operating the small subsidiary. KFC had opened eight restaurants in Brazil but closed them by 2000 because it lacked the cash flow needed to support an expansion program in that market. Franchises were opened in other markets that had good growth potential such as Chile, Ecuador, and Peru. In 2003, KFC signed a joint venture agreement with a Brazilian partner that had a deeper understanding of the Brazilian market. KFC hoped the joint venture would help it reestablish a presence in Brazil.

KFC's early entry into Latin America gave it a leadership position over McDonald's in Mexico and the Caribbean. It also had an edge in Ecuador and

EXHIBIT 6

Latin America Restaurant Count in 2003: McDonald's, Burger King, Wendy's, and KFC

	McDonald's	Burger King	Wendy's	KFC
Mexico	261	154	16	274
Puerto Rico	112	163	46	97
Caribbean Islands	29	55	20	134
Central America	99	104	38	32
Subtotal	501	476	120	537
% Total	31%	82%	68%	83%
Colombia	25	0	3	9
Ecuador	10	13	0	39
Peru	10	12	0	25
Venezuela	129	20	33	5
Other Andean	45	6	0	5
Andean Region	219	51	36	83
% Total	14%	9%	25%	13%
Argentina	203	25	21	0
Brazil	584	0	0	0
Chile	70	23	0	30
Paraguay + Uruguay	28	6	0	0
Southern Cone	885	54	21	30
% Total	55%	9%	15%	5%
Latin America	1,605	581	143	650
% Total	100%	100%	100%	100%

Peru. KFC's Latin America strategy represented a classic internationalization strategy. It first expanded into Mexico and Puerto Rico because of their geographic proximity, as well as political and economic ties to the United States. KFC then expanded its franchise system throughout the Caribbean, gradually moving away from its U.S. base as its experience in Latin America grew. Only after it had established a leadership position in Mexico and the Caribbean did it venture into South America. McDonald's pursued a different strategy. It was late to expand into the region. Despite a rapid restaurant construction program in Mexico during the 1990s, McDonald's still lagged behind KFC. Therefore, McDonald's initiated a first mover strategy in Brazil and Argentina, large markets where KFC had no presence. By 2003, 55 percent of McDonald's restaurants in Latin America were located in the two countries. Wendy's pursued a different strategy. It first expanded into Puerto Rico, the Caribbean, and Central America because of their geographic proximity to the United States. Wendy's late entry into Latin America, however, made it difficult to penetrate Mexico, where KFC, McDonald's, and Burger King had already established strong positions. Wendy's announced plans to build one hundred Wendy's restaurants in Mexico by 2010; however, its primary objective was to establish strong positions in Venezuela and Argentina, where most U.S. fast-food chains had not yet been established.

Country Risk Assessment in Latin America

Latin America comprised some fifty countries, island nations, and principalities that were settled primarily by the Spanish, Portuguese, French, Dutch, and British during the 1500s and 1600s. Spanish was spoken in most countries, the most notable exception being Brazil where the official language is Portuguese. Catholicism was the major religion, though Methodist missionaries successfully exported Protestantism into many regions of Latin America in the 1800s, most notably on the coast of Brazil. Despite commonalities in language, religion, and history, however, political and economic policies differed significantly from one country to another. Frequent changes in governments and economic instability increased the uncertainty of doing business in the region.

Most U.S. and Canadian companies realized that they could not overlook the region. Geographic proximity made communications and travel easier, and the North American Trade Agreement (NAFTA) eliminated tariffs on goods shipped between Canada, Mexico, and the United States. A customs union agreement signed in 1991 (Mercosur) between Argentina, Paraguay, Uruguay, and Brazil eliminated tariffs on trade among those four countries. Other countries such as Chile had also established free trade policies that were stimulating strong growth. The primary task for companies investing in the region was to accurately assess the different risks of doing business in Latin America and to select the proper countries for investment. Miller (1992) developed a framework for analyzing country risk that was a useful tool for evaluating different countries for future investment. He argued that firms must examine country, industry, and firm factors to fully assess country risk.

Country factors addressed the risks associated with changes in the country's political and economic environment that potentially affected the firm's ability to conduct business. They included

1. *Political risk* (e.g., war, revolution, changes in government, price controls, tariffs and other trade restrictions, appropriation of assets, government regulations, and restrictions on the repatriation of profits)

2. *Economic risk* (e.g., inflation, high interest rates, foreign exchange rate volatility, balance of trade movements, social unrest, riots, and terrorism)

3. *Natural risk* (e.g., rainfall, hurricanes, earthquakes, and volcanic activity)

Industry factors addressed changes in industry structure that inhibited the firm's ability to successfully compete in its industry. They included

1. *Supplier risk* (e.g., changes in quality, shifts in supply, and changes in supplier power)

2. *Product market risk* (e.g., consumer tastes and availability of substitute products)

3. *Competitive risk* (e.g., rivalry among competitors, new market entrants, and new product innovations)

Firm factors examined the firm's ability to control its internal operations. They included

1. *Labor risk* (e.g., labor unrest, absenteeism, employee turnover, and labor strikes)

2. *Supplier risk* (e.g., raw material shortages and unpredictable price changes)

3. *Trade secret risk* (e.g., protection of trade secrets and intangible assets)

4. *Credit risk* (e.g., problems collecting receivables)

5. *Behavioral risk* (e.g., control over franchise operations, product quality and consistency, service quality, and restaurant cleanliness)

Mexico

Many U.S. companies considered Mexico to be one of the most attractive investment locations in Latin America. Mexico's population of 105 million exceeded one-third of that of the United States. It was three times larger than Canada's 32 million. Prior to 1994, Mexico levied high tariffs on many goods imported from the United States. Other goods were regulated by quotas and licensing requirements that made Mexican goods more expensive. As a result, many U.S. consumers purchased less expensive products from Asia or Europe. In 1994, the long-awaited NAFTA agreement between Canada, the United States, and Mexico went into effect. NAFTA eliminated tariffs on goods traded among the three countries and created a trading bloc with a larger population and gross domestic product than the European Union. The elimination of tariffs led to an immediate increase in trade between Mexico and the United States. In 1995, only one year after NAFTA was signed, Mexico posted its first balance of trade surplus in six years. A large part of that surplus was attributed to greater exports to the United States. By 2003, almost 85 percent of Mexico's exports were purchased by U.S. consumers. In turn, about 68 percent of Mexico's total imports came from the United States.

U.S. investment in Mexico also increased significantly after NAFTA was signed, largely in the Maquiladoras located along the U.S.-Mexican border. With the elimination of import tariffs, U.S. firms could produce or assemble goods and transport them back into the United States more quickly and at significantly less cost than they could transport goods from Asia or Europe. Mexico's largest exports to the United States were automobiles, automobile parts, crude oil, petroleum products, and natural gas. A large portion of Mexico's automobile and auto part production was produced in U.S.-owned plants. The cost of

transporting automobiles back into the United States was more than offset by the lower cost of labor in Mexico. Today, twenty-six hundred U.S. firms operate in Mexico and account for 60 percent of all foreign direct investment in that country.

Despite the benefits, many Mexican farmers and unskilled workers strongly opposed NAFTA and U.S. investment. The day after NAFTA went into effect, rebels rioted in the southern Mexican province of Chiapas on the Guatemalan border. After four days of fighting, Mexican troops drove the rebels out of several towns the rebels had earlier seized. Around 150 people were killed. The Mexican government negotiated a cease-fire with the rebels; however, armed clashes between rebel groups protesting poverty and lack of land rights continued to be a problem. Another protest followed the signing of NAFTA when 30 to 40 masked men attacked a McDonald's restaurant in the tourist section of Mexico City. The men threw cash registers to the floor, smashed windows, overturned tables, and spray-painted "No to Fascism" and "Yankee Go Home" on the walls.

Most Mexicans (70 percent) lived in urban areas such as Mexico City, Guadalajara, and Monterrey. Mexico City's population of 18 million made it one of the most populated areas in Latin America. Many U.S. firms had operations in or around Mexico City. The fast-food industry was well developed in Mexico's cities. The leading U.S. fast-food chains already had significant restaurant bases in Mexico: KFC (274 restaurants), McDonald's (261), Pizza Hut (174), Burger King (154), and Subway (71). Mexican consumers readily accepted the fast-food concept. Chicken was also a staple product in Mexico and helped explain KFC's wide popularity. Mexico's large population and ready acceptance of fast-food represented a significant opportunity for fast-food chains. Competition, however, was intense.

Despite Mexico's relative economic stability during the late 1990s and early 2000s, Mexico had a history of high inflation, foreign exchange controls, and government regulations. These often affected foreign firms' ability to make a profit. In 1989, President Salinas attempted to reduce high inflation by controlling the peso-dollar exchange rate, allowing the peso to depreciate by only one peso per day against the dollar. He also instituted price and wage controls. Firms like KFC were unable to raise prices and were closely monitored by Mexican authorities. However, smaller firms that supplied KFC and other U.S. firms with raw materials continued to charge higher prices to compensate for inflation. KFC was soon operating at a loss, setting off heated debate in PepsiCo's headquarters. PepsiCo's finance group wanted to halt further restaurant construction in Mexico until economic stability improved. PepsiCo's marketing group wanted to continue expansion despite losses to protect its leading market share in Mexico. PepsiCo's marketing group eventually won the debate, and KFC continued to build new restaurants in Mexico during the period.

When Ernesto Zedillo became Mexico's president in December 1994, one of his objectives was to continue the stability of prices, wages, and exchange rates achieved by ex-president Carlos Salinas. This stability, however, was achieved primarily on the basis of price, wage, and foreign exchange controls. While giving the appearance of stability, an overvalued peso continued to encourage imports that exacerbated Mexico's balance of trade deficit. At the same time, Mexican exports became less competitive on world markets. Anticipating a devaluation of the peso, investors began to move capital into U.S. dollar investments. On December 19, 1994, Zedillo announced that the peso would be allowed to depreciate by an additional 15 percent per year against the dollar. Within two days, continued pressure on the peso forced Zedillo to allow the peso to float freely against the dollar.

By mid-January 1995, the peso had lost 35 percent of its value against the dollar, and the Mexican stock market had plunged 20 percent. By the end of the year, the peso had depreciated from 3.1 pesos per dollar to 7.6 pesos per dollar. In order to thwart a possible default by Mexico, the U.S. government, International Monetary Fund, and World Bank pledged $25 billion in emergency loans. Shortly thereafter, Zedillo announced an emergency economic package called the "pacto" that included lower government spending, the sale of government-run businesses, and a wage freeze. By 2000, there were signs that Mexico's economy had stabilized. Interest rates and inflation, however, remained higher than in the United States, putting continuous pressure on the peso. This led to higher import prices and exacerbated inflation. In sum, optimism about future prospects for trade and investment in Mexico was tempered by concern about continued economic stability.

Brazil

Mexico's geographic proximity and membership in NAFTA partially explained why many U.S. firms with little experience in Latin America expanded to Mexico first. Mexico's close proximity to the United States minimized travel and communication problems, and NAFTA reduced the complexity of establishing production in Mexico and importing goods back into the United States. Many firms overlooked the potential of Brazil. Brazil, with a population of 182 million, was the largest country in Latin America and fifth largest country in the world. Its land base was as large as the United States and bordered ten countries. It was the world's largest coffee producer and largest exporter of sugar and tobacco. In addition to its abundant natural resources and strong export position in agriculture, Brazil was a strong industrial power. Its major exports were airplanes, automobiles, and chemicals. Its gross domestic product of $1.3 trillion was larger than Mexico's and the largest in Latin America (see Exhibit 7). Some firms did view Brazil as one of the most important emerging markets, along with China and India.

In 1990, U.S. President George Bush initiated negotiations on a Free Trade Area of the Americas (FTAA) that would eliminate tariffs on trade within North, Central, and South America. The FTAA would create the world's largest free trade area with a combined gross domestic product of $13 trillion and 800 million consumers. In 1994, the presidents of thirty-three countries met with President Bush to negotiate details of the free trade agreement to go into effect by 2005. Many Brazilians opposed the FTAA because they feared Brazilian companies could not compete with more efficient U.S. firms. Brazil imposed high tariffs of between 10 and 35 percent on a variety of goods imported from the United States such as automobiles, automobile parts, computers, computer parts, engines, and soybeans. Other Brazilian firms, however, stood to gain substantially. To protect U.S. producers from lower cost Brazilian goods, the United States imposed tariffs of between 10 and 350 percent on imported Brazilian sugar cane, tobacco, orange juice concentrate, soybean oil, and women's leather footwear. The FTAA would eliminate these tariffs. This would give U.S. consumers the opportunity to buy Brazilian products at significantly lower prices.

EXHIBIT 7

Latin America—Selected Economic and Demographic Data

	U.S.A.	Canada	Mexico	Colombia	Venezuela	Peru	Brazil	Argentina	Chile
Population (millions)	290.3	32.2	104.9	41.7	24.7	28.4	182.0	38.7	15.7
Growth Rate	0.9%	0.9%	1.4%	1.6%	1.5%	1.6%	1.5%	1.1%	1.1%
Population Data: Origin									
European (non-French origin)	65.1%	43.0%	9.0%	20.0%	21.0%	15.0%	55.0%	97.0%	95.0%
European (French origin)		23.0%							
African	12.9%			4.0%	10.0%		6.0%		
Mixed African & European				14.0%		37.0%	38.0%		
Latin American (Hispanic)	12.0%								
Asian	4.2%	6.0%							
Amerindian or Alaskan native	1.5%	2.0%	30.0%	1.0%	2.0%	45.0%			3.0%
Mixed Amerindian & Spanish			60.0%	58.0%	67.0%				
Mixed African & Amerindian				3.0%					
Other	4.3%	26.0%	1.0%			3.0%	1.0%	3.0%	2.0%
Total	100.0%	100.0%	100.0%	100.0%	100.0%	100.0%	100.0%	100.0%	100.0%
GDP ($ billion)	$10,400	$923	$900	$268	$133	$132	$1,340	$391	$151
Per Capita Income ($U.S.)	$37,600	$29,400	$9,000	$6,500	$5,500	$4,800	$7,600	$10,200	$10,000
Real GDP Growth Rate	2.5%	3.4%	1.0%	2.0%	−8.9%	4.8%	1.0%	−14.7%	1.8%
Inflation Rate	1.6%	2.2%	6.4%	6.2%	31.2%	0.2%	8.3%	41.0%	2.5%
Unemployment Rate	5.8%	7.6%	3.0%	17.4%	17.0%	9.4%	6.4%	21.5%	9.2%
Literacy Rate	97.0%	97.0%	92.2%	92.5%	93.4%	90.9%	86.4%	97.0%	96.2%

Source: U.S. Central Intelligence Agency, *The World Factbook.* Demographic data are 2003 estimate; economic data as of year-end 2002.

Brazil played a leading role in negotiating trade and investment arrangements with other countries in Latin America. In 1991, Brazil, Argentina, Uruguay, and Paraguay signed an agreement to form a common market (Mercosur) that eliminated internal tariffs on goods traded among member countries and established a common external tariff. By 1995, 90 percent of trade among member countries was free from trade restrictions. Member countries were allowed to impose tariffs on a limited number of products considered to be a threat to sensitive domestic industries. The hope was to expand Mercosur to include other countries in the region. Chile and Bolivia, for example, were offered associate memberships. Chile, however, later withdrew because it wanted to negotiate future membership in NAFTA. Like NAFTA, the signing of Mercosur had a dramatic effect on trade among its members. Argentina quickly became Brazil's second-largest trading partner after the United States, while Brazil became Argentina's largest trading partner. Brazilian officials made it clear that making Mercosur successful was their highest priority and that the Free Trade Area of the Americas might have to wait. Many believed Brazil was the major stumbling block to establishing FTAA by 2005.

Historically, the Brazilian government used a variety of tariffs and other restrictions on imports to encourage foreign investment in Brazil. The most highly visible example was automobiles that were taxed at rates up to 100 percent during the 1980s and 1990s. By 2003, almost all global automobile companies, including General Motors, Mercedes-Benz, Toyota, Volkswagen, Honda, Fiat, and Peugeot, were producing cars in Brazil for the Brazilian market. During the 1980s, the Brazilian government attempted to stimulate domestic production in a number of technology industries like computers through an outright prohibition on imports. An example was Texas Instruments (TI), a major computer manufacturer with semiconductor operations in São Paulo. TI was prohibited from using its own computers in its Brazilian production facilities. Instead, it was forced to use slower, less efficient Brazilian computers. The Brazilian government later eliminated such restrictions after it became clear that Brazilian computer firms were unable to compete head-to-head with global computer firms. Strong government regulations and the tendency of the Brazilian government to change regulations from year to year eventually caused TI to withdraw from Brazil, even though its plant was profitable.

During the 1980s and early 1990s, Brazil battled sustained cycles of high inflation and currency instability. Between 1980 and 1993, inflation averaged more than 400 percent per year. Brazil's government attempted to reduce inflation through a variety of new currency programs, price and wage controls, and the policy of indexation, which adjusted wages and contracts based on the inflation rate. In 1994, President Cardoso introduced the Real Plan, which restructured Brazil's currency system. The cruzeiro was eliminated and replaced with a new currency called the real. The real was pegged to the U.S. dollar in an attempt to break the practice of indexation. By 1997, inflation had dropped to under 7 percent. Brazil's ability to successfully peg the real against the dollar was made possible in large part by the large foreign investment flows into Brazil during this period. The inflow of dollars boosted Brazil's dollar reserves, which could be used to buy the real on currency markets, thereby stabilizing the value of the real against the dollar.

By 1998, however, investors began to pull investments out of Brazil. Many investors were increasingly concerned about Brazil's growing budget deficit and pension system crisis. Pension benefits represented almost 10 percent of Brazil's gross domestic product. Almost half of Brazil's retirement payments went to retired civil servants who made up only 5 percent of all retired Brazilians. The heavy demand on public funds for pension benefits diminished Brazil's ability to use fiscal and monetary policy to support economic development and promote stability. The Brazilian Central Bank attempted to reduce the outflow of investment capital by raising interest rates; however, dwindling dollar reserves finally reached a crisis in 1999, when Brazil abandoned its policy of pegging the real. The real was subsequently allowed to float against the dollar. The real depreciated by almost 50 percent against the dollar in 1999.

The fast-food industry in Brazil was less developed than in Mexico or the Caribbean. This was partly the result of the structure of the fast-food industry that was dominated by U.S. restaurant chains. U.S. chains expanded further away from their home base as they gained experience operating in Latin America. As firms gained a foothold in Mexico and Central America, it was a natural progression to move into South America. McDonald's understood the importance of the Brazilian market and was early to expand there. By 2003, it was operating 584 restaurants. Many restaurant chains such as Burger King,

Pizza Hut, and KFC built restaurants in Brazil in the early to mid-1990s but eventually closed them because of poor sales. In one example, Pizza Hut opened a restaurant in a popular restaurant section of Goiânia, a city of more than 1 million people about a two-hour drive from Brasìlia, Brazil's capital. When the restaurant opened, long lines of Brazilian customers wrapped around the block waiting to try Pizza Hut for the first time. Within a few weeks, the lines were gone. Pizza Hut had opened a freestanding restaurant identical to those it operated in the United States. U.S. consumers were accustomed to waiting until a table was opened, sitting down and eating their meal, and leaving. Brazilian consumers did not mind waiting. However, they were accustomed to sitting outside with friends, socializing with a drink and hors d'oeuvres until a table was ready. Pizza Hut restaurants didn't accommodate this facet of Brazilian culture. Rather than change the structure of its operations, Pizza Hut sold the restaurant to Habib's, a popular Brazilian restaurant chain that sold Arab food.

Another problem was eating customs. Brazilians normally ate their big meal in the early afternoon. This could last two hours. It normally included salad, meat, rice and beans, dessert, fruit, and coffee. In the evening, it was customary to have a light meal such as a soup or small plate of pasta. Brazilians rarely ate food with their hands, preferring to eat with a knife and fork. This included food like pizza, which Americans typically ate with their hands. They also were not accustomed to eating sandwiches. If they did eat sandwiches, they wrapped the sandwich in a napkin. U.S. fast-food chains catered to a different kind of customer, one who wanted more than soup but less than a full sit-down meal. U.S. fast-food chains such as McDonald's were more popular in larger cities such as São Paulo and Rio de Janeiro, where business people were in a hurry. In smaller cities, however, traditional customs of eating were still popular. Food courts were well developed in Brazil's shopping malls. They included a variety of sit-down restaurants, fast-food restaurants, and kiosks. In the United States, in contrast, food courts consisted primarily of fast-food restaurants. U.S. restaurant chains were, therefore, faced with a daunting task of changing Brazilians' eating habits—or convincing Brazilians of the attractiveness of fast-food, American style. The risk of not penetrating the Brazilian market, however, was significant given the size of Brazil's economy and McDonald's already significant presence.

Risks and Opportunities

KFC faced difficult decisions surrounding the design and implementation of an effective Latin American strategy over the next twenty years. It wanted to sustain its leadership position in Mexico and the Caribbean but also looked to strengthen its position in other regions in South America, particularly in Brazil. Limited resources and cash flow limited KFC's ability to aggressively expand in all countries simultaneously. KFC also faced the task of adapting its entry strategy to overcome barriers to entry in countries where it had little presence such as Argentina, Paraguay, Uruguay, and Venezuela. In Brazil, KFC hoped a joint venture partner would help overcome cultural barriers that forced it to withdraw in 2000. How should KFC expand its restaurant base in Latin America given differences in consumer acceptance of the fast-food concept, intensity of competition, and culture? Should KFC open company-owned restaurants or rely on franchises to grow its restaurant base? In which markets should KFC approach joint venture partners as a means of more effectively developing the KFC concept? Could KFC approach markets like Brazil and Argentina cautiously in light of McDonald's and Wendy's aggressive first mover advantages in those countries, or should KFC proceed more aggressively? Last, in which countries should KFC establish subsidiaries that actively managed multiple restaurants in order to exploit synergies in purchasing, operations, and advertising? A country subsidiary that was supported by resources from KFC headquarters in Louisville could only be justified if KFC had a large restaurant base in the targeted country. KFC's Latin American strategy required considerable analysis and thought about how to most efficiently use its resources. It also required an in-depth analysis of country risk and selection of the right country portfolio.

REFERENCES

General References

Direction of Trade Statistics, International Monetary Fund, Washington, DC.

International Financial Statistics, International Monetary Fund, Washington, DC.

Miller, Kent D., "A Framework for Integrated Risk Management in International Business," *Journal of International Business Studies* 23, no. 2 (1992): pages 311–331.

Quickservice Restaurant Trends, National Restaurant Association, Washington, DC.

Standard & Poor's Industry Surveys, Standard & Poor's Corporation, New York, NY.

The World Factbook, U.S. Central Intelligence Agency, Washington, D.C.

Periodicals

FIU Hospitality Review, FIU Hospitality Review, Inc., Miami, FL.

IFMA Word, International Foodservice Manufacturers Association, Chicago, IL.

Independent Restaurant, EIP, Madison, WI.

Journal of Nutrition in Recipe & Menu Development, Food Product Press, Binghamton, NY.

Nation's Restaurant News, Lebhar-Friedman, Inc., New York, NY (**http://www.nrn.com**).

Restaurants & Institutions, Cahners Publishing Co., New York, NY (**http://www.restaurantsandinstitutions.com**).

Restaurant Business, Bill Communications Inc., New York, NY (**http://www.restaurant.biz.com**).

Restaurants USA, National Restaurant Association, Washington, DC. (**http://www.restaurant.org**).

Associations

International Franchise Association, 1350 New York Ave. NW, Suite 900, Washington, DC 20005-4709, (202) 628-8000, **http://www.franchise.org**.

National Restaurant Association, 1200 17th St. NW, Washington, DC 20036-3097, (202) 331-5900, **http://www.restaurant.org**.

Books

Dave's Way: A New Approach to Old-Fashioned Success, by R. David Thomas (founder of Wendy's), Berkley Publishing Group, 1992.

The Globalization Reader, by Frank Lechner and John Boli (eds.), Blackwell Publishing, 2000.

Golden Arches East: McDonald's in East Asia, by James L. Watson (ed.), Stanford University Press, Palo Alto, CA, 1998.

Grinding It Out: The Making of McDonald's, by Ray Kroc (founder of McDonald's) and Robert Anderson, St. Martin's, 1990.

I'd Like the World to Buy a Coke: The Life and Leadership of Roberto Goizueta, by David Greising, John Wiley & Sons, 1999.

It's Easier to Succeed Than to Fail, by S. Truett Cathy (founder of Chick-fil-A), Oliver-Nelson Books, Nashville, TN, 1989.

Kentucky Fried Chicken Japan Ltd.: International Competitive Benchmarks and Financial Gap Analysis, by Icon Group Ltd., 2000.

Kentucky Fried Chicken Japan Ltd.: Labor Productivity Benchmarks and International Gap Analysis, by Icon Group Ltd., 2000.

McDonaldization Revisited, by Mark Alfino, John S. Caputo, and Robin Wynyard (eds.), Greenwood Publishing Group, 1998.

The McDonaldization of Society: An Investigation into the Changing Character of Contemporary Social Life, by George Ritzer, Pine Forge Press, 1995.

McDonald's Behind the Arches, by John F. Love, Bantam Books, 1986, 1995, 1999.

The McDonald's Thesis: Explorations and Extensions, by George Ritzer, Sage Publications, 1998.

Selling 'Em by the Sack: White Castle and the Creation of American Food, by David Gerard Hogan, New York University Press, 1999.

Taco Titan: The Glen Bell Story, by Debra Lee Baldwin, Summit Publishing Group, 1999.

Web Pages

Bojangles' (**http://www.bojangles.com**).
Boston Market Corporation (**http://www.bostonmarket.com**).
Burger King Corporation (**http://www.burgerking.com**).
Chick-fil-A (**http://www.chickfila.com**).
Churchs Chicken (**http://www.churchs.com**).
McDonald's Corporation (**http://www.mcdonalds.com**).
Popeyes Chicken & Biscuits (**http://www.popeyes.com**).
Yum! Brands, Inc. (**http://www.yum.com**).
Wendy's International Incorporated (**http://www.wendys.com**).

Nucor in 2005

This case was prepared by Frank C. Barnes, University of North Carolina-Charlotte, and Beverly B. Tyler, North Carolina State University.

Nucor Corporation took first place in the 2005 *Business Week* 50 list of the best performers of the S&P 500 companies. Not bad for a company in an industry often considered unexciting and low tech! In 2004, sales were up 82%, from $6 to $12 billion, and earnings went from $.40 to $7.02 per share. In a little over a year, the stock price tripled. Long-time employees with $300,000 in their retirement stock saw it rise to over $1 million. The tons shipped increased 9%, with the average selling price up 66%. However, scrap prices were up 74%. At the beginning of 2005, prices seemed to be holding up because of the mergers in the United States and the state control of supply in China. And Nucor expected the first quarter of 2005 to double its 2004 results. This was a reasonable expectation, since Nucor began the year with 70% of its flat-rolled steel output for all of 2005 sold, compared to just 25% a year earlier. Furthermore, in 2005 Nucor had two joint ventures with global partners to find alternatives to the use of scrap steel. In Brazil they were working on an environmentally friendly way to produce pig iron. With Mitsubishi and the Chinese steelmaker they were building a facility in Western Australia to use the new Hismelt process to produce iron from iron ore fines and cold fines with less energy and pollution.

The previous three years had been among the worst down cycle in the steel industry's history. During those years Nucor acquired failing competitors, increased its steel capacity, and achieved a profit in every quarter. The world economy and demand had improved recently as prices went from $300 a ton to $640 a ton. Thus, Nucor expected profits to continue to grow for a while. While bankruptcies had eliminated some excess capacity in the United States and state-controlled China could hold back capacity to maintain prices, global competitors were consolidating, suppliers were raising their prices on iron ore and scrap, and buyers were considering alternatives to steel. Nucor, and its new president Dan DiMicco, faced a challenge in continuing Nucor's reputation for excellence.

Background

Nucor could be traced back to the company that manufactured the first Oldsmobile in 1897 and became the Reo Truck Company. As the company declined into bankruptcy in the postwar years, a 1955 merger created Nuclear Corp. of America. Following the "conglomerate" trend of the period, Nuclear acquired various "high-tech" businesses, such as radiation sensors, semiconductors, rare earths, and air-conditioning equipment. However, the company lost money continually, and a fourth reorganization in 1966 put forty-year-old Ken Iverson in charge. The building of Nucor had begun.

Ken Iverson had joined the Navy after high school in 1943 and had been transferred from officer training school to Cornell's Aeronautical Engineering Program. On graduation he selected mechanical engineering/metallurgy for a master's degree to avoid the long drafting apprenticeship in aeronautical engineering. His college work with an electron microscope earned him a job with International Harvester. After five years in their lab, his boss, and mentor, prodded him to expand his vision by going with a smaller company.

Over the next ten years, Iverson worked for four small metals companies, gaining technical knowledge and increasing his exposure to other business functions. He enjoyed working with the presidents of these small companies and admired their ability to achieve outstanding results. Nuclear Corp., after failing to buy the company Iverson worked for, hired him as a consultant to find them another metals business to buy. In 1962, the firm bought a small joist plant in South Carolina that Iverson found, on the condition that he run it.

Over the next four years, Iverson built up the Vulcraft division as Nuclear Corporation struggled. The president, David Thomas, was described as a great promoter and salesman but a weak manager. A partner with Bear Stearns actually made a personal loan to the company to keep it going. In 1966, when the company was on the edge of bankruptcy, Iverson, who headed the only successful division, was named president and moved the headquarters to Charlotte, North Carolina, where he focused the company business first on the joist industry and soon moved into steel production.

He immediately began getting rid of the esoteric, but unprofitable, high-tech divisions and concentrated on the steel joist business he found successful. They built more joist plants and in 1968 began building their first steel mill in South Carolina to "make steel cheaper than they were buying from importers." By 1984, Nucor had six joist plants and four steel mills, using the new "minimill" technology.

From the beginning, Iverson had the people running the various plants, called divisions, make all the major decisions about how to build and run Nucor. The original board was composed of Iverson; Sam Siegel, his financial chief; and Dave Aycock, who had been with the South Carolina joist company before Nuclear acquired it. Siegel had joined Nuclear as an accountant in 1961. He had quit Nuclear but in their crisis agreed to return as treasurer if Iverson were named president. Aycock and Siegel were named vice presidents at the time Iverson was named president.

Dave Aycock had been very impressed with the original owner of Vulcraft, Sanborn Chase. Aycock had started his career as a welder there. He described

him as "the best person I've ever known" and as "a scientific genius." He said he was a man of great compassion, who understood the atmosphere necessary for people to self-motivate. Chase, an engineer by training, invented a number of things in diverse fields. He also established the incentive programs for which Nucor later became known. With only one plant, he was still able to operate with a "decentralized" manner. Before his death in 1960, while still in his forties, the company was studying the building of a steel mill using newly developed minimill technology. His widow ran the company until it was sold to Nucor in 1962.

Aycock met Ken Iverson when Nuclear purchased Vulcraft, and they worked together closely for the next year and a half. Located in Phoenix at the corporate headquarters, he was responsible to Iverson for all the joist operations and was given the task of planning and building a new joist plant in Texas. In late 1963, he was transferred to Norfolk, where he lived for the next thirteen years and managed a number of Nucor's joist plants. Then in 1977 he was named the manager of the Darlington South Carolina steel plant. In 1984, Aycock became Nucor's President and Chief Operating Officer, while Iverson became Chairman and Chief Executive Officer.

Aycock had this to say about Iverson: "Ken was a very good leader, with an entrepreneurial spirit. He is easy to work with and has the courage to do things, to take lots of risks. Many things didn't work, but some worked very well." There is the old saying "failure to take risk is failure." This saying epitomizes a cultural value personified by the company's founder and reinforced by Iverson during his time at the helm. Nucor was very innovative in steel and joists. Their plant was years ahead in wire rod welding at Norfolk. In the late 1960s, they had one of the first computer inventory management systems and design/engineering programs. They were very sophisticated in purchasing, sales, and managing, and they beat their competition often by the speed of their design efforts.

Between 1964 and 1984 the bankrupt conglomerate became a leading steel company in America. It was a fairytale story. Tom Peters used Nucor's management style as an example of "Excellence" while the barons of old steel ruled over creeping ghettos. NBC featured Nucor on television and *New Yorker* magazine serialized a book about how a relatively small American steel company built a team, which led the whole world into a new era of steelmaking. As the NBC program asked, "If Japan Can, Why Can't We?" Nucor had! Iverson was rich, owning $10 million in stock, but with a salary that rarely reached $1 million, compared with some U.S. executive's $50 or $100 million. The forty-year-old manager of the South Carolina Vulcraft plant had become a millionaire. Stockholders chuckled and ununionized hourly workers, who had never seen a layoff in the twenty years, earned more than the unionized workers of old steel and more than 85 percent of the people in the states where they worked. Many employees were financially quite secure.

Nucor owed much of its success to its benchmark organizational style and the empowered division managers. There were two basic lines of business, the first being the six steel joist plants that made the steel frames seen in many buildings. The second line included four steel mills that utilized the innovative minimill technology to supply the joist plants at first and later outside customers. Nucor was still only the seventh largest steel company in America. Over its second twenty years, Nucor was to rise to become the second-largest U.S. steel company. A number of significant challenges were to be met and overcome to get there, and once that horizon was reached even greater challenges would arise. Below are described the systems Nucor built and its organization, divisions, management, and incentive system.

Nucor's Organization

In the early 1990s, Nucor's twenty-two divisions (up to thirty by 2005), one for every plant, had a general manager, who was also a vice president of the corporation. The divisions were of three basic types, joist plants, steel mills, and miscellaneous plants. The corporate staff consisted of less than forty-five people (twenty-five in the 1990s). In the beginning Iverson had chosen Charlotte "as the new home base for what he had envisioned as a small cadre of executives who would guide a decentralized operation with liberal authority delegated to managers in the field," according to *South* magazine.

Iverson gave his views on keeping a lean organization:

> Each division is a profit center and the division manager has control over the day-to-day decisions that make that particular division profitable or not profitable. We expect the division to provide contribution, which is earnings before corporate expenses. We do not allocate our corporate expenses, because we do not think there is any way to do this reasonably and fairly. We do focus on earnings. And we expect a division to earn 25 percent return on total assets employed, before corporate expenses, taxes, interest or profit sharing. And we have a saying in the company—if a manager doesn't provide that for a number of years, we are either going to get rid of the division or get rid of the general manager, and it's generally the division manager.

A joist division manager commented on being in an organization with only four levels:

> I've been a division manager four years now and at times I'm still awed by it: the opportunity I was given to be a Fortune 500 vice-president. . . . I think we are successful because it is our style to pay more attention to our business than our competitors. . . . We are kind of a "no nonsense" company.

The divisions did their own manufacturing, selling, accounting, engineering, and personnel management. A steel division manager, when questioned about Florida Steel, which had a large plant 90 miles away, commented, "I expect they do have more of the hierarchy. I think they have central purchasing, centralized sales, centralized credit collections, centralized engineering, and most of the major functions."

Nucor strengthened its position by developing strong alliances with outside parties. It did no internal research and development. Instead, they monitored other's work worldwide and attracted investors who brought them new technical applications at the earliest possible dates. Though Nucor was known for constructing new facilities at the lowest possible costs; their engineering and construction team consists of only three individuals. They did not attempt to specify exact equipment parameters, but asked the equipment supplier to provide this information and then held the manufacturer accountable. They had alliances with selected construction companies around the country who knew the kind of work Nucor wanted. Nucor bought 95 percent of its scrap steel from an independent broker who followed the market and made recommendations regarding scrap purchases. They did not have a corporate advertising department, corporate public relations department, or a corporate legal or environmental department. They had long-term relationships with outsiders to provide these services.

The steel industry had established a pattern of absorbing the cost of shipment so, regardless of the distance from the mill, all users paid the same delivered price. Nucor broke with this tradition and stopped equalizing freight. It offered all customers the same sales terms. Nucor also gave no volume discounts, feeling that with modern computer systems there was no justification. Customers located next to the plant guaranteed themselves the lowest possible costs for steel purchases. Two tube manufacturers, two steel service centers, and a cold rolling facility had located adjacent to the Arkansas plant. These facilities accounted for 60 percent of the shipments from the mill. The plants were linked electronically to each other's production schedules, allowing them to function in a just-in-time inventory mode. All new mills were built on large enough tracks of land to accommodate collaborating businesses.

Iverson didn't feel greater centralization would be good for Nucor. Hamilton Lott, a Vulcraft plant manager, commented in 1997, "We're truly autonomous; we can duplicate efforts made in other parts of Nucor. We might develop the same computer program six times. But the advantages of local autonomy make it worth it." Joe Rutkowski, manager at Darlington steel, agreed, "We're not constrained; headquarters doesn't restrict what I spend. I just have to make my profit contribution at the end of year."

South magazine observed that Iverson had established a characteristic organizational style described as "stripped down" and "no nonsense." "Jack Benny would like this company," observed Roland Underhill, an analyst with Crowell, Weedon and Co. of Los Angeles, "so would Peter Drucker." Underhill pointed out that Nucor's thriftiness doesn't end with its "spartan" office staff or modest offices. "There are no corporate perquisites," he recited. "No company planes, No country club memberships. No company cars."

Fortune noted, "'Iverson takes the subway when he is in New York,' a Wall Street analyst reports in a voice that suggests both admiration and amazement." The general managers reflected this style in the operation of their individual divisions. Their offices were more like plant offices or the offices of private companies built around manufacturing rather than for public appeal. They were simple, routine, and businesslike.

Division Managers

The corporate personnel manager described management relations as informal, trusting, and not "bureaucratic." He felt there was a minimum of paperwork, that a phone call was more common than memos, and that no confirming memo was thought to be necessary.

A Vulcraft manager commented, "We have what I would call a very friendly spirit of competition from one plant to the next. And of course all of the vice-presidents and general managers share the same bonus systems so we are in this together as a team even though we operate our divisions individually." He added, "When I came to this plant four years ago, I saw we had too many people, too much overhead. We had 410 people at the plant and I could see, from my experience at the Nebraska plant, we had many more than we needed. Now with 55 fewer men, we are still capable of producing the same number of tons as four years ago."

The divisions managed their activities with a minimum of contact with the corporate staff. Each day disbursements were reported to the corporate office. Payments flowed into regional lock-boxes. On a weekly basis, joist divisions reported total quotes, sales cancellations, backlog, and production. Steel mills reported tons rolled, outside shipments, orders, cancellations, and backlog.

Each month the divisions completed a two-page (11″ x 17″) "Operations Analysis" which was sent to all the managers. Its three main purposes were (1) financial consolidation, (2) sharing information among the divisions, and (3) corporate management examination. The summarized information and the performance statistics for all the divisions were then returned to the managers.

The general managers met three times a year. In late October they presented preliminary budgets and capital requests. In late February they met to finalize budgets and treat miscellaneous matters. Then, at a meeting in May, they handled personnel matters, such as wage increases and changes of policies or benefits. The general managers as a group considered the raises for the department heads, the next lower level of management for all the plants.

Vulcraft—The Joist Divisions

One of Nucor's major businesses was the manufacture and sale of open web steel joists and joist girders at seven Vulcraft divisions located in Florence, South Carolina; Norfolk, Nebraska; Ft. Payne, Alabama; Grapeland, Texas; St. Joe, Indiana; Brigham City, Utah; and Chemung, New York. Open web joists, in contrast

FIGURE 1

Illustration of Joists

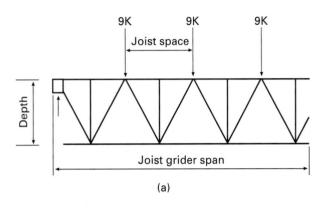

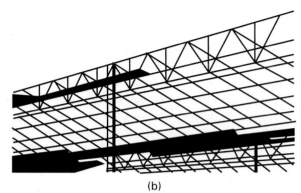

(a)   (b)

to solid joists, were made of steel angle iron separated by round bars or smaller angle iron (Figure 1). These joists cost less, were of greater strength for many applications, and were used primarily as the roof support systems in larger buildings, such as warehouses and shopping malls.

The joist industry was characterized by high competition among many manufacturers for many small customers. With an estimated 40 percent of the market, Nucor was the largest supplier in the United States. It utilized national advertising campaigns and prepared competitive bids on 80 percent to 90 percent of the buildings using joists. Competition was based on price and delivery performance. Nucor had developed computer programs to prepare designs for customers and to compute bids based on current prices and labor standards. In addition, each Vulcraft plant maintained its own Engineering Department to help customers with design problems or specifications. The Florence manager commented, "Here on the East Coast we have six or seven major competitors; of course none of them are as large as we are. The competition for any order will be heavy, and we will see six or seven different prices." He added, "I think we have a strong selling force in the market place. It has been said to us by some of our competitors that in this particular industry we have the finest selling organization in the country."

Nucor aggressively sought to be the lowest-cost producer in the industry. Materials and freight were two important elements of cost. Nucor maintained its own fleet of almost one hundred fifty trucks to ensure on-time delivery to all of the states, although most business was regional due to transportation costs. Plants

were located in rural areas near the markets they served. Nucor's move into steel production was a move to lower the cost of steel used by the joist business.

Joist Production

On the basic assembly line used at the joist divisions, three or four of which might make up any one plant, about six tons of joists per hour would be assembled. In the first stage, 8 people cut the angles to the right lengths or bend the round bars to the desired form. These were moved on a roller conveyer to 6-man assembly stations, where the component parts would be tacked together for the next stage, welding. Drilling and miscellaneous work were done by 3 people between the lines. The 9-man welding station completed the welds before passing the joists on roller conveyers to 2-man inspection teams. The last step before shipment was the painting.

The workers had control over and responsibility for quality. There was an independent quality control inspector who had the authority to reject the run of joists and cause them to be reworked. The quality control people were not under the incentive system and reported to the engineering department.

Daily production might vary widely, since each joist was made for a specific job. The wide range of joists made control of the workload at each station difficult; bottlenecks might arise anywhere along the line. Each workstation was responsible for identifying such bottlenecks so that the foreman could reassign people promptly to maintain productivity. Since workers knew most of the jobs on the line, including the more skilled welding job, they could be shifted as needed. Work on the line was described by one general manager as "not machine type but mostly physical labor." He said the important thing was to avoid bottlenecks.

There were four lines of about twenty-eight people, each on two shifts, at the Florence division. The jobs on the line were rated on responsibility and assigned a base wage, from $11 to $13 per hour. In addition, a weekly bonus was paid on the total output of each line. Each worker received the same percent bonus on his base wage. The Texas plant was typical with the bonus running 225 percent, giving a wage of $27 an hour in 1999.

The amount of time required to make a joist had been established as a result of experience; the general manager had seen no time studies in his fifteen years with the company. As a job was bid, the cost of each joist was determined through the computer program. The time required depended on the length, number of panels, and depth of the joist. At the time of production, the labor value of production, the standard, was determined in a similar manner. The South Carolina general manager stated, "In the last nine or ten years we have not changed a standard."

The Grapeland plant maintained a time chart, which was used to estimate the labor required on a job. The plant teams were measured against this time for bonus. The chart was based on the historical time required on the jobs. Every few years the time chart was updated. Because some of the changes in performance were due to equipment changes, generally the chart would be increased by half the change, and the employee would benefit in pay from the other half. The last change, two years ago, saw some departments' pay increased by as much as 10 percent. The production manager at Grapeland considered himself an example for the Nucor policy—"the sky is the limit." He had started in an entry position and risen to the head of this plant of two hundred people.

Table 1 below shows the productivity of the South Carolina plant in tons per man-hour for a number of years. The year 1999 set a record for overall tonnage,

TABLE 1

Tons per Man-Hour

1977	0.163	1982	0.208	1987	0.218
1978	0.179	1983	0.215	1988	0.249
1979	0.192	1984	0.214	1999	0.251
1980	0.195	1985	0.228	2000	0.241
1981	0.194	1986	0.225	2004	0.222

before a downturn which bottomed in 2002 but had begun to rise again by 2004.

Steel Divisions

Nucor moved into the steel business in 1968 to provide raw material for the Vulcraft plants. Iverson said, "We got into the steel business because we wanted to build a mill that could make steel as cheaply as we were buying it from foreign importers or from offshore mills." Thus, they entered the industry using the new minimill technology after they took a task force of four people around the world to investigate new technological advancements. A case writer from Harvard recounted the development of the steel divisions:

> By 1967 about 60% of each Vulcraft sales dollar was spent on materials, primarily steel. Thus, the goal of keeping costs low made it imperative to obtain steel economically. In addition, in 1967 Vulcraft bought about 60% of its steel from foreign sources. As the Vulcraft Division grew, Nucor became concerned about its ability to obtain an adequate economical supply of steel and in 1968 began construction of its first steel mill in Darlington, South Carolina. By 1972 the Florence, South Carolina, joist plant was purchasing over 90% of its steel from this mill. The Fort Payne, Alabama plant bought about 50% of its steel from Florence. Since the mill had excess capacity, Nucor began to market its steel products to outside customers. In 1972, 75% of the shipments of Nucor steel was to Vulcraft and 25% was to other customers.

Between 1973 and 1981, they constructed three more bar mills and their accompanying rolling mills to convert the billits into bars, flats, rounds, channels, and other products. Iverson explained in 1984:

> In constructing these mills we have experimented with new processes and new manufacturing techniques. We serve as our own general contractor and design and build much of our own equipment. In one or more of our mills we have built our own continuous casting unit, reheat furnaces, cooling beds and in Utah even our own mill stands. All of these to date have cost under $125 per ton of annual capacity—compared with projected costs for large integrated mills of $1,200—1,500 per ton of annual capacity, ten times our cost. Our mills have high productivity. We currently use less than four man hours to produce a ton of steel. Our total

employment costs are less than $60 per ton compared with the average employment costs of the seven largest U.S. steel companies of close to $130 per ton. Our total labor costs are less than 20% of our sales price.

In 1987, Nucor was the first steel company in the world to begin to build a minimill to manufacture steel sheet, the raw material for the auto industry and other major manufacturers. This project opened up another 50 percent of the total steel market. The first plant in Crawfordsville, Indiana, was successful, and three additional sheet mills were constructed between 1989 and 1990. Through the years these steel plants were significantly modernized and expanded until the total capacity was 3 million tons per year at a capital cost of less than $170 dollars per ton by 1999. Nucor's total steel production capacity was 5.9 million tons per year at a cost of $300 per ton of annual capacity. The eight mills sold 80 percent of their output to outside customers and the balance to other Nucor divisions.

By 2005, Nucor had sixteen steel facilities producing three times as much as in 1999. The number of bar mills had grown to nine mills with capacity of 6 million tons by the addition of Birmingham's four mills with 2 million tons and Auburn's 400,000 tons. The sheet mills grew to four and increased capacity one-third with the acquisition of Trico. Nucor-Yamato's structural steel capacity was increased by half a million tons from the South Carolina plant. The new million ton plate mill opened in North Carolina in 2000. Ninety-three percent of production was sold to outside customers.

All four of the original "bar mills" were actually two mills operating side by side. One mill concentrated on the larger bar products, which had separate production and customer demands, while the other mill concentrated on smaller diameter bar stock. Throughout Nucor each operation was housed in its own separate building with its own staff. Nucor designed its processes to limit work-in-process inventory, to limit space, to utilize a pull approach to material usage, and to increase flexibility.

The Steel Making Process

A steel mill's work is divided into two phases, preparation of steel of the proper "chemistry" and the forming of the steel into the desired products. The typical minimill utilized scrap steel, such as junk auto parts, instead of the iron ore, which would be used in larger, integrated steel mills. The typical bar minimill had an annual capacity of 200–600 thousand tons, compared with the 7 million tons of Bethlehem Steel's Sparrow's Point, Maryland, integrated plant.

In the bar mills a charging bucket fed loads of scrap steel into electric arc furnaces. The melted load, called a heat, was poured into a ladle to be carried by an overhead crane to the casting machine. In the casting machine, the liquid steel was extruded as a continuous red-hot solid bar of steel and cut into lengths weighing some 900 pounds called "billets." In the typical plant, the billet, about 4 inches in cross section and about 20 feet long, was held temporarily in a pit where it cooled to normal temperatures. Periodically billets were carried to the rolling mill and placed in a reheat oven to bring them up to 2000°F at which temperature they would be malleable. In the rolling mill, presses and dies progressively converted the billet into the desired round bars, angles, channels, flats, and other products. After cutting to standard lengths, they were moved to the warehouse.

Nucor's first steel mill, which employed more than five hundred people, was located in Darlington, South Carolina. The mill, with its three electric arc furnaces, operated 24 hours per day, 5 1/2 days per week. Nucor had made a number of improvements in the melting and casting operations. The general manager of the Darlington plant developed a system that involved preheating the ladles, allowing for the faster flow of steel into the caster and resulting in better control of the steel characteristics. Thus, less time and lower capital investment were required at Darlington than other minimills at the time of its construction. The casting machines were "continuous casters," as opposed to the old batch method. The objective in the "front" of the mill was to keep the casters working. At the time the Darlington plant was also perhaps the only mill in the country that regularly avoided the reheating of billets. This saved $10–12 per ton in fuel usage and losses due to oxidation of the steel. The cost of developing this process had been $12 million. All research projects had not been successful. The company spent approximately $2 million in an unsuccessful effort to utilize resistance heating. They lost even more on an effort at induction melting. As Iverson told *Metal Producing*, "That costs us a lot of money. Time wise it was very expensive. But you have got to make mistakes and we've had lots of failures."

The Darlington design became the basis for plants in Nebraska, Texas, and Utah. The Texas plant had cost under $80 per ton of annual capacity. Whereas the typical minimill at the time cost approximately $250 per ton, the average cost of Nucor's four mills was under $135. An integrated mill was expected to cost between $1,200 and $1,500 per ton.

The Darlington plant was organized into twelve natural groups for the purpose of incentive pay. Two mills each had two shifts with three groups—melting and casting, rolling mill, and finishing. In melting and casting, there were three or four different standards, depending on the material, established by the department manager years ago based on historical performance. The general manager stated, "We don't change the standards." The caster, key to the operation, was used at a 92 percent level—one greater than the claims of the manufacturer. For every good ton of billet above the standard hourly rate for the week, workers in the group received a 4 percent bonus. For example, with a common standard of 10 tons per run hour and an actual rate for the week of 28 tons per hour, the workers would receive a bonus of 72 percent of their base rate in the week's paycheck. In the rolling mill, there were more than one hundred products, each with a different historical standard. Workers received a 4 percent to 6 percent bonus for every good ton sheared per hour for the week over the computed standard. A manager stated, "Melt-shop employees don't ask me how much it costs Chaparral or LTV to make a billet. They want to know what it costs Darlington, Norfolk, Jewitt to put a billet on the ground—scrap costs, alloy costs, electrical costs, refractory, gas, etc. Everybody from Charlotte to Plymouth watches the nickels and dimes."

Management Philosophy

Aycock, while still the Darlington manager, stated,

The key to making a profit when selling a product with no aesthetic value, or a product that you really can't differentiate from your competitors, is cost. I don't look at us as a fantastic marketing organization, even though I think we are pretty good; but we don't try to overcome unreasonable costs by mass marketing. We maintain low costs by keeping the employee force at the level it should be, not doing things that aren't necessary to achieve our goals, and allowing people to function on their own and by judging them on their results.

To keep a cooperative and productive workforce you need, number one, to be completely honest about everything; number two, to allow each employee as much as possible to make decisions about that employee's work, to find easier and more productive ways to perform duties; and number three, to be as fair as possible to all employees. Most of the changes we make in work procedures and in equipment come from the employees. They really know the problems of their jobs better than anyone else.

To communicate with my employees, I try to spend time in the plant and at intervals have meetings with the employees. Usually if they have a question they just visit me. Recently a small group visited me in my office to discuss our vacation policy. They had some suggestions and, after listening to them, I had to agree that the ideas were good.

In discussing his philosophy for dealing with the work force, the Florence manager stated,

I believe very strongly in the incentive system we have. We are a non-union shop and we all feel that the way to stay so is to take care of our people and show them we care. I think that's easily done because of our fewer layers of management. . . . I spend a good part of my time in the plant, maybe an hour or so a day. If a man wants to know anything, for example an insurance question, I'm there and they walk right up to me and ask me questions, which I'll answer the best I know how.

We don't lay our people off and we make a point of telling our people this. In the slowdown of 1994, we scheduled our line for four days, but the men were allowed to come in the fifth day for maintenance work at base pay. The men in the plant on an average running bonus might make $17 to $19 an hour. If their base pay is half that, on Friday they would only get $8–$9 an hour. Surprisingly, many of the men did not want to come in on Friday. They felt comfortable with just working four days a week. They are happy to have that extra day off. About 20% of the people took the 5th day at base rate, but still no one had been laid off, in an industry with a strong business cycle.

In an earlier business cycle, the executive committee decided in view of economic conditions that a pay freeze was necessary. The employees normally received an increase in their base pay the first of June. The decision was made at that time to freeze wages. The officers of the company, as a show of good faith, accepted a 5 percent pay cut. In addition to announcing this to the workers with a stuffer in their pay envelopes, meetings were held. Each production line, or incentive group of workers, met in the plant conference room with all supervision—foreman, plant production manager, and division manager. The economic crisis the company was facing was explained to the employees by the production manager, and all of their questions were answered.

The Personnel and Incentive Systems

The foremost characteristic of Nucor's personnel system was its incentive plan. Another major personnel policy was providing job security. Also all employees at Nucor received the same fringe benefits. There was only one group insurance plan. Holidays and vacations did not differ by job. Every child of every Nucor employee received up to $1,200 a year for four years if they chose to go on to higher education, including technical schools. The company had no executive dining rooms or restrooms, no fishing lodges, company cars, or reserved parking places.

Jim Coblin, Nucor's vice president of human resources, described Nucor's systems for *HRMagazine* in a 1994 article, "No-frills HR at Nucor: A Lean, Bottom-Line Approach at This Steel Company Empowers Employees." Coblin, as benefits administrator, received part-time help from one of the corporate secretaries in the corporate office. The plants typically used someone from their finance department to handle compensation issues, although two plants had personnel generalists. Nucor plants did not have job descriptions, finding they caused more problems than they solved, given the flexible work force and nonunion status of Nucor employees. Surprisingly, Coblin found performance appraisal a waste of time. If an employee was not performing well, the problem would be dealt with directly. He had observed that when promotional opportunities became available, the performance appraisals were not much help filling the position. So he saw both of these as just more paperwork. The key, he believed, was not to put a maximum on what employees could earn and pay them directly for productivity. Iverson firmly believed that the bonus should be direct and involve no discretion on part of a manager.

Employees were kept informed about the company. Charts showing the division's results in return-on-assets and bonus payoff were posted in prominent places in the plant. The personnel manager commented that as

he traveled around to all the plants, he found everyone in the company could tell him the level of profits in their division. The general managers held dinners at least once but usually twice a year with each of their employees. The dinners were held with fifty or sixty employees at a time, resulting in as many as twenty dinners per year. After introductory remarks the floor was open for discussion of any work-related problems. There was a new employee orientation program and an employee handbook that contained personnel policies and rules. The corporate office sent all news releases to each division where they were posted on bulletin boards. Each employee in the company also received a copy of the annual report. For the last several years the cover of the annual report had contained the names of all Nucor employees.

Absenteeism and tardiness were not problems at Nucor. Each employee had four days of absences before pay was reduced. In addition to these, missing work was allowed for jury duty, military leave, or the death of close relatives. After this, a day's absence cost them bonus pay for that week, and lateness of more than a half-hour meant the loss of bonus for that day.

Safety was a concern of Nucor's critics. With ten fatalities in the 1980s, Nucor was committed to doing better. Safety administrators had been appointed in each plant, and safety had improved in the 1990s. The company also had a formal grievance procedure, although the Darlington manager couldn't recall the last grievance he had processed.

The company had conducted attitude surveys every three years for over two decades. These provided management insight into employee attitudes on twenty issues and allowed comparisons across plants and divisions. There were some concerns and differences but most employees appeared very satisfied with Nucor as an employer. The surveys suggested that pay was not the only thing the workers liked about Nucor. The personnel manager said that an NBC interviewer, working on the documentary "If Japan Can, Why Can't We," often heard employees say, "I enjoy working for Nucor because Nucor is the best, the most productive, and the most profitable company that I know of."

The average hourly worker's pay was over twice the average earnings paid by other manufacturing companies in the states where Nucor's plants were located. In many rural communities where Nucor had located, they provided better wages than most other manufacturers. The new plant in Hertford County illustrated this point as reported in a June 21, 1998, article in *The Charlotte Observer*, entitled "Hope on the Horizon: In Hertford County, Poverty Reigns and Jobs Are Scarce." Here the author wrote, "In North Carolina's forgotten northeastern corner, where poverty rates run more than twice the state average, Nucor's $300 million steel mill is a dream realized." The plant on the banks of the Chowan River in North Carolina's banks coastal district would have their employees earning a rumored $60,000 a year, three times the local average manufacturing wage upon completion. Nucor had recently begun developing its plant sites with the expectation of other companies co-locating to save shipping costs. Four companies have announced plans to locate close to Nucor's property, adding another one to two hundred jobs. People couldn't believe such wages, but calls to the plant's chief financial officer got "we don't like to promise too much, but $60,000 might be a little low." The average wage for these jobs at Darlington was $70,000. The plant's CFO added that Nucor didn't try to set pay "a buck over Wal-Mart" but went for the best workers. The article noted that steel work is hot and often dangerous, and that turnover at the plant may be high as people adjust to this and Nucor's hard-driving team system. He added, "Slackers don't last." The state of North Carolina had given $155 million in tax credits over twenty-five years. The local preacher said, "In 15 years, Baron (a local child) will be making $75,000 a year at Nucor, not in jail. I have a place now I can hold in front of him and say 'Look, right here. This is for you.'"

The Incentive System

There were four incentive programs at Nucor, one each for (1) production workers, (2) department heads, (3) staff people such as accountants, secretaries, or engineers, and (4) senior management, which included the division managers. All these programs were based on group performance.

Within the production program, groups ranged in size from twenty-five to thirty people and had definable and measurable operations. The company believed that a program should be simple and that bonuses should be paid promptly. "We don't have any discretionary bonuses—zero. It is all based on performance. Now we don't want anyone to sit in judgment, because it never is fair," said Iverson. The personnel manager stated, "Their bonus is based on roughly

90% of historical time it takes to make a particular joist. If during a week they make joists at 60% less than the standard time, they receive a 60% bonus." This was paid with the regular pay the following week. The complete pay check amount, including overtime, was multiplied by the bonus factor. A bonus was not paid when equipment was not operating. "We have the philosophy that when equipment is not operating everybody suffers and the bonus for downtime is zero." The foremen are also part of the group and received the same bonus as the employees they supervised.

The second incentive program was for department heads in the various divisions. The incentive pay here was based on division contribution, defined as the division earnings before corporate expenses and profit sharing are determined. Bonuses were reported to run between 0 and 90 percent (average 35 to 50 percent) of a person's base salary. The base salaries at this level were set at 75 percent of industry norms.

There was a third plan for people who were not production workers, department managers, or senior managers. Their bonus was based on either the division return-on-assets or the corporate return-on-assets depending on the unit they were a part of. Bonuses were typically 30 percent or more of a person's base salary for corporate positions.

The fourth program was for the senior officers. The senior officers had no employment contracts, pension or retirement plans, or other perquisites. Their base salaries were set at about 75 percent of what an individual doing similar work in other companies would receive. Once return-on-equity reached 9 percent, slightly below the average for manufacturing firms, 5 percent of net earnings before taxes went into a pool, which was divided among the officers based on their salaries. "Now if return-on-equity for the company reaches, say 20%, which it has, then we can wind up with as much as 190% of our base salaries and 115% on top of that in stock. We get both." Half the bonus was paid in cash, and half was deferred. Individual bonuses ranged from zero to several hundred percent, averaging 75 to 150 percent.

However, the opposite was true as well. In 1982, the return was 8 percent, and the executives received no bonus. Iverson's pay in 1981 was approximately $300,000 but dropped the next year to $110,000. "I think that ranked by total compensation I was the lowest paid CEO in the Fortune 500. I was kind of proud of that, too." In his 1997 book, *Plain Talk: Lessons From a Business Maverick*, Iverson said, "Can management expect employees to be loyal if we lay them all off at every dip of the economy, while we go on padding our own pockets." Even so by 1986, Iverson's stock was worth over $10 million, and the once Vulcraft manager was a millionaire.

In lieu of a retirement plan, the company had a profit sharing plan with a deferred trust. Each year 10 percent of pretax earnings was put into profit sharing for all people below officer level. Twenty percent of this was set aside to be paid to employees in the following March as a cash bonus, and the remainder was put into trust for each employee on the basis of the percentage of their earnings as a percentage of total wages paid within the corporation. The employee was vested after the first year. Employees received a quarterly statement of their balance in profit sharing.

The company had an Employer Monthly Stock Investment Plan to which Nucor added 10 percent to the amount the employee contributed on the purchase of any Nucor stock and paid the commission. After each five years of service with the company, the employee received a service award consisting of five shares of Nucor stock. Moreover, if profits were good, extraordinary bonus payments would be made to the employees. For example, in December 1998 each employee received an $800 payment.

According to Iverson:

> I think the first obligation of the company is to the stockholder and to its employees. I find in this country too many cases where employees are underpaid and corporate management is making huge social donations for self-fulfillment. We regularly give donations, but we have a very interesting corporate policy. First, we give donations where our employees are. Second, we give donations that will benefit our employees, such as to the YMCA. It is a difficult area and it requires a lot of thought. There is certainly a strong social responsibility for a company, but it cannot be at the expense of the employees or the stockholders.

Having welcomed a parade of visitors over the years, Iverson had become concerned with the pattern apparent at other companies' steel plants: "They only do one or two of the things we do. It's not just incentives or the scholarship program; it's all those things put together that results in a unified philosophy for the company."

Building on Their Success

Throughout the 1980s and 1990s, Nucor continued to take the initiative and be the prime mover in steel and the industries vertically related to steel. For example, in 1984 Nucor broke with the industry pattern of basing the price of an order of steel on the quantity ordered. Iverson noted, "Some time ago we began to realize that with computer order entry and billing, the extra charge for smaller orders was not cost justified." In a seemingly risky move in 1986, Nucor began construction of a $25 million plant in Indiana to manufacture steel fasteners. Imports had grown to 90 percent of this market as U.S. companies failed to compete. Iverson said, "We're going to bring that business back; we can make bolts as cheaply as foreign producers." A second plant, in 1995, gave Nucor 20 percent of the U.S. market for steel fasteners. Nucor also acquired a steel bearings manufacturer in 1986, which Iverson called "a good fit with our business, our policies and our people."

In early 1986, Iverson announced plans for a revolutionary plant at Crawfordsville, Indiana, which would be the first minimill in the world to manufacture flat-rolled or sheet steel, the last bastion of the integrated manufacturers. This market alone was twice the size of the existing market for minimill products. It would be a quarter of a billion dollar gamble on a new technology. The plant was expected to halve the integrated manufacturer's $3 of labor per ton and save $50 to $75 on a $400 a ton selling price. If it worked, the profit from this plant alone would come close to the profit of the whole corporation. *Forbes* commented, "If any mini-mill can meet the challenge, it's Nucor. But expect the going to be tougher this time around." If successful, Nucor had the licensing rights to the next two plants built in the world with this technology.

Nucor had spent millions trying to develop the process when it heard of some promising developments at a German company. In the spring of 1986, Aycock flew to Germany to see the pilot machine at SMS Schloemann-Siemag AG. In December the Germans came to Charlotte for the first of what they thought would be many meetings to hammer out a deal with Nucor. Iverson shocked them when he announced Nucor was ready to proceed to build the first plant of its kind.

Keith Busse was given the job of building the Crawfordsville, Indiana, steel sheet plant. The process of bringing this plant online was so exciting it became the basis for a bestselling book by Robert Preston, which was serialized in *New Yorker* magazine. Preston reported on a conversation at dinner during construction between Iverson and Busse. Thinking about the future, Busse was worried that Nucor might someday become like Big Steel. He asked, "How do we allow Nucor to grow without expanding the bureaucracy?" He commented on the vice presidents stacked on vice presidents, research departments, assistants to assistants, and so on. Iverson agreed. Busse seriously suggested, "Maybe we're going to need group vice presidents." Iverson's heated response was, "Do you want to ruin the company? That's the old Harvard Business School thinking. They would only get in the way, slow us down." He said the company could at least double, to $2 billion, before it added a new level of management. "I hope that by the time we have group vice presidents I'll be collecting Social Security."

The gamble on the new plant paid off, and Busse, the general manager of the plant, became a key man within Nucor. The new mill began operations in August of 1989 and reached 15 percent of capacity by the end of the year. In June of 1990, it had its first profitable month, and Nucor announced the construction of a second plant in Arkansas.

In December 1992, Nucor signed a letter of intent with Oregon Steel Mills to build a sheet mill on the West Coast to begin in 1994. This project was later canceled. The supply and cost of scrap steel to feed the minimills was an important future concern to Iverson. So at the beginning of 1993 Nucor announced the construction of a plant in Trinidad to supply its mills with iron carbide pellets. The innovative plant would cost $60 million and take a year and a half to complete. In 1994, the two existing sheet mills were expanded, and a new $500 million, 1.8 million ton sheet mill in South Carolina was announced, to begin operation in early 1997.

In what the *New York Times* called their "most ambitious project yet," in 1987 Nucor began a joint venture with Yamato Kogyo, Ltd. to make structural steel products in a mill on the Mississippi River in a direct challenge to the Big Three integrated steel companies. He put John Correnti in charge of the operation. Correnti built and then became the general manager of Nucor-Yamato when it started up in 1988. In 1991, he surprised many people by deciding to double Nucor-Yamato's capacity by 1994. It became Nucor's largest division and the largest wide flange

producer in the United States. By 1995, Bethlehem Steel was the only other wide flange producer of structural steel products left and had plans to leave the business.

Nucor started up its first facility to produce metal buildings in 1987. A second metal buildings facility began operations in late 1996 in South Carolina and a new steel deck facility, in Alabama, was announced for 1997. At the end of 1997, the Arkansas sheet mill was undergoing a $120 million expansion to include a galvanizing facility.

In 1995, Nucor became involved in its first international venture, an ambitious project with Brazil's Companhia Siderurgica National to build a $700 million steel mill in the state of Ceara. While other minimills were cutting deals to buy and sell abroad, Nucor was planning to ship iron from Brazil and process it in Trinidad.

Nucor set records for sales and net earnings in 1997. In the spring of 1998, as Iverson approached his seventy-third birthday, he was commenting, "People ask me when I'm going to retire. I tell them our mandatory retirement age is 95, but I may change that when I get there." It surprised the world when, in October 1998, Ken Iverson left the board. He retired as chairman at the end the year. Although sales for 1998 decreased 1 percent and net earnings were down 10 percent, the management made a number of long-term investments and closed draining investments. Start-up began at the new South Carolina steam mill and at the Arkansas sheet mill expansion. The plans for a North Carolina steel plate mill in Hertford were announced. This would bring Nucor's total steel production capacity to 12 million tons per year. Moreover, the plant in Trinidad, which had proven much more expensive than was originally expected, was deemed unsuccessful and closed. Finally, directors approved the repurchase of up to 5 million shares of Nucor stock.

Still, the downward trends at Nucor continued. Sales and earnings were down 3 percent and 7 percent, respectively, for 1999 (see Appendix 1 for financial reports and Appendix 2 for financial ratios). However, these trends did not seem to affect the company's investments. Expansions were underway in the steel mills, and a third building systems facility was under construction in Texas. Nucor was actively searching for a site for a joist plant in the northeast. A letter of intent was signed with Australian and Japanese companies to form a joint venture to commercialize the strip casting technology. To understand the challenges facing Nucor, industry, technology, and environmental trends in the 1980s and 1990s must be considered.

The U.S. Steel Industry in the 1980s

The early 1980s had been the worst years in decades for the steel industry. Data from the American Iron and Steel Institute showed shipments falling from 100 million tons in 1979 to the mid-eighty levels in 1980 and 1981. A slackening in the economy, particularly in auto sales, led the decline. In 1986, when industry capacity was at 130 million tons, the outlook was for a continued decline in per-capita consumption and movement toward capacity in the 90–100 million ton range. The chairman of Armco saw "millions of tons chasing a market that's not there: excess capacity that must be eliminated."

The large, integrated steel firms, such as U.S. Steel and Armco, which made up the major part of the industry, were the hardest hit. *The Wall Street Journal* stated, "The decline has resulted from such problems as high labor and energy costs in mining and processing iron ore, a lack of profits and capital to modernize plants, and conservative management that has hesitated to take risks."

These companies produced a wide range of steels, primarily from ore processed in blast furnaces. They had found it difficult to compete with imports, usually from Japan, and had given market share to imports. They sought the protection of import quotas. Imported steel accounted for 20 percent of the U.S. steel consumption, up from 12 percent in the early 1970s. The U.S. share of world production of raw steel declined from 19 percent to 14 percent over the period. Imports of light bar products accounted for less that 9 percent of the U.S. consumption of those products in 1981, according to the U.S. Commerce Department, while imports of wire rod totaled 23 percent of U.S. consumption.

Iron Age stated that exports, as a percent of shipments in 1985, were 34 percent for Nippon, 26 percent for British Steel, 30 percent for Krupp, 49 percent for USINOR of France, and less than 1 percent for every American producer on the list. The consensus of steel experts was that imports would average 23 percent of the market in the last half of the 1980s.

Iverson was one of the very few in the steel industry to oppose import restrictions. He saw an outdated U.S. steel industry that had to change.

We Americans have been conditioned to believe in our technical superiority. For many generations a continuing stream of new inventions and manufacturing techniques allowed us to far outpace the rest of the world in both volume and efficiency of production. In many areas this is no longer true and particularly in the steel industry. In the last three decades, almost all the major developments in steel making were made outside the U.S. I would be negligent if I did not recognize the significant contribution that the government has made toward the technological deterioration of the steel industry. Unrealistic depreciation schedules, high corporate taxes, excessive regulation and jaw-boning for lower steel prices have make it difficult for the U.S. steel industry to borrow or generate the huge quantities of capital required for modernization.

By the mid 1980s, the integrated mills were moving fast to get back into the game: They were restructuring, cutting capacity, dropping unprofitable lines, focusing products, and trying to become responsive to the market. The industry made a pronounced move toward segmentation. Integrated producers focused on mostly flat-rolled and structural grades, reorganized steel companies focused on a limited range of products, minimills dominated the bar and light structural product areas, and specialty steel firms sought niches. There was an accelerated shutdown of older plants, elimination of products by some firms, and the installation of new product lines with new technologies by others. High-tonnage mills restructured to handle sheets, plates, structural beams, high-quality bars, and large pipe and tubular products which allowed resurgence of specialized mills: cold-finished bar manufacturers, independent strip mills, and minimills.

The road for the integrated mills was not easy. As *Purchasing* pointed out, tax laws and accounting rules slowed the closing of inefficient plants. Shutting down a ten thousand-person plant could require a firm to hold a cash reserve of $100 million to fund health, pension, and insurance liabilities. The chairman of Armco commented, "Liabilities associated with a planned shutdown are so large that they can quickly devastate a company's balance sheet."

Joint ventures had arisen to produce steel for a specific market or region. The chairman of USX called them "an important new wrinkle in steel's fight for survival" and stated, "If there had been more joint ventures like these two decades ago, the U.S. steel industry might have built only half of the dozen or so hot-strip mills it put up in that time and avoided today's over-capacity."

The American Iron and Steel Institute reported steel production in 1988 of 99.3 million tons, up from 89.2 in 1987, and the highest in seven years. As a result of modernization programs, 60.9 percent of production was from continuous casters. Exports for steel increased and imports fell. Some steel experts believed the United States was now cost competitive with Japan. However, 1989 proved to be a year of "waiting for the other shoe to drop," according to *Metal Center News*. U.S. steel production was hampered by a new recession, the expiration of the voluntary import restraints, and labor negotiations in several companies. Declines in car production and consumer goods hit flat-rolled hard. AUJ Consultants told MCN, "The U.S. steel market has peaked. Steel consumption is tending down. By 1990, we expect total domestic demand to dip under 90 million tons."

The U.S. Steel Industry in the 1990s

The economic slowdown of the early 1990s did lead to a decline in the demand for steel through early 1993, but by 1995, America was in its best steel market in twenty years and many companies were building new flat-roll minimills. A *Business Week* article at the time described it as "the race of the Nucor look-alikes." Six years after Nucor pioneered the low-cost German technology in Crawfordsville, Indiana, the competition was finally gearing up to compete. Ten new projects were expected to add 20 million tons per year of the flat-rolled steel, raising U.S. capacity by as much as 40 percent by 1998. These mills opened in 1997 just as the industry was expected to move into a cyclical slump. It was no surprise that worldwide competition increased, and companies that had previously focused on their home markets began a race to become global powerhouses. The foreign push was new for U.S. firms who had focused on defending their home markets. U.S. minimills focused their international expansion primarily in Asia and South America.

Meanwhile in 1994, U.S. Steel, North America's largest integrated steel producer, began a major business process reengineering project to improve order fulfillment performance and customer satisfaction on the heels of a decade of restructuring. According to *Steel Times International*, "US Steel had to completely change the way it did business. Cutting labor costs, and increasing reliability and productivity took the company a long way towards improving profitability and competitiveness. However, it became clear that this leaner organization still had to implement new technologies and business processes if it was to maintain a competitive advantage." The goals of the business process reengineering project included a sharp reduction in cycle time, greatly decreased levels of inventory, shorter order lead times, and the ability to offer real-time promise dates to customers. In 1995, the company successfully installed integrated planning/production/order fulfillment software and results were very positive. U.S. Steel believed that the reengineering project had positioned it for a future of increased competition, tighter markets, and raised customer expectations.

In late 1997 and again in 1998, the decline in demand prompted Nucor and other U.S. companies to slash prices in order to compete with the unprecedented surge of imports. By the last quarter of 1998, these imports had led to the filing of unfair trade complaints with U.S. trade regulators, causing steel prices in the spot market to drop sharply in August and September before they stabilized. A press release by the U.S. secretary of commerce, William Daley, stated "I will not stand by and allow U.S. workers, communities and companies to bear the brunt of other nations' problematic policies and practices. We are the most open economy of the world. But we are not the world's dumpster." In early 1999, American Iron and Steel Institute reported in its Opinion section of its web page the following quotes by Andy Sharkey and Hank Barnette. Sharkey said, "With many of the world's economies in recession, and no signs of recovery on the horizon, it should come as no surprise that the United States is now seen as the only reliable market for manufactured goods. This can be seen in the dramatic surge of imports." Barnette noted, "While there are different ways to gauge the impact of the Asian crisis, believe me, it has already hit. Just ask the 163,000 employees of the U.S. steel industry."

The Commerce Department concluded in March 1999 that six countries had illegally dumped stainless steel in the United States at prices below production costs or home market prices. The Commerce Department found that Canada, South Korea, and Taiwan were guilty only of dumping, while Belgium, Italy, and South Africa also gave producers unfair subsidies that effectively lowered prices. However, on June 23, 1999, *The Wall Street Journal* reported that the Senate decisively shut off an attempt to restrict U.S. imports of steel despite industry complaints that a flood of cheap imports were driving them out of business. Advisors of President Clinton were reported to have said the president would likely veto the bill if it passed. Administrative officials opposed the bill because it would violate international trade law and leave the United States open to retaliation.

The American Iron and Steel Institute reported that in May 1999, U.S. steel mills shipped 8,330,000 net tons, a decrease of 6.7 percent from the 8,927,000 net tons shipped in May 1998. They also stated that for the first five months of 1999 shipments were 41,205,000 net tons, down 10 percent from the same period in 1998. AISI President and CEO Andrew Sharkey III said, "Once again, the May data show clearly that America's steel trade crisis continues. U.S. steel companies and employees continue to be injured by high levels of dumping and subsidized imports. . . . In addition, steel inventory levels remain excessive, and steel operating rates continue to be very low."

As the 1990s ended, Nucor was the second-largest steel producer in the United States, behind USX. The company's market capitalization was about two times that of the next smaller competitor. Even in a tight industry, someone can win. Nucor was in the best position because the industry was very fragmented, and there were many marginal competitors.

Steel Technology and the Minimill

A new type of mill, the "minimill," had emerged in the United States during the 1970s to compete with the integrated mill. The minimill used electric arc furnaces initially to manufacture a narrow product line from scrap steel. The leading U.S. minimills in the 1980s were Nucor, Florida Steel, Georgetown Steel, North Star Steel, and Chaparral. Between the late 1970s and 1980s, the integrated mills' market share fell from about 90 percent to about 60 percent, with the integrated steel companies averaging a 7 percent return on equity, the minimills averaging 14 percent, and some, such as Nucor, achieving about 25 percent. In the 1990s, minimills tripled their output to capture 17 percent of domestic shipments. Moreover, integrated mills' market share fell to around 40 percent, while minimills' share rose to 23 percent, reconstructed

mills increased their share from 11 percent to 28 percent, and specialized mills increased their share from 1 percent to 6 percent.

Some experts believed that a relatively new technology, the twin shell electric arc furnace, would help minimills increase production and lower costs and take market share. According to the *Pittsburgh Business Times*, "With a twin shell furnace, one shell—the chamber holding the scrap to be melted—is filled and heated. During the heating of the first shell, the second shell is filled. When the heating is finished on the first shell, the electrodes move to the second. The first shell is emptied and refilled before the second gets hot." This increased the production by 60 percent. Twin shell production had been widely adopted in the last few years. For example, Nucor Steel began running a twin shell furnace in November 1996 in Berkeley, South Carolina, and installed another in Norfolk, Nebraska, which began operations in 1997. "Everyone accepts twin shells as a good concept because there's a lot of flexibility of operation," said Rodney Mott, vice president and general manager of Nucor-Berkeley. However, this move toward twin shell furnaces could mean trouble in the area of scrap availability. According to an October 1997 quote in *Pittsburgh Business Times* by Ralph Smaller, vice president of process technology at Kvaerner, "Innovations that feed the electric furnaces' production of flat-rolled (steel) will increase the demand on high quality scrap and alternatives. The technological changes are just beginning and will accelerate over the next few years."

According to a September 1997 *Industry Week* article, steelmakers around the world were now closely monitoring the development of continuous "strip casting" technology, which may prove to be the next leap forward for the industry. "The objective of strip casting is to produce thin strips of steel (in the 1-mm to 4-mm range) as liquid steel flows from a tundish—the stationary vessel which received molten steel from the ladle. It would eliminate the slab-casting stage and all of the rolling that now takes place in a hot mill." Strip casting was reported to have some difficult technological challenges, but companies in Germany, France, Japan, Australia, Italy, and Canada had strip-casting projects under way. In fact, all of the significant development work in strip casting was taking place outside the United States.

Larry Kavanaph, American Iron and Steel Institute vice president for manufacturing and technology, said, "Steel is a very high-tech industry, but nobody knows it." Today's most productive steel-making facilities incorporated advanced metallurgical practices, sophisticated process-control sensors, state-of-the-art computer controls, and the latest refinements in continuous casting and rolling mill technology. Michael Shot, vice president–manufacturing at Carpenter Technology Corp., Reading, Pennsylvania, a specialty steels and premium-grade alloys producer, said, "You don't survive in this industry unless you have the technology to make the best products in the world in the most efficient manner."

Environmental and Political Issues

Not all stakeholders were happy with the way Nucor did business. In June 1998, *Waste News* reported that Nucor's mill in Crawfordsville, Indiana, was cited by the United States Environmental Protection Agency for alleged violations of federal and state clean-air rules. The Pamlico-Tar River Foundation, the NC Coastal Federation, and the Environmental Defense Fund had concerns about the state's decision to allow the company to start building the plant before the environmental review was completed. According to the *News & Observer* website, "The environmental groups charge that the mill will discharge 6,720 tons of pollutants into the air each year."

Moreover, there were other concerns about the fast-track approval of the facility being built in Hertford County. First, this plant was located on the banks of one of the most important and sensitive stretches of the Chowan, a principle tributary to the national treasure Albemarle Sound and the last bastion of the state's once vibrant river-herring fishery. North Carolina passed a law in 1997 that required the restoration of this fishery through a combination of measures designed to prevent overfishing, restore spawning and nursery habitats, and improve water quality in the Chowan. "New federal law requires extra care in protecting essential habitat for the herring, which spawn upstream," according to an article in the *Business Journal*. Second were the concerns regarding the excessive incentives the state gave to convince Nucor to build a $300 million steel mill in North Carolina. Some questioned whether the promise of three hundred well-paying jobs in Hertford County was worth the $155 million in tax breaks the state was giving Nucor to locate there.

Management Evolution

As Nucor opened new plants, each was made a division and given a general manager with complete responsibility for all aspects of the business. The corporate office did not involve itself in the routine functioning of the divisions. There was no centralized purchasing, or hiring and firing, or division accounting. The total corporate staff was still less than twenty-five people, including clerical staff when 1999 began.

In 1984, Dave Aycock moved into the corporate office as president. Ken Iverson was chief executive officer and chairman. Iverson, Aycock, and Sam Siegel operated as an executive board, providing overall direction to the corporation. By 1990, Aycock, who had invested his money wisely, owned over six hundred thousand shares of Nucor stock, five hotels and farms in three states, and was ready to retire. He was 60, five years younger than Iverson, and was concerned that if he waited, he and Iverson might be leaving the company at the same time. Two people stood out as candidates for the presidency, Keith Busse and John Correnti. In November, Iverson called Correnti to the Charlotte airport and offered him the job. Aycock commented, "Keith Busse was my choice, but I got outvoted." In June 1991, Aycock retired, and Keith Busse left Nucor to build an independent sheet mill in Indiana for a group of investors.

Thus Iverson, Correnti, and Siegel led the company. In 1993, Iverson had heart problems and major surgery. Correnti was given the CEO role in 1996. The Board of Directors had always been small, consisting of the executive team and one or two past Nucor vice presidents. Several organizations with large blocks of Nucor stock had been pressing Nucor to diversify its board membership and add outside directors. In 1996, Jim Hlavacek, head of a small consulting firm and friend of Iverson, was added to the board.

Only five, not six, members of the board were in attendance during the Board of Directors meeting in the fall of 1998, due to the death of Jim Cunningham. Near its end, Aycock read a motion, drafted by Siegel, that Ken Iverson be removed as chairman. It was seconded by Hlavacek and passed. It was announced in October that Iverson would be a chairman emeritus and a director, but after disagreements Iverson left the company completely. It was agreed Iverson would receive $500,000 a year for five years. Aycock left retirement to become chairman.

The details of Iverson's leaving did not become known until June of 1999 when John Correnti resigned after disagreements with the board and Aycock took his place. All of this was a complete surprise to investors and brought the stock price down 10 percent. Siegel commented that "the board felt Correnti was not the right person to lead Nucor into the 21st century." Aycock assured everyone he would be happy to move back into retirement as soon as replacements could be found.

In December 1999, Correnti became chairman of rival Birmingham Steel, with an astounding corporate staff of 156 people. With Nucor's organizational changes, he predicted more overhead staff and questioned their ability to move as fast in the future: "Nucor's trying to centralize and do more mentoring. That's not what grew the company to what it is today."

Aycock moved ahead with adding outside directors to the board. He appointed Harvey Gantt, principal in his own architectural firm and former mayor of Charlotte, Victoria Haynes, formally BF Goodrich's chief technology officer, and Peter Browning, chief executive of Sonoco (biographical sketches of board members and executive management are provided in Appendices 3 and 4). Then he moved to increase the corporate office staff by adding a level of executive vice presidents over four areas of business and adding two specialist jobs in strategic planning and steel technology. When Siegel retired, Aycock promoted Terry Lisenby to CFO and treasurer, and hired a director of IT to report to Lisenby (Figures 2 and 3 show the organization chart in 2000 and 2004, respectively).

Jim Coblin, vice president of human resources, believed the additions to management were necessary: "It's not bad to get a little more like other companies." He noted that the various divisions did their business cards and plant signs differently; some did not even want a Nucor sign. Sometimes six different Nucor salesmen would call on the same customer. "There is no

FIGURE 2

Nucor Organization Chart 2000

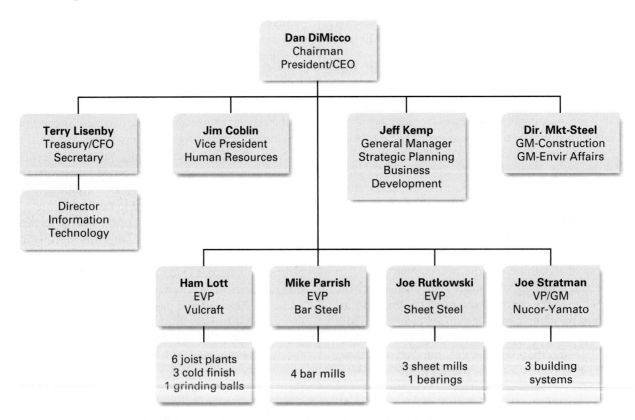

FIGURE 3

Nucor Organization Chart: Executive Management 2004

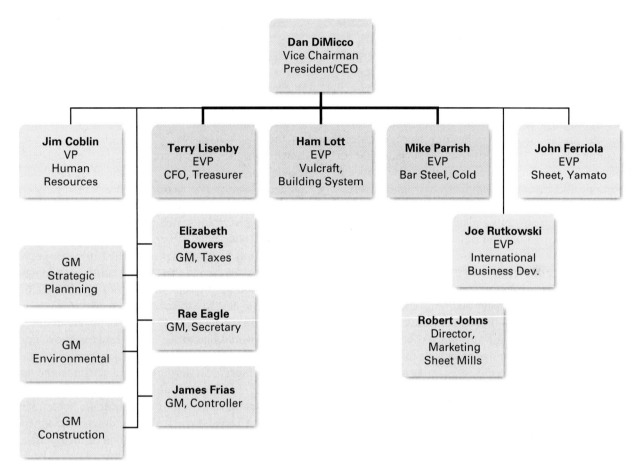

manager of human resources in the plants, so at least we needed to give additional training to the person who does most of that work at the plant," he stated. With these new additions there would be a director of information technology and two important committees, one for environmental issues and the second for audit.

He believed the old span of control of twenty might have worked well when there was less competition. Aycock considered it "ridiculous." "It was not possible to properly manage, to know what was going on. The top managers have totally lost contact with the company." Coblin was optimistic that the use of executive vice presidents would improve management. The three meetings of the general managers had slowly increased from about 1 1/2 days to about 2 1/2 days and become more focused. The new EVP

positions would bring a perspective above the level of the individual plants. Instead of fifteen individual detailed presentations, each general manager would give a short, five-minute briefing, and then there would be an in-depth presentation on the group, with team participation. After some training by Lisenby, the divisions had recently done a pretty good job with a SWOT analysis. Coblin thought these changes would make Nucor a stronger global player.

To Jeff Kemp, the new general manager of strategic planning and business development, the big issue was how to sustain earnings growth. In the U.S. steel industry, there were too many marginal competitors. The U.S. government had recently added to the problem by giving almost a billion dollars to nine mills, which simply allowed them to limp along and weaken the industry. He was looking for Nucor's opportunities within the steel industry. He asked why Nucor had bought a bearing company. His experience in the chemical industry suggested a need for Nucor to establish a position of superiority and grow globally, driving industry competition rather than reacting. He argued that a company should protect its overall market position, which could mean sacrifices for individual plants. Aycock liked Kemp's background in law and accounting and had specifically sought someone from outside the steel industry to head up Nucor's strategic planning. By June 2000, Kemp had conducted studies of other industries in the U.S. market and developed a working document that identified opportunities worthy of further analysis.

"Every company hits a plateau," Aycock observed. "You can't just go out and build plants to grow. How do you step up to the next level? I wouldn't say it's a turning point but we have to get our strategic vision and strategic plans." He stated, "We are beginning Nucor's first ever strategic planning sessions, it was not necessary before." His conclusions were partly the result of an Imaging Study Nucor had conducted.

In early 2000, Nucor had an outside consulting firm conduct a survey of the company's image as seen by the top ten to fifteen managers, including the corporate office. They also gathered the views of a few analysts and media personnel. In looking at the survey, one saw that the managers still agreed that Nucor valued risk taking, innovation, and a lean management structure with aggressive, hardworking employees who accepted the responsibility of failure along with the opportunity for success. They seemed to see Nucor as a way of doing business—not just a way of making steel—in terms of values and personality, not just business terms. When asked to associate Nucor's persona with a public figure, John Wayne was the clear choice.

The managers in the field seemed to believe the new layer of management was needed, and were not concerned about a loss of decentralization. They liked the new management team and the changes so far, particularly the improved communications with the corporate office. However, the corporate managers thought the company was changing much faster than the division managers. They also held a more positive view of the company on such things as how good the company was in their community or with the environment.

The people from the media had positive views of Nucor as hardworking and committed to its employees, an innovative risk-taking economic powerhouse.

Some—those most familiar with the company—believed the company needed to do a better job of communicating its vision during a period of transition.

Aycock believed Nucor needed to be quick to recognize developing technology in all production areas. He noted the joint venture to develop a new "strip caster," which would cast the current flat-rolled material in a more finished form. The impact could be "explosive," allowing Nucor to build smaller plants closer to markets. This would be particularly helpful on the West Coast. Nucor would own the U.S. and Brazilian rights, their partners the rest. He was also looking forward to the next generation of steel mills and wanted to own the rights this time. He praised Iverson's skill at seeing technology and committing to it.

He was very interested in acquisitions, but "they must fit strategically." A bar mill in the upper central Midwest and a flat-rolled plant in the Northeast would be good. A significant opportunity existed in preengineered buildings. Aycock intended to concentrate on steel for the next five to six years, achieving an average growth rate of 15 percent per year. In about seven years, he would like to see Nucor ready to move into other areas. He said Nucor had already "picked the low hanging grapes" and must be careful in its next moves.

Daniel DiMicco assumed the role of Nucor's president and chief executive officer in September 2000 when David Aycock stepped down as planned. Peter Browning was elected chairman of the Board of Directors. Aycock retired from the board a year later.

Sales for 2000 increased 14 percent over 1999 to reach a record level. Earnings were also at record levels, 27 percent over 1999. The year had begun on a strong footing but had turned weak by the years' end. While Nucor remained profitable, other steel companies faced bankruptcy. A Vulcraft plant was under construction in New York. It was their first northeastern operation and expanded the geographical coverage into a new region. They were also attempting a breakthrough technological step in strip casting at Crawfordsville, the Castrip process. They sold their Grinding Ball process and the Bearing Products operation because they were not a part of their core business.

In the company's annual report, DiMicco laid out their plans for 2000 and beyond:

> Our targets are to deliver an average annual earnings growth of 10–15 percent over the next ten years, to deliver a return well in excess of our cost of capital, to maintain a minimum average return on equity of 14 percent and to deliver a return on sales

of 8–10 percent. Our strategy will focus on Nucor becoming a "Market Leader" in every product group and business in which we compete. This calls for significant increases in market share for many of our core products and the maintenance of market share where we currently enjoy a leadership position.

While pointing out that it would be impossible to obtain this success through the previous strategy of greenfield construction, he added, "There will now be a heavy focus on growth through acquisitions. We will also continue growing through the commercialization of new disruptive and leapfrog technologies."

Steel and Nucor in the Twenty-First Century

In early 2001, *The Wall Street Journal* predicted that all but two of the United States's biggest steel makers would post fourth quarter losses. AK Steel Holding Corp. and Nucor Corp. were expected to have profits for the quarter of 2000, while U.S. Steel Group, a unit of USX Corp., was expected to post a profit for the year but not the fourth quarter. By October 1, more than twenty steel companies in the United States, including Bethlehem Steel Corp. and LTV Corp., the nation's third and fourth largest U.S. steel producers, respectively, had filed for bankruptcy protection. Over a dozen producers were operating under Chapter 11 bankruptcy-law protection, which allowed them to maintain market share by selling steel cheaper than non-Chapter 11 steelmakers. On October 20, *The Economist* noted that of the fourteen steel companies followed by Standard & Poor's, only Nucor was indisputably healthy. In the fall of 2001, 25 percent of domestic steel companies were in bankruptcy proceedings, although the United States was the largest importer of steel in the world. Experts believed that close to half of the U.S. steel industry might be forced to close before conditions improved.

The world steel industry found itself in the middle of one of its most unprofitable and volatile periods ever, in part due to a glut of steel that had sent prices to twenty-year lows. While domestic steel producers found themselves mired in red ink, many foreign steel makers desperately needed to continue to sell in the relatively open U.S. market to stay profitable. The industry was hovering around 75 percent capacity utilization, a level too low to be profitable for many companies. Three European companies—France's Usinor SA, Luxembourg's Arbed SA, and Spain's Aceralia

Corp.—merged to form the world's largest steel company. Two Japanese companies—NKK Corp. and Kawasaki Steel Corp.—merged to form the world's second-biggest steel maker. These new mega-steelmakers could outmuscle U.S. competitors, which were less efficient, smaller, and financially weaker than their competitors in Asia and Europe. At this time the largest U.S. steelmaker, USX-U.S. Steel Group, was only the eleventh largest producer in the world, and continued consolidation in the industry was expected.

In addition to cheap imports, U.S. steel producers faced higher energy prices, weakening demand by customer industries, increasingly tough environmental rules, and a changing cost structure among producers. With the declining economy, energy prices began to drop. However, so did demand for construction, automobiles, and farm equipment. Environmental rules led to costly modifications and closings of old plants, which produced coke along with vast clouds of ash and acrid green smoke. In 1990, minimills accounted for 36 percent of the domestic steel market, but by 2000, the more efficient minimill had seized 50 percent of the market and the resulting competition had driven prices lower.

The year 2001 turned out to be one of the worst years ever for steel. There was 9/11, a recession, and a surge of imports. DiMicco broke with Nucor's traditional opposition to government intervention to make a major push for protective tariffs. He stated, "The need to enforce trade rules is similar to the need to enforce any other law. If two merchants have stores side by side, but one sells stolen merchandise at a vast discount, we know that it's time for the police to step in." In March 2002, President Bush, after an investigation and recommendation by the ITC, imposed antidumping tariffs under Section 201 of the Trade Act of 1974. This restricted some imports of steel and placed quotas of up to 30 percent on others. The move was opposed by many, including steel users. Columnist George Will in his editorial on March 10, 2002, criticized Bush for abandoning free trade and pointed out the protection would hamper the necessary actions to restructure the steel industry in America by reducing excess capacity. The European Union immediately threatened reprisals and appealed to the WTO. In December, China imposed its own three-year program of import duties. Steel prices rose 40 percent in 2002 after the tariffs. Within a year hot-rolled steel prices increased 50 percent to $260 per ton over the twenty-year low of $210 during 2002. The price had been $361 in 1980. In November 2003, the WTO ruled against the tariffs, and, under increasing pressure of retaliation, Bush withdrew the tariffs.

While many steel companies floundered, Nucor was able to take advantage of the weakened conditions. In March 2001, Nucor made its first acquisition in ten years, purchasing a minimill in New York from Sumitomo Corp. Nucor had hired about five people to help plan for future acquisitions. DiMicco commented, "It's taken us three years before our team has felt this is the right thing to do and get started making acquisitions." In the challenged industry, he argued it would be cheaper to buy than build plants. They purchased the assets of Auburn Steel, which gave them a merchant bar presence in the Northeast and helped the new Vulcraft facility in New York. They acquired ITEC Steel, a leader in the emerging load-bearing light-gauge steel framing market, and saw an opportunity to aggressively broaden its market. Nucor increased its sheet capacity by roughly one-third when it acquired the assets of Trico Steel Co. in Alabama for $120 million. In early 2002, they acquired the assets of Birmingham Steel Corp. The $650 million purchase of four minimills was the largest acquisition in Nucor's history. In addition to making acquisitions to efficiently increase their market share and capacity, Nucor was actively working on new production processes that would provide them with technological advantages. They acquired the U.S. and Brazilian rights to the promising Castrip process for strip casting, the process of directly casting thin sheet steel. After development work on the process in Indiana they began full-time production in May 2002 and produced 7,000 tons in the last 10 months of 2002.

Moreover, in April Nucor entered into a joint venture with a Brazilian mining company, CVRD, the world's largest producer of iron-ore pellets, to jointly develop low-cost iron-based products. Success with this effort would give them the ability to make steel from scratch by combining iron ore and coke rather than using scrap steel.

As the year ended they were encouraged by the decrease in total steel capacity and what appeared to be a recovery in prices from record lows and expected slight improvement for 2002.

However, 2002 proved to be a difficult year for Nucor. Revenue increased 11 percent and earnings improved 43 percent over weak 2001, but the other financial goals were not met. They did increase their steel-making capacity by more than 25 percent. Looking

ahead to 2003, they anticipated a challenging year. However, they commented, "Nucor has a long-standing tradition of successfully emerging from industry downturns stronger than ever. It will be no different this time."

During 2003, prices of steel rose in the United States and Asia as global demand outpaced supply in some areas. China, with its booming economy, drove the market. An article in *The Wall Street Journal*, October 15, quoted Guy Dolle, chief executive of Arcelor SA of Luxembourg, the world's largest steelmaker in terms of steel product shipped, as saying, "China is the wild card in the balance between supply and demand." World prices did not soar dangerously because the steel industry continued to be plagued by overcapacity. Still steel-hungry China and other fast-growing nations added to their steel capacity.

Imports of steel commodities into the United States fell in August 2003 by 22 percent. A weakened dollar, the growing demand from China, and tariffs imposed in 2002 by Bush drove away imports. Domestic capacity declined, increasing capacity utilization from 77.2 percent to 93.4 percent as producers consolidated, idled plants, or went out of business. Prices for iron ore and energy rose, affecting integrated producers. Minimills saw their costs rise as worldwide demand for scrap prices rose. Thus, U.S. steelmakers boosted their prices. By February 2004, a growing coalition of U.S. steel producers and consumers were considering whether to petition to limit soaring exports of scrap steel from the United States, the world's largest producer of steel scrap. The United States had exported an estimated 12 million metric tons of steel scrap in 2003, a 21 percent increase from 2002. Moreover, the price of scrap steel was up 83 percent from a year earlier to $255 a ton. At the same time, the price of hot-rolled sheet steel rose 30 percent to $360 a ton. One result was that the International Steel Group (ISG) replaced Nucor as the most profitable U.S. steel producer. ISG was created when investor Wilbur Ross began acquiring the failing traditional steel producers in America, including LTV, Bethlehem, and Weirton. These mills used iron ore rather than scrap steel.

When 2003 ended, Nucor struck a positive note by reminding their investors that they had been profitable every single quarter since beginning operations in 1966. But while Nucor set records for both steel production and steel shipments, net earnings declined 61 percent. While the steel industry struggled through one of its deepest down cycles with weak prices and bankruptcies throughout the industry, Nucor increased its market share and held on to profitability. They worked on expanding their business with the automotive industry, continued their joint venture in Brazil to produce pig iron, and pursued a joint venture with the Japanese and Chinese to make iron without the usual raw materials. In February 2004 they were "optimistic about the prospects for obtaining commercialization" of their promising Castrip process for strip casting in the U.S. and Brazil. Moreover, Nucor was optimistic because the administration was using its trade laws to curtail import dumping and Nucor expected higher margins.

Global competition continued. Nucor has good reason to be proactive. According to the *Wall Street Journal,* Posco steelworks in Pohang, South Korea enjoyed the highest profits in the global steel industry as of 2004. Moreover, *Business Week* reported that the company had developed a new technology called Finex, which turns coal and iron ore into iron without coking and sintering, and which was expected to cut production costs by nearly a fifth and harmful emissions by 90%. They had also expanded their 80 Korean plants by investing in 14 Chinese joint ventures. By December 2004, demand in China had slowed and it had become a net steel exporter, sparking concerns of global oversupply.

Global consolidation continued. In October 2004, London's Mittal family announced that they would merge their Ispat International NV with LNM Group and ISG, to create the world's largest steel maker, with estimated annual revenues of $31.5 billion and output of 57 million tons. This would open a new chapter for the industry's consolidation, which had been mostly regional. Although the world's steel industry remains largely fragmented, with the world's top 10 steelmakers supplying less than 30% of global production, Mittal Steel will have about 40% of the U.S. market in flat-rolled steel. Moreover, Mittal, which had a history of using its scale to buy lower-cost raw materials and import modern management techniques into previously inefficient state-run mills, was buying ISG, a U.S. company which already owned the lowest-cost, highest profit mills in the United States. In January 2005, Mittal announced plans to buy 37% of China's Hunan Valin Iron & Steel Group Co.

With output of around 20 million metric tons each, U.S. Steel and Nucor face an uncertain environment as the industry consolidates. Some argue that if they didn't grow quickly, they might be taken over by foreign makers trying to gain entry into the United States. According to *Business Week,* Karlis Kirsis, managing partner of World Steel Dynamics, Inc., an information service, said "everybody's in play these days" in the wake of Mittal's planned merger with ISG. Even as they made bids of their own, South Korea's Posco and Belgium's Arcelor might snap them up.

APPENDIX 1

Financial Report
Balance Sheet 2000–2004 (in millions of USD)

As of:	12/31/2004	12/31/2003	12/31/2002	12/31/2001	12/31/2000
Assets					
Cash	779.05	350.33	219	462.35	490.58
Marketable Securities	n/a	n/a	n/a	n/a	n/a
Receivables	962.76	572.48	483.61	330.86	350.18
Total Inventories	1,239.89	560.4	588.99	466.69	461.15
Other Current Assets	193.26	137.35	157.34	133.8	79.53
Total Current Assets	3,174.95	1,620.56	1,448.94	1,393.69	1,381.45
Property, Plant & Equipment, Net	2,818.31	2,817.14	2,932.06	2,365.66	2,329.42
Property, Plant & Equipment, Gross	2,818.31	2,817.14	2,932.06	2,365.66	2,329.42
Deposits & Other Assets	139.95	54.66	n/a	n/a	n/a
Total Assets	6,133.21	4,492.35	4,381.00	3,759.35	3,710.87

APPENDIX 1 *(Continued)*

Financial Report
Balance Sheet 2000–2004 (in millions of USD)

As of:	12/31/2004	12/31/2003	12/31/2002	12/31/2001	12/31/2000
Liabilities					
Accounts Payable	471.55	329.86	247.23	189.24	203.33
Curr. Long-Term Debt	n/a	n/a	n/a	n/a	n/a
Accrued Expense	565.28	299.73	319.36	294.92	354.73
Income Taxes	28.96	n/a	8.95	n/a	n/a
Other Current Liabilities	n/a	n/a	n/a	n/a	n/a
Total Current Liabilities	1,065.79	629.6	591.54	484.16	558.07
Deferred Charges/Inc.	514.57	439.85	371.27	329.39	260.05
Long-Term Debt	923.55	903.55	878.55	460.45	460.45
Other Long-Term Liab.	n/a	n/a	n/a	n/a	n/a
Total Liabilities	2,503.91	1,973.00	1,841.36	1,274.00	1,278.57
Shareholder Equity					
Minority Interest	173.31	177.28	216.65	283.89	301.34
Preferred Stock	n/a	n/a	n/a	n/a	n/a
Common Stock	73.75	36.43	36.27	36.13	36.04
Capital Surplus	147.21	117.4	99.4	81.19	71.49
Retained Earnings	3,688.56	2,641.71	2,641.58	2,538.88	2,478.79
Treasury Stock	451.96	453.46	454.26	454.74	455.37
Total Shareholders Equity	3,455.99	2,342.08	2,322.99	2,201.46	2,130.95
Total Liab.& Shdr Equity	6,133.21	4,492.35	4,381.00	3,759.35	3,710.87

Income Statement 2000–2004 (in millions of USD)

Period Ended	12/31/2004	12/31/2003	12/31/2002	12/31/2001	12/31/2000
Net Sales	11,376.83	6,265.82	4,801.78	4,333.71	4,756.52
Cost of Goods Sold	9,128.87	5,996.55	4,332.28	3,914.28	3,929.18
Gross Profit	2,247.96	269.28	469.5	419.43	827.34
R & D Expenditure	n/a	n/a	n/a	n/a	n/a
Selling, General & Admin Exps	415.03	165.37	175.59	150.67	183.18
Depreciation & Amort.	n/a	n/a	n/a	n/a	n/a
Non-Operating Income	−79.3	−12.4	−49.57	−82.87	−150.65
Interest Expense	22.35	24.63	14.29	6.53	n/a
Income Before Taxes	1,731.28	66.88	230.05	179.37	493.52
Prov. For Inc. Taxes	609.79	4.1	67.97	66.41	182.61
Minority Interest	n/a	n/a	n/a	n/a	n/a
Realized Investment (Gain/Loss)	n/a	n/a	n/a	n/a	n/a
Other Income	n/a	n/a	n/a	n/a	n/a
Net Income Before Extra Items	1,121.49	62.78	162.08	112.96	310.91
Extra Items & Disc. Ops.	n/a	n/a	n/a	n/a	n/a
Net Income	1,121.49	62.78	162.08	112.96	310.91

Source: Data by Thomson Financial, Nucor webpage.

APPENDIX 2

Financial Ratios
Nucor Valuation Ratios 2004

P/E (TTM)	7.38
Per Share Ratios	
Dividend per Share	0.47
Book Value per Share	21.54
EPS Fully Diluted	7.02
Revenue per Share	71.21
Profit Margins	
Operating Margin	16.23
Net Profit Margin	9.86
Gross Profit Margin	19.88
Dividends	
Dividend Yield	1.13
Dividend Yield - 5 Yr. Avg.	1.28
Dividend per Share (TTM)	0.52
Dividend Payout Ratio	6.66
Growth (%)	
5 Year Annual Growth	35.6
Revenue - 5 Year Growth	23.19
Div/Share - 5 Yr Growth	12.57
EPS - 5 Year Growth	32.58
Financial Strength	
Quick Ratio	1.63
Current Ratio	2.98
LT Debt to Equity	26.72
Total Debt to Equity	26.72
Return on Equity (ROE) per Share	38.57
Return on Assets (ROA)	25.4
Return on Invested Capital (ROIC)	33.33
Assets	
Asset Turnover	1.85
Inventory Turnover	9.7

Source: Data by Thomson Financial, Nucor webpage.

APPENDIX 3

Board of Directors and Executive Management
In 1990
Board: Iverson, Aycock, Cunningham, Siegel, Vandekieft

Executive Office: Iverson, Aycock, Siegel

1991 to 1994
Board: Iverson, Aycock, Siegel, Cunningham, Correnti

Executive Office: Iverson, Siegel, Correnti, Lisenby, Prichard

1995 to 1996
Board: Iverson, Aycock, Siegel, Cunningham, Correnti, Hlavacek

Executive Office: Iverson, Siegel, Correnti, Doherty, Prichard

In 1997
Board: Iverson, Aycock, Siegel, Cunningham, Correnti, Hlavacek

Executive Office: Iverson, Siegel, Correnti, Lisenby, Prichard

In 1998
Board: Aycock, Siegel, Correnti, Hlavacek, Browning, Gantt, Haynes

Executive Office: Aycock, Siegel, Correnti, Parrish, Rutowski, Lisenby, Prichard

1999 to 2000
Board: Aycock, Siegel, Hlavacek, Browning, Gantt, Haynes

Executive Office: Aycock, Lisenby, DiMicco, Lott, Parrish, Rutowski, Coblin, Prichard

2002 to 2003
Board: Browning, Daley, DiMicco, Gantt, Haynes, Hlavacek, Milchovich, Waltermire

Executive Office: DiMicco, Lisenby, Ferriola, Lott, Parrish, Rutkowski, Coblin, Bowers, Frias, Johns, Laxton, Maero, Rowlan, Eagle (new 2003)

APPENDIX 4

Biographies of Selected Board Members and Executive Managers

Peter C. Browning has been the president and chief executive officer of Sonoco Products Company and was senior officer in 1993. He was previously the president, chairman, and chief executive officer of National Gypsum Company. He was elected chairman of Nucor's Board of Directors in September 2000 and became the nonexecutive chairman of Nucor when David Aycock retired from the board in 2001.

Daniel R. Dimicco was executive vice president of Nucor–Yamato Steel, Nucor Steel Hertford (plate division), and Nucor Building Systems before becoming president. He graduated from Brown University in 1972 with a bachelor of science in engineering, metallurgy and materials science. He received a master's in metallurgy from the University of Pennsylvania in 1975. He was with Republic Steel in Cleveland as a research metallurgy and project leader until he joined Nucor in 1982 as plant metallurgist and manager of quality control for Nucor Steel in Utah. In 1988, he became melting and castings manager. In 1991, he became general manager of Nucor–Yamato and a vice president in 1992. In September 2000, he was elected president and chief executive officer of Nucor. In 2001, when Aycock retired, he became vice chairman, president, and chief executive officer of Nucor.

Harvey B. Gantt was a partner in Gantt Huberman Architects for more than twenty-five years. He also served as mayor of the City of Charlotte, North Carolina, and was active in civic affairs. He was the first African-American graduate of Clemson University. He joined Nucor's Board of Directors in 1998.

Victoria F. Haynes is the president of Research Triangle Institute in Chapel Hill, North Carolina. Until 2000, she was the chief technical officer of the B. F. Goodrich Co. and vice president of its advanced technology group. She started with Goodrich in 1992 as vice president of research and development. She joined Nucor's Board of Directors in 1998.

James D. Hlavacek is the managing director of market driven management. Hlavacek was a neighbor and long-term friend of Iverson. He joined Nucor's Board of Directors in 1995.

Terry S. Lisenby is chief financial officer and an executive vice president. He graduated from the University of North Carolina at Charlotte in 1976 with a bachelor of science in accounting. Mr. Lisenby held accounting and management positions with Seidman and Seidman, Harper Corporation of America, and Concept Development, Inc. He joined Nucor in September 1985 as manager of financial accounting. He became vice president and corporate controller in 1991 and assumed the role of chief financial officer on January 1, 2000.

Hamilton Lott Jr. is executive vice president over the Vulcraft operations, cold-finished operations in Nebraska, and the Utah grinding ball plant. He graduated from the University of South Carolina in 1972 with a bachelor of science in engineering and then served in the United States Navy. He joined Nucor in 1975 as a design engineer at Florence. He later served as engineering manager and as sales manager at Nucor's Vulcraft division in Indiana. He was general manager of the Vulcraft division in Texas from 1987 to 1993 and the general manager in Florence from 1993 to 1999. He became a vice president in 1988 and joined the executive office in 1999.

D. Michael Parrish is executive vice president for the four steel plants and Nucor Fastener. He graduated from the University of Toledo in 1975 with a bachelor of science degree in civil engineering. He joined Nucor in September 1975 as a design engineer for Vulcraft and became engineering manager at Vulcraft in 1981. In 1986, he moved to Alabama as manufacturing manager, and in 1989, he returned to Utah as vice president and general manager. In 1991, he took the top job with Nucor Steel Texas and in 1995 at Nucor Steel Arkansas. In January 1999, he moved into corporate offices as executive vice president.

Joseph A. Rutkowski is executive vice president of Nucor Steel in Indiana, Arkansas, Berkeley, South Carolina, and Nucor Bearing Products. He graduated from Johns Hopkins University in 1976 with a bachelor of science in materials science engineering. He held metallurgical and management positions with Korf Lurgi Steeltec, North American Refractories, Georgetown Steel, and Bethlehem Steel. He joined Nucor in 1989 as manager of cold finish in Nebraska and became melting and casting manager in Utah before becoming vice president and general manager of Nucor Steel in Darlington in 1992. In 1998, he moved to Hertford as vice president, general manager to oversee the building of the new plate mill.

Case 19

3M in the New Millennium

This case was prepared by Charles W. L. Hill, the University of Washington.

Established in 1902, by 2002 3M was one of the largest technology-driven enterprises in the United States with annual sales of $16.4 billion, 55 percent of which were outside the United States. Throughout its history 3M's researchers had driven much of the company's growth. In 2002, the company sold some fifty thousand products, including Post-it Notes, Flex Circuits, Scotch tape, abrasives, specialty chemicals, Thinsulate insulation products, Nexcare bandage, optical films, fiber optic connectors, drug delivery systems, and much more. One-third of the company's products in 2002 didn't even exist in 1997. Around 7,000 of the company's 68,000 employees were technical employees. 3M's annual R&D budget exceeded $1 billion. The company had garnered over six thousand patents since 1990, with more than six hundred new patents awarded in 2002 alone. 3M was organized into forty different business units in a wide range of sectors, including consumer and office products; display and graphics; electronics and telecommunications; health care; industrial; safety, security, and protection services; and transportation (see Exhibit 1 for more details).

The company's 100-year anniversary was a time for celebration, but also one for strategic reflection. During the prior decade, 3M had grown profits and sales by between 6 to 7 percent per annum, a respectable figure but one that lagged behind the growth rates achieved by some other technology-based enterprises and diversified industrial enterprises such as General Electric. In 2001, 3M took a step away from its past when the company hired the first outsider to become CEO, James McNerney Jr. McNerney, who joined 3M after heading up GE's fast growing medical equipment business (and losing out in the race to replace legendary GE CEO, Jack Welch), was quick to signal that he wanted 3M to accelerate its growth rate. McNerney set an ambitious target for 3M to grow sales by 11 percent per annum and profits by 12 percent per annum. The question was how to achieve this without damaging the innovation engine that had propelled 3M to its current stature?

The History of 3M: Building Innovative Capabilities

The 3M story goes back to 1902 when five Minnesota businessmen established the Minnesota Mining and Manufacturing Company to mine a mineral that they thought was corundum, which is ideal for making sandpaper. The mineral, however, turned out to be low-grade anorthosite, nowhere near as suitable for making sandpaper, and the company nearly failed. To try and salvage the business, 3M turned to making the sandpaper itself using materials purchased from another source.

In 1907, 3M hired a twenty-year-old business student, William McKnight, as assistant bookkeeper. This turned out to be a pivotal move in the history of the company. The hardworking McKnight soon made his mark. By 1929, he was CEO of the company, and in 1949, he became chairman of 3M's Board of Directors, a position that he held until 1966.

EXHIBIT 1

3M Facts: Year-end 2002

3M is one of thirty companies in the Dow Jones Industrial Average and also is a component of the Standard & Poor's 500 Index.

Sales

Worldwide	$16.332 billion
International	$8.906 billion
55% of company's total	

Net Income*

Net income—reported	$1.974 billion
Percent to sales	12.1%
Earnings per share—diluted—reported	$4.99

*Includes non-recurring net loss of $108 million ($0.27 per share) principally related to 3M's restructuring plan.

Taxes

Income tax expense	$966 million

Dividends

(Paid every quarter since 1916)

Cash dividends per share	$2.48
One original share, if held, is now	1,536 shares

R&D and Related Expenditures

For 2002	$1.070 billion
Total for last five years	$5.339 billion

Capital Spending

For 2002	$763 million
Total for last five years	$5.361 billion

Employees

Worldwide	68,774
United States	35,024
International	33,750

Common Stock Data

Price at 12/31/02	$123.30
52-Week Range	$100.00–131.55
Market Capitalization	$48 billion
Indicated Annual Dividend	$2.48
Dividend Yield	2.0%
Year End	December 31
Ticker Symbol (NYSE)	MMM

Organization

- More than 40 business units, organized into seven businesses:
  - Health Care
  - Industrial
  - Consumer and Office
  - Display and Graphics
  - Electro and Communications
  - Safety, Security, and Protection Services
  - Transportation
- Operations in more than 60 countries—29 international companies with manufacturing operations, 32 with laboratories.
- In the United States, operations in 24 states.

Contributions

From 3M and 3M Foundation

U.S. cash and gifts-in-kind	more than $43 million

U.S. Patents Awarded 2002 608

3M Values

- Provide investors an attractive return through sustained, quality growth
- Satisfy customers with superior quality, value, and service
- Respect our social and physical environment
- Be a company employees are proud to be part of

3M Performance Initiatives

- Six Sigma
- 3M Acceleration
- eProductivity
- Sourcing Effectiveness
- Indirect Cost Control

As part of our everyday business processes, these initiatives will drive improvements in productivity and efficiency, and help us focus even more strongly on customer solutions and growth.

Source: 3M website.

From Sandpaper to Post-it Notes

It was McKnight, then 3M's president, who hired the company's first scientist, Richard Carlton, in 1921. Around the same time, McKnight's interest had been piqued by an odd request from a Philadelphia printer by the name of Francis Okie for samples of every sandpaper grit size that 3M made. McKnight dispatched 3M's East Coast sales manager to find out what Okie was up to. The sales manager discovered that Okie had invented a new kind of sandpaper that he had patented. It was waterproof sandpaper that could be used with water or oil to reduce dust and decrease the friction that marred auto finishes. In addition, the lack of dust reduced the poisoning associated with inhaling the dust of paint that had a high lead content. Okie had a problem though: He had no financial backers to commercialize the sandpaper. 3M quickly stepped into the breach, purchasing the rights to Okie's Wetordry waterproof sandpaper, and hiring the young printer to come and join Richard Carlton in 3M's lab. Wetordry sandpaper went on to revolutionize the sandpaper industry, and was the driver of significant growth at 3M.

Another key player in the company's history, Richard Drew, also joined 3M in 1921. Hired straight out of the University of Minnesota, Drew would round out the trio of scientists, Carlton, Okie and Drew, who, under McKnight's leadership, would do much to shape 3M's innovative organization.

McKnight charged the newly hired Drew with developing a stronger adhesive to better bind the grit for sandpaper to paper backing. While experimenting with adhesives, Drew accidentally developed a weak adhesive that had an interesting quality—if placed on the back of a strip of paper and stuck to a surface, the strip of paper could be peeled off the surface it was adhered to without leaving any adhesive residue on that surface. This discovery gave Drew an epiphany. He had been visiting autobody paint shops to see how 3M's Wetordry sandpaper was used, and he noticed that there was a problem with paint running. His epiphany was to cover the back of a strip of paper with his weak adhesive, and use it as "masking tape" to cover parts of the auto body that were not to be painted. An excited Drew took his idea to McKnight, and explained how masking tape might create an entirely new business for 3M. McKnight reminded Drew that he had been hired to fix a specific problem, and pointedly suggested that he concentrate on doing just that.

Chastised, Drew went back to his lab, but he could not get the idea out of his mind, so he continued to work on it at night, long after everyone else had gone home. Drew succeeded in perfecting the masking tape product, and then went to visit several autobody shops to show them his innovation. He quickly received several commitments for orders. Drew then went to see McKnight again. He told him that he had continued to work on the masking tape idea on his own time, had perfected the product, and got several customers interested in purchasing it. This time it was McKnight's turn to be chastised. Realizing that he had almost killed a good business idea, McKnight reversed his original position, and gave Drew the go ahead to pursue the idea.[1]

Introduced into the market in 1925, Drew's invention of masking tape represented the first significant product diversification at 3M. Company legend has it that this incident was also the genesis for 3M's famous 15 percent rule. Reflecting on Drew's work, both McKnight and Carlton agreed that technical people could disagree with management, and should be allowed to go and do some experimentation on their own. The company then established a norm that technical people could spend up to 15 percent of their own workweek on projects that might benefit the consumer, without having to justify the project to their manager.

Drew himself was not finished. In the late 1920s he was working with cellophane, a product that had been invented by DuPont, when lightning struck for a second time. Why, Drew wondered, couldn't cellophane be coated with an adhesive and used as a sealing tape? The result was Scotch Cellophane Tape. The first batch was delivered to a customer in September 1930, and Scotch Tape went on to become one of 3M's best selling products. Years later, Drew noted, "Would there have been any masking or cellophane tape if it hadn't been for earlier 3M research on adhesive binders for 3M™ Wetordry™ Abrasive Paper? Probably not!"[2]

Over the years, other scientists followed Drew's footsteps at 3M, creating a wide range of innovative products by leveraging existing technology and applying it to new areas. Two famous examples illustrate how many of these innovations occurred—the invention of Scotch Guard and the development of the ubiquitous Post-it Notes.

The genesis of Scotch Guard was in 1953 when a 3M scientist named Patsy Sherman was working on a new kind of rubber for jet aircraft fuel lines. Some of the latex mixture splashed onto a pair of canvas tennis shoes. Over time, the spot stayed clean while the rest of the canvas soiled. Sherman enlisted the help of fellow chemist Sam Smith. Together they began to investigate polymers, and it didn't take long for them to realize that they were onto something. They discovered an oil and water repellent substance, based on the fluorocarbon fluid used in air conditioners, with enormous potential for protecting fabrics from stains. It took several years before the team perfected a means to apply the treatment using water as the carrier, thereby making it economically feasible for use as a finish in textile plants.

Three years after the accidental spill, the first rain and stain repellent for use on wool was announced. Experience and time revealed that one product could not, however, effectively protect all fabrics, so 3M continued working, producing a wide range of Scotch Guard products that could be used to protect all kinds of fabrics.[3]

The story of Post-it Notes began with Spencer Silver, a senior scientist studying adhesives.[4] In 1968, Silver had developed an adhesive with properties like no other; it was a pressure sensitive adhesive that would adhere to a surface, but was weak enough to easily peel off the surface and leave no residue. Silver spent several years shopping his adhesive around 3M, to no avail. It was a classic case of a technology in search of a product. Then one day in 1973, Art Fry, a new product development researcher who had attended one of Silver's seminars, was singing in his church choir. He was frustrated that his bookmarks kept falling out of his hymn book, when he had a "Eureka" moment. Fry realized that Silver's adhesive could be used to make a wonderfully reliable bookmark.

Fry went to work next day, and using 15 percent time, started to develop the bookmark. When he started using samples to write notes to his boss, Fry suddenly realized that he had stumbled on a much bigger potential use for the product. Before the product could be commercialized, however, Fry had to solve a host of technical and manufacturing problems. With the support of his boss, Fry persisted, and after eighteen months, the product development effort moved from 15 percent time to a formal development effort funded by 3M's own seed capital.

The first Post-it Notes were test marketed in 1977 in four major cities, but customers were lukewarm at best. This did not gel with the experience within 3M,

where people in Fry's division were using samples all the time to write messages to each other. Further research revealed that the test marketing effort, which focused on ads and brochures, didn't resonate well with consumers, who didn't seem to value Post-it Notes until they had the actual product in their hands. In 1978, 3M tried again, this time descending on Boise, Idaho, and handing out samples. Follow-up research revealed that 90 percent of consumers who tried the product said they would buy it. Armed with this knowledge, 3M rolled out the national launch of Post-it Notes in 1980. The product subsequently went on to become a bestseller.

Institutionalizing Innovation

Early on McKnight set an ambitious target for 3M— a 10 percent annual increase in sales and 25 percent profit target. He also indicated how he thought that should be achieved with a commitment to plow 5 percent of sales back into R&D every year. The question though was how to ensure that 3M would continue to produce new products.

The answer was not apparent all at once, but rather evolved over the years from experience. A prime example was the 15 percent rule, which came out of McKnight's experience with Drew. In addition to the 15 percent rule and the continued commitment to push money back into R&D, a number of other mechanisms evolved at 3M to spur innovation.

Initially research took place in the business units that made and sold products, but by the 1930s, 3M had already diversified into several different fields, thanks in large part to the efforts of Drew and others. McKnight and Carlton realized that there was a need for a central research function. In 1937, they established a central research laboratory that was charged with supplementing the work of product divisions and undertaking long-run basic research. From the outset, the researchers at the lab were multidisciplinary, with people from different scientific disciplines often working next to each other on research benches.

As the company continued to grow, it became clear that there was a need for some mechanism to knit together the company's increasingly diverse business operations. This led to the establishment of the 3M Technical Forum in 1951. The goal of the Technical Forum was to foster idea sharing, discussion, and problem solving between technical employees located in different divisions and the central research laboratory. The Technical Forum sponsored "problem solving sessions" at which businesses would present their most recent technical nightmares in the hope that somebody might be able to suggest a solution—and that often was the case. The forum also established an annual event in which each division put up a booth to show off its latest technologies. Chapters were also created to focus on specific disciplines, such as polymer chemistry or coating processes.

During the 1970s, the Technical Forum cloned itself, establishing forums in Australia and England. By 2001, the forum had grown to 9,500 members in 8 U.S. locations and 19 other countries, becoming an international network of researchers who could share ideas, solve problems, and leverage technology.

According to Marlyee Paulson, who coordinated the Technical Forum from 1979 to 1992, the great virtue of the Technical Forum is to cross pollinate ideas. To quote:

3M has lots of polymer chemists. They may be in tape; they may be medical or several other divisions. The forum pulls them across 3M to share what they know. It's a simple but amazingly effective way to bring like minds together.[5]

In 1999, 3M created another unit within the company, 3M Innovative Properties (3M, IPC) to leverage technical know-how. 3M IPC is explicitly charged with protecting and leveraging 3M's intellectual property around the world. At 3M there has been a long tradition that while divisions "own" their products, the company as a whole "owns" the underlying technology, or intellectual property. One task of 3M IPC is to find ways in which 3M technology can be applied across business units to produce unique marketable products. Historically, the company has been remarkably successful at leveraging company technology to produce new product ideas (see Exhibit 2 for some recent examples).

EXHIBIT 2

Recent Examples of Leveraging Technology at 3M[6]

Richard Miller, a corporate scientist in 3M Pharmaceuticals, began experimental development of an antiherpes medicinal cream in 1982. After several years of development, his research team found that the interferon-based materials they were working with could be applied to any skin-based virus. The innovative chemistry they were working with was applied topically and was more effective than other compounds on the market. They found that the cream was particularly effective at interfering with the growth mechanism of genital warts. Competitive materials on the market at the time were caustic and tended to be painful. Miller's team obtained FDA approval for its Aldara (imiquimod) line of topical patient-applied creams in 1997.

Miller then applied the same Aldara-based chemical mechanism to basal cell carcinomas and found that here, too, it was particularly effective at restricting the growth of the skin cancer. "The patient benefit is quite remarkable," says Miller. New results in efficacy have been presented for treating skin cancers. His team recently completed phase III clinical testing and expects to apply later this year for FDA approval for this disease preventative. This material is already FDA approved for use in the treatment of genital warts. Doctors are free to choose to use it to treat those patients with skin cancers.

Andrew Ouderkirk is a corporate scientist in 3M's Film & Light Management Technology Center. 3M has been working in light management materials applied to polymer-based films since the 1930s, according to Ouderkirk. Every decade since then 3M has introduced some unique thin film structure for a specific customer application from high-performance safety reflectors for street signs to polarized lighting products. And every decade, 3M's technology base has become more specialized and more sophisticated. Their technology has now reached the point where they can produce multiple-layer interference films to 100-nm thicknesses each and hold the tolerances on each layer to within +/−3 nm. "Our laminated films are now starting to compete with vacuum-coated films in some applications," says Ouderkirk.

Rick Weiss is technical director of 3M's Microreplication Technology Center, one of 3M's twelve core technology centers. The basic microreplication technology was discovered in the early 1960s when 3M researchers were developing the fresnel lenses for overhead projectors. 3M scientists have expanded upon this technology to a wide variety of applications, including optical reflectors for solar collectors and adhesive coatings with air bleed ribs that allow large area films to be applied without having the characteristic "bubbles" appear. Weiss is currently working on development of dimensionally precise barrier ribs that can be applied to separate the individual "gas" cells on the new high-resolution large screen commercial plasma displays. Other applications include fluid management where capillary action can be used in biological testing systems to split a drop of blood into a large number of parts.

Another key to institutionalizing innovation at 3M has been the principle of "patient money." The basic idea is that producing revolutionary new products requires substantial long-term investments, and often repeated failure, before a major payoff occurs. The principle can be traced back to 3M's early days. It took the company twelve years before its initial sandpaper business started to show a profit, a fact that drove home the importance of taking the long view. Throughout the company's history, similar examples can be found. Scotchlite reflective sheeting, now widely used on road signs, didn't show much profit for ten years. The same was true of flurochemicals and duplicating products. Patient money doesn't mean substantial funding for long periods of time, however. Rather, it might imply that a small group of five researchers is supported for ten years while they work on a technology.

More generally, if researchers create a new technology or idea, they can begin working on it using 15 percent time. If the idea shows promise, they may request seed capital from their business unit managers to develop it further. If that funding is denied, which can occur, they are free to take the idea to any other 3M business unit. Unlike the case in many other companies, requests for seed capital do not require that researchers draft detailed business plans that are reviewed by top management. That comes later in the process. As one former senior technology manager has noted:

> In the early stages of a new product or technology, it shouldn't be overly managed. If we start asking for business plans too early and insist on tight financial evaluations, we'll kill an idea or surely slow it down.[7]

Explaining the patient money philosophy, Ron Baukol, a former executive vice president of 3M's international operations, and a manager who started as a researcher, has noted that

> You just know that some things are going to be worth working on, and that requires technological patience. . . . you don't put too much money into the investigation, but you keep one to five people working on it for twenty years if you have to. You do that because you know that, once you have cracked the code, it's going to be big.[8]

An internal review of 3M's innovation process in the early 1980s concluded that despite the liberal process for funding new product ideas, some promising ideas did not receive funding from business units or the central research budget. This led to the establishment in 1985 of Genesis Grants, which provide up to $100,000 in seed capital to fund projects that do not get funded through 3M's regular channels. About a dozen of these grants are given every year. One of the recipients of these grants, a project that focused on creating a multilayered reflective film, has subsequently produced a breakthrough reflective technology that may have applications in a wide range of businesses, from better reflective strips on road signs to computer displays and the reflective linings in light fixtures. Company estimates in 2002 suggest that the commercialization of this technology might ultimately generate $1 billion in sales for 3M.

Underlying the patient money philosophy is recognition that innovation is a very risky business. 3M has long acknowledged that failure is an accepted and essential part of the new product development process. As former 3M CEO Lew Lehr once noted:

> We estimate that 60% of our formal new product development programs never make it. When this happens, the important thing is to not punish the people involved.[9]

In an effort to reduce the probability of failure, in the 1960s 3M started to establish a process for auditing the product development efforts ongoing in the company's business units. The idea has been to provide a peer review, or technical audit, of major development projects taking place in the company. A typical technical audit team is composed of ten to fifteen business and technical people, including technical directors and senior scientists from other divisions. The audit team looks at the strengths and weaknesses of a development program, and its probability of success, both from a technical standpoint and a business standpoint. The team then makes nonbinding recommendations, but they are normally taken very seriously by the managers of a project. For example, if an audit team concludes that a project has enormous potential, but is terribly underfunded, managers of the unit would often increase the funding level. Of course, the converse can also happen, and in many instances, the audit team can provide useful feedback and technical ideas that can help a development team to improve their project's chance of success.

By the 1990s, the continuing growth of 3M had produced a company that was simultaneously pursuing a vast array of new product ideas. This was a natural outcome of 3M's decentralized and bottom up approach to innovation, but it was problematic in one crucial respect: the company's R&D resources were being spread too thinly over a wide range of opportunities, resulting in potentially major projects being underfunded.

To try and channel R&D resources into projects that had blockbuster potential, in 1994 3M introduced what was known as the Pacing Plus Program.

The program asked business to select a small number of programs that would receive priority funding, but 3M's senior executives made the final decision on which programs were to be selected for the Pacing Plus Program. An earlier attempt to do this in 1990 had met with limited success because each sector in 3M submitted as many as 200 programs. The Pacing Plus Program narrowed the list down to 25 key programs that by 1996 were receiving some 20 percent of 3M's entire R&D funds (by the early 2000s the number of projects funded under the Pacing Plus Program had grown to 60). The focus was on "leapfrog technologies," revolutionary ideas that might change the basis of competition and led to entirely new technology platforms that might, in typical 3M fashion, spawn an entire range of new products.

To further foster a culture of entrepreneurial innovation and risk taking, over the years 3M established a number of reward and recognition programs to honor employees who make significant contributions to the company. These include the Carton Society Award, which honors employees for outstanding career scientific achievements, and the Circle of Technical Excellence and Innovation Award, which recognizes people who have made exceptional contributions to 3M's technical capabilities.

Another key component of 3M's innovative culture has been an emphasis on duel career tracks. Right from its early days, many of the key players in 3M's history, people like Richard Drew, chose to stay in research, turning down opportunities to go into the management side of the business. Over the years, this became formalized in a dual career path. Today, technical employees can choose to follow a technical career path or a management career path, with equal advancement opportunities. The idea is to let researchers develop their technical professional interests, without being penalized financially for not going into management.

Although 3M's innovative culture emphasizes the role of technical employees in producing innovations, the company also has a strong tradition of emphasizing that new product ideas often come from watching customers at work. Richard Drew's original idea for masking tape, for example, came from watching workers use 3M Wetordry sandpaper in autobody shops. As with much else at 3M, the tone was set by McKnight who insisted that salespeople needed to "get behind the smokestacks" of 3M customers, going onto the factory floor, talking to workers, and finding out what their problems were. Over the years this theme has become ingrained in 3M's culture, with salespeople often requesting time to watch customers work, and then bringing their insights about customer problems back into their organization.

By the mid 1990s, McKnight's notion of getting behind the smokestacks had evolved into the idea that 3M could learn a tremendous amount from what were termed "lead users," who were customers working in very demanding conditions. Over the years, 3M had observed that in many cases, customers themselves can be innovators, developing new products to solve problems that they face in their work setting. This was most likely to occur for customers working in very demanding conditions. To take advantage of this process, 3M has instituted a lead user process in the company in which cross functional teams from a business unit go and observe how customers work in demanding situations.

For example, 3M has a $100 million business selling surgical drapes, which are drapes backed with adhesives that are used to cover parts of a body during surgery and help prevent infection. As an aid to new product development, 3M's surgical drapes business formed a cross functional team that went to observe surgeons at work in very demanding situations—including on the battlefield, hospitals in developing nations, and in vets' offices. The result was a new set of product ideas, including low-cost surgical drapes that were affordable in developing nations and devices for coating a patient's skin and surgical instruments with antimicrobial substances that would reduce the chance of infection during surgery.[10]

Driving the entire innovation machine at 3M has been a series of stretch goals set by top managers. The goals date back to 3M's early days and McKnight's ambitious growth targets. In 1977, the company established "Challenge 81," which called for 25 percent of sales to come from products that had been on the market for less than five years by 1981. By the 1990s, the goal had been raised to the requirement that

30 percent of sales should come from products that had been on the market less than four years.

The flip side of these goals was that over the years, many products and businesses that had been 3M staples were phased out. More than twenty of the businesses that were 3M mainstays in 1980, for example, had been phased out by 2000. Analysts estimate that sales from mature products at 3M generally fall by 3 to 4 percent per annum. The company has a long history of inventing businesses, leading the market for long periods of time, and then shutting those businesses down, or selling them off, when they can no longer meet 3M's own demanding growth targets. Notable examples include the duplicating business, a business 3M invented with Thermo Fax copiers (which were ultimately made obsolete by Xerox's patented technology), and the video and audio magnetic tape business. The former division was sold off in 1985, and then later in 1995. In both cases the company exited these areas because they had become low-growth commodity businesses that could not generate the kind of top line growth that 3M was looking for.

Still, 3M was by no means invulnerable in the realm of innovation and on occasion squandered huge opportunities. A case in point was the document copying business. 3M invented this business in 1951 when it introduced the world's first commercially successful Thermo Fax copier (which used specially coated 3M paper to copy original typed documents). 3M dominated the world copier business until 1970, when Xerox overtook the company with its revolutionary xerographic technology that used plain paper to make copies. 3M saw Xerox coming, but rather than try and develop their own plain paper copier, the company invested funds in trying to improve its (increasingly obsolete) copying technology. It was not until 1975 that 3M introduced its own plain paper copier, and by then it was too late. Ironically, 3M turned down the chance to acquire Xerox's technology twenty years earlier, when the company's founders had approached 3M.

Building the Organization

McKnight, a strong believer in decentralization, organized the company into product divisions in 1948 making 3M one of the early adopters of this organizational form. Each division was set up as an individual profit center that had the power, autonomy, and resources to run independently. At the same time, certain functions remained centralized, including significant R&D, human resources, and finance.

McKnight wanted to keep the divisions small enough that people had a chance to be entrepreneurial, and focused on the customer. A key philosophy of McKnight's was "divide and grow." Put simply, when a division became too big, some of its embryonic businesses were spun off into a new division. Not only did this new division then typically attain higher growth rates, but also the original division had to find new drivers of growth to make up for the contribution of the businesses that had gained independence. This drove the search for further innovations.

At 3M the process of organic diversification by splitting divisions became known as "renewal." The examples of renewal within 3M are legion. A copying machine project for Thermo-Fax copiers grew to become the Office Products Division. When Magnetic Recording Materials was spun off from the Electrical Products Division, it grew to become its own division, and then in turn spawned a spate of divisions.

However, this organic process was not without its downside. By the early 1990s, some of 3M's key customers were frustrated that they had to do business with a large number of different 3M divisions. In some cases, there could be representatives from ten to twenty 3M divisions calling on the same customer. To cope with this problem, in 1992 3M started to assign key account representatives to sell 3M products directly to major customers. These representatives typically worked across divisional lines. Implementing the strategy required many of 3M's general managers to give up some of their autonomy and power, but the solution seemed to work well, particularly for 3M's consumer and office divisions.

Underpinning the organization that McKnight put in place was his own management philosophy. As explained in a 1948 document, his basic management philosophy consisted of the following values:[11]

> As our business grows, it becomes increasingly necessary to delegate responsibility and to encourage men and women to exercise their initiative. This requires considerable tolerance. Those men and women to whom we delegate authority and responsibility, if they are good people, are going to want to do their jobs in their own way.
>
> Mistakes will be made. But if a person is essentially right, the mistakes he or she makes are not as serious in the long run as the mistakes management

will make if it undertakes to tell those in authority exactly how they must do their jobs.

Management that is destructively critical when mistakes are made kills initiative. And it's essential that we have many people with initiative if we are to continue to grow.

At just 3 percent per annum, employee turnover rate at 3M has long been among the lowest in corporate America, a fact that is often attributed to the tolerant, empowering, and familylike corporate culture that McKnight helped to establish. Reinforcing this culture has been a progressive approach toward employee compensation and retention. In the depths of the Great Depression, 3M was able to avoid laying off employees while many others did because the company's innovation engine was able to keep building new businesses even through the worst of times.

In many ways, 3M was ahead of its time in management philosophy and human resource practices. The company introduced its first profit sharing plan in 1916, and McKnight instituted a pension plan in 1930 and an employee stock purchase plan in 1950. McKnight himself was convinced that people would be much more likely to be loyal in a company if they had a stake in it. 3M also developed a policy of promoting from within and of giving its employees a plethora of career opportunities within the company.

Going International

The first steps abroad occurred in the 1920s. There were some limited sales of Wetordry sandpaper in Europe during the early 1920s. These increased after 1929 when 3M joined the Durex Corporation, a joint venture for international abrasive product sales in which 3M was involved along with eight other U.S. companies. In 1950, however, the Department of Justice alleged that the Durex Corporation was a mechanism for achieving collusion among U.S. abrasives manufacturers, and a judge ordered that the corporation be broken up. After the Durex Corporation was dissolved in 1951, 3M was left with a sandpaper factory in Britain, a small plant in France, a sales office in Germany, and a tape factory in Brazil. International sales at this point amounted to no more than 5 percent of 3M's total revenues.

Although 3M opposed the dissolution of the Durex Corporation, in retrospect it turned out to be one of the most important events in the company's history, for it forced the corporation to build its own

international operations. By 2002, international sales amounted to 55 percent of total revenues.

In 1952, Clarence Sampair was put in charge of 3M's international operations and charged with getting them off the ground. He was given considerable strategic and operational independence. Sampair and his successor, Maynard Patterson, worked hard to protect the international operations from getting caught up in the red tape of a major corporation. For example, Patterson recounts how

> I asked Em Monteiro to start a small company in Colombia. I told him to pick a key person he wanted to take with him. "Go start a company," I said, "and no one from St. Paul is going to visit you unless you ask for them. We'll stay out of your way, and if someone sticks his nose in your business you call me."[12]

The international businesses were grouped into an International Division that Sampair headed. From the get-go the company insisted that foreign ventures pay their own way. In addition, 3M's international companies were expected to pay a 5 to 10 percent royalty to the corporate head office. Starved of working capital, 3M's International Division relied heavily on local borrowing to fund local operations, a fact that forced those operations to quickly pay their own way.

The international growth at 3M typically occurred in stages. The company would start by exporting to a country and working through sales subsidiaries. In that way, it began to understand the country, the local marketplace, and the local business environment. Next 3M established warehouses in each nation, and stocked those with goods paid for in local currency. The next phase involved converting products to the sizes and packaging forms that the local market conditions, customs, and culture dictated. 3M would ship jumbo rolls of products from the United States, which were then broken up and repackaged for each country. The next stage was designing and building plants, buying machinery, and getting everything up and running. Over the years, R&D functions were often added, and by the 1980s, considerable R&D was being done outside of the United States.

Both Sampair and Patterson set an innovative, entrepreneurial framework that, according to the company, still guides 3M's international operations today. The philosophy can be reduced to several key and simple commitments: (1) Get in early (within the company, the strategy is known as FIDO—"First in Defeats Others");

(2) hire talented and motivated local people; (3) become a good corporate citizen of the country; (4) grow with the local economy; (5) American products are not one size fits all around the world—tailor products to fit local needs; and (6) enforce patents in local countries.

As 3M stepped into the international market vacuum, foreign sales surged from less than 5 percent in 1951 to 42 percent by 1979. By the end of the 1970s, 3M was beginning to understand how important it was to integrate the international operations more closely with the U.S. operations and to build innovative capabilities overseas. It expanded the company's international R&D presence (there are now more than twenty-two hundred technical employees outside the United States), built closer ties between the United States and foreign research organizations, and started to transfer more managerial and technical employees between businesses in different countries.

In 1978, the company started the Pathfinder Program to encourage new product and new business initiatives born outside the United States. By 1983, products developed under the initiative were generating sales of over $150 million a year. 3M Brazil invented a low-cost, hot melt adhesive from local raw materials. 3M Germany teamed up with Sumitomo 3M of Japan (a joint venture with Sumitomo) to develop electronic connectors with new features for the worldwide electronics industry, and 3M Philippines developed a Scotch-Brite cleaning pad shaped like a foot after learning that Filipinos polished floors with their feet, and so on. On the back of such developments, in 1992 international operations exceeded 50 percent for the first time in the company's history.

By the 1990s, 3M started to shift away from a country-by-country management structure to more regional management. Drivers behind this development included the fall of trade barriers, the rise of trading blocks such as the European Union and NAFTA, and the need to drive down costs in the face of intense global competition. The first European Business Center (EBC) was created in 1991 to manage 3M's chemical business across Europe. The EBC was charged with product development, manufacturing, sales and marketing for Europe, but also with paying attention to local country requirements. Other EBCs soon followed, such as EBCs for disposable products and pharmaceuticals.

As the millennium ended, 3M seemed set on transforming the company into a transnational organization characterized by an integrated network of businesses that spanned the globe. The goal was to get the right mix of global scale to deal with competitive pressures while at the same time maintaining 3M's traditional focus on local market differences and decentralized R&D capabilities.

The New Era
The DeSimone Years

In 1991, Desi DeSimone became CEO of 3M. A longtime 3M employee, the Canadian born DeSimone was the epitome of a twenty-first century manager—he had made his name by building 3M's Brazilian business, and he spoke five languages fluently. Unlike most prior 3M CEOs, DeSimone came from the manufacturing side of the business, rather than the technical side. He soon received praise for managing 3M through the recession of the early 1990s. By the late 1990s, however, his leadership had come under fire from both inside and outside the company.

In 1998 and 1999, the company missed its earnings targets, and the stock price fell as disappointed investors sold. Sales were flat, profit margins fell, and earnings slumped by 50 percent. The stock had underperformed the widely tracked S&P 500 stock index for most of the 1980s and 1990s.

One cause of the earnings slump in the late 1990s was 3M's sluggish response to the 1997 Asian crisis. During the Asian crisis, the value of several Asian currencies fell by as much as 80 percent against the U.S. dollar in a matter of months. 3M generated a quarter of its sales from Asia, but it was slow to cut costs there in the face of slumping demand following the collapse of currency values. At the same time, a flood of cheap Asian products cut into 3M's market share in the United States and Europe as lower currency values made Asian products much cheaper.

Another problem was that for all of its vaunted innovative capabilities, 3M had not produced a new blockbuster product since Post-it Notes. Most of the new products produced during the 1990s were just improvements over existing products, not truly new products.

DeSimone was also blamed for not pushing 3M hard enough earlier in the decade to reduce costs. An example was the company's supply chain excellence program. Back in 1995, 3M's inventory was turning over just 3.5 times a year, subpar for manufacturing. An internal study suggested that every half point increase in inventory turnover could reduce 3M's working capital needs by $700 million and boost its return on invested capital. But by 1998, 3M had made no progress on this front.[13]

By 1998, there was also evidence of internal concerns. Anonymous letters from 3M employees were sent to the Board of Directors, claiming that DeSimone was not committed to research as he should have been. Some letters complained that DeSimone was not funding important projects for future growth, others that he had not moved boldly enough to cut costs, and still others that the company's dual career track was not being implemented well and that technical people were underpaid. Critics argued that he was a slow and cautious decision maker in a time that required decisive strategic decisions. For example, in August 1998 DeSimone announced a restructuring plan that included a commitment to cut forty-five hundred jobs, but reports suggest that other senior managers wanted ten thousand job cuts, and DeSimone had watered down the proposals.[14]

Despite the criticism, 3M's board, which included four previous 3M CEOs among its members, stood behind DeSimone until he retired in 2001. However, the board began a search for a new top executive in February 2000 and signaled that it was looking for an outsider. In December 2000, the company announced that it had found the person they wanted, Jim McNerney, a fifty-one-year-old General Electric veteran who ran GE's medical equipment businesses, and before that GE's Asian operations. McNerney was one of the front runners in the race to succeed Jack Welsh as CEO of General Electric, but lost out to Jeffrey Immelt. One week after that announcement, 3M hired him.

McNerney's Plan for 3M

In his first public statement days after being appointed, McNerney said that his focus would be on getting to know 3M's people and culture and its diverse lines of business:

> I think getting to know some of those businesses and bringing some of GE here to overlay on top of 3M's strong culture of innovation will be particularly important.[15]

It soon became apparent that McNerney's game plan was exactly that: to bring the GE play book to 3M and use it to try and boost 3M's results, while simultaneously not destroying the innovative culture that had produced the company's portfolio of fifty thousand products.

The first move came in April 2001 when 3M announced that the company would cut five thousand jobs, or about 7 percent of the work force, in a restructuring effort that would zero in on struggling businesses. To cover severance and other costs of restructuring, 3M announced that it would take a $600 million charge against earnings. The job cuts were expected to save $500 million a year. In another effort to save costs, the company streamlined its purchasing processes, for example, by reducing the number of packaging suppliers on a global basis from fifty to five, saving another $100 million a year in the process.

Next, McNerney introduced the Six-Sigma process, a rigorous statistically based quality control process that was one of the drivers of process improvement and cost savings at General Electric. At heart, Six Sigma is a management philosophy, accompanied by a set of tools, that is rooted in identifying and prioritizing customers and their needs, reducing variation in all business processes, and selecting and grading all projects based on their impact on financial results. Six Sigma breaks every task (process) in an organization down into increments to be measured against a perfect model.

McNerney called for Six Sigma to be rolled out across 3M's global operations. He also introduced a 3M-like performance evaluation system at 3M under which managers were asked to rank every single employee who reported to them.

In addition to boosting performance from existing business, McNerney quickly signaled that he wanted to play a more active role in allocating resources between new business opportunities. At any given time, 3M has around fifteen hundred products in the development pipeline. McNerney thinks that is too many, and he has stated that he wants to funnel more cash to the most promising ideas, those with a potential market of $100 million a year or more, while cutting funding to weaker looking development projects.

In the same vein, he signaled that he wanted to play a more active role in resource allocation than had traditionally been the case for a 3M CEO, using cash from mature businesses to fund growth opportunities elsewhere. He scrapped the requirement that each division get 30 percent of its sales from products introduced in the past four years, noting that:

> To make that number, some managers were resorting to some rather dubious innovations, such as pink Post it Notes. It became a game, what could you do to get a new SKU?[16]

Some long time 3M watchers, however, worried that by changing resource allocation practices McNerney might harm 3M's innovative culture. If the company's history proves anything, they say, it's that it is hard to tell which of today's tiny products will become tomorrow's home runs. No one predicted that Scotch Guard or Post-it Notes would earn millions. They began as little experiments that evolved without planning into big hits. McNerney's innovations all sound fine in theory, they say, but there is a risk that he will transform 3M into "3E" and lose what is valuable in 3M in the process.

In general though, securities analysts greeted McNerney's moves favorably. One noted that "McNerney is all about speed" and that there will be "no more Tower of Babel—everyone speaks one language." This "one company" vision was meant to replace the program under which 3M systematically spun off successful new products into new business centers. The problem with this approach, according to the analyst, was that there was no leveraging of best practices across businesses.[17]

McNerney also signaled that he would reform 3M's regional management structure, replacing it with a global business unit structure that will be defined by either products or markets.

Fall 2003

At a meeting for investment analysts, held on September 30, 2003, McNerney summarized a number of achievements to date.[18] At the time, the early indications seemed to suggest that McNerney was helping to revitalize 3M. Profitability, measured by return on invested capital, had risen from 17.6 percent in 2001 to 21.6 percent in the first half of 2003, and 3M's stock price had risen from $42 just before McNerney was hired to $73 in October 2003.

Like his former boss, Jack Welsh at GE, McNerney seemed to place significant value on internal executive education programs as a way of shifting to a performance-oriented culture. McNerney noted that some twenty thousand employees had been through Six-Sigma training by the third quarter of 2003. Almost four hundred higher level managers had been through an Advanced Leadership Development Program set up by McNerney, and offered by 3M's own internal executive education institute. Some 40 percent of participants had been promoted on graduating. All of the company's top managers had graduated from an Executive Leadership Program offered by 3M.

McNerney also emphasized the value of five initiatives that he has put in place at 3M; indirect cost control, global sourcing, e-productivity, Six Sigma, and the 3M Acceleration Program. With regard to indirect cost control, some $800 million had been taken out of 3M's cost structure since 2001, primarily by reducing employee numbers, introducing more efficient processes that boost productivity, benchmarking operations internally, and leveraging best practices. According to McNerney, internal benchmarking highlighted another $200 to $400 million in potential cost savings over the next few years.

On global sourcing, McNerney noted that more than $500 million had been saved since 2000 by consolidating purchasing, reducing the number of suppliers, switching to lower cost suppliers in developing nations, and introducing dual sourcing policies to keep price increases under control.

The e-productivity program at 3M embraces the entire organization and all functions. It involves the digitalization of a wide range of processes, from customer ordering and payment, through supply chain management and inventory control, to managing employee processes. The central goal is to boost productivity by using information technology to more effectively manage information within the company, and between the company and its customers and suppliers. McNerney cites some $100 million in annual cost savings from this process to date.

The Six-Sigma program overlays the entire organization, and focuses on improving processes to boost cash flow, lower costs (through productivity enhancements), and boost growth rates. By late 2003, there were some seven thousand Six-Sigma projects in process at 3M. By using working capital more efficiently, Six-Sigma programs had helped to generate some $800 million in cash, with the total expected to rise to $1.5 billion by the end of 2004. 3M has applied the Six-Sigma process to the company's R&D process, enabling researchers to engage customer information in the initial stages of a design discussion, which, according to Jay Inlenfeld, the vice president of R&D, Six-Sigma tools, "allow us to be more closely connected to the market and give us a much higher probability of success in our new product designs."[19]

Finally, the 3M Acceleration program is aimed to boost the growth rate from new products through better resource allocation, particularly by shifting resources from slower growing to faster growing markets. As McNerney noted,

> 3M has always had extremely strong competitive positions, but not in markets that are growing fast enough. The issue has been to shift emphasis into markets that are growing faster.[20]

Part of this program is a tool termed 2X/3X. 2X is an objective for two times the number of new products that were introduced in the past, and 3X is a business objective for three times as many winning products as there were in the past (see Exhibit 3). 2X focuses on generating more "major" product initiatives, and 3X on improving the commercialization of those initiatives. The process illustrated in Exhibit 3 is 3M's "stage gate" process, where each gate represents a major decision point in the development of a new product, from idea generation to postlaunch.

Other initiatives aimed at boosting 3M's organization growth rate through innovation include the Six-Sigma process, leadership development programs, and technology leadership (see Exhibit 4). The purpose of these initiatives is to help implement the 2X/3X strategy.

As a further step in the Acceleration Program, 3M has decided to centralize its corporate R&D effort. Prior to the arrival of McNerney, there were 12 technology centers staffed by 900 scientists that focused on core technology development. The company is replacing these with one central research lab, staffed by 500 scientists, some 120 of whom will be located outside the United States. The remaining 400 scientists will be relocated to R&D centers in the business units. The goal of this new corporate research lab is to focus on developing new technology that might fill high growth "white spaces," which are areas where the company currently has no presence, but where the long-term market potential is great. An example is research on fuel cells, which is currently a big research project within 3M.

Responding to critics' charges that changes such as these might impact on 3M's innovative culture, Vice President of R&D Inlenfeld notes that:

> We are not going to change the basic culture of innovation at 3M. There is a lot of culture in 3M, but we are going to introduce more systematic, more productive tools that allow our researchers to be more successful.[23]

For example, Inlenfeld has repeatedly emphasized that the company remains committed to basic 3M principles, such as the 15 percent rule and leveraging technology across businesses.

By late 2003, McNerney noted that some six hundred new product ideas were under development and that, collectively, they were expected to reach the

EXHIBIT 3

The New Product Development Process at 3M[21]

2X/3X Strategy: 2X Idea Velocity/3X Winning Products Out

EXHIBIT 4

R&D's Role in Organic Growth[22]

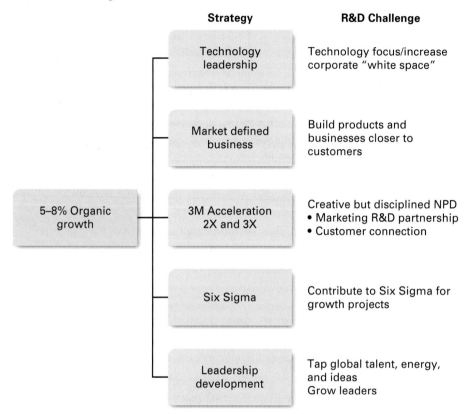

Strategy	R&D Challenge
Technology leadership	Technology focus/increase corporate "white space"
Market defined business	Build products and businesses closer to customers
3M Acceleration 2X and 3X	Creative but disciplined NPD • Marketing R&D partnership • Customer connection
Six Sigma	Contribute to Six Sigma for growth projects
Leadership development	Tap global talent, energy, and ideas Grow leaders

5–8% Organic growth

market and generate some $5 billion in new revenues between 2003 and 2006, up from $3.5 billion eighteen months earlier. Some $1 billion of these gains were expected to come in 2003.

The Acceleration Program was helping to increase 3M's organic growth rate in earnings per share, which hit an annual rate of 3.6 percent in the first half of 2003, up from 1 percent a year earlier and a decline in 2001. To complement internally generated growth, McNerney signaled that he would make selected acquisitions in business that 3M already had a presence in.

REFERENCES

J.C. Collins and J.I. Porras. *Built to Last.* New York: Harper Business, 1994.

Michelle Conlin. "Too Much Doodle?" *Forbes,* October 19, 1998, pages 54–56.

M. Dickson. "Back to the Future." *Financial Times,* May 30, 1994, page 7.

Joseph Hallinan. "3M's Next Chief Plans to Fortify Results With Discipline He Learned at GE Unit." *Wall Street Journal,* December 6, 2000, page B17.

Eric von Hippel et al. "Creating Breakthroughs at 3M." *Harvard Business Review* (September–October 1999).

Rick Mullin. "Analysts Rate 3M's New Culture." *Chemical Week,* September 26, 2001, pages 39–40.

Tim Studt. "3M—Where Innovation Rules," *R&D Magazine* 45 (April 2003): pages 20–24.

3M. "A Century of Innovation, the 3M Story." 3M, 2002. Available at **http://www.3m.com/about3m/century/index.jhtml.**

3M Investor Meeting, September 30, 2003, archived at **http://www.corporate-ir.net/ireye/ir_site.zhtml?ticker=MMM&script= 2100.**

Jerry Useem. "(Tape) + (Light bulb) = ?" *Fortune,* August 12, 2002, pages 127–131.

De'Ann Weimer. "3M: The Heat Is on the Boss." *Business Week,* March 15, 1999, pages 82–83.

ENDNOTES

1. M. Dickson, "Back to the Future," *Financial Times,* May 30, 1994, page 7, **http://www.3m.com/profile/looking/mcknight.jhtml.**

2. **http://www.3m.com/about3M/pioneers/drew2.jhtml.**

3. **http://www.3m.com/about3M/innovation/scotchgard50/index.jhtml.**

4. "3M. A Century of Innovation, the 3M Story." 3M, 2002. Available at **http://www.3m.com/about3m/century/index.jhtml.**

5. Ibid., page 33.

6. Tim Studt, "3M—Where Innovation Rules," *R&D Magazine* 45 (April 2003): pages 20–24.

7. "3M. A Century of Innovation," page 78.

8. Ibid.

9. Ibid., page 42.

10. Eric Von Hippel et al., "Creating Breakthroughs at 3M," *Harvard Business Review* (September–October 1999).

11. From 3M website at **http://www.3m.com/about3M/history/mcknight.jhtml.**

12. "3M. A Century of Innovation," pages 143–144.

13. Michelle Conlin, "Too Much Doodle?" *Forbes*, October 19, 1998, pages 54–56.

14. De'Ann Weimer, "3M: The Heat Is on the Boss," *Business Week*, March 15, 1999, pages 82–83.

15. Joseph Hallinan, "3M's Next Chief Plans to Fortify Results With Discipline He Learned at GE Unit," *Wall Street Journal*, December 6, 2000, page B17.

16. Jerry Useem, "(Tape) + (Light bulb) = ?" *Fortune*, August 12, 2002, pages 127–131.

17. Rick Mullin, "Analysts Rate 3M's New Culture," *Chemical Week*, September 26, 2001, pages 39–40.

18. 3M Investor Meeting, September 30, 2003, archived at **http://www. corporate-ir.net/ireye/ir_site.zhtml?ticker=MMM&script=2100.**

19. Studt, "3M—Where Innovation Rules," page 22.

20. 3M Investor Meeting, September 30, 2003.

21. Adapted from presentation by Jay Inlenfeld, 3M Investor Meeting, September 30, 2003, archived at **http://www.corporate-ir.net/ireye/ ir_site.zhtml?ticker=MMM&script=2100.**

22. Ibid.

23. Studt, "3M—Where Innovation Rules," page 21.

Case 20

The Rise of IBM

This case was prepared by Gareth R. Jones and Susan L. Peters, Texas A&M University.

In 1900 Charles Flint, a financier and arms merchant, owned among many other businesses two business machine manufacturers: the International Time Recording Co. (ITR), a clock manufacturer, and Computing Scale Co. of America, a weighing scale and food slicing machine manufacturer. In the search for new markets for its products, ITR began to produce new kinds of time-measuring machines that, among other things, permitted the rapidly expanding Bell telephone company to time its customers' long-distance calls. By 1910 ITR had become the leader in the time-recording industry with sales over $1 million. Computing Scale's main product was a scale that weighed items and calculated the cost per unit; the company also sold meat and cheese slicers to retail stores.

Toward the end of the nineteenth century, engineer Herman Hollerith invented a tabulating machine that sorted cards by punching holes. Any kind of data could be recorded by punching holes in cards according to a standard procedure and then the data could be analyzed statistically to provide a picture of the overall results. Potential customers for this device were organizations that needed a way of managing and manipulating large amounts of information, such as government agencies, railroads, and retail establishments. The U.S. Census Bureau, for example, saw the potential of this device for handling its national

data collection efforts and Hollerith was awarded a contract for managing the data processing of the 1890 census. Holes were punched in cards to represent different census attributes like age, sex, and national origin. The cards were then sorted by these punched holes and Hollerith's tabulating machine would then supply the requested data such as the statistics for the percentage of people in a certain age group in a certain state.

The punch card machine required a huge number of punched cards—in the census, one for every family unit—that could be used only once, so each machine sale provided card revenue. Nevertheless, the potential uses of the machine were limitless since any kind of data could be recorded on these cards. James Powers, an employee of the U.S. Census Bureau, immediately saw the potential of the tabulating machine and from his experience with Hollerith's machines at the Census Bureau he understood its strengths and weaknesses. Using this information, Powers invented an improved tabulating machine. Using his contacts at the Census Bureau, he managed to secure the contract for the 1910 census beating out Hollerith.

Hollerith was now in a difficult position because he had lost his principal customer and lacked the resources to improve his machine and to find new customers. He approached Flint to get Flint to invest in the business. Flint, seeing the opportunity to broaden his company's line of business machines, decided instead to acquire Hollerith's Tabulating Machine Company. In 1911 Flint merged it with ITR and Computing Scale to form the Computing Tabulating & Recording Company (CTR).

In operating his business, Hollerith had developed the practice of leasing, rather than selling, his machines to customers. He had opted for leasing because his machines were prone to breaking down, and they needed frequent repair as their mechanical components tended to break down with repeated use. By leasing his machines and backing them with an efficient repair service, Hollerith kept his customers happy. Moreover, customers liked the arrangement because it lowered their costs. Using CTR's resources, the Hollerith tabulating machines were continually improved over time, and as new machines were developed, they were leased to customers and replaced the old machines. These leases provided CTR with a continuing source of revenue, but more important, each of CTR's customers was required to buy punch cards from CTR. Seventy-five percent of tabulating revenues and most of the profit came from the sale of the punched cards, while only 25 percent came from the lease of the actual machine itself. In 1912 CTR's profits were $541,000 with 66 percent of this total coming from ITR, its time machine division. By 1913, however, profits rose to $613,000 with most of the increase traceable to revenues from punch cards and tabulators. The revenue produced by its new tabulator business proved very important to CTR because the next year, 1914, profits plunged to $490,000 due to a decline in the time clock sector. Only the tabulating business kept the company afloat.

The Impact of Thomas Watson

In 1914, to build CTR's business, Flint agreed to hire Thomas Watson as the general manager of CTR. Watson was a former employee of National Cash Register (NCR), another major business machine company, which he had joined in 1895 when he was 21 years old. Watson had a passion for selling and began selling pianos, sewing machines, and organs when he was 18. The opportunity to earn large commissions eventually led him to NCR where a mentor took an interest in his career and helped him develop his selling skills to the point where he became the star salesman at NCR within three years. Watson became an NCR branch manager in 1899.

To exploit Watson's talents, NCR assigned him to create an independent company using NCR funds. It was called Watson's Cash Register and Second Hand Exchange and was designed to beat NCR's competitors in the used cash register market. Just as NCR had a virtual monopoly over the sale of new cash registers, so Watson set out to monopolize the used cash register market by deliberately undercutting competitors'

prices. With their businesses failing, NCR would then acquire its competitors. This practice was blatantly illegal, and in 1912, Watson along with 29 other NCR managers were indicted for violation of antitrust laws. Watson was fined and sentenced to one year in jail; however, he won on appeal, and having quarreled with the head of NCR he decided to leave the company. Watson had other offers in the boat, auto, and retail industries, but because he wanted to use his knowledge of business machines, he accepted Flint's offer at CTR.

Watson's experience at NCR was significant for CTR because he implemented many of NCR's sales practices at CTR. Although NCR's competitors had higher-quality cash registers than NCR, NCR consistently beat the competition because of the way it organized and rewarded its sales force. NCR had developed the practice of granting salespeople exclusive rights to a territory and then paying them on commission. Salespeople would pursue all sales opportunities in their territories aggressively and they would call continually on customers in order to build strong, personal relationships with them. This sales strategy had been developed by the leader of NCR, John Patterson, who believed that a product was worthless until it was sold and that salespeople were the key to selling the product. Patterson insisted that NCR salespeople answer repair calls immediately and instilled in them the notion that they were selling a service, not just a product. NCR created a training school in 1894 to train its salespeople; it also established the NCR "Hundred Point Club" which recognized and rewarded salespeople who exceeded their quotas. Members of the club received bonuses and trips to conventions in big cities, coverage in the company newspaper, and personal congratulations from Patterson. Watson took full advantage of his knowledge of NCR's sales practices and transferred them to CTR. He also took full advantage of his entrepreneurial ability to sense unmet customer needs; he was fascinated by the potential of the punch card tabulating machine.

In 1904 Watson saw a friend at Eastman Kodak using a Hollerith punch card tabulating machine to monitor salespeople. Each time a sale was completed, all the data were stored onto a card, which was sorted and tabulated monthly to generate reports indicating what each person sold, which products were selling best in which regions, and so on. The cards were permanent records that could be filed, accumulated, and printed automatically. The punch card system eliminated boring jobs such as copying ledger entries and writing bills. Furthermore, the machines were relatively inexpensive (compared to employing clerks to keep records), dependable, and fast. Thus, as head of CTR, Watson became most interested in the tabulating machine side of the business even though ITR's time measurement business generated the highest sales and profits at the time.

When Watson became president of CTR in 1915 he convinced Flint that CTR should devote most of its resources to developing the tabulator side of the business. Watson implemented a plan to develop new tabulators, recorders, and printers to print the output of the tabulating machine. To achieve this new plan, the company funded the development of a research laboratory to improve the tabulating machines and established a facility to train salespeople. His goal was to create a sales force like NCR's sales force and to make better tabulating machines than CTR's competitors. To help provide the revenue to achieve this, Watson licensed foreign companies to produce and sell the tabulators in foreign markets. The licensees paid a royalty to CTR based on sales. This was the beginning of CTR's international strategy. Within two years, CTR's research laboratory created a new line of tabulators that were easier to use than competitors' models and that were priced below its competitors and offered for lease on favorable terms.

Powers was still CTR's major competitor at this time. To compete with Powers, which had tabulators as good as CTR's, Watson used the strategy that NCR had developed in the cash register business: sell a service, not just a product. Watson, like Patterson, emphasized that the salesperson's role was to provide good quality customer service, not merely to lease and install a machine. What CTR was selling was a way to handle information. This new philosophy was to guide the company's future mission.

Watson established the "100 Percent Club" to reward his best salespeople, and employees were paid generous commissions for meeting and exceeding their quotas. Those who met quotas and joined the 100 Percent Club were honored at conventions and received special status in the organization; 80 percent of employees made the club. In addition, employees received a premium salary and good benefits. The company's policy of internal promotion made it possible for hard-working employees to advance quickly in the organization. These employment practices made

it easy for CTR to attract and retain good salespeople and to gain the commitment of its work force which was famous for championing the company's products.

By 1917 CTR's sales had increased to $8.3 million from $4.2 million in 1914. All three of its divisions were doing well. Computing Scale's products were now used throughout the United States in places such as shipyards and factories to measure the quantity of products such as nuts and bolts. CTR had record sales during World War I. CTR had 1,400 tabulators on lease by the end of the war.

Virtually all big insurance companies, railroads, and government agencies used CTR's tabulators. In addition to the leased machines, the sales of punch cards were increasing and contributing to company revenues. In 1919, CTR launched a new printer that displayed the data collected and analyzed in the Hollerith tabulators and card sorters. The printer was priced below the machine made by Powers and was so successful that CTR had a backorder for the printers and Watson planned to build a new production plant to meet the high demand.

The large expenditures on research and development and on developing and training a skilled national sales force put a severe strain on CTR's resources. The strain was so severe that when sales revenues dropped from a record of $16 million in 1920 to $10.6 million in 1921, due to a slump in the national economy, CTR had to seek outside funds to survive. Fortunately for the company, Guaranty Trust Bank lent CTR the money it needed to meet current liabilities, and in 1922 sales revenues rebounded and the company made a profit. However, the company had to cut costs in every area, including sales and R&D, and CTR learned not to let cash balances go too low and implemented policies of low dividends, high revenues, and careful cost controls. In addition, the company intentionally refrained from introducing its new products until a mass market had developed for its new range of tabulating machines.

Watson became chairman of CTR in 1924 and renamed the company International Business Machines (IBM). This new name not only presented an integrated image of the company's three main product lines but also indicated the direction Watson planned for the company—the company's business was to provide advanced business machines for both the domestic and foreign markets.

IBM's strategy from the 1920s on was to produce and lease business machines that collect, process, and present large amounts of data. From 1924 to 1941, IBM's primary business was the production and lease of punched card tabulating machines and the sale of punch cards; punched cards still contributed most to the revenues of the company. As the technology of punch card tabulators became more advanced, they were able to sort 400 cards a minute and could print paychecks and address labels. Tabulating machines were used increasingly by large companies to keep records on their employees and suppliers and to keep track of their customer accounts. Companies usually leased IBM's machines and IBM would develop a specific punch card system to meet the needs of each individual customer. For example, IBM would help the customer design a coding system appropriate to each client's information processing needs.

The potential of punch card tabulating machines had been recognized by other companies as well. While the Powers Accounting Machine Corp. had long been IBM's competitor, new computers included Burroughs, National Cash Register, Remington Rand, and Underwood Elliot Fisher. Underwood, which was created in 1927, ruled the typewriter industry with its Model 5 and had a sales force as good as IBM's, while Burroughs was the leader in adding machines. At this time, IBM was not interested in mass producing machines like typewriters and adding machines unless such machines could be made part of the tabulating system. Its strategy was to lease its machines and then support the machines with trained service representatives who were available to handle a customer's problems and to make suggestions for improving a customer's information processing as the individual business changed.

Leasing gave IBM several competitive advantages over Burroughs, NCR, and Remington Rand, which all sold their machines to customers. First, it allowed the company to retain control over outdated technology which could not be resold in the used market (a problem NCR had encountered which reduced its profits). Second, leasing made it easier for the customer because they were not committed to a large capital outlay or the threat of purchasing a machine that would be outmoded quickly by technological change. Third, leasing provided IBM with a steady cash flow. Fourth, and very important, by leasing its machine IBM was also able to force customers to purchase the thousands of punch cards they used each month from IBM.

IBM's practice of requiring customers to buy its cards led to an antitrust suit in 1936, and the Supreme Court ruled that IBM should discontinue requiring customers to buy cards from it alone. This ruling had little impact on IBM because IBM was the most convenient supplier of cards and its sales force serviced the machines and made sure that customers were kept happy.

During the 1920s and 1930s IBM also began to develop specialized tabulators to handle specific types of information processing needs for customers. For example, IBM developed a proofing machine to be used by banks that could sort and add checks, a very labor-intensive process. This proof machine, called the IBM 405, was launched in 1932 and became IBM's most profitable product at the time. The 405 consisted of a punch, sorter, and accounting machine. Operators punched holes in cards to represent data; the sorter then put the cards in the appropriate bins; the cards were then taken out of the bins and run through the accounting machines, which generated printouts of the data and which also could print checks. Some customers rented verifiers which attached to the punch to ensure the cards were prepared properly. IBM trained its customers' employees on how to use the 405 machines at no cost to promote customer loyalty and to ensure a demand for its products.

By 1939 IBM was the biggest and most powerful business machine company in the United States. IBM owned about 80 percent of the keypunches, sorters, and accounting machines used for tabulating purposes. By this time Remington Rand and Burroughs were minor competitors and the Powers company had disappeared, unable to match IBM's strengths in sales and research and development.

Also by 1939 Watson had reorganized the company's business divisions to meet the needs to IBM's new focus on tabulating machines. The punch card tabulating division became the center of the company business, and the company's other products were now oriented around this division. For example, Watson decided to keep ITR, which sold time clocks among other things, because customers purchased many time cards that were similar to punch cards. He sold off the largest part of the scale division because it no longer fit the company's new direction. He bought Electromatic Typewriter Co. because it was working on keypunch consoles. This purchase proved very significant; by 1945 IBM had developed this company into the U.S. leader in electric typewriters, which were sold by IBM's large, well-trained sales force.

In 1939 total revenues were $34.8 million and profits were $9.1 million. Sales of punch cards were about $5 million of this and had higher profit margins than any other product. The start of World War II accelerated the demand for IBM's tabulating machines and sales rose to $143.3 million by 1943. However, profits were only $9.7 million due to the wartime excess profits tax. IBM achieved higher sales with mobile punch card units that followed supply controllers across war zones so that bookkeeping could be done on the battlefield. For example, a mobile unit would go to a Pacific Island and compute the soldiers' payroll. The tabulators also recorded bombing results, casualties, prisoners, displaced persons, and supplies. A punch card record was maintained on every man drafted and followed him until he was discharged from the military.

By 1945 IBM had begun aggressively to pursue the idea that just producing business machines was not enough; supplying customers with a way to manage their information processing needs was even more important. This change in focus was very significant; IBM now saw its role as developing new and different kinds of products to suit its customers' needs, rather than in finding new ways to use and improve existing machines. This change in operating philosophy proved very important with the development of the first working computer.

The Computer Age

Toward the end of World War II, a research team at the University of Pennsylvania constructed a computer to solve math problems for the Army; the machine, called the ENIAC, could compute ballistic tables to accurately aim and fire the big guns of World War II. In 1946 the ENIAC was the only working computer in the world. This computer was the size of a small house and had 18,000 vacuum tubes, which were apt to burn out. The machine cost $3 million to build, took a long time to set up, and was very difficult to use. The inventors of the computer, J. Presper Eckert and John Mauchley, realized that computers could perform the same function as punch card tabulating machines only much more quickly because they processed information electronically rather than mechanically. They realized that their computer eventually could replace tabulating machines in business, so they created a company to develop and manufacture their computer for commercial use. Their machine and company was

called Univac. In 1948 they received an order from the U.S. Census Bureau for their computer, just as Hollerith 60 years before had received an order for his tabulating machine. In the same year Prudential Insurance also ordered a Univac. These organizations were two of IBM's largest customers and so IBM took notice of the new technology and became interested in the Univac computer. In 1950 Remington Rand, which also sold typewriters, tabulators, filing cabinets, and electric shavers, forestalled IBM and bought Eckert and Mauchley's company to gain entry into the new computer market. Just as Watson had realized the potential of the punch card machine, so Remington Rand realized the potential of the computer. The race was on between IBM and Remington Rand to become the company that would dominate the next generation of business machines: computers.

IBM's Race to Catch Up

IBM had not ignored technical developments in the tabulating industry. By 1948 it had developed an electromechanical machine called the MARK I that was 51 feet long by 8 feet high and cost $1 million. This machine was more advanced than a punch card machine, but it was still not a true computer because it did not use vacuum tubes, and it was slower than the Univac. The company was still not committed to the new technology, however, and it took the arrival of Tom Watson, Sr.'s two sons, Tom Jr. and Arthur ("Dick") who joined IBM at the end of the war to bring IBM up to speed.

Tom Watson, Jr., convinced his father that IBM would lose everything if it did not embrace the new technology and enter the computer age. He pointed out that large IBM customers such as the Prudential and Metropolitan Life insurance companies had been complaining for a long time that the punch card system required too much storage space and was becoming too slow and cumbersome to handle the volume of information these companies were generating. Under Tom Jr.'s leadership IBM began to check into new kinds of storage systems, such as magnetic tapes, and to look at the machine that used the new electronic circuits to sort data and handle calculations: the computer. After studying the ENIAC computer, Tom Jr. encouraged IBM's research laboratory managers to recruit more electronic specialists. He prodded IBM to incorporate electronic circuits in punch card machines because a primitive electronic circuit could perform 5,000 additions per second compared to 4 per second for the fastest mechanism in a punch card machine.

Working quickly, and with access to the company's large resource base, in 1946 IBM developed a new machine, the 603 Electronic Multiplier, that could compute payroll in one-tenth the time a mechanical punch card machine could do it. The machine was upgraded to the 604 which had electronic circuits that also allowed the machine to divide. The 604 was not a true computer because numbers were still processed from punch cards rather than from signals recorded in the machine's memory circuits. Nevertheless, when it was introduced in mid 1948 it sold by the thousands. Both machines matched IBM's existing punch card equipment which made it easy for IBM customers to upgrade to the new machines. The machine's success convinced Tom Jr. and Sr. that electronics would grow even faster; from this time on, the company committed its resources to the new technology and to the development of an advanced new computer system.

IBM began working on its first family of electronic computers, called the 701 series, in 1949. Tom Jr. became president of domestic IBM in 1952, the same year the 701 was launched. The 701 was a scientific computer for use in laboratories, but it was not as advanced as the Univac. However, although Remington Rand was ahead in technology, the company lacked IBM's vision and Rand would not permit punch card salespeople to sell Univacs. Tom Jr., however, placed IBM's sales force behind its computer and required both senior executives and engineers to help its sales force in operating the new machine. By 1953 IBM had installed 32 701 computers and had 164 on order compared to Remington Rand's 33 installations and 24 orders.

The 702, a commercial computer for general accounting applications, was launched in 1954. This machine was faster than the Univac and with this machine IBM took the technological lead. By 1956 IBM had 87 computers installed at various businesses and 190 on order, compared to all other competitors' combined installations of 41 and combined orders of 40 computers.

Because all its machines were leased, it was easy for IBM to upgrade its customers to its new advanced machines. When the 705 was developed to replace the 702, and the 704 to replace the 701, IBM retained and increased its market share. Between 1950 and

1956, IBM's revenues tripled from $214.9 million to $743.3 million. The average growth rate of the company from 1946 to 1955 was 22 percent. Watson decided to expand IBM's product line as fast as the market would allow.

IBM's technological success was due to the way Tom Watson, Jr., had totally changed the company's research and development thrust. IBM's research laboratory had been dominated by mechanical engineers because its punch card machines operated on mechanical principles. None of its engineers really understood electronics. So Tom Jr. hired a new laboratory director and increased the size of the R&D staff from 500 mechanical engineers and technicians in 1950 to over 4,000 electrical engineers by 1956. Tom Jr. also created a smaller lab in California to specialize in developing advanced information storage devices; in less than three years the laboratory developed a computer disk that stored data on magnetic tape rather than punch cards, a storage system that became the backbone of IBM's future computer systems and a major source of its competitive advantage.

Tom Watson, Jr., also led the development of the IBM 650 in 1956. It provided enough data processing power for most general commercial applications. The 650 was less powerful than the 700 series but it was much cheaper. The 650 introduced thousands of punch card customers to computers. It was designed to work with ordinary punch card equipment but to make the punch card system much more powerful and versatile. For example, life insurance companies compute insurance premiums from actuarial tables based on age, sex, and other customer factors. Using a 650, these actuarial tables could be loaded into the computer memory, and when the punch card containing information of a particular customer was loaded into the machine the computer did the calculations and furnished the total premium. Previously a clerk had to figure the totals and record the information on a punch card for recording purposes.

IBM put its huge sales force behind the 650 machine; as a result of its efforts, within a year almost 1,000 machines were sold. Most computers were used in administrative offices and in factories where the computer was used to control the manufacturing process. By the end of the 1950s, IBM had a 75 percent market share. The remaining market was divided among Remington Rand, Honeywell Electronics, NCR, and a few others. Although Underwood Typewriter and NCR attempted to launch small computers, they were unable to produce as good a performer as the 650.

The Transistor

In 1956 the transistor, which weighed 100 times less than the vacuum tube, was developed by William Shockley at Bell Labs. Compared to a vacuum tube, the transistor required less electrical power, had the potential to miniaturize computing systems, and, most important, could perform calculations at a much faster rate. The transistor made the design of a more complex and powerful computer feasible; it also made it possible to sell the computer at a price that most large companies could afford.

IBM's electronic researchers had been successfully using the vacuum tube, and as the mechanical engineers before them, they were reluctant to change to new technology: a transistor-based computer technology. So Tom Watson, Jr., sent a memo to R&D personnel stating that no more IBM machines would be designed using vacuum tubes. This memo started a whole new thrust in IBM's research efforts that led to the 7000 computer series, IBM's first computer based on transistors rather than vacuum tubes. However, IBM's scientists had a major problem in wiring transistors together to produce the new advanced computer until the integrated circuit was invented in 1959 by a Fairchild Semiconductor engineer. With the arrival of the integrated circuit, thousands of transistors could be joined together on a circuit board the size of a fingernail. In turn, thousands of integrated circuits could be joined together to make the first modern computer. By the early 1960s, IBM computers guided Polaris missiles and Air Force jets. When integrated circuits were mass produced, their cost fell from $1,000 per circuit in 1960 to a few cents per circuit by 1970, and IBM developed successive generations of more powerful machines to exploit the new technology.

Redefining the Industry

As a result of this succession of technological developments, by 1960 IBM's computer division was disorganized and had a product line consisting of eight newer transistor-based computers and several older vacuum tube machines. This mixed product line caused several problems for IBM's customers and its sales force because the computers were not compatible and could not work together. For example, if a customer expanded and wanted to upgrade to a larger or newer computer, the customer had to lease a whole new range of equipment and rewrite all the programs to make the computer work. The disjointed product line also caused problems for IBM's personnel.

Because IBM's product line had grown so large, Watson decided to split the Data Processing Division into two units: one for the newer machines that rented for over the average price of $10,000 a month and one for older, less-powerful machines that rented for less than $10,000 a month. This decision caused competition between managers of the different product lines, each of whom fought to obtain resources to develop and improve their particular product line. It also led to a duplication of research and development efforts.

The diverse range of computers IBM now leased also made it more difficult for IBM's sales force to learn the characteristics of the different systems associated with each computer and to inform customers about the suitability of a given system for the particular business involved. IBM's technological thrust had outpaced the ability of the company to service its products adequately. Its attempt to dominate the industry by being the first mover in technology had resulted in the development of a fragmented product line that was confusing its customers and its employees. The company needed a new strategy to grow.

Watson's answer was that IBM needed to build a new line of computers that would cover the needs of the whole computer market. The project was called the System/360, representing the 360 degrees in a circle, because IBM wanted to meet the needs of every user in both the scientific and business community. The 360 was intended to make all other computers, both IBM's and its competitors, obsolete. All the 360 computers would be compatible with one another. Moreover, they would all use the same operating language, software, disk drives, printers, and so on. The goal of the new design was to lock in customers to IBM's computer systems and to make it very difficult for customers to change to competitors' products—both because of superior product quality and because their incentive would be to upgrade to a more powerful machine that was compatible with their old machines. The other goal of the system was to make better use of IBM's research and development resources and to make it easier for its sales force to sell an integrated package of products to customers.

The project was challenging because hardware and software had to be developed and coordinated across the whole of its product line. This meant that all of the different parts of the mainframe system—storage devices, central processors, terminals, and printers—had to be compatible, as did the components used in the various parts of the system. To ensure the compatibility of the new system, and the supply and quality of the component parts, IBM began producing many of its own electronic components itself. From this point on IBM became involved in all aspects of the mainframe computer business—it would design and manufacture almost all of the components that would be used in its mainframe computers, it would manufacture its mainframes in its own factories, and it would distribute and sell its mainframes itself. IBM opened six new plants around the world to manufacture the System/360 computers. Over a four-year period, $5 billion was invested and 50,000 new employees were hired as part of IBM's ambitious expansion plan.

The System/360 mainframe computer was launched in 1964 and captured 70 percent of the market. The project was an immense success and put IBM way ahead of its competitors. Although before the 360, competitors such as RCA, Burroughs, Honeywell, Univac, and GE sold machines that performed much better than IBM computers for the same price, the compatible design and the power of the System/360 beat all competitors. Moreover, marketing played as large a role in the success of the project as technology. While all its competitors had access to integrated circuits and could produce an advanced computer, only IBM had the capacity to provide a customer a complete information processing service—the machine itself, installation and maintenance, and the quality personalized service that allowed it to retain and tie up its customers.

Due to the technical superiority of the System/360 mainframes and the reputation for quality service established by IBM's sales force, IBM dominated the computer industry. The 360 spurred growth in the whole industry. In 1963 there were only 11,700 computers in the United States; this figure doubled in 1965 and redoubled in 1969. By 1969 IBM leased over 50,000 computer systems which generated sales revenues of $7.196 billion and earnings of $934 million, a staggering figure for the time. A large part of these revenues was generated from IBM's international operations.

Global Development

IBM's movement into global markets began in 1908 when Herman Hollerith made a licensing agreement with the British Tabulating Company (BTC) to produce and sell Hollerith tabulators throughout the British Empire. Tom Watson, Sr., continued with Hollerith's vision of IBM as an international company and established IBM's foreign department. After World War I, he began to build small manufacturing plants in Germany, France, and Great Britain to evade the tariffs these countries levied on foreign imports. Sales and marketing agencies were created throughout Europe, Latin America, and parts of Asia. The branches were called Watson Business Machines and their function, as in the United States, was to provide the high level of customer service that supported IBM's business machines. In 1935 foreign revenue was $1.6 million, with punch cards once again being the biggest contributor. By 1939 over 12 percent of IBM's revenues came from foreign operations.

During World War II, IBM's plants in Europe and Japan were seized. However, even though IBM's German plant, which contributed 50 percent of the foreign department's revenue, was in ruins, by 1945 foreign revenues were almost $2 million. After the war, IBM's British plant became the largest facility outside North America, and in 1949 IBM renegotiated the 1908 agreement with the BTC whereby BTC would receive a free, nonexclusive license on all current IBM products in exchange for letting IBM sell its new products through its own sales organization. This agreement resulted in the creation of a new subsidiary called IBM U.K. which, selling IBM's new advanced computers, soon came to dominate the British and European markets.

In 1949 Dick Watson, who spoke German, French, Italian, and Spanish, was put in charge of IBM's international operations, and in 1950 the foreign department was renamed IBM World Trade Division and became an independent subsidiary that would receive product and financial support from IBM's Domestic Division but would operate on its own. By 1950 the World Trade Division had 10 factories producing machines and over 20 facilities making cards throughout the world. World Trade operated in 58 countries through subsidiaries such as IBM Deutschland, IBM France, and many smaller units in Latin America and Africa.

Of World Trade's 16,000 employees in 1954, only 200 were Americans, because Dick Watson believed that most success would be achieved if each subsidiary was responsive to the needs of its own region or country. Dick Watson set high standards for World Trade, hired good people as country managers, and was responsive to local customs.

By 1967 foreign revenues were $1.6 billion and net earnings were $209 million. World Trade sales were equal to IBM's Domestic Division sales. Although IBM operated in 130 countries, Europe accounted for two-thirds of foreign revenue. In 1970 Dick Watson resigned from IBM to become the U.S. ambassador to France. With his departure, the World Trade Division was further divided into world regions: Europe, the Middle East, Africa, the Americas, and the Far East. By 1970 foreign revenues had increased to $3.5 billion and once again accounted for almost 50 percent of IBM's total revenues.

IBM's Structure

IBM's Domestic Division, which was led by Tom Watson, Jr., was responsible for research and development and for financing the operations of the entire global company. By 1950 not only was IBM Domestic designing and manufacturing a large number of different models of computer, it was also designing and manufacturing many of the component and peripheral parts used in the computers such as disk drives, transistors, printers, and file storage and servers. Many of these products were produced throughout the world and distributed by IBM's international division. The increase in the range of IBM's activities, both domestically and internationally, put considerable strain on IBM's organization structure, which began to cause it many problems.

IBM was run largely by Tom Watson, Sr., until he retired in 1955. Watson oversaw all of IBM's operations, and a line of top managers was always waiting to see him. No formal organizational chart existed in IBM because Watson believed that people should be interested in all aspects of IBM's activities rather than focusing on specific jobs. The company had no clear chain of command, no policy of decentralization which gave lower-level managers the right to make independent decisions, and no formal planning process or business policies. Knowledge was simply in employees' heads and strategy emerged gradually over time from discussion and negotiations between Watson and his top management team.

After Tom Watson, Sr.'s retirement, Tom Watson, Jr., and Al Williams, IBM's president at this time,

decided to construct an organizational chart to see who had reported to Watson and found that 38 to 40 top managers reported directly to him. It was obvious that this highly centralized management style could not continue if the rapidly growing company was to stay on top of the computer industry. Already unmade decisions were accumulating because managers lacked the authority to make decisions, and now they looked to Tom Watson, Jr., to take the lead.

Tom Jr. wanted to break with his father's centralized, autocratic style of management in order to speed communication and decision making, so he and Al Williams reorganized IBM's operating structure to decentralize control to managers who were given the responsibility of managing the different functional areas of the company. The organizational chart they devised put Red Lamotte in charge of sales and R&D and Al Williams in charge of finance, while Tom Jr. would take control of the company's strategy. Unfortunately, this reorganization simply divided the chaos among three people instead of one. There were still far too many managers reporting to the three top managers, and they were unable to control IBM's operations adequately. So in 1956 IBM was reorganized along divisional lines.

IBM Domestic was broken up into five separate divisions: the Field Engineering Division, which primarily served commercial customers; the Federal Systems Division, which primarily served government customers; the Systems Manufacturing Division, which manufactured the computers; the Component Manufacturing Division, which manufactured the components; and the Research Division, which performed the basic research and design activities. In each division a general manager was given the responsibility of making decisions for the division and developing its strategy. The World Trade Division would continue to operate separately from IBM Domestic.

This multidivisional structure ensured that each general manager had a clearly defined task. At the top of the organization, Tom Jr. created a top management team of six people, consisting of himself and the heads of the five divisions, to oversee the company's strategy. Each of the five general managers was responsible for a major part of IBM, and Tom Jr. was to oversee the entire company. He claimed that his ability to choose and retain an intelligent top management team was his greatest contribution to IBM.

Watson also created a corporate staff of experts in sales and marketing, finance, manufacturing, personnel, and communications to advise him and to oversee the activities of the divisions. The corporate staff was seen as staff or advisory managers to the general managers of the division who were the line managers with responsibility for bottom-line operating results. It was the line manager's job (the general manager and other divisional managers) to meet production targets, beat sales quotas, and increase market share. The staff manager's job was to give advice to line managers—the heads of the divisions who were their superiors, to convey policy from corporate head-quarters to the operating divisions, and to ensure that the proper objectives were in place and being met. Each line manager would be evaluated solely on his or her unit's results, and each staff manager would be rated on his or her effort in making IBM a world leader.

IBM's divisional structure produced many tensions between corporate (staff) and divisional (line) personnel. For example, as a part of their role, staff managers often would identify problems that needed to be addressed in the divisions and would write memos to line managers suggesting how to solve them. Line managers, however, viewed these moves as interference and an intrusion into their area of operations. They began to guard their territories from corporate personnel who had no direct authority over general managers in IBM's structure.

To resolve these tensions, Williams created a check and balance system in IBM called *contention management.* This system forced both staff and line managers to meet and encouraged them to debate the merits of an idea. However, no operating plan became final without staff approval. When line and staff managers could not agree, the problem would be sent to the corporate management committee—the top six executives—to resolve the problem. Over time, an increasing number of issues were sent to the top of the organization to resolve because line and staff managers could not agree on priorities and future policy. This slowed communication and decision making; eventually, it became accepted that the top management committee would resolve important strategic issues.

Thus, despite Watson's claimed policy of decentralizing authority to divisional managers and their subordinates, much of IBM's decision making remained centralized at the top of the organization, and managers from IBM's mainframe division—its chief revenue earner—had the most power in shaping corporate decision making.

The IBM Culture

The centralized approach that was developing at IBM had important implications for IBM's culture and the values that guided the company. Because IBM's managers began to rely on their superiors to make important policy decisions, they became very conservative in their approach and became increasingly afraid to take risks and to go out on their own. IBM developed many bureaucratic rules and operating procedures that specified how decisions were to be made and how to resolve disputes. Slowly but surely the entrepreneurial values that had allowed the company to capitalize quickly on new technologies changed to emphasize values of conforming to the IBM way: commitment and loyalty to the company and respect and obedience to superiors.

IBM's conservative culture was reinforced by its policy of long-term employment. The company became known throughout the industry for its job security and good pay. With IBM's high rate of growth, internal promotion was easy to come by, and employees rose rapidly through the corporate ranks. In 1955 employee stock options were offered for the first time. In 1966 managers were required to attend an in-house IBM manager school, where they were trained in IBM's philosophy on communications, sales and service efforts, meetings, and employee treatment such as visiting workers with sick spouses. This policy taught employees the IBM way and helped to cement IBM's corporate culture and its style of doing business.

New Management and New Challenges

In 1970 Dick Watson resigned to become the U.S. ambassador to France and Tom Watson, Jr., suffered a heart attack which resulted in his retirement in 1971. When Tom Watson, Jr., appointed T. V. Learson as CEO in 1971 the period of the Watson family's control over IBM came to an end. IBM was the largest, most successful computer company in the world and had complete domination over the global mainframe computer industry. Each year, its revenues and profit reached record levels; the company plowed back over 10 percent of its revenue to fund future research and development to allow it to maintain its dominance in the mainframe market.

Despite its impressive performance, however, all was not well with the company. Although the situation was masked by increasing revenues from World

Trade, by 1970 IBM was starting to slow down. While the company had grown at an annual rate of 22 percent from 1946 to 1955, its growth was only 16 percent per year from 1955 to 1970. Indeed, its stock price actually declined in 1970 despite record sales. Why? IBM was beginning to face increased competition from other companies in the mainframe computer market and from companies that began to produce computers for other segments of the computer market. The challenge for Learson was to use IBM's vast resources to exploit a computer market that was growing by leaps and bounds. How could the company exploit its privileged position to dominate the computer market of the future? The answers were not long in coming.

REFERENCES

Mercer, David. *The Global IBM*. New York: Dodd, Mead, 1988.

Sober, Robert. *IBM: Colossus in Transition*. New York: Times Books, 1981.

Watson, Thomas, Jr., and Peter Petre. *Father and Son & Co.: My Life at IBM and Beyond*. New York: Bantam Books, 1990.

"The Intimate Tale of IBM's First Family." *Fortune*, June 14, 1990, pp. 92–131.

Case 21

The Fall of IBM

This case was prepared by Gareth R. Jones and Susan L. Peters, Texas A&M University.

T. V. Learson took over as CEO of IBM from Tom Watson, Jr., in 1971 and became the head of a company that had a 75 percent share of the world market for mainframe computers—computers powerful enough to manage the information processing needs of an entire company. Learson had made a major personal contribution to IBM's emergence as the dominant global mainframe manufacturer when he led the development of IBM's highly successful 360 mainframe series, the series that led to the rapid rise in the company's fortunes. IBM's 360 mainframes fully automated a company's manual information processing systems, such as payroll and accounting or customer recordkeeping, and made the punch card obsolete. As the former head of the 360 program, Learson understood the critical importance of research and development in maintaining and defending IBM's preeminent position in the mainframe market, and so he initiated and oversaw the development of IBM's new, more powerful System/370 computer series.[1]

Technical advances lowered the System/370's price per calculation to 60 percent below that of the System/360s, and the 370 had a larger information storage system as well. The 370s still used the software of the 360s, however, so they were primarily an upgrade rather than a replacement of the 360. Nevertheless, the 370 machines became the backbone of IBM's mainframe product line from the early 1970s on. Most of the advances that IBM made to its mainframe computers from this time on were designed primarily to improve the 370 machines' processing power or the performance of the various components of the 370 series, such as its software, printers, and especially its storage capacity. The 370 series became the industry standard that IBM's competitors tried to match and outperform.

Under Learson's control and then under the control of Frank Cary, who became CEO when Learson retired in 1973, IBM continued to enjoy its domination of the mainframe market. By 1980 IBM had a market value of $26 billion, four times its size in 1971.

Increasing Competition

Although IBM's continued domination of the mainframe market produced record increases in revenues and profits every year, its performance masked some major problems that were developing during the 1970s and 1980s. The first major problem, which Cary had recognized as early as 1970, was that the mainframe computer market was starting to mature. Almost every large U.S. business company possessed a mainframe computer, as had most scientific and higher education institutions. IBM also had saturated the international market. As a result, IBM's rate of growth was falling; even though its revenues were increasing, they were increasing at a decreasing rate. In the mature mainframe market, competition was increasing from companies that were trying to find ways to attract IBM's customers and share in the huge revenues in the

[1]D. Mercer, *The Global IBM* (New York: Dodd, Mead, 1988), p. 58.

mainframe computer market. Its major competitors at the time were Amdahl, Honeywell, Burroughs, Univac, NCR, and Control Data.

Many of these companies began offering IBM's customers mainframe systems at a lower cost than the expensive IBM systems. Initially, IBM faced competition only from companies selling IBM-compatible peripheral equipment such as disk drives, storage devices, and printers at lower prices than IBM's products. Its sales force had been able to ward off such threats. Now, however, the nature of competition was changing. IBM's competitors began selling cheaper, higher performing, and IBM-compatible central processing units (CPUs), the brain of the computer and the source of its processing power. For the first time they were offering a low-price alternative to the IBM mainframe while IBM was still pursuing its high-priced leased strategy backed by excellent customer service. Another emerging low-price threat came from leasing companies that would buy old 360s from IBM and lease them on better terms than IBM offered, attracting price-conscious IBM customers. While these competitive threats were small, they nevertheless gave IBM cause for concern.

From 1970 on IBM became concerned about the threat of low-cost foreign competition in the mainframe computer market after witnessing the decline in several U.S. industries, including automobiles, due to the entry of low-cost Japanese competitors. The price of integrated circuits, the heart of a mainframe computer, was plummeting at this time, and Japanese companies had the technical capability to build a powerful computer that could match or exceed the IBM 370. The existence of a low-cost global competitor was a major threat to IBM's domination both of the U.S. market and the global market.

To respond to the threat of low-cost competition, Cary announced that IBM would spend $10 billion to build new automated plants to produce low-cost computers over a six-year period. In this way IBM would be able to meet the challenge of low-priced computers should the threat materialize and its customers start to switch to low-cost competitors. John Opel, who became IBM's CEO in 1981, also was concerned about competition from Japan and he carried on with Cary's low-cost producer strategy. Under his control IBM spent $32 billion from 1980 to 1985 to find ways to reduce manufacturing costs.

IBM's push to reduce manufacturing costs did not fit well with its strategy of offering excellent-quality customer service using its very expensive sales force to sell and service its machines. It was unlikely that IBM would ever be able to compete on price with its competitors because its customer service and support activities raised its costs so much. Moreover, competing on price had never been a part of its strategy; IBM always had competed on its unique ability to provide customers with an integrated full-line computer service. Analysts wondered whether Opel was spending too much to lower manufacturing costs and whether the $32 billion could not be better spent in some other way.

Changes in Technology

Changes in mainframe technology also caused a change in IBM's strategy during the 1970s. As a result of technological innovations, particularly the plunging costs of integrated circuits, the life span of a mainframe computer—the time it could be used until it was technologically outdated—was shortening rapidly and development costs were increasing. Formerly, customers would use the same IBM mainframe for several years, but now IBM was forced to replace its leased computers every two or three years, making it difficult to recoup development costs and obtain the premium price on its machines that it was accustomed to.

Because a computer's life span was getting shorter, and because of the growth of low-cost competition, IBM under Cary and then Opel decided to phase out IBM's system of leasing its machines to customers and instead to begin selling them—a major change in IBM's strategy. Although this move increased revenue in the short term, it had major repercussions for the company in the long term. First, the leasing system had tied IBM to its customers and ensured that when customers upgraded and expanded their computer systems they would look first at IBM machines. Moreover, leasing facilitated IBM's strategy of providing customers with excellent customer service and guaranteed the company a steady cash flow and control of the used machine market. With the end of leasing, IBM would be more susceptible to fluctuations in the demand for its products because its customers would be able to shop around.

From 1980 on, IBM began to face major competition from 370 clone manufacturers, large companies like Amdahl (which had a faster 370 processor than IBM), and Hitachi Data Systems (whose low-price machine generated record sales throughout the 1980s). IBM's customers began to feel more comfortable about buying 370 clones from companies that also promised quality support and service at low cost.[2] IBM's sales growth for its biggest mainframe dropped from 12 percent annually in 1984 to 5 percent annually in 1990 as a result of the increased competition. Increased mainframe competition with Amdahl and Hitachi Data Systems also led to price discounting despite the fact that IBM attempted to offer its customers a unique package that included software and services in addition to hardware. The days when IBM could demand whatever price it wanted for its machines were over.

The end of its leasing program also led to increased competition from independent computer leasing companies which would buy older mainframes and then sell the older processors at a price that was frequently only 10 percent of IBM's newest machine. These companies also disassembled mainframes in order to make smaller computers; for example, they could make two smaller machines out of one larger machine. In response to this price competition, IBM was forced to reduce the price of its machines.

The end of leasing, combined with a growth in low-cost competition, changed the nature of industry competition in ways that the company did not expect. IBM's strategy was now to protect its mainframe market from competitors and to hang on to its customers at all costs. IBM devoted most of its huge resources to developing technically superior mainframe products, to lowering their cost of production, and to supporting its very expensive but very successful sales force.

IBM's focus on protecting its mainframe market blinded it to threats from the emergence of new kinds of computers. Even when it did recognize the competitive threat, IBM's operating structure and culture, shaped by its preeminent position as the world's leading mainframe computer company, made it difficult for IBM's managers to see emerging problems in its environment and to react quickly to the changes that technology was bringing about in the computer industry. The way IBM handled the emerging threat from new kinds of computers such as minicomputers, personal computers, and workstations illustrates many of the problems it experienced

[2]John Verity, "A Slimmer IBM May Still Be Overweight," *Business Week*, December 18, 1989, pp. 197–208.

as a result of a corporate mindset that "mainframes were king."

The Minicomputer Market

One of the new computer markets that emerged in the 1970s was the minicomputer market. Minicomputers are smaller and significantly cheaper than mainframe computers and are priced anywhere from $12,000 to $700,000. The readily falling price of integrated circuits during the 1960s and 1970s made it feasible to build a minicomputer that could be afforded by small businesses or used in specialized technical or scientific applications. IBM had ignored this new market segment, preferring to focus its resources on developing and improving its profitable 360 and 370 series of computers.

It was left to two MIT researchers to pioneer the development of a smaller, powerful computer, and they founded the Digital Equipment Corporation (DEC) which in 1965 launched the PDP-8, a computer that could handle the smaller information processing needs and tasks of companies like small businesses, offices, factories, and laboratories. The venture was very successful, and by 1968 DEC's sales reached $57 million and earnings were $6.8 million. DEC's computer competed with the lower end of the 360 range. The computer sold well in research facilities, but it did not do as well in business because IBM dominated this market with its powerful sales force. DEC had plans to develop a more powerful machine, however, and as it grew it was quickly expanding its own national service network, imitating IBM's.

To meet DEC's challenge, which was still seen as a minor issue, Cary formed the General Systems Division in 1969 to produce the System/3 which was to be IBM's small, powerful minicomputer. IBM did not, however, rethink its technology or invest resources to develop a new minicomputer technology to make a product to suit this new market segment. Rather, IBM tried to adapt its existing mainframe technology to the minicomputer market.

IBM's top managers had risen up the ranks of IBM from the mainframe division, and they were conditioned by the idea that the level of computing power was everything. "The bigger the better" was the philosophy of these managers. Moreover, big machines meant big revenues. IBM's mainframe managers saw the potential earning power of the minicomputer as insignificant when compared to the huge revenues generated by its mainframes. More fundamentally, however, IBM's top managers did not want competition from a new computer division inside the company which would absorb large amounts of the company's resources and might change the company's future direction and strategy.

The result was that when the System/3s were developed they were too big and expensive to compete with DEC's machine and too small to compete with IBM's own mainframes, so they failed to make much inroad into what was becoming a very big market segment. As the minicomputer segment of the market continued to grow rapidly in the 1970s, Cary tried to increase the importance of the minicomputer group inside IBM's corporate hierarchy by reorganizing IBM's Data Processing Division and splitting it into two units: General Systems to make small minicomputers and Data Systems to make the mainframes. He hoped that this change would force IBM managers to change their mindset and support the company's move into the new markets.

So strong was the entrenched position of mainframe managers that Cary's change of structure created huge divisional rivalry between mainframe and minicomputer managers. The mainframe division saw itself as in direct competition for resources with the minicomputer division, and managers in both units failed to cooperate and to share technological resources to develop the new range of machines. When General Systems finally produced a smaller minicomputer called the 8100, it did not have a technological edge over the DEC machine. Nevertheless, it was successful, as many IBM customers had large sums of money tied up in IBM mainframes and were reluctant to switch suppliers. Moreover, IBM's powerful sales force (although at first reluctant to push minicomputers for fear of reducing their commissions) could service the needs of the minicomputer users. By the end of 1980, over 100,000 minicomputers had been sold. IBM and DEC were the industry leaders; the new companies that had sprung up, such as Hewlett-Packard and Wang, were also increasing their market share.

In 1986 DEC introduced its new VAX 9000 minicomputer which shocked IBM's mainframe managers because it had the same speed and capacity as IBM's largest 370 mainframe, the 3090, but cost only 25 percent as much. For the first time, mainframe managers were forced to accept the fact that minicomputers might be feasible substitutes for mainframes

in many applications. Although DEC gained the business of some large financial service companies and corporate data processing centers with its new machine, market segments previously dominated solely by IBM, it still could not seize many of IBM's loyal customers who were locked into IBM systems. Nevertheless, DEC's share of the minicomputer market grew from 19 percent in 1984 to 25 percent in 1988, while IBM's share dropped from 24 percent to 16 percent in the same period.

Finally, in 1988 IBM brought out a minicomputer, the AS/400 series, that was superior to DEC's VAX. The AS/400 series was based on RISC (reduced instruction set computing) technology and fast RISC chips that could equal and exceed the speed of large mainframes, including IBM's own mainframes.[3] Many large companies that had a great deal of money invested in IBM mainframes now moved to adopt the IBM minicomputer system because it was compatible with their IBM mainframe systems. As a result of the success of its new minicomputers, IBM increased its market share from about 16 percent in 1988 to 28 percent in 1992 while DEC's fell.[4] DEC now plans to produce machines based on RISC, but in the interim, it has introduced new machines to compete with IBM's AS/400s on price.[5] IBM now has a $14 billion business in minicomputers, which have gross margins of 56 percent.

The Personal Computer

Another technological breakthrough, the microprocessor or "computer on a chip," sparked the development of the personal computer. The personal computer was developed in 1977 by Steven Jobs and Stephen Wozniak who founded Apple Computer. By 1980 Apple's sales had grown to $117 million.[6] Once again, IBM stood by and watched as a new market segment was created. This time, recognizing the mistakes it had made in the microcomputer market by not moving quickly enough to develop a machine to compete with the industry leader, it decided to move quickly to create its own machine to compete with Apple's.

[3]John Verity, "The New IBM," *Business Week*, December 16, 1991, pp. 112–118.
[4]John Verity, "IBM's Major Triumph in Minis," *Business Week*, March 16, 1992, p. 111.
[5]Gary McWilliams, "Can DEC Squeeze One Last Blast from VAX?" *Business Week*, October 28, 1991, p. 134.
[6]Deidre Depke and Richard Brandt, "PCs: What the Future Holds," *Business Week*, August 12, 1991, pp. 58–64.

In the mainframe market, IBM made its own chips, circuit boards, disk drives, terminals, tape drives, and printers; wrote its own proprietary software for its machines; and helped to develop software to meet the needs of its customers. As a result, its machines were not compatible with those of its rivals which used their own proprietary hardware and software. The machines of different manufacturers would not work together. In 1981, however, in an effort to enter the PC market quickly, IBM outsourced and bought the inputs it needed to make its personal computer from other companies. For example, Intel supplied the 8088 microchip that was the heart of the IBM machine and Microsoft delivered MS-DOS, its programming language and software applications for the new machine. Finally, computer stores, not the IBM sales force, were used to sell the new IBM PCs to get the machines to individual customers quickly.

IBM's first PC was introduced at a price of $1,565 in 1981 and was more powerful than the first Apple computer. Intel's 8088 chip had more main memory and was more powerful than the chip used in the Apple II computer, and Microsoft's operating system, MS-DOS, was better than the current industry standard. These features, combined with the power of the IBM brand name, made the IBM PC an immediate success, and it quickly became the industry standard for all other PCs.[7] Backed by IBM's legendary service, business users turned to the machines in the thousands. By 1984 IBM had seized 40 percent of the personal computer market, but the IBM PC still could not be produced or distributed fast enough to meet the enormous customer demand.[8]

Even the runaway success of the IBM PC became a threat to the company because its competitors rapidly imitated the IBM PC; soon clone manufacturers were selling IBM-compatible personal computers as powerful or more powerful than IBM's own machines. For example, Compaq, founded in 1981, began to clone IBMs and produced a high-powered machine that seized a large share of the high-price business market. In 1986 Compaq beat IBM to the market with a machine using Intel's new powerful 386 chip. At the same time, other clone makers like Zenith and Packard Bell attacked the low-price segment of the computer market and began producing PCs that undercut IBM's.

IBM, threatened both in the high-price and the low-price end of the PC market, fought back with the PS/2 which had a proprietary hardware channel that IBM made sure could not be imitated, as its first personal computer had been. However, customers resisted buying the new PS/2 because they did not want to become locked into a new IBM system that was not compatible with IBM's old system and that was not compatible with their other software or hardware investments. In the face of hostility from its customers, and losing market share, IBM was forced to back down and in 1988 began producing PS/2s that were compatible with the existing industry standard— its own older standard.

It was suddenly clear to IBM that it no longer controlled the rules of the competitive game in the personal computer industry. Nonetheless, it was still slow to change its strategy. Despite the fact that its cheaper rivals had machines that were as powerful as its own, IBM still attempted to charge a premium price for its product and so its customers went elsewhere. IBM's share of U.S. PC sales dropped from about 37 percent in 1985 to 24 percent in 1988. Clone makers continued to improve IBM's older standard, and IBM's market share declined to 16.5 percent in 1990.[9]

In 1991 a major price war broke out in the PC market, brought on in large part because of the steadily dropping price of computer hardware such as Intel's microprocessors. IBM reduced prices three times to compete, and prices of the PS/2 were cut as much as 25 percent.[10] Partly due to price competition, a typical 386 PC which had cost $3,500 in early 1991 cost $1,600 in late 1991 and only $1,200 in early 1992. Also in 1992 IBM introduced new low-priced lines of computers like the PS/Value Point targeted at the fastest-growing segment of the computer market, the home market, and to business customers who do not need all the features of the high-end PS/2. These new models have been very successful and are in great demand. Nonetheless, IBM does not hold a dominant position in the PC market; in 1992 its market share was 12 percent, the same as its rival Apple and about twice that of rivals like Dell, Compaq, and NEC.

The PC price wars continued into 1993. In February 1993, Dell Computer, a rapidly growing clone maker, introduced price cuts of 5 percent to 22 percent across

[7]Ibid.
[8]Mercer, pp. 106–111.

[9]Depke and Brandt.
[10]Ibid.

its entire product line. In response, IBM cut prices as much as 16 percent on some models including PS/Value Point.[11] Apple cut prices five times in 1993 for a reduction of up to 33 percent on its three highest-priced computers in an effort to increase U.S. sales.[12] PC makers also battled over distribution and the offering of extras such as warranties. PCs currently range from $500 clones to $2,000 laptops to $25,000 network hubs.[13] PCs dominate the computer industry with world sales of $93 billion in 1993 compared to mainframe sales of $50 billion.[14] The laptop segment of the PC market alone reached $5.67 billion in 1990. IBM, however, did not have a product for this market segment until 1991 and it faces tough competition from the market leader Toshiba and from Apple.[15]

By 1992 it was clear to IBM and to industry analysts that IBM was just one more competitor in a very competitive market. Since 1990 IBM's PC division has yet to show a profit because of the intense price competition and because IBM's costs are above its competitors like Compaq, which moved quickly to slash costs in 1990 when the price of PCs began tumbling.

IBM's response to competition in the personal computer industry throughout the 1980s clearly was affected by its "mainframe mindset." Even though it was clear that new segments of the computer market were developing and that new uses for computers were being found, IBM managers still discounted the potential threat to mainframes from either the minicomputer or the personal computer. IBM was not alone in being unable to sense the significance of changes in the environment. Kenneth Olsen, one of the founders of DEC, the minicomputer maker, went on record saying that "personal computers are just toys" in discounting the challenge of PCs to minicomputers, just as IBM had discounted the threat of minicomputers to mainframes ten years before. The Olsen philosophy blinded IBM's top management to the prospect that powerful PCs could become a

threat to IBM's main line of business, mainframes. This predicament was somewhat surprising given that the computer industry always had been dominated by technological change, and IBM's success was itself the result of it moving quickly and decisively to exploit the opportunities of new technology—the punch card machine, the transistor, and the integrated circuit.

Throughout the 1980s, IBM's personal computer division (which is the biggest personal computer operation in the world) could not respond quickly to the price-cutting moves of its rivals and could not introduce new kinds of personal computers as a result of its centralized decision-making style. Whenever a competitor reduced prices, managers of the personal computer division had to get approval from the corporate management committee to cut prices, a process that sometimes took months. As a result, the PC division was never able to forestall its rivals. Moreover, just as in the case of minicomputers, rivalry between PC and mainframe managers hampered efforts to exploit quickly the potential of the powerful new microprocessors.

IBM's competitors moved quickly to increase the power of their PCs by exploiting the power of the new generation of microprocessors. They also encouraged the development of powerful new netware software that could link PCs together and to a more powerful computer, such as a minicomputer or workstation, so that a network of PCs could work as effectively as a mainframe—but more conveniently and at only a fraction of the cost.

Workstations

Workstations are the fourth wave of computers following mainframes, minicomputers, and PCs. While PCs are designed for individual jobs like word processing and financial analysis, workstations essentially are very powerful PCs designed to be connected to each other and to a mainframe through software. Workstations can analyze financial results and track inventories much faster than PCs and much more cheaply than minicomputers or mainframes. A network of workstations can also be linked to an even more powerful workstation (or minicomputer) called a file server, which contains a company's files and database which can retrieve them from a company's mainframe computer. Workstations, usually priced from $5,000 to $100,000, were first developed for sci-

[11]Richard Hudson and Laurence Hooper, "IBM Slashes PC Prices in the U.S., Europe, Moving Swiftly to Counter Rivals' Cuts," *The Wall Street Journal*, February 12, 1993, p. B6.

[12]Bill Richards, "Apple Computer Cuts Its PC Prices Fifth Time in 1993," *The Wall Street Journal*, August 12, 1993, p. B1.

[13]Depke and Brandt.

[14]Ibid.

[15]John Bryne, Deidre Depke, and John Verity, "IBM: As Markets and Technology Change, Can Big Blue Remake Its Culture?" *Business Week*, June 17, 1991, pp. 24–32.

entists and engineers but increasingly are utilized by business professionals. New network software links workstations so that many people can work together simultaneously on the same project. These desktop machines have "user-friendly" graphic displays and allow people at different machines to share data and software. By 1988, the workstation market was $4.7 billion.[16] Workstations have a 45 percent profit margin compared to 58 percent for minicomputers.[17]

Prior to 1989 IBM was a small player in this segment. Underestimating the potential power of personal computers and slow to develop powerful minicomputers (its AS/400 series was introduced only in 1988), IBM managers once again failed to see the potential of an emerging market. IBM had only a 3.9 percent market share in 1987 compared to Sun Microsystems's 29 percent and Apollo's 21 percent, the two upstart companies that innovated the workstation. Once they realized the importance of this market segment, both IBM and DEC introduced workstations based on RISC (reduced instruction set computing) processors which make machines two to three times faster by eliminating all insignificant instructions. IBM introduced the IBM RT PC workstation in 1986, but the machine failed due to an underpowered microprocessor. Notwithstanding its problems, IBM launched the RS/6000 workstation in 1989 and captured 18 percent of the market by the end of 1991.[18]

Competition in the workstation market is increasing as a result of market growth. This segment was growing 27 percent annually by 1992, compared to 5 percent for the whole computer industry. As the price of workstations falls, more and more small businesses, which could not afford to use mainframe or minicomputers, can afford workstations. The workstation market also is very important to large computer makers because workstations can be used in networks with larger mainframe computers. Thus controlling the workstation market protects a company's mainframe market. By the end of 1991, the workstation market was $11.3 billion, and IBM was facing severe competition from DEC, Sun, Apollo, and Hewlett-Packard, all of which sell RISC workstations.

[16]Stuart Gannes, "IBM and DEC Take on the Little Guys," *Fortune*, October 10, 1988, pp. 108–114.
[17]Leslie Helm, "DEC Discovers It Can't Live by VAX Alone," *Business Week*, November 21, 1988, pp. 104–105.
[18]Carol Loomis and David Kirkpatrick, "The Hunt for Mr. X: Who Can Run IBM?" *Fortune*, February 22, 1993, pp. 68–72.

Software and Services

Designing software, the instructions that allow computers to perform tasks, and providing customer service, particularly assistance in the design of programs to manage company-specific databases and systems, have been a rapidly expanding segment of the computer industry for the past 20 years. IBM always has realized the importance of developing proprietary software that can link and join its mainframes, minicomputers, workstations, and personal computers to provide customers with a totally integrated computer package. It failed, however, to recognize the developing market for more general operating language and software applications.

By 1981, 33 percent of total computer industry revenue came from software and services, a figure which had risen to an estimated 50 percent in 1993. Although software and services accounted for 33 percent of IBM's total revenues by 1990, 68 percent of this revenue came from supporting customers' IBM mainframe computer systems, which represent a declining share of the computer market. Thus IBM, tied to software that supports mainframes, is not in a strong position to compete in the new software and services market.

IBM's failure to realize the potential for software seems surprising given that it had outsourced the operating language for its personal computer to Microsoft, and saw the success of the MS-DOS operating system. IBM's focus on mainframes and its continuing belief that its own proprietary hardware and software would become the industry standard seems to have been the source of its reluctance to enlarge and expand its software operations. In 1980, when IBM had the opportunity to indirectly control the software market by purchasing a large chunk of Microsoft stock at a low price, it declined to do so.

IBM soon found that developing new applications software was a difficult business to be in. First, IBM had a hard time recruiting talented programmers who were not attracted to IBM's bureaucratic and conservative corporate culture in which centralized decision making limited their opportunities to be creative and to take risks. Second, talented software programmers found they could make more money if they were in business for themselves; any programmer who could develop a new system generally started his or her own company. Microsoft recognized this problem early on; consequently,

Bill Gates, Microsoft's chairman, gives his top programmers large stock options to encourage their best performance. Many of them have become millionaires as a result.

In today's computer market developing better and more advanced software is crucial to selling more hardware, or computers of all kinds. So, late as usual, IBM embarked on a program to forge alliances with many small independent software companies to develop software for IBM machines quickly—mainframes, minis, workstations, and PCs. One of IBM's goals is to rejuvenate sales of its mainframe by encouraging software companies to write programs that make mainframes the key part of a computer network that links personal computers and workstations.[19] IBM spent $100 million in 1989 to acquire equity stakes in twelve software developers, including Interactive Images for Graphics, Inc., Polygen Corporation for scientific software, and American Management Systems, Inc., for mainframe software. Marketing agreements were made with several other firms. IBM loans software developers up to $50,000 for start-up costs and takes a seat on the developer's board.[20] For example, IBM is working on a project called Systems Application Architecture (SAA), which is a set of rules for links between programs and computers. SAA will facilitate the creation of networks with all types of machines, including mainframes and PCs.[21]

In 1988 IBM created a new unit to launch applications software and established a position called "complementary resource marketing manager," with responsibility for connecting software "business partners" with IBM customers. Salespeople are expected to sell the products of these software partners as well as IBM products.[22] Although most of the programs are for mainframes, many can be adapted to work with networks based on PCs.[23] Software and services accounted for 40 percent of IBM's revenue in 1992, and IBM wants to get 50 percent of revenues from software and services by the year 2000.[24]

Systems Integration and Outsourcing

Traditionally, IBM limited its service activities to providing support for its own proprietary software and hardware. It did not use its skills to analyze various aspects of a customer's business, such as its inventory control or warehousing operations, and then custom design and install an appropriate mix of hardware and software to meet the customer's needs, a service known as systems integration.[25] Moreover, it had not recognized the developing market for outsourcing data processing whereby one company agrees to take over and manage all aspects of the data processing function for another company in return for a fee. By 1992, however, the systems integration and outsourcing market generated more revenues than the mainframe market.

IBM's failure to see the developing market segment for systems integration and outsourcing had not been lost on one of IBM's star salesmen, Ross Perot. When IBM capped the amount of money that Perot could earn from commissions in selling computers, and when it ignored his plan to start an IBM division whose function would be to provide data management services to customers to advise them on ways to manage their data files and systems, Perot left IBM and started Electronic Data Services (EDS).

The systems integration market and outsourcing market is now growing at 19 percent annually. IBM's failure to enter this market segment early allowed its competitors—principally EDS and Andersen Consulting, the accounting firm which early established a computer consulting division—to gain a first mover advantage and to dominate the market. Currently, EDS has 50 percent of the outsourcing business of managing a company's data storage and management needs, compared to IBM's 6 percent, while Andersen dominates the market for advising companies on their software and hardware needs. IBM leads primarily in the market for government contracts.

To develop a presence in this lucrative market quickly, IBM began developing alliances with various organizations. It formed a joint venture with Coopers & Lybrand to provide management consulting in selected industries. IBM also teamed with AT&T to make IBM's mainframes work better with AT&T's network management systems.[26] IBM established the

[19]Walecia Konrad, "Information Processing: Survival of the Biggest," *Business Week*, April 2, 1990, pp. 66, 68.
[20]Deidre Depke, "Suddenly, Software Houses Have a Big Blue Buddy," *Business Week*, August 7, 1989, pp. 68–69.
[21]Ibid.
[22]Ibid.
[23]Loomis and Kirkpatrick.
[24]IBM 1992 Annual Report, p. 40.
[25]Lewis, *Business Week*, February 14, 1988, pp. 92–98.
[26]John Verity, *Business Week*, April 8, 1991, pp. 83–84.

Integrated Systems Solutions Corporation subsidiary in 1991 to provide a platform for IBM to enter the data processing outsourcing market. Its business is increasing; for example, in 1992 it received a 10-year $3 billion agreement to run computer systems for McDonnell Douglas Corporation. The subsidiary does outsourcing for 30 companies, including Continental Bank. IBM will run all of a client company's systems from mainframes and workstations to voice and data telecommunications.[27] It is aggressively advertising its strengths and services in this area.

The New Computer Industry

By 1990 IBM received about 50 percent of its gross profit from mainframe hardware, software, peripherals, and maintenance; 6 percent from minicomputers; 18.5 percent from PCs and workstations; and 12.4 percent from non-maintenance software and services.[28] However, the future revenue-generating potential of each of these market segments is uncertain as the boundaries between the segments grow less clear. Will workstations replace minicomputers? Will workstations and minicomputers replace mainframes? Will a network of PCs linked by advanced software to a mainframe eliminate the need for minicomputers or workstations? Obviously, IBM has the most to gain from making mainframes the center of a computer network, but its competitors have as much to gain from making minicomputers and powerful workstations the way of the future.

By 1990 IBM was facing stiff competition in all the developing segments of the computer market from companies that were mainly specialized in one market niche, like Microsoft in the software segment or Sun Computer in the workstation niche. IBM was fighting to increase its market share in each market segment but was suffering because of tough competition from strong competitors that had developed their own loyal customer following.

Moreover, the market for mainframe computers, its principal source of revenue, was declining as machines such as PCs and workstations were able to perform mainframe tasks at a lower cost. It had been estimated that, while 80 percent of 1986 computer industry profits were attributable to mainframe computer sales, by 1991 sales of mainframe computer

[27]James Hyatt, "IBM Signs Pact to Offer Service to McDonnell," *The Wall Street Journal*, December 30, 1992, p. A3.
[28]Byrne, Depke, and Verity.

systems accounted for only 20 percent of industry profits. The PC revolution had reduced costs and allowed customers to buy much cheaper computer systems to do the work previously performed by expensive mainframes and minicomputers.

As a result of this shift, suppliers of computer components such as chips and software have been the winners as their share of industry profits rose from 20 percent in 1986 to 31 percent in 1991. Thus, for example, the share prices of Microsoft and Intel, which control the software and microprocessor markets, respectively, have soared, as have the share prices of Conner, Quantum, and Seagate which dominate disk drives and Andersen Consulting and EDS which are the leaders in system integration. IBM's, however, has fallen dramatically from a high of $160 in 1987 to less than $50 in 1992.

To fight the trend toward PCs and workstations, IBM attempted to make its 370 computer the central component of a network of computers that link individual users to the mainframe. However, it did not succeed, as sales growth for its biggest mainframe, the 370, dropped from 4 percent a year in 1990 to less than 2 percent a year in 1992. Even many of IBM's 370 users began switching to IBM AS/400 minicomputers because they can perform the same task more easily and cheaply. The mainframe market is now the third largest market behind PCs and minicomputers.

IBM Fights Back: Restructuring

In 1985 John Akers became CEO and was charged with the task of using IBM's vast resources to make it the market leader in the new lucrative market segments of the computer industry and to reduce IBM's dependence on mainframes. He took over a company where managers were still arrogant and complacent and believed completely in IBM's preeminence despite all the warning signs that it had lost its competitive edge. Its top management committee, staffed primarily of managers from its mainframe division, seemed unable to make the kind of innovative decisions that would allow IBM to respond quickly to the rapidly changing computer environment. The result was the failure to develop products fast enough and a mistaken commitment to the mainframe computer. Even its renowned salespeople had become a problem for the company. Committed to the IBM product, they had become oriented to selling and

C370 SECTION B Corporate Level Cases: Domestic and Global

servicing the mainframe; they were not oriented toward satisfying customer needs, which might be for a minicomputer or a workstation.

Akers launched a year of the customer in 1987 to refocus the sales force on meeting the needs of the customer rather than on the needs of the mainframe. Most important, Akers realized the need to restructure the company and to change IBM's highly centralized style of decision making if IBM was to be able to innovate the next generation of products and emerge as a market leader in the new market segments. Akers recognized that the biggest problem for IBM was its highly bureaucratic organizational structure which slowed decision making and continually frustrated attempts to be innovative and entrepreneurial.

The 1988 Restructuring

To speed decision making, in January 1988 Akers reorganized IBM into seven divisions based on the main product market segments in which the company was competing: personal computer systems, mid-range systems, mainframes, information systems and communications, technology development (such as microchips), programming, and software. The idea behind the reorganization was to demolish the mainframe mindset by giving the managers of each division the autonomy and responsibility for developing new products for their respective markets. No longer would mainframe managers be able to stifle the pace of change and discourage the development of products that threatened the dominance of the mainframe. The sales force, however, was to remain a separate entity whose job would still be to sell the whole line of IBM products. The logic for this was that the sales force could sell customers an integrated IBM computer system—a network of PCs, file servers, and mainframe—and provide the computer software, service, and systems consulting to tailor the system to the customers' individual needs.

The disadvantage of the single sales force was that each division would not be able to devise a sales strategy specific to its own competitive environment and salespeople would not be able to focus on a single product line. IBM felt that the economies of scale and scope provided by a unified sales force outweighed these disadvantages. Twenty-thousand employees were transferred from staff and lab positions to the sales force and the commission system was revamped so that salespeople were now evaluated on total revenue, not on the number of units rented or sold.[29]

IBM's Contention System

If the first purpose of the reorganization was to focus IBM's activities more closely on the main segments of the computer market, the second purpose was to shorten the product development cycle and to speed products to market. Since the early 1970s, IBM had taken advantage of its dominance in the market to use a "contention" system to control new product development. In this system, two or more project teams designed competing product prototypes and a series of committees at both the divisional level and the corporate level met over a period of months to debate the merits of each project. A project would be approved after six committee members rated the two processes, which could take months or years; then the committee met to finalize the product plan. During this process if any committee member said, "I non-concur," meaning that he or she disagreed with the project, it would be sent back for further review or scrapped.

The result of the contention system was that the projects that were approved were generally successful. However, the time frame associated with making the decision was generally so long that products were late to market, putting IBM at a competitive disadvantage. For example, the small, independent team charged with the development of the first IBM PC launched the product in one year. However, once the PC group was put into the Information Systems & Communications Division and decision making became constrained by IBM's contention system, the speed of the development process slowed significantly. For example, the PS/2 was not introduced until 1987 instead of the 1985 target. This delay allowed clone makers of the older PCs to gain 33 percent of the market share in PCs. Other symptoms of IBM's overly bureaucratic approach to decision making included its failure to enter new market segments quickly. For example, IBM entered the PC market four years late; it was also a laggard in workstations. Similarly, IBM's top managers refused to recognize the importance of the growth of minicomputers and were hesitant to launch products that would compete with the mainframes.

[29]John Verity, *Business Week*, May 29, 1989, pp. 72–78.

The reorganization was designed to shorten the time it took to get a product to market and to overcome the hurdles to product development.[30] In the 1980s IBM no longer had the luxury of taking a long time to make competitive decisions, as smaller and more agile competitors were forging ahead and the product life cycle of computers was shortening.

In an attempt to cut costs, increase profitability, get close to the customers, and reduce bureaucracy, Akers embarked on a major campaign to downsize the organization. The 1985 work force of 405,000 was reduced to 389,300 in 1988 through early retirement and attrition. In addition, overtime and temporary employees, equivalent to 12,500 full-time employees, were cut.[31] Despite the facts that IBM closed plants, cut spending, and reduced capital outlays, costs grew faster than revenues during most of the reorganization. Moreover, analysts could not discern any noticeable change in IBM's strategy or the way it made decisions. Products were still late to market.

The 1988 reorganization was a failure. Although each division was supposed to become more autonomous, in reality most decisions still required approval by IBM's corporate headquarters managers—managers who had risen through the ranks from the powerful mainframe computer division. Products that might have cannibalized the sale of mainframes were still discouraged by corporate managers, who having achieved their success during the mainframe era were hesitant to introduce products to compete with mainframes. One example of the mainframe mindset involved the PC unit's push to get into the laptop market in 1989 by pricing the laptop competitively at $4,995. Corporate headquarters insisted on a price of $5,995 to meet corporate profit margin targets. As a result, many competitors were able to price their products lower than IBM's machines. Even though IBM later priced the machine lower, it never regained lost market share.[32]

To allow the personal computer division to respond faster to the quickly changing PC market, Akers decided to place the PC business in a separate operating unit. In 1991 Akers formed the IBM Personal Computer Co. and gave it control over the design, production, distribution, and marketing of IBM PCs. Prior to this change, distribution was performed by IBM's large sales and marketing division, but 1,200 former marketing and sales employees were transferred to the new PC unit, which also was to handle telephone sales. The corporate sales force was to continue to sell to big corporate customers.[33] In decentralizing authority to managers in the PC division, Akers was showing managers his plans for the IBM of the future.

The 1991 Restructuring

IBM announced another restructuring at the end of 1991 to try to decentralize decision-making authority to the divisions and to reduce the role of IBM corporate headquarters in setting divisional strategy.[34] Akers divided IBM into thirteen separate divisions: nine divisions were based on the company's main product lines and four divisions were to be marketing and service operations organized geographically. The nine manufacturing divisions were to supply the four marketing divisions. The goal of the restructuring effort was to make the divisions independent units operating under a broad IBM umbrella to free the divisions from corporate control.

Aker's plan was that each division would be an autonomous operating unit that could freely negotiate transfer prices of inputs with other divisions and, if a division wanted to, could buy from and sell to outside companies. The divisions were to treat each other the same as they would outside companies, and no favorable prices were to be granted to IBM divisions. Moreover, the performance of each division would be reported separately and each division would be accountable for its individual profits and losses. The heads of the divisions were responsible for developing annual business plans and were to guarantee IBM a certain return on money invested in their division. In the past, most managers did not know the details of an individual division's financial performance such as profit and loss statements.[35] Each divisional manager signed a contract to meet

[30]Lewis.

[31]Aaron Bernstein, "How IBM Cut 16,200 Employees without an Ax," *Business Week*, February 15, 1988, p. 98.

[32]Verity, "The New IBM."

[33]Laurence Hooper, "IBM Set to Unveil Restyled PC Business That Could Operate as a Separate Unit," *The Wall Street Journal*, September 3, 1992, p. A3.

[34]Verity, "The New IBM."

[35]Ibid.

objectives in revenue growth, profit, ROA (return on assets), cash flow, customer satisfaction, quality, and morale.[36] If the divisional heads were successful, they would get a share of the profits; however, if they failed, their jobs were on the line. Financial results for all thirteen units were to be made public by 1994.[37]

The goal of this restructuring was to free up IBM's powerful resources and to make it more competitive. Division heads will have control over long-term development and business-level strategy. For example, the Personal Systems Division's manager can decide how PCs and workstations are produced and designed, and the PC division's research and development function will not compete directly with the mainframe division for resources. The hope is that the divisions will be able to compete with their smaller, more entrepreneurial rivals once they are freed from corporate bureaucracy.

The sales divisions will still be responsible for selling the whole range of IBM products, however, and control over sales will be centralized at corporate headquarters. The logic, once again, is that customers want a sales force that can handle their entire computer needs and that there are synergies from having one sales force provide a full set of products and services. IBM's traditional focus on service is still a strong competitive advantage. Analysts are, however, skeptical of having only one sales force, especially one in which representatives are still biased toward mainframes.[38] Many analysts feel that one sales force is a mistake and that giving each division its own sales force would be a better source of competitive advantage. Moreover, the huge costs of operating the sales force could be hard to allocate between divisions, causing rivalry among them.[39]

To demonstrate to IBM's thirteen operating divisions top management's commitment to IBM's more autonomous and more entrepreneurial approach to doing business, IBM's PC division was given total control over its own sales and named an independent unit in 1992. James Cannavino, the head of the PC unit, took total control over the PC division's strategy and organized the PC division around products instead of functions. The five product groups of the PC

division are the low-cost Value-Points; PS/2; PS-1, aimed at home and small business users; portable products; and Ambra, a line of PCs built by an Asian contractor and sold in Europe. Each product group is in charge of its own brand development, manufacturing, pricing, and marketing.[40] This change was designed to allow the product groups to respond much more quickly to changes in the PC market, where products may have a life span of only six months to a year. In addition, Cannavino met with thirty-two CEOs of Silicon Valley start-ups and told them that he wanted to form alliances with them to speed the development of new hardware and software products such as multimedia and CD-ROM products. The IBM PC division is the world's largest PC company.

New Management and New Plans

Despite the 1991 organization, IBM's profits and revenues continued to decline; 1991 revenues fell 5 percent from 1990, the first decline since 1946. The company's 1991 loss of $2.8 billion was the first loss in IBM's history. In 1992 IBM's losses increased to $5 billion on $65 billion in revenues. In January 1993 the stock went below $46, the lowest price in 17 years, and pressure for change at the top was increasing.

Under pressure from investors and the public, John Akers resigned in January 1993. Although Akers reorganized and restructured, critics claimed that he never went far enough in implementing the reforms that would really turn around IBM. For example, despite the facts that between 1986 to 1990 a total of 100,000 IBM workers were cut mainly through early retirement and that Akers had removed the whole of IBM's former top management team to try to rid IBM of the "mainframe mindset," critics claimed that Akers had avoided initiating the major layoffs that were needed to restore profitability.[41]

In 1993 the board of directors searched for a replacement for Akers and shunning an insider, for fear that he could not bring a fresh perspective to IBM's problems, chose an outsider to be CEO of IBM, the first time an outsider had occupied the top job.

[36]David Kirkpatrick, "Breaking up IBM," *Fortune*, July 27, 1992, pp. 44–58.
[37]Ibid.
[38]Verity, "The New IBM."
[39]John Verity and Arnst, December 21, 1992, p. 32.

[40]Catherine Arnst and Bart Ziegler, "A Freewheeling Youngster Named IBM," *Business Week*, May 3, 1993, pp. 134–138.
[41]Catherine Arnst and Weber, *Fortune*, February 8, 1993, pp. 22–24.

Case 22

The Rebirth of IBM

This case was prepared by Gareth R. Jones, Texas A&M University.

Today, IBM has a market capitalization of over $155 billion and employs over 319,000 people worldwide who operate in over 150 countries. It is also one of the most profitable global computer companies because by 2004 it had become the leader in the global business computer services and consulting industry, surpassing competitors such as EDS, Accenture, Cap Gemini, and HP. What changes in its business model and strategies have allowed IBM to achieve such a dramatic turnaround in performance given its disastrous performance in the 1980s? To answer this question, it is necessary to look at the way changes in IBM's top management and the business model its new CEOs Louis Gerstner, and then Sam Palmisano, crafted have transformed the company over the last decade.

Akers's Last Stand

As discussed in "The Fall of IBM," John Akers's vision of IBM's future was for the corporation to be broken up into thirteen different companies that would be spun off to operate independently—essentially that the IBM empire should be dissolved. While IBM's top managers considered how to go about the mammoth task of dismantling the company, Akers still faced the problem of how to keep it afloat in the short run. In his final desperate attempt to keep IBM viable, Akers continued to make drastic cost reductions, and

between 1991 and 1993, an additional eighty thousand employees were laid off as IBM sought to lower its cost structure—it now had less than half the work force that it had at its peak. The restructuring charges associated with these layoffs and the closing of many of its factories and offices resulted in record losses of over $15 billion for IBM, and its stock price plunged to record lows as investors decided the future lay not in mainframe computers but in networks of servers and client PCs. Moreover, by this time its personal systems group that manufactured its PCs and the small size servers it was developing had become a liability. This was because such competitors as Dell, Gateway, and Sun now had gained a major cost advantage—amounting to hundreds of dollars a computer—over IBM's PCs, and the PC division was losing money.

Another major problem IBM encountered in the early 1990s was the result of a major change in business-level strategy it made during the 1980s in the attempt to prop up its revenues and profits. As discussed in the earlier cases, IBM traditionally offered a complete service to its clients who typically rented its computer hardware and software on a multi-year basis, and then their IT system was maintained and upgraded by IBM service specialists. To boost revenues in the face of growing competition from servers, IBM decided to focus on selling, rather than renting, its computers, and it began offering special deals to its clients to encourage them to buy them.

While this boosted its performance in the short run, by the 1990s, however, the result was that IBM lost its special relationship with clients who now were looking to upgrade their computer systems. Given the rapid advances in IT, they now became more likely to buy the products of other computer companies, especially because servers and PCs seemed to offer considerable cost savings over mainframes.

By the 1990s, sales of network computers were rocketing while sales of mainframes were plunging, and IBM's strategy had inadvertently reduced its clients switching costs. By 1990, sales of computer hardware and software accounted for over 80 percent of IBM's sales and revenues because revenues from its service operations had declined significantly as clients began to build their own IT departments.

In 1993, when the company's performance showed no sign of improving despite his best efforts, CEO Akers resigned and IBM's Board of Directors looked for a successor who could somehow find the right business model to turnaround the ailing company. The person they selected to be IBM's new CEO was Louis Gerstner, an ex-management consultant who, as president of American Express and CEO of Nabisco, had engineered a major turnaround in the performance of these companies. Gerstner had no background in the computing industry, however, and his appointment was viewed by many analysts—and by many of IBM's powerful top managers—as an enormous mistake, and IBM's stock dropped to a new low when Gerstner took over. How could an outsider, with no knowledge of the way IBM operated, know how to compete against its rivals in the rapidly changing computer sector?

Gerstner's Immediate Moves

IBM's board had chosen Gerstner, however, because they wanted a new leader who could take a fresh perspective on the company's problems and one who had not been a part of IBM's slow-moving bureaucratic culture in which slow, centralized decision making and power struggles between divisions had dominated its strategic thinking. Gerstner's task was to decide what the right business model was for IBM. What kinds of products, customers, and distinctive competencies should IBM invest in and pursue in the future or should the company be broken up? In the meantime he also faced the problem of stemming IBM's losses and keeping it afloat.

The major argument Akers had made in support of breaking up IBM into thirteen different and independent companies was that each new company would then be free to decide how best to compete against rivals in its particular industry, PC or storage or particular software application, for example. By doing this, each former IBM division would become more efficient because its newly independent managers

would have greater incentive to make tough decisions and find the best way to compete. Before making this decision, Gerstner decided to closely study IBM's different business divisions and search out their strengths and weaknesses. Also, he wanted to examine the fit between IBM's different businesses—what was the rationale for keeping IBM as a whole versus breaking it up?

Gerstner has a reputation for hands on management that involves frequent visits to all a company's divisions to talk to managers at all levels. He spent his first months as CEO on a whistle stop tour interviewing IBM's divisional managers, searching out those who seemed to have special insight into its problems and analyzing its portfolio of businesses. He also visited many of IBM's largest corporate clients to get a sense of what they wanted from IBM and what they saw to be its future.

Gerstner soon publicly announced that his decision was that IBM should remain as one single united company; the real problem was to find a better way to integrate the products and activities of its different divisions to create more value from its businesses for clients. His strategic analysis led him to conclude that it was IBM's ability to provide clients with a complete and comprehensive collection of computer hardware, software, and services, including business consultancy that could be customized to each client's particular needs that would be the source of its future competitive advantage—just as it had been in the past when it dominated mainframe computing. In his view, what IBM needed to do was to work toward offering clients a complete computer package that suited the realities of the new computing environment, which now had strong competitors in all industries in the computer sector.

Having made the decision to keep IBM intact, Gerstner saw the main challenge as how to speed innovation and decision making both within and across IBM's many divisions. He soon found that IBM's top managers, inured as they were in its slow-moving culture based on consensus decision making, could not respond at the pace he was expecting. One IBM manager described the old IBM's decision-making process as being like "wading through a jar of peanut butter." Gerstner announced that IBM's managers "just didn't have what it takes," and he began to replace many senior IBM executives with managers from lower down in the ranks. He also continued to lay off large numbers of employees in product areas that he felt could not compete successfully in the new advanced IT environment to further reduce IBM's cost structure. He also decided to totally change the way decisions were made.

In the past, meetings to discuss important new product or strategy decisions, which were held at IBM's Armonk, New York, skyscraper headquarters, had often lasted many hours or days. Gerstner issued new rules requiring senior managers to distribute short, ten-page reports that outlined all significant strategy issues to other senior managers in advance of the meeting. Now, with all managers informed of the major issues involved, meetings could focus on the critical issues. Also, the managers championing a new product or project were now aware that they would be facing the probing questions of other managers, including Gerstner, who has a reputation for a blunt, confrontational style of management—one far removed from IBM's old consensus decision making. All managers came to meetings much better prepared and ready to defend or challenge new proposals for new products or services. Gerstner's new rules dramatically shortened meeting time, and unlike previous CEOs he often moved during or even before meetings to unilaterally approve or disapprove of new proposals regardless of the views of other managers. He knew IBM needed an autocratic, hands-on style of governance to challenge managers, to develop better strategies, and to speed decision making.

Finally, to change IBM's culture and decision making Gerstner decided to build a new campus-style IBM headquarters to replace its high-rise office building. In the old building, the more senior managers were, the higher the floor they had their offices on, and this had helped create IBM's centralized, hierarchical culture. In the new building top managers would be located on the same floor next to all the other managers in their operating group to encourage faster communication. Also, it would be easier for managers in different divisions to collaborate and discuss ways to harmonize their products and services and discover new product opportunities. The old headquarters was sold off—one more way Gerstner told his managers the old ways were gone.

Gerstner's New Business Model

Between 1993–1996, Gerstner and his top management team spent their time identifying IBM's core set of distinctive competences and deciding how they could nurture and build these competences to provide a foundation for IBM's future business model. When Gerstner found a product line or division that did not seem to meet IBM's future needs, it was either sold off to another company or closed down, which resulted in still more employee layoffs. But Gerstner's goal was to invest IBM's remaining resources in businesses where they could create the most value—and in so doing save the company. But what was Gerstner's vision for the rebirth of IBM?

His business model was that IBM should (1) provide a complete package of state-of-the-art computing solutions (hardware, software, services, and consultancy) that could be customized to a particular client's needs, and (2) to take advantage of the possibilities created by the Internet to create new markets for IBM's products and services. The whole focus of Gerstner's efforts was to make IBM a customer-driven company by which he meant that every manager and employee had the responsibility to make or provide those products or services that could best meet the needs of IBM's clients. Given that PCs, and even servers, were becoming commodity products with low-profit margins, what IBM had to do was to provide something unique so that customers would be willing to pay a premium price for its products and services. The challenge facing IBM was to learn how to customize products to the needs of customers if it was to be able to succeed in the new highly competitive computing environment.

Changes in Computer Hardware

Gerstner instructed his top managers to begin initiatives in all computer divisions to meet clients' changing IT needs. In its traditional hardware business, it faced two major problems. First, as noted earlier, mainframe sales were declining due to the growing popularity of network servers and PCs. To stem the decline Gerstner instructed the mainframe division, in conjunction with IBM's semiconductor division, to find ways to reduce the costs of mainframe computing, and to increase the scalability of its computers. Scalability means that a computer can be customized and designed and built to suit the needs of any size of company or any size computing task, from managing global databases to operating a small chain of restaurants. IBM began to position its smaller mainframes as "enterprise servers," and sales representatives were told to emphasize to clients that they could be made at a size and price to suit their unique needs, but that a large powerful mainframe computer was still needed at the hub of any company's IT system no matter what its size. Sales representatives were also told to emphasize that managing huge amounts of data and enormous databases on a more powerful enterprise server was not much higher than a network server, and that the enterprise server could satisfy the needs of a growing company. Also, IBM wanted to sell its clients its software and services such as maintenance so that it deliberately set prices of its hardware (enterprise servers) low, knowing that it could make money later on new software and services.

IBM quickly succeeded in lowering the costs of mainframe computing and had a clear cost advantage over competitors in this market. Another bright spot in its PC division was the popularity of IBM's sophisticated problem-solving ThinkPad computing devices among corporate customers. But Gerstner and his managers continued to struggle to develop strategies to increase the efficiency of IBM's server and PC division that was losing even more money as companies like Dell found new ways to slow down the learning curve. Although this division continued to lose money, however, it was difficult for IBM to leave this business because of its desire to offer its clients a complete hardware solution for their computing needs.

Another major change Gerstner made on the hardware side of the business was to take advantage of IBM's acknowledged skills in the development of new and advanced microprocessor chips. Before 1993, IBM only made chips for use in its own high-powered computers to protect its proprietary mainframe technology. Gerstner now instructed the chip division's managers to market these chips to other computer makers and to vigorously solicit contracts to build customized chips to suit the needs of other original equipment manufacturers (OEMs). In this way the division would learn how to build customized chips to suit the needs of clients in a particular industry, for example, which had a particular kind of need from a chip. This change in strategy proved very successful, and revenues from chips sales surged over time.

Changes in Computer Software

The rapid pace of change in the computer software industry resulted in a major challenge for Gerstner and his managers. Before IBM made the mistake of allowing Microsoft to provide the MS-DOS operating system for its own PC, it had been the largest seller of computer software (principally for mainframes and mainframe applications) in the world. Now Microsoft had usurped its position, but there were many other challenges as well from makers of specialized applications software such as companies like Oracle, which is the market leader in database management software, and SAP the German company whose Enterprise Resource Planning (ERP) software was soaring in popularity throughout the 1980s and 1990s. ERP software allows a company to link its value-chain activities and connects mainframes to servers and servers to PCs. It gives a company's managers at all levels extensive real-time information about a company's activities; ERP software has become the backbone of most large companies' IT systems. IBM had little to offer clients in these software applications areas; these companies had gained a first-mover advantage that was difficult for IBM to challenge.

Gerstner instructed the software division to focus its efforts on developing networking software designed to link IBM's new scalable enterprise (mainframe) servers to smaller servers and PCs. To catch up quickly, Gerstner began to buy companies that possessed unique network software that could provide clients with valuable new applications that would allow them to make better use of their computer network—and thus give IBM a competitive advantage. One of the companies IBM acquired at a cost of over $3 billion in 1995 was Lotus, which had developed the popular Lotus Notes collaborative software that essentially created a corporate intranet, an information network inside a company that allows managers at all levels to share information quickly both inside their own department and division and between divisions.

Gerstner early on saw another important way in which IBM could use its resources to develop software that would meet its clients' changing needs. This was to begin the push to develop "middleware" software that links the hardware and software provided by *any* computer company across *all* the levels of computing. In other words, middleware software provides customers with a "seamless" solution to their computing needs regardless of their legacy system. A legacy system is a company's current IT system at any point in time. Clearly, if IBM could develop middleware that could link any kind of computer products now and in the future, it would be in a good position to serve any client that wished to change or upgrade their current legacy system to take advantage of new and advanced IT applications offered by any company. This revolutionary approach was part of Gerstner's "open standards" strategy designed both to make IBM's own services available to all kinds of customers and to lessen the dominance of Microsoft.

Changes in Services and Consulting

Gerstner's drive to focus the efforts of all IBM employees on satisfying the needs of clients had been strongly influenced by the continued success of IBM's computer services group which in 1995 contributed around 20 percent to IBM's revenues. IBM's entry into the computer services business had arisen via the need of the U.S. government to employ the recognized global IT leader to run its major computing systems, such as those involved in national defense and space exploration. Recognizing that many large businesses had a similar need for expert help to install, maintain, and upgrade their computer systems—most of which then ran on IBM mainframes—the company established the Integrated Systems Solution Corporation (ISSC), which was a self-contained division separate from IBM's corporate headquarters and whose employees were service and customer oriented. Their job was to search for new clients and then to contract to manage their IT systems for a period of several years. Essentially this group provided the first computer outsourcing service that had been imitated by such growing competitors as Electronic Data Systems (EDS) and Accenture (which previously had been the consulting division of defunct Arthur Anderson) that had become the leading competitors in the IT outsourcing and services industry.

Gerstner recognized that this division possessed the customer-focused business model that IBM needed to grow its revenues in the future, especially if sales of its hardware and software declined. Moreover, Gerstner was familiar with the business model that Jack Welsh, former CEO of GE, had developed for his company. This was that GE would sell a product such as a turbine or aircraft or diesel engine at a relatively low price to increase sales because each sale would result in a profitable stream of future income from servicing and maintaining the complex equipment it sold. Gerstner recognized this same model was viable in the new IT environment; he also

recognized that in the IT sector clients need expert help to decide which kind of computer solution best meets their current and future business needs. Once again companies like EDS and Accenture were the leaders here and earned huge profits by providing companies with such expert help. And the market was only getting bigger; for example, SAP could not satisfy the demand of large global clients to install its ERP software in its clients companies, and clients were paying billions of dollars to consulting companies like Accenture and Cap Gemini for their expert help.

In 1996, Gerstner renamed the services division Global Services and charged it with the task of spearheading IBM's push into the outsourcing and value-chain management business to go head-to-head with competitors like EDS and Accenture. Gerstner's business model was now that global services would offer clients an outsourcing and business consultancy service based on assessing a customer's current legacy system and its future computing needs. IBM consultants would then design, plan, implement, maintain, and upgrade the client's IT system over time to help reduce the client's cost structure, improve its products, and build its competitive advantage.

Gerstner also hoped that providing such expert services would once again build up switching costs and keep IBM's clients loyal on a long-term basis because of its ability to show them how its comprehensive, customized computing solution could help increase their profitability over time.

Global services experienced continuing success throughout the 1990s, and it established hundreds of outsourcing deals with large corporate clients through the 1990s.

The New Global Services Division

Throughout the 1990s Gerstner continued to invest a large proportion of IBM's capital to strengthen the global services division, which was led by Sam Palmisano, because he believed this was the new foundation on which IBM's future success lay. His business model for IBM was that the company would build such a broad and sophisticated range of computer hardware and software, backed by the best consulting and service competencies in the industry, that it would overwhelm its competitors in the future. EDS and Accenture provide consultancy and service, for example, and HP, Dell, Sun, Oracle, and Microsoft produce computer hardware and software, but none of them had the capability to match the breadth and depth of IBM's growing computer offerings. By the late 1990s the ability to bundle products together was becoming a major advantage to clients seeking a seamless and cost-effective way of managing their IT—it has only become more important since.

In implementing this business model Gerstner recognized that in many specific computer hardware and software product areas IBM was no longer the industry leader. So he and Palmisano embarked on a the strategy of offering IBM's clients the "leading edge" products currently available, such as SAP's ERP software or Peoplesoft's HRM software or Sun's servers and Dell's PCs when they were either clearly better or lower priced than those supplied by IBM's own divisions. Then, and crucially, IBM's consultants, as a result of its focus on developing expertise in middleware that links any computer products together, were able to guarantee clients that they could install, maintain, and integrate them so that they work together seamlessly.

In adopting this strategy IBM was strengthening its commitment to "open standards" in the computer industry by announcing publicly that in the future it would continue to work to make all the *future* software and hardware of all producers—its competitors—compatible by strengthening its expertise in middleware. In doing so, Gerstner and IBM were also assuring clients that when they used IBM's computer consulting services this would not result in them becoming locked into its own proprietary hardware and software—so no switching costs would arise from this source. However, Gerstner hoped at the same time that clients would be so impressed by IBM's ability to provide such a complete service that they would become "locked in" because of the high quality of the service that it could provide.

An additional advantage of the open standards approach was that as IBM's consultants went from client to client assessing their needs they were able to provide detailed feedback to IBM's other divisions about whether their products were adequately meeting clients' needs. So, if a consultant decided that a competitor's software was more appropriate than that offered by IBM's, the division making the software could now clearly recognize why its product was not meeting customer needs—and what was necessary to improve its software to make it the "best of breed" or leading-edge product. Thus, Gerstner's strong focus on being close to clients had the additional advantage of spurring innovation throughout the organization;

managers had a clear goal to achieve, and they knew that Gerstner and his top management team were watching their performance. So, if a division did not meet customer needs its managers might lose their jobs or it might be sold off or shut down.

E-Business at IBM

Another indicator of how well Gerstner was attuned to the changing IT environment was his early recognition that the growth of the Internet and e-commerce would become a dominant force in the direction of computing in the future. IBM coined the term "e-business," and Gerstner established an Internet division in IBM in 1995 before most other computer companies. Its early awareness of the future possibilities of e-business in commerce also allowed it to adapt its software and hardware to serve Internet-related value-chain transactions before its competitors. Once again, being close to its clients helped it to understand their changing needs and built its competitive advantage. Also, its acquisition of Lotus helped IBM understand the potential of the Internet. Lotus Notes was a company-specific or internal software collaboration application, while the Internet provided a major channel for collaboration between different companies. It was by chance that IBM's acquisition of Lotus revealed how the power of the Internet would shape supply chain transactions between companies and their suppliers and distributors, and the Lotus collaborative software provided a model for making IBM middleware software Internet compatible.

IBM embarked on its e-business initiative in 1996 with a global marketing campaign aimed at showing companies how value-chain transactions with other companies and clients could be carried out online. Soon companies recognized that its competency in e-business gave it a competitive advantage over companies such as SAP, Oracle, and HP, which now raced to catch up. As a result, it attracted a growing number of e-business clients that resulted in a major increase in its computer service revenues. First in line to adopt IBM's e-business software were large corporations that needed to manage transactions with hundreds or even thousands of suppliers and distributors. Companies such as Wal-Mart and Goodyear formed contracts with IBM to use its immense computing resources to manage their huge volume of online transactions.

IBM, however, also recognized that small and medium businesses (SMBs) were another important kind of business opportunity to sell its service offerings—especially as it now had computer hardware and software that was scaleable so that it could be sold at a price to meet their needs. IBM had developed less expensive software targeted at the needs of SMB clients, and it now worked with the thousands of new dot.com startups, such as Internet web-design and hosting companies, to teach these companies how to install and maintain its software in SMBs. IBM hoped that once SMBs had made the connection with IBM they would start to buy other kinds of its software, for example, to manage their databases and functional, value-chain tasks such as bookkeeping and inventory control. In 1999, Gerstner announced that IBM had a goal of reaching two million SMB clients by 2001.

A last advantage of IBM's early move to the Internet was that it also helped with its own cost-cutting efforts. IBM claimed to have saved billions of dollars by selling its own computer hardware and software directly to customers online, and billions more by using e-business to purchase the components it uses to make its own products.

Gerstner Transfers Power to Palmisano

By 2000, IBM had replaced EDS as the global leader in computer services; it had a backlog of outsourcing contracts worth over $100 billion. Until he retired as CEO of IBM in February 2002, Gerstner continued to work to strengthen his new services-driven business model across all IBM's U.S. and global operations. To encourage managers, consultants, and salespeople to focus on the customer, Gerstner introduced a new pay-for-performance evaluation system that rewarded employees at all levels based upon their ability to meet the goals and objectives in the business model. In addition, Gerstner imitated EDS and Accenture in making stock options a part of IBM's incentive structure to encourage top managers to pursue IBM's new business model and forget the old IBM ways. In the old IBM, with the exception of its salespeople who had always been paid according to performance, managers and employees had been rewarded based on their time in the company or the level to which they had been promoted. Now, a manager's own performance drove promotions and rewards—and poor performance and the inability to meet goals resulted in termination. In this way, too, Gerstner changed IBM's culture; from being conservative, hierarchical, and product oriented, it now became entrepreneurial, collaborative, and customer oriented.

Sam Palmisano, the executive in charge of global services, became Gerstner's hand-picked successor. A lifelong IBM employee, Palmisano had joined the company straight from college and was known as a "street fighter" who had worked his way up global services' hierarchy. And global services had the entrepreneurial, customer-based culture that Gerstner wished to propagate throughout IBM. Together, Gerstner and Palmisano worked to hasten IBM's transition from primarily a hardware company to one whose growth would be propelled by services and software (see Exhibit 1).

EXHIBIT 1

IBM's Organizational Structure

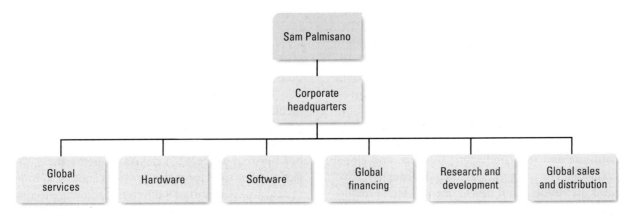

As IBM enjoyed increasing success with its e-business initiative, it became increasingly clear that clients in different industries faced different sets of e-business problems and issues and that increasingly industry-customized solutions were necessary. Also the problems facing large and SMB clients were often quite different. As a result, in 2002 Gerstner and Palmisano decided that a major overhaul of IBM's operating structure was necessary to support its new services-driven business model. At the same time, they wished to strengthen the ability of the software division to produce the kind of software that different industry customers needed. Global Services's intimate knowledge of the software capabilities of competitor's software and hardware provided IBM's software divisions with vital information that could help them improve their products. Gerstner and Palmisano wanted to increase the links between services and software to achieve more synergies. In addition, its consultant's knowledge of competitors' products provided the competitive information that helped top managers select the acquisition targets that would do the most to strengthen IBM's service and software offerings. IBM steadily acquired software and service companies throughout the 1990s to accomplish this goal, and since 2000, IBM has spent over $7 billion on over twenty acquisitions.

IBM's New Operating Structure

To pursue its business model and strategies, Gerstner and Palmisano decided to create a new operating structure to make it easier for its different divisions to cooperate to provide customized solutions to industry customers. First, they decided to divide IBM's clients into six major groups to better cater to their industry-specific needs. These groups are financial services, public, industrial, distribution, communication, and small and medium-size businesses (SMBs). As Exhibit 2 shows, the industries or types of client in each group share a need for a similar kind of computing solution. Second, they grouped IBM's many different individual divisions into six major operating groups or divisions that were instructed to cooperate to serve the needs of each of these client groups. The four main operating groups are global services, hardware and semiconductors, software, and global financing. The two principal functional support divisions are research and development, which provides assistance to the operating groups, and global sales

EXHIBIT 2

IBM's Clients by Sector and Industry

Sector	Industries
Financial Services	Banking
	Financial Markets
	Insurance
Public	Education
	Government
	Health care
	Life Sciences
Industrial	Aerospace
	Automotive
	Defense
	Chemical and Petroleum
	Electronics
Distribution	Consumer Products
	Retail
	Travel
	Transportation
Communications	Energy and Utilities
	Media and Entertainment
	Telecommunications
Small & Medium Business	The majority of businesses in this sector have fewer than 1,000 employees

and distribution, which links the client groups with the operating groups, especially to global services.

Sales and distribution is comprised of a network of internal and external routes-to-market which includes IBM's thousands of salespeople located all around the world, ibm.com, and a staff of experts who help to train and provide support for IBM's army of independent software vendors. IBM's sales force is also grouped into industry-specific global units that specialize in a certain type of client. Typically the sales force discovers a client, meets their immediate needs, but then passes the client on to global services which offers the client its services to analyze its legacy system and the way this legacy system can be improved to meet the client's future business objectives. The sales force also provides another avenue to integrate across IBM's different operating groups, for it provides information that allows the global services, hardware, and software groups to cooperate to provide a customer-specific solution.

IBM's research and semiconductor division has been one of its principal sources of competitive advantage that has allowed the company to differentiate itself from its rivals. In fact, IBM has been awarded more U.S. patents that any other company each year for the last eleven years. IBM spends about $5 billion annually on R&D and concentrates on developing new software, such as e-business, open-source, and middleware software, and new hardware such as advanced storage and memory devices, semiconductors, and autonomic computing. IBM's research and semiconductor group was also instructed to focus on projects that would have the most payoff for the company's clients, especially new projects that would be applicable across the different client groups to increase the return from the capital IBM invests in R&D. It was also charged with finding ways to shorten the time it takes to get new hardware and software to the market to maintain IBM's advantage over competitors.

Recent Developments in the Operating Groups

In the 2000s, IBM has continued to make many changes to its operating groups to strengthen its business model. Many of these changes have also resulted in its competitors altering their business models in order to compete more effectively with IBM. For example, HP's merger with Compaq in 2003 and Oracle's merger with Peoplesoft in 2005 were brought about because these companies perceived the need to offer a wider range of hardware, software, and services to compete effectively with IBM.

Global Services

Today, global services is the lynchpin, the central and most powerful operating group in the new IBM, and since 1992, services revenue has risen steadily to surpass IBM's hardware revenue. Today it is the biggest contributor to revenues and profit (see Exhibit 3). Today, the other operating groups support its activities as it works with clients to deliver solutions that use a complete lineup of IBM software and hardware. However, it still continues to offer clients the "best of breed" hardware and software from its competitors if the solution requires it and they have superior software or hardware such as Peoplesoft's HRM software and SAP's ERP software. In addition, global services has continued to champion IBM's push into open standards software, and like the other divisions, it promotes the use of the Linux open standards software for use by clients especially in linked network server and mainframe applications.

Indeed, in the early 2000s IBM invested over $3 billion to develop Linux-based operating and applications software to reduce Microsoft's hold on the server-PC software market that it dominates. In 2005, it was estimated that 30 percent of servers now run on the Linux platform. In developing countries in Asia such as India and China, IBM's global subsidiaries are strongly promoting IBM's own Linux-based software as an inexpensive alternative to Microsoft's expensive Windows platform. In 2004, Microsoft was forced to respond to this threat by offering customers in Asia stripped-down, low-cost versions of its software to retain its control of the global server-PC market, but clearly global services will promote IBM's own Linux software whenever possible.

As the company's business model continues to evolve, Palmisano's expectation is that global services

EXHIBIT 3

Changes in Percentage Revenues by Operating Group

% of Revenue/Segment	2003	2002	2001	2000	1999	1998	1992
Global Services	48%	45%	42%	43%	43%	44%	23%
Hardware	32%	34%	37%	38%	37%	35%	53%
Software	16%	16%	16%	14%	14%	15%	17%
Global Financing	3%	4%	4%	4%	4%	4%	7%
Other	1%	1%	1%	2%	2%	2%	2%
Total Revenue	100%	100%	100%	100%	100%	100%	100%

will play a larger role interfacing with IBM's customers, perhaps even IBM's sales force will be merged into global services. Global services has three main lines of business: (1) strategic outsourcing services (SO) provides customers with competitive cost advantages by outsourcing customers' processes and operations; (2) integrated technology services (ITS) designs, implements, and maintains customers' technology infrastructures; and (3) business consulting services (BCS) which deliver value to customers through business process innovation, application enablement, and integration services.

SO and ITS allow clients to outsource many different kinds of value chain activities or to outsource management of their entire IT system to IBM. Some contracts with SMB clients may only last for a few years, but contracts with large corporations and in the public client group, such as those with U.S. government agencies, may last for ten years and then be renewed. IBM had over $100 billion of long-term outsourcing deals by the end of 2002—one major reason that explains why it took the lead from EDS. BCS offers six main kinds of business and consulting and service activities for the six different client groups (Exhibit 4). *Strategic change solutions* involve analyzing a client's legacy system from the standpoint of competitive advantage, such as advising how changes in IT can increase efficiency or intraorganizational collaboration. *Customer relationship management* (CRM) is a rapidly expanding software application that provides the information companies need to accurately assess their customers' needs and to alter their products or services to respond to those needs appropriately. *Supply chain and operations solutions* are those typically involved in helping companies better manage relationships with suppliers and distributors, especially when they outsource manufacturing to companies abroad. Frequently, this involves the implementation of ERP systems that help clients collect, process, and analyze more information about their companies' operations so that they can formulate better strategies to increase their profitability.

The final three kinds of solutions IBM offers clients are *financial management, human capital management* or HRM software, such as that provided by Peoplesoft or SAP's HRM module from its ERP package, and *e-business integration.* E-business integration involves showing clients how to move and manage their value-chain activities online. Such e-business integration is often accompanied by one or more of the other solutions IBM offers, for its goal is to get its clients to utilize more and more of its hardware and software in their legacy systems. So, for example, outsourcing and supply chain management are frequently a part of the process of e-business integration.

A major coup for Palmisano occurred in 2002 when IBM was able to acquire PriceWaterhouseCoopers, a leading global business consulting services company, for $2.3 billion. This added more than twelve hundred business consultants to its ranks and gave the BCS group the expertise it needed to better serve the needs of its different industry client groups. Moreover, the

EXHIBIT 4

Global Services Solutions and Clients

BCS Solution Areas	Client Sectors					
	Communication	Distribution	Financial Services	Industrial	Public	SMB
Strategic Change Solutions						
Customer Relationship Management (CRM)						
Supply Chain and Operations Solutions						
Financial Management						
Human Capital Management						
E-Business Integration						

twelve hundred new consultants are also globally based, and this allowed global services to provide an integrated range of solutions for clients in regions around the world. Indeed, one of Gerstner's major goals was for IBM to be able to offer the same complete IBM solution to a client anywhere in the world.

Revenues from abroad account for more than 40 percent of global services total revenues. Global services is broadly divided into three world regions: the United States, Europe, and Asia. In each of these regions, its consultants may be based in one country, such as India or France, but they are always ready to travel to a client in their world region or another should their expert services be required. The goal is always that IBM should offer the best customized solution for a specific client in a specific industry. Of course, today IBM makes full use of its own expertise in global intranet and Internet applications such as online collaboration and global teleconferencing to promote collaboration between its consultants and clients anywhere in the world. Clients are also able to use ibm.com to easily access information on its products so that they can also make informed choices.

Hardware

In 2003, IBM reorganized the divisions in its hardware group to shorten product development time and ensure they offered a seamless computing solution for its different types of clients. The two main hardware segments are the Systems and Technology Group, which deals with large enterprise clients, and the Personal Systems Group, which has been undergoing a major transformation.

Systems and Technology Group

The systems and technology group provides customized hardware solutions to global services for their clients; it also provides the collection of products that IBM's salespeople sell directly to any client to meet their business needs. A large percentage of hardware is also sold directly online through ibm.com to clients that already understand their needs. The main types of hardware are servers such as enterprise (mainframe), midmarket, web, or network servers and large storage systems that manage and store vast amounts of database information. IBM has been devoting considerable

resources to find ways to reduce the costs of its large servers by running them on Linux-based software to reduce their long-term maintenance and operating cost. It has been increasingly pressured by Sun and Dell, which are offering low-cost servers, or in Sun's case, complete midsize network solutions that can be rented rather than bought—the old IBM model.

The systems group comprises eServer and Storage products. eServers are based upon IBM operating systems, as well as UNIX and the Microsoft Windows operating system. All these server lines have the capability to run Linux, a key open standard operating system. Data storage products include disk, tape, and storage area networks. The systems group provides integrated business solutions to customers. Approximately half of the group's sales transactions are through business partners and approximately 40 percent direct to customers, over 20 percent of which take place through the Internet at ibm.com. In addition, the systems group also creates the hardware used internally in support of IBM Global Services offerings and contracts, such as managing clients' IT systems or outsourcing operations.

The Technology Group primarily consists of IBM's Microelectronics Division, which provides leading semiconductor technology, customized solutions, and engineering technology services to original equipment manufacturers (OEM), other computer companies and to the Systems Group. The Microelectronics Division develops and manufactures products in three general categories. First, the technology group manufactures and tests customized semiconductor products for customers. The customers design these customized product solutions using IBM's suite of design tools and portfolio of intellectual property (IP), resulting in faster speeds to market for the customers.

Second, semiconductor customers provide IBM with their product designs based upon the customer's product IP. Using the customer's design, IBM provides a full suite of semiconductor manufacturing and integrated supply chain services to deliver the product to the customer. The technology division is in the business of producing the advanced microelectronic chips both for IBM's own hardware but also for any company that wants a customized chip to support its own product applications. For example, in 2003 IBM signed a contract with Sony to design the new microprocessor that will become the heart of

Sony's new PlayStation 3 when it debuts in 2006. This chip has state-of-the-art graphic and sound capabilities and will permit a seamless integration of the user with other game players on the Internet. The chip will also become the hub of Sony's new wireless home media center whereby a user will be able to control all electronic devices such as televisions, computers, and printers using the chip and its associated operating system.

The technology group makes semiconductors designed primarily for use in IBM's own Power PC platform used in its servers and PCs. In addition, the Technology Group launched in 2002 its new Engineering and Technology Services Division that provides system and component design services, strategic outsourcing of customers' design teams, and technology and manufacturing consulting services.

Personal Systems Group

In 2003, the Personal Systems Group included the company's lines of PCs, printers, and point-of-sale terminals used in retail stores and fast-food restaurants, and IBM's Thinkpad devices. However, in the 1990s the PC business became characterized by a high degree of commoditization, short product life cycles, and intense price competition. As noted earlier, IBM's cost disadvantage compared with companies like Dell, Hitachi, and Samsung, which specialize in manufacturing low-cost computer components, increased dramatically. Despite the personal systems division's attempt to reduce costs, it could not match those of its efficient competitors so major changes have been made to the personal systems group in the 2000s. In 2001, IBM sold its hard drive unit to Hitachi, and then in 2002, it announced that it would sign a three-year outsourcing agreement to allow Sanmina-SCI to make IBM's PCs and low-range servers that would be sold under the IBM name. However, it also said it would continue to design and sell server and PC software.

In 2005, however, despite its outsourcing of production, the division was still losing money and pulling down IBM's profits, and IBM announced that it had sold its computer business to Chinese assembler Lenovo, formerly the Legend Group. Lenovo will pay Big Blue $1.25 billion, with $650 million in cash, and IBM will retain an 18.9 percent stake in the joint venture. Lenovo will be IBM's preferred supplier and retains the right to use the brand for five years. IBM will continue to provide software and technical support for the product lines for the next ten years. Its stake in the joint venture may allow it to benefit significantly from cost reductions that Lenovo hopes to make that will make its PCs competitive with those offered by Dell and Gateway.

As Exhibit 3 shows, IBM's hardware sales have largely remained steady over the last several years, and the fact that they have not declined more is the result of Gerstner's focus on making IBM's mainframe or enterprise servers and storage devices scaleable and compatible with the needs of its global clients, as well as his focus on taking advantage of IBM's expertise in semiconductors and other specialized hardware where operating margins are high. Profit margins are high in these specialized product areas, unlike in PCs which have become largely a commodity product where margins are low and only the huge buying power of companies like Dell and their vast global sales make these companies profitable. A generalist like IBM can never compete against a specialist like Dell in a specific area—and this was Gerstner's insight that led him to promote IBM's ability to provide a complete range of computer products and solutions.

In the 2000s, Dell has also recognized the need to expand its product offerings, and it began to make or sell small servers, printers, computer peripherals, and then electronics in general, such as digital cameras, PDAs, and so on, to provide its customers with a more comprehensive solution. Dell also began to offer computer services such as installation and maintenance and has been trying to develop a consultancy group to meet the needs of small companies that need advice and a customized solution. It has watched IBM and learned how profitable such a customized service can be.

Software

Despite Gerstner's hope that IBM would obtain 2 million SMB clients by 2001, this did not come to pass. The recession of the early 2000s discouraged many SMBs from investing in expensive software that had uncertain returns. Nevertheless, IBM has made increasing SMB accounts a major goal for the future in a vast market currently dominated by BEA systems. Indeed, the software division has been rapidly working to develop the open source middleware solutions that can be scaled to the needs of SMBs.

Other companies such as Oracle, SAP, and Microsoft have followed IBM's lead, recognizing the huge potential revenues from this untapped client area, and have also launched their own software and service packages aimed at this sector. Once the U.S. economy rebounds, the strength of each company's relative product offerings will become clear.

Once again, to strengthen its competencies in applications software IBM has made many strategic acquisitions. After the success of its Lotus acquisition, it followed up by acquiring companies like Tivoli Systems and Rational Software in 2003 for $2.1 billion. Rational provides software tools that allow independent software vendors (ISVs) to effectively capture and analyze requirements to create designs for software applications, test applications, and manage the software development process. Rational's software development tools can be used to develop and upgrade any other company's software products, so this acquisition was a critical part of IBM's open standard strategy.

Throughout the 2000s, the software division has focused on developing two main kinds of operating and middleware software: first, a software that seamlessly connects computers at all levels with all kinds of peripheral devices such as printers and storage devices regardless of which company makes the hardware. IBM backs Linux because it believes the highest returns are achieved when customization of open source software is possible. Second, IBM has focused on extending its rage of customized software packages for different kinds of industry clients. As noted earlier, middleware software integrates IBM's clients' IT systems end-to-end and builds a base for ISVs to install and maintain industry-specific applications that allow IBM to differentiate its products. IBM's middleware brands include WebSphere, which facilitates customers' ability to manage a wide variety of business processes through the Web; data management such as DB2 Database software; Tivoli, which enables customers to centrally manage and efficiently utilize their network and storage; and Lotus, which increases customers' ability to communicate, collaborate, and learn in an effective way. As Exhibit 3 shows, sales of IBM's own software have also held constant over the last decade because sales of mainframe software have been replaced with sales of its middleware, and this operating group contributes significantly to its revenues and profits. IBM hopes that when the economy recovers sales of software will increase dramatically.

Global Financing

IBM's global financing division allows it to provide its clients with the financing they need to purchase its computer products and services, and this division is a major source of IBM's profitability. Indeed, IBM is currently the largest IT financier in the world. Although not a major contributor to total profits, financing is a very profitable operation with high gross margins.

Research and Development

Finally, IBM has an operating division devoted to advanced research. The research division's focus is to contribute to IBM's success by balancing projects that have an immediate impact with those that are long-term investments. Thus, it will help to develop innovations that support customized industry-specific solutions, but it also focuses on emerging technologies like nanotechnologies and autonomic computing that may pay off decades in the future.

E-Business on Demand

Under Palmisano the pace of change at IBM has accelerated as the company works to achieve a sustainable competitive advantage over its rivals. IBM's acquisitions since 2001 to improve its capabilities in software and services are listed in Exhibit 5. The acquisition of PWC was supported by the acquisition of specialized companies such as Mainspring. As noted earlier, Rational Software was a significant acquisition because of its expertise in middleware; it was also an important acquisition because it fit well with Palmisano's new "e-business on demand initiative."

After becoming CEO in 2002, Palmisano faced immediate problems because of the poor economic conditions of the early 2000s. IBM's revenues, like those of all other IT companies, plunged and so did its stock price as its existing and potential clients slashed their IT budgets. With lower IT budgets, all companies worked hard to identify the types of computer hardware and software that would have the biggest impact on their company's profitability in the future. Convincing a potential client to spend millions to buy new kinds of software and hardware, or billions of dollars on outsourcing contracts, was a daunting task facing IBM's sales force and that of any other IT supplier.

Looking ahead, Palmisano searched for new IT business solutions and applications IBM could develop

EXHIBIT 5

IBM's Acquisitions in the 2000s

2005	Corio
	SRD
2004	KeyMRO
	Liberty Insurance Services
	Systemcorp
	Venetica
	Alphablox Corporation
	Cyanea
	Candle Corporation
	Trigo Technologies
2003	Green Pasture Software
	Productivity Solutions Inc.
	CrossAccess Technology
	Think Dynamics
	Rational Software
2002	Tarian Software
	EADS Matra Datavision
	PWC Consulting
	Holosofx
	Access360
	TrelliSoft Metamerge
	CrossWorlds Software
2001	Database Assets of Informix Corporation
	Mainspring

using its growing set of core competencies. He and his top management team identified four major business objectives companies wish to achieve from advanced IT applications: to further innovation, to significantly reduce their cost structure, to integrate activities across a company's value chain, and to more accurately forecast potential return on investment from capital expenditures on new products or projects.

To help clients obtain these goals, Palmisano pioneered "on-demand business," a customized IT platform based on IBM hardware and software that allows clients to (1) be quickly responsive to any and all opportunities, threats, or demands from their customers or from the environment in general, (2) completely integrate their company's value-chain activities, and (3) integrate with external strategic partners, suppliers, and distributors. Palmisano announced that companies that adopted IBM's new on-demand IT would

obtain millions or billions of dollars in savings in operating costs—something very appealing to companies trying to make their IT budgets go as far as possible. Also their companies would be strategically positioned better to meet future business challenges.

To promote on-demand business, IBM told its clients to think of information and computing power as a "fluid" like water that is contained in the hundreds or thousands of computers that are the "reservoirs" or "lakes" of a large company's IT system. This water flows between enterprise and network servers and PCs in a company's IT system through the fiber-optic cables that connect them. Thus, computing power, like water, can be moved between computers both inside and between companies, providing that computer hardware and software are linked seamlessly together and so do not create information "logjams" that disrupt the flow of information and computing power.

IBM's research and software engineers worked together to develop new e-business software to allow computers both inside and between companies to work seamlessly together. Among other things, this software allows computer operators at some remote location to monitor hundreds of different computers at the same time and shift work from one machine to another to distribute a company's computing power to wherever it is most needed. This has several cost saving advantages. First, it allows companies to run their computers close to capacity, which greatly improves IT productivity and reduces operating costs. Second, to ensure that there was never any possibility of its clients experiencing a "drought" IBM proposed to use its own vast mainframe computer capacity as a kind of bank or reservoir that clients could tap into whenever their own systems might become overloaded. For example, IBM's e-business software allows companies to shift any excess workload from their network to IBM's computers which means they do not have to invest tens of millions of dollars in extra computers—a huge cost saving. Third, when a company's computers are seamlessly networked they can function as a "supercomputer," a computer with immense information processing power that can easily cost upward of $50 million to purchase as a stand-alone computer and tens of millions more dollars to maintain.

To show clients the cost saving potential of its new e-business products, IBM decided it would be the first company to use it. Previously, IBM allowed its hundreds of different divisions to choose whatever software they liked to manage their own purchasing and supply chain activities. In 2003, Palmisano appointed star manager Linda Stanford to overhaul IBM's company-wide supply chain—which purchases inputs worth $44 billion a year! Stanford was made responsible for developing software to seamlessly link all IBM's divisions into a single integrated computer network. When implemented in 2004, the new software resulted in a 5 percent gain in productivity, which IBM expects to repeat for the next five to ten years—this will result in cost savings of over $2 billion a year. IBM was quick to tell its clients that they can expect to see similar savings if they purchase its e-business software.

IBM's new e-business system also has many other performance-enhancing benefits. Its thousands of IT consultants are experts in particular industries such as the car, financial services, or retail industries. They have a deep understanding of the particular problems facing companies in those industries and how to improve their business models. Palmisano told IBM's consultants to work closely with software engineers to find ways to incorporate their knowledge into advanced software that can be implanted into a customer's IT system to better manage its business model.

IBM is developing seventeen "expert systems" that are industry-specific, problem-solving software solutions clients can use to make better business decisions as well as reduce operating costs. One of these expert systems is being developed in the pharmaceutical industry, for example. Using IBM's new pharmaceutical expert system, a company's computer network will function as a supercomputer able to simulate and model the potential success of the many new drugs it has under development. Currently, only 5 to 10 percent of new drugs make it to the market. IBM believes its new expert system could raise that rate to over 50 percent which would result in billions of dollars in cost savings for drug companies.

The Future

By 2005, as companies began to increase their IT budgets IBM was working hard to promote its new customized on-demand hardware and software offerings. Palmisano believes all the pieces are in place for IBM to consolidate its leading position over the next decade. However, while IBM has been forging ahead with its new computer services initiative its rivals have also woken up to the advantages of IBM's

new business model and the threats it posed to them unless they also adopted a similar business model.

The need to expand its range of computer products and services prompted the merger between HP and Compaq in 2003, which led it to claim in 2004 that it had a range of products and services that equaled those of IBM. As noted earlier Dell has also been working to increase its product range and offer a low-cost alternative to IBM's hardware and software. Sun, too, abandoned its sales model and adopted a fee-based rental model for its servers and software to try to seize a larger share of the network market. SAP in the meantime had transformed its software so that it was also e-business compatible and made it scaleable so that it could suit the needs of SMB clients. Moreover, SAP had greatly increased the number of its own consultants and was working with EDS and Accenture to train their consultants to better analyze clients' legacy systems and to install and customize its software to better meet the needs of individual clients in order to compete with IBM's business consulting group.

The threat of IBM led many analysts to believe that a wave of future mergers in the computer sector was likely as it was becoming clear clients liked the ability to deal with just only one major computer company, rather than to have to deal with several different ones, to obtain a seamless and cost-effective solution to their IT needs. A merger between Microsoft and SAP would have been a major threat to IBM, but this did not materialize in 2004 as the companies decided that the threat of antitrust regulations and their own quite different corporate cultures would make such an alliance untenable. In 2004, it appeared that HP offered the only real challenge to IBM in its ability to offer a complete computer solution although it lagged behind IBM in the sophistication of its consultancy operations and in its experience of offering customers a seamless open standards computer package. In February 2005, however, HP's failure to realize synergies between its hardware, software, and consulting groups, and the continuing problems with its PC division led its Board of Directors to oust its CEO Carly Fiorina. It was not clear in the spring of 2005 what changes would now occur in HP's business model. Some analysts wanted the company broken up—just as they had wanted to break up IBM in the 1980s; others believe the problem is just to find a better way to execute HP's business model so it can compete effectively with IBM.

As companies jockey for competitive advantage IBM will not find the future easygoing. SAP is potentially a major threat given that its software is the backbone of most large companies' IT systems, and advances in computing power that continually reduce the cost of computer hardware will work in its favor. Similarly, the lucrative SMB segment is becoming increasingly competitive as IBM, SAP, Microsoft, and Oracle compete to become the leader in this area. Nevertheless, thanks to its new CEOs, IBM now has the opportunity and ability to sustain its leading position, and Palmisano is determined that the reborn IBM will never again repeat the mistakes of the past where its success bred the complacency that led to its collapse.

Case 23

Hewlett Packard: The Merger with the Compaq Corporation

This case was prepared by Isaac Cohen, San Jose State University.

On September 4, 2001, Hewlett Packard (HP) CEO Carleton (Carly) Fiorina and Compaq CEO Michael Capellas met in New York City to announce what was expected to become the largest merger ever undertaken in the computer industry: HP offered to buy its arch-rival, the Compaq Corporation, in a stock deal valued at $25 billion. While the announcement sent shock waves throughout the industry, and while Compaq's Board of Directors readily approved the deal, the merger soon became highly contentious. HP board member Walter Hewlett, other members of the Hewlett family, and the HP Foundation opposed the merger, and, as a result, an unusual fight erupted between the HP board and the cofounding family. Assisted by the majority of the HP board members, Carly Fiorina embarked on an extensive six-month campaign to convince investors to vote yes on the deal. Subsequently, in March 2002, HP shareholders had narrowly approved the merger, and two months later, HP and Compaq closed the deal officially. Valued at about $19 billion on the day of its closing, the merger ended a twenty-year-long rivalry between the two companies.

This case was presented at the October 2004 meeting of the North American Case Research Association (NACRA) at Sedona, Arizona. Copyright © 2004 by Isaac Cohen and NACRA. Reprinted by permission of Isaac Cohen and NACRA. All rights reserved. For the most recent financial results of the company discussed in this case, go to **http://finance.yahoo.com**, input the company's stock symbol, and download the latest company report from its homepage.

To Capellas and Compaq's Board of Directors, the deal with HP represented an attractive offer. With Compaq losing market share in two product groups—low-end home personal computers (PCs) and high-end servers—and with both product groups undergoing a steady decline in profits, Compaq was struggling. Subject to a price war launched by Dell Computer in the PC market (home computers and PC servers), and unable to compete successfully with IBM on the supply of information technology (IT) services, Compaq's future existence was precarious. To survive, Compaq needed to either exist in both the home PC market and the high-end computer business or to merge with other firms. Capellas, therefore, was faced with a difficult dilemma: Should Compaq sell its declining businesses and continue operating as a smaller company? Should it buy other firms, or should it merge with a leading computer company to create a global technology leader equal in size and complexity to IBM? Clearly the uncertain prospects of selling its declining businesses and continuing operating on a smaller scale, coupled with Compaq's recent failure to execute successful mergers with Tandem Computers and the Digital Equipment Corporation (DEC), persuaded its Board of Directors to sell the company to HP. "We wanted to be the next IBM," Capellas recalled, noting that the alliance with HP was "intuitively obvious" to all Compaq directors. Following the acquisition, Capellas became HP's president.[1]

To Fiorina and the HP board, the acquisition of Compaq also represented an opportunity. To begin with, Compaq's products and services complemented HP's. HP built up a strong business in Unix-based servers where the market was stagnant, but was weak in the production and sales of window servers where the growth prospects were promising. HP, in addition, built a healthy business in home PCs where competition with Dell was fierce, but lagged far behind Dell in its ability to sell PCs directly to consumers. Compaq, by contrast, was highly competitive in the production of cheap, standard-designed window servers on the one hand, and in selling build-to-order PCs directly to consumers on the other. Compaq was also competitive in making data storage devices—another expanding market where HP sought growth.[2]

Fiorina, furthermore, articulated a strategy that was expected to turn HP into an IT services company comparable to IBM: Combining Compaq's $7 billion IT services revenues with HP's $7 billion was projected to vault HP from a distant competitor into the industry's number four spot behind IBM, Electronic Data System (EDS), and Fujitsu. Additionally, a consulting firm hired by Fiorina and the HP board estimated that by 2004 the merger was expected to save the consolidated company at least $2.5 billion in operating costs, phasing out duplicated products and services.[3] Following the approval of the merger, Fiorina continued serving as HP's CEO.

Although HP's Board of Directors studied the implications of the merger thoroughly, Fiorina's decision amounted to a strategic gamble. Critics of the merger contended that no large-scale merger in the computer/telecom/IT industries had ever resulted in a success;[4] that most of Compaq and HP's IT revenues took the form of low-level support and maintenance services, not high-level consulting and outsourcing, the typical services sought by large corporate customers;[5] and that the new HP was unlikely to compete successfully with Dell—the cost leader of the industry. They predicted, instead, that the merger would undermine HP's worldwide competitive position relative to IBM and Dell Computer, its two main rivals, and result in a failure to integrate the two companies together.

Were the critics right? The present case looks at the merger two years later in an attempt to assess its overall impact on HP's performance.

Compaq and the Computer Industry

The success of IBM's PC gave rise to Compaq. IBM developed its first PC in 1980, brought it to market in 1981, and captured a 50 percent share in PC revenues

three years later. As sales of IBM's PCs exploded, three Texas Instruments engineers started their own company: Compaq was founded in 1982 to manufacture and sell IBM portable computers. Unlike other manufacturers of PCs, Compaq's founders imitated IBM very closely, offering their customers a computer that ran all important IBM PC software programs. Examining an IBM PC at a Houston trade show, the three founders drew a blueprint sketch of the IBM machine on a paper placemat in a local restaurant, and used the sketch later to design Compaq's first portable computer.[6]

Compaq's founders raised an initial venture capital investment of $1.5 million, and subsequently, the company expanded at a remarkable pace. In 1983, its first full year, Compaq recorded $111 million in sales, an unprecedented growth figure for any start-up company; in 1986, its third full year, Compaq became the first company to achieve a Fortune 500 ranking in less than four years; and between 1986 and 1989, Compaq's revenues jumped fivefold to $3 billion.[7]

Compaq's rapid growth may be explained by a combination of several elements. First, focusing on excellence in engineering, Compaq had quickly become the industry's most competent designer and producer of PCs. Second, Compaq managed to develop, manufacture, and market its products faster than any of its competitors; in 1986, for example, Compaq delivered a new PC based on Intel's 386 chip one year before IBM. In addition Compaq built a superior distribution system. While all other manufacturers used direct sales forces, Compaq relied exclusively on an extensive network of dealerships. Never competing directly with its own dealers, and always granting dealers generous profit margins, Compaq provided its dealers with a strong incentive to increase sales.[8]

Compaq's rapid growth was further sustained by global expansion. In 1984, Compaq was one of the earliest American companies to market PCs in Europe, and five years later, it had become the second largest supplier of PCs to the European market. Compaq expanded global sales outside Europe as well. By 1990—a record year of sales ($3.6 billion) and profits ($455 million)—Compaq generated over half of its total revenues abroad, relying on a network of nearly four thousand authorized dealers stationed in 152 countries.[9]

Compaq's first crisis unfolded shortly thereafter. Partly as a result of a worldwide economic recession, and also as a consequence of increased competition with start-up companies such as Dell Computer and AST Research, Compaq experienced its first ever quarterly loss in 1991.[10] The Board of Directors acted swiftly. It fired Compaq cofounder Rod Canion as CEO and replaced him with Eckhard Pfeiffer, the company's chief operation officer and former head of Compaq's European division.

Under Pfeiffer's leadership, Compaq's top management introduced three strategic initiatives that helped turn the company around. First, Compaq launched a ferocious price war against IBM, Dell, and other PC vendors, slashing its profit margins by more than half while increasing revenues threefold in three years, 1991–1994. In 1994, Compaq passed IBM as the world's leading supplier of PCs. Next, Compaq introduced mass merchandizing as well as direct sales, thus abandoning its long-standing policy of relying solely on authorized dealers. By 1992, Compaq sold its products in six hundred U.S. outlets, and in 1994, Compaq began building PCs to order, following the Dell model.[11] A third initiative introduced by Pfeiffer was corporate reorganization. Compaq sold its first server (a powerful computer that "served" data to corporate networks and internet sites) in 1989, but sales were disappointing. To revitalize Compaq's languishing services unit and diversify further into servers, Pfeiffer revamped Compaq's functional structure (manufacturing, sales, engineering) and reorganized the company along three product groups that together made up Compaq's new divisional structure: servers, desktop and portable computers, and network products. By 1996, Compaq had become the world's leading seller of "PC servers."[12]

A year later Compaq posted its largest profits to date: $1.9 billion on $25 billion in sales (Exhibit 1). Using a "Wintel" technology—a combination of Microsoft's operating system and Intel's microprocessors—Compaq managed to keep its research expenses far below its competitors, spending on research just 3.5 percent of sales in 1997 (the corresponding figures for Sun Microsystems and HP were 9.6 percent and 7.2 percent). The largest customer of both Microsoft and Intel, Compaq, in addition, benefited from economies of scale, receiving the best prices, fastest deliveries, and earliest information on product development from its two primary suppliers. In 1997, consequently, *Forbes* magazine selected Compaq as its Company of the Year.[13]

EXHIBIT 1

Compaq: Sales, Net Income, and Stock Prices, 1991–2000

	Sales ($Bil.)	Net Income ($Bil.)	Stock Price FY Close ($)
1991	3.3	0.1	1.76
1992	4.1	0.2	3.25
1993	7.2	0.5	4.92
1994	10.9	0.9	7.90
1995	14.8	0.8	9.60
1996	18.1	1.3	14.88
1997	24.6	1.9	28.25
1998	31.2	(2.7)	42.00
1999	38.5	0.6	27.06
2000	42.4	0.6	15.05

Source: "Compaq," *Hoover's Handbook of American Business, 2000.* p. 399.

Compaq's second and final crisis erupted in 1998. The crisis stemmed first and foremost from Compaq's acquisition of Digital Equipment for $8.4 billion. Under Pfeiffer's direction, Compaq bought Digital in 1998 in order to expand its customer base and offer corporate clients a full range of computer software programs, hardware products, and global IT services. But the merger backfired. In 1998, Compaq lost $2.7 billion (see Exhibit 1) as a result of high restructuring costs related to the merger. Cutting seventeen thousand jobs, dismantling plants, and closing down office buildings, Compaq's losses mounted while revenue growth stalled (Exhibit 2). As it became apparent that integrating the two companies together was getting harder and harder—some two hundred integration committees grappled with the process—Pfeiffer was forced to resign.[14]

Compaq's Board of Directors selected Michael Capellas, a newcomer who had joined the company in 1998, to replace Pfeiffer as president and CEO in 2000. Capellas moved quickly. Infusing Compaq with a true sense of urgency, Capellas introduced two strategic initiatives, the first aimed at focusing "Everything [on] the Internet" and the second sought to speed up Compaq's drive at global services. To facilitate the implementation of both strategies, Capellas reorganized the company around three market-driven "profit centers,"

Market Share and Year/Year Growth of
Worldwide Sales of Wintel Portable, Desktop,
and Server Computers, Third Quarter, 1998

	Market Share	Year/Year Growth
Compaq	14.4%	6%
Dell	9.2%	68%
IBM	9.2%	25%
HP	6.6%	26%

Source: Eric Nee, "Defending the Desktop," *Forbes,* December 28, 1998, p. 54.

the most dynamic of which was "enterprise solutions and services."[15]

Still, Compaq continued to drift. On the eve of the HP-Compaq merger announcement in the summer of 2001, Compaq reported its third successive quarterly decline in sales and profits. In spring 2001, Dell passed Compaq as the world's leading vendor of PCs, capturing 13 percent of the global PC market (compared with Compaq's 12 percent). And in July 2001, Compaq's stock price dropped to $15 a share, down from $35 a year earlier, while its market value sank to $26 billion, its lowest valuation in years.[16] Selling the company had become now a viable option.

The Evolution of HP

Unlike Compaq, HP was an old established company dating back to the Franklin D. Roosevelt era. Founded in 1939 by William Hewlett and David Packard, two electrical engineers and recent Stanford University graduates, HP specialized in the production of test and measurement instruments. HP's first product was an electronic sound equipment test instrument called an audio oscillator, and its first large customer was the Disney movie studios. Assembled by the two partners in a Palo Alto, California, garage, the oscillator was used by Walt Disney Studios to develop a new sound track for the movie *Fantasia.*[17]

As demand for electronic test instruments exploded during World War II, the two partners hired dozens of employees, broadened their product line, and expanded their sales. HP's revenues jumped from $34,000 in 1940 to $2 million in 1950 and $30 million in 1958. In 1957, HP went public, and a few years later, HP diversified into the production

and sales of medical and analytical instruments, acquiring the Sanborn Company, a manufacturer of medical equipment, in 1961, and the F&M Scientific Corporation in 1966.[18]

Diversification went hand in hand with international expansion. HP established its European headquarters in Switzerland in 1959, opening a manufacturing plant in Germany and building an extensive marketing organization that served the European Community. In the 1960s, HP formed a joint venture with a Japanese partner to facilitate the manufacture and sales of HP products in Japan. By 1975, foreign sales accounted for 51 percent of HP's revenues, and in 1995, HP generated 44 percent of its sales at home, 36 percent in Europe, and 20 percent in Asia, Canada, and Latin America.[19]

HP's entry into the computer industry radically changed the nature of the company. In 1965, 87 percent of HP's revenues were derived from the sales of test and measuring instruments, 11 percent from the sales of medical and analytical equipment, and just 1 percent from computer-related products ("data products"). In 1977, computer-related products accounted for 42 percent of HP's revenues, and in 1995, 80 percent of HP's revenues were generated by computers, peripherals, and related products.[20]

HP's original interest in computing stemmed from its need to improve the performance of test and measurement instruments. In the 1960s, as high-end instruments required more and more computing power, HP embarked on the manufacture of electronic calculators—desktop computers that performed scientific functions. One of HP's most profitable and bestselling products was a handheld scientific calculator, the HP 35. Introduced in 1972 and known as the "electronic slide rule," the pocket size calculator was so successful that it persuaded Hewlett and Packard to enter, at long last, the computing business, a field dominated at the time by two large companies, IBM and the Digital Equipment Corporation.[21]

The founders selected John Young to lead HP's diversification into computers. Young was named CEO in 1978, following the retirement of Hewlett and Packard from active management. During Young's first five years at HP's helm, sales tripled, reaching $4.3 billion in 1982. Young introduced several lines of PCs and workstations in the early 1980s, and was responsible for the development of HP's most successful product, the laser jet printer (introduced in 1984). In 1983, Young launched the Spectrum project, a $500 million drive to build a new family of desktop mainframe computers based in Reduced Instruction Set Computing (RISC) architecture which allowed programs to run faster by eliminating routine instructions. To ensure the success of the project, Young restructured HP's computer business, building centralized R&D and marketing organizations that cut across divisional boundaries. Under Young's direction, furthermore, HP purchased Apollo Computers in 1989, a pioneer designer and manufacturer of engineering workstations, in a $500 million deal.[22]

By the late 1980s, however, HP was losing ground. Revenue growth shrank, and HP's stock declined by 50 percent in three years (1987–1990). The Spectrum computer was introduced in 1987, yet initial sales were disappointing as the $60,000 machine failed to compete favorably with a comparable $50,000 workstation offered by Sun Microsystems. HP's merger with Apollo, moreover, resulted in a $750 million loss in new business, as the integration of the two companies proved more difficult than expected. The founders were alarmed. Serving as board members—they owned together one-third of the company stock—William Hewlett and David Packard were convinced that Young's recent restructuring was responsible for HP's underperformance, at least in part. They urged Young to reverse course and decentralize. Young, in turn, disbanded dozens of committees, and empowered executives, once again, to exercise control over their divisions. But he did not keep his job. In 1992, HP's Board of Directors announced the retirement of John Young and his replacement by Lewis Platt.[23]

Initially, HP prospered under Platt's leadership. During Platt's first three years as CEO, 1992 to 1995, HP's revenues doubled from $16 billion to $32 billion, and its rate of return on sales climbed from 3.3 percent to 7.7 percent.[24] Running HP as a collection of autonomous businesses, Platt streamlined the decision-making process, shortened the design cycle of new products, and introduced thousands of new products. By 1996, HP made more than twenty-four thousand products, including PCs, workstations, printers, Unix and NT Window servers, network products, software, and testing and analyzing instruments. HP's growth was fueled by a phenomenal rise in sales of desktop printers and PCs. In 1996, HP generated about one-third of its revenues from the printer business, and the company had clearly become the dominant firm in the industry—HP's global market share ranged from 76 percent of all laser printer sales to 61 percent of all ink-jet printer sales.[25] Under Platt's leadership, furthermore, HP had become a major player in the PC market, deriving over 19 percent of its revenues from PC sales in 1998, up from less than 6 percent in 1992.[26] Other segments of the HP computer business—most notably, Unix workstations and servers—contributed to the growth in revenues and profits as well. In 1993, HP had surpassed Digital as the second largest computer maker in the United States behind IBM.[27]

Still, HP's computer business experienced a slowdown during Platt's last three years in office (1996–1999). One reason for the slowdown was Platt's failure to embrace the Internet. In a stark contrast to IBM, Sun Microsystems, and Microsoft, HP was slow to respond to opportunities offered by the Internet, and had remained a second-tier Web player throughout Platt's tenure. Another source of HP's difficulties was the rise of Dell Computer. Over time, HP had become increasingly dependent on the sales of PCs and printers, but such commodity-like products were subject to fierce competition that drove prices and profits down. Because HP's cost of manufacturing PCs was sharply higher than Dell's, HP's rate of return on PC sales was lower, amounting to 3 percent in 1998 against Dell's 11 percent—hence the decline in HP's market value. In 1998, both Dell and Sun passed HP in stock market valuation, yet each of these two companies generated less than half of HP's revenues.[28]

Platt responded to the crisis with a bold decision that was intended to create a "single identity" for the company and thereby sharpen its competitive focus. He split HP into two: an $8 billion company selling test, measurement, and medical products and services and a $40 billion company selling computers, printers, and IT services.[29] In May 1999, HP announced the spilt and renamed the spun-off segment Agilent Technologies. Key board members, in the meantime, pressured Platt to step down and retire,[30] and sought to replace him with a new chief executive who would embrace the Internet and bring change. For the first time in HP's sixty-year history, the board would consider CEO candidates who had never worked for HP.

Fiorina's HP

Carleton Fiorina was the HP board's first choice. The Board of Director's search committee looked at three hundred candidates, four of whom were selected as finalists. The search committee members were looking for candidates with excellent management and communication skills, the ability to conceptualize complex strategies, the capacity to deliver financial results, and the power to inject a sense of urgency throughout the company. Each of the top four candidates possessed all these qualities. Three of the four were "insiders" working for major Silicon Valley firms, namely, Oracle, Sun Microsystems, and Intel. Fiorina was the outsider. A gifted salesperson with a college degree in medieval history and philosophy, Fiorina rose to become president of Lucent Technologies, an AT&T spun-off telephone equipment company located in New Jersey. In the end, only Fiorina won the unanimous support of HP's board members.[31]

Unlike Platt, Fiorina was a decisive and deliberate leader whose management style combined command and persuasion rather than consensus—the hallmark of HP's decision-making process known as "The HP Way." Not bringing with her a single executive from Lucent, Fiorina relied entirely on her ability to win over HP's employees. Seeking high visibility from the outset, Fiorina traveled from one HP facility to another all around the world, meeting employees in "coffee talks"—an HP practice first introduced by the founders decades earlier—and publicizing the content of these talks in an in-house sheet called "Travels with Carly." Making sure her speeches were posted regularly on HP's website, Fiorina told *Forbes* magazine in 1999, "Leadership is a performance."[32]

Unlike Platt, Fiorina hired managers from rival firms. Throughout Platt's six-year tenure, managers were almost always promoted from the firm's own workforce, and employee turnover rate remained under 5 percent. During Fiorina's early tenure, by contrast, the employee turnover rate more than doubled to 10 percent, and many of HP's top executives were recruited from other technology firms, most notably Motorola, Xerox, and Netscape.[33]

To motivate HP employees, Fiorina restructured HP's compensation system early on. First, across all divisions Fiorina modified the financial incentives paid to HP employees, replacing the company's profit sharing plan with a more rigorous scheme of merit pay that tied compensation directly to company performance. Second, Fiorina revamped HP's sales commission system. In the past, HP paid commissions once a year, and such commissions were often tied to orders rather than sales. To drive HP's sales force harder, Fiorina cut the period over which commis-

sions were paid from one year to six months, and tied all commissions to actual sales. "You can feel the stress her changes are causing," one executive doing business with HP commented in 1999. "These guys know they have to perform."[34] Third, Fiorina altered the financial incentive paid to researchers. In the 1990s, merit pay received by HP engineers was tied to the number of inventions they introduced, not the number of patents they filed. Consequently, engineers had little incentive to work on projects that were likely to result in new products; instead, they strove to produce incremental improvements to existing products. Fiorina, in response, restructured the R&D pay scheme to award engineers a generous bonus for each patent they filed. As a result, the number of patents filed by HP doubled from 1,500 in 2000 to 3,000 in 2001.[35]

To revamp HP's decentralized structure, Fiorina launched a sweeping corporate reorganization in 2000.

William Hewlett and David Packard had originally organized HP as a confederation of independent businesses, each responsible for the engineering, manufacturing, marketing, and sales of its own line of products. A highly decentralized structure, the founders believed, would promote flexibility, encourage entrepreneurship and innovation, and speed up the decision-making process.[36] Notwithstanding John Young's move to centralize control over HP computer business in the 1980s, the founders, as noted, managed to restore HP's highly decentralized structure in the early 1990s. By the time Fiorina took charge of the company in 1999, HP had evolved into a collection of eighty-three vertically integrated, semi-independent, and loosely coordinated divisions.

Because HP's structure was highly decentralized and divisions were vertically integrated, the company experienced difficulties in coordinating product design, pricing, and marketing strategies. Fiorina, a former HP customer at Lucent, experienced the frustration of dealing with HP personally. At the time Lucent was seeking integrated solutions, HP offered the company stand-alone products and services only. Other corporate customers—the Ford Motor Company, Boeing, and the Best Buy Company—also encountered similar difficulties in dealing with HP. In case after case reported by representatives of these companies, dozens of HP salespersons would converge on a single facility and compete against one another over the supply of narrowly designed product lines rather than address the company's overall needs.[37]

Fiorina, consequently, consolidated the company's eighty-three divisions into four large groups or "quadrants" made up of two types of units: a "front end" unit responsible for marketing and sales and a "back end" unit responsible for manufacturing and services. The front end unit was divided, in turn, into two large groups, one dealing with corporate customers, the other with consumers. The back end unit too was made up of two large groups, the first supplied customers with printing and imaging equipment and services, and the second provided clients with a whole range of computer products and services.[38]

Implemented in 2000, Fiorina's reorganization initiative produced mixed results. On the one hand, the new marketing strategy enhanced customer satisfaction. Corporate customers were no longer dealing with competing sales teams but with a single person. Front end marketers were authorized to sign agreements that took into account the total value of the customer's projected needs, granting sales representatives the flexibility to sell some products at lower prices than others and thus maximizing HP's profits over the life of the contract. The new structure, likewise, empowered marketers to authorize discounts to clients who signed long-term consulting contracts.[39]

On the other hand, the new structure undermined accountability, diffused responsibility, and weakened financial controls. Under the new structure, profit and loss responsibilities were shared by both front and back end groups, and as a result, assigning financial responsibilities to individual managers had become nearly impossible. Under the new system, similarly, allocating costs between front and back end organizations had become exceedingly difficult, and consequently, some of the sales authorized by front end sales representatives turned out later to be unprofitable.[40]

Following a two-year experience with the front/back end system, Fiorina eventually acknowledged that her original plan was flawed. Subsequently, in late 2001, she granted executives greater profit and loss responsibilities over their product lines, and replaced the new quadrant structure with a hybrid version that combined product divisions with front/back end groups.[41]

The Fight Over the Merger

Ever since Fiorina had taken charge of the Hewlett Packard Company, the Board of Directors debated the strategy of undertaking a major acquisition. In discussing HP's options with the new CEO, members of the board concluded that IBM was the only company that competed with HP in all markets, and that IBM's most profitable and fastest growing business was the supply of IT services to large corporate clients. An acquisition of a large IT services company by HP, Fiorina and the board members agreed, was therefore likely to improve HP's worldwide competitive position versus IBM.

In early September 2000, accordingly, Fiorina and her team began discussing the purchase of PricewaterhouseCoopers (PwC) consulting division—a unit employing thirty-one thousand consultants who offered a wide range of computer services to large corporate customers—with PwC top executives. Soon thereafter, the *Sunday Times* of London disclosed the merger talks, reporting that PwC set the asking price at $18 billion. Commenting on the merger, industry analysts considered the price too high and wondered whether key PwC consultants would stay with HP throughout the merger or leave to work for other consulting firms, taking with them their lucrative businesses. In the meantime, opposition to the merger was growing among PwC executives. In November 2000, finally, Fiorina backed away from the deal telling investors: "In hindsight I let the PwC opportunity linger far too long."[42]

The Compaq opportunity unfolded next. Since 1999, Fiorina and Capellas had been discussing, off and on, the possibility of an HP-Compaq merger, and following the PwC setback, Fiorina informed HP directors that Compaq was interested in combining forces with HP. The acquisition of Compaq, Fiorina pointed out, was likely to strengthen HP across the board and thereby contribute to its competitive advantage relative to both IBM and Dell. On July 19, 2001, consequently, Fiorina brought the issue before the Board of Directors for discussion and vote. All eight directors present in the meeting supported the deal and instructed Fiorina to proceed with the merger talks. Absent from the meeting was Walter Hewlett, son of the cofounder, and an HP director. He opposed the merger.[43]

HP and Compaq went ahead and announced the merger on September 4, 2001. Following the merger announcement, HP shares fell 22 percent from $23 to $18.[44] Neither Fiorina nor any other HP directors expected Walter Hewlett to oppose the deal publicly, yet within a few weeks he launched a public relations campaign against the merger, declaring, "This isn't what my father would have wanted done with the company."[45] He thought that the merger was likely to hurt HP's profitable printing business and weaken HP's healthy PC business. He scored a major victory on December 7 when the Packard Foundation—HP's largest shareholder—voted unanimously to oppose the merger. Owning 10.2 percent of all shares outstanding, the David and Lucille Packard Foundation unified the heirs in opposition to the deal.[46]

Notwithstanding the Foundation's vote, HP directors continued supporting the merger enthusiastically, empowering Fiorina to proceed with the merger's preapproval preparations. Walter Hewlett fought back, spending $36 million during a proxy battle that raged over three months. Outspending W. Hewlett by more than two to one, the Hewlett Packard Company scored an important victory when the Institutional Shareholder Services (ISS)—a major consulting firm advising institutional investors on proxy votes—recommended a shareholder approval of the deal. The proxy vote was cast on March 19, 2002, and was close: 51.2 percent of the shares were voted in favor of the merger, and 48.6 percent against it.[47]

Walter Hewlett was not ready to concede defeat, however, but sued HP, charging the company with "fraud and misinformation." HP directors decided, in response, to remove Walter Hewlett from the board. The trial was brief, attracted a great deal of media attention, and ended in another victory on behalf of Fiorina and the company directors. A day after the judge issued his ruling, Walter Hewlett's lawyers, speaking for their client, announced that they would no longer challenge the proxy vote.[48]

Integration of the Merged Companies

The fight over the merger and the plan to integrate the two companies together were interrelated. Just as the long contest with Walter Hewlett gave HP ample time to implement the integration plan effectively, so did the company's integration plan help HP win the proxy vote. Consider the following statement. In its decision to recommend an approval of the merger, the ISS, the nation's leading proxy advisory firm, concluded:

> HP and Compaq... appear to have done pioneering work in thinking about and planning cultural integration of the two companies. It appears that management has done everything it can to maximize the chance that integration will be a success....

It is hard to remain unimpressed in the face of such enthusiastic attention paid to the integration efforts. Half a million man-hours of work have thus far been devoted to integration planning, which surely makes the HP-Compaq one of the most exhaustively planned combinations ever.[49]

Long before the approval of the merger, HP board members were involved in devising plans to ensure the success of the deal. Two board members, Boeing CEO Philip Condit and Vodafone former Chairman Sam Ginn, had managed mega mergers themselves and did so effectively—Condit directed the 1998 Boeing acquisition of McDonnell Douglas, and Ginn executed the 1999 combination of Vodafone and Air Touch Communication. Drawing upon their experiences, Condit and Ginn helped develop the blueprints of the HP-Compaq integration plan. Working together with other board members, they set cost reduction goals for each of the combined businesses of the two companies.[50]

While HP board members were preoccupied with the broad outline of the integration plan, HP and Compaq executives were busy drafting the plan's details. In August 2001, a few weeks before the merger was even announced, Fiorina and Capellas each selected a senior executive to oversee the integration plan. Representing HP, on the one side, and Compaq, on the other, the two selected officers recruited a thirty-person integration team and directed its members to study and analyze data from hundreds of mergers in dozens of industries. Team members examined relevant articles published by the *Harvard Business Review* and pertinent documents supplied by McKinsey & Co., a consulting firm contracted by Fiorina to help HP execute the merger properly. Team members, furthermore, interviewed a large number of executives who worked for companies that underwent recent mergers.[51] Lessons were drawn from mistaken deals as well as successful mergers, from failing acquisitions as well as effective combinations.

Among the deals studied by the HP-Compaq integration team were two oil industry mergers that produced distinctly different outcomes. A 1984 merger between the Chevron Corp. and the Gulf Oil Company resulted in long integration delays that led to demoralization among the employees of the combined company and to confusion among customers: new managerial jobs in the combined company remained unfilled for months. Chevron's 2001 merger with Texaco, by contrast, resulted in effective integration efforts that were facilitated by preplanning and speed: key managerial positions in the new Chevron were filled in days. The 2001 merger of Time Warner and America On Line (AOL), to mention another case studied by the team, failed to produce the expected results, and brought about a steep decline in the combined company's stock market valuation. Cultural differences between the two companies created deep divisions among the employees of the combined company, the HP-Compaq team concluded, and added that each company—Time Warner and AOL—was not sufficiently familiar with the business of the other.[52]

Next, the integration team moved on to examine past mergers undertaken by Compaq and HP. During the 1998 Compaq-Digital integration process, the team found out, many employees as well as managers continued occupying overlapping jobs for months, and some products, designed to be phased out, were never discontinued. More important, the combined (Compaq-Digital) company lost many of its customers owing to serious communication problems stemming from the failure of top management to prepare customers for the transition to a new product roadmap. The team, then, turned to HP's 1989 takeover of Apollo Computers, and discovered that Apollo's integration planning did not begin until after the acquisition was approved, a delay that led to both customer defection and a substantial loss in new business. Last, the team examined HP's 1999 spin off of Agilent Technologies, concluding that the move was successful for two reasons: Lewis Platt preplanned the diversification scheme carefully, and he executed the spin off quickly and deliberately.[53] Taken together, these deals, and many others studied by the integration team, offered an additional lesson: To retain key executives throughout the transition period, top management needed to grant these executives generous retention bonuses.

Initially, before the merger was announced, the compensation committees of both boards—HP and Compaq—set aside $55 million for the purpose of paying executives rich retention bonuses and thereby persuading them to stay with the combined company throughout the merger. The bonus plan was later expanded to cover about six thousand HP and Compaq employees, each receiving a bonus of approximately $50,000.[54]

Additionally, in summer 2001 the two CEOs—Fiorina and Capellas—commissioned a large-scale study of HP and Compaq corporate cultures. Based on interviews conducted with 127 executives and 135 focus groups (made up of 1,500 managers and employees) in 22 countries around the world, the study sought to compare and contrast cultural perceptions held by HP and Compaq employees. Subsequently, the two CEOs authorized the creation of a team for the specific goal of uncovering cultural differences among employees of the two companies. The team found, for example, that HP employees used voice mail while their Compaq counterparts used e-mail to communicate, and that HP employees viewed their Compaq counterparts as "cowboys" whereas Compaq employees viewed their HP counterparts as "bureaucrats." To bridge such differences and forge a unified culture, top management created a task force of 650 part-time "cultural consultants" who continued working in their regular jobs in the combined company while tracking the progress of the HP-Compaq integration plan across all business units.[55]

To ensure a smooth and easy integration process, top management filled managerial positions quickly. Before the merger closed, HP appointed its top three levels of executives as well as 150 senior managers. Once the deal closed in May 2002, HP named its highest ranking sales managers—account leaders serving the company's top 200 customers—in addition to 800 other managers. During the summer and fall of 2002, HP continued announcing wave after wave of new appointments, a practice that expedited the integration process and brought it into completion ahead of schedule.[56]

Integrating the product lines of the two companies was another challenge faced by management. During the premerger planning phase, members of the HP-Compaq's integration team inspected the product lines of the two companies, pitting comparable products against each other and choosing the superior product in nearly every product group. Once the selection process was over, integration team members met with each business unit to devise an exit strategy for products designed to be phased out. Executives monitored the exit progress of each product weekly, using color-coded charts. For example, in the handheld PC business, HP selected the Compaq iPAQ PC over the HP Jornada handheld PC. Renaming the Compaq product HP iPAQ, Hewlett Packard phased out its Jornada product line within a year. In the low-end server business, to take another example, the integration team decided to retire HP Netserver and adopt Compaq's ProLiant product instead. The Compaq product performed better than the HP one, benefited from worldwide brand recognition, and held the largest market share in the industry standard server market for about a decade (1992–2001).[57]

HP phased out the Netserver swiftly. It stopped accepting new orders for the Netserver in September 2002. It laid off 50 percent of Netserver's personnel in May 2002, serving the remaining three hundred employees with future dismissal or relocation notices. And it launched a promotion program whereby HP executives traveled around the world offering Netserver customers the better performing Compaq machine.[58]

HP phased out related products as well. The combined company reduced its offering from 33 to 27 business computer product lines during the first year of the merger, and was expected to discontinue 6 more business computer product lines by the end of 2004.[59]

Discontinuing redundant products contributed handsomely to cost saving. During the first year of the merger (May 2002 to May 2003), HP reduced its costs by over $3 billion, well above its expected merger related cost savings of $2.5 billion. During the same period, HP's closed plants, office buildings, and other facilities, cutting nearly seventeen thousand jobs related to the merger.[60]

Last, the successful integration of the two companies was facilitated by the protracted high-tech recession and by HP's effective use of the Internet. First, the long recession of 2000–2003 provided the combined company with sufficient time to complete the merger integration before the economy turned around and before customers were ready to increase their investments in IT products and services. Second, the key to successful planning and communication was the use of the Internet. The Internet furnished the combined company with the means to plan the merger integration extensively, as well as communicate the details of the integration plan, step by step, to employees as well as customers.[61]

The Results of the Merger: Achievements and Opportunities

Upon the completion of the merger, Fiorina took firm command of the combined company. Assuming the title of president, Michael Capellas had become increasingly invisible as Fiorina exercised day-to-day control over HP's operational divisions, instructing department heads to report directly to her. Six months after the merger closed, in November 2002, Capellas left HP to become the CEO of World Com. His departure precipitated a decline of more than 10 percent in HP stock.[62] Following Capellas's resignation, Fiorina decided not to replace him with another executive but run the company herself without a second in command.

Under Fiorina's leadership, HP's financial performance during the first two years of the merger had improved. In 2002—the year in which the merger closed—HP lost nearly $1 billion as a result of restructuring charges related to the merger, on the one hand, and slow sales stemming from the deepening recession, on the other. A year later, in 2003, the combined company generated $2.5 billion in net income. Similarly, the combined company recorded a loss of 31 cents per share during 2002 as opposed to a gain of 83 cents per share during 2003, the first full year of the merger. Between 2002 and 2003, furthermore, the new HP experienced a modest increase in sales (Exhibit 3).

Evaluating the results of the merger, it is useful to examine each product group separately. Of HP's four postmerger product groups, Imaging and Printing had remained the company's fastest growing and most profitable one. In 2003, HP's Printing and Imaging generated $22.6 billion in sales and nearly $3.6 billion in operating income, as shown in Exhibit 4. Seeking to expand its printer business, HP diversified into copiers, introducing in 2003 a multifunction printer—a printer that operated as both a printer

EXHIBIT 3

Highlights of HP's Financial Data Before the Merger with Compaq (1999–2001) and After the Merger (2002–2003)

	Before the Merger			After the Merger	
	1999	2000	2001	2002	2003
Sales (bil.)	42	49	45	72	73
Net Income (Loss) (bil.)	3.5	3.7	0.4	(0.9)	2.5
Income as % of Sales	8.2%	7.6%	0.9%	—	3.4%
Earnings per Share (Loss)	1.68	1.80	0.21	(0.31)	0.83

Source: For 1999–2001, *Hoover's Handbook of American Business, 2003,* p. 713; for 2002–2003, HP Annual Report, 2003, p. 17.

EXHIBIT 4

Highlights of HP's Financial Data, 2003—The Combined Company's First Full Year, Broken Down by Product Groups

	Imaging & Printing	PCs	Servers	Services
Sales (mil.)	$22,623	$21,228	$15,397	$12,305
Operating Income (mil.)	3,570	19	(54)	1,372

Source: HP Annual Report, 2003, pp. 3–7.

and a copier. To build up a strong distribution network for the new product, HP formed an alliance with IKON Office Solution, an office equipment supplier. To persuade corporate customers to purchase the new machine, HP guaranteed clients substantial savings in printing costs.[63]

Hewlett Packard's second most profitable product was HP Services (see Exhibit 4). The merger with Compaq vaulted HP to the industry number four position, and, as such, turned the combined company into a real contender over lucrative IT services contracts. In 2002, HP signed a $1.3 billion outsourcing deal with the Canadian Imperial Bank of Commerce, and a year later, Hewlett Packard signed large-scale IT consulting deals with the Bank of Ireland, the Ericsson Corporation, and the U.S. Department of Agriculture. Competing successfully against both IBM and EDS, HP was awarded a landmark $3 billion ten-year IT services contract by the Procter & Gamble Corporation in 2003.[64]

While HP Services Group posted a respectable rate of return on sales, the combined company's servers unit ("Enterprise Systems Group") recorded a loss of $54 million in 2003 (see Exhibit 4). To help the struggling unit improve its financial performance, HP announced in December 2003 a reorganization move that was intended to combine its services organization with its servers unit and thereby create a new Technology Solution Group. Because corporate customers were looking for solutions, and because HP's hardware sales had increasingly been driven by its consulting services (an HP executive explained), combining the two together in one unit was likely to sharpen the company's customer focus.[65]

HP's fourth product group was responsible for the manufacture of PCs. In 2003, corporate customers

accounted for 60 percent of HP's PC sales and consumers for 40 percent. The second largest product group in terms of revenues, HP's PC unit (Personal Systems Group) had improved its financial performance in 2003, recording a small profit of $19 million (see Exhibit 4) that followed an operating loss in 2002. In 2002, HP held the worldwide leading position in PC sales, delivering 22 million PC units or 1 million units more than the number delivered by its main rival, Dell Computer. In the five quarters ending August 2003, the PC market's top spot switched back and forth four times between HP and Dell.[66]

The Results of the Merger: Disappointments and Concerns

HP's two arch rivals were IBM and Dell. HP competed with IBM over the worldwide supply of servers and services, and with Dell over the global sales of PCs and servers. In 2002, Dell announced plans to enter the IT services industry, on the one side, and the printer business on the other, hence challenging HP's dominance in each of the combined firm's four postmerger product groups.[67] Two years later, in 2004, most industry analysts concluded that the new HP had lost its direction and was being squeezed by its two main rivals, IBM and Dell; HP was unable to compete successfully with either. HP's difficulties were reflected in the company's stock prices. In August 2004, the value of HP shares was lower than their value on the day the merger closed, as well as the day before the merger was announced.[68]

In 2002, HP trailed IBM in the worldwide sales of servers, and a year later, the gap between the market shares of the two companies widened (Exhibit 5).

EXHIBIT 5

Worldwide Server Market Share by Revenues, 2002–2003

	2002	2003
IBM	30%	32%
HP	27%	27%
SUN	15%	12%
DELL	7%	9%

Source: Robert Guth and Don Clark, "Behind Secret Settlement Talks: New Power of Tech Customers," *Wall Street Journal,* April 5, 2004.

A 2002 Merrill Lynch survey of chief information officers employed by large corporations found that HP's technical support for open standard-based servers lagged far behind IBM's. In 2002, for example, Home Depot selected IBM over HP as its long-term supplier of servers,[69] and in 2003, NetCreation Inc., a New York e-mail marketing firm, decided to replace its HP servers with IBM equivalents. Not only did the IBM machine cost $100,000 less than the HP one, but IBM offered its new customer superior product support. "HP did try to coax us to stay with them," a NetCreation executive explained, "but we never got to speak with any decision makers beyond a certain sales level."[70]

HP trailed IBM in the global supply of IT services too, generating just $12 billion in revenues in 2002 compared with IBM's $36 billion and EDS's $22 billion. Unlike IBM, moreover, most HP consulting services offered customers low-end technical support such as the maintenance and repair of the customer's IT system, not high-end outsourcing—that is, the planning, designing, implementing, and running of the client's entire IT system. Only about one-eighth of HP's services revenues came from outsourcing in 2002, yet according to a 2003 estimate, outsourcing was expected to grow at a rate of 8 percent annually whereas the demand for low-end support services was projected to increase at a 3 percent rate.[71]

IBM had one other advantage over HP. In an attempt to expand and diversify its global services division, IBM acquired in 2002 the Pricewaterhouse-Coopers consulting firm, paying $3.5 billion or less than a fifth of PwC's asking price two years earlier, at the time Fiorina considered purchasing the firm. IBM's takeover of PwC helped Big Blue add some 30,000 new services professionals to its global services work force of 150,000 consultants, bringing the total up to about 180,000. Hewlett Packard, by contrast, employed 65,000 IT consultants, most of whom were not nearly as experienced as the consultants working for IBM/PwC.[72]

While IBM waged war on HP Services, Dell battled HP for shares in the low-end server and desktop PC markets. For one thing, during the two-year period 2002–2003, Dell's share in the worldwide server market grew from 7 percent to 9 percent while HP's share stagnated (see Exhibit 5). For another, in 2003, Dell's PC sales produced a healthy rate of return of about 8.5 percent, whereas HP's PC unit generated a profit rate of less than 1 percent (see Exhibit 4).[73]

EXHIBIT 6

Spending on Research and Development as a Percentage of Sales, 2002

	IBM	HP*	DELL
R&D	5.9%	5.4%	1.3%
Sales (bil.)	$81.5	$72.3	$35.4

*Including Compaq.

Sources: For IBM and Dell, John Markoff, "Innovation at Hewlett Packard Tries to Evade the Ax," New York Times, May 5, 2003; for HP, HP Form 10K for 2002, p. 33.

Dell's higher rate of return may be explained by its lower costs. In the second quarter of 2003, Dell spent 10 cents on overhead for every dollar the company generated in PC sales; the comparable figure for HP was 21 cents per revenue dollar. One reason why Dell's costs were lower than HP's was Dell's smaller R&D budget. In 2002, Dell spent less than $0.5 billion or 1.3 percent of its revenues on R&D compared with HP's $3.9 billion or 5.4 percent of revenues (Exhibit 6). Another was Dell's overwhelming reliance on direct sales to customers and HP's heavy reliance on dealers and retailers for its PC sales: while Dell sold directly to customers nearly every machine it shipped in 2003, HP sold directly just 13 to 27 percent of the PC units it delivered.[74]

The Future

Attacked by both IBM and Dell, the new HP was fighting back, seeking to compete simultaneously with both IBM and Dell. Fiorina portrayed Dell as a "low tech, low cost" company, IBM as a "high tech, high cost" company, and HP as a "high tech, low cost" company, asserting that the new HP represented a combination of the best qualities of its two arch rivals.[75] By contrast to IBM as well as Dell, Fiorina pointed out HP was at one and the same time a leading producer of desktop PCs, a leading provider of IT services, and the dominant vendor of printers, and the three were interrelated: Selling desktop PCs to corporate clients was expected to encourage such clients to purchase HP services and printers, and vice versa, and providing corporate customers with IT services was likely to encourage such customers to buy HP printers and PCs too. "We think the PC business is strategic," Fiorina said in May 2004, noting that the company was willing to sell PCs at a very modest profit rate, or sometimes at a loss, in order to gain large corporate customers for its more profitable printers and IT services.[76]

Would Fiorina's strategy work?

Despite HP's 2004 difficulties, Fiorina had not reversed course but remained steadfast. It was still too early to tell whether her long-term strategy would eventually work.

ENDNOTES

1. Quoted in George Anders, *Perfect Enough: Carly Fiorina and the Reinvention of Hewlett Packard* (New York: Portfolio, 2003), p. 117, but see also pp. 126, 133, and Andrew Park, "Can Compaq Survive as a Solo Act?" *Business Week*, December 24, 2001, p. 71.
2. Peter Burrows, "Carly's Last Stand," *Business Week*, December 24, 2001, p. 64; Anders, *Perfect Enough*, pp. 96, 126.
3. Benjamin Pimentel, "Pumped by Big Blue; Strengthened by the Merger with Compaq, HP Prepares to Battle IBM," *San Francisco Chronicle*, August 2, 2002. Online. Lexis Nexis. Academic Universe; "Hewlett Packard," *Hoover's Handbook of American Business, 2003* (Austin, TX: Hoover Business Press, 2003), p. 713; *Business Week*, December 24, 2001, pp. 64, 71.
4. David Yoffie and Mary Kwak, "Manager's Journal: HP and Compaq Should Return to Their Roots," *Wall Street Journal*, December 17, 2001. Online. ABI database.
5. Wendy Zellner and Mike France, "HP's Beachhead in High-Tech Services," *Business Week*, April 28, 2003, p. 40.
6. Charles Ferguson and Charles Morris, *Computer Wars: How the West Can Win in a Post IBM World* (New York: Random House, 1993), pp. 51–52.
7. Ibid., pp. 52–53; "Hewlett Packard Company," *International Directory of Company Histories*, Vol. 50 (New York: St. James Press, 2003), p. 225.
8. Lois Therrien, "Compaq: How It Made Its Impressive Move Out of the Doldrums," *Business Week*, November 1992, p. 147; Julie Pitta, "Identity Crisis," *Forbes*, May 25, 1992, p. 82; Simon Caulkin, "Compaq's Compact," *Management Today*, May 1985, p. 94.
9. "Hewlett Packard," *International Directory of Company Histories*, pp. 225–226; "Compaq," *Hoover's Handbook of American Business, 2002*, p. 398, but see also Robert Heller, "The Compaq Comeback," *Management Today* (December 1994): 66.
10. *Business Week*, November 2, 1992, p. 147.
11. Ibid., pp. 146, 150; "Compaq," *Hoover's Handbook of American Business, 2002*, p. 398.
12. Eric Nee, "Compaq Computer Corp.," *Forbes*, January 12, 1998, pp. 2–3; David Kirkpatrick, "Fast Times at Compaq," *Fortune*, April 1, 1996, pp. 91–92.
13. *Forbes*, January 12, 1998, pp. 93–94.
14. *Wall Street Journal*, December 17, 2001; David Kirkpatrick, "Eckhard's Gone but the PC Rocks On," *Fortune*, May 24, 1999, p. 154.
15. Michael Gelfand, "Can a CIO Turned CEO Save Compaq?" *Chief Executive* (February 2000): 38, 40.
16. Bill Alpert, "Beating the PC Blues," *Barron's*, July 16, 2001, pp. 20–21.
17. Deone Zell, *Changing by Design: Organizational Innovation at Hewlett Packard* (Ithaca, NY: Cornell University Press, 1997), p. 35.
18. "Hewlett Packard," *Hoover's Handbook of American Business, 2003*, p. 712; "Hewlett Packard," *International Directory of Company Histories*, pp. 222–223.
19. Sara Beckman and David Mowery, "Corporate Change and Competitiveness: The Hewlett Packard Company," Working Paper 95/12, Haas School of Business, University of California, Berkeley, pp. 4, 7; Anders, *Perfect Enough*, p. 17.
20. Beckman and Mowery, "Corporate Change and Competitiveness," p. 4.
21. Anders, *Perfect Enough*, p. 20; Peter Burrows, *Backfire; Carly Fiorina's High Stakes Battle for the Soul of Hewlett Packard* (New York: John Wiley, 2003), pp. 72–73; "Hewlett Packard," *International Directory of Company Histories*, p. 223.
22. Anders, *Perfect Enough*, pp. 20–21; Burrows, *Backfire*, p. 74; David Packard, *The HP Way* (New York: Harper, 1995), ch. 8; Julia Pitta, "It Had to Be Done and We Did It," *Forbes*, April 26, 1993, pp. 151–152; "Hewlett Packard," *International Directory of Company Histories*, p. 223.
23. *Forbes*, April 26, 1993, p. 152; Anders, *Perfect Enough*, pp. 22–24; "Hewlett Packard," *Hoover's Handbook of American Business, 2003*, p. 712; Robert Hof, "Suddenly Hewlett Packard Is Doing Everything Right," *Business Week*, March 23, 1992, p. 88.
24. "Hewlett Packard," *Hoover's Handbook of American Business, 2003*, p. 713.
25. Eric Savitz, "Hewlett Packard's Money Machine," *Barron's*, August 28, 1996. Online. ABI database. Start page 25; John Sheridan, "Lew Platt: Creating a Culture for Innovation," *Industry Week*, December 19, 1994, pp. 26, 28; Alan Deutschman, "How HP Continues to Grow and Grow," *Fortune*, May 2, 1994, pp. 90–92, 96.
26. *International Directory of Company History*, p. 227.
27. *Fortune*, May 2, 1994, pp. 90–92.
28. Robert Hof, "Hewlett Packard Made a Tough Decision, but the Right One," *Business Week*, March 15, 1999, p. 32; Eric Nee, "Defending the Desktop," *Forbes*, December 28, 1998, pp. 53–54; Anders, *Perfect Enough*, pp. 39–40.
29. Eric Nee, "Lew Platt: Why I Dismember HP?" *Fortune*, May 29, 1999, p. 167; *Business Week*, March 15, 1999, p. 32; David Hamilton and Scott Thurm, "HP to Spin Off Its Measurement Operations," *Wall Street Journal*, March 3, 1999. Online. ABI database.
30. Anders, *Perfect Enough*, pp. 42–43.
31. Peter Burrows, "The Boss: Carly Fiorina's Challenge Will Be to Propel Staid Hewlett Packard Into the Internet Age," *Business Week*, August 2, 1999, pp. 76, 78; Anders, *Perfect Enough*, ch. 3.
32. Adam Lashinsky, "Now for the Hard Part: Carly Fiorina Sold Investors on the HP Merger," *Fortune*, November 18, 2002, p. 104; Quentin Hardy, "All Carly All the Time," *Forbes*, December 13, 1999, p. 135, but see also pp. 140–144.
33. Anders, *Perfect Enough*, p. 76.
34. Peter Burrows, "The Radical: Carly Fiorina's Bold Management Experiment at HP," *Business Week*, February 19, 2001, p. 78, but see also December 24, 2001, p. 66.
35. *Business Week*, February 19, 2001, p. 78; December 24, 2001, pp. 67–69.
36. Zell, *Changing by Design*, pp. 35–36.
37. Anders, *Perfect Enough*, p. 75; *Business Week*, February 19, 2001, p. 78; August 2, 1999, p. 80.
38. Anders, *Perfect Enough*, p. 75.
39. *Business Week*, February 19, 2001, p. 78.
40. Anders, *Perfect Enough*, pp. 75–76; *Business Week*, February 19, 2001, pp. 73, 78.
41. Anders, *Perfect Enough*, p. 76.
42. Ibid., pp. 93–94; Burrows, *Backfire*, pp. 168–169.
43. Burrows, *Backfire*, ch. 9; Anders, *Perfect Enough*, p. 95 and ch. 7.
44. *Business Week*, December 24, 2001, p. 67.
45. Quoted in Anders, *Perfect Enough*, p. 144.
46. Burrows, *Backfire*, ch. 10; *Business Week*, December 24, 2001, p. 67.
47. Anders, *Perfect Enough*, chs. 9, 10; Burrows, *Backfire*, ch. 11.
48. Burrows, *Backfire*, ch. 12; Anders, *Perfect Enough*, ch. 11.
49. "ISS Recommends HP Shareholders Vote for Merger," Press Release, Palo Alto, California, March 5, 2002. HP.com.
50. Carly Fiorina, "The Case for Merger," a speech delivered at the Goldman Sachs Technology Conference, Palm Springs, California, February 4, 2002, HP.com; *Business Week*, December 24, 2001, p. 66.

51. Pui-Wing Tam, "Merger by Numbers: An Elaborate Plan Forces HP Union to Stay on Target," *Wall Street Journal*, April 28, 2003; Carly Fiorina, "Remarks," a speech delivered in the Information Processing Interagency Conference, Orlando, Florida, March 3, 2003, HP.com; *Business Week*, December 24, 2001, p. 66.

52. *Wall Street Journal*, April 28, 2003; *Business Week*, December 24, 2001, p. 66.

53. Fiorina, "Remarks," December 24, 2001; *Wall Street Journal*, April 28, 2003.

54. Burrows, *Backfire*, p. 228; *Business Week*, December 24, 2001, p. 66.

55. Fiorina, "Remarks," December 24, 2001; *Wall Street Journal*, April 28, 2003.

56. "HP Announces Latest Merger Integration Milestone With Naming 150 Senior Managers," Press Release, Palo Alto, California, April 3, 2002; Fiorina, "Remarks," December 24, 2001; *Wall Street Journal*, April 28, 2003.

57. "HP White Paper: Hewlett Packard Product Roadmaps," press release, undated; *Wall Street Journal*, April 28, 2003.

58. *Wall Street Journal*, April 28, 2003.

59. Ibid.

60. Matthew Fordahl, "Hewlett Packard to Cut More Workers," *Chicago Sun Times*, May 21, 2003. Online, ABI database; *Wall Street Journal*, April 28, 2003.

61. Fiorina, "The Case for Merger," February 4, 2002; Fiorina, "Remarks," December 24, 2001; "Merger Mystery: HP and Compaq," *The Economist*, November 16, 2002, p. 7.

62. Cliff Edwards, "Why Capellas Flew the Coop," *Business Week*, December 23, 2002, pp. 52–53; Anders, *Perfect Enough*, pp. 215–216.

63. Steve Lohr, "Hewlett Now Wants to Be Your Copier Company, Too," *New York Times*, November 18, 2003.

64. *Business Week*, April 28, 2003, p. 40; Bob Keefe, "HP-Compaq Merger So Far a Success," *Palm Beach Post*, May 11, 2003. Online. ABI database; Bill Breen, "The Big Score," *Fast Company*, September 1, 2003.

65. David Bank and Gary McWilliams, "HP to Reorganize Operating Units," *Wall Street Journal*, December 9, 2003.

66. Terril Yue Jones, "Commitment to PC Market Hurts HP's Bottom Line," *Los Angeles Times*, August 25, 2003. Online. Lexis Nexis, Academic Universe.

67. Dell's impending entry into both the IT services market and the printer business posed a potential threat to HP's future earnings. On the one hand, Dell planned to supply small- and medium-size customers with low-end IT services for a price as low as $200. On the other, Dell decided to form an alliance with Lexmark, the former IBM printer company, in order to compete with HP over the supply of small size printers in the short run, and ink and laser printer cartridges in the long run. Cliff Edwards, "The New HP: How's It Doing?" *Business Week*, December 23, 2002, p. 54; Anders, *Perfect Enough*, p. 217.

68. "Losing the HP Way: Hewlett Packard," *The Economist*, August 21, 2004, p. 58.

69. Cliff Edwards, "The New HP: How's It Doing?" *Business Week*, December 23, 2002, p. 54.

70. Cited in Pui Wing Tam, "HP Launches a New Tech Strategy," *Wall Street Journal*, May 6, 2003.

71. *Business Week*, April 28, 2003, p. 40.

72. Anders, *Perfect Enough*, p. 217; Benjamin Pimental, "Pumped for Big Blue: Strengthened by Its Merger with Compaq, HP Prepares to Battle IBM for IT Customers," *San Francisco Chronicle*, August 2, 2002. Online. Lexis Nexis, Academic Universe.

73. *Los Angeles Times*, August 25, 2003.

74. A massive reliance on direct sales allowed, in turn, for greater pricing flexibility. By contrast to HP, Dell could adjust prices daily and thereby launch price wars against its competitors. In August 2003, for instance, Dell announced price reductions that ranged from 6 percent on desktop PCs to 22 percent on network servers. HP was able to adjust prices quickly on the proportion of PCs that it sold directly to customers, but it was unable to do so on the PCs it sold indirectly because it needed to set prices up to six weeks in advance in order to provide dealers and retailers with sufficient time to both advertise and replenish their inventories. Gary McWilliams and Pui Wing Tam, "Dell Price Cuts Put a Squeeze on Rival HP," *Wall Street Journal*, August 21, 2003; Scott Morrison, "Dell Delivers a Salutary Slap in the Face to HP," *Financial Times*, August 22, 2003. Online. ABI database.

75. *The Economist*, August 21, 2004.

76. David Bank and Gary McWilliams, "Picking a Big Fight with Dell, HP Cuts Profits Razor Thin," *Wall Street Journal*, May 12, 2004.

Case 24

Hewlett Packard Ousts Carly Fiorina

This case was prepared by Gareth R. Jones, Texas A&M University.

On February 7, 2005, Hewlett Packard (HP) announced that Carly Fiorina, the person its Board of Directors had handpicked to be the company's new CEO in 1999, would be leaving the company with a severance package of over $20 million. The board, which named Chief Financial Officer Robert P. Wayman, a thirty-six-year veteran, as interim CEO, began the search for a new CEO who could develop a business model that would allow the company to compete with arch rivals IBM and Dell—a CEO who could perform the same miracle that Louis Gerstner accomplished for IBM. One person who may be a likely candidate is former Compaq CEO Michael A. Capellas, who served briefly as Fiorina's second in command after the Compaq-HP merger before he left to become the CEO of troubled telecommunication company MCI.

Clearly, HP's board and major stockholders felt that the merger had not achieved the results Fiorina had predicted. HP's performance has been mixed in the two years since it took place. While the immediate integration of the two companies produced cost savings faster and larger than anticipated and silenced her critics, by late 2003 some analysts began to feel the merger had not done much to improve HP's

ebbing position against key competitors IBM and Dell. However, other analysts felt the company would be worse off in 2005 if the merger had not taken place because its main profit generator is its printer division, which has been under attack from such low-cost competitors as Lexmark, Canon, and Dell, and its uncompetitive PC division might be making much larger losses if the merger had not taken place.

On the news of Fiorina's dismissal, HP's stock jumped 7 percent because investors hoped that the company would spin off its unprofitable PC and network computer operations, and even its money losing software division, to focus on strengthening its highly profitable Printing & Imaging Division. Yet despite Fiorina's dismissal, the board reiterated its support for her business model that is based on offering customers a complete line of computer hardware, software, services, and consultancy. Fiorina had argued that the board was simply not giving her enough time to make her business model work. After all, it took Gerstner over a decade to really turn around IBM's performance and transform that company. However, the board obviously felt the way she was implementing her business model was not resulting either in the lower costs or improved computer solutions that would raise the company's revenues and profits.

Of particular concern to analysts was a series of missed chances and botched implementation efforts that had hurt the company's image and performance. HP's software division lost over $100 million on $900 million in sales in 2004, and Fiorina moved too slowly to acquire a profitable company called Veritas Software, which made enterprise software, that might have been a perfect complement with HP's software division. It was eventually snapped up by Symantec, a major competitor. In its other divisions too, directors were concerned that she was too slow to either acquire companies or change the company's internal operating procedures to improve its competitive position, and when she did, she had made mistakes.

In sales, for example, it was widely acknowledged that HP lagged far behind both Dell and IBM. HP's direct selling model was inferior to Dell's and too little was being done to improve it. HP's marketing and sales operations were also a major problem. Its sales force found it very difficult to offer customers a complete solution, similar to IBM, because there was little coordination between sales and different operating groups. When Fiorina reorganized sales so that each operating division had its own sales force, this led to enormous problems of coordinating between operating groups so the system was changed again. In the third quarter of 2004, the company missed its profit targets because of serious glitches in a new internal order procurement system created to integrate between the different operating groups in their efforts to provide customers an integrated solution. This sign of HP's worsening performance apparently led the board to start questioning Fiorina's ability to control the company and her failure to create a strong top management team that might have forestalled such problems. So, even if her overall business model and strategies for HP were the right ones, they were failing because of poor implementation and control over organizational structure. Indeed, HP's organizational structure and culture had changed dramatically by 2005; the old culture based on values and norms, emphasizing the importance of research and development, was slowing down her attempts to create a customer-focused culture. The clash of cultures was contributing to the problems of integrating between the various operating divisions.

In any event, the jury is out on HP's future; only time will tell what business model its new CEO will choose for the company, that is, if HP's board will allow the new CEO to radically change its current model or find ways to better implement it. The jury is even out on whether the merger will be regarded as a success or failure in the years to come. What is clear is that HP is in a major struggle with its competitors in the computer sector and that more changes are ahead as technology changes and as companies fight to reduce their cost structures to increase their efficiency and effectiveness.

Michael Eisner's Walt Disney Company: Part One

This case was prepared by Gareth R. Jones, Texas A&M University.

It was early 1991, and Michael Eisner, chairman and CEO of the Walt Disney Company, was sitting down with Frank Wells, president and chief operating officer, and Gary Wilson, executive vice president and chief financial officer, to discuss Disney's prospects for the new year. These men were still basking in the glow generated by another record revenue- and profit-breaking year in Disney's history. Disney's businesses were performing at an unprecedented level, and confidence was high. The problem facing the trio who had engineered Disney's turnaround was how to maintain Disney's explosive growth rate and its return-on-investment goal of increasing earnings per share by 20 percent over any five-year period to achieve a 20 percent annual return on equity. Paradoxically, the very success of their strategy, which had originated to protect an underperforming Disney from the rampages of corporate raiders and the threat of takeover, was causing the opposite problem: how to maintain the company's explosive growth in a business environment where attractive opportunities for expansion were becoming increasingly scarce. The men were reflecting on how to develop a five-year plan that would cement the strategy that had led to their present enviable situation and make the 1990s the "Disney Decade."

Disney Before Eisner

When Walt Disney died in 1966, he left a company that was experiencing record revenues and profits. Disney was at its creative peak and forging ahead at full steam on the many ideas generated by Walt Disney's creative genius. However, by the early 1980s all the drive in the Disney Company had evaporated. Although revenues were increasing somewhat, net income and profit were dropping drastically. While top executives believed they were following what "Walt would have wanted," the vision that was uniquely Walt Disney's was gone. Table 1 charts the net income of the Walt Disney Company from 1980 to 1990. How did this situation come about? To understand it, we need to look at the way in which Walt Disney built his company and try to find the pattern in his creative endeavors.

Walt Disney's Company

Walt Elias Disney was born in 1901. Raised on a farm, he early developed an interest in art and drawing, and his ambition was to be a cartoonist. His interest in static cartoons soon waned, however, with the beginning of animated cartoons in movie theaters. At the time, these were extremely crude; the figures bounced rather than moved gracefully around, they were silent, and they were in black and white. He immediately saw the potential for developing high-quality, graphic art cartoons that moved and set about marshaling resources to produce his product.

After a series of early setbacks, Disney had success with a character called Oswald the Rabbit, perhaps the forerunner of Roger the Rabbit. The carefully drawn cartoons were very popular with movie audiences and

TABLE 1

Selected Financial Data (in millions, except per share and other data)

	1989	1988	1987	1986	1985
Statement of Income Data					
Revenues	$4,594.3	$3,438.2	$2,876.8	$2,165.8	$1,700.1
Operating income	1,229.0	884.8	776.8	527.7	345.7
Interest expense	23.9	5.8	29.1	44.1	54.6
Income from continuing operations	703.3	522.0	392.3	213.2	132.3
Net income	703.3	522.0	444.7	247.3	173.5
Balance Sheet Data					
Total assets	$6,657.2	$5,108.9	$3,806.3	$3,121.0	$2,897.3
Borrowing	860.6	435.5	584.5	547.2	823.1
Stockholders' equity	3,044.0	2,359.3	1,845.4	1,418.7	1,184.9
Statement of Cash Flow Data					
Cash flow	$1,275.6	$1,075.4*	$830.6	$668.4	$518.8
Investments					
Theme parks, resorts, and other property, net	749.6	595.7	280.1	174.1	179.8
Film costs	426.7	225.7	178.3	203.7	149.9
Acquisitions	237.3	221.7			
Per Share Data					
Net income					
Continuing operations	$5.10	$3.80	$2.85	$1.57	$.98
Total	5.10	3.80	3.23	1.82	1.29
Cash dividends	.46	.38	.32	.315	.30
Other Data					
Stockholders at close of year	143,000	124,000	101,000	77,000	58,000
Employees at close of year	47,000	39,000	31,000	30,000	30,000

*Excludes $722.6 million unearned royalty advances.

Source: The Walt Disney Company, *Annual Report,* 1989.

provided Disney with the money he needed to expand his operations and to hire additional artists and animators. However, after battles about money and profits, Disney lost control of the Oswald character to Charles Mintz, the cartoon's distributor, which taught him an important lesson. From then on, he would retain all the rights to his characters, to the films produced using these characters, and to the distribution end of the film business. This was the start of Disney's fortune.

With the experience gained from Oswald the Rabbit, Disney set about finding a new character to

hang his fortunes to. He came up with the idea of a mouse, and in 1928 he created Mickey Mouse. He was the voice, but the cartoons were drawn by Ubbe (Ub) Iwerks, an artist and animator who had worked closely with Disney from the beginning. The Mickey Mouse cartoons were immensely popular, and their success provided Walt Disney with the resources to expand his repertoire of characters and improve his animation techniques. He and his company then, and now, were always at the forefront of technological developments. The next decade saw the emergence of Disney's now familiar cast of characters: Donald

Duck, Goofy, and the Three Little Pigs, a cartoon for which Disney won an Oscar. At the same time, Disney became involved in making cartoons in color. Using technicolor's new three-color process, he produced these cartoons in color and won his first Oscar for color in 1932.[1] It was this ability to meld technical developments with his emerging cast of cartoon characters that was the source of Disney's distinctive strength. None of his competitors was able to take this advantage away; although other studios established animation departments, none had the same success.

Full-Length Movies

By the late 1930s, Disney's experience in short cartoons had now developed his studio's skills in the three techniques needed for quality animation and cartoon making: art and drawing, perspective and sound, and color. He had learned the value of using a large number of drawings per second to provide his characters with realistic movements, even though this dramatically increased costs. He had seen the value of color as a way of making his characters more true to life (since one of the virtues of cartoons is that they can extend and amplify reality). Lastly, he had developed a technique that gave depth to the previously flat cartoons. This was the famous Multiplane technique, which involved the use of a camera that could focus in and out of three planes of celluloid drawings: the foreground, the characters themselves, and the background. By photographing these planes at an angle, an impression of depth was achieved in the cartoon that gave the characters life. This technique resulted in another Oscar for Disney.

Taking these techniques, Walt Disney set about advancing his long-term dream: a full-length cartoon motion picture. He was careful in his selection of a subject. From the beginning, he believed that his subjects should be characters that were widely accepted by the public so that little learning by the public was involved. It was with his characteristic genius that he chose Snow White and the Seven Dwarfs as his subject in 1937. *Snow White* cost a fortune to make, but it went on to make animation history as it also grossed a fortune at the box office. It also provided the capital that precipitated Disney into the ranks of the big studios. The money from *Snow White* allowed Disney to build his studio at Burbank and financed the animated films *Pinocchio* and *Bambi*, which were also very successful. Then, in 1940, departing from his own maxim of only choosing "brand-name characters," he made *Fantasia*. Despite being an artistic success, the film was a commercial disaster, which, coinciding with the unpopularity of cartoons during World War II, plunged Walt Disney Productions into debt. When the banks restricted the amount they were willing to provide to fund the company, Walt Disney offered stock to the public for the first time. In 1940 Walt Disney Productions issued 155,000 shares at $25 a share, raising $3,500,000 in working capital.

More Walt Disney Magic

With the end of the war, the public was once again receptive to fun and fantasy. The boom years after the war produced an audience with money in their pockets who were in search of excitement, and Walt Disney was determined to provide them with it. He began the search for new projects to exercise the talents of the Disney studios. By 1950 he had come up with new directions for the Disney studios.

Motion Pictures

Disney realized that animation was not the only way of bringing the public's favorite fantasy characters to the screen. Many popular heroes such as Robin Hood could be depicted in live-action movies. So, Disney took popular fictional characters and turned them into movies. A string of hits resulted as Disney studios came out with *Treasure Island, The Swiss Family Robinson, The Story of Robin Hood and His Merry Men, Kidnapped, 20,000 Leagues Under the Sea*, and a host of films starring such people as Hayley Mills and Maurice Chevalier. He then also decided to create new characters and developed scripts for such projects as *The Shaggy Dog, The Absent Minded Professor, Son of Flubber*, and *The Parent Trap*. Side by side with these developments, Disney embarked on a series of nature or wildlife projects. Between 1950 and 1960, films such as *Water Birds, The Alaskan Eskimo, Bear Country*, and the *White Wilderness* were produced for enthusiastic audiences. These films are still popular today.

At the same time his interest in animation did not lapse and was a major moneymaker for the studio in the 1950s. *Cinderella* was a smash hit as was *101 Dalmatians, Peter Pan, Lady and the Tramp*, and *The Jungle Book*. Moreover, by 1960 he was experimenting with combining animation and live action, and one result was *Mary Poppins*, which was an all-time revenue winner for Disney, one of the greatest hits in the history of motion pictures, and which won five Academy Awards.

Television

Another move that helped Disney studios at this time was Walt's decision to take his products to the television screen. While other movie studios were worrying that television would cut into their profits and reduce their audiences, Walt realized the prospective synergies between the television and movie businesses for Disney. Disney was already producing a wide range of family-oriented entertainment: cartoons, full-length animation, live action, and wildlife. What could be more logical than taking its characters and developing its products to fit into a television format? Not only would this be the source of additional revenues for Disney and allow it to exploit its resources and people to the full, but it would also provide advertising for the Walt Disney name and its future product offerings. The result was that in 1954 Disney brought *The Wonderful World of Disney* to the screen. In 1955 the *Mickey Mouse Club* was introduced, and the Disney name became part of popular American culture as for the next twenty years Walt Disney television became a weekly event for the viewing public.

Theme Parks

Walt Disney had another reason for entering the television market. By itself, television was not a great money spinner for Disney. It would provide some free advertising and permit a more efficient utilization of the Disney resources, but animation was expensive compared to live action. What Walt Disney principally saw in television was a way to promote an idea that had been on his mind for years: a permanent amusement park that could exploit the Disney characters' popularity and which would offer a family a fun-filled day of Disney fantasy. Rather than passively watching a movie, amusement park goers would become a part of the movie; they would become actors in a live Disney entertainment. Television would show viewers how to take part in this experience; it would also show them what they could expect. Disney realized that the combination of theme park, television, and movies would feed on each other, and each would promote the other. He was right. The theme park idea was wildly successful,

and since its opening Disneyland became the backbone of the Disney empire.

After deliberation, Disney chose the Anaheim site in California for the opening of his first theme park. Disneyland opened in July 1955. Anaheim was chosen because of the huge population base of southern California and because with less than 5 inches of rain a year, it could be operated all year round with little threat from the weather. Immense planning went into the creation of the Disney experience and still does. Every ride and attraction was crafted to highlight the Disney theme; all its movies and characters are represented by different kinds of amusements and, of course, by the personal appearances of its characters, too. The number of attractions has grown from seventeen in 1955 to sixty-two now, and exhibits are constantly improved and updated to take advantage of the latest technological developments. Attractions are often connected with a corporate sponsor that buys into a Disney theme and leases an exhibit. For example, AT&T, Sony, and Kodak are some of the many sponsors of Disney's exhibits. The park is divided into seven major areas: Adventureland, Tomorrowland, Fantasyland, Frontierland, Mainstreet, Bearcountry, and New Orleans Square.

Then, in 1965 Walt Disney announced yet another part of his grand plan, the development of Disney World including the EPCOT (Experimental Prototype Community of Tomorrow) Center in Orlando, Florida. As originally imagined by Disney, part of Disney World would include a Magic Kingdom similar to the one already established in Anaheim. However, the EPCOT Center he envisaged was a "living laboratory" where 20,000 to 30,000 people would permanently live, experimenting with advanced technology and literally providing the world with examples of future life on Earth. He did not live to see either dream realized; Walt Disney died in December 1966.

Disney After Walt

When Walt Disney died, he left his company at the pinnacle of its success up to that date. There were new films ready to distribute, plans for Disney World, steadily rising attendance at Disneyland, and a secure television audience. However, nothing seemed to go as well as before in the Disney organization. In the years from 1966 to 1984, when Michael Eisner took over, the company seemed to just be spinning its wheels.

The problem was that nobody emerged to wear Walt Disney's crown; nobody could provide the creative vision to lead a company whose mission was to provide fun and fantasy. There was a void in the organization, and little was accomplished by the company that did not already have Walt Disney's stamp of approval on it.

Walt's brother Roy took over management of the company and supervised the building of Disney World. Most of the advance planning for Disney World had been carried out by Walt. The first step in that plan had been to purchase a huge tract of land outside Orlando, Florida, to hold Disney World. Disney had never liked the situation that had developed outside Anaheim after the opening of Disneyland. Disney only owns the area on which the theme park and its car park is built. As a result, development around the park proceeded unchecked, and the surrounding area became full of motels and hotels that Walt Disney felt detracted from the Disney image. Moreover, on a financial level, the profits being earned by businesses in the vicinity of the park were vastly more than the revenues Disney received from park attendance. Because Walt Disney was determined that this should not happen in Orlando, he arranged, through subsidiary companies, the purchase of 28,000 acres of undeveloped land, an area the size of 34 square miles, enough to hold any number of hotels and amusement parks. Then, when Disney made the announcement of the park in 1965, the value of the land increased dramatically overnight.

The Magic Kingdom was the first part of Disney World to be built, and it opened in 1971 with thirty-five attractions; now there are more than fifty. Just as corporate sponsorship was important in financing the development of the Magic Kingdom, it was also very important in providing the financing for the EPCOT Center, with large corporations paying $25 million for the right to sponsor an attraction. Nevertheless, the plans for EPCOT changed dramatically after Walt's death. The company realized that development costs would be enormous, and the venture as devised by Walt was not commercially feasible. Instead, the company changed EPCOT's mission to provide a showcase of modern technology and of international culture. In essence, EPCOT became a kind of permanent World's Fair when it opened in 1982. It is composed of two main areas. The first,

World Showcase, consists of pavilions sponsored by many different countries demonstrating their national culture and products and offering a wide variety of different kinds of national foods. The second area is Future World, which, in the spirit of Walt Disney's original plan, showcases future developments that can be expected in all areas of human commerce and endeavor. Attractions include the Living Seas, sponsored by United Technologies; a future farming exhibit sponsored by Kraft; and, recently, a journey through the human body highlighting advances in medical knowledge. EPCOT was the first Walt Disney exhibit specifically designed to appeal to adults, although Walt Disney always said everything Disney does is designed for the child in everybody.

The development of EPCOT and Disney World was Disney's principal priority during these years, and the opening of EPCOT attracted record crowds. However, despite high attendance, the profit margin of Disney World was lower than that of Disneyland, and both revenues and profits were disappointing, given Disney's huge investment of $1.5 billion. Moreover, by 1984 attendance at Disney World and Disneyland dropped off from its previous record high, further reducing revenues. Clearly, Disney had problems with its theme parks, but management did not know what to do.

Another problem Disney experienced was that while it had developed three large hotels with more than 2,000 rooms at the theme park to exploit the hotel market that they had missed at Anaheim, luxury hotels chains such as the Hyatt and Hilton were opening new luxury hotels at the park's borders. The result was that Disney was losing potential Disney revenues to these hotel chains, and the situation that had happened at Disneyland was in danger of happening again.

The other areas of Disney's business were also not doing well. Planning for the Disney Channel had begun in the late 1970s, and it came on line in 1983 with 532,000 subscribers. The channel was a natural complement to Disney's other activities because it was an additional vehicle through which the company could exploit its skills and characters. However, the start-up costs of the Disney Channel were enormous, and even though it had more than 1 million subscribers by 1984, it was still losing more than $10 million a year. This was another drain on the company's dwindling resources and a threat to its profit margins.

Home Video and Consumer Products

One bright spot for Disney was its entry into the home video market. It began selling videocassettes of some of its movie hits in 1983. Some of these were contemporary hits from its new Touchstone label, such as *Splash*. However, it also began marketing its old classics, first selecting those that, while popular, were not its greatest hits to see customers' reaction and to protect its rerun movie revenues. *Dumbo* and *Alice in Wonderland* were released in 1983 to enthusiastic demand, and Disney, realizing the revenue potential from video sales was enormous, soon orchestrated the gradual release of all its classics on videotape.[2]

The sale of consumer products bearing Disney's logo had long been one of Disney's major lines of business. However, many analysts felt that Disney was not exploiting the potential of this market and that their strategy of franchising rights to the use of Disney's name and characters to other companies was bringing Disney some money, but making far more money for the actual producers and distributors of Disney's products than for the company itself. They felt the potential market for Disney's books, comics, records, clothing, and all kinds of Disney souvenirs had yet to be exploited.

Moviemaking

Since Walt's death, Disney's movie operations suffered because they failed to find good scripts and projects. The performance of Disney's film business had been lackluster throughout the 1970s, and although the film division accounted for more than 20 percent of Disney's profits in 1979, by 1982 it was losing money. The situation became so bad that Disney's CEO, E. Cardon (Card) Walker, who had taken over after Roy Disney's death in 1971, was talking about closing it down! The division that had been Disney's core business and the source of its success was now in danger. How had this come about? First, Disney was relying on reruns of its classic movies and living on its past glory rather than on the proceeds of its present activities. Reruns were contributing more than 50 percent of the revenues of the film division because Disney was having little commercial success with its new ventures. Although receiving good reviews, animated movies, such as the *Secret of Nimb*, *Watership Down*, and the *Black Hole*, were not big money spinners, and the live-action films Disney had been producing, such as *Something Wicked This Way*

Comes and *Condorman*, lost money; these two, for example, lost more than $20 million each.

Moreover, analysts were claiming that Disney was not making the best use of its film library, which contained more than 700 different titles. They felt that Disney could be making a much more creative use of this resource, and, in part as a response to this pressure to exploit this resource, the company drew up plans for the Disney Channel, its pay-TV channel. Meanwhile, industry analysts did not like Card Walker's attitude toward the film division. They felt a turnaround in this division rather than liquidation was the answer, and in 1983 Ronald Miller became chief executive to implement this turnaround strategy. His answer to the problem was to create a new film division, Touchstone Films, to produce movies that were unsuitable for the family-oriented Disney label. He saw the problem as one of being straight-jacketed by Disney's conservative, family image, which had not allowed filmmakers to exploit the opportunities in the market for new kinds of movies. Touchstone brought out *Splash* in 1983; it was a huge hit and the beginning of a turnaround of the film division. Nevertheless, Disney's top management was worried that Walt would not have liked it, and they actively sought to isolate the Touchstone division from the Disney organization. This conflict over Disney's future was the start of infighting between Disney's managers and stockholders over the best way to manage the company.

Roy Disney II, the nephew of Walt Disney, in particular lost confidence in the management team. He felt it lacked the Disney vision and the skills to exploit the Disney resources; in essence, he felt that it was destroying the legacy Walt had left behind. These open conflicts brought Disney to the attention of corporate raiders, and by 1984 there was an increasing possibility of an unfriendly takeover of the Disney organization. To prevent such a takeover, the Disney family sided with new investors, the Bass family, to oust the old, conservative, management team. The Disney family then set out to recruit somebody who could return Disney to a preeminent position in the entertainment industry. The person they fixed on was Michael Eisner, previously vice chairman of Paramount, and widely regarded as the originator of a massive turnaround in the fortunes of that corporation, due to his ability to find and act on new trends in the marketplace. In September 1984, Michael Eisner took control of

Disney and a new era began. Finally, someone had emerged who could wear Walt's crown.

Michael Eisner's Walt Disney Company

It was December 1984, and Michael Eisner was sitting down with Frank Wells, the person he had recruited to help him turn the Disney Company around, and Roy Disney, the nephew of the founder who had been instrumental in Eisner's appointment to plan Disney's future. They were looking over Disney's resources and the activities of its divisions and subsidiaries, and both Eisner and Wells were amazed at the extent and diversity of Disney's resources. Eisner decided that Disney's strengths were in its three principal business segments:

■ *Entertainment and recreation,* which included all its theme parks and hotel businesses, together with shopping centers, conference centers, and golf courses

■ *Motion pictures and home videos,* which included the Disney studios; Buena Vista Productions, which had the Touchstone label; and Buena Vista Distribution, which distributed Disney's films at home and abroad

■ *Consumer products,* which was the licensing arm of Disney and licensed its characters; literary properties; and songs and music to various manufacturers, retailers, printers, and publishers as well

Why were these businesses underperforming, and what could be done about it? It did not take Eisner and Wells long to realize that the problem was that the potential of these businesses was not being exploited. In none of these business segments was management following any clearly defined strategy to exploit the Disney resources or a vision of what use these resources could be put to in the future. Each division was drifting aimlessly along. For example, despite Disney's raw filmmaking talent, the movie business was losing money. Similarly, due to inaction, Disney had lost its television presence outside its own movie channel.

Moreover, it was apparent that while Disney was not taking advantage of its opportunities, other people were. For every dollar Disney was collecting in revenues from its characters and theme parks, those manufacturers who were licensing Disney's products or those hotel chains housing and feeding Disney customers at the theme parks were getting five. Disney was stagnating, and new ways had to be found to exploit its revenue-generating potential and regain "Disney dollars." First, however, they realized the need to recruit some exceptional executives to provide leadership in the financial planning areas of the company to back up the creative end, which they would lead. Eisner had to find the money to finance his expansion plans and to develop new business ventures. In 1985 he hired Gary L. Wilson as executive vice president and chief financial officer of Disney and made him a director. Wilson, a project finance specialist, had previously performed the same role for the Marriot Corporation, the hotel chain, and had participated in the enormous growth of that corporation. According to Eisner, his responsibility would be to "plan and implement the company's expansion programs, including internal development and acquisitions."[3] With the team set, Eisner began to change Disney.

Entertainment and Recreation

Eisner began to take a long hard look at the theme park business. This was Disney's biggest money spinner, but revenue growth had been slow. How could he revitalize this division's strategy? He started by looking at the customer groups and segments Disney was serving. Was Disney targeting the right segment? What kind of product was Disney really offering? He soon discovered that 70 percent of theme park attendance was repeat business, and that more than anything else what brought people back time after time was the existence of new attractions and new novelties, not the price of the attractions. However, developing new attractions was expensive; it cost millions to develop a new ride, which was why corporate sponsorship was so important. Could he increase the price of attendance to provide the revenue to finance the new attractions and business ventures, or would this drive customers away? Going against the conventional wisdom that higher prices would reduce attendance, Eisner raised admission prices substantially. The result was only a small falloff in attendance and a huge increase in revenues. Essentially, he had discovered that Disney's theme parks had a captive audience. When he raised the entry price again (prices had now risen 45 percent in two years), revenues again dramatically increased with little falloff in attendance. In fact, the increase in theme park prices caused a 59 percent growth in company revenues and accounted for fully 94 percent of earnings growth in 1986. Pretax profits of Disneyland and Disney World rose by 38 percent by September 1985 to $266.4 million from $192.7 million a year earlier. This provided some much needed cash for expansion of Disney's attractions and for its hotel developments and was the source of the turnaround in Disney profits.

Eisner set about revamping the theme park concept to find ways of increasing Disney's revenues and regaining "Disney dollars" from other firms. On the theme park side, Eisner realized that what was needed was first, more kinds of attractions and more rides inside existing theme parks and second, additional theme parks, or "gates," which are new collections of attractions. Moreover, competition was developing at Orlando as other entertainment companies opened attractions to capitalize on tourists' presence. For example, a major water park attraction had been opened called Wet and Wild, which offered a wide variety of water rides. Also, Sea World had opened an Orlando theme park. The popularity of active, physically oriented attractions was accelerating, and Disney, recognizing the possibilities of such an attraction, planned Typhoon Lagoon to recapture revenue. This opened in 1989 to major success. It provided one reason to stay an extra day in a Disney hotel.

Disney sought new "gate" ideas to capture tourists' imagination. In this effort, it was helped by a rival, MCA, which announced that it would build a Universal Studio Tours theme park, similar to the one it already operated in southern California, near Orlando. Eisner, never slow to recognize opportunity, rushed to come out with an alternative. The result was a joint announcement by Disney and MGM that they would build a Disney-MGM Studio theme park on the Orlando site, which would open in 1989. It opened to enthusiastic crowds on time, ahead of Universal's, which was not planned to open until 1990. So popular was the studio tour attraction that Disney announced it would double its size by 1992.

The company began actively searching for a fourth gate at Disney World, and there was speculation that this might take the form of a zoological park. Disney did not ignore shopping and night-time entertainment at Disney World, in an effort to wrest tourists' dollars from the Orlando competition. At night, many of its guests were leaving Disney World to eat and play in the entertainment district of Church Street Station in Orlando. To keep patrons on the site, Disney built Pleasure Island, a huge complex of shops, bars, restaurants, discos, and nightclubs on its land to attract its guests. This has also been very successful and has provided a new dimension to the Disney experience.

Finally, the company looked at the food concession business. At Disney World and Disneyland, food concessions had previously been licensed to other companies that provided the food and paid Disney a percentage of the proceeds. Eisner realized that this was also a source of revenue loss, and as leases and agreements expired, Disney began to take over all the food operations at the theme parks. Not wanting to get into the soft drink business or photography business, however, Eisner was content to make lucrative deals with Coca-Cola and Kodak that they would be the sole suppliers of soft drinks and film products at Disney's theme parks.

Meanwhile, Eisner was not ignoring either the Magic Kingdom or the EPCOT Center at Orlando. New attractions were being constantly announced. For example, Captain EO, a $17 million 3-D music video starring Michael Jackson, was developed for the EPCOT Center at Disney World. Also, the Living Seas exhibit, sponsored by United Technologies, and the Wonders of Life, sponsored by Metropolitan Life, had been opened. Similarly, with George Lucas a new $32 million spaceship ride, Star Tours, was developed for the Disney-MGM Studios theme park. Production of a ride based on the exploits of Indiana Jones was also planned. At Anaheim, too, attractions were coming thick and fast. In 1985 Eisner announced a collaboration with George Lucas of Star Wars fame for a Star Wars attraction at Disneyland, and many additional Lucas attractions followed. In 1988 the company announced plans for Splash mountain at Disneyland, an attraction in which passengers ride replicas of hollowed out logs down huge slides populated with Disney characters. Moreover, in 1989 the company also bought Henson Associates Inc., the originators of the muppet characters, and the Muppet Theater opened at the Disney-MGM Studios to show the exploits of Kermit the Frog and Miss Piggy in glorious 3-D. Under Eisner, the repertoire of Disney's cast of characters constantly increases at its theme parks.

The Imagineering Unit At the source of the new developments in attractions and theme park development is Disney's Imagineering unit. Started by Walt Disney to actualize his ideas, the unit became responsible for all technical advances involving the design and building of Disney's new rides. However, as the company was experiencing problems in the early 1980s, consideration had even been given to closing down this unit to save money. Under Eisner, this unit's budget has been increased dramatically, and it is the source of new adventures and attractions at the theme parks. It was this unit that cooperated with George Lucas to develop the Star Wars attractions at the theme parks. It was also this unit that planned EPCOT Center, the Disney-MGM Studio tours attraction, the rides developed for Tokyo Disneyland, and the new EuroDisneyland outside Paris. Disney is selling the skills of this division to other interested parties. For example, Disney agreed to build a $40 million exhibit on the history of space flight for the Johnson Space Center in Houston, Texas.

Hotel Developments In developing new attractions, Eisner and his team had another moneymaking venture in mind. Disney's guests (it calls its visitors guests) would need somewhere to stay; moreover, if there were many attractions to see, they would need to stay for several days. Here was an opportunity to take advantage of. Disney should get into the hotel business in a big way and build luxury hotels to meet their guests' needs. At Anaheim, but principally in Orlando, this new strategy went into operation. At Disney World, Eisner got his team together to discuss expansion plans for exploiting the vast untapped land and resources in its Orlando site. Eisner realized that Disney was offering far more than eight hours of live entertainment. It could offer a total package of Disney fun whereby its guests could live inside Disney World—eating, sleeping, and breathing Disney. In the years since Disney World had been built, several luxury hotels and convention facilities had been built on the boundaries of Disney, such as the Grand Hyatt Regency Cypress Hotel and the Hilton. Eisner and Wilson planned to steal back the hotel and food dollars for Disney.

They embarked on an ambitious campaign that involved Disney's building not one but many luxury hotels on the Orlando site, each of which would offer a different kind of experience to Disney's guests. Then, each time guests returned, they could stay at a new Disney hotel location and never leave Disney World. In quick succession they opened hotels such

as the Grand Floridian Hotel and the Caribbean Beach Club and Resort, both of which, like the other Disney hotels, enjoyed occupancy rates of more than 90 percent, well above the industry average of 65 percent. They also built budget hotels such as Musicland and Sportsland. Moreover, Disney built major new convention centers and hotels to reclaim the convention trade it had let the Hyatt and Hilton corporations seize. Near EPCOT Center Disney opened four new luxury hotels, including the Dolphin Convention Hotel and the Swan Hotel, which together have more than 2,350 rooms and 200,000 square feet of convention space.

Using Wilson's skills, Disney has found the ideal formula for building hotels without putting a financial debt burden on the company. As with its films, it arranges limited partnerships to finance its hotel building program and then often brings in the large hotel chains to actually run the hotels themselves. For example, a partnership formed by Tischman Realty and Construction Company, Metropolitan Life Insurance Company, and Aoki Corporation financed these hotels. The Dolphin was run by the Sheraton Corporation, while the Swan was run by the Westin Company. Disney puts up the land and its name, and continuing this investment strategy it expected to develop 10,000 more hotel rooms by 1992. The proximity of the hotels and convention centers to Disney World and the Magic Kingdom gives the Disney operations a major advantage over its competitors. To get patrons to use Disney's hotels for longer periods, it was logical that Disney should find new ways of entertaining them, and this is just what Eisner did in finding new "gates" and attractions for his theme parks.

At Disneyland, Eisner's hotel and attraction development strategy was hampered by the fact that Disney did not own much of the land surrounding the park. It owned a small undeveloped tract of land at Disneyland, but this was just barely big enough to contain a new "gate" or hotel complex. Even if there was no room to build hotels, maybe Disney could acquire some. Under the old management team's operating philosophy, Disney had previously licensed the rights to use the Disney name for a hotel. The result was the Disneyland Hotel owned by the Wrather Corporation, a California entertainment corporation. Disney first acquired a large stake in the Wrather Corporation and then finally took over the whole operation in 1989. It then revamped the hotel to upgrade it to the luxury class, carrying on the Orlando strategy.

As a part of this deal, however, Disney also gained control of the Wrather Corporation's Long Beach entertainment complex, which consisted of the liner the Queen Mary, run as a hotel, together with Howard Hughes's Spruce Goose Aeroplane, the largest ever built, and an entertainment village. Disney revamped the liner as a luxury hotel complex, and then Eisner realized that maybe this complex could become Disney's second California "gate," one that tourists could stop at on their way to or from Disneyland. Moreover, there was all the revenue currently going to Sea World and Knottsberry Farm to compete for. In 1990 Disney announced a proposal to develop the Long Beach site as the center for a Disney Sea theme park which would be a water-based attraction. It would contain the largest aquarium in the world, a glass cage in which tourists could go down among the sharks, and many other water-oriented rides and attractions such as Captain Nemo's submarine from *20,000 Leagues Under the Sea*, another Imagineering unit project.

Eisner also began to consider ideas for new theme parks abroad. Disney already had participated in the planning of a Disneyland outside Tokyo, Japan. This had opened in April 1983 and had been wildly successful. However, in this venture Disney has taken no financial stake and, pursuing its old strategy, had licensed its name to a group of Japanese investors in return for 10 percent of the gate receipts and 5 percent of other proceeds. This had cost Disney much loss in profit. Now Eisner was actively considering the idea for a Disney theme park somewhere in Europe to capture the vast European market. After much planning and upfront negotiations with several European countries, in December 1985 Eisner announced the decision to build what became a $2.1 billion EuroDisney theme park and resort complex, modeled on the Disney World concept, about 20 miles east of Paris in a suburb called Marne-La-Vallee. This opened in 1991. Disney owns 49 percent of the park, the other 51 percent being held by a company consisting of French and European investors. Disney receives fees for operating the park and royalties on admissions, rides, food, and other operations, but the French company controls the entire project. Plans were for a Disney World kind of complex where, along with the Magic Kingdom, there will be Disney hotels, shopping centers, golf courses,

and convention facilities to ensure that Disney is capturing all the dollars in related entertainment activities. In short, the whole successful Eisner formula.

The result of these developments on Disney theme park revenues can be seen in Table 2. At the same time as Eisner and his team were revamping their theme park strategy, he was working on plans for a turnaround of the motion picture and television business.

Competition in the Theme Park Industry Disney is by far the biggest of the theme park companies and the most profitable. However, as it has been expanding its "gates" and attractions, it has run into the competition. The new Disney Sea attraction is a prime rival for Sea World, and in California and Florida Sea World will have to compete against an expanding Disney presence into water-related entertainments. The opening of Typhoon Lagoon hurt Sea World's Orlando operation, for example. In addition, Disney has been having a running battle with MCA, the owner of the Universal Studio Tours. Sidney Sheinberg, the president of MCA, claims that his company was the originator of the idea of the Orlando studio tours attraction but that Disney took the idea and ran with it. Competition between the Disney-MGM Studio tour and the Universal will heat up in the coming years. Moreover, after announcing that Disney would build a studio tour on its EuroDisney site, MCA announced that it, too, would open one in Paris or London. Other companies in the industry are those such as Six Flags and Busch Gardens, and Disney's new Orlando "gate" might bring it into direct competition with them. Moreover, Disney's huge expansion into hotels had brought it up against the major hotel companies, and competition could be expected to be fierce there if ever there was a falloff in demand for hotel rooms.

Motion Pictures and Television

When Eisner took over Disney in 1984, Disney executives were just apologizing for the success of their new smash hit movie *Splash,* because even though it was produced by their separate Touchstone label, it was not in the tradition of Walt Disney family entertainment. Eisner had no such problems recognizing that times had changed and that the family of 1985 was not the family of 1965. As head of children's entertainment at ABC, he had recognized the

TABLE 2

Consolidated Statement of Income (in millions, except per share data)

Year Ended September 30	1989	1988	1987
Revenues			
Theme parks and resorts	$2,595.4	$2,042.0	$1,834.2
Filmed entertainment	1,587.6	1,149.2	875.6
Consumer products	411.3	247.0	167.0
	4,594.3	3,438.2	2,876.8
Costs and Expenses			
Theme parks and resorts	1,810.0	1,477.2	1,285.3
Filmed entertainment	1,331.1	962.9	745.0
Consumer products	224.2	113.3	69.7
	3,365.3	2,553.4	2,100.0
Operating Income			
Theme parks and resorts	785.4	564.8	548.9
Filmed entertainment	256.5	186.3	130.6
Consumer products	187.1	133.7	97.3
	1,229.0	884.8	776.8
Corporate Expenses (Income)			
General and administrative	119.6	96.0	70.3
Interest expense	23.9	5.8	29.1
Investment and interest income	(67.4)	(58.9)	(49.0)
	76.1	42.9	50.4
Income From Continuing Operations Before Income Taxes	1,152.9	841.9	726.4
Income taxes	449.6	319.9	334.1
Income From Continuing Operations	703.3	522.0	392.3
Discontinued operations, net			52.4
Net Income	$703.3	$522.0	$444.7
Earnings per Share			
Continuing operations	$5.10	$3.80	$2.85
Discontinued operations			.38
	$5.10	$3.80	$3.23
Average number of common and common equivalent shares outstanding	138.0	137.4	137.8

Source: The Walt Disney Company, *Annual Report,* 1989.

changing trends in viewing habits and had understood that new definitions of family entertainment were possible in the 1980s. Later, at Paramount, he had been involved in many of that studio's huge successes. It was he who had seen the possibility for projects such as *Raiders of the Lost Ark, Airplane,* and *Terms of Endearment,* all of which became blockbuster movies.[4]

At Disney, Eisner used this experience and with Jeff Katzenberg, the creative head of Disney's movie division, began to fashion Disney's new strategy. Katzenberg was also a Paramount veteran, where he was known as the "golden retriever" for his ability to sniff out just the right scripts.[5] He also is a workaholic who makes hundreds of two-minute phone calls a week to producers, directors, and so forth. At Paramount he was attributed with the phrase, "If you don't come in on Saturday, don't bother to come in on Sunday."[6]

By 1984 Disney had only a 4 percent share of box office revenues for its movies. Its movie division was losing money and had become a drain on the company's resources. The problem facing the two men was how to turn around the division. On the financial side, to lessen the burden on Disney and to reduce the fear of failure, Eisner negotiated an agreement to raise money to finance Touchstone's movie productions with Silver Screens Management Inc. The idea was that Silver Screens would sell limited partnerships to outside investors that would put up the money to finance Disney's movies. In return, investors would receive a percentage of the movie's subsequent revenues. By 1985, $193 million had been raised to finance fourteen new movies.

With the financing in place, Eisner and Katzenberg moved to change Disney's strategy. Luring talented people away from Paramount, Eisner quickly approved *Down and Out in Beverly Hills,* which grossed an impressive $62 million. He then focused on signing stars who were then not box office draw, such as Bette Midler and Richard Dreyfus, in order to keep costs low, and he added films to the production schedule that were vehicles for their talents. Disney boasts that while other studios spend $16 million per movie, it spends about $11 million; low cost is the hallmark of Eisner's strategy. Such films as *Stakeout* and *Outrageous Fortune* were the result. By 1987 Disney had captured 14 percent of the $4.2 billion movie market, and the turnaround was clear as its film operations became the fastest-growing part of its operations. By 1987 Disney had turned the $10 million loss in 1984 into a huge profit.

He then turned to the next part of his movie strategy, which involved deals for distribution of the movies to television and videocassette sales. Disney had always distributed its own movies to movie theater chains through its distribution company, a subsidiary called Buena Vista Distributions,

and had in this way captured the profit rather than give it to distributors. In 1985 the company formed a new television division and hired yet another Paramount executive to orchestrate the sale of movies to television networks and to handle video-cassette sales.[7] In 1986 Viacom's Showtime movie channel signed an exclusive agreement to buy cable television rights for movies produced through the Touchstone division through 1990.[8] The deal started with *Down and Out in Beverly Hills* and involved more than fifty movies. Although very expensive for the movie channel, Disney was reported to have received $3 million to $5 million per film when the deal was signed, and both parties have benefited from it. Eisner also went ahead with the videocassette sales. He decided to release one classic a year, and in 1986, for example, 1 million copies of *Sleeping Beauty* were sold. Small wonder Disney's stock price increased by five times between 1983 and 1986. Disney is also vigorously expanding foreign sales of videocassettes.

On the television front, Disney also went through a major turnaround. Eisner moved quickly to exploit Disney's resources. He arranged for syndication of the twenty-nine years of the Wonderful World of Disney material, cartoons, and feature films on the new networks emerging with the advent of cable television. Three packages of material were put up for sale in 1987, which helped to double film revenues. This market had previously been ignored. He also moved to make more product for the small screen. For the adult audience, the hit series *Golden Girls* was developed; he also arranged for a new format for *Siskel & Ebert at the Movies.* Eisner then brought back the Disney Sunday Movie, introducing it himself, and arranged for the development of *Duck Tales, Gummie Bears,* and *The Little Mermaid* new animation series to take advantage of Disney's animation skills. These cartoons shown on afternoon television and then the Disney Channel have proved immensely popular. There were failures, however. For example, two series introduced in 1986, *The Ellen Burstyn Show* and *Sidekicks,* were quickly abandoned. Meanwhile, under the new management, the Disney Channel was doing somewhat better. Competition for subscribers is fierce in the pay-TV industry, but Disney had made some headway. Its subscriber base grew 27 percent to almost 3.2 million by 1986 and 4 million by 1988.

Then, in 1989 came another move in the television market. Disney acquired KHU-TV, a Los Angeles television station, and renamed it KCAL-TV. This takeover gave it a wholly owned distribution outlet for the products of its studios, so it can capture some of the value that is currently being earned by its end users. It had previously tried, but failed, to acquire the 360 screen Mann theater chain bought by Gulf & Western and a New York television station that MCA bought. So expansion into the television station market and movie theater market appears possible. They also approached CBS to buy CBS Records but were spurned by the board, which eventually sold it to the Sony Corporation. As Eisner said, "We are going to be awfully conservative in what we go after, but if there was something out there that could add value to this company, we're going to go for it."[9] The search for new assets is part of Eisner's strategy to reduce its heavy dependence on theme parks and movies for its operating revenues in the future.

By 1987 Walt Disney was number two in share of box office revenues, with 14 percent of revenues after Paramount. Twenty-two of the twenty-three films produced by Disney have made a profit, far higher than the industry ratio of about three in ten. Then came such hits as *Three Men and a Baby,* which grossed more than $160 million; *Good Morning Vietnam,* with $110 million; and *Cocktail,* with Tom Cruise. It also introduced two more animation movies, *Who Framed Roger Rabbit?* which cost $38 million, thus departing from the Disney formula of keeping costs low; and *Oliver and Company.* As a result of these films, Disney took the box office lead from Paramount in 1988 with 22 percent of revenues through Labor Day, the end of the summer film season.

At the beginning of 1989, Walt Disney established a third motion picture company, called Hollywood Pictures, to continue the success story established by Touchstone. It gave charge of this company to Ricardo Mestres, former president of production at Touchstone, and a mega performer in his own right. To finance the intended twenty-four to twenty-eight movies a year, another silver screen partnership was established, which raised $600 million to fund future Disney films. Clearly, Disney was expecting big things from its three divisions. By the end of 1989, expectations were fulfilled; Disney was the market leader with almost 20 percent of box office revenues as a result of more successes such as *The Little Mermaid* and *Oliver and Company.* The change in the revenues and profits of the movie division is given in Table 3.

TABLE 3

Consolidated Balance Sheet (in millions)

September 30	1989	1988
Assets		
Cash	$380.8	$428.0
Marketable securities	662.3	668.6
Receivables	908.5	561.5
Merchandise inventories	224.3	159.9
Film costs	443.3	211.0
Theme parks, resorts, and other property, at cost		
Attractions, buildings and equipment	4,143.3	3,322.5
Accumulated depreciation	(1,217.3)	(1,065.2)
	2,926.0	2,257.3
Projects in progress	407.4	511.1
Land	63.9	53.3
	3,397.3	2,821.7
Other assets	640.7	258.2
	$6,657.2	$5,108.9
Liabilities and Stockholders' Equity		
Accounts payable and other accrued liabilities	$1,011.4	$698.7
Income taxes payable	250.9	204.3
Borrowings	860.6	435.5
Unearned royalty and other advances	912.7	823.3
Deferred income taxes	577.6	587.8
Stockholders' equity		
Common stock, $.10 par value		
Authorized—300.00 million shares		
Outstanding—135.3 million shares and 133.2 million shares	392.8	349.6
Retained earnings	2,651.2	2,009.7
	3,044.0	2,359.3
	$6,657.2	$5,108.9

Source: The Walt Disney Company, *Annual Report,* 1989.

Consumer Products Division

The final area that Eisner turned his attention to was improving revenues from the licensing of the Disney brand name to firms that wished to manufacture and sell products using the Disney characters. Eisner's intention might be summed up as saying he would like to see a mouse or duck on every T-shirt, every wrist, and every toy or piece of baby equipment in every home in every country in the world. He started by developing deals with major manufacturers and retailers, signing an agreement with Mattel, the biggest U.S. toy manufacturer, to sell Disney-brand infant and preschool toys worldwide. In 1987 Disney signed a ten-year agreement with Sears to develop clothing and toys using certain Disney characters. By 1988 Disney had negotiated more than 3,000 agreements with companies to manufacture more than 14,000 Disney-licensed products.

Meanwhile, in 1987 the company announced plans for a large-scale expansion into retailing stores that will sell nothing but Disney products. The Disney stores will market products produced by Disney's manufacturers, so that as in the case of Disney's entry into the television station market, Disney will reap the rewards from selling its own products. These stores sell videotapes of Disney's films, children's clothing, toys, and the whole Disney paraphernalia at premium prices. Given the ability to charge a premium price, each store is proving very profitable, and malls are fighting to attract a store.[10]

In 1988 Disney paid $52 million to buy Childcraft Education Corporation, which sells educational toys and play equipment through direct mail. This move complements Disney's mail-order, catalog sales operation, which sends out more than 6 million catalogs a year and has expanded product offerings by more than 50 percent. Given its move into mail-order and store operations, it seems as if Disney is looking to become the Sears of the entertainment business. One more benefit to Disney from these store and catalog sales is the intangible brand-name loyalty it creates for other Disney ventures. The stores are a marketing vehicle for Disney; they open up the Disney Company to the public and invite attendance at its theme parks and hotels.[11]

International sales of Disney products are extremely important to the company. For example, every year Japanese consumers buy more than $1 billion worth of Disney-brand products. In Italy the Mickey Mouse comic book, *Topolino*, sells 70,000 copies a month, and when Disney took over publishing the comic itself, it made an extra $15 million a year in profits. Videocassette sales and records are major revenue earners for Disney worldwide. In 1989 Eisner pointed to the internationalization of all Disney franchises as the source of the massive gains in the revenues of the consumer products and home video operations.[12]

Another expanding dimension of Disney's business is publishing. While Disney licenses Mickey Mouse Tales and Duck Tales to Welch Publishing, it is planning the publication of *Disney Adventure Digest* to be the official magazine of *Disney Afternoon*, two hours each weekday afternoon of syndicated programming scheduled for the fall of 1990. This has a planned circulation of 100,000. Many more magazine opportunities are being explored, as are books to accompany Disney's movies. For example, many books were planned around Disney's successful *Dick Tracy* movie in 1990, and publishing provides new opportunities for Disney to exploit the linkages between its products. This division will also mastermind international publication and sales of Disney's books and magazines, a market that is likely to increase with the opening of EuroDisney. In 1990 Disney sold more than 500 million books and comics worldwide.[13]

Another venture for Disney involves selling its organizational culture, which is centered on providing high-quality customer service. Disney University in Orlando puts all new recruits through a three-day program designed to bring them into the Disney way of doing things. They learn the history of Disney, its mission, and its emphasis on courtesy to customers to maximize visitors' satisfaction. This is very important to Disney, given that more than 70 percent of visitors are repeats. New employees learn the Disney language in which employees are known as cast members, visitors as guests, and employees are said to be on stage when they are working and off stage when they are not. Now Disney is selling its expertise and its techniques to major companies. So far, more than 3,000 executives from more than 1,200 companies have attended the two-day seminar Disney offers called Traditions in order to learn Disney's techniques so that they can increase the quality of customer service in their own companies. One of the central features of the Disney approach is to empower employees so that they try to solve problems themselves as and when they occur rather than turn for help.[14] According to Disney, the secret to Disney's success is "pixie dust," which is a combination of training, communication, and care.

Disney's Future

As a result of these developments, by 1989 sales had jumped from $1.46 billion in 1984 to $4.59 billion. Net profit rose from $97.8 million to $703.3 million, and earnings per share increased more than ten times during the same period. Everything Disney is doing is designed to capitalize on the incredible progress that it has made. While the annual increase in profit was 46 percent in the 1980s Eisner and Wells have vowed to increase profits by an average of 20 percent a year in the 1990s. To do so, they are constantly expanding the range and scope of Disney's activities as well as building on the base they have established. A new Disneyland theme park somewhere in Asia is in preparation, and a new studio tours park next to the EuroDisneyland is planned, as well as a new theme park in southern California. More new attractions based on its more recent successes are planned, including one designed around Dick Tracy. Similarly, Eisner has announced that Disney will have thirty hotels with more than 26,000 rooms by 1995.

Industry analysts wonder whether or not Eisner and his team can maintain the same growth rate and even whether the company may be headed for a fall. Because most of Disney's revenue comes first from its theme parks and second from its film operations, they wonder whether the pace can be maintained. For example, they point out that a recession or an increase in the price of gas could rapidly affect theme park attendance, since the price of airplane seats and auto travel would increase. They also point out that historically no movie studio has been able to maintain an unbroken string of successes, and they wonder whether the movie division might be in for a rough ride in the future.

They also wonder about the wisdom of Disney's current projects and the direction Michael Eisner's Disney company is taking. After the incredible successes Eisner and his team have achieved, critics claim that the conceit of Disney executives is huge and that they believe they can do no wrong. Eisner has been called an egomaniac, albeit by his archcritic Sidney Sheinberg, the president of rival MCA, and is said to be in search of ever greater opportunities for the expansion of Disney's empire. Already the largest entertainment company in the world, it is now exercising its muscle as it seeks to enlarge its share of the television station market. However, critics wonder whether such expansion is wise.

Since Disney can already sell its existing film products to the networks, does it need the added burden of owning television stations? In 1990 Eisner was looking around for new acquisitions to add to its Los Angeles station, and CBS was mentioned as a possible takeover target. Critics ask whether this would add value to Disney or to CBS.

In 1990 Disney announced that it would open a new record division, called Hollywood Records, to produce records for the general public, not just the Disney audience. This move will bring it into direct competition with huge record companies such as CBS Records, which Disney bid for but lost in the very competitive record business. The huge expansion into the hotel business is justified if occupancy rates stay more than 90 percent, but is the resort market becoming saturated with too many luxury hotels and conference centers being built? Any downturn in the vacation market for whatever cause might put severe pressure on hotel operations. Against opposition from his own team, Eisner also embarked on the concept of a Disney fast-food restaurant. Offering a wide array of food, they would seek to exploit the Disney cartoon characters in a restaurant format. However, this is a relatively new business for Disney. Although Disney operates restaurants in its own theme parks, it would be entering the highly competitive $65 billion fast-food industry currently dominated by big chains such as McDonald's and Burger King. Does Disney have the core skills to compete in this market?

Moreover, while guests may like to eat, sleep, and breathe Disney on their vacations, do they want to do so 365 days a year? Is there a danger of overexposure as children wear Disney clothes, read Disney books, watch Disney television programs, go to sleep in Disney beds playing with Disney toys, and then eat Disney food, too? Will there be a reaction as people turn from Disney to new forms of excitement and fantasy? However, where would they go? Disney has co-opted George Lucas and his characters; bought the muppets; and, in films such as *Dick Tracy*, captured more characters. Is there a place for people to run? For now, it seems that Michael Eisner can force the golden goose to keep on laying golden eggs, but if the environment changes, if the film division falls on hard times, or if his new projects fail to meet expectations, the supply of eggs might stop.

ENDNOTES

1. L. Gartley and E. Leebron, *Walt Disney: A Guide to References and Resources* (Boston: G. K. Hall, 1979).
2. Walt Disney Productions' 1983 Annual Report.
3. *Wall Street Journal*, August 9, 1985, p. 14.
4. "Michael Eisner's Hit Parade," *Business Week,* February 1, 1988.
5. "Disney's Magic," *Business Week,* March 9, 1987.
6. *Time,* April 25, 1988.
7. *Wall Street Journal,* March 16, 1985.
8. *Wall Street Journal,* April 25, 1986.
9. *Business Week,* March 9, 1987.
10. *Wall Street Journal,* December 23, 1987.
11. *Advertising Age,* November 28, 1988, p. 46.
12. Walt Disney Company's 1989 Annual Report.
13. *Folio,* April 1990, p. 57.
14. *Marketing News,* January 8, 1990.

The Walt Disney Company, 1995—2005: Part Two

This case was prepared by Gareth R. Jones, Texas A&M University.

After a long struggle with analysts and board members who were increasingly critical of his performance as CEO of Disney during the last decade, and a bitter fight with Roy Disney, a major shareholder, Michael Eisner announced he would step down as its CEO in 2006 when his contract expired. While the board searched for a successor in 2005, one candidate being his hand-picked successor Robert Iger, president and chief operating officer of Disney, Eisner pondered the events that had first brought him to popular acclaim as one of the most successful CEOs in America, but who was now regarded by many as a "lame duck" CEO whose reign was coming to an end.

Disney's Growing Entertainment Empire

Michael Eisner, with his then top management team of Frank Wells and Gary Wilson, began the 1990s with the same strategy they had previously developed—to build Disney's core strengths in the three areas of entertainment and recreation, motion pictures, and video and consumer products in order to increase the value of Disney's franchises and brand

name. As a reward for all these efforts, the Walt Disney Company made Michael Eisner one of the highest-paid executives in history. In 1993 alone Disney paid Michael Eisner $203,010,590 in salary and stock options as a reward for taking Disney's market value from $2.2 billion in 1984, when Eisner took over, to $22.7 billion in 1993. This huge salary was more than any other CEO of a public corporation had made in a single year at that time, and for many CEOs in an entire career.

Entertainment and Recreation

In the entertainment area, Disney's top managers began by enlarging the size and variety of its theme parks and other entertainment properties. The number of attractions offered by its three Orlando properties—Disney World, EPCOT, and Disney MGM—was increased to seventy-eight in the 1990s. Moreover, three water parks were now in operation together with the Disney Vacation Club, Discovery Island, and the Disney Boardwalk. These properties extended Disney's hotel, restaurant, and shopping empire.

In July 1995, Disney finally announced that it would build a $500 million zoological park as its fourth property in Orlando, but it would be a zoo with a difference. Called Disney's Wild Animal Kingdom, the five hundred-acre park is larger than any of Disney's parks around the world. It has three main areas, showcasing animals that are live, extinct, and mythical. For example, the live animal section of the park features large herds of African animals such as elephants and giraffes in a natural setting; the extinct section of the park features Disney's famous moving models (animatronics) of creatures such as dinosaurs and flying lizards; and the mythical section will feature creatures such as dragons and unicorns. Eisner hoped that the new property would attract both new and repeat visitors to its parks. Repeat visitors now have another reason to return to Orlando. When both new and repeat visitors do come, they now have a reason to spend an extra day in the Disney empire, increasing the revenues that Disney receives from its hotels, catering, and shopping businesses.

The EuroDisney Disaster Some of Disney's entertainment ventures proved less than successful, however. EuroDisney, which opened in April 1992, proved to be a financial disaster through the 1990s. By 1996, Disney, which owns a 39 percent equity interest in the park, had lost more than $500 million on the venture. There were many reasons for EuroDisney's failure. First, Eisner and his team did not explore European customers' needs in enough detail, particularly the needs of its French customers. Modeling EuroDisney on its Orlando property, Disney built six theme hotels with a total of fifty-two hundred rooms and a huge entertainment center offering a full complement of shops and restaurants around its European park. However, it found that Europeans do not have the free-spending ways of their American counterparts and like to make their vacation dollars go much further. Europeans did not like Disney's high prices; they stayed fewer days in the hotels, tried to find less expensive accommodations farther away, and even bought less food and Disney merchandise. Also, fewer visitors came to the park than expected, and, in particular, French citizens did not provide the stream of revenues that Disney expected. Moreover, many Europeans found it not much more expensive to vacation in Orlando than in France; British and German tourists, in particular, flocked to Florida to enjoy its warm climate. Many critics said that Disney would have done better to locate its park in Spain, somewhere on the Costa Del Sol, where the climate is much more temperate than in France, where it becomes cold and wet in the winter.

EuroDisney's stock price plunged in 1993 and 1994 as investors fled. In 1994, Eisner authorized emergency financing to keep the park afloat. In 1995, a Saudi Arabian prince purchased a large stake in the park and, together with Disney, injected some much needed funding. By 1996, the park was showing a small profit after it had adjusted its prices and policies to match the tastes of its European customers.

One entertainment venture that Disney finalized was a revitalization of West 42nd Street in New York City. The ambitious venture turned a near red-light district into a huge entertainment complex full of games, theaters, hotels, shops, and restaurants to attract tourists to New York, which provided $35 million in financing to condemn and clear the buildings so that Disney and other entertainment companies such as Viacom could create a state-of-the-art entertainment complex. (Disney's cost was over $350 million.)

Movies

Disney's movie division also started off the 1990s in full swing. Its Walt Disney Pictures, Touchstone Pictures, Hollywood Pictures, and Buena Vista Pictures movie divisions all began producing a full array of pictures for distribution. Disney also acquired Miramax Pictures, a small company known for its production of high-quality, adult-oriented pictures, for about $60 million. While much of Miramax's movie output is critically acclaimed, Disney received considerable flack when Miramax began to make controversial films such as *Priest*, whose content has nothing in common with traditional Disney themes.

One blockbuster movie put out by Walt Disney Pictures in the early 1990s was *The Lion King*, Disney's highest-grossing animated movie ever. The success of this movie extended into the videocassette market where it sold more than 60 million copies, and then on into the consumer product areas, where Lion King games, clothing, books, and so on generated record profits for Disney. A Lion King attraction was also opened at Disneyland to take advantage of the movie's success and a Lion King theater production has been touring the United States and Europe ever since with great success.

The success of *The Lion King* convinced Disney's executives that they needed to release one new animated movie each year to keep the revenues flowing into the movie division (and eventually into the consumer products division, too). In 1995 Disney released *Pocahontas*, and in 1996, it released *The Hunchback of Notre Dame*, both accompanied by a flood of movie-related Disney merchandise to capitalize on the anticipated popularity of these movies. These movies did not have the blockbuster appeal of *Little Simba*, however, and have not generated the huge stream of revenues that have kept the movie division's profits surging.

In fact, by 1996 Disney's movie division as a whole had run into hard times. Touchstone and Hollywood Pictures produced a string of failures including *White Squall* and *Before and After*, and Eisner announced in 1996 that Disney would close Hollywood Pictures to consolidate movie production in the other divisions. As other movie studios have discovered, Disney learned that repeating major successes year after year is difficult. Also, in common with other studios, Disney has experienced cost increases, as major stars such as Tom Cruise and Jim Carrey demand $20 million a picture. As a result, Disney's former low-cost strength in movie production largely disappeared.

In fact, by 1996 most movie studios were beginning to learn that, collectively, they were making too many movies per year to be profitable. It became increasingly clear that two kinds of movies were usually the most successful: expensive blockbuster movies backed by advertising campaigns amounting to $20 million to $40 million, which could generate $200 million to $500 million in theater revenues worldwide, and inexpensive movies costing about $13 million to $15 million, backed by modest $3 million to $5 million advertising budgets that could find a niche and be profitable. What was costing Disney and the other studios a fortune was the stuck-in-the-middle movies in the $30 million to $40 million range, which often lacked true star appeal and still required a $10 million to $20 million advertising effort. When these movies flopped, as they often did, they ate up the profits from the blockbuster movies, which each studio desperately needed at least one of every year to remain profitable.

Disney, as with other movie companies, announced in 1996 that it would produce fewer movies per year in the future and focus more on the production of the two successful kinds of movie previously described. It also announced a return to its cost-cutting ways and expressed renewed support for Miramax, which specialized in finding and producing the low-budget, niche movies that often prove to be very profitable.

Home Video

Inspired by the early success of its home video releases, throughout the 1990s Disney has forged ahead with promoting this division's business. In 1995, Disney's domestic home video division reached phenomenal sales of $2 billion in revenues, up from just $1 billion in revenues in 1992. Contributing to this increase was *The Lion King*, which sold 30 million copies in 1995 alone. Even *Snow White* sold 25 million copies. Disney then started to release from its library more movies, such as *Sleeping Beauty* or *Dumbo*, that are perennial favorites. In 1996, the introduction of the new DVD digital movie format opened up a new revenue channel for Disney because customers now had to buy their favorite movies in the new format if they wished to obtain the unsurpassed picture and sound quality that the new DVD players provide.

By 1995, the Disney Channel had become the second most popular pay movie channel in the United States after HBO. Increasingly, Disney used the channel to advertise its new movie offerings, such as *The Hunchback of Notre Dame*, and all the new happenings at its theme parks.

Consumer Products

Disney's shopping empire also expanded rapidly in the 1990s. By 1995, Disney had opened 429 specialty Disney Stores worldwide (including 26 in Europe and 15 in the Asia-Pacific area). It also opened a chain of Disney boutiques called the Walt Disney Gallery, which sold high-priced, premium products such as cartoon lithographs or $1,000 reproduction Disney characters to wealthy customers. These boutiques were to be attached to existing Disney stores. Disney also started a catalog mail-order business to reach customers that are not served by Disney stores (which tend to be located only in large, prestigious malls in major cities). These catalogs offer a representative set of its merchandise and also allow customers to book complete Disney vacation packages, often at a discount.

Disney's publishing interests also increased sharply, and it now published more than 500 million books a year worldwide through its Mouse Books, Disney Press, and Hyperion Books titles. These books were intended to publicize its new features, attractions, and movies, which extends the popularity of the traditional cast of Disney characters.

Management Issues

The top management team that has been building Disney's entertainment empire changed significantly during the 1990s. In the spring of 1994, Frank Wells, Michael Eisner's trusted president, was killed in a helicopter accident. This was a major blow to Eisner, well known for the direct, hands-on way he managed the Disney empire and holds his top managers to account. Because of his trust in Wells, Eisner had been able to leave many aspects of Disney's business in Wells's hands. Now he had to manage the whole empire. To compound the matter, Eisner's move to centralize decision making came at a time when he was diagnosed with heart problems, and in 1994, he entered the hospital for quadruple bypass heart surgery.

Although successful, many analysts began to wonder how long Eisner could remain in control at Disney, especially after one executive, Jeffrey Katzenberg, launched a major move in 1994 to obtain more power at Disney. Katzenberg was the creative force behind Disney's major animated movies. It was he who had orchestrated the success of *Aladdin* and *The Lion King*, and he had major input into other movies such as *Beauty and the Beast* and *Pocahontas*. Katzenberg lobbied strongly for Eisner to name him president of the Disney Company, a position from which he could hope to become its CEO if and when Eisner departed. Eisner would not name him to this position, not wanting a powerful rival in his weakened state, some analysts said, and not believing Katzenberg was the right person to head a company such as Disney, others said. A major rift between the two men occurred, and Katzenberg resigned from Disney in 1994, leaving a major gap in Disney's creative leadership. Many other executives followed, including Richard Frank, the head of Disney's television operations.

Katzenberg then joined with David Geffen, a charismatic Hollywood mogul, and Steven Spielberg, the well-known movie producer, to form a new movie studio, Dream Works, which with $2 billion in cash began to produce a whole series of movies (live action and animated) to compete with Disney and the other major studios. Katzenberg recruited several top Disney animators and other executives for his new studio with the intention that Dream Works would become a major competitor to Disney in the years ahead. In 1996, after several rounds of failed negotiations, Katzenberg launched a $300 million lawsuit against Disney, arguing that this was the money he was due under his contract with Disney, which specified that he was to receive a percentage of the royalties associated with each of the creative efforts he was involved with, such as *The Lion King*. Katzenberg finally won his lawsuit and reportedly received a settlement of around the $300 million figure.

Recovering from surgery and under intense pressure to find someone to help him manage the Disney empire, Eisner focused on Michael Ovitz, the head of Creative Arts Agency, the agency that handled the careers of many major stars, such as Tom Cruise and Barbra Streisand, as well as sports figures, such as famous basketball and tennis players. Ovitz had a huge reputation in Hollywood as a consummate deal maker and the person that everybody had to know. In 1995, Eisner made him a lucrative offer to join Disney as its president (an offer that included over $1 million in stock options in Disney and a severance package worth over $100 million), more or less assuring Ovitz that he would be picked as Disney's next CEO. Eisner put Ovitz in charge of overseeing Disney's many divisions, in particular the movie division, and Disney's biggest money spinner. Together with a senior executive vice president and chief financial officer, Stephen F. Bollenbach (who left to become CEO of Hilton in 1996) spent 1995 analyzing all aspects of the Disney Company's operations to create a new blueprint of the company's future. Together they planned a strategy that was to take Disney to the top of the entertainment world: the acquisition of Capital Cities/ABC Inc.

The Disney-Capital Cities/ABC Merger

On July 31, 1995, Michael Eisner astonished the entertainment world when, together with Capital Cities/ABC Inc.'s CEO, Thomas S. Murphy, he announced that Disney would acquire that company for $19 billion in order to make Disney "the world's premier entertainment company, to protect and build upon the Disney name and franchise, and to preserve and foster quality, imagination and guest service." Capital Cities/ABC owned one of the three biggest television networks in the United States, owns 10 television stations that reach 25 percent of the U.S. viewing public, has 224 affiliated television stations, owns 22 radio stations in large cities, and has a network of 344 radio stations. It also owned 80 percent of ESPN and ESPN2, 37.5 percent of A&E television network, 50 percent of Lifetime television—all well-known "branded channels." Furthermore, it had interests in several international television companies, owned 6 newspapers, and had extensive publishing interests, including weekly newspapers and shopping guides.

EXHIBIT 1

Walt Disney's Revenue Breakdown, 1995

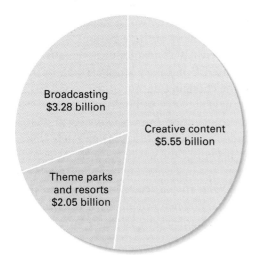

Broadcasting
$3.28 billion

Creative content
$5.55 billion

Theme parks
and resorts
$2.05 billion

After the acquisition, Disney redefined its three main areas of business as creative content (which includes all its movie and television production operations, all licensing activities involving the Disney name and characters, and consumer products), theme parks and resorts, and broadcasting. The revenues that Disney derived from each of these three areas in 1995 in relation to each other are shown in Exhibit 1.

Using its new business area breakdown, 1995 broadcasting revenues were at $3.28 billion, which exceeded the contributions of Disney's theme parks and resorts (making it less dependent on this area) but were still only half of what it obtained from its creative content business area. Moreover, for 1995 operating income for the creative content group was down 37 percent to $262 million, while operating income for broadcasting was flat at $198 million, and income from theme parks rose significantly by 11 percent to $182 million because of good attendance. The reason for the decline in profit of the creative content group was the disappointing sales of *Pocahontas* videotapes compared with *The Lion King* in the year before; several movie flops such as *White Squall, Before and After,* and *Mr. Wrong;* and major write-offs in film development for failed or abandoned ongoing projects.

In championing the merger, Eisner and Ovitz spoke enthusiastically about the synergies that could be obtained. For example, in the future, Disney television programming would be offered primarily through its

own network and then subsequently rerun on the Disney Channel. Moreover, Disney would have a secure outlet for all its new television productions, even marginal ones, in an environment in which major networks had an increasing number of content providers from which to choose. In addition, Disney could feature its new movies on television specials, similar to the one that aired on ABC in 1996 showing the making of *The Hunchback of Notre Dame.* Given the high costs of advertising new movies, the possession of its own network would allow it to publicize its movies at less cost than other studios, cost savings that would be substantial in the years ahead. Finally, Disney's movie library could be shown at low cost over the years on ABC television, and the resources of the new company could even be combined to create new digital cable television channels to strengthen the package of television channels that Disney already owned (such as the Disney Channel, ESPN, and A&E).

As in the case of the other major mergers that occurred between entertainment giants Viacom and Paramount, and Time Warner and Turner, the claimed rational for the merger was that it linked entertainment production with the means of its distribution (by television, videocassette, and so forth). By 1995, he and other top entertainment executives were arguing that in the future companies needed to be involved in both of these sides of the business. Disney's top managers claimed that by acquiring Capital Cities/ABC they had secured Disney's future as the entertainment leader and given it the platform from which it could dominate the industry.

Many critics of the merger existed, however. Some industry analysts questioned the price tag of $19 billion that Disney had paid. They pointed out that Capital Cities/ABC was at the peak of its profitability when Disney made its offer because it was enjoying record advertising revenues (which are the main source of profitability of television and radio broadcasting). Its CEO, Tom Murphy, recognizing the premium that Disney was offering for the network, was therefore happy to jump at the Disney offer. Other critics also argued that the synergies Eisner claimed would result from the merger could easily have been achieved through a strategic alliance between the two companies over such issues as programming content and advertising revenues. In other words, the two companies could just as easily have entered into a written contract with each other to achieve these gains from cooperation. For example, Disney formed an alliance with Coca-Cola to promote that company's soft drinks in its operations and in 1996 formed an alliance with McDonald's under which the latter would be given the rights for ten years to use new Disney movies to promote foods in its restaurants. Disney did not have to merge with these companies to obtain synergies.

Critics even argued that the merger was unnecessary and would lock Disney into an unprofitable situation because the Big Three television networks only attracted 40 percent of the viewing audience by 1996 and this figure was falling because of the proliferation of new cable television channels and the increasing popularity of the Internet as a media resource. Disney's executives responded that by providing their new network with innovative Disney programming they would be able to increase its viewing audience. Moreover, as discussed previously, Disney could create new digital cable channels, opening up another major source of revenue. Finally some critics argued that Eisner was driven by ego, the desire to become the head of the world's biggest entertainment company at a time when other large entertainment companies, such as Viacom and Time Warner, were expanding their empires. Disney would be able to continue to grow its revenues at a fast pace as a result of the merger, they argued, but would its profits also be growing?

Events at ABC

Whatever the merits of each side of the argument, in 1995 the ABC network saw a precipitous drop in its share of the viewing audience as its prime-time ratings plunged. These ratings are vital because they determine how much the ABC network and its owned and affiliated television stations can charge advertisers. Eisner bought ABC when its ratings were very high, so that its advertising revenues were also high. The ratings had now fallen to a new low, and NBC, owned by General Electric, had become the new industry leader.

Another factor reducing the profitability of ABC was that Rupert Murdoch, the owner of the Fox Broadcasting network, had begun a battle with the Big Three networks to convince their television station affiliates to turn their allegiance to him and to switch to the Fox channel in return for large cash payments. Traditionally, the large networks had paid their affiliates nothing, expecting them to get their

revenue from local advertising linked to local news shows and syndications of rerun series. To stop their local television affiliates from jumping ship, ABC and the other Big Three networks had to make large cash payments to many of these stations, something that also drained ABC's profitability. Finally, ABC was under intense industry pressures of its own because of the changing nature of the broadcasting industry brought about by technological changes. The rapid rise in competition from new networks such as Rupert Murdoch's Fox network, Viacom's new United Paramount network, and even the new Microsoft/NBC 24 news channel were all emerging threats to ABC in the 1990s. In particular, since ABC was the most popular evening news channel, the emergence of alternative news channels posed a major threat.

Disney After the Merger

ABC's poor performance in the year following the merger brought its top management team under intense scrutiny from Eisner and Ovitz. Although before the merger it appeared that both organizations had similar cultures (both being managed by a strong CEO who had a hands-on approach), after the merger it became apparent that the two companies were very different. Eisner uses a very centralized management style and expects all his top managers to craft a five-year and ten-year plan for their business divisions to guide their future growth. He then evaluates them on the success with which they reach their division's performance goals, and with a plan to look at he can quickly intervene to take control if a division does not perform up to expectations. Thus, Disney's top managers know they are under constant scrutiny, and it is clear that Eisner is the person in charge of Disney's future strategy.

At ABC, however, the situation had been very different. In the television business, events change rapidly because a network's success depends on how well its shows are received on a week-by-week and month-by-month basis. For example, in 1992 ABC was the most successful of the Big Three networks and NBC was the least successful. Just three years later ABC's fall 1995 new show lineup bombed, while NBC's was a hit; their positions reversed. A television network's success rises and falls rapidly, unlike in the more stable movie business, where major movies may take three years to arrive at movie theaters from their initial conception.

Because of their shorter time horizon, ABC's executives typically used a one-year plan to guide their choices for the next year's programming. This conflicted with Eisner's desire for a longer strategic plan, and in 1996, it became clear that all was not going well between Disney's top management team and the team of managers in charge of ABC. As ABC's performance deteriorated in the fall of 1995, ABC executives came under even closer scrutiny, and they were forced to defend their every move to Disney's managers. As a result, several senior managers left ABC during this time as ABC's stressed-out managers tried to formulate a strategy to turn the division's fortunes around.

Major Problems for Eisner and Disney

It was July 1996, and Eisner and had just finished reading a *Wall Street Journal* article that was highly critical of the way they had handled top executives at ABC. The article argued that their close, hands-on management style resulted in conflict with key ABC executives that had caused their departures, thus delaying the process of obtaining the much needed synergies from the merger between the two companies. Moreover, industry analysts were still questioning whether the merger should have taken place at all.

Eisner was quick to sense that something needed to be done and done soon, and suddenly Eisner decided to oust Ovitz as president. Apparently, at least two of Disney's top managers refused to report to him, rather than Eisner, and he and Eisner had a major falling out over their respective roles at the top of the organization. The contract he had signed with Disney resulted in Ovitz receiving over $40 million in his severance package, and analysts and shareholders were astounded at what had happened. All of a sudden things seemed to have gone from bad to worse at Disney.

In fact, after his first decade of incredible success at Disney, Eisner's next decade as CEO was characterized by a major decrease in its performance and a plunging share price (until it recovered somewhat after 2003). The main reason for this was that Disney's entertainment assets, now organized into four major operating groups—media networks, studio entertainment, consumer products, and parks and resorts—began to perform poorly (see Exhibit 2). This was partly due to poor strategic decision making and partly due to changes in the environment that hurt the company's ability to realize value from its assets.

Problems in Media Networks

Disney's problems in its media properties, particularly its ABC network, continued to worsen over time

EXHIBIT 2

Walt Disney's Organizational Structure

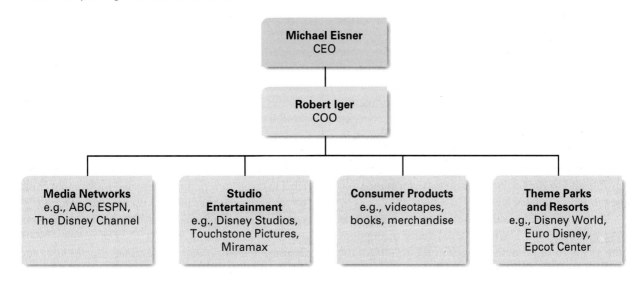

and reached a low point in the summer of 2002, as did its share price. As analysts had expected, hundreds of new cable channels that were established throughout the 1990s further reduced the size of ABC's viewing audience, and the constant screening of Disney's programming on the ABC network was no longer attractive to today's viewing audience. Disney also continued to find it hard to develop hit shows, and it was not until 2004 with the introduction of hit shows such as *Desperate Housewives* and *Lost* that ABC's fortunes began to look up. In addition, the massive increase in the use of the Internet and growing access to broadband further cut into the time people spent viewing television programming. In particular, men between the age of eighteen to thirty-five, a critical audience for advertisers, were reducing the time they spent watching TV. The result was that reality programming grew in popularity, and ABC had its share of hits.

Disney, like all other media companies, was also hurt badly by the recession that occurred in the early 2000s that caused many consumer products companies to reduce their TV advertising budgets. Add to this the unpopularity of its ABC network—a falling, lower viewing audience reduces the amount Disney can charge TV advertisers— its advertising revenues fell by over 10 percent between 2000–2002, which drained its bottom line profitability and sunk its share price. By 2004, as the economy recovered and its evening lineup now contained hit shows, Disney's advertising revenues rose once again, and from its low, Disney's price almost doubled by 2005, although this was still well below its peak price.

In fact the brightest spot in Disney's media networks was its ESPN sports channels, because sports programming was one of the few areas in the 2000s where the TV viewing audience was increasing as the range of different kinds of sports being televised soared, along with the price of tickets to sporting events. Disney was able to charge cable TV companies higher fees to carry its ESPN and associated networks, and its ESPN sports channels largely escaped the problem of the overall decline in advertising revenues. By 2003, ESPN was a major contributor to Disney's profits and to the turnaround in its performance that began in late 2002.

In addition, like other media companies such as Viacom and Fox, Disney worked hard throughout the 1990s to build new cable channels to attract the specialized viewing audiences that advertisers increasingly targeted, such as the ESPN male viewing audience that is a major buyer of cars, pickups, home-delivered pizza, beer, fast food, and so on. Today ESPN is broadcast in over eighteen different languages in over 165 countries; its franchise is booming as the global popularity of many different kinds of sports programming is increasing.

In 2005, ESPN and Electronic Arts (EA), the home video game maker, announced a long-term agreement for the development and integrated marketing of EA SPORTS games containing ESPN content. The relationship will include established EA SPORTS franchises—which will be enhanced by ESPN telecast, print, and online content—as well as new sports games to be published by EA based on ESPN media properties. The agreement gives EA access to ESPN programming, personalities, and integrated marketing opportunities on ESPN television programming and other ESPN properties. The ESPN integration will appear in EA SPORTS console, handheld, PC, and wireless games beginning in 2006.

In sum, the continuing poor performance of the media division from 1995–2002 was a major factor contributing to the company's poor performance in the last decade, although problems also existed in Disney's other operating groups. At the company's annual meeting in February 2005, Disney CEO Michael Eisner and President Bob Iger told investors that Disney's management team is focused on producing world-class creative content across the company to drive growth over the long term in order to increase return on invested capital.

Problems in Studio Entertainment

During the last decade Disney also has experienced major problems in its studio entertainment group, which contains its major movie studios Walt Disney, Touchstone, and Miramax. The profitability of Disney's movies has continued to fall, and for a variety of reasons, it does not seem likely that this division will be a major source of growth in the future.

First, in its core animation movie business, its Disney Studios continued to experience major problems to create new popular animated movies that could be released each year to drive up revenues. *Pocahontas* was a success compared with subsequent movies like *Hercules* (1997), *Fantasia 2000*, *102 Dalmatians* (2000), *Treasure Planet* (2002), and *Brother Bear* (2003), and these releases did little to help its bottom line. In response, Disney turned to releasing regular movies through this studio, such as *Pirates of the Caribbean*, its first PG-13 movie in 2003, and *Hidalgo*, its second PG-13 release in 2004.

Second, the shift to produce animated movies using computer-based digital technology accelerated in the 1990s, and Pixar and DreamWorks became the leaders in this movie genre. Disney had been fortunate to secure its contract with Pixar to distribute its films before the obvious advantages of digital technology became apparent. Its revenues from distributing Pixar movies such as *Toy Story* (1995), *Toy Story 2* (1999), *Monsters Inc.* (2001), *Finding Nemo* (2003), and the hugely successful *The Incredibles* (2004) became the biggest single source of the profits of the studio entertainment operating group. However, the Pixar contract was to expire in 2005, and Steve Jobs, Pixar's CEO, was reluctant to renew the contract with Disney. One major reason was apparently the hostile relationship between him and Eisner that had developed over time. Another reason was Disney's announcement in 2004 that in the future it would only make animated movies using the new computer-based technology, and the company began to layoff hundreds of the animators who had created its past successes. Disney's first digital movie, *Chicken Little*, was due to be released in the spring of 2005.

In early 2005, it was still unclear if Jobs, who had been offering the Pixar franchise to other movie distributors, would renew the contract with Disney. However, it appears that Jobs might be waiting until Eisner's successor had been named. The loss of Pixar's movies would be a major blow for Disney because analysts estimate that over 40 percent or about $1 billion of the operating income of its movie studios have come from its successes with Pixar. The final movie in process, *Cars*, was due to be released in 2005, and like *The Incredibles*, it took over two years to develop and bring to the screen.

Disney also continued to experience poor success with many of its regular feature film releases. For example, in 2003 and 2004 a string of flops, including movies such as *The Alamo*, *Miracle*, *Home on the Range*, and *Around the World in Eighty Days*, drained its movie studio's profits. In its own studios, the brightest spot was Miramax Pictures whose high-quality, but relatively low-budget movies continued to enjoy enormous commercial success and reaped many

Oscars for the studio. In 2005, however, the Weinstein brothers, who have been attributed with producing its successful movies, also decided to leave the studio they founded after major disputes with Eisner and Disney over increasing studio operating costs. So the future success of this studio was uncertain in 2005.

Problems in Consumer Products

Several major developments also led to problems in Disney's consumer products group, which, although not a major contributor to its revenues (see Exhibit 3), helped to significantly reduce its profit margins. First, Disney's success with its ESPN sports networks prompted Eisner to purchase two major sports team franchises, the Mighty Ducks of Anaheim hockey team and the Anaheim Angels baseball team. However, Disney had no experience operating sports franchises, and both these ventures began to lose money. In response, in 2004 Eisner decided to reverse course and find a buyer for these assets; by 2005, only the Anaheim Angels had been divested.

Second, one of the drivers of Disney's profits in Eisner's early years was the decision to release its classic movies on videotape. However, that meant by 2000 Disney was no longer able to rerelease these movies in movie theaters, and with millions of Disney videos and DVDs in circulation, and movie video piracy rampant, its revenues from this source fell sharply. Moreover, its lack of a string of new hit movies that

EXHIBIT 3

Financial Highlights, 2004 ($ in millions)

Operating Group	2004		
	Revenue	Operating Income	Operating Profit Margin %
Media Networks	$11,778	$2,169	18.4
Parks and Resorts	7,750	1,123	14.4
Studio Entertainment	8,713	662	7.6
Consumer Products	2,511	534	2.1
Total	**$30,752**	**$4,488**	**14.6**

could be profitably released on DVD also did nothing to help its consumer product revenues at a time when DVD sales were exploding because consumers, attracted by the falling price of DVDs, began to build their own movie collections. In fact, movie and music digital piracy has reduced the revenues of most major media companies, which is why Disney agreed in 2004 to join the Blu-Ray consortium and use its new digital media encryption technology that is intended to make such activity impossible in the future.

By 2000, it was clear that Eisner's decision to open the Disney Store chain to sell its Disney merchandise at premium prices was also a disastrous investment decision as these stores began to lose more and more money. Disney's management had not understood the specific competitive problems that exist in the retail store industry, such as intense price competition and high inventory holding and store maintenance costs that make profit margins thin. Disney began to search for a buyer for its stores, and in 2004, it finally found a buyer in the Children's Place retail store chain which agreed to buy Disney's 335 stores and the right to sell Disney's merchandise in these stores. The Children's Place hopes that by operating Disney stores in conjunction with its other store chain it will be able to cut operating expenses and so make a profit. Disney will continue to receive a percentage of revenues from the sale of its products in these stores. A better strategy for Disney from the beginning would have been to distribute an exclusive line of its products through one or more specialized retailers like Toys "R" Us, which would have helped the bottom lines of both of these companies.

In sum, while promoting sales of Disney's consumer products had been seen in the 1990s as a way to leverage its resources and reap synergies from its theme parks and movie assets, in practice the way Disney implemented this strategy has proved to be a major liability and hurt its performance in the 2000s. The issue today is which businesses the company should compete in and how to market and distribute its products in a way that will maximize the profitability of sales.

Problems in Theme Parks and Resorts

Disney's theme parks have also turned in mixed performance over the last several years for a variety of reasons. Faced with increasing competition from other theme park companies such as MGM Studios, Six Flags, and the plethora of attractions that have opened up in Orlando, Disney was forced to spend billions of dollars to build new rides and modernize its Anaheim and Orlando properties to protect its famous franchise. However, just after it had spent $5 billion to enhance these franchises in the early 2000s, disasters such as the September 11 tragedy and the SARS epidemic that started in Asia occurred. These events, combined with the general world recession that started in the early 2000s, significantly reduced the volume of world air travel and the number of domestic and overseas visitors to Disney's parks, once again eroding profit margins.

However, Disney's attention to improving the quality of its properties while keeping costs in check started to pay off in 2004 as the number of visitors increased sharply and profit margins once again rose by 2003 as Exhibit 3 shows. Certainly, Disney World, with its four theme parks, remains the number one tourist attraction in the world and is one of its most important assets.

The performance of Disney's overseas theme parks has also been erratic. The Japanese Disney park continues to prosper, but the company only receives a small percentage of the profits of that enterprise. The French theme park has continued to perform poorly, so poorly in fact that Disney has allowed the park to forgo its yearly royalties to the Disney Company to keep the park viable in the hope that it will prosper once the global economy regains momentum. The park is Europe's number one tourist destination, but European vacationers spend less than the tourists that visit its U.S. parks and resorts. Disney's newest theme park is slated to open in Hong Kong. In 2005, Disney and the Hong Kong SAR Government announced that Hong Kong Disneyland is expected to welcome its first guests on September 12, 2005, earlier than originally projected. The world-class theme park and resort, located on Lantau Island, will be Disney's first theme park in China, offering the typical Disney magical experiences and signature attractions such as fireworks and parades. Disney has a significant stake in this venture, and if it enjoys the success of the Japanese park, which seems likely given the rate at which Asian economies are developing and prospering, this will increase the profitability of this operating group in the years ahead.

Finally, Disney's decision to enter the cruise line industry also proved to be a major financial disappointment. Once again the costs of operating a handful of cruise ships are much greater than the cost of operating hundreds, as Carnival Cruise Line does, because of the lack of economies of scale. So, despite Disney's ability to charge customers a premium price for the Disney experience at sea, that venture also did little or nothing to help the company's profitability. However, this operating group is also unlikely to be a driver of the kind of revenue growth that propels a company's value, although it has been and should continue to be a generator of cash for investment that Disney needs to make much better use of in the years ahead.

Governance Problems at Disney

Although it was unlikely that Eisner or any CEO could hope to maintain the rapid growth in revenues and profits that the company experienced in the first decade of his leadership, its relatively poor performance in the last decade has caused many analysts to question the soundness of Eisner's strategy for the company. The debacle over the departure of two seconds in command, Jeffrey Katzenberg and Steven Ovitz; the charge that Eisner's micromanagement of the company has reduced the level of innovation in the company; top management's inability so far to realize real synergies from the ABC/Capital Cities merger; the failure of the many ventures into new industries; and the growing competition from rivals such as Viacom, Fox, and Dream Works has all led to increasing criticism of Eisner. The company is lucky it acquired the ESPN networks as a part of the ABC merger for this seems to be the main source of its current growth in revenues and profits.

Eisner's decision to close down the animation studio in favor of computer animation also brought him into conflict with Roy Disney, who had been the head of that division which he championed because of its links to the past. Roy Disney, with the support of some other major disgruntled investors, began to publicly challenge Eisner's leadership of the company and began a campaign to oust Eisner as CEO. The dispute between Eisner and his opponents became very bitter as the performance of the company continued to suffer in the 2000s, and in February 2004, 43 percent of Disney stockholders supported a vote of no confidence in Eisner's leadership that led him to resign as chairman although he remained CEO.

In the midst of this dissent, Comcast, one of the two largest cable TV providers in the United States, took advantage of Disney's apparent weakness to launch a hostile takeover bid for the company, which Comcast valued at $66 billion. After several months it became clear that investors thought this bid was inadequate, and as noted earlier, Disney's performance began to recover in 2003–2004. So both these events lifted its stock price, and Comcast withdrew its offer for the company although some analysts expect it to try again at some point.

In the meantime, however, Eisner had not been able to escape from the criticism that he was no longer the right person to lead the company. Led by Roy Disney, many investors began to question corporate governance at Disney. As noted earlier, Eisner has always had a hands-on approach to running the business: He wants to be involved in every major business decision, and he keeps a tight reign on his managers. He has been criticized because although past sixty years old he would not publicly lay out a succession plan indicating which managers will assume the top roles in Disney after he steps down.

In addition, Eisner has been criticized for creating a weak or captive Board of Directors that has been unable or unwilling to scrutinize and question his business decisions over the last decade. In the last twenty years, Eisner had created a sixteen-member Board of Directors in the company, at least eight of whom had strong personal ties to him. Over that same period, Eisner has received more than a billion in salary, stock options, and so on from the company and enjoyed all the lavish perks that most CEOs of large companies receive today.

So in 2004 the new chairman of the board of the company began the process of reorganizing its Board of Directors to reduce Eisner's influence over it. For example, two new special outside directors were appointed, one of whom chairs two board meetings a year that Eisner—who used to chair these meetings—is not permitted to attend. While Disney's board now has more freedom to assess Eisner's performance, many analysts claim these changes were still not enough because the majority of the board is still beholden to him and he controls all Disney's important committees. Nevertheless, to avoid another major fight with Roy Disney and his supporters in the fall of 2004, Eisner announced that he would not seek another term as CEO when his contract expired in 2006, as noted earlier.

In the spring of 2005, no successor had been named as the new CEO of Disney, despite an earlier feeling that one should be named before Eisner would be forced to resign as CEO when his contract expired in 2006. His handpicked successor, Robert Iger, is waiting in the wings, and of course should he be appointed, it is very possible that Eisner will turn over the reins to him and become Disney's new chairman. In this case he would continue to have enormous influence over Disney's future strategy. In February 2005, Disney's twelve directors received a vote of support at its annual meeting, and the doubling of its stock price over the past two years has made many investors more receptive to Eisner. However, it seems likely that more fireworks are ahead in the battle over who will become Disney's new CEO and chairman—fireworks that may make Disney's nightly display in its Orlando EPCOT center pale in comparison.

First Greyhound, Then Greyhound Dial, Then Dial, Now Henkel-Dial

This case was prepared by Gareth R. Jones, Texas A&M University.

It was the end of 2003, and Herbert Baum, Dial's CEO, was reflecting on the performance of the company since he had been brought in to engineer a turnaround in 2000. He had sold off underperforming product lines and invested heavily in building Dial's core products like Dial soap. By April 2002, he had been happy to report a rebound in Dial's earnings, which sent its share soaring from the lows it had reached in April 2001, when its earnings plunged by 69 percent due to the poor strategic decisions of his predecessor. Now the question was what to do? Should he continue to build Dial's portfolio of brand name products and strive to keep the company independent? Or should he sell off the company, either as a whole or in parts, to other companies that would now be prepared to pay a high price for its strong brand name products? While pondering this question, Baum thought that the history of the company, which had started out as Greyhound, might provide him with some important clues.

Greyhound's Early History and Growth

Greyhound was founded in Hibbing, Minnesota, in 1914. Its first business was providing bus transportation to carry miners to work at the Mesabi Iron Range.

Because Greyhound was the sole provider of bus service for these workers, it was immediately successful. In its very first year, the new corporation started expanding its routes and acquiring interests in bus companies operating near Chicago. For the next sixteen years, the young company continued purchasing interests in bus companies, extending its route structure from New York to Kansas City. In 1930, the name *Greyhound Corporation* was adopted, and the now-familiar running-dog logo was painted on the buses.

For the next twenty-seven years, Greyhound continued to acquire bus interests in order to consolidate its routes and link its various bus operations. Growth proceeded sometimes by purchase, sometimes by stock swaps, and sometimes by merger. However, the result was always the same to the traveling public: It saw more and more of the familiar running dog. By 1960, Greyhound had substantially achieved its objective of operating a bus system that could carry passengers to most destinations in the continental United States and Canada.

By 1962, however, Greyhound was facing the prospect of increasingly limited opportunities to expand its route system; in the company's favor was the fact that bus operations were generating large sums of excess cash, which could fund expansion into new businesses. So Greyhound's Board of Directors decided to diversify into operations outside the bus transportation industry.

In that same year, Greyhound began the program of acquisition that turned it into a conglomerate. It solidified its bus-manufacturing operations into Motor

Coach Industries, which became the foundation of Greyhound Dial's transportation manufacturing operating division. Also in 1962, the corporation acquired Boothe Leasing Company, an enterprise that specialized in equipment leasing. Boothe Leasing was renamed Greyhound Leasing and became the core business around which Greyhound's financial services division was to be built. Thus, by the end of 1963, Greyhound Corporation was operating in three major businesses: bus transportation, bus manufacturing, and financial services. Bus manufacturing supplied buses to bus transportation as well as to other bus companies.

Acquisitions Between 1966 and 1970

Gerry Trautman was appointed CEO in 1966, and he wasted no time in accelerating Greyhound's new strategy for expansion and growth. From Trautman's installation as CEO until 1970, Greyhound acquired more than thirty widely different companies and formed a new operating division—services—that specialized in managing transportation-related businesses, such as Border Brokerage Company, which operated two duty-free shops at the Canadian border, and Florida Export Group, which also handled duty-free commerce. In addition, the services division included Manncraft Exhibitors, a company that specialized in building displays for major exhibitions; Nassau Air Dispatch, a Caribbean shipping company; and Freeport Flight Services, a Bahamian aircraft-servicing business. Trautman also brought in a line of cruise ships in the Caribbean, the Bahama Cruise Line Company. Then he added companies as diverse as Ford Van Lines of Lincoln, Nebraska, a company specializing in furniture moving; Red Top Sedan Service, a Florida limousine service; two regional intercity bus lines; Washington Airport Transport, a commuter carrier from the Washington, D.C., suburbs to Dulles Airport; and Gray Line New York Tours Corporation, a sightseeing bus line. Furthermore, he added Hausman Bus Parts to the bus-manufacturing unit.

Not all the companies that Trautman acquired proved to be as profitable or as manageable as he had hoped. What he was looking for was value, as well as some synergy with Greyhound's existing transportation activities. However, as the acquisition process continued, synergy became a secondary objective. When Trautman became dissatisfied with an acquisition, he

would divest it as quickly as he had acquired it, and many companies were spun off. Near the end of his tenure as CEO, Trautman would boast that Greyhound had achieved "diversification within diversification." What he meant was that in his view the operating groups had become diversified, so that each individually was recession-proof and all were enhancing the financial strength of the holding company.

Trautman's boldest maneuver and biggest acquisition came in 1970. He acquired Armour & Co., another large conglomerate that had many diverse business interests in food and consumer products. Trautman paid $400 million in cash, notes, and stock to take over Armour, which was primarily a large meat-packing company with more than $2 billion of sales in marginally profitable businesses. However, Armour also had interests in pharmaceuticals, cosmetics, and consumer products such as soap through its very profitable Dial division. Trautman knew that it appeared as though he had overpaid for Armour-Dial. However, he soon reduced the price of the acquisition by selling off, for some $225 million, a number of Armour's divisions that he considered to be peripheral to Armour's core food and consumer businesses. In 1977, he sold off Armour's pharmaceutical division for $87 million, reducing Greyhound's net investment to $88 million. What remained after the divestitures were Armour's food operations and Armour's Dial division, from which would emerge Greyhound Dial's consumer products operating division.

Trautman hoped that his new acquisition would be more recession-proof than the bus business, if not countercyclical to it. However, the Armour acquisition brought to Greyhound new businesses that had management problems of their own in areas in which Greyhound had no experience, such as the price of pork bellies, cycles for meat packers' contracts, and foreign competition.

Trautman's Acquisitions and Divestitures Between 1970 and 1978

For the next eight years, Greyhound under Trautman continued buying businesses and increasing the size of the operating divisions in its corporate portfolio. By 1978, Greyhound's holding company consisted of five operating divisions: transportation, bus manufacturing, food and consumer products, financial, and services/food service. Each of these operating divisions acquired many new businesses, so that Greyhound was still undergoing "diversification within diversification." Many of the new acquisitions, however, were failures. Businesses as diverse as a chicken hatchery, a European acquisition to expand the financial services group, and various transportation businesses (Caribbean Gray Cruise Line, Ltd., VAVO Greyhound N.V. of Schoonhoven, Netherlands, Shannon-Greyhound Coaches, and Hausman Bus Parts) proved unprofitable.

Greyhound's portfolio of businesses kept changing during this period, and Trautman continued to feel that he was shaping a diversified company that would have a powerful base in many lines of business. He was willing to take the risk of acquiring some companies that would be failures as long as the overall health of the company was strengthened. However, Greyhound became more and more distant from its core business—bus transportation.

In April 1978, Trautman engineered another major acquisition by acquiring 97 percent of the stock of Verex Corporation, the largest private insurer of residential mortgages in the United States. The Verex acquisition was intended to strengthen the operations of Greyhound's financial operating division. Verex insured first mortgages on residential real estate generally having loan-to-value ratios in excess of 80 percent.

By 1978, Greyhound had grown nearly as large as it would grow under Trautman's leadership. The collection of businesses that he had assembled—some by acquisition, some by internal growth, and some by selling off pieces of larger businesses—was designed to make Greyhound more resistant to economic downturns. The activities of Greyhound's five major operating divisions are summarized below.

- *Transportation.* This operating division comprised the intercity services division and the travel services division. Transportation operated regularly scheduled passenger bus service between most metropolitan areas in North America and engaged in related operations, such as package shipping, sightseeing services, airport ground transportation, and deluxe tour and charter bus services.

- *Bus manufacturing.* The largest maker of intercity buses in North America, the bus-manufacturing division had operations that were vertically integrated to fabricate bus shells of intercity design, assemble buses, and manufacture bus parts for final assembly. In addition, this operating division warehoused and distributed replacement parts to meet its own requirements and the larger requirements of the bus industry. Greyhound bus manufacturing was the principal U.S. supplier of buses to charter operators and sightseeing companies.

- *Food and consumer products.* The companies in this operating group manufactured and marketed products to independent retailers under private-label arrangements and distributed several products under their own trademarks. These trademarks included Dial, Tone, and Pure & Natural soaps, Armour Star and Armour Tree canned meat and meat food products, Dial antiperspirants and shampoos, Appian Way pizza mixes, Parsons' ammonia, Bruce floor care products, Magic sizing and prewash, and Malina handknitting yarns and needle products.

- *Services/food service.* Companies in this operating division provided a broad range of services directed primarily to business markets, although duty-free shops located at airports and on cruise ships were targeted toward the consumer market. Greyhound convention services (GCS) specialized in designing, fabricating, warehousing, shipping, and setting up exhibits for trade shows, conventions, and exhibitions. GCS also served as a decorating contractor at conventions and trade show sites. The food service division, generally known as Greyhound food management (GFM), served approximately twenty-four hundred locations in industrial plants, bus terminals, airports, office buildings, schools, colleges, and other facilities.

- *Financial.* This operating division consisted of Greyhound Computer Corporation, a company specializing in computer leasing and sales in the United States, Canada, Mexico, and Europe; Greyhound Leasing and Financial Corporation, a company specializing in worldwide industrial equipment leasing; Pine Top Insurance, an entity that reinsured commercial property and provided excess casualty insurance for large policyholders; and Verex Corporation, the leading private insurer of highly leveraged residential mortgages for primary lenders. Travelers Express Company, Inc., another company in the financial division, specialized in providing travelers' checks and check-cashing services in thirty-two thousand retail establishments and financial institutions in the mainland United States and Puerto Rico.

Together, those five operating divisions were generating combined revenues of nearly $4.5 billion. Trautman had accomplished his objective of using profits from the bus operations to move Greyhound into other businesses.

Trautman Selects Teets to Take over Greyhound

Serious problems became apparent at Armour when the food and consumer products operating division went from a profit of $22 million in 1979 to a loss of $1.7 million in 1980. Armour's problems came at a very inconvenient time for Trautman because he had planned to retire in 1980. Trautman wanted to solve Armour's difficulties while he kept business rolling at Greyhound's other groups and prepared a successor to take over the collection of companies that he had assembled. That successor was to be John Teets.

Teets was very different from Trautman. His background did not include Harvard Business School or law practice. Instead, Teets had learned to be an effective hands-on manager by staying as close to the action as possible. He had worked for his father's construction company but decided that he wanted to operate a restaurant. He borrowed money, started his own restaurant, and quickly made it successful. However, soon after he had paid back his loan money and his restaurant was earning a profit, it burned to the ground. In search of a new business opportunity, Teets answered a newspaper advertisement about a position managing a Greyhound food service concession stand at the New York World's Fair in 1964.

After joining the services/food service operating group, Teets quickly distinguished himself as a tight-fisted cost cutter who could make money on a miserly budget. He seemed to have a talent for squeezing every last penny out of everything he managed. Teets moved up quickly, gaining a reputation as an extremely effective manager. By 1975, he was put in charge of the food service group, which primarily operated a conglomeration of marginally profitable, obscure, franchised restaurants. His aggressive management style produced quick results, and in 1980, he was named the outstanding executive in the food industry. Also in 1980, in addition to Teets's responsibilities as CEO of the food service group, Trautman named Teets to head Armour and turn around the division's performance.

In 1981, Armour's major problem, as Teets saw it, was that it was paying 30 to 50 percent more in wages and fringe benefits than its competitors. Teets asked Armour's unions for immediate wage concessions. He told the unions that if he failed to get the concessions, he would have to start closing plants. After a bitter strike, wage concessions in excess of 15 percent were obtained. Given these concessions, the cost cutting from plant closings, and more efficient operating procedures, it looked as though Armour had bought itself some time.

With Armour running more efficiently, the bus business cruising along on excess profits because of the recession and energy crunch in 1979–1980, and high profits in its financial operating division generated by high interest rates in the early 1980s, it seemed that the stage was set for Trautman's retirement. In fact, all that remained was to formally select a successor. It was not difficult for Trautman to make up his mind about who that should be. He was impressed with Teets's successes in managing the services/food service group and also with the way in which Teets had dominated Armour's labor unions.

Teets Seeks Solutions

In 1981, John Teets succeeded Gerry Trautman as the chief executive officer of the Greyhound Corporation. The challenge facing Teets was to manage Greyhound's diverse businesses so that he would be able to achieve at least a 15 percent return on equity. However, many problems on the horizon might hinder the achievement of this goal. Some were the direct consequence of Trautman's ambitious expansion and diversification efforts. Others resulted from changes in environmental factors and consumer preferences. Still others stemmed from internal inefficiencies that Teets hoped he would be able to remedy.

Two challenges in particular caused Teets to feel uneasy about the corporation's overall profit picture. The first problem was Armour's high production costs, which made it a weak competitor. The second was the challenge faced by Greyhound Bus Lines: the need to compete in a newly deregulated bus transportation market. He knew that if he did not find solutions for these two problems, they would seriously diminish the Greyhound Corporation's earnings. The contribution of each operating division to Greyhound's total sales revenues in 1981 is presented in Figure 1.

FIGURE 1

Greyhound in 1981

Source: Data from Greyhound Dial Corporation, Annual Report, 1990.

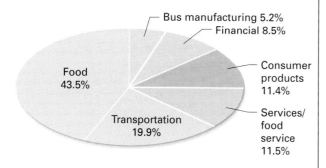

Dealing With Armour's High Production Costs

Having been president of Armour, Teets was very familiar with the division's problems: its high production costs, the reluctance of union leadership and rank-and-file workers to agree with Greyhound's assessment of Armour's problems, and its utter inability to successfully change its marketing orientation to compete effectively. In addition, Teets was concerned about Armour's inefficient plants and the volatility of hog and pork-belly prices, which cyclically depressed Armour's 1981 profit of $9 million and represented a profit margin of less than 0.39 percent on sales of more than $2.3 billion. Teets sensed that it was not going to be easy to make Armour a low-cost leader. Thus, he decided to divest Armour.

In preparation for the sale, he separated the Armour Food Company from Armour-Dial. On December 18, 1983, the food company was sold to ConAgra, Inc., for $166 million. With the Armour sale, Teets was chopping off nearly half of Greyhound's business. Nevertheless, even with Greyhound's revenues dropping from $5 billion in 1982 to less than $3 billion in 1984 without Armour, the sale gave Teets the opportunity to put Greyhound in better shape than it had been in years.

The Bus Line Divestiture

Teets was also concerned about the 1981 passage of House bill H.R. 3663, which deregulated the intercity bus business. Greyhound Bus Lines had based its route system on the competitive conditions that had existed in the earlier business environment. Teets, however, sensed that future success in the bus business would be based not on the extensiveness of Greyhound's route system or its fifty years of experience in operating in a regulated industry but on its ability to make money by charging competitive fares.

With the beginning of deregulated competition in the intercity bus business and declining passenger revenues resulting from the end of the energy crunch, Greyhound found itself paying wages and benefits that were 30 to 50 percent higher than those paid by its competitors. Furthermore, its chief competitor, Trailways, having negotiated significant wage concessions from the Amalgamated Transit Union, had immediately passed the savings on to customers in the form of lower fares. Trailways's action was a frontal assault on Greyhound's most lucrative routes in an attempt to gain market share. Greyhound's response was to match every one of Trailways's price cuts. Although Greyhound preserved its market share, it lost millions of dollars.

For Greyhound Bus Lines, the legacy of deregulation was a total inability to be a low-cost provider of bus transportation. Deregulation had brought about the emergence of lower-cost competitors in regional markets, competitors that were able to be responsive and flexible in pricing and in reacting to Greyhound's actions. As a result, Greyhound lost its competitive edge. In 1986, in an effort to save the bus lines, Teets converted 120 company-owned terminals to commission agencies, trimming a huge overhead burden. He also created four stand-alone regional bus companies and a new travel and charter company. Finally, he franchised several of Greyhound's least profitable routes to independent operators, licensing them to use the Greyhound logo and trademark.

However, the one factor that Teets could not control was winning a new labor contract. In February 1986, an offer to freeze wages was rejected by the union. In October, in a deteriorating market, a second offer involving concessions was presented with the understanding that its rejection would prompt the sale of the company. The offer was subsequently rejected, and fifteen days later Teets announced the sale of Greyhound Bus Lines for approximately $350 million to an investor group headquartered in Dallas. Teets claimed that the actions taken by management in an effort to salvage the bus business were exactly the ones that made it an attractive acquisition for the Currey Group in Dallas.

The sale of Greyhound Bus Lines brought in $290 million in cash and equivalents, including a

22.5 percent interest in a new holding company established by the Dallas investor group.

Divestitures in the Financial Operating Division

Besides selling Greyhound Bus Lines in 1987, Teets also sold Greyhound Capital Corporation (GCC). The decision to sell GCC reportedly reflected Teets's conviction that "some businesses just fit better into Greyhound's plans than others." What this statement really meant was that GCC had become an underperformer in the face of lowered interest rates and changes in the tax laws that disallowed investment tax credits. GCC was sold for $140 million, realizing a one-time gain of $79.7 million for Greyhound.

In early 1987, Greyhound announced its intention to sell Verex. The timing of the acquisition had been a disaster, given the recession in the real estate market caused by the oil bust in the early 1980s. Verex suffered huge losses generated by insurance claims from business generated before 1985. These claims were originating in states where severe downturns in farming, auto production, and oil drilling had led to a widespread inability to keep up with mortgage payments.

Not surprisingly, Teets could not find a buyer for Verex. In January 1988, Greyhound announced that it had stopped taking applications for new mortgage insurance and that it was discontinuing its mortgage insurance business. It also announced that 1987 results would reflect a one-time aftertax charge of $45 million as a result of reclassifying Verex as a discontinued operation; then Greyhound would manage Verex's existing portfolio to minimize continuing losses from the company's operations. Management hoped the remnants of Verex would not be a drain on corporate resources.

With the sale of Greyhound Bus Lines, Greyhound Capital Corporation, and Armour, and with the discontinuation of Verex, Teets announced that he was near the end of his mammoth task of restructuring Greyhound and shedding businesses that seemed to lack sufficient growth potential. By late 1987, Greyhound Corporation was primarily a consumer products and services company. Figure 2 summarizes the contribution of the different operating groups to total revenues in 1988. Compare the Greyhound Corporation that Teets structured (Figure 2) with the corporation he inherited in 1982 (Figure 1).

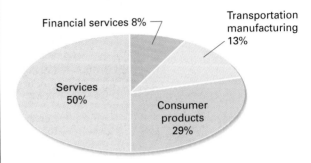

FIGURE 2

Total Revenues: $3.3 Billion

Source: Data from Greyhound Dial Corporation, Annual Report, 1990.

Financial services 8%
Transportation manufacturing 13%
Services 50%
Consumer products 29%

With the restructuring in place, Wall Street looked for an improvement in Greyhound's performance. However, it soon became obvious that the stack of businesses created by Teets was not proving much more profitable than the ones he had divested. There was only an 8.8 percent return on equity in 1987, and net income after nonrecurring losses was $25.1 million, the lowest for many years. Revenue was $2.5 billion. Teets maintained that the problems with Greyhound's various divisions could not have been foreseen as the restructuring was taking place but that Greyhound was set for "substantial profits in the future." Teets began a program of acquisitions and new product developments to strengthen Greyhound's presence in the four business areas identified in Figure 2 and to begin the turnaround process.

Consumer Products

In the midst of the divestiture of Armour and Greyhound Bus Lines, Teets had made one major acquisition. On February 21, 1985, he announced the purchase of Purex Industries and its thirty household cleaning products for $264 million. Teets's aim with this acquisition was to boost profits in Greyhound's Consumer Products operating division (principally composed of the old Dial division) by using the Dial sales force and marketing expertise to sell Purex products—Purex bleach, Brillo soap pads, Old Dutch cleanser, and Sweetheart and Fels-Naptha soap, among others.

The Purex acquisition drew mixed reviews from Wall Street. It did not meet Teets's goal of a 15 percent return, but Teets believed that it would by 1988. Analysts were also unimpressed with the purchase because Greyhound had not been successful in managing Armour. Teets responded that Dial was capable of marketing consumer products, although it had not been successful at developing its own lines. He cited as evidence the fact that Dial was marketing the number one deodorant soap in its Dial brand. Analysts did concede that Teets should be able to realize increased profitability by using the same sales force to sell Purex and Dial products. Along with Purex's household cleaners, Greyhound also got Elio's Pizza as part of the Purex acquisition. Teets was enthusiastic about expanding this frozen pizza business nationwide from its East Coast base. This was to be done by means of the Dial sales force.

The Dial operating division, as it was now known, became the center of Teets's attention and the flagship of the Greyhound Corporation. In the past Dial had not had much success in launching new products, but Teets was determined to change the situation, recognizing that growth in revenue had to come from the manufacture and marketing of new products. The first product introduced by the Dial division was Lunch Buckets, a range of microwavable meals with a stable shelf life of two years. This was a new market segment. Previously all microwavable meals had been frozen. Lunch Buckets meals were very successful and surpassed early expectations by a wide margin. By 1988, they had national distribution. By 1990, they had seized a 30 percent market share, becoming the market leader. In 1990, Dial announced new low-calorie Lunch Buckets.

Another new product introduced in 1987 was Liquid Dial antibacterial soap. This product, too, was very successful, and by 1990, it had achieved a 20 percent market share and was the second best-selling liquid soap in the market, after Procter & Gamble's Ivory liquid. Another successful new product was Mountain Fresh Dial, a highly scented version of Dial's deodorant soap. Additional developments were liquid Purex detergent and other cleaning products.

In 1988, Teets acquired the household products and industrial specialties businesses of the 20 Mule Team division of United States Borax and Chemical Corporation. Teets announced a new advertising campaign to reestablish the market presence of Borax bleaches and cleaning powders. Teets's formula for increasing the Dial division's market share called for further extensions of the Dial brand, further extensions of the Purex brand name, and Parsons' ammonia.

Greyhound Dial, Then Dial

On June 4, 1990, Teets learned that Greyhound Bus lines, the bus transportation company that he had sold in 1987, had declared bankruptcy and Greyhound's stake was now valueless. To distance his "new" company from Greyhound, he changed the company's name to Greyhound Dial in February 1990, and the next year it became simply Dial. The name change also marked the company's new focus on its consumer products division. However, the price of Dial's stock, which had been more or less unchanged for the last six years, started to plunge in 1990 after Dial reported a loss. Analysts wondered whether Teets would ever be able to improve the company's profitability.

In September 1990, another consumer products acquisition was announced: Breck hair care products. Breck had 1989 revenues of $60 million. Teets announced that integrating Breck into Dial would result in annual sales of more than $1 billion for the Dial division. Teets said that "Breck has been a household name for 60 years. It's a perfect fit with our other Dial products and under Dial management the power of the Breck name will flourish." Under its previous owners, Breck had languished. Teets hoped to turn the product around by applying Dial's marketing skills.

From the changes he had orchestrated, Teets was hoping for sizable revenue growth and profit from the Dial division, and in March 1991, as an indication of the company's future strategy, the company's name was again changed, to the Dial Corporation.

Services

By 1987, the restaurant food services division was contributing the most to total revenues. It was natural, therefore, that Teets should seek to strengthen food operations. In 1987, Dial purchased the nation's second biggest airline catering and airline retailing business. The new operation had three units: Dobbs International Services, the nation's second largest provider of in-flight meals for airlines; Dobbs Houses, the operator of restaurants at many airports; and Carson International, which operated the food and beverage concession at Chicago's O'Hare Airport.

In 1990, Teets announced that Dobbs had had a record year—the company had served sixty scheduled airlines in forty cities. Moreover, it had added five new accounts, including Houston International Airport.

Teets strengthened Dial's Travelers Express money order business with the purchase of Republic Money Orders, Inc., of Dallas. This acquisition made Dial the leader in the money order business, ahead of the U.S. Postal Service. Teets had returned to the cruise ship industry in 1984 with the takeover of Premier Cruise Lines. In 1986, he negotiated an agreement with the Walt Disney Company that made Dial's Premier Cruise Line Disney's exclusive cruise ship line, with three- and four-day sailing to the Bahamas from Cape Canaveral in Florida. The cruise line business enjoyed record sales, and in 1989, another line was added.

The New Look of the Dial Corporation

The new look of Dial's businesses after the acquisitions and divestitures is shown in Table 1. Teets acknowledged the wide diversity of businesses in the company's portfolio. However, he contended that the businesses did fit together. In his words, "We are a multiservice business. We operate in niches and were number one or two in most of these niches. From a recession standpoint, I think we're going to feel it less than most major companies." Teets argued that Dial was making acquisitions to strengthen its presence in existing niches. By concentrating on a niche, the corporation avoided going head-to-head with major competitors. Moreover, the niches were recession-proof, small-ticket items such as Lunch Buckets and soap, not refrigerators and cars. Teets argued that Dial was positioned for growth and that management expected revenues to increase steadily over the next few years. See Table 2.

Some analysts, however, felt that the organization was still a hodgepodge of different businesses in need of rationalization. They pointed to the lack of fit between a cruise ship line and hotel operations in Glacier National Park and contract catering, saying that Dial was still a collection of companies with no real connection. They also argued that Greyhound Dial's breakup value was more than $60 a share, while its stock price had been in the range of $25 to $35 for years. Teets agreed that some minor divestitures were

necessary, but he believed that the best way to proceed was to stay in the same niches and manage the existing businesses more efficiently.

Dial, 1990–1996

Finally it appeared that, at last, things were going Dial's way. Dial's share price, which had plummeted to less than $10 a share at the end of 1990, rose to almost $25 a share by the end of 1992. This turnaround occurred for several reasons. First, Dial had finally spun off its loss-making financial services group to stockholders so that the liabilities no longer affected its balance sheet. Second, its consumer products group, and in particular the Dial soap division, was performing strongly. Dial had become the number one selling deodorant soap in the United States, with more than 20 percent of the market. Third, Teets had orchestrated a major downsizing, or what he had called "rightsizing," reducing the number of corporate managers from four hundred to three hundred. Also, all of Dial's different businesses were subjected to close scrutiny to try to reduce costs, and employment was reduced across the board, even in the successful Dial division. Teets also reduced corporate debt from a high of $850 million to $550 million through the sales of certain assets such as Dobbs House, its airport catering company. Analysts hoped that all these events were the first signs of a turnaround in the company's performance.

These hopes were doomed, however, by a series of problems that emerged in Dial's various businesses. In the 1990s, businesses in Dial's transportation manufacturing unit began to perform poorly, draining the company's profits. In 1993, Teets decided to dispose of it. Also, its Purex bleach business was doing poorly and losing money. It began to seem that just when Dial was making strides in one of its businesses, problems in another were wiping out the effects of the improvement. Investors began to wonder again about Teets's claims for his recession-proof niche strategy.

By 1995, major problems were affecting many areas of the company, including the pivotal Dial division. Teets, desperate to increase the company's return on equity and stock price, which had been flat since its high in 1992, began again to slash costs. One way he did this was by reducing the advertising budget for Dial soap products from $8.7 million to $4.9 million. However, this was something that no niche player could afford to do when battling such industry giants as Procter & Gamble and Unilever,

TABLE 1

Greyhound's Businesses

Consumer Products	Services	Transportation Manufacturing	Financial Services

The Dial Corporation
  Food
  Personal care
  Laundry and
  household
	Brewster Transport Company, Ltd.
	Consultants and Designers, Inc.
	Carson International, Inc.
	Dobbs Houses, Inc.
	Dobbs International Services, Inc.
		Motor Coach Industries (MCI)
		Transportation Manufacturing Corporation (TMC)
		■ Custom Coach
			Greyhound Financial Corporation
			Greyhound Financial and Leasing
			Greyhound Financial Services, Ltd.
			Greyhound Bank PLC

Greyhound Airport Services Companies

Greyhound Exhibitgroup Inc.

Greyhound Exposition Services, Inc.

Greyhound Food Management, Inc.
- ■ Faber Enterprises, Inc.
- ■ Glacier Park, Inc.
- ■ GFM Engineering and Design Group
- ■ GFM Fast Food Division
- ■ GFM Public Service Division
- ■ GFM Truckstop Systems
- ■ Restaura
- ■ Restaura, S.A.

Greyhound International Travel, Inc. (GITI)

Greyhound Leisure Services, Inc. (GLSI)
- ■ Florida Export Warehouse
- ■ International Cruise Shops
- ■ Greyhound Leisure Services Duty-Free Shops
- ■ Premier Cruise Lines, Ltd.

Greyhound Lines of Canada, Ltd.

Travelers Express Company, Inc.
- ■ Republic Money Orders, Inc.

Universal Coach Parts, Inc.

Source: Greyhound Dial Corporation, Annual Report, 1990.

whose new soap Lever 2000 made major inroads into sales of Dial soap. Dial soap's market share dropped to 17.6 percent from 19.7 percent of the market in 1995, which was a severe blow to the Dial Corporation's most important product line and a disaster for the company.

The Purex division also was not performing well. The Purex bleach line was phased out in 1995 because of mounting losses. Late in 1995, Purex detergent, the low-priced detergent that had been selling well, came under intense pressure from Procter & Gamble, which introduced a competing low-priced brand, Ultra Bonus, which was aimed directly at Purex. Dial was forced to slash the price of Purex by 10 percent to compete, further cutting into the company's profits. Furthermore, Dial's successful Lunch Buckets, the line of microwave products, had generated a host of imitators from major food companies that quickly introduced their own competing products. Having lost this niche and no longer able to compete, Dial phased out Lunch Buckets in 1995. It began to seem to Dial's managers that even when they found a winning strategy their larger competitors just stole the idea away from them.

TABLE 2

The Dial Corporation: Consolidated Balance Sheet
(000 omitted, except per-share data)

	Year-ended December 31		
	1995	1994	1993
Revenues	$3,575,070	$3,546,847	$3,000,342
Costs and expenses			
Costs of sales and services	$3,271,151	$3,216,627	$2,725,049
Restructuring charges and asset write downs	191,100		
Unallocated corporate expense and other items, net	43,194	43,938	42,734
Interest expense	75,994	61,195	57,292
Minority interests	4,346	3,392	3,618
	$3,585,785	$3,325,152	$2,828,693
Income (loss) before income taxes	$(10,715)	$221,695	$171,649
Income taxes (benefit)	(11,852)	81,384	61,376
Income from Continuing Operations	$1,137	$140,311	$110,273
Income from discontinued operations			32,120
Income before extraordinary charge and cumulative effect of change in accounting principle	$1,137	$140,311	$142,393
Extraordinary charge for early retirement of debt net of tax benefit of $11,833			(21,908)
Cumulative effect net of tax benefit of $7,544 to January 1, 1995, of initial application of SFAS No. 121, "Accounting for the Impairment of Long-Lived Assets and for Long-Lived Assets to Be Disposed Of"			(17,696)
Net income (loss)	$(16,559)	$140,311	$120,485
Income (Loss) per Common Share			
Continuing operations	$0.00	$1.61	$1.28
Discontinued operations			
Income before extraordinary charge and cumulative effect of change in accounting principle	$0.00	$1.61	$1.66
Extraordinary charge			(0.26)
Cumulative effect, to January 1, 1995, of initial application of SFAS No. 121	(0.20)		
Net income (loss) per common share	$(0.20)	$1.61	$1.40

Source: Greyhound Dial Corporation, Annual Report, 1990.

Dial's other businesses were also suffering problems. Its cruise ship line, Premier Cruise Lines, which had formed an agreement with the Walt Disney Company to operate Disney's theme cruises on the Big Red Boat, lost its license in 1995 when Disney decided that it would launch its own cruise line. With four aging ships, and lacking any differentiated appeal in the increasingly competitive cruise ship industry in the 1990s, the company put its ships up for sale and withdrew from the cruise ship business—one more recession-proof niche gone.

Then, Dial's airline food business began to suffer in the 1990s when, to cut down on costs in an increasingly competitive airline industry, the major airlines cut back on the quality of the food they offered their customers. Airlines that had offered full meals began to offer snacks, and airlines such as Southwest offered passengers nothing. In airports, too, there had been a move to allow fast-food chains to set up their franchises on-site to increase the variety of foods offered to customers. All this hurt Dial's catering businesses.

It was becoming increasingly obvious to industry analysts that Dial was nothing more than a hodgepodge of different businesses that had nothing in common, were not recession-proof, and did not even have a secure niche.

Dial, 1996–2002

With its profits flat or eroding and no turnaround in sight, the question became how to create new value from Dial's different businesses. The movement of many diversified companies to break up their operations and let individual businesses go it alone in the early 1990s gave Teets his answer. He would split apart Dial's consumer products and services operations—thus dismantling the empire he had built since 1984—into two different companies. One, which would still be known as the Dial Corp., would consist of all its consumer product interests and would have revenues of about $1.3 billion. The other, to be called Viad Corp., would manage its remaining financial, catering, and exhibition businesses and have revenues of about $2.2 billion.

Initially, analysts thought that the breakup would allow the two new companies to realize more value. For example, since they operated separately, a downturn in the business of one division would no longer hurt the performance of the other. Moreover, after the breakup managers would be able to make decisions that could promote their own businesses, not corporate interests. However, analysts later came to realize that in the future there would be two sets of managers who would have to be paid to manage the two companies and two sets of overhead costs. Moreover, the question arose as to whether there was any value to be created by the breakups, because all of Dial's businesses were under threats from more efficient and aggressive competitors such as Procter & Gamble, Colgate-Palmolive, and Unilever. Analysts came to believe increasingly that more value could be made for shareholders if the company dismantled itself and sold off its assets separately to the highest bidder. A bidder could then merge a particular Dial business into its own operations and thus reduce manufacturing, distribution, or marketing costs or

even use its skills to increase the division's differentiation advantage.

In July 1996, John Teets's plan came under increasing attack from Michael Price, president of Heine Securities Corp. Price was the advisor to Mutual Series Funds, a large mutual fund company that owned 9.9 percent of Dial's stock. Price, along with other analysts, however, argued that Teet's plan would reduce, not increase, value for shareholders and that what Teets should do was to divest Dial's many different businesses and return the proceeds to shareholders. Of course, the sell off would mean that many of Dial's managers might find themselves out of well-paying jobs, including Teets, who had earned many millions of dollars over the years. On the other hand, these managers had not created much value for their shareholders.

In 1996, Teets answered his critics with half-page ads in the *Wall Street Journal* arguing that his strategy was a "strategy for empowered growth" that would allow each of the two new companies to "aggressively pursue acquisition opportunities without worry about upsetting the balance in Dial's existing mix of business." However, he did not explain how new value would be created by the two companies or how the proposed acquisitions might create value. Since Teets's acquisition strategy had met with little success for the last twelve years, what reason would shareholders have to suppose it would improve in the future?

This question remained unanswered, but in 1996, Viad was spun off to stockholders, Teets stepped down as CEO, and a new CEO, Malcolm Jozoff, was appointed to head what was now a consumer products company, albeit one that sold canned beef and shampoo. Jozoff was recruited from Procter & Gamble because Dial's board believed that a P&G veteran would understand how to fashion a business model to promote the profitability of a soap and detergent maker. What they forgot was that P&G is a differentiator whose claim to fame is developing new and improved products and marketing them successfully to consumers. While it is true that Dial, the bestselling antibacterial soap, was their flagship differentiated product, Dial's other main products, such as Purex detergent, Breck Shampoo, and even Armour corned beef, were not bought for their differentiated qualities but because of their low price. Even Dial soap did not command much of a premium price compared with P&G's and Unilever's brands; it sold because of the advertising expenditures used to promote its brand name.

Jozoff, however, given his immersion in P&G's "differentiation" culture, saw Dial's problems as the lack of a differentiated appeal of its products, not the fact that its high-cost structure was eroding the profitability of a low-price cost leadership strategy. Jozoff's efforts were thus directed toward increasing customer demand by differentiating Dial's brands. To promote Purex washing powder, he entered into a joint venture with Germany's Henkel group to use that company's expertise in stain removal to boost Purex's cleaning power (not its strong point); he proposed to call the new powder "Purex Advanced" and to recoup the extra costs it would cost a few dollars more a pack. He felt these moves would position it against Tide, the leading brand. Knowing that P&G was entering the home dry-cleaning market, he introduced a new Purex home dry-cleaning kit, and also knowing that P&G and Unilever were introducing washing powder in tablet form, he put in motion Purex Tablets. To push Dial into higher-end personal care products, he bought two companies, Sarah Michaels and Freeman Cosmetics, that specialized in producing upscale soaps, bath powders, and oils for gift boxes, although he did not propose to sell these under the Dial name. Also, knowing that rivals were developing new kinds of antibacterial soap with more fragrant scents and better foaming qualities, he reformulated Dial soap to position it against tough future competition. Jozoff also agreed to acquire the Plusbelle brand hair care business from Revlon for $46.5 million. Plusbelle was the leader in the Argentinean market. These acquisitions cost over $300 million and pushed up Dial's debt to over $550 million. Teets had left Dial saddled with a $300 million debt during the Viad spinoff, whereas Viad emerged virtually debt free.

In changing Dial's business-level strategy, Jozoff plunged the company into a whole new set of problems. First, the movement to a differentiation strategy raised Dial's cost structure, especially because of the extra debt it had to assume, so he was betting the company's future on consumers' acceptance of Dial's new products and higher-pricing structure. At the same time, Jozoff brought the company into more direct competition with such rivals as P&G and Unilever that had much more money to spend on the expensive business of promoting new brand products. For example, it was estimated that in 1994 it would cost $5 million in fees to retailers to promote a new consumer product in the greater New York area; that figure

had risen to $25 million by 1999 because of increasing competition for shelf space caused by the consolidation both of consumer product companies and of retailers and supermarkets such as Kroger's.

When Dial's new products started to be manufactured and introduced in 1998 and 1999, at first things looked good; sales increased by 12 percent in 1998 and by 13 percent in 1999 to $1.7 billion, and operating profits grew 13 percent in 1998 and 17 percent in 1999. However, it turned out that things were not as good as they seemed. While sales did increase in 1998, largely as the result of a big increase in marketing expenditures to sell the new, wider product range, by 1999 consumers were turning away from Dial's brands. By the middle of 1999, Dial's top managers knew there were problems, but to disguise the issue from the board, the company's sales team was instructed to boost the end-of-year sales figures by "stuffing the channel" with Dial products; that is, sending huge inventories of products, particularly Dial soap, to retailers that counted as sales in the company's books, and by offering retailers big promotions to sell its products at discounted prices to move them off the shelves.

Major errors were also made. First, expecting customers to stock up on canned goods because of Y2K glitches, the company loaded up stores with extra Armor Star Vienna Sausage and then raised prices hoping its competitors would follow. When there was no Y2K panic and competitors didn't raise prices, most of this product was left unsold and was either returned or sold at cost. Second, although it seemed to Jozoff that the Sarah Michaels and Freeman Cosmetics acquisitions were natural, albeit "upmarket," extensions to Dial's product line, Dial was not prepared for the huge manufacturing challenges involved in custom-packing gift boxes and matching them to the needs of the customers. As Baum (see next section) later said, upmarket products such as scented lotions, bath oils, and aromatherapy products are "fashion products," whereas Dial's business was "bread-and-butter" products where low-cost production and distribution were vital. Third, it turned out that the market for home dry-cleaning was far smaller than anticipated, and Dial's dry-cleaning product was simply left on the shelf because of its rivals' higher advertising budgets.

Even in the vital soap business, problems arose. Because Dial had stuffed the channels with its old soap product, when its new improved scented moisturizing soap came out in late 1999, retailers would not sell it until they had sold the old soap product. This gave a leg up to P&G and Unilever, which had also introduced a new range of soap to compete with Dial. Finally, Dial discovered that customers didn't understand the properties of the new improved Purex washing powder or why they should spend a lot more for it. As Baum later commented, he pleaded with Jozoff to introduce it under another upmarket name to differentiate it, but this was not done, and the powder was left stuck in the middle—not differentiated and not low cost.

Dial Gets a New CEO

As a result of all these problems, estimates for Dial's 2000 operating profits dropped from $73 million to $60 million in the summer of 2000, wiping out all its previous gains. The board became increasingly aware of the problems that had been taking place, and in August 2000, they ousted Jozoff as CEO and replaced him with a vocal board member, Herbert M. Baum. Baum, a former Campbell Soup executive and CEO of Quaker State (which he had sold to Pennzoil) and then the COO of Hasbro, the toy maker, was surprised to be asked to take over yet one more turnaround effort at Dial, but he accepted the challenge. Since his experience was with bread-and-butter products—canned soups and oil—he was familiar with the problems of managing a company's cost structure to get the most value out of its products. He also recognized the importance of finding the right strategy to compete against rivals like P&G and powerful retail chains like Kroger and Wal-Mart, both of which were launching private-label low-price washing powders and soaps at the low end of the market. The problem was that he had to move fast because Dial's performance and stock price were collapsing.

Baum took a close look at how Dial's brands were managed internally. He reorganized them into a product structure with five product groups—personal cleansing, washing powders, air fresheners, food products, and Dial International. For the first time, Baum made the product line managers accountable for their own inventory management and profit-and-loss figures. Previously, these had been spread across brands so that each line's relative performance had been hidden. Now it was possible to identify specific underperforming brands and decide what to do about them—turn them around, sell them off, or close them down.

Baum then turned his attention to the various problems that emerged in launching Dial's new products. Recognizing the importance of protecting Dial soap's market share, he pumped money into advertising its improved products to regain their momentum and build their profitability. With Purex, he decided to go ahead with the introduction of Purex tablets, but ended the joint venture with Henkel and went back to the old low-cost strategy. He also decided to sell off the Sarah Michaels and Freeman upscale lines, which had only resulted in losses, and he used the money to reduce Dial's debt. He also withdrew from the home dry-cleaning market and took Purex's product off the shelf. The savings in operating costs from abandoning these product lines provided money to fund Dial's core soap, Purex, and Renuzit air freshener products and lowered its cost structure.

In September 2001, Baum announced that, given the increasing competitive pressures in all its brand categories from companies like P&G and Unilever, he and the board felt that it would be better if Dial were part of a larger enterprise. Various possible acquirers came forward to look at the company's books in the next months, but it appeared that none of them wanted to buy the whole company. In the meantime, Baum's business model and strategies began to pay off for Dial. Its inventory stocking and manufacturing problems were gone; brand managers were squeezing out costs now that they were directly responsible for their brand's performance; and top managers were not distracted by searching for elusive new product opportunities but were focusing, perhaps for the first time, on managing all aspects of the value chain to reduce costs. With its well-known products, sold at the right price, there was no reason why Dial should not be able to increase revenues and profits and build cash flow.

In fact, the company astounded analysts when in April 2002, only six months after it put itself up for sale, it raised its first-quarter earnings estimates, citing stronger-than-expected domestic sales. Dial's share reached $20, up from just $12 only a year before. Baum also announced in April that Dial itself, to strengthen and protect its core businesses, would be looking to make acquisitions in the coming year. Baum emphasized that Dial would be buying brands, not companies—those with high sales volumes and those that used the same sales channels as Dial so it could make better use of the company's resources.

Dial Is Bought by Henkel

By the end of 2002, under Baum's turnaround strategy, Dial reported that it had turned an operating loss of $132 million in 2001 into a profit of $16 million for 2002. Baum's strategy to build Dial's strengths in its core washing powder, soap, and foods brands was apparently working. The company's stock price shot up as investors either hoped for continued operating improvements or a takeover by another company. By the end of 2003, Dial's stock price had doubled since Baum became its CEO.

In 2003, however, it became clear that Dial's worries were not over. In the retail industry, many retailers who were struggling to compete with Wal-Mart began to demand lower prices for products from their suppliers. At the same time, Dial's sales of its products to discount operations such as Sam's and Costco, which expected low prices, were accounting for an increasingly bigger part of its sales. By 2003, Wal-Mart, for example, accounted for 28 percent of Dial's sales, and it was putting pressure on Dial for cost reductions to allow it to maintain its price advantage over retail competitors.

At the same time, Dial was still struggling to compete with its much larger rivals Procter & Gamble and Unilever in an industry increasingly dominated by a few global giants who had the broad product range and financial resources to compete successfully against Dial. Indeed, using its marketing muscle, P&G had now become the leading seller of liquid soap and Dial was in second place. In addition, there had been a major change in customer taste for soap because demand for bar soap had dropped significantly as customers increasingly turned to milder body wash products. Once again P&G and Unilever with their brands such as Dove and Oil of Olay had begun to dominate the market although Baum fought back by introducing and promoting Dial's own Dial, Coast, and Tone body washes.

In this increasingly competitive industry environment, Baum continued to search for a potential takeover partner even as he strengthened the company's core products lines. In 2003, Baum was also successful in rejuvenating Dial's money-losing food

products such as its Armor and Armor Star canned meats, chili, hash, and meat spreads. As a part of this strategy, Dial began to manufacture meat products for third parties under their own private brand labels, and this accounted for 28 percent of their business in 2003 so that with Armor's own 20 percent market share Dial had close to half of the U.S. canned meats business.

With all these ongoing improvements, in December 2003 Henkel—the German company that Dial had previously entered into an alliance with to develop advanced washing powders and dry-cleaning products—announced that it would takeover Dial in a deal worth $2.9 billion or for $28.75 a share which represented an 11 percent premium over Dial's stock price. This merger would bring together two small global players who, even combined, would be dwarfed by P&G and Unilever. However, for Henkel the acquisition of Dial would bring it broader global reach and allow it to enter the profitable U.S. market. Despite the marketing mistakes with Advanced Purex that had hurt Dial's performance, Henkel saw many opportunities for using its expertise in chemicals to innovate new and improved products.

To fund the acquisition, Henkel announced it planned to sell its 29.7 percent stake in Clorox, the profitable U.S. maker of bleach and other household products; however, it would also take over some of Clorox's brands. In May 2004, the merger proceeded as planned, and Dial became an operating unit of Henkel although Henkel has gained Herbert Baum's commitment to stay on as its CEO for the next two years to guide the transition as Henkel integrates its new U.S. operations.

Baum's actions left the Dial unit in a strong position. In 2004, he was able to avoid layoffs and increase sales volume of its Purex laundry detergent to make it No. 2 nationwide. Indeed, although Wal-Mart pressured Dial for lower costs, Baum was able to reduce Dial's cost structure so that it could still maintain good profit margins from its sales of Purex to Wal-Mart.

Henkel has also benefited from the turnaround of its new Dial Unit. In 2005, it reported that its fourth quarter earnings rose nearly 13 percent, beating analyst forecasts, as the strong performance of the Dial unit compensated for slow sales in the European market for toiletries and cosmetics. It also plans to expand the presence of its European brands such as Persil in the U.S. market to better compete with giant Procter & Gamble, which announced in 2005 that it wanted to merge with Gillette to create the biggest consumer products company in the world.

REFERENCES

Moody's Transportation Manual, 1987.

A. Stuart, "Greyhound Gets Ready for a New Driver," *Fortune*, March 3, 1966, pp. 34–38.

Greyhound Corporation, Annual Reports, 1966–1990.

Dial Corporation, Annual Reports and 10K Reports, 1971–2002.

"Greyhound: A Big Sell-off Leaves It Built for Better Speed," *Business Week*, July 25, 1983, pp. 88–90.

"Greyhound's New Strategy: Slimmed Down and Decentralized, It's After More Market Share, 15% on Equity," *Dun's Business Month*, February 1984, pp. 66–68.

S. Toy and J. H. Dobrzynski, "Will More Soap Help Greyhound Shine?" *Business Week*, March 11, 1985, pp. 73–78.

"The Greyhound Corporation," *Wall Street Journal Transcript*, February 5, 1990, pp. 96, 204.

"Dial Corp.: Firm's Loss of $26.2 Million Is Due to Special Charges," *Wall Street Journal*, October 25, 2000, p. B8.

Jack Neff and Kate MacArthur, "Beleaguered Dial Cuts Product Lines," *Advertising Age*, September 25, 2000, p. 128.

"Dial Corp.: Loss of $7.5 Million Posted, Partly from a Restructuring," *Wall Street Journal*, January 25, 2001, p. B5.

Rebecca Flass, "Dial Shifts Direction," *Adweek*, May 21, 2001, p. 8.

"Dial Agrees to Buy Plusbelle," *Wall Street Journal*, March 30, 2000, p. C14.

Steven Lipin and Anna W. Mathews, "Dial Board, Hit by New Profit Shortfall, Ousts Top Executives and Turns to Baum," *Wall Street Journal*, August 8, 2000, p. A3.

Arlene Weintraub and Christopher Palameri, "Wish Everyone Used Dial? Dial Does," *Business Week*, September 25, 2000, pp. 132–134.

Kerri Walsh, "Dial Raises First-Quarter Earnings Estimates; Eyes Brand Acquisitions," *Chemical Week*, April 17, 2002, p. 36.

"Dial Jettisons Underperforming Unit," *SPC Soap, Perfumery, and Cosmetics*, London, September, 2001, p. 4.

Brent Shearer, "Under Competitive Pressures, Dial Puts Itself Up for Sale," *Mergers and Acquisitions*, October 2001, p. 23.

"Dial Corp.: Earnings Forecast Climbs Again to as Much as 25 Cents a Share," *Wall Street Journal*, April 10, 2002, p. A8.

Jack Neff, "Clorox, Dial Exit Dry Cleaning Biz," *Advertising Age*, September 10, 2001, p. 4.

Kerri Walsh, "Dial May Be Broken Up," *Chemical Week*, August 15, 2001, p. 25.

"Dial Puts Itself Up for Sale Despite Portfolio, Analysts Say Company Could Fetch $2 Billion," *Chemical Market Reporter*, August 13, 2001, p. 3.

"Dial Corp.: Quarterly Earnings Surge, Outlook for Year Is Raised," *Wall Street Journal*, July 26, 2001.

Gene G. Marcial, "With Dial, Clorox Could Clean Up," *Business Week*, October 4, 1999, p. 247.

"Dial Corp.: Laundry-Products Venture to Tap Henkel Technology," *Wall Street Journal*, April 21, 1999.

Case 28

Hanson PLC (A): The Acquisition Machine

This case was prepared by Charles W. L. Hill, the University of Washington.

Introduction

Hanson PLC is one of the ten biggest companies in Britain, and its U.S. arm, Hanson Industries, is one of America's sixty largest industrial concerns. A conglomerate with more than 150 different businesses in its portfolio, Hanson PLC has grown primarily by making acquisitions. By the end of 1989, the company had recorded twenty-six years of uninterrupted profit growth, cumulating in 1989 operating income of $1.61 billion on revenues of $11.3 billion and assets of $12.03 billion. The company's shareholders have been major beneficiaries of this growth. Between 1974 and 1989, the price of the company's shares on the London Stock Exchange increased eightyfold, compared with an average increase of fifteenfold for all companies quoted on the London Stock Exchange during this period.[1] Along the way, Hanson has gained a reputation for being one of the most successful takeover machines in the world. Its acquisitions during the 1980s included three American conglomerates (U.S. Industries, SCM Corporation, and Kidde) and three major British companies (London Brick, the Imperial Group, and Consolidated Gold Fields). So high is Hanson's profile that Oliver Stone, in his film *Wall Street*, reportedly used Sir Gordon White, head of Hanson Industries, as the model for the British corporate raider (the one who outmaneuvered the evil Gordon Gekko).

Despite this impressive track record, as Hanson enters the 1990s analysts increasingly wonder about the strategy of the company. There is speculation that the company may be on the verge of breaking itself up and returning the gains to shareholders. The age of the company's founders is fueling this speculation. The two men who built and still run the conglomerate, Lord Hanson and Sir Gordon White, are in their late sixties, and both have promised to consider retiring when they are seventy. As one insider put it, "The guys that started it off will finish it off."[2] Another factor is that Hanson is now so big that it would take some spectacular deals to continue its historic growth rate. According to many, including Harvard Business School strategy guru Michael Porter, there simply are not that many obvious companies for Hanson to buy. Thus, "even Hanson will be faced with poorer and poorer odds of maintaining its record."[3] On the other hand, at the end of 1989 Hanson had $8.5 billion in cash on its balance sheet. That, along with the billions it could borrow if need be (the company reportedly has a borrowing capacity of $20 billion), suggests that if Hanson and White should so wish, they could undertake an acquisition that would rival the RJR-Nabisco deal in size.

Other commentators question the long-term viability of the company. Some claim that Hanson PLC is little more than an asset stripper that in the long run will drive the companies it manages into the ground. According to one investment banker, "I'm not convinced that Hanson runs companies any better than anyone else. But I certainly know it squeezes them for cash, sucking the life from them."[4] Similarly, one former executive noted that "some of the incentive programs that they write for managers actually keep the company from growing. . . . They become so concerned with profit today that they don't re-invest for tomorrow."[5] The company disagrees. Sir Gordon White clearly sees Hanson PLC as reducing inefficiencies in the companies it acquires, not stripping assets. If anything is stripped away from acquisitions, according to White, it is unnecessary corporate bureaucracy, overstaffed head offices, and top-management perks, not assets. He steadfastly maintains that the company treats all acquired businesses as if it were going to keep them.[6]

With these issues in mind, in this case we consider the growth and development of Hanson PLC. We review the administrative systems that the company uses to manage its ongoing businesses, and we look at two acquisitions and their aftermath in depth: the 1987 acquisitions of SCM Corporation and the Imperial Group.

History

The origins of Hanson PLC go back to the port city of Hull in Yorkshire, England, in the 1950s.[7] At that time, James Hanson was learning his family's transportation business (the family operated a fleet of passenger coaches), and Gordon White was selling advertising for Welbecson Limited, a magazine printing company owned by his father. James Hanson's brother, Bill, was White's closest friend, and when Bill died of cancer at twenty-nine, James and Gordon became close friends. In the late 1950s, Hanson and White decided to team up in business. They formed Hanson White Ltd., a greeting card company. Although the company did well, the two soon became bored with the limited challenges and potential that the greeting card business offered, and in 1963 they sold out and began to look for acquisition opportunities.

Their first buy was Oswald Tillotson Ltd., a vehicle distribution company. This company was subsequently acquired by Wiles Group Ltd., a Yorkshire-based manufacturer of agricultural sacks and fertilizers. As part of the takeover deal, Hanson and White were given a substantial ownership position in the Wiles Group. Hanson and White soon gained management control of the Wiles Group, and in 1969, after deciding that James Hanson's name had a nicer ring to it than Gordon White's, they changed the name to Hanson Trust.

Because of a series of small acquisitions, by the end of 1973 Hanson Trust owned twenty-four companies with combined sales of $120 million.

By 1973, however, the British economy was in deep trouble. The stock market had collapsed; the country was paralyzed by labor disputes; inflation was increasing rapidly, as was unemployment; and Prime Minister Edward Heath of the supposedly probusiness Conservative party had blasted conglomerate companies such as Hanson Trust as representing "the unacceptable face of capitalism." All of this prompted Gordon White to rethink his future. As White put it,

> I was disgusted with England at the time. Disgusted with socialism and unions and excessive, antibusiness government, disgusted with the way initiative was being taxed out of existence. . . . I'd done a lot of thinking. I told James (Hanson) that maybe we should just call it a day. I thought I'd try America.[8]

Hanson replied that there was no need to split up, and they agreed that Hanson would run the British operations while White tried to build operations in America.

White arrived in New York in the fall of 1973 in possession of a round-trip ticket, a one-year work visa, and $3,000 in traveler's checks, which was the most that British currency controls permitted a U.K. citizen to take abroad at that time. Moreover, because of British exchange controls, White could not gain access to Hanson's ample treasury without substantial penalties, and he had to struggle to convince banks that he was creditworthy. Despite this, in 1974 White managed to borrow $32 million from Chemical Bank to finance his first major U.S. acquisition, a friendly takeover of J. Howard Smith Company, a New Jersey-based processor of edible oils and animal feed that was later renamed Seacoast Products. The CEO of J. Howard Smith was David Clarke, whose family business it was. Clarke subsequently became White's right-hand man. He is now president of Hanson Industries and the most senior executive in the United States after White.

Over the next ten years, White made another six major U.S. acquisitions, all of them friendly (see Table 1). Then, in 1984, White was ready for his first hostile takeover, the $532-million purchase of U.S. Industries (USI). USI was a conglomerate that had grown by acquisitions during the 1960s and 1970s. White became interested in the company when he read in a newspaper that management was putting together a

TABLE 1

U.S. Acquisitions, 1974–1990

Date	Acquisition	Cost (millions)	Businesses
1974	Seacost	$32	Fish processing, pet food
1975	Carisbrook	36	Textile manufacturing
1976	Hygrade	32	Castings and casing units
1977	Old Salt Seafood	2	Prepared foods
1978	Interstate United	30	Food service management
1978	Templon	7	Textile manufacturing
1981	McDonough	185	Cement, concrete
1984	U.S. Industries	532	33-company conglomerate
1986	SCM	930	22-company conglomerate
1987	Kaiser Cement	250	Cement plants
1988	Kidde	1,700	108-company conglomerate
1990	Peabody	1,230	Coal mining

Source: Adapted from Gordon White, "How I Turned $3,000 into $10 Billion," *Fortune,* November 7, 1988, pp. 80–89; and "Hanson PLC," *Value Line,* July 20, 1990, p. 832.

leveraged buyout at $20 a share for a total purchase price of $445 million. He suspected that the company was worth more than that and quickly worked out how big a loan Hanson Industries could handle, using USI's projected cash flow to cover interest charges. To USI's pretax earnings of $67 million he added $40 million generated by depreciation and $24 million in savings that he thought Hanson could effect by removing USI's corporate headquarters. That yielded a total cash flow of $131 million, or more than $70 million after taxes. With interest rates running at 13 percent, white figured that Hanson Industries could afford a loan of $544 million. In what was to become standard White thinking, he also reckoned that even with a worse-case scenario, he could recoup his investment by selling off the disparate pieces of the company.

Hanson Industries began to buy USI shares and by April 1984 held 5 percent of the company. Hanson then made a $19 per share bid for the company, which was quickly rebuffed by USI management. Three days later White increased Hanson's bid to $22 per share. USI's management, which had yet to raise the financing for its own proposed leveraged buyout, responded by increasing the purchase price to $24 per share. Hanson responded by initiating a tender offer of $23 per share in cash. For stockholders, cash in hand at $23 per share was far more attractive than management's promise of $24 per share if financing could be arranged, and Hanson's bid quickly won the day.

After the acquisition was completed, Hanson Industries President David Clarke spent six months at USI's corporate headquarters reviewing operations. At the end of this period USI's corporate headquarters was closed down, the staff was laid off, and financial control was centralized at Hanson Industries' small headquarters. However, most of the operating managers in charge of USI's constituent companies stayed on, lured by Hanson's incentive pay scheme and the promise that they could run their own shows. In what was also typical Hanson fashion, nine of USI's operating companies were subsequently sold off to outside investors for a price of $225 million.

The acquisition of USI was followed by three other hostile takeover bids in the United States: for SCM Corporation, Kaiser Cement, and Kidde. Of these, the SCM bid was by far the most acrimonious. SCM took a poison pill and tried to protect its position through the law courts before Hanson finally won control over the company. (The SCM takeover is discussed in detail later in this case.)

While White was making these U.S. acquisitions, Hanson was not sitting idle in Britain. During the 1980s

U.K. Acquisitions During the 1980s

Date	Acquisition	Cost (millions)	Businesses
1981	Ever Ready	£95	Dry cell batteries
1983	UDS	£250	Retail operations
1984	London Brick	£247	Brick manufacturer
1984	Powell Duffryn	£150	Engineering, shipping, fuel
1986	Imperial Group	£2,360	Tobacco, brewing, food
1989	Consolidated Gold Fields	£3,610	Gold mining, building aggregates

Source: Various press reports.

the company made a series of acquisitions in the United Kingdom. These are summarized in Table 2. The most notable were the 1984 acquisition of London Brick, Britain's largest brick manufacturer, against vigorous opposition from London Brick's incumbent management; the £2.36-billion acquisition of Imperial, the largest tobacco company in Britain and the third largest in the world; and the £3.61-billion acquisition of Consolidated Gold Fields, the second largest gold-mining business in the world. The acquisitions of Imperial and Consolidated Gold Fields were the two largest takeovers ever undertaken in Britain. (The Imperial takeover is discussed in detail later in this case.)

Acquisitions Philosophy

Hanson PLC's acquisitions on both sides of the Atlantic are primarily overseen by Sir Gordon White. Lord Hanson is primarily responsible for the ongoing administration of the company. As Lord Hanson says of White, "He's the one with the gift for takeovers."[9] In turn, White says of Hanson, "James is a brilliant administrator and really knows how to run a company."[10] White claims that many of his acquisition ideas, including the USI deal, come from the newspapers. Others are suggested to him by contacts in the investment banking community, particularly Bob Pirie, president of the Rothschild investment bank, with whom white has lunch once a week.

Whenever possible, White avoids working at the office, opting instead to work from one of his four houses. Unlike corporate raiders such as Saul Steinberg and Carl Icahn, White rarely reads annual reports or detailed stock reports on a target company, claiming that he can get all of the financial information that he needs from Standard & Poor's two-page summaries. In addition, his three-person takeover staff distills reams of financial data on a target and provides him with a short memo on the target company. Says White, "I'm like Churchill, tell me everything you can tell me. On one page."[11]

Under White's leadership, one of the things that has distinguished Hanson PLC from many other acquisitive conglomerates is its distinctive acquisitions philosophy (which is, in essence, White's philosophy). This philosophy appears to be based on a number of consistent factors that are found to underlie most of Hanson's acquisitions.[12]

1. *Target characteristics.* Hanson looks for companies based in mature, low-technology industries that have a less-than-inspiring record but show potential for improving performance. Normally, the objective has been to identify a poorly performing target where the incumbent management team has gone some way toward improving the underlying performance but whose efforts have not yet been reflected in either the profit-and-loss account or, more importantly, the target's stock price.

2. *Research.* Although White claims that he does little reading on takeover targets, his takeover staff does undertake detailed research into the potential of target companies before any bid is made. The staff routinely investigates companies undertaking leveraged buyouts.

3. *Risk assessment.* One of White's most often quoted edicts is "watch the downside." What this means is that instead of considering the potential benefits of a deal, give consideration to what can go wrong and the likely consequences of a worst-case scenario. White will purchase a company only if he thinks that in a worst-case scenario he will be able to recover the purchase price by breaking the target up and selling off its constituent parts.

4. *Funding.* White was one of the early pioneers of the highly leveraged takeover deal. All of the U.S. acquisitions have been financed by nonrecourse debt, secured on the assets of the target. This

enabled White to engineer substantial acquisitions when Hanson Industries itself had a very small capital base. The British acquisitions have been funded by a mix of cash, equity, convertible securities, and loan stock.

5. *Disposals to reduce debt.* After an acquisition has been completed, Hanson sends some of its own managers along with a group of external accountants to go through and audit the acquired businesses. After a thorough review, Hanson typically sells off the parts of the acquired company that cannot reach Hanson's stringent profitability targets. In the process, Hanson is able to reduce the debt taken on to fund the acquisition. The most outstanding example followed the purchase of SCM for $930 million. After the takeover, Hanson sold off SCM's real estate, pulp and paper, and food holdings for a price of $964 million while holding on to SCM's typewriter and chemicals business, which in effect had been acquired for nothing. Thus, within six months of the takeover's being completed, Hanson was able to eliminate the debt taken on to finance the SCM acquisition. Similar, although less spectacular, disposals have characterized almost all of Hanson's major acquisitions on both sides of the Atlantic.

6. *Elimination of excess overhead.* Another objective of Hanson's housecleaning of acquired companies is to eliminate any excess overhead. This typically involves closing down the corporate headquarters of the acquired company, eliminating some of the staff, and sending other staff down to the operating level. Before Hanson took over, SCM had 230 people in its corporate office, USI had 180, Kidde had 200, and Hanson itself had 30. Today the total headquarters staff for all four is 120.

Hanson also disposes of any management perks found either at the corporate or the operating level of an acquired company. For example, one of Kidde's operating companies had a collection of art and antiques, a hunting lodge, and three corporate jets. Hanson kept one jet and disposed of the rest, including the man at the top who had spent the money.

7. *The creation of incentives.* Hanson tries to create strong incentives for the management of acquired operating companies to improve performance. This is achieved by (a) decentralization designed to give operating managers full autonomy for the running of their businesses, (b) motivating operating managers by setting profit targets that, if achieved, will result in significant profit enhancements, and (c) motivating managers by giving them large pay bonuses if they hit or exceed Hanson's profit targets.

Organization and Management Philosophy

In addition to its acquisitions philosophy, Hanson is also renowned for its ongoing management of operating companies, of which there are more than 150 in the corporate portfolio. Although Hanson does have some interests elsewhere, the strategic development of the group has centered on the United States and Britain, where a broad balance has tended to exist in recent years. Hanson PLC looks after the British operations, and Hanson Industries, the U.S. subsidiary, manages the U.S. operations. Each of these two units is operated on an entirely autonomous basis. Only one director sits on the board of both companies. Hanson PLC is headed by Hanson; Hanson Industries is headed by White.[13]

There are two corporate headquarters, one in the United States and one in Britain. At both locations there is a small central staff responsible for monitoring the performance of operating companies, selecting and motivating operating management, the treasury function (including acting as a central bank for the operating units), acquisitions and disposals, and professional services such as legal and taxation.

Below each headquarters are a number of divisions (see Figure 1). These are not operating companies. Rather, they are groupings of operating companies. In 1988 there were four U.S. divisions (consumer, building products, industrial, and food) and four British divisions (again, consumer, building products, industrial, and food). There are no personnel at the divisional level with the exception of a divisional CEO. Below the divisions are the operating companies. Each operating company has its own CEO who reports to the divisional CEO. The divisional CEOs in Britain are responsible to Lord Hanson; those in the United States are responsible to David Clarke, White's right-hand man. White himself is primarily concerned with acquisitions and leaves most issues of control to David Clarke. Indeed, White claims that he has never visited Hanson Industries' U.S. corporate

FIGURE 1

Hanson PLC Organizational Structure

Source: Hanson Industries, Annual Report, 1986.

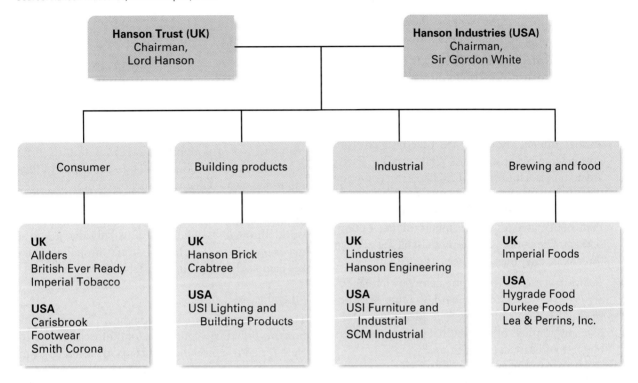

headquarters and as a matter of policy never visits operating companies.[14]

The following principles seem to characterize Hanson's management philosophy.

- ■ *Decentralization.* All day-to-day operating decisions are decentralized to operating company managers. The corporate center does not offer suggestions about how to manufacture or market a product. Thus, within the limits set by centrally approved operating budgets and capital expenditures, operating management has unlimited autonomy. As a consequence, operating managers are responsible for the return on capital that they employ.

- ■ *Tight financial control.* Financial control is achieved through two devices: (1) operating budgets and (2) capital expenditure policies. In a bottom-up process, operating budgets are submitted annually to the corporate center by operating company managers. The budgets include detailed performance targets, particularly with regard to return on capital employed (ROK). Corporate staff reviews

the budgets and, after consultation with operating management, approves a budget for the coming year. Once agreed upon, the operating budget becomes gospel. The performance of an operating company is compared against budget on a monthly basis, and any variance is investigated by the corporate center. If an operating company betters its projected ROK, the figure used as the base for the next year's budget is the actual ROK, not the budgeted figure.

Any cash generated by an operating company is viewed as belonging to the corporate center, not to the operating company. Capital expenditures are extremely closely monitored. All cash expenditures in excess of $3,000 (£1,000 in Britain) have to be agreed upon by corporate headquarters. Capital expenditure requests are frequently challenged by headquarters staff. For example, a manager who contends that an investment in more efficient machinery will cut labor costs must even provide the names of the employees that he or she expects to lay off to achieve the savings.

According to company insiders, when justifying a request for capital expenditure, a manager must explain every possibility. In general, Hanson looks for a pretax payback on expenditures of three years. The quicker the payback, the more likely it is that an expenditure will be approved.

- *Incentive systems.* A major element of the pay of operating managers is linked directly to operating company performance. A manager can earn up to 60 percent of his or her base salary if the operating company exceeds the ROK target detailed in its annual budget. Bonuses are based strictly on bottom-line performance. As White puts it, "There are no bonuses for being a nice chap."[15] In addition, there is a share option scheme for the most senior operating company and corporate managers. More than 600 managers are members of the option scheme. The options are not exercisable for at least three years after they have been granted.

- *Board structure.* No operating company managers are ever appointed to the board of either Hanson PLC or Hanson Industries. The idea is to eliminate any conflicts of interest that might arise over budgets and capital expenditures.

- *De-emphasizing operating synergy.* In contrast to many diversified companies, Hanson has no interest in trying to realize operating synergy. For example, two of Hanson PLC's subsidiaries, Imperial Tobacco and Elizabeth Shaw (a chocolate firm), are based in Bristol, England, and both deliver goods to news agents and corner shops around Britain. However, Hanson prohibits them from sharing distribution because it reckons that any economies of scale that result would be outweighed by the inefficiencies that would arise if each operating company could blame the other for distribution problems.

The SCM Acquisition

SCM was a diversified manufacturer of consumer and industrial products. SCM had twenty-two operating companies based in five industries: chemicals, coatings and resins, paper and pulp, foods, and typewriters.[16] Among other things, SCM was the world's leading manufacturer of portable typewriters (Smith-Corona typewriters), the world's third largest producer of titanium dioxide (a white inorganic pigment widely used in the manufacture of paint, paper, plastic, and rubber products), the sixth largest paint manufacturer in the world through its Glidden Paints subsidiary, and a major force in the U.S. food industry through its Durkee Famous Foods group (see Table 3).

Attractions to Hanson

The SCM group was first brought to White's attention by Bob Pirie, president of Rothschild Inc. in New York. Pirie thought, and Hanson's research team soon confirmed, that SCM had a number of characteristics that made it a perfect Hanson buy.

1. *Poor financial performance.* Summary financial data for SCM are given in Table 4. Pretax profit had declined from a peak of $83.2 million in 1980 to $54.1 million in 1985. The 1985 return on equity of 7.7 percent was very poor by Hanson's standards, and earnings per share had declined by 19 percent since 1980.

TABLE 3

SCM Divisional Results for the Year Ended June 1985

Division	Revenues		Profits	
	$m	Percentage of Change from 1984	$m	Percentage of Change from 1984
Chemicals	$539.0	+49%	$73.7	−100%
Coatings and resins	687.0	+5%	49.9	−3%
Paper and pulp	362.0	+3%	23.1	+10%
Foods	422.0	+7%	23.0	+35%
Typewriters	176.0	−11%	(47.4)*	−200%

*Loss after a $35 million charge for restructuring.
Source: Data from Hanson Industries, Annual Report, 1986.

TABLE 4

Financial Data for SCM

	1980	1981	1982	1983	1984	1985
Net sales ($m)	$1,745.0	$1,761.0	$1,703.0	$1,663.0	$1,963.0	$2,175.0
Pretax profits ($m)	83.2	72.6	35.3	37.8	64.8	54.1
Earnings per share ($)—fully diluted	$4.76	$5.01	$3.20	$2.63	$4.05	$3.85
Return on equity	12.40%	12.00%	5.80%	4.90%	8.00%	7.70%

Source: Data from Hanson Industries, Annual Report, 1986.

2. *Beginnings of a turnaround.* There were signs that incumbent management was coming to grips with SCM's problems, particularly in the troubled type-writer operation, where the 1985 loss was due to a one-time charge of $39 million for restructuring. Financial performance had improved since the low point in 1983, but the benefits of this improvement were not yet reflected in the company's stock price.

3. *Mature businesses.* SCM's presence in mature, proven markets that were technologically stable fit White's preferences.

4. *Low risk.* Some 50 percent of SCM's turnover covered products well known to the U.S. consumer (for example, Smith-Corona typewriters, Glidden paint, Durkee foods). White felt that there would be a ready market for such highly branded businesses if Hanson decided to dispose of any companies that did not meet its stringent ROK requirements.

5. *Titanium dioxide.* Titanium dioxide was dominated by a global oligopoly. Hanson was aware of two favorable trends in the industry that made high returns likely: (a) worldwide demand was forecasted to exceed supply for the next few years, and (b) input costs were declining because of the currency weakness of the major raw material source, Australia.

6. *Corporate overhead.* A corporate staff of 230 indicated to White that SCM was "a lumbering old top-heavy conglomerate with a huge corporate overhead that was draining earnings."[17] He envisioned substantial savings from the elimination of this overhead.

The Takeover Battle

After reviewing the situation, in early August White decided to acquire SCM. He began to buy stock, and on August 21 Hanson Industries formally made a $60 per share tender offer for SCM, valuing the company at $740 million. SCM's top management team responded on August 30 with its own offer to shareholders in the form of a proposed leveraged buyout of SCM. SCM's management had arranged financing from its investment banker Merrill Lynch and offered shareholders $70 per share. On September 4 White responded by raising Hanson's offer to $72 per share.

SCM's management responded to White's second offer by increasing its own offer to $74 per share. To discourage White from making another bid, SCM's management gave Merrill Lynch a "lock-up" option to buy Durkee Famous Foods and SCM Chemicals (the titanium dioxide division) at a substantial discount should Hanson or another outsider gain control. In effect, SCM's management had agreed to give its crown jewels to Merrill Lynch for less than their market value if Hanson won the bidding war.

White's next move was to apparently throw in the towel by announcing withdrawal of Hanson's tender offer. However, in contrast to normal practice on Wall Street, White went into the market and quickly purchased some 25 percent of SCM's stock at a fixed price of $73.5 per share, taking Hanson's stake to 27 percent. Furious at this break with convention, SCM's lawyers drafted a lawsuit against Hanson charging that White's tactics violated tender-offer regulations and demanding a restraining order prohibiting Hanson from making any further market purchases. Hanson quickly filed a countersuit, claiming that Merrill Lynch's lock-up option to buy the two SCM divisions illegally prevented the shareholders from getting the best price.

Hanson lost both suits in federal court in New York. White immediately appealed and on September 30 a U.S. court of appeals ruled in Hanson's favor. This, however, was not to be the end of the matter. On

October 7 Hanson spent another $40 million to increase its stake in SCM to 33 percent, thereby effectively stalling the leveraged buyout plan, which needed approval by two-thirds of the shareholders. The following day Hanson revised its tender offer to an all-cash $75 per share offer, subject to SCM's dropping the "lock-up" option because the option had been triggered by Hanson's acquiring 33 percent of SCM.

Hanson's next move, on October 10, was to file a suit to prevent Merrill Lynch from exercising the right to buy SCM's crown jewels. On October 15 it followed this with a second suit against Merrill Lynch for conspiracy. A U.S. district court ruled on November 26 that the lock-up was legal and that Hanson had triggered its exercise by the size of its stake. Once again Hanson appealed to a higher court. On January 6, 1986, a U.S. court of appeals overturned the lower court ruling, granting to Hanson an injunction that prevented SCM from exercising the lock-up option. The following day Hanson Industries won control over SCM after further market purchases. The final purchase price was $930 million, which represented a price/earnings multiple of 11.5.

After the Acquisition

Having gained control of SCM, Hanson immediately set about trying to realize SCM's potential. Within three months, 250 employees were laid off, mostly headquarters staff, and the former SCM headquarters in New York was sold for $36 million in cash. At the same time, White and his team were using their new position as owners to thoroughly audit the affairs of SCM's operating companies. Their objective was to identify those businesses whose returns were adequate or could be improved upon and those businesses for which the outlook was such that they were unlikely to achieve Hanson's stringent ROK requirements.

At the end of this process, four businesses were sold off in as many months for a total amount that recouped for Hanson the original purchase price and left Hanson with the two best businesses in SCM's portfolio: Smith-Corona typewriters and the titanium dioxide business. In May 1986, SCM's paper and pulp operations were sold to Boise Cascade for $160 million in cash, a price that represented a price/earnings multiple of 29 and was 3 times book value. Hanson felt that the outlook for those operations was not good because of a depression in paper and pulp prices. Boise Cascade obviously thought

otherwise. Shortly afterward, Sylvachem, part of SCM's chemicals division, was sold for $30 million, representing a price/earnings multiple of 18.5.

In August 1986 Glidden Paints was sold to the British chemical giant and Europe's largest paint manufacturer, Imperial Chemical Industries PLC (ICI) for $580 million. This represented a price/earnings multiple of 17.5 and was 2.5 times book value. The purchase of this operation enabled ICI to become the world's largest paint manufacturer. A few days later Durkee Famous Foods was sold to another British firm, Reckitt & Colman PLC, for $120 million in cash and the assumption of $20 million in debt. This represented a price/earnings multiple of 17 and was 3 times book value. This disposal served to withdraw Hanson from an area that was subject to uncontrollable and volatile commodity price movements. For Reckitt & Colman, however, which was already one of the largest manufacturers of branded food products outside the United States, it represented an important strategic addition.

The four disposals amounted to $926 million and were accomplished at an average price/earnings multiple of 19.5. Having recovered 100 percent of the purchase price paid for SCM within eight months, Hanson had effectively acquired for nothing a number of businesses that were projected to contribute around $140 million to net pretax profit for their first full year under Hanson's control.

Hanson retained the titanium dioxide business for two main reasons. First, with the industry operating at close to 100 percent capacity and with projections indicating an increase in demand through to 1989, prices and margins were expected to increase substantially. Although several companies had plans to expand global capacity, given the three- to four-year time lag in bringing new capacity on stream, this sellers' market was likely to persist for a while. Nor did it look as if the additional capacity would outstrip the projected rise in demand. Second, two-thirds of world production of titanium dioxide is in the hands of global producers. SCM's business is ranked third with 12 percent of world capacity, behind Du Pont and Tioxide PLC. Given this oligopoly, orderly pricing in world markets seemed likely to continue.

Hanson also decided to retain SCM's typewriter business, despite the fact that in recent years it had been the worst-performing unit in SCM's portfolio. Hanson quickly realized that SCM management had in effect just completed a drastic overhaul of the

Imperial Divisional Results for the Year Ended October 1985

	Revenues		Profits	
Division	£m	Percentage of Change from 1984	£m	Percentage of Change from 1984
Tobacco	£2,641	+7%	£123.1	+11%
Brewing and leisure	974	+8%	97.0	+20%
Foods	719	+4%	33.0	+5%
Howard Johnson	617	+11%	11.1	−40%

Source: Data from Hanson Industries, Annual Report, 1986.

typewriter businesses and that a dramatic turnaround was likely. In the two years prior to Hanson's acquisition, SCM's management had undertaken the following steps:

1. A new line of electronic typewriters had been introduced to match the increasingly sophisticated Japanese models.

2. Capacity had been reduced by 50 percent, and six U.S. production facilities had been consolidated into a single assembly plant and distribution center in New York to manufacture all electronic models.

3. As a result of automation, economies of scale, and labor agreements, productivity at the New York plant had increased fourfold since 1984, and unit labor costs had declined by 60 percent.

4. The manufacture of electric models had been moved offshore to a low-cost facility in Singapore.

5. Smith-Corona had just introduced the first personal word processor for use with a portable electronic typewriter, and it retailed at slightly less than $500.

As a result of these improvements, the Smith-Corona business seemed ready to become a major profit producer. Hanson forecasted profits of $30 million for this business during 1986–1987, compared with an operating loss of $47.4 million in financial year 1985.

The Imperial Acquisition

On December 6, 1985, while still engaged in the SCM acquisition, Hanson opened another takeover battle in Britain by announcing an offer of £1.5 billion for Imperial Group PLC.[18] Imperial Group was one of the ten largest firms in Britain. Imperial was Britain's

leading tobacco manufacturer and the third largest tobacco company in the world. Its Courage Brewing subsidiary was one of the "big six" beer companies in Britain. Its leisure operations included 1,371 public houses (taverns), 120-plus restaurants, and more than 750 specialized retail shops. Imperial manufactured more than 1,000 branded food products. (See Table 5 for a breakdown of Imperial's divisional results.) In September 1985 Imperial had sold its fourth business, the U.S. motel chain Howard Johnson, to Marriott. Howard Johnson had been purchased in 1980 and was widely regarded as one of the worst acquisitions ever made by a major British company.

Attractions to Hanson

Hanson's interest in Imperial was prompted by the news on December 2, 1985, of a planned merger between Imperial and United Biscuits PLC, a major manufacturer of branded food products. The financial press perceived this measure as a defensive move by Imperial. However, despite its well-documented problems with Howard Johnson, Imperial's financial performance was reasonably strong (see Table 6). What factors made Imperial an attractive takeover target to Hanson? The following seem to have been important.

- *Mature business.* Like SCM's businesses, most of Imperial's businesses were based in mature, low-technology industries. There is little prospect of radically changing fashions or technological change in the tobacco, brewing, and food industries.

- *Low risk.* Most of Imperial's products had a high brand recognition within Britain. Thus, Hanson could easily dispose of those that did not stand up to Hanson's demanding ROK targets.

TABLE 6

Financial Data for Imperial

	1981	1982	1983	1984	1985
Revenues (£m)	£4,526	£4,614	£4,381	£4,593	£4,918
Pretax profits (£m)	106	154	195	221	236
Earnings per share (pence)	12.8	16.4	18.0	20.3	22.4
Return on capital (%)	12.7%	17.9%	20.4%	21.1%	18.1%

Source: Data from Hanson Industries, Annual Report, 1986.

- *Tobacco cash flow.* Imperial's tobacco business was a classic cash cow. The company had 45 percent of the tobacco market and seven of the ten best-selling brands in 1985. Although tobacco sales are declining in Britain because of a combination of health concerns and punitive taxation, the decline has been gradual, amounting to 29 percent since the peak year of 1973. Given Hanson's emphasis on ROK and cash flow, this made Imperial particularly attractive to Hanson. Imperial had arguably squandered much of this cash flow by using it to underwrite unprofitable growth opportunities, particularly Howard Johnson.

- *Failure of Imperial's diversification strategy.* Imperial's recent track record with respect to diversification was poor. In 1978 it bought a construction company, J. B. Eastward, for £40 million. After four years of trading losses, Eastward was sold in 1982 for a total loss of £54 million. In 1979 Imperial paid $640 million for Howard Johnson, the U.S. motel and restaurant chain. In 1985, after six years of declining profits, this business was sold for $341 million. These losses suggested a fundamental weakness in Imperial's top management in an area in which Hanson was strong: diversification strategy. Moreover, the failure of Imperial's diversification strategy probably resulted in Imperial's shares being discounted by the stock market.

- *Inadequate returns in brewing and leisure.* Imperial's brewing and leisure operations earned an ROK of 9 percent in 1985. This return was considered very low for the brewing industry, which was characterized by strong demand and was dominated by a mature oligopoly that had engineered high prices and margins. Hanson thought that this return could be significantly improved.

The Takeover Battle

The planned merger between Imperial and United Biscuits PLC (UB), announced on December 2, 1985, gave rise to considerable concern among Imperial's already disgruntled shareholders. Under the terms of the proposed merger, UB, although contributing just 21 percent of net assets, would end up with a 42 percent interest in the enlarged group. The implication was that Imperial's shareholders would experience significant earnings dilution. In addition, it was proposed that the corporate management of the enlarged group would primarily come from UB personnel. These factors prompted a reverse takeover by UB of the much larger Imperial group. See Table 7.

Hanson's interest was sparked by this controversy. Hanson's corporate staff had been tracking Imperial for some time, so when the for-sale sign was raised over Imperial, Hanson was able to move quickly. On December 6, 1985, Hanson made a 250-pence per share offer for Imperial, valuing the group at £1.9 billion. This offer was rejected out of hand by Imperial's management.

The next major development came on February 12, 1986, when the British secretary of state of trade and industry referred the proposed Imperial/UB merger to the Monopolies and Mergers Commission for consideration. Britain's Monopolies and Mergers Commission has the authority to prohibit any merger that might create a monopoly. The referral was due to the recognition that an Imperial/UB group would command more than 40 percent of the British snack-food market.

On February 17, Hanson took advantage of the uncertainty created by the referral to unveil a revised offer 24 percent higher than its original offer, valuing Imperial at £2.35 billion. On the same day,

TABLE 7

Hanson PLC—Financial Data

Year Ended Sept. 30	Revs.	Oper. Inc.	% Oper. Inc. of Revs.	Cap. Exp.	Depr.	Int. Exp.	Net Bef. Taxes	Eff. Tax Rate	Net[‡] Inc.	% Net Inc. of Revs.
1989[§]	$11,302	$1,609	14.2%	$2,141	$200	$533	$1,718[†]	23.6%	1,313	11.6%
1988[§]	12,507	1,561	12.5%	724	215	485	1,488[†]	23.2%	1,143	9.1%
1987[‖]	10,975	1,230	11.2%	522	172	493	1,217[†]	22.8%	939	8.6%
1986[‖]	6,196	713	11.5%	848	105	359	667	22.5%	517	8.3%
1985	3,771	477	12.7%	84	74	172	356	23.5%	272	7.2%
1984	2,930	303	10.3%	61	55	119	208	25.7%	154	5.3%
1983	2,226	207	9.3%	59	47	81	137	30.2%	94	4.2%
1982	1,952	NA	NA	NA	NA	NA	NA	NA	72	3.7%
1981	1,549	NA	NA	NA	NA	NA	NA	NA	62	4.0%

Income Data (million $)*

Sept. 30	Cash	Assets	Curr. Liab.	Ratio	Total Assets	% Ret. on Assets	Long-Term Debt	Common Equity	Total Inv. Capital	% LT Debt. of Cap.	% Ret. on Equity
1989	$8,574	$12,038	$5,278	2.3	$17,482	8.5%	$8,028	$1,689	$10,683	75.1%	47.6%
1988	6,527	10,413	4,165	2.5	13,210	9.4%	3,592	3,707	7,878	45.6%	33.5%
1987	5,025	8,236	3,422	2.4	10,471	9.3%	2,837	2,841	6,151	46.1%	37.5%
1986	2,509	7,977	3,572	2.2	9,577	7.6%	2,834	2,068	5,252	54.0%	29.1%
1985	1,659	2,908	1,277	2.3	4,021	7.7%	903	1,376	2,563	35.2%	27.7%
1984	641	1,775	925	1.9	2,638	9.0%	981	505	1,540	63.7%	36.7%

Balance Sheet Data (million $)*

*Data as originally reported; prior to 1986 data as reported in the 1985 Annual Report (prior to 1984, data are from the listing application of November 3, 1986), conversion to U.S. dollars at year-end exchange rates.
[†]Includes equity in earnings of nonconsolidated subsidiaries.
[‡]Before specific item(s) in 1989, 1988, 1986.
[§]Excludes discount operations and reflects merger or acquisition.
[‖]Reflects merger or acquisition.

Source: Standard & Poor's, *Standard & Poor's NYSE Stock Reports*, Vol. 57, No. 54, Sec. 12, p. 1096. Reprinted by permission of Standard & Poor's, a division of The McGraw-Hill Companies, Inc.

UB announced a bid of £2.5 billion for Imperial and indicated that, if the offer was successful, Imperial's snack-food businesses would be sold, thus eliminating the need for a Monopolies and Mergers Commission investigation. Imperial's board duly recommended the UB offer to shareholders for acceptance.

Many of Imperial's shareholders, however, were in no mood to accept Imperial's recommendation. Under British stock market regulations, once the Imperial board accepted UB's offer, Imperial's shareholders had two months in which to indicate their acceptance or rejection of it. If the offer was rejected, then the shareholders were free to consider the hostile bid from Hanson. What followed was an increasingly acrimonious war of words between Hanson and Imperial. Hanson charged Imperial with mismanagement. Imperial responded by trying to depict Hanson as an asset stripper with no real interest in generating internal growth from the companies it owned. In the words of one Imperial executive during this period, Lord Hanson "buys and sells companies well, but he manages them jolly badly. He buys, squeezes and goes on to the next one. The only way to grow is by bigger and bigger acquisitions. Like all great conglomerate builders of the past, he's over the hill."[19]

Imperial's management failed to win the war of words. By April 17, UB had secured acceptances for only 34 percent of Imperial's shares, including 14.9 percent held by UB associates. The UB offer lapsed, leaving the way clear for Hanson. On April 18 Hanson secured acceptances for more than 50 percent of Imperial's shares, and its offer went unconditional. At £2.5 billion, the takeover was the largest in British history; it implied a price/earnings multiple of 12.3 on Imperial's prospective earnings.

After the Acquisition

After the acquisition Hanson moved quickly to realize potential from Imperial. Of the 300 staff at Imperial's headquarters, 260 were laid off, and most of the remainder were sent back to the operating level. In July Imperial's hotels and restaurants were sold to Trusthouse Forte for £190 million in cash, representing a price/earnings multiple of 24 on prospective earnings and amounting to 1.7 times book value. That sale was followed in September 1986 by the sale of the Courage Brewing operations, along with a wine and spirits wholesaler and an "off-license" chain (liquor stores) to Elders IXL, an Australian brewing company, for £1.4 billion in cash. The price/earnings multiple for that deal amounted to 17.5 times prospective earnings and represented a premium of £150 million over book value. It was quickly followed by the sale of Imperial's Golden Wonder snack-food business to Dalgety PLC, a British food concern, for £87 million in cash, representing a price/earnings multiple of 13.5 over prospective earnings.

As a result of these moves, by the autumn of 1986 Hanson had raised £1.7 billion from the sale of Imperial's businesses. Effectively, Hanson recouped 66 percent of the total cost of its acquisition by selling companies that contributed slightly more than 45 percent of Imperial's net profit forecasted for the year to October 1986. The net cost of Imperial on this basis had fallen to £850 million, with a consequent decline in the price/earnings multiple on prospective earnings from 12.3 to 7.6.

This was followed in 1988 by the sale of Imperial's food businesses for £534 million, along with the

sale of various other smaller interests for £56 million. By the end of 1988, therefore, Hanson had raised £2.26 billion from the sale of Imperial's assets. It still retained Imperial Tobacco, by far the largest business in Imperial's portfolio, which it had in effect gained for a net cost of £240 million—this for a business that in 1988 generated £150 million in operating profit.

Later Developments

Following the SCM and Imperial acquisitions, in 1987 Hanson acquired Kidde, a 108-company U.S. conglomerate, for $1.7 billion. Kidde seemed set for the "Hanson treatment." Its headquarters was closed within three months of the takeover, and a series of disposals was arranged. These were followed in 1988 by continuing disposals of operations acquired in the Imperial and Kidde acquisitions. In total, they amounted to $1.5 billion.

In mid 1989 Hanson embarked on its biggest takeover ever, the £3.61 billion ($4.8 billion) acquisition of Consolidated Gold Field PLC (CGF). In addition to being the second largest gold-mining operation in the world, CGF also owns a large stone and gravel operation, ARC Ltd., with major holdings in Britain. CGF came to Hanson's attention following an abortive takeover bid for the company from South African-controlled Minorco.

Hanson bought Minorco's 29.9 percent minority stake in CGF and launched its own takeover bid in July 1989. After raising its bid, Hanson won control of CGF in August. CGF also seemed set to be broken up. About half of CGF's value consists of minority stakes in publicly quoted mining companies in the United States, South Africa, and Australia. These stakes range from 38 to 49 percent, enough to hold the key to control in many of the companies. Thus, Hanson should be able to extract a premium price for them. Initial estimates suggest that Hanson should be able to raise $2.5 billion from the sale of CGF's minority holdings.[20] Indeed, by February 1990 Hanson had reportedly recouped about one-third of the purchase price of CGF through disposals and was looking to sell additional operations while gold prices remained high.[21]

The CGF deal led directly to the June 1990 acquisition of Peabody Holdings Co., the largest U.S. coal producer, for a total cost of $1.23 billion in cash. CGF had a 49 percent stake in Newmont Mining Corp., the biggest U.S. gold-mining concern. In turn,

Newmont owned 55 percent of Peabody. In April 1990 Hanson purchased the 45 percent of Peabody not owned by Newmont from three minority owners. Then in June it outbid AMAX Corporation for Newmont's stake in Peabody.

The attraction of Peabody to Hanson lies in two factors: (1) the company owns large deposits of low-sulfur coal, which is increasingly in demand because of environmental concerns; (2) the company has recently invested heavily to upgrade its plant. As a result, in the past four years labor productivity has increased 50 percent.[22] In addition, analysts speculate that the deals, by improving Newmont's financial position (Newmont has used the cash to reduce its debt), may make it possible for Hanson to sell off its 49 percent stake in Newmont for a reasonable premium.

ENDNOTES

1. "The Conglomerate as Antique Dealer," *Economist*, March 11, 1989, pp. 71–73.
2. Quoted in ibid.
3. Quoted in John Byrne and Mark Maremont, "Hanson: The Dangers of Living by Takeover Alone," *Business Week*, August 15, 1988, pp. 62–64.
4. Quoted in Andrew Marton, "The Buccaneer from Britain," *Mergers and Acquisitions* (February 1987), pp. 141–146.
5. Quoted in Byrne and Maremont, "Hanson: The Dangers."
6. Gordon White, "How I Turned $3,000 into $10 Billion," *Fortune*, November 7, 1988, pp. 80–89.
7. The material in this section is based on the following sources: White, "How I Turned," pp. 80–89; Marton, "The Buccaneer from Britain," pp. 141–146; and Hope Lampert, "Britons on the Prowl," *New York Times Magazine*, November 29, 1987, pp. 22–24, 36, 38, 42.
8. White, "How I Turned," p. 81.
9. Quoted in Lampert, "Britons on the Prowl," p. 36.
10. Quoted in White, "How I Turned," p. 81.
11. Quoted in Lampert, "Britons on the Prowl," p. 24.
12. The material in this section is based on the following sources: White, "How I Turned," pp. 80–89; Lampert, "Britons on the Prowl," pp. 22–24, 36, 38, 42; and Mark Cusack, *Hanson Trust: A Review of the Company and Its Prospects* (London: Hoare Govett Limited, 1987).
13. The material in this section is based on the following sources: Cusack, *Hanson Trust*; "The Conglomerate as Antique Dealer," pp. 71–73; Byrne and Maremont, "Hanson: The Dangers," pp. 62–64; and Gordon White, "Nothing Hurts More Than a Bogus Bonus," *Wall Street Journal*, July 20, 1987, p. 18.
14. White, "How I Turned," p. 81.
15. White, "Nothing Hurts More," p. 18.
16. Most of the detail in this section is drawn from two sources: Cusack, *Hanson Trust*; and Lampert, "Britons on the Prowl," pp. 22–24, 36, 38, 42.
17. White, "How I Turned," p. 84.
18. The material in this section is based on the following sources: Cusack, *Hanson Trust*; and Lampert, "Britons on the Prowl," pp. 22–24, 36, 38, 42.
19. Quoted in Philip Revzin, "U.K.'s Hanson Trust Aims for Big Leagues in Takeovers," *Wall Street Journal*, February 25, 1986, p. 30.
20. Mark Maremont and Chuck Hawkins, "Is Consgold Just an Appetizer for Hanson?" *Business Week*, July 10, 1989, pp. 41–42.
21. Joann Lubin, "Hanson to Buy Peabody Stake for $504 Million," *Wall Street Journal*, February 16, 1990, p. A4.
22. "Hanson PLC," *Value Line*, July 20, 1990, p. 832.

Case 29

Hanson PLC (B): Breaking It Up

This case was prepared by Charles W. L. Hill, the University of Washington.

Introduction

During the 1970s and 1980s, Hanson PLC put together one of the most impressive growth stories of any industrial company in the world. Under the leadership of James Hanson and Gordon White, Hanson PLC made its name by acquiring poorly run conglomerate companies in both Britain and America at prices that were often below their book value. In quick order Hanson would then change the senior management of the acquired company, sell many of the company's assets to other enterprises, typically for a considerable profit, and impose tight financial controls on what remained in order to maximize profitability and cash flow. The locus classicus was Hanson's 1986 acquisition of the Imperial Group, a diversified British tobacco, brewing, and food conglomerate, where some £2.4 billion of the £2.5 billion purchase price was recouped from asset disposals, leaving Hanson with the cash-generating tobacco business intact. The results of this strategy were nothing short of stunning. Between 1973 and 1991, Hanson put together twenty-nine years of uninterrupted profit growth to build a diversified company with revenues of £7.69 billion ($12.3 billion) and operating income of £1.33 billion ($2.13 billion). Hanson's stock price appreciation was also spectacular, increasing more than a hundredfold between 1973 and 1991.

However, 1991 may have been the high-water mark of Hanson's growth story. In 1990 Hanson took a 2.9 percent stake in the British chemical and pharmaceutical company, Imperial Chemical Industries (ICI). Many saw this as a prelude to yet another Hanson acquisition, but ICI was not about to be taken over. After a bitter public relations battle during which ICI characterized Hanson's management as having a short-term orientation and criticized them for failure to add value to the companies they acquired, Hanson sold its stake in May 1991. While the stake was sold for a profit of £45 million ($70 million), the public relations battle damaged Hanson's image. A year later Hanson was outbid for a British food company, RHM, by a smaller conglomerate run by a former Hanson manager. These two failures raised questions as to whether Hanson's two founders, who were now both in their seventies, were still up to the rough game of hostile takeovers. To compound matters further, for the year ending in September 1993, with many of its cyclical businesses suffering from the effects of a recession in both Britain and America, Hanson reported a 33 percent decline in after-tax profits to $1.5 billion, the first such decline in its history. Reflecting these problems, Hanson's stock price peaked in early 1991 and remained flat over the next few years, while the equity markets in Britain and America boomed.

A New Direction?

In 1992 the leadership mantle at Hanson started to pass from the company's charismatic founders, the now ennobled (Lord) Hanson and White, to Derek Bonham and David Clarke, who were then forty-eight and fifty, respectively. Bonham took over as CEO with primary responsibilities for Hanson's

British-based operations, while Clarke succeeded White as president of Hanson's substantial American operation. Lord Hanson remained on in the chairman's role, while White continued as the company's senior person in charge of mergers and acquisitions. (White died in 1995.)

Although both long-time Hanson employees, Bonham and Clarke clearly lacked the predatory thirst that had driven Hanson and White. Early in his tenure Bonham admitted that Hanson had become "too much of a mishmash" and stated that he hoped to correct that by focusing management's attention on improving the performance of its core businesses in building materials, chemicals, tobacco, and natural resources (primarily timber and coal). While this might require "bolt on acquisitions," Bonham seemed to be signaling that the swashbuckling days of hostile acquisitions and quick asset disposals to pay down debt were over.[1]

Another signal of a shift in management's philosophy came in May 1994, when Hanson announced that it would lengthen the payback period required of new capital investments from three or four years to five or six years. The company stated that it had lengthened the required payback period to take advantage of low interest rates and continuing low inflation. However, many also saw the shift as an attempt to allay fears in the financial community that Hanson's management style was too focused on the short term. Moreover, the move seemed to be consistent with Bonham's stated goal of increasing internal investments as a way of generating growth.[2] The growth that Bonham was talking about, however, was a far cry from the 20 percent annual rate achieved under the leadership of Hanson and White. According to Bonham, "The reality is that we are living in a low growth, low inflation climate. To suggest that you can continue to grow by 20 percent is out of line."[3]

Both Bonham and Clarke repeatedly stated that they saw Hanson growing at about twice the rate of inflation during the 1990s, which suggested a growth rate of around 6 percent, given British and American inflation rates.

Acquiring Quantum

The first significant strategic move under Bonham occurred on June 31, 1993, when Hanson announced that it had reached an agreement to purchase Quantum Chemical Corp., the largest U.S. producer of polyethylene plastics, in a stock swap that valued Quantum at $20 per share, or $720 million. The purchase price represented a premium of 60 percent over Quantum's closing price of $12.50 on June 30. Hanson also stated that it would assume all of Quantum's $2.5 billion in debt. The acquisition added to Hanson's U.S. chemical operations, which included SCM Chemicals, the world's third largest producer of titanium dioxide.

According to observers, the acquisition represented a strategic bet by Hanson that a protracted cyclical downturn in the polyethylene business was nearing an end. At the peak of the last plastics cycle in 1988, Quantum earned $760 million. However, Quantum had saddled itself with the $2.5 billion debt load in a 1989 restructuring, undertaken while plastics prices were at their previous cyclical peak. Massive debt service requirements and a slump in polyethylene prices had left Quantum with a 1992 loss before accounting charges of $118.4 million, or $3.98 per share. One immediate financial benefit of the acquisition was that Hanson was able to use its superior credit rating to refinance Quantum's debt (much of which was in the form of junk bonds with an average yield of more than 10 percent) at rates closer to Hanson's 5 percent borrowing costs. This move alone cut Quantum's $240 million annual interest bill in half.[4]

In retrospect the Quantum acquisition turned out to be particularly well timed. Prices for low density polyethylene bottomed out in the summer of 1993 at $28 per gallon. By the end of 1994 they had risen to $33 per gallon.[5] Quantum's profits turned out to be highly leveraged to prices. As a result of this leverage and lower interest payments, Quantum's chemical operations earned almost $200 million in fiscal 1994, more than $300 million ahead of its 1992 results. Quantum's results helped Hanson to rebound from its poor showing in 1993. For 1994 it reported a 32 percent rise in pretax profits and a record operating profit of £1.23 billion ($1.92 billion).[6]

1993–1994 Disposals

Throughout 1993 and 1994, Hanson proceeded with a series of relatively minor asset disposals. The objectives of these disposals were twofold: first, to focus the company on its core businesses and, second, to help pay down Hanson's enormous debt load, the legacy of its acquisitions including Quantum. In fiscal 1993 Hanson's long-term debt stood at £7.22 billion ($11.5 billion), and its debt to equity ratio was 1.83

TABLE 1

Hanson PLC—Financial Data

Year Ended Sept. 30	($) Per Pound[†]	Revs.	Oper. Inc.	% Oper. Inc. of Revs.	Cap. Exp.	Depr.	Int. Exp.	Net Bef. Taxes	Eff. Tax Rate	Net Inc.[II]	% Net Inc. of Revs.	Cash Flow
1994	1.509	11,199	1,633	14.6	293	401	545	1,346	20.9%	1,065	9.5	1,466
1993	1.523	9,760	1,288	13.2	301	310	600	1,016	27.8%	734	7.5	1,044
1992	1.822	8,798	1,322	15.0	279	254	777	1,286	15.3%	1,089	12.4	1,343
1991[‡]	1.820	7,691	1,327	17.3	266	216	741	1,319	21.5%	1,035	13.5	1,251
1990[‡]	1.700	7,153	1,236	17.3	247	180	638	1,285	24.4%	971	13.6	NA
1989[‡]	1.690	6,998	996	14.2	192	124	330	1,064	23.6%	813	11.6	NA
1988[‡]	1.770	7,396	923	12.5	198	127	287	880	23.2%	676	9.1	NA
1987[§]	1.560	6,682	749	11.2	151	105	300	741	22.8%	572	9.6	NA

Income Data (million £)*

Sept. 30	($) Per Pound[†]	Cash	Curr. Assets	Curr. Liab.	Ratio	Total Assets	% Ret. on Assets	Long-Term Debt	Common Equity	Total Inv. Cap.	% LT Debt of Cap.	% Ret. on Equity
1994	1.566	6,815	9,933	6,704	1.5	21,536	4.7	5,038	4,598	9,768	51.6	24.9
1993	1.525	8,067	11,636	7,065	1.6	24,057	3.3	7,221	3,953	11,266	64.1	18.0
1992	1.779	8,445	11,204	6,386	1.8	20,541	5.9	5,069	4,224	9,430	53.8	28.9
1991	1.750	7,771	9,955	4,751	2.1	16,583	6.6	4,880	3,325	8,351	58.4	33.6
1990	1.870	6,883	8,993	4,226	2.1	14,754	7.6	4,258	2,834	7,222	59.0	50.1
1989	1.620	5,309	7,454	3,269	2.3	10,825	8.7	4,971	1,046	6,133	81.1	50.1
1988	1.690	3,860	6,158	2,463	2.5	7,812	9.5	2,124	2,192	4,659	45.6	34.1
1987	1.630	3,059	5,014	2,083	2.4	6,375	8.8	1,727	1,730	3,745	46.1	35.5

Balance Sheet Data (million £)*

*Data as originally reported; prior to 1988 as reported in 1987 Annual Report. Based on UK GAAP.
[†]Average exchange rates for income data; fiscal year-end exchange rates for balance sheet.
[‡]Excludes discretionary operations and reflects merger or acquisition.
[§]Reflects merger or acquisition.
[II]Before special items.

(see Table 1). This debt load was beginning to trouble the financial community, who were starting to question the ability of Hanson to maintain its historically high dividend. In a previous era Hanson had quickly paid down debt from acquisitions by raising cash through asset disposals, but there had been little movement in this direction since the late 1980s.

Between January 1993 and August 1994, Hanson sold more than fifteen companies for a total of £815 million ($1.3 billion). These disposals included its Beazer home building operations in both the United States and the United Kingdom; an office supply business; and Axelson, an oil industry equipment group.[7]

Spinning off U.S. Industries

The next big strategic move occurred in February 1995, when Hanson announced that it would spin off thirty-four of its smaller American-based companies into a new entity called U.S. Industries under the leadership of David Clarke. Hanson would retain ownership over several of its larger U.S. operations, including Quantum Chemical and Peabody Coal. The new company was to include such well-known brand names as Jacuzzi whirlpools, Farberware cookware, Ames garden tools, Rexair vacuum cleaners, and Tommy Armour golf clubs. In 1994 the thirty-four companies had sales of $3 billion and operating profits of $252 million.

The company was to be responsible for $1.4 billion of Hanson's debt. According to one analyst,

> For Hanson, it achieves a one shot divestiture of a number of companies they may have struggled to sell independently, not because the individual assets are unattractive, but because it's messy to sell so many of them. They are able to divest in a tax efficient way and at the same time take a lot of cash out, leaving them with the ability to buy something else.[8]

The spinoff was completed on June 1, 1995. At the time, David Clarke stated that the new company's first objective would be to reduce its debt load, primarily by selling off a number of companies valued at $600 million.[9]

Acquiring Eastern Group

Only July 31, 1995, Hanson announced that it would acquire Eastern Group, one of Britain's major electric utilities, for £2 billion ($3.2 billion). Eastern, which was privatized in 1990, has a customer base of 3 million and is responsible for 15 percent of the electricity produced in Britain, primarily for natural gas-fired generating facilities. Eastern is also the seventh largest natural gas supplier in the country. In the year ending March 31, 1995, Eastern's earnings were up 15 percent to £203 million ($324 billion) on revenues of £2.06 billion ($3.2 billion).[10]

Hanson stated that it was attracted to Eastern by its steady earnings growth. However, critics noted that the deal yet again stretched Hanson's balance sheet, which once more had begun to look solid after the U.S. Industries spinoff. The debt-financed purchase of Eastern caused Hanson's debt-to-equity ratio to shoot up from 37 percent to 130 percent, once more raising concerns that Hanson might not be able to service its historically high dividends. A partial response to these concerns came in December 1995, when the company announced plans to dispose of two additional U.S. subsidiaries—Suburban Propane and Cavenham Forest Industries—for £1.5 billion ($2.4 billion). The proceeds were to be used to pay down Hanson's debt load. Analysts calculated that the cash raised from these spinoffs would reduce Hanson's debt-to-equity ratio to around 90 percent.[11]

The Demerger

By late 1995 it was becoming increasingly clear within Hanson's senior management team that dras-tic action would be required to boost the company's lagging share price.[12] As the British and American economies continued in their long recovery from recession, Hanson's cyclical business staged a significant performance improvement, with operating profits increasing by 44 percent for the fiscal year that ended in September 1995. Despite this performance, the company's share price had been essentially flat since the early 1990s (see Figure 1). Over the same period both the London and New York stock markets had increased substantially. By the end of 1995 the price-to-earnings ratio of Hanson's shares was 30 percent below that of the average stock on the London exchange, while Hanson's dividend yield at over 6.5 percent was among the highest offered by any company. It seemed that nothing could move the stock price, not the strong profit performance, not the spinoff of U.S. Industries, not the Eastern acquisition, and not the recently announced disposals.

It was against this background that Hanson stunned both London and Wall Street with its January 29 announcement that it would divide the company up into four independent businesses, effectively dismantling the conglomerate assembled by Hanson and White. Hanson stated that it would split into a chemicals business, an energy company, a tobacco company, and a building materials enterprise. Imperial Tobacco would be the largest company, with sales of £3.57 billion ($5.37 billion). The energy business, which would include Hanson's coal and electric businesses, would have sales of £3.5 billion ($5.27 billion). The chemicals business would have sales of £2 billion ($3.04 billion), while the building materials group would have sales of £2.3 billion ($3.48 billion).[13] Bonham was to run the energy business, while Hanson was to take over the building materials group until his retirement. The company estimated that the demerger would be completed by early 1997.

Hanson's stock price initially surged 7 percent on the news, but it fell later the same day and ended up less than 0.5 percent. The lack of a sustained positive reaction from the stock markets on both sides of the Atlantic puzzled Hanson's managers. Over the last few years, a number of diversified companies had announced demergers—including ITT, AT&T, and Sears—and their stock prices had almost always responded in a very positive fashion. In Hanson's case, however, this did not occur.

One possible explanation for the lack of a favorable reaction came from Moody's Investor Service,

FIGURE 1

Hanson PLC

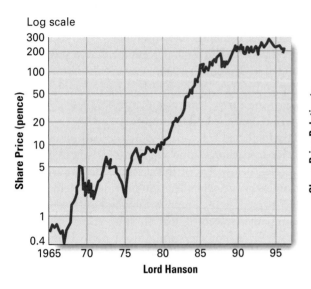

Lord Hanson

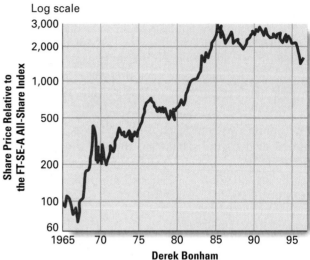

Derek Bonham

which put Hanson's debt under review for a possible downgrade one day after the breakup was announced. Moody's noted that "this is a highly complex sequence of transactions which are at an early stage and which will require various approvals."[14] Among the concerns expressed were that the demerger might raise Hanson's borrowing costs. The tax consequences of the demerger were also not immediately apparent, although there were some indications that there might be some one-time capital gains tax charges. Moreover, several stock analysts commented that the demerged Hanson units might not be able or willing to maintain Hanson's historically high level of dividends. One influential London-based stock analyst also noted that unlike most conglomerates that were demerging, there were few if any hidden assets at Hanson. This analyst calculated that Hanson's constituent parts should be valued at 194 pence, which was below the 212 pence price that Hanson's stock closed at on January 30, 1996.[15]

As a further prelude to the demerger, in March 1996 Hanson announced the sale of its remaining U.S. timberland operations to Willamette Industries for $1.59 billion. This sale followed Hanson's disposal of Cavenham Forest Industries in December 1995, and it completed Hanson's exit from the timber business. The cash generated from the sale was to be used to pay down Hanson's debt.[16]

ENDNOTES

1. R. A. Melcher, "Can This Predator Change Its Stripes?" *Business Week*, June 22, 1992, p. 38; J. Guyon, "Hanson Crosses the Atlantic to Woo Investors," *Wall Street Journal*, December 6, 1983, p. 7D.
2. R. Rudd, "Hanson Increases Investment Payback Time," *Financial Times*, May 16, 1994, p. 15.
3. P. Dwyer and J. Weber, "Hanson Looks for a Hat Trick," *Business Week*, March 14, 1994. pp. 68–69.
4. S. McMurray, "UK's Hanson to Buy Maker of Polyethylene," *Wall Street Journal*, July 1, 1993, p. A3.
5. D. Wighton, "Conglomerate's $3.2 Billion Gamble Pays Off," *Financial Times*, December 2, 1994, p. 23.
6. "Hanson Posts 32% Rise in Pre Tax Profits," *Wall Street Journal*, December 2, 1994, p. B3.
7. P. Taylor, "Hanson Lifted by Quantum Chemical," *Financial Times*, August 17, 1994, p. 13.
8. R. W. Stevenson, "Hanson Plans to Spin Off 34 U.S. Companies," *New York Times*, February 23, 1995, p. C1.
9. L. L. Brownlee and J. R. Dorfman, "Birth of U.S. Industries Isn't Without Complications," *Wall Street Journal*, May 18, 1995, p. B4.
10. D. Wighton, "Hanson Plugs into New Current," *Financial Times*, July 31, 1995, p. 15.
11. D. Wighton, "Hanson Seeks £1.5 Billion from U.S. Disposals," *Financial Times*, December 21, 1995, p. 13.
12. "Widow Hanson's Children Leave Home," *Economist*, February 3, 1996, pp. 51–52.
13. R. Bonte-Friedheim and J. Guyon, "Hanson to Divide into Four Businesses," *Wall Street Journal*, January 31, 1996, p. A3.
14. Bonte-Friedheim and Guyon, "Hanson to Divide into Four Businesses."
15. D. Wighton, "Centrifugal Forces That Pulled Hanson Apart," *Financial Times*, January 31, 1996, p. 18.
16. "Hanson to Sell Mills," *Wall Street Journal: Money & Investing Update*, March 12, 1996.

Case 30

Philips Versus Matsushita: A New Century, a New Round

This case was prepared by Christopher A. Bartlett, Harvard Business School.

Throughout their long histories, N.V. Philips (Netherlands) and Matsushita Electric (Japan) had followed very different strategies and emerged with very different organizational capabilities. Philips built its success on a worldwide portfolio of responsive national organizations while Matsushita based its global competitiveness on its centralized, highly efficient operations in Japan.

During the 1990s, both companies experienced major challenges to their historic competitive positions and organizational models, and at the end of the decade, both companies were struggling to reestablish their competitiveness. At the turn of the millennium, new CEOs at both companies were implementing yet another round of strategic initiatives and organizational restructurings. Observers wondered how the changes would affect their long-running competitive battle.

Philips: Background

In 1892, Gerard Philips and his father opened a small light-bulb factory in Eindhoven, Holland. When their venture almost failed, they recruited Gerard's brother, Anton, an excellent salesman and manager. By 1900, Philips was the third largest light-bulb producer in Europe.

From its founding, Philips developed a tradition of caring for workers. In Eindhoven it built company houses, bolstered education, and paid its employees so well that other local employers complained. When Philips incorporated in 1912, it set aside 10% of profits for employees.

Technological Competence and Geographic Expansion

While larger electrical products companies were racing to diversify, Philips made only light-bulbs. This one-product focus and Gerard's technological prowess enabled the company to create significant innovations. Company policy was to scrap old plants and use new machines or factories whenever advances were made in new production technology. Anton wrote down assets rapidly and set aside substantial reserves for replacing outdated equipment. Philips also became a leader in industrial research, creating physics and chemistry labs to address production problems as well as more abstract scientific ones. The labs developed a tungsten metal filament bulb that was a great commercial success and gave Philips the financial strength to compete against its giant rivals.

Holland's small size soon forced Philips to look beyond its Dutch borders for enough volume to mass produce. In 1899, Anton hired the company's first export manager, and soon the company was selling into such diverse markets as Japan, Australia, Canada,

Brazil, and Russia. In 1912, as the electric lamp industry began to show signs of overcapacity, Philips started building sales organizations in the United States, Canada, and France. All other functions remained highly centralized in Eindhoven. In many foreign countries Philips created local joint ventures to gain market acceptance.

In 1919, Philips entered into the Principal Agreement with General Electric, giving each company the use of the other's patents. The agreement also divided the world into "three spheres of influence": General Electric would control North America; Philips would control Holland; but both companies agreed to compete freely in the rest of the world. (General Electric also took a 20% stake in Philips.) After this time, Philips began evolving from a highly centralized company, whose sales were conducted through third parties, to a decentralized sales organization with autonomous marketing companies in 14 European countries, China, Brazil, and Australia.

During this period, the company also broadened its product line significantly. In 1918, it began producing electronic vacuum tubes; eight years later its first radios appeared, capturing a 20% world market share within a decade; and during the 1930s, Philips began producing X-ray tubes. The Great Depression brought with it trade barriers and high tariffs, and Philips was forced to build local production facilities to protect its foreign sales of these products.

Philips: Organizational Development

One of the earliest traditions at Philips was a shared but competitive leadership by the commercial and technical functions. Gerard, an engineer, and Anton, a businessman, began a subtle competition where Gerard would try to produce more than Anton could sell and vice versa. Nevertheless, the two agreed that strong research was vital to Philips' survival.

During the late 1930s, in anticipation of the impending war, Philips transferred its overseas assets to two trusts, British Philips and the North American Philips Corporation; it also moved most of its vital research laboratories to Redhill in Surrey, England, and its top management to the United States. Supported by the assets and resources transferred abroad, and isolated from their parent, the individual country organizations became more independent during the war.

Because waves of Allied and German bombing had pummeled most of Philips' industrial plant in the Netherlands, the management board decided to build the postwar organization on the strengths of the national organizations (NOs). Their greatly increased self-sufficiency during the war had allowed most to become adept at responding to country-specific market conditions—a capability that became a valuable asset in the postwar era. For example, when international wrangling precluded any agreement on three competing television transmission standards (PAL, SECAM, and NTSC), each nation decided which to adopt. Furthermore, consumer preferences and economic conditions varied: in some countries, rich, furniture-encased TV sets were the norm; in others, sleek, contemporary models dominated the market. In the United Kingdom, the only way to penetrate the market was to establish a rental business; in richer countries, a major marketing challenge was overcoming elitist prejudice against television. In this environment, the independent NOs had a great advantage in being able to sense and respond to the differences.

Eventually, responsiveness extended beyond adaptive marketing. As NOs built their own technical capabilities, product development often became a function of local market conditions. For example, Philips of Canada created the company's first color TV; Philips of Australia created the first stereo TV; and Philips of the United Kingdom created the first TVs with teletext.

While NOs took major responsibility for financial, legal, and administrative matters, fourteen product divisions (PDs), located in Eindhoven, were formally responsible for development, production, and global distribution. (In reality, the NOs' control of assets and the PDs' distance from the operations often undercut this formal role.) The research function remained independent and, with continued strong funding, set up eight separate laboratories in Europe and the United States.

While the formal corporate-level structure was represented as a type of geographic/product matrix, it was clear that NOs had the real power. NOs reported directly to the management board, which Philips enlarged from 4 members to 10 to ensure that top management remained in contact with and control of the highly autonomous NOs. Each NO also regularly sent envoys to Eindhoven to represent its interests. Top management, most of whom had careers that included multiple foreign tours of duty, made frequent overseas visits to the NOs. In 1954, the board established the International Concern Council to formalize regular meetings with the heads of all major NOs.

Within the NOs, the management structure mimicked the legendary joint technical and commercial leadership of the two Philips brothers. Most were led by a technical manager and a commercial manager. In some locations, a finance manager filled out the top management triad that typically reached key decisions collectively. This cross-functional coordination capability was reflected down through the NOs in front-line product teams, product-group-level management teams, and at the senior management committee of the NOs' top commercial, technical, and financial managers.

The overwhelming importance of foreign operations to Philips, the commensurate status of the NOs within the corporate hierarchy, and even the cosmopolitan appeal of many of the offshore subsidiaries' locations encouraged many Philips managers to take extended foreign tours of duty, working in a series of two- or three-year posts. This elite group of expatriate managers identified strongly with each other and with the NOs as a group and had no difficulty representing their strong, country-oriented views to corporate management.

Philips: Attempts at Reorganization

In the late 1960s, the creation of the Common Market eroded trade barriers within Europe and diluted the rationale for maintaining independent, country-level subsidiaries. New transistor- and printed circuit-based technologies demanded larger production runs than most national plants could justify, and many of Philips' competitors were moving production of electronics to new facilities in low-wage areas in East Asia and Central and South America. Despite its many technological innovations, Philips' ability to bring products to market began to falter. In the 1960s, the company invented the audiocassette but let its Japanese competitors capture the mass market. A decade later, its R&D group developed the V2000 videocassette format—superior technically to Sony's Beta or Matsushita's VHS—but was forced to abandon it when North American Philips decided to outsource, brand, and sell a VHS product which it manufactured under license from Matsushita.

Over three decades, seven chairmen experimented with reorganizing the company to deal with its growing problems. Yet, entering the new millennium, Philips' financial performance remained poor and its global competitiveness was still in question. (See Exhibits 1 and 2.)

Van Riemsdijk and Rodenburg Reorganizations, 1970s

Concerned about what one magazine described as "continued profitless progress," newly appointed CEO Hendrick van Riemsdijk created an organization committee to prepare a policy paper on the division of responsibilities between the PDs and the NOs. Their report, dubbed the "Yellow Booklet," outlined the disadvantages of Philips' matrix organization in 1971:

> Without an agreement [defining the relationship between national organizations and product divisions], it is impossible to determine in any given situation which of the two parties is responsible. . . . As operations become increasingly complex, an organizational form of this type will only lower the speed of reaction of an enterprise.

On the basis of this report, van Riemsdijk proposed rebalancing the managerial relationships between PDs and NOs—"tilting the matrix" in his words—to allow Philips to decrease the number of products marketed, build scale by concentrating production, and increase the flow of goods among national organizations. He proposed closing the least efficient local plants and converting the best into International Production Centers (IPCs), each supplying many NOs. In so doing, van Riemsdijk hoped that PD managers would gain control over manufacturing operations. Due to the political and organizational difficulty of closing local plants, however, implementation was slow.

In the late 1970s, his successor CEO, Dr. Rodenburg, continued this thrust. Several IPCs were established, but the NOs seemed as powerful and independent as ever. He furthered matrix simplification by replacing the dual commercial and technical leadership with single management at both the corporate and national organizational levels. Yet the power struggles continued.

Wisse Dekker Reorganization, 1982

Unsatisfied with the company's slow response and concerned by its slumping financial performance, upon becoming CEO in 1982, Wisse Dekker outlined

EXHIBIT 1

Philips Group Summary Financial Data, 1970–2000 (millions of guilders unless otherwise stated)

	2000	1995	1990	1985	1980	1975	1970
Net sales	F83,437	F64,462	F55,764	F60,045	F36,536	F27,115	F15,070
Income from operations (excluding restructuring)	NA	4,090	2,260	3,075	1,577	1,201	1,280
Income from operations (including restructuring)	9,434	4,044	−2,389	N/A	N/A	N/A	N/A
As a percentage of net sales	11.3%	6.3%	−4.3%	5.1%	4.3%	4.5%	8.5%
Income after taxes	12,559	2,889	F−4,447	F1,025	F532	F341	F446
Net income from normal business operations	NA	2,684	−4,526	n/a	328	347	435
Stockholders' equity (common)	49,473	14,055	11,165	16,151	12,996	10,047	6,324
Return on stockholders' equity	42.8%	20.2%	−30.2%	5.6%	2.7%	3.6%	7.3%
Distribution per common share, par value F10 (in guilders)	F2.64	F1.60	F0.0	F2.00	F1.80	F1.40	F1.70
Total assets	86,114	54,683	51,595	52,883	39,647	30,040	19,088
Inventories as a percentage of net sales	13.9%	18.2%	20.7%	23.2%	32.8%	32.9%	35.2%
Outstanding trade receivables in month's sales	1.5	1.6	1.6	2.0	3.0	3.0	2.8
Current ratio	1.2		1.4	1.6	1.7	1.8	1.7
Employees at year-end (in thousands)	219	265	273	346	373	397	359
Wages, salaries and other related costs	NA	NA	F17,582	F21,491	F15,339	F11,212	F5,890
Exchange rate (period end; guilder/$)	2.34	1.60	1.69	2.75	2.15	2.69	3.62
Selected Data in Millions of Dollars:							
Sales	$35,253	$40,039	$33,018	$21,802	$16,993	$10,098	$4,163
Operating profit	3,986	2,512	1,247	988	734	464	NA
Pretax income	5,837	2,083	−2,380	658	364	256	NA
Net income	5,306	1,667	−2,510	334	153	95	120
Total assets	35,885	32,651	30,549	19,202	18,440	11,186	5,273
Shareholders' equity (common)	20,238	8,784	6,611	5,864	6,044	3,741	1,747

Note: Exchange rate 12/31/00 was Euro/US$: 1.074.

Source: Annual reports; Standard & Poors' *Compustat*; Moody's Industrial and International Manuals.

a new initiative. Aware of the cost advantage of Philips' Japanese counterparts, he closed inefficient operations—particularly in Europe where 40 of the company's more than 200 plants were shut. He focused on core operations by selling some businesses (for example, welding, energy cables, and furniture) while acquiring an interest in Grundig and Westinghouse's North American lamp activities. Dekker also supported technology-sharing agreements and entered alliances in offshore manufacturing.

To deal with the slow-moving bureaucracy, he continued his predecessor's initiative to replace dual leadership with single general managers. He also continued to "tilt the matrix" by giving PDs formal product management responsibility, but leaving NOs responsible for local profits. And, he energized the management board by reducing its size, bringing on directors with strong operating experience, and creating subcommittees to deal with difficult issues. Finally, Dekker redefined the product planning process incorporating input from the NOs, but giving global PDs the final decision on long-range direction. Still sales declined and profits stagnated.

Van der Klugt Reorganization, 1987

When Cor van der Klugt succeeded Dekker as chairman in 1987, Philips had lost its long-held consumer electronics leadership position to Matsushita, and was

EXHIBIT 2

Philips Group, Sales by Product and Geographic Segment, 1985–2000 (millions of guilders)

	2000		1995		1990		1985	
Net Sales by Product Segment:								
Lighting	F11,133	13%	F 8,353	13%	F 7,026	13%	F 7,976	12%
Consumer electronics	32,357	39	22,027	34	25,400	46	16,906	26
Domestic appliances	4,643	6	—				6,644	10
Professional products/Systems	—	—	11,562	18	13,059	23	17,850	28
Components/Semiconductors	23,009	28	10,714	17	8,161	15	11,620	18
Software/Services	—	—	9,425	15	—	—	—-	—
Medical systems	6,679	8	—	—	—	—	—	—
Origin	1,580	2	—	—	—	—	—	—
Miscellaneous	4,035	5	2,381	4	2,118	4	3,272	5
Total	**83,437**	**100%**	**64,462**	**100%**	**F55,764**	**100%**	**F 64,266**	**100%**
Operating Income by Sector:								
Lighting	1,472	16%	983	24%	419	18%	F 910	30%
Consumer electronics	824	9	167	4	1,499	66	34	1
Domestic appliances	632	7	—	—	—	—	397	13
Professional products/Systems	—	—	157	4	189	8	1,484	48
Components/Semiconductors	4,220	45	2,233	55	−43	−2	44	1
Software/Services	—	—	886	22	—	—	—	—
Medical systems	372	4	—	—	—	—	—	—
Origin	2,343	25	—	—	—	—	—	—
Miscellaneous	−249	−3	423	10	218	10	200	7
Increase not attributable to a sector	−181	−2	(805)	(20)	−22	−1	6	0
Total	**9,434**	**100%**	**4,044**	**100%**	**2,260**	**100%**	**F 3,075**	**100%**

Notes:
Conversion rate (12/31/00): 1 Euro: 2.20371 Dutch Guilders
Totals may not add due to rounding.
Product sector sales after 1988 are external sales only; therefore, no eliminations are made; sector sales before 1988 include sales to other
  sectors; therefore, eliminations are made.
Data are not comparable to consolidated financial summary due to restating.
Source: Annual reports.

one of only two non-Japanese companies in the world's top ten. Its net profit margins of 1% to 2% not only lagged behind General Electric's 9%, but even its highly aggressive Japanese competitors' slim 4%. Van der Klugt set a profit objective of 3% to 4% and made beating the Japanese companies a top priority.

As van der Klugt reviewed Philips' strategy, he designated various businesses as core (those that shared related technologies, had strategic importance, or were technical leaders) and non-core (stand-alone businesses that were not targets for world leadership and could eventually be sold if required). Of the four businesses defined as core, three were strategically linked: components, consumer electronics, and telecommunications and data systems. The fourth, lighting, was regarded as strategically vital because its cash flow funded development. The non-core businesses included domestic appliances and medical systems which van der Klugt spun off into joint ventures with Whirlpool and GE, respectively.

In continuing efforts to strengthen the PDs relative to the NOs, van der Klugt restructured Philips around the four core global divisions rather than the former 14 PDs. This allowed him to trim the management board, appointing the displaced board members to a new policy-making Group Management Committee. Consisting primarily of PD heads and functional chiefs, this body replaced the old NO-dominated International Concern Council. Finally, he sharply reduced the 3,000-strong headquarters staff, reallocating many of them to the PDs.

To link PDs more directly to markets, van der Klugt dispatched many experienced product-line managers to Philips' most competitive markets. For example, management of the digital audio tape and electric-shaver product lines were relocated to Japan, while the medical technology and domestic appliances lines were moved to the United States.

Such moves, along with continued efforts at globalizing product development and production efforts, required that the parent company gain firmer control over NOs, especially the giant North American Philips Corp. (NAPC). Although Philips had obtained a majority equity interest after World War II, it was not always able to make the U.S. company respond to directives from the center, as the V2000 VCR incident showed. To prevent replays of such experiences, in 1987 van der Klugt repurchased publicly owned NAPC shares for $700 million.

Reflecting the growing sentiment among some managers that R&D was not market oriented enough, van der Klugt halved spending on basic research to about 10% of total R&D. To manage what he described as "R&D's tendency to ponder the fundamental laws of nature," he made R&D the direct responsibility of the businesses being supported by the research. This required that each research lab become focused on specific business areas (see Exhibit 3).

Finally, van der Klugt continued the effort to build efficient, specialized, multi-market production facilities by closing 75 of the company's 420 remaining plants worldwide. He also eliminated 38,000 of its 344,000 employees—21,000 through divesting businesses, shaking up the myth of lifetime employment at the company. He anticipated that all these restructurings would lead to a financial recovery by 1990. Unanticipated losses for that year, however—more than 4.5 billion Dutch guilders ($2.5 billion)—provoked a class-action law suit by angry American investors, who alleged that positive projections by the company had been misleading. In a surprise move, on May 14, 1990, van der Klugt and half of the management board were replaced.

EXHIBIT 3

Philips Research Labs by Location and Specialty, 1987

Location	Size (staff)	Specialty
Eindhoven, The Netherlands	2,000	Basic research, electronics, manufacturing technology
Redhill, Surrey, England	450	Microelectronics, television, defense
Hamburg, Germany	350	Communications, office equipment, medical imaging
Aachen, W. Germany	250	Fiber optics, X-ray systems
Paris, France	350	Microprocessors, chip materials, design
Brussels	50	Artificial intelligence
Briarcliff Manor, New York	35	Optical systems, television, superconductivity, defense
Sunnyvale, California	150	Integrated circuits

Source: Philips, in *Business Week*, March 21, 1988, p. 156.

Timmer Reorganization, 1990

The new president, Jan Timmer, had spent most of his 35-year Philips career turning around unprofitable businesses. With rumors of a takeover or a government bailout swirling, he met with his top 100 managers and distributed a hypothetical—but fact-based—release announcing that Philips was bankrupt. "So what action can you take this weekend?" he challenged them.

Under "Operation Centurion," headcount was reduced by 68,000 or 22% over the next 18 months, earning Timmer the nickname "The Butcher of Eindhoven." Because European laws required substantial compensation for layoffs—Eindhoven workers received 15 months' pay, for example—the first round of 10,000 layoffs alone cost Philips $700 million. To spread the burden around the globe and to speed the process, Timmer asked his PD managers to negotiate cuts with NO managers. According to one report, however, country managers were "digging in their heels to save local jobs." But the cuts came—many from overseas operations. In addition to the job cuts, Timmer vowed to "change the way we work." He established new performance rules and asked hundreds of top managers to sign contracts that committed them to specific financial goals. Those who broke those contracts were replaced—often with outsiders.

To focus resources further, Timmer sold off various businesses including integrated circuits to Matsushita, minicomputers to Digital, defense electronics to Thomson and the remaining 53% of appliances to Whirlpool. Yet profitability was still well below the modest 4% on sales he promised. In particular, consumer electronics lagged with slow growth in a price-competitive market. The core problem was identified by a 1994 McKinsey study that estimated that value added per hour in Japanese consumer electronic factories was still 68% above that of European plants. In this environment, most NO managers kept their heads down, using their distance from Eindhoven as their defense against the ongoing rationalization.

After three years of cost-cutting, in early 1994, Timmer finally presented a new growth strategy to the board. His plan was to expand software, services, and multimedia to become 40% of revenues by 2000. He was betting on Philips' legendary innovative capability to restart the growth engines. Earlier, he had recruited Frank Carrubba, Hewlett-Packard's director of research, and encouraged him to focus on developing 15 core technologies. The list, which included interactive compact disc (CD-i), digital compact cassettes (DCC), high definition television (HDTV), and multimedia software, was soon dubbed "the president's projects." But his earlier divestment of some of Philips' truly high-tech businesses and a 37% cut in R&D personnel left the company with few who understood the technology of the new priority businesses.

By 1996, it was clear that Philips' HDTV technology would not become industry standard, that its DCC gamble had lost out to Sony's Minidisc, and that CD-i was a marketing failure. While costs were lower, so too was morale, particularly among middle management. Critics claimed that the company's drive for cost-cutting and standardization had led it to ignore new worldwide market demands for more segmented products and higher consumer service.

Boonstra Reorganization, 1996

When Timmer stepped down in October 1996, the board replaced him with a radical choice for Philips—an outsider whose expertise was in marketing and Asia rather than technology and Europe. Cor Boonstra was a 58-year-old Dutchman whose years as CEO of Sara Lee, the U.S. consumer products firm,

had earned him a reputation as a hard-driving marketing genius. Joining Philips in 1994, he headed the Asia Pacific region and the lighting division before being tapped as CEO.

Unencumbered by tradition, he immediately announced strategic sweeping changes designed to reach his target of increasing return on net assets from 17% to 24% by 1999. "There are no taboos, no sacred cows," he said. "The bleeders must be turned around, sold, or closed." Within three years, he had sold off 40 of Philips' 120 major businesses—including such well known units as Polygram and Grundig. He also initiated a major worldwide restructuring, promising to transform a structure he described as "a plate of spaghetti" into "a neat row of asparagus." He said:

> How can we compete with the Koreans? They don't have 350 companies all over the world. Their factory in Ireland covers Europe and their manufacturing facility in Mexico serves North America. We need a more structured and simpler manufacturing and marketing organization to achieve a cost pattern in line with those who do not have our heritage. This is still one of the biggest issues facing Philips.

Within a year, 3,100 jobs were eliminated in North America and 3,000 employees were added in Asia Pacific, emphasizing Boonstra's determination to shift production to low-wage countries and his broader commitment to Asia. And after three years, he had closed 100 of the company's 356 factories worldwide. At the same time, he replaced the company's 21 PDs with 7 divisions, but shifted day-to-day operating responsibility to 100 business units, each responsible for its profits worldwide. It was a move designed to finally eliminate the old PD/NO matrix. Finally, in a move that shocked most employees, he announced that the 100-year-old Eindhoven headquarters would be relocated to Amsterdam with only 400 of the 3,000 corporate positions remaining.

By early 1998, he was ready to announce his new strategy. Despite early speculation that he might abandon consumer electronics, he proclaimed it as the center of Philips' future. Betting on the "digital revolution," he planned to focus on established technologies such as cellular phones (through a joint venture with Lucent), digital TV, digital videodisc, and web TV. Furthermore, he committed major resources to marketing, including a 40% increase in advertising to raise awareness and image of the Philips brand and de-emphasize most of the 150 other brands it supported worldwide—from Magnavox TVs to Norelco shavers to Marantz stereos.

While not everything succeeded (the Lucent cell phone JV collapsed after nine months, for example), overall performance improved significantly in the late 1990s. By 1999, Boonstra was able to announce that he had achieved his objective of a 24% return on net assets.

Kleisterlee Reorganization, 2001

In May 2001, Boonstra passed the CEO's mantle to Gerard Kleisterlee, a 54-year-old engineer (and career Philips man) whose turnaround of the components business had earned him a board seat only a year earlier. Believing that Philips had finally turned around, the board challenged Kleisterlee to grow sales by 10% annually and earnings 15%, while increasing return on assets to 30%.

Despite its stock trading at a steep discount to its breakup value, Philips governance structure and Dutch legislation made a hostile raid all but impossible. Nonetheless, Kleisterlee described the difference as "a management discount" and vowed to eliminate it. The first sign of restructuring came within weeks, when mobile phone production was outsourced to CEC of China. Then, in August, Kleisterlee announced an agreement with Japan's Funai Electric to take over production of its VCRs, resulting in the immediate closure of the European production center in Austria and the loss of 1,000 jobs. The CEO then acknowledged that he was seeking partners to take over the manufacturing of some of its other mass-produced items such as television sets.

In mid 2001, a slowing economy resulted in the company's first quarterly loss since 1996 and a reversal of the prior year's strong positive cash flow. Many felt that these growing financial pressures—and shareholders' growing impatience—were finally leading Philips to recognize that its best hope of survival was to outsource even more of its basic manufacturing and become a technology developer and global marketer. They believed it was time to recognize that its 30-year quest to build efficiency into its global operations had failed.

Matsushita: Background

In 1918, Konosuke Matsushita (or "KM" as he was affectionately known), a 23-year-old inspector with the Osaka Electric Light Company, invested ¥100 to start

production of double-ended sockets in his modest home. The company grew rapidly, expanding into battery-powered lamps, electric irons, and radios. On May 5, 1932, Matsushita's 14th anniversary, KM announced to his 162 employees a 250-year corporate plan broken into 25-year sections, each to be carried out by successive generations. His plan was codified in a company creed and in the "Seven Spirits of Matsushita" (see Exhibit 4), which, along with the company song, continued to be woven into morning assemblies worldwide and provided the basis of the "cultural and spiritual training" all new employees received during their first seven months with the company.

EXHIBIT 4

Matsushita Creed and Philosophy (Excerpts)

Creed

Through our industrial activities, we strive to foster progress, to promote the general welfare of society, and to devote ourselves to furthering the development of world culture.

Seven Spirits of Matsushita

Service through Industry
Fairness
Harmony and Cooperation
Struggle for Progress
Courtesy and Humility
Adjustment and Assimilation
Gratitude

KM's Business Philosophy (Selected Quotations)

"The purpose of an enterprise is to contribute to society by supplying goods of high quality at low prices in ample quantity."

"Profit comes in compensation for contribution to society. . . . [It] is a result rather than a goal."

"The responsibility of the manufacturer cannot be relieved until its product is disposed of by the end user."

"Unsuccessful business employs a wrong management. You should not find its causes in bad fortune, unfavorable surroundings or wrong timing."

"Business appetite has no self-restraining mechanism.... When you notice you have gone too far, you must have the courage to come back."

Source: "Matsushita Electric Industrial (MEI) in 1987," Harvard Business School Case No. 388-144.

In the post-war boom, Matsushita introduced a flood of new products: TV sets in 1952; transistor radios in 1958; color TVs, dishwashers, and electric ovens in 1960. Capitalizing on its broad line of 5,000 products (Sony produced 80), the company opened 25,000 domestic retail outlets. With more than six times the outlets of rival Sony, the ubiquitous "National Shops" represented 40% of appliance stores in Japan in the late 1960s. These not only provided assured sales volume, but also gave the company direct access to market trends and consumer reaction. When post-war growth slowed, however, Matsushita had to look beyond its expanding product line and excellent distribution system for growth. After trying many tactics to boost sales—even sending assembly line workers out as door-to-door salesmen—the company eventually focused on export markets.

The Organization's Foundation: Divisional Structure

Plagued by ill health, KM wished to delegate more authority than was typical in Japanese companies. In 1933, Matsushita became the first Japanese company to adopt the divisional structure, giving each division clearly defined profit responsibility for its product. In addition to creating a "small business" environment, the product division structure generated internal competition that spurred each business to drive growth by leveraging its technology to develop new products. After the innovating division had earned substantial profits on its new product, however, company policy was to spin it off as a new division to maintain the "hungry spirit."

Under the "one-product-one-division" system, corporate management provided each largely self-sufficient division with initial funds to establish its own development, production, and marketing capabilities. Corporate treasury operated like a commercial bank, reviewing divisions' loan requests for which it charged slightly higher-than-market interest, and accepting deposits on their excess funds. Divisional profitability was determined after deductions for central services such as corporate R&D and interest on internal borrowings. Each division paid 60% of earnings to headquarters and financed all additional working capital and fixed asset requirements from the retained 40%. Transfer prices were based on the market and settled through the treasury on normal commercial terms. KM expected uniform performance across the company's 36 divisions, and division

managers whose operating profits fell below 4% of sales for two successive years were replaced.

While basic technology was developed in a central research laboratory (CRL), product development and engineering occurred in each of the product divisions. Matsushita intentionally under-funded the CRL, forcing it to compete for additional funding from the divisions. Annually, the CRL publicized its major research projects to the product divisions, which then provided funding in exchange for technology for marketable applications. While it was rarely the innovator, Matsushita was usually very fast to market—earning it the nickname "Manishita," or copycat.

Matsushita: Internationalization

Although the establishment of overseas markets was a major thrust of the second 25 years in the 250-year plan, in an overseas trip in 1951 KM had been unable to find any American company willing to collaborate with Matsushita. The best he could do was a technology exchange and licensing agreement with Philips. Nonetheless, the push to internationalize continued.

Expanding Through Color TV

In the 1950s and 1960s, trade liberalization and lower shipping rates made possible a healthy export business built on black and white TV sets. In 1953, the company opened its first overseas branch office—the Matsushita Electric Corporation of America (MECA). With neither a distribution network nor a strong brand, the company could not access traditional retailers, and had to resort to selling its products under their private brands through mass merchandisers and discounters.

During the 1960s, pressure from national governments in developing countries led Matsushita to open plants in several countries in Southeast Asia and Central and South America. As manufacturing costs in Japan rose, Matsushita shifted more basic production to these low-wage countries, but almost all high-value components and subassemblies were still made in its scale-intensive Japanese plants. By the 1970s, protectionist sentiments in the West forced the company to establish assembly operations in the Americas and Europe. In 1972, it opened a plant in Canada; in 1974, it bought Motorola's TV business and started manufacturing its Quasar brand in the United States; and in 1976, it built a plant in Cardiff, Wales, to supply the Common Market.

Building Global Leadership Through VCRs

The birth of the videocassette recorder (VCR) propelled Matsushita into first place in the consumer electronics industry during the 1980s. Recognizing the potential mass-market appeal of the VCR—developed by Californian broadcasting company, Ampex, in 1956—engineers at Matsushita began developing VCR technology. After six years of development work, Matsushita launched its commercial broadcast video recorder in 1964, and introduced a consumer version two years later.

In 1975, Sony introduced the technically superior "Betamax" format, and the next year JVC launched a competing "VHS" format. Under pressure from MITI, the government's industrial planning ministry, Matsushita agreed to give up its own format and adopt the established VHS standard. During Matsushita's 20 years of VCR product development, various members of the VCR research team spent most of their careers working together, moving from central labs to the product divisions' development labs and eventually to the plant.

The company quickly built production to meet its own needs as well as those of OEM customers like GE, RCA, and Zenith, who decided to forego self-manufacture and outsource to the low-cost Japanese. Between 1977 and 1985, capacity increased 33-fold to 6.8 million units. (In parallel, the company aggressively licensed the VHS format to other manufacturers, including Hitachi, Sharp, Mitsubishi and, eventually, Philips.) Increased volume enabled Matsushita to slash prices 50% within five years of product launch, while simultaneously improving quality. By the mid-1980s, VCRs accounted for 30% of total sales—over 40% of overseas revenues—and provided 45% of profits.

Changing Systems and Controls

In the mid-1980s, Matsushita's growing number of overseas companies reported to the parent in one of two ways: wholly owned, single-product global plants reported directly to the appropriate product division, while overseas sales and marketing subsidiaries and overseas companies producing a broad product line for local markets reported to Matsushita Electric Trading Company (METC), a separate legal entity. (See Exhibit 5 for METC's organization.)

Throughout the 1970s, the central product divisions maintained strong operating control over their offshore production units. Overseas operations used plant and equipment designed by the parent company, followed manufacturing procedures dictated by the center, and used materials from Matsushita's domestic plants. Growing trends toward local sourcing, however, gradually weakened the divisions' direct control. By the 1980s, instead of controlling inputs, they began to monitor measures of output (for example, quality, productivity, inventory levels).

About the same time, product divisions began receiving the globally consolidated return on sales reports that had previously been consolidated in METC statements. By the mid-1980s, as worldwide planning was introduced for the first time, corporate management required all its product divisions to prepare global product strategies.

Headquarters-Subsidiary Relations

Although METC and the product divisions set detailed sales and profits targets for their overseas subsidiaries, local managers were told they had autonomy on how to achieve the targets. "Mike" Matsuoko, president of the company's largest European production subsidiary in Cardiff, Wales, however, emphasized that failure to meet targets forfeited freedom: "Losses show bad health and invite many doctors from Japan who provide advice and support."

In the mid-1980s, Matsushita had over 700 expatriate Japanese managers and technicians on foreign assignment for four to eight years, but defended that high number by describing their pivotal role. "This vital communication role," said one manager, "almost always requires a manager from the parent company. Even if a local manager speaks Japanese, he would not have the long experience that is needed to build relationships and understand our management processes."

Expatriate managers were located throughout foreign subsidiaries, but there were a few positions that were almost always reserved for them. The most visible were subsidiary general mangers whose main role was to translate Matsushita philosophy abroad. Expatriate accounting managers were expected to "mercilessly expose the truth" to corporate headquarters; and Japanese technical managers were sent to transfer product and process technologies and provide headquarters with local market information. These expatriates maintained relationships with senior colleagues at headquarters, who acted as career mentors, evaluated performance (with some input

EXHIBIT 5

Organization of METC, 1985

Note: ( ) = number of people.
Source: Harvard Business School Case No. 388-144.

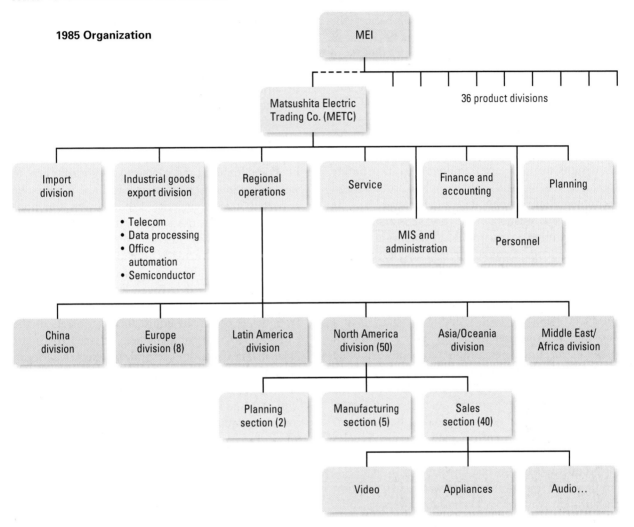

from local managers), and provided expatriates with information about parent company developments.

General managers of foreign subsidiaries visited Osaka headquarters at least two or three times each year—some as often as every month. Corporate managers reciprocated these visits, and on average, major operations hosted at least one headquarters manager each day of the year. Face-to-face meetings were considered vital: "Figures are important," said one manager, "but the meetings are necessary to develop judgment." Daily faxes and nightly phone calls between headquarters and expatriate colleagues were a vital management link.

Yamashita's Operation Localization

Although international sales kept rising, as early as 1982 growing host country pressures caused concern about the company's highly centralized operations. In that year, newly appointed company President Toshihiko Yamashita launched "Operation Localization" to boost offshore production from less than 10% of value-added to 25%, or half of overseas sales, by 1990. To support the target, he set out a program of four localizations—personnel, technology, material, and capital.

Over the next few years, Matsushita increased the number of local nationals in key positions. In the United States, for example, U.S. nationals became the presidents of three of the six local companies, while in Taiwan the majority of production divisions were replaced by Chinese managers. In each case, however, local national managers were still supported by senior Japanese advisors, who maintained a direct link with the parent company. To localize technology and materials, the company developed its national subsidiaries' expertise to source equipment locally, modify designs to meet local requirements, incorporate local components, and adapt corporate processes and technologies to accommodate these changes. And by the mid-1980s, offshore production subsidiaries were free to buy minor parts from local vendors as long as quality could be assured, but still had to buy key components from internal sources.

One of the most successful innovations was to give overseas sales subsidiaries more choice over the products they sold. Each year the company held a two-week internal merchandising show and product planning meeting where product divisions exhibited the new lines. Here, overseas sales subsidiary managers described their local market needs and negotiated for change in features, quantities, and even prices of the products they wanted to buy. Product division managers, however, could overrule the sales subsidiary if they thought introduction of a particular product was of strategic importance.

President Yamashita's hope was that Operation Localization would help Matsushita's overseas companies develop the innovative capability and entrepreneurial initiatives that he had long admired in the national organizations of rival Philips. (Past efforts to develop such capabilities abroad had failed. For example, when Matsushita acquired Motorola's TV business in the United States, its highly innovative technology group atrophied as American engineers resigned in response to what they felt to be excessive control from Japan's highly centralized R&D operations.) Yet despite his four localizations, overseas companies continued to act primarily as the implementation arms of central product divisions. In an unusual act for a Japanese CEO, Yamashita publicly expressed his unhappiness with the lack of initiative at the TV plant in Cardiff. Despite the transfer of

substantial resources and the delegation of many responsibilities, he felt that the plant remained too dependent on the center.

Tanii's Integration and Expansion

Yamashita's successor, Akio Tanii, expanded on his predecessor's initiatives. In 1986, feeling that Matsushita's product divisions were not giving sufficient attention to international development—in part because they received only 3% royalties for foreign production against at least 10% return on sales for exports from Japan—he brought all foreign subsidiaries under the control of METC. Tanii then merged METC into the parent company in an effort to fully integrate domestic and overseas operations. Then, to shift operational control nearer to local markets, he relocated major regional headquarters functions from Japan to North America, Europe, and Southeast Asia. Yet still he was frustrated that the overseas subsidiary companies acted as little more than the implementing agents of the Osaka-based product divisions.

Through all these changes, however, Matsushita's worldwide growth continued generating huge reserves. With $17.5 billion in liquid financial assets at the end of 1989, the company was referred to as the "Matsushita Bank," and several top executives began proposing that if they could not develop innovative overseas companies, they should buy them. Flush with cash and international success, in early 1991 the company acquired MCA, the U.S. entertainment giant, for $6.1 billion with the objective of obtaining a media software source for its hardware. Within a year, however, Japan's bubble economy had burst, plunging the economy into recession. Almost overnight, Tanii had to shift the company's focus from expansion to cost containment. Despite his best efforts to cut costs, the problems ran too deep. With 1992 profits less than half their 1991 level, the board took the unusual move of forcing Tanii to resign in February 1993.

Morishita's Challenge and Response

At 56, Yoichi Morishita was the most junior of the company's executive vice presidents when he was tapped as the new president. Under the slogan "simple, small, speedy and strategic," he committed to cutting headquarters staff and decentralizing responsibility. Over the next 18 months, he moved 6,000 staff to operating jobs. In a major strategic reversal, he also sold 80% of MCA to Seagram, booking a $1.2 billion loss on the transaction.

Yet the company continued to struggle. Japan's domestic market for consumer electronics collapsed—from $42 billion in 1989 to $21 billion in 1999. Excess capacity drove down prices and profits evaporated. And although offshore markets were growing, the rise of new competition—first from Korea, then China—created a global glut of consumer electronics, and prices collapsed.

With a strong yen making exports from Japan uncompetitive, Matsushita's product divisions rapidly shifted production offshore during the 1990s, mostly to low-cost Asian countries like China and Malaysia. By the end of the decade, its 160 factories outside Japan employed 140,000 people—about the same number of employees as in its 133 plants in Japan. Yet, despite the excess capacity and strong yen, management seemed unwilling to radically restructure its increasingly inefficient portfolio of production facilities.

In the closing years of the decade, Morishita began emphasizing the need to develop more of its technology

EXHIBIT 6

Matsushita, Summary Financial Data, 1970–2000[a]

	2000	1995	1990	1985	1980	1975	1970
In billions of yen and percent:							
Sales	¥7,299	¥6,948	¥6,003	¥5,291	¥2,916	¥1,385	¥932
Income before tax	219	232	572	723	324	83	147
As % of sales	3.0%	3.3%	9.5%	13.7%	11.1%	6.0%	15.8%
Net income	¥100	¥90	¥236	¥216	¥125	¥32	¥70
As % of sales	1.4%	1.3%	3.9%	4.1%	4.3%	2.3%	7.6%
Cash dividends (per share)	¥14.00	¥13.50	¥10.00	¥9.52	¥7.51	¥6.82	¥6.21
Total assets	7,955	8,202	7,851	5,076	2,479	1,274	735
Stockholders' equity	3,684	3,255	3,201	2,084	1,092	573	324
Capital investment	355	316	355	288	NA	NA	NA
Depreciation	343	296	238	227	65	28	23
R&D	526	378	346	248	102	51	NA
Employees (units)	290,448	265,397	198,299	175,828	107,057	82,869	78,924
Overseas employees	143,773	112,314	59,216	38,380	NA	NA	NA
As % of total employees	50%	42%	30%	22%	NA	NA	NA
Exchange rate (fiscal period end: ¥/$)	103	89	159	213	213	303	360
In millions of dollars:							
Sales	$68,862	$78,069	$37,753	$24,890	$13,690	$4,572	$2,588
Operating income before depreciation	4,944	6,250	4,343	3,682	1,606	317	NA
Operating income after depreciation	1,501	2,609	2,847	2,764	1,301	224	NA
Pretax income	2,224	2,678	3,667	3,396	1,520	273	408
Net income	941	1,017	1,482	1,214	584	105	195
Total assets	77,233	92,159	49,379	21,499	11,636	4,206	2,042
Total equity	35,767	36,575	20,131	10,153	5,129	1,890	900

[a]Data prior to 1987 are for the fiscal year ending November 20; data 1988 and after are for the fiscal year ending March 31.

Source: Annual reports; Standard & Poors' *Compustat;* Moody's Industrial and International Manuals.

and innovation offshore. Concerned that only 250 of the company's 3,000 R&D scientists and engineers were located outside Japan, he began investing in R&D partnerships and technical exchanges, particularly in fast emerging fields. For example, in 1998 he signed a joint R&D agreement with the Chinese Academy of Sciences, China's leading research organization. Later that year, he announced the establishment of the Panasonic Digital Concepts Center in California. Its mission was to act as a venture fund and an incubation center for the new ideas and technologies emerging in Silicon Valley. To some it was an indication that Matsushita had given up trying to generate new technology and business initiatives from its own overseas companies.

Nakamura's Initiatives

In April 2000, Morishita became chairman and Kunio Nakamura replaced him as president. Profitability was at 2.2% of sales, with consumer electronics at only 0.4%, including losses generated by one-time cash cows, the TV and VCR divisions. (Exhibit 6 and 7 provide the financial history for Matsushita and key product lines.) The new CEO vowed to raise this to 5% by 2004. Key to his plan was to move Matsushita

beyond its roots as a "super manufacturer of products" and begin "to meet customer needs through systems and services." He planned to flatten the hierarchy and empower employees to respond to customer needs, and as part of the implementation, all key headquarters functions relating to international operations were transferred to overseas regional offices.

But the biggest shock came in November, when Nakamura announced a program of "destruction and creation," in which he disbanded the product division structure that KM had created as Matsushita's basic organization building block 67 years earlier. Plants, previously controlled by individual product divisions, would now be integrated into multi-product production centers. In Japan alone 30 of the 133 factories were to be consolidated or closed. And marketing would shift to two corporate marketing entities, one for Panasonic brands (consumer electronics, information and communications products) and one for National branded products (mostly home appliances).

They were radical moves, but in a company that even in Japan was being talked about as a takeover target, observers wondered if they were sufficient to restore its global competitiveness.

EXHIBIT 7

Matsushita, Sales by Product and Geographic Segment, 1985–2000 (billion yen)

	2000		1995		FY 1990		FY 1985	
By Product Segment:								
Video and audio equipment	¥1,706	23%	¥1,827	26%	¥2,159	36%	¥2,517	48%
Home appliances and household equipment	1,306	18	—	—	—	—	—	—
Home appliances	—	—	916	13	802	13	763	14
Communication and industrial equipment	—	—	1,797	26	1,375	23	849	16
Electronic components	—	—	893	13	781	13	573	11
Batteries and kitchen-related equipment	—	—	374	4	312	5	217	4
Information and communications equipment	2,175	28	—	—	—	—	—	—
Industrial equipment	817	11	—	—	—	—	—	—
Components	1,618	21	—	—	—	—	—	—
Others	—	—	530	8	573	10	372	7
Total	**¥7,682**	**100%**	**¥6,948**	**100%**	**¥6,003**	**100%**	**¥5,291**	**100%**
By Geographic Segment:								
Domestic	¥3,698	51%	¥3,455	50%	¥3,382	56%	¥2,659	50%
Overseas	3,601	49	3,493	50	2,621	44	2,632	50

Note: Total may not add due to rounding.
Source: Annual reports.

GE's Two-Decade Transformation: Jack Welch's Leadership

This case was prepared by Christopher A. Bartlett and Meg Wozny, Harvard Business School.

Jack Welch glowed with pride at General Electric's Annual Meeting in March 1999. For the first time, GE's revenues exceeded $100 billion, operating margins were at an all-time high of 16.7%, and earnings per share had increased 14% over 1997's record level. In recognition of this outstanding performance and the company's transformation over the previous two decades, the *Fortune* poll of U.S. corporate executives had voted GE the country's "Most Admired Company" for the second year running, and the *Financial Times* had named it the "Most Respected Company in the World."

While the mood at the annual meeting was clearly upbeat, some shareholders worried about Welch's intention to retire at the end of 2000. The company he would hand over to his successor was radically different from the GE he took over in 1981. The question on many minds was whether anyone could sustain the blistering pace of change and growth characteristic of the Welch era. It would be a tough act to follow. (See Exhibit 1 for financial summary of Welch's era at GE.)

The GE Heritage

Founded in 1878 by Thomas Edison, General Electric grew from its early focus on the generation, distribution, and use of electric power to become, a hundred years later, one of the world's leading diversified industrial companies. In addition to its core businesses in power generation, household appliances, and lighting, by 1978 the company was also engaged in businesses as diverse as aircraft engines, medical systems, and diesel locomotives.

Long regarded as a bellwether of American management practices, GE was constantly undergoing change. In the 1930s, it was a model of the era's highly centralized, tightly controlled corporate form. By the 1950s, GE had delegated responsibility to hundreds of department managers, leading a trend towards greater decentralization. But a subsequent period of "profitless growth" in the 1960s caused the company to strengthen its corporate staffs and develop sophisticated strategic planning systems. Again, GE found itself at the leading edge of management practice.

When Reg Jones, Welch's predecessor, became CEO in 1973, he inherited the company that had just completed a major reorganization. Overlaying its 10 groups, 46 divisions, and 190 departments were 43 strategic business units designed to support the strategic planning that was so central to GE's management process. Jones raised strategic planning to an art form, and GE again became the benchmark for hundreds of companies that imitated its SBU-based structure and its sophisticated planning processes. Soon, however, Jones was unable to keep up with

EXHIBIT 1

Selected Financial Data ($ millions)

	1998	1997	1996	1995	1994	1993	1992	1991	1990	1986	1981
General Electric Company and Consolidated Affiliates											
Revenues	$100,469	$90,840	$79,179	$70,028	$60,109	$55,701	$53,051	$51,283	$49,696	$36,725	$27,240
Earnings from continuing operations	9,296	8,203	7,280	6,573	5,915	4,184	4,137	3,943	3,920	3,689	N/A
Loss from discontinued operations	—	—	—	—	-1,189	993	588	492	383	N/A	N/A
Net earnings	9,296	8,203	7,280	6,573	4,726	4,315	4,725	2,636	4,303	2,492	1,652
Dividends declared	4,081	3,535	3,138	2,838	2,546	2,229	1,985	1,808	1,696	1,081	715
Earned on average share owners' equity	25.7%	25.0%	24.0%	23.5%	18.1%	17.5%	20.9%	12.2%	20.2%	17.3%	19.1%
Per share											
Net earnings	2.84	2.50	2.20	1.95	1.38	3.03	2.75	2.55	2.42	2.73	N/A
Net earnings—diluted	2.80	2.46	2.16	1.93	1.37	2.52	2.75	1.51	2.42	N/A	N/A
Dividends declared	1.25	1.08	0.95	0.845	0.745	1.31	1.16	1.04	0.96	1.18	N/A
Stock price range (1)	103.9–69	76.6–47.9	53.1–34.7	36.6–24	27.4–22.5	26.7–20.2	87.5–72.7	78.1–53	75.5–50	44.4–33.2	69.9–51.1
Total assets of continuing operations	355,935	304,012	272,402	228,035	185,871	251,506	192,876	166,508	152,000	84,818	20,942
Long-term borrowings	59,663	46,603	49,246	51,027	36,979	28,194	25,298	22,602	20,886	100,001	1,059
Shares outstanding—average (in thousands)	3,268,998	3,274,692	3,307,394	3,367,624	3,417,476	1,707,979	1,714,396	1,737,863	1,775,104	912,594	227,528
Employees at year end											
United States	163,000	165,000	155,000	150,000	156,000	157,000	168,000	173,000	183,000	302,000	N/A
Other countries	130,000	111,000	84,000	72,000	60,000	59,000	58,000	62,000	62,000	71,000	N/A
Discontinued operations (primarily U.S.)	—	—	—	—	5,000	6,000	42,000	49,000	53,000	N/A	N/A
Total employees	293,000	276,000	239,000	222,000	221,000	222,000	268,000	284,000	298,000	373,000	404,000

(1) Price unadjusted for four 2-for-1 stock splits during the period.

reviewing and approving the massive volumes of information generated by 43 strategic plans. Explaining that "the review burden had to be carried on more shoulders," in 1977 he capped GE's departments, divisions, groups, and SBUs with a new organizational layer of "sectors," representing macrobusiness agglomerations such as consumer products, power systems, or technical products.

In addition to his focus on strategic planning, Jones spent a great deal of time on government relations, becoming the country's leading business statesman. During the 1970s, he was voted CEO of the Year three times by his peers, with one leading business journal dubbing him CEO of the Decade in 1979. When he retired in 1981, *The Wall Street Journal* proclaimed Jones a "management legend," adding that by handing the reins to Welch, GE had "replaced a legend with a live wire."

Welch's Early Priorities: GE's Restructuring

When the 45-year-old Welch became CEO in April 1981, the U.S. economy was in a recession. High interest rates and a strong dollar exacerbated the problem resulting in the country's highest unemployment rates since the Depression. To leverage performance in GE's diverse portfolio of businesses, the new CEO challenged each to be "better than the best" and set in motion a series of changes that were to radically restructure the company over the next five years.

#1 or #2: Fix, Sell, or Close

Soon after taking charge, Welch set the standard for each business to become the #1 or #2 competitor in its industry—or to disengage. Asked whether this simple notion represented GE's strategy, Welch responded, "You can't set an overall theme or a single strategy for a corporation as broad as GE." By 1983, however, Welch had elaborated this general "#1 or #2" objective into a "three circle concept" of his vision for GE. (See Exhibit 2.) Businesses were categorized as core (with the priority of "reinvesting in productivity and quality"), high-technology (challenged to "stay on the leading edge" by investing in R&D), and services (required to "add outstanding people and make

EXHIBIT 2

The Three-Circle Vision for GE, 1982

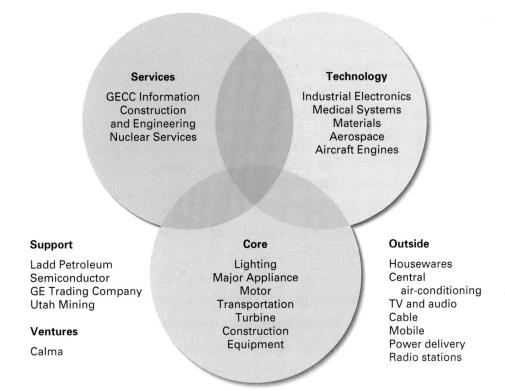

Services
GECC Information
Construction
and Engineering
Nuclear Services

Technology
Industrial Electronics
Medical Systems
Materials
Aerospace
Aircraft Engines

Support
Ladd Petroleum
Semiconductor
GE Trading Company
Utah Mining

Ventures
Calma

Core
Lighting
Major Appliance
Motor
Transportation
Turbine
Construction
Equipment

Outside
Housewares
Central
    air-conditioning
TV and audio
Cable
Mobile
Power delivery
Radio stations

contiguous acquisitions"). To a question about what he hoped to build at GE, Welch replied:

> A decade from now, I would like General Electric to be perceived as a unique, high-spirited, entrepreneurial enterprise.... the most profitable, highly diversified company on earth, with world quality leadership in every one of its product lines.[i]

But as GE managers struggled to build #1 or #2 positions in a recessionary environment and under attack from global—often, Japanese—competitors, Welch's admonition to "fix, sell, or close" uncompetitive businesses frequently led to the latter options. Scores of businesses were sold, including central air-

conditioning, housewares, coal mining, and, eventually, even GE's well-known consumer electronics business. Between 1981 and 1990, GE freed up over $11 billion of capital by selling off more than 200 businesses, which had accounted for 25% of 1980 sales. In that same time frame, the company made over 370 acquisitions, investing more than $21 billion in such major purchases as Westinghouse's lighting business, Employers Reinsurance, RCA, Kidder Peabody, and Thomson/ CGR, the French medical imaging company. (See Exhibit 3.)

Internally, Welch's insistence that GE become more "lean and agile" resulted in a highly disciplined destaffing process aimed at all large headquarters

EXHIBIT 3

Changes in the GE Business Portfolio

Major Acquisitions ($21 Billion Total)	Major Divestitures ($11 Billion Total)
Calma (CAD/CAM equipment)	Central Air Conditioning
Intersil (semiconductors)	Pathfinder Mines
Employers Reinsurance Corp.	Broadcasting Properties (non-RCA TV & radio stations)
Decimus (computer leasing)	Utah International (mining)
RCA (NBC Television, aerospace, electronics)	Housewares (small appliances)
Kidder, Peabody (investment banking)	Family Financial Services
Polaris (aircraft leasing)	RCA Records
Genstar (container leasing)	Nacolah Life Insurance (RCA's)
Thomson/CGR (medical equipment)	Coronet Carpets (RCA's)
Gelco (portable building leasing)	Consumer Electronics (TV sets)
Borg-Warner Chemicals (plastics)	Carboloy (industrial cutting tools)
Montgomery Ward Credit (credit cards)	NBC Radio Networks
Roper (appliances)	Roper Outdoor Lawn Equipment
Penske Leasing (truck leasing)	GE Solid State (semiconductors)
Financial Guaranty Insurance Co.	Calma (CAD/CAM equipment)
Thungsram (light bulbs)	RCA Globcomm (international telex)
Burton Group Financial Services	Ladd Petroleum (oil exploration & refining)
Travelers Mortgage (mortgage services)	RCA Columbia Home Video
Thorn Lighting (light bulbs)	Auto Auctions (auctions of used cars)
Financial News Network (cable network)	
Chase Manhattan Leasing	
Itel Containers (container leasing)	
Harrods/House of Fraser Credit Cards	

Source: The Business Engine.

groups, including a highly symbolic 50% reduction in the 200-person strategic planning staff. Welch described his motivation:

> We don't need the questioners and checkers, the nitpickers who bog down the process.... Today, each staff person has to ask, "How do I add value? How do I make people on the line more effective and competitive?"[ii]

As he continued to chip away at bureaucracy, Welch next scrapped GE's laborious strategic planning system—and with it, the remaining corporate planning staff. He replaced it with "real time planning" built around a five-page strategy playbook, which Welch and his 14 key business heads discussed in shirtsleeves sessions "unencumbered by staff." Each business's playbook provided simple one-page answers to five questions concerning current market dynamics, the competitors' key recent activities, the GE business response, the greatest competitive threat over the next three years, and the GE business's planned response.

The budgeting process was equally radically redefined. Rather than documenting internally focused comparisons with past performance, results were now evaluated against external competitively based criteria: Do sales show increases in market share, for example? Do margins indicate a cost advantage compared with competition?

In 1985, Welch eliminated the sector level, previously the powerful center of strategic control. (See Exhibits 4a and 4b.) By reducing the number of hierarchical levels from nine to as few as four, Welch ensured that all businesses reported directly to him. He said:

> We used to have department managers, sector managers, subsector managers, unit mangers, supervisors. We're driving those titles out... We used to go from the CEO to sectors to groups to businesses. Now we go from the CEO to businesses. There is nothing else. Zero.[iii]

Through downsizing, destaffing, and delayering, GE eliminated 59,290 salaried and 64,160 hourly positions between 1981 and 1988; divestiture eliminated an additional 122,700. Even when offset by the acquisitions, the number of employees at GE declined from 404,000 in 1980 to 330,000 by 1984 and 292,000 by 1989. Between 1981 and 1985, revenues increased modestly from $27.2 billion to $29.2 billion, but operating profits rose dramatically from $1.6 billion to $2.4 billion. This set the base for strong increases in both sales and earnings in the second half of the decade (see Exhibit 5).

This drastic restructuring in the early- and mid-1980s earned Welch the nickname "Neutron Jack," a term that gained currency even among GE managers when the CEO replaced 12 of his 14 business heads in August 1986. Welch's new "varsity team" consisted of managers with a strong commitment to the new management values, a willingness to break with the old GE culture, and most of all, an ability to take charge and bring about change. Despite his great dislike for a nickname he felt he did not deserve, Welch kept pushing the organization for more change. The further into the restructuring he got, the more convinced he became of the need for bold action:

> For me, the idea is to shun the incremental and go for the leap... How does an institution know when the pace is about right? I hope you won't think I'm being melodramatic if I say that the institution ought to stretch itself, ought to reach, to the point where it almost comes unglued... Remember the theory that a manager should have no more than 6 or 7 direct reports? I say the right number is closer to 10 or 15.[iv]

The Late 1980s: Second Stage of the Rocket

By the late 1980s, most of GE's business restructuring was complete, but the organization was still reeling from culture shock and management exhaustion. Welch was as eager as anyone in GE to move past the "Neutron-Jack" stage and begin rebuilding the company on its more solid foundations.

The "Software" Initiatives: Work-Out and Best Practices

Years after launching GE's massive restructuring effort, Welch concluded, "By mid-1988 the hardware was basically in place. We liked our businesses. Now it was time to focus on the organization's software." He also acknowledged that his priorities were shifting: "A company can boost productivity by restructuring, removing bureaucracy and downsizing, but it cannot sustain high productivity without cultural change."

In 1989, Welch articulated the management style he hoped to make GE's norm—an approach based on openness, candor, and facing reality. Simultaneously, he refined the core elements of the organizational

C486

EXHIBIT 4A

GE Organization in 1981

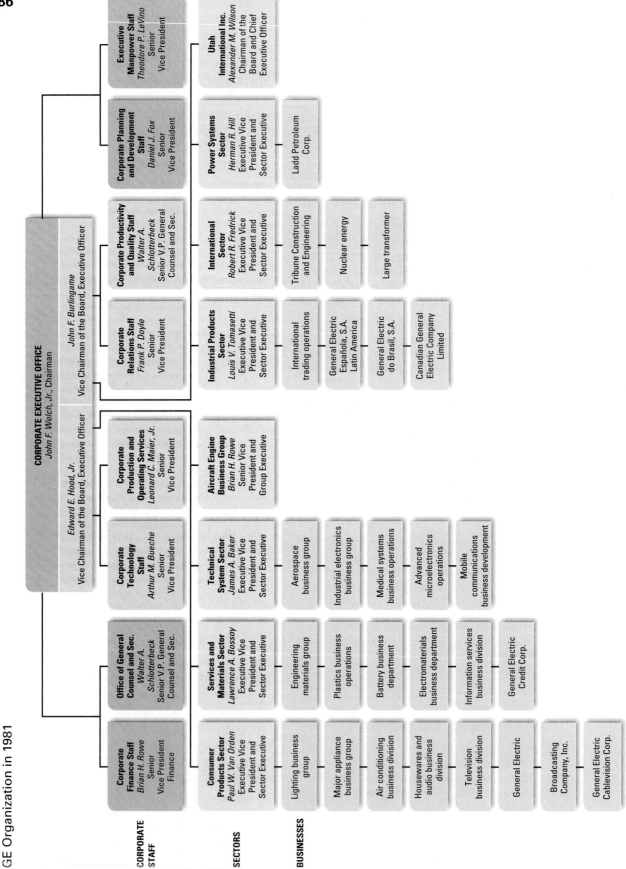

EXHIBIT 4B

GE Organization in 1992

CORPORATE EXECUTIVE OFFICE
John F. Welch, Jr., Chairman

Edward E. Hood, Jr.
Vice Chairman

Frank P. Doyle
Executive Vice Chairman

John F. Burlingame
Vice Chairman

CORPORATE STAFF

Legal Staff
Benjamin W. Herman, Jr.
Senior V.P. General Counsel and Sec.

Business Development
Gary M. Remer
Vice President

Finance
Dennis D. Dammerman
Senior Vice President

Research and Development
Walter L. Ross
Senior Vice President

External and Industrial Relations
Frank P. Doyle
Executive Vice President

GE International
Paolo Fresco
Vice Chairman

Human Resources
Jack O. Peiffer
Senior Vice President

Corporate and Information Technology
Edward J. Skiko
Vice President

Sector layers taken out

BUSINESSES

GE Aircraft Engines
Brian H. Rowe
President and CEO

GE Appliances
J. Richard Stonesiper
President and CEO

GE Financial Services
Gary C. Wendt
Chairman, President and CEO

GE Motors
James W. Rogers
President and CEO

GE Aerospace
Eugene F. Murphy
President and CEO

GE Medical Systems
John M. Trane
President and CEO

GE Plastics
Gary L. Rogers
President and CEO

GE Electrical Distribution and Control
W. James C. McNerney, Jr.
President and CEO

GE Transportation System
Robert L. Mardelli
President and CEO

GE Information Services
Helemen S. Runtagh
President

GE Industrial and Power System
David C. Genever-Walting
President and CEO

NBC
Robert C. Wright
President and CEO

GE Lighting
John D. Opie
President and CEO

EXHIBIT 5

General Electric's Performance in Three Eras (millions of dollars)

	Borch		Jones		Welch		
	1961	1970	1971	1980	1981	1990	1998
Sales	4,666.6	8,726.7	9,557.0	24,950.0	27,240.0	52,619.0	100,469.0
Operating profit	431.8	548.9	737.0	2,243.0	2,447.0	6,616.0	13,477.0
Net earnings	238.4	328.5	510.0	1,514.0	1,652.0	4,303.0	9,296.0
ROS	5.1%	3.8%	5.3%	6.1%	6.1%	8.2%	10.8%
ROE	14.8%	12.6%	17.2%	19.5%	18.1%	19.8%	25.4%
Stock market capitalization	6,283.7	7,026.7	10,870.5	12,173.4	13,073.4	50,344.9	334,236.9
S&P 500 Stock Price							
Index—Composite	65.7	83.0	97.9	119.4	126.4	330.2	1,095.4
Employees	279,547	396,583	402,000	366,000	404,000	298,000	293,000
U.S. GNP ($ billion)	523.0	982.0	1,063.0	2,626.0	2,708.0	5,524.5	8,508.9

Source: GE Annual Reports, Survey of Current Business, Datastream.

culture he wanted to create—one characterized by speed, simplicity, and self-confidence.[1] Over the next few years, he launched two closely linked initiatives—dubbed Work-Out and Best Practices—aimed at creating the desired culture and management approach.

Work-Out In late 1988, during one of Welch's regular visits to teach in the company's Management Development Institute, he engaged a group of GE managers in a particularly outspoken session about the difficulty they were having implementing change back at their operations. In a subsequent discussion with James Baughman, GE's director of management development, Welch wondered how to replicate this type of honest, energetic interaction throughout the company. His objective was to create the culture of a small company—a place where all felt engaged and everyone had voice. Together, they developed the idea of a forum where employees could not only speak their minds about how their business might be run more effectively, but also get immediate responses to their ideas and proposals. By the time their helicopter touched down at GE's headquarters, Welch and Baughman had sketched out a major change initiative they called "Work-Out"—a process designed to get unnecessary bureaucratic work out of the system while providing a forum in which employees and their bosses could work out new ways of dealing with each other.

At Welch's request, Baughman formed a small implementation team and, with the help of two dozen outside consultants, led the company-wide program rollout. Assigned to one of GE's businesses, each consultant facilitated a series of off-site meetings patterned after the open-forum style of New England town meetings. Groups of 40 to 100 employees were invited to share views about their business and how it might be improved. The three-day sessions usually began with a talk by the unit boss, who presented a challenge and a broad agenda. Then,

[1] Interestingly, Welch's first attempts at articulating and communicating GE's new cultural values were awkward. For example, in 1986 he defined 10 desirable cultural "attitudes and policies" which few in GE could remember, let alone practice. Furthermore, he communicated his new organizational model as the GE Business Engine, a concept that many found depersonalizing since it seemed to depict people as inputs into a financial machine. Gradually, Welch became more comfortable articulating cultural values which he continued to refine into what he termed "GE's social architecture." Eventually his concept of The Business Engine evolved to become The Human Engine.

the boss was asked to leave, allowing employees aided by facilitators to list their problems, debate solutions, and prepare presentations. On the final day, the bosses returned and were asked to listen to their employees' analyses and recommendations. The rules of the process required managers to make instant, on-the-spot decisions about each proposal, in front of everyone. About 80% of proposals got immediate yes-or-no decisions; if the manager needed more information, he or she had to charter a team to get it by an agreed-upon decision date.

Armand Lauzon, a manager at a GE Aircraft Engine factory, described to *Fortune* how he felt as his employees presented him with their suggestions in a room where they had carefully arranged the seating so his boss was behind him. "I was wringing wet within half an hour," he said. "They had 108 proposals; I had about a minute to say yes or no to each one. And I couldn't make eye contact with my boss without turning around, which would show everyone in the room I was chickenshit." In total, Lauzon supported all but eight of the 108 proposals.

By mid-1992, over 200,000 GE employees—well over two-thirds of the workforce—had participated in Work-Out, although the exact number was hard to determine, since Welch insisted that none of the meetings be documented. "You're just going to end up with more bureaucracy," he said. What was clear, however, was that productivity increases, which had been growing at an average annual rate of 2% between 1981 and 1987, doubled to a 4% annual rate between 1988 and 1992.[2]

Best Practices As Work-Out was getting started, Welch's relentless pursuit of ideas to increase productivity resulted in the birth of a related movement called Best Practices. In the summer of 1988, Welch gave Michael Frazier of GE's Business Development department a simple challenge: How can we learn from other companies that are achieving higher productivity growth than GE? Frazier selected nine companies, including Ford, Hewlett Packard, Xerox, and Toshiba, with different best practices to study. In addition to specific tools and practices, Frazier's team

also identified several characteristics common to the successful companies: they focused more on developing effective processes than controlling individual activities; customer satisfaction was their main gauge of performance; they treated their suppliers as partners; and they emphasized the need for a constant stream of high-quality new products designed for efficient manufacturing.

On reviewing Frazier's report, Welch became an instant convert and committed to a major new training program to introduce Best Practices thinking throughout the organization, integrating it into the ongoing agenda of Work-Out teams. As a result of the Best Practices program, many GE managers began to realize they were managing and measuring the wrong things. (Said one, "We should have focused more on *how* things get done than on just *what* got done.") Subsequently, several units began radically revising their whole work approach. For example, the head of the corporate audit staff explained: "When I started 10 years ago, the first thing I did was count the $5,000 in the petty cash box. Today, we look at the $5 million in inventory on the floor, searching for process improvements that will bring it down."

Going Global

During the early- and mid-1980s, internationalization had remained a back-burner issue at GE, but strong advocates of globalization such as Paolo Fresco, the Italian-born president of GE Europe, understood why Welch had to concentrate his early efforts on the rationalization of the U.S. operations. "It's very difficult to jump into the world arena if you don't have a solid base at home," said Fresco, "but once the solid base was created, we really took the jump."

The first rumblings of the emerging globalization priority came in Welch's challenges to his Corporate Executive Council meetings during 1986. Reflecting his own early experience in GE Plastics, he did not try to impose a corporate globalization strategy, preferring to let each business take responsibility for implementing a plan appropriate to its particular needs:

> When I was 29 years old I bought land in Holland and built the plants there. That was "my land" for "my business." I was never interested in the global GE, just the global Plastics business. The idea of a company being global is nonsense. Businesses are global, not companies.[v]

[2]In GE, productivity was defined by the following calculation: Productivity = Real Revenue (net of price increases) / Real Costs (net of inflationary increases).

This did not mean, however, that Welch was un-involved in his business managers' globalization plans. In 1987, he focused their attention by raising the bar on GE's well-known performance standard: from now on, "#1 or #2" was to be evaluated on *world* market position. As if to underline his seriousness, a few months later he announced a major deal with Thomson S.A., in which GE agreed to exchange its struggling consumer electronics business for the large French electronics company's medical imaging business, a business in which GE had a leading global position.

To provide continuing momentum to the internationalization effort, in 1989, Welch appointed Paolo Fresco as head of International Operations and in 1992 made him a vice-chairman and member of his four-man corporate executive office. Fresco, a key negotiator on the Thomson swap, continued to broker numerous international deals: a joint venture with German-based Robert Bosch, a partnership with Toshiba, and the acquisition of Sovac, the French consumer credit company. As Eastern Europe opened, he initiated a major thrust into the former Communist bloc, spearheaded by the purchase of a majority share in the Hungarian lighting company, Tungsram. Fresco became the locator and champion of new opportunities. "I fill vacuums," he said. "All these assignments are temporary—once they are complete, I get out of the way."

Like subsequent strategic initiatives, globalization was not a one-time effort, but an ongoing theme that Welch doggedly pursued over the years. Taking advantage of Europe's economic downturn, GE invested $17.5 billion in the region between 1989 and 1995, half on new plants and facilities and half to finance 50 or so acquisitions. Then in 1995, after the Mexican peso collapsed, the company again saw the economic uncertainty as a great buying opportunity. Within six months GE had acquired 16 companies, positioning it to participate in the country's surprisingly rapid recovery. And as Asia slipped into crisis in 1997–1998, Welch urged his managers to view it as a buying opportunity rather than a problem. In Japan alone the company spent $15 billion on acquisitions in six months.

By 1998, international revenues were $42.8 billion, almost double the level just five years earlier. The company expected to do almost half its business outside the United States by 2000, compared with only 20% in 1985, the year before the first international push. More important, global revenues were growing at almost three times the rate of domestic sales. (See Exhibit 6.)

EXHIBIT 6

Growth Through Globalization

Source: GE Annual Report, 1998.

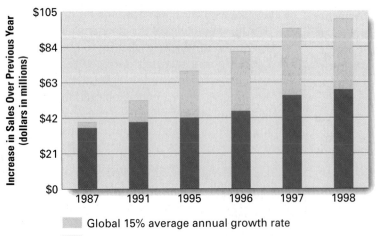

Global 15% average annual growth rate

Domestic 6% average annual growth rate

Developing Leaders

While the global thrust and the new cultural initiatives were being implemented, Welch was also focusing on the huge task of realigning the skill sets—and, more important, the mindsets—of the company's 290,000 employees with GE's new strategic and organizational imperatives. Amidst the grumbling of those who felt overworked in the new demanding environment and the residual distrust left over from the layoffs of the 1980s, he recognized his challenge was nothing short of redefining the implicit contract that GE had with its employees:

> Like many other large companies in the U.S., Europe and Japan, GE has had an implicit psychological contract based on perceived lifetime employment. This produced a paternal, feudal, fuzzy kind of loyalty. That kind of loyalty tends to focus people inward. But in today's environment, people's emotional energy must be focused outward on a competitive world… The new psychological contract, if there is such a thing, is that jobs at GE are the best in the world for people willing to compete. We have the best training and development resources and an environment committed to providing opportunities for personal and professional growth.[vi]

Like all GE managers, Welch grew up in an organization deeply committed to developing its people. He wanted to harness that tradition and use it to translate his broad cultural changes down to the individual level. This would mean adapting GE's well-established human resource systems to his goals. For example, for as long as he could remember, the company's top executives had committed substantial amounts of time to the rigorous management appraisal, development, and succession planning reviews known as Session C. He began using this process to help achieve his objectives, predictably adding his own intense personal style to its implementation.

Starting in April and lasting through May each year, Welch and three of his senior executives visited each of his businesses to review the progress of the company's top 3,000 executives. Welch kept particularly close tabs on the upper 500, all of whom had been appointed with his personal approval. In these multi-day meetings, Welch wanted to be exposed to high-potential managers presenting results on major projects. In an exhaustive 10- to 12-hour review in each business, Welch asked the top executive to identify the future leaders, outline planned training and development plans, and detail succession plans for all key jobs. The exercise reflected his strong belief that good people were GE's key assets and had to be managed as a company resource. "I own the people," he told his business heads. "You just rent them."

As these reviews rolled out through GE, all professional-level employees expected honest feedback about where they were professionally, reasonable expectations about future positions they could hold, and the specific skills required to get there. Managers at every level used these discussions as the basis for coaching and developing their staff. (As a role model, Welch estimated he spent at least 70% of his time on people issues, most of that teaching and developing others.)

A strong believer in incentives, Welch also radically overhauled GE's compensation package. From a system driven by narrow-range increases in base salary supplemented by bonuses based on one's business performance, he implemented a model in which stock options became the primary component of management compensation. He expanded the number of options recipients from 300 to 30,000 and began making much more aggressive bonus awards and options allocations strongly tied to the individual's performance on the current program priority (globalization, for example, or best practices initiatives).

Through all of these human resource tools and processes, Welch's major effort was increasingly focused on creating an environment in which people could be their best. Entering the 1990s, he described his objective for GE in these terms:

> Ten years from now, we want magazines to write about GE as a place where people have the freedom to be creative, a place that brings out the best in everybody. An open, fair place where people have a sense that what they do matters, and where that sense of accomplishment is rewarded in the pocketbook and the soul. That will be our report card.

A key institution that Welch harnessed to bring about this cultural change was GE's Crotonville management development facility. Welch wanted to convert Crotonville from its management training focus and its role as a reward or a consolation prize for those who missed out on a promotion to a powerful engine of change in his transformation effort. In the

EXHIBIT 7

Welch at GE's Crotonville Center

A typical note Welch sent to 30 participants to prepare for his session of GE's Executive Development Course (EDC):

Dear EDC Participants,

I'm looking forward to an exciting time with you tomorrow. I've included here a few thoughts for you to think about prior to our session:

As a group—

Situation: Tomorrow you are appointed CEO of GE.

■ What would you do in first 30 days?

■ Do you have a current "vision" of what to do?

■ How would you go about developing one?

■ Present your best shot at a vision.

■ How would you go about "selling" the vision?

■ What foundations would you build on?

■ What current practices would you jettison?

Individually—

1. Please be prepared to describe a leadership dilemma that you have faced in the past 12 months, i.e., plant closing, work transfer, HR, buy or sell a business, etc.

2. Think about what you would recommend to accelerate the Quality drive across the company.

3. I'll be talking about "A, B & C" players. What are your thoughts on just what makes up such a player?

4. I'll also be talking about energy/energizing/edge as key characteristics of today's leaders. Do you agree? Would you broaden this? How?

I'm looking forward to a fun time, and I know I'll leave a lot smarter than when I arrived.

—Jack

Source: *The Leadership Engine.*

mid-1980s, when he was cutting costs almost everywhere else, he spent $45 million on new buildings and improvements at Crotonville. He also hired some experienced academics—Jim Baughman from Harvard and Noel Tichy from Michigan—to revolutionize Crotonville's activities.

Under Welch's direct control and with his personal involvement, Crotonville's priority became to develop a generation of leaders aligned to GE's new vision and cultural norms. Increasingly, it evolved from a training center to a place where teams of managers worked together on real priority issues and decided on results-oriented action. And this led to the gradual replacement of outside faculty by GE insiders acting as discussion leaders. Leading the

change was Welch, who twice a month traveled to Crotonville to teach and interact with GE employees. ("Haven't missed a session yet," he boasted in the late 1990s.) (See Exhibit 7.) It was during one of these sessions that the idea for Work-Out emerged, and it was at Crotonville that many of the Best Practices sessions were held.

Despite all the individual development and the corporate initiatives, not all managers were able to achieve Welch's ideal leadership profile. (See Exhibit 8.) Of greatest concern to the CEO were those who seemed unwilling or unable to embrace the open, participative values he was espousing. In 1991, he addressed the problem and the seriousness of its consequences:

In our view, leaders, whether on the shop floor or at the top of our businesses, can be characterized in at least four ways. The first is one who delivers on commitments—financial or otherwise—and shares the values of our company. His or her future is an easy call. Onward and upward. The second type of leader is one who does not meet commitments and does not share our values. Not as pleasant a call, but equally easy. The third is one who misses commitments but shares the values. He or she usually gets a second chance, preferably in a different environment.

Then there's the fourth type—the most difficult for many of us to deal with. That leader delivers on commitments, makes all the numbers, but doesn't share the values we must have. This is the individual who typically forces performance out of people rather than inspires it: the autocrat, the big shot, the tyrant. Too often all of us have looked the other way and tolerated these "Type 4" managers because "they always deliver"—at least in the short term.[vii]

To reinforce his intention to identify and weed out Type 4 managers, Welch began rating GE top-level managers not only on their performance against quantifiable targets but also on the extent to which they "lived" GE values. Subsequently, many of GE's 500 officers started using a similar two-dimensional grid to evaluate and coach their own direct reports. And when coaching failed, Welch was prepared to take action on the type 4s. "People are removed for having the wrong values," he insisted. "We don't even talk about the numbers."

To back up this commitment to the new leadership criteria, a few years later GE introduced a 360° feedback process. Every employee was graded by his or her manager, peers and all subordinates on a 1 to 5 scale in areas such as teambuilding, quality focus, and vision. Welch described it as a powerful tool for detecting and changing those who "smile up and kick down." Tied into the evaluation process and linked to the Session C human resource planning exercise, the 360° feedback became the means for identifying training needs, coaching opportunities, and, eventually, career planning—whether that be up, sideways, or out.

Into the 1990s: The Third Wave

Entering the 1990s, Welch felt that GE's new foundation had been laid. Despite the slowdown in the industrial sector in the first few years of the new decade, he was committed to the task of rebuilding the company at an even more urgent pace. The new initiatives rolled on.

Boundaryless Behavior

Moving beyond the earlier initiatives aimed at strengthening GE's individual businesses, Welch began to focus on creating what he called "integrated diversity." He articulated his vision for GE in the 1990s as a "boundaryless" company, one characterized by an "open, anti-parochial environment friendly toward

EXHIBIT 8

GE Leadership Capabilities

- Create a clear, simple, reality-based, customer-focused vision and are able to communicate it straightforwardly to all constituencies.

- Understand accountability and commitment and are decisive ... set and meet aggressive targets ... always with unyielding integrity.

- Have the self-confidence to empower others and behave in a boundaryless fashion... believe in and are committed to Work-Out as a means of empowerment ... be open to ideas from anywhere.

- Have a passion for excellence ... hate bureaucracy and all the nonsense that comes with it.

- Have, or have the capacity to develop global brains and global sensitivity and are comfortable building diverse global teams.

- Stimulate and relish change ... are not frightened or paralyzed by it. See change as opportunity, not just a threat.

- Have enormous energy and the ability to energize and invigorate others. Understand speed as a competitive advantage and see the total organizational benefits that can be derived from a focus on speed.

Source: 1992 Annual Report.

the seeking and sharing of new ideas, regardless of their origins"—in many ways an institutionalization of the openness "Work-Out" had initiated and "best practices" transfers had reinforced. Describing his barrier-free vision for GE, Welch wrote:

> The boundaryless company we envision will remove the barriers among engineering, manufacturing, marketing, sales, and customer service; it will recognize no distinctions between domestic and foreign operations—we'll be as comfortable doing business in Budapest and Seoul as we are in Louisville and Schenectady. A boundaryless organization will ignore or erase group labels such as "management," "salaried" or "hourly," which get in the way of people working together.[viii]

One of Welch's most repeated stories of how best practices could be leveraged by boundaryless behavior described how managers from Canadian GE identified a small New Zealand appliance maker, Fisher & Paykel, producing a broad range of products very efficiently in its small, low-volume plant. When the Canadians used the flexible job-shop techniques to increase productivity in their high-volume factory, the U.S. appliance business became interested. More than 200 managers and employees from the Louisville plant went to Montreal to study the accomplishments, and soon a Quick Response program had cut the U.S. production cycle in half and reduced inventory costs by 20%. Not surprisingly, GE's Appliance Park in Louisville became a "must see" destination for many other businesses, and within a year, the program had been adapted for businesses as diverse as locomotives and jet engines.

The CEO gave the abstract concept of boundarylessness teeth not only by repeating such success stories but also by emphasizing that there was no place at GE for the adherents of the old culture: "We take people who aren't boundaryless out of jobs… If you're turf-oriented, self-centered, don't share with people and aren't searching for ideas, you don't belong here," he said. He also changed the criteria for bonuses and options awards to reward idea-seeking and sharing, not just idea creation. Five years later, Welch had a list of boundarylessness success stories:

> We quickly began to learn from each other: productivity solutions from Lighting; "quick response" asset management from Appliances; transaction effectiveness from GE Capital; cost-reduction techniques from Aircraft Engines; and global account management from Plastics.[ix]

One of the most impressive examples of the way ideas and expertise spread throughout GE was the company's "integration model." Developed on the lessons drawn from literally hundreds of post-acquisition reviews, the model guided the actions of managers in any part of the company responsible for integrating a newly acquired operation: from taking control of the accounts to realigning the organization, and from identifying and removing "blockers" to implementing GE tools and programs. By the late 1990s, GE's integration programs were completed in about 100 days.

Stretch: Achieving the Impossible

To reinforce his rising managerial expectations, in the early 1990s Welch made a new assault on GE's cultural norms. He introduced the notions of "stretch" to set performance targets and described it as "using dreams to set business targets, with no real idea of how to get there."[x] His objective was to change the way targets were set and performance was measured by creating an atmosphere that asked of everyone, "How good can you be?"

Stretch targets did not replace traditional forecasting and objective-setting processes. Managers still had to hit basic targets—adjusted to recognize the world as it turned out to be, not some rigid plan negotiated a year earlier. But during the budget cycle they were also required to set higher, "stretch" goals for their businesses. While managers were not held accountable for these goals, those who achieved them were rewarded with substantial bonuses or stock options. Said Welch: "Rigorous budgeting alone is nonsense. I think in terms of . . . what is the best you can do. You soon begin to see what comes out of a trusting, open environment."

Within a year of introducing the concept of stretch, Welch was reporting progress:

> We used to timidly nudge the peanut along, setting goals of moving from, say, 4.73 in inventory turns to 4.91, or from 8.53% operating margin to 8.92%; and then indulge in time-consuming high-level, bureaucratic negotiations to move the number a few hundredths one way or the other… We don't do that anymore. In a boundaryless organization with a bias for speed, decimal points are a bore. They inspire or challenge no one, capture no imaginations. We're aiming at 10 inventory turns, at 15% operating margins.[xi]

By the mid-1990s, stretch goals were an established part of GE's culture. A senior executive explained: "People like problem solving. They want to go to that next level. That's becoming a bigger driver for the company than Work-Out." But the introduction of stretch targets did not come without implementation difficulties. According to Steve Kerr, the head of Crotonville, "You absolutely have to honor the don't-punish-failure concept; stretch targets become a disaster without that." Unless properly managed, he explained, stretch could easily degenerate into a justification for forcing people to work 60-hour weeks to achieve impossible goals. "It's not the number per se, especially because it's a made-up number. It's the process you're trying to stimulate. You're trying to get people to think of fundamentally better ways of performing their work."[xii]

In early 1996, Welch acknowledged that GE did not meet two of its four-year corporate stretch targets: to increase operating margins from their 1991 level of 10% to 15% by 1995, and inventory turns from 5 to 10 times. However, after decades of single-digit operating margins and inventory turns of 4 or 5, GE did achieve an operating margin of 14.4% and inventory turns of almost 7 in 1995. "In stretching for these 'impossible' targets," said Welch, "we learned to do things faster than we would have going after 'doable' goals, and we have enough confidence now to set new stretch targets of at least 16% operating margin and more than 10 turns by 1998."[xiii]

Service Businesses

In 1994, Welch launched a new strategic initiative designed to reinforce one of his earliest goals: to reduce GE's dependence on its traditional industrial products. In the early 1980s, he had initiated the initial tilt towards service businesses through the acquisition of financial service companies such as Employers Reinsurance and Kidder, Peabody. "Nearly 60% of GE's profits now comes from services," said Welch in 1995. "Up from 16.4% in 1980. I wish it were 80%."[xiv]

To fulfill that wish, Welch began moving to the next stage—a push for product services. During his annual strategic reviews with senior managers, Welch began to challenge his managers "to participate in more of the food chain." While customers would always need high-quality hardware, Welch argued that GE's future challenge would be to offset slowing growth for its products by supplementing them with added-value services. Describing it as one of "the biggest growth opportunities in [GE's] history," he named a cadre of rising executives to focus on the

issue. At the same time, he asked Vice Chairman Paolo Fresco to set up a Services Council through which top managers could exchange ideas.

Soon, all GE's businesses were exploring new service-based growth opportunities. The medical business, for example, developed a concept called "In Site." This involved placing diagnostic sensors and communications capability into their installed base of CT scanners, MRI equipment, and other GE medical devices. The system linked the equipment directly to GE's on-line service center, continuously diagnosing its operating condition in real time. Soon, GE was offering its remote diagnostics and other services to all medical equipment—including non-GE products.

Like other internal "best practice" service examples, the "In Site" story was shared in the Services Council, and soon online diagnostic technology was being transferred to other GE businesses. In Aircraft Engines, critical operating parameters of GE jet engines were monitored by GE Service experts while the engines were in flight, providing the company with a major value-added benefit for its customers. The same real-time diagnostic concepts were also applied in GE's power systems business, and other businesses had plans to develop remote diagnostic capability as well.

According to Welch, the opportunity for growth in product services was unlimited. With an advantage unique in the world—an installed base of some 9,000 GE commercial jet engines, 10,000 turbines, 13,000 locomotives, and 84,000 major pieces of medical diagnostic imaging equipment—he felt GE had an incredibly strong platform on which to build. Commented Lewis Edelheit, GE's senior VP for Corporate Research and Development:

> A few years ago, businesses were seen as a pyramid, with the base as the product and the other elements—services, manufacturing processes and information—resting on that base. We are now looking at turning the pyramid upside down. The product will become just one piece of the picture—the tip of that inverted pyramid. The biggest growth opportunities may come from providing services to the customer: providing the customer with ways to become more productive—and with information so valuable the customer will pay for it.[xv]

By 1996, GE had built an $8 billion equipment services business, which was growing much faster than the underlying product businesses. Equally important, in Welch's view, it was changing internal mindsets from selling products to "helping our customers to win." GE's product services were to be aimed at making customers' existing assets—power plants, locomotives, airplanes, factories, hospital equipment and the like—more productive. Yet while GE was helping its customers reduce their capital outlays, its managers were also shifting demand from low-margin products to their newer high-profit services with margins almost twice the company average.

This initiative led to a new round of acquisitions. In 1997 alone, GE made 20 service-related acquisitions and joint ventures, including a $1.5 billion acquisition of a jet engine service business and the $600 million purchase of a global power generation equipment service company. GE's radical business shift over two decades led Welch to claim, "We have changed the very nature of what we do for a living. Today, services account for two-thirds of our revenues." (See Exhibit 9.)

Closing Out the Decade: Welch's Final Chapter

As he entered the last half of the decade, Welch was aware that he would reach GE's mandatory retirement age in 2001. Yet his commitment to keep building GE was undiminished, despite critics who continued to question if the company could keep adding value to such a highly diversified business portfolio. In the 1995 Annual Report, he tackled the issue head on:

> The hottest trend in business is the rush toward breaking up multi-business companies. The obvious question to GE, the world's largest multi-business company, was, "When are you going to do it?" The short answer is that we're not.... We are a company intent on getting bigger, not smaller. Our only answer to the trendy question "What do you intend to spin off?" is "Cash—and lots of it."

Despite hospitalization for triple bypass surgery in 1995, he showed no signs of slowing down. Indeed, many felt he gained new energy in his post-operative state as the pressure for performance and new initiatives continued.

Six Sigma Quality Initiative

When a 1995 company survey showed that GE employees were dissatisfied with the quality of its products and processes, Welch met with Lawrence Bossidy, an old friend who had left GE in 1991 to become CEO of AlliedSignal Inc. Welch learned how the Six Sigma

EXHIBIT 9

Growth in GE's Service Businesses

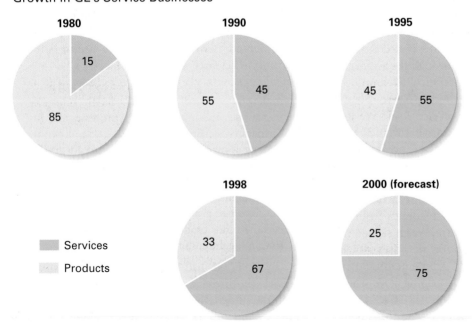

quality program Bossidy had borrowed from Motorola Inc. had helped AlliedSignal dramatically improve quality, lower costs, and increase productivity. Immediately, he invited Bossidy to GE's next Corporate Executive Council meeting. His presentation of the AlliedSignal program won universal rave reviews.

After the meeting, Welch asked Gary Reiner, vice president for Business Development, to lead a quality initiative for GE. Reiner undertook a detailed study of the impact of quality programs at companies like Motorola and AlliedSignal. His analysis concluded that GE was operating at error rates ten thousand times the Six Sigma quality level of 3.4 defects per million operations. Furthermore, he estimated that the gap was costing the company between $8 billion and $12 billion a year in inefficiencies and lost productivity. On the basis of Reiner's findings, at GE's 1996 annual gathering of its 500 top managers in Boca Raton, Welch announced a goal of reaching Six Sigma quality levels company-wide by the year 2000, describing the program as "the biggest opportunity for growth, increased profitability, and individual employee satisfaction in the history of our company."

Like all initiatives announced in Boca (services, globalization, etc.), Six Sigma quality was more than a slogan: it was a well-developed program, with a detailed plan for its implementation. Furthermore, it would be monitored throughout the year in a carefully linked series of management meetings that Welch started to refer to as GE's "operating system"—the series of planning, resource allocation, review, and communication meetings that were at the heart of its management process. The Boca initiative announcement was followed up by a first progress report at the two-day March CEC meeting; then in the April Session C reviews, Welch would check how key human resources had been deployed against the target; the July strategic review sessions would review the impact of the initiative on each business's three-year outlook; October's Officers Meeting tracked progress and showcased best practice; and the November operating plan reviews would fold the impact into the following year's forecasts. (See Exhibit 10.) Said Welch, "We are relentless."

Six Sigma participation was not optional, and Welch tied 40% of bonus to an individual's Six Sigma objectives. To provide managers the skills, Reiner designed a massive training of thousands of managers to create a cadre of "Green Belts," "Black Belts," and "Master Black Belts" in Six Sigma quality. "Green

Belt" training took about four weeks, followed by implementation of a five-month project aimed at improving quality. Black Belts required six weeks of instruction in statistics, data analysis, and other Six Sigma tools which prepared the candidate to undertake three major quality projects that resulted in measurable performance increases. Master Black Belts—full-time Six Sigma instructors—mentored the Black Belt candidates through the two-year process.

At the January 1998 Boca Raton meeting, speakers from across the company and around the world presented Six Sigma best practice and achievements. Managers from Medical Systems described how Six Sigma designs produced a tenfold increase in the life of CT scanner X-ray tubes; the railcar leasing business described a 62% reduction in turnaround time at its repair shops, making it two to three times faster than its nearest rival; and a team from the plastics business described how the Six Sigma process added 300 million pounds of new capacity, equivalent to a "free plant." In all, 30,000 Six Sigma projects had been initiated in the prior year.

At the April 1999 Annual Meeting, Welch announced that in the first two years of Six Sigma, GE had invested $500 million to train the entire professional workforce of 85,000. In addition, 5,000 managers had been appointed to work on the program full-time as Black Belts and Master Black Belts, leading Welch to claim "they have begun to change the DNA of GE to one whose central strand is quality." Returns of $750 million over the investment exceeded expectations, and the company was forecasting additional returns of $1.5 billion in 1999 (Exhibit 11). Clearly delighted by the program, Welch stated, "In nearly four decades with GE, I have never seen a company initiative move so willingly and so rapidly in pursuit of a big idea."

"A Players" with "Four E's"

The closer he got to his planned retirement date, the more Welch seemed to focus on the quality of the organization he would leave to his successor. While he felt he had assembled a first-class team of leaders at the top of the company, he wanted to continue upgrading quality deep in the organization. This implied not only raising the bar on new hires but also weeding out those who did not meet GE's high standards. Modifying his earlier language of four management types, he began describing GE as a company that wanted only "A Players"—individuals with vision,

EXHIBIT 10

The GE Management System

Core Business Processes

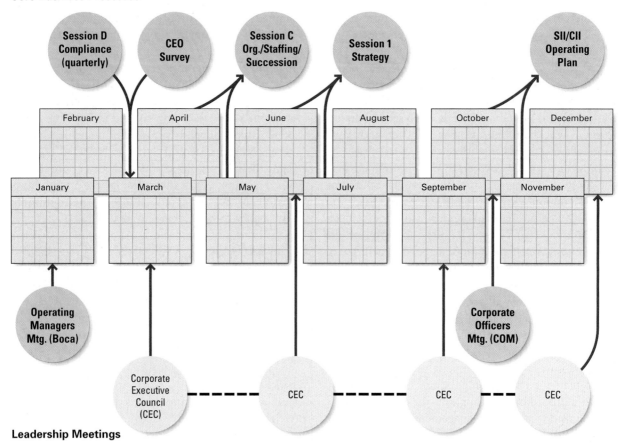

Management System Drives Resource Allocation (People and $) and Accelerates Consistent Best Practice Implementation.

leadership, energy, and courage. He described what he was trying to achieve:

> The GE leader sees this company for what it truly is: the largest petri dish of business innovation in the world. We have roughly 350 business segments. We see them as 350 laboratories whose ideas are there to be shared, learned, and spread as fast as we can. The leader sees that sharing and spreading near the top of his or her responsibilities.

"A Players" were characterized by what Welch described as the 4E's—energy ("excited by ideas and attracted to turbulence because of the opportunity it brings"), ability to energize others ("infecting everyone with their enthusiasm for an idea and having everyone dreaming the same big dreams"), edge ("the ability to make tough calls") and execution ("the consistent ability to turn vision into results").

To meet the company's need for exceptional leadership talent, Welch insisted that GE move to phase three of its globalization initiative. Beyond focusing on global markets and global sources—the earlier two phases of globalization—he urged his managers to expand their efforts in "globalizing the intellect of the company." At the same time, he urged his top management group to take strong action to upgrade the quality of their existing employees:

> We're an A-plus company. We want only A players. We can get anyone we want. Shame on any of you who aren't facing into your less-than-the-best. Take care of your best. Reward them. Promote them. Pay them well. Give them a lot of [stock] options and don't spend all that time trying to work plans to get Cs to be Bs. Move them on out early. It's a contribution.[xvi]

EXHIBIT 11

Costs and Benefits of GE's Six Sigma Program
Six Sigma Results: 1996–1999

Source: GE Annual Report, 1998.

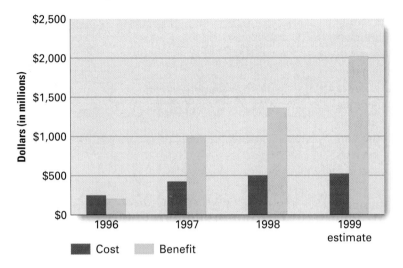

To help clarify those decisions, the company implemented a performance appraisal system that required every manager to rank each of his or her employees into one of five categories based on his or her long-term performance—the "top" 10% as 1s, the "strong" 15% as 2s, the "highly valued" 50% as 3s, the "borderline" 15% as 4s, and the "least effective" 10% as 5s.[3] Every group, even a 10-person team, had to be ranked on this so-called "vitality curve." All 1s and most 2s received stock options but anyone rated a 5 had to go. Welch elaborated on the need to weed out poor performers. "With the 5s it's clear as a bell. I think they know it, and you know it. It's better for everyone. They go on to a new place, a new life, a new start." At the other end of the scale, Welch expected managers to take action on their top performers to develop them: "You send your top 10 on and see how many of them get into the top 10 of the whole business."

Welch knew that nurturing and continuously upgrading the quality of management was one of the main keys to GE's success. He felt that the talent he

amassed over 18 years—especially at the senior management levels—was of a significantly higher quality than in past years. "I've got all A players in the Corporate Council. It wasn't like that before. I'm really pleased about that," he said.

Toward Retirement: One More Initiative

Just when the organization felt Welch had put his final stamp on GE, at the 1999 Operating Managers' Meeting in Boca, the 64-year-old CEO introduced his fourth strategic initiative—e-business.[4] Describing the impact of the Internet as "the biggest change I have ever seen," he launched a program he described as *"destroyyourbusiness.com."* Within two months each unit had a full-time *dyb.com* team focused on the challenge of redefining its business model before someone else did. "Change means opportunity," he told them. "And this is our greatest opportunity yet."

Yet Welch also knew that GE was late to the Internet party. As he acknowledged in his address to shareholders three months after the Boca meeting, "Big companies like us were frightened by the unfamiliarity of the technology. We thought this was

[3]Eventually, the five categories were reduced to three—the top 20%, the high-performance 70%, and the bottom 10%. The practice of counseling out the bottom 10% continued under the philosophy of "improve or move."

[4]The three earlier ones were globalization, services, and Six Sigma.

mysterious, Nobel Prize stuff, the province of the wild-eyed and purple haired." But the more he explored the Internet and talked to people about it, the more Welch came to believe that, through processes like Six Sigma, GE had done the really hard work of building the assets needed to support e-business—like strong brands, top ranked product reliability, great fulfillment capability, and excellent service quality. "It's much harder for a dot com startup to challenge us when they don't have the fundamentals down," he said. "They're popcorn stands without a real business or operating capabilities."

As the organization cranked up to push the new initiative through the monthly schedule of reviews that GE operating system required, Welch was impressed by early results from the *dyb.com* teams. "Digitizing the company and developing e-business models is easier—not harder—than we ever imagined," he said. But others were more sanguine. Said David Mark, a partner at McKinsey and Co., "It's going to take a decade for this to play out. I don't think it's a simple transition." If Mark was correct, building GE's e-business would be a long-term challenge for Welch's successor.

SOURCES AND REFERENCES

Byrne, John A., "Jack," *Business Week*, June 8, 1998.

Cosco, Joseph P., "General Electric Works it All Out," *Journal of Business Strategy*, May-June, 1994.

Filipczak, Bob, "CEOs Who Train," *Training*, June, 1996.

Grant, Linda, "GE: The Envelope, Please," *Fortune*, June 26, 1995.

Hodgetts, Richard M., "A Conversation with Steve Kerr, GE's Chief Learning Officer," *Organizational Dynamics*, March 22, 1996.

Kandebo, Stanley, "Engine Services Critical to GE Strategy," *Aviation Week*, February 23, 1998.

Koenig, Peter, "If Europe's Dead, Why is GE Investing Billions There?" *Fortune*, September 9, 1996.

Lorenz, Christopher, "The Alliance-Maker," *Financial Times*, April 14, 1989.

Norman, James R., "A Very Nimble Elephant," *Forbes*, October 10, 1994.

Rifkin, Glenn, "GE: Bringing Good Leaders to Life," *Forbes*, April 8, 1996.

Tichy, M. Noel and Eli Cohen, *The Leadership Engine: How Winning Companies Build Leaders at Every Level* (HarperBusiness, New York, 1997).

Tichy, M. Noel and Eli Cohen, "The Teaching Organization," *Training & Development*, July 1998.

Tichy, M. Noel and Stratford Sherman, *Control Your Destiny or Someone Else Will* (HarperBusiness, New York, 1994).

Tichy, M. Noel and Stratford Sherman, "Walking the Talk at GE," *Training & Development*, June 1996.

Slater, Robert, *Get Better or Get Beaten!* (McGraw-Hill, New York, 1996).

Smart, Tim, "GE's Brave New World," *Business Week*, November 8, 1993.

Stewart, Thomas A., "GE Keeps Those Ideas Coming," *Fortune*, August 12, 1991.

ENDNOTES

i. "General Electric: 1984" (HBS Case No. 385-315), by Professor Francis J. Aguilar and Richard G. Hamermesh and RA Caroline Brainard. © 1985 by the President and Fellows of Harvard College.

ii. Noel Tichy and Ram Charan, "Speed, Simplicity, Self-Confidence: An Interview with Jack Welch," *Harvard Business Review*, September-October 1989.

iii. Anon, "GE Chief Hopes to Shape Agile Giant," *Los Angeles Times*, June 1, 1988.

iv. Tichy and Charan, op. cit., p. 112.

v. Robert Slater, *Jack Welch and the GE Way: Management Insights and Leadership Secrets of the Legendary CEO* (McGraw-Hill), 1998, p. 195.

vi. Tichy and Charan, op. cit., p. 120.

vii. GE Annual Report, 1991.

viii. GE Annual Report, 1989.

ix. GE Annual Report, 1995.

x. GE Annual Report, 1993.

xi. GE Annual Report, 1993.

xii. "Stretch Goals: The Dark Side of Asking for Miracles," Interview excerpts with Steve Kerr, GE's Vice President of Leadership Development. *Fortune*, November 13, 1995.

xiii. GE Annual Report, 1995.

xiv. Tim Smart, "Jack Welch's Encore," *Fortune*, October 28, 1996.

xv. Lewis Edelheit, "GE's R&D Strategy: Be Vital," *Research Technology Management*, March-April, 1998.

xvi. Slater, op. cit., p. 39.

Case 32

Nike's Dispute with the University of Oregon

This case was prepared by Rebecca J. Morris, University of Nebraska at Omaha, and Anne T. Lawrence, San Jose State University.

Nike's Dispute with the University of Oregon[1]

On April 24, 2000, Philip H. Knight, CEO of athletic shoe and apparel maker Nike Inc., publicly announced that he would no longer donate money to the University of Oregon (UO). It was a dramatic and unexpected move for the high-profile executive. A former UO track and field star, Knight had founded Nike's predecessor in 1963 with his former UO coach and mentor, Bill Bowerman. Over the years, Knight had maintained close ties with his alma mater, giving more than $50 million of his personal fortune to the school over a quarter century. In 2000, he was in active discussion with school officials about his biggest donation yet—millions for reno-

Reprinted by permission from the *Case Research Journal*. Copyright © 2001 by Rebecca J. Morris and Anne T. Lawrence and the North American Case Research Association. All rights reserved. This case was prepared by Rebecca J. Morris, University of Nebraska at Omaha, and Anne T. Lawrence, San Jose State University, as the basis for class discussion rather than to illustrate either effective or ineffective handling of an administrative situation. For the most recent financial results of the company discussed in this case, go to http://finance.yahoo.com, input the company's stock symbol, and download the latest company report from its homepage.

[1]By Rebecca J. Morris, University of Nebraska at Omaha and Anne T. Lawrence, San Jose State University. This case was written on the basis of publicly available information solely for the purpose of stimulating student discussion. All individuals and events are real. An earlier version of this case was presented at the 2000 annual meeting of the North American Case Research Association. The comments of reviewers at that meeting and of three anonymous reviewers for the Case Research Journal are greatly appreciated. All rights reserved jointly to the authors and the North American Case Research Association. Copyright © 2001 by the *Case Research Journal* and Rebecca J. Morris and Anne T. Lawrence.

vating the football stadium. But suddenly it was all called off. Said Knight in his statement: "[F]or me personally, there will be no further donations of any kind to the University of Oregon. At this time, this is not a situation that can be resolved. The bonds of trust, which allowed me to give at a high level, have been shredded."[2]

At issue was the University of Oregon's intention, announced April 14, 2000, to join the Worker Rights Consortium (WRC). Like many universities, UO was engaged in an internal debate over the ethical responsibilities associated with its role as a purchaser of goods manufactured overseas. Over a period of several months, UO administrators, faculty, and students had been discussing what steps they could take to ensure that products sold in the campus store, especially university-logo apparel, were not manufactured under sweatshop conditions. The university had considered joining two organizations, both of which purported to certify goods as "no sweat." The first, the Fair Labor Association (FLA), had grown out of President Clinton's Apparel Industry Partnership (AIP) initiative and was vigorously backed by Nike, as well as several other leading apparel makers. The second, the Worker Rights Consortium, was supported by student activists and several U.S.-based labor unions that had broken from the AIP after charging it did not go far enough to protect workers. Knight clearly felt that his alma mater had made the wrong choice. "[The] University [has] inserted itself into the new global economy where I make my living," he charged. "And inserted itself on the wrong side, fumbling a teachable moment."

[2]"Knight's Statement," by Philip H. Knight, via press release, http://www.oregonlive.com.

The dispute between Phil Knight and the University of Oregon captured much of the furor swirling about the issue of the role of multinational corporations in the global economy and the effects of their far-flung operations on their many thousands of workers, communities, and other stakeholders. In part because of its high-profile brand name, Nike had become a lightning rod for activists concerned about worker rights abroad. Like many U.S.-based shoe and apparel makers, Nike had located its manufacturing operations overseas, mainly in Southeast Asia, in search of low wages. Almost all production was carried out by subcontractors rather than by Nike directly. Nike's employees in the United States, by contrast, directed their efforts to the high-end work of research and development, marketing, and retailing. In the context of this global division of labor, what responsibility, if any, did Nike have to ensure adequate working conditions and living standards for the hundreds of thousands of workers, mostly young Asian women, who made its shoes and apparel? If this was not Nike's responsibility, then whose was it? Did organizations like the University of Oregon have any business pressuring companies through their purchasing practices? If so, how should they best do so? In short, what were the lessons of this "teachable moment"?

Nike, Inc.

In 2000, Nike, Inc. was the leading designer and marketer of athletic footwear, apparel, and equipment in the world. Based in Beaverton, Oregon, the company's "swoosh" logo, its "Just Do It!" slogan, and its spokespersons Michael Jordan, Mia Hamm, and Tiger Woods were universally recognized. Nike employed around 20,000 people directly, and *half a million* indirectly in 565 contract factories in 46 countries around the world turning out Nike products.[3] Wholly owned subsidiaries included Bauer Nike Hockey Inc. (hockey equipment), Cole Haan (dress and casual shoes), and Nike Team Sports (licensed team products). Revenues for the 12 months ending November 1999 were almost $9 billion.[4] With a 45 percent global market share, Nike was in a league of its own.[5] Knight owned 34 percent of the

company's stock and was believed to be the sixth richest individual in the United States.[6]

Knight had launched this far-flung global empire shortly after completing his MBA degree at Stanford University in the early 1960s. Drawing on his firsthand knowledge of track and field, he decided to import low-priced track shoes from Japan in partnership with his former college coach. Bowerman would provide design ideas, test the shoes in competition, and endorse the shoes with other coaches; Knight would handle all financial and day-to-day operations of the business. Neither man had much money to offer, so for $500 apiece and a handshake, the company (then called Blue Ribbon Sports) was officially founded in 1963. The company took the name Nike in 1978; two years later, with revenues topping $269 million and 2,700 employees, Nike became a publicly traded company.[7]

From the beginning, marketing had been a critical part of Knight's vision. The founder defined Nike as a "marketing-oriented company." During the 1980s and early 1990s, Nike aggressively sought out endorsements by celebrity athletes to increase brand awareness and foster consumer loyalty. Early Nike endorsers included marathoners Alberto Salazar and Joan Benoit, Olympic gold medalist Carl Lewis, Wimbledon champion Andre Agassi, and six members of the 1992 Olympic basketball "Dream Team." Later Nike endorsers included tennis aces Pete Sampras and Monica Seles, basketball great Michael Jordan, and golf superstar Tiger Woods.

Nike became the world's largest athletic shoe company in 1991 when revenues soared to $3 billion, but that was only the beginning.[8] Continued development of "cool shoes," aggressive geographic expansion, and the world dominance of Nike-endorsing athletes resulted in record-breaking performances year after year. By 1998, Nike's total revenues exceeded $9.5 billion.[9] Although the Asian economic crisis and sluggish U.S. sales caused revenues to dip slightly in 1999, Nike easily led the athletic footwear industry, outpacing the number two firm (Adidas) by 1.5 times.[10] Key events in Nike's history are summarized in Exhibit 1.

[3]Greenhouse, S. (January 26, 2000). "Anti-Sweatshop Movement Is Achieving Gains Overseas," *New York Times*, Section A, p. 10.
[4]Lee, L. (February 21, 2000). "Can Nike Still Do It," *Business Week*, p. 120.
[5]Martinson, J. (July 8, 2000). "Brand Values: Nike: The Sweet Swoosh of Success," *The Guardian* (London), Guardian City Pages, p. 26.

[6]Anonymous. (October 11, 1999). "The Forbes 400: America's Richest People," *Forbes*, p. 296.
[7]*Our History: BRS Becomes Nike.* (n.d). Nike, Inc. Accessed: February 3, 2000. http://www.nikebiz.com/story/before.shtml.
[8]*Our History: In Our Own League.* (n.d.). Nike, Inc. Accessed: February 3, 2000. http://www.nikebiz.com/story/chrono.shtml.
[9]Nike, Inc. (1999, May 31—filing date). Form 10-K. Securities and Exchange Commission. Accessed: February 5, 2000.
[10]Gellene, D. (April 8, 1999). "Ad Reviews: Adidas," *The Los Angeles Times*, Part C, p. 6.

EXHIBIT 1

Key Events in Nike's History

1957	Phil Knight and Coach Bill Bowerman met for the first time at the University of Oregon.
1959	Phil Knight graduated from the University of Oregon with a BBA degree in Accounting.
1962	Knight wrote the marketing research paper outlining the concept that became "Blue Ribbon Sports" (BRS).
1963	The first shipment of 200 Tiger shoes arrived from Japan.
1966	The first retail store was opened.
1969	Knight left the accounting field to devote his full-time efforts to building the company.
1970	Nike's legal dispute with the Japanese supplier resulted in the exploration of manufacturing in Mexico, Puerto Rico, and Canada.
1971	Nike contracted for the production of shoes in Mexico; however, the shoes were a disaster—cracking when used in cold weather.
1972	The first shoes bearing the Nike brand were sold.
1977	Nike contracted with factories in Taiwan and Korea, ending the manufacturing relationship with the Japanese firm.
1978	The split between Blue Ribbon Sports and their Japanese supplier became final. BRS changed to the Nike name for all operations.
1980	Nike sold the first shares of common stock to the public.
1981	Revenues were $457.7 million and Nike had 3,000 employees.
1982	Phil Knight received the Pioneer Award. The Pioneer Award was given annually by the University of Oregon to a person "whose character places him/her in a position of leadership." The award recognized individuals who led in business, philanthropy, communications, government or the arts.
1986	For the first time, Nike revenues surpassed the billion-dollar mark.
1990	Growth in international sales helped Nike reach $2 billion in revenues. Nike employed 5,300 employees in the United States. The Nike World Campus opened in Beaverton, Oregon.
1991	Revenues reached $3 billion with $869 million in international revenues. Michael Jordan wears Nike shoes while leading the Chicago Bulls to their first NBA championship.
1995	Nike's revenues were $4.8 billion. Nike shoes using the patented Nike-Air system were introduced, radically changing shoe design.
1996	Nike's revenues were $6.5 billion. In the Atlanta Olympics, Michael Johnson became the fastest man in the world wearing a pair of specially designed gold metallic Nike's. Phil Knight donated $25 million to the Oregon Campaign. His gift designated $15 million to the creation of endowed chairs. The remaining $10 million helped finance the construction of a new law school building that was named the William W. Knight Law Center after Phil Knight's father. The $25 million gift was the largest single gift to a university in the Pacific Northwest. Knight's earlier gifts to UO totaled $25 million. Knight funds supported athletics and the university library was named for his family in the 1980s.
1998	Nike's revenues were $9.5 billion. Basketball shoes slumped as Michael Jordan retired and the NBA played a shortened season due to a labor dispute. Nike's international trading partner, Nissho Iwai of Japan, donated an undisclosed "generous" amount to the UO Knight Library to "honor Mr. Knight's great commitment to supporting the University of Oregon." Nissho Iwai had made a donation to the renovation of the library in 1990. One floor of the library was named for the Japanese company.
1999	Nike's revenues dipped to $8.8 billion. Revenue decline was attributed to the "brown shoes" movement in the United States and the Asian economic slump.
2000	Phil Knight withdrew his pledge for a $30 million contribution for the University of Oregon's football stadium.

Sources: Our History. (n.d.). Nike, Inc. Accessed: February 3, 2000. **http://www.nikebiz.com/story/chrono.shtml.** Katz, D. R. (1995). *Just Do It: The Nike Spirit in the Corporate World,* Holbrook, MA: Adams Media Corporation. Nike, Inc. (1995–1999). Form 10-K. Securities and Exchange Commission. Accessed: February 5, 2000. The library floor information is based on the following source:"Trading Firm Makes Gift to UO Knight Library endowment." (June 11, 1998). University of Oregon Press Release. Accessed: March 27, 2000. **http://comm.uoregon.edu/newsreleases/ official/jun98/G061198_1.html.**

Cutting Edge Products

An important element in Nike's success was its ability to develop cutting-edge products that met the needs of serious athletes, as well as set fashion trends. Research specialists in Nike's Sports Research Labs conducted extensive research and testing to develop new technologies to improve the performance of Nike shoes in a variety of sports. Tom McQuirk, head of the company's Sports Research Labs stated, "Our job here in Sports Research is to define human movement in terms of biomechanics and physiology. Our job is to translate activities into a set of performance-enhancing and injury-reducing needs."[11] For example, research specialists studied the causes of ankle injuries in basketball players to develop shoes that would physically prevent injuries as well as signal information to the user to help him or her resist turning the ankle while in the air. Other specialists developed new polymer materials that would make the shoes lighter, more aerodynamic, or more resistant to the abrasions incurred during normal athletic use.

Findings from the Sports Research Labs were then passed on to design teams that developed the look and styling of the shoes. Drawing heavily from trends in popular culture, shoe designers in the Jordan Building of Nike's Beaverton, Oregon, corporate campus blended the technological with the "romance and imagery and all those subliminal characteristics that make an object important to people in less utilitarian ways."[12] Put more simply, the Nike designers took a technologically sophisticated piece of sporting equipment and gave it attitude.

The Making of Athletic Shoes

Although it was the leading athletic footwear company in the world, Nike never manufactured shoes in any significant number. Rather, from its inception, the company had outsourced production to subcontractors in Southeast Asia, with the company shifting production locations within the region when prevailing wage rates became too high. In the early years, it had imported shoes from Japan. It later shifted production to South Korea and Taiwan, then to Indonesia and Thailand, and later yet to Vietnam and China, as shown in Exhibit 2.[13]

[11]Katz, D. R. (1995), *Just Do It: The Nike Spirit in the Corporate World* (Holbrook, MA: Adams Media Corporation), p. 132.
[12]Ibid., p. 130.
[13]Although Nike operated shoe factories in New England in the 1970s and 1980s, Nike's annual U.S. production never accounted for more than one week of demand annually. Later, these plants were closed, and Nike stopped producing shoes in the United States, other than prototypes.

EXHIBIT 2

Location of Shoe Production in Nike Subcontractor Factories, 1995–1999 (Percent of Athletic Shoe Production by Country)

	1995	1996	1997	1998	1999
China	31	34	37	37	40
Indonesia	31	38	37	34	30
South Korea	16	11	5	2	1
Thailand	14	10	10	10	11
Taiwan	8	5	3	2	2
Vietnam		2	8	11	12
Philippines			4	4	2
Italy					2

Source: Nike 10-K statements, 1995–1999.

The reasons for locating shoe production mainly in Southeast Asia were several, but the most important was the cost of labor. The availability of component materials and trade policies were also factors. Modern athletic shoes were composed of mesh, leather, and nylon uppers that were hand-assembled, sewn, and glued to composite soles.[14] Mechanization had not been considered effective for shoe manufacturing due to the fragile materials used and the short life spans of styles of athletic shoes.[15] Therefore, shoe production was highly labor intensive. Developing countries, primarily in Southeast Asia, offered the distinct advantage of considerably lower wage rates. For example, in the early 1990s, when Nike shifted much of its shoe production to Indonesia, daily wages there hovered around $1 a day (compared with wages in the U.S. shoe industry at that time of around $8 an hour).[16]

Along with lower labor costs, Asia provided the additional advantage of access to raw materials suppliers.[17] Very few rubber firms in the United States, for example, produced the sophisticated composite soles demanded in modern athletic shoe designs. Satellite industries necessary for modern shoe production, plentiful in Asia, included tanneries, textiles, and plastic and iron-work moldings.[18]

[14]Nike, Inc. (1999, May 31—filing date). Form 10-K. Securities and Exchange Commission. Accessed: February 5, 2000.
[15]Vanderbilt, T. (1998). *The Sneaker Book* (New York: New Press), p. 77.
[16]Katz, *Just Do It*, p. 162.
[17]Vanderbilt, *The Sneaker Book*, p. 81.
[18]Ibid., p. 90.

A third factor in determining where to locate production was differential tariffs that applied to athletic shoes. The tariffs were determined by the manner in which the upper was attached to the sole of the shoe. The three types—nonmolded, molded, and fox-banded (where a strip of material was applied over the joint of the sole and upper, as in canvas sneakers)—were assessed different tariffs for importation. Variations in the materials used for the uppers also determined the tariff rate. In general, canvas sneakers were assessed higher tariffs than leather molded footwear, such as basketball or running shoes. As a result, differential tariffs prompted shoe companies to outsource higher margin high-technology athletic shoes while sometimes producing low-margin canvas shoes domestically.[19]

The economic reality for many firms in the athletic footwear industry involved balancing consumer demand for new and innovative styles with pressures to improve the profit picture. Manufacturing new high-technology styles in Southeast Asia permitted the firms to take advantage of lower labor costs, lower tariffs and a better-developed supplier network. Many of Nike's factories in Asia were operated by a small number of Taiwanese and Korean firms that specialized in shoe manufacturing, many owned by some of the wealthiest families in the region. When Nike moved from one location to another, often these companies followed, bringing their managerial expertise with them.

Nike's Subcontractor Factories

In 2000, Nike contracted with over five hundred different footwear and apparel factories around the world to produce its shoes and apparel.[20] Although there was no such thing as a typical Nike plant, a factory operated by the Korean subcontractor Tae Kwang Vina (TKV) in the Bien Hoa City industrial zone near Ho Chi Minh City in Vietnam provided a glimpse into the setting in which many Nike shoes were made.[21]

TKV employed approximately 10,000 workers in the Bien Hoa City factory. The workforce consisted of 200 clerical workers, 355 supervisors, and 9,465 production workers, all making athletic shoes for Nike. Ninety percent of the workers were women between the ages of 18 to 24. Production workers were employed in one of three major areas within the factory: the chemical, stitching, and assembly sections. Production levels at the Bien Hoa City factory reached 400,000 pairs of shoes per month; Nike shoes made at this and other factories made up fully 5 percent of Vietnam's total exports.[22]

A second-generation South Korean shoe worker employed by Nike described the challenges of work in the typical shoe factory as the "three D's." "It's dirty, dangerous, and difficult," explained T. H. Lee. "Making shoes on a production line is something people only do because they see it as an important and lucrative job. Nobody who could do something else for the same wage would be here. It's less dirty, dangerous, and difficult than it was in the past—but it's not an easy way to spend a day."[23]

The Chemical Section[24]

Over one thousand natural and manmade materials were used in the factory to produce shoes from scratch. Workers in the chemical or polyurethane (PU) plant were responsible for producing the high-technology outsoles. Production steps in the chemical division involved stretching and flattening huge blobs of raw rubber on heavy-duty rollers and baking chemical compounds in steel molds to form the innovative three-dimensional outsoles. The chemical composition of the soles changed constantly in response to the cutting-edge formulations developed by the Beaverton, Oregon, design teams, requiring frequent changes in the production process.

The smell of complex polymers, the hot ovens, and the clanging of the steel molds resulted in a working environment that was louder, hotter, and had higher concentrations of chemical fumes than allowed by Vietnamese law.[25] Chemicals used in the section were known to cause eye, skin, and throat

[19]Austen, J. and Barff, R. (1993). "It's Gotta Be da Shoes," *Environment and Planning* 25, pp. 48–52.
[20]Greenhouse, "Anti-Sweatshop Movement Is Achieving Gains Overseas," p. 10.
[21]Descriptions of the Tae Kwang Vina factory in Bien Hoa City were derived from the following: Manning, J. (November 9, 1997). "Nike: Track's Across the Globe" (three-part newspaper series originally appearing in *The Oregonian*), online source http://oregonlive.com/series/nike11091.html. Katz, *Just Do It*; Vanderbilt, *The Sneaker Book*; Ernst & Young (January 13, 1997). *Ernst & Young Environmental and Labor Practice Audit of the Tae Kwang Vina Industrial Ltd. Co., Vietnam.* Copy of the audit available at http://www.corpwatch.org/trac/nike/audit.html.

[22]Greenhouse, S. (November 8, 1997). "Nike Shoe Plant in Vietnam Is Called Unsafe for Workers," *New York Times*, Section A, p. 1.
[23]Katz, *Just Do It*, p. 161.
[24]Manning, J. (November 9, 1997). "Nike: Track's Across the Globe" (three-part newspaper series originally appearing in *The Oregonian*), online source http://oregonlive.com/series/nike11091.html.
[25]Manning, J. (November 11, 1997). "Poverty's Legions Flock to Nike," *The Oregonian*, http://www.oregonlive.com/series/nike11103.html.

irritations; damage to liver and kidneys; nausea; anorexia; and reproductive health hazards through inhalation or in some cases through absorption through the skin.[26] Workers in the chemical section were thought to have high rates of respiratory illnesses, although records kept at the TKV operations did not permit the tracking of illnesses by the factory section.

Workers in the chemical section were issued gloves and surgical-style masks. However, they often discarded the protective gear, complaining that it was too hot and humid to wear them in the plant. Cotton masks and gloves also were ineffective in protecting workers from solvent fumes and exposure to skin-damaging chemicals.[27]

The Stitching Section[28]

In a space the size of three football fields, row after row of sewing machines operated by young women hummed and clattered. One thousand stitchers worked on a single floor of the TKV factory, sewing together nylon, leather, and other fabrics to make the uppers. Other floors of the factory were filled with thousands of additional sewing machines producing different shoe models.

The stitching job required precision and speed. Workers who did not meet the aggressive production goals did not receive a bonus. Failing to meet production goals three times resulted in the worker's dismissal. Workers were sometimes required to work additional hours without pay to meet production quotas.[29] Supervisors were strict, chastising workers for excessive talking or spending too much time in the restrooms. Korean supervisors, often hampered by language and cultural barriers, sometimes resorted to hard-nosed management tactics, hitting or slapping slower workers. Other workers in need of discipline were forced to stand outside the factory for long periods in the tropical sun. The Vietnamese term for this practice was *phoi nang*, or sun-drying.[30]

The Assembly Section[31]

Women worked side by side along an assembly line to join the uppers to the outsoles through the rapid manipulation of sharp knives, skivers,[32] routers, and glue-coated brushes. Women were thought to be better suited for the assembly jobs because their hands were smaller and more capable of the manual dexterity needed to fit the shoe components together precisely. During the assembly process, some 120 pairs of hands touched a single shoe.

A strong, sweet solvent smell was prominent in the assembly area. Ceiling-mounted ventilation fans were ineffective since the heavy fumes settled to the floor. Assembly workers wore cotton surgical masks to protect themselves from the fumes; however, many workers pulled the masks below their noses, saying they were more comfortable that way.[33]

Rows and rows of shoes passed along a conveyor before the sharp eyes of the quality control inspectors. The inspectors examined each of the thousands of shoes produced daily for poor stitching or crooked connections between soles. Defective shoes were discarded. Approved shoes continued on the conveyor to stations where they were laced by assembly workers and finally put into Nike shoeboxes for shipment to the United States.[34]

Despite the dirty, dangerous, and difficult nature of the work inside the Bien Hoa factory, there was no shortage of applicants for positions. Although entry level wages averaged only $1.50 per day (the lowest of all countries where Nike manufactured), many workers viewed factory jobs as better than their other options, such as working in the rice paddies or pedaling a pedicab along the streets of Ho Chi Minh City.[35] With overtime pay at one and a half times the regular rate, workers could double their salaries—generating enough income to purchase a motorscooter or to send money home to impoverished rural relatives. These wages were well above national norms. An independent study by researchers from Dartmouth University showed that the average annual income for workers at two Nike subcontractor factories in Vietnam was

---

[26]Ernst & Young Audit. (n.d.). Corporate Watch. Accessed: March 26, 2000. **http://www.corpwatch.org/trac/nike/audit.html.**
[27]Ibid.
[28]Manning, J. (November 9, 1997). "Nike: Track's Across the Globe" (three-part newspaper series originally appearing in *The Oregonian*), online source **http://oregonlive.com/series/nike11091.html.**
[29]Manning, J. (November 9, 1997). "Nike's Asian Machine Goes on Trial," (part 1 of a three-part newspaper series originally appearing in *The Oregonian*), online source **http://oregonlive.com/series/nike11091.html.**
[30]Manning, J. (November 10, 1997). "Poverty's Legions Flock to Nike" (part 2 of a three-part newspaper series originally appearing in *The Oregonian*), online source **http://oregonlive.com/series/nike11091.html.**

[31]Vanderbilt, *The Sneaker Book*, p. 84.
[32]Skivers are cutting tools that are used to split leather. In athletic shoe manufacturing, skivers are used to cut away the excess leather when bonding the upper to the sole.
[33]Ernst & Young Audit. **http://www.corpwatch.org/trac/nike/audit.html.**
[34]Katz, *Just Do It*, p. 160.
[35]Lamb, D. (April 18, 1999). "Job Opportunity or Exploitation?" *Los Angeles Times*, Part C, p. 1.

between $545 and $566, compared with the national average of between $250 and $300.[36] Additionally, workers were provided free room and board and access to on-site health care facilities.

Many Vietnamese workers viewed positions in the shoe factory as transitional jobs—a way to earn money for a dowry or to experience living in a larger city. Many returned to their homes after working for Nike for two or three years to marry and begin the next phase of their lives.[37]

The Campaigns Against Nike

In the early 1990s, criticism of Nike's global labor practices began to gather steam. *Harper's Magazine*, for example, published the pay stub of an Indonesian worker, showing that the Nike subcontractor had paid the woman just under 14 cents per hour, and contrasted this with the high retail price of the shoes and the high salaries paid to the company's celebrity endorsers.[38] The Made in the U.S.A. Foundation, a group backed by American unions, used a million dollar ad budget to urge consumers to send their "old, dirty, smelly, worn-out Nikes" to Phil Knight in protest of Nike's Asian manufacturing practices.[39] Human rights groups and Christian organizations joined the labor unions in targeting the labor practices of the athletic shoes firm. Many felt that Nike's anti-authority corporate image ("Just Do It") and message of social betterment through fitness were incompatible with press photos of slight Asian women hunched over sewing machines seventy hours a week, earning just pennies an hour.

By mid-1993, Nike was being regularly pilloried in the press as an imperialist profiteer. A CBS news segment airing on July 2, 1993, opened with images of Michael Jordan and Andre Agassi, two athletes who had multimillion dollar promotion contracts with Nike. Viewers were told to contrast the athletes' pay checks with those of the Chinese and Indonesian workers who made "pennies" so that Nike could "Just Do It."[40]

In 1995, the *Washington Post* reported that a pair of Nike Air Pegasus shoes that retailed for $70 cost Nike only $2.75 in labor costs, or 4 percent of the price paid by consumers. Nike's operating profit on the same pair of shoes was $6.25, while the retailer pocketed $9 in operating profits, as shown in Exhibit 3. Also that year, shareholder activists organized by the Interfaith Center on Corporate Responsibility submitted a shareholder proposal at Nike's annual meeting, calling on the company to review labor practices by its subcontractors; the proposal garnered 3 percent of the shareholder vote.

Things were to get worse. A story in *Life*[41] magazine documented the use of child labor in Pakistan to produce soccer balls for Nike, Adidas, and other companies. The publicity fallout was intense. The public could not ignore the photographs of small children sitting in the dirt, carefully stitching together the panels of a soccer ball that would become the plaything of some American child the same age.[42] Nike moved quickly to work with its Pakistani subcontractor to eliminate the use of child labor, but damage to Nike's image had been done.

In October 1996, CBS News *48 Hours* broadcast a scathing report on Nike's factories in Vietnam. CBS reporter Roberta Baskin focused on low wage rates, extensive overtime, and physical abuse of workers. Several young workers told Baskin how a Korean supervisor had beaten them with a part of a shoe because of problems with production.[43] A journalist in Vietnam told the reporter that the phrase "to Nike someone" was part of the Vietnamese vernacular. It meant to "take out one's frustration on a fellow worker." Vietnamese plant managers refused to be interviewed, covering their faces as they ran inside the factory. CBS news anchor Dan Rather concluded the damaging report by saying, "Nike now says it plans to hire outside observers to talk to employees and examine working conditions in its Vietnam factories, but the company just won't say when that might happen."[44]

The negative publicity was having an effect. In 1996, a marketing research study authorized by Nike reported the perceptions of young people aged thirteen

[36]Baum, B. (August 27, 1999). "Study Concludes That Nike Workers Can More Than Make Ends Meet," *Athenaeum;* online version available at: http://www.athensnewspapers.com/1997/101797/1017.a3nike.html.
[37]Manning, "Poverty's Legions," http://oregonlive.com/series/nike11091.html.
[38]Ballinger, J. (August 1992). "Nike: The New Free Trade Heel," *Harper's,* p. 119.
[39]Katz, *Just Do It,* p. 166.
[40]Katz, *Just Do It,* p. 187.

[41]Schanberg, S. (June 1996). "Six Cents an Hour," *Life Magazine,* pp. 38–47.
[42]Holstein, W.J., Palmer, B., Ur-Rehman, S., and Ito, T. (December 23, 1996). "Santa's Sweatshops," *U.S. News and World Report,* p. 50.
[43]The *48 Hours* report, however, neglected to mention that the supervisor had subsequently been fired and was later criminally convicted in a Vietnamese court (Katz, *Just Do It,* p. 188).
[44]CBS News, *48 Hours* (October 17, 1996), transcript.

EXHIBIT 3

The Cost of a Pair of Nike "Air Pegasus" Shoes

Source: Adapted from *Washington Post* (May 3, 1995). "Why It Costs $70 for a Pair of Athletic Shoes."

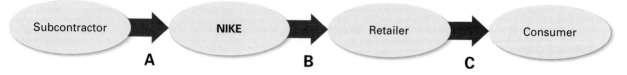

A. Cost to Nike		B. Cost to retailer		C. Cost to consumer	
Materials	$9.00	Nike's operating profit	$6.25	Retail sales personnel	$9.50
Tariffs	3.00	Sales, distribution, and administration	5.00	Rent of retail space	9.00
Rent and equipment	3.00	Promotion/advertising	4.00	Retailer's operating profit	9.00
Production labor	2.75	Research and development	0.25	Other expenses	7.00
Subcontractor's operating profit	1.75				
Shipping	0.50				
Cost to Nike	**$20.00**	**Cost to retailer**	**$35.50**	**Cost to consumer**	**$70.00**

to twenty-five of Nike as a company. The top three perceptions, in the order of their response frequency, were athletics, cool, and bad labor practices.[45] Although Nike maintained that its sales were never affected, company executives were clearly concerned about the effect of criticism of its global labor practices on the reputation of the brand they had worked so hard to build.

The Evolution of Nike's Global Labor Practices

In its early years, Nike had maintained that the labor practices of its foreign subcontractors—like TKV—were simply not its responsibility. "When we started Nike," Knight later commented, "it never occurred to us that we should dictate what their factor[ies] should look like, which really didn't matter because we had no idea what a shoe factory should look like anyway."[46] The subcontractors, not Nike, were responsible for

wages and working conditions. Dave Taylor, Nike's vice president of production, explained the company's position: "We don't pay anybody at the factories and we don't set policy within the factories; it is their business to run."[47]

When negative articles first began appearing in the early 1990s, however, Nike managers realized that they needed to take some action to avoid further bad publicity. In 1992, the company drafted its first Code of Conduct (Exhibit 4), which required every subcontractor and supplier in the Nike network to honor all applicable local government labor and environmental regulations, or Nike would terminate the relationship.[48] The subcontractors were also required to allow plant inspections and complete all necessary paperwork. Despite the compliance reports the factories filed every six months, Nike insiders acknowledged that the code of conduct system might not catch all violations. Tony Nava, Nike's country coordinator for Indonesia, told a *Chicago Tribune* reporter, "We can't know if they're actually complying

[45]Manning, "Poverty's Legions," http://wwworegonlive.com/series/nike11101.html.
[46]Philip Knight, Speech to the National Press Club, May 12, 1998.
[47]Katz, *Just Do It*, p. 191.
[48]Ibid.

EXHIBIT 4

Nike's 1992 Code of Conduct

Source: Code of Conduct. (n.d.). Nike, Inc. Accessed: November 18, 2000. **http://www.nikebiz.com/labor/code.shtml**.

NIKE Inc. was founded on a handshake.

Implicit in that act was the determination that we would build our business with all our partners upon trust, teamwork, honesty, and mutual respect. We expect all of our business partners to operate on the same principles.

At the core of the NIKE corporate ethic is the belief that we are a company comprised of many different kinds of people, appreciating individual diversity, and dedicated to equal opportunity for each individual.

NIKE designs, manufactures, and markets sports and fitness products. At each step in that process we are dedicated to minimizing our impact on the environment. We seek to implement to the maximum extent possible the three "R's" of environmental action—reduce, reuse, and recycle.

There is No Finish Line.

MEMORANDUM OF UNDERSTANDING

Wherever NIKE operates around the globe, we are guided by our Code of Conduct and bind our business partners to those principles with a signed Memorandum of Understanding.

Government Regulation of Business (Subcontractor/supplier) certifies compliance with all applicable local government regulations regarding minimum wage; overtime; child labor laws; provisions of pregnancy, menstrual leave; provisions for vacation and holidays; and mandatory retirement benefits.

Safety and Health (Subcontractor/supplier) certifies compliance with all applicable local government regulations regarding occupational health and safety.

Worker Insurance (Subcontractor/supplier) certifies compliance with all applicable local laws providing health insurance, life insurance, and worker's compensation.

Forced Labor (Subcontractor/supplier) certifies that it and its suppliers and contractors do not use any form of forced labor—prison or otherwise.

Environment (Subcontractor/supplier) certifies compliance with all applicable local environmental regulations, and adhere to NIKE's own broader environmental practices, including the prohibition on the use of chloro-flouro-carbons (CFCs), the release of which could contribute to the depletion of the earth's ozone layer.

Equal Opportunity (Subcontractor/supplier) certifies that it does not discriminate in hiring, salary, benefits, advancement, termination, or retirement on the basis of gender, race, religion, age, sexual orientation or ethnic origin.

Documentation and Inspection (Subcontractor/supplier) agrees to maintain on file such documentation as may be needed to demonstrate compliance with the certifications in this Memorandum of Understanding, and further agrees to make these documents available for NIKE's inspection upon request.

with what they put down on paper."[49] In short, Nike required its subcontractors to comply with existing labor laws, but did not feel it was the firm's duty to challenge local policies that suppressed worker rights or kept wages low in order to attract manufacturing.

In 1994, Nike tried to address this problem by hiring Ernst & Young, the accounting firm, to independently monitor worker abuse allegations in Nike's Indonesian factories. Later, Ernst & Young also audited Nike's factories in Thailand and Vietnam. Although these audits were not made public, a copy of the Vietnam audit leaked to the press showed that workers were often unaware of the toxicity of the compounds they were using and ignorant of the need for safety precautions.[50] In 1998, Nike implemented important changes in its Vietnamese plants to reduce exposure to toxins—substituting less harmful chemicals, installing ventilation systems, and training personnel in occupational health and safety issues.

In 1996, Nike established a new Labor Practices Department, headed by Dusty Kidd, formerly a public relations executive for the company. Later that year, Nike hired GoodWorks International, headed by former U.S. ambassador to the United Nations Andrew Young, to investigate conditions in its overseas factories. In January 1997, GoodWorks issued a glossy report, stating that "Nike is doing a good job in the application of its Code of Conduct. But Nike can and should do better." The report was criticized by activists for its failure to look at the issue of wages. Young demurred, saying he did not have expertise in conducting wage surveys. Said one critic, "This was a public relations problem, and the world's largest sneaker company did what it does best: it purchased a celebrity endorsement."[51]

Over the next few years, Nike continued to work to improve labor practices in its overseas subcontractor factories, as well as the public perception of them. In January 1998, Nike formed a Corporate Responsibility Division, combining the Labor Practices, Global Community Affairs, and Environmental Action Teams under the leadership of former Microsoft executive Maria S. Eitel, hired to be Nike's new vice president for corporate and social responsibility. Nike subsequently doubled the staff of this division. In May of that year, Knight gave a speech at the National Press Club, at which he announced several new initiatives. At that time, he committed Nike to raise the minimum age for employment in its shoe factories to eighteen and in its apparel factories to sixteen. He also promised to achieve OSHA standards for indoor air quality in all its factories by the end of the year, mainly by eliminating the use of the solvent toluene; to expand educational programs for workers and its microenterprise loan program; and to fund university research on responsible business practices. Nike also continued its use of external monitors, hiring PricewaterhouseCoopers to join Ernst & Young in a comprehensive program of factory audits, checking them against Nike's code. At the conclusion of his speech Knight said,

> At the end of the day, we don't have all the answers. Nobody has all the answers. We want to be the best corporate citizens we can be. If we continue to improve, and our industry colleagues and people interested in these issues join in our efforts, the workers are the ultimate beneficiaries.[52]

Apparel Industry Partnership

One of Nike's most ambitious social responsibility initiatives was its participation in the Apparel Industry Partnership. It was this involvement that would lead, eventually, to Knight's break with the University of Oregon.

In August 1996, President Clinton launched the White House Apparel Industry Partnership on Workplace Standards (AIP). The initial group was comprised of eighteen organizations. Participants included several leading manufacturers, such as Nike, Reebok, and Liz Claiborne. Also in the group were several labor unions, including the Union of Needletrades, Industrial, and Textile Employees (UNITE) and the Retail, Wholesale and Department Store Union; and several human rights, consumer, and shareholder organizations, including Business for Social Responsibility, the Interfaith Center on Corporate Responsibility, and the National

[49]Goozner, M. (November 7, 1994). "Nike Manager Knows Abuses Do Happen," *Chicago Tribune*, p. 6.

[50]Hammond, K. (November 7, 1997). "Leaked Audit: Nike Factory Violated Worker Laws," *Mother Jones*. http://www.motherjones.com/news_wire/nike.html.

[51]Glass, S. (August 25, 1997). "The Young and the Feckless," *The New Republic*, online source: http://www.corpwatch.org/trac/feature/sweatshops/newprogressive. html. Glass was later fired by *The New Republic*, which charged that Glass had fabricated some of his sources for this and other articles.

[52]Federal News Service. (May 12, 1998). National Press Club Luncheon Address by Philip Knight, Chief Executive Officer, Nike. LEXIS-NEXIS Academic Universe, Category: News. Accessed: August 27, 2000. http://web.lexis-nexis.com/universe.

Consumers League. The goal of the AIP was to develop a set of standards to ensure that apparel and footwear were not made under sweatshop conditions. For companies, it held out the promise of certifying to their customers that their products were "no sweat." For labor and human rights groups, it held out the promise of improving working conditions in overseas factories.[53]

In April 1997, after months of often-fractious meetings, the AIP announced that it had agreed on a Workplace Code of Conduct that sought to define decent and humane working conditions.[54] Companies agreeing to the code would have to pledge not to use forced labor, that is, prisoners or bonded or indentured workers. They could not require more than sixty hours of work a week, including overtime. They could not employ children younger than fifteen years old, or the age for completing compulsory schooling, whichever was older except they could hire fourteen-year-olds if local law allowed. The code also called on signatory companies to treat all workers with respect and dignity; to refrain from discrimination on the basis of gender, race, religion, age, disability, sexual orientation, nationality, political opinion, or social or ethnic origin; and to provide a safe and healthy workplace. Employees' rights to organize and bargain collectively would be respected. In a key provision, the code also required companies to pay at least the local legal minimum wage or the prevailing industry wage, whichever was higher. All standards would apply not only to a company's own facilities but also to their subcontractors or suppliers.

Knight, who prominently joined President Clinton and others at a White House ceremony announcing the code, issued the following statement:

> Nike agreed to participate in this Partnership because it was the first credible attempt, by a diverse group of interests, to address the important issue of improving factories worldwide. It was worth the effort and hard work. The agreement will prove important for several reasons. Not only is our industry stepping up to the plate and taking a giant swing at improving factory conditions, but equally important, we are finally providing consumers some guidance to counter all of the misinformation that has surrounded this issue for far too long.[55]

The Fair Labor Association

But this was not the end of the AIP's work; it also had to agree on a process for monitoring compliance with the code. Although the group hoped to complete its work in six months, over a year later it was still deeply divided on several key matters. Internal documents leaked to the *New York Times* in July 1998 showed that industry representatives had opposed proposals, circulated by labor and human rights members, calling for the monitoring of 30 percent of plants annually by independent auditors. The companies also opposed proposals that would require them to support workers' rights to organize independent unions and to bargain collectively, even in countries like China where workers did not have such rights by law. Said one nonindustry member, "We're teetering on the edge of collapse."[56]

Finally, a subgroup of nine centrist participants, including Nike, began meeting separately in an attempt to move forward. In November 1998, this subgroup announced that it had come to agreement on a monitoring system for overseas factories of U.S.-based companies. The AIP would establish a new organization, the Fair Labor Association (FLA), to oversee compliance with its Workplace Code of Conduct. Companies would be required to monitor their own factories and those of their subcontractors for compliance; all would have to be checked within the first two years. In addition, the FLA would select and certify independent external monitors, who would inspect 10 percent of each firm's factories each year. Most of these monitors were expected to be accounting firms, which had expertise in conducting audits. The monitors' reports would be kept private. If a company were found to be out of compliance, it would be given a chance to correct the problem. Eventually, if it did not, the company would be dropped from the FLA and its termination announced to the public. Companies would pay for most of their own monitoring.[57]

The Clinton administration quickly endorsed the plan. Secretary of Labor Alexis Herman said, "[We are] convinced this agreement lays the foundation to eliminate sweatshop labor, here and abroad. It is workable for business and creates a credible system

[53]"Companies Agree to Meet on Sweatshops," *Washington Post*, August 3, 1996.

[54]For the full text of the Fair Labor Association Workplace Code of Conduct, see **http://www.fairlabor.org/html/amendctr.html#workplace**.

[55]Philip H. Knight, statement released to the press, April 14, 1997.

[56]Steven Greenhouse, "Anti-Sweatshop Coalition Finds Itself at Odds on Garment Factory Code," *New York Times*, July 3, 1998.

[57]For a description of the monitoring process, see: **http://www.fairlabor.org/html/amendctr.html#monitoringprocess**.

that will let consumers know the garments they buy are not produced by exploited workers."[58]

Both manufacturers and institutional buyers stood to benefit from participation in the Fair Labor Association. Companies, once certified for three years, could place an FLA service mark on their brands, signaling both to individual consumers and institutional buyers that their products were "sweatshop-free." It was expected that the FLA would also serve the needs of institutional buyers, particularly universities. By joining the FLA and agreeing to contract only with certified companies, universities could warrant to their students and others that their logo apparel and athletic gear were manufactured under conditions conforming with an established code of fair labor standards.[59] Both parties would pay for these benefits. The FLA was to be funded by dues from participating companies ($5,000 to $100,000 annually, depending on revenue) and by payments from affiliated colleges and universities (based on 1 percent of their licensing income from logo products, up to a $50,000 annual cap).

Criticism of the Fair Labor Association

Although many welcomed the agreement—and some new companies signed on with the FLA soon after it was announced—others did not. Warnaco, a leading apparel maker that had participated in the AIP, quit, saying that the monitoring process would require it to turn over competitive information to outsiders. The American Apparel Manufacturing Association (AAMA), an industry group representing three hundred fifty companies, scoffed at the whole idea of monitoring. "Who is going to do the monitoring?" asked a spokesperson for the AAMA, apparently sarcastically. "Accountants or Jesuit priests?" The FLA monitoring scheme was also attacked as insufficient by some Partnership participants that had not been part of the subgroup. In their view, companies simply could not be relied upon to monitor themselves objectively. Said Jay Mazur, president of UNITE, "The fox cannot watch the chickens. If they want the monitoring to be independent, it can't be controlled by the companies."[60] FLA critics believed that a visit from an

external monitor once every ten years would not prevent abuses. And in any case, as a practical matter, they stated that most monitors would be drawn from the major accounting firms that did business with the companies they were monitoring and were therefore unlikely to seek out lapses. Companies would not be required to publish a list of their factories, and any problems uncovered by the monitoring process could be kept from the public under the rules governing nondisclosure of proprietary information.

One of the issues most troubling to critics was the code's position on wages. The code called on companies to pay the minimum wage or prevailing wage, whichever was higher. But in many of the countries of Southeast Asia, these wages fell well below the minimum considered necessary for a decent standard of living for an individual or family. For example, the *Economist*[61] reported that Indonesia's average minimum wage—paid by Nike subcontractors—was only two-thirds of what a person needed for basic subsistence. An alternative view was that a code of conduct should require that companies pay a *living wage*, that is, compensation for a normal workweek adequate to provide for the basic needs of an average family, adjusted for the average number of adult wage earners per family. One problem with this approach, however, was that many countries did not systematically study the cost of living, relative to wages, so defining a living wage was difficult. The Partnership asked the U.S. Department of Labor to conduct a preliminary study of these issues; the results were published in 2000 (Exhibit 5).

The code also called on companies to respect workers' rights to organize and bargain collectively. Yet a number of FLA companies outsourced production to nondemocratic countries, such as China and Vietnam, where workers had no such rights. Finally, some criticized the agreement on the grounds it provided companies, as one put it, "a piece of paper to use as a fig leaf." Commented a representative of the needle trades unions, "The problem with the partnership plan is that it tinkers at the margins of the sweatshop system but creates the impression that it is doing much more. This is potentially helpful to companies stung by public condemnation of their labor practices, but it hurts millions of workers and undermines the growing antisweatshop movement."[62]

[58]"Plan to Curtain Sweatshops Rejected by Union," *New York Times*, November 5, 1998.
[59]For a list of signatory companies, universities, and other organizations, see: http://www.fairlabor.org/html/affiliat.html.
[60]*New York Times*, November 21, 1997.
[61]Anonymous. (June 15, 1991). "Indonesia: Staying Alive," *The Economist*, p. 38.
[62]Alan Howard, "Partners in Sweat," *The Nation*, December 29, 1998.

EXHIBIT 5

Wages, Minimum Wages, and Poverty Lines for Selected Countries (in U.S. Dollars)

Country	Year (Latest Available)	National Poverty Line	Minimum Wage	Prevailing Wage in Apparel and Footwear Industries
China	1997	$21–$27/cap/mo*	$12–$39/mo	$115–$191/mo
Indonesia	1999	$5–$6/cap/mo	$15–$34/mo	$15–$42/mo
South Korea	1999	$182/mo	$265/mo	$727–$932/mo
Thailand	1999	$22/cap/mo	$93–$109/mo	$106/mo
Taiwan	1998	$214–$344/mo	$476/mo	$690–$742/mo
Vietnam	1997	$27–$29/mo	$35–$45/mo	$47–$56/mo
Philippines	1999	$26/cap/mo	$150/mo	$150/mo
Italy	1998	$390/cap/mo	$949–$1,445/mo	$1,280–$1,285/mo
United States	1998	$693/cap/mo	$858/mo–$1,083/mo	$1,420–$1,488/mo

National Poverty Line: Poverty measures reflect an estimate of absolute poverty thresholds based on some specified set of basic needs. Opinions differ as to whether the poverty line should reflect mere physical subsistence levels or sufficient income to provide for a nutritious diet, safe drinking water, suitable housing, energy, transportation, health care, child care, education, savings and discretionary income. Comparability between countries is difficult because the basis for establishing the poverty level usually differs across countries.

Minimum Wage: The minimum wage fixing system differs according to the country's objectives and criteria. It is usually set by striking a balance between the needs of the worker and what employers can afford or what economic conditions will permit. A range for minimum wage indicates that the country has differential minimums based on the region, often differing for urban and rural regions.

Prevailing Wage: The prevailing wage reflects the "going rate" or average level of wages paid by employers for workers in the apparel or footwear industries. Positions requiring greater skills, supervisory responsibilities or workers with longer years of employment typically earn more than the wage reported. Nonwage benefits such as access to health care, paid vacations, supplementary pay or training are not included in the prevailing wage.

Sources: The wages, minimum wages, and poverty lines for selected countries are from the U.S. Department of Labor (February 2000). "Wages, Benefits, Poverty Line and Meeting Workers' Needs in the Apparel and Footwear Industries of Selected Countries." **http://www.dol.gov/ilab/ public/media/reports/oiea/main.htm.** The information on Vietnam is from Canada NewsWire (October 16, 1997). "Nike Factory Workers in SE Asia Help Support Their Families and Have Discretionary Income, According to Preliminary Findings of Study by MBA Team From Dartmouth's Tuck School."

*Per capita per month.

The Worker Rights Consortium

Some activists in the antisweatshop movement decided to chart their own course, independent of the FLA. On October 20, 1999, students from more than one hundred colleges held a press conference to announce formation of the Worker Rights Consortium (WRC), and called on their schools to withdraw from, or not to join, the FLA. The organization would be formally launched at a founding convention in April, 2000.[63]

[63]The website for the WRC is http://www.workersrights.org. Further material on disagreements within the FLA that led to the WRC's founding may be found at http://www.sweatshopwatch.org.

The Worker Rights Consortium differed radically in its approach to eliminating sweatshops. First, the WRC did not permit corporations to join; it was comprised exclusively of universities and colleges, with unions and human rights organizations playing an advisory role. In joining the WRC, universities would agree to "require decent working conditions in factories producing their licensed products." Unlike the FLA, the WCA did not endorse a single, comprehensive set of fair labor standards. Rather, it called on its affiliated universities to develop their own codes. However, it did establish minimum standards that such codes should meet ones that were, in some respects, stricter than the FLA's. Perhaps most significantly, companies would have to pay a living wage. Companies were also required to publish the names and addresses of all of their manufacturing facilities, in contrast to FLA rules. Universities could refuse to license goods made in countries where compliance with fair labor standards was "deemed impossible," whatever efforts companies had made to enforce their own codes in factories there.

By contrast with the FLA, monitoring would be carried out by "a network of local organizations in regions where licensed goods are produced," generally nongovernmental organizations, independent human rights groups, and unions. These organizations would conduct unannounced "spot investigations," usually in response to worker complaints; WRC organizers called this the "fire alarm" method of uncovering code violations. Systematic monitoring would not be attempted.

The consortium's governance structure reflected its mission of being an organization by and for colleges and universities. Its 12-person board was composed of 3 representatives of United Students Against Sweatshops, 3 university administrators from participating schools, and 6 members drawn from an Advisory Board of persons with "expertise in the issues surrounding worker abuses in the apparel industry and independent verification of labor standards in apparel factories." No seats at the table were reserved for industry representatives. The group would be financed by 1 percent of licensing revenue from participating universities, as well as foundation grants.

The Universities Take Sides

Over the course of the spring semester 2000, student protests were held on a number of campuses, including the University of Oregon, to demand that their schools join the WRC. By April, around forty-five schools had done so. At UO, the administration encouraged an open debate on the issue so that all sides could be heard on how to ensure that UO products were made under humane conditions. Over a period of several months, the Academic Senate passed a resolution in support of the WRC. In a referendum sponsored by the student government, three-quarters of voters supported a proposal to join the WRC. A committee of faculty, students, administrators, and alumni appointed by the president voted unanimously to join the consortium.[64] Finally, after concluding that all constituents had had an opportunity to be heard, on April 12, 2000, University of Oregon president David Frohnmayer announced that UO would join the WRC for one year. Its membership would be conditional, he said, on the Consortium's agreement to give companies a voice in its operations and universities more power in governance. Shortly after the University's decision was announced in the press, Phil Knight withdrew his philanthropic contribution. In his public announcement, he stated his main disagreements with the Worker Rights Consortium:

> Frankly, we are frustrated that factory monitoring is badly misconstrued. For us one of the great hurdles and real handicaps in the dialogue has been the complexity of the issue. For real progress to be made, all key participants have to be at the table. That's why the FLA has taken so long to get going. The WRC is supported by the AFL-CIO and its affiliated apparel workers' union, UNITE. Their main aim, logically and understandably, however misguided, is to bring apparel jobs back to the U.S. Among WRC rules, no company can participate in setting standards, or monitoring. It has an unrealistic living wage provision. And its "gotcha" approach to monitoring doesn't do what monitoring should—measure conditions and make improvements.[65]

[64]Sarah Edith Jacobson, "Nike's Power Game" [editorial page letter], *New York Times*, May 16, 2000.
[65]"Knight's Statement," by Philip H. Knight, via press release, **http:// www.oregonlive.com.**

Etch-A-Sketch Ethics

This case was prepared by Charles W. L. Hill, the University of Washington.

The Ohio Art Company is perhaps best known as the producer on one of the top selling toys of all time, the venerable Etch-A-Sketch. More than 100 million of the familiar red rectangular drawing toys have been sold since 1960 when it was invented. The late 1990s, however, was a troubled time for the toy's maker. Confronted with sluggish toy sales, the Ohio Art Company lost money for two years running. In December 2000, it took the strategic decision to outsource production of the Etch-A-Sketch toys to Kin Ki Industrial, a leading Chinese toy maker, laying off one hundred U.S. workers in the process.

The closure of the Etch-A-Sketch line was not unexpected among employees. The company had already moved the production of other toy lines to China, and most employees knew it was just a matter of time before Etch-A-Sketch went too. Still, the decision was a tough one for the company, which did most of its manufacturing in its home base, the small Ohio town of Bryan (population eight thousand). As William Killgallon, the CEO of the Ohio Art Company noted, the employees who made the product "were like family. It was a necessary financial decision we saw coming for some time, and we did it gradually, product by product. But that doesn't mean it's emotionally easy."

In a small town like Bryan, the cumulative effect of outsourcing to China has been significant. The tax base is eroding from a loss of manufacturing and a population decline. The local paper is full of notices of home foreclosures and auctions. According to former employees, the biggest hole in their lives after Etch-A-Sketch moved came from the death of a community. For many workers, the company was their family, and now that family was gone.

The rationale for the outsourcing was simple enough. Pressured to keep the cost of Etch-A-Sketch under $10 by such big retailers as Wal-Mart and Toys "R" Us, the Ohio Art Company had to get its costs down or lose money. In this case, unionized workers making $1,500 a month were replaced by Chinese factory workers who made $75 a month. However, according to Killgallon, the main savings came not from lower wages, but from lower overhead costs for plant, maintenance, electricity, payroll, and the ability to get out from the soaring costs of providing health benefits to U.S. manufacturing employees.

The choice of Kin Ki as manufacturer for Etch-A-Sketch was easy enough—the company had been making pocket-sized Etch-A-Sketch toys for nearly a decade and always delivered on cost. To help Kin Ki, the Ohio Art Company shipped some of its best equipment to the company, and it continues to send crucial raw materials to Kin Ki, such as aluminum powder, which is hard to get in China.

The story would have ended there had it not been for an exposé run in the *New York Times* in December 2003. The *Times* reporter painted a dismal picture of working conditions at the Kin Ki factory that manufactured the Etch-A-Sketch. According to official Kin Ki publications: "Workers at Kin Ki make a decent salary, rarely work nights or weekends and often 'hang out along the streets, playing Ping Pong and watching TV.' They all have work contracts, pensions and medical benefits. The factory canteen offers tasty food. The dormitories are comfortable." Not so according to Joseph Kahn, the *Times* reporter. He alleged that real world Kin Ki employees, mostly teenage migrants from internal Chinese provinces, work long hours for 40 percent less than the company claims. They are paid 24 cents per hour, below the legal minimum wage (33 cents an hour) in Shenzhen province where Kin Ki is located. Most do not have pensions, medical benefits, or employment contracts. Production starts at 7:30 A.M. and continues until 10 P.M., with breaks only for lunch and dinner. Saturdays and Sundays are treated as normal workdays. This translates into a work week of seven 12-hour days, or 84 hours a week, well above the standard 40-hour week set by authorities in Shenzhen. Moreover, local rules allow for no more than 32 hours of overtime and stipulate that the employees must be paid 1.5 times the standard hourly wage, but Kin Ki's overtime rate is just 1.3 times base pay.

As for the "comfortable dormitories," the workers sleep head to toe in tiny rooms with windows that are covered with chicken wires. To get into and out of the factories, which are surrounded by high walls, workers must enter and leave through a guarded gate. As for the tasty food, it is apparently a mix of boiled vegetables, beans, and rice with meat or fish served only twice a month.

The workers at Kin Ki have apparently become restless. They went on strike twice in 2003, demanding higher wages and better working conditions. The company responded by raising wages a few cents and allotting an extra dish of food to each worker per day (but still no more meat)! However, Kin Ki simultaneously made "fried squid" of two workers who were ring leaders of the strike (fried squid is apparently a popular term for dismissal). Johnson Tao, a senior executive at the company, denies that the two ring leaders were dismissed for organizing the strikes. Rather, he noted that they were well-known troublemakers who left the factory of their own accord. Tao also acknowledges the low wages at the company, stating, "I know that I need to increase wages to comply with the law. I have the intention of doing this and will raise all wages in 2004."

Meanwhile, back in Ohio, William Killgallon, Ohio's CEO, stated to the *Times* reporter that he considered Kin Ki's executives to be honest and that he had no knowledge of labor problems there. But he said that he intended to make a visit to China soon to make sure that "they understand what we expect."

REFERENCES

Carol Hymowitz. "Toy Maker Survives by Moving an Icon From Ohio to China," *Wall Street Journal*, October 21, 2003, page B1.
Joseph Kahn. "An Ohio Town Is Hard Hit as Leading Industry Moves to China," New York Times, December 7, 2003, page A8.
Joseph Kahn. "Ruse in Toyland: Chinese Workers Hidden Woe," *New York Times*, December 7, 2003, pages A1, A8.
John Seewer. "Etch A Sketch Enters Fourth Decade," *Columbian*, November 22, 2001, page E3.

Case 34

Western Drug Companies and the AIDS Epidemic in South Africa

This case was prepared by Charles W. L. Hill, the University of Washington.

In December 1997, the government of South Africa passed a law that authorized two controversial practices. One, called parallel importing, allowed importers in South Africa to purchase drugs from the cheapest source available, regardless of whether the patent holders had given their approval. Thus, South Africa asserted its right to import "generic versions" of drugs that are still patent protected. The government did this because it claimed to be unable to afford the high cost of medicines that were patent protected. The other practice, called compulsory licensing, permitted the South African government to license local companies to produce cheaper versions of drugs whose patents are held by foreign companies, irrespective of whether the patent holder agreed.

The law seemed to be in violation of international agreements to protect property rights, including World Trade Organization agreements on patents to which South Africa is a signatory. South Africa, however, insisted that the law was necessary given its own health crisis and the high cost of patented medicines. By 1997, South Africa was wrestling with an AIDS crisis of enormous proportions. It was estimated that over 3 million of the country's 45 million people were infected with the virus at the time, more than in any other country. However, although the

AIDS epidemic in South Africa was seen as the primary reason for the new law, the law itself was applied to "communicable diseases" (of which AIDS is just one, albeit a devastating one).

Foreign drug manufacturers saw the law as an unbridled attempt to expropriate their intellectual property rights, and thirty-nine foreign companies quickly filed a lawsuit in the country to try to block implementation of the law. Drug manufacturers were particularly concerned about the applicability of the law to all "communicable diseases." They feared that South Africa was the thin end of the wedge, and if the law was allowed to stand, other countries would follow suit. Many Western companies also feared that if poor countries such as South Africa were allowed to buy low-priced generic versions of patent protected drugs, in violation of intellectual property laws, American and European consumers would soon demand the same.

In defense of their patents, the drug companies argued that because drug development is a very expensive, time-consuming, and risky process, they need the protection of intellectual property laws to maintain the incentive to innovate. It can take $800 million and twelve years to develop a drug and bring it to market. Less than one in five compounds that enter clinical trials actually become marketed drugs—the rest fail in trials due to poor efficacy or unfavorable side effects—and of those that make it to market, only three out of ten earn profits that exceed their costs of capital. If drug companies could not count on high prices for their few successful products, the drug development process would dry up.

The drug companies have long recognized that countries such as South Africa face special health challenges and lack the money to pay developed world prices. Accordingly, there is a history in the industry of pricing drugs low in the developing world or giving them away. For example, many AIDS drugs were already being sold to developing nations at large discounts to their prices in the United States. The South African government thought this was not good enough. The government was quickly supported by various human rights and AIDS organizations, which cast the case as an attempt by the prosperous multinational drug companies of the West to maintain their intellectual property rights in the face of desperate attempts by an impoverished government to stem a deadly crisis. For their part, the drug companies stated that the case had little to do with AIDS and was really about the right of South Africa to break international law.

While the drug companies may have had international law on their side, the tie-in with the AIDS epidemic clearly put them on the public relations defensive. After a blizzard of negative publicity, and little support from Western governments who were keen not to touch this political "hot potato," several leading manufacturers of AIDS drugs, while still opposing the South African law, started to change their policies. In May 2000, five large manufacturers of AIDS medicines—Merck, Bristol-Myers Squibb, Roche, Glaxo, and Boehringer Ingelhiem—announced that they would negotiate lower priced AIDS drugs in developing countries, primarily in Sub-Saharan Africa (some 25 million of the 36 million people infected with the HIV virus in 2000 lived in that region). Still the protests continued.

In February 2001, an Indian drug company, Cipla Ltd., offered to sell a cocktail of three AIDS drugs to poor African nations for $600 per patient per year, and for $350 a year to Doctors without Borders (AIDS is commonly treated with a cocktail that combines up to ten different antiviral drugs). The patents for these drugs were held by Western companies, but Indian law allowed local companies to produce generic versions of patent protected drugs.

The Cipla announcement seemed to galvanize Western drug companies into further action. In March 2001, Merck announced that it would cut the prices of its two AIDS drugs, Crixivan and Stocrin. Crixivan, which sold for $6,016 per year in the United States,

would be sold in developing countries for $600 a year. Stocrin, which cost $4,730 a year in the United States, would be sold for $500. Both drugs were often used together as part of an AIDS cocktail. Officials at Doctors without Borders, the Nobel Peace Prize–winning relief agency, welcomed the announcement, but pointed out that in a region where many people lived on less than a dollar a day, the price was still out of reach of many AIDS patients.

A few days later, Bristol-Meyers Squibb went further, announcing that it would sell its AIDS drug Zerit to poor nations in Africa for just $0.15 a day, or $54 a patient per year, which was below Zerit's costs of production. In the United States and Europe, Zerit was selling for $3,589 per patient per year. This was followed by an announcement from Abbot Labs that it would sell two of its AIDS drugs at "no profit" in Sub-Saharan Africa.

None of these moves, however, were enough to satisfy critics. In April 2001, the drug companies seemed to come to the conclusion that they were losing the public relations war, and they agreed to drop their suit against the South African government. This opened the way for South Africa to start importing cheap generic versions of patented medicines from producers such as Cipla of India. The decision to drop the suit was widely interpreted in the media as a defeat for the drug companies and a reaffirmation of the ability of the South African government to enforce compulsory licensing. At the same time, the pharmaceutical companies appear to have gotten assurances from South Africa that locally produced generic versions of patented drugs would only be sold in Sub-Saharan Africa, and not exported to other regions of the world.

In 2003, Aspen Pharmaceuticals, a South African drug maker, took advantage of the 1997 law to introduce a generic version of Stavudine, and it asked the South African authorities' permission to produce up to six more AIDS drugs. Aspen had licensed the rights to produce this drug, and several others, from Bristol-Meyers Squibb and Glaxo, the large British company. Bristol and Glaxo had waved their rights to royalties from sales of the drugs in Sub-Saharan Africa. At the same, the companies noted that Aspen was only able to sell the drugs within the Sub-Saharan Africa region.

Despite these moves, critics still urged Western drug companies to do more to fight the global AIDS epidemic, which by 2003 was estimated to afflict some

50 million people. For example, in a 2003 *New York Times* Op-Ed article, noted playwright and AIDS activist, Larry Kramer, stated, "It is incumbent upon every manufacturer of every HIV drug to contribute its patents or its drugs free for the salvation of these people.... I believe it is evil for drug companies to possess a means of saving lives and then not provide it to the desperate people who need it. What kind of hideous people have we become? It is time to throw out the selfish notion that these companies have the right not to share their patents."

Meanwhile in South Africa, the AIDS epidemic continued on its relentless course. By 2004, some 5.3 million South Africans were estimated to have been infected with HIV, and 600 people a day were dying from AIDS-related complications. In 2003, the South African government had committed itself to offering at low or no cost antiviral drugs to everyone with AIDS. By working with pharmaceutical companies such as Aspen and three Indian producers of generic drugs, the government was able to purchase a cocktail of antiviral HIV drugs for $65 per patient per month. However, by late 2004 only one out of fifty AIDS patients who were ready for the drugs were getting them, according to news reports. The problem now was distribution and particularly a chronic shortage of clinics, doctors, and nurses. Estimates suggested that it would still be years before cheap AIDS drugs were available to all those who needed them in South Africa.

REFERENCES

R. Block, "Big Drug Firms Defend Right to Patent on AIDS Drugs in South African Courts," *Wall Street Journal*, March 6, 2001, p. A3.

H. Cooper, R. Zimmerman, and L. McGinley, "Patents Pending—AIDS Epidemic Traps Drug Firms in a Vise," *Wall Street Journal*, March 2, 2001, p. A1.

J. Jeter, "Trial Opens in South Africa AIDS Drug Suit," *Washington Post*, March 6, 2001, p. A1.

L. Kramer, "The Plague We Can't Escape," *New York Times*, March 15, 2003, p. A17.

J. Nurton, "Overcoming the AIDS Hurdle," *Managing Intellectual Property*, June 2002, pp. 39–40.

T. Smith, "Mixed View of a Pact for Generic Drugs," *New York Times*, August 29, 2003, p. C3.

C. Timberg, "South Africans with AIDS See a Ray of Hope," *Washington Post*, November 30, 2004, p. A1.

Index